WASHINGTON
GONE CRAZY

WASHINGTON GONE CRAZY

Senator Pat McCarran
and the
Great American Communist Hunt

Michael J. Ybarra

STEERFORTH PRESS
HANOVER, NEW HAMPSHIRE

For information about permission to reproduce
selections from this book, write to:
Steerforth Press L.C., 25 Lebanon Street
Hanover, New Hampshire 03755

Library of Congress Cataloging-in-Publication Data

Ybarra, Michael J.
Washington gone crazy : senator Pat McCarran and the great American Communist
hunt / Michael J. Ybarra.— 1st ed.
p. cm.
Includes bibliographical references and index.
ISBN 1-58642-065-8 (alk. paper)
1. McCarran, Pat, 1876-1954. 2. Legislators—United States—Biography.
3. United States. Congress. Senate--Biography. 4. Anti-communist movements—
United States—History—20th century. 5. United States. Congress. House.
Committee on Un-American Activities. 6. United States—Politics and government—1901-1953. 7. Nevada—Politics and government—20th century. I. Title.
E748.M142Y33 2004
328.73'092—dc22

2004006627

FIRST EDITION

To my parents

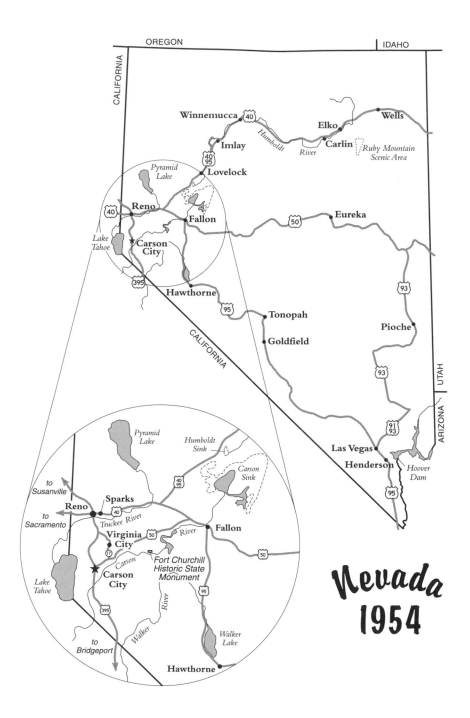

Nevada
1954

CONTENTS

The Road to Wheeling

Monday, October 6, 1952

Pat McCarran waved the U.S. marshal to approach. McCarran sat in the middle of the table in the federal courthouse in Salt Lake City. Nat Witt sat facing him at the witness table.

"I'll order you in the custody of the marshal now in just about a minute," McCarran warned.

"I am just appalled at the form of that question," Witt said.

"All you have to do is answer, Yes or No," McCarran said.

"Not *that* question, Mr. Chairman. I just can't. *I just can't.* I wasn't taught this kind of law in law school."

McCarran had never graduated from college. Witt had gone to Harvard Law. Each arrived in Washington in 1933. Witt was the son of a Jewish immigrant tailor in New York; McCarran, the son of an Irish immigrant farmer in Nevada. Witt came to change the world; McCarran, to keep it the way it was. Both despised Franklin Roosevelt's New Deal — Witt because it didn't go nearly far enough, McCarran because it went too far.

"Do you know Alger Hiss?" McCarran's aide Don Connors asked.

"Yes."

"Did you serve in the Communist Party with Hiss?"

Another McCarran aide, Jay Sourwine, started to ask Witt a question. Witt pleaded with McCarran to limit his interrogators to one at a time as is usual in court.

"You are not in court and this is not a trial," McCarran snapped.

"I don't know what's happening to me," Witt said, "if I'm not being put on trial here."

What was happening was a hearing of the Senate Internal Security Subcommittee, the least remembered but most fearsome of the congressional investigating committees in mid–twentieth-century America. Once, in a much different decade, Nat Witt had been one of the most powerful figures in the great union movement of the New Deal years: the secretary of the National Labor Relations Board. Then he had sat on the other side of the table, asking the questions, issuing the subpoenas, and wielding the coercive power of the federal government to move, however slightly, the nation in a new direction. Now it was McCarran's turn.

I

"Answer that question," McCarran insisted.

"It's a simple thing to tell me, but I'm under pressure, and under your threats, and I am going to protect myself," Witt replied.

"*I,*" McCarran thundered, "am running this committee."

"I know you are. I am running — "

"You are not running — "

"I am running my testimony in the light of my constitutional rights."

Witt was at sea. What was happening to him? To the country? His old friend Alger Hiss was in prison for lying to Congress about his Communist past; his friend Lee Pressman, whom he could no longer bring himself to look at when they passed each other in the street, had testified to Congress that Witt, too, had been a party member almost twenty years before. Witt was the lawyer for a union that had recently been kicked out of the CIO, the labor movement that both Witt and the union had helped to build. Witt was not even supposed to be a witness today. He had walked into the hearing room to represent a client when a federal marshal handed him a subpoena and Witt found himself facing McCarran. Almost a decade before, Witt had worked to drive McCarran from office; now McCarran was trying to drive Witt from the bar.

"May I be confronted with any testimony referring to an espionage ring in Washington?" Witt asked. "I think I am entitled to that before this gets out in the press."

"I am sorry," McCarran replied, "but this is not a trial. I am sorry, but you are excused."

"You are depriving me of my rights," Witt said.

"You are excused," McCarran said. "Will you please be excused before the marshal takes you out!"

Twenty years earlier Nat Witt had come to Washington to change the world. And the world had indeed changed — but not in the way that he thought it would.[1]

Patrick Anthony McCarran, seventy-six, looked like he could have stepped out of a Titian portrait of a fierce doge: a mountainous body topped by a great shock of white hair over an impassive face dominated by a hawkish nose and two small blue eyes as sharp as daggers. Most people called him Pat. Friends called him Patsy. Those who worked for him called him, their voices rising like a salute, *The Senator*. His enemies, of whom there were many, called him a son of a bitch. "A political mad dog and a subversive influence in the United States Senate,"[2] said broadcaster Norman Corwin. "He has hounded educators, writers, artists, actors, scientists, diplomats and trade unionists," read an ad in that morning's *Salt Lake City Tribune*. "He has struck fear in the hearts of millions of foreign born Americans. He has helped to destroy one article of the Bill of Rights after another. And for those who refuse to 'conform,' for those who see in his reign of terror the ingredients which Hitler poured into his own poison brew, McCarran has brought concentration camps to America."[3]

In the Senate McCarran was one of the half a dozen most senior Democrats. Senators, the young majority whip Lyndon Johnson noted, were either whales or guppies. McCarran was a whale. "He was sixth in seniority among United States senators," wrote *Las Vegas Sun* publisher Hank Greenspun, "but first in power."[4] McCarran was a lifelong Democrat, but he was also the least loyal party man imaginable. "Why don't you go along with the president?" his wife, Birdie, asked once — and it didn't matter which president she was talking about. "Can't you get along with anybody?"[5]

McCarran had fought Franklin Roosevelt from the fifth day of the New Deal to the last, and twenty years later he was no more accommodating to Dwight Eisenhower. But mostly he battled Harry Truman. McCarran and Truman hated each other, and for eight years — the formative period of the Cold War — they slugged it out over what kind of country America was and would become. They fought over the laws that would shape immigration and internal security policy for a generation, and they fought over how those laws would be carried out. These were not abstract debates: People lost jobs, were locked up, were deported, and even died as a result. And unfortunately for the country, Truman did not often win. "McCarran," wrote the *Progressive* magazine earlier in 1952, "has licked the president from start to finish."[6]

For most of Truman's presidency McCarran was the chairman of the Judiciary Committee and the chairman of the appropriations subcommittee that controlled the budgets of the State and Justice Departments — a résumé that barely began to describe McCarran's might. "As chairman of the Judiciary Committee," Senator Paul Douglas recalled, "he terrified the Department of Justice, whether Republican or Democratic, and as a powerful member of the Appropriations Committee he threw fear into many government agencies. Exercising his power like a despot, he could imperil any witness who came before his committees."[7]

McCarran wrote and passed bills. He approved — or disapproved —

the appointments of the people who would carry out *his* laws. And he controlled the budgets of the departments that implemented those laws. The net result was that Truman often found that he seemed to have little control over his own government. "Certain personnel in the Office of Security and Consular Affairs, particularly in the Visa Division, have been working in close conjunction with Senator McCarran and are really not responsive to executive control," White House aide David Lloyd told Truman that summer. "These people have tried to carry out the wishes of Senator McCarran and they have little or no sympathy with the administration program. . . . I had a report yesterday that the regulations were being drafted, at Senator McCarran's suggestion, in such a way as to be even more severe than the letter of the McCarran Act."[8] It was even worse in the Justice Department. "McCarran," wrote *New York Post* columnist Murray Kempton, "was de facto attorney general during the last year of the Truman Administration."[9]

On February 9, 1950, Joe McCarthy blustered his way into American history. McCarthy was a young freshman senator from the minority party, a virtual nonentity in the gerontocracy that was the Senate. Yet with almost a single speech in Wheeling, West Virginia, McCarthy thrust himself into the national narrative with such force that only Harry Truman and Dwight Eisenhower could compete with him for headlines over the next five years. McCarthy said that the State Department was full of Communists and that the Truman White House was tolerating them — if not worse. He gave a specific number, 205, and mentioned names. Both the number and the names would change from speech to speech, but the central charge — that the government was crawling with Communists and that Truman wasn't willing to do anything about it — would reverberate for half a decade. Within a month of Wheeling, *Washington Post* cartoonist Herbert Block drew a caricature of McCarthy slinging tar from a bucket and labeled it McCarthyism. The name stuck.

   McCarthyism quickly became a synonym for indiscriminate, unsupported charges, and the senator became an icon for the entire period in American history. As a descriptive term, *McCarthyism* had force and power, but as an explanatory concept the word bore more weight than it could support, especially when the man was confused with the ism. McCarthyism the phenomenon had been flourishing for years before McCarthy the senator made his speech; it dragged on for years more after the senator fell into obscurity. McCarthy said almost nothing that others hadn't said before. But

the force with which he voiced his charges and the moment — the tremulous interlude between the Soviet Union testing an atomic bomb and the
outbreak of the Korean War — combined to make him the focus of the
phenomenon. Truman — unlike many historians — understood the difference between McCarthy and McCarthyism. "He is only important,"
Truman said after leaving office, "in that his name has taken on a dictionary
meaning of the word."[10]

One speech did not start a witch hunt. The road to Wheeling was a
long one. McCarthyism, in fact, would have existed even if the senator had
made a success of his first vocation, chicken raising, and never come to
Washington. Although no politician was more reckless or colorful or successful in seizing national attention than McCarthy, the senator's actual
contributions to the age that bears his name were nearly negligible. "He
was its creature," George Kennan remarked, "not its creator."[11] For the first
three years of McCarthy's crusade, publicity was his only weapon. The
laws, the investigating committees, and the bureaucratic actions that
formed the institutional scaffolding of the McCarthy era were the work
of other men. Who or what, then, was responsible for McCarthyism? The
subject has been hotly debated for decades, with blame falling variously
on President Truman, his conservative political rivals, his anti-Communist
liberal supporters, the FBI, even the Communists themselves. "Why," asked
columnists Joseph and Stewart Alsop in July 1950, "Has Washington Gone
Crazy?"[12] This book offers one explanation.

McCarthyism, in this telling, was essentially a conservative reaction to
the New Deal, a long-simmering series of resentments and antipathies that
boiled over into an awful, scalding mess during the late 1940s. The sources
of bitterness that fueled this reaction were many: rural rancor toward
urban elites, nativist dread of encroaching minorities, fundamentalist anx-
iety over the spread of secular values, Jeffersonian scorn for a growing and
activist government. Pat McCarran was harried by all these fears.

Something terrible and wrenching happened to American society during
the middle of the past century. The country seemed gripped by a long fit,
a *status epilepticus* that convulsed the body politic for the better part of a
decade. The spasm was at least a decade in the coming, but the proximate
cause was the appearance of two unprepossessing witnesses before congressional investigating committees in August 1948: Whittaker Chambers
and Elizabeth Bentley, former Communists who had left the party. In
those and many subsequent appearances, Chambers and Bentley told the

country much of what it would come to know about Communism and its secret history across two decades of American life. As a result, many people suffered, more than a few went to jail, others lost jobs, some even killed themselves. And much of what they said was greatly disputed, at the time and for decades to come.

During these years there were three main factions contending for the truth: liberals, conservatives, and Communists. The liberals were led, more or less, by President Harry Truman in an uneasy coalition with the anti-Communist left, largely represented by the activist organization Americans for Democratic Action. The liberals believed that the American Communist Party was a small but tractable domestic problem, while the Soviet Union represented a real external threat; they strove to balance liberty and security. The conservatives believed that domestic Communists were the real problem, that the liberals themselves were either blind to this menace or actually in cahoots with the party, and that the solution was a thorough, coercive scouring of left-wing influence from every corner of American life. The Communists, and their allies on the American left, contended that both liberals and conservatives were wrong: The party was a radical political organization but independent of the Soviet Union; its members were loyal Americans, not subversives; and any curtailment on the liberty of the party would be the first step on the road to fascism that would lead inexorably to a crackdown on everyone's freedom.

Debate is too mild a term to describe this argument; *three-party political civil war* would be better. Since the end of the Cold War, however, it has become more and more clear what happened in America during those years. Chambers and Bentley were telling the truth. The Communists were lying. With the opening of U.S. and Soviet archives, many of the interminable Cold War debates can finally be settled. Alger Hiss *was* a Soviet agent. The Rosenbergs *were* guilty. The Soviet Union ran an extensive intelligence network in the United States involving hundreds of operatives, most of whom were recruited from the Communist Party of the U.S.A. Not all Communists were subversives, but in ways small and large, many of them were.

There is still perhaps one great unresolved question: whether the liberals or the conservatives had a better solution for dealing with domestic Communism. Truman represents the liberal anti-Communist approach; McCarran, the conservative. The conflict between the liberals and the conservatives was often fiercer than that between each and their mutual enemy, the Communists. That struggle, which stretched back twenty years to the first days of the New Deal, is the heart of this book.

To comprehend what happened in America in the 1940s and 1950s, then, it is necessary to know what happened in America during the 1930s. The prism through which this book views that period is Pat McCarran, who arrived in Washington at the dawn of the New Deal in 1933. He sat in the Senate until the twilight of McCarthyism in 1954, dying barely a month before Joe McCarthy was censured by his colleagues and disappeared from the headlines. To understand McCarran it is also necessary to understand his enemies, both liberals and radicals. Illusions shape history as much as anything else, and so this is a book about illusions: the liberal illusion of the 1930s and the conservative illusion of the 1950s.

It is no accident that perhaps the single best book on the McCarthy era remains Murray Kempton's *Part of Our Time,* which was published virtually contemporaneously with the history it records and saw no need to even mention Joe McCarthy. Kempton focused on people whose lives intersected in some way with the history of their period, exploring how those individuals and events affected each other. The approach here is similar, focusing mostly on Pat McCarran's life but also exploring many others for what they say about McCarran and the time through which he moved.

Pat McCarran walked into the Senate once when his Democratic colleagues Paul Douglas and Herbert Lehman were talking. "There," Douglas said to Lehman, "goes an evil man."[13]

Douglas and Lehman were two of the most decent, best-intentioned men ever to sit in the Senate. "The radical left wing clique in Congress," McCarran called them.[14] Douglas and Lehman were great liberals who distinguished themselves with their convictions and courage and brought honor to the body they served so valiantly. But they were not great lawmakers. Whatever else McCarran was, he was one hell of a lawmaker. Few senators in the history of the republic have amassed so much power or used it with such determination.

McCarran's ends were often outrageous but his means, like a shark's on the hunt, were magnificent to behold, a stunning display of directed purpose. "Pat McCarran was an earth-shaking force," Lyndon Johnson said once. "He lived in the midst of great controversy. And he himself was one of the controversial figures around which the storm raged . . . who impressed his personality deeply and indelibly upon the institution of the Senate and upon the history of the nation."[15]

Paul Douglas did not hate many men. He hated McCarran. "As I watched him at work," he wrote, "I often recalled the lines from *Measure for Measure:*

> *Oh, it is excellent*
> *To have a giant's strength, but it is tyrannous*
> *To use it like a giant.*[16]

McCarran was obsessed with Communists and immigration, and more than anything he feared that the former would infiltrate the country by the latter. "This plan and this program," McCarran told a reporter, "are so big as to stagger the imagination."[17] Years before Joe McCarthy ever opened his mouth in public, McCarran believed — *really* believed — that the Democratic Party was controlled by the Communists and that one mysterious person especially had managed to exert a malign influence that could be felt at the highest levels of government. "It seems like heresy,"[18] McCarran confessed to his friend Pete Petersen in 1944. "I feel his influence all over Washington," he told Norm Biltz, another friend. "If I throw up a hundred false balloons, if I make a hundred efforts that fail, if I make a hundred mistakes, and do eventually find that one, I will have served my country well."[19]

The search for the one heretic consumed McCarran's last decade in Washington. It consumed more than that, as well. "This was the thing that he worked on and dreamed of day and night," Biltz recalled, "to block it every way possible."[20] McCarran, it turns out, was half right. There actually were Communists in Washington. But it was the hunt for them that did the real damage.

PART ONE

STRUGGLE

"Mary, you know I'm gonna need Bill to help me in my business. Why do you want to start putting things like that in the boy's head?" protested Lonigan.

"Patrick, you know that if God wants a boy or a girl for His work, and that boy or girl turns his back on the Will of Almighty God, he or she won't never be happy and they'll stand in grave danger of losing their immortal souls," she said.

"Isn't it the truth?" said Mrs. Reilley.

"But Mary . . ."

"Patrick, the Will of God is the Will of God, and no mortal can tamper with it or try to thwart it," his wife replied.[1]

— James T. Farrell, *Young Lonigan*

CHAPTER 1

Unruly Spirits

You do not know what a great big, broad, magnificent
country we have up here, full of sunshine, full of hope,
and full of big hearted, open handed people.[1]
— Pat McCarran

From nowhere the railroad tracks came, stretched through the hardpan little valley, past low hills covered with a pale stubble of sagebrush, and disappeared into the vastness beyond. A few hundred feet down the south slope of the railbed the Truckee River bubbled eastward, flowing from the unseen Sierra Nevada in the west. Riding against the river was a slight, dark-haired boy on a pony. He followed the glinting parallel lines of rail and river on a relentless, plodding journey past a monotonous landscape that seemed as immune to the seasons of the East as it was forbidding to all but the hardiest of plant or animal life. Even the improbable green ribbon — aspen, willow, and cottonwood — that clung to the riverbank soon grew dull as the sun climbed behind the boy in overalls, chasing away the morning shadows, its glare washing the color from this tiny rift in the huge Nevada desert.

Harsh and stark as it may have been, Pat McCarran loved the land, loved the subtle change in hue as the sage freshened into olive green in spring and then faded to olive brown long before fall, loved the Truckee as it raced its banks, dark and rapid and full in winter, clear and slow and sometimes barely there at all in summer. It was a route McCarran saw a lot of between the ages of ten and fifteen. Every morning after milking a dozen cows on the family ranch in the little river canyon, he set off for the ten-mile ride to a one-room school in the railway village of Glendale, five miles outside the big city of Reno, where more than three thousand people lived. The school year was short — the interval between the end of the fall harvest and the start of lambing season in spring, when McCarran quit his studies to attend to the bloody, tiring work of mid-wiving sheep. His attendance flickered even more when winter rains turned the dirt road to school into an impassable track of muck and the warming new year sent snowmelt flooding down the river, whitecaps marching on the Truckee, Sierra pines shooting down the rapids, turning bridges into overflowing dams and widening the waters beyond belief.

But on this brilliant autumn day in the late 1880s the Truckee just trickled, and nothing threatened to break the boredom of the ride to school until McCarran spotted a handcar standing lonesomely on a siding. Hitching his horse to a fence, the boy climbed aboard and began pumping his way down the track, past the scrub of sagebrush and greasewood, down a grade to the base of a narrow pass.

The train came from nowhere. Over the hill from the next valley, the locomotive steamed down on the little handcar. McCarran jumped off; the train trundled past, smashing the car to splinters. Then the section men of the Central Pacific Railroad appeared and grabbed the boy who had reduced their handcar to kindling. They were marching him off to the sheriff in Sparks when Margaret McCarran arrived in her buggy. Pat's mother demanded to know where they were going with the boy. Just out of her teens, Mrs. McCarran had worked her way across the Atlantic Ocean from Ireland and then crossed most of the continent on this same railroad, stopping in Reno where she met a taciturn fellow countryman who had come down the steep mountains from California to dig a life out of the thin soil of Nevada. In this scorched land both nature and nurture were harsh, and their son knew work before he knew anything else. When Pat rose at 4 A.M. to start the day's chores, his mother was already up and busy. Maggie McCarran was built like one of Michelangelo's sibyls and was as unyielding as the Nevada desert. She was not the kind of woman anyone wanted to argue with.

Mrs. McCarran ordered Pat back on his pony and off to school, promising the railroad crew that she would personally take him to the sheriff later to work out a settlement and then see to it that the boy got his real punishment at home. Maggie McCarran could neither read nor write, but she was sending her boy to school to get an education, and she would be damned if she let anything get in the way of that. She had not crossed an ocean to raise a farmer. In his long life Pat McCarran feared little. He feared his mother.[2]

Long before the railroad existed, a man crossed the mountains on a horse. In the waning summer of 1862 he rode along the Truckee, following the rushing river as it fell from the alpine splendor of Lake Tahoe, at 6,200 feet above sea level, down the piney eastern slope of the Sierra and into the new territory called Nevada. The trail dropped through slot canyons so narrow that their sheer walls seemed to meet overhead, zigging and zagging across the cold river two dozen times. In forty miles the road fell twenty-three hundred feet. Great trees gave way to shrunken; Jeffrey, pon-derosa, and sugar pines were replaced by piñons and junipers. And by the time the canyon disappeared and the river slowed and the hills flattened out, only a fringe of foliage clung to the Truckee, the land to the horizon covered by nothing but scratchy sagebrush. At the edge of the world rose another set of mountains, smaller and smoother, dull and dry as bones, the Virginia Range. Patrick McCarran liked what he saw. He would stay.

McCarran was twenty-seven, an illiterate Irish immigrant with fiery red hair and a temper to match. He was born in Londonderry County in 1834, part of the cottier class that survived on small patches of rented land and twelve pounds of potatoes a day. When McCarran was twelve, a great blight wiped out the potato crop; over the next several years a million Irish died from famine and disease, and another million fled the isle. A quarter of the country's population disappeared in half a decade, including McCarran. He found a hiding place in the hold of a sailing ship and crossed the Atlantic to Quebec — a route notorious as the "coffin ship cruise," because one in five passengers died on the voyage. McCarran arrived in 1848. He worked his way to New York, then to the Missouri River frontier.

In 1857 McCarran joined the U.S. Army in Fort Leavenworth, Kansas, and rode into the immense unknown region between the Rockies and the Sierra Nevada. Out there Brigham Young and his Mormon pioneers were drifting toward war with the United States, whose authority they thought they could escape in the wide desert of the Utah territory. President James Buchanan dispatched fifteen hundred troops to show the Mormons otherwise. But by the time the army reached Salt Lake City in June 1858, the Mormons had reached a modus vivendi with Washington, and McCarran and the cavalry passed through town without even stop-ping. The troops continued west, crossing a sea of sagebrush three times as large as McCarran's homeland before reaching the lee of the Sierra Nevada. As the first snow of winter began to fall, the troops climbed high into the steeply rising mountains and rode down the more gradual western slope into California's enormous Central Valley. Following the Sacramento River to where it flowed through the Carquinez Straits into San Pablo Bay northeast of San Francisco, the troops finally arrived at the barracks of Benicia — 2,128 miles and the better part of a year after they had left Kansas.

Less than four years later, in the fall of 1862, McCarran found himself riding back into the great desert. The year before, the Confederate States had broken away from the Union, and the western half of Utah had become the territory of Nevada. President Abraham Lincoln called for volunteers to help protect the western flank of the nation. Almost seventeen thousand men signed up, including McCarran, who enlisted in the Second Cavalry Regiment that November in San Francisco. Private McCarran was posted to Fort Alert in San Francisco, where the 225 men of Company L drilled day after day for most of the next year and then headed east toward Nevada. "They are all under a rigid course of discipline and instruction,"[3] General George Wright told his superiors in Washington. Military life proved too rigid for some. Thirty-one men deserted the company before it was ordered across the Sierra in August; another six slipped away en route to Nevada. The company was headed to a new adobe garrison rising from the sagebrush along the Carson River called Fort Churchill. McCarran was going to fight Indians.

In the spring of 1860 settlers kidnapped two Paiute Indian women. The Paiutes then killed the settlers and burned down their trading post. A ragtag army of 105 men formed at the Virginia City mining outpost, riding down from the hills and galloping along the Truckee River toward its terminus at Pyramid Lake to teach the Indians a lesson. Twenty-nine men returned. For the Indians it was a fleeting victory. Two hundred and seven cavalry troops poured over the mountains from California, joined up with 549 Nevada volunteers at the big bend where the Truckee doglegs north to Pyramid Lake, and drove the Indians into the desert. Bloody skirmishes continued for years, and McCarran's regiment was assigned to protect the trade route across the desert. It was an ugly business. "I told two of the Indians, through the interpreter, that if they would go and bring in Indians who were engaged in the massacre of emigrants I would release them, but that if they did not return that night I would kill all the Indians I held as prisoners in camp," reported Major Edward McGarry not long after McCarran's company entered Nevada. "Hearing nothing from the Indians I had sent out the day previous, I put to death four of those remaining, and released the squaws and child, telling them that we were sent there to punish Indians who were engaged in the massacre of emigrants, and instructed them to tell all the Indians that if they did not desist from killing emigrants that I would return there next summer and destroy them."[4] And the settlers were not much easier to manage. "There is no law or government there at all," General Edwin Sumner informed Washington, "and the Territory is a place of refuge for disorganizers and other unruly spirits."[5]

One such spirit was McCarran. But in Nevada, for the first time since he had fled Ireland fourteen years before, he found something that soothed him. In the swales alongside the Truckee, a river other men cursed because it cut a canyon so narrow in places that they had to walk in the water on rocks sharp enough that the feet of their horses bled, he was smitten. Under the poplars and cottonwoods that marked the banks of the river there grew bunchgrass and alfalfa. It was not green like his homeland. But it was green enough. He deserted the calvary before the troops reached Fort Churchill.

On the map it was a void, hostile to life, best avoided altogether, or raced through if there was no other way. Between the Rocky Mountains and the Sierra Nevada lies what John Frémont called the Great Basin — two hundred thousand arid square miles that could seemingly swallow the runoff from the two greatest mountain ranges on the continent and still remain the driest place in the United States. The name *Nevada* (Spanish for "snow covered") was as wrong as it was cruel. Water simply avoids Nevada. Not a single river spans the state, although more than 160 mountain ranges run from north to south, dividing the land into some ninety basins and making a topographic map of Nevada look like what geographer C. E. Dutton called an "army of caterpillars crawling toward Mexico."[6] The Colorado River skirts the southern edge of the state, while the Sierra Nevada forms a granite wall that blocks rain from entering the basin. Three rivers carry snowmelt into Nevada from the west, but none get far: The Truckee and the Walker puddle into lakes (the only two in the state's lowlands), and the Carson disappears into a sink. Nevada is one of the hottest and the coldest places in the country, with the temperature in its southern tip sizzling up to 120 degrees Fahrenheit in summer and the northern peaks plunging to 50 degrees below zero in winter. Eighty-eight percent of the land is desert, vast oceans of sagebrush, broken in the south only by the gnarled figure of the Joshua tree, its thick and fuzzy branches contorted as if driven crazy by the search for moisture. So much sagebrush. Never, marveled Thomas Edison, had the Lord put so much of anything anywhere with so little purpose. In Nevada, added Mark Twain, Satan would be homesick for hell. "Everything here," wrote one explorer, "seems to declare that, 'Here man shall not dwell.'"[7]

And yet people did. Small bands of Paiute Indians wandered the kinder reaches of the basin, scratching for sustenance from a place reluctant to give it. They pounded grasshoppers and crickets into a mash mixed with animal fat, and skimmed fly larvae from riversides and rolled them into balls to eat in the lean winter. "Humanity," said explorer John Frémont, ". . . in its lowest form and most elementary state."[8]

It was the last great unexplored region of the United States. In 1826 rival fur traders Jedediah Smith and Peter Ogden began a series of excursions into the area, and what they discovered almost killed them. Smith's party had to eat its mules to survive, digging holes in the ground and burying themselves under dirt to escape the heat of the day. Explorers named things for the pain they caused or the disgust they evoked: Barren River, Dead Mule Canyon, Lousy Ravine. Clarence King, an early and energetic surveyor, was struck by lightning while charting the fortieth parallel from a peak, as if God were warning him not to try to measure this vastness. "The whole country appeared so dreary and dismal, so forsaken and cursed of the Almighty, that it reminded me every day of the curse pronounced against Babylon," one traveler remarked.[9]

One day in January 1848 something bright caught John Marshall's eye while inspecting a newly dug millrace on a sawmill on the South Fork of the American River on the California side of the Sierra. It was gold. Suddenly thousands of fortune hunters were hellbent to cross the desert to reach California. Many took the Humboldt Trail, which started in the northeast corner of Nevada and followed an alkaline river that taunted the thirsty as it lazed across much of the desert before draining into a sink forty miles short of the Truckee. "A 'river' in Nevada is a sickly rivulet which is just the counterpart of the Erie Canal in all respects save that the canal is twice as long and four times as deep," Twain wrote. "One of the pleasantest and most invigorating exercises one can contrive is to run and jump across the Humboldt river till he is overheated, and then drink it dry."[10] Few were tempted to drink deep of the Humboldt, whose water tasted like lye. One sojourner from Iowa was moved to write to Mary's River (as the Humboldt was originally called):

> Meanest and muddiest, filthiest stream,
> most cordially I hate you;
> Meaner and muddier still you seem
> since the first day I met you.
> Your namesake better was no doubt,
> a truth, the scriptures tell,
> Her seven devils were cast out,
> but yours are in you still.

What mean these graves so fresh and new
along your banks on either side?
They've all been dug and filled by you,
thou guilty wretch, thou homicide.
Now fare thee well, we here shake hands
and part (I hope) to meet no more,
I'd rather die in happier lands than longer live
upon your shore.[11]

Then the journey got worse. The wasteland between the rivers was the most awful part of any trip across the continent. Men stuck their hands into anthills and licked the insects off for food, roasted the soles of moccasins for dinner, drank the blood of fallen horses to quench their thirst. One traveler counted 934 graves along the way, many simple crosses with no names, some dug up by wolves, exposed bones whitening in the sun. "The stench was horrible," said Bennett Clark. "All our traveling experience furnishes no parallel to this."[12] "From one extremity of this desert to the other, the road was white with the bones of oxen and horses," added Twain almost a decade later. "It would hardly be an exaggeration to say that we could have walked the forty miles and set our feet on a bone at every step! The desert was one prodigious graveyard. And the log-chains, wagon tyres, and rotting wrecks of vehicles were almost as thick as the bones."[13] It was a place to be gotten through as fast as possible.

But in 1859 two prospectors dug into a seemingly endless vein of silver in the eastern slope of Sun Mountain in the Virginia Range. They had struck a bonanza that over the next quarter century would yield $293 million in gold and silver and become famous as the Comstock Lode. Suddenly thousands poured back through the mountain passes from California. In a year Nevada's population doubled, reaching sixteen thousand in 1861, the year it became a U.S. territory. Three years later it became the thirty-sixth state. Mining towns were popping up in every corner of the land, their inhabitants as rough as the rock they raised picks against. "There are about 1,200 people here, half of whom have been in the state prison and the rest ought to be," reported a miner from Pioche in eastern Nevada. "Our graveyard has forty-one graves, of which two were filled by death from natural causes."[14]

It was the fall of 1862. Rude settlement had recently come to the Truckee Meadows, an oasis amid the aridity of the Great Basin, the place where

Patrick McCarran had decided to settle. Three years earlier C. W. Fuller had begun ferrying miners headed to the Comstock Lode across the Truckee; then he built a log bridge over the river and charged a toll. Myron Lake built a better bridge and then something to cross to: a trading post and a hotel, the first structures of what would become Reno. Men poured into the meadows, then rushed up to the barren mountains to the southeast where the boomtown of Virginia City promised easy wealth.

McCarran, unlike most who were attracted to the territory, never scratched deeper than the topsoil. All he wanted, he saw along the banks of the Truckee: land and water. He found work cutting grass and driving a bull team up to Virginia City, where hay was needed for livestock feed. By 1863 he had a piece of his own land in a small canyon downriver from the meadows. That same year, on the other side of the Sierra Nevada, Leland Stanford's Central Pacific Railroad began to crawl its way east from Sacramento; by 1867 the railroad was following the Truckee down into Nevada. In May 1868 the railroad auctioned off four hundred lots in the newborn town of Reno, named for a Union general killed during the Civil War. The first building to go up was a saloon. Soon track was sloping into McCarran's valley. In another year the Central Pacific would meet the Union Pacific at Promontory, Utah, where a gold spike from California and a silver spike from Nevada were driven into the ties bridging the transcontinental railroad. Before long young Reno had a thousand residents, while the entire state had swollen to more than forty-two thousand people. Men outnumbered women sixteen to one.

One of the passengers from the East to step off the new railroad at Reno was a young Irishwoman named Margaret Shay. The daughter of tenant farmers in County Cook, Shay came to the United States in 1872, working as a domestic to pay her way through steerage. In 1875 the dark-haired twenty-three-year-old who loved to sing stopped in Nevada on her way to San Francisco. She was working as a cook on a farm five miles south of Reno when she met an Irishman twenty-two years her senior named Patrick McCarran. A dozen years after arriving in Nevada McCarran had acquired land in Reno and down the river, $1,150 worth of real estate, and could afford to pay his seventy-five-year-old mother's way to the United States from Ireland. That October, McCarran married Maggie Shay, and on August 8, 1876, she gave birth to a baby boy. They named him Patrick Anthony McCarran.

McCarran took his bride back to a little river canyon she had first passed through on the train, fifteen miles down the Truckee near a railroad siding that would come to be called Patrick. There, between the gleaming tracks and the shining river, McCarran built a small house and a ranch that would eventually swell to two thousand acres. Even on the thin margins of the Truckee, Nevada was niggardly. Brutal frosts kept the hills from turning green until May; by June the sun and the wind had turned them brown again. McCarran cleared sagebrush, marked his land with a rock fence, and dug irrigation ditches. He planted an orchard and put up chicken coops. And when his house burned down while the family was out in the field gleaning potatoes he built another one, this time carving a wooden shamrock that he painted green and nailed above the front door for good luck. The land by the river yielded enough for Maggie McCarran to fill up a horse-drawn wagon with fruits and vegetables, drive the winding mountain roads up to Virginia City to arrive by dawn, and return home to drop clanking silver coins into a mason jar in the dining room cupboard. "The people of Nevada have forgotten the miraculous quality of their soil and the rare flavor of the apples, plums and big peaches that could be the product of the canyon," remembered Margaret McCarran, Patrick's granddaughter. "McCarran cabbages were huge and crisp and the corn and immense potatoes of a flavor long lost but unforgettable."[15]

Also unforgettable were McCarran's temper and his loose way of handling money, especially other people's — traits his young son would inherit in spades. More than once he rode into Reno for elections, spent the night, and returned to the ranch the next day with a broken nose. When McCarran shot at a sheepherder who grazed his flock across the ranch, the Irishman was charged with "assault with intent to kill" but acquitted by a jury. A neighboring rancher dug a ditch across McCarran's land; he filled it up. McCarran was hauled into court again. The judge agreed that his land had been trespassed, but he still fined McCarran eight hundred dollars for interfering with someone else's water rights — by far the greater crime in Nevada. Another time the illiterate Irish immigrant hired an Italian who didn't speak English to dig a ditch, and the dispute over the payment sent McCarran back to court (the going rate for an Italian digger was $1.50 for every sixteen feet of ditch, while a Chinese laborer got 90 cents for the same work). When McCarran couldn't pay the seven-hundred-dollar judgment, the court confiscated some of his land. Margaret McCarran, too, ran afoul of creditors. After nursing a relative's son through typhoid and giving the family milk, cream, butter, and hay, Maggie borrowed five hundred dollars from her kin to buy some cows —

only to wind up being sued for the money. McCarran had to mortgage the ranch to pay off the claim and interest. "Poverty," the granddaughter wrote, "marked the whole life of the family."[16]

Soon poverty marked the whole state. In 1880 Nevada's population peaked at 62,266 people, almost 11,000 of them crowded into Virginia City alone. But the endless veins of precious metal were not so endless after all. In 1876 the Comstock Lode produced $36.8 million worth of ore; five years later miners would be lucky to gouge $1.2 million out of the mountain. The demise of a mine, which always happened sooner or later, came to be called a *borrasca*, Spanish for "ill wind." By the turn of the century fewer than 2,700 people remained in Virginia City, and the state's population had dwindled to about 42,300 — somewhat less than it had been thirty years earlier. The Comstock bonanza had built great banking fortunes in San Francisco and mansions high atop its Nob Hill, but all Nevada had to show for producing the silver in the first place was sagebrush growing in the streets of ghost towns. "Shall Nevada Be Deprived of Statehood?"[17] asked William Ellsworth Smythe in the publication *Forum,* and soon the national press was echoing suggestions that the state should be absorbed by one of its neighbors. "Nevada is one of the very youngest and wildest of the States," observed John Muir. "Nevertheless, it is already strewn with ruins that seem as gray and silent and time-worn as if the civilization to which they belonged had perished centuries ago. . . . Wander where you may throughout the length and breadth of this mountain-barred wilderness, you everywhere come upon these dead mining towns, with their tall chimney-stacks, standing forlorn amid broken walls and furnaces, and machinery half buried in sand, the very names of many of them already forgotten."[18]

Hundreds of luckless men passed the McCarran ranch, walking the rails to someplace they hoped would be better than where they had come from. Some stopped to earn a dollar a day, a meal, and a bunk in the cellar of the burned-down house. It was not a sight likely to make a young boy believe that the world was a kind place.

In winter the sheep appeared high on the sage-covered ridge above the McCarran ranch, flowing down the hills like white lava until thousands filled the canyon with their bleats. The banks of the Truckee sheltered the sheep from the harsh winters of their summer range in the high country. On cold mornings they huddled together for warmth, steam rising from their breath, mounds of stirring snow foraging for sagebrush in the frozen earth. The handful of men who led the sheep were the only regular visitors to the lonely ranch. "The sheep owners and sheepherders were my almost constant companions . . . my pals and friends," McCarran recalled. "And I was their errand boy for everything and anything that they wanted."[19]

Reno was fifteen miles upstream, a hard day's journey over rough roads to get there and back by dark. It was a trip that young McCarran could only be sure of making on the Saturday before Easter when he hitched two horses to an old spring wagon and drove his mother to town for Mass, the two of them dressed in their best clothes ("none too good," he remembered) as they rattled up Virginia Street to a little church on the bluff where the new state university had broken ground when he was nine. Together they knelt and read prayers before filing into the confessional. "Where," McCarran recalled, "the freckled faced boy told all the terrible sins which a freckled faced boy with only a dog for a playmate might be guilty of committing." That evening was a rare chance for him to play with other boys. On Sunday he was up before dawn and already in church when the sun came streaming through the stained-glass window as the old priest raised the sacramental body and blood of Christ above the altar. "Have mercy on us," his mother whispered.[20]

But for most of the rest of the year McCarran saw almost no one except his parents until the sheepmen appeared at the ranch. In spring came lambing season. All day long and then into the kerosene-lit night, lanterns trailing off oily smoke and throwing orange shadows on everything, ewes gave birth. A constant chorus of mothers moaning, *ma-a-ma-a-a;* the newborns answering with thin *baa*s. Several hundred lambs could drop in a day. Not all easily. In difficult births the corralman would roll up his sleeves, scrub his hands and arms in hot water and bathe them in olive oil, thrust his fist into the ewe's womb, and pull out the lamb. If the lamb appeared stillborn he'd have to peel the birth membrane off and try to give mouth-to-mouth and a good thump over the knee. Twins had to be tied to one another and the mother so the ewe wouldn't reject one of her own. Then came the sad search for dead lambs, which were skinned and their hides tied onto newborns that had become orphans, or bummers, because a ewe would rather kick a lamb in the head than nurse one that didn't smell like her offspring. Three months later the males matured sexually and had to be castrated, which the shepherd did by slicing the scrotum open with a knife, grabbing the testicles in his teeth, and biting them off. Sheep ranching was hard, bloody work, but it stirred something inside the boy. Every spring McCarran roamed the lambing camps, collecting bummers and nursing them by bottle until he had a flock of his own, the sheep as devoted to McCarran as any lamb to a ewe. "I grew," he said, "into a liking for the sheep business."[21]

McCarran started school at the age of ten, four years behind most of his peers. Rising at 4 A.M., he milked a dozen cows before setting off on the ten-mile ride to Glendale, a railroad stop up the Truckee that later came to be called Sparks. There he studied in a one-room white-clapboard school. On the ride back in the evening McCarran rounded up the cows and milked them one more time. One day McCarran showed up at school in his overalls as usual, only to find a performance scheduled and the other children dressed for the occasion. He went straight home. Still, the schoolhouse was a glimpse of a larger world, a place where he discovered a realm of ideas and possibilities that had never drifted down the Truckee to the ranch. "My first love is with the little white schoolhouse at the turn of the road," McCarran remembered. "It was there that I spent my happiest boyhood days. It was there that I received my first ambitions, and I look back to the little white schoolhouse as the scene of my fondest recollections."[22] McCarran's attendance was sporadic. It started only after he was done with the harvest in late October. In winter snow choked off the road; in spring the Truckee flooded over bridges. Lambing season in March killed whatever was left of the school year.

When he was fifteen, McCarran's father promised to send him to live in Reno and go to school there after the boy finished helping him with the harvest. October was almost over before the crops were picked and McCarran showed up to belatedly start the school year, wearing a new pair of overalls, new shoes, and a chinchilla coat. "My garb evidently was a matter of much comment, as it should have been," he recalled, "but I knew no different and was content."[23]

Maggie McCarran was far from content. She could neither read nor write, but her only son was going to do better. He was born in America; he could be president. He worked every day of his life on the ranch; he could work as hard at school. And she would work hard, too, if that's what it took. She got a job as a cook in a hotel to earn the money to pay for Pat's room and board (six bits and a sack of potatoes).

The last thing on her son's mind was work. While the overall population of Nevada had shrunk by a quarter in the past decade, Reno had grown to hold more than thirty-five hundred residents in 1891. It was becoming a real city; lynching victims no longer dangled from the Virginia Street Bridge. But there was still plenty of excitement: horse carts clomping up and down Virginia Street, crossing the bridge over the Truckee, as well as the comings and goings of the train a few blocks up from the river where two-story brick buildings lined Commercial Row. Farther up Virginia buildings fell off and the street grew steep where a four-story structure, built in 1885, loomed over the lonely edge of town. Perched on a bluff overlooking an irrigation ditch, the redbrick edifice topped by a clock tower housed the entire University of Nevada. Herd animals grazing across the campus outnumbered students.

The city was a wonder to McCarran. "When I came to Reno to live," he recalled years later, "the town nearly took possession of the boy."[24] McCarran did poorly, skipped classes, didn't get along with the other boys. "The other kids couldn't feel sorry for him, because he wasn't the kind you felt sorry for," recalled one teacher. "So they fought him."[25] One day teacher Libby Booth caught him playing hooky and gave him a good talking-to. He had it in him to be more than just another rancher, she told him. McCarran began going to her house for tutoring after school. "For the first time in my life I was brought to a realization by this good woman that I had something in me that was worth while," he remembered.[26] When Maggie McCarran showed up to pay her son's board, Booth told her the boy was too old for his grade; that he needed more work. McCarran soon found himself studying shorthand, telegraphy, and typing, and his mother hung the certificates from those classes on the ranch house walls. "The lessons taught, and the rules you laid down, have been with me constantly, and I look back to you as the beginning of my public career," McCarran wrote Booth years later. "It is with extreme gratitude that I always look back to the one who gave me the first words of encouragement, to the one who awakened me to the realization that it was possible for me to achieve something in life."[27] When McCarran graduated from high school in June 1897 he was the valedictorian of a class of sixteen. He was almost twenty-one years old.

That fall McCarran entered the University of Nevada, which by now consisted of eleven brick buildings and twenty-five teachers, three of whom had doctorates, one honorary. Cows and sheep kept the lawns clipped between the well-spaced buildings and skinny tree sprigs. Lincoln Hall was the brand-new dorm for ninety-five male students, while Manzanita Hall housed forty-five females. Half the three hundred students lived off campus. Many were farm folk more than a little disoriented by town. One freshman tried to ignite the school's new electric lights with matches. Some students worked their way through school by lining up at Dolph Shane's butcher shop on election day to vote repeatedly for candidates. McCarran earned his school money by shoveling coal into the university furnaces at four in the morning.

McCarran's best subject was political science, part of the History Department, which consisted of two professors. One was Joseph Stubbs, who was also president of the university and a classicist by training. Stubbs believed that the school's first mission was the moral education and ethical uplifting of its students — and he led a crusade against Reno's gambling halls, bars, and brothels. "To serve the government faithfully is one of the noblest of callings," he once explained. "Is there time for such teaching? Far better to take the minutes from any other subject taught in our public schools than to neglect in the slightest degree this all important foundation stone in the characters of our children: The teaching of patriotism."[28]

McCarran's other political science instructor was Anne Martin. She was a year older than McCarran himself, a product of the University of Nevada who had picked up a master's degree at Stanford and started teaching in Reno when McCarran was a freshman. Martin taught McCarran history, but she also tried to change it herself: She would become a leader of the fight to win women the right to vote, getting arrested for protesting at the White House and twice running for the Senate from Nevada. Martin was as radical a social critic as the state's soil ever produced. Nevada, she wrote in 1922 in *The Nation,* was the ugly duckling, the disappointment, the neglected stepchild, the weakling in the family of states. "With no large cities and a largely rural population, why has she a greater percentage in her jails and prison, her almshouses and insane asylum than certain of her neighbors?" she asked.[29] Her answer was that big livestock had a monopoly on the water rights and de facto control of federal rangelands. Called "Nevada: Beautiful Desert of Buried Hopes," the incendiary article went unnoticed in Nevada until the following year when the publisher of a book that was reprinting the piece approached Governor James Scrugham for a blurb. "Gross libel," he replied.[30] Martin's views did not rub off on her most famous student. Between Stubbs's patriotic verities and Martin's ceaseless questioning of the established order, there was no contest between whose outlook McCarran would mirror.

McCarran joined the football team, which had no coach and had to turn out early for games to pick rocks off the field. He won medals for shotput, javelin, and hurdles. He got picked to join the university's debating team, which went to Salt Lake City to compete against the state university there; the team lost, but McCarran was named the best debater at school. He was the sports editor of the student paper. Busy as McCarran appeared, he could never shake the feeling that he was not quite a part of things. "I was never sufficiently popular to become a member of any fraternity," he said years later. Having grown up practically by himself and having always been older than his classmates, McCarran was distrustful of clubs and cliques. "I am a great believer in the democracy of life," he said. "I believe that there is no man or no woman so insignificant, or even so bad, but that contains within himself or herself a scintillating light, as it were, a something worthy of the recognition and admiration of every other."[31] It was a light that was not easy for many to see. "He was rather peculiar," a fellow student remarked about McCarran, "and no one liked him much."[32]

By McCarran's third year his grades slid from fair to poor, and he pulled out of a number of classes. All the while he was a sheepman, having turned his bummer lambs into a flock of seven hundred breeding ewes, which he mortgaged to buy another seven hundred. While he was at school, McCarran's father took charge of the sheep. But in 1901 the old man, pushing seventy, fell from a wagon at the start of lambing season. His son had to take over both the sheep and the running of the ranch. In April of his senior year he quit college.

On the June night that his class was graduating McCarran was out working in the sheepfolds. Bleating lambs had stampeded a flock of ewes, mixing the two together. McCarran grew disgusted as he struggled to separate the flocks. Finally he gave up and left the sheep. He hitched up the wagon and took his mother to the university graduation. They sat in the auditorium watching his twenty-six classmates walk across the stage in their caps and gowns and pick up their diplomas. Maggie McCarran was not a woman given to tears, but that night she cried.

One day in 1902 McCarran was sweating in the corrals, separating some gummers (old sheep) that he wanted to put out to pasture from the rest of the flock, when a buggy drove up. Out stepped William E. Sharon, campaign manager for Francis Newlands, who had been the state's single congressman for the past decade and had his sights set on the Senate. Because that officeholder was still appointed by the state legislature,

Newland's elevation depended on his party controlling the votes in Carson City. McCarran had a passing acquaintance with Sharon but was surprised to see him that day. He hadn't shaved in two weeks. Sharon asked him to run on the Silver Democrat ticket for the assembly election. McCarran said he didn't know if he could spare the time from his sheep. Sharon persisted; McCarran agreed. He would join the Silver Democrats. The white metal, after all, was in his blood.

Nevada was not called the Silver State for nothing. "By and by I was smitten with the silver fever,"[33] Twain remembered, describing his short and unspectacular career in mining. "The human animal must be educated up to a just appreciation of gold," added Dan De Quille, "but silver by its brilliant white luster and flash in the light of the sun recommends itself to him as soon as its sheen strikes his eye."[34] For many in the West silver was more than just a precious metal; it was a grail, a lost covenant between agrarian America and its government. Congress originally created a currency backed by both silver and gold — based on a ratio of fifteen ounces of silver to one of gold. Later the ratio changed to sixteen to one — a phrase that gained totemic status in the West, the virtual birthright of free-born men. Gold was scare, hence expensive, beloved of eastern bankers and those insisting on a tight credit supply; silver was relatively plentiful, almost cheap, the metal of the little man, favored by farmers and the producing classes who wanted loose credit. "As the two legs are necessary to walk and two eyes to see, so were these two monies necessary to the prosperity of the people,"[35] William Hope Harvey, an avowed silverite, claimed.

Then, suddenly, silver dollars disappeared. In 1873 Congress, trying to clean up the monetary system, decided to stop minting silver dollars. Within three years the price of silver had fallen 21 percent. At the same time agricultural prices had been dropping since 1865, and by 1896 the dollar had trebled in value, meaning that a loan a farmer could have paid off with a thousand bushels of wheat at the end of the Civil War would cost him three thousand bushels thirty years later. To silverites the economic turbulence besetting America in the last quarter of the nineteenth century was not an accident; it was part of an international conspiracy by British bankers and Jewish financiers to demonetize silver and thus drive up the value of gold, enriching Wall Street while impoverishing Main Street. "The Crime of '73," they called it. "A crime," explained the aptly named Coin in William Hope Harvey's enormously popular *Coin's Financial School,* "because it has confiscated millions of dollars worth of property. A crime, because it has made thousands of paupers. A crime, because it has made thousands of suicides. A crime, because it has brought tears to strong men's eyes, and hunger and pinching want to widows and orphans. A crime, because it is destroying the honest yeomanry of the land, the bulwark of the nation. A crime, because it has brought this once great republic to the verge of ruin, where it is now in imminent danger of tottering to its fall."[36]

Silver was the cure. Make dollars from silver again and more money would slosh across the country, raising the incomes of farmers and miners and those who worked for a living. "The elixir that will restore Nevada to her former youth and freshness," declared the *Carson City Morning Appeal,* "is the restoration of silver."[37] General James Weaver carried this message across the country when he ran for president in 1892 as candidate of the People's (or Populist) Party. "It is a fight between labor and capital," he declared.[38] But it was not a fair fight, an aboveboard match; rather, it was the secret machinations of Wall Street and Lombard Street that were turning American farmers into serfs. "A vast conspiracy against mankind has been organized on two continents, and it is rapidly taking possession of the world," Ignatius Donnelly explained in his preamble to the People's Party platform. "If not met and overthrown at once it forebodes terrible social convulsions, the destruction of civilization, or the establishment of absolute despotism."[39]

No state was more receptive to this gospel than Nevada, where silverites by the thousands took an oath not to support any politician who didn't pledge his all for the white metal. "A subject of more interest to the people of the state of Nevada and every poor man in the United States than any other question of public policy,"[40] noted a newly arrived lawyer named Key Pittman. "I was always led to look at a silver man as a fanatic," added Tasker Oddie, the son of a partner at a Wall Street firm, after scarcely a year in the state, "but since I have been among them for so long, I have learned to respect their arguments."[41] In 1892 the silverites formed their own party, and when Weaver's train pulled into Virginia City that August the station was draped in bunting and flags; a brass band thundered its greeting, and bonfires blazed in celebration. Two thousand people filled the Piper Opera House and spilled into the surrounding streets to listen to a candidate who could not have been more popular if he had gone to Newcastle preaching a monetary system based on coal. The next day two rising state politicians, Francis Newlands and William Stewart, joined the state's Silver League. That November, Nevada gave its electoral votes to Weaver, who won only 8.5 percent of the popular vote nationally, and sent

Newlands to Congress besides giving the Silver Party control of the state assembly and a working majority in the Senate. "We are simply a homogenous mass of silver people," proclaimed Nevada's C. C. Wallace.[42]

In 1896 a young congressman whose hair was already disappearing at the temples took the stage at the Democratic National Convention in Chicago. William Jennings Bryan was thirty-six, the son of a stern, devout judge from Illinois whose boyhood Sabbaths had been filled with Sunday school (he went to a Baptist one to please his father and a Methodist one for his mother but eventually became a Presbyterian himself) and who grew up with an intense moral fervor, a crusading zeal that would have carried him into the pulpit if the prospect of a baptismal dunking hadn't scared him away. Bryan never lost his righteous fury and in school turned to secular oratory with a religious vengeance, speaking with marbles in his mouth to improve his pronunciation, rehearsing speeches to trees in the woods — where he once sent a group of picnickers fleeing when they mistook him for an escapee from an insane asylum. His diversions, his wife recalled, were Sunday school, church, prayer meetings, an occasional church social, and once in a while a good circus. Bryan became a lawyer, moved to Nebraska, and quickly established himself as a masterful speaker whose moral surety and rich, booming voice captivated crowds. "He smiled," Mary Bryan remembered, "and the smile rippled away over his listeners; he frowned, and so did they; he grew tense with emotion, they bent forward and sat upon the very edge of the seats." "I could move them as I chose,"[43] he told his wife and then prayed that he would never abuse his power. Bryan quickly gained a national reputation when he arrived in Washington in 1892 and delivered a bewitching three-hour speech on the binding twine tariff.

But it was his oration four years later at the Chicago Coliseum that would make Bryan the presidential candidate of both the Democrats and the Populists. "You come to us and tell us that the great cities are in favor of the gold standard," he roared. "We reply that the great cities rest upon our broad and fertile prairies. Burn down your cities and leave our farms, and your cities will spring up again as if by magic; but destroy our farms and the grass will grow in the streets of every city in the country. . . . You shall not press down upon the brow of labor this crown of thorns, you shall not crucify mankind upon a cross of gold."[44]

Bryan stretched out his arms and threw back his head, and the largest exhibition building in the world was quiet as a church; then twenty thousand people thundered their approval. "God has sent you amongst our

people to save the poor from starvation and we no [*sic*] you will save us,"
marveled a letter writer from Indiana.[45] Bryan campaigned with a preter-
natural passion, traveling eighteen thousand miles in three months, sometimes giving thirty speeches a day. He won twenty-two states, virtually all
of the West and South, and more votes than any presidential candidate ever
had before — although not enough to beat William McKinley. Nevada
gave him 8,376 of its 10,314 votes. Bryan might have lost the election, but
he became a hero to an entire generation, including a twenty-year-old
farm boy going to school in Reno and earnestly trying to master the art
of oratory himself.

McCarran had left the ranch to study in the city the year before
Nevada's Silver Party held its founding convention in the Reno Opera
House in 1892. For much of the rest of the decade, as McCarran went
to high school and college, he inhabited a hothouse of silver theology.
"The dominant party in Nevada is neither Republican, Democratic nor
Populist," noted the *Review of Reviews,* "its sole raison d'être is its
demand for free silver."[46] McCarran grew up in a home in which the
British were hated (his father ran a Sinn Fein flag up at the ranch) and
in a state where an international banking conspiracy conveniently
explained Nevada's twenty-year depression. The silverite weltan-
schauung tied up these twin antipathies into a nice bundle, revealing that
the privations America endured as it stumbled out of the nineteenth
century and into the industrial age were not random dislocations or the
results of demographic and historical trends, but rather part of some
grand plan. "I am here to destroy the United States,"[47] a British Jewish
banker in Coin Harvey's *A Tale of Two Nations* announced forthrightly.
Harvey was the literary impresario of silver par excellence, and his book
made clear that the foreign plot to turn America into a serf nation could
only succeed with the help of the enemy within (his banker bribed a
senator to push the United States onto the gold standard). "The United
States," Harvey added in a later book, *The Patriots of America,* "has been
honeycombed by foreign influences and our property is rapidly passing
into their hands."[48] It was a lesson that McCarran would learn well. "The
greatest value in the world is human energy, and brain, brawn and
muscle are represented in every ounce of silver we produce," he said
once. "But there is no human energy represented in printing presses.
Remonetization of silver is not inflation, but the printing of billions of
paper money with no metal backing is inflation."[49]

McCarran would carry the silver gospel in his heart for the rest of his life, its tropes and truisms providing him a worldview that would explain not only monetary policy but, later, international Communism as well.

In 1902 McCarran joined the Silver Democrats and ran for one of the seven seats representing Washoe County. He took out a two-thousand-dollar mortgage on the ranch and campaigned in a buckboard with his fellow candidate Herman Cooke, who passed out cigars while McCarran gave speeches urging the passage of an eight-hour workday for miners, millers, and smelters. McCarran finished sixth.

On a Sunday in late January 1903 McCarran took the train to Carson City, which was filling up with assemblymen for the brief legislative session, held once every two years. Even for the several weeks of its existence there often wasn't enough business to give the lawmakers anything to do in the afternoon except hang out at the Arlington Hotel with lobbyists. "Wine and punch were as free as water," McCarran noted.[50] He had made a deal with the *Reno Evening Gazette* to become its assembly correspondent in Carson City. When the assembly met at 11 A.M., McCarran's first act as a lawmaker set the tone for the rest of his life as a legislator: He objected to the expense of the assembly hiring a minister to open its session. He lost this first fight, but another came quickly. Assembly Bill Number 1 was introduced and would have prevented the grazing of sheep within two miles of dwellings. McCarran was on the floor at once. "The red hand of foreign power is very evident in it," he declared.[51] The bill would stop a man from grazing sheep on his own land if someone else had a house nearby. What authority does the legislature have to interfere with a man's property rights like that? McCarran fought the bill with arguments and amendments, but it carried 21 to 12. McCarran managed to get the bill reconsidered. He tried more amendments, and he tried delaying the vote in the hope that some of the members wouldn't show up — all to no avail. The bill passed again, but McCarran's fight against it dominated his dispatches from the capital. "It was from the first," he wrote, "a scene of strife."[52]

The session lasted two months. Then it was back to the ranch.

Before McCarran set off for Carson City he had to make another trip. He took the train most of the way across Nevada to the northeastern corner of the state, where purple sage and green junipers covered the land, and in a cleft between the snow-topped Humboldt Mountains blue haze filled a valley. There in a one-room school in a town too small to have either a post

office or a general store, McCarran sat at a desk and asked a young teacher
to go to the inaugural ball, where five hundred of the state's elite would
gather in the Carson City Opera House to shake hands with the governor
and dance into the early hours.

Her name was Martha Harriet Weeks, Birdie to her family. She was six
years younger than McCarran and had been in the class behind him at the
university. Her family had settled in Clover Valley in 1872. The fourth of
seven children of Samuel Tyler and Martha Ann Wood Weeks, Martha
Weeks was a short, timid, dark-eyed woman whom McCarran had met at
a school dance. She'd come with someone else. Her smile felt like sunshine
on his face. He took her to the next dance. She graduated and returned
home to teach in the valley. He wrote her letters.

When the rancher and politician with the thick dark hair and wide
smile came calling to Clover Valley, Birdie was thrilled. She hired a dress-
maker for the ball, who created a pale lavender grown that Weeks never
got to wear. As soon as her brothers found out that the young woman was
planning to journey across the state by herself to go to a gala with a
Catholic, they made her call off the date.

McCarran went back to the valley. In the sitting room of the Bulls
Head Hotel, McCarran took out an engagement ring and asked Birdie to
marry him. "I remember you cried," he wrote to her forty years later, "and
I wondered why you would cry and you said because you were happy and
I was happy."[53] The couple drove to her house, where her father and sisters looked over the young man and teased her. Then they went to the
train station in Wells. She wished the train would never come.

In August 1903 the couple was married by an Episcopal bishop in
Clover Valley before they caught the train at Wells for a honeymoon in San
Francisco, where they were remarried in a Catholic church. Later Birdie
would convert to her husband's religion. "Dear Girl," he told her forty
years later, "I never really know how much you are to me until I am away
from you. Then you come to seem so lovely, more lovely even than in the
old days when we sat at the old wall and you said yes, more lovely than
when your hair and mine was dark and yours was so beautiful. Now the
gray mixed with the dark crowns your lean face and I know as you must
know that to me you are now the girl I knew and the mother I know
crowned by the glory of fine years — years that have matured us both,
years through which we endured, you endured all my failings and faults
and short comings and I endured to learn to love my sweetheart of the
yester years more, and to miss her more when she is away from me because

there is no one who knows me so well nor who would endure and forgive so much."[54]

In spring the walking began. The constant work of lambing season was over,
the hired hands had drifted away, and McCarran was alone with his sheep,
wandering the vast public grazing lands of the West until it was time to
return to the ranch for the fall shearing. It was just about the loneliest life a
man could imagine. McCarran would rise with the stars, eating breakfast
before the sheep began stirring at first light. Then it was on to the trail,
grazing the animals across the sagebrush before the buds got too hot for the
sheep to nibble. At noon came a break, followed by more grazing until sundown. Wherever the sheep stopped, the shepherd stopped, throwing down
a bedroll beneath the stars, sleeping with an ear open for the clang of the
sheep bells: A slow, solitary peal meant a ewe wandering off, a faster toll signaled a run, a riot of rings the alarm that something was attacking the flock.
Now and then a ewe would bleat for a lost lamb, but mostly the sheep were
a silent presence, a sea moving without a sound. "In a year we would walk
thousands of miles," one sheepman remembered. "But that wasn't the hard
part. The hard part was the loneliness. You would almost die from the loneliness, just to hear a human voice."[55]

McCarran walked endlessly, trudging through the Truckee Meadows,
hiking up the foothills of the Carson Range, higher still into the Sierra,
where smooth granite domes stood guard over glacial valleys patched with
snow until late summer, then down the other side of the mountains into
Plumas County where the flock grew heavy on the grass of the California
high country. Every couple of weeks a camptender would come looking
for McCarran with a new supply of food. Sometimes they would miss one
another and McCarran would move on; the sheep still had to eat. "On
through the forest ever higher we go, a cloud of dust dimming the way,
thousands of feet trampling leaves and flowers, but in this mighty wilderness they seem but a feeble band," wrote John Muir, who also herded
sheep in the Sierra. ". . . Poor, helpless, hungry sheep, in great part misbe-
gotten, without good right to be, semi-manufactured, made less by God
than man, born out of time and place, yet their voices are strangely human
and call out one's pity."[56]

Most of those on the sheep trail were Basques. Many came to the New
World with a job waiting in the West and not a word of English, other
than the name of their destination pinned to a beret. Out on the range
they might bump into a cousin without recognizing the man, his face so

sun blackened that he looked almost African. Few would have taken the job had they known how howlingly lonely it would be. "You would have to see that country to believe it, but it was so big that even from the top of the highest hill I couldn't see a town or a house, except one little cabin and a corral . . . ," recalled Dominique Laxalt, a Basque contemporary of McCarran's. "Oh, how cruel a country that was. It wasn't like the Pyrenees, . . . For as far as you could see, there was sagebrush and rocks, and the only trees were rutted little junipers. Herding in that country was something I never dreamed could be. There was so little feed that the sheep would wake up before daylight and never stop until it was dark, and it was all even a young man could to keep up with them. If I didn't have the dog, I couldn't have done it. . . . They were so tough you wouldn't believe it, with strong legs and feet like leather, even though sometimes after a couple of days on the hillsides where it was rocky I would have to wrap my dog's feet in burlap to keep them from bleeding. Those slopes with the rocks were something, even for a man. A pair of boots wouldn't last you two weeks, they would be so torn up."[57]

This was not the future Maggie McCarran wanted for her boy, trailing sheep across the scrub like some Bosco just off the train who couldn't even speak English. She hadn't worked her fingers to the bone so her son could walk the wastes of the range until he went mad — getting sage-brushed or sheeped, the Basques called it. It might be good hard work to the elder Patrick McCarran, but to his wife sheepherding was beneath her only son. The boy had brains. If he would just apply himself he could do anything. McCarran's old teacher Libby Booth agreed. "These were two people," McCarran recalled, ". . . who were bound and determined that I should not persist in the sheep business and should take up what to their mind was my real bent, law."[58] So McCarran began asking lawyers in town what he should do to study the subject. He borrowed legal books and, after bedding his flock for the night, held Blackstone close to the camp-fire and read into the small hours. During the day he taught himself the art of public speaking, standing before his flock and declaiming law and philosophy to the incurious sheep, a livelier audience to be sure than the trees that Bryan had spoken to. "If the individual would be strong, he must rely on himself," McCarran boomed in a typical speech. "He must trust himself. He must have implicit confidence in his own power to perform, never for a moment doubting himself. Self-reliance is not self-sufficiency or conceit. . . . Self-reliance, as contrasted with empty conceit, is daring to stand alone. Be an oak, not a vine. Be ready to give support, but never crave it, never depend on it. Say and do and declare what you believe to be right; openly and frankly condemn what you honestly believe to be wrong. . . . It should matter not what anybody thinks or says so long as the central altar of our own motive is clear and clean. Life is a battle which the individual must fight for himself. He must be his own soldier. He cannot buy a substitute. He cannot win a reprieve. He can never be placed on the retired list — the retired list of life is death."[59]

There was no applause when he finished, only a few indifferent bleats. It was enough to try even the most self-reliant of men.

As the Sierra summer waned, McCarran recrossed the mountains, melting snow forming small pools by the hundreds that spangled the granite heights above the tree line like diamonds cast from the heavens. Late-blooming carpets of wildflowers covered pastures with lilies, columbines, larkspurs, and lupines. "Flowers everywhere . . . acres of them . . . fields of them," McCarran remembered. "Our forests of wild lupines that grow knee-high are prettier than the tame lupines that gardeners know. Then, over all the wild flowers the sky takes on delicate colors — unbelievably wonderful colors."[60] Down into the cooling desert McCarran trailed his flock, heavy with their summer feast, their wool hanging like dreadlocks so thick that you couldn't see their hooves.

Back at the ranch on the Truckee it was shearing season, when dogs chased the wool-blind sheep through chutes and into the skilled arms of traveling trimmers, who shaved the wool to the pink with sharp oversized barber clippers, holding a ewe with one hand and a knee, their palms as soft as a baby's bottom from being exposed to lanolin day after day. The weather was critical. On warm, sunny days the wool slid off easily, but when it turned cold the sheepskin puckered and the fleece came off grudgingly — and the sheep wound up nicked worse than a drunk trying to shave. Then the shearing had to stop and the unshorn got mixed back with the naked sheep to keep them warm. After spending the better part of a year trying to protect his flock, it was time to put some of the plump sheep on the train to San Francisco. One fall McCarran shipped his yearling wethers west, where they turned out to be the heaviest on the market, fetching top dollar. "Mr. McCarran," the *Nevada State Journal* proclaimed, "is the youngest sheep man in Nevada, and is one of the most successful."[61] The writer might as well have been mocking Maggie McCarran.

One day as Maggie McCarran sat on the small porch of the ranch house with her son, her prayers were answered. A hired hand was driving

McCarran's prized flock of black-faced Merinos across the tracks. A Southern Pacific locomotive shrieked down into the valley. The train plowed through the flock like a bullet through a bale of wool. Ewes flew through the air.

Pat McCarran's sheep days were numbered.

CHAPTER 2

To the Last Ditch

> In such a wilderness, the tempo is — always has been —
> that each man should be capable of looking out for him-
> self. If he is not capable he can get out, he can go "over
> the hill," meaning over the Sierra to California. If he
> wants to gamble, the prerogative is his own. But he must
> not hang around whining if he loses, nor ask the state for
> recompense, nor for a free living ever afterwards. But in
> this Nevada the word gambling is a broad term. The
> word reaches beyond the Methodists' conception of it.
> Cattlemen are gamblers. Each season in this dry land is a
> gamble with them. The same with sheepmen, miners,
> and certainly with prospectors. Not to gamble in Nevada
> would mean not to be working for a living.[1]
>
> — Max Miller

Old Patrick McCarran swung the lantern as soon as he heard the train. When the locomotive groaned to a stop at the siding he helped his two grandchildren and their mother aboard. It was good to do something. Old age was not an easy time for McCarran. After the fall from the wagon he could no longer do much heavy labor on the ranch, sitting instead for hours on a buckboard seat fitted on two stumps next to the house he had built. There he whittled until the pile of shavings was knee high; then he swept up and started again.

McCarran's hair and beard had gone white but were both still thick, and his frame had stayed wiry long after he'd given up digging ditches and cutting sagebrush. And the McCarran temper still flared brightly when-ever the old man was crossed. When the U.S. government planted forty telegraph poles along the railroad tracks and across his ranch in 1904, McCarran had them cut down and stacked in his yard like an outsized woodpile. A government engineer came by and told McCarran to replace the poles or face charges for stealing eight dollars' worth of federal prop-erty. Go to hell, McCarran told him. The next visitor to the ranch was a U.S. marshal, who arrested the septuagenarian. McCarran was released on five hundred dollars' bail (he signed the form with his X) and went on trial in Carson City in July 1905.

His lawyer was his son, Pat. Young McCarran, his knees shaking, had passed the oral bar exam the month before. His first client was his father, who had to be restrained by two men in court during the two-day trial. McCarran put himself on the stand and testified that he, not the older man, had actually cut down the poles. The jury acquitted the elder McCarran. The prosecutor accused young McCarran of lying and announced that he would seek to indict him for perjury. Charges, however, were never filed. McCarran had found his calling. McCarran sold his sheep and decided to set up shop in the fastest-growing part of the state, a new boomtown 230 miles to the south, high in the desolate mountains of central Nevada where fortunes were being made and lost and a young man could easily make a name for himself. After opening an office and finding a small house, McCarran sent for his wife and two daughters — two-year-old Margaret and the newborn Mary — to join him. And on this day in 1906 old man McCarran put the young family on the train.

They were going to Tonopah.[2]

This, Tasker Oddie wrote to his mother in September 1900, might be it. For the past two years Oddie had been scratching around the wastes of central Nevada, looking for a fortune. The son of a partner at a Wall Street firm, Oddie was born in Brooklyn in 1870, grew up in New Jersey, and spent two years as a teenager on a ranch in Nebraska, where he fell in love with horses and wide-open country. After graduating from night law school, Oddie took a job with a real-estate company that dispatched him to oversee its mining interests in Nevada. Arriving in Austin, a town almost sixty-six hundred feet high in the Toiyabe Mountains in the dead center of the state, Oddie was instantly smitten. "It is very romantic in every way and the most ideal place to live in I can imagine," he told his mother. "The air is simply delightful and the climate is as fine as any that can be found."[3]

Oddie decided he wanted to be a miner himself. Central Nevada was studded with abandoned mines — claims that had discouraged the less hopeful but which a prospector with the proper perseverance might turn to profit. "Instead of looking forward to being a clerk all my life," Oddie wrote home, "I will have a chance to make myself somebody."[4] He invested fifteen dollars in geology books, enrolled in a mining engineering correspondence school course, bought a tent, a heavy piece of duck cloth to wrap around his blankets at night, and a rubber mat to sleep on, and set off into the wilds of Nye County — 18,294 square miles that was home to

1,140 residents, not counting Indians. Following rude roads or cattle trails on his horse, Oddie rode up one range of mountains and down another for hundreds of hard miles in search of a suitable mine. In places the path was more tunnel than trail, and Oddie had to press himself almost flat against the horse to pass under the brush. His mules seemed to rub up against trees on purpose, sloughing off their heavy packs and spilling gear in their dusty wake. When Oddie inspected a claim high above the tree line and turned the mules out to graze with their front legs tied together, the beasts hobbled down the mountain; he had to track them into the night. "More perverse, stubborn, mean devils never lived," he said. "Their sole aim in life was to torment the soul out of me every day."[5] Meanwhile his fine horse grew thin and broken from constant labor and little but sage grazing. "I had to cross two summits which were holy terrors as they were covered with snow and ice and it took me four hours to get across," he told his mother. "The snow had melted some during the day and frozen in the road in the evening, so my horse slid around like a girl learning to skate."[6]

The hard work really started when Oddie went into a mine that had been someone else's bad luck. Holding a drill bit with one hand, Oddie swung a four-pound hammer again and again and again, often whacking his hand with what felt like a ton of bricks. Fine rocks and dirt collected in his collar and sleeves, his socks and his shoes. And after ninety minutes he would have a hole deep enough to pack two sticks of blasting powder. But blowing up rock was an art, and knowing where to stuff the charges to follow the slopes and bends of a vein of ore was a skill that was slowly mastered. Once Oddie lit a fuse and ran out of the tunnel only to see ore fly out after him, raining down on his camp in the canyon below, rattling onto his dishes and pans and kettle, and sending up a cloud of ash from the firepit. Another time he swung the hammer into his nose and almost knocked himself out. Some stone was so hard that Oddie was lucky to gain twelve inches after a whole day of hammering and blasting, dulling a dozen drills that he would have to sharpen himself before attacking the rock again. "A man mining earns all he gets out of it," Oddie told his mother.[7]

The work was ceaseless. When a shaft needed timbering to keep it from caving in, Oddie climbed back below the tree line, hacked down whatever scrub wood he could find, and dragged the trunks up the mountain over his shoulder. In the tunnels he shoveled loose rock into a wheelbarrow and pushed it along a wooden track, frequently running off the narrow plank and into the mud of the mine. He filled buckets with two hundred pounds of rock and then leaned into the hand crank of a windlass to raise the rubble out of the ground. One day he tripped on a board while pushing out a load of granite and pitched himself into the wheelbarrow, bashing his arm badly, gashing himself over his eye, and covering his face with blood. After a while the air grew so bad in the tunnels that a candle wouldn't burn. Then it was time to collect stunted mountain mahogany and kindle a fire that burned so hot that whatever Oddie dropped into his pan blackened before it cooked. A meal of baking powder bread, bacon, and coffee and then Oddie would lie on his back and look up at the stars filling the vast Nevada sky like a million promises. It was, he thought before drifting off to sleep around eight in the evening, a beautiful country.

After two years of hard labor Oddie had little to show but black fingernails and thickened hands. He was tall and lean and tan, pushing thirty, bald, broke, and eternally optimistic. He borrowed money to keep going and had his widowed mother take a mortgage out on her house. "It means much hard work and worry, but it also means that I may strike it rich and make a good deal of money," he tried to reassure her. "If I fail it will not be because I did not try."[8]

Then luck found Oddie. His friend Jim Butler needed some help. Butler had picked up promising ore samples along a windswept cleft in the San Antonio Mountains, but he didn't have the money to get an assay. He offered Oddie a share in the mine if he could get the ore examined. Oddie, too, was broke. He promised a slice of his slice to another friend, Walter Gayhart, a principal who moonlighted as an assayist. "If these assay well," Oddie wrote home, "we will go down right away and look at the property, because it may turn out to be a rich one."[9]

The sample was loaded with gold and silver — the first glimmer of a $110 million bonanza.

Oddie and friends borrowed twenty-five dollars to buy food and supplies and subdivided another share to get a wagon and a team; then they made the two-day trek south from the town of Belmont to the place that would become known as Tonopah. Oddie walked ahead of the wagon with a pick, clearing brush and rocks out of the way. Even by Nevada standards Tonopah was barren and remote. Roughly south of Austin, north of Death Valley, east of Yosemite, and west of hell, Tonopah was a moonscape six-thousand-feet high in the San Antonio Mountains. The nearest spring was three miles away, trees fifteen. "It is a hard country to rustle in for man and beast," Oddie told his mother, "but as long as the mines turn out well, I will not care."[10]

They dug two tons of ore from the rock then sent it in a wagon rum-
bling down the hill to a narrow-gauge railroad sixty miles away. It fetched
five hundred dollars. The word spread: A huge silver strike was on in
Tonopah, followed two years later by a massive gold find thirty miles
south across the Esmeralda County line in Goldfield. Nevada's twenty-
year depression, in which it had lost a third of its population, was over. In
the next decade the number of people in the state almost doubled, to
81,900, with Goldfield becoming Nevada's largest city: It had more than
15,000 residents in 1907. "Our camp has been a source of great good to
the surrounding country for several hundred miles," Oddie boasted. "All
this country was in a dormant, stagnant state, and Tonopah has set it all
ablaze with excitement."[11]

Located in a high gap in a bleak range of sawtooth mountains, between
Mount Butler and Mount Oddie, Tonopah had no water, no trees, nothing
but blowing sand and, in winter, deep drifts of snow. Then a tent city
popped up. Nights were so cold that people slept with clocks under their
pillows to keep them from freezing. Soon men were crawling over the
hills like ants, and otherworldly mountains of tailings grew high like the
scat of the gods. The new residents dug holes in the ground or built
shanties of tin cans, packing crates, glass bottles — anything that could be
cobbled together into rude shelter. By 1902 there was a post office, a
newspaper, and a local chapter of the Western Federation of Miners.

Night and day the dull thunder of underground blasting rocked the
town, while a donkey engine filled the dim hours with a steady wheezing.
As the town grew, another sound was added: three blasts of a whistle and
the roar of an ambulance up to the mines when an accident took place.
Three shifts kept the mines running twenty-four hours a day. "If you had
millions under the ground," Hugh Brown explained, "wouldn't you be in
a hurry to get them out?"[12]

Not all fortune seekers were welcomed. The Chinese were banned
from the mines and had to cook or clean for a living (although the better
restaurants would boast "No Chinese employed"). Even that proved too
much for some townsfolk to endure. One night in 1903 dozens of men
invaded homes in the Chinese part of town on the west end of Tonopah,
pulled people from their beds, and told them to leave by noon or face a
public hanging. A smaller mob marched a group of Chinese immigrants a
mile out of town in their pajamas and beat them. The next day the bruised
body of one was found. Eighteen men, all members of the Tonopah Labor
Union, were arrested. But the only ones to get punished were two

deputies, fired by the Nye County sheriff for investigating the case too zealously. "It might now be in order," opined one newspaper editor, "to bring the Chinamen into court — all but the one who happened to die — and prosecute them for taking up so much of the public's time over this trivial matter."[13]

Tonopah might be sitting atop a fortune, but the town soon resembled a slum. Dead horses were dragged to the edge of town and left to rot on the road, packs of dogs snuffed through mounds of garbage, and tin cans skittered down the streets in the raking winds. The young district attorney, William Pittman, got sick just walking around and declared that he was going to clean up Tonopah. "There will be no more rivers of swill and slime," he promised.[14]

Butler and his partners sold out in July 1901 to an eastern firm, and Oddie became general manager of the Tonopah Mining Company. "It makes me wild to think that we sold out the mines when we did, but Butler held the controlling interest, and so I told him I would do what he did, and he wanted to sell," Oddie lamented. "The mines have increased in value fully 500% since they were sold."[15] Oddie prospered. He invested in mines and real estate. He built a rambling house in town, hired a Chinese cook, imported fresh fruit and oysters by train from San Francisco, and once threw a candlelit dinner party deep in the Mizpah mine, where three hundred feet below the surface miners played accordions and a banjo while twenty guests danced. He gave money to the library fund-raising campaign in Tonopah, brought his mother and two sisters out from the East, and married a New York divorcée.

But his real passion was ranching. In 1902 Oddie purchased Pine Creek Ranch in Monitor Valley, about sixty miles northeast of Tonopah at the base of twelve-thousand-foot Mount Jefferson. "The ranch itself is the prettiest one in the county," he said proudly.[16] Located at the mouth of a canyon, it was well watered by trout-filled streams that tumbled down steep gorges into the valley. Oddie raised blooded cattle, prize Hereford bulls, and thoroughbred horses. At eight thousand feet, the ranch was an oasis from Nevada's brutal summers. Oddie's nine-room house filled with friends who rode horses in the hills and spent warm evenings on the wide porch while the dying sun enveloped the crags of the valley in warm colors and shadows. All the years of work seemed worth it. "Later on in life I will feel that I will always have a fine ranch to go to," Oddie beamed. "I love such a place."[17]

When a rail-thin lawyer named Key Pittman climbed off the stage at
Tonopah after a grueling sixty-mile, eighteen-hour ride from the train station at Sodaville, he found one pathetic hotel, the Mizpah, but there were
thirty-two saloons, two dance halls, and six faro parlors. Pittman was in
heaven. "I am thinking of making our home in Nevada, and growing up
with the country," he wrote to his wife, Mimosa, in San Francisco. "I see
many opportunities here both in law, mines and polytics [sic]."[18]

Pittman was born in 1872 in Mississippi, the eldest son of a prosperous
attorney. He attended Southwestern Presbyterian University in Clarksville,
near Nashville, but was a so-so student and dropped out during his third year.
He wound up in Seattle, working as a lawyer. When gold was discovered in
the Klondike in 1897, he headed north to Alaska with a friend. Landing in
Skagway Bay, seven hundred miles from the mining town of Dawson, they
hauled one hundred pounds of gear each over a tortuous forty-mile path, so
treacherous that the bloated bodies of pack animals lined the way, giving it
the name Dead Horse Trail. At Lake Bennet they cut trees and built a boat,
sailing up the Yukon past the wrecks of those who came before, Pittman
rowing into rapids that sent most scrambling to the river's edge. Eighty miles
from Dawson the river froze; the two hiked the rest of the way, arriving six
weeks after they had left Seattle. Pittman didn't get rich, but he did earn a
reputation as a wildman, a heavy drinker who was said to have killed a man
and impregnated a woman. Pittman also found his bride, Mimosa, whom he
met when their dogsleds almost collided. "It took more courage for her to
marry Key Pittman than to face the Yukon trail," recalled a friend.[19]

Pittman came to Tonopah in 1902 still seeking his fortune. This time he
found it, setting up a thriving law practice that kept him busy thirteen hours
a day; he worked for corporate clients such as Charles M. Schwab, picked up
lucrative mining holdings, and sat on the boards of more than one hundred
mining, banking, and utility companies, all of which made him a wealthy
man but did little to assuage his persistent self-loathing. "I never was right and
never can be," he once confessed. "God created me to be a horrible mistake."[20] Pittman was often separated from his wife and by more than mere
geography. "I am so miserable and lonesome," he wrote her. "I can't live
without you — come back to me, say what you want to me — treat me with
contempt, ridicule me, tell me every day that I am a liar and a coward and
though I will suffer, I am ready to endure it. . . . I deserve nothing."[21]

Alcohol helped, and Pittman was soon one of the most famous rummies in the state, his drunkenly waved pistol a familiar sight. "He'd get lit and he was heartless, reckless, and he was apt to do anything," noted one observer. "Shoot up in the air and shoot at anything."[22] Pittman and his wife, who also had a fondness for the bottle, even signed a contract, in front of witnesses, that "drinking alcoholic liquor with all of its dissatisfaction and consequences and that dissipations of any sort no matter what they may lead to — shall not be grounds for complaint or divorce."[23] Theirs was a stormy, tortured marriage, but it would endure. Mimosa lied to her husband about her age and hid financial investments from him. He longed for her affection, hated her for denying it. "You are killing my love and my ambition — Of course it is useless to say anything and impossible to do anything," he raged at her once. "You discourage me, humiliate me and destroy in me every desire."[24]

Pittman sought approval in politics, and soon after arriving in Tonopah was talking about running for the legislature. He joined the Silver Party and later jumped to the Democratic Party. "Bryan at my age had been two terms in Congress and two years later was the nominee for President of the United States," he wrote his wife on his thirty-second birthday. "I realize that I am not mature, not suited, not determined."[25]

Pittman underestimated himself. A decade after arriving in Nevada he would win his first elective office — the U.S. Senate. But politics, he would discover, did not soothe his demons, either. "For months my mind worked ceaselessly, and with a feverish energy," he explained. "My willpower was at such times taxed to the extreme by every form of self-denial. My temper was subjected to my mind and every act was marked by patience and clarity — Then came the reaction. The breaking of the other chain — The surrender and abandonment. A mania seized me, you cannot understand it, and no one can explain — and my growing desire was to escape from myself, from my thoughts, from my will. All of the savage in man asserted itself in me. I longed for, and nothing satisfied me but the most intense excitement — I longed to murder, kill and howl with delight at the sound of death dealing instruments and the sight of human blood."[26]

Key Pittman was often wobbly on his feet with drink, but he could stand firmly enough to block Pat McCarran's greatest goal for years.

Not long before dawn on April 7, 1906, Walter Barieau walked into a brothel called the Jewel — "a notorious house" as the newspapers would soon label it — in the mining camp of Manhattan. Barieau, whose

handlebar mustache looked ready to fly off his face and made up for the hair
he was losing on his head, had been born in Boston in 1869, came west as
a child, spun the roulette wheel in a club in nearby Tonopah for a while, and
now pretty much lived by gambling in the mining towns of Nye County.
His was not the most welcome face in a bar in central Nevada. A year earlier, it was rumored, he had pulled a knife in a bar fight and dodged three
shots fired at him; several weeks before he had been chained to a tree by a
deputy for public drunkenness.

Now, as the sun lit the eastern edge of the Nevada desert, Barieau
wanted a drink. He downed a glass and flopped onto a sofa. The man at
the piano stopped playing. May Biggs, the proprietress of the establishment, walked over and ordered Barieau to beat it. He dragged himself
toward the door. She gave him a shove. Barieau jabbed back at Biggs with
his elbow, hitting her arm, and Biggs screamed. Bouncing out of bed in
another room, a man in a nightshirt rushed up to Barieau and punched
him. Barieau tried to back out of the saloon doors as the man whacked
him in the head with something hard and heavy. Barieau could see the
butt of a pistol beating down on him. He pulled out his own gun, fired,
stumbled out the doors, and fired four more shots. The two grappled in
front of the saloon. Like a bad movie it ended with the piano player
conking Barieau over the head with the butt of a pistol.

Walt Barieau's troubles were just beginning. He had killed Tom Logan,
the county's beloved sheriff. Logan was forty-five, a Nevada native with a
wife and eight children who had been sheriff for seven years. He was
friends with Oddie and Pittman and indeed virtually everyone in Tonopah.
"Logan," one contemporary recalled, "was one of the most popular men
in Southwestern Nevada."[27] A week after his shooting, thousands flocked
to Tonopah's opera house to view Logan's body, piling flowers high around
the casket. The large hall was packed long before the service began,
mourners spilling into the surrounding streets. Shops and mines closed for
the day, and for once the dull roar of underground blasting ceased. Few
could remember a longer funeral procession in the state. A band beat a
bleak dirge as the bereaved followed Logan's coffin on the fire department's truck, slowly winding its way through the sad streets of Tonopah to
the cemetery on the edge of town. The sun had set before the last
mourner dragged himself away. "The cold blooded murder of Nye
County's popular sheriff, by an absinthe fiend last Saturday," the weekly
Bonanza newspaper reported, "has been the sole topic of conversation by
the people of Tonopah during the past week and on every hand the opinion

was expressed that the inhuman wretch who committed the foul deed should be given a speedy trial and a chance to dangle at the end of a rope."[28]

Lawyers were not lining up to save Walt Barieau from the gallows. Pat McCarran had been in Tonopah for nearly eight months. He opened an office in the new Broker's Exchange building, a block off Main Street, but clients were scarce when he jostled into the packed courtroom for Barieau's arraignment.

Judge Peter Breen asked Barieau, whose face was bruised and his eyes swollen from the fight, if he had counsel. No, he replied. Did he have the means to retain a lawyer? No. Did he want the court to appoint one for him? Yes. Breen looked at McCarran. "I had heard that there might be occasions in one's life when his knees would go out from under him but I never believed it to be true until that moment," McCarran recalled. "And then for the first time I realized what it was to be possessed of fear, embarrassment and consternation."[29]

McCarran was picked to defend the man who killed Tom Logan. The words of an old attorney who had given him guidance when he was studying law popped into McCarran's mind. "When you enter into a man's case, never give up," the lawyer said. "Go through with him to the last ditch."[30]

On Monday, July 9, 1906, a hush fell over the courtroom when Judge Breen gaveled the murder trial to start. Heads turned, necks stretched, and people whispered to one another as a deputy led Barieau to the defense table where McCarran and cocounsel S. P. Flynn stood. District Attorney William Pittman, friend of Logan, brother of Key, put May Biggs on the stand. Waving her arms excitedly, the proprietress of the Jewel described how Barieau had refused to leave, struck her, and then brawled with Logan before shooting the sheriff. When it came time for the cross-examination, McCarran questioned Biggs about the gifts that the married Logan had showered on the madam. Logan had given her expensive vases and a pair of diamond earrings worth six hundred dollars; he even bought the lumber used to build the brothel. McCarran's strategy was to show that Logan had been led astray by a temptress, and he passed lightly over the actions of the sheriff, who was also the tax collector for the county, the coffers of which were discovered to be missing nine thousand dollars after Logan's death. On Wednesday, Barieau took the stand and explained how a man started beating him without saying a word. "I did not know that he was Thomas Logan, the sheriff of this county," he testified. "I had never seen the man before."[31]

In his closing argument McCarran attacked the two prosecution witnesses, charging that the piano player and the madam were lying. May Biggs, McCarran implied, actually bore some responsibility for Logan's death, for corrupting the sheriff, causing him to neglect his family and lavish time and money on her. "An enchantress," McCarran called her, "who had wound herself into the life of a man inclined to do right and making him a slave to her every will and wish."[32]

Pittman broke down during his summation and cried his way through his closing argument. The jury, many of whom knew Logan, too, cried as well. By Friday lunchtime the trial was over. The jury went into deliberations at twelve-thirty, broke for dinner, and slept in cots in the courthouse. On the streets of Tonopah no one talked about anything but the trial. The smart money was on at least a verdict of manslaughter. All day and evening and early the next morning people stopped by the newspaper office and the sheriff's office asking for news.

At 9 A.M. on Saturday the judge called the court to order and the sheriff escorted Barieau into the room. His wife and daughter were already there, and Mrs. Barieau broke into tears when she saw her husband. Barieau stood next to his lawyers, his fingers twitching and his feet shuffling. The jury foreman read the verdict: Barieau was not guilty.

McCarran's career was off to a good start. "It was the unanimous opinion of those present in the courtroom," reported the *Tonopah Sun,* "that no finer argument, from the standpoint of eloquence and logic, has ever been delivered in the courthouse. During the course of the argument, Attorney McCarran demonstrated that as a dealer in sarcasm and invective, he is without a peer at the local bar."[33]

May Baric wanted a divorce. McCarran, despite being a Catholic, was more than happy to take her case. The only problem would be proving that she was actually married to George Wingfield, who was well on his way to becoming the richest man in the state. For McCarran, it was the kind of juicy case that could make his career — or break it.

Born the same year as McCarran, George Wingfield grew up on a cattle ranch in Oregon and arrived in Nevada when he was twenty. Three years later his skill at poker had netted him forty thousand dollars, which he bet on a saloon that went bust. He had better luck with George Nixon, a telegraph-operator-turned-banker who had helped organize the Silver Party. Wingfield asked Nixon to grubstake his move to Tonopah; the banker never made a better investment. Wingfield arrived in town in 1901 and got a job dealing cards at the Tonopah Club; five years later he had given up on a small gambling fortune (although always kept the habit of shuffling stacks of silver dollars with one hand) to concentrate on a much bigger mining and banking fortune. In 1906 Wingfield and Nixon (who had been elected a U.S. senator) pulled together their scattered mining holdings to create the Goldfield Consolidated Mines Company, which was capitalized at fifty million dollars and eventually controlled all but one mine in town. By his early thirties Wingfield's personal worth was a reputed thirty million dollars. Eventually Wingfield, who was a Republican, would own most of the banks in the state, the majority of the hotels in Reno, and many of the politicians of both parties.

Wingfield had the perfect poker face of a born gambler. His expression never changed; even his lips didn't seem to move when he talked. But beneath his placid exterior burned a fury. He broke his wife's nose and did the same to a newspaper editor. At a dinner party he once regaled the wife of a prominent attorney with a colorful story, poking her in the ribs with his beloved .48-caliber revolver, which he called Betsy (when he sobered up he sent her son a Chevrolet sportster to make amends). "His motto," claimed his bodyguard, Diamondfield Jack Davis, "is to use anyone that he can and then throw them aside like a broken branch."[34]

Wingfield, McCarran's new client told him, had been her common-law husband for four years. Baric (she used the name *Wingfield*) claimed that the two had had a turbulent relationship; she nursed him through smallpox but said he beat her badly enough to call a doctor, threatened her life, and forced her to have sex with him when he had syphilis. "He broke me down physically and left me without a cent after living with me as his wife . . . ," she said. "Wingfield used to beat me terribly."[35] In 1906, after a one-night reconciliation ended with Baric put on a train to California, she decided to sue Wingfield for divorce — not to mention three thousand dollars a month in alimony and half his property.

No lawyer in his right mind would take such a case, Baric claimed Wingfield scoffed at her. He could buy any attorney she could find. And his friend the judge would never find him guilty. Baric found McCarran. "She knew that because of her husband's high political position," the complaint stated, "she had reason to believe that he would buy the judgment."[36] The local papers, which normally couldn't write enough about Wingfield, didn't even mention the suit.

Judge Breen ruled that Baric had not produced any evidence to prove her case, reaching the rather extraordinary conclusion that not only had

Wingfield not done any of the terrible things alleged by Baric, but he had never in any way abused or even insulted her. Certainly, the judge wrote, Wingfield did not treat her in a cruel or inhuman or beastly manner, nor did he beat or curse or abuse or abase her, or call her vile or lewd or indecent or opprobrious names, or beat her over the head or on the body with the butt of a pistol or with a chair or any other weapon or instrument or fist or kick or point a loaded pistol at her and threaten to blow her goddamn head off. And he definitely did not say, "How I like to see an old whore like you suffer." "The court further finds," Breen added somewhat gratuitously, "that each and all the allegations contained in the defendant's answer are true, and that each and all of the allegations set forth, made and contained in plaintiff's complaint are untrue."[37]

Whatever the truth of Baric's allegations — and she does seem to have been rather unstable — the judge went to great lengths to absolve Wingfield of all charges, including, Breen noted mysteriously, those not included in the lawsuit. While Baric was ordered to pay Wingfield's legal fees, he actually paid off thousands of dollars in Baric's bills and dropped six thousand dollars on a house for her in San Jose — safely, he hoped, on the other side of the Sierra. None of which stopped Baric from showing up in Nevada now and then in a rage, still claiming to be Wingfield's wife, demanding the diamonds he had given her but had taken back. After Wingfield announced his engagement to a San Francisco banker's daughter, Maude Murdoch, Baric called the bride's mother and told her that her daughter was engaged to a married man. The day before his wedding, Wingfield showed up at Baric's house and promised that he would continue to help her. "If you had acted differently," he told her, putting his hand on her shoulder, "you might now be in the place of the woman I am about to marry."[38]

One night shortly after he arrived in Tonopah in the fall of 1905, McCarran heard laughter spilling out of a second-story window downtown and climbed up the stairs to find a large party going on. A man wearing a monocle stepped in front of McCarran and looked him up and down with a stare colder than the wind whipping through Sawtooth Pass. The young lawyer was not invited in.

As with school, which he'd started four years behind his peers, McCarran was a late arrival in Tonopah. Fortunes had already been made, empires built, allegiances forged. Tonopah was the smelter that fused the political and economic elite of Nevada for the first half of the twentieth century; the place where men who would loom large in the state's destiny got their start. Key

Pittman and Tasker Oddie might belong to different political parties but they also shared a sense of belonging to a select fraternity, a Harvard Club of the Great Basin, that transcended partisanship. McCarran, as always, was the outsider. He belonged to no club then or ever. "Keep your own counsel," he once advised a friend. "Don't allow anyone to know what you are going to do next. You never know who your friends are and there is one person only whom you can implicitly trust."[39]

Yet McCarran's skill as a lawyer was undeniable, and in the fall of 1906 the Democratic convention picked him to run for Nye County district attorney. The Republicans didn't field a candidate, and McCarran trounced his socialist opponent 914 votes to 159. "He is a fine orator, a shrewd lawyer and a worthy gentleman," said the *Tonopah Bonanza,* "and no better selection could have been made by the Democratic convention."[40]

McCarran went from defending murderers to prosecuting them. It was a role that he never felt completely comfortable in. When Elsie Cronin shot her husband McCarran tried her for murder. She claimed that she had shot her husband in self-defense while he was beating her in a drunken rage. Defense attorney Bert Gibbons called the trial a persecution. McCarran was wounded. He was deeply hurt, he told the court, that a fellow lawyer could say such a thing about someone who was just doing his sworn duty.[41]

Gibbons won the case, but more than that he had already won the kind of acceptance in Tonopah that McCarran never would. Gibbons, who arrived in town after McCarran, was a Republican, although his two law partners were prominent Democrats: Congressman George Bartlett and George Thatcher. He was also a frequent guest at Bartlett's palatial house, perched on a hillside and the scene of some of the town's most memorable parties, where women's hats towered and their jewels glittered and the men talked politics late into the night. "The elite of local society was there and it was in the wee small hours of the morning before the affair broke up,"[42] reported the *Sun* after one soiree during McCarran's third year in Tonopah.

The DA, however, wasn't on the guest list.

On an early morning in December 1906 Wingfield got word that a heavy shipment of gold was being loaded on the baggage car of the Reno-bound train at the Goldfield depot: Forty-four sacks of rich ore worth twenty thousand dollars was on its way to a Wells Fargo office in California. It was, Wingfield immediately thought, *his* gold.

For years local saloons had been filled with miners who made four dollars a day but still managed to drop hundreds of dollars a night, bragging about the rich pieces of ore they had secreted out of the tunnels, a mountain of pebbles that cost mine owners millions. The practice was called high-grading — that is, smuggling out high-grade ore, the extremely rare and rich jewelry rock that was the stuff of miners' dreams. And many miners considered high-grading an unwritten part of their union contract, an unofficial bonus for their brutal work: A misstep might send a man spiraling hundreds of feet down a shaft, his body bashed to pulp by the timbers before it plunged into the scalding water that collected at the bottom, where other miners would have to fish it out with grappling hooks; a single mucker could shovel a ton of rock into a car a dozen times a shift and push it out a tunnel — or just as easily get crushed beneath its wheels; a driller might swing his pick into an unexploded blasting cap or find that the fuse that was supposed to burn fifty-eight seconds to the foot was running faster — in either case he was lucky to find himself thrown only thirty feet down a tunnel and might someday hope to get his hearing back. But to the mine owners high-grading was just theft. Wingfield sent watchmen into the mines, where their arrival was greeted by a dynamite explosion. Strongboxes had been broken into, and three miners had just been caught trying to walk off their shift several pounds heavier than when they started.

Now, Wingfield thought, his stolen gold was leaving town. He quickly telegraphed his attorneys in Reno, then hopped on the train. As soon as the train pulled into the Sierra Street station the sheriff climbed into the baggage car and seized the gold, which was taken to the Nixon National Bank, owned by Wingfield's partner. A week later the miners demanded an immediate raise from four dollars a day to five. The next day fifteen hundred miners went out on strike. The labor wars had come to Nevada.[43]

Mac McCreary had barely stepped off the train in Goldfield before a man bounded up to him wanting to know what he was doing in town. Selling schoolbooks, he said. "I guess you're all right," the man replied. "You see we're looking out for these goddamn agitators, the I Won't Work outfit."[44] In fact, the hero of John Dos Passos' *The 42nd Parallel* was a card-carrying member of the Industrial Workers of the World who had rushed to central Nevada to join what in 1906 seemed like an American revolution in the making.

A year earlier two hundred battle-scarred socialists, anarchists, and radical labor organizers had gathered in Chicago to form a different kind of union. They were fed up with the conservative approach of the American Federation of Labor, which for almost twenty years had been organizing skilled workers into Balkanized guilds that politely asked for better wages and conditions instead of bringing together the laboring masses and demanding their fair share. One of these groups was the Western Federation of Miners, which had been active in Tonopah since 1901 to little effect. In Colorado the WFM had learned to its peril what going it alone could mean: In 1903 the union went on strike in Cripple Creek, and Governor James Peabody declared martial law, calling in the state militia (paid for by the Mine Owners' Association). "It is better to suppress wrong-doing, without loss of life and destruction of property," he declared, "than to wait until damage is accomplished and then attempt to punish the offenders."[45] The next year a train of strike-breaking miners pulled into the station at Cripple Creek and a bomb exploded, killing fourteen and setting off an anti-union rampage through the town. The federation's headquarters was sacked while scores of unionists were pushed onto trains and sent out of state. Thus was framed the Chicago convention in 1905 when the WFM joined the newly organized Industrial Workers of the World, whose name proclaimed its strategy of forming One Big Union, uniting all the laboring classes together into a single unbeatable force. "The working class and the employing class," the Wobblies declared, "have nothing in common."[46]

Soon the Wobblies were testing their theory in Goldfield, thirty miles south of Tonopah and the site of an even bigger mining boom. Led by Vincent St. John (The Saint), a veteran of the Colorado struggles, the Wobblies tried to sign up every worker from prostitute to engineer. One IWW organizer walked into the office of the *Goldfield Sun* and told the printers to join the union or expect to be run out of town in twenty-four hours. The printers didn't join, and the Wobblies boycotted the paper. "Before the advent of the IWW in Tonopah there was absolutely no labor trouble," wrote Lindley C. Branson, the owner of the *Tonopah* and *Goldfield Sun* newspapers, which largely served as mouthpieces for Wingfield. "Everything was peace and harmony and all were satisfied with the conditions which were more favorable than anywhere in the whole world. . . . The trouble makers have not obeyed their own injunction to work but eight hours but have gone on for twenty-four hours arraying friend against friend and brother against brother. They have been unceasing in their efforts to wind this town up in bloodshed."[47] When a member of a rival AFL union tried to break the boycott by selling copies of the *Sun* on the street, a crowd of Wobblies pressed around him. *Scab, scab, scab,* they chanted. Wingfield waded into the crowd and declared that he was no scab, pulling out his pistol and firing into the air.

But Wingfield seemed to be firing blanks that December when the Wobblies struck his mines after he declared war on high-grading. Three weeks later the miners went back to work, having won most of their demands for better wages and hours. As 1907 dawned, the IWW appeared to be running Goldfield. That January the Wobblies shut down all business one day for a boisterous parade through town to commemorate their Russian socialist brothers who had been mowed down by the czar's troops two years earlier, as well as to protest the coming trial in Idaho of Big Bill Haywood and two other union stalwarts accused of assassinating former governor Frank Steunenberg. Waving red banners ("Our flag is the banner that is dyed red with the martyrs' blood of our class!"), three thousand workingmen marched behind St. John to the Miners' Union Hall. "We will sweep the capitalist class out of the life of this nation and then out of the whole world," he vowed.[48] The Wobblies decreed an eight-hour day for all employees in Goldfield. "The highest point of efficiency for any labor organization was reached by the IWW and WFM in Goldfield," St. John wrote. "No committees were ever sent to any employers. The unions adopted wage scales and regulated hours. The secretary posted the same on a bulletin board outside of the union hall and it was the LAW."[49]

Enforcing the law was more difficult. On March 10, IWW organizer Morrie Preston was standing vigil in front of the Nevada Restaurant, which the Wobblies were boycotting, when owner John Silva came running at the union man with a pistol. Preston shot Silva, claiming self-defense. Silva died. The businessmen of Goldfield were more than willing to take the Wobbly boasts of revolution aborning at face value, claiming that Silva was the first victim on a union hit list that included Wingfield and other mine owners. The sheriff quickly swore in 175 extra deputies, some of them millionaires, and armed patrols prowled the town on horses with instructions to shoot to kill at the first sign of trouble. "There is scarcely a citizen who is not armed," the *Sun* reported, "his gun held in his hand in his overcoat pocket ready for action and let one overt act be committed and merry hell will be to pay."[50]

Four days later Wingfield and the other ostensible targets of the assassination plot formed the Goldfield Businessmen's and Mine Owners' Association and shut all businesses in town on March 15 — reopening the next day but refusing to rehire any Wobblies. "Goldfield Declares Its

Freedom From The Anarchists' Rule," the *Sun* screamed.[51] The mine owners and the miners' union, whose buildings were across the street from one another, turned their offices into bunkers. Windows bristled with Winchesters. "Compromise be damned," Wingfield declaimed. "The Goldfield mines will stay closed down until hell freezes over before we open them to let a lot of anarchists tell us how we are to run our property."[52] The mines opened again on April 22, and shortly thereafter Preston was convicted of second-degree murder. Soon the town quieted down, which the *Sun* took as a sign that the Wobblies were only massing their strength for a new assault. "When a man of known shrewdness is quiet in the face of seeming utter rout," the paper said of St. John, "that is the time he is most dangerous for he is laying deep plans that will later burst upon the town with almost overwhelming suddenness."[53]

In October 1907 two of Goldfield's three banks failed. "During the boom days," Wingfield recalled, "you could go to a bank here and borrow a thousand dollars on a paper napkin with I.O.U. written on it."[54] These were not boom days. Across the country interest rates had been rising, choking off credit and forcing the veritable Knickerbocker Trust in New York to close its doors. A depression soon spread across the country. On October 15 there was a run on one of the Wingfield and Nixon banks — part of a conspiracy by the militant miners' union, it was alleged, to close the institution. Governor John Sparks declared a banking holiday. Wingfield and Nixon pledged their personal fortunes to prop up their Goldfield bank, borrowing money and selling stock at fire-sale prices to raise more cash. They reopened the bank with one million dollars in gold coins stacked on the counter.

But when Goldfield Consolidated announced that it could meet only half of its payroll with cash and would offer scrip for the remainder, the Wobblies voted to strike. The mine owners vowed to keep the tunnels closed until they could break the union. Suddenly Goldfield had almost two thousand unemployed miners idling about — and more than seven tons of dynamite had disappeared from Goldfield Consolidated. Wingfield hopped on a train to Carson to urge Governor Sparks to ask President Theodore Roosevelt for federal troops to prevent an armed uprising. Senator Nixon and Representative George Bartlett agreed. The governor, without checking with authorities in Esmeralda County, telegraphed the president for help in quelling a threatened insurrection. "There does now exist domestic violence and unlawful combinations and conspiracies," Sparks claimed.[55]

On December 6 Roosevelt ordered five hundred troops from California to Goldfield. "There is not a dollar's worth of property in danger," the WFM's Bill Haywood complained, "and the only possible use for soldiers would be to inaugurate a reign of terror with the ultimate purpose of reducing the wages in the mines."[56] Haywood was right. Two days after the troops arrived the mine owners announced that the mines were reopening — but filled with men recruited from out of state earning one dollar less a day than their predecessors. "We have started in to win and we will win," Wingfield said. "With the protection afforded us by the United States soldiers," he added, "we propose to run our mining properties on any basis we choose."[57]

Roosevelt dispatched a three-man commission to investigate the dispute. The commission reported that the threat of violence was a pretext used by the mine owners, who were determined to break the union and wanted federal troops for protection. Roosevelt wired Sparks that if the state wanted a garrison in Goldfield, it would have to supply its own. Faced with the withdrawal of the army, Sparks called a special session of the legislature to create a state police force.

One of the few politicians to speak out against the bill was the young district attorney in Nye County who favored arbitration. "The plan of Governor Sparks to equip a body of Texas Rangers and vest these horsemen with power to use their shooting irons at will in the settlement of labor controversies would be more than a state disgrace," McCarran said. "Instead of stopping trouble the adoption of the ranger system would start trouble that would be never-ending in Nevada and it would set us back several notches in the scale of civilization."[58]

The bill passed. State troopers were quickly sworn in and sent to Goldfield to replace the army. The strike collapsed. The union was crushed.

In early August a man showed up at a polling place in Tonopah to vote in the Democratic primary. One official thought he looked a bit young to be casting a ballot and asked him how long he had been voting. "I started early this morning," he replied, "and I've been voting ever since."[59]

A mining camp loves nothing better than a good fight, and the primary battle between Pat McCarran and Congressman George Bartlett wasn't disappointing. "The hottest political contest ever waged in Tonopah," noted the *Sun*. ". . . The whole populace turned out and is taking a hand in the fight. Republicans, independence party men, socialists, members of the miners' union and all other unions are joining in with the democrats to help them settle the question of supremacy of George A. Bartlett and P. A. McCarran."[60]

McCarran wanted to go to Washington. His months in the assembly six years earlier had lit a fire for politics. The district attorney's job — a post so unimportant that the Republicans couldn't even be bothered to field a candidate when McCarran ran — was only a way station to higher office. The year before, Governor Sparks had offered to make McCarran a district judge, which would seem not bad for a self-educated lawyer who had only been practicing for two years. But McCarran turned down the job. It was the last time the Democratic Party in Nevada would offer McCarran anything. "That was the first and only appointment that was ever offered to me," he recalled years later. "I have always had to fight for everything I have received."[61]

In April, McCarran made his first fight for the goal that would consume him for the next quarter century: getting to Washington. Standing in his way was Bartlett, the toast of Tonopah, a wealthy, well-connected lawyer who worked for Wingfield and was partners with local party boss George Thatcher. Bartlett's first term in Congress was undistinguished, but his visit to Carson City to help Sparks pass the state police bill had endeared him to the conservatives in the party while angering the rank-and-file workers. "He is one of the best-known men at Washington," the *Sun* dubiously reported, "and there is none more popular personally in either house of Congress."[62]

Bartlett was anything but popular in Goldfield. And the Nye County district attorney spent a good part of the spring crossing the line into Esmeralda County to stir up support for repealing or amending the police law. McCarran had made it clear at the beginning of the year when he opposed the bill that his sympathies were with the men who dug the gold and silver out of the earth, not the men who owned the mines.

In light of his later obsession with Communism, McCarran's equanimity in the face of the mine-country Red Scare might seem remarkable. After all, the local papers had been filled with horror stories about the devilishly clever and bloodthirsty Wobblies, who themselves made no secret of their desire to see capitalism perish in the flames of its own greed. But McCarran, not long off the sheep trail, was in his bones more a peasant than a prosecutor. It was the Wingfields, the Pittmans, and the Oddies — the men of fame and fortune — who clung so tightly to what they had that made McCarran's stomach turn. When he ran for the assembly McCarran supported the eight-hour day for miners, but it was the Wobblies who — briefly — made that a reality. In the contest between miners and mine owners it was not the landlords who needed police protection. To a perpetual outsider, populism came as naturally as breathing. And McCarran's hero in oratory, action, and, above all, persistence remained William Jennings Bryan, the Great Commoner who that summer was making a fourth run for the White House. "The greatest living exponent of Jeffersonian principles," McCarran called him at the Jefferson Day dinner in Goldfield. "I come as a Democrat," he added in Bryanite fervor, "free from all entanglements."[63]

McCarran's bid angered the Democratic poohbahs, who began to view him as a demagogue, perhaps even a radical, certainly not a loyal party member. "Those," Bartlett said, "who are decrying the state police and seeking a repeal of the bill must have ulterior motives."[64] The *Sun* agreed, charging that McCarran and his backers were not sincerely opposed to the police bill but only using it as a club to beat Bartlett and attract the votes of workers. "It is dangerous business and men should have more sense than to take such chances," the paper wrote. "The state police law was passed to get rid of agitation and give honest miners a chance to work. The agitators left because of it, and now the McCarran faction wishes to bring them back."[65] The paper began a carping campaign against McCarran, complaining that his seventy-five-hundred-dollar-a-year salary was twice that of a U.S. senator and holding him personally responsible for rising taxes. Privately, party leaders had already come to despise McCarran. "Nearly all who know him doubt his sincerity," Key Pittman remarked, "and believe that he would sacrifice everything for his own political ambition."[66]

Publicly, however, Pittman was supposed to be leading the McCarran delegation to the state convention — which he led into an ambush. The convention opened at 10 A.M. on August 31, and the mood of delegates was so acrimonious that proceedings were immediately adjourned until 7 P.M. to give the factions a chance to reach a backroom deal and avoid a public bawl. McCarran's hopes were soon gutted when the credentials committee refused to seat a dozen of the thirty-nine delegates whom the district attorney had lined up from Esmeralda County. McCarran's supporters threatened to bolt the convention, and Bartlett's backers vowed to vote Republican if their candidate was denied the nomination. Beneath the flag- and bunting-draped buildings of Tonopah, loud arguments carried into the night. "Pandemonium reigned on the streets," the *Sun* reported.[67] The next day didn't go much smoother, with a protracted fight over a plank to support the police law. The day dragged to a close at two-thirty in the morning, but not before Pittman had come out for Bartlett.

"McCarran," Pittman explained privately, "has no strength because his reputation as a double-crosser is too well established throughout the state."[68] The McCarran forces were in a rout even before the voting began. After Francis Newlands was renominated for the Senate, he gave a forceful speech in support of the militia law and, implicitly, Bartlett and party unity. "This state will not be the scene of civil strife," he warned, "and no internal warfare will be tolerated."[69]

Bartlett was renominated on the first ballot, 136 to 46. Even before the convention met, Democratic activists were writing McCarran's political obituary. "I think," one told Pittman, "we may fairly consider McCarran's fight lost."[70]

George Dugan was in his wagon about forty miles east of Tonopah when he saw the dust. A car was coming toward him. He reined in his team when he saw the familiar bald head of the driver. The car stopped. It had once been a beautiful Thomas Flyer touring car, but now it was dirty and dingy; the rear passenger compartment had been sawed off, turning it into a flatbed that was loaded down with mining tools, food, and blankets. It was Tasker Oddie's home. They talked politics for two hours, Oddie's sunburned head turning redder in the desert sun. He was, Oddie explained, running for governor.

The lawyer-prospector who had helped Jim Butler dig the first ore out of the Tonopah hills had lost it all. Tonopah, at first, had been good to Oddie. He had enough money to throw $250,000 at a gold-digging wife to get rid of her and still sink $100,000 into his beloved ranch in Monitor Valley. But after the stock market collapse of 1907 Oddie found himself holding the paper on five worthless mines and owing seventy-five thousand dollars to the bank. He had gone from beans to oysters and back to beans. He sold everything but his brand-new Thomas Flyer and a pair of pearl shirt studs, and in 1909 he drove out of Tonopah virtually as poor as the day he'd arrived almost a decade earlier.

The road out of Tonopah was seeing a lot of traffic. As in all boomtowns, the losers far outnumbered the winners, and when Tonopah's mines declined both headed back to Reno, suddenly the state's political and economic center once again. Among them was McCarran, who had launched a successful law career but alienated many of the prominent players in his party. He had lunged for Congress and lost; he had invested in mines but found no fortune. Maybe he would have better luck back in the city of his birth. He certainly wasn't going to be alone. Most of the town seemed to be leaving.

Few exits, however, were more poignant than Oddie's. He went back into the desert, looking for another mining fortune. ". . . I cannot stop because things fail," he insisted. "I must keep on and get a winner. I have gotten them before and will do it again."[71] But his pick struck no second bonanza, and Oddie turned to the only other thing he ever won at: politics. He had served a term in the state Senate. Now he would run for governor. He hit up friends and collected $150; he pawned his shirt studs. It was a threadbare campaign. Camping in the desert, Oddie followed wagon ruts from place to place, passing his hat at each campaign stop to get to the next. "I tell you, old man," Oddie wrote to a friend, "it has been worse than hell, and I will be glad when it is all over."[72] Oddie campaigned on personality more than policy. "I am a Progressive or Insurgent Republican," he explained. And he won. On election night after his victory was clear, Oddie pulled from his pocket a postcard of the governor's mansion in Carson City to show a friend. "That's my new home," he beamed. "It was either that or a tent."[73]

CHAPTER 3

Night, Noon, and Morning

> Overabundant zeal, spiced with that ever impelling ele-
> ment, personal ambition for success, is too often the
> shrine of excessive devotion, where wild tongues are
> loosed. . . .[1]
>
> — Pat McCarran, chief justice,
> Nevada Supreme Court

Key Pittman stumbled out of Democratic Party headquarters in the Golden
Hotel in downtown Reno, rounded a corner, and came face to face with
Pat McCarran. It was 11 A.M., a week before the 1914 congressional elections, and Pittman was drunk off his ass. He had already punched three
prominent Democrats at party headquarters, including his friend U.S. marshal A. B. Gray and state senator William F. Sharon, before he bumped into
McCarran. Pittman pulled the cigar out of his mouth.[2]

Two years earlier Pittman had become Nevada's junior U.S. senator on
his second try. In 1910 Pittman was playing poker with the leaders of the
state Democratic Party when he found himself ahead by five thousand dollars. Pushing his winnings across the table, he offered to bet it all for the
Senate nomination. He won the hand, and one of the state's wealthiest
lawyers and corporate directors went on the campaign trail, speaking in
front of a silk banner proclaiming KEY PITTMAN, MINER. The Republican
incumbent was George Nixon, George Wingfield's millionaire partner who
allegedly spent $250,000 of his own fortune, as well as almost as much of
the Southern Pacific Railroad's money, on the campaign. The Democrats
won control of the statehouse that year and were free to appoint their candidate to the Senate — except that Pittman had challenged Nixon to
accept the judgment of the popular vote, which the banker won by a 1,105
majority. "I would have beaten him in spite of all this had it not been for
the extensive bribery indulged in on election day," Pittman complained. "It
was simply $5 before and $10 after election if Nixon won."[3] Eighteen
months later Nixon died and Pittman won a special election to fill out the
term by eighty-nine votes — his first elective office and one that he would
keep for the next twenty-eight years of his life.

Pittman struck McCarran. The tall, thin, tottering Pittman grappled with
the short and stout McCarran, and then Pittman got loose and staggered

down Virginia Street, lurched up to a deputy sheriff, and reeled at him with another pathetic punch. The lawman pushed off Pittman, who then weaved over to an elderly man, grabbed his hand, and asked him to have a drink. The man begged off. Pittman responded by hitting him in the jaw, knocking off his glasses. A crowd had gathered, and Pittman began to randomly throw blows. One of the unlucky bystanders smacked Pittman back good, sending the senator spilling into the gutter and ending his campaign on behalf of the Democratic Party.

"I worked every saloon wherever I spoke before and after the speaking, and was entirely successful in such campaiging until I had a physical col-lapse in Reno caused by the great strain that I was under for two weeks," Pittman explained to supporters a little while later. "It was not the speaking or campaigning that was too much for me, but it was doing the saloons all over the state. I think it was quite remarkable that I was able to do the saloon electioneering that I did and retain perfect equilibrium throughout the whole campaign until I arrived at Reno."[4]

McCarran, in a sense, always seemed to be getting beaten by Pittman and his friends. After his bid for Congress sputtered out in Tonopah (thanks in part to Pittman's duplicity), McCarran picked up his family and moved back to Reno. Tonopah's silver was petering out, and the state's center of gravity had shifted to the town on the Truckee, once again the largest city in the state, home to ten thousand of Nevada's eighty-two thousand resi-dents. McCarran quickly established himself as a successful criminal attorney, a resolute defender of murderers, prostitutes, bank robbers, and even abor-tionists. McCarran, the *Nevada State Journal* quipped, had the reputation "sometimes claimed by surgeons of never sending a man to the cemetery."[5]

He also earned a reputation as one of the state's great orators, a tireless speaker who could talk passionately to a small seventh-grade civics class or a stockmen's convention of thousands, a dependable stemwinder for every occasion from St. Patrick's Day to the Fourth of July or no occasion at all, whipping up speech after speech for anyone who would listen, sometimes several a day. "He was a William Jennings Bryan orator and a wonderful, wonderful speaker, one of the best you could ever hear," remembered Reno newspaperman Joe McDonald. "You just loved to listen to him because he was an orator. It was beautiful, the way he talked! And yet he could take any subject, no matter what it was, and paint rosy pictures. It just made you feel good to listen to him. So maybe in the course of the whole thing, he never said anything very important, but it was well worth listening to. And people would go a long ways just to hear him talk on politics and anything else."[6]

Like his soliloquies before his sheep in the Sierra, McCarran was still only practicing. Two years after returning to Reno, McCarran looked to his future — and once again he saw Congress. This time he decided to court favor with influential Democrats, not spurn them, as he had in Tonopah. In the fall of 1911, a year before the election, McCarran tried to enlist Pittman's support in the upcoming congressional contest. Pittman was evasive. "I have at all times held the success of the party superior to my own ambitions or the ambitions of my friends," he told McCarran.[7]

It had been quite a few years since McCarran had made his living out of doors, and his once lean frame had bulked up considerably. At thirty-six his hair was still thick and dark, but his face had grown wide, his chin drooped, his neck thickened. When he folded his arms he had the immensity of Rodin's monument to Balzac, his short stature offset by a physical density that matched his inner drive and implacable personality. McCarran's physique mirrored his temperament. Built like a steamroller, he moved through politics with the same subtlety.

McCarran was not a patient man, but he was preternaturally persistent. His ambition was tremendous, his resolve unshakable. He had walked across the Nevada desert and climbed over the Sierra on foot. He knew about crossing vast distances. If the party would not smile upon him for this campaign, McCarran would work to make himself strong enough to succeed without the party's help. He decided to sit out the congressional race; instead he would run for the state Supreme Court, which would give him a platform to build prestige and influence and position himself as the front-runner for another go at Washington. "I am out for the supreme bench and I am out to win," McCarran promised Pittman.[8] "Should you get the nomination," Pittman responded with studied ambiguity, "I will make the same fight for you as you made for me."[9]

Mainstream Democrats, again, did not back McCarran. A poll of Democratic lawyers by the *Nevada State Journal* found that 51 percent supported attorney A. A. Heer for the party's nomination, while only 7 percent went for McCarran.[10] But when the votes were counted in September, McCarran rolled over Heer 3,577 to 2,650. With the election eight weeks away and no Republican candidate of any note, McCarran looked like a sure bet for the bench. Then George Bartlett showed up.

George Bartlett was on a crusade. Four years earlier he had beaten the tar out of McCarran when the young district attorney challenged him for a second term in Congress. Bartlett went on to rack up the largest vote ever in Nevada for a congressional race, winning every county but one. Now he was practicing law in Reno. Long a Democratic darling, he had announced in March that he was running for the Supreme Court on the party's ticket. But it wasn't until after the primary that Bartlett actually jumped into the race. Suddenly he was calling himself the nonpartisan candidate and running on the sole issue of raising the bench out of the mire of politics. McCarran, Bartlett implied, was nothing but a party hack, a machine politician whose election to the Supreme Court would defile the temple of justice. McCarran, the least party-minded Democrat imaginable, abruptly found himself the symbol of partisan ossification.

The progressive movement was sweeping over the United States, with reformers trying to bust trusts, break the iron oligarchies of political machines, and make government again the servant of the people and not the tool of the powerful. Amendments to the Constitution for the income tax and the direct election of senators were working their way through Congress. Even remote Nevada was touched by the spirit of change. Two years earlier Tasker Oddie had won the governorship as a progressive Republican. In the statehouse he called for giving women the right to vote and found himself allied with McCarran's old college teacher Anne Martin, who was leading the state's Equal Franchise Society. Nevada legislators — long viewed as the hirelings of the railroad and mining interests — changed the state constitution to give voters the right to hold referenda, sponsor initiatives, and recall their representatives. Gambling was made illegal and even easy divorce, the most sacrosanct of frontier freedoms, was threatened. Now, Bartlett declared, it was time to remove the taint of politics from the judiciary. "Nevada," he said, "must join the ranks of all progressive states that have declared for the non-partisan selection of members of courts."[11]

The Democratic Party, finding itself with McCarran as its unwanted candidate, seemed to agree. The state's leading Democratic newspaper, the *Nevada State Journal,* suddenly found itself troubled by the idea of partisanship. It enlisted in Bartlett's campaign with the fervor of a reformed sinner. "He dared to cut loose from politics," the paper marveled, and in a supposed news story dubbed Bartlett "the next succeeding justice."[12] The newspaper began to run almost daily stories about the lawyer's quest. Most read like press releases from Bartlett campaign headquarters. "The certainty," the *Journal* divined more than a month before the election, "is that Bartlett will have more votes than all opponents combined."[13] Who Bartlett's main opponent was the paper usually declined to tell its readers. When the *Journal* did bother to mention McCarran's name, it was only to point out that his practice largely involved criminal law while the Supreme Court decided mostly civil cases, an area in which Bartlett had gained more experience during the nineteen years that he had been an attorney. "Seven years' time is brief, very brief," added the *Reno Evening Gazette,* which also jumped on the Bartlett bandwagon, "for a lawyer to qualify himself for the highest court in the state."[14] All of which made McCarran furious. "Had I been defeated in the primary contest I would have supported the man who might honorably have defeated me," he fumed.[15]

In October, Bartlett announced that he would travel the state, talk with every nominee for the legislature, and lobby each one to change the constitution to ban party identification from judicial ballots. Arriving in Tonopah, the longtime Democrat was greeted with a huge banner strung across Main Street that read BARTLETT, NON-PARTISAN CANDIDATE FOR JUSTICE OF THE SUPREME COURT. "Bartlett is performing a patriotic public service," the *Journal* applauded.[16] From Carson City to Eureka, from Goldfield to Battle Mountain, Bartlett traveled the state as if on a holy mission. "Every place I have visited," Bartlett said, "I have met with gratifying assurance of support for the independent judiciary idea."[17]

A week before the vote the *Evening Gazette* was declaring victory for Bartlett. "From all over the state, Bartlett is receiving telegrams and letters from scores of friends, commending his non-partisan attitude and pledging support at the polls," the paper noted under the headline "Looks Bright for Bartlett." "Newspapers which are partisan in all other respects, have declared unequivocally for the complete separation of the courts and politics and are manifesting their approval by advocating the election of Bartlett."[18] The *Journal* proclaimed Bartlett the only independent candidate in Nevada to ever overtake a party's nominee. His friends predicted that he would carry fourteen of the state's sixteen counties. "Nothing," a *Journal* reporter said, "will prevent the election of George A. Bartlett."[19]

This was too much for McCarran. "Mr. Bartlett," McCarran noted, "has been, according to the Republican press of this state, a practitioner in the law for the last nineteen years, but never once during those nineteen years has he declared himself in favor of non-partisan judiciary until the time had expired in which candidates should file their nominating certificates."[20] McCarran campaigned hard, traveling the state, taking out large ads in newspapers that wouldn't cover his speeches. "I believe that I am going to be elected," he claimed, "and if elected I propose to hold every man and every interest upon an equal basis."[21]

McCarran trounced Bartlett, winning 9,721 votes to his old rival's 4,466. It was an expensive victory, McCarran told a friend who hit him up for a loan several months later. "The fact is that after the campaign I had scarcely money enough to buy a lunch for a canary bird," he said, "and it will take me at least a year to get out of debt, hence I am flying rather low."[22]

It was good to finally beat Bartlett. But it wasn't really the victory McCarran wanted.

McCarran had barely moved to Carson City in 1913 to sit on the court for a six-year term before he started talking about running for the U.S. Senate the next year. It was an audacious idea. First, the state constitution forbade judges to run for other offices while sitting on the court and went so far as to render any such election void (although how this would apply to a federal office was an open question). Second, the Senate seat was held by Francis Newlands, a two-term veteran.

Newlands was the most effective and successful statesman Nevada had ever sent to Washington. A lawyer with a predilection for plaid suits, he had gone to Yale, married into a Comstock Lode fortune, helped organize the Silver Party, and built an impressive house on the south side of the Truckee in Reno. He'd served ten years as a congressman, twelve in the Senate, personally bankrolled much of Nevada's Democratic Party for years, and put his name on the Newlands' Reclamation Act, which turned forty thousand acres of barren desert into productive cropland and created the towns of Fallon and Fernley. In fact, it was Newlands's 1902 Senate bid that had first drawn McCarran into state politics. McCarran had seconded Newlands's nomination in the legislative session that appointed him to the Senate.

Newlands did have some liabilities: He was old — turning sixty-six in 1914 — and he was allergic to sagebrush, rarely returning to Nevada. He was almost completely uninterested in local issues — a potentially crippling weakness in a state where a politician could expect to meet every one of his constituents and wasn't supposed to forget any of them.[23]

Nevada didn't demand much from the men it sent to Washington, but it did expect a little pandering now and then. But the aloof and distant Newlands was so busy playing statesman that more than a few voters were upset. "That there is a better opportunity to defeat him this fall than for the past twelve years is acknowledged by both Democrats and Republicans alike," claimed the *Elko Free Press*. "In every county in the state there is a majority of the Democratic Party who are known — and take pride in the name — as the anti-Newlands faction, and every day this faction is being swelled by discontented followers of Newlands, who are simply disgusted with the senator's actions."[24]

McCarran agreed. "I am candid to confess," he told a friend, "that in my judgement Senator Newlands is weaker today than he ever was in the history of his public career."[25] It was not personal ambition, McCarran hastened to point out, that was making him consider challenging Newlands. It was the fact that people from all over the state were constantly telling him that he would be the stronger candidate, he told people all over the state. "By the way, Jim," McCarran wrote James Finch, "there are just three men of prominence in the State of Nevada, who have not written to me personal letters requesting me to run for U.S. Senate. You are one of them. What's the matter?"[26]

Not all McCarran's supporters shared his optimism. "Many of your friends think that you will be committing political suicide," warned one.[27] While professing that the health of the party was his overriding concern, McCarran made it clear that he wasn't about to follow the opinion of party regulars on the matter. "There is no one who can bring me out in this fight and there is no one who can cause me to stay out of it," McCarran wrote. "I am not controlled by any individual or element."[28]

Ultimately, however, McCarran quailed before the united opposition of his party. "His attempts to initiate a boom for himself are quite amusing," one of Newlands's supporters wrote to the senator. "[A. B.] Gray told me that after he heard of this, as he went about the state, if he met a prominent Democrat, he would state to him that he understood the latter had urged McCarran to run, whereupon, after prompt denial, Gray would advise the party that every Democrat but three had urged him to run. It would appear that a number of your friends in Reno did some very agile and effective work in procuring McCarran to lie down. Many of his Reno friends and supporters, who are also yours, frankly told him that he would not receive their support if he ran. These statements came around quite numerous and emphatic, as a result of which . . . he gave it up. You will doubtless find a number of people who will claim the sole credit for having procured McCarran to give up the race."[29]

There were good reasons for McCarran to opt out. For one, Newlands could spend him into the poorhouse. Newlands dropped fifty thousand on his first election in 1892 and another hundred thousand electing the rest of the Silver Party slate. More recently — in 1912, when he wasn't even running — Newlands had given four thousand dollars to the party for national and state campaigns. All of which endeared him to the party hacks in a way McCarran could never hope to challenge. Some of McCarran's enemies thought that the aborted campaign was a mere feint. "The schemer in Pat's brain is to pretend to be a candidate against Newlands and then agree to withdraw if all hands will agree to support him two years hence against you," Gray told Pittman.[30] But McCarran had been right that Newlands was weak. The state's senior senator won re-election by a mere 40 votes.

William Woodburn Jr. put out his hand. Pat McCarran shook it. Billy, if you've come to ask me to withdraw, McCarran said first thing, forget about it.[31] Woodburn couldn't. Woodburn was the U.S. attorney for Nevada, a wheelhorse for the Democratic Party, the son of a beloved congressman, a former secretary to Newlands, and a friend of Pittman. He was the latest in a parade of Democratic leaders who marched up to McCarran in the summer of 1915 to plead with the judge not to challenge Pittman for his Senate seat the following year. Former governor Denver Dickerson had already had a long talk with McCarran, urging him to withdraw in the interest of Democratic harmony, telling him that he would be a hero to the party and could count on its support for the Senate some other time. Dickerson was encouraged; he thought McCarran might be coming around.

Nothing could have been farther from the truth. "If reports and rumors and assertions made from nearly every locality in the state amount to anything," McCarran assured a friend, "I have every chance in the world to win this nomination."[32] Why not? McCarran had won election to the court by a two-to-one margin. Pittman squeaked into office by eighty-nine votes. McCarran had spent the past six years assiduously courting supporters throughout the state, gaining a fine reputation as a skillful attorney and spellbinding speaker. Pittman spent most of his time in Washington and was seldom seen at home when he wasn't listing with drink.

Timing seemed crucial. As a replacement for Nixon, who had died in office, Pittman would have half a term under his belt by the election, but so far he had yet to make much of a name for himself as a legislator. If McCarran waited for another run, Pittman would gain seniority and the spoils that came with it in the Senate. True, Pittman, for all his faults, was a revered figure. Unlike Newlands, who always seemed like a carpet-bagger, Pittman clearly loved Nevada, and whatever he did in the Senate he did for the state. So what if he liked to unwind with the occasional drunken rampage? The Tonopah mafia, relocated to Reno, still ran the Democratic Party. Pittman was a founding member. And McCarran was still the pushy interloper. Going into the election year McCarran was so on the outs with his fellow Democrats that he had to ask the state's Republican congressman to put him on the mailing list for the *Congressional Record.* And when a friend wrote asking for an endorsement for a political appointment, McCarran replied that his name would not be a help with the Democratic powers-that-be. "My mere act of endorsement would, in all probability, be the first sign for them to refuse to appoint you," McCarran replied.[33] If McCarran went after Pittman's seat and didn't get it, he would surely earn the party's undying enmity. But he still found himself compelled to try. McCarran was about to turn forty. It was time to go to Washington.

Woodburn was worried. Which was why he had sought a meeting with the judge on this day in Reno. He had spoken to seventy-five friends in the past few days on Pittman's behalf and found that McCarran had already talked to every single one. They didn't have a problem with Pittman's ability or record, but he was a distant figure while McCarran was familiar. "McCarran," observed the *Evening Gazette,* "is known from one end of the state to the other, and his personal popularity is undeniable."[34] "McCarran is prodigiously active," Woodburn informed Pittman. "He is on the go every minute, spending his money, and campaigning day and night. I venture to state he has seen pretty nearly every voter in this county."[35]

He would not quit under any circumstances, McCarran told Woodburn. He'd rather be defeated than desert the friends who had stood by him. In fact, he was leaving for his third trip this year to eastern Nevada to see some of his supporters. He said he was absolutely confident that the fight was already won. The man is completely obsessed with his own importance, Woodburn thought; he thinks he's the only hope for the party. What, Woodburn suggested, if he could bring leading Democrats from every part of the state, including most of McCarran's own friends and supporters; would the judge then listen to their pleas not to split the party?

Nothing, McCarran said, could make him withdraw.

Pittman was furious. "McCarran," he sputtered to Woodburn, "has nothing to recommend him for this position except his nerve, energy and social qualities. He is violating the policy, if not the constitution, of our state. He is degrading the dignity of the bench. He is threatening the success of our party, and he is selfish and ungrateful. He is utilizing the great office that has been conferred upon him for the purpose of intimidation. . . . Every leading Democrat in the state has got to take a stand on this issue sooner or later, and the sooner they take the stand, the better. I am in this fight to win, and I don't intend to spare any energy or resource to accomplish it. McCarran will know that he is in a fight before he gets through with it."[36]

In July, McCarran defiantly announced his bid. "I am in this contest to win, if fair and honest effort will gain that end," he wrote. "There will be no withdrawal by me until the convention of my party has named its candidate."[37]

Pittman's three years in Washington had been uneventful. He didn't say much, dutifully voted for Woodrow Wilson's programs, and diligently introduced resolutions to keep the folks at home happy. Silver, irrigation, and federal land grants commanded his attention, while most domestic and international issues never crossed his horizon. "I am thoroughly in accord with the administration," he told a friend, "and am pleased that I am in a position where I can assist in carrying out its policies."[38] Pittman's major concern was keeping his job, which meant constantly reminding the citizens of Nevada of all that he was doing for them. "Publicize the amendment," he told his brother Vail, who was the editor of the *Tonopah Miner.* "Summarize it under the heading, 'Senator Pittman wins another victory in the cause of humanity.'"[39]

Then, early in the year when he would face reelection, Pittman suddenly became interested in foreign affairs (a subject he had commented on exactly twice publicly during the two years that World War I was tearing Europe apart and threatening to engulf the United States). When a vacancy unexpectedly opened up on the prestigious Foreign Relations Committee in March, Pittman tore up a prepared speech to deliver a paean to Wilson's handling of international relations. He was rewarded by getting a seat on the committee — ahead of seven other applicants. Thus as the summer primary campaign heated up in Nevada, Pittman begged off from even putting in an appearance in the state. "There are matters of too great importance pending to permit me to go to Nevada or devote much time to politics," he explained. "Wilson needs me here."[40] And Wilson repaid Pittman's loyalty by sending him a letter of endorsement. "It would be a very serious loss to the Senate were you not returned," the president wrote.[41]

McCarran went through the roof. He dashed off a furious telegram to the president, telling him to forget about the state electing a Democrat. He didn't send the wire, but its contents were leaked and his enemies used it as further evidence that he was a bad Democrat. Campaign issues were almost nonexistent. Pittman based his campaign on his support for the state's livestock and mining industries. McCarran mounted his challenge on the platform that he would do the same, only more so. "I believe," McCarran announced, "that an hour spent in defense of that which will insure to the prosperity of this state is worth a term spent in an endeavor to assist some other state in a matter of its own internal concern."[42] To Pittman, McCarran was a mere annoyance, a bug to be swatted away. "I am not afraid of McCarran," he confided. "...Waiving all personal interest, it seems to me to the interest of the Democratic party to nip in the bud the primary aspirations of any senatorial candidate so long as I satisfactorily represent the state and the Democratic Party."[43] Reports of McCarran's popularity didn't faze him. In 1915 the Nevada legislature had changed the law for nominating candidates from popular vote back to the convention system. The nomination was in the hands of the party regulars. "Am safe in saying that fully 70% of the Democrats in Lander County with whom I have talked are for you," one adviser from Battle Mountain reported to McCarran. "But all are agreed that inasmuch as the organization is for Pittman and the nomination made in convention that the odds are heavily against you."[44]

Belatedly this dawned on McCarran. "Lined up against me I find Newlands, Dickerson, Bartlett, and Thatcher, as well as Pittman," he acknowledged. "This is the old machine."[45] And the clogs of the old machine were ready to grind McCarran to dust. "He will fall so hard that he will never recover and you need expect absolutely no help, and probably secret opposition from him," Gray wrote to Pittman. "It looks to me like political suicide for Pat but he is bringing it on himself."[46]

McCarran's campaign got nowhere. "In my early days," he confided to a friend, "I was told that 'He aims too low who aims beneath the stars,' but I have later found out that to keep up such an aim requires a mountain of vanity."[47] Shortly before the August convention McCarran wrote Pittman an effusive letter of concession. "That the Democratic Party is big enough and strong enough to endure a contest within its own ranks and come forth strengthened as the result of the contest is a fact that will, in my judgment, be made manifest by your re-election," he wrote. "Whenever a party becomes so solidified and self-centered that it cannot endure a wholesome contest for the honors which that party affords, the first sign of weakness is made manifest. The contest between us is over."[48]

Pittman, who easily sailed back to office, didn't think so. "He will have my fight inside of the party as long as I am in the State of Nevada, and I have no intention of every leaving it . . . ," he told Woodburn. "I do believe that Judge McCarran's selfishness has endangered the success of the whole party in the State. I do believe that he has forfeited the support of the party for anything that he may ever aspire to."[49]

When Woodrow Wilson was elected in 1912, the former president of Princeton University became the first Democrat to sit in the White House in sixteen years. The son of a Presbyterian minister (he had practiced speech making in front of his father's empty pews), Wilson came to the office with a keen intellect, a missionary's zeal, and a well-honed disdain for Congress. ("The President is at liberty, both in law and conscience, to be as big a man as he can," he had written. "His capacity will set the limit; and if Congress be overborne by him, it will be no fault of the makers of the Constitution."[50]) Wilson reluctantly appointed McCarran's hero William Jennings Bryan as his secretary of state. But Bryan was a pacifist, and increasingly the world was not a pacific place. After Europe slid into the Great War in 1914, Bryan watched tremulously as the Anglophile Wilson spoke about America's mission to be a moral beacon above war, while at the same time sidling up to the Allies. After Germany sank the *Lusitania* in 1915 — killing 1,198 people, including 128 U.S. citizens — Wilson threatened to break off diplomatic relations with Germany. Bryan, an ardent anti-imperialist and a puritan even more pinched than his president (he served only grape juice at state banquets), quit in protest.

Wilson was reelected in 1916. "He kept us out of the war" was a campaign slogan. But increasingly, he found it hard to reconcile the duty of being a moral exemplar among nations with the responsibility to protect the democratic ideals that seemed at risk if the Allies lost. On April 2, 1917, Wilson went to Congress for a declaration of war. "The right is more precious than peace," he said, "and we shall fight for the things which we have always carried nearest our hearts . . . for a universal dominion of right by such a concert of free peoples as shall bring peace and safety to all nations and make the world itself at last free."[51]

The shooting ended in November 1918, but the conflict's ramifications were just beginning. The war had bled Europe white, killing some ten million men, wounding double that number, toppling empires, redrawing maps. In Russia the war ate away at the already rotten throne of the Romanov dynasty, bringing to power in the spring of 1917 a reformist government. Eight months later Vladimir Lenin and a small band of Bolsheviks seized control of the largest country on the continent, proclaimed the world's first socialist republic, and pulled Russia out of the war, making the new Union of Soviet Socialist Republics a pariah among nations. The victorious Allies declared Germany solely responsible for the war and heaped a crushing reparations burden on top of national humiliation. A German corporal named Adolf Hitler vowed to avenge his country's defeat.

The United States started the war with the world's seventeenth largest army, smaller than Portugal's; it ended by sending an Allied Expeditionary Force of two million men to war. More than one hundred thousand Americans died in the fighting, while Britain lost one million lives and Germany almost two million. The war was a shattering event for many young people. "I had been deeply distressed and shamed," lamented a New York college student named Bert Wolfe, who watched in horror and indignation as America slipped into the war and Russia climbed out and thought he saw where the hope of humankind lay, "by the feeling that all of our institutions for maintaining peace, our churches, our unions, our Hague Conferences and Arbitration Treaties, had failed us."[52]

In Europe the old world seem to be dying. In Russia a new one was being born.

McCarran was unperturbed by the war. His father had flown a Sinn Fein flag at the ranch, and the fact that the British could lose twenty thousand soldiers on the first day of the four-month-long battle of the Somme didn't trouble him — especially after Britain demonstrated its commitment to democracy by violently suppressing the 1916 Easter uprising in Ireland and executing its leaders. At a time when all things German had become verboten (sauerkraut was renamed Liberty Cabbage, and Beethoven and Brahms disappeared from symphony repertoires), McCarran privately exulted in the triumphs of the entente. "It is pretty hard to trust these British and especially for an Irishman to place confidence in a Britisher is something unheard of," he told a friend. "But in view of the fact that civilization will shortly dawn on the British isles, and the Kaiser will be comfortably located in Birmingham Castle, we can look forward to the hour and the time when the British lion will be domesticated."[53] Have you started taking German lessons yet? McCarran asked one correspondent. "Won't it be fine when they grow sauerkraut in Piccadilly Square or make weisswurst at Trafalgar Square," he asked another. "They are going to convert the Tower of London into a beer garden."[54]

Then one of McCarran's closest friends went into the army. Joe McNamara was a young attorney in Elko whom McCarran had tutored for the bar exam five years earlier, sending McNamara books to read and constantly reassuring him that he would do fine on the test — encouraging advice considering that Judge McCarran was one of the bar examiners. "We will have some secret sessions and I will try to get you acquainted with the ways of the court as much as possible so as to take away the newness of the thing," McCarran told him. ". . . If it is necessary I will have a roll of blankets here so that you can sleep on the court room floor to overcome this awe inspiring sense."[55] McCarran showed the same solicitude for McNamara when the young attorney went off to Camp Lewis in Washington in 1918. McNamara was thirteen years McCarran's junior; the judge took a paternal interest in the younger lawyer. McNamara had first studied law while driving a stage between Elko and Tuscarora, and McCarran saw more than a little of himself in the young man.

Private McNamara wanted to get a commission as an officer, and McCarran hounded Nevada's congressional delegation with letters and wires and personal implorings to make it happen. "I will never let go on this thing until it is accomplished," McCarran promised.[56] For months McCarran lobbied Pittman and his colleagues and nudged a Nevada acquaintance, James Scrugham, who was serving as a colonel in the War Department. "I am going to keep after this thing night, noon and morning," McCarran assured McNamara. "We will make it an issue in the campaign, if necessary. We will do anything."[57]

McNamara got his lieutenant's bars.

In July 1919 Wilson presented the Treaty of Versailles to the Senate, declaring that it was a moral duty for the United States to join the League of Nations and World Court. "The stage is set, the destiny disclosed," Wilson told Congress. "It has come about by no plan of our conceiving, but by the hand of God who led us into this way."[58]

But the hand of God had also placed Henry Cabot Lodge in the chairmanship of the Senate Foreign Relations Committee. Wilson and Lodge got along not much better than France and Germany. Wilson demanded that the treaty be approved as written; Lodge stalled and spiked it with

Downstream from Reno, Pat McCarran's immigrant father cleared sagebrush from the banks of the Truckee River where he built the family house and nailed up a shamrock for good luck.

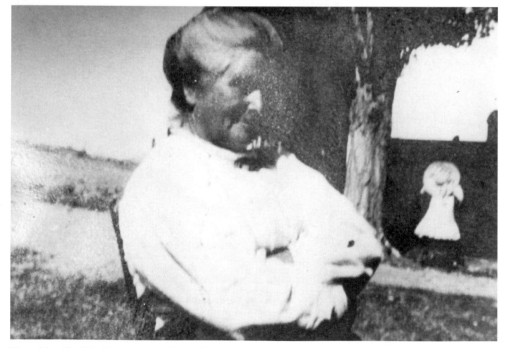

The elder Pat McCarran sometimes shot at trespassers; he passed his temper on to his only son. Margaret McCarran couldn't read or write, but she pushed her son to study law and leave the farm.

Born in 1876, Pat McCarran (above, second row, third from left) was four years older than his classmates when he started school. He would never play well with others. McCarran married Martha (Birdie) Harriet Weeks in 1903.

In 1900 a huge silver strike was
discovered in the barren mountains
of central Nevada, giving birth to
the boomtown of Tonopah —
which eventually became the
smelter that forged the political
and economic elite of the state for
the next generation. McCarran
was a latecomer to Tonopah,
where he opened his first law
office in 1906.

Republican Tasker Oddie
found a bonanza in Tonopah,
then lost everything, before
striking it rich in politics, first
as governor and then as a U.S.
senator — the job McCarran
longed for.

Democrat Key Pittman (right) launched a political career in Tonopah that sent him to the U.S. Senate for twenty-six years — and put him in a position to block McCarran's dearest goal. George Wingfield (below) went from playing cards in the boom-town to building a banking and real-estate empire that made him the richest man in Nevada — and the head of a bipartisan political machine that ran the state from his office in Reno.

In the 1930s Reno was the largest city in Nevada, with more than eighteen thousand inhabitants — not counting the divorce colony that took up temporary residence at the Riverside Hotel.

McCarran (above, center) served as Chief Justice of the Nevada Supreme Court. After losing reelection to the bench, McCarran went into private practice, helping clients such as actress Mary Pickford get a divorce. But more than anything he wanted to go to Washington.

amendments that Wilson would not accept, especially one designed to keep the United States from going to war on behalf of other countries.

Truculence from the leaders of the Republican opposition might be expected, but the war also opened a chasm between the western progressives in Congress, who had long been among the most energetic of liberal reformers, and Wilson. Less numerous but more vocal than the reservationists, the progressives became known as the irreconcilables. Their leader was Idaho senator William Edgar Borah, a liberal Republican who supported Wilson domestically and voted for the war resolution — which he regretted for the rest of his life. Borah was one of six senators to vote against the Espionage Act and became so disillusioned with the domestic repression during the war that he almost left the Senate. "I am unwilling to Prussianize this country in order to de-Prussianize Germany," he said. ". . . I would rather quit and shovel dirt the rest of my life."[59]

The treaty, *any* treaty, Borah believed, would be a betrayal of American sovereignty. To enter the league was to step into disaster. To give up George Washington's foreign policy of no entangling alliances would not make the world more liberal and peaceful but would only leach liberty and peace from the United States. "These distinguishing virtues of a real republic you can not commingle with the discordant and destructive forces of the Old World and still preserve them," Borah told the Senate. "You can not yoke a government whose fundamental maxim is that of liberty to a government whose first law is that of force and hope to preserve the former."[60] He would oppose the treaty, Borah said, if Christ himself were to return to earth in support of the league.

In September, Wilson took his case to the American people, hoping that public pressure would translate into the sixty-four votes that he needed in the Senate for the United States to join the league. Wilson spent twenty-two days crossing the country, traveling eight thousand miles, giving forty speeches on behalf of the treaty without reservations — followed everywhere by a tag team of irreconcilables made up of Borah and Senator Hiram Johnson, a progressive Republican from California. The trip broke Wilson's health. Shortly after returning to Washington the president suffered a stroke from which he never recovered. In November the Senate finally voted on the treaty, Wilson's Democrats and the irreconcilables both voting against Lodge's version, 39 to 55. When Wilson's version came up for a vote it went down 38 to 53. "The greatest victory," Borah exulted, "since Appomattox."[61]

Back in Nevada, McCarran was bored and frustrated. Six years on the bench
— the length of a Senate term. It was, he told a friend, like being buried alive.
"There is no place on earth that constitutes so fine a political burying ground
as the bench," he said.[62] Sitting in his high, stiff-backed leather chair between
his two judicial colleagues in a tiny courtroom on the second floor of the
sleepy Carson statehouse, McCarran felt like he was the one in prison.
McCarran worked hard (as chief justice for the last two years of his term he
wrote thirty-two decisions out of seventy-three, on top of thirteen concur-
rences and four dissents), but deciding the constitutionality of the Nevada
Employer Liability Act of 1907 did little to challenge his powers or focus his
energies. In that small room McCarran's mind often drifted to a much larger
chamber very far away. "In the Senate of the United States today the vice president is president of that body," he advised a correspondent who had just been
elected to the state assembly, "but the greatest single power, the greatest representation of individual influence, is neither in the president of the Senate nor
in the majority side of the house, but on the contrary is a single individual on
the minority side of that body, Robert M. La Follette. The sole and only
reason for this is his wonderful knowledge of legislative affairs, his wonderful
grasp of the law, and above all his wonderful standing with the men of affairs
who recognized that he is beyond reproach and that he has a keen conception of right and wrong. This man is but a single individual. He has not been
in recent years even in touch with the power of his own great party, but stood
head and shoulders above that party in the estimation of the people."[63]

Like a man obsessed with a beautiful woman, McCarran could not keep
his thoughts off the object of his longing or what he would do if he ever
obtained it. "The greatest influence, the greatest honor, and the greatest
power that can come to a member of this legislature is to be an active, energetic, conscientious, studious worker on the floor," he rhapsodized. "If I
were a member-elect of the legislature, I would not aspire to any position,
save that perhaps of chairmanship of some important committee. My
reason for this is that the speaker is but a functionary, governed by the
power of the majority, limited by rules of action. His greatest power is in
the appointing of committees, and when that has been performed his force
has practically spent itself. The fellow on the floor, with a knowledge of
legislative affairs, who makes it a special point to verse himself in statutes
already in existence in this state and with the decisions of the court of last
resort of this state will be the greatest power in any legislative body. He will
be a power that the speaker himself will be afraid to challenge."[64]

One could dream, anyway.

In 1919 a great wave of strikes broke out across the country. "Every strike," proclaimed the Wobblies, "is a small revolution and a dress rehearsal for the big one."[65] In Seattle, an IWW stronghold, thirty-five thousand shipyard workers walked off the job in January. The next month a general strike paralyzed the city, closing schools, stalling streetcars, shuttering businesses. Mayor Ole Hanson led a column of federal troops into town in a car draped with an American flag. "The anarchists in this community shall not rule its affairs," he proclaimed.[66] The strike collapsed. Then in April, a bomb was mailed to Hanson's office. No one was injured, but the next day another mail bomb blew the hands off the maid who opened it for former senator Thomas Hardwick. Thirty-four more bombs were intercepted in the mail — addressed to everyone from the postmaster who had banned the radical magazine *The Masses* from the mails to Oliver Wendell Holmes Jr., who had written a decision that sent socialist and antiwar activist Charles Schenk to jail. On May Day riots broke out between radicals and police in Boston, New York, and Cleveland. In June a bomb blew up a porch (and an anarchist bomber) at the home of Attorney General A. Mitchell Palmer — followed within the hour by explosions in eight other cities, one of which killed a night watchman outside a judge's house. "Palmer," Woodrow Wilson warned his Quaker attorney general, "do not let this country see red."[67]

The attorney general created a new General Intelligence Division inside the Bureau of Investigation and put a twenty-four-year Justice Department lawyer named J. Edgar Hoover in charge. The former librarian soon had a card catalog of sixty thousand radicals. On November 7, the second anniversary of the Russian Revolution, the Justice Department raided the offices of the Union of Russian Workers in a dozen cities, catching a grab bag of thousands of immigrants and anarchists, between which Hoover and his minions saw little difference. The next month Hoover put 249 foreign-born radicals, including Emma Goldman and Alexander Berkman, on the USS *Buford* and sent the ship sailing to Russia. "Other 'Soviet arks' will sail for Europe," Hoover promised, "just as often as it is necessary to rid the country of dangerous radicals."[68]

The most dangerous radicals seemed to be the brand-new Communist Party, which had formed in 1919 to bring the Bolshevik revolution to America but had so far spent most of its time fighting itself. Young Hoover had found his life's work. On January 2, 1920, government agents swept up four thousand members of the fledgling Communist Party in raids in thirty-three cities. "Each and every adherent of this movement," Palmer said, "is a potential murderer or a potential thief."[69] In Congress that winter, some seventy sedition bills were proposed. Within two years thirty-five states and two territories also had their own sedition or criminal syndicalist laws, such as the one in California making failure to salute the flag punishable by twenty years in prison. Thirty-two states and numerous cities also banned red flags or the display of other banners supporting anarchy or revolution. Five socialists elected to the New York legislature were denied their seats.

No more Soviet arks, however, would sail. Louis Post, an assistant secretary of labor, decided that mere membership in a radical organization was not sufficient cause for deportation. Palmer tried to have Post impeached. Post won the fight, and hundreds of jailed immigrants were released. Hoover then had his investigators investigate Post for ties to the Wobblies. The tide, however, had turned. A dozen prominent lawyers — including Harvard Law School dean Roscoe Pound and his colleagues Felix Frankfurter and Zechariah Chafee Jr. — released a sixty-seven-page brief (Report Upon the Illegal Practices of the United States Department of Justice) that charged the attorney general's office with wholesale violations of the Constitution, from inflicting cruel and unusual punishment to arrests without warrants and coercing witnesses into incriminating themselves. Hoover responded by opening a file on each of the twelve lawyers who signed the report.

The Red Scare soon faded. The Republicans regained the White House, and it was left to Warren Harding and Calvin Coolidge to pardon most of the antiwar protestors imprisoned by Wilson's government. Hoover, however, kept his job. And his lists. By 1921 he had 450,000 names in his radical index file.

McCarran was not moved by the Red Scare. A decade earlier he had seen the Wobblies crushed in Tonopah and Goldfield, and he knew that the rhetoric of revolution was a useful excuse for mine owners like George Wingfield to strangle labor organizers. During the war Nevada, like the rest of the nation, was caught up in a frenzy of patriotism. The Lutheran church at Minden, for example, called off services in German, and the local high school stopped teaching the language. A smelter worker in Belmont named Al Shidler was fired for opposing the draft, then found a job as a deputy sheriff but lost it after the Tonopah Loyalty League complained about his politics; eventually he was sentenced to federal prison for sedition. After the war Nevada, too, was rocked by a series of strikes, most blamed on the resurgent Wobblies. In 1919 the state responded by passing a Criminal Syndicalism Act, making it a crime to advocate violent revolution. Governor Emmet Boyle used the law to help break an IWW strike in Tonopah that finally squashed what was left of the union in Nevada. Boyle was a Democrat. But McCarran so hated the governor that when he ran for reelection in 1918 McCarran promised to vote for an anarchist, a socialist, a Wobbly, or even a Republican before Boyle. "Anybody," he fumed, "but Boyle."[70]

The mere whiff of radicalism did not yet set McCarran atremble. In fact, he soon formed a law partnership with Grant Miller, a Nevada socialist who had run for the Senate several times (he had polled 25 percent of the ballots going against Newlands in the race McCarran sat out in 1914 and won almost 29 percent of the vote against Pittman two years later) and was drifting into the Republican Party. Later in life McCarran would grow much more circumspect in his associations. But during the long years in which he pined to go to Washington, McCarran's greatest enemies were those in his own party who blocked his way. Out of power, his heart went to the powerless. His feelings on the lawlessness of the Palmer Raids can be inferred from one of his early Supreme Court decisions. "It is commendable for district attorneys to be vigorous in the prosecution of crime, but they should not forget that their duty is not solely to convict," he wrote. "The defendant has rights which the prosecuting attorney is . . . bound to respect, and even protect. . . . When a prosecuting officer seeks to take advantage of public sentiment to gain an unjust conviction or seeks to take an unfair advantage in the introduction of evidence or in any other respect, he is failing in his duty as the state's representative. The duty of district attorneys to be fair to defendants on trial is scarcely less obligatory than the duty which rests upon the courts, whose officers they are. Both are bound, while holding a defendant accountable for his acts, to protect him in his substantial rights."[71]

McCarran sounded more like Felix Frankfurter than J. Edgar Hoover. Time would change that.

As McCarran's six-year term on the bench drew to a close in January 1918, he wanted nothing more than to be someplace else. Let someone else have the job. "I am very much inclined not to run," he said. "The work and confinement are in no wise compensated for by the salary; and

whatever of honor or prestige there may be in the position, one gains it
all his first term."[72] A few weeks before — on Christmas Eve 1917 —
Newlands had died, and McCarran immediately grasped for an appointment to serve out the senator's term. Instead, Governor Boyle named Elko
Democrat Charles Henderson, a veteran of the state assembly and a regent
at the university, to the seat. McCarran was forlorn. "Conditions in Carson
never changed," he lamented. "There is little to be heard, save the ceaseless wrangle of the official family. Factions being formed and broke; plans
being laid and wrecked; political intrigue ever uppermost; thus we spend
the time in the capitol."[73]

In the fall McCarran could have another shot at the Senate, when
Henderson would have to face voters to stay in office. Henderson, however, was the anointed of the party. It would be safer for McCarran to stay
on the bench. But McCarran's enemies were already plotting to get rid of
him by encouraging District Judge Edward Ducker to challenge McCarran
for his seat. "I am of the opinion that Ducker will beat Pat if he makes the
race for the judgeship and that Henderson will beat him if he tries for the
Senate, so let our beloved friend practice law," his old nemesis A. B. Gray
chortled. "It is a noble profession."[74] For months McCarran dithered. He
knew a crowd was gathering to watch him fall but seemed gripped by a
strange lassitude, moving as if he were wrapped in gauze. "The Capitol is
about as usual," he reported. "Everybody hates everybody else and political
knives are being ground and whetted."[75]

When McCarran first ran for the court six years earlier he was
emphatic that he would not make it a career. "I will never again be a candidate for this office," he had declared.[76] At the time McCarran was sure
he would not be long on the bench; he would move fast, and the promise
cost him nothing. Six years and half as many thwarted campaigns for the
Senate later his prospects looked far different. He didn't really want to stay
on the bench, but it still looked better than sliding back into his own practice and private frustrations. In June he finally announced for the court
again. "I concluded to try for one more term," he told a friend. "If I am
successful in this I am through with politics."[77]

It was too late. The wheels on the party machine were already moving,
and McCarran fell beneath them. Ducker beat him at the polls 12,101 to
11,566. Five hundred and thirty-five votes. Ducker would serve on the
bench for the next twenty-seven years. McCarran hardly seemed to mind.
"One who cannot accept defeat has no business playing the political
game," he said.[78] His foes were ecstatic. "We have given our beloved friend

Pat McCarran a drubbing that he will not forget soon," rejoiced Gray.[79] McCarran had spent a decade struggling to get to Washington. At every turn a familiar face seemed to block the way. His ceaseless striving alienated and angered those in his own party; enemies collected like tumbleweed in a ditch. Sprung from the prison of the court, perhaps he could find satisfaction elsewhere. "Another six years on the bench would mean six years retirement from active life," McCarran concluded after his defeat, "whereas, I hope I am free to enter into life with a new determination and a new activity."[80]

McCarran's political career seemed finished. All that was left was the law.

CHAPTER 4

Where Is Your Blood?

All about him the city was hustling, for hustling's sake.
Men in motors were hustling to pass one another in the
hustling traffic. Men were hustling to catch trolleys,
with another trolley a minute behind, and to leap from
the trolleys, to gallop across the sidewalk, to hurl themselves into buildings, into hustling express elevators.
Men in dairy lunches were hustling to gulp down the
food which cooks had hustled to fry. . . . Men who had
made five thousand, year before last, and ten thousand
last year, were urging on nerve-yelping bodies and
parched brains so that they might make twenty thousand this year; and the men who had broken down
immediately after making their twenty thousand dollars
were hustling to catch trains, to hustle through the
vacations which the hustling doctors had ordered.

Among them Babbitt hustled back to his office, to sit
down with nothing much to do except see that the staff
looked as though they were hustling.[1]

— Sinclair Lewis, *Babbitt*

McCarran was waiting when the train from California rumbled into Reno
on Sunday, February 15, 1920, rattling the windows along Commercial
Row as it whistled past Virginia Street and clattered to a stop at the depot
off Center Street. He was looking for a client. She wasn't hard to find. For
one thing, she was a pretty twenty-seven-year-old (although she claimed to
be only twenty-six) who stood a little taller than five feet and didn't weigh
more than a hundred pounds, traveling with her mother, a business manager, and a maid. For another, she was Mary Pickford, the most popular
actress in the country, the star of *Rebecca of Sunnybrook Farm* and *A Poor Little
Rich Girl*. Born Gladys Smith in 1892, she had made her first stage appearance when she was six; at fourteen she hit Broadway and became Mary
Pickford. At nineteen she married actor Owen Moore. Her career soared;
his swooned. By 1920 Pickford was commanding more than two hundred
thousand dollars a film. But "America's Sweetheart" had a problem: She

wanted to ditch her tosspot husband for her lover, actor Douglas Fairbanks. McCarran was going to help.

After the double humiliation of not running for the Senate and losing his seat on the Supreme Court, McCarran returned to private practice in Reno. He added his name to the firm of Miller and Mashburn, and the partnership did a thriving business, much of it in the divorce trade. Reno had become the national mecca for those desiring to slip the bounds of holy matrimony. Laura Corey had put the town on the map when she moved there in 1906 for half a year in order to dump her husband of twenty years, William Ellis Corey, president of U.S. Steel Corporation. Most states required at least a year's residency before a person could apply for a divorce; some, like California, required a year's waiting period before getting remarried. In Nevada it was six months. The Silver State never had many citizens, and it did whatever it could to encourage people to reside within its borders — even if for only twenty-six weeks. Nevada had averaged less than one hundred divorces a year, but the Corey case became a national scandal. She easily won a divorce and walked away with custody of her son and two million dollars.

Once again there was a gold rush in Nevada. One lawyer printed up a flyer ("Are You Seeking DIVORCE? Do You Want Quick and Reliable Action?"[2]), touting Nevada as the cure for marital troubles, which he had inserted in New York theater programs and newspapers. By the early 1920s the state was granting around fifteen hundred divorces a year, the vast majority to temporary residents, most of whom spent their time in Reno hotels or nearby dude ranches. The flood of mostly female, mostly well-off divorce seekers gave Reno a cosmopolitan cast far greater than one would normally expect in a cow town of twelve thousand people. Beauty parlors and boutiques did a good business, even if the faces of the clientele constantly changed. Reno developed its own slang: The noon train from the East was the Divorce Special, the courthouse became the Separator, seeing a client off after the decree was called pouring a divorcée on the train. The divorce colony had its own mythology: Newly cured women would kiss the columns of the courthouse and pitch their wedding rings off the Virginia Street Bridge into the Truckee. During the nadir of the Depression, Nevada earned up to five million dollars a year from divorce, more than from mining. Much of the country was shocked by the state's eagerness to rend marriage asunder. "The two great danger centers that threaten American society,"[3] claimed New York University chancellor

Elmer Ellsworth Brown, were Moscow and Reno. But to the practical-minded citizenry of Nevada, the state was merely offering a public service. "If I were compelled to fly in an untested airplane," as George Bartlett, McCarran's old foe and a longtime Reno divorce judge, put it, "I should certainly want to wear a parachute."[4]

Pickford and her entourage piled into McCarran's car and drove south to the Campbell Ranch near Genoa, the state's oldest town, in a valley down the steep eastern slope below Lake Tahoe. For the next two weeks Pickford and her mother went riding every day in the shadow of the Sierra and impressed the Campbell family with their generous tipping.

On March 2 McCarran escorted Pickford and her mother to the court-house in the nearby town of Minden. Another Reno attorney, Albert Ayres, met them there. Ayres represented Pickford's estranged husband, Owen Moore, who had crossed into Nevada for twelve hours the day before and stopped for dinner at the Minden Inn — just long enough for McCarran to have him served with divorce papers. It was late in the day — already after five — but Judge Frank Langan agreed to hear the case. Moore wasn't contesting the divorce.

"If the court please," McCarran started, "this case is Number Three hundred and Sixty-two, Gladys M. Moore versus Owen E. Moore."[5] A Nevada divorce involved as much ritual as any church wedding — and the outcome was usually just about as certain. First the lawyer had to establish that his client was a bona fide resident of the state. Then the attorney had to provide grounds for the action, which was usually either desertion (Pickford's claim) or extreme cruelty (which in Nevada divorce courts covered a lot of marital territory). McCarran put James Campbell, whose family owned the ranch Moore was staying at, on the stand.

"No arrangements have been made for their leaving?" the lawyer asked.

"No," Campbell replied.

"And so far as you know it is her intention to remain at your home?"

"Yes, sir."

"Have you ever been informed by the plaintiff, Mrs. Moore, or by her mother, Mrs. Smith, as to her remaining in Douglas County and a resident of the county?"

"No, sir."

"That is all."

Then McCarran put Pickford — or Mrs. Moore, as she was referred to in court — on the stand. Clad in a simple black dress, her blond hair pinned up under a hat and large glasses covering her eyes, the actress recounted her torturous relationship with Moore — how she'd married at seventeen and went to Cuba with her husband, who got drunk the first day in Havana and then disappeared for the next three. And that was the honeymoon. "From the time of my marriage I was forced to support myself, my mother, my brother and sister," she sobbed to the court, "and I was forced to work and my husband said that a wife was a luxury and that he did not intend buying my clothes."

Moore told his wife that she was the cause of his failure, that she was the reason he drank, and that he was sorry he ever married her. He left her repeatedly and hadn't returned in the last three years. She hadn't even spoken to her husband in more than a year. She sent Moore letters and presents and begged him to return — all to no avail. At Christmas she had a nervous breakdown, and her doctor told her she needed a change of climate. So she moved to Nevada.

"Where do you live?" McCarran asked.

"At Genoa."

"Have you any other residence?"

"No."

"Is it your intention to make this your permanent residence?"

"It is."

McCarran asked his client if she had anything to do with her husband coming into the state. No. The first she knew about Moore's visit was when she had heard from her manager that he was heading to Virginia City to scout coal mine locations for a movie.

"You mean gold mines," suggested Judge Langan.

"Yes, gold mines."

"No arrangements were made between yourself and your husband whereby he was to come into this state?" McCarran asked.

"No, sir."

The judge then questioned the plaintiff.

"You have spoken several times of your company," Langan asked. "What is your work?"

"Motion pictures."

"You have been engaged in this work for some time?"

"Yes, sir."

"Is it your purpose to build here?"

"Well, if I can find a place to suit me I will."

"And you have given up Los Angeles as your residence and your permanent residence is Genoa, Douglas County, Nevada?"

"Until I regain my health, but this will be my home."

"Do I understand that you have come into this state in good faith, seeking health and nothing else?"

"Yes, sir."

"That you have not come into the state of Nevada for the purpose of instituting divorce proceedings?"

"No, sir."

"That is absolutely so?"

"Absolutely so."

"I think," concluded the judge, "I have gone into this question pretty thoroughly. I feel that I should do so in all of these matters in view of the fact that our statute requires a six months residence."

Divorce granted!

Pickford's friends later claimed that it cost the actress one hundred thousand dollars for Moore to turn up in Nevada on cue.

The next afternoon a large car, curtains drawn, drove up the highway from Genoa, entered Reno just after sundown, and stopped at McCarran's house. Mary Pickford (wearing a veil), her mother, and her maid climbed out and spent an hour playing with McCarran's children while the judge went downtown to attend to some urgent business. Then McCarran took the women to the depot and put Pickford on the Number 5 train to San Francisco. Pickford, it seemed, had regained her health. But even as Pickford's train was climbing into the Sierra, the *Reno Evening Gazette* was screaming in an eight-column banner headline that the state's most famous resident had just been divorced. "Maybe," the paper hoped, "Reno will see her tomorrow or next week."[6]

When the train pulled into the station in Oakland, a horde of reporters was waiting. Two women jumped from the train into a waiting car, and the media posse chased them down to San Jose. The reporters had followed decoys. Pickford and her mother had escaped to San Francisco. But the next day when they arrived in Los Angeles, reporters hounded them again; Pickford broke into tears and stumbled and fell as she tried to run away. "Why can't you leave the poor little girl alone," her mother scolded.[7] "I never in my life felt so much like a hunted animal," Pickford later complained.[8] Pickford held a press conference and proclaimed that she would never marry again. Then on March 28, barely three weeks after her divorce, Pickford wed Douglas Fairbanks at a dinner party at his house.

Nevada was the laughingstock of the country. The state's six-month divorce law was scandalous enough, but now even that requirement was a joke. McCarran's enemies didn't waste time. Three days after Pickford's wedding, the Washoe County Bar Association passed a resolution asking the state attorney general to investigate the case and set aside the judgment, which would make the actress a bigamist. Gray Mashburn, McCarran's law partner, was at the meeting and jumped up in protest, arguing that the Pickford case was no different from most others. "In divorce cases practically every attorney knew that the testimony of plaintiffs that they intend to make this county their place of permanent residence was not true," he said.[9] If we're going to investigate one divorce case, Mashburn suggested, we should investigate them all. The bar association had a sudden change of heart, voted to reconsider the resolution, unanimously defeated it, and expunged all mention of the idea from the minutes of its meeting.

For a while Nevada judges enforced the six-month residency requirement more stringently. Then the legislature cut it down to three months. By 1931 it took only six weeks to get a divorce in Nevada. Cartoonists had a field day. *Pic* magazine, for instance, ran a drawing of a busty young woman leaving the Washoe County Courthouse with her rotund lawyer. "Boy," she enthused, "I feel like a new man!"

Two months after getting Pickford unhitched, McCarran turned a key and opened the door on his beautiful new house on a bluff above the Truckee. The house sat at 401 Court Street, a few blocks down the road from the Washoe County Courthouse, on the same street where George Wingfield lived. McCarran had seen the house being built in 1913 for Lewis "Bert" Gibbons. Bert Gibbons was only two years older than McCarran, but he represented everything McCarran wasn't: An attorney trained at Hastings College of Law in San Francisco who had come to Tonopah in 1906, Gibbons was a Republican who had been law partners with prominent Democrats and McCarran haters George Bartlett and George Thatcher in Nye County, all of whom joined the exodus to Reno. Gibbons personified the kind of wealthy and successful lawyer that McCarran had always aspired to be, and his house was the most austerely elegant in town.

McCarran lived in a two-bedroom house on unfashionable Belmont Road. Most of Reno's elite lived in a six-block neighborhood south of the

Truckee and west of Virginia Street called Newlands Heights. The area took its name from Senator Francis Newlands, who'd built a sprawling Queen Anne mansion overlooking a bend in the river. Bert Gibbons settled down the street, and George Wingfield just half a block farther. In this neighborhood of Victorians and Tudor mansions, the Gibbons house stood out for its Palladian simplicity: a two-story rectangle with paired Doric columns supporting a first-story porch and a classical frieze running under a peaked roof. Hawthorn and linden trees shaded a backyard that ran down toward the rocky bank of the Truckee. When Gibbons died earlier that year, McCarran was determined to buy the house. He might not be part of Reno's clubby ruling class, but he could at least live among them, a prospect that some of the town's oligarchy found unpleasant. "Pat McCarran," Gibbons's widow sniffed, "couldn't buy one of my little hawthorne trees."[10] When McCarran offered her thirty-five thousand dollars she changed her mind. Soon the rumor spread that Mary Pickford had given the property to her lawyer as part of his fee. In truth McCarran had to take out a bank loan to buy the house.

Now McCarran seemed literally surrounded by his enemies. Thatcher had just purchased the old Newlands mansion at the end of the block, and Wingfield lived on McCarran's other side. And he paid dearly for the privilege. It was a lot of money for McCarran to spend on a house. He had a wife, four children — two of whom were in Catholic school in California — a fifth on the way, and two elderly parents to support. But for McCarran 401 Court Street was more than a house; it was a symbol of his success and his hard-earned place among the Nevada aristocracy. His dream of going to Washington might seem hopeless, but the sheepherder son of illiterate immigrants had become one of the state's most eminent jurists, and in the house above the Truckee in the neighborhood of senators and bankers he would live where he belonged. And who knew? Someday he might run for office again. "I'm going to be a candidate again," McCarran vowed. "I don't know just when. Whenever the time is right."[11]

And when McCarran came home from the office on the lengthening days of spring after he bought the house and walked out the back and through the scrim of fifty-foot-tall trees down to the river that meant so much to him and his family, it all seemed worth it. The branches were still bare from the winter, but when the late-afternoon wind blew down from the mountains, the rustling was a musical counterpoint to the constant murmur of the river. Across the Truckee he could see two of the towers of his church, St. Thomas

Aquinas, both crowned with the cross of his faith, still shining in twilight. From the east the darkening river rounded a bend and softly forked past a long sliver of land just below McCarran's house before curling together again and flowing west under the double stone arch of the Virginia Street Bridge. The tree-studded islet was called Belle Isle. A few years earlier it held a small amusement park that had gone bankrupt and fallen, like so much else in Nevada, into George Wingfield's hands. McCarran's new neighbor had just given the land to Reno for its first park, and the city had renamed it in the banker's honor. Now George Wingfield Park literally parted the waters behind McCarran's house. If he thought about it too long, it was enough to cause the smile to drop from McCarran's face.

He really was surrounded.

A year after moving into the new house, Birdie McCarran finally gave her husband a son, Samuel Patrick. His daughter Margaret had been born in 1904, followed by Mary (1906), Norine (1911), and the baby Sylvia Patricia (1919). McCarran doted on his family, which was to be both a source of strength and repeated anguish to him over his long life. None of the children save perhaps Margaret would live a happy life — and in her case she found contentment only in a stern submission to her twin gods: the Catholic Church and her father.

From an early age Margaret, who inherited her father's fierce will and unyielding nature, was fascinated with the Church. When the McCarran family went to nine o'clock Mass on Sundays at St. Thomas Aquinas the girls would stare up at the city's three nuns high in the choir loft, their dour visages like dark gargoyles. Little Mary, who had been named for a nun in the hospital where she was born, trembled at the sight. Margaret was enthralled.

When the family moved to Carson City while McCarran sat on the court, Margaret found a tree house in their yard and called it a convent. Then, in 1915, McCarran drove his brood over the Donner Pass to the Panama–Pacific International Exposition. On the way back they stopped at the Holy Names Convent in Oakland, where Margaret's friend went to school. When McCarran turned the crank and drove away two hours later, Margaret was not in the car; she stayed at the school. By her senior year Margaret had decided to become a nun. McCarran was not pleased. The family might give up steak for salmon to observe meatless Fridays, but giving up his eldest daughter to the cloister was something else. Margaret was as sharp and unbending as steel; she could have a brilliant career in politics or public affairs. Why not try going to the University of Nevada for a year? McCarran pleaded. Margaret agreed. She joined a sorority and dated boys. She bobbed her hair and tried to comb and spray the thick McCarran waves into the straight lines of a flapper. She wore frilly dresses and long strands of beads. When Margaret wanted to throw a party, McCarran was all too happy to pull back the rugs on the hardwood floor in the Court Street house for dancing. Then on a summer morning after Margaret finished school with honors, she told McCarran over breakfast that she still wanted to enter the convent. Mary, who had also gone off to school at the Holy Names and wore her hair just like her big sister's, had just come home from Oakland and walked her desolated father to his office holding his hand.

In August 1923 McCarran and Birdie took Margaret back to Oakland to enter the Holy Names novitiate. McCarran's heart was broken. "Every place, everything here brings you back to me," he wrote Margaret. "We returned here Saturday evening, the miserable old house was there, a shell, empty and horrible. Most men need die but once but that dissolution which takes one home would be most welcome — it isn't fair to have to go through it twice. . . . Margie dear in all my sorrow I rest on your promise given to me that you will in God's name come to me on the very first occasion of regret or unhappiness. Your promise Margie, remember it. In all my heartache, in this all this awfulness, I am proud of you. Proud that I am what I am to you. Proud that you are my daughter. I am going through this as God gives me strength to bear it. This is my cross, a cross I made for myself, constructed with no end of diligence and I will bear it. Margie pray for me! I know it is cowardly to talk to you but I just must explode and to what other source may I go with my heart ache and feelings. I don't dare show them at home because the blame is mine."[12]

In her senior year at high school Mary decided that she, too, wanted to be a nun. Birdie McCarran was not thrilled to lose a second daughter to the Church. "Over my dead body," she exclaimed.[13] McCarran offered to buy her a car and a fur coat and send her to Stanford University if she would not enter the convent. Please, Papa, she said, don't. McCarran was crestfallen that she wanted to become a nun, but when Mary struggled over finding a religious name he wrote his daughter a letter. "For years," it began, "you were called Mary, until we had another little child who couldn't say her R's very well, and slurred it into 'Mercy.' Soon we all

began to call you Mercy, so that you went into the convent with a nickname. A little child gave you that beautiful name of Mercy, and an old man
would have you keep it, for out of the mouths of babes and fools comes
truth. If you will live your life in the spirit of that word, you will have no
fear, my daughter, because you will save your soul."[14]

When McCarran walked out his front door and took the short stroll to his
office downtown he traversed the entire power structure of Nevada. Turning
left he ambled down Court Street, passing Wingfield's house in half a block
and catching glimpses of the Truckee between homes and trees until he
arrived at the corner of Virginia Street three blocks down the road, where
the Washoe County Courthouse stood. The building, like many in Reno,
was the work of local architect Frederic DeLongchamps. The courthouse
was not his masterwork: A poorly proportioned classical pile fronted by six
large Corinthian columns and topped by a too-small dome, the whole thing
crowded hard against Virginia Street. Next door rose the new Riverside
Hotel, a six-story brick DeLongchamps building that Wingfield had just put
up in 1927 for $750,000 — the same year the state halved its residency
requirement for divorce seekers to three months. In Reno such coinci-
dences as the richest man in Nevada opening a huge new hotel full of suites
perfect for a ninety-day stay the same year that the state passed a law guar-
anteeing a flood of new visitors happened all the time.

Heading north up Virginia Street, McCarran crossed the Truckee and
in two blocks came to the Reno National Bank building, another
DeLongchamps creation. The building was a four-story gleaming-white
neoclassical temple with fluted pilasters standing at the corner of Virginia
and Second Streets. The second floor housed Wingfield's office, room 203,
which was adjacent to the offices of his law firm, Thatcher & Woodburn.
Wingfield was also head of the state Republican Party; Thatcher, national
committeeman, and Woodburn, state chairman, ran the Democratic Party.
The office was called the cave; all three shared the same phone number,
4111, and reception area. "Every little thing that went on around," newsman John Sanford recalled, "everybody said, 'Well, now, how's that gonna
get along with the boys up there in the cave?'"[15]

And *4111* became a shorthand expression for what came to be called the
bipartisan political machine, through which, it was assumed, Wingfield
influenced most important decisions in Nevada. Back in 1912 Governor
Tasker Oddie had offered to appoint Wingfield to the remainder of George
Nixon's Senate term after Wingfield's old partner died. Wingfield turned

him down. He preferred to stay in Reno. While he was the state's most prominent Republican, Wingfield was hardly bent out of shape when the Democrats did well. "I would have liked one or two more Republican senators," he wrote after one state legislative election. "However, with [Democrat] Fletcher playing the game right, which I am sure he will, there will be nothing to it anyway."[16] In 1922 Wingfield briefly resigned as the state's Republican national committeeman. He claimed poor health, but most people suspected that he didn't want to be involved in the contest against his friend Key Pittman.

"The people of the state are interested in able representation at Washington," explained the *Nevada State Journal*. "It is not so much that the senator is a Democrat or a Republican, so long as he safeguards the interests of his constituents, whether they be Democrats or Republicans. The senators from Nevada must represent the state and not the party. The state comes first, the party second."[17]

If McCarran kept walking up Virginia Street he would finally hit the university, his alma mater, where Wingfield became a trustee. Wingfield, it seemed, was everywhere.

On the Fourth of July 1926 McCarran stood on a platform in Ely, in eastern Nevada's copper country, and insisted that the United States declare its independence from the rest of the world. The annual Nevada State Federation of Labor convention had drawn thousands to the dusty mining outpost. And the town had gone all-out: parades, boxing matches, and a bathing-beauty contest. The only minor mishap took place when a parachute jumper aiming for the town's baseball park was blown off course, over a hill, and came down on a hard patch of desert. For McCarran it was a bad omen.

McCarran shared the podium with a gaggle of other politicians, all running for the Senate. There was the Republican incumbent Tasker Oddie, his old Tonopah acquaintance, who had lost his fortune, moved into the governor's manson, only to return to the hardscrabble life of prospecting before Wingfield finally helped him win election to the U.S. Senate in 1920. There was E. E. Roberts, Reno's liberal mayor, a former Republican congressman, who was hoping to take Oddie's place on the GOP ticket. And there were three other Democrats: C. H. "Bert" McIntosh, Dr. William H. Brennan, and Ray Baker.

Baker was the only one to worry about. He was rich, well connected, an intimate of Pittman. Baker had been born in Nevada three years after

McCarran. Although his father was a successful lawyer in Eureka, Baker lit out for Tonopah, where he found work driving a mule train to mining camps in Death Valley. Baker became Pittman's secretary in Washington, then went to Russia as an assistant to the American ambassador. Returning home, he was appointed director of the U.S. mint in Carson City, married a Vanderbilt, and became a Washington lobbyist for the Dollar Steamship Line and chairman of the Wingfield United Nevada Bank in Reno. In Ely, Baker's speech sounded like he was reading the state Democratic platform, with a few lush references to Pittman thrown in. "Baker is in complete accord with the views and plans of Senator Pittman," his campaign declared. "He is a Democrat and the only candidate standing squarely on the Democratic platform."[18]

When it was McCarran's turn to talk, it was hard to tell what party he belonged to. He devoted his speech to attacking the World Court, a non-issue in Nevada. The country should never have joined the court, he said; Congress had made a grave mistake, and the United States should pull out immediately. "The interest and prosperity of America does not depend on alliances with alien power," his platform stated. "This nation should avoid participating involvement with any court, compact or league which may endanger our being drawn into foreign wars."[19]

After the speech Reno attorney William McKnight asked McCarran not to go so far out against Baker that he couldn't support him if he won the nomination. "McCarran is a peculiar fellow," McKnight reported to Pittman. "He told me that he intended to force Baker to take a positive stand upon the World Court issue, and that unless Baker's position was the same as McCarran's he would not support Baker if nominated."[20]

To McCarran there was no more important issue facing the country than whether it would join the World Court. To McCarran's enemies the more important question was whether he would ever really join the Democratic Party. "Pat's effort to establish his party loyalty is by far his hardest obstacle to overcome," noted the *Journal*.[21] "Pat is running ostensibly on the Democratic ticket but in reality, if we take his word for it and the word of the Democratic leaders, he is an independent as he likens himself to Borah," added the *Elko Free Press*. "At a previous election Pat and the Democratic leaders fell out and Pat went his own way and at that time dire threats were made that if he ever ran for office again he would not have the support of the party; and from all appearance the Democratic machine and all the influence of the party leaders is being exerted to this end."[22] Privately, William Woodburn told Pittman that the machine was doing its best to finally crush McCarran once and for all. "Thatcher and I both took a solemn oath that we would not be active in this campaign, but as usual we could not resist the lure and are actively supporting Baker," Woodburn said. "Of course, our desire to pay our respects to McCarran may have something to do with it."[23]

McCarran and Baker both circled the state courting voters. Baker concentrated on telling crowds how rough he'd had it in his mule-skinning days. "Ray says he has been broke in every mining camp in the state," the *Journal* reported.[24] McCarran focused on the World Court and criticized Baker for being too busy talking about his donkey days to take a stand on the most important issue before the country since the ratification of the Constitution in 1789. The state's Democratic newspapers hammered McCarran for his seeming obsession with the court. "Nevada does not need and does not want its representatives in Congress following in the steps of Borah or Johnson or Reed," the *Journal* opined. "Idaho and California may be willing to sacrifice the services of one of their senators for the enlightenment of the world in general, but Nevada cannot afford it."[25] "Pat has his World Court and Ray has his burros," added the *Tonopah Bonanza*. "Ray doesn't interfere with Pat's court and Pat shouldn't bother Ray's burros. Pat says that he doesn't lead any Jackasses but he does lead a World Court around. . . . Ray doesn't make people cry over his burros the way Patty does over his World Court."[26]

On the Saturday before the primary election three hundred people gathered in Powning Park across from the courthouse in Reno. A brass band played; a Stand Pat for Pat banner hung in front of the platform. As the Truckee flowed past, McCarran said that he had lived on the banks of the river for forty-nine years. "If I go to Washington I won't have to bring back a search warrant to find my own home," he said. "McCarran," one of his ads went. "He has always lived in Nevada. He has always been a taxpayer in Nevada. He has always maintained his family in Nevada. He has always been a home builder in Nevada. He is one of us!" But the real issue in the election, he said once again, was whether the United States would corrupt itself by joining the World Court or preserve its liberty and independence. "Whenever the question arises where a young man may be called abroad to die on foreign soil," McCarran roared, "it is an issue."[27]

By eight o'clock on election evening it was clear it was over as the returns flashed on a screen outside the *Journal* building in downtown Reno. Baker walloped McCarran, 4,732 to 2,755. Oddie trounced Roberts. Two months later Oddie would whip Baker and go back to Washington. McCarran's enemies had been hoping to see him obliterated. "Am hopeful," McKnight had written, "that he will be so decisively defeated in the primary that he cannot possibly do much harm hereafter."[28]

On the evening of April 27, 1927, George Wingfield was at home visiting with his friend Jimmy McKay, who controlled most of the gambling and prostitution in Reno and shared an avid interest with his host in thoroughbred horses and prizefighting. Two men came calling. In walked George Cole and Ed Malley. Both men were well known in the state, Democrats who had been elected to office in 1914: Cole had become the state controller and Malley the treasurer. But Cole had finally lost his position in the past year's election. Wingfield thought Cole had come for a loan to start up a business. People were always asking him for something.

Wingfield owned thirteen of Nevada's thirty-two banks, controlling 57 percent of all deposits in the state. He controlled the credit of newspapers. When a U.S. attorney spent too much time enforcing Prohibition, Wingfield complained to Oddie, and the offending lawyer was soon in private practice. Wingfield personally picked the new U.S. attorney, who set up his office next door to his sponsor in the Reno National Bank building. Wingfield purchased property along Virginia Street and the Truckee, selling parcels to the city and county so that Reno could build another bridge over the river and Washoe County could expand the courthouse. "Politics in this state," Jim Farley would later report to Franklin Roosevelt's chief strategist after he embarked upon a cross-country intelligence-gathering mission for the governor of New York in 1931, "are in a sense under the dominance of one man by the name of George Wingfield, who seems to control through his lawyers who represent him, the politics of both parties."[29]

Wingfield had his indulgences, but in middle age he seemed to settle into a placid existence far removed from his rowdy frontier days. He liked horses and vintage wine, but his four-bedroom house was far from the grandest in town (his wife and kids lived in a much more elaborate home in San Francisco). Wingfield rolled his own cigarettes, answered his own letters, and most days walked to work, stopping by the Hotel Golden and the Riverside to check occupancy rates and the manners of the elevator boys. He was famous for his largesse, giving to church construction funds, footing the bill for the cleanup of the city-owned Wingfield Park, helping to pay for a new building for St. Mary's Hospital, dropping seven thousand dollars on a summer camp up at Lake Tahoe.

So Wingfield assumed that his visitors wanted some help. He offered drinks. Then McKay, who did most of his business at night, departed. The duo seemed nervous. "Well," Wingfield said, "what do you boys want?"[30] It turned out to be about money after all. "We are in a hell of a fix," Malley began. The state treasurer mentioned H. C. Clapp. Wingfield knew Clapp well: He had worked for him at his Carson Valley Bank since 1913, but the banker had recently fired the cashier for drinking too much. What Wingfield didn't know, the state treasurer said, was that for the past eight years Clapp had been helping Malley and Cole use state money to invest in mining and oil stocks. They were not good investments. About half a million dollars of Nevada's money was gone. Or maybe it was Wingfield's money, since it was in his bank. Not to mention the fact that Wingfield also owned the Nevada Surety and Bonding Company, which was insuring Malley and Cole for one hundred thousand dollars each in liability. In any case, the three men had spent years building up an elaborate edifice of fraud that had cost somebody a lot of money and that now seemed to be on the verge of toppling.

Let's keep this quiet, Wingfield suggested. Then the banker went into action. He borrowed half a million dollars from Crocker Bank in San Francisco to cover the shortfall, which finally added up to $516,322.16, mortgaging his new Riverside Hotel and putting up his bank stock as collateral. Then he held a dinner party, inviting the governor, the attorney general, and the state bank examiner over to his house. Nine days after learning about the defalcation Wingfield told the authorities and announced the news publicly the next day. "Nevada was shocked, probably as it had never previously been shocked," reported the *Journal*. "The names of the men, their reputations and the magnitude of the alleged swindle caused the state to gasp."[31] "The wonder of it all is that so huge a shortage should have so long escaped detection," added the *Evening Gazette*. "Seemingly there has been an inexcusable amount of looseness in the financial administration of the state."[32] "This is a hell of a mess," Wingfield told Oddie, "and I think in the wind up you will find a good many people in jail."[33]

One day in early August, McCarran walked into the Ormsby County Courthouse in Carson City smelling blood in the dry summer air. For twenty years he had seen his hopes and dreams thwarted by the small group of men who ruled Nevada politically, economically, and socially. Between George Wingfield and his Republican Party, and his lawyer George Thatcher and his Democratic Party, not much happened in Nevada without the approval of someone on the second floor of the Reno National Bank building. The state treasurer had gone to Wingfield and not the governor to report the biggest financial fraud in Nevada history, and Wingfield had told the governor how *he* was going to clean up the mess. Fred Balzar was the first Republican governor in a dozen years, but he wasn't eager to blame the chicanery on his predecessor, James Scrugham, a Democrat who was now publisher of the *Nevada State Journal* (which Wingfield held the bank loan on). In Nevada sooner or later all streams of power seemed to flow back to the same place. Blatant crime, of course, had to be punished. Clapp was indicted, pled guilty, and was sentenced to five to fifteen years in prison. But Malley and Cole were also indicted. That, they claimed, wasn't supposed to happen. Wingfield, they said, had promised to take care of everything. "Where does this double crossing come in!" Malley yelled at Thatcher.[34]

The duo hired McCarran to defend them, and McCarran jumped into the task with extraordinary zeal. At the start of the trial McCarran declared his clients innocent, which was a hard claim to sustain, so he spent the bulk of his time in court trying to spread the blame around. The Carson Valley Bank, he pointed out, was capitalized at $50,000 but held $750,000 in state money — a violation of Nevada law. So who was going to have to cough up the missing money? If his clients were innocent, the state was not liable. Wingfield was. And Wingfield knew this, which was why he was pushing for Malley and Cole to take the fall.

The state's case was simple: Clapp, who testified for the prosecution, had conspired with Malley and Cole to steal half a million dollars from Nevada and Wingfield's bank. McCarran popped up with the regularity of a metronome to object to Clapp's recital. Did Clapp know, McCarran asked him on cross-examination, that the charges he had faced could have put him in prison for a century instead of the mere five to fifteen years he was finally sentenced to? No, Clapp replied, he didn't. McCarran could do little to dispute the basic facts, as spelled out by thousands of deposit slips, cashier's checks, and bank ledgers that piled up as documentation of a decade's worth of embezzlement. Although the courtroom saw a parade of notables take the stand — Governor Balzar, former governor Scrugham, George Thatcher, William Woodburn, and George Wingfield — the prosecutor displayed little curiosity over how so many of the state's movers and shakers could have been taken in for so long by Malley, Cole, and Clapp. McCarran managed to bring up the fact that bank examiner, Gilbert Ross, was allowed to cash bad checks totaling almost seven thousand dollars. "Why was Ross treated any different than any other customers?" the attorney asked. "Well, he was the bank examiner," Clapp answered.[35]

McCarran put his clients on the stand. They denied having confessed any illegal actions to Wingfield and Thatcher; they had only alerted Wingfield to the problem with Clapp. But they also said that Wingfield had offered them immunity — a claim Wingfield denied when it was his turn to testify. Only at this point did the boldness — even recklessness for a man with any political ambition — of McCarran's strategy became clear. McCarran went into Wingfield's history as a professional gambler; his current friendship with James McKay, who ran most of Reno's illegal gambling and liquor trade; and what he'd done for the nine days that he keep the shortfall secret. McCarran made much of the fact that the banker said he didn't have to issue specific orders to his attorneys Thatcher and Woodburn because they knew what he wanted. The banker spoke in such a low voice that McCarran had to ask him to talk louder. McCarran's own voiced boomed through the room. "They know what I want," McCarran repeated, again and again. Everyone, he implied, knew what George Wingfield wanted.[36]

The four-week trial came to a close on Saturday, September 10. "Nevada's greatest legal drama," the *Journal* called the case.[37] Prosecutor Norman Barry summed up by praising Wingfield, calling him a great man. "It is a far cry from an ordinary vaquero to the chief financial leader of a great state," Barry said. He reminded the jury that Wingfield wasn't on trial. Malley and Cole were. "Give these men the benefit of every reasonable doubt," he concluded. "My heart goes out to them, but there is no excuse."[38]

McCarran followed him with a three-hour-and-twenty-five-minute blast at Wingfield. Would Cole and Malley go to jail or would Wingfield pay the half a million dollars in missing funds? The greedy multimillionaire, McCarran raged, treated the entire state like a little boy playing in a sandbox, building castles and wiping away anything he didn't like with a swat of his hand. The case, he said, came down to standing up to George Wingfield. Cole and Malley could have gone straight to the attorney general. Wingfield's banking empire would have tottered. They had tried to save the state from financial ruin. They could have pretended to know nothing about the whole thing. "Can human liberty go into bondage and come out? Can liberty of state go into bondage of gold and come out? If so, free men, where is your blood?" McCarran told the jury. "I want wealth in this state, but I want liberty more — even if there is not a dollar in the state. . . . Can this sovereign state go into the bondage of gold and come out?

"There is one thing to decide — which is greater, the gold of life or the gold of George Wingfield."[39]

"Miserable trash," Wingfield muttered to his attorney.[40]

At 9:30 P.M. the jury finally went out. "McCarran," the *Journal* wrote, "made tears come to the eyes of spectators with his impassioned pleas."[41] Just after midnight the jury came back. "We the jury find Ed Malley and George A. Cole guilty as charged," the foreman read.

Malley's wife fell to the floor. She was carried from the court, muttering, "The murderers, my God, the murderers." Cole's wife hugged him and sobbed. Cole collapsed. Two members of the jury were also so overcome that they almost fainted. McCarran remained stern. "This case will be appealed," he said.

McCarran's clients were sentenced to five to fifteen years but served only three and a half before being paroled. The state legislature had to be called into emergency session to deal with the matter. Wingfield paid 30 percent of the loss (a little more than $150,000). The state got stuck with a tab for more than four hundred thousand dollars, which the legislature had to pass a special tax to pay.

George Wingfield had won again.

CHAPTER 5

A Time for Surprises

You could never know the true circumstances as politics
are swayed in this state. It would delight me to inform
you of the terrible circumstances that we are confronted
with and the great effort that we will have to make to
purge the Democratic Party.[1]

— William Boyle, chairman of the
Nevada Democratic state committee,
to Governor Franklin Roosevelt

All day I talked and talked to people, saw many and many
a porch piled up with dirty diapers and old shoes and
even tin cans — what white trash we have in the small
towns of this county! . . . I am almost disgusted with politics. . . . I am not thrilled at the thought of representing
such inferior people.[2]

— Clel Georgetta, running for
the Nevada state Senate

In May 1932 Pete Petersen stopped for gas in the tiny town of Beatty,
almost halfway between Tonopah and Las Vegas. Petersen, thirty-nine, was
a Danish immigrant, a baker who had come to the country in 1915 and
lived on liver and onions and ham and eggs because those were the only
words he knew in English. Arriving in Nevada in 1919, Petersen worked
at the Purity French Bakery in Reno, becoming secretary of the Bakers
and Confectionery Workers Union and then president of the Nevada
State Federation of Labor. Now he was on the five-hundred-mile drive to
Las Vegas, where Democrats from around the state were meeting.

At the gas station another car pulled up, and out stepped a short, portly
man with a mane of white hair. It was Pat McCarran, who was also headed
toward Las Vegas. The talk, as always, turned to politics. McCarran,
Petersen knew, was running for the Senate. But what the attorney told
him next was a surprise. Six years earlier McCarran had been beaten in
the primaries by Ray Baker, who had then been whumped by more than
four thousand votes by Tasker Oddie. The Republican senator was probably going into the election with at least as great a margin this year,

McCarran told Petersen. The baker nodded. "It's the wotes that count," said the Dane. The only chance, McCarran continued, that the party had to beat Oddie and the Republicans was to pull together like never before. That, he added, is why I'm going to propose that the convention pass a resolution recommending that I get no primary opposition. Petersen said he didn't think it could be done. Well, said McCarran, neither do I.[3]

The Democrats, in truth, were hard up for a Senate candidate in 1932. Republican Oddie was running for a third term, and everyone expected him to get it. He wasn't a great senator, but he was good enough: He was friendly and popular, had landed the state plenty of highway construction money, could claim a share of the credit for the massive Hoover Dam building project on the Colorado River near Las Vegas, and was promising that a new post office in Reno would break ground any day now. Few of the state's leading Democrats, most of whom were his friends, wanted to run against Oddie. George Thatcher was a natural, but he was happy to run for national committeeman and keep his influence behind the scenes. Thatcher's law partner, William Woodburn, also begged off. Same with former governor James Scrugham, who was renting a house from Oddie in Reno and whose newspaper, the *Nevada State Journal,* was mortgaged to Wingfield for fifty-six thousand dollars. Scrugham had his eye on the Senate but decided to aim for the House instead and challenge five-term Republican congressman Sam Arentz. At first the only person who seemed to want to go against Oddie was Belle Livingstone, a Reno nightclub hostess. In January she had announced that she would run for the Senate as an independent, on a platform of lower taxes and an end to Prohibition. "I would make prohibition agents go out and get jobs and work for a living like other people have to," she said. "What we need is more bars and fewer jails."[4]

To many in Nevada, McCarran's odds didn't look much better than those of a madam. McCarran was about to turn fifty-six. He had spent almost half his life struggling to get to Washington. Now, with everyone else shying away, he might be able to get the party's nomination, if not the complete confidence of its leaders. "It is just barely possible that the existing feeling of political unrest may bring about the defeat of the junior senator," W. A. Kelly, a party official, told Key Pittman. "Personally I am certain that we can beat him if we had the proper candidate, and while I do not think that McCarran is the man to do it, yet it is a time to be prepared for surprises."[5]

For McCarran, like many in the country, 1932 was not shaping up as a good year. He had taken to pacing his office floor, fretting over his finances.

He had lots of clients, but few could afford to pay him. He talked many of them out of filing lawsuits: No one had any money to pay a judgment. McCarran was never good about paying his own bills. Now he got worse. He owned a small second house in Reno that he wanted to rent out, but tenants were scarce and squatters moved in. His elderly mother had to go into St. Mary's Hospital. One client gave him a bankrupt cafeteria in Reno in lieu of cash. He sold property in Reno at a loss. He lost real estate in California because he couldn't make payments. He couldn't even pay the life insurance policies for his children. McCarran was one of the lucky ones.

Another *borrasca* had come to Nevada; indeed, to the whole country. Nevada had the highest per-capita unemployment in the nation, and the Salvation Army fed more people per thousand there than in any other state.[6] The price of silver had tumbled by two-thirds in a decade, while a drought in 1930 dried up water holes and killed thousands of stock animals. In three years the state's mining revenues had fallen from $31.5 million to $4.3 million. In four years farm and ranching income dropped from $22.1 million to $6.4 million. "Darkness is enveloping us," lamented Pittman.[7]

Men began to tumble off freight trains passing through Reno and collect under the Park Street Bridge, bathing in the Truckee, begging scraps from back doors, and turning up their palms on downtown street corners. Families moved into shanties down along the river, while the more hard-up built sagebrush forts and drank the alcohol out of tins of canned heat. Donations to the Salvation Army dwindled as lines at its Sierra Street soup kitchen grew. The men had to chop wood from a grove down the Truckee in exchange for a meal of pig knuckles and cabbage or beef stew and bread but no butter. That winter the trees by the river virtually disappeared.

It was the third year of the Great Depression. One out of every four workers was out of a job. Farmers lost their land. Bread lines snaked through city streets. Protestors marched for work and clashed with police. America was a cheerless place in 1932, and increasingly people blamed a single man: Herbert Hoover, the living embodiment of the American Dream and, in this long winter, the unsmiling symbol of its utter failure. Hoover was born in 1874 in West Branch, Iowa, a Quaker town of less than a hundred people. He grew up in a two-room house with a family of five. When his father died, the villagers rebuked his mother for putting up too big a tombstone. By the age of ten Hoover was an orphan. He enrolled in the first class at Stanford University when it opened in 1891.

When Hoover graduated he went to work as a miner. He was one of the few young men of his generation completely unmoved by William Jennings Bryan. "It was," he scowled, "my first shock at intellectual dishonesty as a foundation of economics."[8] At twenty-three he went to Australia to manage a new gold mine; by forty he was worth ten million dollars and had become known as the Great Engineer. When World War I broke out Hoover went to Belgium and organized a billion-dollar relief effort that clothed and fed millions. In 1922 he published a book called *American Individualism,* warning of the dangers of communism. Only the American tradition of enlightened individualism could offer hope for social progress. "The crowd only feels," he wrote, "it has no mind of its own which can plan. The crowd is credulous, it destroys, it consumes, it hates, and it dreams — but it never builds."[9]

Building was something Hoover understood; dreaming wasn't. One friend who knew Hoover for thirty years couldn't ever recall him laughing. Perhaps it was because Hoover always seemed so busy. When Warren Harding became president in 1922, Hoover became his commerce secretary. He added to the department new divisions dealing with housing, radio, and aeronautics, insisted that runways install landing lights, and saw his unsmiling features broadcast in the first public demonstration of television. But there was always something solitary and out of step about Hoover. During the happy times of the Harding administration he ducked White House dinners because the drinking and card playing offended him. During the sleepy tenure of Calvin Coolidge he protested to the president about the stock market madness and warned that a great collapse was looming.

There was nothing, Hoover assumed, that he couldn't handle. When he became the Republican nominee for the White House in 1928, he saw no reason why he couldn't manage the country as effectively as he had managed everything else in his life. "We in America today are nearer to the final triumph over poverty than ever before in the history of any land," he promised. "The poorhouse is vanishing from among us. We have not yet reached the goal, but, given a chance to go forward with the policies of the last eight years, we shall soon with the help of God be in sight of the day when poverty will be banished from this nation."[10]

Hoover was elected with 58 percent of the vote, a forty-state sweep that was the greatest electoral triumph in American history. Half of Washington's population turned out to hear Hoover's inaugural address in March 1929. "In no nation are the fruits of accomplishment more secure," he declared. "In no nation is the government more worthy of respect. . . . I have no fears for the future of our country. It is bright with hope."[11]

Seven months later the stock market ran off the cliff. Within three weeks a decade of ever-expanding riches had turned to ashes. The New York Stock Exchange lost more than 40 percent of its value, twenty-six billion dollars disappearing almost overnight. By early the next year there were four million unemployed in the country. A year later twice as many. By 1932 twelve million Americans were looking for work.

In the fourth year of Hoover's presidency the police used blackjacks and tear gas to clear away a Communist-organized unemployment protest in front of the White House. In New York thirty-five thousand men and women who had gathered to listen to Communist leader William Foster in Union Square were scattered by a police riot that left crumpled figures and pools of blood. In Dearborn, outside Detroit, thousands of unemployed auto workers marched on the Ford Motor Company's River Rouge plant, where they were greeted with tear gas and fire hoses and finally bullets. Four demonstrators were killed. When the Red Cross in England, Arkansas, tried to turn away a mob of hungry men, they stormed the center and seized their own supplies. In New York, Amtorg, the Soviet trading corporation, got 350 applications a day from Americans wanting jobs in Russia.

The Great Engineer was now the Great Funeral Director. Hoover's name became a synonym for misery. Shantytowns were Hoovervilles, newspapers stuffed into the coats of the homeless Hoover blankets, boxcars crowded with men fleeing hard times Hoover Pullmans, autos pulled by mules Hoovercarts, empty pockets turned inside out Hoover flags. During the boom Hoover had been cool and collected; in the bust he just seemed cold and unconcerned. "You will find that when I say a thing is a fact it is a fact," Hoover once said.[12] As the American economy reeled and collapsed, Hoover kept telling the public that it wasn't so. The business of the country is sound, he had tried to reassure the nation in the first week of the disaster. "We have now passed the worst and with continued unity of effort we shall rapidly recover,"[13] he said six months later. "The depression," he added in June 1930, "is over."[14] "Look how I have risen,"[15] he once told a friend, and Hoover often seemed to be saying as much to the country. In early 1931 he told the nation that the federal government was not the place to look for help. "The moment that responsibilities of any community, particularly in economic and social questions, are shifted from any part of the nation to Washington then that community has subjected itself to a removed bureaucracy," he lectured. "It has lost a large part of its voice in the control of its own destiny."[16]

In this election year Hoover's own destiny seemed as gloomy as the country's. He became a virtual prisoner of the White House, refusing to campaign, working long hours at his thankless job, chain-smoking cigars, and importuning visitors to help uplift the country's morale. He asked writers and songsters who stopped by to come up with poems and tunes that the nation could find hope in. That hope could come from the White House seemed never to have occurred to Herbert Hoover.

In 1932 Tasker Oddie, a man who had been beaten plenty in life, finally looked unbeatable. At sixty-one the state's junior senator was tall and thin with a long, smooth oval face that by rights should have been as cragged and as seamed as the baked desert he long labored in. He was easygoing and popular, and no one could imagine that McCarran would stand a chance against him. "I find that you are very strong in all parts of the state among both Republicans and Democrats," reported one correspondent. "I can see no reason why you should not be re-elected by a larger majority than ever before."[17] The editor of the *Elko Daily Free Press* informed Oddie that in a straw poll at the Rotary Club he trounced McCarran 11 to 2. "The fact that Pat is your opponent should warm the cockles of your heart," he crowed.[18] "I think it is a lead-pipe cinch," rejoiced another adviser.[19]

Oddie found and lost one of the great silver strikes in history. Then he won one term as governor, but lost a bid for a second, borrowed to the limit on his life insurance, and struck out in the wilds of Nevada — once more a penniless prospector. He had traded in the Thomas Flyer for a Model T and scoured the land for copper and tungsten instead of gold and silver, but had no better luck. He lived in a wooden shack that his brother and sister helped him pay the rent on and borrowed from George Wingfield. In 1918 Oddie decided to run for governor (and the free house) a third time, lost again, and wound up further in debt than before. "I am in real need of some money now, and have borrowed all that I can here," he complained. "I would get some more if I could, but there is nobody here that I can go to. I must get some for actual living expenses right away, and don't know where to get it."[20]

Oddie got lucky twice in his life: first in Tonopah, then in George Wingfield. The Tonopah fortune had long since evaporated, but in 1920 Wingfield came to Oddie's rescue yet again. There was a Senate race that year. Sure, you had to find your own house in Washington, but at least it was a regular paycheck for *six* years. Wingfield had become a Republican national committeeman, and when he represented the Nevada delegation at the Chicago convention he traded the state's presidential votes for a five-thousand-dollar contribution from the national committee for Oddie. "I want to give you some straight advice, and I talked it over with George as to what I would write you," Tom Miller told Oddie. "You have made mistakes in your past political performances, the same as all of us, and I think that one of your greatest faults is not taking advice as to the policies to be followed from those of your friends who know how to give advice in matters political. If nominated, I would place myself absolutely in the hands of your State Committee or in Wingfield, and confer with them and follow along the lines suggested by them in your campaign."[21]

Oddie followed the advice, and won. At the age of fifty, Oddie had his first real job since being turned out of the governor's mansion six years before. But the hard years had taken their toll. The small army of bill collectors that had followed him into and out of the governor's mansion (McCarran among them: "I do not want to take this into court. . . ."[22]) and the fruitless years of scratching in the desert for a second bonanza gave Oddie a bleeding ulcer. He went to Washington by train, bedridden, spending his first seven weeks in the capital convalescing.

Oddie easily won reelection in 1926, and despite his grumblings ("The salary is the most miserable, inadequate one paid to any public official and I cannot get by with it,"[23] complained the man who had spent much of the past two decades living in a tent) he could imagine growing old in office. Nevada's senators often found the job a lifetime sinecure. Oddie brought a mild competency to the post, which was more than Nevada usually asked of its representatives in Washington. His most passionate cause was getting the federal government to knit together Nevada's far-flung towns with a skein of decent highways. Having spent more time bouncing over Nevada's miserable roads than probably anyone else in the state, Oddie knew the value of decent grading and gravel. And he knew the value of getting along. His nickname wasn't Easy Oddie for nothing. It was lucky Tasker wasn't born a girl, his friends in Tonopah used to say, because he could never say no. "The most lovable man I have ever met," Governor Denver Dickerson called him.[24] Added Tom Miller, "He always did what he was told."[25] Early in the year Oddie had occasion to write McCarran on a business matter, and you could almost see his wide, genuine smile in the letter. "I hope," he told his rival, "that you are enjoying good health and happiness and that you will be successful in all your ventures but one."[26] McCarran was anything but genial in return. "I am very grateful to you for your very kind wish," he replied, "and regret exceed-

ingly that you inserted the last two words on the last line."[27] In memory
McCarran was more magnanimous. "One of God's noblemen and a lovable character,"[28] McCarran called Oddie years later.

Oddie certainly had a soft spot for his friends and benefactors. In his
Senate office he hung a picture of Wingfield's First National Bank of
Reno. That was one bonanza, he thought, that would always be there.

In late May, McCarran drove into Las Vegas on a day when the temperature hit eighty-nine degrees and headed to the coolness of the new
Apache Hotel on Fremont Street. Open just two months, the Apache was
the town's best hotel, possessing the city's only elevator and its most plush
meeting space, the third-floor banquet room that was filling with scores of
Democrats from all the distant towns of Nevada. Perhaps not coincidentally, the Republican Prohibition enforcer had recently raided a score of
bars and gin shops in the area. "Good Democrats, however," newsman Earl
Leaf joked, "were winning bets that they could find hard drinks within
twenty minutes after reaching the town."[29]

Las Vegas was born as a railroad depot in 1905, but it wasn't until 1925
that the town paved its main drag, Fremont Street, and it took until 1930
before the city had more than five thousand residents. The next year
Nevada legalized gambling, and Las Vegas took to it like crazy. "It is a bit
startling, at first," *The New Republic*'s Bruce Bliven reported, "to walk down
the main street at eleven A.M. and see in almost every block one or more
gambling houses, doors open to every passerby, crowded with men and
women, old and young, playing Keno, roulette, poker, shooting craps, or
betting on horse races. . . . Every second or third man you meet has had
about three drinks too many, and is glad of it."[30]

The real jackpot in southern Nevada, however, was the construction of
Hoover Dam. Over the next decade Washington poured more than seventy million dollars into the area. By 1932 the population of Las Vegas shot
up to seventy-five hundred. New streetlights, sewers, a hospital, and a high
school all appeared. As did men looking for work. Families camped along
the Colorado River in tents and shanties, forty-two thousand people
applying for fewer than six thousand jobs. Vagrants soon collected like
sagebrush. Those who ran afoul of the police found themselves packed
into a holding cell meant for a dozen men but crammed with ten times
that many and no plumbing — just a hole in the floor.

In Black Canyon, where workers were boring massive, fifty-foot-wide
tunnels to divert the river while the dam was going up, it was a hundred

degrees at night and twenty-eight degrees hotter in the shade of the day. Silverware was often too hot to touch; men dusted their sheets with cornstarch to absorb their sweat or soaked them in the river to keep them cool and sometimes had to rise in the night to soak them again after they dried. Heat exhaustion sent men to the hospital in Las Vegas by the dozen where they were dumped into bathtubs filled with ice water. In one month alone twenty-four men died on the dam. Men drowned, were crushed by rocks blown up in explosions. All for $3.50 a day — less than miners had made in Tonopah a quarter century earlier. In the summer of 1931, fourteen thousand men walked off the job to protest a pay cut. The contractors responded by loading the strikers on buses, driving them into the desert, and letting those who wanted to come back to work return. Whole families arrived at the dam site, mattresses and baby cribs tied to the roofs of their cars, an entire Depression household packed into a single auto. One young man showed up with nothing but the clothes on his back; while others sought surcease from the Nevada sun in tents or under blankets hung from poles, he sat in the shade of a big boulder, moving as its shadow moved. Johnny-behind-the-rock they called him. The hopeful and bedraggled spilled over into Las Vegas, where a Hooverville sprouted near the cemetery and men bedded down by the train station. "The open space in front of the station," noted Edmund Wilson, "is so full of sleeping men at night that it looks like a battlefield."[31]

McCarran was certainly ready for a battle when he rolled into town. He had spent months scheming and plotting so that the convention would unfold according to his plan. On Saturday, March 21, 150 Democrats filled the Apache dining room. Working out a platform (for silver, against Prohibition) was a snap. Key Pittman's name was tossed around for president. Hoover's name, some suggested, should be stripped from the dam. Henry Bogan, a black laborer, gave a fiery speech charging that the Republicans claimed to be the colored man's friend but weren't hiring him to work on their new dam. "In a marked negro dialect," newspaper publisher and congressional candidate James Scrugham wrote, ". . . Bogan stated that the great masses of the negro race asked for no social equality but only wanted opportunity to earn an honest living."[32]

Then it was time for McCarran's speech. In his last race for the Senate, six years earlier, he had struck out alone, running as an isolationist candidate who belonged to a nominally internationalist party. This time McCarran gave the safest speech of his life: He called for the remonetization of silver. I am in this race, he declared, until Tasker Oddie congratu-

lates me. "One of the most stirring addresses of the evening," reported the
Las Vegas Review-Journal.[33] At the last minute Joseph O'Brien, who had
come to town from Beatty (where McCarran had lingered longer than
needed to fill his gas tank), popped up and asked the gathering not to let
the reactionaries dominate the party, to support independent thought and
endorse Pat McCarran for the Senate. Tables buzzed with chatter, but the
good feeling of party unity was flowing like bootleg liquor — and there
were no other candidates. McCarran won the nomination he had been
longing for since he'd left the sheepfolds thirty years before. "More like a
kissing bee," observed one veteran Democrat, "than a convention."[34]

A month later the party held another convention in Carson City. Again
the Democrats voted to endorse McCarran for the Senate. His plan had
worked. There would be no primary contest to worry about. All he had
to do was to beat Oddie. "These endorsements," McCarran later explained
to his daughter, "were worked out with painstaking, diligent thought.
They did not come spontaneously. Every endorsement came as a result of
an organization laid carefully months before, and plans that were carried
out. These endorsements discouraged any other party from attempting to
file in the primary. Hence, I was saved the expense and annoyance and
heartache of a primary campaign."[35]

All it cost him was a five-thousand-dollar donation to the state
Democratic Central Committee.[36]

On the night of July 1, the same day that a weary Democratic convention
in Chicago had nominated Franklin Roosevelt for president on the fourth
ballot, McCarran flew to the Windy City to meet the governor. On the
ride to the hotel he saw crowds of men pawing through garbage cans like
animals. The next day Roosevelt flew from Albany to Chicago, accepted
the nomination, spoke to the Democratic National Committee, and shook
hundreds of outstretched hands. "I pledge you, I pledge myself," Roosevelt
declared, "to a new deal for the American people."[37]

What exactly the New Deal was, Roosevelt didn't say. At the beginning
of the year when the governor had announced himself for the presidency,
Roosevelt pretty much summed up his political philosophy by saying he
would do almost anything to end the Depression. "The country," he said,
"demands bold, persistent experimentation. . . . Above all, try something."[38]
As far as Roosevelt could be tied down to specific prescriptions for fixing
the economy, he sounded pretty much like Hoover: Let the states, not
Washington, handle relief, and cut government spending. Before Roosevelt

appeared at the convention, many of the party's leading lights assaulted Hoover for being too liberal. John Davis, the party's candidate for president in 1924, trashed Hoover for "following the road to socialism at a rate never before equaled in time of peace by any of his predecessors."[39] House Speaker (and presidential hopeful) John Nance Garner agreed that the trend toward socialism and Communism was the greatest threat to the republic and flayed Hoover for increasing the size and scope of the federal government. "Had it not been for the steady encroachment of the Federal Government on the rights and duties reserved for the states," he said, "we perhaps would not have the present spectacle of the people rushing to Washington to set right whatever goes wrong."[40]

Roosevelt's task, then, was to reconcile his personal pledge to try anything with his party's marching orders to try anything but Big Government. If any politician ever had a genius for reconciling the irreconcilable, it was Roosevelt. Handed two diametrically opposed speeches on the tariff, Roosevelt handed the drafts back to his advisers and told them to combine them. Roosevelt hated nothing more than to send someone away unhappy. For a politician he always seemed preternaturally contented. Almost nothing perturbed him: Ambition as much as gentility seemed a birthright. Both had always been there, just like the house he was born in, a ramshackle mansion of shutters and porches high on a woodsy bluff above a bend in the Hudson River near the hamlet of Hyde Park, New York. Born in 1882, Roosevelt was the adored only son of Sara Delano, the young wife of James Roosevelt, a ne'er-do-well businessman and local squire. At fourteen he belatedly entered Groton, then went on to Harvard (after the death of Roosevelt's father in his freshman year, his mother took an apartment in nearby Boston). Never much of a student, Roosevelt went to law school at Columbia, drifted into a desultory law practice, married his horse-faced but intriguing cousin Eleanor, and moved into twin town houses with his mother in Manhattan. When his older cousin Theodore Roosevelt became a progressive Republican president, the younger Roosevelt decided that he, too, should spend some time in the White House someday. He wandered into state politics, became assistant secretary of the navy during Woodrow Wilson's presidency, and casually imbibed the progressive politics of the muckrakers and trustbusters and the budding internationalism that grew out of the ashes of the First World War. In 1920 Roosevelt became the running mate of James Cox, who was trounced by Warren Harding.

The next summer Roosevelt was vacationing at Campobello, New

Brunswick, boating and swimming when he came down with a chill and a fever — and then his legs would not move. Roosevelt had polio. He spent the next seven years trying to learn to walk again, and then could only laboriously drag himself a few feet on braces, clutching the arms of others. In 1928 he staged a comeback, winning election as the governor of New York. To some he seemed a different Roosevelt, more serious, more empathetic. "Roosevelt underwent a spiritual transformation during the years of his illness," Frances Perkins observed. "I noticed when he came back that the years of pain and suffering had purged the slightly arrogant attitude he had displayed on occasion before he was stricken. The man emerged completely warmhearted, with humility of spirit and a deeper philosophy. Having been to the depths of trouble, he understood the problems of people in trouble. Although he rarely, almost never, spoke of his illness in later years, he showed that he had developed faith in the capacity of troubled people to respond to help and encouragement."[41]

Others were not so impressed, especially when he announced his run for the White House in January 1932. "A man," Elmer Davis said, "who thinks that the shortest distance between two points is not a straight line but a corkscrew."[42] "He is no enemy of entrenched privilege," declared Walter Lippmann. "He is a pleasant man who, without any important qualifications for the office, would very much like to be President."[43] But in 1932 the most important qualification for being president was merely not being Herbert Hoover. As John Garner told Roosevelt after he won the nomination and the Texan became his running mate: "All you have got to do is to stay alive until election day."[44]

In late May the eastbound Southern Pacific train stopped just past Reno in the town of Sparks and four hundred men spilled out of five freight cars. They were ditchdiggers, loggers, miners, ranch hands, bookkeepers, an editor, and a doctor — veterans all, and like thousands of other ex-servicemen they were heading to Washington. Congress had promised them a bonus for serving in wartime — to be paid in 1945. But they needed the money now. Marching and riding rails from all over the country, a ragtag army gathered on the mudflats across the Anacostia River from the Capitol. Fifteen thousand camped and waited for Hoover to do something or even send word that he cared. Instead the president helped pass a bill to loan the veterans money to return home, deductible from their bonus. On July 28, after the District police skirmished with veterans squatting in abandoned buildings on Pennsylvania Avenue, local authorities asked for federal help.

General Douglas MacArthur led four troops of cavalry, six tanks, and a column of infantry against the bonus marchers. The troops tossed tear gas at the veterans, burned shanties, and chased their former comrades into Maryland. "If the Army must be called out to make war on unarmed citizens," sputtered the *Washington News*, "this is no longer America."[45]

On July 7 Oddie left Washington on the train to New York where he boarded the SS *President Grant* and sailed to San Francisco. "I am sure you will have no trouble in beating McCarran," Noble Getchell, the manager of the Gold Circle Consolidated Mines and the state Republican chairman, reassured him. "My theory on your campaign issues, would be for you to stand squarely on your past record which speaks for itself, and not dwell too much on Hoover's accomplishments or the administrations; just make it a personal campaign, avoiding any explanations for the other fellow."[46] A straw poll in Las Vegas still found him beating McCarran two to one, and he had many supporters, even among Democrats. "When Mr. McCarran was in our office today we told him we would support you, editorially," the manager of the *Fallon Standard* informed Oddie. "Despite the fact that we have been flying the Democratic flag and propose to continue so to do, we believe that one Republican and one Democratic in the United States Senate will best serve Nevada."[47]

Despite this encouragement, Oddie went into the campaign feeling nervous and unappreciated. "I have worked harder this year than I ever have in my life, and I can tell you frankly that I have been carrying a heavier load than any other Nevada senator has carried," Oddie complained to Wingfield. "Yet, scarcely any mention is made of it. The *New York Times* has carried far more about my work this winter on its first page than the *Gazette* has. The *Times* is the largest paper in the United States but it does not reach Nevada. I have been wearing my soul out, which I am glad to do, for the state and its interests, and to be put down as a tenth rater hurts quite a little."[48]

The trip back to Nevada took more than two weeks. Oddie's campaign didn't move any faster. "I have been through bedlam since reaching Nevada," he told his staff back in Washington. ". . . We have not had one minute to prepare data for my campaign on my accomplishments and I do not see where we can get this time."[49] Soon Oddie discovered that Nevada was much unhappier than he had imagined. A sixty-year-old widow from Sparks who was in poor health and nearly blind pleaded for help in getting her five-thousand-dollar savings out of two banks that had closed.

"My boys want you to help to get their mother back to home,"[50] demanded another constituent whose wife had left him. "I need a food immediately," an Indian chief wrote Oddie. "I am starved now. I am old now. I can't work. . . . Please help me immediately."[51] Oddie did nothing for any of them. "The political situation from our standpoint is far more serious than you have any idea of," Oddie wrote back to Washington.[52]

McCarran was driving his Cadillac coupe near Winnemucca, out in the eastern desert beyond Reno, when a hitchhiker jumped in his way. McCarran swerved, then stomped on the brakes, and the car flipped into a ditch. He wasn't hurt, but he cursed his wrecked car. He was already almost three years behind in paying for auto repairs; he didn't have time for accidents. Since Las Vegas, McCarran had seldom stopped moving. Over the next five months, by his odometer, he traveled twenty thousand miles. "I made five laps of this state," he told his daughter Margaret. "I visited every water hole, town, hamlet, valley and place within the state. There was scarcely a man, woman, or child in that state that I did not see personally. Every time I would turn away from a place I thought I had wasted time in, I would think of the motto, 'If you go in, go in to win.'"[53]

Nevada was a bitch of a state to campaign in. A loop of its major cities was a twelve-hundred-mile trip from Reno, but the traveling was much more grueling because the population was so sparsely settled over so vast an area: ninety-one thousand people — fewer than fifty-five thousand of whom were registered voters. Eighteen thousand people lived in Reno, fifty-two hundred in Las Vegas — leaving more than 60 percent of the state's population scattered throughout rural Nevada. Hoping for a 70 percent turnout meant thirty-eight thousand votes were up for grabs. About half the votes were concentrated in opposite ends of the state: Washoe County (Reno) in the north and Clark County (Las Vegas) in the south. Republicans outnumbered Democrats in Washoe, but in Clark the Democrats had the edge, thanks to the dam workers pouring into the area who were overwhelmingly Democrats. Whether they would vote was another question. "In the opinion of the Republican leaders," reported the *Reno Evening Gazette,* "many of these Clark county registrants will never vote because they are transients."[54]

One week McCarran spoke in Reno on a Monday evening, traveled 237 miles to Tonopah for a speech the next night, continued on 206 miles to Las Vegas, ran up to Elko 484 miles to the north, then skipped over to

Fallon 252 miles away — and was still 61 miles from home. Towns like Goldfield, which had fewer than seven hundred people, were significant stops. Even politicians who had just a single county to campaign in found the townships trying. "I am just afraid that most of what I said went over the heads of my listeners," Clel Georgetta, who was running for the state Senate in White Pine County in eastern Nevada, noted in his diary. "I am really surprised to find so very many uninformed and purely illiterate people in this county. They ask me the dumbest questions and a great many people do not even know what the state Senate is. There are hundreds of people in this county who believe Branson, Wheeler and I are running for United States senator."[55]

The man who *was* running for the U.S. Senate was taking no chances. For years McCarran had railed against the League of Nations (the League of Notions, he sneered), the World Court, and other manifestations of Wilsonian internationalism. Suddenly he was silent on foreign affairs, except to mention that he favored giving diplomatic recognition to the Soviet Union and any other country that offered a potential market for American products. He found himself publicly touting men he could not stand, Democratic stalwarts and Wingfield henchmen like George Thatcher who made his skin crawl. "I want the world to know I am for George Thatcher,"[56] McCarran said at one event, and never was he less sincere. His basic platform was to run as a Roosevelt New Dealer, even if he didn't exactly know what that entailed. "Don't hamstring the new president by giving him a hostile Congress," McCarran pleaded on one stop in Las Vegas, where an overflow crowd listened in the street over a loudspeaker. "This is a government where Congress and the president are of equal power. One cannot function efficiently without the support of the other. If you must vote for Oddie and Arentz, vote for Hoover and be consistent. If, on the other hand, you intend to cast your vote for Franklin D. Roosevelt, give him the support of a Democratic senator and congressman from this state."[57]

Not long after Oddie reached Reno and set up headquarters, he received some bad news. Five years before, Reno had been promised a post office building, Congress had approved the funds, a site on the corner of Virginia Street and the Truckee River had been chosen, and plans had been drawn up by eminent local architect Frederick DeLongchamps. The budget was $437,027 — almost a half-million-dollar shot in the arm for the local economy that would stand as a monument to Oddie's ability to do for the people of the state.

Then came the telegram from Washington. Under the Economy Act the project had to have $56,500 cut from it, reducing the building to $380,527 — some $37,000 less than the low bid. That meant the building specs would have to be redrawn, and the whole thing put back out to bid. "This means that work cannot be started this fall," Oddie complained to President Hoover. "I have promised people of Nevada time and again for long time past that this building would start promptly. I will be condemned and punished severely by people of this state because of this unnecessary delay and the administration will be subject to severe attack."[58]

Three days later Hoover, apparently having other problems with running the country and trying to save his own job, had still not responded to Oddie. "This will be disastrous," the senator pleaded in another telegram.[59] "I sympathize with your troubles greatly," the president finally replied, "but as a senator you must realize that no authority has been placed in the president of the United States by the Congress in this matter. If my colleagues on the Hill wish me to take responsibilities of this kind they should give me authorities to deal with them. . . . This is not a complaint; it is merely a statement of fact. I am, however, doing my best for you."[60]

Oddie was not reassured. "This is vital and means my very life," he wailed. "I cannot afford to be defeated."[61]

Shortly after sunset the torches began to burn above the dry riverbed of the Truckee, shrunken by the summer to a lazy stream poking its way through boulders. Hundreds converged on the lot across from the Riverside Hotel on Virginia Street, the site of the new post office Oddie had been long promising. A more perfect place in Reno to mock Republicans would be hard to find. The American Legion drum corps beat out a march and the lights began to move, bouncing torches carried across the Center Street Bridge, flames flickering in the cold wind blowing down from the Sierra. Driven by three different bands, the procession paraded up Center Street, past the train tracks to Fourth Street, men, women, and children holding torches and banners proclaiming ROOSEVELT, MCCARRAN, SCRUGHAM. Hitting Virginia Street they turned back toward the river, the long line of lights stretching into a huge U through the downtown streets. Crossing the bridge, the marchers stubbed out the torches and filed into the Washoe County Library, two thousand people stuffing the auditorium with their placards and hopes.[62]

On a flag-draped stage, standing before a rostrum hung with a large photo of Roosevelt, William Woodburn introduced the party's candidate for the Senate. McCarran and myself, Woodburn admitted, have had more than a few differences in the past, but we are now fighting for the same cause. In the crowd people murmured that Woodburn was laying it on a little too thick. "The story has been going around for weeks that several of the highly influential leaders of Nevada democracy are concerned but little, if at all, about McCarran's candidacy," the *Reno Evening Gazette* had just reported. "Evidently McCarran and his friends are not being fooled very much about the situation as the senatorial candidate has not bolstered up the Democratic treasury with any large contributions."[63]

Roosevelt, McCarran said, was going to win by a landslide. Placards waved and voices shouted in approval for several minutes, and McCarran waited for the noise to subside. Silver, he began, is the metal of the masses; the Democrats are the party of silver. The Republicans propose to do nothing for the white metal. "The Hoover-Oddie-Arentz policy has been tested for three and one half years," he said. "It has resulted in an army, staggering in size, totaling twelve million men, suffering and out of work. Will you hinder Roosevelt with a Senate that will be a stumbling block to his every effort?" He had nothing personal against Oddie, he added. "Senator Oddie is one of the finest men you ever met," he said. "He is a clean lovely gentleman. I like to meet him. I like to call him T. L. I like to shake his hand and say 'Good luck to you,' but not this time. Not one word will ever pass my lips derogatory of the character or private life of Tasker L. Oddie, but T. L. Oddie wed himself to a reactionary party. Senator Oddie has wed himself to Hoover."

Then it was Key Pittman's turn. "Never was there a time in our history when a president needed more loyal, hearty, sympathetic and courageous support from Congress. The Democrats of Nevada have nominated two able and efficient Democrats for Congress," he said. "They are men who are in complete and hearty accord with Franklin Roosevelt, the next president of the United States. Without a substantial majority in both branches of Congress, Roosevelt may be delayed, if not defeated, in carrying out his principles, policies and programs. It is in the interest of every citizen in Nevada who holds to the principles and policies of Roosevelt to vote for Pat McCarran and Jim Scrugham."[64]

A few days later the Republicans held a rally in the library auditorium, this time the floor only two-thirds full and spectators just two rows deep on the balcony. McCarran had been flaying the Republicans for the Smoot-Hawley tariff, and Oddie responded by asserting that the only ones opposed to the tariff were international bankers, Wall Street interests, and the Soviet Union — which one McCarran was, Oddie didn't say. "I am in a position to know the plans of Soviet Russia," Oddie added. "Russia is trying to break down American institutions. It is only people who do not understand the provisions of the Smoot-Hawley tariff bill and three interests I have named that are attacking the Republican tariff provisions."[65]

Oddie's office scrambled to get reaction from veterans groups such as the American Legion on McCarran's statement that Soviet Russia should be diplomatically recognized so that the United States would have another market for exports. "My opponent is advocating cause of Soviet Russia publicly and attacking me because I oppose it," Oddie complained.[66]

It was the last time in his life that anyone would accuse McCarran of being soft on Communism.

Oddie, once again, was broke. "Things have been very slow getting started and, in fact, have not actually started yet but we are getting ready to have cuts made of his latest photograph, talking about having cards printed, the personal accomplishment pamphlet printed," Oddie's aide Eleanor Tientz reported three months after he had arrived in Reno and barely a month before the election. "This may be optimism at that, because the financial help needed hasn't taken any definite form. I do hope they do something soon because there are so many rumors of the opponents being financially assisted."[67]

McCarran, in truth, wasn't much better off. McCarran had never been very good about paying his bills. As Nye County DA he had been sued by a couple of his assistants for not paying them. A local joke had it that the first few rows at any McCarran speech were always filled with creditors. "Really it is most unusual that you not only do not remit us the amount that you owe us for your subscription to the Bench & Bar of Nevada," complained one bill collector when McCarran was on the state Supreme Court, "but you never answer any of our letters on the subject."[68] During his Senate race McCarran found himself more hard-up than ever. The Depression had whacked his business, and he was so behind on paying for car repairs that his mechanic was about to sue him. And then there was the five thousand dollars he had to borrow to fork over to the state's Democratic Central Committee.

As the campaign progressed Oddie did a much better job of fund-raising than McCarran. The Republican National Committee gave Oddie two thousand dollars, while he raised another fifteen hundred on his own.

The Democratic National Committee gave McCarran one thousand dollars; he reported no other contributions. But he did outspend Oddie, $5,215 to $3,870. (The Republicans in general spent twenty-two hundred dollars and the Democrats thirty-three hundred; in the congressional contest, Arentz spent nothing and Scrugham seventy-one dollars.)[69]

Still, Oddie was reduced to borrowing from his staff. "I regret very much to have this load thrown on you and will repay it later on when I get things straightened out," Oddie promised.[70] Oddie, who was already in debt to Wingfield for thirty-one thousand dollars, found that even his rich friend was too hard hit by the Depression to be of much help. "It looks pretty blue for me in getting help that I need very badly," Oddie moaned. "McCarran has lots of money and is spending it like water and going fast all over the state and going everywhere and meeting loads of people while I am without money and tied up with official duties. . . . I am desperate and do not know which way to turn for help in my campaign."[71]

On November 1, George Wingfield left his office in an oddly quiet Reno National Bank building, walked down Virginia Street, waded through the evening crowd, made his way across the Truckee, and turned right onto Court Street to arrive at home, the twin peaks of Mount Rose in the west poking out above the treetops. As usual Wingfield wasn't smiling. He finally had a reason to look so glum. Wingfield was in trouble. Big trouble. For years the Depression had been nibbling on his empire; today the Depression swallowed it. Cattle that fetched almost ten cents a pound three years earlier were now going for four cents a pound, and years of drought and meager feed meant that the animals were skinnier than ever. Seventy percent of Nevada livestock owners had loans with Wingfield's banks, which gave the former cowhand effective ownership of most of the ranchland in the state — land that was worth less and less as the Depression kept deepening. Wingfield hadn't been able to bring himself to foreclose on the loans when it might have done some good. Now it was too late.

He had other worries as well. His hotel rooms were empty, and cash was gushing out of his banks. Net deposits had dropped nine million dollars in fifteen months. Wingfield had to trim the salaries of his managers, sell property on the cheap, and even stop giving personal loans to the many people (such as Oddie) whom he had regularly helped out. The banker soon found himself borrowing from other institutions, racking up $850,000 in personal debt. At the same time he had to cough up twenty-five hundred dollars a month in alimony for his ex-wife, pay for his son's Stanford education, and keep his current wife in caviar and foie gras. Five days after Hoover signed into law the Reconstruction Finance Corporation in January 1932, Wingfield was writing to Oddie to find out how to get a loan to keep his banking empire afloat. Before the year was out, Wingfield had borrowed five million dollars and the RFC was holding the mortgage on the Reno National Bank building; the richest man in Nevada no longer owned the office that had once seemed the star around which the solar system of the state revolved. The banker famous for never showing emotion began to crack, drinking to excess, tearing up in front of others. "I can understand that you have been through hell on earth this year," Oddie wrote him. "You have kept the state going under the most terrible conditions it has ever had to face and I hope the people of the state generally will realize what you have accomplished and what you mean to them."[72]

By the end of October the bank was almost out of money. Governor Fred Balzar flew to Washington to personally plead for more RFC funds from Hoover. Sixty-five percent of all the money in Nevada, including virtually all the government's funds, was held in Wingfield's dozen banks, he explained. The deposits, theoretically, were backed by the Nevada Surety and Bonding Company — which was also owned by Wingfield and in as bad a shape as the rest of his fraying empire. Hoover, once again, could do nothing. The governor then declared a voluntary, two-week banking holiday — the first news most of Nevada had that the marble-columned edifice on Virginia Street was as shaky as the rest of the American economy. On Tuesday, November 1, one week before the election, the doors stayed shut on George Wingfield's banks. "Not a word of blame or censure is heard against this man who has for so long carried the burden of practically the entire state," wrote the *Nevada State Journal*. "Now that burden has become temporarily too great for any one man."[73]

The holiday proved permanent. Wingfield's banks would never reopen. "I want the depositors protected if it takes my shoes off,"[74] Wingfield said — and soon he was left with little but his shoes. He sold his beloved race-horses and everything else he could easily get rid of; by the time he was done economizing he was left with ten thousand dollars in assets and more than three million dollars in debts. Finally Wingfield turned his car, guns, watch, jeweled rings, and trophies over to bankruptcy court. When Wingfield's personal property went on sale George Thatcher bought the trophies and jewelry and gave them back to the family.

Few others had much solicitude for the fallen Wingfield. Garbage was dumped on his doorstep, threats made against him and his family, doggerel penned to insult him (You've got yours and / You've got mine. / If you'll keep yours / And give me mine / Then we'll both / Get along very fine). At the Riverside Hotel dozens of women who were residing in the state until they could qualify for a divorce found that the Wingfield bank in the hotel was closed; they had to line up to telegraph their husbands to wire funds to one of the non-Wingfield banks in town. The state itself had to borrow money from the RFC to stay solvent. "The closing of the Wingfield banks destroyed the financial and industrial life of the state," McCarran told his daughter Margaret. "The Wingfield banks, by reason of political affiliation and by reason of political power had in their custody some one million, two hundred thousand dollars of public funds. This crippled every form of life. State employees were unable to receive their monthly salaries. The business life of the state was the recipient of a solar plexus. Immediately following this, the San Francisco wholesalers issued an order that no credit would be extended for shipment of goods at wholesale to the merchants of Nevada. Cash must be on hand before shipments are made, hence the credit extended by retailers in northern Nevada to the consumers was immediately curtailed — in fact, destroyed entirely."[75]

Picking over the ruins, the *Sacramento Bee* earned a Pulitzer Prize for a four-part series charging that Wingfield had looted his own banks, defrauded his depositors, and was still scheming to regain his throttlehold on Nevada. "The sagebrush caesar," the newspaper called him. Even Wingfield's daughter wrote to carp about the family's fortune disappearing. "I at least expected a word of sympathy and encouragement," Wingfield snapped back. ". . . What you have had in the past and what you will have in the future is due to me, because even though you are now nearly twenty-one, you have yet to earn a cent. I have at least taken good care of you up to this date."[76]

Wingfield could have said as much to his friend Oddie. "Wingfield kept out of politics entirely this time," one Republican noted. "He was too worried and pressed I guess to think anything but his own troubles."[77]

This time Oddie was on his own.

The banking holiday, Oddie told a crowd in Tonopah, was not a big deal. The banks would probably open sooner than in twelve days. But his mind was more on the past than on the present. He wistfully recalled how bad the roads used to be and how effortless his first election to the district attorney's office had been. "I did not have to make any campaign," he said. "All I had to do was to go out early on election morning and vote for myself, and I was elected."[78]

This election was not going to be so easy, but Oddie certainly had plenty of allies. The unions came out for him. "Oddie has been a staunch supporter of labor measures . . . ," AFL president William Green wrote. "He has been of incalculable benefit to the organized wage earners and their friends."[79] And while most of the state's newspapers split along partisan lines, the normally Democratic *Fallon Standard* broke ranks. "The *Standard*, which has long supported the Democratic party and its candidates, is not alone in taking this position," the paper opined. "Thousands of Democratic voters, who normally support the nominees of that party, have been impressed with the highly successful manner in which Senator Oddie has represented Nevada. . . . In other words they do not propose to lose the services of a valuable public official after having secured them."[80]

But Oddie couldn't count on loyalty alone. He was desperate for some grand gesture that would impress the voters. He lobbied the navy to dispatch a squadron of planes for the state's Admission Day celebration at the end of October, but the navy wanted him to pay for the fuel. "I was in hopes some showing could be made by Navy on this day possibly as a practice cruise," he pleaded.[81] Oddie had to dig into his own pockets for one hundred dollars to pay for local radio spots that the national party had promised to pick up the tab for. Even organizing a rally in front of the Goldfield Hotel a week before the election proved difficult. "We will not be able to get a very large crowd," a party official told Oddie. "People are in a very restless frame of mind."[82]

Some Oddie stalwarts began to sense trouble. "I have been very confident up to the present time that you would carry this county, but am beginning to have some doubts," the editor of the *Elko Daily* wrote to Oddie. "McCarran's friends are as busy as a dog with fleas and their efforts are beginning to have their effect. Up to the present time you have done practically nothing except to depend upon your friends. This is not enough and if you need a majority in this county you must use some publicity and get busy at once."[83]

Oddie, McCarran told a crowd in Pioche, was no friend of the workingman. When he was governor he'd vetoed the eight-hour day law, declared martial law, and sent troops to Ely when the miners went out on strike in 1912 — and two workers were killed in the tumult. In the Senate he'd voted against the Wagner relief bill and for the confirmation of a judge who had ruled that employers could ban workers from joining unions — "the worst enemy labor ever had." Even Oddie's friends were impressed. "The speech by Pat McCarran cannot be dismissed so lightly," one Oddie supporter noted. "It is my honest opinion that this man is an able and fully qualified successor to W. J. Bryan; he is a finished orator, and is very adroit in following the attitude of the audience. I sat there spellbound, not because of any solid reasoning or logic placed before me, but because the man is a master of oratory."[84]

"McCarran has lied most viciously about me in different parts of the state," Oddie snapped to a friend.[85]

Oddie was still betting that if he could just get the ground broken on the new post office before the election, the people of Reno would see what he could do for them. DeLongchamps had been furiously reconfiguring his art deco design, trying to cut costs by lopping off the building's top story, facing the structure in limestone instead of terra-cotta, and replacing aluminum interior details with iron and steel. A new bid went out, but with the election only weeks away there was no word yet from Washington. "Imperative that it start soon,"[86] Oddie wired the assistant secretary of the treasury. "Our Democratic opponents will probably carry this state for Roosevelt rather than for Hoover because of it," Oddie fumed the next day. "The starting of this building was the one bright spot I had looked forward to for some time past in helping to carry this part of the state at least for Hoover. One-third of the vote of the state is here. I have been jeered and ridiculed by the people because of this long, exasperating and unnecessary delay until I am angry all through. . . . In heaven's name, do what you can to have a showing made before election. It looks impossible now."[87]

"Contract signed," Oddie's Washington office finally announced two weeks before the election. "Construction company wired to proceed immediately."[88] November came and the Chicago construction company still hadn't shown up in Reno. When Oddie demanded to know when the building would start, the reply broke his heart. "Our representative," the company informed Oddie four days before the election, "arrives in Reno next week."[89]

The Sunday before the election, the Democrats staged another parade through the streets of Reno, a mile-long procession of torches and bands and ROOSEVELT-GARNER-McCARRAN-SCRUGHAM banners. Thousands filed into the auditorium, crowding the floor and filling the balcony, cheering and shouting, booing and catcalling. Hallelujahs rang out. George Thatcher made his first appearance of the campaign. "We are gathered here tonight in a spirit of dedication," he said. "We come to dedicate our next administration to Governor Franklin D. Roosevelt and John Nance Garner. On Mr. Roosevelt and Mr. Garner will lie the responsibility for the rehabilitation of this nation. We must have a Congress to work with them and I am going to introduce you to our next senator, Patrick A. McCarran."

McCarran promised to fight for silver. "Oddie has aligned himself with the enemies of silver," he said. "He is a supporter of the administration that does not believe in the remonetization of silver. . . . Silver is the coin of the poor, the coin of the masses, the coin of the multitude throughout the world. Gold is the coin of the hoarder. Oddie says that any man who does not believe in the single gold standard has something wrong with him. Then I guess there must be something wrong with me."

> *Row, row, row with Roosevelt*
> *On the good ship USA*

"Hoover declared in 1928 that his administration would give us a chicken in every pot, two cars in every garage. We'll be lucky if we have an egg in every omelette. And if we have four years more of Hoover and Gandhi should come to this country, he'd be the best dressed man in America."

> *Sail with Franklin D.*
> *To Victory and to real prosperity*

"We are confronted with an army today as never before. We sent our sons into the trenches to die for the country in 1917 and 1918. They went gladly to sacrifice themselves for our country and now we refuse them the bonus they deserve. We chase them out of our national capital with bayonets and bombs."

> *He's honest, he's strong, he's steady*
> *A chip off the old block that gave us Teddy*
> *Come one and row, row, row with Roosevelt*

"I have tried to cajole and plead and beg and tease and challenge Oddie into a defense of the administration and his silver and tariff policies, but he will not, by word or deed, say one word in defense of the administration he supports. I sometimes think he is trying to get on my horse in the middle of the stream."[90]

After the rally McCarran jumped into a car and headed to Las Vegas. The last four hundred miles on a very long journey.

Almost as soon as the Chicago convention had ended, Roosevelt began campaigning at full throttle, crisscrossing the country in a private railcar. In September, Roosevelt headed west and invited Pittman to join the train. Pittman lobbied for a stop in Nevada, but the train circled the state without ever entering it, climbing from Utah up into Idaho and Montana, then over to Washington, down to Oregon and California, and east through Arizona, New Mexico, and Colorado. Along the way Roosevelt picked up Republican politicians like hitchhikers. In New Mexico, Roosevelt invited progressive Republican senator Bronson Cutting out of the crowd and onto the platform with him, and the lawmaker ambled up to the candidate and shook his hand with a big smile. "I have never traveled on a trip of the kind that was as happy and as successful," Pittman marveled. Everywhere crowds joyously greeted the candidate. "They come as those seeking salvation," Pittman noted. "They were in distress and despair and were looking for hope and encouragement. They left knowing that happy days will soon be here."[91]

At two o'clock on the eve of election day Oddie climbed into a plane for a two-hour flight to Wells, near the Utah border, where he joined President Hoover's train. Hoover hadn't started campaigning until a month before the election. His first stop had been Des Moines, where farmers in his home state greeted him with banners reading IN HOOVER WE TRUSTED; NOW WE ARE BUSTED.[92] He read them a seventy-one-page speech telling them they should stop complaining. "Let no man tell you it could not be worse," he said. "It could be so much worse that these days now, distressing as they are, would look like veritable prosperity."[93] Hoover hated campaigning, hated the thought of selling himself like soap, but in the dying days of the race he found a certain dutiful sense of satisfaction in fulfilling his mission to warn the American people that the republic was headed for ruin if they didn't reelect him. "This election," he sputtered at a Madison Square Garden rally given over to foretellings of doom, admonitions that

Roosevelt would spend the country into bankruptcy, destroy the Supreme Court, and build a monstrous bureaucracy that would overawe the individual, "is not a mere shift from the ins to the outs. It means deciding the direction our nation will take over a century to come."[94] Hoover's gloom was too much even for some Republicans, such as Nevada governor Fred Balzar, who snubbed his president and refused to meet the train when it crossed into the state.

Oddie boarded the train in Wells and rode fifty-one miles with the president to Elko. A haggard Hoover spent most of the time locked away by himself working on a speech even as the train pulled into Elko at six-thirty, greeted by twenty-one sticks of dynamite blowing sagebrush into the sky, the town band beating out songs. It was no use. Even the president said he hadn't been on such a depressing trip since he'd ridden on Harding's funeral train nine years earlier.

Oddie introduced Hoover to the largest crowd ever gathered in Elko, calling him the man who had done more for America in the past few years than people would ever appreciate. Hoover and his wife, Lou, walked onto the platform. Hoover praised Oddie and then disappeared back into the train to give his last speech of the election to the country via a radio hookup. "We have again resumed the road toward prosperity," the president said once again.[95] At seven-thirty Oddie jumped back on a plane and flew across the dark desert to Reno, landing two hours later and hurrying to the county library for one last rally.

Pulling out of Elko, Hoover's train was stopped for twenty minutes when a watchman at an overhead crossing was attacked by two men and shot in the hand. He returned the fire and the men ran away, dropping two sticks of dynamite. Investigators found a bundle of twenty more sticks nearby. Soon the president's train was rolling west again, heading toward Palo Alto where Hoover would spend election day. A bigger bomb was waiting.

Tuesday, November 8, dawned clear and blue and warmer in Reno than it had been for a while: a springlike day with temperatures hitting sixty-five degrees, a day full of hope. At Reno High School a straw poll of students had Roosevelt beating Hoover but Oddie whipping McCarran, 362 to 269. "The people of Nevada would be losers, not Mr. Oddie, if another should be chosen in his stead," labored the *Reno Evening Gazette*.[96]

Last-minute bets jumped from three to one in Roosevelt's favor to four to one and then finally six to one. Even at those odds, few were willing to drop any money on Hoover. Scrugham's odds went from two to one to two and a half to one. Oddie was even money to beat McCarran.

The scuttlebutt had it that local Republicans were ready to sacrifice clear losers like Hoover if the Democrats would cross lines for Oddie. "The Republicans in Nevada are now offering to trade Hoover and Congressman Arentz to save Senator Oddie," one Las Vegas Democrat whose party loyalty was stronger than his spelling wrote to Roosevelt. "We must elect to the Senate the Hon. PA McCarran, if posible to do so. A word from you to the Democrat State Sentral Commity at Reno mit aid us in material way in the suport of McCarran as he semes to be the only one in the state that the Republicans have any hopes of defeeting."[97]

In the southern tip of Nevada workers were days away from diverting the Colorado River from its ancient route and into four massive tunnels that would carry its water downstream so they could begin building the largest human-made structure since the Great Pyramid. Another great shift was also under way. The industrial proletariat that had gathered in Black Canyon to build the great dam named for a Republican was about to make clear which American political party it believed had its best interest at heart. And among no workers would that assertion be more dramatic than black Americans who for generations had given their unquestioning loyalty to the party of Lincoln. All across the country urban workers and ethnic minorities were also discovering that their hopes were focused on the same politician — and it was not the one whose name would be given to a seven-hundred-foot wall of concrete. The dam, to be sure, would stand as the great civic engineering feat of the American republic, but the treatment of the handful of black workers on the project was a reminder of how far yet the country had to go before its democratic mores matched its monuments.

"A bunch of us went to work on the dam early in August and were immediately informed by our foreman, Mr. Davis, that we were not to drink from any hydrants used by whites," J. P. Liddell, the president of the Colored Citizens Labor Protective Association in Las Vegas, had written to Oddie earlier in the campaign. "We were not to use the toilets the whites were using. That forced us to walk nearly a mile to the toilet provided for Negroes. . . . Mr. Davis also informed us that he was from Georgia where he worked 1,500 'Niggers' on one job and was therefore used to 'Niggers.' He told us we would get along OK if we would call all white men with whom we come in contact 'Mister' instead of by their given names. . . . We

shall express our appreciation and gratitude for your aide and consideration in a more tangible way by remembering you favorably at the polls
this November."[98]

Oddie didn't lift a finger to help. And they remembered.

As dusk settled on Reno a large screen lit up on the *Gazette* building on
Virginia Street flashing election returns, while KOH radio carried the results
over the airwaves: A Democratic landslide was moving across the country.

Joyous Democrats paraded through downtown Reno, waving red flares,
shouting and singing. "A New Deal," they chanted. "A New Deal."[99]
Hoarse voices croaked news of the ever-accumulating electoral avalanche
over loudspeakers. Drunken men screamed that Prohibition was dead;
they'd be drinking beer by winter. Jim Scrugham wandered the streets, the
newly elected congressman shaking hands and drinking in the good cheer.

A New Deal. A New Deal. A New Deal.

In Las Vegas hopeful Democrats gathered at 7 P.M. at Fifth and Fremont
Streets and McCarran led a parade to Elks Hall. The *Las Vegas Review-
Journal,* which was still running an ad that misspelled McCarran's name
("McCarren: a new deal for America"), hired scores of extra help. Returns
started to pour in at five. At 10 P.M. the paper published an extra:
"Roosevelt Wins!" A second extra followed: "Demos Win State."

The Senate race was too close to call. "McCarran, but according to the
latest returns available at the time of going to press," the *Las Vegas Age*
hedged in its edition the next morning, "had but a slim chance of winning the election."[100] Returns seesawed all evening. Oddie was carrying
Washoe by 128 votes; then the Democratic wave crashed in the county,
and McCarran bobbed to the surface with a 124-vote lead. About 1 A.M.
McCarran pulled ahead statewide, leading with 224 votes. Clark County
widened his lead to a thousand votes. Then the returns from Nevada's hin-
terlands came in: Oddie swept the cow towns. "Senator Oddie may be
reelected," flashed the *Age* when a 3 A.M. bulletin had the incumbent
pulling ahead by 148 votes.

But the next morning, McCarran had won by 1,692 votes. He carried
Washoe by a slight majority, claimed Clark County by a strong margin, and
really cleaned up in Boulder City, where dam workers voted for him
almost three to one. Roosevelt bulldozed the state 28,756 to 12,674 (and
nationally he won 22.8 million votes to Hoover's 15.8 million, sweeping
forty-two states). Scrugham beat Arentz by almost nine thousand votes.

McCarran won barely 52 percent of the vote. Oddie didn't concede until the afternoon, as if he couldn't finally face the thing he had feared all along.

A week later, when it no longer mattered, Oddie would preside over the long-awaited groundbreaking of the new post office in Reno.[101] Businesses closed, school was let out early, and government workers were given time off to attend the ceremony, carried live over the radio, a rare bit of good news in Depression Nevada. But when the first shovel hit dirt it seemed more like a gravedigging than a groundbreaking. Oddie had worked enough mines to know when his luck was gone. This was one piece of Wingfield land where no fortune would be found.

McCarran, at long last, was a senator. "I propose to dedicate my life in the future to the welfare of my nation and to the welfare and development of my native state," he announced.[102] And, whatever his promises of loyalty to Franklin Roosevelt and his New Deal, he was headed to Washington as unencumbered as when he'd tumbled off the train in Tonopah a quarter century earlier, a young lawyer bright with promise and free from any obligations. "I go into the Senate of the United States independently," he told his daughter Margaret. "I owe my success to no faction and to no power. I owe my success to the masses of the people of this state and espe-cially to the laboring element; to the toilers and to the men in the mediocre walks of life. They were my backers. They put me over in this. The powers that be, so to speak, those who placed themselves in high regard, were not, without a single exception, for me."[103]

McCarran's entire life had been a lesson in what the powerful could do to the powerless. Imperial regimes like the British, he believed, enslaved the Irish, Jewish British bankers like the Rothschilds undermined the American economy by tricking it off bimetallism, a plutocrat like George Wingfield ensnared miners and ranchers and politicians in his many webs. But power also invited its own destruction.

"Too much power was vested in one individual," McCarran told Margaret, "and whenever too much power is vested in one human being, that power usually turns in the form of a flame to destroy the political, financial and moral power of the state — as for the last fifteen years has been vested in George Wingfield. He was an avaricious controller, demanding the pound of flesh in every line in which he bent his efforts. The God of nature seems to destroy such a condition, and it has come here. You may wonder why I should say that. It is a blessing of purification, so to speak. The power that controlled the throttle of this state is at an end, and though the people may go back into the throes of impoverishment, they nevertheless will reap the benefit in many ways."[104]

Suspicious of power in others, McCarran ardently sought it for himself. Only force could bring power to its knees.

After supper, the nuns at Our Lady of Lourdes on Lake Merritt in Oakland gathered around the radio to listen to the election results. The black-robed figures huddled together, their habits bent toward the unseen announcer whose voice crackled three staccato syllables over and over again throughout the evening: *Roo-se-velt, Roo-se-velt, Roo-se-velt.* News from other races drifted over the radio now and then, but never the contest Sister Mary Mercy was hoping to learn about. When her father told her he was going to run for the Senate one more time, Mary Mercy vowed to God that she would not tell a soul so that by the sacrifice of her pride He might grant her father his greatest desire.

The nine o'clock bell tolled. Bedtime was approaching. The nuns scattered to offer their final prayers of the day. Sister Mary Mercy rapped on the Sister Superior's door, asking for permission to listen to the radio for just a few extra minutes. Yes, she could. Mary Mercy almost ran down the hall back to the community room, forgetting the years of her novitiate training to move with quiet tread and moderate pace and never to swing her arms. She turned on the radio. "In Nevada there seems to be an upset in the Senate race," the voice coming from the box intoned. "The incumbent is trailing Patrick A. McCarran."

Mary Mercy turned off the radio. She went to her room and knelt down to say prayers of thanksgiving. The next day after rising and saying morning prayers and dressing and kissing her habit before placing it over her head, Mary Mercy found that a telegram had arrived. "We win," it read. "Love, Pops." Later in the day Mary Mercy saw the pastor in the schoolyard. He offered backhanded congratulations. "Your father was elected to the U.S. Senate," he told her, "but Nevada is so small he will hardly be heard from."[105]

PART TWO

OPPOSITION

The soot, the smoke, the blindness. He is going somewhere, that much he knows. But where he is, he does not
know. They have their way, the horses.[1]

— Ovid

CHAPTER 6

The Awakening Comes

"Two ideas are set upon a collision course, that's all. He believes government must do everything, and I don't see how it can do much more than it does if we're to keep any sort of private freedom. Neither of us is really right, but I think that what I believe is closer to the good life, to the original idea of the country, than what he believes, or is."

"But perhaps he's closer to the way people are now."

Burden studied Clay thoughtfully. Then he nodded.

"That's my nightmare, of course."[1]

— Gore Vidal, *Washington, D.C.*

It was the biggest room Pat McCarran had ever seen. Walking off the train platform into Union Station in December 1932, McCarran's head snapped back as his glance tried to take it all in: More than ninety feet above him soared an enormous barrel-vaulted ceiling, so huge that it seemed to be pushing the single-story wall below into the ground, its coffered surface dimpled with twenty-two-karat gold leaf, its loggia guarded by forty-six stone Roman legionnaires, their shields delicately hiding their nether regions from the innocent eyes of detraining passengers or those passing time in deep wooden seats set amid a massive marble floor. Daniel Burnham had modeled Union Station on the Baths of Diocletian, and when his terminal was finished in 1908 it was the largest train station in the world, a fitting portal to the capital of a republic that had recently just acquired an empire. That was the year McCarran first tried to run for Congress; now, after almost a quarter century of striving, he was finally heading to the Senate.

The month after his election McCarran went down to the ranch on the Truckee, picked up his frail mother, and took her to St. Mary's Hospital in Reno where the nuns would take care of her while he crossed the continent ("Always in good spirits — always looking upon the bright side, but a continuous and continual sufferer," McCarran told his daughter Margaret. "She is a martyr to the cause of optimism. Nothing is as bad as it might be. Everything is good. I often wish that I could have her spirit."). Then he went to the small Center Street depot, where he used a complimentary pass from Southern Pacific to board a train to Washington and emerged a day later into the enormity of Union Station. McCarran was used to the vast range of Nevada but had never laid eyes on such a large interior space, nor on such lavish ornament. The majestic expanse could have swallowed the only faux classical structure in Nevada, George Wingfield's Reno National Bank building, which for McCarran had long represented the hub of power and influence in his home state. Here, McCarran realized, power was on an entirely different scale. Then suddenly all the gilt and marble and echoing space shrank to insignificance as McCarran saw it gleaming through the arch at the far end of the concourse: the dome of the U.S. Capitol, half a mile away. He was almost there.

Saturday, March 4, 1933, was a bleak winter day in Washington. At one o'clock, Franklin Delano Roosevelt hobbled to the speaker stand in front of the Capitol on the arm of his son James, placed his hand on the family Bible, and recited the oath of office to become the thirty-second president of the United States. "Let me assert," Roosevelt intoned, "my firm belief that the only thing we have to fear is fear itself — nameless, unreasoning, unjustified terror which paralyzes needed efforts to convert retreat into advance."[3]

Roosevelt's own uncharacteristically grim face belied his reassuring words. That afternoon the country itself seemed paralyzed: In thirty-eight states banks had been closed; in the other ten, financial institutions were barely clinging to life and limiting transactions. In the past week frightened people had yanked $732 million from banks; the day before the inauguration $109 million in gold gushed out of the Treasury to cover withdrawals. As U.S. dollars disappeared, people began to exchange scrip, Canadian dollars, Mexican pesos, subway tokens, or soda pop bottles as tender. A quarter of the population was still jobless; industrial production was half of what it had been three years earlier. Wheat growers burned grain for heat; cotton planters stayed cold. And the Depression was not confined to the United States. Around the world every industrial power was reeling. In Europe, Adolf Hitler had just become chancellor of Germany and was getting ready to seize absolute power; in Asia, Japan had announced that it was quitting the League of Nations while its troops were marching across northern China. Democracy nowhere seemed strong. Even in the United States some found reason to fear for its continuance. "You may have no alternative but to assume dictatorial power," the pundit Walter Lippmann told the president-elect.[4] Perhaps democracy could not heal itself. Stronger methods might be necessary. Military metaphors at least offered hope, promising power and purpose instead of weakness and drift.

"If we are to go forward," the new president said, "we must move as a trained and loyal army willing to sacrifice for the good of a common discipline." Roosevelt compared the Depression to a war and said that the nation would have to muster the same unity and resolve as if it were in actual combat. In these extraordinary times the normal fine balance between branches of government might need to be adjusted. The Constitution would endure, he promised, but it might be necessary to temporarily give the executive sweeping power if all else failed. "I shall ask," a still-unsmiling Roosevelt concluded, "the Congress for the one remaining instrument to meet the crisis — broad executive power to wage a war against the emergency, as great as the power that would be given to me if we were in fact invaded by a foreign foe."[5]

A crippled country looked at a crippled president promising strength and action, and for the first time in his speech applause came from the one hundred thousand hopeful people crowded before the Capitol. At last Roosevelt smiled.

Less than an hour before Roosevelt's inauguration McCarran took his first steps down the red-carpeted center aisle of the Senate chamber: a large rectangular room on the second floor of the north wing of the Capitol, home since 1859 to the most exclusive club in the world. Overhead a thirty-five-foot-tall cast-iron ceiling bejeweled with twenty-one brilliant glass panels glowed from skylights. Gleaming mahogany desks for the ninety-six senators fanned out on both sides in curving rows. Sitting above the room's rich marble and damask-covered walls, six hundred visitors packed the galleries like spectators at a Roman amphitheater. Above the galleries the busts of twenty vice presidents filled marble niches — a celestial chorus gazing down toward the follies on the floor. John Nance Garner, who had just adjourned the House where he had served for thirty years and risen to Speaker, took the oath of vice president from his predecessor Charles Curtis, both men speaking so low that people in the galleries strained forward to hear them. Then Garner, whose only legal duty in his new position was to preside over the Senate, weakly banged his gavel, a handleless piece of ivory that John Adams had first pounded in 1789; he then swore in the new senators in groups of four.

Walking up the aisle with McCarran was Key Pittman, who, as tradition directed, escorted his junior colleague to the dark wooden rostrum

where the vice president stood framed by red marble pilasters, above which
E PLURIBUS UNUM (out of many, one) was carved in white marble. On
McCarran's left sat his Democratic brethren, fifty-nine senators in all, who
covered the political spectrum from Virginia's Carter Glass, a Democrat
only because Lincoln had been a Republican, to Montana's Burt Wheeler,
whose party regularity was so irregular that he ran as the Progressive Party's
vice presidential candidate in 1924. On McCarran's right were the
Republicans, thirty-seven legislators of almost less cohesion, ranging from
roaring western progressives such as Nebraska's George Norris, who was
farther to the left than most of the Democrats across the aisle, to hidebound
reactionaries like Oregon's Frederick Steiwer. McCarran was one of nine
Democrats swept into the Senate with Roosevelt; ninety new Democrats
were crowding the House.[6]

But it was less the difference between right and left than that between
the back rows and front rows that best defined the Senate's topography.
Majorities, after all, could come and go, but seniorities just kept accumulating. Work ethic, brilliance, and oratorical skill were all assets to a senator, but reelection was what really counted. To the longest-serving
members of the majority party went the choice committee chairmanships
and assignments and leadership posts and the seats in the front of the
chamber. Which explains why after twenty years of conscientious but
hardly distinguished service in the Senate, Pittman was about to become
chairman of the Foreign Relations Committee; that Pittman was almost
totally indifferent to foreign affairs with the exception of silver price supports meant little compared to the fact that he had been on the committee
for sixteen years. "It is like a club rather than a legislative body,"[7] Pittman
had observed when he joined the Senate in 1913. Actually, the Senate was
two clubs: the one you could get elected to and an even more select one
of insiders. To gain access to the Senate's inner club, party loyalty helped,
but even more crucial was a reverence for the institution itself. "I would
rather live and compromise than die for a principle,"[8] Pittman said, perfectly expressing the ethos of civility that had not only brought him the
chairmanship of the Foreign Relations Committee but also made him the
Senate's new president pro tempore, charged with presiding over the body
in the absence of the vice president.

At the age of only fifty-nine, however, Pittman was still something of a
whippersnapper by Senate standards. The Constitution required a senator to
be at least thirty years old; it said nothing about a retirement age. Thus the

Senate was less a meritocracy than a gerontocracy. The average age was fifty-eight, but the Senate's barons tended toward Old Testament longevity. South Carolina's Ellison "Cotton Ed" Smith, for example, was sixty-eight, a senator since 1909; he would stay on the job until he dropped dead in 1944, a few months before his eightieth birthday. And Tennessee's Kenneth McKellar, sixty-four, a sixteen-year veteran, would serve another twenty years, finally retiring at the age of eighty-four — but only after losing an election.

In such a mausoleum, tradition was not easily broken. It was only the year before that Hattie Caraway became the first woman elected to the Senate (and her political career had begun eight weeks before that, when she was appointed to the body as a caretaker for her dead husband's term). Among the Senate's traditions, none was more revered than the deference that new members were expected to pay to their elders. "Like children," one first-term senator said, "we should be seen and not heard."[9] Pittman, for example, had kept deliberately silent for his first month in the chamber ("I want to deceive my colleagues into believing I am satisfied with silence and peace"[10]). The year was almost over before he took part in his first major debate; it was four years before he landed a spot on a prestigious committee. Sexennial terms, not years, marked a member's progress. Senator Joseph S. Clark once began a speech by saying, "After a relatively brief sojourn here — I am now in my seventh year. . . ."[11] And infractions of decorum appalled even the body's most unruly members. When a freshman rose to praise William Borah on the senator's birthday after a parade of dinosaurs had already done so, the object of admiration could only mutter, "That son-of-a-bitch, that son-of-a-bitch,"[12] so offended was the ancient lawmaker by the presumptuousness of his young colleague. After giving a speech, another freshman sat down next to one of the chamber's patriarchs and asked what major changes the august statesman had seen in the Senate in his long career. "Freshmen," he replied, "didn't use to talk so much."[13]

McCarran was in a hurry. Tasker Oddie had gone to Washington confined to bed with a bleeding ulcer and spent his first seven weeks in the capital recovering; Pittman slogged through four years with such unimportant assignments as the Committee on Territories and the Indian Affairs Committee before landing a spot on a prestigious panel. After McCarran's December scouting trip to Washington he came back to Reno but could barely contain himself before he left again for the capital, not even crossing town to visit his mother in St. Mary's Hospital. "I find it imperative that I should go on to Washington at once," he explained to his daughter Margaret. "The reason for this is that the power of the individual of the Senate of the United States is largely vested in the committees that he may be a member of."[14] And McCarran knew the panel that he wanted to sit on above all others: the Judiciary — a committee with vast power and even more potential. The Judiciary Committee was the clearinghouse for a great deal of legislation and controlled the patronage of federal judgeships, a valuable currency to win friends and influence people in both Nevada and every other state in the union. "I wanted to leave no stone unturned to get the best assignments I could," McCarran remembered.[15]

On his first trip to Washington, McCarran met one of his heroes: Senator William Borah. At sixty-seven, Borah was the outgoing chairman of the Foreign Relations Committee, a progressive Republican from Idaho, a fiery orator who had been elected in 1907 and proved one of the more hyperactive foes of the League of Nations and World Court. "Borah befriended me from the start," McCarran recalled. "He gave me a great deal of valuable advice, told me much about the inner workings of the Senate, and helped me in other ways to get my feet on the ground. Borah offered to do what he could to help me get an assignment to the Committee on the Judiciary."[16]

McCarran's choice of senatorial mentors was instructive. For one thing, Borah was a Republican. For another, he was as prickly and independent a lawmaker as the Senate had ever seen. "There are," journalist Ray Tucker once claimed, "four distinct political factions in the United States — Republicans, Democrats, Progressives and William Edgar Borah. . . ."[17] Borah was a natural role model for McCarran. An Illinois farm boy who gave his first speeches to a mule in a cornfield, Borah passed the bar in Kansas and then jumped on a train until he ran out of money and settled in Idaho, where he became a famed attorney. He had prosecuted George Wingfield's future bodyguard, Jack Davis, for murdering two sheepherders (convicted but pardoned) and also tried (unsuccessfully) William "Big Bill" Haywood and two other Western Federation of Miners firebrands for assassinating the state's governor.

Borah's political career furnished a blueprint for McCarran's. Going to Washington from one of the least populated states in the country, Borah turned himself into a national figure, a passionate liberal on domestic issues, but also an Anglophobe and a friend of Irish nationalism who trailed Woodrow Wilson on the president's ill-fated speaking tour in 1919, denouncing the League of Nations as suicide for America and leading the

Senate's "Battalion of Death" against the treaty. To Borah, loyalty to party paled beside loyalty to principle. "If you ask me if I am a Republican, I answer 'Yes,' as I understand Republican doctrines," he once explained. "I am a Progressive, but I want to fight inside the old party."[18] He was also possessed of a towering ego. In 1924 Calvin Coolidge asked Borah if the senator was interested in a place on the ticket. "Which place, Mr. President?" Borah replied.[19] In 1926 Borah turned on his own president and party when the United States fumblingly tried to join the World Court. Running for the Democratic nomination for the Senate that year, McCarran mentioned Borah's name and anti-court stand more than he mentioned Pittman, the Democratic colleague he purportedly wanted to join in Washington. Borah's principled belligerence earned him the nick-name "the Great Opposer." His protégé would aspire to at least as much.

At the dais McCarran looked up at the vice president looming above him, raised his right hand, and listened to Garner read the oath of office.

"I do solemnly swear that I will support and defend the Constitution of the United States against all enemies, foreign and domestic," the Texan drawled.

"There was never a time in the history of this country when so much devolved upon an incoming administration," McCarran had told his daughter Margaret the month before the inauguration. "Democracy is in the balance. A great test is being put forth from which it will be deter-mined whether or not a Republican form of government can endure."

". . . that I will bear true faith and allegiance to the same; that I take this obli-gation freely, without any mental reservation or purpose of evasion . . ."

"I would," McCarran had promised, "break from my party in a minute if I thought that my party was not doing the right thing."[20]

". . . and that I will well and faithfully discharge the duties of the office on which I am about to enter: So help me God."[21]

"I do," said McCarran. And never did words mean more to him.

Five years before the U.S. economy turned into a train wreck, a lonely, quarreling group gathered in the bucolic setting of Camp Tamiment in Bushkill, Pennsylvania — a workers resort run by the socialist Rand School — to argue over how to dynamite the tracks of American capitalism. How do we destroy the system? asked a tall, gangly, sharp-faced man in his midthirties. It was June 1928, and about the only thing the grab bag of rad-icals assembled under the auspices of the League for Industrial Democracy could agree about was that capitalism was evil. A Communist revolution, averred the speaker, was not the answer. "If the capitalists," Paul Douglas said, "are as strong as the Communists declare them to be and if the majority of the working class as apathetic and weak-spirited as they assume, is there any likelihood that a plebescite of force would be any more favorable to the cause of socialism than a plebescite of votes?"[22] A Communist seizure of power, then, could only produce another authoritarian regime that would delay the coming of true democracy. "Since the democratic way," he concluded, "is, therefore, more effective and more humane both as an end and as a means, it follows that the socialist movement should resist the temptation to resort to methods which may seem immediately to be more effective but which ultimately would be disastrous."[23]

Paul Douglas was born in 1892, grew up poor in the Maine woods, and went on to earn a Ph.D. in economics at Columbia University. But his real education was on the streets of Manhattan, where Douglas began a long life of social commitment by trying to organize shopgirls outside Stern's department store; he was arrested for blocking traffic. In court the police officer lied that Douglas had tried to incite a crowd and pushed a cop. "For the first time," Douglas recalled, "I saw how the law could be used to prevent the weak from peacefully trying to redress their grievances."[24] Douglas became a socialist, and a Quaker. As an economist at the University of Chicago he authored numerous articles, along with a book every other year. In his spare time, he worked on behalf of groups ranging from the National Association of Colored People to the International Ladies' Garment Workers. About the only left-wing group he recoiled from was the Communist Party.

In 1927 Douglas went to the Soviet Union with a union delegation. The United States still did not recognize the Bolshevik government, but the Russian experiment had become the shining hope of many liberals and leftists around the world. "One feels so normal and strong in Russia," Mike Gold told Upton Sinclair, "and all things one only theorizes about here and feels a little bitter and savage in defending, are so simple and real in Russia. It's a great new amazing place, everything beginning, life young and hopeful and strong . . . it is the earth and not heaven; the earth in the throes of the birth of a new race of giants."[25] Douglas and his delegation were not quite so smitten, but they were still impressed. Unemployment had vanished. Trotsky could still publicly quarrel with Stalin. Perhaps men really could build a better society than the one they were born into.

To Douglas, however, the means were as important as the end. One night in an aircraft factory a worker shouted "Sacco and Vanzetti" at him.

"You Americans have no justice," one English speaker said. Douglas grabbed a translator by the arm and related how he had signed petitions and given money on behalf of the two anarchists, how their appeals had stretched out for seven years, and how the ultimate mistake of executing them was the fault of men and not the system itself. But, Douglas continued, two months ago in the Soviet Union a group of bank clerks was arrested at two o'clock in the morning — the interpreter stopped, Douglas shook him, and his voice continued in trembling Russian — tried at four, and executed at six. "If you demand justice for those with whom you sympathize," Douglas said, "you must be prepared to give justice to those whom you dislike."

A year after his trip to the Soviet Union, Douglas argued at the Camp Tamiment conference that American radicalism had to find its own path. Douglas, countered Solon DeLeon, the perennial presidential candidate of the microscopic Worker's Party, was living in a fantasyland. "The idea of legal, peaceful solution of the society problem, in the face of the powerfully entrenched American capitalist class, is an illusion," declared DeLeon. "... Credulous talk about constitutionality and peace creates effective barriers against real preparation. Who will trouble to learn marksmanship if he never expects to use it?. . ."[26]

Such was the chasm across which radicals shouted at each other in the late 1920s. Revolution, they agreed, needed to come to America. But could drastic change come about peacefully or would it take a violent and bloody upheaval like the Russian Revolution? On one side stood Douglas and various liberals and socialists whom he gathered together in 1929 to form the League for Independent Political Action, a radical alternative to both mainstream parties; its chairman was philosopher John Dewey, and its national committee mixed liberals such as Morris Ernst with socialists like Norman Thomas and theologian Reinhold Niebuhr. On the other side stood hard-core revolutionaries and the Communist Party.

The American Communist Party was born in 1919, two years after the Bolsheviks had demonstrated that a tiny band of committed revolutionaries could start the year as a fringe group with only about eleven thousand members and end it in charge of a country covering one-sixth of the earth. "Capitalism is in collapse," the American Communist Party proclaimed in its first manifesto.[27] A decade later the party claimed nine thousand members — two-thirds of whom didn't speak English, while many of the rest spoke it as a second language. In the 1924 presidential election the party ticket headed by William Z. Foster pulled thirty-three thousand votes, trailing even the Prohibitionist candidate and Socialist Labor Party. Four years later forty-eight thousand souls voted for Foster; twenty-one million voted for Herbert Hoover.

Then the American economy collapsed. "We had a low opinion of the system when it worked," said Granville Hicks, "and we could not be expected to think well of it when it proved a failure."[28] Reinhold Niebuhr offered the system its last rites. "Capitalism is dying," he wrote. ". . . it ought to die."[29] Suddenly Communism with its promise of a more just distribution of wealth and rational economic planning loomed as the only real alternative to the chaos and cruelty of capitalism. Foster and his doctrinaire zealots might be the wrong people to trust to bring the revolution, argued Edmund Wilson, but they had the right idea. "Take Communism away from the Communists," he wrote in *The New Republic* in 1931.[30] Instead, the Communists seemed to take the liberals away from liberalism. When the determined Foster ran again for president in 1932, he won more than 102,000 votes — including those of many intellectuals and artists, such John Dos Passos, Sidney Hook, and Edmund Wilson. Joining any other lefty party, Dos Passos quipped, would have the same effect as drinking a glass of near-beer. "Nobody in the world proposes anything basic and real except the Communists," said Lincoln Steffens.[31]

Staring over one precipice at the injustice of American society and over another at the harshness of Communist practice, many liberals and radicals swallowed deeply and chose the direction that at least seemed to offer hope. "I believe," a friend wrote to Granville Hicks, "we can spare ourselves a great deal of pain and disenchantment and even worse (treachery to ourselves) if we discipline ourselves to accept proletarian and revolutionary leaders and even theorists for what they are and must be: grim fighters in about the most dreadful and desperate struggle in all history. . . . My fundamental conviction about the whole thing, at this stage, is that everything gives way before the terrible social conflict itself: that the power of imperialism must be fought at every turn at every moment with any weapon and without quarter."[32]

Those on the other hand who, like Douglas, scrupled over methods seemed callow and ineffective, the kind of timid creatures who let Sacco and Vanzetti die. Even a pacifist like Roger Baldwin, a founder of the ACLU, believed the prospect of bloodshed better than the alternative of stasis. "I would rather see violent revolution than none at all, though I would not personally support it . . . ," he had said at Camp Tamiment. "Even the terrible cost of bloody revolution is a cheaper price to humanity than the continued exploitation and wreck of human life under the settled violence of the present system."[33]

At the desk in the back row of the U.S. Senate chamber Pat McCarran stood up. "I doubt," he started in his high, quavering voice, "if there is any bill that will come before this body during this session that strikes so vitally at the fundamental principles of our government as does the bill now before the Senate."[34]

Newspapermen rocked to drooping by days of gentle unanimity bolted upright. "The time-honored tradition that new members should be seen and not heard has been in the process of being broken down gradually ever since the direct election of senators was adopted," scribbled the *Washington Herald* correspondent. "Now it has been tossed out of the window."[35]

It was March 13. Four days earlier Roosevelt had called Congress into a special session to enact emergency legislation — the New Deal's famous Hundred Days. The first day had been a whirlwind. Gaveled into session at noon, Thursday, March 9, the Seventy-third Congress was greeted with a plea from Roosevelt to pass an emergency bill to revamp the country's banking system. In the House there was no spare copy of the proposed legislation, so a folded newspaper was pushed into the hamper where new bills were normally deposited. No one spoke against the legislation, and just after four the bill that most members had not laid eyes passed the House unanimously on a voice vote. The bill shot through the Senate (73 to 7) inside of another four hours, with only Huey Long raising any questions. At eight-thirty that evening Roosevelt signed it into law. "Capitalism," Ray Moley later wrote, "was saved in eight days."[36]

An hour later Roosevelt was telling congressional leaders that he wanted to deliver on a campaign pledge to cut federal spending by slashing the budget, that with Congress delegating him the power he would whack half a billion dollars out of congressional pay, federal salaries, and veterans' benefits, which were to be sliced in half. Two days later an economy bill slipped out of the House, 266 to 138, pushed by conservatives including sixty-nine Republicans, and opposed by liberal Democrats.

Now, on Monday, March 13, the bill was in the Senate. No sooner did it hit the floor for discussion than McCarran rose to suggest that the bill be referred to the Judiciary Committee, where he was the newest member, for further study. Six months before on the campaign trail McCarran had vowed to vote for paying the veterans their bonus early; he wasn't about to cut it. "At a time when the government's money is being given in generous quantities to the banks, the railroads, insurance companies and other aggregations of the wealthy," McCarran said, "the compensation veterans are getting represents the only benefits coming from the Treasury for the poor and lowly." But what really bothered him was that the bill would require Congress to delegate its authority to set veterans' pay to the White House and the Veteran's Bureau and limit appeals to administrative review instead of the courts — a dangerous upsetting of the delicate constitutional tripod on which the entire American system was balanced. "There may be those here who think that I am impelled by the flood of telegrams that come to the various senators," McCarran said. "I am impelled by something that is higher than is expressed in any telegram. I am impelled by a desire to maintain the integrity of the three divisions of our government."[37]

Pat Harrison, a Mississippi senator and party leader, popped up and asked the Senate to table McCarran's motion. McCarran demanded a roll-call vote. He lost 60 to 20. "While the bill does contain a grant of certain powers which senators and representatives would not, in ordinary times, desire to delegate," Harrison said, "I need not remind this body of the tragic happenings throughout this country which call for exceptional action."[38]

McCarran was not the only lawmaker who found the bill unsettling. Fellow Democrat Huey Long, the wildman from Louisiana who had delighted in upsetting the folkways of the body since his swearing-in the year before when he'd walked up the Senate aisle with a lit cigar, also argued against the measure. But the most withering criticism came from Oregon Republican Frederick Steiwer. "We are now asked to take a definite step toward dictatorship," he began. ". . . This is a day of dictatorship. Italy is under dictatorship; Russia is under dictatorship; Germany is under dictatorship; and those who are here pressing this legislation are seeking to put the United States of America under a dictatorship just as rapidly as they can."[39]

Barely a week after Roosevelt's inauguration and the trenches were already being dug in Congress. On one side were those who believed the president's declaration that the economic emergency was the equivalent of war requiring bold experiments and the temporary setting aside of constitutional qualms. On the other were those who feared that too many departures from precedent would ultimately destroy the system rather than save it. McCarran had been elected to support Roosevelt, but he discovered himself at loggerheads with the president on his second piece of legislation. "Almost from the outset of my service in the Senate, I found myself at odds with the administration," he later reflected. "This was, in a sense, a matter of my own choice. And yet I do not see how I could have chosen otherwise."[40]

The Democrats tried to rein in the rebels by invoking a party caucus pledge to support the president by voting as a bloc. This, too, brought McCarran to his feet. Of fifty-nine Democrats, McCarran was the only one to stand up and proclaim that he would not be bound by his party's caucus. "There are some in the majority," McCarran said, "who do not propose to be harnessed by any rule of the majority that would force us into voting against our consciences and I for one do not propose to vote for this measure."[41]

Undaunted, McCarran piled another half a dozen amendments upon the bill. He asserted that the bill would relegate to obscurity the judicial branch of government. "We are considering legislation here the nature of which and the like of which have seldom passed the Congress of the United States. The law is not the people. The people are not the law. The law is the spirit of justice governing the people."

"There is," added Alben Barkley acidly, "nothing new in that."

"In all the history of legislation, when was there more drastic power demanded?" McCarran shot back. "In all the history of legislation in this country, when was the individual struck at more seriously?"[42]

Two days later the bill passed 62 to 13. The Senate moved on to more pressing business, such as legalizing beer. McCarran, it seemed, had lost his first fight.

The first time McCarran walked out the west front of the Capitol the view was breathtaking. From atop the marble stairs he looked down the slight hill to the snow-covered Mall, where the Washington Monument poked into the gray sky for more than five hundred feet, the tallest structure in the flat city, beyond which stood the massive Greek temple housing the Lincoln Memorial, barely a decade old. To his left, the icy Potomac curled past the Tidal Basin, beyond which stretched Virginia's lush woods. To his right, Pennsylvania Avenue shot out toward the White House, which was flanked by the solemn Greek Revival Treasury building and the ugly Second Empire building that was big enough to house both the State and War Departments. The government for the entire country (including the military) employed not much more than a million people and spent $4.8 billion a year, less than 12 percent of the $58 billion gross domestic product.[43] In the winter air McCarran could visualize his philosophical precepts as clearly as his clouded breathing.

The bedrock was the Constitution, the granite foundation on which all of Washington's monuments rested. The organic law, McCarran always called it. And McCarran had begun to fear for its future.

The Washington Monument was just one mile away and the Lincoln Memorial only another mile farther — but the span between the two shrines represented a much greater distance, the polar extremes of executive authority in American history. Washington's obelisk literally towered over the town, but the nation's first president was anything but a giant in office. Having shucked off the tyranny of George III, the framers of the new government were determined that no single vessel of government would overflow with power; rather they shaped three leaky bowls of governance. Congress could raise an army, but only the president could command it — after a declaration of war by both houses. Congress could pass laws, but only the president could enforce them. And the Supreme Court would adjudicate disputes over constitutional issues. The powers were separate in principle but conjoined in practice. Where boundaries blurred even the framers could fix no horizon. "Experience," James Madison wrote in Federalist Number 37, "has instructed us that no skill in the science of government has yet been able to discriminate and define, with sufficient certainty, its three great provinces — the legislative, executive, and judiciary; or even the privileges and powers of the different legislative branches. Questions daily occur in the course of practice, which prove the obscurity which reigns in these subjects, and which puzzle the greatest adepts in political science."[44]

The Constitution that Madison more than anyone else wrote wound up giving a long list of express duties to Congress, from taxation to regulating commerce, and for good measure added a "necessary and proper" clause elastic enough to stretch legislative power far and wide. The president, on the other hand, was given specific writ only to act as commander in chief of the armed forces, dole out government jobs, and make treaties with other countries — and even the last two prerogatives were constrained by the requirement to seek the advice and consent of the Senate, where a one-third minority of the chamber could torpedo a treaty it disliked. The president, of course, could refuse to sign any bill, but Washington set the tone for most of his successors by promising not to veto measures that he disagreed with, only ones that struck him as clearly unconstitutional. He used the power once in eight years.

Washington's followers did not force the issue. John Adams felt himself so inessential to the government that he left the capital for eight months straight when his wife was ill. Even when presidents did flex their muscles it tended to be to restrain a hyperactive Congress, such as when James Monroe vetoed a bill to construct roads and canals — something legislators always seem to want to build but that president after early president could find no authority for in the Constitution. Even this lean conception of the office was too much for some of its holders, such as James Buchanan, who rejected the idea of southern secession but threw up his arms claiming that as president he had no power to prevent it since only Congress could order military action. When John Tyler actually began to veto bills, he was read out of the Whig Party that elected him for usurping the powers of Congress. "If the federal government will confine itself to the exercise of power clearly granted by the Constitution," Franklin Pierce announced in his inaugural address, "it can hardly happen that its action upon any question should endanger the institutions of the states or interfere with their right to manage matters strictly domestic according to the will of their own people."[45] Zachary Taylor came into office vowing never to use the veto. But the very vagueness of the president's authority also offered a substantial opportunity for an executive with a large vision. "The laws allow him to be strong," Alexis de Tocqueville observed, "but circumstances have made him weak."[46]

Abraham Lincoln transformed the presidency. As a representative Lincoln had made his name by attacking James Polk for exceeding his authority by starting the war with Mexico. In 1861, the year he was inaugurated, Lincoln favored keeping the White House out of legislation. "As a rule," he said, "I think it is better that Congress should originate as well as perfect its measures."[47] But when the South began to break away the next month, Lincoln went to war with the Confederacy without seeking congressional approval, launching a blockade of southern ports and suspending the writ of habeas corpus. "Popular demand and public necessity," Lincoln told Congress when he retroactively sought approval, had forced him to act. Congress belatedly agreed. War, it was clear, could compel the president to suspend some laws to preserve the nation itself. "A limb," Lincoln said, "must be amputated to save a life, but a life is never wisely given to save a limb."[48] The Supreme Court, however, ruled in *Ex parte Milligan* that Lincoln had acted unconstitutionally — but the decision came only after the war was over.

Congress soon clamped down on executive authority. When Andrew Johnson tried to wreck congressional plans for reconstruction, including vetoing the Fourteenth Amendment, Congress responded with the Tenure of Office Act, forbidding the president from removing officials who had been confirmed by the Senate. Johnson tried to ignore the act. Congress put him on trial for impeachment, and the president stayed in office by a single vote. "The bravest battle for constitutional liberty and for the preservation of our institutions ever waged by an executive," Claude G. Bowers wrote in his best-selling 1929 book, *The Tragic Era*.[49]

Presidents got the hint until William McKinley went to war with Spain and turned a continental republic into a global empire, with colonies from the Philippines to the Caribbean. Theodore Roosevelt then forcefully pushed the federal government into national life by reining in huge corporations through antitrust suits, empowering the Interstate Commerce Commission to set shipping rates, and putting the government into the business of inspecting meat and making sure that the food and drugs that people consumed would not kill them. Woodrow Wilson went even farther, creating the Federal Reserve to regulate the economy and the Federal Trade Commission to regulate big business. And even Herbert Hoover created the Reconstruction Finance Corporation, which the government used to bail out failing banks, railroads, and insurance companies. What kind of president Franklin Roosevelt would be was anyone's guess.

Now as McCarran looked across the bleak but beautiful landscape of Washington's winter, he felt a reverence for his country's institutions that bordered on the religious. The snowy Mall and its gleaming monuments seemed a civic crèche, the embodiment of all that he had been brought up to believe in and all that he always tried to fight for. He knew that the country had changed much since its beginnings, that even his sainted Jefferson had bent the Constitution on occasion, and that recent presidents had poked bigger and bigger holes through what Madison called the parchment barriers of that hallowed document — men dazzled by a vision of what they were after and heedless of what they risked losing in its pursuit. But the organic law was still the law. McCarran knew that as well as he knew anything.

Gardner Jackson was sitting with his wife, Dorothy, in the garden behind their home in Chevy Chase, just across the District line in Maryland, when the doorbell rang one day in the spring of 1933. Jackson answered the door and found two young men who said they wanted to meet him. They had admired his commitment, they explained, during Sacco and Vanzetti. The last three words said it all: Five years later and the six sharp syllables still stabbed at the heart.

Pat Jackson had been a young reporter at the *Boston Globe* in 1921 when two anarchist immigrants from Italy, Nicola Sacco and Bartolomeo Vanzetti, a shoemaker and a fish peddler, were sentenced to death for two murders committed during a payroll robbery. "I wasn't really a good newspaper man," Jackson once admitted. "I always tried to make causes out of every set of circumstances I was sent to cover."[50] The case consumed Jackson. The underdog, a friend later observed, has him on a leash. He quit his job (although as the son of the largest landowner in Colorado, working was never much of a necessity) and became the secretary of the Sacco-Vanzetti Defense Committee, which contended that the trial had been unfair and demanded a new one. After Felix Frankfurter published a scathing dissection of the trial, "Case of Sacco and Vanzetti," in the *Atlantic Monthly* in 1927, the pending executions became an international cause célèbre. Anguished appeals poured in from everyone from Gandhi to Albert Einstein.

As the execution approached in August 1927, protestors from around the country marched across the Boston Common and into one of those rare crucibles of communal experience that fires an entire generation. "How can you stand it?" Mary French asked a reporter in Dos Passos' *The Big Money.* "If the state of Massachusetts can kill those two innocent men in the face of the protest of the whole world it'll mean that there never will be any justice in America ever again."[51] For many in Boston that summer their belief in America died with the two anarchists. "Don't you see the glory of this case," said Betty Alvin in Upton Sinclair's novel *Boston,* "it kills off the liberals! Before this, it was possible to argue that injustice was an accident, just an oversight — in a country that was busy making automobiles and bathtubs and books of etiquette. But now here's a test — we settle the question forever!"[52] Although they died in the electric chair, artist Rockwell Kent painted a picture of the pair as a secular version of John the Baptist, the severed heads of two revolutionary prophets dripping blood that offered redemption for those who would head their call to action. For Dos Passos, who was arrested while peacefully protesting and found himself sharing a jail cell with a passionate Communist organizer named Bertram Wolfe, it was as if the earth had opened at his feet:

> they have clubbed us off the streets   they are stronger   they
> are rich   they hire and fire the politicians the newspapereditors
> the old judges the small men with reputations the collegepresidents
> the wardheelers (listen businessmen collegepresidents judges
> America will not forget her betrayers) they hire the men with guns
> the uniforms the policecars the patrolwagons

all right you have won   you will kill the brave men our friends
tonight

America our nation has been beaten by strangers who have turned
our language inside out who have taken the clean words our fathers
spoke and made them slimy and foul

their hired men sit on the judge's bench they sit back with their feet
on the tables under the dome of the State House they are ignorant
of our beliefs they have the dollars the guns the armed forces the
powerplants

they have built the electricchair and hired the executioner to throw
the switch

all right we are two nations[53]

The two men at Pat Jackson's door introduced themselves as Lee
Pressman and Nat Witt. They told Jackson they had both been at Harvard
Law School during the final agony of Sacco and Vanzetti. Jackson took
the young men out back to meet his wife, Dode. The two men said they
had come to Washington to join the New Deal. They weren't getting paid
yet, but they had already started working on the legal staff of the new
Agricultural Adjustment Administration.

Pressman was twenty-six, the son of Russian Jewish immigrants who
had climbed out of the garment trade in the Lower East Side where talk
of social revolution filled the air like steam pouring out of street grates. As
a child he was afflicted with polio; doctors said that he would never walk.
His mother didn't want her son to feel inferior to other children by using
crutches, so for the first five years of his life she carried him everywhere.
Pressman never did feel inferior. He went to Cornell on a scholarship,
then Harvard Law, where he was an editor on the *Law Review* along with
his friend Alger Hiss. He stood six feet tall with dark curly hair and a sharp
face. "He had eyes like a squirrel's after a nut," remembered Murray
Kempton.[54] *Arrogant* was the word that even his friends used to describe
him. Pressman was hired by the New York law firm of Chadbourne,
Stanchfield, and Levy and started work in 1929 — a month before the
stock market collapse. His mentor at the firm was Jerome Frank, although
it soon seemed to many that Frank was the more awestruck of the two.

"The best lawyer that I've ever met," Frank remembered. "The quickest legal mind I ever encountered."[55] And when Frank (through the good offices of Felix Frankfurter) came to Washington to join the New Deal, Pressman was right behind him. "I am exceedingly anxious to get to work with you," Pressman told Frank.[56] When Frank wound up as the general counsel for the new Agricultural Adjustment Administration (he was one of the main drafters of the bill), he tapped Pressman as his assistant. And in turn Pressman recruited his law school friend Witt.

Dode Jackson took an instant dislike to Pressman. Many did. Both Jacksons were personally more taken with Witt. Another product of a Jewish immigrant sweatshop background, Witt left high school for three years to help support his family, won a scholarship to New York University, drove a cab for two years to pay his way through Harvard Law, then spent an unhappy year at a Wall Street law firm. Witt, thirty, was all jokes and smiles, lacking Pressman's sharp edges and blunt words. Witt was clearly more like the good-natured Jackson. At thirty-seven, Jackson was already something of an icon to the young and idealistic who were flocking to Washington. Some of his left-leaning friends couldn't walk up his driveway and pass his Essex coupe without thinking of the same car piled high with boxes of petitions, three hundred thousand signatures imploring clemency for two Italians, headed on a fruitless mission to the Boston State House. Stout and hearty, Jackson was a great big unwrapped package of emotion. He had a square face, a broad nose, and a dimpled chin. He wore rimless eyeglasses that were as transparent as his feelings. Pressman, in all his steely assurance, was altogether different. And yet Jackson found something intriguing about Pressman that day. What others saw as arrogance, Jackson admired as surety of purpose and direction. "Certainty in human form," Jackson called Pressman.[57]

The two young lawyers told the veteran crusader that they were going to remake the world. Jackson told them that he had given up on such dreams. "Have set my face firmly against allowing myself to be drawn in deeply into any further causes,"[58] he had written his sister.

It was time to start acting like an adult. Money, as always, kept slipping through Jackson's fingers like sand. He had to pull his children out of private school and send them to public school. He owed back taxes and an eighteen-thousand-dollar mortgage on his Chevy Chase house, the value of which had plummeted in the Depression. He was in debt for a country-house renovation. "I have at last come to the place where I absolutely have to drop all extended concern with causes and devote myself religiously to the arduous task of trying to chisel five and ten dollar payments out of news items and articles for my papers and magazines," he told his brother. "Not until this time have I really faced the fact that I have been entirely reckless and careless in the matter of my family's welfare in terms of the level of living to which they have been accustomed. Whenever I had a bit of money in advance I have counted myself well off and have dispersed it in an open-handed and easy way to almost all comers."[59]

Discipline was not Jackson's strong suit. Born to wealth, he was always broke. Many days he was drinking by noon. His friends were after him to start acting more responsibly. "By all that is sensible and by all the things that you have most at heart, do for Heaven's sake, hang on to that job," Felix Frankfurter told him. "Which means make it a full-time job in the way some of the rest of us who like irresponsibility and adventure and the thousand and one excitements of life as much as you do, attend to our jobs. . . . If you seek for freedom in every direction you will get it in one but will simply be the slave of your own diffuse romanticism."[60]

The young visitors urged Jackson back to battle. "They saw an opportunity of really doing great things in reforming our economic and social organization through government," he recalled.[61] They wanted Jackson to join the New Deal, to work with them in the AAA. To help them change the world.

He couldn't say no.

On March 16 Roosevelt sent Congress a farm bill. Eight days earlier Agriculture Secretary Henry Wallace and his new assistant, Rexford Tugwell, had taken a stroll from the department's massive building on the Mall, looping around the Washington Monument and coming back with an ambitious plan to reshape agriculture in America. Farmers, who made up almost a quarter of the population, had been staggering under the weight of declining agricultural prices for years before the Depression knocked them silly. Their problem, starkly put, was that they produced too much. A superabundance of farm products drove prices down. Gross farm income had collapsed from seventeen billion dollars in 1919 to five billion in 1932 — the year wheat prices dived to a three-hundred-year low. As a result, in little more than a decade farmers had lost half of their purchasing power. Now, in the Depression, they were losing their farms, with mortgage foreclosures running at twenty thousand a month. Impoverishment was breeding desperation and violence. One farmer told a Senate committee that if his fellow farmers could buy planes they would bomb Washington. "I am as conservative as any man could be," added A. N. Young, president of the Wisconsin Farmers' Union, "but any economic system that has it in its power to set me and my wife in the streets, at my age — what else could I see but red."[62] In early March three thousand farmers marched behind their firebrand leader, Milo Reno, to the state capital in Des Moines, Iowa, and threatened to lead a national agricultural strike if they didn't get relief by May 3.

Racing the calendar to help farmers before the spring planting season evaporated, Roosevelt's brain trust cobbled together a farm bill in less than a week. The proposed Agricultural Adjustment Act declared that a state of emergency existed, asserting in so many words that the free market between farmers and industrial producers had broken down and that radical government action was required to restore parity in purchasing power so that crop prices would rise to the level where farmers could once again afford to buy consumer goods. The bill granted Agriculture Secretary Henry Wallace sweeping powers to limit crop production, buy up surplus commodities, regulate marketing, impose excise taxes to pay for the program, and set up a special Agricultural Adjustment Administration to implement the act. "I tell you frankly," the president told Congress, "that this is a new and untrod path, but I tell you with equal frankness that an unprecedented condition calls for new means to rescue agriculture."[63]

The bill outraged many in Congress. "More Bolshevistic than any law or regulation existing in Soviet Russia," foamed Illinois representative Fred Britten.[64] "We are on our way to Moscow," added Massachusetts representative Joe Martin.[65] "The most revolutionary proposal that has ever been presented in the history of government," Michigan senator Arthur Vandenberg called it.[66] Still, the House passed the bill without amendment in just over a week.

The Senate took its time. Burt Wheeler proposed an amendment remonetizing silver, which devotees of the white metal claimed would raise the purchasing power of farmers overnight. "Give back to the poor the coin of the poor," McCarran cried. "Give back to the masses the coin of the masses."[67] The amendment was narrowly defeated. Then in late April a mob in Le Mars, Iowa, pulled a judge out of his courtroom, yanked off his pants, tied a noose around his neck, and demanded that he promise no further foreclosures. On May 12, after two months of delays and debate, the Senate passed the measure 64 to 20 and Roosevelt signed the bill. McCarran voted for the bill but against the conference report. The farm strike was called off.

Hope Hale and her soon-to-be paramour Hermann Brunck walked into the Washington Newspaper Club, a drinking dive with bare bulbs and roaches on the walls. "It's the 'in' place for New Dealers," Brunck said.[68] Before Hale could even settle in at a table, Pat Jackson was waving her across the room. The Press Club was another of Jackson's good causes: His money opened the speakeasy. On Hale's way back a redhead from Jackson's office named Mary Taylor grabbed her hand and pulled her into the seat next to her. A cigarette belched smoke from a long holder clamped between Taylor's teeth, red with lipstick. Before Hale got back across the room to Brunck she had promised to show up for work at the Agricultural Adjustment Administration's consumer counsel office on Monday.

Washington was like that in the early, dizzy days of the New Deal. You bumped into someone and wound up with a job at an alphabet agency that had just been created. "The shy young man," remembered Marion Bachrach, whose husband Arnie and brother John Abt both worked for the AAA, "brought to dinner by someone whose name you didn't catch, turned up in next week's headlines as one of Professor Felix Frankfurter's 'hot dogs,' assigned to help Harry Hopkins spend a half-billion dollars."[69]

And no place was more exciting than the AAA, which took on the aspect of a crusade with twenty thousand volunteers racing across the country to sign up farmers for the agency's crop reduction program. The Agriculture Department had swollen into the biggest agency in the federal government and was still growing by hundreds of employees a week. But behind the marbled columns of the Agriculture building, Hale soon discovered fissures deeper than mere office politics. There seemed to be some sort of invisible barrier between people who on the surface seemed to have similar politics, like Mary Taylor and Nat Weyl. The difference, Hale would learn, was that one was a Norman Thomas socialist and the other a Communist. Even the more politically experienced were confused. "The whirl of events is so fast that I am left without any balance and with little ability to set down and quietly reason out any given situation," Pat Jackson told Frankfurter. "The clash of forces in this administration is so much greater than the clash in preceding administrations. . . . Decisions are made and are changed with such rapidity here that a story you write in the afternoon for use the next day may and is often wrong by the next morning."[70]

The slow southern town of Washington suddenly became a vertiginous city, filled with young idealists and reformers. "I want to get out of this Wall Street racket," Jerome Frank had pleaded to Frankfurter, who was acting as an unofficial headhunter for the New Deal. "More important, this crisis seems to me to be the equivalent of a war, and I'd like to join up for the duration."[71] To many Frank seemed like the prototypical New Dealer. At forty-four he was an accomplished attorney with a voracious appetite for all things avant garde who rarely slept more than five hours a night and seldom seemed to have time to get to the barber. For a while he went to see a psychoanalyst twice a day. He read shelves of physics books for fun. He talked so excitedly when he drove that his friends feared for his (and their own) safety. He wrote a book while commuting on trains: *Law and the Modern Mind*, in which he applied Freudian theory to jurisprudence. Frank's powers of concentration were legendary. Once when his wife grew annoyed that he was too absorbed in working at home, she went to a movie to scare him; when she returned several hours later he hadn't noticed that she had ever left. Eventually, Frank's inability to pay attention to what was happening around him would cause him great trouble.

One thing Frank (and his recruits) knew almost nothing about was agriculture. Adlai Stevenson's first assignment was to draft a marketing agreement for the deciduous-tree fruit industry. What's *deciduous* mean? Stevenson asked. When Pressman found himself negotiating with macaroni producers, he asked, What does the agreement do for the macaroni farmers?

To Jerry Frank it didn't matter. He was a technician, a legal craftsman whose job it was to take the instruments of the law and wield them on behalf of the farmer. And that was the sense of mission that Frank impressed upon his young recruits when he raided the country's best law firms and schools. The men Frank attracted to Washington would wind up as some of the most powerful lawyers in town (Thurman Arnold and Paul Porter), a Supreme Court justice (Abe Fortas), and a two-time Democratic nominee for president (Adlai Stevenson).

Frank hired more lawyers (around sixty) than he had desks. They worked impossible hours, then regrouped for boozy dinners and heated arguments over poker, which then spilled into the next day and carried over to the weekends when they played tennis together or galloped through the Virginia countryside on horses. Some government offices started to look more like freshman dorms in Cambridge, and popular Washington eating places began to resemble Harvard dining halls. To Donald Hiss, Alger's younger brother, the atmosphere of Washington reminded him of the Harvard-Yale game. Within the languid universe of old Washington, the young New Dealers lived in their own world. One day Alger Hiss actually left the office around five o'clock instead of midnight and was amazed at all the people leaving normal jobs and filling the streets. Is there a parade or something? he wondered.

Older members of the administration were simply flabbergasted. "A plague of young lawyers settled on Washington," recalled George Peek, who was the nominal boss of the AAA but found himself bewildered by the stampede of Ivy League attorneys twenty to forty years his junior, most of whom resembled no animal he had ever seen back on his farm or in business in the Midwest. "They all claimed to be friends of somebody or other and most of all Felix Frankfurter and Jerome Frank. They floated airily into offices, took desks, asked for papers and found no end of things to be busy about. I never found out why they came, what they did or why they left."[72]

For young refugees from Wall Street firms, it was stirring in a way they would never experience again. John Abt, for example, was a Chicago native from a middle-class Jewish family who had gone to the University of Chicago Law School and then to work at Jerry Frank's firm, where he spent three years floating bond issues before the Depression and then three more years foreclosing on the same bonds. One day Abt watched in shock as Communists protesting the invasion of Manchuria tried to march across the Michigan Avenue Bridge to the Japanese consulate, only to be driven back by mounted police swinging clubs like American Cossacks. The sight made him sick. In 1932 Abt voted for William Z. Foster for president. Then he heard Roosevelt's inaugural speech. "Fired by the spirit of high purpose that charged the atmosphere in Washington," Abt recalled, "I committed myself to the New Deal."[73]

Never before had the drafting of codes and regulations, covering everything from Atlantic oysters to California oranges, the holding of hearings and departmental meetings, been so thrilling. Heady days gave way to giddy nights, lubricated by cocktails at Jerry Frank's house, more work, and maybe a nap on the office couch. It was possible to be idealistic and opportunistic at the same time. A man as cool and cautious as Alger Hiss, who thirsted for intellectual excitement but quailed before buying a copy of Joyce's *Ulysses* in Paris because the U.S. Customs might confiscate it as obscene, could finally tremble with excitement. "I was conscious of a feeling of kinship with a host of like-minded fellow citizens," Hiss said. "The feeling was exhilarating and new to me."[74]

"Everybody I met claimed to be a New Dealer," added his friend Abt, "but what this meant nobody quite knew."[75]

Two weeks after Congress adjourned on June 15, McCarran climbed into an army plane and settled in for the seventeen-hour trip back to Nevada, his briefcase stuffed with papers and his mind bulging with questions. Barely three months — the famed Hundred Days — had passed since Roosevelt had taken the reins of government and jerked the country into a new direction. Where was it going? Like millions of others, McCarran didn't know.

In a frenzy of legislation Congress had passed fifteen major laws, overhauling everything from the banking system to farming and industrial relations. Some of the measures were essentially conservative, such as the banking bill (prepared largely by Hoover's aides); others boldly experimental, such as the AAA and NRA. The last two bills basically tried to reinvent the American economy, inviting the federal government into the management of agriculture and industry as never before in the nation's history. The president didn't think he had a choice. When Roosevelt came to office, farmers were burning corn instead of trying to sell it, while manufacturing was half of what it had been four years earlier. "You realize, then, that you're taking an enormous step away from the philosophy of equalitarianism and laissez-faire?" Ray Moley asked Roosevelt before he signed the National Recovery Act. "If that philosophy hadn't proved to be bankrupt," the president replied, "Herbert Hoover would be sitting here right now."[76]

If Roosevelt's plan to pay farmers for not farming was a big step away from the usual rugged individualism of American capitalism, then his industrial policy was an even wider stride. The first part of the National Recovery Act (Title I) envisioned a government-business partnership (and antitrust exemptions) that would eliminate the chaos and cutthroat competition of capitalism by introducing codes of conduct regulating everything from the production of autos to the making of corks. And to make sure that workers as well as businesses benefited from this new partnership, Section 7a gave workers the right to form unions, guaranteed minimum wages, set maximum hours, and outlawed child labor. The second part of the bill (Title II) implicitly proclaimed that if the economy couldn't generate jobs, then the government would by creating the Public Works Administration and giving it $3.3 billion to spend hiring the unemployed to build schools, clean parks, and paint murals in public buildings. "History probably will record the National Industrial Recovery Act," Roosevelt said, "as the most important and far-reaching legislation ever enacted by the American Congress."[77]

To more than a few, however, there was something a little frightening about how fast and big government seemed to be growing, not to mention the zeal and undisguised anger of many New Dealers. In September more than a quarter million people paraded down Fifth Avenue behind the lofted banners of the Blue Eagle, the symbol of the NRA. Some watching the biggest demonstration in New York's history, with platoons of young men in the olive-drab uniforms of the Civilian Conservation Corps, thought they saw disturbing parallels with Germans marching behind their new bent-cross symbol. "Away slight men!" NRA chief Hugh Johnson blustered. "You may have been Captains of Industry once, but you are Corporals of Disaster now. A safe place for you may be yapping at the flanks but it is not safe to stand obstructing the front of this great army."[78]

Liberal icons such as Supreme Court justice Louis Brandeis were alarmed. "Brandeis was terribly concerned about the bigness of these administrations and how much we were trying to take on," Pressman recalled. ". . . I was explaining to him about these marketing units and licensing pertaining to the milk processing, how we were attempting to regulate and curtail the production and how we were trying to fix the prices on the retail end — and his only response after hearing me out very nicely and patiently was: 'There's something wrong with these big agencies.'"[79]

Pat Jackson agreed. "Under the New Deal the executive branch of the government has become virtually a law-making agency by reason of the great powers granted to it by Congress," he told Brandeis. "Under such a condition it has developed that the consumer agencies are the only agencies within the executive side which act as checks in the public interest upon the executive's operations."[80]

Roosevelt even made some of the Senate's most fiery progressives a little nervous. Shortly before the inauguration, the president of the American Silk Spinning Company had written to William Borah to urge Congress to bestow upon Roosevelt unlimited power. "Dozens of men I have conferred with — both Republicans and Democrats — fully endorse this," the businessman claimed. "A *leader* — whoever he is, irrespective of party — to lead us out of the wilderness! Affairs are rapidly growing worse — action — and *direct action* — is needed."[81] Borah demurred, noting that there was no evidence Roosevelt even wanted such power. "He entertains no such views and nurses no such desire," the senator replied. "Should Congress undertake to confer upon him dictatorial power, I would hope, I would expect, him to fling it back in the chattering teeth of a pusillanimous Congress with the reminder that he was the president of the United States and not its dictator."[82] Barely two months later Borah had changed his mind. "It is unpleasant, even painful, to be called upon to differ in these times with a president who enjoys great popularity and whose sincerity of purpose I do not assume to question," he wrote. ". . . I think we have granted powers to the president that we have no authority under the Constitution to grant."[83]

The president himself was a mystery. As a young man FDR had fretted over cousin Teddy's expansive vision of the presidency. "His tendency to make the executive power stronger than the houses of Congress is bound to be a bad thing," young Franklin said.[84] But by 1920 Roosevelt's experience under Woodrow Wilson persuaded him that executive authority was the motor of creative government. "Washington would not have led us to victory in the revolution if he had merely followed the actions or lack of action of the Continental Congress," he declared in a speech. "Lincoln would not have issued the Emancipation Proclamation if he had heeded the leaders of the Senate. Cleveland would not have maintained the Monroe Doctrine in the Venezuela affair if he had first asked the advice of mere party leaders."[85] Entering the White House, Roosevelt had no grand plan. "Let's concentrate upon one thing," he told a friend, "— save the people and the nation and, if we have to change our minds twice every day to accomplish that end, we should do it."[86] When a reporter once asked Roosevelt about his political philosophy, he reacted as if he were hearing a word in a foreign language for the first time. "Philosophy?" he said. "I am a Christian and a Democrat — that's all."[87] Thus armed with a rather expansive set of first principles, Roosevelt launched a New Deal so riddled with inconsistencies and contradictions that only the most single-minded thinker could find a coherent pattern.

McCarran was such a thinker. The common thread, he thought, running through each act seemed to be a delegation of authority from Congress to the White House and its various bureaus and agencies, which seemed to be popping up faster than clover after a spring rain. The federal government was suddenly striding across vast areas of American life where it had previously seldom trod. The AAA, for instance, was paying farmers one hundred million dollars to plow under a quarter of their planted cotton crop, which helped agricultural income jump 30 percent in a year.

But what was the federal government? Originally it was a small collection of bureaucrats who carried out the polices of the president and Congress, whose own purview was largely concerned with matters too big to be handled by state or local governments, such as national defense. Over the years the government had grown much bigger, and so had its presumed responsibilities. Now, it seemed to McCarran, Roosevelt had used the Depression as an excuse to grossly inflate the bureaucracy, making government so immense that a quarrelsome Congress could no longer practically guide its operations, thereby endowing the president and his unelected minions with powers never dreamed of by the writers of the Constitution.

As the plane droned close to Nevada, the pilot nosed the unheated aircraft up to twelve thousand feet to cross the Ruby Mountains and McCarran could feel the bite of the cold in his bones. Nevada newspapers had already begun to wonder what manner of man they had sent to Washington. "Right now the entire United States is back of Franklin Roosevelt, and it does not sit very well to have somebody throw a monkey-wrench in the new machinery hardly before it is even in operation," opined the *Tonopah Daily Bonanza*.[88] "The majority of Nevada's people," added the *Reno Gazette,* "are with the president."[89]

The plane touched down in dusty Elko, the heart of Nevada's cattle country, the dry air and earthy smells flooding McCarran with boyhood memories of a world so sure, of a path as clear as a well-stamped sheep trail. At the airstrip he was greeted by a city councilman, reporters, and friends. Could he really tell these people what was happening on the other side of the country? Perhaps he would, for the moment, pull his punches. "Congress accomplished more than had ever been accomplished in a similar space of time in the history of the country," McCarran finally told a local editor. "Critics of this session used the word 'revolutionary,' in other words, revolutionizing every thing American. What was really accomplished was just this — a bloodless revolution in which the people were rescued from the throes of depression and despair and uplifted to the summit of optimism and hope."[90]

The next day McCarran headed to Sparks, near Reno, where he delivered a Fourth of July speech at the Roosevelt Jubilee. "The president and Congress achieved a revolution without shedding a drop of blood," he said.[91]

One day Hal Ware invited Lee Pressman to lunch. Tall, lean, all earnestness in heavy brown pressed suits and matching brushed fedoras, Ware was commonly sighted in the endless halls of the massive Agriculture Department building. He'd been there on and off since the Coolidge administration, when he was hired as a dollar-a-year consultant. A dwindling thatch of hair was all that stood between Ware's forehead and a hairline in full retreat, which coupled with his pince-nez made him seem older and wiser and somehow more knowing than his forty-three years.

Normally terribly shy, more comfortable working in a field than in an office, Ware could grow effusive and outgoing when talk turned to his twin passions: agriculture and socialism. "He had a startlingly vivid imagination, and an urge and talent for organizing. . . ." observed his mother. "He forgot his shyness when engaged in one of his organizing ventures, and a flow of colorful, stirring talk would come from him, so persuasive that those who heard him were completely carried away."[92]

Pressman, as unlikely as it may have seemed to some of his colleagues, was waiting to be carried away. A striver as only someone who has crawled his way up from Lower East Side immigrant origins and childhood polio to the top rank of Harvard Law and a promising position at a tony legal firm could be, Pressman was not given to easy sentimentality or squandering compassion. Yet within his tightly knotted soul was a need to yield to something sterner than himself, a desire to submerge his own stubbornness into a cause greater than any individual undertaking could ever be. While toiling days at his Wall Street law firm on behalf of corporate behemoths such as Anaconda Copper and American Tobacco, Pressman had given his nights to the International Juridical Association, whose *IJA Bulletin* was the bible of radical lawyers — those defending immigrants who shouted revolution and faced deportation as a result, unions trying to organize workers, and a group of young blacks accused of raping a white woman in the South and soon known as the Scottsboro Boys. Pressman's friends Alger Hiss and Nat Witt were also drawn to the IJA, and all of them thrilled at the chance the New Deal offered to move close to the levers of power. "I am sitting on edge just waiting for news from you as to what's occurring,"[93] Pressman wrote to Jerry Frank when the New Deal seemed to be starting without him. When he finally got an appointment, Pressman worked a month without getting paid.

Being close to power, however, was not the same thing as actually having any. Already his colleagues at the AAA were talking about Pressman's raw antagonism toward agribusiness; about how he had looked straight at a bullheaded lawyer for the dairy producers and told him that his intransigence might lead to the government taking over the sale of milk. You might as well take over all business, the lawyer snapped. "Why not?" Pressman shot back.[94] At one hearing Pressman could barely contain himself at the table, mumbling under his breath to Pat Jackson as the dairy companies presented their case. "Lying sons of bitches," he grumbled.[95]

Pressman didn't feel much more affection for George Peek, head of the Triple A. Jerry Frank, who was in charge of the AAA's legal section, was turning out to be bad enough. "A timid liberal," Abt called him,[96] and in his circle there was no worse insult. But Peek, who headed the entire agency, was a pure reactionary. At sixty-six Peek had already had a long career in agriculture, having been raised in rural Illinois and then making a living selling farm equipment. The first time the gruff Peek met Frank was in bankruptcy court, where as the president of the Moline Plow Company he faced off against the lawyer selling off the assets of his company. They didn't get along any better in the AAA, and when Peek couldn't get rid of Frank as general counsel he dug into his own pocket to hire a private lawyer as his personal attorney for department business. The boys with their hair ablaze, Peek called Frank's young lawyers. Peek complained so much that eventually Roosevelt was forced to find him another job. The new head of the AAA, Chester Davis, wasn't any better. And when the young lawyers in Frank's office insisted to Davis that they needed to check the books and records of producers to make sure they were sharing profits from their licensing agreements with farmers, the head of the AAA was unpersuaded. He didn't want to drive agribusiness away from the bargaining table. "In the AAA, the big growers, big processors, big dairies were really in command," Pressman's friend Abt recalled. "The tenant farmers, the sharecroppers, the small farmers received the short end of the stick, if they received anything at all."[97] Thus it was that every good idea that the lawyers came up with seemed to be thwarted by the old managers at the top. "Well, my God," Pressman complained, "the Civil War was a picnic compared to this."[98]

There was one place in the world, Ware told Pressman at lunch, where real change was happening: the Soviet Union. In a sense Ware had been waiting all his life for the Russian Revolution. "His interest in socialism began as early as I can remember," his mother recalled.[99] That wasn't surprising, since Ware's mother was Ella Reeve Bloor — better known as Mother Bloor — who had started reading Marx in her thirties in the 1890s, raised six children, worked as a labor activist, and, after hearing a firsthand report from John Reed about the building of socialism in the Soviet Union, became a founding member of the American Communist Party in 1919. "A whole new vista of glorious living opened before me," she remembered. "I knew that all my development, all my strivings to bring about a better society, on this day laid a course I could finally subscribe to with all my heart and mind. I felt that our new party, firmly rooted in American soil, would be capable of leading the workers to final victory because of its faith in the workers themselves."[100]

Ware, too, was a charter member of the party. A graduate of Pennsylvania State College, where he studied agriculture, Ware had been a mushroom grower and a dairy farmer when he heeded Lenin's call for help in building socialism. Ware found nine other radical farmers, collected twenty carloads of equipment and rye seeds, and hauled it all over to the Soviet Union. He came back with twenty-five thousand U.S. dollars stuffed into a money belt to help in organizing American farm workers. During the Depression, Ware and his seventy-year-old mother traveled thousands of miles through the heartland trying to stir up revolutionary consciousness. Then at the dawn of the New Deal the party dispatched Ware to Washington to scout for talent among the idealists pouring into town. "Ware was a man without personal ambition," remembered his friend Whittaker Chambers. "The purpose of his life lay in promoting Communism."[101] And Communists had few illusions about the New Deal. "Reaction sought through Roosevelt to breathe life into the dying capitalist system by giving it a semblance of liberalism," is how Mother Bloor put it.[102]

A few months in Washington was all it took to convince Pressman that this was true; that Roosevelt wanted nothing more than to prop up the system, and that even the New Deal's timorous efforts to make capitalism more just were doomed to be foiled by industry and agribusiness. So when Hal Ware asked Pressman to join the party, the Harvard lawyer said yes. The party was perfectly legal, Ware added, but Pressman would have to keep his membership secret unless he wanted to wreck his career.

Lee Pressman could keep a secret.

One day in August, McCarran stood before the American Bar Association in Grand Rapids, Michigan, and recited a history lesson: an explication of how Jefferson and Hamilton had fought over whether governmental power ought to be centralized or dispersed and how Jefferson violated his own principles by making the Louisiana Purchase without any explicit authority to do so. Ever since then things had been going downhill. "The innovations," McCarran said, "of executive power indulged in by Jackson, promoted by Lincoln, expounded by Garfield, declared righteous by Roosevelt and philosophically promulgated by Wilson, appear to have been but forerunners, rivulets, as it were, contributing to a flood that now sweeps on, submerging the utopian doctrines and theories of Jefferson and conferring unheard-of and unfettered expansion to the executive." Looking over the landscape of the special session — the Banking Act, the

Agricultural Adjustment Act, the National Recovery Act — McCarran could only shake his head. "These acts and others of their kind, all couched under the declaration of 'national emergency,' constitute an avalanche that sweeps away the structures fought for and reared by the great Jefferson and his adherents," he continued. "New powers, never dreamed of by the framers of the organic law, never ventured even in the imagination of Hamilton, never claimed by the arrogant Jackson, never espoused by even the studious Wilson, are now the prerogatives of a democratic executive."[103]

McCarran was still holding back. "I honestly believed," he said later, "that it was far better for the party to be criticized from friends within than be condemned by enemies without."[104] On one hand McCarran had quickly emerged as one of the prickliest, most independent members of Congress; on the other, he supported enough New Deal legislation to conceal his overarching philosophical break with his president and party. While the month before he had dripped honey over the way Roosevelt had staved off revolution, McCarran privately believed that the president had surrounded himself with dangerous radicals who had not only usurped legislative authority but actually turned their bureaucratic fiefdoms into citadels of revolution. "Mr. Wallace is in fact and in reality a socialist," McCarran told a friend, days before he left to give his speech in Michigan. "This Farm Bureau, instructed and trained under recent lines of education, is in fact and in reality a Soviet organization, deriving its whole sustenance from our present federal government. . . . This growth in America threatens the democracy of this country more than anything that has ever developed in the nation."[105]

While McCarran was less blunt in public, there was no mistaking the warning in his words to the bar association. "Today," McCarran thundered, "the awakening comes, when a new form of government is found seated on the throne of democracy. . . . The road back may be more destructive than the avenue forward."[106]

CHAPTER 7

Rise Up and Stamp This Thing Out of Existence

With a few fellows like Alger Hiss you can really show
'em.[1]
— Felix Frankfurter to Jerome Frank

Unless you were in Washington in '33 and '34 I can't
describe why.[2]
— Lee Pressman

Pat McCarran picked up the phone. Jim Farley was on the other end. Pat, he said, I need a favor.

James Aloysius Farley was a man that even Pat McCarran wanted to keep happy. The big, bald, Irish Catholic New Yorker was the chairman of the Democratic National Committee who had tirelessly traveled the country to swing the party's nomination toward Roosevelt in 1932 and was rewarded with a job in the cabinet as postmaster general. But it was Farley's unofficial title as patronage chief, the man who held the tap on the New Deal job spigot, that more precisely described his power. And however philosophically opposed McCarran might be to the wild growth of the federal bureaucracy under the New Deal, he was not practically opposed to grabbing as many of those new jobs as possible for Nevada. Especially not when Reno needed a new postmaster.*

McCarran was fifty-eight, bulky, not in great health, his face often florid with outrage on the floor of the Senate — but he was also filled with a passion and zest for work that he hadn't felt in years. Usually in the office by eight, he spent mornings in hearings, afternoons on the floor, and evenings catching up on everything else in the office. Many nights he worked until midnight. McCarran was in Washington for almost a year before he even got around to replacing the pictures on the office walls left by his predecessor. There was simply too much to do. Not least of which was keeping an eye on Roosevelt. "For Mr. Roosevelt I have unbounded

---

*In 1936 McCarran would get Pete Petersen, the former baker and Nevada labor leader, appointed as the Reno postmaster. Petersen would hold the job for two decades, turning the post office into a virtual Senate field office for his patron. McCarran's enemies claimed that letters critical of the senator always seemed to get lost in the mail.

admiration," McCarran claimed to one reporter. "I cheerfully support him when my intelligence permits, otherwise I oppose his policies. I am keeper of my own conscience; I cannot delegate that job to anybody."[3]

When Congress returned to Washington in January 1934, McCarran once again stood out as one of the body's more defiant members. He attempted to reassert the authority of the legislative branch (and at the same time bolster his own authority in Nevada politics) by tacking onto an appropriations bill an amendment that would force the president to seek senatorial approval for state relief administrators. The amendment died in the House. Then McCarran went to work chipping away at the Economy Act that Roosevelt had rammed through Congress during the first week of the New Deal the year before, which had sliced the pay of all government employees by 15 percent and cut veterans' benefits. In February, McCarran led a successful assault on the act by amending it to restore the pensions of Spanish-American War vets.

McCarran's middle initial, reporters joked, must stand for "Amendment."[4] "There are so many McCarran amendments in the 73rd Congress that the press galleries long ago lost count," wrote reporter Kirke Simpson.[5] "He does not rate as a conservative, nor as a radical, nor as an opponent of the president," observed *Time* magazine. "Already one of the best liked members of the Senate, he is considered intellectually honest, frank, logical, and has a way of coming to the point without a smoke screen of oratory. Therefore he is potentially a bigger upsetter of administration plans than almost any other member of the Senate."[6]

McCarran lived up to his potential. In March he announced that he wasn't going to stop amending the Economy Act until all 1.2 million federal government employees were back on full pay. The White House responded by agreeing to phase in a two-thirds pay restoration, with the final third to come at the president's discretion. When an appropriations bill hit the Senate, McCarran attached an amendment to restore government salaries in full by July, larding the president's bill with an extra sixty-three million dollars. With the government spending billions to create jobs and raise private wages, McCarran didn't see any reason federal employees should be forced to work on the cheap. Most of the Senate's Republicans and a dozen Democrats quickly lined up to vote for McCarran's amendment, which passed 41 to 40. When the House passed Roosevelt's original bill by invoking its gag rule and not letting any amendments come up, McCarran bellowed that he would filibuster in the Senate and stop all other legislative business until the conference committee reported out his version. "If the conference produces anything less than one hundred percent pay restoration," McCarran said, "I assure you that I will hold the floor until next January, or until hundred percent pay restoration is accepted by both houses and the president."[7] But when the conference committee deadlocked, McCarran caved, and the Senate went for the president's plan. "I believe that two-thirds of a loaf is better than none and the working class in this country certainly need bread," McCarran said.[8]

Then Farley called. During the Hundred Days when Majority Leader Joe Robinson was having trouble whipping some of his Democrats in line on the bonus bill, the president asked Farley to talk with the more troublesome senators. Several of the legislators were worried about facing voters the following year but said that they'd go along if the president really wanted them to. A couple said they couldn't go on record at the moment, but if it came down to a close call they'd support the president. McCarran was the only one Farley chatted up who absolutely refused to go along. But this time, when Farley asked McCarran to go up to Maine to give a speech at the state Democratic convention, McCarran agreed.

In late April, McCarran traveled to Bangor, Maine, gave his speech, and made his way through snowy streets back to his hotel. He was ready to turn in when his office called. Roosevelt had unexpectedly vetoed the pay restoration bill, the House had overridden the president, and the Senate was going to take up the matter the next day. Farley, McCarran realized, had set him up. McCarran's amendment had passed by a single vote; now the Senate was getting ready to vote, and McCarran was stuck in Maine.

He had to get back to Washington. But the airport was snowed in and the trains were backed up. McCarran hired a car and drove through rain and fog to Portland, where he boarded a train to New York, jumped a plane to Washington, and then drove straight from the airport to the Capitol. Unshaven and rumpled, McCarran shambled into the chamber at 1:30 P.M. Bennett Champ Clark, a Democratic rebel from Missouri, rushed over to shake his hand. The debate dragged on for another five hours. "It soon began to look," noted the *Washington Post,* "as though McCarran could have come down from Maine in an ox cart and been in plenty of time."[9] Finally, at 7 P.M., the Senate voted 63 to 27 to override the veto. There were three votes to spare.

It had taken a year, but McCarran had won his first fight in the Senate.

John Abt felt that something strange was going on. After six months of working together in the general counsel's office at the Agricultural

Adjustment Administration, Abt considered Lee Pressman one of his best friends. "As close a friend as Lee would allow himself," Abt said later, "given his competitive and domineering streaks."[10] But Abt began to notice that Pressman and some of the other young lawyers in the Triple A would get together occasionally without inviting him. Then Pressman suddenly asked Abt to write an urgent critique of the dairy industry's exploitation of the AAA's milk program. Abt turned in the report but didn't hear anything. Not until one day in 1934 when a tall, thin man turned up uninvited at Abt's home. He introduced himself as Hal Ware.

Ware was, he told Abt, the leader of the Communist Party in Washington. Secret party members in the AAA had recommended Abt. Ware wanted him to join. Like many in the Triple A, Abt's early enthusiasm for the New Deal had given way to the realization that Roosevelt was more interested in saving the system than transforming it, and that if fundamental change were to come it would have to be by other means. Abt said yes. A few weeks later Ware told Abt that he had also recruited his sister Marion, who was married to Abt's AAA colleague Artie Bachrach. "We were," Abt remembered, "the closest of friends, neighbors in the same building, yet neither of us discussed the party or the possibility of joining it with the other."[11]

Abt finally figured out what his colleagues in the Triple A were doing behind his back. Besides Pressman, Abt discovered who the other Communists in the AAA were: Nat Witt, Charlie Kramer, Nathaniel Weyl, Hope Hale (whose husband, Hermann Brunck, was also a member), and Alger Hiss. And over in the NRA Vic Perlo and Henry Collins were also members. The exact number of secret Communists working for the government was a closely held secret. All told they numbered several score, but most members only knew about half a dozen in their own cell — in case, Kramer told Hale, of interrogation or torture. The Triple A cell dubbed itself the "cling peaches" after a recently concluded marketing agreement that the lawyers had drafted. Much later they would become known as the Ware Group.

The group met once a week at night in a violin studio above a florist shop on Connecticut Avenue, near Dupont Circle, which was run by Ware's sister Helen. They talked about Marx and Lenin, discussed what was going on in various New Deal agencies, forked over 10 percent of their salaries for dues — and increasingly they collected reports and documents that the party might find interesting. It didn't seem like much of a betrayal.

Above all they were supposed to keep the group a secret. Kramer admonished newcomers like Hale to stay away from leftists, even liberals like Pat Jackson. Do nothing to draw any attention to your political beliefs, he told her. Don't even think of buying the *Daily Worker* or the *New Masses* at the newsstand. Copies will be for sale at meetings. Even spouses were not supposed to know. Writer Josephine Herbst, for example, followed her husband, John Hermann, to Washington. He was doing something with Hal Ware and the party, she knew, but she didn't know what. "It was very much in the nature of a secret society," Herbst recalled many years later, "and these people took great pride in their sense of conspiracy and in the little unimportant assignments that they were given to perform."[12] Even within the cell there were things that could not be talked about. During one meeting Kramer told Hermann Brunck that he had a special task to discuss with him privately. "On the way home Hermann was silent at first," his wife remembered. "I wondered what Charles had asked him to do. But from now on we would have to have secrets from each other."[13]

The torture Charlie Kramer expected never came. The interrogation did. Years later Lee Pressman would remember that the party cell in the AAA was basically a Marxist study group. On another occasion, however, Pressman would admit that he had never read Marx. After twenty years, his faith shattered, his career in ruins, jail a possibility, Pressman would admit that the group had once existed. But he would keep its secrets.

On April 9 Alice Barrows showed up for an appointment at her hairdresser's. This is all very mysterious, her hairdresser started to say. Then he said something about a woman waiting upstairs who claimed to be a friend of Barrows, but didn't want to visit her at the office because of a federal investigation. Barrows walked upstairs and found Mildred Wirt, the wife of William A. Wirt. Things were about to get a lot more mysterious.

Barrows was an education specialist in the Interior Department, where she had worked since 1919. Wirt was sixty years old, the superintendent of schools in Gary, Indiana, a nationally known expert who had gained prominence for his theory that modern schools were failing students because they failed to inculcate the virtues and discipline that Americans had traditionally learned from farm work and manual labor. Barrows had once been Wirt's secretary; for twenty years they had been friends. That friendship would soon be severely tested.

Two weeks earlier, Wirt had stumbled into the national spotlight when James H. Rand Jr. read a letter from the educator before a House panel that was considering a stock market bill. Rand and Wirt were both members of the Committee for the Nation, a group that was lobbying for a return to the gold standard, and Wirt's letter recounted a dinner party he had attended the previous fall full of New Dealers openly talking about over-throwing capitalism. "We believe that we can keep Mr. Roosevelt there until we are ready to supplant him with a Stalin," one of the guests report-edly told Wirt. "We all think that Mr. Roosevelt is only the Kerensky of this revolution. . . . We are on the inside. We can control the avenues of influence. We can make the president believe that he is making decisions for himself."[14] The dinner party, it turned out, had been held at the Barrows house in Virginia.

Wirt's story became a sensation. Columnist Walter Winchell wired postmaster Jim Farley to tell him that economist Paul Douglas was the brainchild of the plot. The House created a select committee under North Carolina congressman Alfred Bulwinkle to investigate the charges. Then, the day before Wirt was scheduled to testify, Mrs. Wirt turned up at the hairdresser and told Barrows that her husband couldn't remember all the names of those who were at the dinner party. Barrows gave her the names: Robert Bruere of the NRA, David Cushman Coyle of the Public Works Administration, Hildegarde Kneeland from the Agriculture Department, Mary Taylor, the editor of the AAA's Consumer's Guide, and Laurence Todd, a correspondent for Tass, the Soviet news agency.

The next day Wirt walked through a throng of spectators and reporters to a witness table in the packed House Caucus Room and proceeded to both bore and baffle almost everyone there. Chairman Alfred Bulwinkle tried to get Wirt to tell his story and Wirt tried to tell his story, but it seemed as if they were speaking different languages: Wirt related that he had talked for three hours at the dinner party, and the revolutionary rhetoric he quoted had been uttered by three guests. Well, two guests actually, while a third nodded approvingly. His letter, he admitted, was really an interpretation of the writ-ings of Rexford Tugwell, the brain truster who had become assistant secre-tary of agriculture. "I never said," Wirt noted, "that anybody was planning to overthrow the government; they were planning to overthrow the established social order. . . . So many people are misled when you talk about revolution; they think it means an armed force coming into Washington and blowing the dome off of the Capitol and maybe driving out our president."[15]

Barrows remembered an altogether different evening. "After dinner, at about, I think, eight o'clock, he began talking on the devaluation of the dollar," she recalled, "and talked continuously on that subject until, I should say, about eleven o'clock. . . . At no time during that whole evening or dinner did I hear the names of Kerensky or Stalin or Dr. Tugwell, or Secretary Wallace or the president mentioned. At no time did Dr. Wirt ask any questions."[16] The other dinner guests all offered similar accounts. Overnight Wirt was a national laughingstock. "The lowest form of public burlesque," sniffed Arthur Krock in the *New York Times*.[17] "A cuttlefish squirt," the NRA's Don Richberg joked. "Nobody hurt / From beginning to end: / Dr. Wirt."[18] "Flatter than a crepe suzette," said *Time* in its weird Lucian syntax, "fell the Red Scare of 1934."[19]

But Harold McGugin, one of the two minority members of the committee, wasn't satisfied. The Kansas Republican quizzed Barrows about her guests. Did she know that Bruere had defended the IWW and criticized the Wilson administration during the Red Scare? Did she know that Mary Taylor worked at the AAA for Fred Howe, who was the commissioner of immigration during the Wilson years but defended anarchists instead of deporting them? "Your beliefs," he inquired, "are kindred to their beliefs, I suppose?"[20]

The committee report, written by the three Democrats, found that Wirt's charges were false and that there was no revolutionary group in the government. The Republicans balked and filed a dissenting report written by McGugin, who faulted the committee for not undertaking a broader investigation of internal subversion. "A determined effort throughout the entire proceedings to discredit Dr. Wirt and to suppress the truth," McGugin called the hearings.[21] It was clear, he implied, that the government employees at the dinner party represented the radical thinking of their superiors. "It is significant," McGugin noted, "that these five people holding key positions in our government should be in such close social relationships with Laurence Todd, one of the foremost propaganda agents of the Soviet government in America."[22]

The dark warnings, however, were lost in the roar of laughter that greeted Wirt's fuzzy idea about revolution. Yet as ridiculous as Wirt's subversive plot was, he was closer to the truth than many of his critics realized. There *was* a secret fraternity worming its way into the government that did not want the New Deal to succeed in saving capitalism. While Wirt named the AAA's Mary Taylor as one of the purported conspirators, the real Communists in the agency dismissed her as a mere socialist, which was virtually as bad as being a fascist. Wirt, by complete happenstance, was within spitting distance of naming Communists in government.

And Washington dinner parties were certainly abuzz with talk of revolution, about who was or wasn't a secret Communist. When Jonathan

Mitchell arrived in the capital the next year to become the Washington editor of *The New Republic*, he quickly began to hear rumors about a Communist underground over drinks at Pat Jackson's Newspaper Club. Lee Pressman, Nat Witt, Alger Hiss, and Jackson himself were all said to be members. Much later Mitchell would tell the FBI that Jackson confessed to him that he was a member of the group. Jackson admitted that he had been asked to join but claimed that he never did.[23]

The Wirt hearings, in short, became the paradigm for the festering argument over Communist subversion that liberals and conservatives engaged in for the next twenty years: A ridiculous-sounding charge would be hurled, liberals would scoff that rumors and gossip about hidden Communists were baseless and malicious, and conservatives would fume, the former believing that their political enemies were dreaming about Reds under the bed, while the latter grew sure that their antagonists had no interest in even checking — and perhaps for good reason. Delusion and derision twined around each other like fighting snakes. In all the commotion the real Communists escaped attention.

McCarran said nothing about Wirt at the time, but twenty years later, at the height of his power, he devoted his life to proving Wirt right.

In June, after Congress went home for the summer, Roosevelt took to the airwaves to tell the American public how the New Deal was progressing in its second year. He talked about the bankruptcy and farm relief acts, the securities and exchange regulation, the reciprocal trade agreement, and monetary reform. But more than the sum of various laws, Roosevelt told his radio audience that the federal government was positively asserting itself as a force for good in the lives of individuals. Which, he noted, was scaring the hell out of some people. "Have you as an individual paid too high a price for these gains?" the president asked. "Plausible self-seekers and theoretical die-hards will tell you of the loss of individual liberty. Answer this question also out of the facts of your own life. Have you lost any of your rights or liberty or constitutional freedom of action and choice? . . . Read each provision of that Bill of Rights and ask yourself whether you personally have suffered the impairment of a single jot of these great assurances. I have no question in my mind as to what your answer will be."

The New Deal was far from complete, he continued. Americans needed better housing, the country's natural resources needed conservation, the old and sick needed social security. "A few timid people, who fear progress, will try to give you new and strange names for what we are doing," Roosevelt said. "Sometimes they will call it 'Fascism,' sometimes 'Communism,' sometimes 'Regimentation,' sometimes 'Socialism.' But, in so doing, they are trying to make very complex and theoretical something that is really very simple and very practical. I believe in practical explanations and in practical policies."

What the government was actually doing, Roosevelt said, was similar to the renovation of the White House that was going to happen when he left town for the summer. The White House and the Old Executive Office Building were going to get modern wiring, plumbing, and air-conditioning. But the basic structures would not be changed, only adapted to the times.

"If I were to listen to the arguments of some prophets of calamity who are talking these days," he concluded, "I should hesitate to make these alterations. I should fear that while I am away for a few weeks the architects might build some strange new Gothic tower or a factory building or perhaps a replica of the Kremlin or of the Potsdam Palace. But I have no such fears. The architects and builders are men of common sense and of artistic American tastes. They know that the principles of harmony and of necessity itself require that the building of the new structure shall blend with the essential lines of the old. It is this combination of the old and the new that marks orderly peaceful progress — not only in building buildings but in building government itself."[24]

In the summer of 1934 a party member from New York turned up in Washington. He had been sleeping at Helen Ware's violin studio, and looked it. Short and heavy and rumpled with a fleshy face and sad eyes, he had the shabby look of someone who wore clothes with a complete indifference. He was like a man without an umbrella walking with his head down in the rain: oblivious to everything but his destination. He said his name was Carl.

Carl collected cash-stuffed envelopes at party meetings and carried the dues back to New York. Increasingly, he also collected whatever reports or documents party members could lay their hands on at work. Even by the standards of the Communist underground, Carl was mysterious. Melodrama seemed to run in his blood. In restaurants he always sat with a view of the door. Going anywhere with him involved a circuitous route dodging into and out of buildings, switching buses, and doubling back. He checked for tails the way some men compulsively glanced at their watches. He seemed to know several languages. Some party members were sure that he was a Russian. This made them respect him more.

For Josephine Herbst, Carl was just a headache. She couldn't understand all the sneaking around and childish spy games. Carl, for instance, would show up at her door with a small suitcase demanding to see John, and the next thing she knew her husband was asking her to leave her own apartment. Then Carl would take out his camera.

Years later Herbst would learn Carl's real name: Whittaker Chambers.[25]

In September, Democrats from all over Nevada gathered in Ely for their state convention. William McKnight, a Reno attorney and the chairman of the state Democratic committee, opened the convention and then handed the gavel over to the chairman, Jack Robbins. "I think," Robbins said, "William McKnight was treated shamefully."[26]

In the coded words of Nevada politics this was a dagger thrown straight at McCarran. Key Pittman's friends — which is to say those who had long controlled the Democratic Party in Nevada — were furious with McCarran for humiliating the senior senator several months earlier. McCarran and Pittman had been enemies for ages, but as much as Pittman hated McCarran at times, he always put party unity above personal animosity. So when McCarran finally turned up in Washington, Pittman did more than the ritual courtesy of walking his new colleague up the aisle for his swearing-in; he escorted McCarran around the Senate, introducing him to other lawmakers. Pittman had been there twenty-one years and was now president pro tempore, chairman of the Foreign Relations Committee, and one of the president's most loyal followers.

Pittman was also a bad drunk, and more and more often he was drunk all the time. At the London Economic Conference during the summer of 1933, for example, he drank to blind excess, chasing one fellow delegate down a hotel hallway with a hunting knife, tickling a lady onto the floor at a dinner party, and shooting out streetlights with a pistol. About the only accomplishment of the conference, however, was Pittman's doing: an international silver agreement, which in effect committed the U.S. Treasury to buy the yearly production of American silver for four years — de facto free coinage of silver. In Nevada's mining towns there was free beer and dancing in the streets.

McCarran couldn't wait for a chance to embarrass Pittman. It came when Nevada needed a new U.S. attorney in 1934. Pittman recommended William McKnight to the president. McCarran threatened a floor fight over the nomination. Pittman quailed, withdrew the name, and submitted another candidate, A. L. Scott, an undistinguished party hack from Pioche.

McCarran suggested Elko judge Edward Carville. Pittman, who had no stomach for a fight, capitulated. It got worse. When Pittman nominated his friend Robert Douglass as internal revenue collector for Nevada, McCarran insisted on the right to name all of his subordinates. The two senators worked out a similar arrangement with the U.S. marshal: Pittman got to name the marshal, and McCarran named all the deputies. Thus while Pittman could claim the loyalty of high-ranking officials through the state, the staffs of many offices owed their jobs to McCarran. "Pat," Governor Richard Kirman said, "wants every job in the state."[27]

But Pittman's friends still controlled the state convention, and after Robbins's veiled slight, they gave a more direct one to McCarran. Representative James Scrugham, not the junior senator, would give the keynote speech. Toward the end of the day, Robbins finally got around to asking McCarran to come up on stage. No thank you, McCarran replied, I've been insulted by the convention. Later McCarran argued so vocally with Pittman loyalists that one of them asked him to step outside. He declined. McCarran's enemies were quick to write his political obituary. "He inexorably divorced himself from the regular Democratic Party and can never hope to be re-elected to the United States Senate," opined the *Elko Daily Free Press*.[28] Even the always friendly Al Cahlan agreed. "Pat is a dead one," he wrote in the *Las Vegas Review Journal*, "or will be after his term expires in 1938."[29]

Publicly McCarran claimed to support the party, and because Pittman was running for a fifth term, his junior colleague even appeared at a rally for the senior senator. Backstage, however, political observers were sure that McCarran was instrumental in the fact that Pittman was facing his first real primary challenge in years, this time from H. R. Cooke, an old friend of McCarran's. Pittman didn't have any problem winning the nomination, but he was sure that McCarran was actively backing his Republican rival George Malone. In the final days of the election an anonymous pamphlet appeared in Nevada accusing Pittman of being in the pay of Wall Street silver speculators. This, too, Pittman blamed on McCarran. "There is no doubt that he intends to continue his fight against the president and his policies," Pittman said privately. "He has probably come to the conclusion that he can not be renominated four years from now unless I am defeated. McCarran made several speeches during the campaign similar to those he made before the American Bar Association in which he charged that we were drifting away from the Constitution, and that unless we returned to the Constitution there would be anarchy in this country. In other words, it was the same attack being made upon the president that is being made by the new Liberty League."[30]

Pittman knew his enemies. Back in July, Jim Farley arrived in Reno, dedicated the new post office, and spoke to a Democratic luncheon. Before the meeting, McCarran took Farley aside and asked him not to mention Pittman in his speech. Even by McCarran's standards this was nervy: a novice junior senator telling his party's national chairman not to stump for one of the most senior and loyal Democrats in the Senate. Farley demurred. "I did speak for Pittman, however, much to Pat McCarran's discomfort," Farley recorded in his diary, "as I believe Pittman to be loyal and entitled to that consideration from me."[31] After Farley told him of his plans to endorse Pittman, McCarran skipped the lunch.

McCarran was also a no-show in January when Pittman was expecting the traditional courtesy of having his colleague escort him up the aisle to his swearing-in. McCarran claimed that he had suddenly taken ill. McCarran, however, was well enough to answer the next roll call.

One gray, fall day in 1934 William H. O'Donnell Jr. and a black comrade drove into Port Norris on the New Jersey shore. In the flood tide of oyster season more than fifteen hundred workers stood long hours at tables piled high with rough shells, prying open the reluctant bivalves and slicing out the meaty mollusks, a repetitive and often painful process that left hands scarred and bleeding but at least let a man earn a living, however meager. But in the Depression there were more hands than work. Wages, never great to begin with, slipped even lower. This bleak autumn families in the shacks down the road from the oyster factory swore that if it wasn't for that minister from northern New Jersey bringing down truckloads of donated food, they would have starved.

To Bill O'Donnell these men were the raw, the very raw, material of the revolution. O'Donnell was a veteran of the bloody union-organizing struggles in the Kentucky coalfields who was now consumed by the fight to establish the Agricultural and Cannery Workers' Industrial Union at the sprawling Seabrook Farms in Bridgeton, New Jersey. If he could make the shuckers see that the canners' struggle was also theirs — that all the disparate and divided workers were really fighting the same fight, and that together they had more power than all the bosses in the world — then he would be doing something.

The smell of brine hung heavy in the damp air, and their feet crunched on a macadam made from years of broken shells as O'Donnell and his comrade walked up to the building where workers were shucking away. Company guards like barking dogs chased them away. Then they drove to the shacks to talk to those who didn't have jobs. A state trooper pulled up and arrested the two. After two hours they released him. O'Donnell's friend, however, was detained for disorderly conduct and given thirty days in the local jail. Too late, O'Donnell realized his mistake: When a black and a white came to town together, all the cops saw was red. "Here it will be necessary to work 'illegally' — i.e., underground for some time," O'Donnell told his friend Pat Jackson. "To organize openly now would be like walking up to the county jail and asking for a six months sentence to get a rest."[32]

By 1934 the fields and factories of the United States had become battlegrounds. In Minneapolis the police tried to break a strike by Trotskyist Teamsters and fired into a crowd, wounding sixty-seven people and killing two. In Toledo National Guardsmen killed two in a clash with strikers at the Electric Auto-Lite Company. In the South and Northeast almost four hundred thousand textile workers laid down their needles and walked away from their looms. In San Francisco street fighting broke out between police and striking longshoremen who were part of a labor dispute that virtually paralyzed shipping on the West Coast for eighty-three days, which culminated in a general strike led by a stubborn Australian named Harry Bridges that shut down the entire city for four days.

And in Bridgeton, New Jersey, three hundred Italian and black workers walked off their jobs on the Seabrook Farm. "I say, if we can't get anything for working," said one worker, "let's see what we can get for fighting."[33] It was a fight that Pat Jackson thought the Agricultural Adjustment Administration should get involved in. On his own, Jackson was doing as much as he could. He sent money to O'Donnell and his South Jersey Committee in Defense of Labor and Farmers Rights — and in turn O'Donnell sent his friend five copies of Lenin's tract on American agriculture. ("The best analysis of capitalist development in agriculture available in the English language," O'Donnell enthused.[34])

O'Donnell, of course, was a Communist — perhaps only a little-c believer and not an actual, card-carrying, dues-paying member of the party, although that is unlikely. But the difference didn't matter. Not to conservatives like McCarran who saw no philosophical space between American Bolsheviks and American liberals. Not to progressives like Jackson who cared not a wit whether someone read Jefferson or Marx as long as he boiled with outrage over the fact that a man could work like a mule all day and still earn barely a buck, which would disappear with interest as soon as he stepped into the company store to buy clothes and food and rotgut from his boss.

And in southern New Jersey — where, O'Donnell told Jackson, townships were banning strike demonstrations and buying machine guns — the only hope of averting fascism seemed to be the building of a broad coalition among workers and their middle-class supporters. "The mayor of one of the towns here (I am not at liberty to divulge his name) is very sympathetic to this aspect of our work although he is opposed to Communism with equal ardor as he understands it now," O'Donnell reported to Jackson. ". . . Ordinarily we maintain that thought without action is abortive and when thought has revolutionary or even progressive directions without action, that it is a betrayal of the working class. However in these cases temporary tolerance is the keynote. Many of these elements, and more to come will learn further and as the crisis in the system advances come over to a united front against reaction. . . ."[35]

Officially the Communist Party was still stuck in its strident Third Period phase, in which it denounced the New Deal and liberals (and socialists) as the agents and abettors of fascism. "One often wanted to work with them," recalled socialist leader Norman Thomas. "But their tactics were completely unscrupulous. The great Lenin had taught them that anything is ethical which advances the interests of the Communist party. This was, I thought, a monstrous doctrine."[36] None of the party's enemies on the left were more hated than the tiny band of Trotskyists. Six years after Stalin had vanquished his rival Lev Trotsky, the brilliant and militant revolutionary headed a sect that on a good day approached five hundred members. Still, nothing bearing Trotsky's name was too small for Stalin to stomp to death. The first public meeting of Trotskyists in the United States was rushed by Communists waving lead pipes and knives. "In the early thirties," recalled Max Shachtman, the party's leader, "there was hardly a Trotskyist meeting that I spoke at from coast to coast, and the same held true for other speakers, that did not suffer from the same threats of violence at Communist hands."[37]

But unofficially, radicals such as O'Donnell were finding that the New Deal was full of sympathetic souls. Still, working with the Communists wasn't easy. They were stern and censorious and, as Pat Jackson learned, never looked for ashtrays or offered to help with the dishes when you had them over to the house. During Sacco and Vanzetti, Jackson, who had spent a good chunk of his inheritance and even more of his heart on the cause, had been derided by the Communists as practically one of the duo's murderers. Yet, he was convinced that good liberals had to pull together with Communists if they were going to keep the country from tipping into fascism. "We all were distressed at your having issued the leaflet you did condemning the radical organizers in the fields," he scolded one liberal ally.[38]

The real enemy, Jackson believed, was not anyone who was trying to help farm workers but those who oppressed them — or a government that was indifferent to their struggle. The NRA was supposed to help factory workers and the Triple A was meant to assist farmers but agricultural workers, the seasonal hired hands who did the actual picking and processing and then moved on, seemed to have slipped between the acronyms. "Agricultural laborers," wrote *The Nation* that fall, "continue even under the New Deal to be America's worst-exploited workers."[39] And the government didn't seem to care. "The Department of Agriculture has never admitted that there is such a group as agriculture labor demanding attention,"[40] Jackson told a friend.

Jackson tried to interest Jerry Frank in setting up a section in the AAA to deal with ag workers. Frank said it was political dynamite; Chester Davis, the head of the AAA, was already tired of all the wild ideas his underlings kept suggesting. "If the Consumer's Counsel were to determine the policies of the Agricultural Adjustment Administration," Davis dressed down Frank, "this organization would have an exceedingly interesting life, but, I am afraid, a brief one."[41]

So Jackson found himself going behind the backs of his superiors to stir up public pressure. "I have to be non-official since the Consumers' Counsel office of which I am a member is supposed to have nothing whatever to do with agricultural labor," Jackson explained to a friend. "Writing you this way raises the whole problem of one's personal loyalty to individuals and the administration. I have thought the thing through and feel justified in placing loyalty to ideals and principles above the former."[42]

To Pat Jackson the one person in the AAA who really seemed to care about the downtrodden was Lee Pressman. That fall Pressman was burning indignant with tales from Scioto Marsh in Hardin County, Ohio, where he had gone as part of a Labor Department investigation into conditions in the onion fields. "The first time the department of Agriculture had ever consented to look officially into an agricultural labor strike," Jackson beamed.[43]

Over the summer Ohio's onion workers created the first ag workers' union ever to win a charter from the conservative American Federation of Labor. The newly formed Agricultural Workers' Union then demanded a raise for its members. The bosses refused, the workers struck, and a local judge issued an injunction limiting picketing to groups of two. Deputies called strikers together in a group and promptly arrested them for illegally congregating. When strike leader Okey Odell was arrested by the sheriff, a group of two hundred vigilantes abducted Odell. He was lucky to escape with his life.

While Agriculture Secretary Henry Wallace and Frank listened to Pressman's report, neither of them was willing to expose the Triple A to more controversy. It was already all Frank could do to keep Pressman from being dismissed. "Lee was the center of attack . . . ," Frank recalled. "Twice he was all but fired. His alleged free-spoken statements were a constant source of vicious criticism against him."[44]

Jackson was smitten. "Lee supplied a lack in me which I needed,"[45] Jackson acknowledged, calling him "my closest crony in the AAA."[46] And Jackson certainly had a lot of friends. "At the Jacksons, one never knew whether one might meet a Supreme Court justice, a fledgling trade union editor, one of the Garst brothers in transit from Russia to Iowa, or a Bolivian political exile," recalled William V. Shannon.[47]

So it just seemed natural that Pressman kept telling Jackson about bright young men whom he should help find jobs in the government. Which was how Charlie Kramer, then using his given name, Krivitsky, got hired in the consumer counsel office. The sullen young economist seemed the antithesis of the usually vocal New Deal type, but Pressman told Jackson he was their kind of liberal. So he was hired. Then Pressman mentioned that Alger Hiss, his colleague in the legal division, would be perfect to become the counsel for a new Senate committee being put together by Jackson's friend Senator Gerald Nye to investigate the international munitions trade. Hiss was loaned to the committee.

The attacks from the big ag producers only got worse. The milk magnates couldn't get Pressman fired, but they did convince Henry Wallace to sack Einar Jensen, the federal milk administrator in Boston, whom almost no one thought was much of a firebrand. "His thinking," Jackson told his friend Supreme Court justice Louis Brandeis, "is nowhere nearly as radical as mine."[48]

Jackson, whose personality was perpetually teetering between elation and despair, tried to get Tom Blaisdell, Jensen's boss, to put up a fight. He wouldn't. So Jackson went out and got blasted, tearing through a restaurant roaring against Blaisdell as a weak-kneed sycophant to anyone who would listen. Dode had to ask Jerry Frank to bring her husband home.

"Confusion, confusion, confusion," Jackson wailed. "Increasing fascism around the corner. F. D. a false hope. No strong leader in sight. Capitalism doomed as hell without war."[49]

The reporters were waiting outside Senator Robert Wagner's office when McCarran walked out one day in February 1935.

Earlier in the month Roosevelt had sent the Senate a public works bill that would take three and a half million workers off relief rolls by pumping $4.9 billion into construction projects. To spread the money around, the president's bill would limit each worker to no more than fifty dollars a month. To critics on the left, the bill was too little, the money too meager for each worker, which might even inspire private industry to slash its own wages to the government level. McCarran was one of these critics. "It will tear down the wage structure of the country in private enterprise," he said.[50]

McCarran offered an amendment that would force the government to pay the prevailing local wage for any public works project. But raising the government wage without increasing the budget for the program would mean either tossing a million workers off projects or ending the whole thing four months early. It would, in other words, wreck the centerpiece of the president's recovery plan for 1935. The White House threatened to veto the whole bill if the McCarran amendment passed and warned that it would spell the end of federal relief, forcing the government to shut down its CCC camps and turn 350,000 men out onto the streets. Fears that the bill would drive down private wages, the president said, were nonsense. "I have enough faith in the country to believe that practically one hundred percent of employers are patriotic enough to prevent the lowering of wages," Roosevelt told the Senate.[51]

The McCarran amendment passed by a single vote, 44 to 43. Nineteen-thirty-five wasn't starting out to be such a great year for the president. In January, Roosevelt asked the Senate to let the United States join the World Court. In Detroit, Father Charles Coughlin, whose weekly radio sermon reached millions and earned him more mail than anyone else in the country, urged his listeners to deluge Congress with telegrams protesting any surrender of U.S. sovereignty. They did. In the Senate, William Borah and the progressives were coming to realize that their fear of the U.S. sliding into another European conflict outweighed their support of the New Deal. McCarran joined their ranks, and the court proposal died. "I will never vote to send the boys of America across the water again," McCarran vowed.[52]

McCarran was proving equally adept at attacking the president from either the right or the left. "The New Deal's preeminent Nemesis," the *Washington Herald* called him.[53] "No member of Congress," added Max Stern in *Today,* "whether New Dealer, Son of the Wild Jackass or Black Republican, has given the Administration more worry, not even the pestiferous Huey Long himself. . . . Just as shooting clay pigeons is his favorite outdoor sport, sniping the New Deal program seems to be his most relished indoor diversion."[54]

Now McCarran's amendment threatened the public works bill, and hence the entire New Deal recovery effort. "The gross stupidity and crass demagogy of the McCarran amendment to the relief appropriations act has caused a nation-wide storm of indignation," wrote the *Washington Herald.* "Senator McCarran and Senator Wagner have now joined the Huey Long crowd of destructive demagogues."[55]

But Wagner, one of the most revered liberals in the Senate, wanted to find some middle ground between McCarran and the White House. So he invited McCarran to his office to discuss a compromise. It was a long meeting. Afterward they walked into the hall and a pack of reporters pounced upon them. Is there any room for compromise? they wanted to know.

"Of course there is an area," Wagner said.

McCarran glared. "There will be no compromise," he said.[56]

Pat Jackson came rushing into Lee Pressman's office, clutching a letter. It was February 5, 1935, and Jackson had just come back from lunch to find an envelope on his desk marked PERSONAL. He tore it open. "I have asked Mr. Howe to advise you that I would like to have your resignation in my hands today," he read.[57] Signed, Chester Davis.

Jackson waved the letter at Pressman. Is there any way to challenge this? he asked. Pressman opened the letter, read it coolly, refolded it carefully, and handed it back. There's nothing you can do, he told his friend. Jackson looked like he was on the verge of tears; he trembled toward the door. Wait a minute, Pressman said. He pulled out his own dismissal letter. "He was obviously getting a saturnine chuckle out of the whole thing,"[58] Jackson recalled.

Pressman, too, had just come back from lunch, where he and John Abt had joked about whose neck would get the ax at the Triple A. For a long time it had been clear that Chester Davis and Jerry Frank didn't agree on the basic policy of the agency, but lately things had gotten really thorny over the AAA's cotton program, which paid growers not to grow cotton. Farmers eagerly pocketed the government's money, but they often didn't share it with the sharecroppers who worked their land and suddenly found themselves without either crops or cash. The sharecroppers responded by forming the Southern Tenant Farmer's Union (one of whose financial angels was Pat Jackson). The farmers responded by forming vigilante groups that shot up union meetings. "They said," wrote the wife of one black union activist, "they gonter brake this union up if I was you I woulden rist my life here among these heathen people here they will hurt or kill you you know if they shoot in white man house they will do the same thing for us."[59]

When the AAA lawyers insisted that landowners had to pass along some of the government payments to their tenants, the farmers responded by evicting their sharecroppers. The legal division shot back with a directive that sharecroppers had the right to stay on their land as long as the government contracts were in force. Alger Hiss, who was on loan to the Nye Committee during the day but still giving his nights to the AAA, drafted the opinion. Jerry Frank signed it and (while Chester Davis was out of the office) prevailed upon the acting director to issue it as an official ruling. Davis canceled the order as soon as he got back and stormed off to Henry Wallace demanding that the secretary fire the radicals in the agency. Wallace readily agreed.

The next day dismissal letters fell like ripe fruit. Frank and Pressman were of course sacked. So was Jackson, who didn't work in the legal division and had nothing to do with the cotton opinion but had made himself such a pain in the ass that the only surprise was how long he had actually lasted. Hiss, the author of the order, wasn't fired. Nor was John Abt, who was disappointed that he wasn't purged. "Perhaps," Abt thought, "my behavior was somehow defective that it should appear so unthreatening to those I heartily opposed."[60] Rumors flew that Hiss had been on the list but wriggled off. When he was offered Frank's old job as counsel and considered accepting it, his friends were livid. Hiss might be as radical as any of his friends, but he was proving very skilled at concealing his views from his superiors. "The purge spells the end of an era,"[61] wrote *The Nation*. "Something approaching despair has seized scores of young men and women in the New Deal," Jackson later wrote in *the Boston Globe*. ". . . Mr. Wallace's treatment of Mr. Frank and the others has done more to undermine the young New Dealers' morale than any other single episode in the New Deal."[62]

Frank's office filled with young lawyers on their last day. Frank walked back and forth behind his desk like a dog in a new cage. He looked out his window at the indifferent Potomac curling past. This cannot be, he said. Then he said it again. We worked so closely with Wallace. Frank chain-smoked and puffed that they were only carrying out Wallace's wishes. Pressman mocked Frank's faith and naïveté. Jerome, Pressman said, you're crazy. You're a romantic. Of course Wallace did this. He had to. I would, too, if I were in his place.

Barely a week after being shown the door at the AAA, Jackson was leading a picket line of twenty black sharecroppers and southern ministers singing spirituals in front of the Ag Department building.[63]

When the public works bill came to the floor in March, McCarran turned to the one man in the Senate whom he knew would never cave in: Huey Long. Long was enough of a contrarian to make McCarran look like a loyal Democrat. He was also perhaps McCarran's favorite colleague. Coming to the Senate the year before McCarran, Long was the first Democrat to break with Roosevelt, when he opposed the New Deal's first measure, the Banking Act. Both of them opposed the Economy Act. From the first week of the New Deal they were allies. Long told anyone who would listen in the Senate cloakroom that there would soon be a mob storming the chamber to hang members from the rafters — "And I'm undecided," he said, "whether to stick here with you or go out and lead them."[64] The Democrats and the Republicans, he thundered, were the same medicine in different bottles. Long ran his home state of Louisiana like a third-world dictator and by the middle of 1935 was scaring the bejesus out of many people who thought he had the same thing in mind for the whole country.

At forty-two Long was as bold a rebel as ever sat in the Senate. McCarran liked him instantly. They cosponsored the prevailing wage amendment. They spelled each other on a filibuster against the NRA. "A splendid intellect, a wonderful memory and an untiring nature," McCarran said of Long in words that he could have applied to himself. "A good man to have with you and a dangerous man to have against you, but when you get close to him, you discover that he is really a lovable character."[65]

On March 15 McCarran wasn't feeling much love for most of his fellow party members. Long had wanted to filibuster (his specialty); McCarran insisted on letting his amendment come to a vote. He was sure that he could count on the progressives and liberals to back him. He was almost instantly sorry. "I don't want to wreck the whole program,"[66] Wagner said. McCarran could feel the earth beneath his feet shift. Most of his allies ran out on him: Wagner, La Follette, Hugo Black.

The galleries were packed, the floor thick with senators. Everyone had come to see a good show. Long delivered. "The hand of the tempter is strong," he drawled, fixing his wrath on Wagner, "and the flesh is weak. There were only two left when Moses reached the Promised Land. And we will equal his record. The senator from Nevada and myself will vote for his amendment."[67]

The amendment lost 50 to 38. "Whom do we represent?" McCarran asked. "Do we represent the executive? If we do, then I think it's about time to reform our organic law."[68]

Roosevelt got his way. He eventually forced through a cascade of legislation that made 1935 almost the equal to the Hundred Days: Social Security, the National Labor Relations Act, a utilities bill, a Federal Reserve bill, and tax overhaul.

McCarran did not take defeat well. "In God's name," he shouted on the Senate floor, "isn't there a man here?"[69]

On July 3, 1935, McCarran got word that his mother was near death. He hopped into an army plane and stopped in Cleveland, where he found a telegram telling him that Mrs. McCarran had died at the age of eighty-nine. He bumped into a reporter. He was angry and bitter and not just about his mother. "I supported many of their measures at first," McCarran said, "but I find myself forced to take issue with them on many points now and I expect to be forced increasingly into this position in the future. . . . Democracy, as I conceive it, is being killed by the New Deal."[70]

Communism was much on McCarran's mind in the summer of 1935. In the Senate he tore into Secretary of State Cordell Hull's reciprocal trade agreement with Russia. The secretary's so-called trade agreement was either a treaty, McCarran said, which needed the Senate's approval, or a tariff act, which required legislation. McCarran introduced an amendment to the Agricultural Adjustment Act banning the State Department from negotiating trade agreements. "This pact, with a nation that floods our country with Communist propaganda and tears up its promises to settle its legitimate debts with us," McCarran said, "is the crowning blow of Secretary Hull's ruinous and fantastic mania for free trade."[71]

McCarran gave speeches across the country decrying the danger of Communism, warning that subversives were teaching in schools and slipping propaganda into textbooks. "If you will only read the current press word," he told a national convention of federal employees, "you will see that just across the ocean channel, over in Russia they have been holding a convention where they boasted about the inroads they have made into American life, boasted about the manner in which they have planted and will plant the seeds of Communism over in America, in contradiction to their own given promises. . . . I say it is not for you or for me to stand idly by if today in the schools of this country there is being taught something that would tear down the fundamental principles of this country. It is for you and me to rise up as an army and stamp that thing out of existence."[72]

In the summer of 1935 Earl Browder walked proudly into a conference room in Moscow. The walls were papered with the publications of the CPUSA, many written by Browder, most of them assailing Roosevelt as America's leading Nazi, a fascist warmonger eager to attack the Soviet Union. For the past year Browder had been the American party's undisputed leader, a Middle Border Bolshevik used to being ignored at home but expecting today that his Russian patrons would smile once again on his dogged efforts to bring Communism to the heartland of capitalism.

Raised on Kansas corn and his father's socialism, Browder came early to despise the American system, but as a milquetoast radical he looked to the revolutionary movement as a source of job security for a long time to come. Browder had labored by day as a bookkeeper then — like Penelope with her knitting — spent his nights trying to undo the same system he served from nine to five. A stint in Leavenworth for opposing conscription during World War I gave Browder the leisure time to study Lenin, and after leaving prison he joined the American Communist Party in 1921. Browder became a frequent visitor to Moscow, where he struck up a friendship with a forbidding Bulgarian named Georgi Dimitrov. Now as Browder took his seat in the conference room he looked hopefully toward Dimitrov, the head of the Comintern, the association of international Communist parties.

Dimitrov began speaking in rapid German. As soon as the words were translated into English, Browder's face fell. "One must indeed be a confirmed idiot not to see that it is the most reactionary pro-Nazi circles of

American finance capital which are attacking Roosevelt," Dimitrov said. "...The anti-Nazi forces must rally around Roosevelt."[73]

Any questions? Dimitrov asked. An ashen Browder shook his head no. The Communist Party had just pulled one of the sharpest U-turns of its unsteady existence. A few days later, on August 2, Dimitrov addressed the Seventh World Congress of the Comintern and officially announced the creation of the Popular Front. No longer would Communists regard anyone to their right as fascist enemies, whether they were Socialists or New Dealers. The real fascists had grown into such a monstrous threat that it was time for the Communists to join with *anyone* who would help fight them. The party's Third Period program was over. Since the dawn of the New Deal, the party's official position had been that Roosevelt was merely the smiling face of fascism; that mild reform was as bad as reaction because it pacified the masses just enough to keep them from revolting but failed to adequately address any of the real inequalities of the capitalist system. Objectively speaking, then, liberals and socialists were class enemies, never allies. Then everything turned upside down.

While Browder at first trembled that his leadership role in the party was finished, he soon realized that Moscow had handed him a great gift, greater even than when it had elevated him to the head of a pariah party a year earlier: Under the Popular Front, the party's membership exploded. In 1932 the party claimed around fourteen thousand members; four years later it would boast forty-three thousand. And for the first time since the party's founding, a majority actually spoke English. "We were not only Communists," George Charney recalled, "we were also Americans again."[74]

Before long Browder was filling Madison Square Garden on a few days' notice, orating to crowds that mixed comrades with the curious, proclaiming that the Declaration of Independence foreshadowed the Communist Manifesto. George Washington, Browder pointed out, favored a one-party system. "Communism," he insisted, "is Twentieth Century Americanism."[75]

On December 17, 1935, McCarran was in Chicago when he was taken ill, rushed to a hospital in an ambulance, and treated for a bleeding ulcer. He didn't leave the hospital until February, ventured back into the Senate for a few sessions, and then suffered a relapse. Long ago McCarran had traded the sheepman's life for the sedentary pursuit of politics, and now his five-foot, seven-inch frame buckled under 235 pounds. His heart was also in bad shape. The Senate physician ordered McCarran back to Nevada for bedrest.

Leaving his family in Washington, McCarran set out for his in-laws' ranch in Clover Valley, in the shadow of Ruby Mountain on Nevada's eastern flank. McCarran's health improved. "I am out sitting at a card table in the yard and the big willow is budding as the bees are in the willow and the honey is in the bees and the birds are singing and the creek is babbling by," he wrote to his daughter Mary, ". . . and the calves are cooing and the doves are mooing and the sky is bluing and the mountain is covered with snow and the grass is green all round all round."[76]

McCarran steadily shed weight, dropping forty pounds, although his silhouette remained far from thin. Soon his suits were loose, his pants suddenly baggy and hanging like drapes from his suspenders. Exhaustion wrote itself in his face, in forced smiles and sad, hanging jowls.

"You look exceptionally well, Senator," a friend said one day. "Considering that . . ."

"Yes, I know," McCarran sighed. "The trouble with me is I always look well, even when I'm very ill. So I get no sympathy. . . . The doctors won't let me smoke. . . . I'm lost without a cigar. And eat? Listen, I eat a diet of nothing three times a day."[77]

But doctors could only help with so much. The real cause of McCarran's illness, his oldest daughter, Margaret, believed, was family stress. "His health had been undermined more by sad circumstances in his family life than by his strenuous work," Margaret recalled. "No one . . . knew the grief which undermined his rugged constitution and made his personal life a series of hospitalizations."[78]

McCarran's worries were legion. His mother had recently died. His wife felt neglected. "It is beyond mama's power to control her head . . . ," Margaret once advised her father. "If she is treated with kindness and gentle firmness now she will come through a normal woman. Attention seeking, a desperate clinging to her rights, jealousy all mark her age. Ask any doctor. You have a patient on your hands."[79]

Margaret (Sister Margaret Patricia) herself was as tough as the Nevada range and happily submitted to the discipline and abjurations of life in a convent, asking for nothing but copies of the *Congressional Record* to follow her adored father's progress. With her fierce, if narrow, intellect and rawhide tenacity she could have been a politician, but to her father's continuing disappointment she had chosen to confine her mind and independence in the tight spaces of the cloister. At thirty-two she was happily in orbit around the double star of her father and her church and never would either move an inch in her affections. "You are the best friend I ever had," she told her father.[80]

But Mary McCarran (Sister Mary Mercy) was not having such an easy time of it. At thirty, she was in ill health herself and quite unhappy with the rigors of life in a nunnery. On her birthday, her father tried to console her. "I love you on your thirtieth birthday as I loved you on every birthday since August 31, 1906," he began. Then rage crept into his words. "You are working yourself to premature age," he continued. "It's a shame. I could kill some people who want to let you do it all. I hope they lighten your work for you. It's a shame to work a free horse to death."[81] At times McCarran even regretted his religion, feeling that his church had cost him his daughter. "How I wish I had been born a Mormon or a mason," he told her, ". . . or something other than what I am. Then you wouldn't be where you are and as you are."[82]

Norine McCarran, too, was a continual concern to her father. At the age of twelve she had come down with encephalitis and never fully recovered. Now twenty-five, she lived at home and worked in the Library of Congress where she paged books for the next twenty-five years. "Norine is quite well but has but little ambition," McCarran fretted.[83] Ever unsteady on her feet, falls and bruises marked her life and filled her father with an ever-present low-level dread.

Then there was Patty. Sylvia Patricia McCarran was the beauty and heartbreak of the family. Even in their younger days, Margaret and Mary had been nothing to look at; their habits only made things worse, forcing attention to Margaret's pinched and stern features and Mary's wide and rubbery face. Norine, too, was no beauty, even stouter than the average McCarran female. Patty McCarran seemed born of different stock altogether. At seventeen, McCarran's fourth daughter was a trim brunette with gently waving hair that almost touched her slim shoulders, large brown eyes, and a slightly sad look that never failed to melt her father's heart (or that of many other men). "She is brilliant," McCarran said, "has a splendid mind and a wonderful memory, learns readily and retains well, but she treads on air. She is as pretty as a picture and really is a credit to any family or to any circle."[84]

But she was terribly unhappy at the Immaculata Seminary in Washington. She was one McCarran daughter who would never be tempted to become a nun. In 1934, at fifteen, she ran away from home, ditching her mother in Reno and hitchhiking toward Washington using a fake name. McCarran sent the FBI after the girl, and the agents reinstalled her at the hated boarding school. "Well, where are you?" she wrote her father that spring. "We haven't heard from you in quite some time now. . . . I am busy writing to a cute little fat fellow way out west. He isn't going to stay fat though. Tsk! Tsk!"[85]

Now, in the summer of McCarran's returning health, she almost gave him a heart attack. In August, Patty turned up in Carson City with John D. Breckenridge. He was the stepson of a Reno stockbroker, had recently worked for the capital police in Washington, and currently was unemployed. They took out a marriage license, listed both their ages as twenty-one, and were wed in a quick ceremony. McCarran was actually seventeen. "The wedding," as the *Reno Gazette* noted in a vast understatement, "came as a surprise to friends and relatives of the young couple."[86]

The couple took off for San Francisco. Nine months later Patricia was back home in Washington. "She seems to have no idea of responsibility," her father fumed to Mary. "She is just back home again with no particular aim or ambition. She is running around with the boys whom she went with before she married John. I am fearful of the result. I am anxious lest perhaps a wholesale scandal come of the thing."[87] When Patty finally got divorced in Nevada a few months later, McCarran got stuck with the court costs. "The gentleman did not seem to think that his association for months with the little girl was worth paying the costs for her," he complained to Margaret.[88] "It seems exceedingly sad that a little child's life should be wrecked in this manner," McCarran wrote to Mary. "If I stop to think on it, I would go crazy. I keep my mind intent on other things."[89]

The only bright spot in McCarran's family constellation was his treasured son, Sam. At fifteen Sammy was the baby of the family, dark and lean with the long-lost good looks of his father, but enjoying limitless opportunities that McCarran had never dreamed about as a boy. Possessing a sharp mind and a doting, powerful father, Sammy McCarran fairly glowed with promise. "He is a fine looking boy — you will be very proud of him," his father raved to Margaret. "He has a splendid character and many beautiful traits. He is a good clean kid and I want to keep him so."[90] When Sam came out to the Clover Valley ranch and got stung by a bee on his chest, the usually isolationist McCarran suddenly became a war-whooping militant. "Hence forth a state of strict neutrality no longer exists — I am against every bee from now on, and I'll gladly furnish the munitions of war," he wrote to Mary. "We will bomb them from the air and blow them from the water and gas them from the land — damn them. They have no business molesting my Sam."[91]

But great expectations can also be great weights, and Sammy McCarran would never be a man for heavy lifting. In a few years he would crush his father's hopes flatter than the rest of McCarran's children combined.

Hede Massing stared in disbelief at her friend Noel Field, who was standing at the top of the Lincoln Memorial singing. What he was singing took awhile to make out.

Vstavaj, prokljat'em zaklejmennyj,
Ves' mir golodnyx i rabov!

It was "The Internationale," she finally realized, the Communist anthem. In bad Russian. This was not good. Massing was a Soviet agent sent to Washington to recruit New Dealers to work for the NKVD; Field was a young man going places in the State Department. "I was embarrassed and alarmed," she recalled. "It was pathetic and ludicrous. He had studied the Russian words diligently so that he could surprise me. Poor dear Noel! My heart went out to him."[92]

Arise ye workers from your slumbers
Arise ye prisoners of want

In October 1933 Massing had arrived in New York on an ocean liner carrying the top half of a cigarette box. Her NKVD contact would be holding the other half. Massing, née Gumperz, was a tall, redheaded Austrian with American citizenship. At seventeen she met a short man with lovely eyes named Gerhart Eisler. The second day she knew him, Eisler told her that he was going to make the world a better place, and that he was looking for a woman to help him. She wed him and made his cause her cause. The marriage didn't last long. Communism did.

For reason in revolt now thunders
And at last ends the age of cant.

Harold Ware showed Massing around Washington. Massing's third husband, Paul, soon joined her. He had just escaped from a German concentration camp and was writing an antifascist book called *Fatherland*. When a chapter was printed in the *New Masses,* Massing found herself very popular at dinner parties. "As the wife of an anti-fascist hero," Massing noted, "my social stock skyrocketed among the left liberals. With anybody who had read parts of Paul's book, it was easy enough to discuss the anti-fascist fight; the need for help and co-operation."[93]

Away with all your superstitions
Servile masses arise, arise

Noel and Herta Field were eager to meet Massing. Field, tall and lank, was a cultivated man, a foreign service officer since 1926 who loved to talk about psychoanalysis, Wagner, and the illnesses that he imagined he had. He swallowed phenobarbital like popcorn. The trio became quick friends. Massing would stay with the couple when she visited Washington.

We'll change henceforth the old tradition
And spurn the dust to win the prize.

Field wanted to join the party. Some of his colleagues at the State Department already thought he was a Communist. Field used to stop by the Eastern Europe desk to read the office copy of the *Daily Worker.* He couldn't wait, he explained, to get home to look through his subscription copy of the *Worker.* Field was discreet enough to hide his stack of old *Worker*s under a pile of clothes in his closet; proud enough to tell friends about it. When the bonus marchers passed the State Department building in 1932, Field stepped into line, marched to the Capitol, and pelted MacArthur's troops with sticks and stones.

So comrades, come rally
And the last fight let us face
The Internationale unites the human race.

The American party could really use someone as decent as Field, Massing thought. You'd be misplaced in the party, was what she told him. Her assignment was to recruit him for secret work, not open membership. Field tried to join the party anyway. "A stupid child in the woods," Earl Browder called him.[94] "Noel was an aesthete," Massing recalled. "He was hypersensitive. He was a neurotic. He was worried by politics, by his sex life, by preoccupation with his destiny. Ideologically, he was ready for bold deeds; in practice he shrank from decisions. His attitude toward life was extremely unrealistic."[95]

No more deluded by reaction
On tyrants only we'll make war

When Massing suggested that Field slip her documents from the State Department, he was taken aback. "What about loyalty to my country?" he asked. What about loyalty to humanity? she responded. He finally agreed to give her verbal reports. "What he produced in this fashion was of no value at all," Massing remembered.[96]

The soldiers too will take strike action
They'll break ranks and fight no more

Then one day Field mentioned that a friend of his in government was pressing him to join another secret cell. Who? Massing asked. Alger Hiss. She wanted to meet him. Field invited both friends over for dinner, after which Massing took Hiss aside. I understand that you are trying to get Noel away from my organization into yours, Massing said. Hiss smiled. So you are this famous girl? What is your apparatus, anyhow? Now, Alger, Massing said, you should know better than that. I wouldn't ask you that kind of question. Well, whoever is going to win, we are working for the same boss. Which one said the last line? Years later Massing couldn't remember. It could have been either one of them. They were, after all, on the same side.

And if those cannibals keep trying
To sacrifice us to their pride

Field's conscience bothered him. When he was offered a job at the League of Nations in Geneva, he told Massing that he could serve the party better working for the international agency than for the U.S. government. She tried to talk him out of leaving the State Department. He bought a set of Linguaphone records to teach himself Russian so he could listen to Radio Moscow in Europe. In 1936 the Fields moved to Switzerland.

They soon shall hear the bullets flying
We'll shoot the generals on our own side.

Noel Field introduced Massing to his best friend, Larry Duggan. Duggan worked in the Latin American division of the State Department. He shared Field's dreamy romanticism but had a more practical side as well. "Very liberal," noted John Hermann, who was trying to recruit him for the Ware Group, "but not entirely of a mind to be with us."[97] But when Massing sounded him out about helping her apparatus, Duggan agreed. He hated his job at State, which mostly seemed to entail wearing a tuxedo to diplomatic receptions. The only thing that made it bearable was the idea of helping *the cause.* Still, he wouldn't hand over documents, Duggan explained, but he would furnish oral reports. When Massing told him that she would not be the one to take the information, Duggan was pleased. Sounds like a well-organized group, he said.

E'er the thieves will out with their booty
And give to all a happier lot.
Each at the forge must do their duty
And we'll strike while the iron is hot.[98]

In May, after three months of rest, McCarran left Clover Valley and crossed the state to visit Reno, where he checked on his ranch along the Truckee and visited the graves of his parents in town. "I am feeling fine," he told his daughter Mary. "Weigh 184 pounds today and win my dollar bet. Wouldn't take the kid's dollar — told him I'd take one dollar's worth of interest in his future."[99]

Then McCarran headed to Lovelock, on the shore of the meager Humboldt River, where the state Democratic convention was being held. "There is no more chance of defeating Franklin D. Roosevelt for president this year than there is of me flying to the moon," McCarran told the convention. ". . . Our great leader, yours and mine, gave security to the people of this nation when people craved security."[100]

To those in the audience it must have seemed as if McCarran had come back from his long illness a different man altogether, a Lazarus risen from the cold crypt of anti–New Deal conservativism. McCarran tried to convince Roosevelt of as much. Four years after they both arrived in Washington together and almost two years since he had last visited the White House, McCarran finally got around to asking the president for an autographed picture for his office. "I regret that because of illness I have been compelled to be absent from the Senate nearly all of this session," McCarran informed Roosevelt. "Improved health makes it now possible to assure you that I will be at the convention to assist in your re-nomination and will gladly put forth my best efforts for your re-election."[101]

Of course, McCarran had been putting forth his best efforts to defeat much of the New Deal ever since his arrival in the Senate. But by the middle of 1936 Roosevelt was coasting toward a second term, and McCarran knew that if he hoped to do so as well in two more years, he had better get back into the good graces of his party. "I am such a sound believer in the New Deal," McCarran told one reporter. "The New Deal and I went in together. . . . I helped make the New Deal. . . . I ought to think well of it, oughtn't I? I do. I'm very proud of it, and I think it is destined to go on to still greater heights. Not only America but all the rest of the world is calling for the New Deal now."[102]

Roosevelt has done more for the workers of America in the past three years than has been done for them in the previous century, McCarran told the crowd in a jammed Clark County courtroom. "Roosevelt saved the nation with a single stroke of the pen," McCarran said. ". . . Some say that the president takes his methods from foreign fields, but they are wrong. He is only a courageous American and America stands first with him."[103] "My chief," McCarran began to call the president, something he had never said of any man before. "We were faced with a serious situation, the most serious perhaps in the nation's history," McCarran said at another rally. "We had to do something. We didn't have time to determine whether our various plans were constitutional or not — we had to try them out, let the Supreme Court pass upon them and if they were ruled out, to try something else."[104]

But McCarran could only dissemble so much. The day before he was supposed to catch a plane for an eastern speaking tour on behalf of Roosevelt, McCarran gave a talk at the University of Nevada. "While the legislative and judiciary have remained within their respective domains, the executive has expanded beyond all expectation," he said. ". . . The fear of unhampered executive power, repeatedly declared and made manifest by Jefferson and the realization of his prediction which realization he frequently declared would destroy the democracy and would threaten the existence of individual, human liberty, have, and each of them has, stealthily and silently but nevertheless emphatically become realities."[105]

A week before the election a reporter asked McCarran about Roosevelt and Communism. "Here's the way I answer that," McCarran replied. "Look at his name. There's too much behind that name to believe that he would be sympathetic toward that kind of a movement. You hear them talk about dictatorship. That's always the case when progressive men take the lead. They find reason to cry dictatorship."[106]

On September 29, Roosevelt kicked off his campaign for reelection with a speech to the Democratic state convention in Syracuse. Almost exactly three years earlier, at the end of the Hundred Days, McCarran had made a passionate speech to the American Bar Association assailing the tendency of U.S. presidents to grab more and more power. Now Roosevelt offered a rejoinder to McCarran and the conservative chorus that had been singing the same gloomy song for most of his presidency.

"A malicious opposition charged that George Washington planned to make himself king under a British form of government," the president said, "that Thomas Jefferson planned to set up a guillotine under a French revolutionary form of government; that Andrew Jackson soaked the rich of the eastern seaboard and planned to surrender American democracy to the dictatorship of the frontier mob. They called Abraham Lincoln a Roman Emperor; Theodore Roosevelt a destroyer; Woodrow Wilson a self-constituted Messiah."

The Republicans, he said, couldn't run on issues. Unemployment was down by four million. Six million new jobs existed. Stock prices, ag prices, industrial production — all had doubled or come close to it. So the Republicans invented the diversionary issue of Communism.

"Here and now, once and for all, let us bury that red herring, and destroy that false issue . . . ," he said. "I have not sought, I do not seek, I repudiate the support of any advocate of Communism or of any other alien 'ism' which would by fair means or foul change our American democracy. . . . There is no difference between the major parties as to what they think about Communism. But there is a very great difference between the two parties in what they do about Communism. . . . Conditions congenial to Communism were being bred and fostered throughout this nation up to the very day of March 4, 1933. Hunger was breeding it, loss of homes and farms was breeding it, closing banks were breeding it, a ruinous price level was breeding it. Discontent and fear were spreading through the land. The previous national administration bewildered, did nothing. . . . Wise and prudent men — intelligent conservatives — have long known that in a changing world worthy institutions can be conserved only by adjusting them to the changing time. . . . I am that kind of conservative because I am that kind of liberal."[107]

On October 31 Roosevelt wrapped up his two-month campaign at Madison Square Garden. His nominal opponent was Alf Landon, the Republican governor of Kansas, who supported much of the New Deal. But Roosevelt ignored Landon and lashed out at his conservative enemies. "Never before in all our history have these forces been so united against one candidate as they stand today," he said. "They are unanimous in their hate for me — and I welcome their hatred. . . . I should like to have it said of my first administration that in it the forces of selfishness and of lust for power met their match. . . . I should like to have it said of my second administration that in it these forces met their master."[108]

The election was a landslide. Roosevelt crushed Landon by the biggest plurality in history, almost twenty-eight million votes to less than seventeen million, sweeping every state but Maine and Vermont. The Democrats picked up nine seats in the House and five in the Senate.

McCarran, too, seemed to have been sucked into the slipstream of Roosevelt's victory. Days before the election, McCarran's utterances could have come from the most starry-eyed New Deal acolyte. "Those who would tear down the New Deal," he said, "are the ones who encourage anarchism, Communism and other Red programs bent upon the destruction of Democratic government."[109]

He sounded like he almost believed it.

CHAPTER 8

Copperheads Among Us

The things he had come to know in this war were not
so simple.[1]

— Ernest Hemingway, *For Whom the Bell Tolls*

Rain soaked Washington on inauguration day in January. Hatless and wet, Roosevelt stood beneath the colorless Capitol dome and raised his hand. Chief Justice Charles Evans Hughes, whose Supreme Court had spent the past two years tossing one New Deal law after another off the books as unconstitutional, recited the oath of office. *Promise to support the Constitution of the United States,* the justice said with stress. Roosevelt repeated the oath with just as much intensity. Yes, he thought, but it's the Constitution as I understand it.

The downpour continued. Roosevelt went on to promise the millions struggling for decent lives — "one-third of a nation ill-housed, ill-clad, ill-nourished" — that their government would heed their cries. "I assume," he said, "the solemn obligation of leading the American people forward along the road over which they have chosen to advance."[2]

On February 10, 1937, McCarran walked into the White House for the third time in barely a week. After more than two years when McCarran couldn't get into the Oval Office, Roosevelt was suddenly generous with his time. Indeed, over the past week there had been a virtual parade of lawmakers summoned to visit the president — ever since February 5, when the White House secretarial staff had been ordered to report to work at 6:30 A.M. to start the mimeograph machines. Later that morning a smiling Roosevelt was wheeled into the Cabinet Room where he had invited the congressional leadership, including the chairmen of both Judiciary Committees, for a special announcement. He began to read a message that he was sending to Congress in an hour. The Supreme Court, the president said, was working too hard. He wanted to add a few new members to help ease the load and make the Court more efficient — one new justice for each who worked past the age of seventy, up to six new members. And with the average justice now seventy-one, this meant that Roosevelt, who had yet to appoint a single justice to the Court, would soon be able to pick half a dozen new judges. The president smiled and then wheeled off for a press conference.

The Republicans didn't have a prayer of defeating the proposal on a straight party vote. In the House there were 334 Democrats and 89 Republicans; in the Senate 75 Democrats and 17 Republicans. So they kept quiet. They figured the Democrats would rip each other to shreds. They were right. "Of course I shall oppose it," snapped Virginia's Carter Glass. "I shall oppose it with all the strength which remains to me, but I don't imagine for a minute that it'll do any good. Why, if the President asked Congress to commit suicide tomorrow they'd do it."[3]

A week after his announcement, Roosevelt asked McCarran and three other Democratic members of the Senate Judiciary Committee to visit the Oval Office, its pale green walls hung with pictures of the president's beloved ships. Roosevelt sat behind his large desk, flanked by the flag, and pitched his plan. For the past two years the Supreme Court had mowed through the legislation of the New Deal like an overgrown field: The Railroad Retirement Act, the NRA, the Farm Mortgage Act, the AAA — all fell before the Court's blade. In decision after decision the justices declared the legislative pillars of the New Deal unconstitutional. Congress could not delegate its lawmaking authority to the NRA *(Schechter Poultry Corporation v. U.S.)*. Nor could it usurp the regulatory power of the states through the AAA *(U.S. v. Butler)*. Nor could New York state violate the freedom of contract with a minimum wage law *(Morehead v New York ex rel. Tipaldo)*. What exactly, one had to wonder, *could* government do?

Roosevelt knew what he would have to do. If the Court wouldn't change, then he would change the Court. Nowhere in the Constitution was the size of the Supreme Court fixed. Who was to say that the president couldn't add a few more justices? "We live in a nation where there is no legal power anywhere to deal with its most difficult practical problems — a No Man's Land of final futility,"[4] Roosevelt would eventually declare to the public. But not today. To the members of the Judiciary Committee, Roosevelt was more tactful, hiding behind the fig leaf of improving efficiency by making it easier for overworked justices to retire.

The president spent thirty minutes laying out his plan, then excused himself for another appointment. "No one was asked if he had approved or disapproved of the program," McCarran said.[5]

Jim Loeb was shocked by the booing. He didn't understand why his fellow socialists were hissing at Louis Fischer. This was supposed to be a rally for the Spanish Loyalists, and Fischer was the first U.S. citizen to join the International Brigades.

"There would not be a Spanish Republic," Fischer said, *"if the Russians hadn't come."*[6]

In February 1936 a Popular Front government was elected in Madrid; in July, Francisco Franco and other right-wing generals rose up in revolt. The fascist rebels asked for help from Germany and Italy, which sent bombers and troops. The elected government looked to the democracies for help, which looked away. Of the major powers, only Russia would sell arms and send military advisers to the Loyalists. It was, in a sense, the opening battle of World War II, the first time liberals and fascists were shooting at each other. And if the democracies quailed at the prospect of taking sides, fearful that the Iberian Civil War might flame up into an all-out European war, many individuals did not. George Orwell, for example, went to Spain as a reporter and almost immediately joined a Loyalist militia. "At that time and in that atmosphere," he recalled, "it seemed the only conceivable thing to do."[7]

Some thirty thousand volunteers raced to Spain, including thirty-three hundred Americans, many of whom had never picked up a gun before. When the United States forbade its citizens from traveling to Spain, they walked over the Pyrenees to join the International Brigades. "You felt that you were taking part in a crusade," said university-professor-turned-partisan Robert Jordan in Ernest Hemingway's *For Whom the Bell Tolls*. "That was the only word for it although it was a word that had been so worn and abused that it no longer gave its true meaning. You felt, in spite of all bureaucracy and inefficiency and party strife something that was like the feeling you expected to have and did not have when you made your first communion. . . . It gave you a part in something that you could believe in wholly and completely and in which you felt an absolute brotherhood with the others who were engaged in it. It was something that you had never known before but that you had experienced now and you gave such importance to it and the reasons for it that your own death seemed of complete unimportance; only a thing to be avoided because it would interfere with the performance of your duty. But the best thing was that there was something you could do about this feeling and this necessity too. You could fight."[8]

Fischer came to fight. He had been living in Moscow, writing for *The Nation*. When the Civil War erupted he rushed to Spain. Fischer was not a party member, although 80 percent of those who joined the Brigades were, but he was a fervent admirer of the Russian Revolution. Now, in early 1937, he was on publicity tour in the United States, trying to rally support for the Loyalist government.

"Vive Russo! is written on all the streets and portraits of Stalin are everywhere . . . ," Fischer said. *"Everyone, even the anarchists, loves the Russians."*[9]

The boos confused Jim Loeb. Weren't the fascists the real enemy? he wondered. Loeb was new to politics, and there was a lot he didn't understand. Why, for instance, did the socialists heckle Fischer every time he said something good about the Russians? Loeb had only been a socialist for a couple of months, not much longer than he had lived in Greenwich Village, but he knew that what was happening in Spain was terrible and that everyone on the left should put aside their differences and fight the fascists with a united front.

Loeb had grown up in the suburbs of Chicago, where his father was in the insurance business, a business Loeb was supposed to join after graduating from Dartmouth. Instead, Loeb decided to spend his savings on a year in France; when he came home he went to graduate school at Northwestern, earning a Ph.D. in French literature in 1936. Loeb and his wife, Ellen, then moved to New York, where they found themselves reading the Socialist Party's *Call.* One day Ellen went down to party headquarters when she saw an ad for volunteers and came back a member. Jim followed. The couple passed out leaflets, tried to recruit members, helped organize rallies for sundry causes. "Most of all," Loeb recalled, "we argued . . . at the branch meetings, in factional caucuses, in our homes or, best of all, with coffee and Danish pastry at Stewart's Cafeteria after meetings."[10]

And sooner or later that winter every argument seemed to come around to Spain. Why, Loeb wondered, did only the Russians help the Loyalists while the Germans and Italians backed Franco and the democracies did nothing but dither? Eleanor Roosevelt was a passionate supporter of Republican Spain but couldn't get her husband to challenge Congress over the Neutrality Act that prevented the United States from selling arms to nations at war — even duly elected governments fighting armed insurrection. "Intervene," cried W. H. Auden in "Spain 1937," "O descend as a dove or / A furious papa or a mild engineer: but descend."[11]

"I met many of the Soviet Russians who had been sent to do their best for the Loyalists," Fischer recounted. *"In all the Spanish War, there were no more tireless workers, valiant fighters, and devoted partisans. They seemed to pour into the Spanish struggle the pent-up revolutionary passion which no longer found application in Russia."*[12]

Loeb was so embarrassed by the reception given to Fischer that he wrote to the journalist to apologize. Help the North American Committee to Aid Spanish Democracy, Fischer replied. The NAC was an umbrella group with chapters in Hollywood, at universities, and within unions. The committee had collected hundreds of tons of food, clothing, and medical supplies and raised more than one million dollars. Loeb volunteered as an assistant to publicity director Varian Fry, who had quit his job as an editor to devote all his energy to the cause. Fry was an oddity in the NAC: an avowed anti-Communist. "Almost everyone connected with the staff was either a Communist or a close fellow-traveler," Loeb observed.[13]

Fry soon left the committee. Slowly Loeb began to understand how deep the divide was between Communists and socialists. He learned that socialist leader Norman Thomas had never forgiven the Communists for physically attacking his followers at Madison Square Garden before the Popular Front. And he also learned that the Civil War seemed to be turning into a war within a war. Since Loeb was fluent in Spanish, Thomas asked him to compile a weekly digest of the Loyalist press. As editor of the *Spanish Labor News,* Loeb discovered that most of the reporting coming out of the Civil War was terribly flawed. Nine-tenths of everything written about the Spanish Civil War, as Orwell put it, was a lie. In May, for instance, street fighting broke out in Barcelona when the Communists tried to disarm the anarchist POUM, which the Communists brutally suppressed. The party press tried to portray the conflict as an attempted coup by the POUM — an interpretation that Communists on the North American Committee board wanted NAC to publicly affirm. Only the threatened resignations of non–party members such as Roger Baldwin prevented the committee from supporting the purge of non-Communists from the Loyalist ranks. "It is clearly impossible for Socialists to remain part of an organization which is being slowly eaten up," Loeb told Baldwin.[14]

Loeb was beginning to learn a few things.

A week after his visit to the White House, McCarran headed up a meeting of a Judiciary subcommittee that discussed the Court bill. As soon as McCarran walked out of the conference room, a gaggle of reporters tailed him back to his office. McCarran invited them in for a statement. The newsmen eagerly settled into seats, pulling out their pads and pencils. McCarran picked up his glasses, touched them to his nose, frowned in concentration.

"We think," he said, "the tariff provision as regards Brazil —"

Then he looked up at the reporters. "Nuts," said one.

McCarran smiled. "Yes, that's it. Brazil nuts. What do you want anyway?"[15]

What they wanted was to know how McCarran was going to vote on the Court plan. McCarran was one of only three members of the Judiciary Committee who hadn't yet indicated what they thought of the bill. Nine had announced themselves opposed to the plan; six were in favor. The three undecided members could deadlock the committee, leaving hope for a single defection, or tip the balance hard to the opposition. A lot of Democrats didn't like the idea, but if Roosevelt was going to make the bill a litmus test of support for the New Deal, then they were going to back the measure. The country, too, seemed narrowly divided, the Gallup poll finding a slim majority (53 percent) opposed to the idea.

Every fiber of McCarran's being knew that the NRA and the AAA were hideously unconstitutional. He could have written the Court decisions overruling the acts himself. "Delegation run riot" Justice Benjamin Cardozo had called the NRA.[16] McCarran had been shouting as much in the Senate and across the country for five years now. "To be advised by the court of last resort that it is exceeding the Constitution is the best thing that could happen to the administration at this time," he'd said in Salt Lake City two years earlier.[17] To McCarran the trinity of government (his expression) was as sacred as that of his church. "The Supreme Court is the infallible interpreter of the law," he proclaimed during the campaign, "It is the last word."[18]

But now McCarran was keeping strangely silent. He was, after all, planning to run for reelection the next year. Openly breaking with an enormously popular president over what was quickly becoming *the* key measure of support for the New Deal could prove hard to explain even to Nevada's independent-minded voters. Key Pittman, who was also on the Judiciary Committee and supported Roosevelt's Court plan without question, privately noted that the only threat to McCarran's reelection was the question mark about his party loyalty. "If Pat will stop making personal enemies I don't believe he will have any opposition at all for the nomination," Pittman told a friend. "If he gets the nomination, his election is assured, that is, provided he does not make half the Democratic Party his personal enemies."[19] For once in his life McCarran was chary of making enemies. "It is too important a matter to rush in and declare one's self," McCarran said publicly and dishonestly. "I want to hear the evidence of both sides, weigh it and then make up my mind how I should vote."[20]

Roosevelt's Court plan was like throwing red meat to starving pit bulls. "Every Communist in America is solidly behind the president's program to take over the Supreme Court,"[21] growled North Dakota representative Usher Burdick. "The court will become as ductile as a gob of chewing gum," wrote H. L. Mencken.[22] Even moderate Republican opinion was incensed. "President Roosevelt has brought forward a proposal which, if enacted into law, would end the American state as it has existed throughout the long years of its life . . . ," wrote the *New York Herald Tribune.* "The paper shell of American constitutionalism would continue if President Roosevelt secured the passage of the law he now demands. But it would be only a shell."[23] "Hands off the Supreme Court,"[24] added Herbert Hoover. Conservative Democrats, too, were predictably outraged. "I have lived too long,"[25] wailed Carter Glass.

Roosevelt expected as much from his usual enemies, but then the progressives ran off the reservation. Burt Wheeler had been the first Democrat to back Roosevelt in 1932; now the liberal wheelhorse took the lead in organizing opposition to the plan among erstwhile New Dealers. Wheeler wanted the same end as the president but favored amending the Constitution to make the Court less powerful, not stuffing it with hacks. "Many of these same liberals, who agree with his aims, disagree with his packing of the Court because we believe it is fundamentally unsound, undemocratic, and reactionary in principle," Wheeler said. "Create now a political court to echo the ideas of the executive and you have created a weapon. A weapon which, in the hands of another president in times of war or other hysteria, could well be an instrument of destruction. A weapon that can cut down those guaranties of liberty written into your great document by the blood of your forefathers and that can extinguish your right of liberty, of speech, of thought, of action, and of religion. A weapon whose use is only dictated by the conscience of the wielder."[26]

Not long after returning from a six-week trip to Reno, where she had been a legal resident just long enough to divorce her husband, Mary McCarthy was invited to a cocktail party in Greenwich Village that was being given in honor of Art Young, a cartoonist for the Communist *New Masses* magazine.

McCarthy was a pretty, fiercely smart Vassar graduate who reviewed books for liberal magazines such as *The New Republic.* McCarthy was, in the manner of the times, something of a radical. She gave up silk stockings for lace to protest the Japanese invasion of China. She smoked only union-made cigarettes. She supported Earl Browder for president — although she didn't actually vote for him because she never got around to registering.

She wasn't a party member but respected those who were, especially those reputed to be in the underground. "We looked up to those who were close-lipped and stern about their beliefs," she recalled, "and we disparaged the more voluble members — the forensic little actors who tried to harangue us in the dressing rooms. The idea of a double life was what impressed us. . . . It is hard not to respect somebody who has an alias."[27]

The book party was not much fun. Everyone seemed ill at ease. Small groups formed and re-formed into different groups but never seemed to include certain other clusters of people, as if some invisible force like meeting magnets were pushing them apart.

McCarthy anchored herself at the drinks table and fell into an uninteresting conversation. Do you think Trotsky is entitled to a hearing? interrupted a struggling novelist McCarthy vaguely knew.

What had Trotsky done? McCarthy replied. The novelist looked at McCarthy as if she were from the moon. Then he explained. In August Grigori Zinoviev, Lev Kamenev, and fourteen other Old Bolsheviks whose names were synonymous with the Russian Revolution walked into a courtroom in Moscow and confessed to being part of an incredible conspiracy. They had been plotting with Stalin's exiled rival Trotsky to kill the Soviet leader. There was no evidence. No defense lawyers. Just the confessions. And then, three days after sentencing, bullets to the head in the basement of the Lubyanka.

Do you believe that Trotsky should have the right of asylum? the novelist pursued. Yeah, sure, whatever. "I went home," McCarthy remembered, "with the serene feeling that all these people were slightly crazy."[28]

Four days later she found an envelope in the mail from something called the Committee for the Defense of Trotsky. We demand, the letter began. Who demands? she wondered, looking down a list of signatories until she stumbled upon her own name. She decided to write in protest. Then the phone calls started. Acquaintances called late at night to tell her to get off the committee, not to mix with reactionaries or to stick her nose into the internal affairs of the Soviet Union. Curious at last, McCarthy started reading up on the trials. "Everywhere you touched the case," she recalled, "something crumbled."[29]

A week after Zinoviev and the other Old Bolsheviks were shot, in the summer of 1936, the NKVD executed five thousand prisoners sitting in the Gulag for antirevolutionary crimes. The year before Stalin had lowered the age for the death penalty to twelve. Over the next four years three-quarters of a million Soviet people would be shot as traitors. Millions more were arrested and imprisoned. The Great Purge had begun.

The Moscow trials opened a fissure between liberals and Communists that threatened to swallow the Popular Front. The show trials, as Mary McCarthy quickly learned, didn't bear even casual scrutiny. But observers such as the *New York Times*'s Walter Duranty and Roosevelt's ambassador Joseph Davies shined up the proceedings for readers. Others preached agnosticism. "The simple fact is that we do not know enough to be sure of our ground," weaseled *The New Republic.* "We should therefore be content to let opinions differ and turn our attention to matters near at home."[30]

For those outraged by the violence of economic injustice in the United States, the revolutionary violence of the Soviet system was something altogether different, something so awesome to behold that it defied comprehension and simply demanded acceptance — like the purity of a forest fire cleansing the woods of rotten underbrush. "One of the greatest causes for rejoicing on the twentieth anniversary of the revolution was the wiping out of the nest of traitors in the treason trials of 1936 and 1937,"[31] exulted Mother Bloor in her autobiography, which was ghostwritten by John Abt's wife, Jessica.

Those whose friends were killed on Stalin's orders had a different opinion. Hede and Paul Massing, for example, found a letter in their mailbox one day from a man they knew as Ludwig. His real name was Ignace Reiss, thirty-nine, a Polish-born veteran of Soviet intelligence who had been one of Hede Massing's contacts in the underground. Ludwig was breaking with the Soviets. He included a copy of a letter he'd written to Stalin. "He who keeps silent at this hour becomes an accomplice of Stalin," the letter read, "and a traitor to the cause of the working class and of Socialism."[32] A month later Reiss was murdered.

The Massings had come to doubt the Soviet Union. "It is a slow, painful process," Hede Massing wrote. "It is not a decision one makes, but a decision that grows. It grows slowly in the beginning. It is nourished by disillusionment. And then finally come the days when one is sick enough. And still it is like renouncing your religion, your family, your life's work, the taking leave from all your friends — all at once."[33]

The couple was ordered to visit Moscow, where their passports were taken and they spent eight months being questioned about their loyalty. Eventually they managed to leave Moscow, but not before bumping into Yury Fischer, the teenaged son of Louis Fischer, the American correspondent and fellow traveler.

What would you say, Yuri, Paul asked, if you were to come tomorrow to our rooms and find that I had been arrested? Fischer was quiet for a long time.

Paul, he said finally, if you are arrested, you are guilty.[34]

In March, Attorney General Hommer Cummings and Assistant Attorney General Robert Jackson sat in the ornate Senate Caucus Room answering questions from members of the Judiciary Committee about the Court plan. The committee should have been a snap. The Democrats held fourteen of the eighteen seats, the Republicans a mere three — and one of these belonged to progressive William Borah, who had come close to openly endorsing Roosevelt the previous fall. The last seat was held by George Norris, the Nebraska independent, a former Republican whom Roosevelt had supported over the Democratic nominee in the previous election.

Although Chairman Henry Ashurst didn't like the bill ("A prelude to tyranny"[35] he called it), he endorsed it. Another seven members of the committee quickly lined up behind Ashurst. Seven declared themselves opposed. That left three officially undecided — McCarran among them.

McCarran slid to the center of the committee table and wondered if the plan might destroy the confidence of the American people in its Court. "Don't you think," he asked the assistant attorney general, "that if the six new judges went on the bench now, the people would say they were six new justices selected by the New Deal — to use a harsh word, they would be stultified before they went on the bench, even though they might hold against the New Deal to show their independence."

No, Jackson replied. "I believe this country can produce six men in whom the public would have confidence," he said. "If not, the situation is pretty bad and then we are pretty nearly over the dam, anyway."[36]

Senator Burt Wheeler, who had became the leading Democrat to oppose the Court plan, then read a letter from Chief Justice Hughes asserting that the Court was not inefficient or remiss in its duties. More justices would actually mean more work. "There would be," the justice wrote, "more judges to hear, more judges to confer, more judges to discuss, more judges to be convinced and to deride."[37]

Bad news continued to fall on the Court plan like freezing rain. On March 29 the Court upheld a Washington State minimum wage law *(West Coast Hotel v. Parrish)* similar to the New York one it had struck down a year earlier. And on April 12 it voted to sustain the Wagner Act *(NLRB v. Jones and Laughlin)*, holding that the government's power to regulate interstate commerce gave it the authority to stop companies from firing people because they joined a union. This was good news for the New Deal, but not so good if Roosevelt had any hope of passing his Court bill. If the aged Court could accept such a bumptious piece of legislation as the Wagner Act, then Roosevelt's plan seemed to lack much of a rationale.

The president didn't despair. He went fishing. "I haven't a care in the world," he told William Bullitt, "which is going some for a president who is said by the newspapers to be a remorseless dictator driving his government into hopeless bankruptcy."[38]

In April 1937 John Lewis walked into a meeting in Detroit. Lee Pressman followed like a puppy. A former coal miner with a gift for Shakespearean declamation, a hulking presence with a great mane of thick, dark hair combed straight over his huge head as if blown back by his own velocity, Lewis was the lion of American labor. His most recognizable features were his massive, furry, angry eyebrows, which looked as if they wanted to leap off his wide brow. In October 1935 Lewis had jumped over a row of chairs to slug a rival union leader at the AFL convention in Atlantic City.

Lewis knew the power of metaphor. The AFL had been led for a dozen years by William Green, a former coal miner as conservative and plodding as Lewis was colorful and confrontational. Lewis saw the New Deal as a golden opportunity. Under Section 7a of the NRA, workers were finally given the right to form unions without asking the permission of their employers. Labor's magna carta, Lewis called it, and in a year he tripled the membership of his United Mine Workers. He then wanted to go out and unionize whole industries. Green didn't. The AFL preferred to form unions along craft, not industrial, lines. The AFL convention voted down Lewis's proposal for a mass industrial union drive. Lewis went ahead anyway. His United Mine Workers joined with a handful of other defiant unions and formed the Committee for Industrial Organization (later called the Congress of Industrial Organizations). Inside two years, the CIO would grow larger than the AFL, claiming more than 3.4 million members.

Pressman was not the sort to go gaga over much. He went gaga over Lewis. As soon as Lewis formed the CIO, Pressman wanted to work for him. Pressman asked Pat Jackson for an introduction to his friend, and in the summer of 1936 Pressman became the counsel of the CIO's Steel Workers Organizing Committee. Pressman soon came to look at Lewis the way Jackson looked at Pressman. "His ordinary features, his nose and his mouth, are very, very sensitive features," he once swooned. "The ruggedness is given by virtue of his jowls, but look at each individual feature, when he smiles, his eyes, his nose, his mouth are the features of a very sensitive soul."[39]

In December 1936, autoworkers at the massive General Motors plant in Flint, Michigan, staged a sitdown strike, seizing factories and crippling production at the company that made half of the cars in America. After three months GM signed an agreement recognizing the CIO's United Auto Workers as the exclusive bargaining agent for the strikers. The next month U.S. Steel capitulated as well. Then a sitdown strike paralyzed Chrysler, and Lewis met with K. T. Keller, the company's vice president. Keller raged and glowered at the union organizers, who said nothing. Finally he asked Lewis why he was so quiet. Lewis rose and said that he wanted to come around the table and wipe the sneer off Keller's face. "Lewis' voice at that moment was in every sense the voice of millions of unorganized workers who were exploited by gigantic corporations." Pressman said. "He was expressing at that instant their resentment, their hostility, and their passionate desire to strike back. There just was no question that Lewis' threat was not against Mr. Keller as a person, but against the Chrysler Corporation and every other giant, soulless corporation in the country. It was a moment of real greatness because Lewis transcended his own person and was speaking out of the deep yearning of millions to force a great, sneering arrogant corporation to bend its knee to organized labor. I cannot remember when I have been so moved in my life. I have never before experienced anything so completely devoid of individual personality, for those two voices of Lewis and Keller were really the spokesmen of opposing fundamental forces."

Chrysler soon gave in. "I do not worry about dealing with you," Walter Chrysler told Lewis as soon as he signed the contract recognizing the union, "but it is the Communists in these unions that worry me a great deal."[40]

John Lewis was not a man to worry much. "I do not turn my organizers or CIO members upside down and shake them to see what kind of literature falls out of their pockets," he said.[41] That many of the most energetic and experienced organizers might be party members did not overly concern Lewis. Who gets the bird, he asked, the dog or the hunter? "To contemplate him being aware of somebody else's power or influence over the organization that he had given birth to, that's something you just couldn't contemplate," Pressman explained. "I mean, it would be like talking to him about the atmosphere on Mars."[42]

As much as Pressman worshiped John Lewis, when his idol offered him the job as general counsel to the CIO he agonized over whether to take it. Pressman told Whittaker Chambers that the party's central committee had instructed him not to accept the post. Pressman was too much of a lone operator, too impulsive, too difficult to control, J. Peters explained to Chambers. Chambers told Pressman to accept the job. "I was convinced that the job of general counsel for the CIO was of first importance to the Communist Party," Chambers later told the FBI.[43]

In the Agricultural Adjustment Agency, Pressman could threaten the producers with nationalizing their industries, but he was the one who lost his job. With John Lewis, Pressman could watch as American workers seized the means of production from the capitalists and exult as Lewis threatened violence when the industrialists dared to ask for their plants back. Pressman took the job.

McCarran tried to compromise. In April he introduced a substitute bill that would increase the Court from nine to eleven justices. That way Roosevelt could finally name a couple of justices but not enough to really dilute the Court's concern for the unconstitutionality of the New Deal. The idea was greeted coldly. "Mathematically," Senator Arthur Vandenberg said, "the proposal to add two new justices simply reduces by two-thirds the degree of wrong in the president's proposal."[44] The president's supporters were no more welcoming. "Why should we compromise," wondered Senator James Byrnes, "when we have the votes to enact the president's measure?"[45]

Less than two weeks later, on April 28, McCarran announced that he was going to vote against the Court plan. The last two holdouts (O'Mahoney and Hatch) followed McCarran into the opposition. "The Supreme Court," McCarran told the Senate, "should not be a department of government subject to the will of either of the other two branches of government."[46]

Walking out of the White House one day in May, Jim Farley was dogged by a *Washington Post* reporter. How is the Court fight going? he asked. Off the record, Farley replied, McCarran and the rest will have to vote for the bill if they ever want anything from the administration. "When Senator O'Mahoney comes down here wanting help on a sugar bill," Farley said, "his conscience won't be bothering him, will it? Or when Senator McCarran wants aid for his state?"[47]

The *Post* ran Farley's comments, and McCarran promptly withdrew his compromise bill. "I knew I had made it impossible for either of them to vote for the president,"[48] Farley recalled.

For McCarran, for all of his Hamlet-like posturing and halfhearted attempts at compromise, it never had been possible. "Farley says no compromise," McCarran told a reporter, "and there will be no compromise."[49]

On May 18 the eighteen members of the Judiciary Committee were filing into a room to vote on whether to endorse the president's bill when the news came: Justice Willis Van Devanter announced his retirement. Roosevelt would get to name his own justice at last.

"The proposals contemplated in the president's bill open the way to dictatorship," McCarran wrote in a memo to his colleagues. ". . . The procedure employed in the pending bill might also be used to strike down every right which labor and farmers enjoy as free American citizens."[50]

George Norris made a motion to report the Court bill favorably. It failed. McCarran moved to report the bill negatively. This passed 10 to 8. King, McCarran, and O'Mahoney were named to a subcommittee to draft the majority report.

"Let us," the report began, "of the 75th Congress, in words that will never be disregarded by any succeeding Congress, declare that we would rather have an independent court, a fearless court, a court that will dare to announce its honest opinions in what it believes to be the defense of the liberties of the people, than a court that, out of fear or sense of obligation to the appointing power, or factional passion, approves any measure we may enact. We are not the judges of the judges. We are not above the Constitution."

It was a devastating document. The bill, the report said, would not accomplish its objectives, would undermine the independence of the Court, and would traduce the Constitution.

"Its ultimate operation would be to make this government one of men rather than one of law, and its practical operation would be to make the Constitution what the executive or legislative branches of the government choose to say it is — an interpretation to be changed with each change of administration."

After the vote, McCarran walked over to Borah, put his arm around his congressional mentor, and both broke into wide smiles. "We've got them licked," McCarran enthused.[51]

"It is a measure which should be so emphatically rejected that its parallel will never again be presented to the free representatives of the free people of America."[52]

Congress, however, still had to vote on the bill. "The war," McCarran confided to his daughter, "is on."[53]

John Abt watched the terrible images again and again. In slow motion, the black-and-white film flickered ghastly scenes that looked like outtakes from an Eisenstein movie:

Hundreds of men and woman and children marching. A line of uniformed police raising weapons and firing at point-blank range. People running, police chasing and swinging, billy clubs rising and falling. The haze of tear gas giving way to a field littered with the dead and wounded. Three officers beating a man with his arms raised in surrender to the ground, then beating him some more. A nightstick swung like a baseball bat into a face. Garbled sounds of guns and screams and two clear words: *"God Almighty!"*

Abt was the chief counsel to the La Follette Committee (formally the Subcommittee to Investigate Violations of Free Speech and the Rights of Labor), and he was watching footage taken on Memorial Day 1937 in Chicago by a news agency when striking workers marched peacefully toward the Republic Steel Company plant. Ten of them died. Scores were injured, many shot in the back. Abt had to subpoena the film from the news agency, which thought that it was too graphic to show to the public.

The committee had its origins more than a year before, in February 1936, when Pat Jackson organized a dinner at the Cosmos Club and invited more than a dozen lawmakers to listen to a black sharecropper who wore a bandage from a recent beating and a white liberal who had gone to the South to organize a union and was tarred and feathered. Jackson wanted Congress to investigate what was happening in the South. Senator after senator told him it was impossible. Finally Wisconsin progressive Bob La Follette said that he would.

Lee Pressman suggested to Jackson that his old buddy from the Triple A, John Abt, would make a good counsel. La Follette hired Abt, who hired Charlie Kramer as his investigator. At first Pressman tried to get the counsel's job for himself — in addition to his post at the CIO. To some observers, it was hard to tell where the CIO stopped and the committee began. On December 18, for example, the CIO announced that it would demand a collective bargaining agreement with General Motors. The next day the La Follette Committee announced it would investigate labor conditions at GM plants. "All through early CIO years, all over the field, I ran into men from the La Follette Committee doing their brave, shrewd, and conscientious work," recalled Len De Caux, the editor of the *CIO News* and a longtime party member. ". . . The men from the La Follette Committee were good guys with the same kind of flame in their hearts, the same kind of song (sotto voce) on their lips, as all the other youngsters (and oldsters) daring and fighting for the workers' freedom on a hundred fronts in those glory days."[54]

Abt and his staff handed out subpoenas left and right. They trawled through the garbage of Pinkerton and the Burns Detective Agency and spent weeks pasting together shredded documents showing how corporate America spied on its workers and infiltrated their unions. "Not only is the worker's freedom of association nullified by the employers' spies," Abt wrote in a committee report, "but his freedom of action, of speech and of assembly is completely destroyed. Fear harries his every footstep, caution muffles his words. He is in no sense any longer a free American."[55]

Abt, like his friend Pressman, delighted at turning the tables on the titans of American industry. At committee hearings he gathered all the witnesses together around a table, where La Follette would ask questions and the witnesses would answer and confront one another. The idea, Abt recalled, came from the Moscow trials.

It never crossed Abt's mind that years later he might be the one sitting on the other side of the table answering questions from congressional investigators.

July 10 dawned hot in Washington and quickly grew intolerable, hitting a heavy and sticky ninety-five degrees. In the packed Senate chamber the air-conditioning labored lamely to make it more bearable. People stood in the galleries, thick with Boy Scouts on jamboree; House members crowded onto the floor, three deep against the wall. Behind a row of desks, McCarran paced back and forth, speaking in a low voice that built to a crescendo. "We constitute ourselves a battalion of death," he shouted, "that this bill may not pass and that the Constitution shall be protected."

He stopped and raised a fist toward the leadership platform. It was the fifth day of the floor debate over Roosevelt's Court plan. McCarran had not made a major speech in the chamber in eighteen months.

"There is a philosophy that gave sanction to this bill," he said, "a rampant philosophy that is going the rounds of this country, that if it starts with sufficient fury will sweep this country off its feet. Because today, from without, there come the enemies, enemies greater than any army that ever challenged our existence."

For two hours McCarran raged. His voice grew high pitched, trembled. He attacked Farley for threatening to cut off White House patronage to Nevada. "He wrote my death warrant and he knew it," McCarran said, "and I may today be delivering my valedictory by reason of a mandate of Mr. Farley."

Packing the Supreme Court, McCarran warned, was not the last grasp for greater executive power; only the first. "The Supreme Court can be destroyed and if the Supreme Court can be destroyed in that way, the judicial branch of the government can be destroyed," he said. "And if the judicial branch of the government may be thus destroyed, it is only tomorrow that an effort may be made to destroy the legislative branch of the government. That has been done in other lands."

Given McCarran's history in the Senate, no one should have doubted where he would stand on the Court bill. Now no one did. "The time has come," McCarran roared, "for the people of this country to rise in defense of their own government."[56]

A year earlier the Supreme Court had moved from the cramped old Senate chamber in the Capitol across the street to a sprawling new Greek temple. The Court got a new home but, for the time being, Roosevelt wasn't going to get a new Court. The Senate voted 70 to 20 to send the bill back to the Judiciary Committee, where it was entombed. "Glory be to God," exclaimed Hiram Johnson.[57]

There was something more than a little tragic about the entire episode: Roosevelt won the most smashing electoral triumph in American history and immediately overreached. What could have been a reasonable plan to enlarge the Court (no specific number of justices, after all, was carved on a tablet anywhere) turned into an epic debacle. Seduced by his love of secrecy and the dramatic, Roosevelt hurled the plan at Congress and the public like a thunderbolt from Olympus. And, like a Greek hero, he slew his own: fracturing the New Deal coalition, empowering his conservative enemies, and leaving himself embittered and frustrated.

Like any tragedy, the ramifications lingered. In another year Roosevelt's fury would lead to a quest for revenge as ill considered and fruitless as the Court plan. "I do not believe President Roosevelt ever forgave me," McCarran recalled, "for my part in bringing about his defeat on the court packing issue."[58]

It hit McCarran in the middle of the night. In August a blood vessel burst in his intestinal tract. The Senate doctor immediately sent him to the Naval Hospital. "I'm worn out by this strenuous session of Congress," he said.[59]

He was in bed for three weeks. Doctors gave him a glass of milk and cream every hour to coat his ulcer. They stuffed a fluoroscope tube down his throat and into his stomach. "On Tuesday my gallbladder is to be x-rayed," he told his daughter Margaret. "That should be all right because I am noted for having plenty of 'gall.'"[60]

Shortly after becoming the secretary of the National Labor Relations Board in November 1937, Natt Witt sent two assistants to visit the board's regional offices, where they told field officers how to do their jobs better. Special examiners, Witt called them. "The goon squad" others at the agency labeled them. To those who casually knew the friendly Witt, such a transparent power play seemed completely out of character; to those who really knew Witt, it made all the sense in the world.

In the labor wars of the late 1930s, no government agency was more important than the NLRB, which for the first time exerted the government's authority to compel companies to deal with unions and also decided which among the rival AFL and CIO unions was the legitimate bargaining agent. The NLRB's actual decisions were made by three board members appointed by the president; almost everything else that happened at the agency was Witt's doing.

Unlike his friend Lee Pressman, Nat Witt did not move through the world like a knife. His inner steel was sheathed in an even temper and an imperturbable pleasantness. "His calm soothing manner, so sure and reasonable in his convictions," recalled Len De Caux.[61] People liked him. He was the kind of man who if he forgot to leave a tip at lunch while on a business trip would send a telegram asking a friend to deliver the gratuity. Witt knew what it was like to work for a living.

The son of an immigrant Polish tailor, Witt (né Witkofski) grew up in New York's Lower East Side. His father was fired for trying to start a union, and his mother had to support the family by selling chickens. High school was interrupted by three years of work. Many of the boys from Witt's neighborhood wound up in jail. Witt, with the help of a scholarship and a night job, wound up at New York University. Afterward he spent two years driving a cab and saving every penny. Then he went to Harvard Law. "It was his early experience as a worker that gave Nat his working-class point of view," John Abt remarked, "and imbued him with a mighty sense of outrage at every manifestation of injustice."[62]

Law school classmate Pressman brought Witt to Washington and the Triple A in 1933 (and thence to the Communist Party). The next year Witt moved over to the new NLRB. The board had originally been created in

1934 and revamped under the Wagner Act a year later but was largely impotent until the Supreme Court declared the act constitutional in 1937. Witt became the board's secretary, the top administrative post, which put him in charge of the 250-person Washington office as well as almost two dozen regional offices. Witt handled everything from hiring and budgets to scheduling hearings and the timing of board decisions. "This," recalled one board lawyer, "was a Witt organization."[63]

The regional directors soon revolted. They complained en masse to the board that their authority was being usurped. Regional Director Elinore Herrick, for example, said that Witt's examiners acted like political commissars sent to enforce a party line. "It is the procedure one might expect from the OGPU," she griped, "but not from fellow administrators of an agency of the American government."[64]

The AFL was even more upset. In 1937 the AFL lost three out of every four elections contested by the CIO. So desperate was the AFL that its officials were soon talking about repealing the Wagner Act, the most pro-labor law ever passed in the country. Then things got worse. In June 1938 the NLRB named Harry Bridges and his International Longshoremen and Warehousemen's Union the designated bargaining agent for every stevedore from Alaska to San Diego, a devastating blow to the rival AFL International Longshoremen Association — especially since the Labor Department was trying to deport Bridges as a Communist.

Witt could relate to Bridges's ordeal. "The conservatives and Redbaiters were always after me," he recalled.[65] But even when Roosevelt became concerned about the leftward tilt of the NLRB and appointed a liberal anti-Communist board member to clean house, Witt was hard to dislodge.

If the president couldn't move him, how could Witt dream that one day federal marshals would drag him from a congressional hearing room at the behest of a mere senator like Pat McCarran?

On November 7, 1937, Pat and Dode Jackson walked into a grand Italianate mansion on Sixteenth Street, NW, a few blocks from the White House. They were going to the Soviet embassy to celebrate the twentieth anniversary of the Bolshevik revolution. "They always threw a great party . . . ," Jackson recalled. "Everybody went. You saw everybody there who was anything in the liberal, political, intellectual or labor fields."*[66]

Russia had purchased the old Pullman mansion in 1913, but only an

---

*McCarran was on the guest list. He didn't attend.

unpaid caretaker occupied it from the Bolshevik revolution in 1917 until Roosevelt recognized the Soviet Union in 1933. Ambassador Alexander Troyanovsky, the son of a czarist officer, soon charmed official Washingotn with lavish parties and good humor.

Clad in acres of mahogany and marble, the embassy drawing room rang with the sound of Metropolitan Opera singers and famous violinists. Enormous, whole sturgeons decorated tables; small mountains of beluga caviar filled punch bowls and were heaped onto plates with silver soup ladles. Hammers and scythes crowned cakes; champagne and vodka flowed like the Volga. Society matrons who didn't trust the Reds enough to check their minks carried their coats over their arms and had second helpings of roe. "If we could swallow the New Deal," one remarked between bites, "we can certainly swallow the Bolsheviks."[67] J. P. Morgan, thought one guest, would not look out of place. "The entire New Deal was there with the exception of the president," Josie Herbst told her husband, John Hermann, a member of the Ware Group, after one party. "Tugwell, Frank, Howe and etc."[68]

At the twentieth-anniversary celebration, however, not everyone was there. Pat Jackson's old friend Boris Skvirsky, who had been Russia's unofficial representative before diplomatic relationships were established, was not at the party. He had been recalled to Moscow. "None of us have ever been able to find a trace of Skvirsky," Jackson lamented.[69] Also missing was Vladimir Romm, the Washington correspondent for *Izvestia*. Before long even Ambassador Troyanovsky was ordered back to Moscow. When U.S. diplomat Charles Bohlen bumped into Troyanovsky and his wife at a Moscow dinner party, the former ambassador was not laughing anymore. "I have rarely been through as painful an experience," Bohlen remembered. ". . . When a question was directed to them, they would jump as if startled, mumble a reply, then lapse into silence. Both were desperately afraid."[70]

Troyanovsky managed to survive the Great Purge. Skvirky and Romm did not.

In March 1938 twenty-one Old Bolsheviks went on trial in Moscow for being part of a vast Trotsky–directed conspiracy. They plotted to kill Lenin and Stalin. They murdered Maxim Gorki. They spied for the British, the Japanese, and the Germans. They tried to destroy socialism by sabotage, by derailing trains and mixing nails and broken glass into butter. Nikolai Bukharin had once been one of the party's star theorists; now he stood accused of plotting to kill his beloved Lenin. He confessed.

"A case involving the gravest crimes directed against the well-being of our country, against our socialist father, the fatherland of the working people of the whole world . . . ," Prosecutor Andrei Vyshinsky said.

Reading the newspaper accounts Whittaker Chambers thought that something terrible was happening. Then John Sherman, an American Communist just back from Moscow, told him a frightening tale of Americans sequestered in Russia. Sherman was sent back to the States on assignment for the underground. Instead he was planning to move to California and attach himself to the open party. "I will not work one hour longer for those murderers," he said.[71]

"The chain of shameful, unparalleled, monstrous crimes committed by the accused, the entire abominable chain of heinous deeds before which the base deeds of the most inveterate, vile, unbridled and despicable criminals fade and grow dim. . . ."

Chambers was working harder than ever. His contacts in the Washington underground were steadily rising in government service. Alger Hiss, whom Chambers considered a great friend, worked for Assistant Secretary of State Francis Sayre. Harry Dexter White was assistant to the secretary in the Treasury. Chambers needed three photographers to copy all the secret memos and summaries of confidential documents that these and other sources gave him.

"A gang of murderers, spies, diversionists and wreckers, without any principles or ideals. . . ."

Chambers started to make plans. I studied the mistakes by which the deserters were trapped as a man might study the chart of a minefield, he recalled. He began to carry a knife to meetings with his Soviet handler. He needed a car. Alger Hiss offered his.

"Criminals who have sold themselves to enemy intelligence services, criminals who even ordinary felons treat as the basest, the lowest, the most contemptible, the most depraved of the depraved. . . ."

For years Chambers had lived like a ghost, an incorporeal being who moved among the living without leaving footprints. He needed to establish the fact that he had once existed. He asked George Silverman, who worked at the Railroad Retirement Board, to get him a job in the government. He was soon paying taxes. He stashed away copies of documents from his most productive source: Hiss.

"A foul-smelling heap of human garbage. . . ."

Sitting in a jail cell Bukharin wrote a final plea to Stalin. He promised not to recant his confession but insisted that he was innocent of everything. Let me drink poison, he pleaded, but don't shoot me. Or send me to America and I'll wage war against Trotsky and campaign in support of the purges.

"Our people are demanding one thing: crush the accursed reptile!"

"If the charge was true, then every other Communist had given his life for a fraud," Chambers later wrote. "If the charge was false, then every other Communist was giving his life for a fraud. This was a torturing thought. No Communist could escape it."[72]

"Over the road cleared of the last scum and filth of the past, we, our people, with our beloved leader and teacher, the great Stalin, at our head will march as before onwards and onwards, towards Communism!"[73]

A month after Bukharin was shot, Chambers disappeared. You know, he told his wife, we are leaving the winning world for the losing world.

On a hot June evening in Washington, Roosevelt took to the airwaves to tell the nation that he was declaring war on those in his own party who didn't support the New Deal.

"Never in our lifetime has such a concerted campaign of defeatism been thrown at the heads of the president and the senators and congressmen as in the case of this Seventy-Fifth Congress," Roosevelt said. "Never before have we had so many Copperheads among us — and you will remember that it was the Copperheads who, in the days of the Civil War, the War between the States, tried their best to make President Lincoln and his Congress give up the fight in the middle of the fight, to let the nation remain split in two and return to peace — yes, peace at any price. An election cannot give the country a firm sense of direction if it has two or more national parties which merely have different names but are as alike in their principles and aims as peas in the same pod."

For months Roosevelt's advisers had been telling him not to do this. And for as many months the president kept muttering about which Democrats had to go. Don't get involved in the primaries, Farley begged. Don't worry, the president replied, the American people would defeat his opponents. "I knew from the beginning," Farley said later, "that the purge could lead to nothing but misfortune."[74]

"As head of the Democratic Party, however, charged with the responsibility of carrying out the definitely liberal declaration of principles set forth in the 1936 Democratic platform, I feel that I have every right to speak on those few instances where there may be a clear issue between candidates for a Democratic nomination involving these principles, or involving a clear misuse of my own name."

There were, the president said, nine Democrats he really wanted to see defeated, among them the junior senator from Nevada. Can we beat

McCarran? the president kept asking. No, Farley kept insisting. "I tried to tell him why this or that candidate could not dent one of his targets," Farley recalled, "but each time I found him determined to go through with the purge."[75]

"Do not misunderstand me, I certainly would not indicate a preference in a state primary merely because a candidate, otherwise liberal in outlook, had conscientiously disagreed with me on any single issue. I would be far more concerned about the general attitude of a candidate toward present day problems and his own inward desire to get practical needs attended to in a practical way. We all know that progress may be blocked by outspoken reactionaries and also by those who say 'yes' to a progressive objective, but who always find some reason to oppose any proposal to gain that objective. I call that type of candidate a 'yes, but' fellow."[76]

But finding viable candidates would not be easy. Roosevelt was undeterred. "I am going to endorse someone," Roosevelt told Farley, "if I have to pick my tenant farmer."[77]

So began Roosevelt's version of the Great Purge.

At 6:11 on the morning of July 13 Roosevelt's Pullman car chugged out of Ogden, Utah, thirty-five miles north of Salt Lake City. The high-desert day was dawning hot, heading toward the nineties, and the train had been delayed by an hour while extra ice was loaded aboard for the air-conditioning system. Sitting in the train's dining car was Pat McCarran, whom Roosevelt was hoping to keep on ice as well for the long ride across Nevada.

Three weeks earlier Roosevelt had declared war on the copperheads in his party, like McCarran, who opposed most of the New Deal. Now as the president rolled toward a Pacific fishing trip, he was heading to Nevada to pick up the man who was challenging McCarran in the state primary. Al Hilliard was a young Reno attorney, a political novice running on a single-issue platform — that he, unlike McCarran, would support Roosevelt unstintingly. "I am one hundred percent for Roosevelt,"[78] Hilliard declared when he announced his bid in May. "I am for Roosevelt and shall support him whether in the Senate or in private life," he added. "And I don't mean whether he is right or whether he is wrong. In this battle between the people, represented by the president on the one hand and the old emaciated forces of reaction, Democratic and Republican on the other, the president has never been wrong and never will. . . . The people know that enemies of the president are not their friends."[79]

Roosevelt wanted to make clear who his friends in Nevada were. A week earlier the administration slapped McCarran by appointing William ("I will leave no stone unturned until I defeat McCarran") Boyle, a friend of Farley and Pittman, as the U.S. attorney for Nevada. Four years earlier McCarran had sunk two of Key Pittman's nominees for the post and finally got E. P. Carville the position. Carville did an excellent job. Just before he left Washington for Nevada, McCarran talked to the Justice Department and was assured that Carville would be reappointed. When he arrived in Nevada a few days later, though, McCarran was greeted with the news that the president had instead appointed Boyle. And at the train's first stop in Nevada, the townlet of Carlin, Roosevelt had invited Hilliard on board for the three-hundred-mile ride to Reno. "I had thought of running, but did not care to do so without some word from Washington," Hilliard boasted in private. "While there I spent two days with a first assistant secretary of one of the departments, and was assured that the administration would rejoice in McCarran's defeat."[80]

When McCarran found out that Hilliard was getting on in Carlin, he arranged to board the train in Utah. For six hours McCarran rode in the dining car, separated from the president's Pullman in the rear by one car of reporters and another of Secret Service agents. It was closer to Roosevelt than he'd been in months. The ten car train rounded the Great Salt Lake and crossed into Nevada, where it crawled up the Pequop Mountain pass at seven thousand feet, soon to be dwarfed by the eleven-thousand-foot peaks of the Ruby Mountains to the south. Through Elko the train trundled, hundreds lining the tracks for a glimpse of the president, who obliged with smiles and waves from the back of his Pullman.

At eleven-thirty the train pulled into Carlin, a dusty railroad stop where four hundred people had gathered from the wastes of eastern Nevada to see the president. Al Hilliard boarded the train with George L. Swartz, the chairman of the state Democratic committee, a further reminder of McCarran's status with the party regulars. Workers attached loudspeakers the size of car tires to the side of the train. Women in their best hats and men in their Sunday suits eddied around the stern of the Pullman, flowing over the tracks and engulfing the train.

Using the arm of his son-in-law John Boettiger like a cane, Roosevelt hobbled onto the platform. A man lifted a restless boy onto his shoulders; the child squirreled around, finding the sea of faces more interesting than the old man on the train. Roosevelt, wearing a dark suit, gripped the lectern above the seal of the Baltimore & Ohio Special. Hilliard stood in the background. McCarran was nowhere to be seen. Someone, it seemed, had forgotten to tell him that Roosevelt was speaking. "Good morning," the president began. "I'm glad to get back in Nevada — "

McCarran nosed out on the platform in a light, unbuttoned summer suit. "Hello, Pat," someone in the crowd yelled. Applause rippled through the audience. Roosevelt stopped speaking, smiled (or was it a frown?) at McCarran, and shook his hand. "Three cheers for Pat," another voice chimed. "Speech, Pat," a third said.[81] McCarran inched over to the edge of the train, put his hand on the rail, and looked over the crowd, his head turned away from Roosevelt. "I am having a grand trip," Roosevelt wrote to Pittman as the train lurched on. "The governor and Scrugham are with me and your colleague pops in and out!"[82]

The train crossed the middle third of the Nevada desert, groaning to a halt in Imlay, another miserable railway town, midway between Winnemucca and Lovelock, where a crowd of fifteen hundred people waited. Governor Richard Kirman and Representative Jim Scrugham boarded. "I'm glad to be back on the desert and tell you that I appreciate the fine cooperation the state government of Nevada has given me from the governor on down," Roosevelt said.[83] Governor Kirman was one potential candidate whom many people thought could beat McCarran. The president then introduced both declared Senate candidates. "The senator," said Roosevelt, then — putting his hand on Hilliard's shoulder — "and Al Hilliard."[84]

The train continued on, the track crossing the Truckee and then running along the river, past the McCarran ranch and into Sparks for a twenty-minute service stop. A crowd of thirty-five hundred clustered around the back of the train, and the president came out. Roosevelt introduced McCarran with a wave of the hand that could have been swatting away a fly. "The senator," he said stiffly. Then he turned toward Hilliard, put his hand on his shoulder, and smiled. "Brother Hilliard," he cooed. Before the train left the station, McCarran saw a local clergyman talking to the president's secretary, Marvin McIntyre. Later the priest told McCarran that he had asked McIntyre why Carville wasn't reappointed. "To take a slap at Pat," McIntyre replied.[85]

A few miles later the train clacked into Reno, where fifteen thousand people jammed the Center Street station, straining for a glimpse of the president during his five-minute stop. The city band blasted into song. Police- and firemen struggled to keep people twenty feet away from the train. Once again, the president buttered up Kirman. "I have been especially interested in studying with your governor the problem of water in your state," Roosevelt said.[86] McCarran, once again, was virtually ignored. "McCarran," Roosevelt told his son James, "is being treated with 'due courtesy.'"[87]

The visitors piled off the train before it pulled out of the station and made the long climb up the steep side of the Sierra Nevada. On the twelve-hour trip across Nevada, McCarran had fifteen minutes of small talk with Roosevelt in the president's parlor car — in the company of Hilliard and Swartz. Hilliard later claimed to have had a private talk with Roosevelt on the train. "I have never asked a senator to vote one way or another," Hilliard said Roosevelt told him. "But I do expect, and the people have every right to expect, that Democratic senators will play ball with the administration. Senator McCarran has consistently and stubbornly refused to play ball. That is why I am against him and that is why I wish you the best of luck in your campaign."[88]

Sailing in the Pacific, Roosevelt took time off from fishing to plot against McCarran. "Joe Keenan and Key Pittman talked to me today," Harry Hopkins told Roosevelt. "They are confident that Richard Kirman, the governor, can win in primary for senatorship, but that he will run only if gets confidential message from you. Other two friendly candidates hopelessly out of it. I will deliver any confidential message you may wish to give to Governor Kirman."[89] Roosevelt was pleased. "I would be very happy," the president replied, "and before primary I am wholly willing to make my position clear beyond any doubt."[90]

But Kirman never entered the primary, and Roosevelt didn't offer Hilliard any overt support. The attorney trudged down to Las Vegas to campaign but found it easier to get coverage in the eastern press than in Nevada newspapers. "The administration is opposed to the return of Senator McCarran," Hilliard told one rally. "He has opposed the administration at every turn."[91]

No one listened. McCarran's anti–New Deal stand enticed hundreds of Republicans to switch party registration. "If we cannot defeat the president through the Republican Party," said Judge Thomas Moran, who joined the Democrats after forty-five years in the GOP, "then we shall have to fight him from within the Democratic Party."[92]

McCarran ran on what he did for Nevada. The federal government, he claimed, had spent $1,150 for every person in the state during the past six years. The price of silver jumped from 27.25 cents an ounce when McCarran took office, he noted, to almost 65 cents. "A friend of silver," one campaign handout called him.

Although Labor's Non-Partisan League gave McCarran's voting record a mere C, the CIO had no presence in Nevada and the AFL was solidly behind the senator. The Railroad Brotherhood publication *Labor* printed up fifty thousand copies (more than one per voter) of a special issue dedicated to McCarran. "He's an honor to Nevada," the paper declared. ". . . His is a magnificent record, unsurpassed by any member of the Senate."[93]

McCarran easily won the primary, 17,921 votes to Hilliard's 5,329, and carried every county in the state.

It wound up being the Not So Great Purge. Roosevelt picked challengers in three races, channeled patronage away from their opponents, and put aides, money, and his own moral authority into the contested battlegrounds. In Georgia he stood on a stage with incumbent Walter George and challenger Lawrence Camp. He looked into the senator's face, called him a friend, but said he wasn't a liberal and that he couldn't vote for him. In South Carolina, Roosevelt invited the state's governor, Olin Johnston, to lunch and then invited him to run against Cotton Ed Smith. And in Maryland the president stumped against Millard Tydings, dragging a reluctant Jim Farley along for the show. All the incumbents thumped their rivals. The Republicans trounced the Democrats, not losing a single seat, but gaining eight in the Senate and eighty-two in the House. Only New York's John O'Connor lost to a Roosevelt-blessed challenger. "An escalator to dictatorship," O'Connor called the purge.[94] In reality it wasn't even a stepladder.

There was one last chance for the Democrats to defeat McCarran: support the Republican candidate in the general election. "We must get Oddie to run," William Boyle implored Pittman before the primary. "We can put him over. Our Democratic line up is hopeless."[95]

So was the Republican one. Six years earlier Tasker Oddie had lost to McCarran by a mere five hundred votes. Oddie, in his midsixties, went back to mining, setting off once again to search for a fortune like the one he had found and lost thirty years before in Tonopah. In August, Oddie, sixty-eight, announced against McCarran, running on a platform calling for economy in government, old-age pensions (he could use one himself), unemployment insurance (ditto), and social security. Oddie seemed not to have noticed that the New Deal had already happened. On election morning an airplane rained "Oddie for Senator" handbills over Reno. Farley sent an open letter to Democrats urging them to vote for

McCarran. That day McCarran beat his old rival mercilessly. McCarran won 59 percent of the vote, trouncing Oddie 27,406 to 19,078. Oddie went back to his cabin, where he lived until 1950 when he died of a heart attack, looking for another bonanza almost to the end.

McCarran was going back to Washington. "I will sustain and support the executive of the nation as I have sustained him in the past when he was right," McCarran said. "I will oppose him when he is wrong. I will be true to my oath to uphold and defend the Constitution."[96]

On January 9, 1939, the Veterans of the Abraham Lincoln Brigade marched in Washington. A few weeks before, the Republican government in Spain had started evacuating the foreign militias of the International Brigades as Franco's troops continued to advance. The only thing that might save Spain's elected government was for the United States to sell arms to the Loyalists. Eleanor Roosevelt, Harold Ickes, and other liberals had been urging Roosevelt to do just that ever since the war started in 1936. But Roosevelt claimed that his hands were tied by the Neutrality Act, which prohibited the United States from supplying weapons to either side in a conflict. "Catholic opposition to any move that might help the Loyalists immobilized the president," Joe Lash recalled.[97] The protestors from the Lincoln Brigade, most of whom were Communists, demanded that Congress repeal the law. "Lift the embargo on Loyalist Spain," they shouted.

Keep the embargo, McCarran declared in the Senate two days later. "We immediately encourage a Communistic form of government on the Spanish peninsula which would put the rest of Europe between the two millstones of Communism with Russia on one side and Spain on the other," he said. "This would do more to make Europe Communistic than anything I know of. But aside from these views, and based purely on precedent, our neutrality law as to Spain should not be changed."[98]

Roosevelt did nothing. "Leaders of a Senate group favoring repeal agreed it would be unwise to launch their move now," reported the *New York World Telegram*.[99]

Fifteen days later Barcelona fell to Franco's forces.

Spain was dying. The Republic would hold out until March but the end was in sight. "We were morally right, but too weak," Eleanor said to a guest at the White House. She turned to her husband. "We should have pushed *him* harder," she said.[100] Roosevelt didn't say a word.

Spain was a dividing line. For many of those who rushed into the

International Brigades it was the greatest struggle and worst defeat of their lives. Some would never forgive the democracies for not taking sides. "The Republic's struggle against Fascism in Spain was probably the zenith of political idealism in the first half of the twentieth century," Louis Fischer recalled. "Even in the best years, the outside sympathy for Soviet Russia was political and cerebral. Bolshevism inspired vehement passions in its foreign adherents but little of the tenderness and intimacy which Loyalist Spain evoked. . . . Only those who lived with Spain through the thirty-three months from July, 1936, to March, 1939, can fully understand the joy of victory and the more frequent pang of defeat which the ups and downs of the Civil War brought to its millions of distant participants."[101]

For others the lesson was different. It was not the democracies they grew to hate but the Russians. Stalin sent hundreds of military advisers to Spain; eventually he shot most of them as traitors. The terror of the Great Purge reached deep into the Iberian Peninsula. The Russians also executed American Loyalists as accused deserters or Trotskyists. To some, like George Orwell, the Soviet brutality in Spain was a final shattering of illusions, a betrayal so great that nothing the Russians ever touched could remain unsullied again.

The contradiction between the public celebration of the Civil War as a heroic endeavor and the private horror grew to be too much for American supporters such as Jim Loeb. Yet even by 1939 the socialists were not ready to pull out of the North American Committee. "Official and public withdrawal from the N.A.C. seems impossible," Loeb concluded. ". . . Those liberals who still retain sympathy for the Socialist Party would never understand an act which would split the movement for Spain."[102]

Before the Republic fell, however, Loeb had bolted from the North American Committee. Henceforth he would work no more with the Communist Party, no matter what the cause. "Sometimes, as a Socialist, I feel ashamed of myself for having been instrumental in keeping the North American Committee together as a 'united front' all these months," Loeb lamented.[103]

He was not alone. Louis Fischer, whose account of Communist heroics in Spain had first moved Loeb, had known all along what the Soviets were like. He had come to Spain from Russia, where the first chill of the purges had convinced him that after fifteen years in Moscow he no longer wanted to live there. Yet in Spain he had the hope that the Russians could redeem the promise of the revolution — which he soon realized was doomed. And yet Fischer, the reporter, would not tell the world what he knew.

"I had no doubts about what had happened and why, and I was even fairly certain that an improvement in Soviet policy was unlikely," Fischer admitted much later. "But since it was possible, I waited and remained silent."[104]

Hundreds of visitors packed themselves into the Caucus Room in the Senate Office Building, overflowing the seats and pressing themselves against the wall on January 12, 1939. Capital police cut through the crowd so that a short, square-faced man in owlish glasses could make his way to the witness table. Felix Frankfurter, fifty-six, Harvard Law School professor, Roosevelt confidant, and, for the past week, Supreme Court nominee, took a seat next to his former student and current counsel Dean Acheson. Applause crackled through the room. Senator Matthew Neely gaveled the Judiciary's subcommittee into session and asked the audience to refrain from any further demonstrations.

A week earlier Frankfurter had declined the subcommittee's invitation to appear, sending Acheson in his place. The last two days had changed his mind. "He corresponds more to the theories of Russian Communism, instead of upholding the liberal ideals of the founder of this country,"[105] asserted the first witness before the subcommittee, Collis O. Redd, the national director and only member of the Constitutional Crusaders of America. Another witness, Allen A. Zoll, vice president of the American Federation Against Communism, objected to Frankfurter "because of his race."[106] That is, because he was Jewish. Then there was Elizabeth Dilling. She was a graduate of the University of Chicago, a concert harpist and the wife of an attorney, but she was best known for *the book*. In 1934 Dilling published (at her husband's expense) *The Red Network,* which explained how tiny islands of liberal thought like the Garland Foundation and *The Nation* magazine were all connected by a vast undersea mountain range of conspiracy. Frankfurter, of course, was part of the conspiracy, as were Roosevelt, Mrs. Roosevelt, several members of the Supreme Court — and a couple of members of the Senate Judiciary Committee itself. "Frankfurter," Dilling told the subcommittee, "has long been one of the principal aids to the 'Red' revolutionary movement in the United States."[107]

Dilling was, to put it mildly, insane. McCarran, alone among his colleagues on the subcommittee, took her seriously. Two years after Roosevelt's failed gambit to enlarge the Supreme Court, the president was getting to remake the bench anyway. Roosevelt's first appointment had been Hugo Black, a fiery New Dealer from the Senate. Then came the bland but dutiful

Stanley Reed. Now Frankfurter was tapped. Liberals were overjoyed. "No other appointee in our history has gone to the court so fully prepared for its great tasks," gushed *The Nation*.[108]

McCarran had more than a few questions for Dilling. During his first term in the Senate, McCarran had repeatedly warned against growing government centralization; increasingly he also railed against encroaching Communism. But he had done little more than speechify. Now, with a second term ahead of him, McCarran began to exercise the power that his seat on the Judiciary Committee gave him — the power to question, harass, and even block presidential appointees. An opposer and contrarian by temperament, McCarran would develop his disposition toward obstructionism to a rare level of skill. He asked Dilling to closely trace Frankfurter's liberal footsteps. He was especially interested in the law professor's role in the Sacco and Vanzetti case and his work with the ACLU. "I believe this situation should be explored by this committee," McCarran said, "and I believe that we should go to the bottom of it and find what it means."[109]

Thus at a quarter past ten on January 12, 1939, Felix Frankfurter walked into the Caucus Room and became the first nominee in the Supreme Court's 150-year history to have to defend himself before a Senate panel. Two days of crackpots, as Frankfurter's friend Oliver Wendell Holmes might have put it, was enough. Frankfurter began by asserting that he did not wish to testify on his own behalf. "My attitude and outlook on relevant matters have been fully expressed over a period of years and are easily accessible," he said. "I should think it not only bad taste but inconsistent with the duties of the office for which I have been nominated for me to attempt to supplement my past record by present declarations."[110]

Senator William Borah led Frankfurter through his personal history: his work as an assistant to the attorney general in Theodore Roosevelt's administration; his appointment to a presidential commission that concluded that labor leader Tom Mooney had been sentenced to death for a bomb blast in a San Francisco parade based on perjured testimony; his efforts to defend aliens who had been arrested in the Red Scare following the war but had been denied due process; his signing of a clemency petition for three men convicted under the Espionage Act for distributing subversive leaflets. In each case, Frankfurter noted, he was only making sure that people were enjoying the rights guaranteed to them under the Constitution, which was all that the American Civil Liberties Union ever did. The ACLU, he added, even came to the defense of Liz Dilling when a radio station tried to ban her after she attacked a Methodist minister as a subversive. "It makes no difference whether a man is a Communist or a Republican or Progressive or Democrat," Frankfurter said, "he is entitled to the protection of the American Civil Liberties Union."[111]

Then it was McCarran's turn. *"Doctor,"* he said, "you were born abroad?"[112] What an amount of poison he put into that term, Frankfurter thought, as though *doctor* were a contagious disease.[113]

Frankfurter, indeed, had been born in Austria and came to the United States with his father when he was twelve. McCarran had heard a rumor that the elder Frankfurter took the naturalization oath a year before he was legally qualified, thereby mooting his son's citizenship and rendering him ineligible to sit on the Supreme Court. Frankfurter's friends had to burrow deep in the government archives before they could find documents to prove that Frankfurter *père's* naturalization was legit.

Doctor, McCarran continued, did you know that Communist leader William Z. Foster had been on the ACLU board? Yes. *Doctor,* McCarran asked, have you read the reports of the Dies, Fish, and Lusk Committees or the American Legion, all of which have charged the ACLU with aiding the Communist cause? No. "There are only twenty-four hours in a day," Frankfurter said. ". . . I shall only say that the repetition of an error does not make it true."

"No," McCarran shot back. "The repetition of an error does not make it true. But I should think it would cause one of your high place to investigate his associates."

McCarran asked Frankfurter if he agreed with his friend, socialist Harold Laski.

"I have many friends who have written many books and I shouldn't want to be charged with all the views in books by all my friends," the professor replied.

"You can answer that question simply," McCarran continued.

"No," Frankfurter snapped. "I cannot answer it simply."

McCarran persisted, demanding to know if Frankfurter had read Laski's book *Communism*. "If you have read this small volume," McCarran persisted, "you can surely answer whether you subscribe to the doctrine."

"Have you read the book?" parried the professor.

"I have just casually glanced at it," McCarran sputtered.

"What would you say is its doctrine?"

"The advocacy of Communism."

"You see," Frankfurter said, "we could debate all day on whether that is in fact the doctrine of that book."

"Do you believe in the doctrine set forth in this book?"

"I cannot answer. . . . You have never read it. . . . It is impossible to define what the doctrine is."

"If it advocates the doctrine of Marxism would you agree with it?"

"Senator," Frankfurter said, "I do not believe you have ever taken an oath to support the Constitution of the United States with fewer reservations than I have or would now, nor do I believe you are more attached to the theories and practices of Americanism than I am. I rest my answer on that statement."

Clapping and cheering rippled throughout the room. Neely gestured for Acheson to approach him. McCarran, Neely said in a low voice, was making Frankfurter look like a dangerous radical, maybe even a Communist, and the law professor's sparring and parsing wasn't making him look any better. Neely told Acheson that he wanted to get the matter out into the open. Acheson agreed. He told Frankfurter that the next time McCarran asked him a question about Communism, he should not split hairs.

"Doctor," McCarran continued, "do you believe in the Constitution of the United States?"

"Most assuredly."

Neely asked Frankfurter directly if he had ever been a Communist.

"I have never been," he replied, "and I am not now."

Do you mean that you have never been enrolled as a member of the Communist Party? McCarran added.

"I mean much more than that," Frankfurter said. "I mean that I have never been enrolled and have never been qualified to be enrolled because that does not represent my view of life, nor my view of government."

Applause broke like thunder, people jumped onto chairs, waved, shouted. Neely gaveled to no effect. It was noon. The hearing was over. Frankfurter was engulfed by well-wishers.[114]

Frankfurter and Acheson went to lunch with Judiciary Committee chairman Henry Ashurst. The teetotaling chairman passed out chilled brandies to his guests. "Tell me about McCarran?" Frankfurter asked. "He seems a hardheaded, shrewd sort of man, but obsessed about Communism. Explain it. Are there Communists in Nevada?"

"No, no," Ashurst replied, "he's never seen one. How can one explain obsessions. If you probe deep enough you will find that everyone is a little cracked on some subject."[115]

After lunch, the subcommittee met in executive session to consider the nomination. McCarran walked out of the room just before the vote was taken. The chairman dispatched a clerk to look for McCarran and found him sulking in the Senate restaurant. When McCarran declined to return, a ballot was sent for him to mark. It came back blank.

Frankfurter was unanimously approved.[116]

CHAPTER 9

Mass Murder Again

The trouble with bein' a dogooder is you find yourself in
some strange company.[1]
— John Dos Passos, *The Grand Design*

The switchboard at the *Daily Worker* lit up like a Christmas tree.

It was August 22, 1939, and the Soviet news agency Tass had just announced that German foreign minister Joachim von Ribbentrop would fly to Moscow to sign a nonaggression pact with his Russian counterpart, Vycheslav Molotov. One incredulous caller to the *Worker* after another could not believe it. For years the party had been leading the fight against fascism. Just the previous month Comrade Browder had told an audience that there was nothing to rumors of an impending pact. There was, he said, as much chance of an agreement between Stalin and Hitler as there was of Browder being elected president of the chamber of commerce. And now, five years to the month after the Popular Front had allowed the party to make common cause with liberals in the fight against Nazism, the motherland of socialism had cut a deal with the fatherland of fascism. The next day Browder invited reporters into his office on the ninth floor of party headquarters on Twelfth Street in New York. He rocked back and forth in his chair, furiously chain-smoked, and called the agreement "a wonderful contribution to peace."[2]

On September 1 German tanks overran Poland from the west. Two weeks later Russian tanks invaded from the east. World War II had come.

On September 21 Roosevelt went to the House and told a joint session of Congress that it was time for the United States to repeal the Neutrality Act and sell arms to the Allies.

"*I am wholly willing to ascribe an honorable desire for peace to those who hold different views from my own . . . ,*" the president said. "*I trust that these gentlemen will be sufficiently generous to ascribe equally lofty purposes to those with whom they disagree . . . the mantle of peace and of patriotism is wide enough to cover us all. Let no group assume the exclusive label of the 'peace bloc.'*"

Roosevelt had signed the original Neutrality Act in 1935, which made it illegal for the United States to provide arms to *any* of the belligerents involved in a conflict, whether they were the aggressor or the attacked.

"This Government must lose no time or effort to keep our nation from being drawn into the war."

In his somber State of the Union speech in January, Roosevelt had asked for the annulment of the act. The only way to keep out of combat, he said, was to help the Allies defeat the Nazis if war should come; otherwise the United States would eventually find the waves of totalitarianism lapping at its own shore. Over the summer both houses beat down the repeal effort. Then Hitler invaded Poland, and Britain and France declared war on Germany. Roosevelt proclaimed a state of limited national emergency and called Congress into a special session, once more demanding that Congress untie his hands.

"I regret that the Congress passed that Act. I regret equally that I signed that Act."

The morning of Roosevelt's speech, a group of senators met in Hiram Johnson's office. Mostly they were progressive Republicans: William Borah, eighty-four, who (with Johnson) had trailed Woodrow Wilson across the country to fight against the United States joining the League of Nations two decades earlier; Johnson, eighty-three, the former governor of California who had helped get women the right to vote in his state but blocked Asians from owning property and ran with Teddy Roosevelt on the Bull Moose ticket; Gerald Nye, forty-seven, whose hearings five years before blamed international arms merchants and Wall Street financiers for the First World War ("war and preparation for war is not a matter of national honor and national defense, but a matter of profit for few"[3]), which stirred up sentiment for the Neutrality Act; Robert La Follette Jr., forty-four, the son of Wisconsin's legendary reformer (and hence known as Young Bob). In the early days of the New Deal this same group gathered frequently in the White House to cheer on the president. But the Court plan sent most of them bolting into the opposition — except for La Follette, who swallowed his fear and backed the president. Now the question of whether to get involved in the European war brought the progressives into Johnson's office to plot strategy.

"These perilous days demand cooperation among us without trace of partisanship. Our acts must be guided by one single hard-headed thought: keeping America out of this war."

Less than a week earlier, late on the evening of September 15, Charles Lindbergh had walked into a New York hotel room with a heavy heart. A dozen years before, Lindbergh flew across the Atlantic and into the maelstrom of celebrity, suffered through the kidnapping and death of his young son, and then fled to Europe. Now, reluctantly, he was about to thrust himself back into public life. Earlier in the day, the White House had offered the aviator a cabinet post not to utter the words he was about to say. "These wars in Europe," Lindbergh said into a thicket of radio microphones that carried his flat voice across the nation, "are not wars in which our civilization is defending itself against some Asiatic intruder. . . . This is simply one more of those age old quarrels within our own family of nations."[4]

"May you by your deeds," Roosevelt concluded, "show the world that we of the United States are one people, of one mind, one spirit, one clear resolution, walking before God in the light of the living."[5]

Roosevelt was never more wrong about anything in his life.

Two weeks later the Keep America Out of War Congress drew thirty-five hundred people to a rally at the Manhattan Opera House. "The press of this country is against us," McCarran told the crowd. "You are going to see us denounced. They are going to call us pro-this and pro-that and pro-any-other-thing. I want you to know that we who have banded ourselves together in the Senate of the United States are pro-American and nothing else."[6]

Growing up far from the world on his family's little ranch on the Truckee, McCarran's mother's milk was the Irish nationalism of his immigrant parents. His father once shut a door in a man's face when he told him that his name was Cromwell. When World War I came, McCarran hoped that the British would lose. When he ran in the Senate primary in 1926, McCarran campaigned on a platform to keep the United States out of the World Court — an issue as obsessive to McCarran as it was obscure to Nevada voters. In the Senate he vowed never to send American troops to foreign battlefields long before anyone considered that a remote possibility. Now, with the Europeans at each other's throats again and another U.S. president siding with the British, McCarran was in full panic. Selling arms to Great Britain, he knew, would be the first step onto a loose cliff; war would follow like rocks down a hill.

"I think one American boy," McCarran said, "the son of an American mother, is worth more than all Central Europe."[7]

It came to be called the Great Debate. For the next two years the country would virtually go to war on the question of getting involved in the war. "You could get away from the war for a little while," the protagonist thought in J. P. Marquand's novel *So Little Time,* "but not for long, because it was everywhere, even in the sunlight. It lay behind everything you said or did. You could taste it in your food, you could hear it in music."[8]

On one side were the internationalists — or the interventionists, as their critics labeled them — led however haltingly by the president. Roosevelt had come to the White House two months after Hitler came to the chancellory in Germany. While McCarran and others were braying about Roosevelt grasping for dictatorial power during the Hundred Days, Hitler actually seized it, taking away legislative power from the Reichstag, destroying German unions, and banning all political parties except for the Nazis. When conservatives and progressives banded together to defeat Roosevelt's Court plan as an attempt to rape the Constitution, Hitler had already shot his rival SA leader Ernst Röhm, stripped Jews of their citizenship with the Nuremberg Decrees, violated the Treaty of Versailles by sending troops into the demilitarized Rhineland, signed pacts with fascist Italy and imperial Japan, and dispatched bombers to help Franco in the Spanish Civil War. Before this gathering storm, Roosevelt could only tack this way and that, never directly sailing into the wind or honestly proclaiming his feelings.

Roosevelt grew up in a cosmopolitan class where cruises to Europe were as common as Sunday picnics and an Anglophile worldview was as natural as a Groton-Harvard education and a Wall Street job. As an assistant secretary for the navy in Wilson's administration, Roosevelt had been an early advocate for intervention ("We've got to get into this war"[9]), but afterward, as he saw his president's hopes and health crushed by the brutal struggle to bring the United States into the League of Nations, he learned the futility of trying to push public opinion too far, too fast. If he had to turn his back on the League of Nations to get elected, he would. If he had to wreck the London Economic Conference and put to fire hopes of international cooperation in order to save the New Deal, he would. But when Roosevelt finally tried to nudge a mulish nation into taking a bigger role in world affairs by joining the World Court in 1935, his erstwhile progressive friends reared and kicked and stomped the idea to death. So Roosevelt signed the first Neutrality Act later that year and sat on his hands as Italy invaded Ethiopia. When the Spanish Civil War erupted in 1936, Roosevelt signed another version of the act, extending its reach to domestic wars as well. Even when Japanese troops bayoneted and raped their way through Nanking in 1937 and sank a U.S. gunboat, the *Panay,* killing two sailors, public opinion seemed to think that the country was already *too* involved

in foreign affairs. A Gallup poll found that 73 percent supported a constitutional amendment requiring a national referendum for the country to go
to war — and a bill to that effect was only narrowly defeated in the House.

Late in 1937 Roosevelt tried to rouse a slumbering public to the fact
that no democracy would be long safe in a world where fascist states
invaded their neighbors and cowed the other great powers into acquies-
cence. War is a contagion, he asserted, and those spreading it must be quar-
antined by peace-loving nations. "There is," the president said, "no escape
through mere isolation or neutrality."[10] Roosevelt himself, however, was
willing to push no farther; he would not ask for sanctions against Japan or
a repeal of the Neutrality Act — at least not yet. "It's a terrible thing," he
confided to a friend, "to look over your shoulder when you are trying to
lead — and find no one there."[11]

On the other side were the isolationists — or noninterventionists, as
some preferred to be called. It was as wild a group as can be imagined,
ranging from right-wing nuts like *Chicago Tribune* publisher Colonel
Robert McCormick to socialist Norman Thomas. If they could agree on
nothing else they could agree that the First World War had been a disaster
for the country — more than one hundred thousand Americans dead and
Europe thrown back into its eternal bickering and warring within a generation. Another conflict would be another disaster. "War," said Ohio senator Robert Taft, "is even worse than a German victory."[12]

Where Roosevelt saw innocent nations like Poland invaded and friendly
countries such as France and Great Britain menaced by the brutal Nazi
regime, the isolationists saw little moral distinction between the British
Empire and its foes. Gerald Nye filled ten pages of the *Congressional Record*
with the crimes of the English. "Paint me a picture of the six years of persecution of the Jews, the Catholics and Protestants in Germany," added
Idaho senator D. Worth Clark, "paint it as gory and bloody as you please,
and I will paint you one ten times as brutal, ten times as savage, ten times
as bloody in the five hundred years of British destruction, pillage, rape, and
bloodshed in Ireland."[13]

The isolationists argued that the best way to protect American democracy was to nourish it at home. "You cannot end war by waging war,"
wrote *The New Republic*. "On the contrary, nothing is more likely than that
the United States would go fascist through the very process of organizing
to defeat the fascist nations."[14] And helping the Allies beat Hitler instead
of fighting him directly would only be a sideways step into war. "If we go

into the war on the economic front," John T. Flynn noted, ". . . we will end by going to war on the military front."[15]

For the older isolationist leaders events were disturbingly familiar: An idealistic and progressive president was preaching neutrality but nudging the country toward war. And war was only the beginning. Regimentation, intolerance, hysteria — all would follow. Democratic government would be abridged, civil liberties suspended, unions emasculated. "The one way we can assure our going totalitarian quickly," lamented pacifist Oswald Harrision Villard, "will be by going to war ourselves to defeat Hitlerism."[16]

And all had been in vain, great hopes ground to fine dust, noble intentions betrayed. To Hemingway it was like the slaughter of the Chicago stockyards, only with the meat buried in the ground. "Those to whom evil is done," wrote poet W. H. Auden, "Do evil in return."[17] Cecil Day Lewis, too, was embarrassed by the grand words used to dress up gory war. "Where Are the War Poets?" he asked.

> They who in folly or mere greed
> Enslaved religion, markets, laws,
> Borrow our language now and bid
> Us to speak up in freedom's cause.
>
> It is the logic of our times,
> No subject for immortal verse —
> That we who lived by honest dreams
> Defend the bad against the worst.[18]

Aside from the pacifist fringe (Thomas, Villard), many isolationists did not stint from spending whatever it took to protect America — as long as the troops stayed on this side of the ocean. "I stand," as McCarran put it, "for the greatest navy in the world — the greatest army in the world, that we may ever be ready to defend the republic against its enemies. But I shall never vote to send those forces into battle in foreign waters or on foreign fields."[19]

There were plenty, moreover, on the left and the right who distrusted Roosevelt mightily, seeing in his constant tucking and trimming not pragmatism but expediency and deviousness that could lead to disaster. How far would he go to whip up a war frenzy? Would an American Expeditionary Force become the biggest make-work program in the history of the New Deal? "Confronted by the difficulties of a deepening domestic crisis and by the comparative ease of a foreign war, what will President Roosevelt do?"

asked Charles Beard, the eminent historian. "Judging by the past history of American politicians he will choose the latter."[20]

Given such irreconcilable premises, such diametrically opposed world-views, the interventionists and the isolationists entered into the Great Debate with a mutual distrust and suspicion that soon soured and curdled into bad faith and outright hatred. "There have been," recalled historian Arthur M. Schlesinger Jr. many years later, "a number of fierce national quarrels in my lifetime — over Communism in the later forties, over McCarthyism in the fifties, over Vietnam in the sixties — but none so tore apart families and friendships as the Great Debate."[21]

When he returned from a Comintern meeting in Moscow in late 1938, Earl Browder gave his chauffeur a tedious task: turn on a shortwave radio once a week at night. For the better part of a year there was nothing but static. Then, a week after the Hitler-Stalin pact came coded instructions. "The CPUSA should stop following Roosevelt's lead and instead take independent positions on all fundamental domestic and foreign policy issues," the cable directed. "American Communists are against involving the American people in the war because they do not want the masses to die to benefit their imperialist exploiters."[22]

The Popular Front was dead. All the energy and invective that had been hurled at Hitler in the fight against fascism was now flung at Roosevelt in the fight against imperialism. "We cannot deny the possibility, even the probability," Browder had declared less than a year before, "that only American arms can preserve the Americans from conquest by the Rome-Berlin-Tokyo alliance."[23] Now Roosevelt was a warmonger and any talk of intervention hysteria. "The Communist Party's first task," Browder would instruct the party's national convention the next spring, "is to . . . keep our country out of the European war."[24]

For professional revolutionaries such as Browder this was a painful but his-torical necessity. The September 13 *Worker*, for example, carried a front-page interview with Browder reciting the new line that both sides were equally responsible for war, while the inside pages featured an anti-Nazi speech that he had given two days earlier to twenty thousand party members in Madison Square Garden *before* receiving the latest Soviet cable. Now almost nothing was too ridiculous for Browder to say with a straight face. "The Jewish people . . . ," he declared, "have nothing to gain from taking sides. They have nothing to gain from an Allied victory, just as they have nothing to gain from victory by Hitler."[25] Even the party songbooks had to be revised. "Now is the time to get together / This is anti-fascist weather," was changed to, "Now is the time to get together / Be prepared for stormy weather."[26]

Some party members took the news like a physical blow. It sent Peggy Dennis to the floor, howling like an animal. Say it isn't so, she wailed. Think before you shout, her husband, Gene, a rising star in the party, commanded. What better way, he explained, to prevent the Nazis from ganging up with the British to attack the Soviet Union than to make peace with Germany?

But many of those drawn to the Popular Front by the party's tireless work in support of New Deal goals were repelled by Stalin's realpolitik. They scattered like pigeons before a car. One hundred thousand party members became fifty thousand members over the next two years. The front groups, too, were wrecked. These organizations attracted mass members to some noble cause, but their boards and staffs always seemed to be dominated by Communists or fellow travelers who steered the group down the party line. "The liberals were lazy," Auden explained, "while the Communists did all the work and, in consequence, won the executive power they deserved."[27] After the pact, the front groups dutifully followed the new line, but most of their members were left by the wayside. The Hollywood Anti-Fascist League became the Hollywood League for Democratic Action; the American League Against War and Fascism trans muted itself into the American Peace Mobilization. Most of their members didn't make the switch.

The Comintern offered Browder some talking points to explain the new line. "Poland was a reactionary multinational state built on the oppression of Ukrainians, Belorussians, and Jews," one secret cable explained. ". . . The international proletariat has no interest in the existence of such a parasitical state. The Soviet Union, in coming to the aid of western Ukrainian and Belorussian workers, saved eleven million people from a capitalist hell, brought them into the ranks of socialism, assured their national and cultural development, and with all of its might secured them from foreign enslavement."[28]

After decoding the cable, Browder faced a more challenging problem: How to translate this into English? Party members were soon in the streets of New York, handing out leaflets. "USSR," one flyer read, "Defends Poland."[29]

November 11, 1939, Armistice Day. Outside the Clark County Courthouse, McCarran stood below a new flagpole on the square in Las Vegas, at the base of which was a bronze plaque inscribed with the names of the state's sons who had died in the First World War.

"Let us here agree," McCarran began *". . . that the armistice then signed shall for America be an armistice for all time and that we shall not under any circumstances send American manhood to die on foreign battlefields."*

The Neutrality Act repeal had easily passed through Congress, and Roosevelt signed it into law. And then . . . nothing. Months would drag on without the German army moving an inch toward the Allies. "The phony war," William Borah called it.

"The threats to our form of government are more likely to come from unworthy agencies and undemocratic propaganda here in our very midst . . . ," McCarran continued. *"The greatest enemies of our republic may not be foreign foes, but rather domestic termites, who enjoy the spirit and atmosphere of our liberties, while at the same time they bore from within, to destroy the foundation of the very liberties they enjoy."*

American Communists, in other words, were still more of a threat to the United States than German Nazis would ever be.

"In place," McCarran finished, *"of that familiar jingle of 1917: 'The Yanks are coming,' we are announcing to the warring peoples: 'The Yanks are not coming.'"*[30]

That, as it happened, was also the latest slogan of the Communist Party.

In late November, Eleanor Roosevelt walked into a hearing room where Representative Joe Starnes of Alabama was leading the House Committee on Un-American Activities into one of its investigations of the Communist conspiracy. Starnes invited Roosevelt to sit at the committee table. "Oh, no thank you," she smiled. "I just came to listen."[31]

The president's wife then sat down in the audience with members of the American Youth Congress, a radical student group that was being investigated by the committee. The hearing soon broke for lunch, and Roosevelt invited half a dozen of the AYC members to come to the White House to eat. Among them was Joe Lash, thirty, who had quit graduate school at Columbia to become a socialist revolutionary, journeyed to Spain to fight in the Civil War (although he never saw combat), became a leader of the American Student Union (an affiliate of the AYC), and now had drifted so far to the left that, until just recently, he considered himself a nonparty Communist. At the end of the day Mrs. Roosevelt took the same group back to the White House for dinner with the president and then invited them to spend the night. It was a jolly evening, with plenty of jokes about the reactionary Un-American

Committee, the only somber note occurring when the first lady's friend Aubrey Williams, head of the National Youth Administration, took the Youth Congress group aside. "Don't let her down," he told them. "It will break her heart."[32]

Eleanor Roosevelt was a big fan of the AYC — she had spoken at its meetings, given money to its members, been invited to their weddings. She was not a fan of HUAC. "I think," she told a friend, "the Dies Committee is doing work which the Federal Bureau of Investigation could do a great deal better."[33]

HUAC had been created as a temporary panel in 1938, charged with investigating subversive activities. Under its chairman, Texas representative Martin Dies, the committee poked into the Nazi doings of German American Bund leader Fritz Kuhn, who could draw twenty thousand swastika-waving zealots to Madison Square Garden, but quickly turned most of its energy to looking for Communists, which it had no trouble finding. After the Hitler-Stalin pact, looking for Communists was like fishing at a trout farm; the pact had few defenders, and almost all of them were party members. HUAC summoned Earl Browder to its hearing room, where he justified the outlawing of political parties in the Soviet Union and admitted that he had traveled on a false passport. The Justice Department arrested Browder for passport fraud.

The more the committee looked at the Communists, the more it saw the New Deal. When the committee raided the Washington office of the American League for Peace and Democracy, it found (and published) a membership list that featured the names of 563 government officials, including New Dealers such as assistant interior secretary Oscar Chapman (who wasn't a Communist) and the National Labor Review Board's Nat Witt (who was). Soon Dies was waving around an even longer list of 1,121 Communists purportedly on the government payroll and demanding that Roosevelt fire them. When Labor Secretary Frances Perkins decided not to try to deport Australian-born longshoreman labor leader Harry Bridges as a Communist because of a pending Supreme Court challenge to the law, HUAC's J. Parnell Thomas introduced a resolution to impeach her. Was it a coincidence, Thomas wondered, that Mrs. Roosevelt and cabinet members such as Ickes and Wallace had sent greetings and spoke to so many front groups such as the American Youth Congress? "It seems," he concluded, "as though the New Deal was hand in glove with the Communist Party."[34]

The irony is that Roosevelt and many liberals, and even socialists like

Joe Lash, had just decided that they wanted nothing more to do with the Communists. But did that mean that demolishing all the good works that the party had been involved in building? The Youth Congress was a good example. Under its umbrella were groups as diverse as the YMCA and the Young Communist League. Joe Lash's American Student Union was far closer to the latter than the former, but he believed that he could fight the party members in the leadership and save the organization. Thus when HUAC called him to testify, Lash was not prepared to share his inner turmoil with the committee. He would combat the Communists, he vowed to himself, but he would not Redbait. "I would fight them on the basis of policy," he recalled. "I would not set myself up as a private Dies Committee."[35] Instead, Lash insulted Dies with an inane ditty that compared the chairman to Alka-Seltzer. Lash didn't deny that there were Communists in the youth movement, but he told the committee that they should not be attacked. "It is the job of those of us who believe in democracy," he said, ". . . to show them how democracy works."[36]

Watching from the press table, Eleanor Roosevelt saw something in the young man that drew her to him. Lash seemed to be struggling, swimming in strange waters, and Roosevelt instinctively wanted to help him. She, too, had concerns about the Youth Congress. Are you Communists? she asked her young friends. No, they assured her, they were not. "Undoubtedly there are some people in any group that we would not approve of," she told her friend Bernard Baruch, who had helped the AYC at her behest but grew suspicious of the organization after HUAC's investigation, "but as long as the work done is creditable work, I think we must go ahead and help this group."[37]

Three months later, in February 1940, the Youth Congress held its national convention in Washington. Once again, Eleanor Roosevelt invited the youth group home, arranging for her husband to address four thousand AYC members on the White House's rear lawn. The young people, however, were a walking reproach to her husband's defense policy. In the rain they waved soggy isolationist signs (SCHOOLS NOT BATTLESHIPS) and sang antiwar songs ("No Major, no Major, we will not go / We'll wager, we'll wager, this ain't our show"). For an hour they waited outside the White House in the drizzle, and Mrs. Roosevelt waited with them.

The president appeared on the rear portico. His wife joined him. Roosevelt defended the New Deal and extolled democracy and excoriated the Youth Congress because its New York chapter had passed a resolution supporting the Soviet invasion of Finland. "Unadulterated twaddle," he said. Boos rippled through the crowd like distant thunder. Roosevelt denounced the Soviet Union. "A dictatorship as absolute as any other dictatorship in the world," he called it.[38] The boos grew louder.

Finally the soaked and sullen youths trudged off and with them went a piece of Eleanor Roosevelt's broken heart.

In December 1939 Pat and Dode Jackson threw a small dinner party and had a few New Dealers over, including Alaska territorial governor Ernest Gruening and Senator Lew Schwellenbach. The talk turned to Communism. Gruening insisted that government officials and labor leaders ought to sign non-Communist oaths and dared Jackson to sign one; Schwellenbach said it would be better to take away the constitutional rights of people proved to be acting as the agents of foreign powers. Jackson didn't think much of either idea. "I have no patience," he retorted, "with my many friends who now take the position that because a person or persons refused to condemn the Soviet action in Finland he or they are therefore Communists."[39]

In the ashes of the Popular Front another Red Scare was smoldering. In Congress anti-Communist bills — the Foreign Agents Registration Act, the Hatch Act, the Smith Act — were popping up almost every day. Earl Browder was about to go on trial and faced four years in federal prison for passport violations. The rest of the party leadership was getting ready for a government crackdown, hiding mimeograph machines and preparing to go underground.

Liberals were at one another's throats. In the National Lawyers Guild, Jerome Frank, Morris Ernst, and other liberals had tried to seize control of the organization from the Communists and their friends, such as Lee Pressman, but failed to pass a resolution equating fascism and Communism. Then the battleground shifted to the American Civil Liberties Union. The ACLU had long been a favorite target of conspiracy-mongers such as Elizabeth Dilling, but with the end of the Popular Front, the organization suddenly found itself more threatened than it had been in twenty years, when the government raided its offices. Martin Dies focused HUAC's attention on the organization, and Browder didn't help when he told the committee that the ACLU was one of the transmission belts that the party used to influence public opinion (the ACLU returned the favor when it declined to join the Earl Browder Defense Fund). Dies demanded that the Justice Department indict the ACLU for failing to register as an agent of a foreign power.

Dies then had a curious change of mind. In October 1939 he had a few drinks with the ACLU's Morris Ernst and Arthur Garfield Hays at the Hay-Adams Hotel in Washington. No one present revealed what they talked about, but Dies soon issued the ACLU a clean bill of health. The fact that a draft ACLU report with unexpected praise for HUAC started circulating after the cocktail meeting convinced many liberals that Ernst had cut an unholy deal with Dies. Pat Jackson was one of many who was furious. "Any attempt to play ball with Martin Dies must spring either from absolute immaturity politically, or from a desire to utilize the kind of dirty tactics which he employs . . . ," Jackson fumed to Ernst. "I cannot for one minute go along with you in the belief that any good can come to anyone from palavering or cajoling with so completely an unprincipled person as Martin Dies."[40]

To Jackson, Martin Dies and HUAC were a bigger threat to civil liberties than the feeble Communist Party. To appease Dies, Jackson thought, was as bad as appeasing Hitler. "Morris," Jackson insulted his old friend, "you really are pulling a Dies on me."[41] And after a few drinks, Jackson began to tell anyone who would listen that that's just what Ernst was doing. "There are large numbers of us who will publicly withdraw from the ACLU if it shifts its role," Jackson threatened Hays, "as the projected report on the Dies Committee implies it intends to do. . . . In these disturbing days we feel more than ever that there is a need for absolute and unwavering devotion to the Bill of Rights, regardless of how unpopular the propagandists are who we, in our role as civil libertarians, seek to protect in the exercise of their civil rights."[42]

Jackson's boozy talk soon got back to Ernst. "I am a little hesitant about even writing this frankly to you for fear that you will gossip on this new score," Ernst scolded Jackson. ". . . I was hurt by your promiscuous and unfounded talk, but my hurt was not beyond anything but the fact that one Pat Jackson, who could have written a letter or picked up a telephone to get the truth, went screwy in the same manner as the Dies Committee. It is difficult to know just why I still have a deep affection for you, but I have . . . maybe you were just tight."[43]

"I have been tight off and on in the past several weeks,"[44] Jackson admitted.

Just before eight o'clock on the evening of May 7, 1940, a stout woman with sad Irish eyes walked into the City Club in New York. Once she had been the Rebel Girl. Wobbly songster Joe Hill crooned:

There are blue blooded queens and princesses,
Who have charms made of diamonds and pearl;
But the only and thoroughbred lady
Is the Rebel Girl.[45]

Thirty years and a hundred pounds later, Elizabeth Gurley Flynn was a Stalinist matron. Twenty years before she had helped found the ACLU. Tonight the organization's board was meeting to decide if she was fit to remain an officer of the civil liberties group. No one accused Flynn of any wrongdoing; her mere membership in the Communist Party — her political affiliation — was enough to bring her before the board for an expulsion trial. A great and terrible reckoning had come to American liberalism. The question split the sky of the left like lightning: Was it possible to cooperate with the Communists?

In 1917 Roger Baldwin and Max Eastman had formed the National Civil Liberties Bureau to defend men who refused to be drafted into the Great War. No state, they believed, should have the power to compel men to kill against their conscience. And freedom of conscience was meaningless without freedom of speech. That was not a popular idea during the war. The Wilson administration attacked antiwar groups such as the Socialist Party and the Industrial Workers of the World, banning their publications from the mail and arresting their leaders — including 169 Wobblies, one of whom was Elizabeth Gurley Flynn.

Flynn had been first arrested for activism at fifteen; at sixteen she quit high school to become a Wobbly organizer. In 1915 she penned a pamphlet called "Sabotage" ("Its necessity is its excuse for existence"[46]), which formed the basis for her indictment two years later under the Espionage Act, which made it a crime to interfere with the war effort. Some Wobblies got twenty years in prison, but Flynn's case was dismissed. In 1920 she helped found the American Civil Liberties Union.

When the Supreme Court first began to hear free speech cases triggered by socialist opposition to World War I, the justices blandly supported the government's right to curb dissent. In 1919, for example, the Court upheld (*Schenck v. United States*) the conviction of a socialist who passed out leaflets urging conscripts to write to Congress to repeal the draft. But over the next decade Oliver Wendell Holmes ("Every idea is an incitement"[47]) and Louis Brandeis ("silence coerced by law — the argument of force in its worst form"[48]) wrote a series of eloquent dissents that created the framework for protecting radical speech as long as it fell short of incitement to immediate revolution. In 1931 the Court ruled *(Stromberg v. California)* that just because a Communist raised a Russian flag at a radical summer camp, she could not be convicted for advocating subversion. Then in 1937 the Court *(Herndon v. Lowry)* reversed the conviction of a black Communist busted for recruiting party members in Atlanta.

That was the year that Flynn joined the Communist Party. In 1939 Flynn was reelected to the board of the ACLU. Also on the board were two other charter members whose sharp political differences were submerged by the high tide of the Popular Front: Harry F. Ward and Norman Thomas. Ward, an ethics professor at the Union Theological Seminary and head of the fellow-traveling American League for Peace and Democracy, never met a Communist he couldn't cooperate with; Thomas, the perennial socialist candidate for president, had been trying to bar Communists from the board since 1934, when they had violently raided a socialist rally in Madison Square Garden. But with the Communists supporting the New Deal, the ACLU found it easy enough to work with the party in important civil liberties cases, such as the Scottsboro trial. Indeed, ACLU director Roger Baldwin seemed to be involved with every Popular Front group that could afford a mimeograph machine.

In 1934 the ACLU set down its credo that even totalitarian groups that would deny freedom to others deserved constitutional protections. "Shall We Defend Free Speech for Nazis in America?" the group asked in a booklet and answered in the affirmative. Five years later the anti-Communist members of the board succeeded in revising the booklet to: "Why We Defend Free Speech for Nazis, Fascists — and Communists." Lumping in Communists with Nazis infuriated many in the ACLU who continued to insist on a moral distinction between left and right totalitarians.

But even if the ACLU would fight for free speech for the odious, did it have to admit them to its leadership council? How could someone who supported Stalin's denial of liberty in Russia be taken seriously as an advocate for freedom of conscience in the United States? "Communists," Norman Thomas wrote after the Hitler-Stalin pact, "belong on the board of the Civil Liberties Union as much or as little as fascists who also want the protection of the Bill of Rights — until they seize power. To argue the contrary seems to me to be either conscious or subconscious hypocrisy, the product of the sloppiest sort of thinking."[49]

On February 5, 1940 — a couple of weeks after a federal judge sentenced Earl Browder to prison for four years — the ACLU board voted to deny leadership positions to totalitarians. Flynn was asked to resign.

Harry Ward quit as chairman in protest. Many non-Communist liberals were outraged. "By the purge resolution the American Civil Liberties Union encourages the very tendencies it was intended to fight," read an open letter to the board signed by seventeen liberals, including Pat Jackson. "It sets an example less liberal organizations will not be slow to imitate. It places the prestige of our foremost defender of civil liberties behind the idea that Communists or Communist sympathizers or that infinitely extensible category of the 'fellow-travelers' are properly to be barred from certain types of offices and treated as less than first-class citizens."[50]

So on this May night a bitterly divided ACLU board met to decide what to do about the Rebel Girl. For six hours arguments raged. The board as much as Flynn was on trial, claimed Corliss Lamont. "I refuse to resign," Flynn said, "because I will not be a party to saving the face of this anti-civil-liberties majority nor to whitewashing their Red-baiting. . . . Ernst playing with the Dies Committee is harmful to the prestige of the ACLU."[51]

Flynn did not take an unequivocal stand for civil liberties. She did not assert that Nazis had a right to sit on the board. Instead, she argued that there was no conflict between her beliefs in Communism and civil liberties. She introduced a copy of the Soviet constitution to prove her point. "The USSR is not a totalitarian dictatorship," she said. "It is a socialist state of workers and peasants."[52] There is more democracy in the Soviet Union than in the American South, she added. The Supreme Soviet has a far greater proportion of women than the U.S. Congress. "The USSR," she said, "guarantees and the majority of her vast population enjoy a larger degree of civil liberties than are enjoyed by the population of the British Empire."[53]

Flynn had implicitly conceded that if the Soviet Union was a totalitarian country, then a Communist would not be morally fit to sit on the board. Flynn, like many Communists, was a great humanitarian but not such a great human. She once compared Earl Browder to Jesus and Stalin to Moses. Eleanor Roosevelt, she thought, was a Wall Street whore. She forgot her son's birthday.

Arthur Hays got to the crux of the issue. "Do you believe in civil liberties and democracy or the Bill of Rights as a way of life, or merely as a means to bring about a Soviet system in this country?" he asked.

"A point of order!" challenged Abe Isserman, one of Flynn's most devoted defenders. Years later it would be disclosed that Isserman was one of three secret Communists on the board.

Flynn didn't answer the question. The debate dragged on until after two in the morning, when the board finally voted, 10 to 9, to expel Flynn.[54]

"You are," Flynn said, "killing the ACLU."*[55]

Roosevelt had a gift for J. Edgar Hoover.

On May 16, 1940, Roosevelt had gone to the Capitol to ask Congress for a massive military buildup. In April, Hitler had lunged into Denmark and Norway. The next month Germany invaded Holland, Belgium, and France. Britain seemed likely to be next. "We expect to be attacked,"[56] Prime Minister Winston Churchill wrote to Roosevelt. The next day the president implored Congress for a billion dollars more for defense, for an army twice its present size, and for at least fifty thousand new fighter planes a year — a tenfold jump in production. Congress thundered its approval in a barrage of applause. Not everyone was thrilled. Telegrams flooded into the White House opposing the arms buildup. Two days after the speech, Roosevelt handed a bundle of critical letters to Steve Early. Give them to Hoover, he said. "It was the president's idea," Early told Hoover, "that you might like to go over these, noting the names and addresses of the senders."[57]

The president knew his man. Like Roosevelt with his stamp collection, Hoover loved nothing more than to add to his intelligence files. Hoover had been an inveterate collector and cataloger of information since his days as a clerk in the Library of Congress. In 1917 he brought his passion for the Dewey decimal system to the Justice Department, where he became chief of the newly created General Intelligence Division, stuffing file cabinets with index cards listing radical organizations and their members. Two years later Hoover's men were taking notes at the founding of the American Communist Party. When Felix Frankfurter and other legal eminences protested the illegalities of the Palmer Raids, Hoover opened dossiers on the law professors. All of which was supposed to end in 1924 when the attorney general ordered Hoover, who became the head of the Bureau of Investigation, to stop spying on political groups and to confine his investigations to violations of federal law. Hoover continued to fatten his files, but kept them in secret, the first items in an immense "Do Not File" archive that would swell and bulge for another fifty years.

Then one day in 1936 Roosevelt invited the director of what was now called the Federal Bureau of Investigation to the White House to talk about fascism and Communism. Roosevelt was growing increasingly alarmed by fascism; Hoover had never stopped being alarmed by Communism.

---

*The ACLU posthumously reinstated Flynn in 1976.

Hoover explained that the FBI was barred from political investigations, but pointed out that under an old wartime law the bureau did have the authority to conduct intelligence probes if requested to by the State Department. The next day Roosevelt mentioned this to Secretary of State Cordell Hull, who turned to Hoover and made the request. Should I put it in writing? Hull asked. No, Roosevelt shook his head, let's keep it between the three of us. "Obtain from all possible sources," clattered tele-type machines in FBI field offices around the country, "information con-cerning subversive activities being conducted in the United States."[58]

In March 1939 Hoover sent Attorney General Frank Murphy a memo suggesting that a State Department plan to coordinate various espionage investigations could result in a repeat of the postwar Red Scare. Instead of having different federal agencies chasing after spies, Hoover recommended that various departments forward any possible leads to the bureau for investigation — which, by the way, would require that the FBI be granted the specific authorization to conduct ongoing intelligence investigations. Murphy passed the memo on to Roosevelt, who signed it. The FBI hired 150 new agents, opened ten additional field offices, and asked Congress for an emergency $1.5 million appropriation. Then days after the German invasion of Poland, Hoover assembled a custodial detention list of subversives who were to be arrested in an emergency situation. He didn't get around to men-tioning the list to the attorney general until ten months later.

So when Roosevelt gave Hoover the stack of telegrams protesting his rearmament program, the director was only too happy to dig through his files and send the president reports on his critics. Roosevelt forwarded more letters. "The two men," recalled Solicitor General Francis Biddle, "liked and understood each other."[59] In two weeks the FBI conducted background checks on 131 of the president's opponents, including Senator Burt Wheeler and Charles Lindbergh. "Prepare a nice letter to Edgar Hoover," Roosevelt told his secretary, "thanking him for all the reports on investigations he has made and tell him I appreciate the fine job he is doing."[60]

Roosevelt had yet another gift for Hoover. On May 21, three days after he first sent the director names to investigate, Roosevelt issued a secret wiretapping directive. Congress had banned wiretaps, and the Supreme Court had twice ruled that taps were unconstitutional. Nonetheless Roosevelt told Attorney General Robert Jackson, who had replaced Murphy, that he could grant the FBI, on a case-by-case basis, the power to eavesdrop on people suspected of subversive activities, especially aliens. The attorney general then delegated the authority to Hoover.

In February the FBI arrested twelve veterans of the Abraham Lincoln Brigade, charging them with recruiting for a foreign army — which they had done three years earlier. Although the charges were dropped, the old progressives in the Senate were alarmed. "Unless we do something to stop this furor of adulation and praise as being omnipotent," George Norris warned, even as his old friend Roosevelt was encouraging Hoover, "we shall have an organization — the organization of the FBI — which, instead of protecting our people from the civil acts of criminals, will itself in the end direct the government by tyrannical force, as the history of the world shows has always been the case when secret police and secret detectives have been snooping around the homes of honest men."[61]

Later that month McCarran called over to the FBI but couldn't reach Hoover. Instead he arranged a meeting with one of the director's deputies, at which McCarran denounced his Senate colleagues for attacking the chief. "If Mr. Hoover has been wrong, then it ought to be brought out," McCarran said. "If Mr. Hoover has not been wrong, Mr. Hoover ought to defend himself and furnish information to his friends in the Senate who would be glad to defend him."[62]

It was the beginning of a long relationship between McCarran and Hoover.

On Tuesday night, July 16, Senate majority leader Alben Barkley took to the stage at the Chicago Stadium. Standing in front of a huge picture of Roosevelt that literally hovered over the convention, Barkley delivered a message from FDR. "The president has never had, and has not today, any desire or purpose to continue in the office . . . ," Barkley said. "All the delegates to this convention are free to vote for any candidate."[63]

"We want Roosevelt!" a voice boomed through loudspeakers around the hall.

The previous month the Republicans had nominated utilities magnate Wendell Willkie to run for the president. The morning before the start of the convention Jim Farley, postmaster, head of the Democratic National Committee, and presidential candidate, had called the convention to order not knowing if Roosevelt was running for a third term. For the past couple of years Roosevelt had been encouraging the presidential ambitions of a number of possible successors. The president pleaded that what he really wanted to do was go back to Hyde Park, to live the life of a gentleman squire. "I want to take care of my trees," he said.[64] Then there was the unwritten rule of American politics that limited the president to two terms. George Washington drew the line there, and no president since had dared to run for a third term. And polls found that a majority of Americans didn't want Roosevelt to break it. Just before Farley left for Chicago, he tried to get Roosevelt to issue a firm no. "Jim," the president said, "if nominated and elected, I could not in these times refuse to the inaugural oath, even if I knew I would be dead within thirty days."[65]

"Everybody wants Roosevelt!" boomed the amplified voice, which belonged to a henchman of Chicago mayor Edward Kelly, who was hiding in the basement with a microphone.

"The world wants Roosevelt!"

Not everybody. McCarran came to Chicago as the de facto leader of Nevada's dozen delegates. Key Pittman was chairman in name, but the senior senator had only been elected to the delegation at McCarran's behest, so tight was his control over the state party. Since his reelection, McCarran had systematically consolidated his power, rewarding his friends with patronage and purging his enemies. At the same time, Pittman was losing his grip. In his drunken dotage, it was all the senior senator could do to remain standing up. At sixty-eight Pittman looked a decade older, years of alcoholism having eroded both his body and spirit. Once the greatest threat to McCarran's political hegemony, Pittman was now only a danger to himself. Recently, for example, Pittman had drunkenly pawed at Roosevelt, insisting that the president order the British fleet to steam for American harbors to escape Nazi capture. The president worried that Pittman would repeat his advice to reporters. "But it appeared," Ickes noted, "that Pittman was either too drunk to do that or not drunk enough."[66]

Roosevelt!

McCarran walked out of a door marked LADIES REST ROOM with a smile on his face. It was Wednesday, a month after Paris fell to the Nazis and a week after Luftwaffe bombers lumbered across the English Channel and began the battle of Britain. Fourteen hours earlier McCarran had gone into a platform drafting meeting threatening a floor fight if the party didn't adopt a peace plank. He also wanted a plank putting the party on record against a third term. South Carolina senator James F. Byrnes told the committee that the president wanted a free hand in foreign affairs. McCarran and Burt Wheeler and Massachusetts senator David Walsh balked. Two months before, the president had declared that the United States needed a massive defense buildup and then declared seventy thousand tons of planes and tanks and guns as surplus, and sent it to England. What would he do with *more* power?

The platform committee bickered for hours. Finally McCarran, Byrnes, Wheeler, and Walsh left the committee room to work out a compromise. The only place they could find to talk was the ladies' rest room. They locked the door. Finally Byrnes suggested that Roosevelt might accept a peace plank if it contained an exception in the event that the United States was attacked. "The American people are determined that war, raging in Europe, Asia and Africa, shall not come to America," they wrote. "We will not participate in foreign wars, and we will not send our army, naval or air forces to fight in foreign lands outside of the Americas — *except in case of attack.*"[67] McCarran was pleased. "If we follow the principles of this platform," he said, "there's no danger of getting into war."[68]

Roosevelt! came the cheers that night when Alabama's Lister Hill nominated the president for a third term, and this time the fervor was real.

Bedlam broke loose on the convention floor. People jumped and clapped and waved and yelled. McCarran didn't budge from his seat. Wearing a light summer suit and a plaid tie, he glumly held the Nevada standard like a medieval knight riding into combat. Then Farley was nominated; McCarran stood and clapped. More nominations followed: the estranged vice president John Garner, the anti–New Deal senator Millard Tydings, and the elderly secretary of state Cordell Hull. The balloting began. McCarran cast four of Nevada's six votes for Farley; Pittman gave two to Roosevelt. It was an avalanche: Roosevelt 946½, Farley 72½, Garner 61, Tydings 9, Hull 5. Farley then moved to make it unanimous.

Roosevelt! it was.

On Thursday evening it was time to pick the vice president.

Propped up on the speaker's platform, Key Pittman, who in his cups had legs weaker than the president's, was prepared to nominate McCarran for the vice presidency when it came time to poll the Nevada delegation. When the state's turn came, McCarran picked up the megaphone. "Nevada," he said, "has no nominations and no second to make."[69] House Speaker William Bankhead was nominated and cheered wildly. Federal loan administrator Jesse Jones and Federal Security Agency head Paul McNutt were also nominated and heartily applauded. Henry Wallace was nominated and booed.

In the wee hours of the morning Roosevelt finally tapped his agriculture secretary as his running mate. "He thinks right," Roosevelt told Farley.[70] As unpopular as Roosevelt's renomination had been with the party's conservative wing, Wallace's elevation to the White House threatened to give heart attacks to anti–New Deal Democrats. "Three years of bitter factional war, purges and personal grudges, have honeycombed all ranks with dissension and animosity," reported Drew Pearson and Robert S. Allen in their "Merry-Go-Round" column. "New Dealers hate the Old Guarders, who reciprocate with interest."[71] Wallace, said Oklahoma governor Leon Phillips, was my second choice. Who was your first? asked another governor. "Any son of a bitch — red, black, white, or yellow — who can get the nomination," he replied.[72] McCarran had thought Wallace a socialist from the moment he met him. "Wallace," he said, "frowns on the Congress."[73]

Wallace was a lapsed Republican, a man of both science and mysticism; he invented a hybrid corn that vastly increased yields, and he studied Theosophy (copies of his "Dear Guru" letters to a Russian occultist were circulating in Washington). He once tried to live on experimental cow feed; on his wedding day he almost drove off from church with his bride still standing on the sidewalk. The hissing continued for Wallace. His wife, Ilo, was close to tears. "Why are they booing my Henry?" she said.[74] Wallace, as usual, stared into space.

Eleanor Roosevelt walked up to the podium and gave the convention a tongue-lashing. "This is no ordinary time," she lectured, "no time for thinking about anything except what we can best do for the country as a whole, and that responsibility is on each and every one of us as individuals."[75]

The voting started. McCarran gave Bankhead four votes. Pittman, usually as loyal as a dog to his president, tossed Jones a vote and Wallace half a vote. By the final tally Wallace won by almost two to one. "I was, frankly, amazed," Roosevelt told George Norris, the one progressive in the Senate not to break with him over foreign affairs, "by the terrific drive which was put on by the old-line conservatives . . . what you and I can privately call 'The Hater's Club' — strange bedfellows like Wheeler and McCarran and Tydings and Glass and John J. O'Connor. . . ."[76]

A few weeks later McCarran was back in Chicago, steaming on a stage in the brutal summer sun. He was supposed to speak. He was threatening to leave.

It was a blistering August day at Soldier Field, a classical-styled stadium on the city's southern lakefront named for the fallen of World War I. Fifty thousand people crowded into the stands to see Lindy. At two-thirty Colonel McCormick's limo pulled up to the stadium and a lanky man in a dark suit stepped into the bright afternoon: Charles Lindbergh, who was almost immediately mobbed by fans. Across the nation Lindbergh was increasingly vilified, but in Chicago he was more of a hero than ever.

New York and Chicago were the London and Berlin of the Great Debate. New York was the interventionist heart of the country, where *New Yorker* and *Time-Life* veteran editor Ralph Ingersoll had recently launched a radical, unabashedly pro-British newspaper called *PM* that refused advertising, bludgeoned isolationists with glee, and attracted some of the great writers and photographers of the day. "This is an anti-fascist paper," Ingersoll declared. "If this is a call to war, perhaps the facts demand it."[77] As Dr. Seuss (the pen name of Theodor Seuss Geisel) wrote under one drawing of a bird sitting peacefully amid the exploding bombs of a battle:

> Said a bird in the midst of a Blitz,
> "Up to now they've scored very few hitz,
> So I'll sit on my canny
> Old Star Spangled Fanny . . ."
> And on it he sitz and he sitz.[78]

The epicenter of the interventionist movement was the aptly named International Building in Rockefeller Center, where several floors housed the offices of some of the more vociferous pro-war groups: Fight for Freedom (twenty-second floor), whose members included columnist Joe Alsop, as well as lawyers Dean Acheson and Allen Dulles; British Security Coordination (thirty-eighth), which ran London's covert operations in North America; and the British Press Service (forty-fourth).

Chicago, on the other hand, was the citadel of isolationism. On Michigan Avenue, just north of the river, Colonel Robert McCormick's spiky Tribune Tower rose like a Gothic cathedral of the nonintervention movement. McCormick, who had been at Groton one class ahead of Roosevelt, was so conservative that he thought Herbert Hoover a socialist. Roosevelt he despised: "That bastard in the White House," he called him.[79] The McCormick empire included the flagship *Chicago Tribune,* the largest paper in the country, with a circulation of more than one million, the *Washington Times-Herald,* the largest paper in the capital and published by his cousin Cissy Patterson, and the *New York Daily News,* published by his cousin Joe Patterson. The McCormick–Patterson Axis, Roosevelt dubbed the chain.

Lindbergh made his way to the speaker's platform. Uniformed veterans decorated the stage like so many flags. A ninety-year-old vet was saying something at the podium, but Lindbergh was too distracted to listen. There was, as ever, a whirl around the aviator. People thronged Lindbergh with greetings, autograph books, pleas to speak at other gatherings. He agreed to have dinner after the rally with a Yale Law School student named Bob Stuart who wanted to tell him about a new antiwar group he was forming called America First.

Then Lindbergh had to mollify McCarran, who was scheduled to speak after him. The senator was livid when he found out that the radio networks were planning to broadcast Lindbergh's speech but not his. He threatened to leave. Couldn't Lindbergh shorten his speech? the organizers implored. No, Lindbergh said, he could not, but he would switch places with the senator and give him his air time. No, the organizers said, the networks had already touted a Lindbergh broadcast. McCarran eventually agreed to stay.[80]

Lindbergh spoke for twenty minutes. "In the past," he said, "we have dealt with a Europe dominated by England and France. In the future we may have to deal with a Europe dominated by Germany. . . . Cooperation is never impossible. . . . But if we refuse to consider treaties with the dominant nation of Europe, regardless of who that may be, we remove all possibility of peace."[81]

The aviator towered over the senator by his side. Tall and thin in a heavy suit, his hair closely cropped and thinning at the temples, Lindbergh stood a head taller than McCarran, short and plump and rumpled in a light summer suit, his face fleshy, his thick white hair whipped around by the merciful breeze blowing in from Lake Michigan. McCarran pulled out the reading glasses that he usually kept hidden in his jacket pocket when in public.

"Watch out for propaganda which may lead us into the new world war," McCarran warned. ". . . The last war we fought did not end wars. It settled nothing, but it bewildered men, and made it possible for mediocre men to become dictators. Despair and helplessness made it possible for egomaniacs to gain control. Mass murder is on again."[82]

McCarran kept talking for an hour as if his words alone could hold off the terrible thing that he feared so much. Before long the crowd melted away like ice on this hot summer day. Evaporating, it seemed, like the chance for peace.

It was a frightening fall. In London men, women, and children cowered in subway tunnels while their city burned above; in two weeks the Royal Air Force lost almost a quarter of its fighter pilots in combat. In September, Congress passed the first peacetime conscription bill in the nation's history, and soon sixteen million men, ages twenty-one to thirty-five — Sammy McCarran among them — were registered for the draft.

Then Roosevelt announced that the United States was swapping fifty old destroyers with the British in exchange for bases in Newfoundland and Bermuda. Roosevelt knew Congress would never approve of such a deal, so, after sounding out Willkie to make sure that his rival would not oppose the deal, he issued an executive order to effect the trade. Willkie supported the move but sniffed at the method. "The most arbitrary and dictatorial action ever taken by any president," he said.[83]

The Great Debate flipped old friends and foes and made for a very strange election.

The Republican candidate — who in fact had been a Democrat until very recently, agreed with most of the New Deal's social legislation, and was an ardent internationalist — had so far refrained from talking trash about Roosevelt. Now, with the election just around the corner, Willkie began to call Roosevelt a warmonger. "If his promise to keep our boys out of foreign wars is not better than his promise to balance the budget," he said, "they're already almost on the transports."[84]

The Communist candidate — who four years earlier ran a stealth campaign for Roosevelt — now lamented the fact that the president ("An unlimited military dictator"[85]) had helped Willkie steal the nomination from isolationist senator Robert Taft. "Can anyone doubt that the result would have been such a Republican landslide that it would have wrecked the Democratic Party for all time?" Browder brayed.[86]

John Lewis — whose CIO members functioned as Democratic foot soldiers in the last election and whose dues bankrolled the campaign — took to the radio and said that labor must oppose Roosevelt or he would resign as president of the union. "America needs no superman. . . ," he roared. "You who may be about to die in a foreign war, created at the whim of an international meddler, should you salute your Caesar? . . . Lead the revolt against the candidate who plays at a game that may make cannon fodder of your sons."[87]

On election night journalist John Flynn gave a radio speech on behalf of Writers for Willkie. Although Flynn was unable to say a word in favor of the Republican, he said quite a few against Roosevelt. "If you vote for him . . . ," he said, "the blood of your sons will be not merely upon his, but on your own hands. . . . I would be against Christ himself if he were running for a third term."[88]

Roosevelt, his temper frayed, his ears ringing with charges of dictatorship and warmongering, shot back. He attacked appeasers and foreign propagandists, those who called themselves Americans but whose counsel would destroy America. "Your boys," he promised the week before the election, "are not going to be sent into any foreign wars."[89]

McCarran, back in the Naval Hospital, voted for Willkie. "Tomorrow night is the big night," he exulted on election eve to his aide Eva Adams. ". . . It is a beautiful day in Washington. It is going to be a beautiful day Wednesday morning. You watch what I say."[90] Adams warned her boss to be discreet with his Republican sympathies. "I'm frankly hoping . . . that you will continue this silence," she told him. "I think it is quietly eloquent to those who know you."[91]

Roosevelt won, 27 million votes to 22 million, 55 percent to 44 percent, the smallest plurality since 1916. FDR was convinced that Willkie's backers and Germany had cut a deal to force the British to make peace in return for the Nazis leaving the Western Hemisphere alone. Late on election night, Joe Lash was with the first family in Hyde Park. "We seemed to have averted a putsch, Joe,"[92] Roosevelt said.

Soon after the election Roosevelt went fishing in the Caribbean on a navy cruiser. The president, John Flynn noted, had a strange love for vacationing on military ships.

In October 1940 Key Pittman made a rare visit to Nevada. He did this every six years or so when he had to run for reelection. He stayed at the Riverside Hotel and haunted its Corner Bar like some long-forgotten ghost. The less the voters saw of Pittman, the better. Once he dallied in the bar too long before a Rotary Club luncheon, and when he was finally dragged up to the podium he seemed to think that he was at the racetrack. "The horses — I got the horses started," he slurred, "and they go around the track, and around the track, and around the track, and around the — oh, hell, I can't get 'em stopped."[93]

Pittman looked worse than ever. Always gaunt, he now seemed positively skeletal, black holes where his cheeks had once been, his eyes gone to slits. "I am as weak as a sick cat . . . ," he told a friend. "I am run ragged here with all kinds of trouble."[94]

Trouble came in a bottle. Pittman was one of the most loyal yet ineffectual of Democrats. As chairman of the Foreign Relations Committee he could have been a powerful force in the Senate to help his president. But Pittman found it easier to quietly sip whiskey during committee hearings than to take the reins. Back in Nevada he seemed thirstier than ever. "He continues to try to drink the entire supply of John Barleycorn and keeps making a fool out of himself . . . ," Reno postmaster Pete Petersen reported to McCarran. "He has been drunk practically every day he has been in the state."[95]

Running, or more precisely stumbling, for a sixth term, Pittman could barely stand up during his speeches. Once he wet himself in front of a room of supporters. "In Sparks, hardly anyone could hear him, which probably was lucky," Eva Adams wrote to McCarran.[96] At another rally Congressman James Scrugham announced that Pittman couldn't appear because of a "sore throat," just before the candidate stumbled onto the stage and called his colleague a "liar." Some Democrats carped that Pittman seemed to be trying to elect the Republican challenger; in Sparks he had to be carried off the platform.

Four days before the election, Pittman woke up ill at the Riverside. On election eve he was taken to Washoe General Hospital. He never checked out. On November 5 Pittman beat Republican Sam Platt by six thousand votes, the largest margin of his career. On November 10, just after midnight, he died. The rumor in Reno was that Pittman had actually died before the election and that Democrats had put his body in a tub of ice so they could say he died after the polls closed and name his successor. Platt went to his own grave believing that he had lost to a dead man. In a way, he had.

McCarran himself was in a sickbed at the Naval Hospital when he heard the news. His condition suddenly improved. On a special train carrying the congressional delegation out west, McCarran was jolly and smiling. He was finally rid of the man who had blocked his way for four decades. McCarran checked into the Riverside like a conquering king seizing a palace and held court in Pittman's old throne room, the Corner Bar. Some of McCarran's colleagues had never seen him so happy. "It was the most jolly affair I ever attended," remembered Rhode Island senator Theodore Green.[97]

Reno never saw a larger funeral. Hundreds packed the Municipal Auditorium across from the Riverside. McCarran praised Pittman as a man whose abiding thought was the cause of silver — and in Nevada there was no higher praise. McCarran's eulogy was the obverse of what his own would have been. "Key Pittman was an unswerving party man . . . ," McCarran said. "He carried the banner of the administration regardless of his own convictions. This was his policy in all things political. He stood high in the councils of his party at all times from the occasion when he first entered the Senate until the day of his passing."[98]

The honorary pallbearers that led the procession to Mountain View Cemetery on the edge of town constituted a phalanx of McCarran's enemies: men such as William Woodburn, the state Democratic chairman who'd done his best to keep McCarran off every ballot, and George Bartlett, who'd beaten him out of the nomination for the House decades earlier.

It didn't matter. McCarran was now the state's senior senator. They might as well be buried with Pittman.

CHAPTER 10

An Act of War

The thought struck me that ten or fifteen years from now when writers sit down to put together the sorry story of these times, our side of this controversy will be rather poorly represented.[1]

— John Flynn to Charles Lindbergh

Pat McCarran squirmed. He fidgeted. He frowned.

Like a boy dragged to church against his will, he wanted, desperately, to be somewhere else. McCarran looked up at Roosevelt.

"At no previous time has American security been as seriously threatened from without as it is today," the president told a joint session of Congress. "...The democratic way of life is at this moment being directly assailed in every part of the world — assailed either by arms, or by secret spreading of poisonous propaganda by those who seek to destroy unity and promote discord in nations that are still at peace. During sixteen long months this assault has blotted out the whole pattern of democratic life in an appalling number of independent nations, great and small. The assailants are still on the march, threatening other nations, great and small. Therefore, as your president, performing my constitutional duty to 'give to the Congress information of the state of the Union,' I find it, unhappily, necessary to report that the future and the safety of our country and of our democracy are overwhelmingly involved in events far beyond our borders."

In the third-row aisle seat, amid a sea of solons with respectfully folded arms or politely clasped hands, McCarran was an island of insubordination. He crossed his legs and screwed his body away from the president, clenching his armrest with one hand and bringing the other to his mouth as he listened with dismay and contempt. McCarran's animus smoldered like a volcano.

"We must always be wary of those who with sounding brass and a tinkling cymbal preach the 'ism' of appeasement. We must especially beware of that small group of selfish men who would clip the wings of the American eagle in order to feather their own nests. ..."

It was January 6, 1941. Fifteen months after Congress had given the president the authority to sell arms to the Allies, Roosevelt was asking for authority to give arms away — to lend or lease under any terms he saw fit any weapon or ship or other sort of matériel to any country whose

fight he deemed in the national interest. The United States would become
the arsenal of democracy.

*"The first phase of the invasion of this hemisphere would not be the landing of
regular troops. The necessary strategic points would be occupied by secret agents and
their dupes — and great numbers of them are already here."*

No president had ever dreamed of such power. And only Woodrow
Wilson had dared announce such transcendent goals for national policy as
Roosevelt was now proclaiming. The four freedoms, FDR called them:
freedom of speech, freedom of religion, freedom from want, and freedom
from fear. History would remember these ringing phrases. But the president's enemies heard only his stern words.

*"We will not be intimidated by the threats of dictators that they will regard as
a breach of international law or as an act of war our aid to the democracies which
dare to resist their aggression. Such aid is not an act of war, even if a dictator should
unilaterally proclaim it so to be. When the dictators, if the dictators, are ready to
make war upon us, they will not wait for an act of war on our part. They did not
wait for Norway or Belgium or the Netherlands to commit an act of war."*

Roosevelt wanted Congress to give him a vast grant of power. "A blank
check," he told Treasury secretary Henry Morgenthau. He would send
Congress the legislation; it would become known as Lend-lease.

*"A free nation has the right to expect full cooperation from all groups. A free
nation has the right to look to the leaders of business, of labor, and of agriculture to
take the lead in stimulating effort, not among other groups but within their own
groups. The best way of dealing with the few slackers or trouble makers in our midst
is, first, to shame them by patriotic example, and, if that fails, to use the sovereignty
of government to save government."*[2]

The Great Debate was about to become the Great Brawl.

The reaction in the Senate was as if Roosevelt had burned a copy of the
Constitution on the Capitol steps. "I think it may constitute an act of war,
either directly or indirectly and I'm against it," McCarran said. "Never
before," put in Burt Wheeler, "has the Congress of the United States been
asked by any president to violate international law. . . . Never before has the
United States given to one man the power to strip this nation of its
defenses." "It is simply," added Bennett Champ Clark, "a bill to authorize the
president to declare war so far as international affairs are concerned and to
establish a totalitarian government so far as domestic affairs are concerned."

And those were the Democrats. "Monstrous," declared Hiram Johnson.
"I am neither an appeaser nor a Hitlerite. I want to see Hitler whipped and

Britain triumphant. But I decline to change the form of my government on the specious plea of assisting one belligerent. The bill presents squarely to the Congress of the United States whether it shall create a dictatorship."

"No Congress except a rubber stamp Congress would enact such a bill," snapped Robert A. Taft. Even Robert M. La Follette, who almost alone among progressives had stood with Roosevelt on the Court plan, found that he had reached the point, so unimaginable in the flush and rush of the early New Deal, at which he could not take another step with the president. "This is not a bill to give the president power," he claimed, "it's a bill for Congress to abdicate."[3]

Some of those who heard John T. Flynn speak in 1941 feared that he might burst a vein.

"Let me tell you what war will do for us . . . ," Flynn said. "A half million will die. A million may be wounded and a vast, melancholy legion of them will live out long, tortured, frustrated lives in veterans' hospitals."[4]

Robert Douglas Stuart Jr. spent the year between Princeton and Yale Law traveling around Europe; after graduation he wanted to work for the National Labor Relations Board. His father, the vice president of the Quaker Oats Company, called him a New Dealer. In the spring of 1940 young Stuart grew worried that the United States would be sucked unthinkingly into war. He talked with friends at Yale (Potter Stewart, Gerald Ford), and they sent to other schools in the East petitions pledging to keep the U.S. neutral. The petitions came back crammed with signatures and requests for more petitions. Stuart went to the Republican and Democratic conventions; he made friends with Robert Taft and Burt Wheeler. His father gave him office space in the Chicago Board of Trade Building. He signed up Sears, Roebuck chairman Robert E. Wood, a retired brigadier general, a veteran of the Philippines conflict and World War I, and a former quartermaster general of the army, as temporary head of a new anti-intervention organization. They called the group the America First Committee.

"Every man, woman and child . . . will have to pay the incalculable costs of this mad adventure. . . . Taxes will consume your earnings and cripple your business. . . . A great army of bureaucrats will help to manage every man's affairs. . . . You will spend half your time seeking permits, getting visas, answering questions, making reports and satisfying the thousand and one demands of the supervisors. . . ."

John T. Flynn was fifty-eight. He had thick iron-gray hair, a deep well of energy, and a passionate belief that the worst day in American history was the day that Franklin Roosevelt's parents met. He was a journalist who had written the "Other People's Money" column for *The New Republic* since the dawn of the New Deal. He also worked for the Pecora Commission, which investigated Wall Street in 1933, and the Nye Committee, which looked into the munitions trade. He despised Herbert Hoover and cheered Roosevelt's election. Within a year he had changed his mind about the new president. "This New Deal . . . is a fraud," he fumed. He voted for Norman Thomas in 1936 because he thought that Roosevelt would lead the country into war. In May 1938 Flynn helped found the Keep America Out of War Congress. When America First formed, Flynn became the chairman of its New York chapter.

"And when the war is over and the terrible bills come due and the illusions have fallen from our eyes, we will look around for some scapegoats. . . . Amidst these disorders we will have the perfect climate for some promising Hitler on the American model to rise to power with promises of abundance and recovery. The peace, the security, the liberties of a whole generation will be destroyed."[5]

Roosevelt was furious.

At eight o'clock on January 12 the American Forum of the Air featured John Flynn and Burt Wheeler debating Oklahoma senator Josh Lee and Herbert Agar, the editor of the *Louisville Courier Journal* and a member of Fight for Freedom. Lee shouted that Germany was about to invade the United States. Flynn claimed that Lee wanted the government to control the press. "Watch your blood pressure, John," Lee said. "My blood pressure is way below normal," Flynn replied. It was less a debate over the Lend-lease bill than a verbal slugfest over the president's leadership. "The New Deal's Triple A foreign policy," Wheeler said, "— it will plough under every fourth American boy."[6]

Two days later Roosevelt blew up in front of a room full of reporters. "The most untruthful, the most dastardly, unpatriotic thing that has ever been said," the president sputtered. "Quote me on that. That really is the rottenest thing that has been said in public life in my generation."[7]

Roosevelt had the rage of a man who knew his opponents were right. He *did* want to bring the country into war, but he could never say so. His opponents could and did, and it made Roosevelt livid. The isolationists in this respect were more candid in the debate than the president. As early as the fall of 1938, when Harry Hopkins sat with the president listening to Hitler rant on the radio about his right to seize Czechoslovakia, Roosevelt knew the United States would be forced to fight someday. "President was sure then that we were going to get into war," Hopkins recorded.[8] But how could he tell the nation, short of an attack, that there are some things worth dying for and that stopping a monster like Hitler is one of them? Even his own son Jimmy didn't think the U.S. had a dog in the fight in Europe. He would, James Roosevelt told his mother, leave his job in Hollywood and go into the army if he had to but didn't think this war would be any different from the last one. Please tell Pa, John Roosevelt told his mother another time, that the United States should not get involved on either side. If Roosevelt couldn't persuade his own boys, how could he convince a nation to send its youth across the ocean once more?

"What worries me, especially, is that public opinion over here is patting itself on the back every morning and thanking God for the Atlantic Ocean (and the Pacific Ocean)," Roosevelt told William Allen White in 1939. "We greatly underestimate the serious implications to our own future. . . . Therefore, my sage old friend, my problem is to get the American people to think of conceivable consequences without scaring the American people into thinking that they are going to be dragged into this war."[9]

Few public figures have ever been more thoroughly or relentlessly or unfairly attacked than Roosevelt. For eight years the abuse piled up against the president like ice in the Arctic winter: Roosevelt wanted to be a dictator, he was leading the country to socialism (or fascism), he treated Congress like a cheap hooker and the Constitution like something to wipe himself with. And this was just what was said in public by respectable people — by politicians in his own party (McCarran), former mentors (Al Smith), leaders of the non-Communist left (Norman Thomas), a former president (Herbert Hoover), former New Dealers (Hugh Johnson, Ray Moley, Stuart Chase). Conservatives, of course, had always hated him, and leftists had seldom trusted him, but now the progressives (with the notable exception of the saintly George Norris) had gone on the warpath against the war. Burt Wheeler, the first Democrat to back Roosevelt in 1932, was now accusing him of wanting to send off the nation's sons to fight and die in someone else's conflict. To his detractors, Roosevelt was a mad Abraham, eager to offer up all the Isaacs of the nation to the god of war. The Great Debate dissolved party lines. There were, said the isolationists, the peace party and the war party. There were, countered the president, those who would help democracy survive and those who would appease the Nazis.

More and more, those who talked with the president saw less of his affability and more of his hostility. "According to a well informed individual from Washington who visited Nevada this week," noted the *Elko Independent,* "President Roosevelt lists his pet senatorial hates thusly: Senator Burton K. Wheeler, No. 1, Senator P. A. McCarran, No. 2. And they say in Washington that the president does things about his pet peeves."[10] He who had been hated for so long was now hating back. "John Flynn," the president wrote to the editor of the *Yale Review,* ". . . should be barred hereafter from the columns of any presentable daily paper, monthly magazine, or national quarterly."[11] Roosevelt's opponents were no longer honorable men with reasonable differences of opinions but the agents or dupes of foreign powers. "If I should die tomorrow," Roosevelt told Morgenthau, "I want you to know this. I am convinced Lindbergh is a Nazi."[12]

McCarran was sweating, his hair damp, a long white forelock curling to the right. "If this bill is enacted into law, it is war," he said, his voice trembling. "War never approved by Congress."

He had not planned to speak. He was just out of the hospital. He sat at his desk, the galleries filled with sightseers, listening as the Senate celebrated Washington's birthday by reading the first president's farewell address with its famous plea for the United States to stay aloof from the eternal cycle of continental war. "The mischiefs of foreign intrigue," Washington told his countrymen during another European war, ". . . our country, under all the circumstances of the case, had a right to take, and was bound in duty and interest to take, a neutral position. Having taken it, I determined, as far as should depend upon me, to maintain it, with moderation, perseverance, and firmness."

McCarran was moved to stand. "Every boy who goes into the army from every state next month will go for good," McCarran said, his voice rising and straining, for he, too, had a boy of draft age, dear Sammy, only twenty. "He may think he's going for a year, that's the happy promise, but he is going out to die."

Above McCarran the great cast-iron- and stained-glass-paneled ceiling was obscured by a latticework of steel girders that workmen had installed in January to keep the chamber's ninety-ton roof from collapsing. The fate of the republic seemed no more secure.

"This is a program that begins in peace," he shouted, "and ends in hell — *in worse than hell!* . . . You will not be given that opportunity. It will be gone and on its way. Your cannon and your tanks and your planes and your boys will be in the battle lines before you ever get a chance to declare war."[13]

On January 10 Roosevelt sent Congress his Lend-lease bill. In the House gallery a Vassar graduate and a member of the American Youth Congress in a black dress pulled on a death mask, stood up, and started chanting. "I will walk through the land," she said. "Oh, oh! Death will follow you all."[14] Three days later Jack McMichael, the chairman of the American Youth Congress, rose during a Senate Foreign Relations Committee hearing. "American young people have sent me here —" he said, before the Capitol police dragged him out of the room. Dozens of protestors in the audience started yelling and whistling. "Don't lend or lease our lives," McMichael shouted.[15]

Realizing that they could not defeat the bill, opponents offered up a barrage of amendments — amendments to ban aid to Russia, to deport Harry Bridges, to forbid government employment to Nazis or Communists. Administration supporters ignored them. On March 8 the bill passed the Senate 60 to 31, with only 14 Democrats defecting. The House followed suit on March 11, 317 to 71. Half an hour later Roosevelt signed the Lend-lease bill into law. Then he set off for a ten-day fishing trip to Florida.

"Well, we gave him $7 billion to go all out to Britain," McCarran lamented to his daughter Margaret. "We raised the national debt limit to $65 billion and we will raise it to one hundred billion before the year is over if this war keeps on. We conscripted the boys, took them out of the schools and fields and homes to teach them to kill and smile while they do it. (We will make them tough and hard so they can draw blood and dream of more blood.) We gave 'cost plus' contracts so we can give more money to the powerful and then pay an army of revenue collectors to take it away from them again in taxes. We raised the workers daily earnings by double and then raised the cost of the workers food and clothing and other essentials of life by four times. We have enacted labor laws and created mediation boards to settle labor disputes and then withheld action so that there are more strikes than ever. All this and more we accomplished in the sacred name of the New Deal. But we are now where we are at war with friendly nations and bestowing favors on the most Communistic country in the world — so this is Easter vacation, and we will sing and see the sun rise on Easter morn for Christ will have risen to look upon our devastation of his divine ordination.

"Well," McCarran concluded, "what's the use in talking or trying."[16]

The day after McCarran delivered a speech against Lend-lease on the floor, the Democratic Steering Committee met to decide who was going to be the new chairman of the Judiciary Committee.

It was an open secret in Washington that the president was pulling for Fred Van Nuys. The Indiana senator might be a foe of the New Deal, he might have yanked the president's portrait off his office wall after FDR put him on the purge list, but he was a practical man. "The White House began making discreet overtures to Van Nuys," reported the *Indianapolis Star.* "These took the tangible form of undercover help in his fight with Senator Pat McCarran."[17] "He had the White House blessing in his battle with Senator McCarran," added the *Washington Daily News.* ". . . His appointment is regarded as the first step in a truce between him and the president."[18]

As the committee began balloting, it soon became clear that McCarran was going to lose. Burt Wheeler argued that McCarran's seniority was already established. Pat Harrison snapped that Indiana was a state before Nevada and that decided the matter. "This has long been the accepted yardstick here," Harrison said, "and you know it."[19] Wheeler then proposed settling it with a coin toss. He was rebuffed again. Then the committee voted, 14 to 3, to make Van Nuys the chairman. McCarran was given the consolation prize of the chairmanship of the District of Columbia Committee, a dog of a panel that almost no senator wanted and that three members with more seniority than McCarran had already turned down — a post in fact that McCarran had told the Senate leadership back in November that he would not accept.

"I can't believe it," McCarran sputtered when a reporter told him the news. "I haven't heard a word of it. But I positively will not accept appointment to the District Committee under any circumstances."[20]

In May, however, McCarran finally accepted the chairmanship. Before the year was out, he would pick up the chairmanship of the appropriations subcommittee that vetted the budgets of the Departments of State, Justice, Commerce, and Labor. "This is the most powerful subcommittee in the U.S. Senate because it controls the money for these departments so vital to the government . . . ," McCarran told his daughter Margaret. "One can raise merry havoc with these departments by the control of their purse strings."[21]

Van Nuys, meanwhile, put Roosevelt's picture back on the wall in his office.

Hundreds of mounted officers rode through people crowding the streets around Madison Square Garden. Twenty-five thousand poured into the arena before ticket takers began turning them away. Another ten thousand pooled around Eighth Avenue and spilled over Forty-ninth and Fiftieth

Streets, hoping to hear Lindbergh on speakers set up outside. It wasn't easy with the jeering and shouting. Protestors from the Committee to Defend America by Aiding the Allies waved signs and lobbed epithets: *Nazis! Commies!* Small fistfights erupted.

America Firsters were getting used to it, but they still didn't like it. "I confess," Norman Thomas said, "it hurts me to find old friends in the ranks of labor and among the Jews who condemn me as fascist for no other reason they say than because I have spoken on American First platform."[22]

Walter Winchell called it "America Last." Ickes dubbed it "America Next." Communist leader William Z. Foster called it subversive. "The voice of American fascism," John Roy Carlson branded the committee in his book *Under Cover.* "Dupes of the enemies of the United States," echoed Michael Sayers and Albert Kahn in their book *Sabotage!*[23]

The Great Debate was already cleaving old friendships. Villard resigned from *The Nation* after four decades because of its interventionist politics. *The New Republic* began publishing disclaimers to Flynn's columns ("his opinion is nonsense") and then dropped him altogether. Soon *Collier's* magazine also ditched Flynn, the Scripps-Howard newspaper chain canceled his column, and *Harper's* stopped accepting submissions from him. "I was liquidated," Flynn fumed.[24]

No figure was more vilified than Lindbergh. "The Number One United States Nazi fellow traveler," Ickes called him.[25] The aviator, to be sure, was an easy target. He had gone to an American embassy reception in Berlin where Hermann Göring surprised him by pinning a medal on his jacket. The photo was a godsend for interventionist propaganda. As was Lindbergh's strange reluctance to denounce the crimes of the Nazis. To Lindbergh's critics this was proof of his bad faith and nefarious intentions. Lindbergh, charged Friends of Democracy director the Reverend L. M. Birkhead, had been picked by Hitler to be the führer of America. The group printed a twenty-eight-page pamphlet called "Is Lindbergh a Nazi?" pairing a quote from Lindbergh pledging his fidelity to constitutional methods with a similar one by Hitler. "Millions would vote today to hang Lindbergh or to exile him — as enthusiastically as they cheered and extolled him," wrote the *Richmond News Leader.*[26] Libraries yanked his books; cities that had christened streets and parks for the aviator renamed them. His hometown painted over his name on its water tower. "In just fifteen years he had gone from Jesus to Judas!" said his sister-in-law Constance.[27] "I am now the bubonic plague among writers and C. is the anti-Christ!" Anne Lindbergh told her diary.[28]

It didn't matter that both Nazis and Communists were barred from America First membership. John Flynn even tried to organize Jewish and black America First chapters but found little interest. Both fascists and Communists turned up at the group's rallies. When Flynn recognized a fascist in the audience at one speech, he heckled his uninvited guest. The haters, Burt Wheeler noted, were as hard to shake off as maggots.

One day Roosevelt handed an America First pamphlet to his secretary. "Will you find out from someone — perhaps F.B.I. — who is paying for this?" the president asked.[29]

Roosevelt never inquired where Fight for Freedom or Friends of Democracy got their money. Since these groups maintained covert ties with both the British government and the White House, Roosevelt didn't really have to ask. "I'm your biggest undercover agent," Roosevelt allegedly joked to Sir William Stephenson, the head of British Security Coordination, which was waging a covert campaign from its office in Rockefeller Center to get the United States into the war. Fight for Freedom's Ulric Bell even showed the president critical comments before uttering them. "If you're going to give me hell," the president advised, "why not use some really strong language?"[30]

Harry Hopkins had recently told Churchill that American public opinion was divided into four groups. "A small group," he explained, "of Nazis and Communists, sheltering behind Lindbergh, who declared for a negotiated peace and wanted a German victory; a group, represented by Joe Kennedy, which said 'Help Britain, but make damn sure you don't get into any danger of war': a majority group which supported the president's determination to send the maximum assistance at whatever risk; and about 10 percent or 15 percent of the country, including Knox, Stimson, and most of the armed forces, who were in favor of immediate war."[31]

There was, one might notice, no legitimate opposition to Roosevelt in this division, only Nazis and Communists. "Will the Nazis considerately wait until we are ready to fight them?" asked Roosevelt speechwriter and Fight for Freedom member Robert Sherwood in a full-page ad in the *New York Times* and other leading papers. ". . . Anyone who argues that they will wait is either an imbecile or a traitor."[32]

Roosevelt was sure that America First and those in its orbit were traitors, and he badgered his new attorney general, Francis Biddle, to indict them for sedition. "Will you speak to me about the possibility of a grand jury investigation of the America First Committee?" Roosevelt prodded.

"It certainly ought to be looked into and I cannot get any action out of Congress."[33]

Florida's Claude Pepper was practically foaming at the mouth on the floor of the Senate. Grab Greenland, Dakar, Singapore, he frantically urged. Get to these strategic chokepoints before the Nazis or the Japanese. Declare a state of national emergency. Seize Axis assets. Bomb Tokyo.

McCarran jumped up to answer. Pepper bolted the chamber. Stay, McCarran implored. Pepper waved him away and walked into the cloak-room. "Although the senator is going out the American people are not going out with him," McCarran said.[34]

Does Pepper, McCarran asked, speak for the White House?

Three weeks later, on May 27, Roosevelt broadcast a speech from the East Room of the White House declaring an unlimited national emergency. In three months U-boats had sunk 142 merchant ships ferrying supplies to Britain. Germany was sinking ships three times faster than Britain could replace them. The president said that he was putting the armed forces on alert. "Some people seem to think that we are not attacked until bombs actually drop in the streets of New York or San Francisco or New Orleans or Chicago," Roosevelt said. "But they are simply shutting their eyes to the lesson that we must learn from the fate of every nation that the Nazis have conquered. . . . It would be suicide to wait until they are in our front yard."[35]

And the next day at his press conference the president backpedaled once again. No, he insisted, he wasn't going to ask for any more legislation.

U.S. Army trucks drove through the predawn streets of Los Angeles and stopped at the North American Aviation Company plant in Inglewood, where twenty-five hundred armed soldiers assembled and marched toward a Communist picket line.

North American Aviation made one out of every four fighter planes in the country, cranking out ten a day. The company made a bundle from defense contracts; its workers didn't. They earned fifty cents an hour, while the going rate in the area was seventy-five cents. They demanded another dime an hour. The company balked. On June 4 the Communist-led United Auto Workers local called a strike — the latest strike in a year when one out of every dozen workers walked off their jobs, the most widespread labor stoppage since the CIO's great organizing drive in 1937. The chairman of the House Judiciary Committee threatened to write a bill to send strikers at defense plants to the chair. In Milwaukee the Communists organized a strike at the Allis-Chalmers plant, where turbines and generators for navy destroyers were built. Secretary of War Henry Stimson demanded that Roosevelt call out the army. Instead a settlement was finally reached, but only after seventy-six days of production were lost.

The international UAW didn't support the Los Angeles strike. Richard Frankensteen, hero of the bloody Ford organizing drive and UAW vice president, pleaded with the workers to return to the assembly line while the National Defense Mediation Board considered their case. He was booed. The UAW then suspended the local's charter and fired union representatives who sided with the strikers. Police clashed with strikers, and tear gas blotted out the smog. Secretary of State Hull wanted to deport the union leaders. Roosevelt wanted to dump them on a remote beach. Secretary Stimson wanted again to call in the army. This time the president listened.

At dawn on June 10, army troops walked strikers back to work at bayonet point. If they didn't go back to work, Washington warned, they would be reclassified under the Selective Service Act and drafted. Eventually the mediation board ordered the company to cough up the raise.[36]

The marine began to unbuckle his belt.

"Commies!" he yelled.

The protestors tried to ignore him.

"The Yanks are not coming," they shouted.

Night and day, they marched in front of the White House waving picket signs. No CONVOYS, their signs read. No AMERICAN EXPEDITIONARY FORCE. One held a railroad lantern labeled KEEP THE LIGHT OF PEACE ALIGHT. The year before they had been urging the U.S. to fight the Nazis as members of the American League Against War and Fascism. Then the Popular Front turned to ashes and out of the ashes of the league came the American Peace Mobilization. Twenty-two thousand people turned out for the group's founding conference in September 1940. The new organization's national committee looked suspiciously familiar: Representative Vito Marcantonio, novelist Theordore Dreiser, singer Paul Robeson, American Youth Congress chairman Jack McMichael, journalist George Seldes, Mine-Mill union president Reid Robinson. Earl Browder asked Frederick Vanderbilt Field to take the job as executive secretary *before* the founding convention. "They had evidently been told that I was to have the job,"[37] recalled Field, an heir to the Vanderbilt fortune, a secret Communist and financial angel for party causes. After the convention, two thousand members immediately jumped on a train to Washington to protest against the conscription bill. The group organized peace councils across the country, enlisting thousands of volunteers to ring doorbells and pass out antiwar literature. Hundreds waded through Saturday-afternoon shopping crowds, waving banners, calling Lend-lease a blueprint for fascism. They picketed meetings of the Committee to Defend America. And for forty-three days and nights they marched in front of the White House.

"The Yanks are not —"

The lantern smashed against the ground. The marine snapped his belt like a whip. He began to punch protestors. Police pulled him off.

"The Yanks are not coming!"

The marchers continued their vigil until June 21 when they temporarily called off the picket to observe National Peace Week. The next day Germany invaded the Soviet Union. The protestors never came back.

The light of peace had gone out.[38]

On June 20, two days before Germany attacked Russia, the Comintern dispatched its latest instructions to the CPUSA. "The party," the Comintern declared, "is continuing to wage the most systematic struggle and gathering the workers and the people to struggle against the aggressive imperialist policies of the Roosevelt administration and the ruling circles of monopolistic capital which are prepared to bring the country totally into the war in the near future."[39]

On June 26, four days after the invasion, the Comintern sent a different directive: Never mind. Forget the past two years of propaganda. "The aggression of the German fascism against Soviet Union has basically changed the whole international situation and character of the war itself . . .," the Comintern instructed. "The main task now is to exert every effort in order to secure the victory of Soviet people and to smash the fascist barbarians. Everything must be subordinated to this main task."[40]

Fred Field immediately turned the America Peace Mobilization into the American People's Mobilization. "For Victory Over Fascism" was the new slogan. Black outfits changed to white. Party members carried war petitions through Manhattan. Balloons were scattered along New York beaches reading, STOP HITLER, FIGHT APPEASEMENT, MAINTAIN DEMOCRACY, JOIN APM.[41]

The editorial staff of the *New Masses* raced back from a retreat in upstate New York to Manhattan to stop the presses on the next issue, which called Roosevelt and Churchill warmongers. After some last-minute rewriting Hitler became a warmonger and Roosevelt was once again a democrat.

Two weeks after the German invasion, Soviet ambassador Constantine Oumansky walked into the White House to ask Roosevelt for help. "Of course we are going to give all the aid we possibly can to Russia," Roosevelt told the press.[42]

The *New York Times* reported that military analysts expected a German victory inside a month; the *Washington Post* quoted another expert as saying that only an act of God could save the USSR. McCarran didn't want anything to save the Soviet Union. "I despise Mr. Hitler and all he stands for, and equally I despise Mr. Stalin and all he stands for," he said. "I want those two dogs to come together and destroy each other. It would be well for democracy. But I would not lend a word to either one of them, because neither of them is a friend of this country. If Stalin succeeds, then God help democracy, and God help Christianity."[43]

Helping the Russians, many Catholics believed, was a pact with the devil. In 1937 a papal encyclical *("On Atheistic Communism, Divini redemptoris")* decreed that the Soviet Union was untouchable. "Communism is intrinsically wrong," the Church had declared, "and no one who would save Christian civilization may collaborate with it in any undertaking whatsoever."[44] It was, said the isolationists, less America's war than ever. "If Russia defeats Germany, Germany will go Communist," John Flynn said. "If Germany wins, Russia will go Fascist. There is no choice for us at all. The question now is, are we going to fight to make Europe safe for Communism?"[45] "I would" added Lindbergh, "a hundred times rather see my country ally herself with England, or even Germany with all her faults, than with the cruelty, the Godlessness, and the barbarism that exist in the Soviet Union."[46]

Churchill, on the other hand, was more than willing to help anyone fighting the country that was bombing his island. "If Hitler invaded Hell," the prime minister noted, "I would make at least a favorable reference to the Devil in the House of Commons."[47] Roosevelt, too, was happy to have someone *else's* troops fighting Hitler. "Russia is governed by a dictatorship as rigid in its manner of being as is the dictatorship of Germany," he explained to Pope Pius XII. "I believe, however, that this Russian dictatorship is less dangerous to the safety of other nations than is the German form of dictatorship. The only weapon which the Russian dictatorship uses outside of its own borders is Communist propaganda which I, of course, recognize has in the past been utilized for the purpose of breaking down the form of government in other countries, religious belief, et cetera. Germany, however, not only has utilized, but is utilizing, this kind of propaganda as well and has also undertaken the employment of every form of military aggression outside of its borders for the purpose of world conquest by force of arms and by force of propaganda. I believe that the survival of Russia is less dangerous to religion, to the church as such, and to humanity in general than would be the survival of the German form of dictatorship."[48]

Roosevelt ordered the State Department to give all the help it could to Stalin under the Lend-lease program and grew impatient when the bureaucracy moved slowly. At one cabinet meeting he raged for forty-five minutes on the subject. "Step on it!" he ordered.[49]

Not long before Germany invaded Russia, Pat Jackson went to New York for a board meeting of the Robert Marshall Civil Liberties Trust. The American Committee for the Protection of the Foreign Born and the League of American Writers, both of which were party front groups, were asking for money. In his will Bob Marshall had left a good chunk of his estate to the "safeguarding and advancement of the cause of civil liberties in the United States."[50] Could Communists be trusted to advance civil liberties?

One trustee, Ed Smith, a member of the National Labor Relations Board, strongly opposed any political litmus test. "The works of the cause should speak for themselves," he said.[51] Smith, of course, was often accused of being either a Communist or a die-hard fellow traveler himself; after he was forced off the NLRB by Roosevelt, he became a paid lobbyist for the Soviet Union. Jackson had found himself facing the same issue many times in the past two years. Usually he answered like Smith. Now he was no longer so sure. "A difficult question," he equivocated.[52]

The vicissitudes of the New Deal years broke many hearts, not least of which was the large one beating within Pat Jackson. The troubles came in bitter succession: The Triple A purge. The failure of the La Follette Committee to take up the cause of the sharecroppers. The death of the Spanish Republic. The demise of the Popular Front. The Moscow purges. The Hitler-Stalin pact. The flop of Labor's Non-Partisan League to become a viable independent political force. The CIO's headlong rush into isolationism. "I cannot do other than have a profound sense of shame at the futility and unworthiness of some of the individuals and causes in that record," Jackson confessed to his sister. ". . . I firmly believe that I am now ready in middle age to pull out of the personal-great-cause operations and hew to a line of action limited to a simpler and smaller sphere about which I am more likely to have something approaching comprehension."[53]

Jackson had become a poster boy for fellow traveling. The Constitutional Education League put out a tract supporting HUAC featuring a large picture of Jackson over the caption FIFTH COLUMN AGENT. Benjamin Stolberg called him a Stalinist in the mass-circulation *Saturday Evening Post*. Things had gotten so bad that when Jackson had blown through most of his family fortune, and finally needed a government job for pay, the only prospect the friend of Felix Frankfurter could find was working at the Surplus Marketing Administration's school lunch program. "The reputation attributed to me by some is not one which certain of the politicians on the Hill think should allow the fellow possessing it to work in the government," Jackson lamented to Arthur Schlesinger.[54]

Nothing hurt more than the break with Lee Pressman. "Lee stands the test of all Dode's and my standards better than any other individual with whom we have been thrown in the New Deal," Jackson enthused to Frankfurter after the AAA purge.[55] At times it seemed Pat Jackson was the only person in Washington who didn't know that Pressman was a Communist. Then the purges opened a space between the two; the Hitler-Stalin pact widened the breach. But it was the ice that seemed to cover Pressman's heart that really pained Jackson. Once, when Jackson came into an unexpected cash windfall, Charlie Kramer bullied him for four grand for some new front group while Pressman looked on without saying anything; Jackson felt physically threatened and verbally intimidated and couldn't understand why Pressman would sit there and do nothing to help. "Every conception of the relationship between two human beings with which I was brought up were violated by the consummately ruthless disregard of friendship which Lee exhibited," Jackson fumed to Jerry Frank.*[56]

Jackson's pain was also the price of experience that many kind people paid in the 1930s — what Eugene Lyons labeled the Red Decade, the title of a book that came out later in the year. "Our own American Popular

---

*Pressman, as usual, knew just how to hurt Jackson: "As far as I was concerned, it was just his getting drunk and bleating and talking all around town about things which never did happen which made it easier for one's life to just let him alone. That itself probably irked him considerably, even more so than if I had become angry. I think what he minded most was just simply that I had no concern about the situation. . . . He became extremely bitter. . . . I don't believe I ever lifted a finger against him. . . . I don't think he was sufficiently important in my life that I would go out and do any injury to him." (Pressman, Columbia Oral History Collection, p. 40.)

Front," Lyons wrote, ". . . penetrated, in various degrees, the labor movement, education, the churches, college and non-college youth movements,
the theatre, movies, the arts, publishing in all its branches; it bored deep
into the federal government and in many communities also into local government; it obtained a strangle-hold on great sectors of national and local
relief setups. . . . At its highest point — roughly about 1938 — the incredible revolution of the Red Decade had mobilized the conscious or the
starry-eyed innocent collaboration of thousands of influential American
educators, social workers, clergymen, New Deal officials, youth leaders,
Negro and other racial spokesmen, Social Registerites, novelists,
Hollywood stars, script writers and directors, trade union chiefs, men and
women of abnormal wealth. Its echoes could be heard, muted or strident,
in the most unexpected places, including the supposed citadels of conservatism and respectability."[57]

Several of these abraded souls had begun gathering in Reinhold
Niebuhr's apartment on Claremont Avenue, near the Union Theological
Seminary in New York where the Protestant minister taught ethics. There
was Lewis Corey (né Louis Fraina), a founding member of the American
Communist Party, who became a pariah to his comrades but flirted with
socialism for decades, only gradually drifting to the center. There was Jim
Loeb, still smarting from Communist duplicity in the Spanish Civil War.
There was Freda Kirchwey, the editor of *The Nation,* who had pleaded
agnosticism on the Great Purge but finally blew her top over the Hitler-
Stalin pact. And there was Niebuhr, who had started the New Deal as a
socialist believing that capitalism not only was doomed but *deserved* to die,
only to end the decade believing that the system could and *should* be
saved. What brought the group together were four interrelated beliefs:
New Deal liberalism could save America, the New Deal must be extended
to the rest of the world, the United States must go to war to fight the fascist powers, and the Communists were as bad as the fascists. "I have myself
worked in dozens of organizations with Communists," Niebuhr noted,
"but their present orientation is so completely under the control of
Russian policy that I will not again knowingly have anything to do with
any organization in which they function."[58]

That May the group from Reiny Niebuhr's apartment created a liberal
interventionist organization called the Union for Democratic Action. Pat
Jackson, who had gone from sneering at Roosevelt to hanging a picture of
the president in his living room, wanted to join. "I have a reputation of being
a Communist, a reputation gained because I went along with the CIO

organizationally all the way up until the crisis really hit," Jackson told Jim Loeb. "If you could only hear the Commies themselves fume about me!"[59]

A year earlier Jackson had threatened to lead a mass resignation from the ACLU if the organization expelled Communists like Liz Flynn from its board. Now he was trying to join a group that treated party members like lepers, morally equal to Nazis.

The Red Decade was over.

In August 1941 McCarran changed trains in Chicago and stopped to chat with a reporter from the *Tribune*. Congress had just extended the peacetime draft — by a single vote. If the president couldn't get the war he wanted, McCarran proclaimed, he would settle for any war. "There is a bunch of Washington advisers to the president, led by Harry Hopkins, Harold Ickes, and their fellow travelers who hope to take us into war," McCarran said. "Their strategy is a cowardly one. They do not dare submit the issue directly to Congress or the people because they know the great majority are against war. Instead their strategy is to stage a condition that will provoke an attack — probably on the American Navy in the Far East — and thus stir up war hysteria."[60]

While Roosevelt believed that the United States needed to fight Germany, it was with Japan that conflict seemed more likely. Hitler went out of his way to keep the United States on the sidelines, ordering his U-boats not to return fire from U.S. warships escorting lend-lease convoys to Britain. The Nazis needed nothing from the United States except neutrality. The Japanese, on the other hand, got 80 percent of their high-octane fuel from the United States. America was the gas station for the Japanese war machine. After the Japanese rolled into Indochina in July, Harold Ickes, who had just been appointed petroleum coordinator, cut off high-octane fuel shipments to Tokyo. Roosevelt, not wanting to anger the Japanese, rescinded the order.

McCarran was sure that sooner or later Roosevelt would do something to rile the Japanese into war. "Our State Department has already by its statements and acts repeatedly provoked Japan," he said. "It is no tribute to our government but rather to Japanese restraint, that Japan has not already declared war on us."[61]

On the morning of September 11, 1941, the Des Moines chapter of America First was celebrating the fact that it had won a contest for signing up the most new members and was to be honored with Charles Lindbergh speaking at a rally that day. The celebration didn't last long.

"The three most important groups who have been pressing this country toward war are the British, the Jewish and the Roosevelt administration . . . ," the aviator said. "Instead of agitating for war the Jewish groups in this country should be opposing it in every possible way. . . . for they will be among the first to feel its consequences. Tolerance is a virtue that depends upon peace and strength. History shows that it cannot survive war and devastation. A few farsighted Jewish people realize this and stand opposed to intervention. But the majority still do not. Their greatest danger to this country lies in their large ownership and influence in our motion pictures, our press, our radio, and our government."[62]

A hurricane of condemnation hit Lindbergh and the committee. "The most un-American talk made in my time by any person of national reputation," said Willkie.[63] "An inexcusable abuse of the right of freedom of speech," added Tom Dewey.[64] White House press secretary Steve Early compared it to comments coming from Berlin.

"If C. speaks again," feared Anne Morrow Lindbergh, the aviator's wife, "they'll put him in prison."[65]

"America has been attacked!"

The president's urgent words came out of radios across the country on October 27. "We have wished to avoid shooting," he said. "But the shooting has started. And history has recorded who fired the first shot. In the long run, however, all that will matter is who fired the last shot."

Eleven days earlier, on October 16, a U-boat fired a torpedo at the USS *Kearny* on patrol near Iceland. Eleven sailors were killed. Roosevelt then announced that he was in possession of a German map showing Nazi plans for taking control of South America.

"The USS *Kearny* is not just a Navy ship. She belongs to every man, woman, and child in this nation. . . . Hitler's torpedo was directed at every American."[66]

Important details soon dribbled out. The attack was not unprovoked. The *Kearny* had been chasing German subs. Even more important details stayed secret. The German map, for instance, was actually a forgery made by British intelligence. [67]

A storm was coming in over Lake Michigan where it lapped at the northern edge of Indiana. The wind whistled and sang through the sand dunes and the trees, and all that Paul Douglas could think about was war.

Six years earlier, in 1935, Douglas and his wife, Emily, were roused from their pensione in Rome by church bells summoning the city to assembly. After years of trying to form a third party with the League for Independent Political Action, Douglas had reconciled himself to the Democratic Party. Douglas was a rare liberal who would have nothing to do with the Popular Front. When Minnesota governor Floyd Olson insisted on inviting Earl Browder to a meeting to organize a national Farmer-Labor Party in 1936, Douglas refused to attend. Then with the passage of the National Labor Relations Act and the Social Security Act, the University of Chicago economist could finally give his heart to Roosevelt as a true liberal.

Douglas had already given his heart to his second wife, Emily, the daughter of a sculptor, who shared her love of art with her bookish, activist husband. Which bought them to a crowded plaza in Rome, where they watched fascist troops goose-stepping through the Eternal City and Mussolini strutting onto a balcony to announce that he had invaded Ethiopia. The sight made Douglas physically sick. He gave up almost twenty years of Quaker pacifism and joined a volunteer military organization back in Chicago, drilling weekly to train for the day when he might need to physically fight fascism. He joined the Committee to Defend America and the Friends of Democracy. He ran for alderman in Chicago in 1939. In Irish pubs he recited lines from Yeats; in Greek taverns he tossed off Byron's verse about the islands. He was actually elected. He took walking tours of the South Side slums. He sponsored a Spanish war orphan. Conservatives called him a Communist; the Communists called him a warmonger.

Douglas jumped in the lake. If he could pass this test, he would do it. He swam two miles in the choppy sea and then ran along the dunes on the beach. He felt good. He was pushing fifty.

Douglas took the fall quarter of 1941 off from the University of Chicago. He toured the state to support Roosevelt's foreign policy and push for U.S. intervention in the war. He decided to run for the U.S. Senate seat held by Republican Curly Brooks, an isolationist supporter of Colonel McCormick. The Democratic Kelly-Nash machine backed Congressman Raymond McKeough in the primary. Douglas lost the race, 570,000 votes to 285,000. "I am free now," he told his wife late on the night of his defeat.

The next morning Paul Douglas enlisted in the marines.[68]

On the morning of December 7, Japanese planes swarmed over Pearl Harbor. When the attack ended an hour later, 2,403 men were dead, 1,178 wounded, three hundred planes destroyed or crippled, and eight battleships sunk or heavily damaged. The month before a Gallup poll found that hard-core interventionists and isolationists each claimed about a quarter of public opinion; half of Americans were undecided.[69] Pearl Harbor ended the Great Debate.

McCarran was on a train in Nevada, heading out to visit his daughters ("my little nuns") in California. He jumped off at the first station and caught the next train in the other direction to Washington. "The Japs spit in our face and the game was off," McCarran wrote to his daughter Margaret. "The little rats we have petted and pampered them for half a century and we deserve to get what we got. They never should have received the kindness we extended to them. However it's war all out war and how. When we get though we will be two hundred billion in debt and more and God only knows what we will be like when we recover. It's going to take more than armies and men and guns to save democracy because democracy has its greatest enemies within its own midst."

For McCarran war was worse than anything. Nothing would give the president more power, which he might or might not give back after the war, and absolutely nothing was more horrible to contemplate than his son Sammy, twenty, going off to fight. "Well our boy must go in the draft — a fine kid and worthy of a better fate," McCarran brooded to Margaret. "I am trying to arrange for him to get into a branch of the service where his fine head will be of most value to his country and to him."[70]

McCarran didn't get to Washington until after Congress had already hastily assembled and voted to declare war. For years McCarran had vowed never to send American troops overseas. He didn't break his word.

CHAPTER 11

Crude Enough for McCarran

Was anyone immune altogether? In times like these?
There were so many treasons; they were a medium, like
air, like water; they passed in and out of you, they made
themselves your accomplices; nothing was impenetrable
to them.[1]

— Saul Bellow, *Dangling Man*

On December 11, four days after Pearl Harbor, Japanese planes roared out
of the sky over Wake Atoll. Twelve hundred construction workers were
racing to finish a major air and sub base, among them Joe F. McDonald Jr.,
the twenty-five-year-old son of the editor of the *Nevada State Journal*. The
construction workers and five hundred marines held out for more than
two weeks. Then on December 27, the Japanese stormed ashore in a
bloody wave and siezed the island.

Back in Reno the elder Joe McDonald ripped wire copy with nervous
hands looking for information about his son. When he couldn't find any,
he called McCarran. "It is with sad heart that I am compelled to advise
you that your fine boy has given his life to his country," McCarran
reported back. "May God give you and his fine mother strength to bear
the loss. Sincerest condolences from your friend."[2]

Once McCarran had been a sheepherder with few prospects. He went
to a lawyer and asked him what to read to become an attorney. With the
guiding hand of the older man, McCarran passed the bar; ever since he
had taken great pains to help others learn the law and climb in the world.
When he'd come to Washington, he'd helped young men from home get
into the capital's many law schools and gotten them jobs running elevators or working in offices in the Senate. These young men went back to
Nevada and became judges and governors and eventually senators themselves, but they were always known as McCarran's boys. McCarran would
do anything for them. And they would do anything for McCarran.

When Joe McDonald Jr. was reported killed on Wake, his father almost
seemed to be consoling McCarran. "I know it was a sad mission for you
as Joe was one of your boys and thought the world of you and you did so
much for him," McDonald told McCarran. "There is consolation in the

thought that he was not wounded and forced to suffer in that desolate place and he would have been so unhappy as a prisoner of the Japs."[3]

The next day an airmail letter arrived from the navy. McDonald knew what it said. McCarran's boys were already dying.

Two days after Pearl Harbor the lights went off at the Capitol, the Washington Monument, and the Lincoln Memorial. The gleaming, floodlit city plunged into darkness. War was changing Washington's landscape. The spacious Mall soon resembled an overcrowded warehouse district: Cheap office structures sprang up like toadstools after a rain, the ugly temp buildings lining both sides of the Lincoln Monument's reflecting pool, connected by two bridges spanning the water. Pennsylvania Avenue was closed to traffic. The roof of the White House bristled with anti-aircraft guns — but so barren was the nation's arsenal that some of the guns were wooden replicas. Men disappeared from offices, swallowed by recruiting stations open twenty-four hours a day and replaced by several times as many women (government girls, they were called) pouring into the city through Union Station, a continual rush hour of new uniforms and shuffling, uncertain feet. Seventy thousand people moved to Washington in a year; the government payroll doubled. The sleepy southern town with one theater and half a dozen movie houses suddenly had a million residents and not nearly enough of anything: offices, hotels, cars, trolleys, phones, sugar.[4] A civil service commissioner told a House panel that another five hundred thousand government employees were needed. In one month the government annexed 358 buildings across the region. The White House Bureau of the Budget announced that it wanted to move a dozen government agencies and more than twenty-one thousand employees outside Washington.

In the Senate, McCarran rose to block the move, calling it illegal and introducing a measure to stop it. "There are," he said, "those in this country who want to tear down this government and set up a super-government."[5] McCarran's measure failed by four votes, a barometer of how chilly the mood in Congress was toward the administration even in the first flush of wartime unity. "We have got to trust the president," Majority Leader Alben Barkley pleaded on the floor. "If we can't trust him then we are in a bad way. It is most unfortunate that so soon after getting into this war we are questioning the authority and good faith, of the president."[6]

Those who had not trusted the president before the war trusted him even less as the wartime bureaucracy grew like kudzu, a weed that McCarran feared would be hard to hack back after peace returned. "I pray that in winning this war we do not lose the fine things of our country," McCarran said. "Will we lose the democracy when we win the battle?"[7]

McCarran was both right and wrong. Roosevelt was not tearing down the government but he *was* erecting, like the temp buildings swallowing up the Mall, an enormous new structure atop the old one. Ironically, however, while the government was growing beyond even the most fervid dreams of the New Dealers, the New Deal itself was withering.

War did what Roosevelt never could: It pulled the country out of Depression. Unemployment practically disappeared. The gross domestic product, which had slumped to $56.4 billion in Roosevelt's first year in office, grew faster than any time in history, jumping from $161.8 billion in 1942 to $223 billion three years later. In 1932, the year Roosevelt and McCarran were sent to Washington, the federal government spent $4.8 billion. In 1940 Washington spent $9.6 billion; four years later, $94 billion. Federal employment went from one million in 1932 to seven million in 1942, then doubled in three more years. During the four years of the war the government produced more paper than in all the previous years of the republic combined.

But like Phaethon's chariot ride, Roosevelt found that although he held the reins he could not choose his destination. As early as 1940 the president was telling intimates that there was not much more he could do domestically. In December 1943 he admitted as much to the American people: Dr. New Deal, he told reporters, had been replaced by Dr. Win-the-War. Increasingly, it looked like the voters wanted to replace the Democrats as well. In the midterm elections in 1942, the Democrats lost fifty seats in the House and eight in the Senate, trimming the party's majority to ten and twenty-one, respectively. By the end of the next year, the New Deal was a cut forest: Congress felled the Civilian Conservation Corps, the Works Progress Administration, the National Youth Administration, and most of what else remained of Roosevelt's grand experiment. Once it was the Supreme Court that foiled Roosevelt's plans; now it was Congress. "The whole New Deal accomplishment to date has been placed in grave jeopardy,"[8] fretted Harold Ickes.

The liberal noninterventionists who feared that war would kill reform were right. The government grew, but it grew less progressive, less of a countervailing force against the bigness of industry that liberals had longed for than an agglomeration of its own special bureaucratic interests. The Office of Price Administration, for example, told Americans what

they could buy in stores and what they would have to pay. "The democracy of capitalist society is on the way out, is, in fact, just about gone,"
James Burnham wrote in *The Managerial Revolution,* published in 1941,
"and will not come back."⁹

Those on the right, like McCarran, who had long decried the expansion of the bureaucracy found cold comfort in the fact that their old intellectual antagonists were also adopting a more critical view toward the
state. "There is a lot of shivering going on around here," McCarran told
his administrative assistant, Eva Adams. "The Republicans are getting
'uppish' and the Democrats are trembling. It is strange how true the old
saying is — rats desert a sinking ship. Around through the halls and in the
offices of the many who have been the recipients of gratuities at the hands
of this administration there is whispering going around that the administration is going too far to the left; that it is becoming too bureaucratic; that
we must get rid of Harry Hopkins and Felix Frankfurter."¹⁰

Stephen Spingarn held the phone away from his ear. The torrent of angry
words continued. Spingarn wasn't making anyone happy these days.

The irate caller was a colleague in the Treasury Department who
wanted to fire Gertrud Schicht, a clerk in the office of foreign funds control — what they were calling around town a G-girl. Schicht was born in
Germany, came to the United States when she was fifteen, and then
became a naturalized citizen. Spingarn was the chairman of the Treasury's
Un-American Activities Committee. The caller was an angry official from
the department's general counsel office. He told Spingarn that the word
in the funds office was that Schicht had spoken favorably about Hitler.

Spingarn interviewed the two women in the funds office who had
allegedly complained about Schicht's praise of Hitler. Neither remembered the purported incident. This wasn't enough for Spingarn. The government had to protect itself, but individuals still had rights that must be
respected. "Once these suspicions are raised," Spingarn told his colleague,
"it is difficult, if not impossible, to ever wholly quiet them."¹¹

The war was swelling Washington like a flooding river, a deluge of government recruits that made the inundation of the New Deal look like a
trickle. In the Treasury Department, for instance, the new offices — foreign funds control, defense savings — hired people first and conducted
background checks afterward. Until recently the government had never
bothered to screen its employees. But with Martin Dies and others raising
hell about alleged subversives in high places, Congress passed the Hatch

Act in 1940, making it illegal for the government to hire Communists or Nazis or members of other groups that advocated the violent overthrow of the government. Congress gave the FBI a hundred thousand dollars to investigate federal employees for subversive activities, but the bureau's investigations often raised more questions than they resolved. How close, for instance, did people have to be to the Communists before they were considered a security risk?

Treasury's foreign funds office, for example, hired an eighteen-year-old named Irene Wenglarz as a junior clerk. Previously, it turned out, Wenglarz had been the treasurer of Lodge 1576, Ukrainian Branch, International Workers Order, in Ambridge, Pennsylvania. The IWO was a fraternal association that offered its members life insurance and other benefits; it was also a Communist front group. Spingarn read the FBI report on the IWO and found that the bureau made a convincing case that the organization was dominated by the party — but he wasn't sure that everyone who was involved with the group was necessarily a party member or under the party's direction. Because she was hired subject to a background check, Wenglarz was not entitled to a hearing; the department could just fire her. But Spingarn thought decency required that the woman be confronted with the allegations against her and given a chance to tell her side of the story. "Miss Wenglarz's extreme youth," he said, "and the danger that an unwarranted stigma might haunt this eighteen-year-old girl throughout her life in case she is dropped, necessitate caution in reaching a conclusion."[12] Gertrude Schict was treated with the same solicitude. Spingarn wanted to make sure that her personnel files didn't paint her as a Communist, and so called the Treasury colleague who had wanted to fire her. "At some future date any record we make now might well rise to haunt Miss Schicht," Spingarn explained. "As a liberal and civil libertarian, I am sure you will agree that even in time of war the basic elements of fair play should not disappear from our procedure."[13]

Treasury's Un-American Activities Committee, in other words, had almost nothing in common with the one run by Martin Dies. One was concerned with a balance between government security and individual rights; the other put its thumb down on the government's side of the scale. One deliberated in bureaucratic anonymity and explored nuances; the other preferred headlines and bold accusations, seeing little if any difference between Communists and liberals. In October, for instance, HUAC's chairman gave the attorney general a list of 1,121 alleged subversives on the federal payroll — most of whom, upon FBI investigation, turned out to have done nothing more to attract HUAC's attention than have left-wing affiliations.

And Dies, William Hinckley told Spingarn, was a traitor to his country. "The committee and its chairman are sabotaging politically the war effort with the same methods with which they have consistently fought the government's social programs . . . ," he said. "Concession to any demand of Martin Dies is domestic appeasement, as ruthless as the Munich agreement, and of the same character. Submission to the pressure of the Dies committee on one issue will lead to the abrogation of the Treasury's authority to make its own personnel decisions."[14]

Hinckley was in Spingarn's office trying to convince the Treasury lawyer that he wasn't a Communist. He wasn't doing a good job. Hinckley, thirty-two, had been the chairman of the American Youth Congress for four years and appeared before HUAC in 1939 to deny that he was a party member or that the AYC was a front group. Since then he had held a number of minor government jobs at agencies such as the Railroad Retirement Board before landing a position on the Treasury Department's defense savings staff, working with youth groups to peddle government war bonds. But a background check quickly turned up Hinckley's record. Spingarn read the HUAC hearings, looked at four years' worth of stories about the AYC in the *Times,* interviewed Hinckley and people who knew him, and came to the conclusion that Hinckley at the very least had been a hard-core fellow traveler and hence a risk to the department if the Soviet line should swing away from the Allies again. "His private utterances and behind-the-scene activities since that date would indicate that his convictions have not changed,"[15] Spingarn noted.

Spingarn bounced Hinckley from the Treasury. On his job application Hinckley had listed Eleanor Roosevelt as a reference. He didn't mention the friend who had sponsored his membership in the Communist Party in 1935. Her name was Elizabeth Bentley. She was a party member and the future girlfriend of Jacob Golos, a Soviet NKVD agent who was in charge of a secret cell of Communists and fellow travelers in Washington. Bentley furnished him with confidential government documents. One of her sources was Harry Dexter White, the number two person in the Treasury. The department's Un-American Activities board seems to have done a fair job of keeping Communists out the government. But it couldn't do anything about the Communists already there.

On March 3, 1941, Roosevelt nominated Gregory Hankin, a respected attorney on the Federal Power Commission, to a seat on the District of Columbia Public Utilities Commission. Almost two months later McCarran, who was chairman of the subcommittee formed to vet the routine appointment, announced that Hankin wasn't qualified for the post. Two more months passed, and the term that Hankin was supposed to fill expired without a confirmation hearing ever taking place.

After eight years in the Senate, McCarran was finding his legs. From the first week of the New Deal, he had proved himself one of the most outspoken and tenacious critics of the president and his policies. He was also a clever parliamentarian who quickly mastered the maneuvers and amendments that are the block and tackle of lifting and moving legislation. And he could filibuster with the best of them. But legislative brain and brawn would carry a senator only so far. What he needed above all was the chairmanship of a committee — the feudal baronies of the body, where the chairman was liege lord, ruler of all that he could schedule or delay, impervious to the slings and arrows of committee majorities, party leadership, or even the overwhelming hostility of the entire Senate. In the tradition-bound body, two traditions towered above all others: unfettered debate (hence the power of the filibuster) and the sovereignty of committee chairmen. Technically there were rules to get a senator to shut up or wrest a bill from a committee's death grip (either a cloture vote, which required a two-thirds majority, to end debate, or a discharge petition to pry a bill or nomination away from a chair). But in practice a senator never knew when he might have to avail himself of one of these crucial privileges, so most were loathe to curtail their use by their colleagues. Nothing, then, was more important to becoming a power in the Senate than owning one of the chairmen's seats, which, in another bow to tradition, were handed out based on seniority. In the gerontocracy of the Senate, the ability to get reelected and stay alive was what mattered most.

McCarran became a chairman toward the middle of his second term. He was almost sixty-five years old, the age at which most men get ready to retire but which in the Senate constituted a solon's teenage years. A chairmanship was like learning to drive: an exhilarating feeling of freedom, theoretically circumscribed by laws but realistically curbed only by the individual's common sense. Unfortunately for McCarran, the committee that he inherited was the legislative equivalent of Grandma's old car: the District of Columbia Committee, which made the chairman the mayor of Washington, a community of voteless citizens, most of whom were black and poor and lived in dilapidated dwellings lining the alleyways of the capital and mocking the promises of the American republic.

When McCarran took over the committee in May 1941 he immediately stuck his tongue out at Roosevelt and the party leadership by opposing the president's nomination of Hankin to the Public Utilities Commission. When the nomination expired, Roosevelt renominated Hankin. He seemed a superb candidate for a minor position: Hankin had been a government attorney since the administration of Calvin Coolidge. He was endorsed by Supreme Court justices Harlan Stone and Louis Brandeis and Harvard Law School dean Roscoe Pound. McCarran publicly opposed Hankin for his lack of qualifications. Slowly, however, the real reason emerged: Hankin had been born in Russia, as were his wife's parents. He was, McCarran insinuated, a Communist.

Roosevelt asked his aide James Rowe to look into the matter. Rowe examined McCarran's files, as well as those of the FBI, the Dies Committee, and the State Department. "I am absolutely convinced in my own mind that Hankin is not a Communist," Rowe told the president. "McCarran has actively opposed only three of your nominations," Rowe added. "They were Felix Frankfurter, Jerome Frank and Gregory Hankin. These three have nothing in common except they are Jews. There is no question of McCarran's anti-Semitism. As you may remember he tried to make out Frankfurter to be a Communist."*[16]

McCarran was a casual anti-Semite. Words like *kike* fell easily from his lips, but his prejudices were largely of his time and place. What Hankin really was to McCarran was his rook to FDR's king: a way to block the president's wishes and reassert the authority of the legislative branch. McCarran, for instance, soon sent word to the president through Senator James Byrnes that he would withdraw his objection if Roosevelt really wanted him to do so.

Rowe advised Roosevelt to play it tough. "Frankly I have not the slightest faith in McCarran's future behavior and Byrnes agrees with me." Rowe noted. "I think this is too unimportant to allow McCarran to give the impression he is doing you a favor. . . . This morning you signed a nomination of U.S. marshal for Nevada. However the nomination has not yet been sent to the Senate. I would suggest this nomination be held. . . . This procedure is crude enough for McCarran to get the point."[17]

---

*Earlier in the year Attorney General Robert Jackson had made the same allegation to Harold Ickes. "Bob told me that Jerome Frank's nomination as a member of the Circuit Court of Appeals of the New York district, was being held up by McCarran because Frank is a Jew," Ickes recorded in his diary. (Ickes, diary, 8 March 1941, Library of Congress.)

This hurt. The marshal's office was a key position that McCarran wanted purged of Pittman appointees. Marshal Frank Middleton, whose term expired in the summer of 1942, had been a close friend of Key Pittman's, which made him a marked man. McCarran recommended to the president that he name Ely machinist James Whalen to the position. McCarran knew he could count on Whalen. "Your counsel will guide my actions,"[18] he assured the senator.

So as Hankin's confirmation struggle dragged on without a hearing in sight, so too did the appointment of a federal marshal for Nevada. McCarran suspected that Democratic National Committee chairman Ed Flynn, who had a ranch in Nevada, was behind the delay, and he struck back at him. "I have returned the compliment, as a pet of his was nominated to be judge of North Dakota," McCarran told Reno postmaster Pete Petersen. "I had that tied up; so it is a case of tie versus tie. I don't know who will come out first and it doesn't make much difference anyway."[19]

Three appointments, then, were being held up in a confirmation chess match — two of them by McCarran. After the impasse dragged on for two months, McCarran was ushered into the Oval Office. The president told him he wanted Hankin appointed, then he pulled out the nomination for Whalen to become the U.S. marshal. "I have your U.S. Marshal here," Roosevelt said. "I am holding it for a day or two on the request of the department as they want to make a little more investigation."[20]

Finally, in October, Hankin went before the committee. He was a small, bespectacled man with a bad comb-over. "You native-born Americans don't realize to what extent you take the liberties and institutions of this country for granted," Hankin said, his voice breaking and his eyes welling with tears. "I have seen a country where life and liberty count for nothing."[21] The committee voted 4 to 2 to approve Hankin. "I shall vote against the confirmation of Mr. Hankin,'" McCarran vowed, "so long as the record stands in the FBI as it does."[22]

Almost eight months after he was first nominated, Hankin was confirmed. Roosevelt had beaten McCarran. But if McCarran could use one of the least powerful committees in the Senate to obstruct the president's will for the better part of a year, Roosevelt's loyalists in the party leadership were wise to keep McCarran out of the chairman's seat on the Judiciary Committee.

In the Senate, however, longevity was its own revenge. And McCarran would live a long time.

Traffic backed up for half a mile on Foxhall Road as virtually all of A-list Washington vied to get to the social event of the season. Joseph and Marjorie Davies were throwing a party for the new Soviet ambassador, Maxim Litvinov, and his British-born wife, Ivy. The Davies mansion was stuffed with Russian art: sixteenth-century religious icons, a magnificent gold-and-enamel Fabergé clock, a vast horde of imperial gold, silver, and porcelain, not to mention socialist-realist paintings of collective farmers selflessly toiling to build a workers' paradise — several truckloads of treasure scooped up by Davies when he had been the U.S. ambassador in Moscow five years before. Davies had recently thanked the Soviets for letting him haul his loot home by publishing a book called *Mission to Moscow.* "All of these trials, purges, and liquidations," he wrote, "which seemed so violent at the time and shocked the world, are now quite clearly a part of a vigorous and determined effort of the Stalin government to protect itself from not only revolution from within but from attack from without. They went to work thoroughly to clean up and clean out all treasonable elements within the country."[23]

The mansion reverberated with the sonorous sounds of a string quartet playing Russian chamber music. Vice President Henry Wallace, never much one for parties, showed up; so, too, did members of the cabinet and the Supreme Court. And over it all presided an elaborately framed and autographed picture of Stalin. Litvinov and Ivy made a very big splash in the capital's notoriously frigid social pool. "The two have already run away with the town,"[24] noted one gossip columnist.

The Russians, once again, were the good guys. Most of the time they weren't. When the Russian Revolution broke out in 1917, Woodrow Wilson called the Bolsheviks worse than the tsars and said that he would not recognize the new regime until it agreed not to incite revolution. Instead, in 1919, the Russians had created the Comintern (Communist International) to spread their ideology around the world. When Roosevelt came to office in 1933, the United States had not had diplomatic relations with the USSR for sixteen years. "If I could only, myself, talk to one man representing the Russians," Roosevelt told Henry Morgenthau, "I could straighten out the whole question."[25]

That turned out to be Roosevelt's basic philosophy for dealing with the Soviets for the next dozen years: Personal diplomacy could overcome any ideological impasse. Shortly after coming to Washington, Roosevelt made a deal with Boris Skvirsky, Russia's unofficial representative in the capital and a friend of Pat Jackson's. In exchange for recognition, the Soviet Union would agree to repay the tsarist debts and not to support revolutionary movements within the United States. "Boris is cautiously optimistic over recognition,"[26] Jackson told Frankfurter a few months into the New Deal. But when Soviet commissar of foreign affairs Maxim Litvinov journeyed to Washington in November to sign the agreement, he balked at the noninterference clause. William Bullitt, who was representing Roosevelt, handed Litvinov the accord along with the schedule for ships back across the Atlantic. Litvinov signed. When Roosevelt and Litvinov met in the White House, the president told the Old Bolshevik that he was willing to bet that five minutes before Litvinov died, he would be thinking of his parents and would want to make his peace with God. Litvinov looked at Roosevelt and didn't say a word.[27]

Litvinov was more talkative at the National Press Club. "The Communist Party of America," he claimed, "is not concerned with the Communist Party of Russia and the Communist Party of Russia is not concerned with the Communist Party of America."[28]

Bullitt went to Moscow as the first U.S. ambassador to the Soviet Union. In 1935 American Communists Earl Browder and William Foster turned up for a Comintern congress, preaching fiery revolution and infuriating Bullitt. The Comintern meeting was such a brazen violation of the recognition agreement, Bullitt reported to Roosevelt, that Washington should consider breaking diplomatic relations with Moscow. "The Soviet foreign office," Bullitt wrote, "does not understand the meaning of honor or fair dealing but it does understand the meaning of acts. . . . We shall never find a better moment to act against the direction of the Communist movement in the United States by the dictator in the Kremlin."[29]

Bullitt soon found himself with a new job. His replacement was Joseph Davies, a wealthy lawyer and prominent Democrat (he had given $17,500 to the party in 1936) who had married cereal heiress Marjorie Post. Davies arrived in Moscow in January 1937, filling an entire train with his entourage of servants and household items. He sat through the purge trials with a brilliant and moody foreign service officer named George Kennan as his translator. During breaks in the proceedings he told Kennan to fetch him lunch. "Had the president wished to slap us down," Kennan recalled years later, "and to mock us for our efforts in the development of Soviet-American relations he could not have done better with this appointment."[30]

For Davies, being ambassador was something of a distraction from his favored pursuits, sailing his yacht around the Baltic and collecting art. When *Izvestia*'s Washington correspondent Vladimir Romm was recalled to Moscow and purged, many of his friends in the American press corps pleaded his innocence and asked Davies to help. The ambassador accepted Romm's confession that he had schemed with Trotsky. "After all he is a Soviet citizen," Davies told the *New York Times*'s Arthur Krock, "knew Soviet law and entered into the situation with his eyes open."[31]

Almost nothing the Soviets could do offended Davies. When an electrician found a microphone hidden above Davies's desk, the ambassador told his staff not to worry. "If the Soviets had a dictaphone installed," he said, "so much the better — the sooner they would find that we were friends, not enemies."[32]

Not all American diplomats were so friendly. In Washington Ambassador Constantine Oumansky invited State Department official Loy Henderson to lunch at the embassy, smiled a smile full of gold teeth, and suggested that they meet privately from time to time, so that the American diplomat could give the Russian names of people in the government to work with and pointers on how to get industrial and military supplies. In exchange, Oumansky would use his influence with high government officials and well-known columnists to help Henderson. You could be ambassador to Moscow, Oumansky suggested. You would be amazed to know how many influential American friends I have, he added.

It was perhaps a measure of either Oumansky's audacity or past success that he would try to recruit one of the better known anti-Communist officials in the State Department as an intelligence asset. "A walking insult,"[33] Secretary of State Cordell Hull called the Russian. But Oumansky's bragging was not wholly without foundation. A few months after lunching with Henderson, Oumansky met with Roosevelt and Ickes in the summer of 1939. The president, Oumansky reported to Moscow, promised him that anti-Soviet bureaucrats in the State Department would have no influence.

Many of the Russian experts in the department certainly believed that this was the case. The department, for example, had already folded its Russian division into the European division, diluting the efficacy of its best-trained (and most skeptical) Soviet experts and even giving their books and documents away to the Library of Congress. George Kennan called it a purge. He and Charles Bohlen suspected that Eleanor Roosevelt and Harry Hopkins were behind it. "There is strong evidence that pressure was brought to bear from the White House," Kennan recalled. "Here, if ever, was a point at which there was indeed the smell of Soviet influence or strongly pro-Soviet influence, somewhere in the higher reaches of government."[34]

The Hitler-Stalin pact obliterated that influence. Official Washington suddenly treated the Russian embassy like a plague house. The only ones who bothered to show up anymore for the October Revolution parties were the Germans. The Justice Department began arresting various Communists, such as Earl Browder, who was sentenced to four years for a case of passport fraud.

Hitler's invasion of the Soviet Union got the Russian embassy back into the society columns. Roosevelt commuted Browder's sentence. The skeptics in the State Department bit their tongues. Bohlen, whose Russian neighbors had disappeared from his Moscow apartment in the middle of the night during the purges, knew as well as anyone the reality of Soviet Communism. "With the fate of the world hanging on the outcome of the Russian-German fighting, I had no inclination to emphasize the odious parts of the Soviet system," he recalled. "On the contrary, I went right along with everyone else, doing everything I could to help our embattled ally."[35]

And so while Russian troops battled the Nazis, Washington's elite lined up in Joe Davies's mansion to shake Maxim Litvinov's hand. A year earlier Litvinov had been suddenly summoned to see Stalin. Ivy Litvinov never expected to see her husband again. But instead of being sent to the basement of Lubyanka, Litvinov was sent to Washington. He was sixty-six and had been in tsarist prisons and British jails. He had negotiated with presidents and prime ministers around the world and recently had more than a little reason to expect to be shot by the boss he'd served faithfully for years. Now he was the toast of Washington, a devoted Communist feted by a millionaire capitalist. Stranger things had happened to him. *Life* magazine photographers covered the gala like a Hollywood premier. "Washington's biggest blowout since the war began," *Life* called the bash. "More celebrities than I have seen under one roof,"[36] added a *Washington Post* society writer.

The train rundled and rocked its way west, the bleakness of the Nevada desert giving way to purple mountains and fields of clover as the track climbed into the Ruby Mountains near the town of Wells. McCarran had gone to Denver on the government's dime to hold hearings, then canceled the meeting and jumped on a train to California to see his daughters. He wrote to his wife:

> Dear Girl,
> I never really know how much you are to me until I am away
> from you. Then you come to seem so lovely, more lovely even

than in the old days when we sat at the old wall and you said yes, more lovely than when your hair and mine was dark and yours was so beautiful. Now the gray mixed with the dark crowns your lean face and I know as you must know that to me you are now the girl I knew and the mother I know crowned by the glory of fine years. Years that have matured us both years through which we endured, you endured all my failings and faults and short comings and I endured to learn to love my sweetheart of the yester years more, and to miss her more when she is away from me because there is no one who knows me so well nor who would endure and forgive so much. Gold bless my little mother sweetheart that's my thought even when I am farthest away. My little "Grandmother" sweetheart now. Yes?

He had to visit his daughters because the Church would not let them come East. "I think when two sisters give their lives to the church the least that the church can do is to give them and those who reared them the consolation of being in proximity," McCarran fumed to Mary. "Well I never did go much on the wisdom of your 'seniors.'"[37]

We are now in sight of dear old Clover Mountains, great patches of snow on their tops and slopes, their spines and peaks reaching into the bluest blue sky. Here in the foreground the purple sage and the green juniper — no sight like that any other place only in Nevada. I can see the opening to the valley now — the old chicken ranch and the hill side; the valley is filled with a blue haze today that seems to reach everywhere and over all a few tufts of white clouds — nice.

McCarran was especially upset that Margaret seemed to be wasting her life teaching music. Politics, he always thought, was what she would excel at. Maybe a nun couldn't run for office, but she could at least study and write on current affairs. Protestants like Reinhold Niebuhr could spout off constantly about the need for socialism; why couldn't a good Catholic talk a little sense? "She has given too much already to the teaching of music, and it seems to me that one becomes stale, if one is forever bending his efforts in one line," McCarran told Mary. "There is too much in Margie to permit her to become warped."[38]

I can see my road in Angel Lode winding up the hill — it looks good. The old house is still there and the old building that was the Bull's Head Hotel. Do you remember what happened in the sitting room of the Bulls Head Hotel? You have the little ring yet. I remember you cried and I wondered why you would cry and you said because you were happy and I was happy and then we drove out to the valley and your father and sisters and all looked me over and teased you about me. Then when I was leaving, as we drove into Wells, you said you wished the old train would never come. You liked me then, didn't you, pal?[39]

When the train arrived in Berkeley, a forest service car, as always, was waiting to drive McCarran around the northern edge of San Francisco Bay to Marin County, to the small convent in San Anselmo in the nape of Mount Tamalpais, where redwoods shaded the lower reaches and manzanita crowned the heights and the sky was as pure and as blue as a newborn's eyes. It was a beautiful place to live; a terrible place to keep his daughters. Sometimes he hated his church.

In May, days before Roosevelt freed Browder, two FBI agents visited Whittaker Chambers in his office in the Time-Life Building, where he was an editor at *Time* magazine. The agents wanted to talk about Communists in government, a subject Chambers was reputed to know something about. Chambers, for whom crossing the street was an act fraught with great moral peril, called Adolf Berle to ask the assistant secretary of state if it was okay. Go ahead, Berle assured him.

Chambers then told the agents the same story that he had related to Berle the day after the Soviet Union invaded Poland, almost three years earlier. On that evening Chambers and journalist Isaac Don Levine went to Berle's for dinner and afterward sat on lawn chairs outside in the warm, honeysuckle-scented Washington evening. Chambers had wanted to talk to the president, but Levine couldn't get past his secretary. So they went to Berle, and Chambers outlined his career in the Washington Communist underground. At midnight they wandered inside and Berle scribbled notes under the heading of "Underground Espionage Agent,"[40] jotting down names Chambers had given him: Pressman, Witt, Abt, Charles Kramer, Elinor Nelson, Laurence Duggan, Noel Field, Julian Wadleigh, Vincent Reno, Solomon Adler, Frank Coe, Lauchlin Currie, and Alger Hiss. Levine also scrawled some notes later that night, picking up one name that Berle missed: Harry White.

Berle, did little with the information. He apparently made a few calls but didn't press the issue very far or even send his notes to the FBI until 1943. By then the bureau had already interviewed Chambers in his office and dismissed the veracity of his tale. "History, hypothesis, or deduction," the agents concluded in 1942.[41]

Sunday, September 12, 1943, broke gorgeous and hopeful in Washington. The summer heat and humidity finally disappeared. McCarran could actually wear a suit again without being uncomfortable. He drove from his house in northwest Washington and crossed the bridge over nearby Rock Creek, where the trees below were ablaze with autumn. On the hill above the other side of the stream perched the campus of the oldest Catholic college in the country, where the gothic spires of Georgetown University bristled in the cool air. So did McCarran. *Would Sam show up?*

McCarran entered the massive gray stone Healy Building, just off the quad, and climbed to the third floor, where Gaston Hall was filling for the commencement exercises that had been postponed from the spring. Stained-glass windows glowed softly with light, flowers filled the stage, an orchestra played, and three score graduates squirmed in their gowns. *Was that Sam in the back?*

McCarran could be very sentimental. He never forgot how, when he'd dropped out of the University of Nevada to help out on the farm, his mother had insisted on going to commencement with him and watching his former classmates pick up their degrees. She wept. Oh, how she would have loved to have seen her boy this day, standing on the stage at Georgetown, dressed in a scholar's robes and mortarboard. The president of the university intoned the Latin words, draped a purple velvet sash over the senator's large neck, and handed Patrick Anthony McCarran the honorary degree. In the audience McCarran's family beamed: Birdie. Norine. Patty (as always the stylish one in a chartreuse silk dress) and her husband down from New York. *Where the hell was Sam?*

"I surely hope Sammy will take time out and attend the exercises," Eva Adams said. "I know it would mean a lot to the senator."[42]

Sam was a no-show. Even through he was going to medical school at Georgetown, he couldn't be bothered to stop by and see his father receive his honorary degree. With Patty living with her husband out on Long

Island, Sam had replaced his sister as the ever-present source of worry and fret in McCarran's life. When Birdie McCarran wanted to join her husband on a trip, Sam threw a fit, refusing to be left alone with his handicapped sister, Norine. He often seemed to want nothing from his father, except help getting rid of parking tickets or beer that he wasn't supposed to get under wartime rationing. "I'm worried about Sam," Margie McCarran told her mother. "The depression is the natural result of too much study. He ought to have a girl. Try to get him out of that shy 'inferior' feeling. I'm praying hard that you won't have too hard a job with Sam now."[43]

McCarran gave a gloomy speech. "Dictatorship is not always a creature of war," he said. "Sometimes it comes tiptoeing stealthily upon an unsuspecting people in time of peace. . . ." Once, McCarran explained, Congress made laws. Now the president appointed bureaucrats who issued directives that had all the force of law, except the bureaucrats were responsible to the president, not (like Congress) to the people. "This is more than a temporary tilting of the scales," McCarran said. "It is a derangement of the fundamental balance which has maintained our form of government for over one hundred and fifty years as the outstanding example of a free democracy. It may be a tipping of the chute down which, if it be not righted, we may eventually plummet toward the abyss of fascism. May God forbid!"[44]

To the graduating college seniors, the elderly white-haired senator must have sounded like a man from outer space. Roosevelt had been president for a decade, almost half a young lifetime; few had any memory of anyone else in the White House. Many of the young men in the audience had been drafted or volunteered for the military and would soon be going overseas to fight German and Japanese soldiers — and here was McCarran, warning that the greatest threat to U.S. freedom came from government bureaucrats. The applause was polite, if that. "The speech, I am sorry to say, did not go over any too good," one of McCarran's staff noted. "It was beautifully prepared but indirectly attacked the administration, of course, and seemed a little heavy, too long, and not suited to a graduation. I think the senator sensed this although everybody was very flattering to him about it."[45]

Afterward McCarran and his family returned home for a party, the house crowded, the table groaning with crab salad and tomatoes, sandwiches, nuts, cakes, homemade ice cream. Birdie baked a pink iced cake. Cocktails were poured. Patricia, as always, had more than she should have.

Sam stayed upstairs. He had to study, he whined. Two days of whiskers gruffed his face. He asked one of McCarran's staffers to send up some food. "He did not even come down while the company was there," sputtered one of the secretaries. "I would like to take him by the back of the neck and shake some sense of decency into him. I know the senator must have been terribly disappointed, but there seems to be no way to arouse him to any sense of what a son should be."[46]

Sam McCarran, twenty-two, did not have to fight in the war. He stayed in medical school. And McCarran passed a bill exempting doctors from gasoline rationing. Sam liked to drive the coupe that his father had given him.

Most of the marines in boot camp with Paul Douglas at Parris Island, South Carolina, were around nineteen. He was fifty, a Quaker who yearned to go to war. The economics professor from the University of Chicago lost thirty pounds in basic training. "I think, therefore, that I am a good military risk," he told his friend Harold Ickes, "and would not weaken the war effort by getting overseas. I feel a deep and constant urge within me for this type of action."[47]

The months dragged on and Douglas could not get assigned overseas. His name topped the list of those taking the test for private first class. He was more thrilled than he had been when he got his Ph.D. He wrote to Secretary of War Frank Knox for a combat assignment. He asked Ickes to help.

In 1943 Douglas shipped out to the Pacific. He read Somerset Maugham and Robert Louis Stevenson on the long voyage and saw the ports they saw but no combat. While young bodies rushed Japanese positions on Bougainville and Tarawa, Douglas haunted old bookstores behind the lines in New Caledonia, where he served as a staff officer at headquarters and read Diderot and Comte de Saint-Simon, delighting in the rationalism of the Enlightenment in a world gone mad. "I must confess that in many respects I feel almost as remote from the actual field of combat as I did in the United States," Douglas wrote Ickes. "I am still hoping that sometime before the war ends I may experience personally some of the hardships and dangers of the men in the front lines."[48]

Finally Douglas was assigned to a front-line unit. By May 1945 the marines had landed on Okinawa, and Douglas was reading Dante in a watery foxhole. He took off his major's oak leaves and went to the front with the enlisted men. Advancing on a hill, he hit the ground under fire and couldn't get up. Blood poured from his left arm. With his right hand he tied a tourniquet as best he could and struggled to his feet. "A deep wave of exaltation swept through me," Douglas recalled, "that at my age I had shed blood in defense of my country."[49]

He moved forward. Toward the hill. Other marines dragged him back.

United Press correspondent Allen Drury stepped into the elevator to go up to the Senate press gallery on January 25, 1944. "You won't be doing anything in the Senate today," the elevator boy said. "Van Nuys is dead."[50]

The Senate met at noon. For eleven years Fred Van Nuys had been a senator, having been sworn in minutes after McCarran; for three years he had been the chairman of the Judiciary Committee, having nudged out McCarran for the position. Members took to the floor to mourn the loss of their colleague and then, after less than half an hour, went into recess in his honor. "In an institution composed in the main of elderly men," Drury noted in his diary, "death is a topic of vital interest and moves invisible but all-dominating through the halls."[51]

No one was more interested than McCarran, who at sixty-seven was two years younger than Van Nuys. In ill health again and needing extensive dental work, McCarran had just returned from a stay in the Bethesda Naval Hospital ("a wonderful place to get a rest") when his old nemesis died. McCarran joined the senatorial mourning party for the train trip to Indiana for the funeral and then returned to Washington, where he sat in his deceased colleague's chair. "An unfortunate death,"[52] McCarran told his daughter Mary, dictating a letter from his new perch at the center of the committee's large table. "There was some revolution here in the Senate,"[53] he told his daughter Margaret.

McCarran was right. A president, especially one elected by a huge majority during a national crisis, comes to Washington like a butterfly bursting his cocoon: ready to fly. A senator, especially one who barely squeaked into office from the smallest state in the Union, comes to the capital like a larva: ready to crawl. After a decade or so their life cycles intersect: the beauty and power of the presidency wanes with age, while the potency and perquisites of the senator grow with seniority. After eleven years in the Senate, McCarran was finally chairman of a major committee. "It is," he exulted to Mary, "by far the most powerful and influential committee in the Senate and its verdict is looked to constantly in all matters of law. I am going again on all eight cylinders — in fact I am doubling the cylinders sometimes."[54]

Soon after taking over the Judiciary Committee, McCarran gave a speech to the Federal Bar Association. "An interesting character," Drury observed, "with his huge square figure, his diamond ring, his perfectly tailored suits, his cynical face like one of Hans Holbein's, and his shock of white hair swirling upward like a cockatoo's."[55] With Attorney General Francis Biddle looking on, McCarran launched into an attack on the "new ideology" of the New Deal. "I have revered our Constitution as long as I can remember," McCarran said. "Let no one have the temerity to come before the committee of which I am chairman to try to tear it down. If we abandon constitutional principles for a minute, we are straying from Americanism."[56]

Biddle had expected as much. When Van Nuys died, Biddle told Harold Ickes that he was desperate enough to keep McCarran out of the chairmanship that he was considering offering McCarran a lifetime appointment to the Ninth Circuit Court. "McCarran," noted Ickes, "has always made trouble for the administration and now he is in a position to cause even more. He is a particular thorn in my side. . . . I told Francis that while, ordinarily, I thought it was terrible to use a federal judgeship to buy a man off, I was in favor of it in this instance."[57]

Some people were *really* sorry that Van Nuys was dead.

On February 22 Roosevelt vetoed the 1944 tax bill. The president had asked Congress to increase taxes by ten and a half billion dollars. Congress gave him a two-billion dollar raise. "A tax relief bill providing relief not for the needy but for the greedy,"[58] Roosevelt called the bill. The next day Senate majority leader Alben Barkley resigned his post in protest. He had gone to the White House twice to argue against the veto, and the president's gratuitous slap was more than he was willing to endure. Reporters had never seen the genial and loyal Barkley in such a fury. "His anger is typical of that of the rest of the Senate," Drury noted. "This is the last time the Roosevelt administration will get anything but the most essential war measures out of the Congress of the United States. There is, in fact, serious doubt now that it will get even those."[59]

Congress was in open revolt. Barkley was immediately reelected as majority leader and Congress quickly overrode Roosevelt's veto, the first time a president had been overruled on a revenue bill. Wartime unity had proved elusive; now even Roosevelt's most loyal Democrats were on the warpath against *him*. The president's majority in Congress had been steadily slipping since the heady days of the second term when so many Democrats thronged the chamber that they had to sit amid the lonely Republicans. "The coalition of Republicans and Southern Democrats is in the saddle now,"[60] Drury wrote.

In addition to killing off the New Deal programs, Congress enacted the Smith-Connally or War Labor Disputes Act, which curbed labor's right to strike and slashed funding to hated wartime agencies such as OPA and OWI. "Congress seems to behave worse daily,"[61] Eleanor Roosevelt lamented. "Liberals," added Archibald MacLeish, "meet in Washington these days, if they can endure to meet at all, to discuss the tragic outlook for all liberal proposals, the collapse of all liberal leadership, and the inevitable defeat of all liberal aims. It is no longer feared, it is assumed, that the country is headed back to normalcy, that Harding is just around the corner."[62] In the Senate press gallery, Drury was equally gloomy. "There is," he wrote, "growing between the Hill and the White House a real, deep and ugly hatred that can have the most serious consequences for the country."[63]

At five minutes before ten on April 27, 1944, Sewell Avery walked into his office at the Chicago headquarters of Montgomery Ward and found Attorney General Francis Biddle waiting for him with half a dozen army troops. Avery was the chairman of the board and president of the huge retailer, which sold six hundred million dollars' worth of goods annually, employed seventy-five thousand people, and operated six hundred stores across the country. Avery was also a devoted Roosevelt hater, a member of the Liberty League and America First. Biddle said that he was carrying out an order from the president to take over Montgomery Ward. Would Avery mind leaving his office? "To hell with the government,"[64] Avery sneered.

Avery had been saying as much for the past two years, ever since early 1942 when the CIO's United Mail Order, Warehouse and Retail Employees Union won an election to represent the company's workers. Montgomery Ward refused to deal with the union, the War Labor Board stepped in, twice the president ordered the company to sign a contract, and finally the union went out on strike. Roosevelt ordered the strikers to return to work and the company to recognize the union; the workers obeyed, the company didn't.

"This reckless old man was paralyzing the national war effort . . . ," Biddle recalled. "Seventy-five percent of Ward's customers were farmers engaged in the government's war-food program. Substantially the entire economy of the nation was a war economy, delicately balanced and synthesized. The resistance to the War Labor Board's decision by such a powerful corporation would necessarily affect the stability of all labor relations and therefore jeopardize the continuity of war production."[65]

So Roosevelt ordered the army to seize the Chicago plant. Avery refused to go. "Take him out," Biddle told the soldiers. Avery glared at the attorney general and spat out the most venomous words that came to mind: "You New Dealer!"[66]

Two GIs linked hands to form a seat and carried Avery — hands folded across his lap, his face tight and impassive — out of his office, into the elevator, and outside to the parking lot. A news photographer snapped a picture, which covered front pages across the country the next day. "Government not by law but by bayonet,"[67] roared the *Fort Wayne News Sentinel*. Senator Harry Byrd wondered if Biddle wanted to become an American Himmler. Illinois Republican representative Leo Elwood Allen demanded the attorney general's impeachment. A Gallup poll found that 60 percent believed the government to be in the wrong.

McCarran was outraged. The month before, he had sponsored a Senate resolution (SR 252) to investigate the constitutional or statutory authority of every executive order (some 3,374 of them) and federal rule and regulation issued since March 1933 — in essence a mandate to scour the legal basis of the entire New Deal. The day after Avery was carried out of his office, McCarran dispatched an investigator to Chicago and created a subcommittee to look into the legality of the government's action. The subcommittee — which besides McCarran included West Virginia Republican reactionary Chap Rivercomb and Arizona Democrat Ernst McFarland — declined to let Biddle testify. "There is nothing new the attorney general could tell us," McCarran snapped. "This is a government of law. Men have no right to take unto themselves more than is authorized by law."[68]

With McFarland dissenting, the subcommittee slammed the attorney general for illegally seizing control of the retailer. McCarran recommended that every executive order should contain citations for the constitutional or statutory authority being invoked — something Biddle admitted didn't exist in the Montgomery Ward case, although the attorney general insisted that other wartime presidents had established the precedent. A district court ruled against the government, but an appeals court reversed the judgment, and the Supreme Court declined to take up the matter.

McCarran, Biddle thought, was able "like some malevolent spider, to spin the web of his own facts and law out of the depths of his belly."[69] Most newspaper editorialists agreed with the attorney general. "McCarran apparently considers himself competent to decide one of the most complex emergency wartime disputes the country has faced," sniffed the *Chicago Sun*.[70] The *Washington Sunday Star* ran a cartoon of the bald, thinly mustachioed Biddle carrying Avery out of Montgomery Ward himself, with McCarran waving a finger at him. "You take him right back where you found him," he barks.

Joe McDonald was alive, after all. There had been two Joe McDonalds on Wake Island, and it was the one from Cody, Wyoming, not Reno, Nevada, who was killed when the garrison on the atoll surrendered. The International Red Cross told the editor of the *Nevada State Journal* that his boy was being held a prisoner in Shanghai.

If Joe Junior were alive, McCarran told Joe Senior, he would get him back. "He had been on my mind," McCarran wrote, "many, many times, and I can't tell you how happy I feel and how glad I am that my feeling that night when I looked at his picture, on that occasion when you were so kind as to have me for dinner, has been verified. I refer to that deep conviction that he was still alive."[71]

McCarran pulled every string he could. He called the secretary of state. He contacted the Vatican. He tried to get young McDonald, who had done some stringing for United Press from Wake, declared a war correspondent. "He speaks of young Joe so often," Adams told McDonald.[72] "We are leaving no stone unturned on your behalf," McCarran wrote to the younger McDonald. "Keep your chin up and take good care."[73]

Then McCarran heard the good news. "In strictest confidence," McCarran told the elder McDonald, "I have had a talk with a party who has been trying to help me in the State Department, and Joe's name is on the list of those who are supposed to come out on the next boat . . . this is the deepest, darkest secret I have ever given you, and you must not mention it to anyone."[74]

It was not to be. McDonald stayed in prison until the end of the war. McCarran could do nothing more.

CHAPTER 12

Hell Popping

The most powerful political activity in the world is the quiet whisper in the ear of someone who will listen and take heed.[1]

— Pat McCarran

On the evening of July 12, 1943, a plane appeared above a small town outside Las Vegas, flying over a huge industrial park, past neat rows of homes and apartments and several stores and churches, before finally dipping low as it approached a baseball field where three sheds suddenly burst into brilliant flames as incendiary bombs exploded. The plane was the *Memphis Belle,* which logged twenty thousand combat miles and dropped more than sixty tons of bombs on Europe before the B-17 Flying Fortress was reassigned to the homefront to promote the war effort. The hamlet was Basic Townsite (soon to be called Henderson), home of the largest magnesium factory in the world, Basic Magnesium Incorporated, which processed the light metal for bombs. Earlier in the day the crew of the *Belle* toured the plant, or BMI as everyone called it. "We have dropped a heck of a lot of your product on Germany,"[2] *Belle* pilot Robert Morgan told cheering workers.

Two summers before the townsite was nothing but a two-lane road cutting through the sagebrush when Pat McCarran wrote a letter to Franklin Roosevelt. The Office of Production Management, McCarran pointed out, had recommended increasing magnesium production, and Nevada just happened to have one of the largest deposits of the ore in the country. The president replied that Nevada would get a plant. In July 1942 the government's Defense Plant Corporation signed a contract with a new company called Basic Magnesium. The government would fund the construction of the plant and own the operation, while BMI would manage the $150 million project. "The biggest thing given to any state,"[3] Edwin Watson, Roosevelt's secretary, assured McCarran.

Nevada was a place that hid its treasure well. Below the rough, empty landscape was the state's only real resource: a fortune in metals — gold, silver, and copper. And when the war created an insatiable hunger for light alloys that burned quick and bright and caused fires that could not be put out with water, the ugly wastes of Nye County turned out to be hiding the world's largest deposit of magnesium. The white alkaline dust that poisoned water and tormented miners and settlers was even more deadly when refined into magnesium and packaged into incendiary bombs.

War was hell but it was also an opportunity. While McCarran labored like Sisyphus to keep his country from rolling into war, he still grabbed as many defense contracts as he could for Nevada. Reno got an air signal training base (later Stead Air Force Base), Las Vegas cadged an army air corps gunnery school (later Nellis AFB), and Fallon picked up a naval air station. While McCarran was happy to get anything that would bring jobs and dollars to his state, he had far bigger dreams.

McCarran wanted to transform Nevada. The state's economy was nothing but extractive: It took things — rocks from the earth, money from the pockets of gamblers, lawyers' fees from divorcees — but never made anything. Indeed, Nevada defined itself, unlike most places, not so much by what it did or had but by what it didn't have: It was a void, the least populated state in the nation, a wide-open expanse without obstructions or barriers. In 1927, for example, Nevada got its first major military project — the Naval Ammunition Depot at Hawthorne — simply because the whole arsenal could blow up and almost no one would know. Similarly, it made sense to put gunnery and air bases in the state because you could fire off sixteen-inch artillery shells at random or crash a plane and not have to worry about disturbing anything but sagebrush. McCarran wanted to change all that. He had a dream of a new Nevada, a place that made things besides fortunes for absentee mine owners and sold things besides sin and attracted residents for longer than six weeks.

And in the heat waves of southern Nevada, the magnesium plant glimmered like a portent of that vision. BMI would give Nevada a shot at everything it needed: industry and population. It was not an idle fancy. Nevada had great mineral resources and all the space in the world; Boulder Dam offered an endless supply of water and power. All the state needed was a smelter, a catalyst to create the fusion that would give birth to industry. Something like BMI. "The whole area will be built up into one great city," BMI's president Howard Eells promised. "The Pittsburgh of the west."[4]

But industry would never really come to Nevada. A proxy war would — a two-year brawl between the conservative AFL and one of the Communist-dominated CIO unions that would escalate into a national fight threatening McCarran's political survival as never before. It was one of the last — and least known—of the great clashes of the New Deal era.

The plane over BMI that night was not really the *Belle,* which was parked at the Las Vegas airport; it was a stand-in. And the baseball field had not really been bombed; the explosives were set off from the ground. McCarran's vision, too, was an illusion.

In October 1942 Ken Eckert flew from Los Angeles to McCarran Field in Las Vegas.* He met John Bell, and the two of them drove out of town on the Boulder Highway heading southeast. On both sides of the road the barren desert was broken by an odd assortment of slapped-together dwellings, hot dog stands, beer joints, and Clark County's ubiquitous casinos. After about fifteen miles the road dipped into a valley dominated by a series of buildings sprawling over twenty-eight hundred acres. One building alone stretched almost a mile long and half a mile wide. A little more than a year earlier the area had been nothing but empty desert. Then the Defense Plant Corporation built the largest magnesium plant in the world, a monster of a factory sucking up more kilowatts of energy than Arizona, Colorado, New Mexico, and Wyoming combined and capable of producing ten times as much of the light metal as all of Germany. Running such a huge operation, however, proved too much for President Howard Eells, and in October, just as production was starting, the government turned over the plant's management to the giant Anaconda Copper Mining Company. With water and power from Boulder Dam, ore from Gabbs in the middle of the state, and thousands of workers from all over the country, the plant churned out more than 166 million pounds of magnesium ingots over the next two years, which were put on railcars in Las Vegas and sent to Los Angeles to be turned into tracer bullets and bomb casings. And the desert became Basic Townsite, where fourteen thousand workers — 10 percent of the state's population, almost triple the workforce that built Boulder Dam — crowded into prefab houses, trailers, tents, and then spilled over into Las Vegas.[5]

The work was arduous. Alchemizing brucite and magnesite into magnesium was a dangerous process. Workers had to tread carefully around electric cells in rubber shoes to avoid shocks in rooms where the temperature topped 130 degrees during the summer; like troops in World War I they kept gas masks at their sides in case of deadly chlorine leaks. More than two thousand workers were treated for chlorine poisoning in the first six months of production. The smell of bleach was everywhere.

---

*The airport had been named in honor of the senator in 1941.

Bell gave Eckert a tour. On one side of the highway sat Victory Village, a housing complex for whites. Across the road Carver Park, a housing project for blacks, would soon be built. Bell was an old-time member of the CIO from Consolidated Edison in New York, and when he got a job at Basic he was told that the AFL represented all seventeen craft unions recognized at BMI. If he wanted to keep his job, he would have to join the AFL. Bell contacted the CIO, which sent Eckert out from Los Angeles. Bell introduced Eckert to some of the plant workers.

Eckert was thirty-five. His father had been a railway telegrapher, an ardent admirer of Gene Debs, and a union activist in Toledo, Ohio. Young Eckert became a railroad brakeman and a union man himself until he lost his job in the Depression. He joined the local unemployment council, which he later learned was organized by the Communist Party. Eckert was soon the head of the council. He organized an unemployment camp on the courthouse lawn and led a thousand protestors into a large department store, where the crowd smashed windows and hauled away everything they could carry. In 1932 he joined the Communist Party, which sent him to the Lenin School in Moscow, where he learned how to fire guns and throw grenades, as well as more subtle tactics. Returning to the United States, Eckert wound up as the Los Angeles regional director of the National Association of Die Casting Workers. The staff of the union, Eckert later testified, was almost exclusively made up of party members. In 1942 the Die Casters merged with the International Union of Mine, Mill and Smelter Workers.

Before long Eckert gathered forty-nine signatures from BMI employees, and that month the plant was chartered as Local 629 of the International Union of Mine, Mill and Smelters Workers. Then the hard work started.

Bob Hollowwa, a Mine-Mill organizer, drove into Las Vegas with fifty dollars in his pocket and a mimeograph machine in the trunk of his car. He spent the better part of three hours looking for a room without any luck. Las Vegas was Nevada's latest boomtown. Two years earlier, eighty-four hundred people had lived in the town; now almost as many were working just at BMI. Like a mining camp, everything was in short supply and everything cost an arm and a leg. Steaks fetched five dollars, and breakfast for two could cost half as much. When Hollowwa eventually found a room it was four dollars a night, and dinner — a sandwich and a glass of milk — set him back almost a buck. His expense allowance from the union was three dollars a day. In a couple of days he was down to five dollars in his pocket. "Living conditions in Las Vegas impossible,"[6] he complained to union headquarters in Denver.

Hollowwa called BMI's manager, E. O. Case,[7] for an appointment to talk about Mine-Mill's intention to start a union at the plant and got the brush-off. When he finally did get to meet Case, the manager was adamant that the union couldn't pass out flyers at the plant gate. Nothing personal, Case said, he was new to Anaconda and didn't know anything about Mine-Mill, but the plant had a deal with the AFL and that was that.

And that was a lie. Case, in fact, had worked for the company since 1921, there wasn't yet any deal with the AFL, and anyone who spent any time at Anaconda knew all about Mine-Mill — or WFM, as old-timers still sometimes called the union, referring to its original name as the Western Federation of Miners. The two were old enemies. Anaconda had been incorporated in Montana in 1891, a mine that gave its name first to the town sitting atop the biggest discovery of copper in the world and then to a corporate colossus. The Western Federation of Miners was formed in nearby Butte two years later, soon establishing itself as the most radical union in the country. ("Labor produces all wealth," went its slogan. "Wealth belongs to the producer.") Like the constantly fuming smokestack of the smelter that towered above the denuded hill in the town of Anaconda, the mining company dominated Montana, owning great swathes of forest, a sawmill, water companies, a railroad, and every daily newspaper in the state. In the demonology of the mining industry, the WFM loomed almost as large, its leaders avowed socialists, its organizing drives marked by violence and death: thirteen scabs blown up by a bomb at a train station in Independence, Colorado, in one case; its militant leader Big Bill Haywood put on trial for assassinating the governor of Idaho in another (he was acquitted but later served time for calling a strike during World War I, skipped bail, and defected to the Soviet Union, where he died). Anaconda became one of the biggest companies in the world; in 1922 the mining concern spent forty-five million dollars to buy the American Brass Company and a year later paid seventy-seven million for Chile Copper, the largest cash deal in Wall Street history. In 1905 the WFM helped found the Industrial Workers of the World ("The working class and the employing class have nothing in common"), but by 1916 the union had fallen on hard times and changed its name to the International Union of Mine, Mill and Smelter Workers. The union limped along — down to half a dozen locals, some existing on paper only — until 1934, when it went on strike for four months against Anaconda Copper. The union was rejuvenated, more vociferous and political than ever. "The American people," Mine-Mill president Reid Robinson thundered at the union's 1940 convention, "refuse to go to some foreign land to make profits for some of the great industrialists such as the Anaconda Copper Company."[8]

No, Case repeated again and again during the ninety-minute meeting with Hollowwa, you can't pass out flyers. "There would be trouble," the manager said. "The AFL wouldn't like it."[9]

War turned out to be a huge boom for Mine-Mill. The union had taken part in more collective bargaining elections in the past year than it had in the previous six. And Mine-Mill won more than three out of four contests against the AFL, adding thirty thousand workers, which pushed its total membership to more than one hundred thousand. "We are now among the nation's great unions," President Robinson had boasted at the union's convention the previous month.

The Anaconda Copper Mining Company had been named for a boa constrictor, a huge snake that coils around its prey and squeezes the life out of it. Mine-Mill was about to discover that the company still lived up to its name.

The first time the AFL's Ragnald Fyhen took a contract to E. O. Case, the BMI manager told the union organizer to take it away. "Case refused to sign it and refused to go along with any union agreement," Fyhen recalled.

Fyhen had come to southern Nevada in 1932 to work on the Boulder Dam project, earning sixty-five cents an hour and holding furtive union meetings behind the camp barbershop. Soon he had formed Lodge 845 of the International Association of Machinists Union, only the third AFL local in southern Nevada. Then he helped organize the Clark County Central Labor Council, an umbrella group for the unions in the area. Worried that the company would fire him once his organizing activity became known, Fyhen took a part-time job as a salesman with Mutual Benefit Health and Life. A few months later he was laid off from the dam. Then, in 1935, five men were killed in an accident. Fyhen had sold them seventy-five thousand dollars' worth of insurance. His friends, it turned out, had been working for thirty-six hours straight. McCarran was in town, and Fyhen woke him up at the Apache Hotel. McCarran was outraged at the deaths. It was the start of a long friendship between the AFL organizer and the senator.

In 1941, Representative Scrugham told Fyhen that a huge defense plant was coming into the area; he wanted the AFL to guarantee that there would be no work stoppages. After talking to AFL president William Green, Fyhen agreed. Then he negotiated a contract with the Howard

Eells. "I told them," Fyhen remembered, "the situation looked very bad and we had some revolutionary organizers coming into the project and they may expect a strike any time and if there was a work stoppage the AFL could not be blamed."[10]

Fyhen got Eells to agree to a contract and sent it back East for approval by the various AFL union presidents. By the time the contract returned to Nevada for Eells's signature, he had been replaced by Case and Anaconda Copper. Case told Fyhen to take a hike. Then the CIO showed up. Fyhen asked AFL president Green for help, and the union sent dozens of organizers to Nevada. A month after Case met with Hollowwa, he called Fyhen into his office on December 16. Case signed the AFL contract.

Robert Hollowwa showed up outside the main gate at BMI at seven in the morning the day after he met with Case and began handing out leaflets to arriving workers. "O.K. Boys, You Asked for Your Own Union — It's Here!" proclaimed the hand-lettered mimeographs. The union's initiation fee was $2, and monthly dues were $1.50 (compared to the AFL's $27 and $4). "Why pay more?" asked the flyers.

A guard bounded up to Hollowwa. Is that a CIO letter? the guard asked. You can't pass it out here. Hollowwa kept handing out leaflets. The security chief, arrived and took Hollowwa to his office, detaining him for forty-five minutes. I know the old Commie tactic, the chief growled at him. You want to be arrested and made a martyr. He was released.[11]

Hollowwa went back to the gate and began handing out more leaflets. He was picked up again. For a third time Hollowwa went back to the gate and again he was detained. He decided to call it a day.

A veteran organizer, Hollowwa was the new rep of Mine-Mill Local 629. He couldn't find a meeting hall to rent, so union meetings took place at members' homes. Hollowwa worked from seven in the morning to two in the morning virtually every day.

AFL organizers roamed the plant at will, tacking their letters and notices on bulletin boards. CIO organizers were chased away from the plant, harassed outside the gate, and had their literature torn down as soon as it was posted.

Hollowwa was back in the morning. This time the guards knocked the leaflets out of his hands, yelled at approaching cars to run him over, and threatened to beat his head in. Finally they dragged him down the dusty road away from the gate. "The war is on,"[12] he whooped to Eckert.

For once the manager didn't have to wander into rooms and turn on lights at random and tell his employees to park out front to make it look like the Last Frontier was busy. Pat McCarran was in town. In the days when Las Vegas entertainment consisted of Gus Martell and his Fifth Avenue Orchestra or a USO charity rodeo, a visit to southern Nevada by the state's senior senator was enough to fill the Frontier's Canary Room on a Tuesday night in February and make it the hottest place on the Strip. Of course, in 1943, there were only two hotels on the Strip.

And, truth be told, the town could use the business. In December the neon signs that had burned continuously along Fremont Street in downtown Las Vegas since gambling had been legalized in 1931 began going dark at midnight. Bar and casino owners, who had previously kept their doors open around the clock, agreed to adopt voluntary closing hours under threat of a military curfew. The police had been picking up more than a hundred drunks a night on the streets downtown, many of whom were supposed to report the next day for work at BMI, where absenteeism was running as high as 25 percent. Part of the problem was that judges in Los Angeles were sentencing petty criminals and vagrants to "thirty days or BMI." The scofflaws would then report to BMI, cash their first paycheck, and not show up to work again. So the Las Vegas police began picking up itinerants and sending them off to the plant as well. One night, for instance, the police arrested one hundred men and shipped forty-two who could stand under their own power over to BMI, which as hard as the work could be was still preferable to the hellhole of the Las Vegas jail, where a holding cell designed for twenty men sometimes held five times that number and the guards were known to pistol-whip unruly guests.

Things weren't nearly so boisterous out on the Strip, a dusty stretch of the road to Los Angeles just beyond the city limits, where strange and sprawling structures had recently begun appearing. Five years earlier hotel builder Thomas E. Hull stood on this road next to his broken car and watched the parade of autos with California license plates flowing into Las Vegas and the bright lights of Fremont Street. In 1941 Hull opened the first resort on the Strip, El Rancho, where a neon-trimmed windmill and a shimmering swimming pool beckoned parched drivers like an oasis. A year later and a mile down the Strip, the Last Frontier appeared: a sprawling, low-rise complex that looked like a fort. At a time when war shortages made building materials almost nonexistent, the Frontier had somehow found the wherewithal to construct a huge resort, with forests of split-log woodwork, acres of flagstone, 170 air-conditioned rooms, a banquet hall seating six hundred, and a paved parking lot that could fit four hundred cars.

This plush, faux-rustic palace, rising suddenly from the dry wastes of southern Nevada, was the perfect place to pay tribute to the man who'd helped make it all possible: Pat McCarran. Overnight, it seemed, a sleepy if sinful railroad town had come alive. On one side of town the burgeoning Strip signaled the emergence of a tourist mecca; on the other, the giant BMI plant promised a future of heavy industry and thousands of jobs. So it was no surprise to see the Canary Room packed with businessmen, politicians, labor leaders (which in Las Vegas meant the AFL), and the top brass from the new army base — all assembled to pay homage to McCarran. "He appeared to enjoy the vast development in this area," noted Al Cahlan, the editor and publisher of the *Las Vegas Review-Journal,* "much of which was brought to realization under his guiding hand."[13]

Three decades earlier McCarran had come to another Nevada boomtown only to receive a far less warm welcome. A young lawyer who had just passed the bar, McCarran arrived in Tonopah all on fire to make a name for himself. He rose no higher than Nye County district attorney, a job so unimportant that no one else ran for it. He was invited to no parties. The community's elite, like mine and bank owner George Wingfield, looked down on him. McCarran almost seemed to court unpopularity. He defended the man who shot the county's beloved sheriff; he represented the woman who claimed Wingfield gave her VD and beat her. When Wingfield and his cronies persuaded President Theodore Roosevelt to dispatch federal troops to crush an organizing drive by the WFM in nearby Goldfield, McCarran's was a rare voice raised in support of the union. McCarran was an outsider and powerless and he championed those who had neither wealth nor position — and in Tonopah that was enough to get him branded as something of a radical. Now, however, Wingfield was a McCarran supporter, and McCarran found himself philosophically more in tune with those running BMI than with those working for the company. Thirty-seven years after his arrival in Tonopah, no one was going to mistake McCarran for a Red.

A dozen years in Washington made all the difference. Almost every day the post office delivered tribute to his suite in the Senate Office Building: crates of whiskey, boxes of cigars, bottles of maple syrup. Once McCarran had to ignore the bill collectors who came to his speeches and stood in the front and tried to heckle him about his unpaid debts. Now he found himself staying in the best rooms in hotels in Reno and Las Vegas — and he rarely had to worry about the tab, because most of the time it never came. For years

McCarran had railed against the Wingfield political machine in Nevada, sputtering at the intrigues hatched in the banker's second-floor office in the Reno National Bank at First and Virginia Streets, where power brokers of both parties came to plan who would run for office and who would win. "The boys on the corner," McCarran called them. Then Wingfield lost his bank and his fortune but clawed his way back to prosperity and hung onto the second-story office even if the name on the bank was no longer his. And suddenly one of the politicians intriguing with Wingfield in that office was McCarran. "Wingfield became as great an admirer of McCarran as I became,"[14] recalled Norm Biltz, a wealthy Republican.

In Las Vegas McCarran had no more ardent admirer than E. O. Case — Frank, to McCarran. Case was the manager of BMI and the host of the party for the senator at the Last Frontier. If BMI was a gift for Nevada, it was even more of a prize for Anaconda Copper: a cost-plus contract, which meant that the giant mining company was guaranteed a healthy profit at absolutely no risk. Case had been in Las Vegas less than half a year but was already well on his way to becoming a pillar of the community and president of the Rotary Club. A chemical engineer by training, a twenty-year veteran of Anaconda Cooper, Case liked to call himself a humanities engineer. "That is," remembered Berkeley Bunker, "he dealt with people   He was a very personable individual. He mixed right in immediately. . . . And he played a very important part in the affairs of southern Nevada and was a very fine man."[15]

McCarran spent a lot of time at the Frontier during the week he was in town. Most of it with Case. The next night there was a smaller, more intimate dinner in McCarran's honor at the resort, hosted by Walter Bracken, head of the Las Vegas Land & Water Company, the major developer in southern Nevada. With the federal government buying up land left and right around town, Bracken also had a lot to be thankful for. Birdie McCarran, too, was quite busy that week. Mrs. Case threw Mrs. McCarran a tea party and escorted the senator's wife to her own dinner at the Frontier, as well as to a luncheon and a breakfast. On Thursday the McCarrans joined the Cases for a visit to the BMI plant.

While BMI was being built McCarran had wondered if the company was going to be properly appreciative of his help. "That magnesium outfit is coming to me frequently for favors," he told Eva Adams. "If they want any favors from me, they had better play fair in this thing."[16]

After his week in Las Vegas, McCarran no longer had any doubts.

Bob Hollowwa was out on the highway by the plant asking men to sign
union cards when a group of workers started hitting him, then knocked
him down and kicked him.[17] Blood ran from his scalp, his nose, his mouth.
Three days later Hollowwa and two plant workers were back, handing out
leaflets near the gate when more than a dozen men set upon them with
baseball bats. The three jumped into Hollowwa's car, which was pelted
with rocks and whacked with bats. The men tipped the car into a ditch
and were trying to pull Hollowwa out through the broken window when
BMI guards showed up. Hollowwa went to the police and identified some
of the gang as AFL representatives, but the DA declined to press charges.
Just a labor dispute, he told Hollowwa.

Five days later Hollowwa was back at the plant, the windows of his car
shattered, its body pocked as if he had driven through a hailstorm of base-
balls. One CIO plant worker showed up with a pistol, another with a rifle.
Hollowwa sat in the car folding leaflets with Ralph Sargent, whose union
activity had cost him his $1.10-an-hour a job as a chlorinator and who
had been chased by a group of men recently. Sargent had a pistol tucked
into his pocket. Someone said that police were searching cars. Sargent
slipped his pistol under the front seat, where the police found it and
arrested Hollowwa on a concealed weapons charge, a felony that could
earn him up to five years in prison. John Bell cashed in a war bond to post
bail. As it happened, a union lawyer and party member named Abraham
Isserman was residing in Las Vegas long enough to dissolve an unsuccessful
marriage. But since Isserman wasn't licensed to practice in Nevada, he
searched for a local attorney. Finding a lawyer willing to take on the case
in Las Vegas proved almost impossible. The closest competent attorney he
could locate was in Reno, fourteen hours by bus. "The charge was
unfounded and was really designed to strike at the union rather than
Hollowwa,"[18] Isserman noted.

Hollowwa went back to BMI yet again. He was giving out leaflets when
scores of construction workers suddenly poured through the gate, beating
up the CIO men, tearing the clothes off one of them, and stoning the
others with handfuls of rocks. BMI security looked on but did nothing.

"We had a battle battalion of regulars with pipe wrenches and spud
wrenches and all other tools which were handy for labor wars," the AFL's
Ragnald Fyhen remembered. "For weeks we had a regular battle ground
outside the gate every afternoon."[19]

And the sounds of those skirmishes soon carried to Washington. "There
is trouble brewing at Basic Magnesium," McCarran told Reno postmaster

Pete Petersen. "I just was called on the phone. It looks like hell popping down there in the labor lines — CIO and AFL at it again."[20]

Hollowwa soon left Las Vegas for the military. At least in the army he would have a gun.

No union benefited more from the defense ramp-up than Mine-Mill. In one year membership jumped 20 percent. And no union had been more opposed to U.S. involvement in the war. Mine-Mill president Reid Robinson was a founder and vice president of American Peace Mobilization and a fierce opponent of lend-lease. "The labor movement is sternly resolved that no self-appointed national leader shall take this nation into a foreign war," Robinson said in the middle of June 1941. "American labor today is in danger of losing all that it has already gained. The machinery is set up in Washington to change our government to a form of fascist state. . . . Social legislation was gained by years of struggle by American labor. . . . Yet it can all be wiped out with a single stroke of the pen by one man in the White House — President Roosevelt."[21]

Robinson was born in Butte in 1908, the year the Western Federation of Miners was driven out of Nevada. His father was a longtime member of the WFM and secretary-treasurer of Mine-Mill. The young Robinson followed his father into the copper mines and the union; by the age of twenty-six he was president of Mine-Mill. That was 1936, the same year that Mine-Mill heeded the summons of John Lewis and became one of the founding unions of the CIO. Four years later Robinson was a CIO vice president as well.

While Robinson's rise in the labor movement was steady, his feelings about war and international events followed more of a switchback trail. In 1935, for example, when he was a leader of the American League Against War and Fascism, he introduced a resolution at the AFL convention (before the formation of the CIO) calling on union president William Green to immediately call for a general strike of all workers if the United States went to war. Two years later, when the antiwar group had changed its mission to lobby for collective security under the name of the American League for Peace and Democracy, Robinson urged the repeal of the Neutrality Act and a boycott of Japan and German goods. Two more years and Robinson was again a leader in the anti-interventionist movement, sitting on the executive committees of three left-wing isolationist groups. "We hate war," he said at an American Peace Mobilization meeting in 1940, "because we go into the bowels of the earth to mine the copper and the zinc for the bullets which find their resting place in the bowels of other workers."[22]

When Hitler invaded the Soviet Union on June 22, the Mine–Mill newspaper had just gone to press featuring a story about Robinson telling a group of miners that America must stay out of the war. Robinson's view of the war turned upside down once again. "Now Hitler has made unmistakable his thirst for world domination by launching war upon another sixth of the globe, the vast territory of the U.S.S.R.," Robinson said. "In so doing he has disposed of the hope that powerful nations remaining out of the war might be the instrumentalities for bringing about a real people's peace."[23]

Increasingly peace was also elusive on the union's executive board, where more conservative members were accusing Robinson of being a Communist. At the union's 1942 convention, Robinson didn't exactly deny the charge; instead he noted that the same accusation was often hurled at the CIO's president. "If Philip Murray is a Communist or a Red then I want to walk side by side with him in that program," Robinson said. ". . . If the Communists believe that we should organize the unorganized to better the conditions of the workers in this country so that we can better prosecute the war effort — and if you want to call anyone who supports such a program a Communist, you have that right to call me a Communist."[24]

The prow of the dusty Hudson Super 6 sedan bounced over the ruts of the desert road like a boat battering its way through rough waves. It was only fifteen miles from Basic Townsite to Las Vegas but it took Estolv Ward the better part of an hour to make the journey, which he did every time he needed to make a phone call. He wouldn't dare touch the single pay phone in the company town, where he was sure that his calls would be monitored; instead he drove into Las Vegas, where union lawyer Abe Isserman was living in a hotel room while waiting for his divorce to finalize. He also drove into the city for union meetings on the Westside, where many of the black workers at BMI lived; they couldn't come calling at his house in the whites-only townsite without drawing attention. So Ward found himself driving back and forth on the wretched Boulder Highway four or five times a day. And the drive often stretched out because he kept stopping to offer rides to the black men he saw straggling alongside the road. Most of them came from the South; almost all of them worked at BMI. I'm an organizer for the CIO, Ward announced to each. "My mammy done tol' me," one of his riders told Ward, "if I ever should meet up with that CIO I should j'in it."[25]

Estolv Ward arrived in Las Vegas early in 1943. He thought he would be there for a few weeks; he stayed almost a year. Reid Robinson had sent Ward to Las Vegas to do PR for the BMI struggle, but when Bob Hollowwa went into the army, Ward found himself running the union campaign.

Ward was forty-four, with dark wavy hair flecked by gray, a thick mustache, and a craggy, careworn face that looked like a road map of the troubles he had seen: His father was a socialist, his mother a doctor; he'd never gone to high school but wound up as a reporter at the *Oakland Tribune*. In 1934 he covered the general strike in San Francisco when the longshoremen shut down the city after two of their own had been killed by the police; one night he saw police brutally clubbing peaceful unionists, and he knew which side was good and which was bad. And when the photographer's pictures of the carnage disappeared from the newsroom, he knew which side the press was on. Ward founded the Newspaper Guild unit at the *Trib*, which ended his newspaper career. By the time he was asked to join the Communist Party officially in 1936, it was less a decision than a fait accompli.

Two years later he was a delegate at the CIO convention in Los Angeles bent over proofs of resolutions at a print shop at two o'clock on a Sunday morning when he looked up and saw another delegate doing the same; she was twenty-eight, eleven years his junior, and every ounce his equal in commitment. Her name was Angela Gizzi and she, too, had been moved beyond words in 1934 when she ignored the threats of her boss, left her office at the Bank of America, and stood in awed respect on Market Street as the river of longshoremen flowed by. It took two hours for the parade to pass; nothing she saw in her life impressed her more. And when she went back to her office and saw her coworkers still punching their adding machines like the moving parts of some vast inhuman contraption, nothing seemed more inconsequential. "That's how I became a radical,"[26] she said.

They married in 1939, the year Estolv became the executive secretary of the Harry Bridges Defense Committee. The next year he published a book about the hearing called *Harry Bridges on Trial*. The year after that they were living in Los Angeles, both working for Mine-Mill. When Ward went to Nevada, Angela soon followed. And when Ward and other union men were set upon by AFL Teamsters swinging baseball bats outside the BMI gate, Angela Ward and other wives showed up at the gate the next morning to pass out handbills. Even Teamsters would not beat women.

The Wards moved into a small house in Basic Townsite with another radical couple, who became party members as well. They opened an office

in a vacant schoolhouse nearby that had been moved there from somewhere else, cast off like so many of the workers they hoped to woo. Then
the international sent an organizer named Joe Houseman (who brought
his wife) to help with the campaign. "We set up a little group," Ward
recalled, "and we made one recruit, a black man well known and liked in
the plant and in the black community of Las Vegas."[27]

That made seven Communists in Las Vegas.

When Senator Mon C. Walgren got off the plane at McCarran Field in
Las Vegas on a Monday morning in May, Pat McCarran was waiting for
him. Two days earlier McCarran had raced from Washington to Vegas so
he could greet his colleague. Walgren, a Democrat from Washington, was
a member of the Truman Committee, which was investigating waste in
war production. For months the CIO had been bombarding the Truman
Committee with allegations of unsafe conditions at the BMI plant, and
now Walgren was making a quick inspection trip. McCarran escorted him
out to BMI, where the two met with E. O. Case.

That night the elite of Las Vegas turned out again at the Last Frontier.
This time the party was for Walgren. The host was McCarran. "If I ever
had a pal, it is this man," McCarran enthused. "That's is why I am giving
this dinner tonight. I want him to know Nevada. I want him to know
Nevadans. And I want him to know the industrial life of Nevada."[28]

One of the Nevadans whom McCarran wanted Walgren to know was
the AFL's Ragnald Fyhen, who told the senator that the CIO "agitators"
were disrupting the war effort with their unreasonable demands. The AFL,
he added, had promised both plant management and McCarran that there
would be no strikes or work stoppages. "The CIO boys got bolder and
braver every day," put in Wesley King, an organizer who had been recently
assigned to Las Vegas by AFL president William Green. "They attacked our
members and forcefully ripped off the AF of L buttons and told our members to sign pledge cards 'or else.'"[29]*

Walgren wore a Stetson and western shirt (gifts from McCarran) and
said that his tour of the BMI plant was impressive. "Frank Case and his
assistants are doing a fine job,"[30] he said.

---

*The CIO version was somewhat different. "The AFL has adopted a policy of terroriza-
tion and violence which put one CIO member in the hospital and a number of others
badly beaten up," organizer Carl Holderman wrote to Reid Robinson on April 22.
"This was an organized attack, which was led by Wesley King." (BMI file, Western
Federation of Miners Papers.)

Although the CIO had prodded Walgren to visit Las Vegas, the senator found himself too busy to meet with any of its organizers. And judging from the way BMI's Frank Case and his assistants mingled at the Last Frontier party with the AFL's Ragnald Fyhen and Wesley King, you'd never guess that three days earlier the CIO had won the union election at the plant.

The first time Jessica Rhine met Pat McCarran she did not even try to hide her anger. It was late May, and Mine-Mill's Washington representative had gone to McCarran's office to tell him that the union had nine locals in his state and the membership was very concerned about what was happening at BMI — or, more precisely, what wasn't happening.

After more than half a year of hard effort, Mine-Mill finally convinced the National Labor Relations Board to order an election at BMI on May 7. It was an ugly campaign. "The revolt of the BMI workers against the AFL and the workers' spontaneous, overwhelming demand for the CIO," Mine-Mill labeled its struggle in an ad in the *Review-Journal*. ". . . Men are choking with dust, dying of gas, outraged by bad working conditions and intolerable living conditions."[31] The AFL screamed back that the CIO was treasonable and un-American. "You and your COMMUNISTIC PROGRAM of divide and conquer have resulted in turmoil in a vital war plant,"[32] an AFL ad declared.

The CIO beat the AFL 1,422 votes to 683. The AFL contested the election, and six hundred of its workers walked off the job for a union meeting in the middle of the day — a bit of muscle flexing that came close to shutting down the plant. The regional NLRB office in San Francisco rushed an investigator to Las Vegas, who upheld the election results and recommended to Washington that the board certify the CIO as the winner. Then Washington did nothing.

Rhine pulled out a newspaper clip and waved it at McCarran. It was an account of the party he'd thrown at the Last Frontier for Senator Mon Walgren. McCarran and BMI both got a lot of coverage in the *Las Vegas Review-Journal,* which was published by McCarran's friend Al Cahlan. The CIO got virtually no coverage, except for Bob Hollowwa's arrest on the weapons charge. "Any of these people who were trying to do anything that would give Las Vegas a bad name," Al's brother John Cahlan recalled, "they would not be covered."[33]

The party was three days *after* the CIO won the election, Rhine fumed, yet there wasn't a single person from the union there, while the guest list was full of AFL organizers.

The AFL folks were old friends, McCarran explained.

You have queer friends, Rhine said.

Are you trying to tell me who to be friends with? McCarran shot back, his voice rising.

I don't give a damn who your friends are, Rhine said, but we resent you entertaining thugs who only a few days before led physical attacks on our organizers.

Rhine mentioned that she was putting together a memo for the Truman Committee and would be happy to discuss it with him.

McCarran said it would be highly improper for him to interfere with the committee.

You've already interfered with the committee, she snapped.

Later Rhine dropped off a copy of the union newspaper. "He must begin to take a definite interest in Mine-Mill and what it is doing,"[34] Rhine wrote to Estolv Ward.

McCarran did develop a very strong interest in the union — an interest that would last a decade and send one member of Mine-Mill to jail.

In June Estolv Ward was fired by Mine-Mill, a victim of what his comrades called the Pittsburgh Purge. Mine-Mill members called each other brother and signed letters "fraternally yours," but the union was a viper's pit of politics. For years the union had been split into left- and right-wing factions (and even some of the left-wingers were barely on speaking terms with one another). By late 1942 the division had grown so wide that the Connecticut local was close to bolting from Mine-Mill. In early 1943 the union's leaders met with CIO president Philip Murray in his Pittsburgh office. "What's wrong with your union?" Murray asked.[35]

Nothing but a few dissenters and disruptionists, President Robinson replied.

"What was wrong with our organization," countered board member Ralph Rasmussen, "was that we have too many Communists in it."

"If you have a cancer on your hand," Murray said, "you better cut it out before it destroys your body."

The union wound up firing half a dozen of its more radical staff members, including the research director, Robinson's personal assistant, and a number of organizers. But as purges go, it was halfhearted at best. Ward, for example, was fired by the international (a hatchetman for Robinson, one board member called him) but stayed on in Las Vegas by becoming the local's rep.[36]

Phil Murray didn't take his own advice. His own right hand was Lee Pressman.

In July, McCarran summoned Jessica Rhine back to his office. Since the last time he'd seen her, he had been inundated with letters and telegrams from Mine-Mill members asking him to help the union get NLRB certification. More than two months after the election, the board was still dragging its feet for some inexplicable reason. McCarran told Rhine that he had nothing to do with the NLRB. "I knew he was a damned liar,"[37] Rhine wrote to Ward.

Once the CIO never had to worry about the National Labor Relations Board. Roosevelt created the board to act as a referee in disputes between management and labor, but it soon found itself acting as a referee *within* labor as the CIO's great organizing drive challenged the AFL's hegemony. "You have gone definitely on the side of the CIO," AFL president William Green complained to NLRB chairman J. Warren Madden.

"I am very sorry that you feel that way about it," Madden replied. ". . . The conflict that is going on within the labor movement, of course, puts the board in a very difficult position."

"There is an impression gaining every day among the officers and members of the federation," Green continued, "that your board is definitely CIO and that your agents are definitely CIO."[38]

That impression was not wrong. The board's secretary and its executive officer was Nat Witt, whose best friends were his former comrades from the Triple A: Lee Pressman, who was CIO general counsel, and John Abt, counsel to the La Follette Civil Liberties Committee (all three, of course, were also secret Communists). And board member Edwin Smith was sympathetic enough to the hard left that after being forced off the board by Roosevelt, he became a paid lobbyist for the Soviet Union.

Conservative complaints about the board reached a crescendo in 1939 when Virginia's Howard Smith filled nearly eight thousand pages of congressional hearings with allegations of left-wing bias at the NLRB. Smith's chief target, however, was not the Communists on the board, but rather its chief economist David Saposs, who was a socialist and who soon found himself without a job. Witt, too, was eventually forced out, going into private practice in New York, where he represented some of the more radical CIO unions, such as Mine-Mill, which he was advising on the BMI campaign. "Brother Witt's suggestion should be followed closely,"[39] President Reid Robinson had instructed Hollowwa.

Still, a number of secret Communists survived in the NLRB, such as Herbert Fuchs (who had previously belonged to the same Washington Communist cell as Jessica Rhine) and Frank Donner. "We told ourselves," Fuchs recalled, "and were told that to be good Communists at the National Labor Relations Board, the better job that we did for the board and for the government, that was it. That was the best thing, and to do a good trustworthy job was a good Communist's job in that area."[40]

But by the time the United States was at war, even members of the NLRB who remained sympathetic to Mine-Mill could do little when the chairman of the Senate appropriations subcommittee that controlled its budget took an interest in a specific case. That chairman was Pat McCarran. "He questioned the board members at great length about the BMI election and indicated that they had no right coming into Nevada where everything was peaceful and creating a scene," Rhine told Ward after talking to one of her sources on the board. "Very definitely we cannot use this incident in talking with the senator because although he discussed the BMI case for nearly an hour, he very cleverly had all reference to it stricken from the record of the committee meeting. Therefore, if we discuss this incident with him at all it will be very easy for him to find out from whom we heard about it and this would be disastrous as far as the future of the NLRB is concerned."

So Rhine steamed out of McCarran's suite in the Senate Office Building and over to the CIO building across from Lafayette Park and the White House. In the back of the narrow building in the left corner she squeezed into Pressman's small office. They talked about McCarran. "Lee said that the board members had told him that McCarran sent the AFL committee over to see them," Rhine later related to Ward.

But Rhine also had some leverage of her own: Berkeley Bunker, who had served in the Senate after Key Pittman's death and narrowly lost the primary special election in 1942. Bunker was young and relatively liberal and itching to go back to Washington — and Nevada's *other* Senate seat was coming up for election in 1944. Bunker was flirting with the CIO about supporting him in the Senate race.

Rhine called McCarran from Pressman's office. When she dropped Bunker's name into the conversation she found that the senator was suddenly more solicitous. She asked him to get in touch with the NLRB and tell the board to decide the case on its merits. McCarran agreed.

"He is a bit concerned now about the growth of the CIO in his state," Rhine informed Ward. "He is particularly vulnerable because he is up for

re-election in 1944 and is very aware of the fact. . . . He definitely is worried about what impression we have of him and is particularly concerned
over the fact that we have been in touch with Bunker. I think it is
extremely important to maintain some relationship with Bunker for the
beneficial effect it has on McCarran."[41]

Two days later, on July 15, the NLRB certified Mine-Mill as the winner
of the election.

The morning after the CIO's victory Ragnald Fyhen flew from Las
Vegas to San Francisco and went to the Fairmont Hotel, where the AFL's
Metal Trades Department was holding a meeting. Fyhen found John
Frey and told him that he needed his help to stop the CIO. He had
come to the right man. Frey was seventy-two, the president of the Metal
Trades Department since 1934, and one of the most vigorous anti-
Communist crusaders in the labor movement. In 1936 Frey helped run
the CIO out of the AFL; two years later he testified before HUAC, reading
the names of 280 CIO organizers whom he said were Communists,
including a number of Mine-Mill reps and attorney Abe Isserman. The
CIO's sitdown strikes, Frey claimed, were practice for the day when
Moscow would command Communists to seize power in the United
States. Frey also excoriated the NLRB for leaning toward Communist-led
unions. After the U.S. went to war, the AFL and CIO signed a nonaggression pact promising to put their differences aside for the duration. The deal
didn't last very long, and the CIO launched an organizing drive in the
Kaiser shipyards that were already under AFL contract. Frey called for the
Wagner Act to be suspended. When that idea went nowhere, Frey came
up with another one: No federal agency should be allowed to get involved
in a jurisdictional dispute when a contract has been in effect for more than
ninety days. This proviso (known as the Frey Rider) was attached to the
NLRB's appropriations bill in the Senate in 1943. The chairman of the
subcommittee that adopted the Frey Rider was Pat McCarran. Frey, as it
happened, was also a friend of BMI manager Frank Case.

Fyhen told Frey that Case had promised not to recognize or negotiate
with the CIO until he could speak to the Metal Trades president. If Frey
could persuade Case to ignore the NLRB ruling, he explained, the
agency would have no way to enforce the certification. When Fyhen
repeated his plan to a group of presidents from various metal trade
unions, they hugged him.

Frey flew back to Las Vegas with Fyhen and headed straight out to

BMI. He had a meeting with Frank Case. "I will beat this election,"[42] Fyhen had promised his AFL colleagues before he left Las Vegas.

At ten in the morning on August 19, Senator Harry Truman and Senator Mon Walgren sat down in the Las Vegas federal building with Abe Isserman and Estolv Ward. Truman had recently shot into the national news as a crusader against defense waste and profiteering. The Missouri Democrat had a reputation for being blunt. He lived up to it. "We can only spend one hour on this hearing," he told Isserman and Ward.[43]

For months Ward and the Washington office of Mine–Mill had been lobbying Truman to bring his celebrated committee to Nevada. Now they had sixty minutes. Isserman started to explain the background of the CIO–AFL fight over which union got to represent the workers at BMI. "We are not interested in jurisdiction," Truman snapped. "What we are interested in is getting magnesium."[44]

Even after the NLRB certified Mine–Mill as the winner of the election, Isserman continued, BMI refused to recognize the union. It would, manager Case said, take a Supreme Court ruling to change his mind.

Ward testified that the plant was discriminating against blacks, paying them less than whites for the same work. Doctors and nurses at the plant hospital were being fired if they didn't return sick workers to the production line, food poisoning was rife in the cafeteria, exorbitant rent was charged for shoddy housing. "Morale is bad," Ward insisted. ". . . I know hundreds of cases of workers, both white and colored, who have left that plant feeling that their lives are being endangered."[45]

No one from the AFL showed up, although the union did file a written rebuttal to the CIO's accusations. "Mr. Ward and the CIO in an attempt to stir up racial friction have not only spread these rumors generally throughout the country, but have fathered such activities as may exist . . . ," claimed Ragnald Fyhen. "There can be no greater act of sabotage to industry, production, and a coordination of effort than to create strife, suspicion and distrust among people."[46]

The Truman Committee (officially, the Special Committee Investigating the National Defense Program) was brutal on the plant in its final report.[47] "This was one of the most unjustified contracts which was proposed in connection with the war program," the report said, "and represented a wholly unwarranted advance of government funds to a newly organized corporation which had no financial resources and only the most meager experience and talent."[48]

But the committee wasn't about to get involved in a labor dispute. "We are continuing to have troubles on BMI in spite of certification,"[49] Jessica Rhine complained to Lee Pressman. If the union wanted help it would have to go someplace else.

In late September, Estolv Ward scraped up thirty dollars, purchased a plane ticket from Las Vegas to Salt Lake City, and had two bucks left in his pocket when he reached Utah, expecting to find a ticket to Washington waiting for him. It wasn't there. So he got on a train to Denver, and when the conductor tried to throw him off near the Continental Divide for not having a ticket, the army troops filling the compartment escorted the ticket taker out of the car. He arrived in Denver on a Saturday; the head-quarters of Mine-Mill was closed. He tried to track down President Reid Robinson, who was at a ball game. Ward finally found Robinson, who got the union's grumbling treasurer to open the office safe and give Ward enough money to buy a ticket to Washington.

Getting to Washington was the easy part. Once in the capital, Ward made the rounds of various government offices, pleading for help in making BMI deal with the union. "Everywhere I found the answer lay with McCarran," Ward recalled. "Occasionally some friendly but scared underling would whisper that things might go better for me if I could secure McCarran's support. When I brought up the subject of McCarran with more prominent officials, they made no bones of the fact that they deeply respected his opinions in such matters."[50]

BMI was still adamant in its refusal to deal with Mine-Mill, claiming that the AFL contract had not been superseded. The NLRB said it was now up to the War Labor Board; the WLB said it lacked jurisdiction. "McCarran," Rhine had explained to Ward, "was behind our difficulties, as of yore."[51]

Ward went to the Senate Office Building to see McCarran. The senator reached into his desk and pulled out a flyer. Ward's stomach clenched. It was copy of a Mine-Mill leaflet that Ward had put out after McCarran had begun crowing about how he had served the cause of labor by getting the NLRB to certify the CIO's victory at BMI. "He had been the villain until forced to act otherwise . . . ," Ward wrote. "Such a rank piece of hypocrisy."[52]

"A most serious mistake," Ward now admitted.

Ward said that the handbill was based on the AFL's Ragnald Fyhen boasting that the senator had called him and assured him that the CIO would never be certified by the NLRB. McCarran rolled his eyes. "Lord protect us from our friends," he said.

Ward pleaded, said that he thought that the information was correct but that if it wasn't he would take the senator's word for it and tell the membership back in Las Vegas. McCarran said that of course it was not true, that he would never spend the taxpayers' money on a long-distance call. "I was nearer to being on my knees before McCarran than I have ever been to any man," Ward remembered years later, "and even in retrospect I do not relish the scene."[53]

Ward got nowhere with McCarran. Late that evening he finally got into see the chairman of the War Labor Board, William H. Davis. There was nothing he could do, Davis said. Your only chance to get the WLB to intervene in the case is to call for a strike vote.

Ward was shocked. No union was more zealous in supporting the war effort than Mine-Mill, Ward explained, and the CIO had pledged not to strike.

You don't have to strike, Davis explained, just hold a strike vote, which might force the WLB to get involved in the dispute.

It was late in the day as they spoke, but the lights had not yet been turned on in the office. Gloom descended upon the room. And upon Ward.

Angela Ward[54] and Joe Houseman were the only white faces in the very crowded, very angry black church on the Westside of Las Vegas. Walking down the aisle toward the pulpit, Ward felt as alone as she looked. She had become a Communist because every bone in her body told her that the party was on the side of right, and now she was supposed to tell the aroused workers to do something that she knew with all her heart was wrong. While her husband was in Washington pleading with McCarran, the workers had taken matters into their own hands. Earlier that day in late October more than two hundred blacks had walked off the job at BMI.

> *Come all you good workers,*
> *Good news to you I'll tell*
> *Of how the good old union*
> *Has come in here to dwell.*[*][55]

---

*In 1931, during the brutal Harlan County coal strike in Kentucky, the sheriff came looking for union leader Sam Reece and ransacked his house in front of his wife, Florence, and her seven children. Afterward Florence Reece tore a piece of paper from a calendar and scratched out the words to "Which Side Are You On?"

Across the seas the United States was fighting for freedom, but at home one-tenth of the nation was still living as second-class citizens. War was dramatically underscoring the contradictions of American society: segregation in the armed forces and Jim Crow in the South, where blacks were killed by vigilantes while the threat of filibusters from Dixiecrats killed any attempt to pass a federal anti-lynching law. And only when the NAACP threatened a march of one hundred thousand blacks on Washington in the summer of 1941 did Roosevelt ban discrimination in defense plants with Executive Order 8802. But the order was frequently ignored, and in the summer of 1943 race riots had broken out all over the country, from Harlem to Detroit.

From its founding in 1905, Las Vegas had been laid out for segregation. The city plans called for blacks to be confined to Block 17, next to Block 16, where bars and brothels were located. In 1940 there were only 178 blacks in the county (out of a total population of 8,422), and most of them lived on the Westside, seventy-two blocks of squalor across the railroad tracks from downtown Vegas. Segregation grew more rigid with the war. Blacks were barred from casinos and restaurants, unless they were porters or maids, prohibited from buying property or getting a business license outside the ghetto. Shops hung signs reading WE DO NOT CATER TO COLORED. Some did. They would sell clothes to blacks but not let them try anything on or let them buy food if they took it to go. Blacks could not swim in the public pools and were restricted to side seats in movie theaters. "The Mississippi of the West," they called the town.

Crossing into the Westside was like leaving the country. E Street, the main drag, was unpaved, plagued by dust storms when the wind blew, turning to muddy tar when rain fell. While the casinos of Fremont Street twinkled like Christmas trees at night, the Westside went virtually dark at sundown, since there was no electricity. Nor was there running water or sewerage. People fetched water from community taps and dug holes in the ground for outhouses. With the war things got worse. In three years more than three thousand blacks poured into the Westside, most attracted by jobs at BMI. The 160-acre ghetto looked like a refugee camp. Already shabby housing grew unbearably overcrowded, shacks sprung up, families huddled under lean-tos made from scavenged wood. Over the summer a coal-oil stove had blown up, quickly burning down a one-room shack in which seven people were living before spreading to three more shanties. A fifth structure was close to catching fire when a group of men picked up the dwelling and carried it out of danger.

At BMI, where two-thirds of the plant employees were black, conditions were not much better. Blacks found themselves paid less than whites for the same job; those with skills could only get work as laborers while less qualified whites moved upward. "I was told emphatically by management that they could not make me a superintendent or foreman because they would lose the people under me," a black BMI worker named Woodrow Wilson recalled. "They wouldn't want to work for a black man. . . . Oh, God, I was told that so many times."[56] In the plant cafeteria workers segregated themselves: Blacks sat on one side and whites on another. "There have been rumors in Las Vegas that race riots might occur at any time," Ward had warned the Truman Committee months earlier. ". . . Angry groups of white and colored workers gather frequently and only the greatest alertness of CIO stewards has thus far prevented racial violence."[57]

Then one day in October black workers showed up for a shift to find that BMI had put up walls up to segregate the dressing facilities, leaving more showers for whites, even through blacks outnumbered them two to one. Separate but equal facilities did not violate the president's nondiscrimination order, Case explained. The Supreme Court, after all, had sanctioned segregation in its 1896 *Plessy v. Ferguson* decision. When a large group of black workers went to complain to management, they were escorted from the plant, stripped of their company badges, and fired. So blacks walked out en masse.

> *Which side are you on?*
> *Which side are you on?*
> *Which side are you on?*
> *Which side are you on?*

As Ward reached the front of the church and turned toward the crowd, she knew that what the workers had done was magnificent. Yet she was supposed to tell them to go back to their jobs. In her heart she wanted them to walk; in her head she knew they had to work. What else could she do?

For a year Mine-Mill had been walking a knife's edge: vigorously trying to organize workers at BMI while at the same time being absolutely committed not to strike. It was like walking into a boxing ring with both hands tied behind one's back. The union, not surprisingly, got pummeled. Ever since Hollowwa first drove into Las Vegas the workers had been asking the union for help. "When will we get action?" one asked Hollowwa. "Use your excess energy for organizational work and let me worry about the action,"[58] Hollowwa replied.

But action was the last thing the union wanted. "Almost impossible for CIO to combat walkout hysteria,"[59] Hollowwa wired the War Production Board on one occasion. "The majority here are rebels at heart," he reported to union headquarters. "They have been run off from far better jobs than what they have here and they don't give a damn about their job and won't stay long any place unless a good fight is in the offing for betterment of working conditions. . . . This gang would throw Case out of his own office if I said the word."[60]

Early in the year work stoppages broke out; the plant was on the verge of being shut down. "Frankly, their unrest is again approaching the explosion point, and in spite of all we can do, repetitions of the work stoppages of two or three weeks ago are highly probable," Hollowwa told the NLRB. "There is a spontaneous combustion among these workers that is hard to quench, and we are afraid they will go farther this time than they ever have before."[61]

> My daddy was a miner,
> And I'm a miner's son,
> And I'll stick with the union
> 'Til every battle's won.

For Communists nothing was more important than winning the war. In a matter of months, Hitler appeared on the verge of doing what the capitalist countries hadn't been able to do in twenty years: snuff out the flame of the Russian Revolution. Suddenly all the goals of the proletarian revolution — not least of which was the emancipation of labor — were subordinated to beating back the Nazis. So when Roosevelt ordered Japanese Americans relocated to remote camps as a security threat in 1942, the party supported the action. When John Lewis led his coal miners out on strike three times in a single year — creating two-thirds of the labor disruptions in 1943 — the Communists called him a traitor.

All-out for the war became the virtual Hippocratic oath of party members: Do not strike. "The business of defeating Adolf Hitler is the most serious task," Reid Robinson told his miners at the union's 1941 convention. ". . . Every other problem we have passes into insignificance when posed against this central duty of supporting every conceivable step that will bring Hitler to his downfall."[62] At the union's 1943 convention, the month before the BMI walkout, Robinson reiterated the no-strike pledge. "We will work without stopping to produce the weapons to destroy fascism," he stated. "We gave our word with full realization that a strike today is a strike against ourselves, against our fellow workers, against our members in the armed forces and accomplishes nothing for our members."[63]

> *They say in Harlan County*
> *There are no neutrals there.*
> *You'll either be a union man*
> *Or a thug for J. H. Blair.*

Ward faced the dark sea of the crowd, expectant faces turned toward her and Houseman. Almost a decade before the police had killed two striking longshoremen in San Francisco and the funeral march along Market Street shut down the city, thousands of men and women insisting on their dignity and rights as human beings. The sight made Ward a radical. Now she was seeing another moving demonstration of the poor and powerless demanding respect. "It was a beautiful manifestation of a wild cat strike," she thought. "Nobody urged them. They urged themselves."[64]

> *Oh workers can you stand it?*
> *Oh tell me how you can?*
> *Will you be a lousy scab*
> *Or will you be a man?*

Angela and Estolv Ward were used to difficult tasks. After he had been fired by the international union and put on the local's payroll, he had to fight with union members to reduce his salary. The local wanted to pay him the same as a senior skilled BMI worker; he insisted on getting paid the same as a newly hired laborer. They went months forgoing even that pay to spend more money on the campaign. They stayed up late into the night working and rose early the next morning to start again.

For years Communists in the labor movement (and the government) had been able to assuage the tinge of guilt they felt at keeping party membership secret by telling themselves that it didn't matter: There was no conflict between what a good Communist and a good unionist (or New Dealer) would do. Yet here was a blatant contradiction as rank as the sharp stench of bleach at BMI: Angela Ward was supposed to organize and help the workers, but she must not let them strike.

Franklin Roosevelt's cheerful demeanor and activist administration inspired millions during the Depression — and terrified conservatives like McCarran (below, pictured with Eva Adams) who feared that his grand experiment would destroy representative government.

Pat Jackson's idealism pushed him to the radical fringe of the New Deal (left) but his faith in politics — and his friends — would be sorely tested by the end of the Red Decade. Jackson's friend, Lee Pressman, secretly joined the Communist Party and became a major force in the labor movement as the legal counsel for the CIO (Pressman, below, right, talks with long-shoreman and CIO vice president Harry Bridges, who was also a party member).

Nathan Witt (right) followed Pressman into the Communist Party, and as the secretary of the National Labor Relations Board was one of the most powerful figures in the labor movement. Pressman and Witt worked to defeat McCarran during the 1944 primary election. McCarran never forgot.

During the 1938 campaign FDR put McCarran on his purge list and tried to ignore the senator as he traveled across Nevada. McCarran popped up on the president's train anyway.

During the Great Debate over U.S. involvement in World War II, McCarran shared the stage with aviator Charles Lindbergh at an anti-intervention rally in Chicago in 1940. Pearl Harbor ended the debate.

McCarran's eldest child, Margaret, (top left), shared his conservative political philosophy and spent her adult life as a nun; Mary followed her sister into the convent but with less happy results. After McCarran's youngest daughter, Patricia (bottom), ran away, the senator had the FBI bring her home. At Patty's marriage McCarran prayed that she would settle down. She didn't. When Sammy (top right), McCarran's youngest child, was in medical school during the war and complained about gas rationing, the senator passed a law making an exemption for doctors.

Pete Petersen (top left) ran the Reno post office as a virtual Senate field office for McCarran. The senator's enemies claimed that critical letters about McCarran always seemed to get lost in the mail. Norman Biltz (top right) was a Republican real-estate developer who marketed Nevada as a tax haven to millionaires — and collected cash contributions for his friend the senator. Many people in Washington preferred to deal with McCarran's administrative assistant, Eva Adams (right), rather than the senator; those who didn't often found themselves being yelled at by McCarran.

In the early 1940s the Las Vegas Strip consisted of two motels, both pictured above, but the building of the BMI defense plant outside of town caused the city's population to swell with workers — and set off a fierce organizing battle between the CIO and the AFL.

McCarran (above) was friendly with BMI's manager, E.O. Case (pictured with silver bar), as well as with the AFL union that claimed to represent the plant's workers. CIO organizer Estolv Ward (top, right) was a Communist who came to Nevada to help with the BMI fight; he stayed to try to defeat McCarran in the 1944 election. Berkeley Bunker (right) was a devout Mormon who flirted with the CIO to scheme against McCarran.

For the better part of a decade, Ward had put the party before principle. She could stomach Stalin shooting Old Bolsheviks and shaking hands with Hitler because these reversals were supposed to be in the ultimate interests of the workers. But when she was asked to let a rapacious corporation exploit its workers she turned to jelly on the inside. Which side are you on? went the folk song that every party member knew. The upturned faces were waiting for Angela.

> *Don't scab for the bosses,*
> *Don't listen to their lies.*
> *Us poor folks haven't got a chance*
> *Unless we organize.*

Ward's duty as a party member was to tell, demand, beseech the strikers to go back to work. Do not strike, she had to tell them. "Neither one of us could get up there and tell those blacks to go back to work," Ward thought. "We just couldn't."[65]

> *Strike, she said.*
> *Strike. Strike. Strike.*

On October 31[66] Roy Hudson went to Philadelphia and checked into the St. James Hotel. Hudson was forty-two, a party member since 1930, a former seaman and maritime unionist who was in charge of labor issues for the CPUSA. "A prototype proletarian character out of a socialist realist painting,"[67] John Abt called him. The CIO convention was taking place that week, and during the course of the day various union leaders, such as Harry Bridges, came by to talk about what was being discussed during the executive board meetings. That night CIO general counsel Lee Pressman showed up. Pressman proceeded to share with Hudson drafts of various resolutions that were going to be introduced at the convention. Hudson told Pressman to change the phrasing on several resolutions, spelling out the exact wording in some cases. The lawyer scribbled down the new language. Pressman wasn't the only one taking dictation: In the next room FBI agents were listening and writing their own notes.

Convention resolutions were of little importance except to those who wrote them, but occasionally the party gave Pressman some instructions that mattered. Earlier in the year, for example, Pressman and John Abt had met with Eugene Dennis, one of the party's leaders, who suggested that the

CIO create a political action committee to help labor's friends and punish its enemies in the 1944 election. "Frankly, a good number of our ideas of what the CIO should be doing came from the party," Abt recalled. "And I can't remember any time when we disagreed with the party, although in retrospect I can see moments when perhaps we should have. But in life, there seemed to be no difference between the best interests of the CIO and the best interests of the Communist Party. Certainly it was my experience that the party had the best interests of the CIO in mind and heart."[68]

Since they had worked together at the AAA a decade earlier, Pressman and Abt had become two of the most influential figures in labor. Pressman was at John Lewis's side during the CIO's great organizing drive; when Lewis resigned, Pressman sidled up to new president Phil Murray and was just as influential. Abt had gone from the La Follette Committee to the Justice Department, where he was a special assistant to the attorney general. Being a secret Communist high in the Justice Department meant keeping some things hidden, such as his wife, Jessica. Abt met Jessica at at Pat Jackson's when she was married to Hal Ware, who had recruited both Abt and Pressman into the party. After Ware's death Abt married Jessica. But because of her open ties to the party (she was editor of *Soviet Russia Today*) and his position in the government, they had to keep their relationship secret. When Abt, for example, hosted a cocktail party attended by senators, the attorney general, and NLRB board members, his wife was nowhere to be seen. Eventually the couple went to Earl Browder asking for an assignment where they could live together openly. Abt mentioned that his father was friendly with Sidney Hillman, the head of the Amalgamated Clothing Workers' Union and one of the most prominent labor leaders in the country. "That's what you should do," Browder exclaimed. "You ought to be Hillman's attorney. Sidney would be delighted to have a Pressman of his own."[69]

Murray and Hillman never asked their lawyers about their politics. They didn't have to: Pressman and Abt were two of the best-known secret Communists in the country. And if Hillman, who had known Jessica Abt since the days when she had lived in the Soviet Union, had any doubts, they were dispelled early in 1943 when Abt showed up at his apartment saying that he had a message from Browder. Hillman asked Abt to step into his bedroom closet, where they could talk out of range of any listening devices. Browder, Abt said, wanted Hillman to know the plans of Mike Quill, a New York labor leader and city council member, in the upcoming elections. That the head of the American Communist Party could authoritatively predict the actions of a labor leader who never admitted to being a party member did not surprise Hillman. Nor did the fact that his right-hand man would be the one to relay the promises of the party's leader.

So later in the year when Pressman and Abt went to their bosses with a nervy idea of creating a labor coalition to skirt campaign spending laws, push for Roosevelt's renomination, and extract vengeance on unfriendly politicians, the union leaders had no doubt that they could once again count on the Communists for energetic support. Hillman became the chairman of the CIO PAC. Abt was its general counsel (although Pressman insisted on being cocounsel on PAC letterhead). Abt suggested Beanie Baldwin for national director. Baldwin had been Henry Wallace's administrative secretary in the AAA. He was also a secret party member. "Some anti-Communist historians have accused Pressman and me of maintaining a kind of placement bureau for Communists and leftists in the CIO and, upon its creation, the CIO-PAC," Abt remembered years later. "To this, I confess that it is true."[70]

More than a year before the 1944 election the CIO created its Political Action Committee to help its friends and hurt its enemies.

On its hit list: Pat McCarran.

The strike vote failed. After Angela Ward defied the party and the CIO and told the BMI workers to strike, the union bigwigs — Phil Murray, Lee Pressman, and Reid Robinson — belatedly backed her up in a final bid to rout the AFL. Over the summer Congress overrode Roosevelt's veto to pass the Smith-Connally Act, which gave the government the authority to seize a plant to prevent a strike. The act was yet another fetter on unions, but Mine-Mill was willing to use its provision for calling a strike vote as a way to get the War Labor Board to intervene, hopefully compelling BMI to recognize the CIO election victory. Mine-Mill was desperate. For a year the union had thrown everything it could into the fight, sending its best organizers, spending itself into debt, and raising more than six thousand dollars in contributions from other CIO unions. Yet every seeming victory was turned against it. The only thing left was the tortured logic of using the Smith-Connally Act against itself. "A strike vote to prevent a strike,"[71] Ward wrote in his newsletter *Basic Facts.* In the end the workers voted 1,700 to 1,217 against the strike. "A tribute to the patriotism of the BMI workers,"[72] Mine-Mill's newspaper, *The Union,* called the vote, somehow forgetting that the CIO was allegedly supporting a yes vote.

BMI fired those who walked out. The War Labor Board, citing the Frey rider, refused to get involved. The CIO might have won the election against the AFL, but it lost the union. "We didn't win anything," Angela

Ward recalled. "It just sort of disintegrated. After a while we could see there was noting to do; the union was broken."[73]

The Wards were pariahs. Ward's friend Paul Eckert introduced a resolution censuring the couple for calling a strike vote during the war. "Everybody was mad at us," Angela Ward said. "The Communist Party was very angry with us because we had condoned strike action in wartime. We were criticized by a lot of the CIO leaders who were following the line."[74]

But even after he had lost all hope for the union, Estolv Ward lingered in Las Vegas. "Mainly for the purpose of building up the political fight against Pat McCarran," he later remembered, "our international union kept the BMI local alive."[75]

McCarran wasn't the only one who saw an illusion in the desert of southern Nevada.

CHAPTER 13

Who Will Rule Nevada?

People who gamble every day probably learn not to
expect too much of life.[1]
— A. J. Liebling, after visiting Las Vegas

In March 1944 Pat McCarran took part in a radio debate about the future
of aviation policy.

"You good Republicans . . . ,"[2] California Democratic representative
Harry Sheppard began.

"Wait a minute, wait a minute!" McCarran interrupted. "I'm a
Democrat."

Days before, McCarran thought that he might be able to get through
the 1944 election without any primary opposition. "I am not afraid of the
general election at all," he wrote to his daughter Mary. "Although one can
never tell, as there is a wild confusion running through the people. The
mass of the people are mad; they are mad at everyone and everything.
They are especially mad at the 'ins' and think there is some hope if they
can put the 'ins' out and the 'outs' in."[3]

"I'm a Democrat!" McCarran repeated. "I may not belong to a certain
group of Democrats, but I'm a Democrat out and out."[4]

It was a bad harbinger for an election year when members of your own
party mistook you for a Republican.

That same month the House Un-American Activities Committee published a report attacking the CIO Political Action Committee as a
Communist front. "Sidney Hillman will soon succeed Earl Browder as
head of the Communists in the United States,"[5] HUAC chairman Martin
Dies predicted.

Dies, as usual, was half right. The Communists may have come up with
the idea for the PAC, as John Abt claimed, but the organization was less a
subversive plot than the last great fling of the Popular Front. Congress
seemed to be growing more conservative each day. In 1943, for example,
both houses overrode Roosevelt's veto to pass the Smith-Connally Act,
which curbed labor activities and forbade unions from contributing to
political campaigns.

The 1944 election was looking like it might be the left's last chance to fight back. "The day is over when labor can afford to take the position that in congressional contests it will support its friends and oppose its enemies," the PAC's Thomas Amlie told Hillman. "Unless labor takes the responsibility of bringing its friends into the political arena to run for office by undertaking to carry the financial load involved, labor will have no friends to support."[6]

The CIO had five million members, and if the union wanted to help candidates, there must be *some* way. The PAC was designed not to contribute *directly* to campaigns, Abt pointed out, but only *indirectly* — that is, registering voters, printing literature, sponsoring speakers. Even if all of the indirect activity was aimed at supporting or opposing specific candidates, it was not illegal. And after the union's dollar-a-member fund-raising drive ("A dollar you won't miss to elect a man you can't afford to lose," ads read) yielded a war chest of close to seven hundred thousand dollars, the PAC could do a lot of indirect contributing, indeed.* And Abt convinced Hillman to name Beanie Baldwin, Henry Wallace's administrative secretary from the Agricultural Adjustment Administration and later head of the Farm Security Administration, as the PAC's national director. Baldwin was also a secret Communist.[7] "He was not reluctant to consult with the Communist leadership," Abt remembered. "Actually, he considered it an imperative."[8]

But even as Hillman and Abt traveled around the country together to support the PAC, the labor leader privately worried about some of his allies. "Although he was again working closely with the CIO left, primarily the Communists," Abt recalled, "he remained quite suspicious and fearful that it might take over CIO-PAC."[9]

In public Hillman concealed his fears and attacked his critics. "Dies is a liar . . . ," Hillman charged after HUAC released its report calling the PAC a party front. "He has again delved into the recesses of a warped mind and come up with the same shopworn smears which he has been peddling to the American people for the past eight years."[10] Mine-Mill president Reid Robinson, whom Dies had accused of being a Communist, was less restrained. "He is a pro-fascist, a defeatist and a liar," Robinson claimed. "I

---

*Decades later corporations would seize on the PAC idea and use the Communist-inspired model to funnel capitalism's largesse into the coffers of more conservative candidates. "The device that I invented to benefit working people in their political action has come back to haunt us in the service of labor's antagonist," Abt groaned years later. (See John J. Abt [with Michael Myerson], *Advocate and Activist: Memoirs of a Communist Lawyer.* Urbana, Ill.: University of Illinois Press, 1993; p. 104.)

call upon the American people to get more active than ever in politics in order to sweep such Hitlerian disciples from the floor of Congress. Mr. Dies is a menace to our national safety."[11]

Dies did not put up much of a fight. In May — after his HUAC colleague Joseph Starnes, an Alabama Democrat, lost a primary fight — Dies announced that because of poor health he would not run for reelection. Then another HUAC member, California Democrat John Costello, failed to win renomination. "Three down and four to go,"[12] exulted *The Union*.

Back in 1943, at its national convention, Mine-Mill had declared war on McCarran. "Victory for Local 629," the union resolved, "will stimulate war production, bring industrial democracy to the four thousand workers at BMI, open great organizational opportunities to the CIO in Southern Nevada, and pave the way for the defeat of Nevada's reactionaries."[13]

Long before the PAC organized any Nevada chapters, Estolv Ward was busy plotting how Mine-Mill and the CIO could get rid of McCarran. "McCarran is known as the 'AFL Senator' from Nevada . . . ," Ward observed. "McCarran has voted against the administration on almost all important issues, except where AFL organizations in Nevada have indicated a strong preference. Senator McCarran generally is to be found supporting the mining companies, which are fundamentally anti-labor."[14]

McCarran had vowed to drive the CIO out of Nevada. The CIO, in turn, vowed to drive McCarran from office. On the face of it, this seemed like a tough task. Ward estimated that the AFL had between six thousand and twelve thousand members in Nevada, while the CIO had only about thirty-five hundred, all affiliated with Mine-Mill, the largest group of which was the thousand workers at BMI. But Nevada's population had grown like crazy — 22 percent in three years — and most of the gain was in the Las Vegas area. In a state with barely 133,000 people, a shift of just a small bloc of votes could be decisive. And Clark County was crawling with new residents who had no loyalty to any particular candidate.

The ramshackle Westside of Las Vegas, where most of the black BMI workers lived, had almost nothing: no electricity, running water, or paved streets. It did, however, have votes.

In May 1944 Robert Hannegan,[15] the chairman of the Democratic National Committee, stopped in Reno for a luncheon at the Golden Hotel. Tall, dark haired, boyishly handsome, Hannegan sat in the center of the head table. Short, plump, white-haired McCarran sat next to him. One seat over was

Lieutenant Governor Vail Pittman, thin, slight, with short white hair and
great black eyebrows. McCarran had traveled across the country for this
lunch, virtually to sit between the representative of his party and the representative of the hated Pittman clan, to keep the two as far apart as possible.
Talking to the luncheon, Hannegan praised McCarran's record, said that he
thought Roosevelt would let himself be drafted for a fourth term, and con-
fidently predicted a sweep at the polls if Democrats pulled together — even
as McCarran seemed to physically recoil from Pittman.

McCarran would turn sixty-eight in August and face voters in the
Democratic primary the following month. The general election was not a
problem: Democrats easily outweighed Republicans in Nevada. The only
trick was winning the nomination, which could prove tough given the fact
that not only was McCarran on the outs with his national party, but he had
also systematically alienated most of the powers in the Nevada party.

While no Democrat had yet announced against McCarran, three
names were on everybody's lips: Vail Pittman, Governor Edward Carville,
and Berkeley Bunker. All loathed McCarran. Not long before, the governor had been a friend and ally, but McCarran's habit of treating him
like an office boy grated (McCarran, for example, called for a special session of the state legislature without asking the governor's opinion); by
1944 Carville was openly tormenting McCarran by refusing to squelch
rumors that he was going to run for the nomination. Bunker, too, had
started out on McCarran's good side when he was named to finish out
Key Pittman's Senate term after the senior senator died in 1940. But
McCarran quickly became enraged when Bunker insisted on following
Pittman's pro-Roosevelt policies instead of deferring to the positions of
the *new* senior senator. McCarran took to calling his colleague Junior and
wouldn't even talk to Bunker when he passed him in the street.
McCarran was glad to be rid of Bunker when he lost the special Senate
election in 1942. Then there was Vail Pittman.

Just before McCarran, Hannegan, and Pittman sat down for lunch, a
photographer for the *Nevada State Journal* snapped a picture: McCarran's
arm reached out imploringly to Hannegan, his head turned toward the
chairman, showing perhaps a bit more of the back of his head than necessary to Pittman. It was as if McCarran could not stomach standing next
to Pittman for even a second.

Berkeley Bunker was broke. When he'd lost the 1942 election, some of his
friends in the Senate promised him a sinecure as the chamber's sergeant at

arms; someone else got the job. "I'll always think that McCarran spiked it," Bunker recalled. "In fact, I'm sure he did."[16]

It was the lowest time of Bunker's life. He tried to get a commission in the army but couldn't. He had no job. And he owed four thousand dollars from the campaign. He was in debt to newspapers all over the state. One editor told him not to worry about a three-hundred-dollar advertising bill. Bunker told him he would send him ten dollars a month until it was all paid. "I paid every dime of that back," he remembered, "paid it like the cat ate the grindstone, a little at a time, but I paid it back."[17]

Bunker was born in Nevada in 1906, grew up on a farm that was submerged behind the rising waters of Boulder Dam, and moved Las Vegas. After high school, he went off as a Mormon missionary to Georgia during the Depression. He had never seen so many trees, nor so much water. Green and wet everywhere, and clouds that carried rain! Bunker had a lot of time to enjoy the scenery, hitchhiking from town to town, waving his Book of Mormon on street corners, walking rural roads, knocking on farmhouse doors and asking the deeply religious southerners if he could share the good news of his upstart church. "They didn't believe what you taught," he recalled, "but they'd invite you in to speak."[18]

For the first time in his life, Bunker met black people. Although the church accepted black members, it did not go looking for them, nor would it appoint them priests. Eventually Bunker believed that blacks would be priests, but, like all great things, it was not for man to say when. "It cannot come from earthly sources," he said. "It'd have to come by divine revelation. . . . The prophets have said the day will come and the Negroes will hold the priesthood. And actually, we feel and know, that we have more to offer the Negroes than any other denomination."[19]

Blacks in the meantime could sit in the same pews as whites. All were God's children. In the South that was a revelation. Once Bunker was staying with a man when a white woman was allegedly raped by a black man and a lynch mob was supposed to gather at dawn. Bunker stayed up all night with his host, telling him that it was wrong to take the law into his own hands. The next morning the man joined the posse, and that day another southern tree bore strange fruit: a black man dangling by a noose. "That was such a horrifying experience to me," Bunker said years later. "But you couldn't talk 'em out of it. You couldn't reason with them."[20]

When he returned to Las Vegas, Bunker[21] opened a gas station and then filled out Pittman's Senate term before losing the special election. Bunker's main campaign issue: He ran against BMI as a war boondoggle. "An agency of the government that is so corrupt that it would make profiteering in the last war look like petty larceny by comparison," he called the magnesium plant. After his narrow defeat, Bunker went into the mortuary business, although public service kept tugging at him. He served on a grand jury that investigated the awful conditions at the Las Vegas jail. Then he met someone who shared his antipathy toward BMI and his concern for civil rights. And, most important, his desire to stop McCarran.

Estolv Ward and Berkeley Bunker were unlikely friends. Ward was an atheist, a revolutionary who wanted to upend the social order. Bunker was a Mormon bishop, a devout believer whose life was devoted to his deeply conservative church. And yet they had more in common than many would suspect. They both belonged to secretive, largely despised sects that required unquestioning faith, strict theological adherence, and heroic acts of labor and perseverance to prepare for an apocalypse that would redeem humankind. Both were upset by the way BMI (and Las Vegas in general) was treating its black workers. And both hated Pat McCarran. That, in an election year, was more than enough to make them fast friends. Bunker, Ward reported to union headquarters, was the CIO's best hope in Nevada. "He has," Ward wrote, "cooperated closely with the CIO in Las Vegas."[22]

At first Bunker had gotten on well with McCarran. When Bunker was appointed to the Senate days after Key Pittman died, McCarran insisted that the new senator ride back to Washington on the same train and then escorted him down the aisle for his swearing-in. There was only one favor he would like, McCarran told his new colleague. He wanted a woman in his office to become Bunker's secretary. Sure, Bunker said. It was practically the last thing the two agreed upon. McCarran wanted to purge all the men Key Pittman had appointed to patronage jobs. Bunker didn't think that was fair, but reluctantly agreed to go along. Then Bunker decided that since he had been named to serve in Pittman's place, he ought to continue his record of voting with the administration on foreign and military policy. Bunker was invited into the Oval Office three times during his brief two-year term—more than McCarran had been during the past six years. "I don't know why Senator McCarran and I don't get along," Roosevelt told Bunker, "but we don't."[23] Bunker went over to McCarran one day before a debate and tried to assuage his feelings. "Don't give me that tommyrot," McCarran snapped. "Go on and leave me alone. I don't want to listen to any of your flattery."[24]

McCarran, then, was only too glad to see Representative Jim Scrugham beat Bunker by one thousand votes in the Senate election in 1942. McCarran didn't like Scrugham (the two had almost come to blows not that long ago); he despised Bunker. "Little Boy Blue was Johnnie-at-the-rat-hole," McCarran spewed when Bunker voted to repeal the Neutrality Act. "I often wonder what that bird thinks about. I have come to the conclusion that he hasn't much to think about, so he shouldn't be blamed too much. At least I always believe in applying a full measure of charity."[25]

Bunker, Ward thought, would make the best candidate to oppose McCarran in the primary. He was young and relatively liberal. He wasn't McCarran. "Bunker would represent a definite advance over McCarran," Ward wrote to union headquarters. "Bunker says he will probably not run unless he is assured of CIO support. He gives private assurances that if he is so supported and is elected, he will give appropriate recognition in his voting and his appointments. If the CIO desires to bring Nevada definitely and strongly into the pro-administration column in 1944, it can do so; but it must move without undue delay."[26]

A man with the fortitude to proselytize for the Latter Day Saints in the Bible Belt might have the gumption to go up against McCarran. But then to cross McCarran openly was to invite a degree of hostility far greater than the casual enmity he bestowed on those who only disagreed with him. "If you didn't like him and he knew it," Bunker acknowledged, "God forbid him ever taking after you because he was a vindictive individual."[27]

Bunker decided not to oppose McCarran. He would run for the state's seat in the House instead. But that didn't mean he wouldn't help Ward.

When McCarran was in Reno, he liked to join his friend Norm Biltz for breakfast at the Riverside Hotel. Most mornings Biltz was in the Corner Bar by eight-thirty, at his regular table, dressed in an open-necked plaid shirt, placidly sipping coffee and smoking other people's cigarettes while the universe seemed to reel about him: Businessmen and politicians and ranchers and waiters with more coffee and phones swirled around Biltz like planets in orbit. Biltz was the most influential businessman in Nevada. McCarran liked to call him Boy.

The Riverside was convenient for both men: McCarran stayed there whenever he was in town (the house he owned blocks away was rented out), and Biltz took care of most of his business there. A hotel had been here longer than the town. Reno was born as a toll bridge across the Truckee in 1859; the next year a hotel appeared on the southern bank of the river. Various hotels (most called the Riverside) were built and burned on the spot until George Wingfield had put up the current six-story, red-brick building in 1926 to house the city's divorce colony. The Riverside stood next to the county courthouse; across the street was the art deco post office, which the devoted Pete Petersen ran as a virtual Senate field office for McCarran. Across the Virginia Street Bridge was downtown Reno, although most of Nevada's important business was usually taken care of in the Corner Bar.

McCarran and Biltz were a salt-and-pepper pair: the senator, short and stout in a suit and topped by his great thicket of white hair; the businessman, tall and trim, dressed like a ranch hand, his hair battleship gray and brushed back from a forehead apparently furrowed by years of squinting for livestock on the range. Biltz, indeed, looked like the rancher McCarran had once been, while the senator resembled the small-town businessman that Biltz claimed to be. Biltz, in fact, was worth millions. He owned tens of thousands of acres of land in the state, grazed thousands of head of cattle, held oil and mining interests, and was a major real-estate developer at Lake Tahoe. At one point Biltz owned twenty-seven miles of Tahoe's shoreline. He was forty-two.

Born in Connecticut, Biltz had gone west as a young man, worked as a dishwasher, a strikebreaker on the San Francisco waterfront, and a shaving brush salesman. In 1927 he found his way into the real-estate business at Tahoe, and because there were no hotels at the lake he took up residence in Reno at the Riverside. One of the benefits of living at the hotel was that every six weeks or so (the length of the state's residency requirement for divorce) a new contingent of women arrived without their estranged husbands. One of these was Esther Auchincloss Nash, a granddaughter of the Standard Oil fortune, who wound up staying in Reno after her divorce and becoming the third and final Mrs. Biltz.

At first Biltz sold lakefront property to wealthy easterners; he once carried a crippled advertising tycoon on his back through the snow for a mile to inspect a parcel. "I wanted the dough," Biltz explained. "I wasn't going to be stopped by anything."[28] Then Biltz began selling Nevada itself. The state was not overly fond of taxes — whether on income, sales, gifts, inheritances, or anything else. Nevada skimmed none. For the superrich, Biltz thought, this could be a big deal. He drew up a list of two hundred very wealthy people in the United States and proceeded to pitch them on the benefits of moving to Nevada. Scores did. Biltz, counting only those worth more than five million dollars, put the number at eighty. During the Depression Biltz started buying up land that had fallen into receivership; 90

percent of the foreclosed property in the state passed through his hands. Eventually Biltz found that his small table at the Riverside had become the center of a constantly expanding universe of business interests and connections, spanning from shipping magnate Stanley Dollar (who had a summer place at Tahoe) to Bank of America president Carl Wente (who had also run the First National Bank of Nevada). Among his millionaire friends, Biltz liked to play the poor cousin. "If I need to," he said, "I can raise real *dough,* fast, from *real* capitalists."[29]

When McCarran came to breakfast, Biltz picked up the tab. That was just the start. Biltz also picked up the room bill and was constantly sending McCarran gifts, such as expensive double-breasted suits. More importantly, Biltz had lured to the state scores of multimillionaires whose aggregate wealth topped a billion dollars. They liked Nevada the way it was. McCarran promised to keep it that way. "In the Nevada elections what most of us are interested in is getting the right kind of people," Biltz explained, "and we don't give a damn whether they are Democrats or Republicans."[30]

Biltz himself was a Republican, a fact that didn't deter him from serving as the de facto finance chairman of McCarran's reelection campaign. "Whenever we needed money," Pete Petersen recalled, "I would tell him how much we needed and he would come up with it."[31]

He wasn't the only one. A dozen years in Washington had given McCarran a wide array of business contacts, from Juan Trippe, the founder of Pan American Airways, to big Democratic backers such as financier Bernard Baruch. "I hope you are not having any trouble," Baruch told McCarran that summer. "If so and I can help let me know."[32]

McCarran did. "Serious opposition filed against me Saturday," McCarran responded. "I have great gratitude for your past fine expressions. Anything you may see fit to do for me now will be most appreciated."[33] Actually, expenses were easy to keep down. McCarran's Las Vegas campaign headquarters, for example, was set up in the El Cortez Hotel, in the heart of downtown's casino district on Fremont Street. Rent was free.

But McCarran still had a ravenous appetite for campaign money. "I was always collecting funds for him,"[34] Biltz remembered. This summer Biltz was practically a one-man postal service for McCarran. "This can be handed to Pat in cash so that he need not make any acknowledgement,"[35] yeast baron and Tahoe resident Max Fleischmann told Biltz when he gave him five hundred dollars for McCarran.

McCarran was twenty-six years older than Biltz, whom he came to love like a son. "I have had a great joy and rare privilege in feeling close to you," McCarran told him. "I have a confidence in you which is rare and I know would never be misplaced. You never ask anything for yourself and I wonder if you know that the greatest happiness I could have would be to do something for you, my friend."[36] Biltz felt the same way about McCarran. "Pat is as stubborn as a mule and he and I have lots of arguments," Biltz said. "On the other hand, he is the greatest senator Nevada could possibly have."[37]

Breakfast with McCarran was usually interesting. It was never cheap.

From Reno, on Nevada's western flank, Highway 50 ran across the desert, wending up into ranges and falling into basins, again and again, for some three hundred miles, before the road finally sliced through the Egan Mountains and dipped toward the state's eastern edge. Here the mountainous terrain yielded glimpses of a weird human-made landscape: huge open-pit mines pocking the ground, mile-wide wounds in the earth surrounded by barren hills of diggings that dwarfed belching steam shovels and locomotives crawling over the vast wastes like ants. This Hieronymus Bosch scene in the American West told you that you were in Nevada's copper country. You were almost to Ely.

In Ely, as in every city in Nevada, the highway became the main drag (Aultman Street), and the first thing you noticed was the six-story Hotel Nevada, the tallest building in the state, towering over the small, mountain-cradled town. Nearby was the two-story White Pine County Courthouse, topped by a small copper dome and fronted by thick copper doors — reminders of why the town existed. While the red metal ultimately yielded more wealth than the Comstock Lode (a billion dollars in half a century), little prosperity clung to Ely, its three thousand residents, or Vail Pittman, the editor and publisher (and writer and pressman) of its newspaper, the *Daily Times,* located a block and a half down the road from the Hotel Nevada. Pittman lived on the other side of town, about a mile away, in a simple two-story house.

Ely was a backwater and seemed to be becoming more so all the time. Three years before, the local train stopped connecting to the transcontinental railroad, 140 miles due north. About the biggest thing to happen lately was a windstorm that ripped the roof off a chicken coop and dropped it on three people planting a victory garden, killing one. Yet in the spring of 1944 most of the political gossip in Nevada centered on Vail Pittman, the Hamlet of White Pine County.

If any man in Nevada wanted to see McCarran kicked out of office, it was Pittman. Born in Mississippi, the youngest of four brothers, Vail Pittman had followed his eldest sibling, Key, to Tonopah in 1903. Young Pittman sold coal, spent a stint as Nye County sheriff (when McCarran was the district attorney), dabbled in mining, and passed time as a bank teller before getting bit by the journalism bug. In 1920 Pittman moved to Ely, where he put out the *Daily Times.* Unlike his wild and drunken older brother, Vail Pittman was temperate and moderate, though just as devout a Democrat.

When Key Pittman died five days after winning his sixth term in the Senate in 1940, his widow handed his gold watch to Vail. The younger Pittman thought he should have gotten more. He was an eminent figure in the Nevada Democratic Party, had served in the Nevada State Senate, was politically and philosophically close to his brother, and believed that by rights he should have been appointed to fill out Key's term and hold his seat in Washington until a special election could be held. But the last thing that McCarran was going to put up with was *another* Pittman in Washington. Governor Ed Carville obliged McCarran and named political novice Berkeley Bunker to the spot. Pittman was uncharacteristically furious. "The governor chose to give the high post to a filling station owner,"[38] he fumed. In front of a friend, Pittman flushed, his jug ears reddening, his great dark eyebrows shaking like angry hawks, his southern accent deepening with outrage. Key's memory was insulted, he sputtered.

The insults kept coming. Mimosa Pittman wanted to build a memorial chapel and campanile at the University of Nevada campus, a tribute to her late husband. But raising money for the Pittman memorial in McCarran's Nevada proved an impossible task. Men who would have flung money at Pittman when he was alive felt much different when he was gone and his great rival McCarran was suddenly the state's undisputed political power. Soon Mimosa was in arrears on the crypt rental she was paying while her husband's remains moldered. "It is my understanding that a body should not be kept there over two years at the outside, and really not that long,"[39] Vail prodded Mimosa. Finally the Pittman family settled for a new crypt in the Mountain View Masonic Cemetery. No bell tower would chime Key's memory. If Pittman were to have a tribute it would have to be by someone reclaiming his senatorial legacy.

In 1942 Vail Pittman ran for lieutenant governor, beating his closest rival by 8,604 votes. Being lieutenant governor in Nevada wasn't much of a job, because the legislature met for only two months every other year. The best part was the fifteen dollars a day he got for being acting governor when Carville left the state. And God knew he could use the money.

Running a provincial paper during wartime was a tough job. Rationing dried up advertising. Other dailies in the state dropped Monday issues or went weekly. Pittman slogged on, putting out the paper with the help of his wife and an assistant. Whenever he could, Pittman hired deskmen to help with editorial work, but they always turned out to be drunks or gambling fiends or incompetent or all three and sooner or later he had to fire them. "I have had plenty of grief," he told a friend. ". . . From week-to-week we never know whether or not some printer will walk out on us."[40]

Pittman was thinking of challenging McCarran for the nomination. "Show the old hog up,"[41] urged a supporter. Rule Number One in Nevada politics was to travel around the state before making any move for high office. But for more than a year Pittman had not been able to leave Ely except for a quick trip to Reno — and that was only a stopover on a business trip to San Francisco. He arranged speaking engagements in Las Vegas, Carson City, and Reno but had to pull out each time because he couldn't get away from work.

In April, Pittman finally thought that he found someone to unshackle him from the *Daily Times,* a new assistant editor named George Lynn. "Somehow, I think he may be the man I have been seeking for all these many years," Pittman told a friend. "I sincerely hope so. I am inclined to believe he will handle his liquor fairly well, as I told him what I had heard about his one possible failing, and he discussed the matter very satisfactorily in a letter to me."[42]

Yet Pittman vacillated. In May, Pittman left Lynn in charge of the paper and went to Reno to speak to the Nevada Peace Officers Association. "He was seriously weighing the advisability of seeking the Democratic nomination," reported the *Reno Evening Gazette.* "At the same time, he is considering the potentialities of his present position as a stepping stone to either the governorship or the United States Senate in 1946."[43]

On May Day in Ely, CIO members were out in force, handing out tracts urging people to sign up to vote. "Things You Should Do To Be Sure You Can Vote,"[44] read one flyer.

The year before, the CIO's Mine-Mill had lost the union fight in Las Vegas, but at the same time it had managed to quietly beat the AFL in elections in White Pine's major mining centers: Ely, Ruth, and McGill. So while the Clark County local existed only on paper (and for the purpose of opposing McCarran), the White Pine locals boasted actual workers, more than thirteen hundred. Which was why the CIO had picked Ely for its state PAC convention in April. Organizers from five Nevada counties gathered in the basement of the Nevada Hotel to listen to George Roberts, the PAC regional director from Los Angeles. "Roberts says that the CIO adheres strongly to the idea of free enterprise as the mainspring of our democratic government,"[45] Pittman's *Daily Times* reported. Other accounts of the meeting were more informative. "Plans were made for action in the crucial election contests of 1944," added Mine-Mill's *The Union* newspaper, "in cooperation with all groups who want international cooperation and who support legislation for the benefit of the majority of people."[46]

All around the country, PAC volunteers were zealously trying to sign up new voters.[47] In Detroit the CIO hired two sound trucks to prowl housing projects and dispatched fifteen full-time workers to go door to door. In less than a week the union registered 3,445 new voters. In Duluth, Minnesota, the CIO registered every member on its books, the organizers manning desks outside steel mills at the end of each shift and marching individual workers down to city hall to sign up. In Dayton, Ohio, three thousand workers lined up to register on the last day, standing in line in front of the courthouse during a rainstorm. In Los Angeles the CIO claimed credit for helping to swell voter rolls by four hundred thousand new names.

Pittman's newspaper applauded the PAC's registration drive. "The CIO, in launching a campaign to get citizens registered to vote in the coming elections, set a fine example," noted the *Daily Times,* ". . . when, in holding an election within its own organizations, eighty-five percent of the members took the time to cast their ballots. . . . And if all the decisions at the ballot box in this country were based on such a high majority of expressed opinion, then we would have democracy at its best."[48]

Scores of delegates from every corner of Nevada poured off trains at the Southern Pacific station in downtown Reno on June 22, picking their way through forty-two Basque sheepherders who'd arrived the same morning, recruited in Spain to cross the Atlantic and fan out across the range tending livestock. The state Democratic convention was not going to be so easy to herd.

The next day the two hundred delegates gathered in a hall on South Virginia Street across from the courthouse. More than half came from just two counties — Washoe (Reno) and Clark (Las Vegas). A week earlier the Washoe County Democratic convention had gone as predictably as a Soviet election. The platform, delegates, and officers were all selected in advance, and only the formality of voting took place. The only oddity at the meeting was that an unusually high number of delegates were women. Perhaps this had something to do with a thirty-two-page pamphlet from Washington that had just been mailed to all federal employees in Nevada, reminding them that the Hatch Act forbade government workers from engaging in campaign activity. So Reno postmaster Pete Petersen, for example, was not a delegate to the county convention for the first time that anyone could remember. He did pop in to watch some sessions, how-ever. His wife, after all, was a delegate — as were the wives of many other federal officeholders in the state.

The Clark delegation, on the other hand, was made up of faces that were largely unfamiliar to McCarran's supporters. Electing representatives to the state convention was usually a pretty sleepy affair in Clark County. The voting took place in backyards and garages all over the county, and few people normally turned up to cast a ballot. But this year the CIO PAC had flooded the polling places with its supporters and elected its own slate, laying claim to thirty-four of the forty delegates. The delegates in turn elected a chairman: Berkeley Bunker. It was a shocking defeat for McCarran's forces, which had planned to walk away with the delegation. "The victory in Clark County is unprecedented," crowed Mine-Mill's newspaper, *The Union,* "and virtually wipes McCarran off the political map."[49]

The distance between the two rival delegations was evident from the opening of the convention. Washoe nominated Harley Harmon, a McCarran man, for the key post of convention chairman. Clark put forward its own candidate, H. W. Young. The factions squabbled through the evening. The White Pine delegation (which was led by Vail Pittman and included PAC organizer Ed Church) tilted toward the opposition. Still, Harley won the next morning, putting the McCarran forces in strategic control of the proceed-ings. Then Washoe renominated Ed Clark, a McCarran loyalist from Las Vegas, to serve again as the Democratic national committeeman. Clark's own delegation tried to thwart him by suggesting a different candidate. Again Clark County lost the contest. Clark County also tried to oust E. C. Mulcahy, a McCarran stalwart, as state party chairman, nominating James Johnson to take his place. Yet again Clark County lost. "Revolt in democratic ranks,"[50] screamed the *Las Vegas Review-Journal.*

In the afternoon the gathering listened to the report of the resolutions committee, which was headed by two local newspaper publishers (and devoted McCarran backers), E. C. Mulcahy and Joseph McDonald. They recommended a fourth term for Roosevelt; cheers filled the hall. Then they read a resolution commending McCarran for the job he was doing in the Senate. "Sincere, able, fearless, his record of achievement is a matter of pride to the Democratic Party,"[51] the proposed resolution read.

Jeers erupted. Clark County delegate James Johnson objected. McCarran's record, he said, gave him no right to be lauded along with the president. He moved that the section be cut since McCarran had opposed the president on every defense measure. "We cannot approve McCarran's conduct in Congress," noted L. O. Hawkins, another Clark delegate. "I believe for the past twelve years he has been against everything the president has stood for," he added. "I think he will continue that way."[52]

For hours debate raged over the support McCarran had given to the president. "Let's not attempt to stage a political rally at this convention," Mulcahy said.[53] Cliff Devine accused the Clark delegation of trying to tear the Democratic Party apart by attacking McCarran. "Certainly he differed with Roosevelt," Devine said, "but that doesn't make him un-American."[54]

Finally the resolution came to a vote. McCarran's forces won, 110½ delegates to 91½, but it was disconcertingly close. "The bitterest attack in years on a holder of high public office,"[55] the *Reno Evening Gazette* chortled.

McCarran didn't attend the convention. Instead he hunkered down across the street in a suite at the Riverside Hotel dispatching orders. "It looks as though I may have some serious opposition in the primary," McCarran complained. "The CIO has set out to find a candidate to run against me, and they are flirting with the Lieutenant Governor, Pittman; so I may have to put on my sword and buckle, but I have never been very lucky in having anything handed to me. I generally have to fight my way for whatever I get. It doesn't seem to make a continental bit of difference how hard I work, or how much I accomplish; when it comes to getting something for myself, I have to take on the battle — but I approach it without fear and with a hellish determination."[56]

The CIO PAC had held another meeting in Ely. Mine-Mill International vice president Ralph Rasmussen came from Washington. PAC regional director George Roberts came from Los Angeles. Clark County organizer Joe Houseman arrived from Las Vegas. Later in the month Rasmussen wrote to union members urging them to do whatever they could to defeat McCarran. "The record speaks for itself," Rasmussen wrote. "It is a record that even a most reactionary Republican would have cause to be ashamed of. . . . McCarran must be eliminated in the primary. . . . Labor cannot afford to allow McCarran to return to the Senate."[57]

It didn't take McCarran long to get a copy of the letter. In fact, three days after Rasmussen sent his missive out, Al Cahlan, McCarran's satrap in southern Nevada, was thundering away at the union in the *Las Vegas Review-Journal*. "Who's running the Democratic Party — the Democrats or the CIO?" asked the paper. "In this state it is common knowledge the CIO committee has consulted with several leading Democrats, trying to persuade them to make the race against McCarran."[58]

Anyone who would dare run against McCarran, Cahlan implied, must be part of a CIO-Communist plot. Rasmussen, ironically, was one of the nonparty board members in Mine-Mill's leadership and was often fighting against the Communists in the union. Unwittingly, he had just given McCarran his campaign theme.

The night of July 19 was a pleasant sixty-five degrees as the Democratic National Convention opened in Chicago Stadium. Everyone knew that Roosevelt would be the nominee, but no one knew who his running mate might be. Typically, Roosevelt had offered encouragement to a number of prospects, including his current vice president, Henry Wallace. Many of the president's intimates were alarmed by Roosevelt's weary appearance. "There is not a chance in the world for him to carry on for four years more,"[59] Jim Farley noted in his diary. The party pros, however, were dead set against the increasingly left-leaning Wallace. "I would like to have one thing on my headstone — that I was the man who kept Henry Wallace from becoming president of the United States,"[60] Democratic national chairman Bob Hannegan later quipped.

Hannegan and others prevailed upon Roosevelt to dump Wallace and suggested Senator Harry S. Truman as his replacement. "Clear it with Sidney,"[61] the president told Hannegan. PAC chairman Sidney Hillman was officially a Wallace supporter. Indeed, the vice president was something of a CIO pin-up boy, a political idol whose unstinting progressive views made him the New Deal's heir apparent. Still, Hillman was enough of a realist to know a done deal when he saw one. He gave labor's nod to Truman.

The next night Senate majority leader Alben Barkley gave the nominating speech for Roosevelt's unprecedented fourth term. Before Barkley finished, McCarran stood up and walked out.[62]

On July 21 Truman was nominated for vice president on the second ballot. Later McCarran bounded up to him on the floor. Truman was sitting down, munching a snack and having a drink. McCarran bent over and reached out a beefy paw. Truman shook hands. McCarran had a small favor to ask.[63]

—

Vail Pittman came to Chicago as the chairman of the Nevada delegation. Before sitting out for the Midwest, Pittman had tried to arrange an appointment in Washington with the president. Pittman's new assistant editor, George Lynn, followed up with a second plea to the White House for an interview. "McCarran, because of his unsympathetic attitude toward the president and toward what the administration has sought to accomplish, inevitably will face opposition for reelection," Lynn wrote to Stephen Early. "Labor wants a candidate that favors Roosevelt and Democrats throughout the state want the same thing."[64]

Early said he would do what he could for Pittman ("Key was one of my old friends — one of the best"[65]) but didn't hold out much hope. Pittman did not get to see the president.

On July 22, as the temperature inched toward the nineties in Chicago, McCarran sat down on the left side of a long table with the other members of the resolutions committee. On the other end of the table sat Harry Truman, Roosevelt's running mate. Sitting before the panel were CIO president Philip Murray and PAC chairman Sidney Hillman, followed by their lawyers, Lee Pressman and John Abt. It was a standing-room-only crowd that gathered to hear labor pitch its program.

Murray started with an attack on the Republicans. "The people of America will overwhelmingly reject a return to the discredited policies of the past," he said. ". . . They want no part of any narrow nationalism or any thinly disguised imperialism that can only lay the basis for another world slaughter in our lifetime."[66]

Murray then complained about the cost of living. "Your statement," McCarran interrupted, "will be supported by every housewife in America."

It was a convivial meeting, considering that Murray and Hillman (and Pressman and Abt) were trying to drive McCarran from office. But McCarran had an even friendlier meeting in Chicago with AFL president William Green. "Be assured," Green told McCarran, "it is our firm and determined purpose to drive with all the influence at our command to bring about your re-election."[67]

McCarran could joke with the CIO in Chicago. Nevada was something else. As soon as the convention adjourned, McCarran left for home.

—

On Saturday, July 29, Vail Pittman climbed onto a stage in the crowed high school gym in Ely. Pittman should have been smiling from ear to ear. He was about to finally announce that he was running against McCarran in the senatorial primary five weeks away. Almost all of political Nevada packed into the gym for the state's AFL convention. Not to mention a number of national AFL officials sitting on the stage. At sixty he was still trim and vigorous. McCarran was only seven years older, but his frequent ill health and paunch constantly reminded voters that he was slouching toward seventy. And with the nation rallying behind its wartime president, McCarran's long and bitter opposition to Roosevelt was more than a little dismaying to many in the state. Pittman, on the other hand, was nothing if not loyal to his party and president. He was a popular lieutenant governor, the brother of the beloved Key Pittman, a man who finally seemed poised to reclaim his family's political legacy.

Pittman looked dour. "I am going to broach a matter that is very distasteful to me," he said, "but I feel constrained to deal with it. It has been reported to me that a statement is being circulated that the CIO union has offered to place ten thousand dollars at my disposal for use, if and when I become a candidate for United States senator. It would seem that these statements are being spread about for the purpose of making it appear that my candidacy will be sponsored and financed by the CIO."[68]

That was putting it mildly. "Who will rule Nevada?" asked full-page ads in newspapers around the state. "The people or the C.I.O.? . . . Who will wear the CIO collar? Who will be the CIO candidate?"[69] The ads reprinted Mine-Mill's Ralph Rasmussen's letter urging CIO members to dump McCarran. And in case anyone missed the point, the ads also reprinted an editorial written by McCarran's henchman Al Cahlan, the editor of the *Las Vegas Review-Journal*. "Nevada does not want and will not stand for a CIO-Communist party dictatorship,"[70] Cahlan thundered.

"I take this occasion to brand that statement as completely false and without a semblance of fact or truth," Pittman continued. "No one connected with the CIO has offered me a dime and I am under no more obligation to the CIO than I am to the AF of L. . . . I have lived in this state for thirty-eight years and I believe the people who know me — and they number in the thousands — have confidence in my integrity and independence. I am perfectly willing to have my life and my deeds, both good and bad, compared with those of any other candidate or man in Nevada."[71] Finally, Pittman attacked his rival. "McCarran, in his opposition to President Roosevelt and the war effort as a whole, must be replaced with some Nevada citizen who is sympathetic to the course of war and the specific effort to bring peace about as soon as possible," he said. ". . . Look what has been happening in Guam the last few days. We have lost hundreds of men out there in the vital and all essential effort to retake the island — but Senator McCarran resisted every effort in Congress to fortify Guam so that the Japs could not take it. Look at what the Russians are doing. We have supplied them through Lend-lease, with thousands of planes, tanks and tons of ammunition — and they are nearer to Berlin today than anyone of our Allies. But Senator McCarran was against Lend-lease — he was opposed to furnishing our Allies the very supplies that would break down the enemy. . . . McCarran, perhaps unwittingly, has opposed almost every fundamental war demand that will hasten the day of victory for us."[72]

Sunday morning opened with a McCarran blitzkrieg. A third of the delegates to the convention were still sleeping off the Saturday-night festivities when McCarran's backers rushed through an unexpected resolution commending the senator's record and advocating his renomination. Among these supporters was Joe Ozanic, one of the mysterious men from the AFL's national staff who had been sitting on stage during Pittman's speech the day before. AFL president Bill Green had promised to help McCarran win reelection, and Joe Ozanic was part of that promise.

Joseph Ozanic Sr. was fifty-four. He had gone to work in coal mines in Illinois when he was fifteen years old; he spent the better part of the next twenty-seven years underground working like a mule. "Sweating in that damn mine until there wasn't a dry stitch of clothes on me,"[73] as he put it. He emerged from the earth to become president of the Progressive Miner Workers of America, an AFL affiliate that fought a bloody jurisdictional fight with the CIO's United Mine Workers of America. The CIO, Ozanic thought, was just about the worst thing to ever happen to American labor. "If you're a Commie, damn it, go to Russia," he said. "That's where you belong. . . . If there's anybody who hates Communists or who detests anything they stand for, it's me." Ozanic spent nights sitting in the dark at home with a shotgun in his lap hoping UMW men would try to break in. "I'm a rabble-rouser type and I can flex my muscles just as good as any

of you," he told his union brothers. "Anybody who mined coal had muscles and guts or he wouldn't be a coal miner . . . you sons-of-bitches."[74]

But battling your way through Nevada politics took more than brawn,
as Ozanic soon discovered. Ozanic had arrived in Nevada weeks before
McCarran had any declared opposition. He appeared at the Reno Trades
and Labor Council convention in early July to tell the various AFL locals
that President Green wanted them to form a united front to support
McCarran — after he privately cleared the idea with Frank J. Bacigalupi,
the president of the Nevada State Federation of Labor. Tumult broke out.
Many state AFL members thought that the union shouldn't take sides in
the primary — at least before other candidates had time to announce.
Bacigalupi, it turned out, was not a McCarran backer.

The Reno resolution failed, which was worse than if it had never been
proposed because it demonstrated vocal opposition to McCarran. "Ozanic is
a very nice fellow," Pete Petersen told McCarran. "He is sincere and he
worked hard, but to use his own statement, he had never been around a labor
group who promised one thing and would do another. . . . He is a much
wiser boy today than he was when he first came to the state of Nevada."[75]

Ozanic learned fast. On a swing through Las Vegas he read a letter from
Bill Green to the Clark County Central Labor Council, which covered all
AFL members in the area, and walked away with a unanimous endorsement for McCarran's reelection. "One of the best friends labor ever had
in the national Congress,"[76] the endorsement read.

In Ely, on Sunday morning, Ozanic's timing was impeccable. Even then
the motion hailing McCarran faced significant opposition, slipping through
by a vote of 46 to 19. But by the time the other forty delegates arrived for
the morning session, they were surprised to discover that the convention
had already gone on record supporting McCarran for another term. "It
doesn't mean anything!" fumed Pittman's newspaper. "Green is a great labor
leader, but he should learn from this experience, at least, that he can't run
the West from the East."[77]

The primary campaign was short but brutal. For five weeks McCarran and
Pittman hammered at each other in newspapers, in speeches, and on the
radio. McCarran had set the stage for a bitter fight, implying that anyone
who might run against him was a frontman for the CIO PAC and hence
either a Communist or the party's dupe. McCarran all but ignored Pittman
and acted as if he were running against the CIO itself. Conservative allies
amplified his charges across the country. "The CIO candidate,"[78] the

Chicago Tribune called Pittman. "Some of the lies about Senator McCarran, circulated by Sidney Hillman's Communist-controlled CIO committee, were so grotesque as to be laughable,"[79] echoed the AFL's *Labor* newspaper.

Pittman was merciless in return. "Had the McCarrans, the Wheelers and the Nyes been able to dictate their program of unpreparedness, the United States already would have lost the war," one Pittman ad claimed.[80] He kept reminding voters that their sons and brothers were dying in a war that the country was ill prepared for and likening McCarran's sentiments before Pearl Harbor to those of American Nazis. "McCarran has the right to be an isolationist," Pittman allowed, "but he hasn't the right to try and choke down our throats an isolationism that has brought us only disaster, death and despair."[81]

As the Allies were sweeping toward Germany from the west and the east, in Nevada it was 1941 all over again. McCarran virtually called Pittman a Communist, and Pittman practically labeled McCarran a fascist. And from the beginning the fight took on the overtones of a national struggle, with the AFL, HUAC, and *Chicago Tribune* lining up behind McCarran, while the CIO, various liberal groups, and muckraking columnist Drew Pearson championed Pittman.

The AFL and the CIO both poured money and men into the campaign. "President Green is reported to have sent more organizers from the international AFL into Nevada to work in Senator McCarran's behalf," reported the *Reno Evening Gazette.* "One AFL member estimated this week that there were at least ten outside organizers in the state engaged in this project. Another placed the number at twenty-five."[82]

Pittman's candidacy, McCarran's backers alleged, was less a campaign than a conspiracy. "Having secured a candidate, the Communists proceeded to develop their campaign," averred AFL's *Labor* newspaper. "Apparently, they had money to burn. They sent into Nevada thirty-five or forty paid 'agents.'"[83]

McCarran's campaign had more of everything: money, men, patronage, experience. But the campaign against McCarran had an excess of one vital quality: passion. "PAC," recalled Len De Caux, a party member who was editor of the CIO's *Labor News,* "revived on the political field some of the unit spirit of early CIO. . . . Enthusiasm spread throughout and beyond the labor movement. Wealthy reaction, responding with frantic Redbaiting and mudslinging, was not alone in seeing the possibility of a great popular movement that might sweep it into the discard . . . an emotional plus-factor conspicuous in mass movements, in revolutions, in wars deemed to be just — the exuberance of being one of many sweeping on united

against the foe, through immediate gains, toward glowing if vague and distant goals. Idealists, romantics, cause-addicts, devotees, feed the flame."[84]

And no PAC campaign was more ardent than the Nevada primary,
which Estolv Ward had been working on for months. "Volunteer political
workers were organized and trained . . . ," he recalled. "Thousands were
rallied to the support of McCarran's opponent."[85]

By the end of August, McCarran was clearly nervous. "Judging by the
telegrams and phone calls colleagues are getting from Nevada's Senator
Pat McCarran, he is racing against political death," Drew Pearson
reported. "He has been frantically calling senators, some of whom vigorously disagree with him, imploring them to endorse him for reelection."[86]

Surprisingly, some Democrats who seldom agreed with McCarran
wrote him encouraging letters. "I sincerely hope the voters of Nevada
return you to the United States Senate," wrote Roosevelt's running mate
Harry Truman, who probably intended that the letter would be used
against McCarran's Republican rival in the general election. "You are
chairman of one of the most important committees of the Senate — the
Judiciary Committee and it would be a sacrifice to the great state of
Nevada to the lose that most important chairman."[87]

Key Pittman's widow, Mimosa, was livid. "McCarran is using Truman's
letter in full page ads all over state," she wired the White House. "Inference
is that President Roosevelt approves of McCarran. This is creating tremendous amount dissension among loyal Roosevelt supporters. . . . Nevada can
defeat McCarran if Truman will wire that he did not intend letter to be
used in primary election."[88]

The wire was passed to DNC chairman Bob Hannegan, who responded vaguely. "Yes," he scribbled, "I knew about it."[89]

Vail Pittman tried to attack McCarran jujitsu-style for bringing AFL out-
siders into the race after the senator spent most of the summer decrying
CIO interference in the campaign. "Just Who Is Going to Run Nevada's
Election — Easterners or Nevadans?"[90] Pittman asked.

But even as he was trying to run against McCarran, Pittman found
himself unexpectedly struggling to run his newspaper as well. The editor
whom he had hired a few months before to take care of the *Daily Times*
so that Pittman could take care of McCarran was turning out to be a disaster. "George Lynn, our editor, is only about fifty percent as efficient as
when he came," Pittman confided to a friend. "He thinks only of drink

and is in a 'fog' most of the time. He started off with a bang but soon drifted into a state of indifference. He tries to shove his work off. . . . He overlooks news everyday if we don't watch him. He never reads a paper or keeps posted on state, national and international developments. With the exception of Roosevelt, Churchill, Stalin and Chiang Kai-shek, he knows few of the war leaders. Amazing, in view of the fact he handles the telegraph. It appears to me that if he continues to drink like he does he will have apoplexy — and if he stops suddenly he will fold up. He shows no desire to regulate his drinking."[91]

Pittman's load wasn't about to get any lighter.

The week before the primary the *Salt Lake City Tribune* broke a story about HUAC's continuing investigation into the CIO PAC, which had been dragging on for the better part of the year. "Telegrams Indicate Fight Against McCarran by PAC,"[92] the paper reported. The Dies Committee had subpoenaed Western Union for telegrams charged to the account of the PAC's California regional office, which included Nevada. "If at all possible please prevail upon Vail Pittman to run against McCarran," Helen Gahagan Douglas, an actress and Democratic activist who was running for Congress in Los Angeles, wrote to U.S. senator Claude Pepper. "Everything is in his favor and he is the most electable."[93]

This wasn't much of a news flash. Nevertheless McCarran had the story reprinted from one end of Nevada to the other, forcing Pittman to once again deny that he was the PAC's stalking horse. "They have never put up a dime for my campaign," Pittman insisted. "They are simply against McCarran. They would have supported any candidate who might have filed against McCarran."[94]

During the last days of the election, Pittman was reduced to taking out full-page ads disputing that he had taken money from the CIO.

Las Vegas had a lot to thank the New Deal for. The federal government paved more than fifty-eight blocks of the city, planted trees, groomed base-ball fields, put in a public golf course, built schools, a post office, a federal building, and a convention center. Then came the wartime boom, when Washington showered the city with even more money and projects: BMI and new roads and infrastructure and the army air base and gunnery range.

The New Deal, however, did nothing for the Westside — the Las Vegas ghetto packed with defense workers who lived like refugees. They built shacks from scrap wood stolen from construction sites at the air base; they lit their hovels with oil lamps that sometimes started fires. Residents dug latrines and dumped lime to cover the stink; they ported water from communal taps. During the day white visitors were rare on this side of town. At night some crossed the railroad tracks to gamble at an interracial casino, but then the city shut it down; others came for the gin joints or the prostitutes. But if you saw a white face before dark, chances were that it belonged to a CIO organizer. "Most of the members who really went all out for the CIO were the minorities," recalled Woodrow Wilson, the black BMI worker. ". . . The CIO program was attractive to blacks because the CIO would promise them anything but the moon. The AFL hadn't been active in participating and communicating with their membership, in doing some of the things like eliminating segregation that would have reduced the possibility of the CIO taking hold. Segregation: that was the key."[95]

Then in late 1943 McCarran developed a sudden interest in the Westside, meeting with Las Vegas mayor E. W. Cragin and the Reverend Henry Cook to talk about the neighborhood. Soon thereafter BMI and the AFL pledged to help improve conditions. "This area will be provided with community shower baths, toilets, wash bowls and laundry facilities,"[96] promised the *Review-Journal*.

The timing struck Mine-Mill's Estolv Ward as more than coincidental. "Jimmie Anderson, the AFL Negro organizer, is back up here and plans an extensive program in the Westside on housing and general civic betterment," Ward noted. "This is to be pushed by the AFL with the backing of Guernsey Frazer, the BMI press agent and political boss. The move is obviously to build up a back-log of AFL colored votes for the dual purpose of winning next year's election at BMI and of securing victory for reactionary candidates in the public elections of 1944. It is a long range, clever program which will undoubtedly place us in a difficult position unless we succeed in doing something for the Negroes and retaining their loyalty."[97]

The Westside, almost overnight, had become an electoral battleground. Blacks (and their votes) were largely negligible in Nevada until the war boom. Then the population of Clark County swelled more than sixfold. All of a sudden two of the three biggest cities in the state were in the south: Las Vegas (population thirty-nine thousand) and BMI's company town, Henderson (twelve thousand), compared with long-dominant Reno (twenty-one thousand). Thousands of these new residents were blacks recruited in the South for work at BMI. In the Westside they created a little patch of home, growing collard greens and raising opossums and throwing a great party on the Nineteenth of June, the date when word of the Emancipation Proclamation finally reached the South — half a year after Lincoln had freed the slaves.

Even by local standards, the Westside was a raucous place. Marijuana cigarettes went for a buck apiece (ask for the man known as Eagle Eye in any Westside nightclub). In May alone the police arrested 313 people for felonies, a disproportionate number on the Westside, where drunken brawls and stabbings were as common as casinos on the other side of the tracks. "A good honest-to-God fight is a different matter," Judge A. G. Blad scolded one resident, whom he fined a hundred dollars for slashing a man in a street brawl. "But one thing we will not tolerate here is using of knives, guns or other similar weapons. With the old time colored people of this community we have had little trouble but that is not true of some of the recent arrivals."[98]

Actually, there wasn't a whole lot that judges would tolerate when it came to the town's black residents. One black man who allegedly threatened a white woman got fifty days in jail and was fined one hundred dollars (by way of contrast, when one black beat another and caused him to lose an eye, the attacker got a suspended sentence when he agreed to enlist in the military). The result was that the daily average number of prisoners in the hellish Las Vegas jail jumped from 25 to 132, about a quarter of whom were black. When the already overcrowded police station holding cells could take no more, the city turned the basement of the War Memorial building into a second jail — although not a very good one, because three men in one cell discovered that they could ungrout the mortar with a can opener and push out enough bricks to squeeze through.

For the military authorities in the area, the Westside (and Las Vegas in general) was a headache. Soldiers were constantly reporting for duty drunk or hungover, and *GI* became a synonym for *VD*. Bars within the city limits were supposed to close at midnight, but many didn't. At the Harlem Club in the Westside, for example, the outside lights were turned off at twelve, but the doorman still welcomed guests at all hours. Outside the city limits no one even bothered with the pretense. A city commissioner got up early one morning to go fishing and drove out on the Boulder Highway toward BMI; he noticed that most of the club parking lots were still crammed with cars at dawn. The army tried issuing a directive to bartenders not to serve military personnel after hours, but few saloon keeps were willing to say no to a man in uniform. The army started sending MPs to round up soldiers. When the military threatened to declare Las Vegas off limits, the city cracked down. Mostly on prostitutes. One weekend the police arrested eight women for prostitution, most of them black. When all of them were found to have venereal disease, the police put them in a jail ward at the county hospital and announced that they would not be released until they were cured. Yet despite the abject poverty of the Westside, money was sloshing around. When police arrested Marion Watson, sixty-two, for pimping his wife, Estelle, fifty-seven, they found seven thousand dollars in cash on him.

Heading into the primary, however, it wasn't just johns who were visiting the Westside. The CIO, of course, had been active on the Westside ever since it came to Las Vegas in late 1942. Less than a year earlier two hundred blacks had walked off the job at BMI rather than accept segregated dressing rooms. The AFL told them to go back to work; the CIO told them to stand up for their rights. And now Westside ministers like the Reverend Lester Cruise, whose Church of Christ Holiness was a gathering place for the strikers, remembered which union talked about racial equity and which union talked about not making a fuss. "The blacks flocked to CIO," recalled Woody Wilson, a rare black who didn't. "I stayed with the AFL, but I really had a lot of respect for these CIO people."[99]

To Estolv Ward and other CIO organizers it was clear that these seventy-two forlorn blocks could tip the election to Pittman. "The CIO has practically complete influence in the large Negro community that has grown up since the war in Las Vegas," Ward told union headquarters. "There are approximately eight thousand Negroes there, of which fifteen hundred to two thousand can be turned into CIO voters with a little educational campaigning."[100]

On the evening of August 16, just hours before the 9 P.M. registration deadline, more than four hundred people rushed to sign up to vote in Clark County. The CIO had been busy. "The workers need political action community organizations as much as they need their trade unions,"[101] a PAC booklet called "Every Worker a Voter" explained.

Clark County was only one of two counties in the state where the number of registered voters increased. Overall, the number of voters in Nevada declined from sixty thousand to fifty-seven thousand. But in Clark County the number jumped by 16 percent. The PAC campaign signed up seven thousand voters in the county. And Democrats outnumbered Republicans more than three to one. The most dramatic registration results were in precincts in the Westside and Carver Park, the segregated housing project at BMI. On the Westside, Democrats outnumbered Republicans by almost six to one, while in Carver Park, the ratio was almost thirty-two to one. WESTSIDE FOR ROOSEVELT CLUB and the ROOSEVELT-PITTMAN CLUB signs were everywhere in the neighborhood. Pittman himself made a swing through the Westside in August. McCarran never found the time.

"Several hundred, perhaps as many as a thousand new colored citizens of this county will cast their ballot for the first time in Nevada," observed the *Review-Journal*. "Coming from the Deep South most of these men and women have never been allowed to register and vote before. Here, they are not only allowed to register and vote, but are encouraged to do so."[102]

The only question was for whom.

Guernsey Frazer was keeping his secretary busy. First he wanted a list of all registered voters in Clark County; then he wanted two sets of index cards filled out for each voter. One set was placed in a file box with three trays. All the cards were put in the first tray. Then, as Frazer checked up on the voter, the card was moved into the middle tray if the individual was deemed "good" or the last tray if he or she was "bad." Good or bad depended upon whether they intended to vote for McCarran. Frazer was running McCarran's campaign in Clark County; he was also one of the top officials at BMI. Officially, Frazer was in charge of publicity for BMI; in reality he was spending practically all of his time trying to ensure McCarran's nomination. "I was on the payroll of BMI and more or less my own boss with an expense account and the power to select and draft many people from BMI plant if and when needed for outside activities," Frazer reminisced a few years later to McCarran. "The circumstances permitted me to devote my full time to your 1944 campaign without expense or worry to you."[103]

As the election drew closer, Frazer had his secretary put together a duplicate card file. The second set noted whether the voter needed a ride to a polling place, his or her phone number, and other information. This set was given out to precinct captains throughout the county. On election day the idea was to send cards back to headquarters as soon as someone voted; that way, the campaign could keep track of "good" voters who hadn't showed up at the polls and have someone call the delinquents or go drag them to the polling place.

"I had been one hundred percent loyal to you at all times even to the point of antagonizing certain groups and individuals. . . . Pat McCarran came Number One with me to the exclusion of any and all others," Frazer told McCarran. "If you personally at any time in any way want me to do anything within reason, you, I think, realize you have but to command me."[104]

BMI was the largest employer in the county. And the highest concentration of BMI employees was in the Westside.

In the last days of the campaign, as the temperature climbed into the hundreds in Las Vegas, things got ugly on the Westside. Each candidate accused the other of racism. "Mister Poll Tax Pittman," blared one flyer, "How about this?" On the other side, the leaflet was divided into two columns. One for McCarran (born: Nevada; education: worked his own way through school; legislative record: voted for bill against poll tax) and one for Pittman (born: Mississippi; education: University of the South; background: part owner and manager of a large cotton plantation; legislative record: voted for the Nevada poll tax bill). It was distributed by the Westside League Against Poll Tax, a group no one had ever heard of before.

"Why is Pat McCarran throwing mud at last minute???" wondered a leaflet from the Westside Roosevelt for President Club. "Because he twice voted against the anti poll tax bill. . . . Because he offers no program and wants us to forget the bad housing conditions on Westside. . . . Do we want to continue this program of slums, poverty, race hatred, and poll taxes as supported by McCarran? No, Mr. McCarran, your last minute smear campaign against our honorable Lt. Governor Vail Pittman is a flop. The Nevada poll tax, as we well know, does not have to be paid in order to vote."[105]

Neither candidate had a sterling record on civil rights. McCarran had voted in support of the poll tax. Pittman was not above casual racism, and his southern accent probably didn't do him any good on the Westside. But Pittman had the CIO seal of approval, and no other group was working harder for civil rights in Las Vegas. And by the eve of the election, Pittman's supporters were sure that they would win the county.

McCarran's supporters grimly agreed. "We had every reason to believe that we would lose Clark County quite heavily,"[106] Norm Biltz recalled.

In Ely the mountain air smelled of pine and optimism. It was Tuesday, September 5, primary day. The temperature climbed toward eighty-five degrees.

On Aultman Street people descended into the basement of the Nevada Hotel to cast their ballots, then knocked back highballs in the bar upstairs waiting for the *Daily Times* to start broadcasting returns at 8 P.M. (state law banned all liquor sales from eight to six). As twilight fell and the temperature quickly dipped into the thirties, loudspeakers blared early results out onto the street. Despite the CIO's campaign, a fifth of the county's twenty precincts saw voter numbers only in single digits; one polling place reported that *no one* had cast a ballot.

Pittman swept the county, 1,238 votes to McCarran's 753. "Pittman," Pittman's paper reported that evening, "appeared to be the leading favorite both to win White Pine County and the state as a whole."[107]

McCarran was sulking. Eva Adams tried to lift his mood. She passed out drinks and sandwiches and reassuring words to the small group that had gathered in campaign headquarters in Reno. The day started with a morning chill that soon burned away, leaving a clear and hot day, with the mercury inching into the nineties, before darkness cooled the desert and the temperature plunged back into the thirties. McCarran was inconsolable.

The local Washoe County returns came in first. Pittman swept Reno. Then he took Elko as well. McCarran won a few cow counties, areas the size of some eastern states: Pershing, Ormsby, and Nye — places that had more square miles than voters. By eight o'clock Pittman's lead had stretched out to four hundred votes — a significant distance in Nevada politics.

McCarran bowed his head, a thatch of white hair falling over his face. He didn't bother to brush it aside. He knew that his career in the Senate was over. Each vote was like a physical blow. The power that he had spent years accumulating was slipping from his grip with every precinct report. "He was convinced he was defeated," Biltz recalled. "He was unbelievably distressed."

Biltz tried to cheer his friend.

"Well, Patsy," he said, "let's wait and see about Clark County."

"You're more of an optimist than I thought you were," McCarran grumbled. "We have no chance in Clark County."

"Well," Biltz said, "let's wait."

The Las Vegas returns began to trickle in. Then something unexpected happened. McCarran pulled even with Pittman. Then he passed him by fifty votes.

McCarran perked up. "Boy," he asked Biltz, "you got a comb?"

For the next four hours it was an even race. At midnight McCarran rushed past Pittman by 685 votes. McCarran combed his hair and headed toward the door.

"Boy," he told Biltz, "let's go out and meet our constituents."[108]

Pittman conceded the next day at noon. "I accept with good grace, the will of the voters of Nevada,"[109] he said.

The final vote was 11,152 for McCarran and 9,911 for Pittman — a

1,241-vote majority supplied by Clark County, where McCarran unexpectedly trounced Pittman. Clark County — Las Vegas, the BMI company town at Henderson and Boulder City — gave McCarran a 1,523-vote lead over Pittman, 3,892 to 2,369.

Pittman was convinced that McCarran had stolen the election. "I was supposed to get the Negro vote—1,200 to 1,500 — solidly, but it went to McCarran — primarily, I am informed, because it was bought," Pittman told one friend. "There is no doubt about this, but proving it is another thing. . . . The support of the CIO hurt me to some extent, because some of the voters did not know the truth and the circumstances: That the CIO was sore at McCarran and would support anyone who opposed him in the primaries. I did not accept financial aid from the PAC, and whatever they did, if anything, was unknown to me."[110]

The CIO organizers also thought that they had the voters in the Westside lined up for Pittman. But McCarran's supporters could play rough. After making a speech for Pittman, for example, a Las Vegas business owner walked out of a radio station and was arrested for violating an OPA price ceiling in his store. "The McCarran forces resorted to all sorts of open intimidation,"[111] Estolv Ward recalled.

McCarran won the black vote — two Westside precincts and Carver Park, the segregated housing unit at BMI — by more than two to one, 341 votes to 148, although almost four hundred people didn't vote.

McCarran certainly outspent Pittman. McCarran reported $2,797.47 in primary expenses and $1,950 in contributions. Pittman reported $1,117.32 in expenses and no contributions. Of course, McCarran didn't count things like the three-thousand-dollar personal loan that Guernsey Frazer took out for campaign expenses or the cash contributions that Norm Biltz's friends secretly funneled into the race. A more realistic estimate was that McCarran actually spent eighty thousand dollars — or four dollars for each voter in the primary. "Many a 'friend' who worked in the campaign had to have 'expense money' and plenty of it,"[112] Frazer told McCarran.

At the very least, McCarran had an enormous financial advantage. On election day one observer counted twelve cars carrying McCarran voters to the polls and only three for Pittman. Then there were reports that McCarran voters were getting forty dollars a head. Pittman had no doubt that the allegations were true.

"I really had the election in the bag . . . ," Pittman seethed. "They spent a very large sum of money in Las Vegas. . . . That block was against McCarran and for me, but on election day something happened — and of course it is not difficult to guess what it was, knowing the set up. There are about twenty-five Negro leaders, mostly preachers, who control the 'thinking' of their respective flocks, so you can readily understand how a 'presto' change could come about all of a sudden."[113]

Pittman's supporters were outraged. "It was a great disappointment to me and hurt me deeply but we will keep the old chin up and look for another chance to sock the 'Old Billy Goat' later on," Frank Middleton told Pittman. "It will be the McCarran Party from now on instead of the Democratic Party in Nevada. I feel that Nevada is disgraced in the eyes of this nation."[114]

Charles Richards, a Reno lawyer and former Democratic congressman, was angry enough to complain to Roosevelt. "Our senior United States senator, through his opposition to your policies, had incurred the enmity of the Roosevelt Democrats of the state to the point where they were willing to sacrifice him and all he stands for as a Democrat," he wrote to FDR. "The Democratic Party of Nevada defeated him for the nomination, but his success was due to the fact that, through a Republican trick engineered by BMI gang of Clark County (Las Vegas) he received the Democratic nomination. This gang of economic royalistic Republicans used about fifteen hundred of the colored workers by registering them as Democrats, transporting them to the polls in automobiles and voting them for McCarran. . . . I, and many others, cannot be truly represented by that kind of Democrat."[115]

McCarran's backers didn't exactly dispute the charges. "We found a way," Biltz said years later, "to get the Negro vote."[116]

McCarran certainly appreciated Guernsey Frazer's efforts among BMI workers. "I owe a great deal to Guernsey Frazer, much more than most people know," McCarran told Petersen. "The real truth of the matter is Guernsey Frazer is the only politically live-wire in Clark County."[117] After the election McCarran struggled to find his friend a federal job. Then when his old Senate colleague Harry Truman became president the following year, McCarran unsuccessfully urged him to appoint Frazer to four different federal posts in as many months — assistant secretary of labor, the Federal Trade Commission, the Civil Service Commission, and the War Claims Commission — none of which he was remotely qualified for. "One of the finest Democratic workers we will ever know,"[118] McCarran told Truman. McCarran seemed to feel that he owed Frazer a lot.

McCarran opened his official campaign in October with a radio broadcast. "Communism is not just knocking at the door of our democracy — it is using a battering ram on the portal of our democratic home," he said. The Communists, he added, had marked him for political annihilation. "I have felt their sting," McCarran cried. "They failed, but they are not yet content."[119]

McCarran made a quick lap of the state, defending his isolationist voting record ("Who among you wanted this war?"), never mentioned Roosevelt by name, and constantly repeated his fear that subversive influences were running riot in America. "There is a Trojan horse working here at home trying to undermine this country,"[120] he said.

McCarran trudged through the campaign with a bad cold and spent the weekend before the election in a hospital. There were rumors that he was seriously ill. McCarran whipped his Republican rival George Malone, 30,595 votes to 21,816.

Estolv Ward drove back to Los Angeles long before the election. The trunk of his car was stuffed with his personal archive of a year's struggle in Las Vegas: The *Basic Facts* newsletter he'd written for the organizing campaign, tracts he'd composed against McCarran, and reams of CIO literature as dated as last week's newspaper. His car was full but Ward felt as empty as the surrounding desert.

"It was more than a defeat at Basic Magnesium," Ward recalled. "We had indulged in dreams, that I think originated and that were certainly supported by the top leadership of that union, that if we could carry Basic Magnesium that we would very shortly overshadow the AF of L setup in Southern Nevada, and eventually possibly the whole state of Nevada. . . . In which case we could get rid of Senator McCarran and the other senator and elect our kind of senators. It was all smoke, of course, but it was a lot of fun to think about. So those dreams were buried in Nevada and we came home."[121]

McCarran's election notwithstanding, the CIO PAC considered the 1944 election a great victory. Conservative Democrats fell in droves: three members of HUAC, not to mention South Carolina's Cotton Ed Smith, Missouri's Bennett Champ Clark, Idaho's D. Worth Clark, Arkansas's Hattie Connoway. "November 7, was our Battle of Britain, our Stalingrad,"[122] Sid Hillman beamed at the CIO convention in November.

Yet McCarran survived. Battered and embittered, he would go back to Washington. "There seems to be an atmosphere of confusion prevailing here and a decided atmosphere of uncertainty," McCarran told Eva Adams. "Some people are waking up. Our beloved England may not be so beloved, and our much admired Russia may still be only Russia. These are the things that some of us predicted in 1940 and 1941, and we have since been called isolationists; and that isn't all we have been called. Well, we won't go into that."[123]

January 20 was frigid in Washington. At noon Roosevelt appeared on the White House south portico. A few hundred people gathered in the slush and the mud on the lawn below. Roosevelt took the oath of office for a fourth time — the only American president ever to do so.

Roosevelt had beaten New York governor Tom Dewey, 54 percent of the popular vote to 46 percent, the slimmest majority in a presidential race since 1916. He spoke for five minutes. Some days it was all Roosevelt could do to make it into his own backyard. The president was rising at noon, turning in by dark. His hands shook so badly that he could barely sign his name, light a cigarette, or pour a drink. His face and frame were haggard. His cousin Margaret (Daisy) Suckley thought he had aged a decade in a year. He started asking friends which of his belongings they would like. Other days, he was his old jocular, assured self. It was like the last stirring of strings in a Mahler opus, a final flickering of flame before the dark.

On January 22 Roosevelt set sail on the USS *Quincy*, where he celebrated his sixty-third birthday a week later crossing the Atlantic en route to Yalta on the Black Sea, where he met with Stalin and Churchill to plan the shape of the postwar world. On March 1 Roosevelt was back in Washington, being rolled down the aisle of the House chamber to address a joint session of Congress. For the first time in his political career since polio took away the use of his legs, Roosevelt did not even make a pretense of being anything other than a cripple. Now he was too tired to pretend. He was sleeping late and taking long naps and still couldn't work more than a few hours a day. "This time," Roosevelt told Congress, "we are not making the mistake of waiting until the end of the war to set up the machinery of peace."[124]

On April 12 Roosevelt sat to have his portrait painted at his cottage in Warm Springs, Georgia. He complained of a headache, then slumped over, felled by a stroke. Roosevelt was dead.

PART THREE

POWER

Senator doesn't forget a grudge.[1]
— Eva Adams

CHAPTER 14

The Edge of Hell

I like to think that at Yalta the calm dictator and his associates shared our hopes of cooperation.[1]
  — Alger Hiss, American diplomat

One day in April 1945 Assistant Secretary of State Dean Acheson found himself sitting across a desk from Pat McCarran in his suite in the Senate Office Building. McCarran wanted to attend the upcoming founding of the United Nations in San Francisco. He wanted to go with his wife. He wanted official status. "The senator," Acheson recalled, "was not a person who in the eighteenth century would have been termed a man of sensibility."[2]

Acheson was. The son of the Episcopalian bishop of Connecticut, Dean Gooderham Acheson, fifty-two, had gone to Groton and Yale and Harvard Law, clerked for Supreme Court justice Louis Brandeis, joined the Washington law firm of Covington & Burling and then the New Deal. Acheson was everything that McCarran was not: wellborn and connected, tall and trim, with a meticulously groomed mustache and a sense of superiority that he wore like a bespoke suit. "Acheson was always dignified, but there was a certain condescension," recalled Minnesota representative Walter Judd. "It was like he was sorry for us hayseeds."[3] Even Acheson's friends could feel his hauteur. "He was the most self-confident man I ever encountered,"[4] remembered Clark Clifford. Acheson made the hair on the back of McCarran's neck stand up.

The UN delegation, Acheson told McCarran, had already been selected, and there was a long line of senators who wanted to go. McCarran said that he was sure a bright fellow like Acheson could find a way to overcome such a problem. Especially, McCarran added, if Acheson considered the alternative. The alternative was the fact that McCarran was the chairman of the appropriations subcommittee considering the State Department budget. Acheson said that he would see what he could do.

Acheson appealed to the chairman of the Appropriations Committee, Tennessee's quarrelsome Kenneth McKellar, a friend of McCarran's. If McCarran gutted State's budget, McKellar told Acheson, the committee didn't have time to redo the subcommittee's work. Acheson went to see Vice President Harry Truman. "I went to him for help," Acheson recalled, "and received, instead, consolation."[5]

Two days later, on April 12, Franklin Roosevelt died and Harry Truman became president. Among the headaches Truman inherited from Roosevelt was McCarran. Before he was reelected in 1944, McCarran had seriously considered leaving the Senate. "To me," he confessed to Pete Petersen, the Reno postmaster and a trusted friend, "it seems like heresy for one who has belonged during all his entire adult life to the Democratic Party . . . to again ask for the nomination of that party, knowing when he asks for that nomination that he cannot support those who call themselves Democrats, but who in reality are nothing but Communists to the very core. To give out to the public information that he is one who serves and supports the administration when he knows he cannot do so in his own conscience is a false front that I cannot tolerate."[6]

Once McCarran decided to stay in the Senate, however, there was no moving him. The month before he died, Roosevelt had tried again to get rid of McCarran, offering to make him a district court judge in Nevada. "Roosevelt seemed to feel pretty strongly that it would be a bad appointment," Interior Secretary Harold Ickes recorded in his diary. "I told him while it would be, nevertheless, on balance it might be worth doing when it was considered that McCarran is chairman of the Judiciary Committee of the Senate. The man is thoroughly a bad actor."[7] McCarran grandly rejected the overture in a press release, averring that he should serve out the term he had just been elected to. "Pat reminded me of a woman lying on the bed with her nighty up over her head protesting that she did not want to be raped,"[8] Ickes noted. "It was no surprise to see McCarran turn the judgeship down," added Nevada's congressman Berkeley Bunker. "It is rather easy to follow his line of reasoning. It would benefit too many other people."[9]

In his Capitol office, Vice President Truman told Acheson in typically salty terms just what he would say to put McCarran in his place. It was the first time Acheson had had to take the measure of the man. Truman, Acheson realized, was nothing like the president who had led the country for a dozen years. "He is straight-forward, decisive, simple, entirely honest," Acheson wrote to his son.[10]

Yes, Acheson agreed, he could chew McCarran out, but what could he do to salvage the State Department's budget? Truman became practical. He knew McCarran.

Truman grew up in Independence, Missouri, and served in France during World War I as an artillery officer. After a lackluster business career, including a failed stint as a haberdasher, he hitched his wagon to the

Kansas City political machine run by Tom Pendergast. In 1934 Truman was elected to the U.S. Senate.

He got along well with most of his new colleagues — except Pat McCarran. Truman disliked his colleague, and McCarran liked Truman less. On paper the two should have been a good match: Both came from hardscrabble farming backgrounds, had little formal education, knew business failure, and were used to being underestimated. But in temperament they were opposites. Truman was a consummate party man, loyal to the marrow; McCarran could abide no discipline save for his own, accept no organization that he did not hold in his hand. Truman was a fighter, but he knew when to give up. McCarran was relentless, a master parliamentarian with the patience of Job; he refused to yield, coming back again and again to the same issue or bill and persisting until his tenacity wore down the opposition and his legislative skill turned his will into deed. "I never compromise with principle," he explained once, "but almost everything is principle to me."[11]

Both men loved the Senate, but in very different ways. Truman was a fervent believer in the institution of the Senate; McCarran, in the myth of the Senate. The institution was the flesh and blood of its members at any given time, practical men bound by traditions, chief among which was the collegial nature of the body, the sense that whatever individual political differences divided senators were ultimately less important than the kinship they shared. The myth was the Platonic ideal of the Senate as an absolute coequal branch of government with the presidency, a sovereign body fixed in its constitutional orbit regardless of the gravitational pull exerted by the occupant of the White House. The institution's embodiment was the inner club. You could get elected to the Senate, but you had to be invited to join the club, which loosely speaking wasn't confined to the north side of the Capitol. The day, for instance, that Truman was summoned to the White House to be told of Roosevelt's death, the vice president was found in House Speaker Sam Rayburn's Capitol hideaway enjoying a bourbon and water. The myth admitted no such conviviality. Its symbol was the Constitution — "the organic law," McCarran called it, as if it were something that grew only from American soil, a document so pure and perfect that it was less a set of guiding principles than an inviolable principle itself, a charter subject to no interpretation save the interpretation that the limit of all permissible governmental action was to be found inscribed on its dry parchment.*

It was this Grand Canyon of American political philosophy more than anything else that separated the New Deal from its enemies. And for Truman and McCarran it became personal in 1938 when they quarreled over the future of commercial aviation. McCarran had long been passionately interested in aviation policy and had sponsored the Civil Aeronautics Act, which overhauled federal regulation of the airways, including the creation of an independent Civil Aeronautics Administration. Truman sponsored the administration alternative, which put the CAA under the control of the White House. "Not only will I not vote for the bill if the Truman amendment prevails," McCarran roared, "but I will ask that my name be stricken from the measure and I will fight it as long as I can stand on my feet. It destroys the entire theory of the bill and the entire principle of freedom."[12] It was a bitter contest, which McCarran won — although Truman claimed credit for the bill. But two years later the White House managed to swallow the CAA under a reorganization plan, which McCarran continued to fight in vain for the next dozen years.

Sitting in the vice president's office, Truman and Acheson decided that the best course was to appease McCarran and send him to the UN conference. "Both of us concluded," Acheson remembered, "that under the circumstances exposure of the senator to an international conference of such lofty purpose might soften his isolationism and, hence, prove in the public interest. The senator went to San Francisco."[†13]

For Truman and Acheson it was a small defeat — the first of many, some not so small, that they would endure from McCarran over the next decade. Two days before he became president, the pattern of Truman's relationship

------

*But even such an ardent New Dealer as Truman sometimes fretted that Congress was too overawed by the White House. "It is really an alarming situation," Truman told his wife during the war. "The Congress has given away all its powers of control and then wonders why people hold it in contempt. I want to be specific in the delegation of powers and have them terminate at a specific time." (Truman, Harry S. *Dear Bess: The Letters of Harry to Bess Truman, 1910–1959,* edited by Robert H. Ferrell. New York: Norton, 1983; page 479.)

†"Nevada's rotund Senator Pat McCarran has got himself another free trip to the West Coast . . . ," columnist Drew Pearson wrote. "McCarran, incidentally, is a past master at getting junkets to the West. For three years he was chairman of a committee investigating forest grazing permits, the future of fishing, placer mining claims, conservation of wildlife, and crowding of ranges and various subjects which took him — at government expense — back to the vicinity of Nevada. So, now that the future of fishing has been worked to the bone as a source of investigation, McCarran will investigate the diplomats and what they do at San Francisco." (*Philadelphia Record,* 28 April 1945.)

with McCarran was already set. On April 12, the day that Roosevelt died, Truman was presiding over the Senate, scribbling a note to his mother about a tedious debate on the floor and some of the senators taking part. "A very disagreeable one from Nevada,"[14] he called McCarran.

Jack Service walked out of his office at the State Department on June 6 and noticed two strange men standing outside. He asked if he could help them. No, they replied, they were waiting for someone. Service left the State Department to go to lunch; the same men followed him out of the building. That evening Service heard a knock on his door. It was the two men again. It was Service they had been waiting for all day. FBI, they announced. You're under arrest for violating the Espionage Act. Where, the agents asked, are the papers?

At thirty-six, John Stewart Service was already what was called an Old China Hand. The son of a missionary family, Service was born and raised in China, went to college in the United States, and joined the foreign service in 1935, spending the next decade in various posts in China. "Service in my opinion is one of the best equipped and most able of the younger officers . . . ," Ambassador Clarence Gauss wrote in an evaluation. "He is the outstanding younger officer who served with me over my thirty six years of service."[15]

Service didn't get along quite so well with the next ambassador, Patrick Hurley, who took over in 1944. Hurley tried and failed to make peace between Chiang Kai-shek's Nationalist government and Mao Tse-tung's Communists, so that they would stop fighting each other and battle the Japanese. Service and other young diplomats thought Chiang was hopelessly corrupt and urged Washington to arm the Communists. Hurley accused Service of insubordination and had him recalled to Washington, where he was waiting for a new assignment when the FBI showed up. Service had been out of China for two months, but he was still worried that the United States was making a tragic mistake by giving unqualified support to Chiang. "I probably should have quit the foreign service then and there," he said years later, "and spoken up."[16]

Service, in fact, was doing a lot of talking — just not in public. In Washington he began to hang around with a small group of friends that shared his feelings about China. One of them was Andrew Roth, who worked for the Office of Naval Intelligence, whom Service had met the year before at a conference put on by the Institute for Pacific Relations — an Asian studies think tank, the ghost of which would loom large over the lives of many China experts during the next decade. Roth invited Service to dinner and suggested that he pick up a friend of his who was staying at a hotel. The friend was Philip Jaffe, the editor of a small left-wing journal called *Amerasia*. Service agreed to give copies of his State Department reports to Jaffe to use as background material.

When Service walked into Jaffe's hotel room, he also walked straight into an FBI investigation — agents were in a nearby room taking notes from a listening device. The FBI had recently become very interested in the magazine editor and his friends. Back in February, Kenneth Wells, an Asian specialist at the Office of Strategic Services, read a striking article in *Amerasia* about British colonial policy. Wells immediately went to the security chief of the OSS, the wartime spy agency. The article, Wells explained, was practically ripped straight from a classified report that *he* had written. The OSS had a leak.

OSS agents broke into the *Amerasia* office on Fifth Avenue. They discovered a darkroom. The magazine didn't print pictures. Still-damp photos of pages of government reports stamped TOP SECRET were spread on a desk to dry. A table was tottering with additional documents. Yet more classified material was stuffed into briefcases and satchels. The *Amerasia* office seemed to be a veritable archive of records from the OSS, the State Department, the War Department, the army, the navy, and British intelligence — several filing cabinets' worth of material. The FBI took over the case and broke into the magazine's office as well. Then Jack Service wandered into the picture.

In June the government arrested six suspects on charges of conspiracy to commit espionage. Three worked for the government: Jack Service, the State Department's Emmanuel Larsen, and navy reserve officer Lieutenant Andrew Roth. Three were journalists: *Amerasia* editors Philip Jaffe and Kate Mitchell and freelance writer Mark Gayn. The sextet insisted that they were only trying to further public debate about foreign policy.

At the center of the case was Jaffe, who was not only the editor of *Amerasia* but also its financial angel — as well as a frequent visitor to both the Soviet consulate in New York and Communist Party headquarters. Jaffe was a Ukrainian-born greeting-card tycoon and a good friend of American Communist leader Earl Browder, whose politics in fact were too moderate for Jaffe's taste. "A good Marxist but a bad Leninist,"[17] Jaffe called him.

Service wasn't a spy; Jaffe wanted to be one. A good Leninist, Jaffe believed, would do anything for the Soviet Union. So when a former colleague, Joseph Bernstein, came to Jaffe and said that he was working for

Soviet intelligence, asking Jaffe to pass on to him any classified material that he could get, the editor didn't flinch. "The first test of a real radical is, do you trust the Soviet Union through thick and thin, regardless of what anybody says?" the FBI recorded Jaffe telling Roth. ". . . It's the worker's government, the one shining star in the whole damned world, and you've got to defend that with your last drop of blood."[18]

Jaffe never had the chance to shed any blood. A grand jury indicted only three of the six — Jaffe, Larsen, and Roth — charging them with unlawful possession of government documents instead of espionage. Jaffe copped a plea and paid a twenty-five-hundred-dollar fine as well as a five-hundred-dollar fine for Larsen, who lost his State Department position. The charges were dropped against Roth, who had learned that the FBI had broken into his apartment without a warrant. Jack Service was cleared by a State Department investigation and soon posted to Japan.

From the moment it hit the headlines in June, the *Amerasia* case became a political Rorschach test: Conservatives saw it as proof that Communists had a pipeline into government and that the government wasn't very eager to prosecute them. Leftists saw it as Redbaiting and a witch hunt. The debate over the case set the tone for much that was to come over the next decade: Each side believed the worst about the other, while the government fumbled, knowing more than it was willing to reveal in court but less then it needed to disarm its critics. The FBI, for example, didn't want to disclose its wiretaps showing that Jaffe was willing to spy for the Soviets. But the bureau was willing to leak tidbits to such sympathetic lawmakers as Michigan representative George Dondero, who promptly denounced the failed *Amerasia* prosecution as a whitewash. "Had this same thing happened in certain other governments," Dondero said, "these people would undoubtedly have been shot without a trial."[19]

Dondero spoke too soon. It would take years, but Jack Service and his fellow China Hands would become the center of a raging controversy over the State Department's action in China. Conservative critics, such as McCarran, would hold this group of junior foreign service officers personally responsible for one of the biggest debacles in American diplomatic history and hound them as traitors. They would not be shot — only endure repeated vilification from the floor of the Senate, face government prosecution, and eventually lose their jobs and reputations. "This was the beginning of a seizure," recalled John Paton Davies, another Old China Hand, "a gnawing at its vitals, that afflicted the American government for a decade and more."[20]

The echoes and reverberations of the *Amerasia* case sounded for years, one congressional committee after another endlessly reexamining the case, McCarran's included. Even then charges and countercharges of conspiracies and cover-ups continued to glow, like the light of a long-dead star, shining in the sky but leading back to nothing.

On June 26 Harry Truman took the stage at the Veterans Building in San Francisco. The flags of fifty nations hung from gilded poles, and a large circular table displayed a huge blue leather book, the United Nations charter. A parade of delegates strode across the stage to affix their signatures. "We can build a better world," Truman told the crowd. ". . . What you have accomplished in San Francisco shows how well the lessons of military and economic cooperation have been learned. You have created a great instrument for peace and security and human progress in the world."[21]

Two months earlier, on April 26, 1945, delegates from around the world gathered in the San Francisco Opera House for the founding conference of the United Nations. "The huge crowds outside, the floodlights within, the popping of camera flashlights," I. F. Stone observed, "recalled an opening night in Hollywood."[22]

Missing from the audience in the Opera House was a representative from Poland, where the United States and the USSR were backing rival governments. On his way to San Francisco, Soviet foreign minister Vyacheslav Molotov stopped in Washington to meet the new president. Truman pointed out that the Soviets were dragging their feet on their promise at Yalta to hold free elections in Poland. Molotov said that he had never been spoken to like that before. Truman told him to carry out his agreement and he wouldn't have to be. "How I enjoyed translating Truman's sentences," State Department Russian expert Charles Bohlen remembered. "They were probably the first sharp words uttered during the war by an American president to a high Soviet official."[23] In San Francisco, Molotov shook hands with Secretary of State Edward Stettinius and casually mentioned that sixteen leaders of the liberal Polish underground that Washington had been trying to locate had been arrested by the Red Army. Then the Russian smiled and turned around to shake another hand. Even the Soviet Union's allies were exasperated by Moscow's blunt dealings. "You can be on your knees and this is not enough for the Russians,"[24] Czech foreign minister Jan Masaryk complained to Bohlen in the bar of the Fairmont Hotel.

Averell Harriman, the American ambassador in Moscow, was so alarmed that he flew to San Francisco. Harriman commanded a huge penthouse suite atop the Fairmont, where he offered his grave assessment of U.S.-Soviet relations to reporters in a series of background briefings. "I was there," he said, "to make everyone understand that the Soviets had already given every indication that they were not going to live up to their postwar agreements."[25] Columnist Walter Lippmann left in a huff and wrote a story critical of the anti-Soviet sentiment in the State Department. Before long Lippmann would popularize a new phrase for what he saw developing in San Francisco: *Cold War.*

Not all U.S. diplomats had such a critical view of the Soviet Union. "Among the younger and more progressive men attached to the American delegation," noted I. F. Stone, "there is increasing apprehension over the extent to which the conference begins to take on the aspects of an attempt by our delegation to build an anti-Soviet world coalition."[26]

One of these was Alger Hiss, who was standing behind Truman on the stage. Hiss was a protégé of Secretary of State Edward Stettinius and the founding secretary general of the conference. "The Russians ... were surprisingly cooperative and conciliatory,"[27] he recalled. And the Russians found Hiss just as amiable. Andrei Gromyko volunteered to Stettinius that Hiss would be a good person to lead the UN. "He would be very happy to see Alger Hiss appointed temporary secretary general," the secretary wrote in his diary, "as he had a very high regard for Alger Hiss, particularly for his fairness and his impartiality."[28] These were qualities that the Russians did not normally admire.

"Let us not fail to grasp," Truman told the audience, "this supreme chance to establish a world-wide rule of reason — to create an enduring peace under the guidance of God."[29]

In late July the Senate ratified the United Nations charter 89 to 2.* McCarran voted for it. "I left San Francisco with a firm belief that the men who mingled there will bring about a program to bring peace to the world," he said. "And I want my country to join in that program with all of its might and all of its power."[30]

It was, McCarran later rued, the worst vote he ever cast in his two decades in the Senate.

In San Francisco diplomats put their confidential reports in code and transmitted the cables home via Western Union. The telegraph company also sent

---

*North Dakota's William Langer and Minnesota's Henrik Shipstead voted against the charter.

copies of all the messages over secure teletype lines to a former girls' school in Virginia called Arlington Hall, where codebreakers labored over the cables around the clock. Some of the codes were easy to break. The Russian wasn't. American analysts weren't sure that they would ever be able to crack it.[31]

In July, McCarran's Judiciary Committee met to vote on the nomination of Nathan Margold to the U.S. District Court. It should have been an easy call: The Democrats controlled the committee, and one of its members, Kentucky's Happy Chandler, strongly supported the nominee, who had been a classmate at Harvard Law School. Born in Romania, Margold came to the United States as a child and lived the immigrant's dream: City College to Harvard to Washington, where he worked as solicitor for Interior Secretary Harold Ickes, who became a powerful patron. Margold became a municipal court judge, and then Roosevelt named him to the federal bench. But from the start Ickes was worried about McCarran. "According to Margold, McCarran had promised to support him . . . ," Ickes told his diary in January 1945. "Probably there will be a nasty fight over this nomination and I don't look forward to it with any degree of pleasure."[32]

Ickes normally enjoyed a good scrap the way some men enjoy a fine cognac. But he was getting tired. Long a bad sleeper, he could now only grab a few hours of shuteye by swallowing Seconal washed down with whiskey. He was seventy-one; his beloved Roosevelt was dead. Ickes didn't like Truman and Truman didn't like him. "Shitass Ix,"[33] Truman called him behind his back. "Never for anyone but Harold," the new president jotted down soon after coming into the Oval Office; "would have cut FDR's throat or mine for his 'high-minded' ideas of a headline — and did."[34]

Ickes and McCarran got along even worse. The two had known each other since the first days of the New Deal. Ickes was one of the most powerful figures in Washington, a Roosevelt devotee who handled vast amounts of patronage through the WPA and whose Interior Department managed most of the public land in Nevada, a state where 85 percent of the land was owned by the federal government. Ickes hated Nevada and its two senators. In 1933 McCarran had gone to Ickes to ask him to transfer control of Boulder City (the townsite at Boulder Dam) from the federal government to Nevada. Ickes exploded. "I don't propose to allow Nevada to inject her policy of gambling and prostitution in Boulder City," he proclaimed. "I am going to keep that place clean."[35]

To Ickes, Nevada and its representatives in Washington were of a piece: selfish, rapacious, and venal, the antithesis of his own puritan progressivism. On a visit to Las Vegas, Ickes dropped $5.50 in quarters into a slot machine and won 50 cents. That told him all he needed to know about the soul of Las Vegas. "A wide open ugly little town where gambling dens and saloons and prostitution run wide open day and night," he observed. "...Three quarters of an hour was all the time we needed to get the savor of this rotten little town."[36]

For the rest of the decade they fought over Nevada. "McCarran, I think, does not like me,"[37] Ickes observed with some understatement. Temperamentally, however, the two were quite alike — both stubborn, bellicose brawlers who elevated minor disagreements to matters of principle and demonized opponents. Ickes had, Francis Biddle once noted, "an unfairness equal to that of Senator Pat McCarran."[38]

Margold's nomination quickly became a test of will between them. "McCarran is going to find it difficult to defeat him," Ickes noted. "They have nothing to fall back upon except prejudice and anti-Semitism."[39]

Then Roosevelt died. "McCarran may urge Truman to withdraw his name," Ickes feared. "It would be perfectly cruel to hold up Margold's nomination simply because of McCarran. Margold tells me that a majority of the committee are for his nomination and that there won't be any question if it is brought to the floor of the Senate."[40]

The problem was that after almost six months there was no sign that the nomination was ever going to make it to the floor. So in May, Ickes had a fifteen-minute meeting with Truman — who unlike his predecessor actually held such appointments to fifteen minutes, if not less. After a dozen years of Roosevelt's meandering and inconclusive meetings, where the president talked about anything that struck his fancy, Ickes was almost taken aback by the new president's punctuality and rapidfire way of getting to the point. Ickes told Truman that he'd heard that McCarran wanted him to withdraw Margold's name. "He said he had no such intention and would not withdraw the nomination although he said that he did not like Margold," Ickes recorded. The president said that he didn't think it would do any good to discuss the matter with McCarran. Ickes agreed. "I was critical of the way McCarran has handled this nomination," Ickes remembered. "He has been as 'bitchy' as a human being could well be."[41]

McCarran eventually appointed a three-member subcommittee with himself as chairman to investigate Margold's nomination. Not surprisingly, the subcommittee recommended against confirmation. Ickes was furious. "McCarran is a son of a bitch from practically every point of view," he told his diary. "It is outrageous that he should be a senator."[42]

In July the Judiciary Committee finally voted, splitting on party lines: five Republicans opposed the nomination, six Democrats supported it. McCarran sided with the Republicans. A deadlock meant no recommendation, which meant that the nomination would stay bottled up in the committee. "This is as dirty a performance on the part of a member of Congress as I have ever seen," Ickes raged.[43]

Hap Chandler and the Democratic leadership tried to wrest the nomination from McCarran's death grip — to no avail. Then on August 1, as the Senate rushed toward a midnight recess, Majority Leader Alben Barkley asked unanimous consent for the nomination to come to a vote. McCarran had been sitting at his desk for nine hours, waiting for just such a move. He objected. Margold's nomination would go back to the White House. It would not come back to the Senate.

"The Judiciary Committee of the United States Senate ought to be the last body to deny any man the right of a fair hearing," Chandler fumed to reporters. "A member of the Senate Judiciary Committee ought to be the last person to bring such an unfounded and unwarranted charge against the committee,"[44] McCarran snapped back.

McCarran won, establishing early on in the new administration his power to obstruct and thwart the will of both his party and his president. Truman did not renominate Margold. The next month McCarran cut the appropriation for Ickes's grazing service by 60 percent and suggested that the secretary resign. "McCarran has once more made my life as secretary of the Interior worth living . . . ," Ickes responded. "If he could only have set up for himself a few more subcommittees with the honorable Pat as chairman he could encroach even more upon my executive duties and responsibilities."[45]

Ickes didn't last long in Truman's cabinet. In 1946 McCarran sponsored the Tidelands Oil bill, which transferred control of offshore oil fields from the federal government to the states. McCarran saw it as a matter of local control; Ickes saw it as a huge favor to the oil industry and its lobbyists, especially because Nevada had no tidelands of its own. Truman opposed the bill but supported Edwin Pauley, an oilman and major Democratic bankroller whom the president nominated to become secretary of the navy. When Truman asked Ickes to take it easy on Pauley in congressional testimony, the secretary publicly accused the president of asking him to commit perjury. Ickes resigned, offering to stay in office for six weeks. Truman told him to be out by Friday.

Ickes became a columnist; one of his favorite subjects was McCarran. "It is wonderful what can be accomplished by a man who could not be elected alderman of a river ward in Chicago . . . ," Ickes grumbled. "What Pat can do on occasion to his Judiciary Committee, of which he is chairman, is equaled only by the ease with which a monkey at the end of a string can fill its tin cup."[46]

In 1947 when Margold died, Ickes wrote a long letter to the *Washington Post* praising his friend as a man fit for the Supreme Court but thwarted by prejudice. "Pat McCarran of Nevada, whom I do not regard as an admirable member of the United States Senate, was allowed, without protest from the newspapers, to smear and crucify a man who had honored the Municipal Court and who would have more greatly honored the District Court . . . ," Ickes wrote. "Anti-Semitism raised its ugly head. . . . Here was a great judge and outstanding citizen, who was cruelly punished because he had had the misfortune of being born as a member of the wrong race. He had not humiliated himself by bowing and scraping before the chairman of the Judiciary Committee."[47]

In July 1945 Earl Browder found himself looking for work for the first time in two decades. Back in April the journal *Cahiers du Communisme* published an article by one of the leaders of the French Communist Party, Jacques Duclos, who assailed Browder's guidance of the American party. In 1944 Browder had dissolved the CPUSA and created in its place the Communist Political Association, a far less militant, milky Popular Front version of the old party that promised to expel anyone who advocated overthrowing the government by violence or force. Lenin must have been rolling over in his tomb. The Duclos article referred to Browder as the American party's *former* secretary. This, as Stalin liked to say, was not an accident; rather, it was an instruction. The article had actually been written in Moscow and sent to the French to be published. The conservative *New York World-Telegram* printed the Duclos article before the *Daily Worker* did.

By the end of July, Browder really was the former general secretary. "An apologist for American imperialism,"[48] the *Daily Worker* called him. The CPA was quickly abolished and replaced by the CPUSA. At party headquarters in Lower Manhattan they had to throw away all the stationery for the second time in eighteen months. Eugene Dennis, Browder's most trusted lieutenant, took over his old boss's office and turned his name into a curse. Browderism became an official heresy. Soon he would be expelled from the party itself.

Being a Communist in America was never easy. But there were two periods when it was least difficult: the New Deal days of the Popular Front and the war years of the grand alliance with the Soviet Union — times when Stalin gave the longest leash to the CPUSA and let it run largely in its own direction. The Duclos article was a sharp tug on the party's chokechain. "The first public declaration of the Cold War,"[49] Browder later called it.

On August 6 the United States dropped an atomic bomb on Japan — revealing both the most closely guarded secret of the war and a terrible new weapon that cast a pall over civilization itself. Eight days later Japan surrendered. The war was over.

On August 23, 1945, a woman walked into a building in New Haven, Connecticut, rode the elevator to the top, and then slipped back down three flights of stairs before walking into the FBI field office. After listening to the woman for two hours, Special Agent Edward Coady still didn't know why she was there. She kept talking about a man named Peter Heller, whom she had been dating. He said that he was a government spy. Did Heller really work for the government? she wanted to know. What should she do?

It was a question that Elizabeth Bentley would ask the bureau over and over again for most of the rest of her life: What should she do? Then, as later, the FBI had few answers for Bentley. Only questions. She left.[50]

Early in the year McCarran spent five days in the Bethesda Naval Hospital, having all his upper teeth removed and replaced by dentures. "I don't say they are so comfortable," he told his daughter Mary. ". . . But I guess I'll get used to these after a while."[51]

Compared to McCarran's family life, getting his teeth pulled was a picnic. He had five children. Two were unhappy nuns, two were drunks, and one was a cripple.

The oldest was Sister Margaret, forty-one. She longed to be a conservative intellectual, to write books tracing the slide of modern democracy into socialism; she taught piano to girls. She had to fight with her mother superior for permission to earn a master's degree; the Ph.D. she desired was out of the question.

Sister Mary Mercy, thirty-nine, was even less happy. She had fallen in love with a priest, who fled to a different diocese to keep from violating his vows. She was physically ill, in and out of the hospital. "Well, such a year, oh my, as has passed," she wrote to Margaret. "Never have I experienced such darkness, disillusion, trials, abandonment, failure, pain (physical and mental). I do not seem to have the trust I should have, either in Father, in God, in Our Lady, in anything. I just hang on and there is nothing to hang on to! It just seems as though God has taken everything."[52]

Sam, twenty-four, was a second-year medical student at Georgetown. As a youth he had been spoiled and coddled, smashing up cars, drinking heavily, and waving away traffic tickets by saying that his father was chairman of the District of Columbia Committee in the Senate — in other words, the virtual mayor of Washington. Not a lot had changed. Sam almost knocked his father out of his hospital bed by suddenly getting married and very quickly after that becoming a father. They named the boy Patrick Anthony. "I was shocked," McCarran told Mary.[53]

Patty, twenty-six, was the mother of two small children and a bad drinker. McCarran had briefly put her on the office payroll and then found a job for her husband with Pan American Airways. She was always asking her parents for money and went in and out of hospitals trying to stop drinking. McCarran called her every day — until she didn't pay the phone bill and the line was disconnected. Her husband, Edwin Hay, told McCarran to stop sending her money ("It will be spent for drink only"[54]). That fall Edwin moved out of their Long Island house. "No one of us had failed Patricia in any way," he wrote McCarran. "You, Pop, have done *everything* a father and father-in-law could possibly do to improve or assist us. . . . Our only hope is that someday Patsy will help herself to the extent that is necessary to overcome this curse. . . . Please do not condemn me for this since having tried every other way to straighten her out and failed. I'm trying this. I love Patricia and will never love anyone else and am only resorting to this in an effort to help her and have no intention of getting any kind of a legal separation. If you two will back me sufficiently this may work. Pray that it will."[55]

Patty began going to Alcoholics Anonymous. "I've seen little of her lately she's gone to so many A.A. meetings," her husband told McCarran.[56] "With God's help and the help of the A.A.," Patty told her father, "I pulled out of the tailspin I was about to go into and am now on the beam again."[57]

In Alcoholics Anonymous, Patricia made a friend whose brother owned property on Long Island that he thought would make a good location for a Veterans Administration hospital. "And I get a cut," Patricia chirped to her father. "I will get a cut of the commission if it is sold and you know without my saying so that that means a nice new home for me. I know you will want to help me all you can."[58]

McCarran took up the matter with the head of the VA, General Omar Bradley, who said that a site had already been chosen but promised to survey the land in case the hospital needed to be expanded.

Only Norine, thirty-four, the encephalitic, who worked in the Library of Congress retrieving books, was apparently untroubled. She lived at home, a perpetual ward of the family. "The load on Pop," McCarran told Mary, "isn't getting any lighter as the years get along."[59]

September 5 was hot and muggy in Ottawa, Canada's sleepy capital, when Igor Gouzenko came back to work at the Soviet embassy early after dinner. He climbed to the second floor, where he pulled aside a velvet curtain, revealing a steel door with a peephole, behind which an eye blinked and then the door opened. The guard said hello to Gouzenko and then unlocked another steel door, which led to a corridor lined with more such doors. Gouzenko entered a small office, the windows painted white and lined with bars. He sat at his desk and began going through files.

Gouzenko, according to the embassy, was a civilian translator. In reality he worked for the GRU, Soviet military intelligence. He was a cipher clerk. He spent his days decoding instructions from Moscow and encoding telegrams from the embassy. Among the many documents Gouzenko coded were reports from Sam Carr, the secretary of the Canadian Communist Party; Fred Rose, a member of parliament; and Alan Nunn May, an atomic scientist. The Russians were especially interested in the new atomic bomb. "Now that the Americans have invented it," one GRU officer told Gouzenko, "we must steal it."[60]

Recently Gouzenko had begun to fold over the corners of interesting documents. On this night, he went through the office files, pulling out the dog-eared telegrams and stuffing them inside his shirt. Padded with 109 Russian documents detailing Soviet espionage in Canada, Gouzenko walked out of the embassy and went to the *Ottawa Journal*. He wanted to defect and figured that the police would have KGB informers, so he decided to take his evidence to a newspaper. He went to the door of the paper's editor and then had second thoughts. What if the paper has a Soviet agent working for it? He turned around.

At home Gouzenko pulled the sweat-soaked documents out from his shirt. His wife, Svetlana, told him to go back to the paper. This time Gouzenko wandered into the newsroom, where he spread Cyrillic documents over a table and told the night editor that his country was trying to steal atomic secrets. The editor suggested that Gouzenko go to the Royal

Canadian Mounted Police. He went to the Ministry of Justice. It was almost midnight. A guard told him to come back in the morning. Gouzenko slept with the documents under a pillow. The next morning Gouzenko, his pregnant wife, and their young son trudged off to the ministry. They spent the day wandering from office to office and visiting two newspapers. They wound up at their apartment more frustrated than ever. Two men seemed to be watching the apartment.

Gouzenko took his family to a neighbor's. By this time he was ready to talk to the police. That night four KGB agents broke into his apartment. When the police arrived, the KGB ordered them to leave Soviet property. The Russians eventually sulked off.

The next morning the police escorted Gouzenko back yet again to the Justice Ministry. This time the authorities listened to him for five hours. By the end of the month, on September 30, Prime Minister Mackenzie King was in Washington telling Truman about Gouzenko and his charge that a high State Department official was working for the Soviets.

On February 4, 1946, Drew Pearson broke the Gouzenko story on his radio show. The next day King appointed a royal commission to investigate Gouzenko's story — five months after he'd defected. On February 15 the Royal Canadian Mounted Police arrested twelve people implicated by Gouzenko in espionage, which eventually included parliament member Fred Rose. Seven were ultimately convicted. When the *Report of the Royal Commission* was released that summer it stretched to 733 pages. "They were trying to establish a fifth column in Canada," Gouzenko testified. "What transpired is only a modest or small part of all that is really here. You may have discovered fifteen men but it still leaves in Canada this dangerous situation because there are other societies and other people working under every embassy, under every consul in each place where there is a consulate."[61]

Ottawa was a backwater. In Washington, for example, Gouzenko said that the Soviet embassy had five cipher clerks.

Dick Cooke Jr. spent his spare time in the Library of Congress. He was thirty-two, married, the father of two small children. He was born in Nevada and educated at Harvard, where he had earned a Ph.D. in geology before enlisting in the Marine Corps. He was stationed in Washington, while his family lived in California. The frustrations were boiling: He was a corporal and had to take orders from former elevator boys with no more education than high school. The only thing that calmed his furies was *the book*: the Dictionary of Geology. He spent every free minute on it. Flipping through volumes in the Library of Congress, he devoured tables, charts, graphs, maps. For months he took notes, but he couldn't write fast enough to keep up with the rush of information. Then one day a graph stopped him dead. It looked impossible to copy. Yet he needed it. So he tore it out of the book. Then he found other pages. There was so much information he needed. He cut and tore and stuffed away. But that was not enough. So he slipped books into his clothing. Hundreds.

The telegram reached McCarran at home on a Sunday. Dick Cooke had been arrested by the FBI in Great Falls, Montana, where he had worked for the U.S. Geological Survey since his discharge from the marines in March. "I took some books and clippings from Library of Congress," the wire read. "If you can convince Library of Congress and U.S. Attorney that reparations better than imprisonment, senator it will save my family and me from disaster."[62]

McCarran had been friends with Dick Cooke's father, Herman Richard Cooke Sr., since they had served together in the Nevada legislature more than forty years before. "Dick's sins of theft have at last caught up with him in a big way," noted Jay Carpenter, a professor at the University of Nevada. "We had definite proof at our school of his theft of books years ago but never went further than to inform his father who took no action."[63]

McCarran called the U.S. attorney, Edward Curran. The next morning he called Curran again. He also called J. Edgar Hoover. McCarran then called the librarian of Congress and the head of the U.S. Geological Survey, to whom Cooke had sent in his resignation. McCarran asked the survey to return Cooke's resignation as a personal favor. "My immediate problem was to stop the case in its tracks," he told the father.[64]

McCarran reassured Richard Cooke that he was in a good position to help Dick. "Curran is a very warm friend of mine," McCarran wrote. "I have had his confirmation up on two different occasions. . . . The head of the FBI, Mr. J. Edgar Hoover, and his fine assistant, Mr. Tamm, are close personal friends of mine, and frequently come to see me."[65]

McCarran managed to keep Cooke out of jail, although he couldn't save his job.

Cooke and his wife, Wini, were grateful. "Wini," Cooke told McCarran, "has just become the first Democrat in a staunch Republican family."[66]

In October, Special Agent Frank Aldrich had one more week to go before he retired from the FBI when his supervisor asked him to look into something. It was a letter written by a woman in Connecticut, who said that someone had contacted her claiming to be an FBI agent. Aldrich asked her to visit him at the New York field office. The woman complained that she was being followed by someone and thought that it might be the FBI. She mentioned that she was involved with some people whom she thought might be Russian spies. She had worked for Amtorg, the Russian trading agency. She had been a Communist.

Why was this woman in his office? Aldrich wondered. She went on for more than two hours. "Possibly," he thought, "she was a psychopath rambling."[67] Aldrich wrote up a memo about a possible espionage case and suggested that the bureau interview the woman further.

Elizabeth Bentley was back.

At four-thirty on the afternoon of November 7, Elizabeth Bentley walked into the FBI's New York field office in Foley Square and sat down with Special Agent Edward Buckley. It was Bentley's third visit to the bureau in as many months. This time she finally revealed what was on her mind. She spoke for eight hours and signed a thirty-one-page statement before she went home around midnight. Then, at 1:55 A.M., the teletype machine in FBI headquarters in Washington started clattering: "A RUSSIAN ESPIONAGE RING . . . IS PRESENTLY OPERATING IN THIS COUNTRY."[68]

J. Edgar Hoover sent the White House a top-secret memo. "A number of persons employed by the government of the United States," Hoover wrote, "have been furnishing data and information to persons outside the federal government, who are in turn transmitting this information to espionage agents of the Soviet government."[69]

The FBI director included a list of fourteen names, one of which was Harry Dexter White, the number two person in the Treasury. And that was just the beginning of Bentley's story. She had given the bureau the names of more than one hundred people helping the Soviets, twenty-seven of whom were currently working for the government. For the bureau it was a double embarrassment: Not only had a large espionage network penetrated the government, but the FBI had actually put Bentley under surveillance four years earlier without discovering that the man she was sleeping with was the major Soviet spy runner in the country.

Elizabeth Bentley was thirty-seven, rather plain looking, and a bit dumpy. She had been born in Connecticut, educated at Vassar and Columbia, where she received a master's degree and where she met a young woman whose life seemed filled with purpose; her new friend brought Bentley to a meeting of the American League Against War and Fascism. "My life," Bentley recalled, "took on a new zest."[70]

Bentley joined the Communist Party in 1935. Four years later she met a man seven inches shorter than herself with red hair and piercing blue eyes. The next several years were possibly the only time in Elizabeth Bentley's life when she was happy. Just sitting next to the intense little man in a car sent Bentley into raptures. "I settled back," she remembered, "and let myself float away into an ecstasy that seemed to have no beginning and no end."[71]

His named was Jacob Golos (né Raisin). He was a Russian immigrant, eighteen years older than Bentley, with a wife and child in the Soviet Union. She became his helpmeet, her apartment a mail drop where letters meant for him arrived bearing foreign postmarks. His day job was as the head of World Tourist, a travel agency that specialized in tours to the Soviet Union, a niche that drew the attention of the Justice Department, which raided the offices and arrested Golos for failing to register as an agent of a foreign government. He pled guilty and got off with a five-hundred-dollar fine. While FBI agents lurked outside, the couple spent romantic evenings in Bentley's Greenwich Village apartment snuggling in front of a fireplace ablaze with fake passports. The bureau gave up surveillance after a few months in August 1941.

That same month Bentley began making regular trips to Washington. When it turned out that being a Communist travel agent wasn't such a great cover for Golos, he came up with another front: the U.S. Service and Shipping Corporation, which specialized in sending packages to the Soviet Union. Golos put Bentley in charge. Then he introduced her to some of his friends. One was Nathan Gregory Silvermaster, a Russian-born, Berkeley-educated economist (Ph.D. dissertation: "Lenin's Economic Thought") who worked for the Board of Economic Warfare in Washington.

Bentley soon began to visit Silvermaster every couple of weeks, bringing copies of Earl Browder's latest tracts or copies of *Pravda* that it was a bad idea for government employees to be seen buying. Helen Silvermaster would cook a fine meal, and she and Gregory and their good friend (and housemate) William Ullmann would sit down to eat and talk politics with Bentley. Afterward they sipped milky Russian tea and Silvermaster handed her the party dues he collected from a group of secret Communists in Washington, most of whom worked for the government. Not all of Silvermaster's friends were party members. Some, like the Treasury's Harry White and White House aide Lauchlin Currie, never officially joined but still furnished Silvermaster with secret documents, which Ullmann, who worked at the Pentagon, photocopied in the basement and gave to Bentley.* Some days when Bentley returned from visiting her friends in Washington her knitting bag bulged with dozens of rolls of microfilm. What have you got? Golos asked Bentley once. "I think I've brought you the entire Pentagon,"[72] she beamed.

Bentley's domestic bliss was fleeting. On Thanksgiving Day 1943 Golos looked like hell. He mumbled something about needing to check with a source at the Institute for Pacific Relations, an Asian studies think tank. That evening he slumped in a chair and died. Bentley gave his clothes to Russian War Relief and went to his office to burn his papers. She swore that she would carry on his work. She met regularly with Earl Browder, who was publicly the leader of the American Communist Party and privately a conduit between the Communist underground and Soviet intelligence.

One day in March 1944 Browder sent Bentley to meet John Abt and some of his friends in his apartment on Central Park West. Abt was a prominent union lawyer (and secret Communist) who was about to become even more visible this election year with the CIO Political Action Committee. Abt introduced Bentley to his friend Victor Perlo. The son of Russian immigrants, Perlo was a Columbia graduate who had come to Washington during the New Deal, joining the National Recovery Administration — and also the Ware Group of secret Communists. Perlo now worked for the War Production Board and had Communist contacts in a host of government agencies, from the Office of Strategic Services to the Treasury. "They are reliable Fellowcountrymen [Communists]," Bentley told Moscow, "politically highly mature. They want to help with information."[73]

But by the end of the year the KGB was growing concerned that Golos had been too sloppy and compromised Bentley's cover; she was eased out of the underground. By 1945 Bentley was afraid that the FBI was following her. She decided to turn herself in before the bureau arrested her. The FBI at first had no idea who she was, although of course it turned out that four years earlier it had identified her as working with Golos when he was being followed.

---

*Silvermaster's friends were useful in other ways as well. When counterintelligence officials suspected Silvermaster of being a secret Communist and wanted to fire him as a security risk, White and Currie personally vouched for him to Undersecretary of War Robert Patterson, who overruled his security investigators. Patterson didn't know that Whittaker Chambers had previously identified both White and Currie as working with Soviet intelligence. Silvermaster was the only American featured in the KGB's Hall of Fame in Moscow. (See Harvey Klehr and John Earl Haynes, *Venona.* New Haven, Conn.: Yale University Press, 1999; p. 132.)

The FBI checked out her story. Agents showed Bentley a stack of photos. She picked out one picture and said that he was her Russian contact, whose name she knew as "Al." It was a photo of Anatoli Gromov, the first secretary of the Russian embassy in Washington. She picked out other photos of people whom the FBI suspected of being KGB agents.* Agents broke into the Silvermaster home and found a photo lab in the basement.

When the bureau looked through its files it found that Whittaker Chambers had mentioned many of the same people on Bentley's list as active in the Communist underground before the war. Then there was the Perlo letter. In 1944 the White House forwarded an unsigned letter to the FBI, which claimed that a government employee named Victor Perlo was involved in secret Communist activities along with Harry White, John Abt, Charles Kramer, and several others. The bureau traced the letter back to Katherine Perlo, who had married Victor Perlo in 1934 and divorced him in 1943. The FBI now had three overlapping lists of alleged secret Communists working for the government.

Hundreds of FBI agents began trailing suspects, including Treasury's Harry White, State's Alger Hiss, and Charles Kramer, Abt's old Ware Group friend who had been at his apartment the day that Bentley visited and who now worked for the Senate subcommittee on wartime health and education. The bureau quickly learned that many of the alleged Soviet agents seemed to know each other very well — but almost no incriminating evidence was discovered. One day the FBI followed Kramer out of his house, then watched him walk to a faraway bus stop and throw a package in the trash. The bureau dug the package out of the garbage and found that it was full of party literature. "Obviously this whole group is wrong and as far as I am concerned they could be shot," Hoover's deputy Lou Nichols noted, "but that is not legal proof."[74]

Somehow Charlie Kramer seemed to know that he was under suspicion. Elizabeth Bentley gave the FBI scores of names of Communists and fellow travelers who worked for the government. But she didn't know that the Soviets also had a source in the Justice Department as well as in the British embassy. With two weeks of Bentley telling her story to the FBI, the Soviets knew as well. They began to plot the best way to kill her.

The day after Harry Truman entered the White House, J. Edgar Hoover searched the FBI's ranks for anyone who had a connection to the new

---

*Soviet intelligence changed its name frequently. Only the two most common are used here: NKVD (until 1943) and, after that, KGB.

president. When he found an agent whose father had been a lifelong friend of Truman's, the FBI director dispatched the man to the Oval Office to offer the bureau's help to the president whenever he needed it. "Anytime I need the services of the FBI," Truman snapped, "I will ask for it through my attorney general."[75]

Truman's attorney general was Tom Clark. Six weeks after becoming president, Truman had fired Roosevelt's attorney general, Francis Biddle, a patrician liberal, and replaced him with Clark, a plainspoken, plain-thinking Texas lawyer who had been in the Justice Department since 1937. Biddle was shocked — not so much by the fact that he was losing his job but by the idea that Tom Clark, whom he had tried to fire for being incompetent, would be the nation's top law enforcement official.

Biddle was just the sort of effete Eastern Establishment type that Truman disliked, but ideologically he was much more in tune with the new president than Clark would ever be. Biddle, like Truman, had an abiding concern for civil liberties, something neither Roosevelt nor Clark shared. Under FDR, Biddle found himself pressed to stifle dissent, and the Justice Department undertook a number of dubious sedition prosecutions, not to mention the wartime detention of Japanese Americans (which Clark was in charge of). Before long Truman would regret his choice. "Tom Clark," he said years later, "was my biggest mistake."[76]

Clark, in effect, became Truman's ambassador to the FBI. J. Edgar Hoover, fifty, nominally worked for the attorney general but in fact ran the FBI like a sovereign kingdom. Hoover was the only director the bureau had ever known, and the bureau was virtually the only life that the director had. Hoover had joined the Justice Department in 1917 after graduating from night law school; in 1919 he spearheaded the mass arrests of thousands of radicals, known as the Palmer Raids, which developed into a lifelong obsession with Communism. In 1924 Hoover was named the director of the department's Bureau of Investigation, the forerunner of the FBI, a title he would hold for almost half a century.

Hoover was a simple but exacting man: He had a passion for collecting information, a reverence for order and stability, and a sense of fastidiousness that bordered on the pathological. He washed his hands so frequently that his personal assistant once estimated he'd spent half of his twenty-five years at the bureau handing towels to the director. Hoover was equally obsessed with keeping the bureau's reputation spotless — and to Hoover the bureau's reputation was indistinguishable from his own. When, for instance, a Washington baker reported to the bureau that he had heard someone making disparaging remarks about Hoover ("Have you heard that the director is a queer?"[77]) a full field investigation was launched. Two agents tracked down the man, discovered that he worked for the National Labor Relations Board, checked his government loyalty file, visited him at home, and asked him in front of his wife if he were homosexual himself. "Because of the vigorous interrogation . . . ," Assistant Director Mickey Ladd told Hoover, "he appeared to be badly frightened. . . . His criminal and civil liability for the making of such statements was clearly and forcefully pointed out to him. . . . He was informed that immediate and positive action would be taken if it again came to your attention that he was engaging in this type of gossip."[78] Hoover also instructed Ladd to make sure that the man's boss at the NLRB knew how much he had displeased the director.

Hoover was no less terrifying to his own agents. "We in the FBI did fear him,"[79] counterintelligence agent Robert Lamphere remembered. Supervisors never left headquarters for the night until Hoover did. They wrote him obsequious letters on his birthday, his anniversary at the bureau, or anytime he was given an award. A summons to the director's office, where Hoover's desk was mounted on a platform so that his stony visage gazed down on his agents like a gargoyle, was always an occasion to get a shoeshine and a suit pressed, if not a haircut. And when Hoover sent a memo to an agent with a question, everything else that the agent was working on stopped. One day Lamphere found himself stumped when Hoover sent him four different queries at the same time. "I asked a superior which of them I was to work on first," Lamphere recalled, "and was told that my humor was not appreciated and that I was to find a way to get all of them done at once."[80]

Hoover expected similar treatment on Capitol Hill. "All congressmen and senators are afraid of him," Truman complained to his wife, Bess. "I'm not and he knows it. If I can prevent it, there'll be no NKVD or gestapo in this country. Edgar Hoover's organization would make a good start toward a citizen spy system. Not for me."[81]

The director more than returned the president's scorn. "Hoover's hatred of Truman," recalled FBI agent William Sullivan, "knew no bounds."[82]

This mutual suspicion would prove costly to the nation. The day after Bentley's November debriefing, Hoover had a courier carry to the White House a summary of her charges, including a list of the ranking suspects. He got no response. Three weeks later Hoover sent a seventy-one-page follow-up report to the president, with the same result. The FBI chief refused to budge from his office in the bunkerlike granite fortress of the Justice

Department and travel half a dozen blocks to the White House to personally try to impress upon Truman how significant Bentley's revelations were.

Hoover was a man of fierce pride. He had already seen Truman's Justice Department lackadaisically prosecute the *Amerasia* case, basically letting everyone involved walk. "Certain aspects of this matter 'smell,' "[83] Hoover complained. Now the president seemed to be paying little if any attention to creditable charges that the Soviets had penetrated virtually every important government department. Then, in January 1946, Truman nominated Harry White to become the head of the International Monetary Fund. Hoover fired off a twenty-eight-page report reminding Truman of the charges against White, which Truman later recalled was the first he'd heard of the whole thing. Hoover was livid. White was the highest-ranking suspected Soviet spy in the government and he was getting promoted. Why not just make Earl Browder secretary of state?

Infuriated, Hoover decided to start secretly giving information to those who would listen: conservative members of Congress and the media. In 1940 when liberals in Congress were complaining about the FBI's crackdown on Communists, McCarran had volunteered his assistance. "Mr. Hoover ought to defend himself," McCarran wrote, "and furnish information to his friends in the Senate who would be glad to defend him."[84]

For the past dozen years conservatives such as McCarran had thought the worst of Roosevelt and the New Deal, believing that Washington was full of Communists who were steering the country toward socialism. Now Hoover had finally found *real* Communists and fellow travelers in positions of influence in the government. But the damage that the Communists did to the country would turn out to be far less than that caused by Hoover and McCarran over the next decade. In February 1946 Hoover authorized a covert program to leak information from the bureau's files ("educational material"[85] he called it) to those who were willing to use it without revealing the source. McCarran, for one, was more eager than ever.

In June, McCarran attached a rider to the State Department appropriations bill giving the secretary the authority to summarily fire any employee. Under the McCarran rider, no stated reason or hearing would be necessary, as long as the firing was in the national interest. "The McCarran rider," reported Jerry Kluttz in the *Washington Post,* "is believed to be another device to get at members of CIO's United Public Workers who actively supported the Communist line, anti-American foreign policy adopted by the union convention."[86]

Actually the McCarran rider was aimed at Alger Hiss and other suspected Communists in government — the opening shot in a decade-long
battle over loyalty and security in Washington. "The atmosphere and
everything about this place," McCarran told Pete Petersen, "has for many
weeks been just on the edge of hell."[87]

Not long before he introduced the rider, McCarran asked his friend
J. Edgar Hoover about Hiss. In 1946 a lot of people were whispering about
Hiss. He'd come to Washington in 1933, the same year as McCarran, but
from a very different world. Hiss worked in the Agricultural Adjustment
Administration with his Harvard Law School classmate Lee Pressman, and
they both traveled in the more radical circles of the New Deal, giving their
days to fighting Big Ag and battling for sharecroppers and their nights to
left-wing groups like the International Juridical Association. But while
Pressman and his friends John Abt and Nat Witt found it hard to reconcile
their revolutionary views with government service and left for the labor
movement, Hiss seemed to give up on his youthful radicalism as he steadily
advanced in the government, moving to the Justice Department and later
State. At Yalta he sat behind Roosevelt when the president negotiated with
Stalin; he'd then managed the United Nations founding, where he stood
on stage with Truman. Competent and cautious, Hiss was forty. He seemed
destined to go far in the State Department.

Then Elizabeth Bentley defected. One of the names she mentioned to
the FBI was Hiss (although she remembered his first name as Eugene).
Bentley didn't know Hiss herself but had been told about him by Charles
Kramer, who had known Hiss since the AAA. "She was questioned at
length concerning this information but admitted that the information
concerning Hiss is very vague," noted the FBI, "and because of this, she
was reluctant to make any definite statements."[88]

It wasn't the first time the FBI had heard the name. During the war, the
bureau had learned about Whittaker Chambers's charge that Hiss was a
secret Communist. Then Igor Gouzenko told Canadian officials that there
was talk in the Russian embassy in Ottawa that the U.S. secretary of state
had an aide who was a spy. In November, Bentley added her recollection.
By the end of the month the FBI had Hiss under surveillance; agents read
his mail and listened to his phone calls (including one in which his mother
worried that people were saying that her son was a Communist).

Before the end of the year people were publicly calling Hiss a
Communist. Carl T. Curtis, a Republican representative from Nebraska,
demanded that the secretary of state fire Communists and fellow travelers

from the department, naming Hiss, Jack Service (who had been cleared of espionage for his involvement in the *Amerasia* case), and fellow Old China Hand John Carter Vincent.[89]

By early 1946 the whispering had grown so loud that the new secretary of state James Byrnes suggested to Hiss (at Hoover's behest) that he talk to the FBI to clear his name. In March, Hiss went to FBI headquarters and told Assistant Director Mickey Ladd that he had never been a Communist or even close to the party. He wasn't much of a joiner, he added. And he hadn't kept in contact with Lee Pressman since he'd joined the CIO the better part of a decade ago. "He had heard many people say that Lee Pressman was either a party member or followed the party line," Ladd told Hoover, "but Hiss did not know this to be a fact."[90]

Although Hiss didn't know it, his career was over. An assistant to Secretary of State Jimmy Byrnes told the FBI that Hiss would not be considered for any more promotions or positions of authority and wanted to know if he could be summarily fired under civil service regulations. "Byrnes is of the definite opinion that Alger Hiss should be disposed of," the bureau's R. R. Roach told Assistant Director Ladd, "but is now concerned over the best manner in which to do it."[91]

The State Department had a real problem on its hands. Two creditable witnesses had named Hiss as a Communist, but it had no proof. Under civil service regulations the department could not fire Hiss without giving him a hearing, yet to keep him in a high-level job was a threat to national security. And while Hiss was in an especially sensitive spot, he was only one of numerous potential security threats swamping the department as it tried to absorb a flood of some four thousand new employees transferred to State from temporary wartime agencies such as the OSS.

By the summer of 1946 McCarran and other conservatives in Congress were attacking State for its lax security. In June, Attorney General Tom Clark briefed McCarran on the investigation. "He informed Senator McCarran that the bureau had no direct proof that Alger Hiss was a Communist," one of Hoover's minions reported, "although there were strong indications of this fact."[92]

Later that month McCarran introduced his rider and told the State Department that it had better get rid of its Communists. "McCarran, chairman of the committee, and Senator Bridges, then ranking Republican member, told me in no uncertain terms that they expected the department to use the power,"[93] remembered J. Anthony Panuch, deputy assistant secretary.

Over the next year Secretary Byrnes used the rider only twice. In

December 1946 Hiss resigned to become the director of the Carnegie Endowment for International Peace. "I was reluctant," Byrnes remembered, "without positive evidence, and with Hiss' positive denial of even knowing Chambers, to ask for a resignation that would ruin a man's life."[94]

To the dismay of conservatives, the McCarran rider seemed to solve nothing. "Stalin's fifth column in America is entrenched in all the policy-making branches of the federal government," Isaac Don Levine wrote in October 1946, in the premiere issue of a magazine called *Plain Talk,* where the lead article was titled "Another Pearl Harbor." "It has even infiltrated our departments of national defense. It controls many pivotal labor unions and critical industries, such as shipping and communications. The report of the Canadian Royal Commission and the evidence gathered by our own congressional inquiries show that legislators, journalists, scientists, educators, publishers, radio commentators, prominent figures of the stage and screen, public servants as well as businessmen are enrolled in the Soviet secret brigade."

Levine, a Russian immigrant and an anti-Communist journalist, had gone with Whittaker Chambers to visit the State Department's Adolf Berle in 1939. Chambers had given Berle the outlines of a Soviet espionage ring in Washington that included Harry White, Alger Hiss, and Lee Pressman — and seven years later all had advanced far in their careers. White was executive director of the IMF, Hiss about to become the head of the Carnegie Endowment, Pressman the CIO's general counsel.

"There is no time to lose in forestalling another and greater Pearl Harbor," Levine continued. "The elementary prerequisites of our national safety require the ruthless exposure and the elimination through democratic processes from our national life of the Soviet fifth column. . . . The Soviet fifth column is in position to strike a savage and paralyzing blow from within, prostrating the nation before the enemy unleashes its rain of atomic weapons. Unless we clean house at once, American will be dragged down, carrying civilization with her into the totalitarian abyss."[95]

McCarran agreed. "It is our duty to make sure that those forces seeking to destroy the American form of government — and I am sorry to say they exist in high places — shall not succeed," McCarran told the San Francisco Bar Association in September. "We cannot meet this threat by arms alone. We must meet and conquer the enemy in our homes, and in the classrooms of our institutions of higher learning."[96]

At a dinner in Las Vegas, McCarran raised his glass and made a toast. "To the next senator from Nevada," he said, "Berkeley Bunker."[97] That simple gesture belied the labyrinthine complexities of Nevada politics. McCarran, of course, had spent most of Bunker's temporary appointment to the Senate insulting his colleague, both behind his back and to his face, and was happy to see him defeated by James Scrugham in 1942. Berkeley returned the favor by slyly siding with the CIO in 1944 when the union worked against McCarran and Bunker was elected to the House. Then in June 1945 Scrugham, who was seriously ill during most of his time in the Senate and rarely in Washington, died. Governor Edward Carville quickly resigned, leaving as the state's new chief executive Lieutenant Governor Vail Pittman, who appointed Carville to fill out the Senate term. With enemies now entrenched in the governor's mansion *and* the Senate, McCarran suddenly found that Bunker wasn't so objectionable after all. In fact, he urged Bunker to challenge Carville in the Senate primary in August. "McCarran was after me to run for the Senate," Bunker remembered. "And I never could really figure out whether he was more interested in electing me or defeating Carville."[98]

The first year of peace was hell. Twelve million soldiers flooded the job market. Eight million workers were laid off. More than four million went out on strike. Trains didn't run, coal wasn't mined, power faded out, the price of beef doubled overnight. Truman's early popularity quickly evaporated.

By the time the midterm elections rolled around in 1946, the president was so unpopular that DNC chairman Bob Hannegan convinced Truman to stay off the campaign trail. Instead, the Democrats rebroadcast old FDR speeches. In September Truman fired Commerce Secretary Henry Wallace, the last New Dealer in the cabinet and to many a living symbol of liberalism, for a Madison Square Garden speech attacking the administration's hard line on the Soviet Union. A month before the election, J. Edgar Hoover warned that there were one hundred thousand Communists in the country and ten fellow travelers for each one. The election, Representative B. Carroll Reece claimed, was a contest between Communism and Republicanism.

The election was a disaster for the Democrats. The party lost control of Congress for the first time since 1930, giving up seven seats in the Senate and thirty-seven in the House. California sent Richard Nixon to the Senate; Wisconsin, Joseph McCarthy.

Nevada, too, went Republican. Bunker had beaten Carville in the primary but lost to George Malone in the general election — McCarran had so split the Democratic Party that Nevada sent a Republican to Washington for the first time in sixteen years. That was fine with McCarran. He would rather have a Republican colleague and be rid of two Democratic rivals.

On balance, however, the election was a disaster for McCarran. First his archrival Vail Pittman was elected governor. Then, even worse, McCarran lost his cherished chairmanship of the Judiciary Committee. For the first time since he'd arrived in Washington in 1933, McCarran was a member of the minority; for the first time in three years he was bereft of his powerful chairman's seat. "I never saw a group of fellows who could do nothing so well, as our Republican friends in charge of the Senate and House," McCarran told Petersen. "They are a complete success. The Democrats don't make much fuss so the Republicans fight among themselves. The Republicans are all generals, and no privates. They all want to be leaders and they all take a turn at it, and when one fellow is leading the others are all throwing turnips and cabbages at him. It's a real circus to watch."[99]

A few months before the election McCarran had incensed Truman by holding up the nomination of the president's friend Carl Vinson to the Supreme Court. "Some day I'll have an opportunity to level him off," Truman fumed to his wife. "Probably won't do it but it should be done."[100]

CHAPTER 15

On All Evidence

The Commission has further information to the effect
that from 1929 to 1947 you continued to follow the
Communist Party line and that this is evidenced by your
full support of the Keep America Out of War Congress.

— State Department loyalty board
interrogatory to Bertram Wolfe

The program of the Keep America Out of War Congress
was drafted by Norman Thomas and the undersigned, after
consultation with and incorporation of the views of such
diverse American leaders of public opinion as Senators
Vandenberg, Taft and McCarran, Herbert Hoover, Thomas
Dewey, Hugh Johnson, William Green of the AF of L and
William [sic] Murray of the CIO.[1]

— Wolfe's reply

At seven twenty-eight on the morning of September 22, 1948, the president's sixteen-car train pulled into Imlay, a tiny railroad town in the middle of Nevada. As soon as the train groaned to a stop a slight man with thin hair, a polka-dotted bow tie, and thick glasses jumped off. About 150 people stood around the depot. By presidential standards it was a pathetic crowd. Harry Truman didn't care. He was in the fight of his life and needed every vote he could grab. "You folks," Truman said, "must have gotten up before daylight."[2]

One of the early risers was Pat McCarran, who came up to Truman and shook the president's hand. "Pat," he said, "it's good to see you again."[3] McCarran believed him. As uncooperative as McCarran had always been, the Republican Congress of the past two years was worse. Seventy-five vetoes, five overrides, most ominously the Taft-Hartley Act, which attempted to undo much of the New Deal's labor legislation. After being out of power for sixteen years the Republicans wanted things the way they used to be before Franklin Roosevelt had come to Washington and changed everything. "You've got the worst Congress," Truman said, "you've ever had."[4]

For McCarran, too, it had been a terrible time. His health was poor, he had suffered two heart attacks in a year, there were family worries aplenty, and, worst of all, he had lost his cherished Judiciary Committee chairmanship. McCarran felt so unimportant as the ranking minority member of the committee that he took a month off in the fall of 1947 and set sail for Hawaii with Birdie.

This fall McCarran had the chance to end his inactivity and regain his chairmanship — but only if the president could lead the Democrats back to power in Congress. If only the sun would rise in the West. Truman was running against liberal Republican Tom Dewey, the popular governor of the country's most populus state. At the same time the hard right and hard left of the Democratic Party had sheared off to run their own candidates: South Carolina governor Strom Thurmond and former vice president Henry Wallace, both of whom promised to steal millions of votes from Truman. Two weeks earlier Roper had stopped its campaign polling because Dewey kept defeating Truman by double digits.

Truman was still working the crowd when an aide said that the train was ready to leave. "I don't think it'll start before I get on," Truman said. In the afternoon the train pulled into Sparks, where more than two thousand people turned out to greet Truman, including Governor Vail Pittman and Walter Baring, who was running for Congress on the Democratic ticket. Truman stood between McCarran and Pittman, slipping his hand into the governor's arm. McCarran was left to hold his Stetson in his hands. "Everybody knows where I stand," Truman told the crowd. "You don't hear any double talk from me. I'm either for a thing or against it. I hope you can find out what the other people are for but I'm afraid you won't for a long, long time."

The president got into a dark convertible with whitewall tires and American flags flying from the bumper. McCarran and Pittman squeezed into the seat beside him. The motorcade raced the few miles into Reno and turned south onto Virginia Street, where crowds turned their backs to the casinos and lined the sidewalk for a glimpse of the president. A Secret Service agent in sunglasses and a too-short tie trotted behind the president's car as it slowly drove down the street, under the Reno Arch (THE BIGGEST LITTLE CITY IN THE WORLD) and across the Truckee to Powing Park, opposite the courthouse.

Truman walked to the stage, draped in stars-and-stripes bunting with a WELCOME TO RENO sign for a backdrop. He looked out at the crowd, which filled the small park, spilled across the street — an estimated twenty-five thousand people, which if true would have been almost everyone in the city. Truman stood in front of a thicket of microphones with McCarran behind him. The Sierra peaked out behind the Washoe County Courthouse; the Truckee bubbled by on his right. Light glinted off the president's Coke-bottle-bottom glasses. It was a glorious fall day and the president lit into the Republican Eightieth Congress. "I want you to fire that Congress," Truman yelled. "A bunch of old mossbacks living back in 1890. Give me one I can work with."

McCarran hadn't wanted Truman to run. Few in the Democratic Party did. Three years after Truman had inherited the White House, he was one of the least popular men in the country. Strikes and shortages and Washington scandals and a war scare had taken their toll. Liberals pined for a new leader, rallying behind General Dwight Eisenhower, although he wasn't a liberal and didn't want to be president. But Truman surprised the convention by winning the nomination after all, ordering Congress into a special session, and then heading out on a vigorous campaign. Now he was six days into his latest cross-country whistle-stop tour. Today he would give six speeches in two states — a light day.

"If you don't want the country run by men who want to turn the clock back," Truman said, his voice growing hoarse, "do something about it on November 2."[5]

Even though McCarran was standing next to Truman, their faces were turned in different directions. It was as close as they would ever be.

When the Eightieth Congress had convened in January 1947, McCarran found himself sitting to the side of the new chairman of the Judiciary Committee, Wisconsin's Alexander Wiley. McCarran, now the ranking minority member, began to pester Wiley about how large a staff the Democrats could have.

"Hold your horses," Wiley snapped.

"I am holding my horses," McCarran replied, "but I can't hold them forever while you make up your mind."

"I guess I should have said, 'hold your jackassess.' "

"When I think of jackasses, I think of you."

"You'd better be careful."

"I'm not worried. I've always been able to step back out of the way in time."[6]

Stephen Spingarn asked his secretary to stay late. It was eight at night, already long dark on this short winter day, normally the time her hyperactive boss might let her go home. But on this January evening in 1947 the Justice Department had just sent over the draft version of a proposal to create a government loyalty program. Spingarn glanced at the document, and his secretary could tell by his face that it was going to be a long night. She left the office at midnight. Spingarn stayed through the night, knocking off at 4:30 A.M. for few hours of sleep. "This report is worthless," Spingarn fumed, "and we must start again."[7]

Spingarn was thirty-nine, a bear of a man standing six feet tall and weighing 250 pounds. As big as he was, Spingarn felt that he never quite measured up to his father. The elder Spingarn was a distinguished professor of American literature at Columbia University who had been a founder and president of the National Association for the Advancement of Colored People. The younger Spingarn went to Yale for two years, spent a year in France, and then came down with a serious sinus problem. After several operations he went west to avoid further surgery. Spingarn finished school at the University of Arizona. In 1934 he went to Washington, armed with a law degree from the University of Arizona. Drew Pearson recommended him to Jerome Frank for a job in the AAA; Frank was unimpressed.

The Treasury hired Spingarn, where he worked for the next eight years, including serving on the department's loyalty board when the government first began to weed out Communists and Nazis as security risks at the start of World War II. In 1942 Spingarn went to war, serving as the commanding officer of the Fifth Army's counterintelligence corps in Africa and Italy. His unit caught 525 German spies. "It was more," he liked to say, "than the FBI had caught in the whole forty years of its history."[8] Spingarn learned a lot about trailing spies and interrogating suspects; he also learned how willing villagers in Italy were to denounce their neighbors as fascists. Almost fifty men whom Spingarn found to be spies were executed. "We had power to arrest without cause, to search without writ or reason, to imprison indefinitely without trial," he recalled in an article in the *Saturday Evening Post*. "With these powers, which we learned to hate, we were, in our way, the first American Gestapo."[9]

Early in 1946 Spingarn returned to Washington, where he became the Treasury's assistant general counsel. Washington was jittery about Communists. A House civil service subcommittee recommended overhauling the government loyalty program, which had been thrown together in haste at the start of the war. Truman ignored the subcommittee report for four months. Then the Republicans drubbed the Democrats in the midterm elections and Truman suddenly faced a GOP Congress that was likely to take matters into its own hands. On November 25 Truman issued Executive Order 9806, creating the President's Temporary Commission on Employee Loyalty. The chairman of the panel was A. Devitt "Gus" Vanech, an assistant attorney general. Spingarn was one of the Treasury members.

The committee met in December 1946 and asked FBI director J. Edgar Hoover to give a presentation on the scope of the problem. Hoover sent Assistant Director Mickey Ladd. It was a very serious problem, Ladd said. The Communist Party, he added, had created a special group to infiltrate the government. He didn't elaborate. Did the FBI have a list of subversives to be picked up in case of war? Spingarn wanted to know. It's none of the committee's business, Ladd replied.

Attorney General Tom Clark also made an appearance and said that there were only two dozen Communists in the government, including several at the Treasury. "I do not believe that the gravity of the problem should be weighed in the light of numbers," he stated, "but rather from the viewpoint of the serious threat which even one disloyal person constitutes to the security of the government."*[10]

A military intelligence officer from the War Department suggested one day that all liberals were potential security risks. "A liberal is only a hop, skip, and a jump from a Communist," the officer asserted "A Communist starts as a liberal."[11] And a conservative, Spingarn wanted to say back, is only a hop, skip, and a jump from a fascist.

How big is the problem? Spingarn kept asking. "We ought to know how big a war this is," as Spingarn put it later. "Is it a one division war, a five division war or a twenty division war? We therefore need to know the real facts, the secret information of the Department of Justice, on how widely infected with subversives they believed the government is. Facts, not speculation."[12]

J. Edgar Hoover loved to gather facts. He didn't especially like to share them. Thus even while the FBI was vigorously, if belatedly, investigating the Communist cells in Washington that Whittaker Chambers and Elizabeth Bentley had revealed, it was refusing to disclose the fruits of those investigations to the president's commission. Hoover was sending worrying letters to the president, naming suspected Communists high in the government; to

---

*Years later Clark would have another view. "I think the Communist scare was highly exaggerated," he said. (Clark oral history, Harry S. Truman Library.)

the president's commission his minions suggested they read a U.S. Chamber of Commerce report for specifics about subversives in government. The bureau had helped Father John F. Cronin prepare the report, but Hoover was unwilling to give similar help to a presidential commission. And Vanech wouldn't even let the committee have copies of the letters Hoover sent it, insisting that the members read the documents at Justice. Spingarn despised Vanech. "A worse choice I have never known," Spingarn said. "He was incompetent and stupid. . . . He was an ignorant, semi-illiterate. He spoke, *dese, dem* and *dose* English. Perhaps you shouldn't hold that against a man, but you expect a senior lawyer at the Justice Department to be able to speak English. . . . He was unbelievably stupid."[13]

Then Vanech sent Spingarn a draft proposal for a new government loyalty program. Spingarn thought that it looked more like a plan to catch liberals than Communists. "The problem is a very serious one regardless of the number of disloyal employees there may be," Spingarn wrote to Vanech, "but that the Temporary Commission has no evidence before it indicating that this number is very great and that the best way to start a witch hunt of the post–World War I variety is to overpaint the picture in terms of numbers. We are as determined as the majority of the subcommittee to bar all Communists and other subversives from government work and to weed out any such person who may already be on the payroll, but we favor the methods of vigorous, effective counter intelligence rather than appeals to emotion and hysteria, and we do not want to extend the prohibition to include, for example, everyone who reads *PM* or the *New Republic.*"[14] Spingarn started rewriting the document almost immediately. "A small number of federal employees today are known to be subversive or are strongly suspected of being disloyal or subversive," Spingarn wrote. "The number is surprisingly small in the light of the hue and cry which has arisen about the matter."[15]

He then spent most of the next couple of weeks arguing with Vanech. The committee blew its deadline and had to ask for an extension. Eventually Spingarn and Vanech hammered out a compromise proposal. "I frankly shudder to think what the final report might have been like," Spingarn noted, "if we had not been represented, and had not expressed our views often and forcibly."[16]

The committee sent Truman its report on March 2, 1947. It recommended that all government agencies should create their own loyalty boards to investigate alleged subversives. Among the evidence the board should weigh was whether the employee was a member of (or in "sympathetic association with") a group designated by the attorney general as subversive, totalitarian, fascist, or Communist. A central loyalty review board should serve as an appellate authority. "The underlying standard," the committee suggested, "for the refusal of employment in loyalty cases shall be that, on all evidence, reasonable grounds exist for believing that the person involved is disloyal to the government of the United States."[17]

Nineteen days later the president issued Executive Order 9835, establishing a loyalty program for all two million federal workers. "The final report represents a lot of compromising by everybody," Spingarn noted. "It is not as good as it should be by a long shot, but at the same time it is far from being as bad as it might have been if Treasury and State had not gone to the mat on issue after issue. I imagine that the final report will be attacked by the extreme left as a witch hunt and by the extreme right as a whitewash. . . . In any event, for better or worse the thing it over."[18]

In February 1947 Arthur Schlesinger stopped in at the office of *The New Republic* on Forty-ninth Street in Manhattan. He was supposed to have lunch with Henry Wallace — Roosevelt's dumped vice president, Truman's fired commerce secretary, and now the nominal editor of the liberal magazine. Wallace wasn't there. The other editors weren't surprised. Wallace didn't much read the magazine he supposedly edited; he sometimes passed his editors in the halls without recognizing them. To Michael Straight, the owner and publisher of *The New Republic,* Wallace was the great hope of American liberalism. To Schlesinger, a young historian and organizer of a new liberal organization called Americans for Democratic Action, he was just hopeless. That chasm of opinion was the Great Debate of postwar American liberalism.

Lunch started without Wallace and soon turned into a shouting match. "What we want to find out," asked Theodore White, Schlesinger's classmate from Harvard and a celebrated China correspondent, "is what ADA has against the *New Republic?*"[19]

Arthur M. Schlesinger Jr. was not a man you had to ask twice for his opinion. "Can't I say what I believe?" his mother once admonished him at the dinner table. "No, mother," he replied, "not when you don't know what you are talking about."[20] The son of an eminent Harvard historian, Schlesinger was not yet thirty, slight of height, thin of hair, thick of glasses. But somehow he exuded a sense of gravitas in inverse proportion to his own physical fragility. "He never quite resembles a prodigy," his friend James Wechsler noted, "because he always sounds a little older than most people in the room."[21] After graduating from Harvard in 1938, Schlesinger served in the OSS during World War II, and in 1945 won a Pulitzer Prize for his second book, *The Age of Jackson*. Without bothering to earn a Ph.D., he was offered jobs at Yale, the University of Chicago, and Johns Hopkins. After a stint writing for Henry Luce's *Fortune* and *Life,* Schlesinger started teaching at Harvard and began work on an epic series of books about the New Deal called *The Age of Roosevelt*. In his spare time Schlesinger decided to drive Communists from public life. He had grown up hearing about the machinations of American Stalinists from Pat Jackson (one of his father's best friends) while Jackson was still a fellow traveler. "Appalling stories of Communist influence in the CIO,"[22] Schlesinger wrote to his family after one dinner with Jackson.

After Lee Pressman broke Jackson's heart, he set out to expose the Communists as passionately as he had once apologized for them. He joined the Union for Democratic Action, the interventionist group founded by Jim Loeb and Reinhold Niebuhr in 1941, which barred Communists and other totalitarians from its ranks (young Schlesinger was also a member). In 1944, while working as reporter for *PM,* Jackson was jumped by a group of long-shoremen from the Communist National Maritime Union, including Vice President Jack Lawrenson. Jackson was beaten to a pulp, wound up in the hospital, and lost the sight in one eye. "It will be interesting to see whether those persons who are so profoundly shocked when anything happens to a Communist are shocked correspondingly when the Communists commit such an outrage," young Schlesinger wrote to Jackson. "This episode rein-forces everything I have seen on this side: that fifth columns and totalitari-anism are pretty much the same, whether marching under a swastika or a hammer and sickle. I intend to devote a good deal of my energy in the next few years to fighting against the attempts of these people to gain a foothold in our country."[23]

More and more liberals began to feel the same way. In May 1946 Jim Loeb, the executive secretary of the UDA, published a letter in *The New Republic* suggesting that the time had finally come for liberals and Communists to part ways. "No united front organization will long remain united," he wrote. "It will become only a 'front.' "[24] Loeb had been moved to write by the "Win-the-Peace Conference," which had just taken place in Washington the month before. On its face the conference was a gathering of liberals — senators and congressmen, writers and artists — rededicating themselves to fulfilling Frank Roosevelt's New Deal. There were condem-nations of imperialism and resolutions to send food to Europe. But a discerning eye noticed something else: There were denunciations of British imperialism, but not Russian imperialism; resolutions against the United States interfering in the affairs of other countries but nothing about the growing control that the Soviet Union was exerting in Eastern Europe. "It is increasingly clear that an effort is being made to form," a UDA memo stated, "an organization that, although designed to appeal to liberals and progressives, has as its basic purpose complete apology for the Soviet Union and consistent opposition to the policies of the Western democracies."[25]

In his *New Republic* letter Loeb urged all progressives to pull out of Popular Front groups and bar Communists from membership in liberal organizations. "Nothing that I have ever done in public life brought that kind of attention . . . ," Loeb remembered. "I was called many names, both good and bad."*[26] A couple of months later Schlesinger said much the same thing in a *Life* magazine story about the CPUSA. "The Communist Party," he concluded, "is no menace to the right in the U.S. It is a great help to the right because of its success in dividing and neutralizing the left. It is to the American left that Communism presents the most serious danger."[27]

Loeb invited Schlesinger to a conference in Washington in the first week of January 1947. The week before, the left-wing Progressive Citizens of America was founded, a merger of two Popular Front groups.† The featured speaker at the PCA conference was Henry Wallace. Later that month the right-wing Eightieth Congress opened. And so it was that the Americans for Democratic Action was born between the extreme left and the extreme right of U.S. politics.

On January 4, in the Willard Hotel across form the White House, the Union for Democratic Action transformed itself into the Americans for Democratic Action. The elegant hotel glittered with the leading lights of politics, labor, and journalism: Eleanor Roosevelt, Reinhold Niebuhr, Minneapolis mayor Hubert Humphrey, Walter Reuther, David Dubinsky, Marquis Childs, Stewart Alsop. "This crowd," cracked Elmer Davis, "looks very much like the United States government in-exile."[28]

From the get-go the ADA had two purposes: to fight for liberalism and to fight its enemies, especially the Communists who claimed to share similar

---

*The letter was actually the idea of Bruce Bliven, editor of *The New Republic*, who suggested it to Loeb at a UDA board meeting. Loeb recalled. "I always accused him of getting an article for nothing." (Loeb Papers, Wisconsin State Historical Society.)

†The PCA was founded from the merger of the ICCASP, or Independent Citizens Committee of the Arts, Sciences and Professions, and the NCPAC, or National Citizens Political Action Committee. The initialization, at least, was an improvement.

goals. "It explicitly rejected all entangling alliances with members, fellow travelers and front organizations of the American Communist Party," Schlesinger declared in a draft statement. "It regards Communist activity as a major source of confusion and paralysis in the liberal movement and feels that the energies of American progressivism cannot be released for the achievement of American ends until the progressives themselves destroy Communist influence in the labor and liberal movements."[29]

Alliances were one thing; lunch was another. So a month after Schlesinger talked himself hoarse denouncing those who would not denounce Communists, he sat down to eat with the editors of *The New Republic,* the house organ of the Popular Front. "From everything we can gather," observed editor Penn Kimball, "ADA is obsessed with the Communist problem to the neglect of all the great fascist and war-making forces which are the real enemy of liberals."[30]

Wallace finally showed up. Tall, shambling, with a thick shock of unruly steel-gray hair, Henry Agard Wallace was never more happy than when he was growing something. Wallace had been a registered Republican and an agricultural journalist who developed a pioneering corn hybrid when Roosevelt made him secretary of agriculture and then vice president. In 1942 Wallace electrified liberals with his speech "A Century of the Common Man," which claimed that a new age of widespread liberty and democracy was dawning. Wallace himself was a most uncommon man. "I am neither a corn breeder nor an editor," he wrote to a friend before he went to Washington, "but a searcher for methods of bringing the 'inner light' to outward manifestation and raising outward manifestation to the inner light."[31] And that was one of his more lucid attempts to explain a long spiritual quest that took him from Indian sweatlodges to Eastern mysticism, which he combined with his temperamental disposition toward being an Old Testament prophet — a hybrid far less successful than his corn. Wallace earned more than $150,000 a year just in dividends from his corn hybrid but never paid his share of a lunch bill, left a skinflint tip when dining on his *New Republic* expense account, and couldn't come up with a buck to chip in for a dinner at a supporter's house, hitting up John Abt for a loan ("One dollar I'd never again see,"[32] Abt noted).

Until recently Schlesinger, like many liberals, had viewed Wallace as the last hope to revive the New Deal. They saw Roosevelt's decision to replace Wallace with Truman in 1944 as the president's final surrender to the right. And when Truman entered the White House, they viewed Wallace as FDR's real heir. "The chief spokesman of the New Deal, the liberal conscience of the administration, the living symbol of its enduring values,"[33] the UDA called Wallace in 1945. Then Truman fired Wallace for criticizing his foreign policy in a speech at Madison Square Garden in September 1946, and Wallace went on the warpath against the Democratic Party. "We are captives of no party," Wallace wrote in his first editorial in *The New Republic*. "If the Democratic Party is incapable of change we shall strike out along other lines."[34] Wallace said that he would rather see a reactionary Republican elected president than a lukewarm liberal Democrat. "If it is traitorous to believe in peace," he had told the founding PCA conference, "we are traitors. If it is communistic to believe in prosperity for all, we are Communists."[35]

As Wallace moved ever more to the left, many liberals began to see him as a threat to liberalism itself: a populist demagogue drunk on his own righteousness. Wallace was never more compelling than in the abstract; in person he somehow still seemed absent. Wallace could orate movingly about humanity, but rarely could he relate to an actual human. "As inarticulate and uncommunicative as ever," Schlesinger noted after lunch. ". . . His comments were ignorant and doctrinaire. His emotions, however, were compelling and his bashful charm remains."[36]

During the lunch argument over Communists, Schlesinger noticed, Michael Straight said little. Straight was rich; his parents had helped found the magazine. What Schlesinger didn't know — what almost no one knew — was that Straight had joined the Communist Party while studying at Cambridge University in 1935 and had been recruited for underground work by the art historian and spy Anthony Blunt. In Washington Straight used family connections to get a couple of make-work government jobs. He passed material to the Soviets but grew increasingly disillusioned with Communism — although unlike Chambers or Bentley, Straight would not feel compelled to unburden himself until the lapse of two decades.

Straight walked Schlesinger out. The publisher said that he was interested in starting a dialogue with the ADA about turning *The New Republic* into *the* publication for the next New Deal. Schlesinger said that he thought there was little chance of that as long as Wallace was associated with the magazine. Straight's face fell. "He looked," Schlesinger remembered, "very depressed but said nothing."[37]

On March 12, 1947, Harry Truman walked into the House chamber and addressed a joint session of Congress. Less than two years after the fighting had stopped, Truman told the nation that the war was not really over.

Poland, Yugoslavia, Romania, and Bulgaria had all fallen into the Soviet orbit. Communism was threatening Greece and Turkey. Italy and France could be next. Great Britain was broke. If the United States hoped to halt Soviet expansion, it would have to give military aid to Greece and Turkey. Truman asked Congress for four hundred million dollars to prop up those two wobbly governments. "The free peoples of the world look to us for support in maintaining their freedoms," Truman said. "If we falter in our leadership, we may endanger the peace of the world — and we shall surely endanger the welfare of our own nation."[38]

The applause was slight, only three times in twenty-one minutes, as if Congress were stunned by what it had just heard. In less than half an hour Truman had radically reoriented the compass of American foreign policy. The true north of U.S. policy was no longer protective isolationism, but active, potentially limitless engagement in world affairs. Truman had pledged the United States as the guarantor of international stability, a Pax Americana designed to forestall a Pax Sovietica. The Truman Doctrine, it would be called.

Conservatives thought that Truman had it exactly backward: The only way to preserve American democracy was to keep it from becoming sullied in the messy affairs of other states. "This is the crossroads where we decide whether we are to strengthen America's position in a democratic world by refraining from conflicts abroad or whether we are to go the other way," McCarran told reporters. "Money alone won't be enough to sustain Greece and Turkey. We will have to go in there with men and materials, if we go at all."[39] Still McCarran voted for the aid bill. "Not that I believe it will do any good," he told Reno postmaster Pete Petersen, "but it will probably do less harm than some other things."[40]

The strongest opposition came from the left, from progressives such as Henry Wallace, who were alarmed by the scope of Truman's commitment and the amorality of his approach. "There is no regime too reactionary for us provided it stands in Russia's expansionist path," Wallace said. "There is no country too remote to serve as the scene of a contest which may widen until it becomes a world war."[41]

"The American Crackpots Association,"[42] Truman called his progressive critics.

White House aide Clark Clifford was in his office one day when Harry Truman popped in. Presidential visits were rare, so Clifford thought it must be important. It was. "Let's be sure that we hold the FBI down,"

Truman told Clifford. "If we leave them to their own devices and give them what they want, they will become an American Gestapo."[43]

Truman was more afraid of the FBI than he was of the American Communist Party. "People are very much wrought up about the Communist 'bugaboo,'" he wrote to Pennsylvania governor George H. Earle in February, "but I am of the opinion that the country is perfectly safe so far as Communism is concerned — we have too many sane people."[44]

Then, on March 21, Truman signed Executive Order 9835. Nine days after the president had announced the Truman Doctrine, he proclaimed its domestic corollary: the government loyalty program. Under the 1939 Hatch Act it was already illegal to employ Communists in the government, but the new program would search for hidden party members and fellow travelers by investigating all current or new federal workers. Anyone suspected of being a Communist (or in "sympathetic association with" the party) would be subject to a full field investigation by the FBI and then given a hearing before a departmental loyalty board. The attorney general would publish a list of subversive organizations, membership in which would be evidence of possible disloyalty. The first attorney general's list ran to ninety-three organizations, from the Communist Party to the North American Committee to Aid Spanish Democracy, which had become defunct almost a decade earlier.

The White House requested $24.9 million to carry out the program, with two-thirds of the money going to the Civil Service Commission and a third to the FBI. Congress stalled on funding the program for three months as J. Edgar Hoover quietly lobbied for more authority. "J. Edgar will in all probability get this backward-looking Congress to give him what he wants," Truman told Clifford. "It's dangerous."[45]

Hoover did get what he wanted. Congress reversed Truman's budget request, giving two-thirds of the money to the FBI and a third to the Civil Service Commission. Decades later, Clifford lamented that the White House didn't put up more of a fight. "My greatest regret," he recalled, "is that I did not make more of an effort to try to kill the loyalty program at its inception."[46]

Shortly before dawn on July 25, 1947, as Congress was struggling toward adjournment, a strange thing happened in the Senate: Pat McCarran defended Harry Truman. The Republicans, McCarran said, were trying "to tear down the great prestige of a great president to lead the people astray in the 1948 elections."[47]

The Senate had been in session for seventeen hours. The Republicans were demanding a Senate investigation of alleged vote fraud in the Kansas City Democratic primary the year before — a rather unwonted solicitude for voting rights, especially considering that the winning Democrat (Truman's candidate, by the way) had lost to a Republican in the general election. The Democrats, led by McCarran, were determined to stop any probe. In May the Judiciary Committee appointed a three-man subcommittee to look into the matter. Attorney General Tom Clark had already ordered the FBI to investigate, and the bureau didn't find a prosecutable case. Missouri Republican senator James Kem called Clark's inquiry a whitewash. The subcommittee, led by Michigan's irritable Homer Ferguson, was expected to reach a similar conclusion, since it was made up of two Republicans and a Democrat (McCarran) who often voted like a Republican. But the second Republican was William "Wild Bill" Langer, a North Dakota maverick who lived up to his nickname. Langer and McCarran filed a blistering report that supported the attorney general and called the proposed probe a partisan attack. "It would amount to political harassment,"[48] they concluded.

Ferguson took his fight to the floor. McCarran blocked him at every move. The battle dragged on for a day, then consumed a night and threatened to eat into another day. The two shouted at each other at the tops of their lungs. Ferguson accused the Democrats of a cover-up. McCarran accused the Republicans of partisan politics.

"That's all that's keeping the Senate in session at 3:30 in the morning," McCarran said. "It's just personal ambition — the desire of someone to be a candidate for president."

McCarran was right — and his own personal ambition played no small part in his unaccustomed role as a defender of the administration. An election was coming up the following year, and only a resounding Democratic victory would put McCarran back in the chairman's seat of the Judiciary Committee. McCarran hated being out of power. Now he needed his party like he had not needed it since 1932.

"Let no one think I'm tired," McCarran yelled, "for I'm not."[49]

The Republicans finally gave up at a quarter after six in the morning. McCarran walked out of the Capitol at sunrise with his aide Hal Lackey, a head taller and half a century younger. A newspaper photographer snapped a picture of the two against the dome of the Capitol. Buttoned up in a double-breasted suit, portly and smiling, McCarran looked on top of the world. Lackey looked tired as hell. McCarran loved a good fight.

Later Attorney General Tom Clark sent McCarran a Saint Christopher medal that had been blessed by the pope. "With this Christopher goes not only my heartfelt appreciation," Clark wrote, "but my prayers for your continued good health in the service of our country."[50]

McCarran didn't feel so good.[51] Seventy people were waiting downstairs in the dining room of the Mizpah Hotel. They could wait some more. Four decades earlier when McCarran had started his legal career in the boomtown of Tonopah, he never got invited to social events. Then the town went bust, McCarran became a senator, and now the biggest employer in the area was the Tonopah Army Air Field, the most powerful patron of which was McCarran. And on this Saturday night in August 1947, the leading lights of this sad little town gathered for a testimonial dinner on McCarran's behalf. He never made it.

At first the pain felt like indigestion. Then it got worse. McCarran was rushed to the hospital at the Naval Ammunition Depot at Hawthorne, seventy miles away. He had suffered a heart attack — his second one in less than a year. In December 1946 McCarran had a heart attack on a train crossing Nevada, got off in Imlay, and boarded the next train going back to Reno, where he was admitted to St. Mary's Hospital for ten days. Now, after a few days at the naval hospital and several transfusions, McCarran was back at St. Mary's. This time he spent three months in the hospital.

His doctor cut McCarran back to a thousand calories a day, ordered him to eat less meat, and told him to give up sugar, butter, milk, cream, oil, and fried foods. Other than that, the doctor said, the senator could eat whatever he wanted. McCarran had just turned seventy-one. Congress was out of session, but when it resumed in the fall McCarran slipped away for a month to cruise to Hawaii with Birdie. "I am feeling fine now," McCarran told his administrative assistant, Eva Adams, "in fact much better than I felt when I left Washington."[52]

Health problems were the least of his worries. Patricia, his youngest daughter, was drinking and having money problems again. "I am naturally very much disappointed and frightfully disturbed at everything that has come about," McCarran told her. "I think you would have known by this time that nothing good can come out of liquor. You should come down here and continue with the treatment. You did not complete the treatment, although you told me you had done so and that the doctor had discharged you. I am sending you the enclosed check for fifty dollars. . . . We are all frightfully disturbed about your condition."[53]

McCarran had gotten her husband, Edwin Hay, a job at Pan American Airways. Then he got him a raise. Then he tried to get him a better job at United Airlines. And McCarran still found himself paying her bills. "It has been hoped that her husband would assume some of the responsibility for this and other outstanding obligations," McCarran told Patricia's doctor, "but evidently he does not see fit to do so."[54]

Hay asked her for a divorce and offered a three-thousand-dollar settlement. "I laughed in his face and said 'I'd take ten times that much,'" she told her parents. ". . . You can't imagine the tension I am under when he is around. . . . His constant needling has caused every bit of my trouble."[55]

Sister Margaret, too, was unhappy. She wanted more than ever to go to graduate school, but her superiors refused. McCarran took the matter up with his friend Cardinal Francis Spellman, who visited the mother general of the Sisters of the Holy Names order. "She told me that the matter rested with the provincial of the California province and that the mother general would ask reconsideration of the case," Spellman told McCarran. "The reason that the sisters did not wish Sister Margaret Patricia to continue her studies for the doctorate was because her present degree fully qualified her to teach the classes required of her and it was the opinion of the authorities of the order that further graduate studies at this time were unnecessary."[56]

Sam had gone into the U.S. Army medical corps as an anesthesiologist (first lieutenant) but didn't like military life. "I had a call on the phone from Sam," McCarran told his wife. "He was in tears. I called the Surgeon General and begged him to pull Sam out of there. I think I'll succeed soon but Sam must be a little patient. He has had the best breaks possible to date."[57]

McCarran's family was keeping him busier than the Senate. While he spent the fall months recovering in Nevada, McCarran ran his office by correspondence and long-distance phone. One staffer worked full time helping Sister Margaret; others attended to Sam's and Patty's problems. Then as he prepared to set sail for Hawaii in October, McCarran ordered his office to take it easy. "May I suggest that during my absence and until I return again the office be closed on every Friday afternoon at the closing hour and remain closed until the following Monday morning,"[58] McCarran told Adams.

Sailing across the Pacific toward the territory of Hawaii with his wife the month after his seventy-second birthday, McCarran could well have been retired. He hated it.

In October overflow crowds thronged the House Caucus Room to watch the House Un-American Activities Committee hold hearings on Communism in Hollywood. Ten screenwriters and directors were summoned before J. Parnell Thomas and his committee. The witnesses insulted the committee; the committee insulted the witnesses. More than three hundred reporters covered the hearings. Seldom has something less important commanded more attention — then or even decades later.

The ten were or had been party members, and while loudly avowing their political beliefs ("This is the beginning . . . ," Dalton Trumbo yelled, "of an American concentration camp."[59]), they refused to answer questions about their political affiliations. They were cited for contempt. They went to jail. Studios stopped employing them.

The Hollywood blacklist had begun, and with it the myth that movie industry Stalinists were somehow martyrs for the cause of freedom. Later, those who recanted — admitting to having been party members and naming their comrades — would be ostracized as moral lepers. It was perhaps Communism's greatest accomplishment in America that it was able to make telling the truth seem disreputable.

On December 29, 1947, Henry Wallace announced that he was running for president as an independent candidate. "The people are on the march," he said. "We have assembled a Gideon's Army, small in number, powerful in conviction, ready for action."[60]

Actually the army had been assembled for Wallace — by the Communists. Wallace wasn't a Communist, as he often pointed out. He was more of a Christian mystic. Wallace, in fact, had fired the radicals in the AAA in 1935, many of whom actually were secret party members. But a dozen years later many of these same men would run his campaign. Chief among them was C. B. Baldwin, Beanie to his friends, who had not been purged from the Agriculture Department and had gone on to become head of the CIO PAC. Baldwin was a prime mover behind a third-party movement, convincing Wallace that it was his destiny to save American liberalism, which wasn't hard to do. "He was a self-intoxicated man," noted Teddy White, who had worked with Wallace at the *New Republic,* "with but two subjects of conversation — botanical genetics and himself."[61]

Baldwin's first campaign advice for Wallace was to hire John Abt as his counsel. For a scientist Wallace was a rather incurious person. You could practically *confess* to Wallace that you were a Communist, and he still wouldn't get it. "I told him that I'd recently been subpoenaed before the federal grand jury, that I was married to Jessica, the editor of *Soviet Russia Today,* and that my sister Marion was public relations director for the Communist Party," Abt recalled. "Wallace was no more alarmed than he would have been had I informed him of my admittance to the Illinois bar."[62]

For many, the Wallace campaign became the crusade of a lifetime. Lee Pressman quit his job as the general counsel of the CIO to join — and later, at the prompting of Communist leader Gene Dennis, decided to run for Congress from Brooklyn. Nat Witt, Charlie Kramer, and Vic Perlo all signed on as well. Pretty soon the Wallace campaign resembled nothing so much as a Ware Group reunion. Wallace wasn't a Communist, but he was practically the only one in the inner circle of the Progressive Party who wasn't.

In July, McCarran checked out of the Mayo Clinic in Rochester, Minnesota, where he had had his prostate removed, and took a train to Reno — skipping the Democratic National Convention in Philadelphia, the first that he had missed in twenty years. "I want to soak up a little good Nevada sunshine," he said, "before I start spending any time in smoke-filled rooms."[63]

McCarran didn't miss much. In June the Republicans had gathered in Philadelphia, where the streets were hung with bright red, white, and blue bunting and the GOP held its most joyous convention in decades, nominating New York's Thomas Dewey and California's Earl Warren to lead their ticket. Both were liberal Republicans, governors of huge states, supremely able and confident men who had every reason to assume that they would be elected just because neither one was Harry Truman.

The next month the Democrats came to Philadelphia, where the bunting now hung faded and tattered by summer storms. The heat was stifling, and delegates broke out in hives at the thought of renominating Harry Truman. "You have," Harold Ickes lectured the accidental president, "the choice of retiring voluntarily and with dignity or of being driven out of office by a disillusioned and indignant citizenry."[64] Days before the convention opened, ADA liberals were still trying to dump Truman and replace him with General Dwight Eisenhower, whose party preference wasn't known, or Supreme Court justice William O. Douglas — or anyone else, for that matter. "It looks like Truman is going to get the gate and God knows who may be nominated," McCarran told Pete Petersen. McCarran himself favored Secretary of State George Marshall. "Marshall is the biggest man in the outfit to my way of thinking," McCarran continued. "There isn't a chance for Eisenhower to take it and I don't know that he would run so awfully high if he did. Marshall has the best experience and is the soundest individual of the outfit."[65]

The convention even tried to repudiate the strong civil rights stand Truman had committed himself to earlier in the year — the first time a president had ever addressed the subject. The platform committee endorsed a mild civil rights program instead.

On the night of July 14 the liberals revolted. Hubert Humphrey, the young mayor of Minneapolis and a Senate candidate, told the convention that some were worried that the party was moving too fast. "I say we are a hundred and seventy-two years late," he said. ". . . The time has arrived for the Democratic Party to get out of the shadow of states' rights and walk forthrightly into the bright sunshine of human rights."[66] Paul Douglas grabbed the Illinois standard and led a thrilling procession through the hall, and the convention adopted the most explicit civil rights platform in American history.

Southern delegates unfurled a Confederate flag and stormed out, later nominating South Carolina governor Strom Thurmond as the Dixiecrat candidate for president. Neither the Progressives nor the Dixiecrats had any chance of winning, but they could prevent the Democrats from doing so. "Harry Truman has never been elected president of the United States," Thurmond said, "and he never will be."[67]

Into the cavernous, sweltering gloom of Philadelphia's Convention Hall, at the ridiculous hour of 2 A.M., Harry Truman took the stage to give one of the most important speeches of his life. A woman presented the president with a Liberty Bell made out of flowers, concealing a cage of pigeons, which she released into the airless hall: The birds careened crazily about, crashing here, diving there, speckling the audience with their droppings — avatars for the chaos of the Democrats.

Truman then announced that he would call the Eightieth Congress back into a special session in two weeks, a challenge to the Republicans to live up to their convention promises. "I will win this election," Truman promised, "and make these Republicans like it."[68]

J. Edgar Hoover had other ideas.

On July 20 government agents arrested General Secretary Eugene Dennis and another eleven top leaders of the Communist Party, charging them under the Smith Act with conspiring to advocate the violent overthrow of the government. The next day the conservative *New York World Telegram* published a sensational story about a Communist espionage network run by a woman it called Mary. "Red Ring Bared by Its Blond Queen,"[69] read the headline. The spy queen was really Elizabeth

Bentley. The two events, like islands on the rim of submerged volcano, were linked below the surface.

When Bentley defected to the FBI in November 1945, she offered the bureau nothing but her word to prove her story. While the FBI soon found corroboration for her account, hundreds of agents were unable to unearth any evidence that could be used in court in more than a year of investigation. In early 1947 the bureau finally began questioning suspects; some admitted knowing Bentley, but none confessed. In March a federal grand jury in New York opened secret hearings on the espionage allegations. Bentley told her story (Chambers had been so tight lipped with FBI interviewers that he wasn't even called as a witness). Scores of other witnesses (including Alger Hiss, Harry White, Nathan Gregory Silvermaster, Victor Perlo, and John Abt) were subpoenaed, all of whom either denied the allegations or refused to answer questions under the Fifth Amendment. The grand jury wasn't having any better luck than the FBI, an assistant attorney general told Stephen Spingarn. "He said that candidly he did not think that they had enough evidence to get indictments on the merits," Spingarn recorded, "although in the present climate of relations between Russia and ourselves, he felt sure that indictments could be obtained if Justice wanted to dramatize and color the case sufficiently, but that he did not feel they ought to do that."[70]

The grand jury struggled on for a year, then suddenly turned its attention to the Communist Party itself. The FBI had compiled a massive brief arguing that the party was an ipso facto conspiracy and subject to indictment under the Smith Act. If the grand jury couldn't indict the secret Communists of the Silvermaster and Perlo Groups for espionage, it could at least true-bill the open party for its seditious behavior. At the same time, Bentley went to Frederick Woltman, a columnist for the *World Telegram* whose wife she knew from Vassar. She had an interesting story to tell him.

On July 20 the grand jury indicted a dozen of the Communist Party's leaders.* The next day the *World Telegram* published Bentley's story.

On July 23 the Progressives met in Philadelphia for their convention. To the self-proclaimed peace party, the world seemed more and more poised for war. The month before, the Soviets had cut off road and rail access to Berlin; the United States responded by organizing a massive airlift. And

---

*The American Communist leader most involved in espionage had been the deposed Earl Browder, who was not indicted.

just two days earlier the Justice Department arrested a dozen leaders of the Communist Party under the Smith Act. A Gallup poll found that 51 percent of those surveyed believed that Communists controlled the new party. The convention did nothing to change that opinion. "Three years after the end of the Second World War," the party's platform stated, "the drums are beating for a third. Civil liberties are being destroyed. Millions cry out for relief from unbearably high prices. The American way of life is in danger. The root cause of this crisis is Big Business control of our economy and government."[71]

The ADA's Jim Loeb appeared and appealed to the delegates to demonstrate their independence from the Communists by more or less adopting the Democratic platform. "Your movement is a dangerous adventure undertaken by cynical men," he said.[72] Even new party members had trouble raising the issue of Communist influence with Wallace. One morning Williams College professor Frederick L. Schuman handed Wallace a statement that he wanted to insert into the platform. Two lines made Wallace choke. "We condemn the totalitarianism of the Left no less than the totalitarianism of the Right," it read. "Both are denials of human dignity and freedom."[*][73]

The party, Wallace said, must not tolerate any form of Redbaiting.[†] The statement was retyped without the offensive sentences. "They will Redsmear us," Wallace's running mate Glen Taylor added, "no matter what we say or do."[74]

On the convention floor three delegates from Vermont made a last-ditch attempt to declare the party's independence by introducing a resolution ("it is not our intention to give blanket endorsement to the foreign policy of any nation"[75]). The proposal was soundly defeated. "The Communists," wrote I. F. Stone, "are doing a major part of the work of

---

[*]In Reno the Progressive Party opened an office, the International Union of Mine, Mill and Smelter Workers launched a petition drive, and the party got on the ballot. George Springmeyer, a liberal Republican and longtime McCarran antagonist, became state chairman. He didn't last long. At the state convention in June, Springmeyer wanted the party to go on record opposing Communism, Nazism, and any other totalitarian philosophy. He was shouted down. "Unless you declare yourself opposed to Communism you will get only a few hundred votes in this state," he said.

Springmeyer walked out. "Our whole history," Yale law professor Thomas Emerson said, "was that of people leaving." (Curtis D. MacDougall, *Gideon's Army*. New York: Marzani and Munsell, 1965; pp. 459 and 628.)

[†]In 1951 Wallace had a different view: "I didn't actually realize how strong the Communists were in the Progressive Party. I think now they were out to knife me." (MacDougall, *Gideon's*, p. 280.)

the Wallace movement, from ringing doorbells to framing platforms. Okay if you want it that way, so they 'dominate' the party. So what?"[76]

> Huge thunderheads threatening rain scudded across the hot Washington sky as late July slid into August . . .

Monday, July 26. The special session of Congress opened, lasted twelve days, and accomplished nothing. At the time it looked like a brilliant and bold move on Truman's part. From a distance it seems an act of hubris that begat a national disaster. Back in April, Truman had grown alarmed that HUAC was too reckless in attacking federal employees and issued an executive order forbidding government departments from providing confidential records to congressional committees without the president's approval. The blunt-spoken president could not imagine what a vengeful FBI director seeking to preserve his reputation and destroy that of his nominal boss might do.

Friday, July 30. Michigan senator Homer Ferguson called the Committee on Expenditures in the Executive Departments into session. A dumpy woman in hat and black dress took the witness chair as flash-bulbs popped and klieg lights blazed.* Elizabeth Bentley swore an oath, mopped her brow, and then told the committee an incredible tale: She had graduated from Vassar and gone on to study at Columbia, where she joined the Communist Party in 1935 and three years later slipped into the party underground. She fell in love with a Russian spy named Jacob Golos, who put her to work as his courier, sending her to Washington every couple of weeks. There she met with a group of secret Communists and sympathizers and returned to New York with a knitting bag stuffed with microfilm rolls full of classified government documents. Bentley recited an astounding list of departments catacombed with Communists: War, State, Treasury, the OSS, even the White House. But she named only two of her contacts: Mary Price, who had been columnist Walter Lippmann's secretary and was now head of the Progressive Party in North Carolina, and William Remington, who had worked for the War Production Board before moving to the Commerce Department. Remington, she said, gave her Communist party dues and aircraft pro-

---

*Attorney General Tom Clark later complained that Homer Ferguson received more cooperation from the FBI than the Justice Department did. "He was getting reports before I got them," Clark said. (Roger Morris, *Richard Milhous Nixon*. New York: Henry Holt, 1990; p. 384.)

duction figures. "Woman Links Spies to U.S. War Offices and White House," ran the one-column headline in the *New York Times* the next day.[77]

Saturday, July 31. Bentley appeared before the House Un-American Activities Committee and revealed more of her story. She mentioned two separate Communist cells operating in Washington (the Perlo Group and the Silvermaster Group, she called them) and named a score of people involved with both. She named White House aide Lauchlin Currie and the Treasury's Harry White as sources who furnished information to her contacts, although she admitted she had never met either one. Both men issued denials. "This is the most fantastic thing I ever heard of,"[78] White said.*

Monday, August 2. Louis F. Budenz, a longtime Communist and former managing editor of the *Daily Worker* who broke with the party in 1945, testified before Ferguson's Senate committee. Budenz recalled that Jacob Golos had introduced him to Bentley in 1943; that Communist leader Gene Dennis, who had recently been arrested, was head of a Washington spy ring; and that the party had secreted thousands of members in government jobs. "Some Communist Party members are confused and think they may be loyal to both," Budenz said. "But I repeat the Communist Party is the real fifth column. It is an actual enemy."[79]

Tuesday, August 3. Whittaker Chambers testified before HUAC, talking so quietly that he had to be told to speak up. The *Time* magazine editor recalled the Ware Group of secret Communists in Washington during the 1930s — and how he had warned the government about this nine years earlier. He named Alger Hiss, his brother Donald, Nat Witt, Lee Pressman, John Abt, Vic Perlo, and Charles Kramer, among others, as members. "The purpose of this group at that time was not primarily espionage," Chambers said. "Its original purpose was the Communist infiltration of the American government. But espionage was certainly one of its eventual objectives. Let no one be surprised at this statement. Disloyalty is a matter of principle with every member of the Communist Party. The Communist Party exists for the specific purpose of overthrowing the government."

John Abt pointed out that the FBI had heard the same "cloak and dagger tales" three years earlier and that the New York grand jury had spent more than a year on the matter — and neither investigation had resulted in any charges. "The Thomas Committee," he said, "has once again disinterred an

---

*Harry White testified on August 13, vehemently denying the allegations, and three days later died of a heart attack. "A victim of the Un-American Thomas Committee," Henry Wallace said. (Curtis D. MacDougall, *Gideon's Army*. New York: Marzani and Munsell, 1965; p. 687.)

old and particularly malodorous red herring which it is endeavoring to warm up and serve as a substitute for price control, public housing and civil rights legislation demanded by the American people."[80]

Wednesday, August 4. Nathan Gregory Silvermaster appeared before HUAC, complaining that he had been hounded from government for his progressive politics. When asked if he was a Communist, he took the Fifth Amendment. "The stale and lurid mouthings of a Republican exhibitionist," Lee Pressman called Chambers's testimony. ". . . I am sure that the American people will see through this shameful circus now going on in Washington."[81]

Thursday, August 5. Alger Hiss, dignified and dapper, testified. "I am not and never have been a member of the Communist Party," he said. "I do not and never have adhered to the tenets of the Communist Party. I am not and never have been a member of any Communist front organization. I have never followed the Communist Party line directly or indirectly. To the best of my knowledge none of my friends is a Communist."[82]

At a White House news conference that morning a reporter asked Truman if he thought that the hearings were a red herring to distract the country from the failure of the special session. Truman often wrote venomous letters to people he was mad at but never sent them; other times he vented to his wife Bess. ("Pearson and Winchell are lying again," he told her once. "Some day I'll have to shoot 'em both."[83]) The day before, Truman's trusted aide Clark Clifford told him that the hearings had not disclosed any new information. "The public hearings now under way are serving no useful purpose," Clifford wrote. "On the contrary, they are doing irreparable harm to certain people, seriously impairing the morals of federal employees and undermining public confidence in the government."[84]

"They are simply a red herring," Truman told his news conference. "They are using this as a red herring, as an excuse to keep from doing what they ought to do."[85]

And then came the downpour . . .

In a closed session later that day the members of the House Un-American Activities Committee were dazed. "We've been had," South Dakota's Karl Mundt whined. "We're ruined."[86]

The committee's investigation seemed to have run aground. The spectacular charges had been met with emphatic denials, especially in the case of Chambers and Hiss. Someone was obviously lying — but *who*? One committee member suggested turning over the transcripts to the Justice Department to decide who had committed perjury. "Let's wash our hands of the whole mess,"[87] said Louisiana's Edward Hébert.

Richard Nixon disagreed. Chambers, Nixon thought, was the shabbiest-looking man he had ever seen. But that didn't mean that he wasn't telling the truth — or at least more of the truth than Hiss. Nixon, thirty-five, had taken an instant dislike to Hiss, forty-three, who seemed to be everything that the California congressman wasn't: an urbane exemplar of the Eastern Establishment. After Harvard Law School Hiss found every door open: the clerkship with Supreme Court justice Oliver Wendell Holmes, the fast-rising job at the State Department, the presidency of the Carnegie Endowment. After Duke Law School Nixon found that life was what it had always been for him: a struggle. He could barely talk his way into the reception rooms of New York law firms, none of which was eager to hire the alumnus of Whittier College and a southern law school. Nixon went home to California.

In 1946 Nixon won a bruising campaign against liberal representative Jerry Voorhis ("Voorhis is a Communist,"[88] anonymous phone callers repeated days before the election) and was elected to the House. In Congress Nixon sought a seat on the House Un-American Activities Committee and devoted his maiden speech to introducing a contempt citation against Gerhart Eisler, a German Comintern agent with immigration problems who had been summoned before HUAC and proved less than cooperative. In 1948 Nixon joined with his HUAC colleague Karl Mundt to sponsor a bill requiring the Communist Party and front groups to register with the government. The freshman congressman spent a lot of his early days in Washington going for long walks with Father John Cronin, a young priest who had been active in the Catholic trade union movement and who shared what he learned about Communist labor organizing with the FBI. The bureau, in turn, shared its files with Cronin. Long before he turned up in HUAC's committee room, Alger Hiss was no stranger to Richard Nixon.

Nixon was appointed head of a HUAC subcommittee to find out who was lying. Twenty-hour days were given over to the task. Nixon studied the hearing transcripts like a Talmudic scholar; he began driving out to Chambers's farm in Westminster on Maryland's Eastern Shore, asking for more information, more recollections, more details. He collected leaks from the FBI by the bucket.

Nixon arranged for Chambers and Hiss to secretly meet, and Hiss

admitted that Chambers might have been a man whom he knew in the
1930s: a reporter named George Crosley, a guest in his house, a deadbeat
to whom he gave a car and from whom he received a rug. Hiss dared
Chambers to repeat his allegations outside a congressional hearing so that
he could sue him for slander. The committee restaged the confrontation
in a hearing room overflowing with reporters.

Two days later, on August 27, Whittaker Chambers went on *Meet the
Press.* "Are you willing," asked a reporter, "to say now that Alger Hiss is or
ever was a Communist?"

"Alger Hiss," Chambers replied, "was a Communist and may be now."[89]
A month later Hiss filed suit for slander.

Whittaker Chambers had been a reluctant witness. The Justice Department
originally declined to present him to the New York grand jury because he
had been so reticent in his interviews with the FBI. When HUAC hauled
Chambers into the committee room, he was only slightly more forthcoming, denying that he or others in the Communist underground were
involved in espionage. Then Hiss sued Chambers, and Chambers reached
into a dumbwaiter shaft where a decade before he had secreted evidence
of his treason: typewritten copies of State Department documents, four
pages of notes written by Hiss, eight pages written by Harry White, and
several rolls of microfilm, which contained more government documents.
In December the New York grand jury indicted Hiss on two counts of perjury: lying about having known Chambers and denying that he had given
him any documents.

Both men had lied. Then Chambers was forced into telling the truth.
Hiss never would. "That goddamned Hiss!" Nixon raged at one point.
"He's a lying son of a bitch."[90]

Richard Nixon knew a liar when he saw one.

The ringing phone woke Steve Spingarn in bed at the Beverly Wilshire
Hotel. Earlier in the year he had written three articles for the *Saturday
Evening Post* about his spy-catching work with army counterintelligence
during the war. Then came book offers from publishers and invitations to
go on a lecture tour. Now he was in Hollywood on his vacation trying to
pitch a movie deal. He hadn't yet seen any of the movie people with
whom he had appointments when the ringing interrupted his dreams.

Spingarn pawed at the phone. It was his boss: Treasury general counsel
Tom Lynch. In January the Treasury loaned Spingarn to the White House

to write Truman's civil rights message. Spingarn then found himself assigned as an assistant to White House aide Charles Murphy. "He was bubbling over and bursting with energy," Murphy remembered. "He is a prodigious worker and he is a very able fellow. He's kind of an overpowering young man."[91]

The president, Lynch told Spingarn, wants you to get back to the White House. Truman told Spingarn that he was putting him in charge of coordinating internal security policy. That was, Spingarn thought, like trying to coordinate a barrel of snakes.

Truman had called Congress back in session to embarrass the Republicans, but the Republicans wound up embarrassing the president. Since William Wirt's fantastic charges in 1934 that the New Deal was a gigantic Communist plot, conservatives had been hinting and sometimes saying much the same thing. In the fall of 1945 Elizabeth Bentley walked into the FBI and offered confirmation that Communists indeed were in the government. For the next three years, the FBI leaked the disclosures from Bentley and Chambers to right-wing politicians and reporters, who dribbled enough of the details to make the public realm slippery with unease and distrust. And then in August the two witnesses testified before Congress: Years of suspicion, rumor, and innuendo burst over Washington in a frightening cloudburst, a summer storm of spectacular fury. "New Deal Coverup Told,"[92] blared the *Chicago Tribune* the day after Chambers testified.

Now Truman wanted Spingarn to clean things up. The president, someone later told Spingarn, had never seen such a big man look so scared. For much of the last two years Spingarn had been beating his head against the granite wall of the FBI, trying to grapple with the problem of Communists in government — both as a member of the presidential commission designing a loyalty program and as Treasury's point man trying to figure out how far the party had penetrated the department. Now the president was telling him to take charge of the whole mess. "What in the hell am I supposed to do?"[93] Spingarn wondered.

The first thing Spingarn did was to visit Attorney General Tom Clark to find out if the Ferguson and HUAC hearings had discovered anything the Justice Department didn't know. Clark was friendly but vague. "I didn't get anywhere," Spingarn recalled. "He wasn't about to tell me any more than I already knew."[94]

It was like trying to drag information out of Hoover and the FBI all over again. In late 1946, more than a year after Bentley's defection, the Treasury assigned Spingarn to investigate a list of eleven people named by

Bentley who had worked in the department, six of whom were still employed. The most serious allegation was that Victor Perlo was head of a Communist cell. Perlo had joined the New Deal in 1933, working for the NRA and moving through different agencies until he landed at the Treasury's division of monetary research in December 1945 — a month *after* Bentley had given his name to the FBI. The Treasury's background check didn't find anything amiss, and it wasn't until September 1946 that the FBI told the department that two unnamed sources had implicated Perlo as a Communist. Harold Glasser was told to ask for Perlo's resignation — two weeks later the Justice Department told Treasury that Glasser, *too,* was a suspected Communist. The general counsel's office overruled the decision, insisting on an internal investigation before forcing a man out of his job. "What would you do if you were a fair-minded man," Spingarn said, "and a man who . . . has worked ten years in your department, and looks you in the eye and under oath states there's not a word of truth in that. And all you know is that an anonymous report from an anonymous informant whom you have never seen says he is a Communist. Now you're on a loyalty board, what do you do?"[95]

What Spingarn did was to ask the FBI for all its material on the suspects. He got nothing. He went to Attorney General Tom Clark. Still, all Spingarn could get was FBI summaries, no raw investigative materials. He wanted to interview Bentley and Chambers himself, but was rebuffed. In March 1947 Perlo resigned, followed by Glasser and most of the other suspects.

By the time Bentley and Chambers testified publicly only two of those implicated by them still worked for the government: Commerce's William Remington and Treasury's Solomon Adler. Remington was soon indicted for perjury and eventually convicted and jailed — where he was killed by another prisoner. Adler clung to his job for two more years until he was pressured into resigning; he later moved to Communist China.

Now Spingarn wanted the president to address the issue head-on, to make a powerful speech setting out the facts, and reassuring the American people that the government was protecting national security. For weeks Truman's advisers rejected the idea. They didn't want to draw more attention to the Communist issue. But instead of burning itself out, the Communist problem just seemed to burn brighter with each passing week. When, for example, the White House (following Truman's executive order) refused to give Ferguson's committee Remington's confidential records, the senator called for the president's impeachment. Truman, Ferguson said, had lowered on "an iron curtain between Congress and the public business."[96] "It is getting worse, not better," Truman's aide George Elsey scratched out on a piece of paper in late August. ". . . The administration's most vulnerable point is Communism. . . . Our hopes that this issue will die are ill-founded. There is paydirt here and the Republicans have no intention of being diverted by appeals from anguished liberals who see the Bill of Rights transgressed. . . . Bentley and Chambers are credible. The confused testimony of Hiss has shaken the faith of many liberals."[97]

Finally, the White House relented. Clark Clifford asked Spingarn to write a rebuttal to the Republican charges. Spingarn plunged into writing with his usual zeal. "I believe it will be the kind of fighting speech," Spingarn told Clifford, "that will have more impact on the air than in print."[98]

Police cleared the way so that the half a dozen cars could drive through the crowd waiting for Henry Wallace and reach the town square in Burlington, North Carolina. The crowd soon surged back on the Progressive Party motorcade. They were not Wallace supporters. People climbed onto the hoods, kicked the doors, banged their fists upon the windows. "Go back to Russia," they shouted. Wallace climbed out of his car. An egg splattered on the person next to him. Two tomatoes hit Wallace in the face, the red juice running down his white shirt. Wallace tried to speak. The crowd howled and cursed. More produce flew. "Am I in America?"[99] yelled the stunned former vice president.

On August 29 Wallace took his campaign to the South, speaking in seven states in six days, visiting twenty-eight cities, and making a dozen radio broadcasts. He was never more noble or courageous. Not long after Henry Wallace fired Pat Jackson from the Agriculture Adjustment Administration for being too radical, Jackson led a group of black sharecroppers to the Ag building to protest the department for not doing anything for them. Wallace refused to meet the group. More than a dozen years later, no candidate was more fearless than Wallace in attacking segregation. "Because they pay taxes," Wallace said in Hickory, North Carolina, "Negroes should be allowed to vote. They should have as free use of their tax money, in building schools and hospitals, as whites."[100]

Wallace was met by a hailstorm of rotten eggs. Crowds were small and often unfriendly, sometimes dangerous. Wallace refused to stay in segregated hotels, which meant staying with supporters, often black, in their homes. He avoided whites-only restaurants and dined in his car or in a park. Progressive Party members and campaign workers were harassed, beaten, occasionally abducted from their homes, and even murdered. In

Birmingham Glen Taylor, the Progressive vice presidential candidate who was also a U.S. senator, was arrested for trying to enter a speaking hall through the colored entrance, roughed up, and thrown into the drunk tank. "This," Wallace wired Taylor, "dramatizes the hypocrisy of spending billions for arms in the name of defending freedom abroad while freedom is trampled on here at home."[101]

After a week in the South, where he had little chance of getting any votes, Wallace came back to New York, where about half of the Progressive Party's members lived. On September 10 he spoke to forty-eight thousand people in Yankee Stadium. "To me," he said, "fascism is no longer a second-hand experience — a motion picture, a photograph, or the deeply-moving words of a great writer. . . . No, fascism has become an ugly reality — a reality which I have tasted."[102]

On September 17 Truman left Union Station on the sixteen-car presidential special, the *Ferdinand Magellan*. "Mow 'em down, Harry," Vice President Alben Barkley told Truman. "I'm going to give 'em hell," the president replied.[103]

Crisscrossing the country for two weeks, Truman campaigned like crazy, giving speeches from first light until well after dark and even wandering out onto the rear platform in his pajamas in the middle of the night to see people. Dewey wouldn't wave to supporters from a window during the day. He didn't need to. Rarely had a presidential election seemed so foreordained. Reporters on the president's train hadn't taken such a gloomy trip since the *Ferdinand Magellan* carried Roosevelt's casket back to Washington from Warm Springs. In Washington the Democratic National Committee didn't bother to rent a ballroom for a victory celebration. *Newsweek* surveyed fifty leading political reporters, who responded fifty to zero that Dewey would defeat Truman. The *Chicago Tribune* would go to press with the same headline on election night.

The only person who seemed to think Truman had a chance was Truman. When Clark Clifford reluctantly showed the president the *Newsweek* story, Truman was unfazed. "I know every one of those fifty fellows," he said, "and not one of them has enough sense to pound sand into a rathole."[104]

Dewey left Albany on September 19 on a train modestly called the *Victory Special*. He told crowds across the country he had a cheaper way of dealing with Communists than Truman's loyalty program: Elect a Republican administration that wouldn't put them there in the first place. Dewey was anything but a firebreather. "In this country we'll have no thought police," he said in Los Angeles. "We will not jail anybody for what he thinks or believes. So long as we keep the Communists among us out in the open, in the light of day, the United States of America has nothing to fear."[105]

Dewey's advance team timed the candidate's steps with a stopwatch, brought along a throat specialist to spray his vocal cords each morning, and engaged a masseuse to rub his muscles. His handlers gave reporters copies of his speeches twenty-four hours in advance, kept the coffee hot, the sandwiches plenty, made hotel reservations for the press corps, and sent out their laundry. On the Truman campaign reporters bunked on the train, washed their clothes in sinks, and considered themselves lucky if the train didn't leave without them. When Truman called the Republicans friendly to Communists, Dewey wanted to slash back. But he first polled his advisers, then had his aides poll the reporters on the train, and finally had his campaign manager, Herbert Brownell, survey the entire GOP National Committee. By the time Dewey got around to making the speech, his temper had cooled. "He comes out," observed reporter Richard Rovere, "like a man who has been mounted on casters and given a tremendous shove from behind."[106]

The whole campaign was an exercise in coasting. The polls were clear: Dewey was the next president. Dewey left the rough stuff to others. "The FBI helped Dewey during the campaign itself by giving him everything we had that could hurt Truman, though there wasn't much,"[107] recalled FBI official William C. Sullivan. Nixon hit the campaign trail in support of the ticket in California, praising the FBI and accusing Truman of following a line laid down by the *Daily Worker*. "The record of the administration," Nixon told John Foster Dulles, "is completely vulnerable and should be attacked without question during the campaign."[108]

The Republican Congress passed a generous appropriation for a grand inaugural celebration. The editors of *Who's Who* sent Dewey an advance copy of the 1949 edition, listing his address as 1600 Pennsylvania Avenue.

The train was forty minutes late. A crowd estimated at one hundred thousand people was waiting for Truman in Oklahoma City on the afternoon of September 28 when the *Ferdinand Magellan* finally crawled into the station. The presidential caboose was an armor-plated bunker on wheels, weighing 142 tons, as heavy as a locomotive, with three-inch bulletproof glass. Truman bolted the Pullman, wearing glasses almost as thick as its windows, and for once didn't linger to shake hands or trash the Republicans. He jumped into a car and sped off.

Truman had already given a dozen speeches since his morning started at half past six. Now it was close to three and he had ten minutes to get across Oklahoma City to the state fairgrounds where twenty thousand people and a radio hookup were waiting. Truman's threadbare campaign had just managed to scrape up a contribution from a New York businessman to reserve the airtime, but now the president was close to missing his slot.

It was supposed to be Truman's first nationally broadcast speech of the campaign. For two weeks Steve Spingarn had been laboring to make the administration's major statement on the Bentley-Chambers disclosures and the spreading furor over domestic Communism. Spingarn sent half a dozen versions of the speech from the White House to the communications car on the train, where Clark Clifford hacked away at drafts three times longer than they were supposed to be. Four days earlier, in the Hollywood Bowl, Dewey had finally given a speech that made it sound like the candidate had some blood in his veins. "Millions upon millions of people," Dewey said, "have been delivered into Soviet slavery while our administration has tried appeasement one day and bluster the next."[109]

Careening across Oklahoma City, the president's motorcade raced onto the fairgrounds one minute before airtime. Truman lunged toward the microphone. "I am happy to be in Oklahoma City today," the president said. It was the last thing he was happy about for the rest of the speech. Truman was blunt, angry, and accusatory, his words like thrown fists. "I charge that the Republicans have impeded and made more difficult our efforts to cope with Communism. . . . I charge that they have hindered the efforts of the FBI, which has been doing wonderful work. . . . I charge that the Republicans have attempted to usurp the constitutional functions of federal grand juries and courts. I charge that they have not produced any significant information about Communist espionage which the FBI did not already have. . . . I charge them with having recklessly cast a cloud of suspicion over the most loyal civil service in the world. I charge them with having trampled on the individual freedoms which distinguish American ideals from totalitarian doctrine. . . ."

Truman attacked the House Un-American Activities Committee by name ("By its irresponsible publicity, this committee already has done damage to the work of the FBI. . . . With reckless disregard for the Bill of Rights, this committee has injured the reputations of innocent men by spreading wild and false accusations."); he defended his loyalty program ("I have given the FBI complete charge of this part of the program . . . their check showed that the loyalty of 99.7 percent of all federal workers was not even questionable."); he bragged that the Justice Department was deporting subversive aliens and getting ready to put the leaders of the Communist Party on trial ("We have prosecuted and we shall prosecute subversive activities wherever we find them. But we must have real evidence. We cannot use the speeches of Republican politicians."); and he defended civil liberties ("I am determined that Communists shall not work for the government. I am equally determined that loyal employees against whom unfounded charges are made shall not suffer injustice.").[110]

Truman's speech was accurate as far as it went: Communists were no longer a real problem in government. Exactly *two* likely party members were left, and they were about to suffer for their pasts. But Truman could have, should have, gone much further. The president had a chance to tell the nation exactly what the government knew what about Communist espionage — and what it didn't know but only suspected. The day before Alger Hiss had sued Chambers for fifty thousand dollars for slander. "Whichever one of you is lying," HUAC member Edward Hébert had said, "is the greatest actor that America has ever produced."[111]

The American people were equally in the dark. HUAC was obviously partisan and almost thuggish in demeanor. Truman's curt dismissal of the whole proceeding was neither reassuring nor convincing. In some respects both sides were right: The White House, especially under Roosevelt, had been lax — although so had the FBI, which was now leaking like a sieve to discredit the Democrats while working to help elect Dewey. The Republicans were opportunistic and overzealous. A miasma of mistrust hung over Washington, a bitter fog that would only grow thicker and more stifling with the passing years. The espionage probe had already fizzled out, but the reckoning was just beginning.

"The Republican Party is the unwitting ally of the Communists in this country . . . ," Truman said. "I have been fighting Communism not merely where it is a contemptible minority in a land of freedom, but wherever it is a marching and menacing power in the world."[112]

Truman flubbed his chance. His speech was as partisan as anything any member of HUAC would say. It was, as Spingarn promised, a tough speech, but it was not the one Truman needed to give.

Back at the station, Truman's campaign was flat broke. "We found that we did not have enough money to get the train out of the station,"[113] Truman's daughter Margaret recalled. Oklahoma governor Roy Turner staged a quick fund-raising party on the train, and the *Ferdinand Magellan* pulled away.

The campaign was back on track. The country wasn't.

At fourteen minutes after ten at night on November 2, 1948, Independence, Missouri, exploded in pandemonium, an eruption of car horns and whistles and the suddenly reassuring whine of the town's air raid siren signaling that contrary to all expectations everything was right with the world. Dewey had just conceded. Truman had done the impossible: The president had been reelected with more than 24 million votes, or almost 50 percent, Dewey managing only 22 million votes, or 45 percent. Southern racist Strom Thurmond won more than a million votes (less than 2 percent), trailed by Henry Wallace, who inched past the million mark but couldn't pick up a single electoral vote — a defeat so resounding that it destroyed what was left of the postwar Popular Front. John Abt forked over $250 to a friend whom he had bet that Wallace would win ten million votes. From now on, the hard left of America huddled under the banner of an Unpopular Front.

And the Democrats were back in charge of Congress. In the front row on the left side of the Senate chamber would be McCarran, eighth in seniority among the Democrats, once again the chairman of the Judiciary Committee. But the Senate seating chart barely hinted at the power McCarran could command. No other Democrat in Congress was as heedless of the party leadership, as single-minded in his vision, or as determined in his obsessions. "The Fair Deal didn't win the 1948 election," McCarran said. "The people just didn't like Dewey and his mustache."[114]

The month before the election McCarran gave a campaign speech over the radio. "If we get enough Communists in the United States," McCarran said, "and enough poor, deluded fools of fellow-travelers who will give aid and comfort to the Communists, and enough people who are so blinded by prejudice, or hatred, or misery, that they can't see the Communist booby-trap, this will *be* a Communist country. Please God that day never comes."[115]

The fall days were growing shorter and darker. McCarran's words were like the skittering of fallen leaves before a storm.

CHAPTER 16

A One-Man Un-American Activities Committee

No committee chairman has wielded power more strictly
or effectively than Senator Pat McCarran.[1]
> — Stephen K. Bailey and Howard D. Samuel,
> *Congress at Work*

He has tried to take over foreign relations, the judiciary,
and a large field of domestic policy.[2]
> — Senate majority leader Scott Lucas

The McCarran Committee became more of an inquisition than an investigation.[3]

> — Harry Truman

On January 1, 1949, a massive cold front crawled across the Sierra Nevada
from the West Coast and settled over a great swath of the mountain and
plains states in the middle of the country. From Nevada to Kansas, from
North Dakota to New Mexico, the barometer dropped like a rock and
snow fell without stopping. Three feet of snow soon covered much of the
Nevada range, blotting out roads, clogging mountain passes, stopping
trains, and isolating already distant towns from the rest of the world. Over
the next three weeks two more blizzards dumped even more snow.
Temperatures plunged to thirty degrees below zero and winds gusted up
to seventy-five miles an hour, heaping snowdrifts higher than homes.

Out on the winter range of northeast Nevada snow fell so thick that
sheep barely moved. Only their heads stuck out of the powder. After days
the animals grew so hungry that they tried to eat each other's wool. Their
eyes clouded over with ice cataracts; they bled from the mouth. Sheep
died on the hoof and didn't fall over. Sheepherders wept. "The worst I've
ever seen,"[4] remembered Louis Beltran, sixty-one years old, a Basque
sheepman who'd spent forty years on the Nevada range.

The sheepmen of Ely organized a truck convoy behind snowplows to
bring feed to their flocks. The plows got stuck. The sheepmen spent the
night in their trucks running heaters until first light. Then they tried to
cut straight across the range. At the end of the day they saw tracks: their

own. They had plowed in a circle. Clear roads drifted up almost as soon as the tractors passed. Ranchers lost trucks under snow and didn't see them again for days. The cold clotted up diesel lines like cornstarch.

Then, on January 24, the big planes came. Beltran had never been in the air before. The world looked so different from above; at first he was lost in the sky. He could hardly believe how fast they covered ground flying. Almost forty years earlier he had arrived in New York from Spain and boarded a train going west, his destination written on a piece of paper and pinned to his beret; he spent three days crossing the continent, not knowing a word of English, eating nothing but some sheep cheese he had with him. Six years later he had his own business and sixteen hundred acres of land in Nevada. In the brutal winter of 1932 it snowed for forty-four hours without stopping, and when it did Beltran used a horse sleigh to drag a thousand pounds of hay to a remote sheep camp. He did this every day for forty days. Beltran lost twenty-nine hundred sheep that winter. So many died that he sent men out onto the range to skin the corpses, most of which were rotten by the time they got there, not yielding enough wool even to pay their wages.

Finally Beltran recognized a mountain range and told the pilot where to fly. The planes dropped to two hundred feet and opened their cargo doors. Crewmen tethered to bulkheads shoved bales out the back in a whirlwind of flying hay. Beltran was scared that the bales would hit and kill his sheep. Instead they hit rocks and exploded into dust. Others landed deep in drifts and disappeared, to be found only in the spring after the snow melted. Still, enough feed fell from the sky that Beltran lost just two hundred sheep and 150 cows that winter.

In Operation Haylift, U.S. Air Force C-82 flying boxcars flew thirty flights a day, dropping half a million tons of food on eastern Nevada. "Within an hour of the time that I got it," McCarran explained to a rancher who had requested help, ". . . I had the Air Corps on the phone and within three hours from that time I had sixteen planes standing by."[5]

The old sheepherder was now ordering the U.S. Air Force around. After two years of virtual inactivity McCarran was again picking up phones and making things happen. He was seventy-two years old, well past the age when most men retire. But he was also the eighth most senior Democrat in the Senate, that weird gerontocracy where longevity equaled potency. Now in his sixteenth year in the chamber, McCarran had one of the coveted mahogany desks in the front row, and when Congress met in January he was given plum committee assignments. For the second time, McCarran was appointed chairman of the Judiciary Committee; he also became head of the appropriations subcommittee that handled the budget for State and Justice and chairman of the Joint Foreign Aid Watchdog Committee, which oversaw the Marshall Plan. It was a powerful combination: Four out of ten bills had to go through Judiciary to get to the floor, as did every nomination for the Supreme Court, the federal bench, and the U.S. attorney's office. From the White House to the Senate, from Foggy Bottom to Embassy Row, McCarran was once again a very important personage.

And McCarran buttressed his committee prerogatives with uncommon parliamentary skill, great tenacity, and utter ruthlessness. Untroubled by the superego of party loyalty or public opinion, answerable only to the paltry population of Nevada, over the next four years McCarran would wield more power and influence in Congress than all but a handful of legislators ever exerted. His name would become a byword and a curse.

In Nevada the snow stopped falling in late February. Two days before the end of the month a new moon rose, a herald, the old sheepmen believed, of changing weather. The next day the skies cleared up, the wind stopped, and the sun came out. In Washington a long winter was just starting.

On January 5, Truman gave a triumphant State of the Union speech. He had made the greatest political comeback in American history, his party was in control of both houses, and his approval rating climbed to 57 percent. Truman spelled out a bold program for the Eighty-first Congress, the most vigorously liberal agenda in a decade: Repeal the Taft-Hartley Act, raise the minimum wage, extend social security, create a national health insurance plan, open the doors of America to more war refugees, enact civil rights legislation, increase public housing. "Every segment of our population and every individual," Truman finished, "has a right to expect from your government a fair deal."[6]

Truman had made it back to the White House by campaigning against the Republican Eightieth Congress. "The worst Congress,"[7] he called it. The Democratic Eighty-first Congress would turn out not to be much better.

When the Democrats came back to power, the elevator boys appointed by the Republicans were suddenly out of work. In a boardinghouse half a block from the Senate Office Building there was a lot of cheer. This was where a group of young men from Nevada lived while going to law school in Washington and supporting themselves by working patronage jobs. The Nevada Embassy, they called the house. McCarran's boys, they

called themselves. Eventually most of them returned to Nevada, where
they practiced law and became judges and then governors and even senators themselves — and never did they forget who brought them to
Washington, gave them jobs, and pestered them to keep up their grades.

Ralph Denton, twenty-four, was one. When Denton came to Washington
from Caliente, Nevada, he got a job running the elevator reserved for senators, which was better than operating the regular elevator but not as good
as the night elevator. A job in the regular elevator was stressful since the
operator was supposed to stop whatever he was doing when he heard the
buzzer ring three times, which meant that a senator was calling, and other
passengers would have to wait while the elevator picked up the member and
delivered him to his floor. And woe be to any operator who offended a senator, especially a testy one like McCarran who once rang three times only
to see the elevator pass him without stopping. "He just turned on his heel,"
recalled an aide, "and went back to his office and called the Sergeant-at-
Arms and the kid was fired on the spot."[8]

The best elevator jobs were the night ones, which most of the time
involved doing nothing. Once the Justice Department decided that it
didn't need a night elevator operator since almost no one was in the
building, whereupon McCarran, who chaired the appropriations subcommittee that gave Justice its budget, decided that the department didn't
need quite such a large appropriation. Justice decided to keep employing
night operators after all. "Any of the Senate office elevators will give you
a chance to study between five o'clock and midnight," McCarran
explained to his son when he got Sammy a job in the Capitol. "As a rule
everything is quiet after six."[9] Occasionally someone would make the mistake of complaining that McCarran's boys weren't working hard enough.
"He didn't come back here to go to work," McCarran would roar. "He
came back here to go to law school. Now leave him alone."[10] And when
Sammy McCarran was working in the Senate, McCarran was even more
solicitous than usual. "Tell him to come to the office for *anything* he wants
at *anytime*,"[11] McCarran instructed one of his staffers.

Denton soon learned which firebreathers on the Senate floor were
really nice guys and which nice guys on the floor were cold in person and
which aging lawmaker patted him on the ass when they were the only
two in the elevator (Massachusetts's David Walsh). When Denton went
into the army, McCarran continued to look after him, finding him a job
as a guard at Arlington Hall, across the river in Virginia, where the Army
Security Agency was trying to break Soviet codes. Denton found himself

summoned before a lieutenant general at the Pentagon. "Would you do me a favor?" the general asked. "Now, would you keep that gray-haired old son-of-a-bitch off my back?" Then when the Democrats regained control of Congress, McCarran had a better job for Denton: working in the Senate sergeant at arms's office, where one of his main tasks was to stock whiskey for members. Patronage jobs didn't get any sweeter. "Best job I ever had," Denton recalled.[12]

Many of McCarran's boys eventually grew to detest his politics and his disruptive influence on their nation and state, but they had seen a side of McCarran that few ever did; whatever anyone would say about the senator, they would retain a stirring sense of loyalty to him. "I'd see quite a bit of McCarran," Denton recalled, "and he always took the time to be pleasant, ask about Caliente, my mom and dad. Always, Is there anything I can do for you? Do you need a few dollars? He'd reach in his pocket. On a couple of occasions, he said, 'Well, here, take five dollars anyway. Go out and have dinner or something.'"[13]

And McCarran really would do almost *anything* for his boys. In 1939 he had all but called Felix Frankfurter a Communist to his face when the distinguished Harvard law professor came before the Judiciary Committee as a Supreme Court nominee. "He did his damndest by all sorts of devices and schemes to prevent my confirmation," Frankfurter recalled.

But six years later when a Nevada boy wanted to go to Harvard Law, McCarran didn't hesitate to call over to the Supreme Court and ask Frankfurter for his help.

"He wants to go to the Harvard Law School?" the incredulous justice responded. "Senator, you're going to save him from that horrendous fate, aren't you?"*[14]

More and more young men from Nevada began going to Harvard.

"Contacted my good friend Frankfurter," McCarran told Eva Adams, "and he is calling on his friends at law school to have boys admitted."[15]

Agnes Smedley — stocky, broad-shouldered, hair cut like a boy's — was on the stage when she spotted him in the crowd in the conference room at the Roosevelt Hotel in New York in January: the short, bald, quietly

---

*"One of the few remarks in my life I cherish," Frankfurter recalled. ". . . There are pleasurable experiences in my life and Senator McCarran asking me to help him get the son of 'an important constituent' into the Harvard Law School is certainly one of them." (Felix Frankfurter, *Reminisces Recorded in Talks with Dr. Harlan B. Phillips*. New York: Reynal, 1960; pp. 286–87.)

insistent man who was becoming such a pain. Alfred Kohlberg had just turned sixty-two, stood five foot five in heels, and had an impish smile that seemed to take over his whole face when he was amused by some foolishness. He was amused a lot lately. Especially when he slipped into a lion's den like the Action Conference on China Policy, where Smedley was speaking. The handkerchief king was his nickname. To Smedley, Kohlberg was a satanic elf. To an increasing number of militant anti-Communists, however, Kohlberg was something else: a prophet. Kohlberg had one great love in life (China) and one great hate (Communism), and in 1949 they were becoming more and more linked every day.

In 1915 Kohlberg had gone to the Panama Pacific Exposition in San Francisco and was smitten by the beautiful laces and silks that he saw in the Chinese exhibit, a country that so intrigued him that he borrowed on his life insurance to travel there. "China," he recalled, "with its good-natured laughing street coolies . . . immediately took itself to my heart."[16] Kohlberg started a textile-importing business: Kohlberg Inc., which operated out of a building on West Thirty-seventh Street in New York, its large plate-glass window painted black with an AK logo. Inside, display cases showed off fine Chinese needlework. The business (mostly transhipping Irish linen to China to be embroidered in sweatshops and then sold in the United States) made Kohlberg wealthy.

The most populous country in the world had been in turmoil for decades. After the Qing empire collapsed in 1911, China shattered into provinces controlled by rival warlords, the best known of whom was Chiang Kai-shek, whose Nationalist, or Kuomintang, government claimed to rule the country of four hundred million people, while Mao Tse-tung and his Communists waged a guerrilla war. In 1931 Japan invaded Manchuria; full-scale war broke out in 1937. The Nationalists and Communists made an uneasy alliance during the war but were at each other's throats as soon as it was over. "There are no Communists left in China," Chiang Kai-shek said in 1939.[17] A decade later there were almost no Nationalists left. In 1945 the Nationalists had more than twice as many troops as the Communists, controlled every major city and most of the vast country, and enjoyed the patronage of the world's greatest power: the United States. Less than four years later, in January 1949, the Communists rode into Peking (Beijing) in captured American tanks and trucks. The Nationalists continued to fight in the south, but Chiang's situation appeared more bleak with every passing day.

To Alfred Kohlberg this seemingly stunning reversal did not look like an accident. During the war he had become alarmed that the Nationalists were not being defeated so much by the Communists on the battlefield as by their supposed allies in the United States, especially an Asian affairs organization called the Institute of Pacific Relations. In 1944 Kohlberg tried to get IPR, whose magazine was edited by Owen Lattimore, to fire those whom he considered Communists. He failed, but the cause consumed him. Kohlberg dedicated himself to warning the public about what he saw as a disaster in the offing in China. His mimeograph machine spat out a torrent of letters, press releases, and memos, which he sent to a mailing list of eight hundred people. He wrote 466 letters to the *New York Times* before one got published. William F. Buckley Jr. once said that if he ever went to hell he was sure that he would find a letter from Kohlberg posted on the gates pointing out that Satan belonged to twenty-three Communist fronts. "I myself count it a day lost," Buckley observed, "when I do not see a letter Mr. Kohlberg has written to the president . . . etc."[18]

Kohlberg was nothing if not determined. If IPR wouldn't change, he would create his own Asian affairs think tank, which he did, founding the American China Policy Association. If the press continued to print nonsense about the Chinese Communists, he would start his own publication, which he did, putting fifty thousand dollars into a new magazine called *Plain Talk*. If the *New York Times* and the *New York Herald Tribune* kept giving good reviews to the books of Owen Lattimore and assigning him to review other people's books about Asia, he would expose Lattimore, which he first did in 1945, writing in the *China Monthly* that the editor filled his magazine's pages with articles by Communists. Two years later Kohlberg claimed that Lattimore himself was a Soviet agent.

Like stones thrown in a pond, Kohlberg's writings and warnings created spreading circles of influence, which included journalists, lawmakers, and military men. The president of the American China Policy Association, for example, was Clare Boothe Luce, the former congresswoman and wife of Henry Luce, the founder of *Time* magazine, whose parents had been missionaries in China and whose publishing empire promoted Chiang Kai-shek like a Hollywood movie star.

Kohlberg's biggest stone was *Plain Talk,* which began publishing in 1946. The magazine was edited by Isaac Don Levine, the journalist who in 1939 had taken Whittaker Chambers to warn the State Department's Adolf Berle about the Communist underground in Washington, only to see the very men that Chambers had named rise in the government. The premiere issue featured an exposé on the *Amerasia* case; the following year

Levine wrote a veiled account of the Hiss case without mentioning him by name. Kohlberg, too, wrote for *Plain Talk,* although Levine usually took his seven-page articles, edited them down to a page, and still complained about his publisher's verbosity. Still, Kohlberg insisted that the magazine published only a fraction of what it knew. "If we told more than fifteen percent of the truth," Kohlberg said, "nobody would believe us and the magazine would not be useful."[19]

Now, as the Nationalists lost one city after another to the Communists, Kohlberg desperately wanted to be useful. Which is why he walked into the Roosevelt Hotel where the Action Conference on China Policy was taking place. Kohlberg wanted to know what the enemy was saying. One of the group's main objectives was to demand a congressional investigation of the China Lobby in Washington, a loose group of right-wing journalists and politicians who demanded more aid for the besieged Nationalist government. Then Agnes Smedley spotted Kohlberg. He *was* the China Lobby.

Smedley, almost fifty-seven, had been enamored by China almost as long as Kohlberg. But where Kohlberg was charmed by China's ancient ways ("good-natured laughing street coolies"[20]), Smedley was appalled ("My rickshaw coolie silently running like a tired horse before me, his heaving breath interrupted by a rotten cough"[21]). Smedley spent most of her life appalled. She grew up poor in Colorado's mining country. Her father deserted the family when she was eleven; three years later she went to work to help support her family. Smedley was married at twenty, divorced at twenty-five. She drifted into radical politics, becoming a socialist, a birth control crusader, and a vocal advocate of driving the British out of India, which resulted in her arrest in 1918 under the Espionage Act for incitement. "Our chief first impressions of Agnes," recalled John King Fairbank, "were of her broad human warmth, an often earthy sense of humor, and an outspoken rebelliousness against political tyranny — also of her living in a conspiratorial world of real danger."[22]

In 1928 Smedley arrived in China. "One of the few spiritually great people I have ever met," recalled Freda Utley, a Communist who later broke with the party. "Agnes Smedley had that burning sympathy for the misery and wrongs of mankind which some of the saints and some great revolutionaries have possessed. For her the wounded soldiers of China, the starving peasants and the over-worked coolies, were brothers in a real sense. She was acutely, vividly, aware of their misery and could not rest for trying to alleviate it."[23]

Smedley spent most of the next dozen years in Asia, writing for the *New*

Masses and *The Nation,* publishing books and becoming an unabashed partisan of the Chinese Communists, with whom she lived in caves in the party's redoubt in Yenan. Smedley tried to join the Chinese Communist Party but was rejected — one of the great disappointments of her life. In the Nationalist capital of Hankow she went around in an Eighth Route (Communist) Army uniform. "She wished," remembered U.S. diplomat John Paton Davies, "she were an Eighth Route soldier."[24] Among the Communists, Smedley found a sense of community and commitment that she had never experienced anywhere else. "I've a calmer, more marvelous life than I have ever dreamed of," she wrote.[25]

Calm was not a word most people used in the same sentence as *Agnes Smedley.* "Smedley is fanatical," observed Malcolm Cowley in 1934. ". . . When she talks about people who betrayed the Chinese rebels, her mouth becomes a thin scar and her eyes bulge and glint with hatred."[26] That same year Owen Lattimore met Smedley on a ship to China. "She's very intense and extraordinarily naive," Lattimore noted. ". . . Has a spy-phobia, detecting detectives behind every pillar and peepers at every porthole. She sees the world in what I can only describe as folklore terms — capitalist consuls, police and other officials are all agents of the Devil; Soviet generals, instead of being militarists, are servants of the Kingdom of God."[27]

When Smedley saw Kohlberg at the conference, she pointed him out to the audience and called him a spy. That was somewhat ironic. Kohlberg was many things, but a spy wasn't one of them. Smedley was — or at least had been. In *Plain Talk* the year before, Kohlberg had accused Smedley of being part of the Sorge spy ring, which was true. In Shanghai she had become the lover of Richard Sorge, a Soviet spy later executed by the Japanese. In the 1930s Smedley had been involved in underground Communist work, although party operatives found her *too* much of a zealot and difficult to control. "She pulled a revolver and threatened to commit suicide unless our friend Alec agreed to do certain work for her,"[28] Comintern agent Rudy Baker reported to Moscow in 1936.

Smedley glared at Kohlberg. She denounced the China Lobby, the first time Kohlberg had heard the term. He would hear it a lot over the next few years. She insisted that Congress examine the financing and propaganda activities of those who supported the Nationalist government. "Be it therefore resolved," the meeting concluded, "that we go on record demanding: That there be a congressional investigation."[29]

It would take two years, but Congress would become interested in how and by whom America's China policy was shaped. Unfortunately, for Smedley's friends, it would be Pat McCarran who was doing the investigating.

On February 25, 1949, McCarran introduced the China Aid Act (S. 1063), a bill to give one and a half billion dollars to the Nationalist government. "I trust my bill will start something," McCarran wrote to New Jersey Republican senator H. Alexander Smith, "and may lead to concertive and constructive action."[30]

What it started was a big headache for Dean Acheson, who had become secretary of state just a month before. "Chiang was in the last stages of collapse," Acheson recalled. "I arrived just in time to have him collapse on me."[31] The previous November Major General David Barr, who directed the U.S. military advisory group helping Chiang, had reported to Washington that the Nationalists were all but defeated. "Only the active participation of United States troops could effect a remedy," he wrote. ". . . No battle has been lost since my arrival due to lack of ammunition or equipment. Their military debacles in my opinion can all be attributed to the world's worst leadership and many other morale destroying factors that lead to a complete loss of will to fight."[32]

By the time Acheson took office on January 20, Chiang had already transferred China's foreign reserves to the island of Formosa (Taiwan); the Communists were in Peking. Acheson was trying to figure out how to wash his hands of China when McCarran proposed loaning the failing government one and a half billion dollars. McCarran was the first Democrat to join a congressional voting bloc of conservative Republicans who had been sniping at the administration for years for not giving enough aid to the Nationalists. McCarran asked his colleagues to sign a petition urging the Foreign Relations Committee to hold hearings on the bill. The results surprised the administration. "Fifty senators, half of them Democrats, supported this bizarre idea," Acheson recalled.[33] The secretary took his case to Foreign Relations chairman Tom Connally. "Such a move as proposed in the McCarran bill," Acheson told Connally, "would involve this country in an undertaking so great in magnitude it would almost surely be catastrophic."[34] The measure died in Connally's committee. So did a resolution sponsored by McCarran and two Republicans (Styles Bridges and William Knowland) calling for an investigation into Truman's China policy.

"What do you think of Dean Acheson?" Mary McCarran asked her father before Acheson's confirmation hearing. "He looks a bit too pink for me."[35] McCarran agreed. He had first tussled with Acheson in 1939 when the lawyer accompanied his mentor Felix Frankfurter to his Supreme Court confirmation hearing, where McCarran tried to portray the Harvard Law School professor as a Communist. A decade later McCarran went after Acheson (who still walked to work with Frankfurter every day) and his State Department. "I cannot explain it," McCarran said in a press release in April, "but the State Department Division of Far Eastern Affairs is definitely soft to Communist Russia. When our own State Department peddles the Communistic propaganda line as in the case of the Department's assertion that Mao Tse-tung, the Chinese Communist leader, is not a real Communist, it is time something was done about it."[36]

McCarran's vitriol was remarkable. Rumors were soon spreading around Washington that not all of it was his own. "David Lu tells us privately that there is every evidence in the wording of McCarran's releases and statements that the material is being written by some Chinese source," reporter Frank McNaughton told his editors at *Time* magazine, "probably Kung's son who is hanging around Washington at the nearby Congressional Hotel. This can't be proved."[37]

H. H. Kung was Chiang Kai-shek's brother-in-law and the former finance minister for the Nationalist government. His two sons lived in the United States, where they were endeavoring to burnish the faltering regime's reputation. After the Nationalist government finally collapsed, Drew Pearson told his diary that he had been offered ten thousand dollars to make a favorable mention of Kung in his column. "More money had been spent on the bribes on behalf of the China Lobby than any other major matter in Washington," he wrote.[38]

There was a certain circularity with U.S. aid to China. Over the past decade the United States had given the Nationalists billions of dollars with virtually no strings attached — no small amount of which allegedly flowed secretly back to Washington. When McCarran wanted to give Chiang another billion and a half dollars, he called his bill the China Aid Act. It could, critics thought, just have well been called the McCarran Aid Act.

In March, Wellington Koo, Chiang's ambassador in Washington who had been educated at Columbia University and spoke fluent English, visited McCarran in the senator's office. The ambassador praised McCarran's bill and the support he seemed to have in Congress. "It was a wonderful achievement," Koo said. McCarran said that he didn't think he could get all the money he wanted for China but that he was sure he could get some. "The attitude of the administration and that of the secretary of state toward the bill . . . were not helpful," McCarran groused.[39]

Koo recalled that the last time he had seen McCarran was in a Chinese restaurant a year earlier. The ambassador said that he would be delighted if the senator would give him the pleasure of entertaining him at a small dinner party at the embassy.

McCarran said that he would love to go.

Hubert Humphrey rose from his schoolboy desk in the back row of the Senate to speak. This by itself was something of a presumptuous move, if not downright arrogant. Humphrey was a freshman senator, serving in his first session of Congress. By tradition he should have stayed silent on the floor for at least a year and even after that not make much noise until he had been in the chamber for some time. Humphrey wasn't very good at being quiet.

The year before, Humphrey had electrified the Democratic National Convention with his rousing civil rights speech. In November he was elected to the Senate, along with Illinois's Paul Douglas and Tennessee's Estes Kefauver. They were soon joined by Herbert Lehman, William Benton, and Frank Graham. Together this loose group of energetic anti-Communist liberals was determined to fight for civil rights and civil liberties. Too determined, some of their fellow Democrats thought. Truman called them crackpots and overeducated SOBs; Lyndon Johnson called them crazies. When he arrived in Washington in January, *Time* magazine put Humphrey on its cover. "Not since the early days of the New Deal," Drew Pearson wrote in his diary, "has there been such a group of youngsters elected on a clear-cut liberal platform."[40] Only in the Senate was a fifty-seven-year-old man a youngster.

On paper the Democrats had a dozen-vote majority; in reality they only had a majority when the South let them. Southern Democrats were a minority in the Senate but an unstoppable one. Liberals tended to come from the North, where two-party states existed, elections were fiercely contested, and tenure in the Senate often didn't last long. Southern Democrats (virtually all of whom were conservatives) came from a region with no real second party, where election to the Senate was tantamount to lifetime tenure. And seniority automatically equaled choice committee assignments. Out of the Senate's fifteen committees, a dozen were chaired by either southerners or their allies. Tennessee's Kenneth McKellar, the eighty-year-old chairman of the Appropriations Committee, for example, was first elected to the Senate in 1916. "The South's unending revenge upon the North for Gettysburg," *New York Times* reporter William White called the Senate.[41]

Next to seniority, the most hallowed of Senate traditions was unfettered debate. A senator could say whatever he wanted for as long as he wanted. Huey Long once held the Senate floor for fifteen hours, although that didn't break Robert La Follette's eighteen-hour record.* In the Senate you could read the New York City phone book and no one could stop you. The only rules were that you had to keep standing and talking. The filibuster was the anaconda of parliamentary tactics: A big enough one could choke to death almost anything. In 1942, for example, McCarran launched a one-man filibuster against a bill supported by the president and both parties to let the Treasury lease its silver stockpile to war industries (which would have caused the price to fall). All the other senators walked out of the chamber to snub McCarran while he was talking, whereupon he asked unanimous consent to have a clerk continue reading his stack of documents. McCarran gave his consent and sat down. Returning senators were shocked at the move but helpless. The bill was dropped. "Silver fight is won," McCarran crowed to Eva Adams. "Filibuster wins."[42]

As long as the South could filibuster, the liberals had no hope of passing any civil rights law, which was why none had been passed since the end of Reconstruction. In theory two-thirds of the Senate could choke off debate by filing a cloture petition (Rule 22). In thirty-two years this had happened once. And it would never happen while the South had dependable allies like McCarran. There were philosophic reasons for McCarran to stand with the South against limiting debate. He *really* did believe in states' rights — in senators as sovereign representatives who should not yield local authority to the rapacious Moloch of the federal government. And there were practical reasons. McCarran was not a member of the Senate's inner club; he was a senior Democrat but not part of the party's policy or steering councils. He needed allies where he could make them.

This summer, for example, McCarran wanted to force the State Department to give aid to fascist Spain as well as the European democracies that were benefiting from the Marshall Plan. McCarran asked Georgia's Richard Russell for help. Russell *was* the Senate's inner club, an erudite, widely respected legislator who also led the Southern Caucus like a general. "It is scarcely necessary for me to say," McCarran reminded Russell, "that I have most happily and with great satisfaction sustained you

---

*Wayne Morse did in 1953, holding the floor for twenty-two hours and twenty-six minutes, a record in turn lost to Strom Thurmond, who spoke for twenty-four hours, eighteen minutes in 1957.

in nearly every activity in which you have engaged on the floor of the Senate."[43] Russell was only too happy to return the favor. "I have not had a great deal of interest in the amendment providing a loan to Spain," Russell replied, "but in view of your unusual interest, I shall be happy to support you as strongly as I can. Your assistance in matters vitally affecting the people of my area is deeply appreciated."[44]

It was in such a mannered realm that Hubert Humphrey rose to speak and did something totally unprecedented. The freshman lawmaker attacked a Senate elder — one who wasn't even present, which was even more of a breach of decorum — Harry Flood Byrd, chairman of the Joint Committee on Reduction of Nonessential Federal Expenditures. The committee, Humphrey suggested, was somewhat nonessential itself; he introduced a resolution to abolish it. "A wanton waste and extravagance," he called it.[45]

Byrd had been a senator since 1933; Humphrey since January. Lèse-majesté was just about the worst crime a senator could commit. You could call the president a Communist, but even suggesting that a colleague was slightly pink was a breach of etiquette so severe as to bring down universal condemnation.

Less than a week later, Byrd rose to respond. "The senator speaks like the wind," he drawled.[46] And for the next four hours, Byrd's colleagues howled like a storm. Elder after elder — Walter George, Pat McCarran, Robert Taft, Eugene Milliken — heaped praise upon Byrd and abuse upon Humphrey. Two dozen senators, Democrats and Republicans alike, beat down the upstart in front of a packed chamber. When the battery was over, Humphrey rose to defend himself. Virtually every senator stood and walked out. Only Paul Douglas remained, sitting silently in support.

Judith Coplon walked[47] in the wrong direction. Most Friday evenings when the petite young woman arrived in New York's Penn Station after taking the train from Washington, she hopped on the subway to Brooklyn, where her parents lived in Flatbush. But on March 4, 1949, when Coplon got off the train in Manhattan she took the subway far uptown instead.

The FBI agents watching Coplon had seen her do this before. The first time was on January 14, when she took the subway to Washington Heights, where she met a short man with dark hair. They walked to an Italian restaurant. He had dinner, she drank coffee and dropped a steady stream of nickels into the music box on the table. Then they got on the subway headed downtown. At 125th Street the doors started to close when the man suddenly jumped out. Inside the subway car two FBI agents could only watch in dismay as the man disappeared. The next day the agents flipped through stacks of photos until they recognized a picture of the man: Valentin Alekseevich Gubitchev. He was a Russian engineer who had come to the United States three years earlier as a part of the Soviet delegation to the United Nations and now worked for the UN secretariat, helping to build the massive headquarters building going up on Manhattan's East Side. The agents already knew where to find Judith Coplon: the Department of Justice building in Washington, the home of the FBI, where she was a political analyst in the foreign agents registration section. Coplon was also a Russian spy — which the FBI had discovered because it was spying on the Russians.

Several weeks before[48] Coplon's January meeting, FBI agent Robert Lamphere had made one of his regular trips across the Potomac to the former girls' school in Virginia called Arlington Hall, where he visited Meredith Gardner in his office every few weeks. Gardner wasn't much for small talk, although he could speak half a dozen languages. A former college teacher, Gardner had been recruited into the Army Signals Intelligence Service during the war as a codebreaker in a supersecret program later called Venona. Gardner taught himself Japanese for the job. Then he learned Russian, which for years seemed like a waste of time.

The Russian code seemed unbreakable. During the war Western Union and other telegraph companies had been turning over to the government copies of the cables sent by the Soviets from their diplomatic missions in the United States. These cables piled up at Arlington Hall, stacks of gibberish: The messages had first been written in code, then scrambled into seemingly random strings of numbers with an elaborate encryption system known as a one-time pad. The only clue Gardner had was a partially burned Soviet code book that had been recovered during the war. For three years Gardner could do nothing with the numbers. Then, in 1946, he began to chip away at the cipher. During the war the Soviets had been forced to reuse the one-time pads instead of destroying them. That mistake was Gardner's big break. Fragments from the cables were suddenly readable. One of these was a list of scientists working on the Manhattan Project, the secret wartime effort to build the atomic bomb. More than a year after Elizabeth Bentley had defected, the United States was able to confirm the outlines of the spy ring she had described. It was Lamphere's job to take what the bureau knew from Bentley and other sources and match it up with Gardner's decrypted cables.

In late 1948 Gardner greeted Lamphere with one of the shy smiles that meant a big breakthrough. Gardner had decoded a message from 1944 reporting to Moscow that a KGB agent working for the Justice Department in New York was being transferred to Washington. Lamphere went back to his office and soon had the name of a Justice Department employee who fit the details: Judith Coplon. She was twenty-seven, a Barnard College graduate who had joined the Young Communist League at school but still managed to get hired by Justice during the war. Coplon was smart and personable and rose through the ranks to become a political analyst in charge of evaluating internal security data forwarded to Justice by the FBI. It was a spy's dream job.

The FBI began following Coplon to meetings with Gubitchev. This time the couple led the bureau on a wild four-hour chase across Manhattan before the FBI finally moved in and arrested them. In Coplon's handbag they found a FBI memo folded down to the size of a postage stamp and several other documents. On Gubitchev they found a white envelope with $125 in small bills. Coplon claimed that she was having an affair with Gubitchev and that the classified documents that she was carrying around were source material for a novel she was writing called *Government Girl*. In June she was found guilty of stealing government documents; the next year in another trial Coplon and Gubitchev were both convicted of espionage, each getting fifteen years in prison. Gubitchev was allowed to leave the country. Coplon appealed, won a retrial, and was convicted again. But the appeals court ruled that the FBI had lacked probable cause to search Coplon, meaning that the documents in her purse were inadmissible. The FBI refused to reveal the existence of Venona.

Judith Coplon walked.

The tall, dark mahogany door opened in the long, dim corridor of the Senate Office Building. A heavy man in sunglasses and a hat pulled low over his face slipped out. The reporters were on him in an instant. Are you the mystery witness? they asked. McCarran's staffers had told the press that the Judiciary Committee's immigration panel would hear important testimony on this morning, May 12, from a witness whose identity could not be revealed without risking his life. McCarran's aides, however, didn't have any qualms about alerting congressional correspondents to the secret hearings in the first place.

No, the man said in a heavy accent, he was not a witness. A little while later McCarran came out. The reporters pressed around him, asking who the mysterious witness was and what he'd said. "I honestly don't remember what his name was," McCarran said. "If you were to shoot me at this moment I couldn't spell it."[49]

In the afternoon the hearing opened to the press. Kirill M. Alexeev, who had defected from the Soviet embassy in Mexico City, testified through an interpreter that every Russian diplomatic mission included a KGB agent assigned to work with the local Communist Party to spy on the host country.

The testimony proved, McCarran said, that the country's immigration laws urgently needed to be changed to keep out subversives — even if they were diplomats. "We are holding hearings on one of the most important subjects affecting the life of this nation," McCarran declared. "We will try to give Congress convincing reasons why it should pass legislation to safeguard this country against foreign diplomatic agents and others who might have ideas subversive to our democratic country."[50]

Such legislation would wreck the UN — which, of course, was the idea. "The United States," the *Washington Post* pointed out, "can scarcely insist that Communist countries choose anti-Communists to fill their diplomatic posts over here without inviting a reciprocal demand that all our emissaries be anti-republican."[51]

It was not the first time that McCarran had warned against spies masquerading as diplomats — a preoccupation with foreign Communists sneaking into the country that would soon turn into a virtual monomania. The year before Judith Coplon was arrested passing secrets to the UN's Valentin Gubitchev, McCarran had touched off a small furor over diplomats from Communist countries. In 1948 McCarran's immigration subcommittee conducted an investigation into the country's visa system — including visas given to diplomats. "Every representative of an Iron Curtain country," William McGrath Harlow, the chief of the State Department's diplomatic visa section, testified, "is a threat to the security of the United States."[52] Another State Department official — Robert C. Alexander, the assistant chief in the visa section — furnished the subcommittee with a list of 164 Russians working for the UN who were suspected spies. The UN protested the accusations, and Secretary of State George Marshall appointed a committee of distinguished citizens to look into the charges. The committee found the allegations baseless.

The story soon dropped from the headlines, but the subcommittee didn't give up. "It can be proved beyond contradiction," immigration subcommittee director Richard Arens reported on Election Day 1948 to McCarran's aide Jay Sourwine, "that many subversives, including a substantial number of actual Communist spies are to be found among those here on United Nations visas and on the visas of other international organizations . . . that several important officials of the United Nations are Communists and are using their official positions to further Communist objectives and that the United Nations desk in our own State Department definitely is Communist-dominated."[53]

The next year McCarran was back in charge of the Judiciary Committee and appointed himself chairman of the immigration subcommittee. And when Coplon and Gubitchev were arrested, McCarran quickly resumed hearings on spies in the UN. "Red Embassy Is Center of Spy Network, Russian Says," the *Washington Post* reported.[54] On May 21 McCarran issued subpoenas to Attorney General Tom Clark and Assistant Secretary of State John Peurifoy to produce the security files on 168 UN employees (the list had grown in the past year) — the first, McCarran added, of several hundred he wanted to see. "It is high time for a showdown on whether or not the people can be told the facts," McCarran said, "and I am confident that when the facts are revealed, the American people will insist on decisive action."[55]

Clark and Peurifoy declined to produce the files, citing Truman's 1948 order not to divulge confidential personnel information to Congress without his express approval. McCarran summoned a legal opinion from the Library of Congress, which supported his request and hinted that jailing the two officials was a possibility if they continued to refuse.

Hauling Peurifoy before the subcommittee, McCarran asked him how many State Department officials had access to the files.

Eighty or ninety, Peurifoy said.

Are they better security risks than ninety-six senators? McCarran demanded. Yes or no.

"I would trust the five members of this committee personally with any information," Peurifoy said, "but I would say some are more competent in their field than in other fields."[56]

When McCarran couldn't get the security files from State to prove his case, he began releasing testimony taken in closed session. Elizabeth Bentley, for instance, had identified to the subcommittee forty-six people whom she said had worked with the Communist underground, several of whom were employed by the UN. Fifteen of those had never been named in public before. McCarran released all the names to the press. Then McCarran released testimony from the mystery witness (identified only as Witness Number Eight), who claimed that UN secretary general Trygve Lie was being terrorized by Communists and should be fired. The UN filed a formal protest with the State Department. "This is the nuttiest story I have heard yet," Lie's deputy Byron Price replied. [57]

Acheson told Price that he was sure that the UN would not tolerate such a situation. McCarran said that neither of them knew what they were talking about. "I would suggest," McCarran said, "that before any official of this government or of an international organization gives himself to irresponsible utterances attacking the investigation, he ask the secretary of state to see the files on the list of hundred and fifty names I submitted to him." [58]

McCarran then publicly named two UN employees as subversives: Ludwig Rajchman, from Poland, chairman of UNICEF, whom McCarran said State had tried to deport as a subversive and who didn't actually work for the UN but for the Polish government, and Norman Corwin, a well-known radio broadcaster working in the UN's information department who had a long record of belonging to front groups. For months businessman Alfred Kohlberg had been urging McCarran to investigate Corwin and supplying him with material about the broadcaster. "Corwin may not be a Communist Party member," Kohlberg told McCarran. "If he is not, it will be a surprise to me because all his actions, his activities, his connections and his broadcasts are more than that of a fellow traveler." [59]

Corwin denied that he was a Communist and attacked McCarran. "A political mad dog and a subversive influence in the United States Senate," Corwin called him. [60] "McCarran," the *Washington Post* editorialized, "has constituted himself a one-man Un-American Activities Committee in the Senate." [61]

Most mornings Jay Sourwine left his house in Silver Spring, Maryland, and took a roundabout way to his office on Capitol Hill. At the District line, Sourwine veered west toward Sixteenth Street, which he followed to Blagden Avenue, a leafy neighborhood perched above Rock Creek. Sourwine picked up Pat McCarran and they drove past the White House and down Constitution Avenue, pulling into the parking lot at the Senate Office Building across the street from the Capitol.

Sourwine was thirty years younger than McCarran, but he still had to work to keep up with his boss as they strode into the huge marble-and-granite Beaux Arts building fronted with a row of great Doric columns. Into the light-filled rotunda they walked, eighteen Corinthian columns rising from the polished floor to support a massive coffered dome.

McCarran was slowing enough that they avoided the two majestic staircases coiling toward the building's higher reaches and instead took the elevator to the fourth floor, where they followed the dimly lit corridor to Room 409, McCarran's office suite. Inside the tall, dark door, the reception room was long and narrow, filled with filing cabinets and pictures of Nevada. The inner office belonged to Eva Adams, who was always there when McCarran and Sourwine walked in around eight, usually with a couple of secretaries already busy answering constituent mail. Then came McCarran's private office, with a fireplace and bathroom and a large window looking over Connecticut Avenue, the Supreme Court off to the left and the Capitol to the right. Next door was the Bull Pen, a room crammed with desks for the Nevada boys to work at. When any of McCarran's young protégés wanted to see the senator, they walked out into the hallway, passed McCarran's door, and entered Adams's office to ask her. But late at night the boys in the Bull Pen could open the direct door to McCarran's office and take naps on his sofa and sometimes read the letters on his desk (anything to or from Harold Ickes was usually good for a chuckle).

The Judiciary and its subcommittees had more office space in the building and in the Capitol. Altogether McCarran had forty people working for him, almost three-quarters of whom were from Nevada. "The largest and one of the most carefully chosen and loyal staffs on Capitol Hill,"[62] Stephen K. Bailey and Howard D. Samuel noted in their study of the legislative branch, *Congress at Work,* which was published in 1952. McCarran often hired two people for one job, paying each half a salary but extracting a full workload from both and doubling his patronage points. And work they did, long days, nights, and weekends. "To him there was no such thing as anything being impossible," Adams recalled. "So you learned to be persistent, you learned to overcome hurdles. In most instances we *had* to get things done. . . . There were a few things we gave up on, but not very many."[63]

And no one worked harder than Adams and Sourwine. Adams was McCarran's right hand. Sourwine was his left. Adams signed his name to letters, attended committee meetings in McCarran's stead, and collected campaign funds for him. "Eva was the smartest girl on the Hill," Norm Biltz remembered.[64] Sourwine wrote McCarran's bills, communicated with other staffers on the Hill for him, and ran his hearings like a Wagner conductor with something to prove. "Sourwine's abrasive interrogations terrified witnesses," recalled lawyer Frank Donner.[65] "Sourwine," added Sylvia Bernstein, one of those witnesses, "is a vicious bastard."[66]

Adams was like a wife. She was forty-one and had worked for McCarran since 1940, when McCarran convinced her to leave teaching in Nevada to run his office in Washington.★ She soon became his alter ego: She paid his bills, apologized for his outbursts, and doted on his family — and looking after the McCarrans was almost a full-time job itself. Birdie, for example, needed someone to drive her to the horse track in Delaware. Sam needed someone to get him extra beer during wartime rationing. Norine needed someone to do her taxes. Sister Margaret needed someone to type her master's thesis or send her books or mail her Christmas cards. "They couldn't even put a stamp on a letter," one of McCarran's boys recalled. "McCarran just babied everyone terribly."[67]

Adams lavished love and attention on all of them, but most of all she loved McCarran. She stroked his ego and soothed his soul. And when she was out of the office, the rest of the staff always noticed that McCarran was more surly than usual. Adams letters to McCarran often read like the mash notes of a love-struck high school girl. "I'm hoping to hear from you tomorrow . . . ," she wrote him during one separation. "I miss, terribly, being able to run up the stairs and see my good friend and talk to him. . . . Maybe I don't knock there on your door very often these days in actuality, but I surely knock many times to open the door of mental telepathy, when I send cheery thoughts back to you! I wish I could share all of these things more clearly with you in words . . . but you know, I hope, what I mean by the sketchy picture I perhaps draw."[68]

And McCarran, too, seemed more than a little taken by his young secretary. "I thought all day yesterday of you driving between Ely and Las Vegas," he wrote to her. "I could see you going through the juniper forest between Ely and Pioche. I always think that is such a beautiful drive. And then through Pioche and Caliente, and over the hill into Pharranegat Valley, and on to Glendale and across the raging, roaring Muddy River to dear old Las Vegas."[69]

McCarran encouraged Adams to go to law school at night at American University and take the bar. Before long, Washington was buzzing with rumors that McCarran wanted Adams, who had never practiced law, to be appointed a judge. "She had all kinds of boyfriends but she never let him know," one McCarran boy recalled. "He always called her at nine at home and she always had to be home for the call but after that she could go out for the rest of the night."[70]

★Around the time McCarran's former secretary left, painters were called to touch up a wall in the office splattered with ink. Birdie, one of the McCarran boys recalled, had walked in on her husband and his secretary in a compromising position and hurled an inkwell at them.

On the Hill many preferred to deal with Adams, rather than McCarran. "I sort of was fortunate in that people were so fearful of Senator McCarran that they were very happy to talk with me . . . ," Adams said. "He would just lay in on the line and cuss 'em out if it took that, where I would reason and discuss things better."[71] And those who didn't want to deal with her usually wound up regretting that decision, as did Graham Morison, the head of the antitrust division in the Justice Department. Once Adams called Morison to deliver a message (a command, really) about several pending federal cases. Morison told Adams that he couldn't talk to an intermediary about such a delicate subject; the next thing he knew McCarran was screaming at him over the phone. "Why in the hell didn't you listen to what my secretary told you?" McCarran roared.[72]

The only person people liked dealing less with than McCarran was Sourwine. Julian Sourwine was forty-one, a large man with a mop of curly hair and a thick mustache, soft of body and voice but strong in mind and conviction. Sourwine was from Reno; he'd gone to the University of Nevada but left before graduating and headed to Washington, where he went to work for Woolworth, then turned to journalism, becoming a reporter at the Washington News Service (although he never learned to type worth a damn). At night he went to National University law school, graduating in 1936. In 1943 McCarran hired Sourwine as his aide on the District of Columbia Committee. Two years later when McCarran became chairman of the Judiciary Committee he took Sourwine with him as his counsel.

Sourwine was as cold and distant as Adams was motherly. "He is a quiet person and not easy to know," Eva Adams admitted to one of McCarran's confidants, "but his capabilities are amazing."[73] Behind his back, McCarran's junior staffers called him Teddy Roosevelt. "Wasn't very civil to anybody, all business," Ralph Denton recalled.[74] "He was anti-social to the ninth degree," another McCarran boy remembered, "but he was smart as hell. I never saw a guy who could dictate a bill off the top of his head."[75]

Sourwine, like his boss, didn't get along well with others. As the Judiciary Committee began to function more and more as an informal internal security committee, McCarran let the Justice Department officials sit in on executive sessions in case any witness revealed leads worth pursuing. But Sourwine was often at odds with the Justice officials. "The Judiciary Committee of the Senate is not an adjunct to the Department of Justice," Sourwine fumed to McCarran. ". . . He is out of bounds when he presumes to bawl out a member of the committee staff. . . . It would be nice to have your permission to become slightly vocal."[76]

And like McCarran, Sourwine came to depend on Adams as well, especially when his fondness for gambling got the better of him. "It was mighty good of you to offer to extend a monetary lifeline again if I should need it," Sourwine told Adams in 1943. "At the time I got your offer, I had no thought of bothering you again, certainly not so soon. . . . I need some sort of expedient which will give me six months or more in which to get a little ahead of the game. . . . If you are in shape to put out about $500 at 6%, for installment repayment, I would be most happy to borrow it."[77] Sourwine never did get much ahead of the game. "I am afraid that Sourwine has been borrowing a little more money from your friends than he should,"[78] Pete Petersen told McCarran seven years later.

With all Sourwine's faults, McCarran was quite fond of him. The worshipful younger lawyer shared the older lawmaker's prickly conservative political philosophy and became a skilled craftsman of his bills and speeches. "He is a fellow that will not impress you on first blush," McCarran once told Petersen, "but he will unfold splendidly."[79] Sourwine was also ambitious and dreamed of someday taking over McCarran's Senate seat. "My shepherd," Sourwine called McCarran. McCarran put a photo of Sourwine on the wall of his private office.

Then, in the summer of 1949, it looked like McCarran was going to get Sourwine made a judge. In July, Truman nominated Attorney General Tom Clark for the Supreme Court. To win McCarran's support, the White House agreed to appoint Jay Sourwine to the bench of the district court in Washington. Two months earlier, when the attorney general had ignored McCarran's subpoena to hand over files on Communist aliens in the country, the senator had threatened to send the attorney general to jail. Moreover, Clark was a bad attorney general and blatantly unqualified for the high court. Yet the nomination sailed through the Judiciary Committee, Clark wasn't even called to testify, and in August the Senate approved him. Then the White House reneged on Sourwine. "I am very sorry about losing out for Julian," McCarran told Adams. "I am only sorry because I built up his hopes and the promise didn't materialize. I am not sorry in other respects because it has been a great worry to me as to how I would fill the place and as to how I would get along with the Judiciary Committee and Julian not there."[80]

In June, McCarran spoke at a testimonial dinner for Nanking archbishop Paul Yu Pin. McCarran accused the State Department of tilting toward the Communists in China but insisted that the United States could still save the Nationalist government. If it didn't, he warned, the entire world would eventually be overwhelmed by Communism. "China is today standing at the crossroads of her future," McCarran said. "She will emerge from the present conflict either a communistic vassal of the Kremlin, or a democratic nation, wedded to the concept of freedom, and a formidable force among the free peoples of the earth. Which road she will take has not yet been determined."[81]

McCarran's speech was ludicrous. Mao was already in Peking; Chiang in Formosa. What was left of the Nationalist forces would follow inside of half a year. Yet McCarran was in good company. Another speaker at the dinner was Patrick J. Hurley, who had been Truman's ambassador to China until he quit in a huff in 1945 and denounced the State Department for being full of Communists. Alfred Kohlberg had put the dinner together. None of these men could accept the fact that the Chinese Civil War was virtually over and that the Nationalists had lost.

On August 5 the State Department released a massive White Paper to try to explain this reality to the American public. "The unfortunate but inescapable fact," Acheson's cover letter said, "is that the ominous result of the civil war in China was beyond the control of the government of the United States. Nothing that this country did or could have done within reasonable limits of its capabilities could have changed the result."[82]

Acheson had told Truman that much of the criticism over China stemmed from a lack of information. So the department unloaded a trainload of information on the public: four hundred pages of text describing the evolution of U.S. policy toward China, with another six hundred pages of documents. The reception was predictable. "A smooth alibi for the pro-Communists in the State Department who had engineered the overthrow of our ally,"[83] Pat Hurley called it. "A 1,054-page whitewash of a wishful, do-nothing policy which has succeeded only in placing Asia in danger of Soviet conquest," added Nebraska senator Kenneth Wherry.[84]

Acheson was wrong. The American public had plenty of information. What it didn't have was the reassurance of its leaders or even much faith in them. And when Truman tried to calm the country, he only seemed to make things worse. Two days after McCarran's China speech, the president told a White House news conference that the nation was passing through a trying time reminiscent of the bruising political battles between the Jeffersonians and the Federalists in the eighteenth century, which resulted in the Alien and Sedition Laws, a sweeping governmental assault on dissent. But the hysteria, Truman said, didn't last long. "The country did not go to hell at all," he insisted, "and it isn't going to now." The headline in the next day's paper, however, did not exactly bespeak reassurance. "Truman Declares Hysteria Over Reds Sweeps the Nation," the *New York Times* announced.[85]

One day at an Appropriations Committee hearing[86] McCarran had a question for Josh Lee, a former senator from Oklahoma who was chairman of the Civil Aeronautics Board. What, McCarran wanted to know, had become of the Bonanza Air request?

Bonanza was a small Nevada airline that had started business in 1945 and had recently applied to the CAB for permission to fly interstate passenger service between Las Vegas and Phoenix. Lee explained that the application was still pending.

McCarran pointed out that all the members of the board were at the hearing. Why not go to the back of the room and consider the application right now while the hearing stopped? After the CAB settled the Bonanza request, McCarran's subcommittee would consider the board's budget request. Lee went to the back of the hearing room with his fellow board members for ten minutes and then returned to the witness table.

We've considered the matter, Lee announced, and have decided to approve Bonanza's application. The hearing continued.

On August 15, 1949, McCarran visited the White House. In Truman's first term McCarran had been in the Oval Office at least eleven times. Now he was in the White House for the first time since the president's reelection — and also for the last time. Truman still had more than three years in office, but after this fifteen-minute meeting (the subject of which is not recorded) he never spoke to McCarran again. "If there was one of these negative thinkers whom he disliked both personally and politically," remembered Margaret Truman, the president's daughter, "it was Senator Pat McCarran."[87]

When McCarran and Truman stopped talking, it made some routine matters of governance rather difficult, such as nominating federal judges. Eva Adams became, in effect, McCarran's emissary to the White House. "Mr. Truman didn't talk to Mr. McCarran — Mr. McCarran didn't talk to Mr. Truman," recalled White House aide Joseph G. Feeney. "So it became a round-about merry-go-round to get messages back and forth and quite often Mr. McCarran was against Mr. Truman."[88]

McCarran, however, had no reservations about picking up the phone and ordering Truman's subordinates around. "Tom Clark was in McCarran's office nearly every damn day," recalled McCarran aide Chester Smith.[89] And when writer Alfred Steinberg stopped by McCarran's office to interview him for a *Harper's* magazine profile, the senator called Peyton Ford, the number two person in the Justice Department, to ask him about a job for one of his boys.

"Hello, Ford," McCarran said. "What about that young fellow I referred to you for a job?"

Ford offered a long excuse.

"That's no excuse," McCarran interrupted. "If you haven't got any money left to put him on, you certainly know where to come for a deficiency appropriation. Who controls your budget?"

Ford promised to find a job later.

"Two months from now will be too late," McCarran said. "Ford, put him on the first of the month."

Ford agreed.

"That's better, Peyton," McCarran continued. "Now let's make a deal. Say, 'Cross my heart.'"

McCarran laughed. Eva Adams clapped her hands in delight. "Did you hear the senator make him say, 'Cross my heart'?" she asked.

"McCarran," Steinberg concluded in *Harper's* magazine, "has emerged as a greater threat to his party's program than the combined forces of the Dixiecrats and the Republicans."[90]

CHAPTER 17

Turbulent Populations

Fervent prayer carries with it a mystic power that pene-
trates heaven and calls down supernatural light and divine
impulses to illumine men's minds and incline their wills to
good, to persuade and move them to charity.[1]
— Pope Pius XII, *Quemadmodum,*
A Plea for the Care of the World's
Destitute Children, January 6, 1946

Finally, at dawn, I fell asleep,
I dreamt that we escaped from the DP camp,
That we crossed borders
And arrived in America,
Away from the cursed European soil.[2]
— Susan Strauss Taube,
American Zone of Germany, August 1946

Cal Cory, McCarran aide: Were you issued oral instruc-
tions that anybody could claim Jewish blood?
John Cutler, Displaced Persons Commission: Constantly.
McCarran: What is the order?
Cutler: You can immediately go to the United States.[3]
— Testimony, Munich, 1949

On August 8, 1949, the day he turned seventy-three, Pat McCarran made
a rare appearance at a meeting of the Democratic Policy Committee.
Majority Leader Scott Lucas surprised McCarran with a huge cake to celebrate his birthday. "A birthday party," Lucas said, "might produce in the
distinguished senator a mellow mood."[4]

Five years after the end of the war, there were more than four hundred
thousand people still living in refugee camps in Europe. The war had displaced millions, creating a massive refugee crisis, which Congress finally
responded to in 1948 by grudgingly agreeing to accept just over two hundred thousand refugees for resettlement in the United States. It wasn't
nearly enough, Truman said, and in his State of the Union speech in 1949
the president called on Congress for a more generous displaced persons

bill. The leaders of both parties agreed. In June the House passed a new DP bill that would let an additional 134,000 refugees into the country. In the Senate nothing happened. The bill had disappeared into McCarran's Judiciary Committee and showed no signs of reappearing. "McCarran," the *Washington Post* noted, "happens to be in a position where he can block DP legislation all by himself until hell freezes over the DP camps in Europe."[5]

Getting the bill to the floor was Lucas's job. Scott Lucas, fifty-seven, had been a senator for a decade, had served as the party whip for the past two years, and was now the majority leader, the nominal head of Democrats in the Senate. The first six months of the job had already given Lucas a bleeding ulcer and sent him to the hospital for three weeks. The southerners (with McCarran's help) had filibustered the civil rights bill to death, and most of the rest of Truman's Fair Deal program wasn't faring much better. McCarran was threatening to give Lucas another ulcer.

"The truth is that Pat McCarran doesn't give a damn about DPs or the party pledges," Lucas exploded to *Time* magazine's Frank McNaughton in an off-the-record conversation. "He wants to kill the bill. He's conducting a two-bit Un-American activities committee hearing, dragging his heels, and trying to beat the DP bill every way possible."[6]

After eight months of arguing and cajolery, Lucas tried cake. It was huge and delicious and changed nothing. "The cake," Lucas admitted, "had no effect upon the senator from Nevada whatever."[7]

The stench was awful. Long before the British soldiers saw the horror they could smell the dying.

On April 15, 1945, British forces drove through the gates of the Bergen-Belsen concentration camp in northeast Germany. They found fifty-eight thousand prisoners still alive and more than ten thousand dead bodies, some piled in great heaps, others lying where they had fallen. Telling the living from the dead was not easy. For days there had been no food or water, a typhus epidemic was raging, and those who could walk looked more like living skeletons than human beings. The Nazis had killed more than fifty thousand people before the British arrived; almost fourteen thousand more died from malnutrition and disease over the two months following their liberation. The dead were buried in mass graves, and the British burned the camp to the ground.

The survivors were almost immediately back behind barbed wire, moved into German military barracks and guarded by Allied troops. More than two-thirds of the camp survivors soon melted away, going home or someplace else, leaving twelve thousand people, mostly from Poland and Hungary — making Belsen, as the Jews continued to call their lodgement, the largest of several score of displaced persons camps in Germany, Austria, and Italy. "There was no ecstasy, no joy at our liberation," Hadassah Bimko Rosensaft recalled. "We had lost our families, our homes. We had no place to go to, nobody to hug. Nobody was waiting for us anywhere."[8]

The arithmetic of the war was staggering: six million Jews killed, seven million people from across Europe homeless and adrift, torn from their countries by the Nazis and forced into slave labor battalions or concentration camps. Even after the war the dislocations continued. So many refugees trudged across the war-ravaged landscape of Germany that U.S. troops blew up bridges to keep them in place. And in 1946, when a pogrom erupted in Kielce, thousands of Polish Jews fled their cursed homeland and poured into the DP camps in Germany, where other waves of persecuted Jews from Russia and Eastern Europe were already swamping relief efforts.

Many of the DP camps were miserable. Jews were mixed in with collaborators, housed in horse stalls or camps deemed unfit for prisoners of war, sometimes given the choice between wearing their prison rags or cast-off Nazi uniforms, fed little but gruel and coffee. One camp had three toilets for almost two thousand people.

President Truman dispatched Earl Harrison, a former commissioner of immigration and dean of the University of Pennsylvania Law School, to investigate the refugee crisis. What he saw made him weep. "We appear to be treating the Jews as the Nazis treated them," Harrison told Truman, "except that we do not exterminate them."[9]

Truman was shocked by the Harrison report, and in December 1945 announced that he wanted to give displaced persons priority in immigrating to the United States. "The grave dislocation," Truman wrote, "of populations in Europe resulting from the war has produced human suffering that the people of the United States cannot and will not ignore."[10]

Plenty in Congress wanted to do just that. "We have," South Carolina Democratic senator Burnet R. Maybank said, "too many foreigners here already and I think we should get rid of them rather than bring in additional ones."[11] Patriotic groups such as the Daughters of the American Revolution and the American Legion wanted to ban immigration to the United States for a decade. "Every representative," Eleanor Roosevelt noted, "in Congress with whom I have talked has told me that the general feeling is that they wish to stop all immigration."[12]

In 1946 Truman asked Congress for legislation to admit refugees, but it wasn't until April 1947 that anyone in either house responded. Representative William G. Stratton introduced a bill to allow four hundred thousand DPs into the United States. It was not a popular bill. In the House legislators lined up to denounce displaced persons. "The scum of the earth,"[13] Georgia Democrat Eugene Cox called them. "Bums, criminals, subversives, revolutionists, crackpots and human wreckage,"[14] added Texas Democrat Ed Gossett.

By the time a bill reached Truman's desk in 1948, Stratton's liberal proposal had been hijacked and turned into the Wiley-Revercomb bill. Alexander ("We don't want any rats. We've got enough of them already"[15]) Wiley was the Wisconsin Republican who had replaced McCarran as the chairman of the Judiciary Committee after the 1946 Democratic rout. Chapman Revercomb was an even more conservative Republican from West Virginia who was chairman of Judiciary's special immigration subcommittee. The subcommittee had been created in 1947 as a two-man panel charged with investigating the country's immigration laws. Its other member was Pat McCarran, whose name was not on the bill but whose fingerprints were all over the legislation.

McCarran was actually opposed to letting *any* displaced person into the country. He preferred to resettle refugees in the territory of Alaska. "A country to challenge the courage of humanity,"[16] he called it. But faced with the inevitability of some bill, McCarran helped write one according to his lights. The Wiley-Revercomb bill that emerged from the subcommittee allowed one hundred thousand DPs into the country over two years but limited admission to those who had been in a refugee camp before December 22, 1945 — a date that excluded the vast majority of Jewish refugees.

Truman grumbled that the bill was almost worse than no legislation at all, signed it, and urged Congress to liberalize the law the next year — a view that Tom Dewey echoed on the campaign trail that fall. When the Democrats regained control of Congress, it looked like Truman would be in a good position to ask for more humane immigration legislation. The *New York Post* surveyed incoming congressmen and found that a large majority favored amending the law. "It seems fairly certain," the American Jewish Committee's Irving Engel wrote to journalist Herbert Bayard Swope, "that the inequities and unworkable provisions in the Displaced Persons Act will be eliminated."[17]

Engel forgot about McCarran.

On April 26, 1949, McCarran pulled himself up from his small mahogany desk in the front row of the Senate to talk about refugees. This was what the president and the leaders of both parties had been waiting months to hear. When Congress opened in January, the White House already had a new displaced persons bill ready to go. Brooklyn representative Emmanuel Celler introduced the bill in the House; Rhode Island's J. Howard McGrath sponsored it in the Senate. Over the next four months the House Judiciary Committee held hearings on the bill and was close to passing a measure increasing the number of refugees that the United States would accept by more than 50 percent and extending the cutoff date. In the Senate nothing happened. McGrath had made a serious mistake. He forgot to show the bill to the chairman of the Judiciary Committee before he introduced it. Most committee chairmen would consider this a slight. McCarran was less forgiving than most.

McCarran appointed a subcommittee to vet the bill. In selecting the panel he bypassed every liberal and moderate on the Judiciary Committee, picking rock-ribbed conservative isolationists like Mississippi Democrat James Eastland and Indiana Republican William Jenner. Four of the five members (including McCarran) had opposed the restrictive 1948 DP law as being *too* liberal. The subcommittee was supposed to be considering McGrath's bill to increase the number of refugees let into the U.S. Instead, it spent its time investigating the lax enforcement of the law and looking for ways to make it *more* exclusive.

It was not exactly surprising, then, when McCarran broke his silence on the new DP bill. The measure, he said, was a bad idea. The bill would create more refugees, impoverish American workers, and undermine immigration law. The motive force behind the bill, he added, was a powerful, unnamed lobbying group that had spent more than eight hundred thousand dollars on propaganda to push its agenda. "Are we going to be guided by the facts," McCarran asked, "or are we going to be led by the dictates of those who employ highly paid publicity men to devise platitudes for the purpose of using a grave humanitarian problem as a lever to destroy our immigration system?"[18]

The lobbying group — or, as McCarran usually called it, the pressure group — was the Citizens Committee on Displaced Persons. The Citizens Committee had been formed in 1946 by the American Jewish Committee and the American Council for Judaism. Although 90 percent of its budget came from Jewish groups (Herbert Lehman was a major fund-raiser), the Citizens Committee did its best to put forward a gentile face, listing

Eleanor Roosevelt, Fiorello La Guardia, and other prominent non-Jews on its letterhead and emphasizing the fact that 80 percent of all displaced persons were Christians (non-European refugees including millions of dislocated Asians didn't concern the committee). The committee launched a massive publicity campaign in support of admitting four hundred thousand refugees to the United States and wrote the bill that Representative William G. Stratton had introduced in the House in 1947.

"The facts, Mr. President, mean nothing to this pressure group," McCarran continued, "which has virtually unlimited money, most of which incidentally has been contributed by a relatively few persons."[19]

It was, in other words, Jew money. In private McCarran called them kikes. In public he never called them anything. A decade earlier McCarran had fiercely opposed a series of Roosevelt nominees, all Jewish. "There were Felix Frankfurter, Jerome Frank and Gregory Hankin," White House aide Jim Rowe told Roosevelt. "These three have nothing in common except they are Jews. There is no question of McCarran's anti-Semitism."[20] In 1945 he strenuously fought another judicial nomination: Nathan Margold, who also happened to be Jewish. "Anti-Semitism," Harold Ickes complained to the *Washington Post,* "raised its ugly head."[21]

Now McCarran was opposing some hundred thousand Jews. McCarran's anti-Semitism grew worse with age. "You say you want to go to Holy Land," he would later tell his daughter Mary. "The Jews and Arabs are at war over there. And you can't see the barn where He was born any way. They tore it down and the Jews sold it for firewood and made one hundred percent profit on it a long time ago. . . . And the sheep that the shepherds were tending are all old bucks and made into baloney long ago, and they don't herd sheep there any more. Under the Taylor Grazing Act all grazing rights have been allotted to the Jews and all the Arabs can do is tend camp for the kikes so what's the use."[22]

McCarran, of course, never openly fought anyone because he was a Jew. There was always some *other* reason.* More and more being a foreigner was enough. For most of the year, McCarran's immigration subcommittee had been too busy working on a bill to keep subversives out of the country to

---

*Privately McCarran could be more blunt, as Interior Secretary Oscar Chapman discovered. "McCarran once summoned Chapman to his office," Jack Anderson told Drew Pearson. "McCarran then ordered Chapman to fire the Jewish solicitor-general; otherwise McCarran threatened to cut the Interior Department's budget. . . . Chapman warned that he would deny it if it ever leaked out." (Jack Anderson to Drew Pearson, 28 December 1950, DP Papers, Lyndon B. Johnson Library.)

work on the bill to let Jews into the country. To McCarran they were two sides of the same coin. Every diplomat from a Communist country, McCarran said, was a potential spy. He believed the same about displaced persons — many of whom were not, in fact, concentration camp survivors, but rather refugees from Russia and Eastern Europe. "Unassimilable blocks of aliens with foreign ideologies,"[23] McCarran called them.

McCarran had a mind that would seize on a single, overriding idea to the exclusion of virtually everything else. From his first week in Congress he was gripped by a monomaniacal worry that Roosevelt wanted to be a dictator; he spent much of the next dozen years warning and fighting against that specter. Recently McCarran had become fixated on another great and terrible idea: the threat of immigration. This son of Irish immigrants became obsessed with immigration. "This was the thing that he worked on and dreamed of day and night," recalled his friend Norm Biltz, "to block it every way possible."[24]

In place of the McGrath bill, McCarran introduced his own proposal, which was denounced by administration supporters as too niggardly. "We simply cannot solve the chaotic condition of the world by mass immigration into the United States," McCarran told the Senate. "I shall not yield to the demagoguery of those who would disregard the best interests of this nation."[25]

In July, McCarran asked the Senate to approve a bill to let 250 Basque sheepherders into the country. "There is no more important bill on the calendar than this one,"[26] he said.

No lawmaker was more opposed to wholesale changes in American immigration law than McCarran. Piecemeal changes were another matter. Even as McCarran fought for tighter immigration laws, he was a prodigious proponent of private immigration bills — measures that applied only to a specific person, such as a constituent's relative who overstayed a visa. When an immigrant didn't meet federal requirements to become a U.S. citizen, an obliging lawmaker could bypass the immigration service by sponsoring a private bill to the same effect — bills that McCarran handed out like Halloween candy.

"I am introducing a bill for Marlia's boy, nephew, cousin, or uncle, whatever he is," McCarran told Pete Petersen. "Whether the bill goes through or not, they will not be able to touch the Marlia sprout until the Congress refuses to do anything. You might tell Marlia that if he has any desire to hold his lineal relative in America, he had better get busy organizing his relatives and other sons of Italy in Sparks for the great drive in 1950 — the McCarran drive, that is. Tell Marlia that his honorable relative doesn't have a Chinaman's chance of staying in America unless I can retain my well-upholstered seat in the Senate."[27]

As chairman of the Judiciary Committee, which handled all immigration legislation, McCarran usually didn't have much trouble getting his private bills passed. But this time New Jersey's Robert Hendrickson rose to block McCarran's bill.

"As I understand," Hendrickson said, "there are in some of the displaced persons camps over five thousand sheepherders."[28]

On August 10, two days after McCarran's surprise party, Scott Lucas was reduced to going to the Republicans for help. Despite urgings from the White House, the Democrats had gotten nowhere with McCarran. Not that all of them were trying that hard. Senator Howard McGrath, for example, was supposed to be the administration point man on the bill but had done next to nothing to lobby for its passage. "I understand he has been a little hesitant to push McCarran," White House aide Steve Spingarn told Charles Murphy, "because of the pending judgeship bill now in conference."[29]

The Republicans, who never minded embarrassing the Democrats, had been the first to complain loudly about McCarran's inaction on the DP bill. Now New York senator Irving Ives invited the Democratic majority leader to talk a meeting of the Republican Policy Committee. "This matter," Lucas said, "doesn't involve politics. It involves human beings, their lives and their futures. And it involves the prestige of this nation. Both parties are pledged to a more liberal law."

Policy chairman Robert Taft agreed to help Lucas. Six Democrats and six Republicans signed a petition to pry the bill out of the Judiciary Committee. A discharge petition needed only a bare majority of votes in the Senate to take effect but it was a measure of absolute last resort — so loath were senators to infringe on the prerogatives of chairmanship that the last successful discharge petition had been in 1932.

"Either McCarran budges," Lucas confided to *Time*'s Frank McNaughton, "or the Senate will blast him off the bill."[30]

On September 12 McCarran rose in the Senate and asked for a three-week leave of absence to investigate the displaced persons situation in Europe.

Scott Lucas interrupted to point out that leaders of both parties urgently wanted to get the displaced persons bill out of McCarran's committee and onto the floor for a vote and that they would use a discharge petition to wrest the bill away from McCarran if necessary.

"I hope the Senator from Illinois will not bring up the motion during my absence," McCarran replied, "but that he will give me time to get back here, for I certainly want to be on the floor."

"So it might be possible to get the bill out while the senator is gone?" Lucas said hopefully.

"I doubt it very much," McCarran replied.[31]

Three days later, on September 15, McCarran and Birdie sailed from New York on the *Queen Mary* to Cherbourg, where they entrained to Paris, arriving on September 21. Waiting in Paris for McCarran were two of his staffers, Calvin Cory and Hal Lackey (and their wives). The McCarrans checked into the Hotel de Crillon on the Place de la Concorde, a massive classical edifice built for Louis XV, a building older than McCarran's country.

Walking out of the hotel was like stepping into a postcard: The majestic square stretched wide, a three-thousand-year-old Egyptian obelisk standing at its center flanked by splashing fountains. Beyond the plaza, where the French royal family had been beheaded, flowed the broad, dark Seine River. To the left the Tuilerie Gardens led to the glorious paintings in the Louvre, and to the right the Avenue des Champs-Élysées stretched toward the Arc de Triomphe. The Place de la Concorde itself could have easily swallowed downtown Reno, with its dinky brick Riverside Hotel and the Truckee, so insubstantial a river that you could skip a stone across it. McCarran was unimpressed.

"I wouldn't give one block of Reno for this whole city," McCarran wrote to his daughter Mary. "Its old houses and ancient palaces and antiquated squares and monuments are all right but they are a century behind the times."[32]

McCarran and Birdie spent a month traveling around Europe, visiting Germany, Switzerland, Italy, then the French Riviera before heading back to the Île de France.

"We are having a wonderful time," Birdie told Mary. "Patsy has been working awfully hard." McCarran himself was less enthusiastic. He enjoyed the floor show at the Lido in Paris ("very nice but boy the price of a dinner there"), was uninspired by the south of France ("awful dull here, but very pretty"), and was altogether disappointed by Mount Vesuvius ("no smoke, nothing"). In Pisa, McCarran brought a postcard of the Leaning Tower for Margaret. "I tried to straighten this thing up, not much luck," he scribbled on the back. "Still leans a little . . . still standing anyway."

After several weeks of sight-seeing, Birdie was far less cheerful. "I am so tired I don't know anything," Birdie wrote to Mary, "am saturated with churches and castles, etc., tea, luncheons, dinners, etc."

By the end of October, McCarran was back in Paris. "We have had a nice trip," McCarran told his daughter Margaret, "aside from the Displaced Persons."[33]

In the Funk Kaserne Emigration and Repatriation Camp outside Munich, McCarran interviewed John W. Cutler Jr., who had worked for the Displaced Persons Commission for almost a year screening refugees. Cutler had previously testified before McCarran's immigration subcommittee that the commission was lax. Nothing, he told McCarran in Germany, had changed. "It probably takes thirty seconds to select someone," Cutler said. "We were told that black marketing was of no offense and never mind. We should still say he was of good moral character."[34]

McCarran heard a lot of testimony like that — the only kind he was looking for. An American consular official, for instance, told McCarran that ten displaced persons had been issued visas over the past half a year based on their statements that they had arrived in Germany before the cutoff date in December 1945 — only for evidence to turn up later indicating that they had not arrived until 1946. With more than ten thousand people a month leaving for the United States, this kind of technical violation of the law might not unduly trouble many people. It bothered the hell out of McCarran.

"We have seen DP's galore . . . ," he told Eva Adams. "The story of what goes on in the DP movement is not a pleasant one to listen to. It involves, fraud, violations of the law, perjury, forgeries of instruments, and what-not. It involves the racketeer who makes hundreds of thousands in black marketing and then applies for placement in the DP ranks and then when placed in a DP camp gets access to transportation to America. . . . It involves the purchase of birth certificates from the police force, it involves the purchase of residential certificates from the police force, this in many instances done by a carton of cigarettes."[35]

McCarran cabled his findings back to Washington, sending almost a dozen wires telling his colleagues in the Senate about abuses in the displaced persons program and urging them not to act on the bill until he returned. "There is no necessity for any immediate change in existing laws," he wired. "United States Displaced Persons Commission, United States Consular Service and United States Immigration Service all agree. . . . My investigation indicates need to tighten existing law." McCarran also mentioned that he had spoken with officials from most of the major relief groups. "All officials agree that present act will have taken care of the person actually displaced," he wrote.[36]

McCarran was lying. As soon as McCarran's allies began reading these cables to the Senate, the relief groups fired off telegrams disputing McCarran's assertions. "We do not agree," wrote James J. Norris of the National Catholic Welfare Conference, "with a single statement in the message of Senator McCarran."[37]

Even the Catholics, it seemed, were being misled by the Jews.

McCarran was being followed, it turned out, by the Jews — or at least *a* Jew. Everywhere McCarran went in Europe, a tall, talkative man with a dark mustache soon turned up. His name was Harry Rosenfield.

When Congress passed the 1948 DP Act, Truman appointed a three-member Displaced Persons Commission to run the program. Truman hated the law. He appointed commissioners who felt the same way. Rosenfield was one of them. He was also Jewish.*

The law was complex and rigid, designed by McCarran and other conservatives to make it easier to keep out potential subversives than to let in refugees, especially Jewish ones. The commission that administered the law, however, was unabashedly liberal, more concerned with alleviating suffering and helping immigrants come to America then in screening out Communists. When McCarran discovered laxity in the resettlement program, he was convinced that it was a plot to sneak Communists into the country. Actually, it was only a connivance among liberals to stretch the law as far as it would go. "All of us who were attached to the U.S. program were like people possessed,"[38] recalled Kathryn Hulme, an official with the International Refugee Organization.

Rosenfield was thirty-eight, a Columbia Law grad and a protégé of New York mayor La Guardia. He had worked for the Farm Security Administration in Washington and then the UN Economic and Social Council before Truman appointed him to the DP Commission in 1948.

---

*The other two commissioners were Ugo Carusi, a Protestant, and Ed O'Connor, a Catholic.

Rosenfield jumped into the job, working harder than he had ever worked before. "The most exciting experience I ever had," he recalled. "I have a feeling that in dealing with these human beings we helped not only them but we helped Europe with a very serious geopolitical problem, and we helped the United States by bringing into the United States a lot of absolutely wonderful people."

McCarran, however, refused to hold confirmation hearings for any of the DP commissioners, so that even after more than a year on the job the appointments were still provisional. "McCarran was not very happy with the program and was not very happy with the commission," Rosenfield said. ". . . None of us really cared. We were trying to do our job, not that we would not have wanted to be confirmed, obviously, but we weren't going to give up our souls, so to speak, for confirmation."

When McCarran sailed to Europe to investigate the displaced persons program after nine months of trench warfare against revising the law, Rosenfield was worried. "I was sure he was going to come back with all sorts of stories detrimental to the program," he recalled.

Rosenfield took off to Europe himself, shadowing McCarran at every camp he visited, reinterviewing everyone McCarran spoke to, and taking copious notes in a large black binder. "I was very earnest with them," he remembered. "I said, 'Senator McCarran saw you on such and such a date; what did he ask you and what did you say to him,' and I made notes in front of them, so there was no attempt to deceive anybody."[39]

This should have ended any chance that Rosenfield had of being confirmed as a member of the Displaced Persons Commission by McCarran's Judiciary Committee. But while McCarran was in Europe, the acting chairman of the committee was Harley Kilgore, a liberal Democrat and steadfast Truman loyalist. Kilgore sent the nominations of the three commissioners to the Senate, which quickly approved them.

As the first session of the Eighty-first Congress staggered toward adjournment, Truman's Fair Deal program was in tatters. Getting his nominees confirmed at long last by the Senate was a rare victory for the president that fall.

Kilgore was just getting started.

Just after 2 P.M. on October 15 Senate aides frantically started making long-distance phone calls. It was finally coming to a vote. At 7 P.M. tonight. Robert Taft was in Ohio picking up an honorary degree; he caught the next flight back. John Foster Dulles broke off campaigning in New York and rushed to the Capitol. Henry Dworshak, who had been appointed days before to fill a vacancy caused by a death, hurried to Washington and took the oath of office just in time to cast a vote. "Why all this haste?"[40] wondered North Dakota's William "Wild Bill" Langer.

The haste was because after ten months of delay, the DP bill was finally on the floor. Three days earlier, on October 12, Harley Kilgore, the acting chairman, called the Judiciary Committee to order. Homer Ferguson made a motion to send the DP bill to the floor without a recommendation. The committee voted 7 to 3 in favor. That day Herb Block drew a cartoon in the *Washington Post* showing a skinny girl with DISPLACED PERSONS BILL written on her dress standing with a broken chain hanging from one ankle outside the door to a brick fortress labeled SENATE JUDICIARY COMMITTEE. "The smallest state in the union from the standpoint of population has the distinction of having contributed a one-man monkey wrench to the legislative process in Washington," the *Washington Post* editorialized. ". . . Other members of the Senate are heartily sick of McCarran's domineering but they are afraid to offend him."[41]

McCarran's allies rose to defend him. Washington Republican Harry P. Cain held the floor for six hours. He attacked the Citizens Committee on Displaced Persons. "I wish the senior senator from Nevada were here," cried Cain, "with his mane of white hair, to fight for himself, as he could do so ably."[42]

Majority Leader Scott Lucas called the current law shameful and decried the delaying tactics. "It's a filibuster, of course,"[43] he snapped.

James Eastland called McCarran's treatment outrageous. "Uphold his hand," he said, "instead of insulting him by taking the bill from his committee."[44]

"The world is watching," countered Majority Whip Francis J. Myers. "By rejecting the bill we give rise to the feeling that we do not intend to carry out our pledges to aid in bringing about a better and a peaceful world."[45]

"We have provided too much help for too many," Cain snipped. "We have required from the DPs nothing."[46]

"What this comes down to," observed Bill Langer, "is a personal question of whether the Senate will repudiate Pat McCarran."[47]

It would not. After three days of drawn-out debate, Cain and Eastland moved to send the bill back to the Judiciary Committee, with the proviso that committee report it out by late January. The Senate voted 36 to 30 to recommit. "The Senate," noted *Newsweek*, "was less afraid of Mr. Truman than of Pat McCarran."[48]

In Rome, on October 18, McCarran and Birdie crossed the Tiber River, entered the Vatican, and were escorted through the Stanza della Segnatura with its wonderful Raphaels, then into the pope's private library. Pope Pius XII, an elderly stick figure beneath his skullcap and white robe, rose to greet them. McCarran kissed his ring. The senator then presented the pope with a pile of rosaries to bless. "I did not know," the pontiff smiled, "there were so many Catholics in America."[49]

Pope Pius XII was seventy-three, as spindly as McCarran was ample and the same age. "His manner is most gracious and lovely," McCarran told his daughter Mary, "and he seemed to be in no haste to conclude with us although there were many outside waiting for the public audience."[50]

The pope, in his heavily accented English, asked McCarran about his family — which was just what McCarran wanted to talk about. McCarran had given his first two daughters to his Church, and now he wanted a favor from that church. Both daughters were teachers in California, but McCarran wanted them closer. He wanted them to go to graduate school in Washington. The mother superior of their order had refused. McCarran enlisted the assistance of New York cardinal Francis Spellman, who had no luck either. So McCarran asked the pope for help. The pontiff said he would do what he could. "All that you wanted is granted," McCarran beamed to Mary, "but don't tell anyone."[51]

Then the pope praised the United States for helping to rebuild Europe. During the war the Nazis had arrested more than a thousand Jews in Rome and sent them to their deaths in Auschwitz without the pope saying a word, yet the Church also sheltered Jews in monasteries and chapels. After the war, in 1946, the pope issued an encyclical *(Quemadmodum)* that called on the faithful to help the refugee children. "Those who live in luxury should reflect and remember," the pope said, "that the indigence, hunger and nakedness of these children will constitute a grave and severe indictment of them before God, the Father of mercies, if they harden their hearts and do not contribute generously. All, finally, should be convinced that their liberality will not be loss but gain, for we can safely say that one who gives from his means to the poor is lending to God Who, in His own time, will repay his generosity with abundant interest."[52]

McCarran seems never to have read the document. He said good-bye to the pope. "The audience granted us by His Holiness was the highest form of audience granted to anyone," McCarran bragged to Mary. "Kings, presidents or emperors get no more. It was grand."[53]

—

In late October McCarran took a train from Paris to the Spanish border, where Pablo Merry del Val was waiting. McCarran knew Merry del Val from the Spanish embassy in Washington ("He speaks splendid English"[54]). For the next nine days, Merry del Val showed McCarran around the country — frozen in time since the 1930s by its authoritarian government, snubbed by the rest of Europe for its tacit alliance with the Axis powers during the war, and parched by years of drought. The trip across Spain told McCarran everything that he needed to know about the country: in every town the signs shouted the same slogan (VIVE FRANCO), in every tavern and café hung the same picture, and in every pocket the money featured the same profile. CAUDILLO BY THE GRACE OF GOD read the coins.[55] Once they reached Madrid, Merry del Val drove McCarran to a vast, wooded estate on the northern edge of town: El Pardo Palace, built by Carlos I in the sixteenth century and decorated by Goya, who filled room after huge room with tapestries depicting hunting parties and happy peasants. Now it was Francisco Franco's home.

Franco welcomed McCarran with a handshake. Short and stout, stuffed into his bemedaled military uniform and riding boots, a sash trussed across his waist, his thin hair slicked back over his bald head, a thin mustache under a large nose — Franco looked like a caricature of a dictator. His demeanor was altogether different. Shy and reserved and painfully polite, Franco spoke in a low voice, but his words were sure and firm. He was, Franco believed, a man of destiny who had saved his country from Communism so that Spain could fulfill its mission. "The history of our nation," he once said, "is inseparably united to the history of the Catholic Church, its glories are our glories and its enemies our enemies."[56]

McCarran beamed. "My visit with Franco was exceedingly interesting," he told Eva Adams, "and I was most agreeably surprised to learn the nature and kind of man that he is. He has been frightfully slandered and maligned. . . . I found the sentiment of the people in Spain from the lowest in stature to the highest, outspoken in praise of Franco's regime and of Franco himself."[57]

Franco was an international pariah. When the United Nations formed it 1945, it refused to admit fascist Spain. Franco had bombed his own people in the town of Guernica, smashed the Republican government with Hitler's help, and crushed the hopes of a whole generation of leftists and liberals who saw in the Spanish Civil War a stark contest between good and evil — a contest that evil won. In 1946 the UN General Assembly passed a resolution calling on all member states to withdraw their ranking diplomats from Spain. Although the United States did not officially sever relations with Madrid, Truman didn't bother to replace the ambassador who left in 1945. "I don't like Franco," Truman said, "and I never will."[58]

Spain didn't have an ambassador in Washington, either — at least officially. In 1945 Franco sent José Felix de Lequerica, who had been Spain's ambassador in occupied France, to Washington. Washington sent him back. Three years later Franco appointed Lequerica as a temporary inspector of the embassy; he stayed for more than two years. Lequerica's real mission was managing what became known as the Spanish Lobby, an informal group of politicians and reporters who advocated that the United States normalize relations with Franco. Lequerica hired the well-connected Washington law firm of Cummings, Stanley, Truitt and Cross (Max Truitt was the son-in-law of Vice President Barkley) and also enlisted the help of James Farley, a well-known Catholic who had been Roosevelt's postmaster and patronage boss. Supporting Spain, Lequerica liked to say, was good for thirty million Catholic votes in America. It was also good for cash. Before one big UN vote, Lequerica spent more than one hundred thousand dollars on politicians and reporters and urgently cabled Madrid for almost a quarter million dollars more. "Anyone," Franco said, "can be bought."[59]

No politician was a bigger supporter of Spain than McCarran. In May, for example, Dean Acheson appeared before the appropriations subcommittee that approved the State Department budget, whose chairman was McCarran. Why hadn't the United States exchanged ambassadors with Madrid? McCarran demanded. Why wasn't Spain part of the Marshall Plan? Why wasn't Spain invited to join NATO? "What has Spain done except fight Communism?" McCarran asked. "What has made her the offspring on whom the door is shut?"[60]

Acheson explained that the United States was trying to honor the UN resolution and that Spain had not been made part of the Marshall Plan or NATO because the Western European allies despised Franco. "It's no secret that the Spanish regime was a fascist regime," he said.[61]

"The secretary of state," McCarran said in the Senate a few days later, "was exceedingly evasive. . . . Why is it, I ask, that our State Department refuses to recognize diplomatically a nation that has been fighting Communism for the past twenty-five years? . . . I for one — and I say it humbly — would never have voted in favor of having the United States sign the United Nations charter if I had thought for a moment that thereby we were giving up our sovereignty to recognize diplomatic attachés."[62]

When the White House declined to change its foreign policy, McCarran took matters into his own hands. In July 1949 he slipped a fifty-million-dollar loan for Spain into the Marshall Plan appropriation. The morning after the bill passed, Lequerica showed up at the State Department and went to the office of Assistant Secretary Willard Thorp. "Where do I go to get my fifty million dollars?" he asked.[63] Thorp tried to explain that Congress had voted to give aid — that is, pay for programs and projects, not give out cash. The next thing Thorp knew McCarran was on the phone. "Why isn't the Spanish ambassador getting his fifty million dollars?" the senator bellowed. McCarran later took up the matter with Acheson. "Are you giving them what they want?" he asked the secretary.[64] "Spain," McCarran once told Truman, "is ready, willing and anxious to place all of her fighting resources by the side of the democracies. . . . Spain is the only country in Europe that has successfully conquered Communism."[65]

Before McCarran sailed from New York in September, he told reporters that he was going to meet with Franco and discuss aid for Spain. The senator, Truman snapped, doesn't have any right to conduct his own foreign policy. "Ambassador from Nevada," the *Reporter* magazine called McCarran.[66]

As McCarran traveled, the news got worse and worse. On September 23 Truman announced that the Soviet Union had exploded an atomic bomb — years earlier than anyone had expected. In October, Mao Tsetung declared the founding of the People's Republic of China — the largest country in the world was now officially Communist. "The Spanish authorities and the Spanish people cannot understand the attitude of America," McCarran told Adams. "They seem depressed with the fact that we would recognize and aid Tito and not recognize and aid Spain."[67]

McCarran would do his best to change that. In the Senate, McCarran eventually lost the Spanish loan after a bitter floor fight. But in 1950 McCarran came back with another hundred-million-dollar loan for Spain, which was cut to sixty-two and a half million dollars in conference and signed by Truman. That November the UN voted to let members send diplomats back to Spain, followed by the United States appointing a new ambassador to Madrid. In 1951 McCarran would finally get Congress to loan Spain one hundred million dollars, and Truman shook hands (grudgingly) with Franco's new ambassador: Lequerica, whom the president had refused to recognize six years earlier. In 1953 the United States and Spain signed the Madrid Pact, which gave the U.S. military bases in Spain in exchange for $226 million in military assistance. In 1955 Spain was finally admitted to the United Nations. "The world needs Spain," Franco said, "more than Spain needs the world."[68]

On August 25, 1954, at noon, McCarran went to the Spanish embassy on Sixteenth Street, where Ambassador de Lequerica presented him with the grand cross of the order of Isabella la Catolica. "It would seem," he said, "that Senator McCarran in his country is rather a controversial fellow, but diplomats know nothing about the internal controversies of the country to which they are accredited."[69] McCarran's wife and his two nun daughters looked on in delight. "McCarran," wrote Madrid's *El Mundo Visto*, "era un gran amigo de espana."[70]

In the Pardo Palace, amid the Goyas and the gilt furniture, McCarran and Franco got to know each other a little bit. They had a lot in common: Both were devout Catholics, despised Communism, and loved to hunt and fish (although Franco liked to shoot goats with a machine gun and chase whales with the Spanish navy). "I will not give Spain any freedom in the next ten years," Franco said not long after his visit with McCarran. "Then, I will open my hand somewhat."*[71]

McCarran left Spain beaming about the country's progressive ruler. "My audience with Franco was very pleasant," McCarran told his daughter Margaret. "He is not the man he is pictured to be but a very tolerant humane man."[72]

Then it was back to Paris, across the Channel to England, a stop in London, and a ferry to Dublin. McCarran journeyed south to Cork, where his mother had been raised before immigrating to America. In Doughmore, McCarran found the house where his mother had been born and met her nieces. The parish priest dug up her baptismal records, and finally he knew the date of his mother's birth: August 25, 1850. "So for the first time," McCarran told Mary, "I know her age — eighty-five. You remember she always said she was as old as her little finger and her birthday was the 17th of March."

Seeing the country that his father had fled a hundred years earlier, followed by his mother, was a profoundly moving experience for McCarran. "I have trod the holy ground where dear old grandma was a girl," he told Mary.

---

*McCarran's critics were outraged by the visit. "Chief volunteer public relations counsel to Europe's Number One Fascist dictator," Drew Pearson called McCarran. "Dictator Pat ought to feel perfectly at home with Dictator Franco," added Harold Ickes. "The latter, in addition to exiling and murdering better Spaniards than himself, is another gnat that has been trying to become an elephant." (*Washington Post*, 23 November 1949; *The New Republic*, 3 October 1949.)

"I had a little silent cry all to myself. It seemed holy ground to me, even though a stranger was in the door. The old walls heard her first made sound and the old floor felt her bare feet. I looked over the fields where she went bare footed and played and starved. They all told me a story of a girl, a woman who had slaved and worked and suffered for her boy, and *I* was that boy. It seemed to me I heard her voice calling me and urging me to go on and on."[73]

The fact that his own parents had been famine refugees in the nineteenth century before they sought a better life in America did nothing to make McCarran the least bit sympathetic toward the refugees of another awful dislocation in the twentieth century. "They are displeased persons rather than displaced persons," McCarran told Eva Adams. "Eighty-seven percent are of one blood, one race, one religion. You know what that is without my telling you."[74]

The Ukrainian refugee had been in the resettlement center near Frankfurt in the American Zone of Germany for a dozen days. The center, like many of the DP camps, operated out of an old Wehrmacht barrack; but unlike the camps, it was a place of hope, the final stop on the long bureaucratic road out of Allied-Occupied Germany. The Ukrainian refugee and his family were lucky: After years in a DP camp in Bayreuth they had been matched up with a sponsor in Detroit. They were going to America.

"Achtung! Achtung!" a loudspeaker blared, calling the Ukrainian back to the medical office. Maybe his medical clearance was ready.

As hard as it was for many refugees to get into a DP camp in the first place, it was even harder to get out. For every visa that Congress agreed to provide under the DP Act, a sponsor had to be found in the United States to guarantee that the arriving immigrant would have a job and a place to live. Once a sponsor was lined up, the would-be immigrant had to pass a series of checks: literacy, medical, security. The whole process was supposed to take four months; twice as long was not uncommon. Some cases lengthened to more than a year. One International Refugee Organization worker pulled out the documents in a single case file and the paperwork went on for seventeen yards. "Watching the machinery of the U.S. program . . . was like watching an enormous merry-go-round without music," recalled Kathryn Hulme, an official with the IRO in Germany, "on which all of the DP's you had ever known seemed to be permanently stuck. And, if you managed to unseat one and get him started in a straight line toward a ship, you very often saw him back again on the merry-go-round, perhaps transfixed on a different technicality this time, but there all the same — doleful, despairing and going around and around."[75]

The security barrier was the highest hurdle. Army Counter Intelligence Corps carried out the screening, which included interrogating the displaced person, interviewing three neighbors, obtaining clearance from the local police, and checking for Nazi Party membership in the Berlin archives. If an immigrant was delayed more than six months (because of a medical problem, for example), the security clearance lapsed and the process had to start over. "Rigorous protective screening processes have been instituted by the Displaced Persons Commission," the agency noted in a report that summer. ". . . The security measures employed under the Displaced Persons Act far exceed those applied in any other immigration program. They involve at least seven major security protective checks. . . . In all cases of doubt as to the admissibility for security reasons, the doubt is resolved in favor of the security of the United States and against the admission of the displaced person."[76]

The Ukrainian reported to the X-ray room. The doctor explained that he could not read the first X ray. They took another one. The Ukrainian went back to his wife and two children in their small room. He told his wife he was convinced that the doctors had found a spot on his lungs. He was sure they weren't going to Detroit.

That night he slipped into the basement and hung himself from a steam pipe. His wife and children were sent back to the displaced persons camp where they had come from. "We had not realized the extent of the emotional strain our DP's were laboring under," Hulme recalled.[77]

Some people never did.

On December 2, his three-week trip already grown to ten weeks, McCarran sailed from England for New York on the *Queen Elizabeth*. "Oh! I'll be glad to get home," McCarran told his daughter Mary. "I'm tired, dear. I'm tired, awful tired. I must get out to Nevada before January 3rd when Congress reconvenes. I'm not going to be in Washington for Christmas. I'm going to be in God's desert where there's rest for this weary soul and peace — the desert out in the nowhere near to God."[78]

Five days later, the *Queen Elizabeth* nosed into New York Harbor, passed the Statue of Liberty, and docked. Reporters were waiting to ask McCarran about his investigation of displaced persons camps. "Far better than living conditions of the average inhabitant of many areas in the United States," McCarran said.[79]

A reporter asked about the January 25 deadline that the Senate had voted on when it returned the DP bill to the Judiciary Committee.

"What deadline?" McCarran said.[80]

On January 4, 1950, Truman gave his State of the Union speech. Tom Connally yawned. McCarran crossed and recrossed his legs like a man with a weak bladder on a long trip. Truman spoke for barely half an hour, calling for much of the same Fair Deal program that he had a year earlier, including a more liberal DP bill. McCarran smirked. "Nevada's one-man roadblock," *Time* called him.[81]

Two days later in the Senate McCarran warned that the current law was being flagrantly violated. He charged that security screening was weak and that an unnamed pressure group was spending a million dollars a year to break down the law — more or less the same speech he had given almost a year earlier. "The floodgates of this nation are being pried open for the entrance of millions of aliens," he said. ". . . Their ultimate objective the destruction of our immigration barriers. . . . There is a complete breakdown in the administration of the law. Inadequate screening of applicants, with little or no regard for background, political beliefs . . . has opened the gates to persons who will not become good citizens and who will become ready recruits in subversive organizations. . . . Help hold the dikes of our protective immigration system."[82]

"The same old baseless charges again," fumed James J. Norris of the National Catholic Welfare Conference. "Untruths, half truths and simple lies," added Ugo Carusi, the chairman of the Displaced Persons Commission. "For the first time in my career in public life I have been called a liar by a federal official," McCarran responded.[83]

The next month McCarran attended a naturalization ceremony in Washington where forty immigrants became U.S. citizens. "If any of you come with the ulterior motive," McCarran said, "of tearing down our government it were better a thousand times if a millstone had been tied around your neck."[84]

Welcome to America.

The immigration subcommittee meetings were getting more and more ugly. At one hearing counsel Richard Arens questioned Senator Kilgore over whether the DP Commission had ghostwritten the dissenting committee report, implying that the outnumbered liberals on the committee were scheming with the liberal commissioners. Kilgore was offended that a congressional *staffer* would dare take such an attitude with a senator. Under McCarran's patronage, Arens had become a force on Capitol Hill, leading the Nevada senator's various investigations into the State Department, the Justice Department, the United Nations, and now immigration policy. "Few elected members of the upper chamber wield the influence he seems to," noted the *Washington Post*.[85]

Indiana senator William Jenner roared to Arens's defense, insisting that the counsel had to work against a million-dollar DP lobby.

Kilgore jumped to his feet. "Is the senator implying that any money has changed hands?" he said. Jenner started shouting. "I stand back of Mr. Arens one hundred percent," he said.[86]

Kilgore turned red and huffed out of the committee room. Then DP commissioner Harry Rosenfield jumped into the fray. "You have been conducting a star chamber proceedings," he said. "You are afraid of the facts."[87]

Arens glared. "Every patriotic American in this country," he said, "ought to get on his knees every night and thank the Good Lord that we have the senior senator from Nevada who had been waging this fight against tremendous odds and against a million dollar lobby that has been defaming him from one end of the country to the other."[88]

On January 24, the Judiciary Committee finally reported out a DP bill. The liberal Celler bill (HR 4567) had gone into the committee, but what came out was completely different, a bill so bristling with McCarran amendments as to be almost unrecognizable. "Less pernicious than might have been expected from Senator McCarran," the *Washington Post* called the bill.[89] "A sham," Celler labeled it.[90]

Liberals quickly wrote a substitute measure. Almost daily they met in Harley Kilgore's office, where the regulars included DP commissioner Harry Rosenfield and Herbert Lehman, who had just been elected to the Senate. Lehman, seventy-two, was almost McCarran's polar opposite: a New York Jew from a wealthy family who had been Roosevelt's lieutenant governor and then governor himself before becoming director of the United Nations Relief and Rehabilitation Administration, which ran the first DP camps in Europe. Lehman was a kindly man, short and stocky with a bull head, thin white hair, and thick dark brows. McCarran was one of the few men whom Lehman ever really hated. "There goes an evil man,"[91] his friend Paul Douglas said once as McCarran walked by. Lehman would spend much of the next five years fighting McCarran on immigration bills.

On February 28 McCarran started the floor debate, which lasted eight days and several times threatened to turn into a melee. James Eastland, the Mississippi senator and champion of segregation, called the DP Commission members traitors. "Guilty of moral treason," he explained, "because they have set up a system there, as a result of which they know that Communist saboteurs and agents and officers of the Russian secret police have been filtered into the United States."[92] Lehman all but called Eastland a liar. "More misstatements and more inaccuracies than he ever thought it possible to be made on the floor of this great deliberative body," he said.[93] "A tissue of lies," Eastland replied.[94]

"Sometimes," Lehman said, "a man can be proud of the enemies he makes."[95]

One day William Jenner was droning on against the bill ("We are bringing in subversives, Communists, robbers, criminals of all kinds, black-marketers, perjurers, defrauders. . . ."[96]) and the floor was empty except for one Republican and one Democrat. Republican Bill Langer then interrupted Jenner and moved to adjourn. Jenner agreed. Democrat Russell B. Long was talking to an aide and turned around too late to object. The Senate shut down for the day, the recess bells ringing throughout the Capitol. Majority Leader Scott Lucas came running in, fuming against his own party for its fumbling. McCarran strolled in smiling. "Where was the Judiciary Committee," Lucas snapped. "You fellows should stick around here." McCarran looked at Lucas. "Where," he asked, "was the majority leader?"[97]

Another day McCarran made a motion to delay the vote because hearing transcripts had not yet been prepared (although Jenner was leafing through transcripts that day as he gave a speech). "Of course," McCarran said, "if I were to make the motion, then the Communists and some others would say I was stalling. . . . I have never stalled this bill."[98]

That was too much for Lucas. "The truth of the matter is that he has never desired to have any kind of bill passed other than the one he wants," he said. "And that is the attitude of the senator on everything, namely, unless he can have what he wants, he will not play on the team."[99]

Lucas agreed to one more delay. It wouldn't be the last.

On Wednesday morning, April 5, McCarran had agreed to start the final debate on the displaced persons bill. He didn't show up.

Vice President Alben Barkley sent the sergeant at arms to look for McCarran. For fifteen months McCarran had defied the leadership of both parties by bottling up the bill in his Judiciary Committee. He had stalled for all of 1949. He had run off to Europe to delay the vote; from across the Atlantic he pulled strings to keep the legislation in abeyance. After he returned to Washington, McCarran dragged his feet for a few more months. Finally he had consented to a vote this day in April. The Senate had adopted a resolution to go into continuous session, which meant that no other business would be taken up until the DP bill was finished. This was supposed to be a way of expediting debate. In McCarran's hands, however, it became a way of paralyzing debate. McCarran was the floor manager for his own DP bill; Kilgore was managing the liberal substitute. They had agreed to divide up their time, with McCarran leading off, which meant that nothing could start that morning until McCarran showed up. And on the morning of the debate no one could find him.

Eventually the sergeant at arms located McCarran and escorted him to the Senate. McCarran took his seat — and did nothing. From his front-row desk McCarran stared up at Barkley on the podium and Barkley stared back at McCarran and the greatest deliberative body in the world ground to a halt. McCarran refused to speak or yield to his colleagues. Kilgore could have broken the impasse by using some of his time and giving his opponent the last word. But he was determined not to back down. So the Senate stopped. Unlike a filibuster, there was not even a pretense of action, only mutterings from the body, pleas from the podium, and stony silence from the two antagonists. After a while Democrat Dennis Chavez tried to get the chamber to consider some other business, but neither McCarran nor Kilgore would yield. "Perfectly preposterous," Barkley sputtered. Chavez then asked Kilgore if he could move for a recess. He said no. "We appear before the country . . . ," Chavez complained, "in a peculiar way." Other Democrats began piling on Kilgore, begging Barkley for a parliamentary ruling that would force the vote. Kilgore yielded.[100]

McCarran and his allies still managed to put off the vote for thirteen hours with a blizzard of 130 amendments to his own bill; then he offered 130 amendments to Kilgore's bill. Most of the amendments were disposed of by voice vote; twenty came to a roll call, a record for a single day. The key vote was to substitute Kilgore's bill for McCarran's, which came just before midnight, passing 49 to 25. Finally, almost two hours later, the roll was called on the DP bill, which was approved 58 to 15.

Shuffling onto the elevator after the defeat, McCarran bumped into William Bernard, the head of the Citizens Committee on Displaced Persons, the nondenominational but largely Jewish group that had been fighting vigorously for a more liberal refugee policy — the same pressure group, as McCarran had loudly been complaining, that was out to destroy the country's immigration system. It was a silent ride down to the ground floor. McCarran was first out the Capitol door, lumbering down the steps, followed by Bernard. Suddenly, the senator stopped, turned around, and exploded.

"You son of a bitch," he yelled.

"Thank you, senator," Bernard replied.[101]

McCarran turned and walked down the steps.

McCarran actually voted for Kilgore's bill on the final roll call, which gave him the right to serve on the conference committee that would iron out differences between the Senate and House versions of the legislation. McCarran even nominated several of his colleagues to sit on the committee with him: All of them were fiercely opposed to the bill. Majority Leader Lucas picked a more balanced slate of conferees, but as the ranking member on the committee McCarran still had the prerogative to set the date for the meeting. Weeks went by and no conference was called. Eventually Representative Celler threatened to arrange the meeting himself. In conference McCarran continued to stall and to lobby for more restrictions. "The only limitation on the number of Communist agents who will be sent into the United States," he said, "will be the number which the Kremlin wants to send to this country."[102]

In early June the bill was sent to Truman to sign — eighteen months after the president had asked for it. "I met the enemy and he took me on the DP bill," McCarran told his daughter Mary. "It's tough to beat a million or more dollars and it's something worth while to give the rotten gang a good fight anyway and they know they have been to a fight for it's not over yet."[103]

McCarran was right. His continued assault on the Displaced Persons Commission destroyed the agency's morale, frightening many of its staff into either resigning or getting tougher with immigrants. McCarran was also successful in reducing the percentage of Jews allowed to come to the United States, from roughly 25 percent of all refugee immigrants to 16 percent And hemanaged to barb the new law with some additional security requirements that created havoc in the European resettlement centers. "The cases of some fifty thousand documented, cleared and read-for-visa DP's . . . were pulled from processing," recalled the IRO's Kathryn Hulme, "and bucked back for a second check by Counter-Intelligence."[104]

Then, three months after he lost the legislative fight for the DP bill, McCarran managed to pass the Internal Security Act, which, among much else, greatly tightened immigration laws. "The passage of the Internal Security Act of September 1950 seemed to paralyze the security agents on our side of the water," remembered Hulme, "making them fearful to recommend a single alien for entry to the states unless he appeared before them shining white like an angel."[105] By the time the U.S. program ended in 1952, almost half a million refugees had come to America. Fewer than one hundred thousand were Jews.[106]

In the fall McCarran was running for reelection. "Emphasize the fact that the Jews were after you," Reno postmaster Pete Petersen suggested.[107]

Actually, it seemed the other way around.

CHAPTER 18

Chamber of Horrors

No president is going to tell me what to do. His job is to execute the laws Congress passes. It certainly is not his business to tell Congress what laws it must pass.[1]

— Pat McCarran

Late on a sluggish Thursday, August 10, 1950, Pat McCarran stood up in the front row of the Senate. "At long last," he began, "those of us who have been striving for legislation which is urgently needed to meet the threat of Communists and other subversives in this country have received a token of encouragement from the administration."[2]

Two days earlier, on McCarran's seventy-fourth birthday, Harry Truman had inadvertently sent a gift to his least favorite senator: a message to Congress asking for some slight tinkering in existing laws that would make it easier to prosecute espionage and sabotage. At the same time, the president warned against succumbing to unreasoning fear and endangering the liberties that the United States was fighting to protect. Communism, he said, was an external threat but not much of a domestic danger. The message was calm, measured, and meant to soothe the unsettled soul of a nation shocked and tremulous since the Korean War had broken out six weeks earlier.

Instead it set off a feeding frenzy. As soon as the message was read, HUAC alum Senator Karl Mundt was on the floor thanking the president for endorsing the Communist registration bill that he had been flogging for three years and moving that the chamber finally take the measure up for debate. Senator Herbert Lehman jumped up to object, blocking the move. This gave the Democrats more time to write the kind of bill Truman wanted, which the president's friend Senator Harley Kilgore was already working on.

But unknown to either his fellow Democrats or the Republicans with whom he more often sided, McCarran had set Jay Sourwine and his staff furiously to work on a different sort of internal security bill. "Beat Kilgore to the punch," McCarran barked.[3] "He is putting together just about all the legislation of that nature that is pending in Congress, which is along his line of thinking,"[4] Sourwine told Eva Adams. Sourwine finished two days of breakneck drafting just before 4 P.M. on this Thursday afternoon.

And as the evening fell and the Senate thinned, McCarran surprised his colleagues on both sides of the aisle with news of yet another anti-Communist bill.

Is this the bill the Democrats have been talking about? wondered Senator Homer Ferguson, a conservative Republican who'd had a hand in the Mundt measure.

No, McCarran said.

Majority Leader Scott Lucas, the administration's voice in the Senate, added that the Democrats hadn't finished their bill, that he didn't know what was in McCarran's, but he commended him for introducing it anyway.

Lucas spoke too soon. What McCarran had actually done in a few minutes was hijack the anti-Communist legislation that HUAC had been pushing for three years (and which Truman and Lucas had been fighting just as long), attach a train of similar bills (including several of his own), and steer the whole unwieldy thing onto the legislative fast track. The move was vintage McCarran: bold, daring, and defiant, a seemingly innocuous parliamentary motion that turned out to be utterly audacious upon inspection. McCarran's omnibus bill wrapped up virtually all of the pending anti-Communist legislation in the Senate into one sprawling internal security package. Never mind that the president's message had clearly criticized several of these proposals as overly broad, unconstitutional, ineffective, and repressive — a threat not just to Communists but to all Americans. Now McCarran was in effect saying that he was going to force these bills down the president's throat anyway. And that was only the beginning. Over the next six weeks McCarran's bill (S. 4037) would grow even bigger and more fearsome, energizing the hard right of the Republican Party and dividing the Democrats, as Congress was carried away on the very flood tide of anti-Communist hysteria that the president had sought so eagerly to avoid. Seldom have the contours of history been as visible on a piece of legislation as they would be on the McCarran Act, a law so shaped by the times as to define them.

Almost six months to the day before McCarran introduced his bill — on February 9, 1950 — a little-known junior senator from Wisconsin named Joseph McCarthy had made a speech in Wheeling, West Virginia, accusing the government of being riddled with traitors. With the onset of the Korean War in June the already gloomy national mood turned even blacker. While the Wisconsin senator would give his name to the era, the phenomenon of McCarthyism was already well under way. The Internal

Security Act of 1950 would turn out to be almost the perfect expression of McCarthyism: the greatest peacetime sedition law in the country's history, a marker of a perilous moment in world politics, and a shameful departure from the American ideals of law and liberty. And McCarthy would have nothing to do with it.

The manager of Harold's Club in Reno marched his six hundred employees — pit bosses, showgirls, janitors — behind a brass band down Virginia Street, across the bridge over the Truckee and up the Washoe County Courthouse steps to sign non-Communist loyalty oaths. Down the block at Brodsky's saloon the owner also handed out loyalty forms to his employees. "Either sign or get out,"[5] he barked.

From the beginning 1950 was a troubling year. On January 6 McCarran blasted the administration for its lax enforcement of immigration laws that threatened to send a flood of subversive aliens washing over the republic. On January 21 a jury convicted Alger Hiss of perjury at his second trial. Hiss was, Nixon added darkly, only "a small part of the whole shocking story."[6]

On January 31 Truman told the nation that he had given the go-ahead for the development of a hydrogen bomb. Soon there was talk of digging mass graves in Central Park in case of a Soviet attack. New York City schools handed out dog tags to children so their bodies could be identified.

McCarran summoned Secretary of State Dean Acheson to a hearing of the appropriations subcommittee that controlled the department's budget. McCarran liked to summon Acheson. "He looks pleased," observed Richard Strout in *The New Republic*. "And why not? He is holding Secretary of State Acheson captive. . . . McCarran insists on Acheson's presence. He must sit and hear his policies attacked. He was here yesterday, too. . . . Few people in Washington are quite so crass and crude as McCarran. . . . McCarran glances covertly at Acheson. The latter sits bland and impassive; this won't do at all. Can the secretary come back again this afternoon?"[7]

This time McCarran wanted Acheson to explain what he'd meant when he'd told a room full of reporters in January that he would not turn his back on Alger Hiss after his conviction. The son of the bishop of Connecticut obliquely referred the reporters to the Gospel of St. Matthew, chapter 25, verse 34, for elaboration ("I was in prison and ye came unto me"). After the news conference Acheson offered his resignation to the president. Truman said forget it. McCarran didn't. "This of course was only a thin excuse to agitate the controversy over again,"

Acheson later remarked, "but could not be evaded and offered a chance to strike a blow for common sense."

For a year Acheson had been sitting placidly while McCarran and the Republicans on the committee impugned his policies and motives. The primitives, he called them. "One must be true to the things by which one lives," Acheson told McCarran. ". . . One must live with one's self; and the consequences of living with a decision which one knows has sprung from timidity and cowardice go to the roots of one's life. It is not merely a question of peace of mind, although that is vital; it is a matter of integrity of character."

But Acheson knew McCarran well enough to know that he wasn't getting out of the room without at least a minor act of supplication. "For the benefit of those who could create doubt where none existed," Acheson concluded, "I will accept the humiliation of stating what should be obvious — that I did not and do not condone in any way the offenses charged, whether committed by a friend or by a total stranger, and that I would never knowingly tolerate any disloyal person in the Department of State."[8]

That was just what McCarran wanted to hear from Acheson. But he didn't believe him for a minute. "Our State Department should be cleared out from top to bottom," he told his daughter Mary. "It's a mess."[9]

On the last weekend in January political, religious, journalistic, and business leaders representing sixty different organizations gathered at the Hotel Astor in New York City for the first All-American Conference, sponsored by the American Legion.[10] One of the featured speakers was Senator Karl Mundt,[11] who said that traitors such as Alger Hiss were created by the liberalism taught at Harvard University. He urged that every high school teach a course called "What's Right with America." To Mundt not much had been right with America since Herbert Hoover left the White House. For eighteen years, he declared in another speech, the United States had been "run by New Dealers, Fair Dealers, misdealers and Hiss dealers, who have shuttled back and forth between freedom and Red Fascism like a pendulum on a cuckoo clock."[12]

Mundt was born in South Dakota in 1890 and imbibed his father's agrarian discontent and distrust of eastern big business as the elder Mundt stropped his straight-edged razor and spoke his mind each morning. He went to Carleton College in Minnesota, got a master's in economics at Columbia University, and taught speech at a state university. Mundt ran twice for the House, both times against incumbents whom he painted as Communists; the second time he was successful. After his 1938 election Mundt spent the better part of a decade serving in anonymity. In 1943 he landed a long-sought assignment on the House Committee on Un-American Activities. When Lawrence Duggan tumbled to his death from a window in New York after a HUAC appearance, Mundt released committee testimony accusing him of having been a Communist agent and promised to reveal the names of other spies as quickly as they could jump out of windows. His ideal presidential candidates were Martin Dies and J. Edgar Hoover.

For years Mundt had been trying, rather haplessly, to pass a bill forcing the Communist Party to register with the government. First introduced in 1947, the bill died in committee but was resurrected the next year by Richard Nixon, Mundt's HUAC colleague. By 1950 Mundt had been struggling for three years to get his bill enacted. His election to the Senate two years earlier hadn't helped, knocking him to near the bottom of the seniority totem pole in a chamber controlled by the opposition party. Not long after the All-American Conference, his frustration with both Communists and Democrats — and to Mundt there was not much space in between — came to a boil.

When a friend sent him a picture of Stalin, Mundt promised to hang it on his wall. "I may want to hang it up alongside a likeness of Alger Hiss," Mundt wrote, "and, perhaps, as unfolding history reveals additional disclosures I may even have to add a president to that galaxy of royal rogues."[13]

On February 7, J. Edgar Hoover testified before McCarran's appropriations subcommittee. The director told Chairman McCarran that while there were only twenty-three Communists in Nevada, there were fifty-three thousand in the whole country, and for each party member there were ten fellow travelers willing to do their bidding. In effect, then, there were already a half million enemy troops within the United States.

Do the Russians deny visas to deportable aliens to keep them in the United States? McCarran asked.

Yes, the director replied, if the Russians won't take them back you have to grant them bail unless they've committed a crime. "I think it is almost a travesty upon our democratic processes that you can have people in this country who have been found to advocate the violent overthrow of your form of government, yet you cannot deport them or hold them at Ellis Island," Hoover continued. "We do not have any law by which we can hold them."[14]

If Hoover wanted a law, McCarran would give him one.

On Thursday, February 9, Wisconsin senator Joseph McCarthy went to Wheeling, West Virginia, to give the Lincoln Day speech to the Ohio County Women's Republican Club. McCarthy attacked the Truman administration, speaking of traitors in high places, including foreign service officer John Service, whose part in the *Amerasia* case made him something of a poster boy for right-wing conspiracy charges. "I have here in my hand," McCarthy said, "a list of two hundred and five — a list of names that were known to the Secretary of State and who nevertheless are still working and shaping the policy of the State Department."[15]

By the standards of the day, it was an unremarkable Mulligan's stew of a speech: a little lift from a Nixon speech about Alger Hiss, a couple of dashes of venom from the *Chicago Tribune* and the *Washington Times-Herald* about Service, some testimony from McCarran's Judiciary Committee about the State Department's refusal to fire subversives. But even the plagiarized material was mangled, the facts jumbled, the numbers wrong. McCarthy's list, it would turn out, was four years old and not really a tally of Communists at all but merely a preliminary tabulation of security risks, ranging from suspected party members to drunks. An Associated Press stringer wrote 110 words about the speech. A couple of dozen newspapers picked up the brief.

On Friday, McCarthy flew to Salt Lake City and gave another speech attacking the State Department. This time he mentioned a list of fifty-seven Communists. This list was a little more recent than the previous one: It was only three years old. While the numbers of Communists seemed to change with the time zone, the number of newspapers paying attention was also growing.

On Saturday, McCarthy landed in Reno. Reporters were waiting for him. He went to Republican senator George Malone's office downtown. McCarthy let the two reporters — Frank McCulloch from the *Reno Gazette* and Ed Olsen of the AP — listen as he talked on the phone. "You gotta give me more names," McCarthy said into the receiver, scratching notes out on a pad. "I want more names."[16]

That evening McCarthy walked to the Mapes Hotel, twelve stories towering above the Truckee River, by far the highest point on Reno's cityscape. He spoke to a crowd of four hundred, again denouncing the State Department, this time naming four people: One had never worked for State, two were former employees, and the fourth was diplomat John Service. McCarthy didn't actually call them Communists, although that seemed to be his purport. The reporters scratched their heads. "The man just talked circles," sighed AP's Ed Olsen. "Everything was by inference, allusion, never a concrete statement of fact. Most of it didn't make sense. I tried to get into my lead that he had named names but he didn't call them anything. AP New York didn't know what to do with it and they asked me to file the whole text, which I did. But they couldn't do any better with it."[17]

After the speech Olsen and McCulloch sat down with McCarthy in the Mapes Sky Room bar. Bourbon and water flowed like the Truckee after a winter storm. They drank and argued. What was he really saying? the reporters pressed. The audience had understood what he said, McCarthy insisted. McCarthy offered to show them the list of Communists, digging into his pockets and pulling out nothing but lint. He accused the reporters of stealing the list. The owner came by to ask the three to keep it down or leave. They stumbled out after three in the morning. McCarthy's story would never get any clearer.

By the time McCarthy returned to Washington at the end of the week he was a sensation; he would stay in the headlines for most of the next five years, commanding more attention than any other public figure save for the president. Those first three days set the pattern for the next few years: McCarthy would say something outrageous, then change his story without recanting the previous one; reporters panted after McCarthy, challenging him but always repeating his charges. "If he said it," remembered reporter Charles Seib, "we wrote it."[18]

Journalists would have a lot to write about, indeed. It would be a terrible time for the nation, but a great time to be a reporter. On February 20 McCarthy made his debut before the national press corps, presenting his case to the Senate. For five hours he spoke almost incoherently, denouncing treachery in Washington, brandishing yet another list of Communists. Majority Leader Scott Lucas and freshman senator Herbert Lehman heckled him like the town drunk. By the time he was done, near midnight, it looked to many smart observers like McCarthy had burned himself badly.

Instead, it was the nation that he lit afire.

After she read the telegram, Angelina Angelides dropped to her knees and threw her hands to the sky, crying blessings to the Lord, the Virgin Mother, and the senator. And not necessarily in that order. For it was not heavenly intercession but senatorial that was bending the immigration rules to let her husband get a visa to enter the United States. Under ordinary circumstances Constantinos Angelides (or Danny Angel, as they called him in Sparks) would have had to wait years for permission, since the quota for Greek immigrants was, as the bureaucrats at the State Department put it, oversubscribed. But the chairman of the Judiciary Committee could simply dash off a bill to exempt Angelides from the normal workings of the law. He did it all the time.

When it came to responding to constituents McCarran was as quick as he was caring. Woe be it to the secretary who forgot the office dictum to respond to every letter the same day, even if just to acknowledge that the senator was working on the problem. "I will tell you this," a grizzled prospector recalled, "the thing I like about McCarran is that no matter who you are, or what your politics are, if you ask him for help, by gosh you always get it."[19] Once McCarran called Norm Biltz, the Nevada real estate tycoon, to ask if he had any wood at his ranch in Winnemucca. Why? Biltz asked. McCarran said there was an old miner with a broken leg up that way who couldn't chop his winter's wood. "Will you load up a truck and a take a load of wood to Tuscarora?" McCarran asked.[20]

Such favors were not forgotten. Eleven months after McCarran's telegram to Mrs. Angelides in January 1950 she was still worshipful. "I will always pray for God to keep you in health and happiness, for people and our country as a whole need you as the outstanding statesman of our nation," she gushed.[21] And McCarran didn't forget either. "I, of course, know that I have your support for reelection," he wrote to another family for whom he had crafted an immigration bill, "but it would be greatly appreciated if you would put in a good word for me now and then with your friends."[22]

McCarran was running for a fourth term in the Senate. In January, long before anyone looked crazy enough to challenge him, he sent instructions to Pete Petersen, the Reno postmaster and McCarran's political lieutenant, about preventing his rivals from having *any* role in the Democratic caucuses. "I don't want those birds to have a chance to show their noses in the State Convention, or any of their friends," McCarran instructed. "This can be done if we just get the matter arranged as to a favorable place to hold the mass meetings and then have our friends so organized that they will fill the places plumb full so that nobody else can get in and then have the motions all ready to put over and adjourn P.D.Q. with all the delegates nominated and elected. It may be necessary to rent five, ten or twenty buses so as to have them loaded up and take them to the respective mass meetings where they can take over. We want to do this thing and do it right."[23]

Not a single voter was to be missed. McCarran wrote to city halls, chamber of commerce offices, and American Legion posts throughout the state asking for lists of members and employees. He had copies of the

Nevada phone book mailed back to Washington. "A political convention is not a social gathering, nor is it a tea party," he wrote, "it is a real fight."[24]

"No one," promised Guernsey Frazer, "will dare oppose you on the Democratic side, except a screwball or two."[25]

That spring internal security bills surfaced in Congress like bubbles in hot tar. A little more than a week after McCarthy's February speech, McCarran introduced a bill to create an independent bureau of passports and visas inside of the State Department — a rebuke on Foggy Bottom for letting subversives into the country. McCarran already had a handful of anti-Communist bills pending: two aimed at tightening immigration restrictions against subversives and making it easier to revoke the citizenship of naturalized aliens, and a third measure beefing up espionage and sabotage laws. On March 21 McCarran's Judiciary Committee reported out S. 2311, the latest version of Mundt's bill (now cosponsored by Michigan Republican Homer Ferguson and South Carolina Democrat Olin Johnston) to force Communists to register with the government. Only liberal Republican William Langer, one of the great contrarians of American politics, voted against it. His minority report blasted the bill as the greatest threat to liberty since the Alien and Sedition Laws of 1798, a recipe for the regimentation of thinking and a bridle on speech and association. "It is the product of hysteria and frantic, unthinking fear," he wrote. "Like that bill, it would strike at the very foundations of our democratic institutions — the right of the people to speak their minds, to hear every viewpoint on public questions, and to associate together freely to advance their common views. Like that bill, it merits the opposition of all who cherish liberty."[26]

By June the number of internal security bills in Congress would swell to thirty-two.

The job of sitting on legislation fell to Scott Lucas. Lucas was born in 1892 on a farm outside of Chandlerville, Illinois. He'd been a star athlete in high school, played semipro baseball, and taught in a one-room country school before opening a law office in Havana (population four thousand). He enlisted in the army in 1918, later becoming a commander in the American Legion. After serving as a state's attorney he went to Congress in 1934 and jumped to the Senate in 1938. Tall, affable, rotely loyal, and of thoroughly middling ability, Lucas became party whip in 1947, making him the waterboy for a president who shared his humble Midwest origins but not his conservative political leanings. Although a bumbling parliamentarian, Lucas stuck with the unpopular Truman while many others in the party, including Hubert Humphrey and Paul Douglas, were trying to dump him from the ticket in 1948. Lucas was rewarded by being made majority leader, which tied him closer than ever to a liberal president with whom he often differed. Still, Lucas tried to put up a fight for Truman's civil rights proposal in 1949, battled the filibustering southern Democrats — and spent three weeks in the hospital recovering from a bleeding ulcer.

Now, at the age of fifty-eight, Lucas was facing the fight of his life for a third term in the Senate. His Republican opponent was Everett Dirksen, four years younger, who had served in the House from 1933 to 1948. A vigorous stump speaker with an instinct for the jugular, Dirksen was running his campaign against Truman and twenty years of Democratic liberalism.

Lucas began distancing himself from Truman's health-care and agricultural programs. "I have flexed my conscience a bit on some things," he told a supporter.[27] And he picked a campaign slogan guaranteed to resonate with his conservative supporters: Lucas leads the fight against Communism at home and abroad. But this theme also emphasized the impossibility of his position: Lucas was running as an anti-Communist against an even more fervid Red hater, while trying to follow his president's instructions to keep all internal security legislation on ice. It would have been a tough dance for even the shrewdest politician or most nimble-minded strategist. Lucas was neither.

On March 28, a week after the Judiciary Committee reported out the Mundt-Ferguson bill, the South Dakotan wrote to his friend Ev Dirksen. "Scuttlebutt around here," Mundt noted, "has it that Scott Lucas whispered the word to left-wing newspaper friends of his that he expects to put this bill on ice and sit on it until late enough in the session so that even though it passed the Senate the House will not have time to act upon it since it is recognized that in all probability Truman will have to veto it and they don't want to have the added embarrassment in this way with the country having its prevailing sentiment against Communism. I am sure that you can do an awful lot of good for yourself and the cause of freedom generally by getting a number of friends of yours throughout the state to inspire a lot of letters and telegrams insisting that Lucas put this bill on the Senate calendar for action."[28]

Mundt wasn't leaving matters up to Dirksen. For the past year Mundt had been trying to drum up support for his friend's challenge to Lucas.

Now with the majority leader trying to kill his bill through inaction, Mundt began a furious letter-writing campaign to assail Lucas as soft on Communism and pressure him to bring up the measure. He wrote to acquaintances all over the country, supplying them with form letters attacking Lucas and giving assurances that even if the first letter got nothing but a mimeographed response, the majority leader would damn well take notice when second and third letters started flooding in. He fed anti-Lucas stories to conservative papers in Illinois and Washington, began making speeches against his colleague, and even prevailed upon the national commander of the American Legion to lobby its loyal member Lucas, as well as to dispatch telegrams to every member of the Senate. "It would appear," Mundt wrote to Dirksen, "that if you can keep the feet of brother Lucas on the hot fires of Communism and get enough people to realize that he, individually, has blocked the Senate from acting on legislation to curtail the activities of communists at home, you should be able to walk in standing up."[29]

The ornate Caucus Room in the Senate Office Building was packed, the audience crowded up against the walls. Klieg lights blazed; newsreel cameras rolled. More flashbulbs popped than at a Hollywood premier. The unlikely center of attention was a middle-aged professor with glasses and a small mustache. Owen Lattimore hardly looked worth the hoopla. Then he opened his mouth.

Joe McCarthy, Lattimore said, had violated his responsibility as an U.S. senator. "He has violated it by impairing the effectiveness of the United States government in its relations with its friends and allies and by making the government of the United States an object of suspicion in the eyes of the anti-Communist world and undoubtedly the laughing stock of the Communist governments," he said. "He has violated it by instituting a reign of terror among officials and employees in the United States government, no one of whom can be sure of safety from attack by the machine gun of irresponsible publicity in Joseph McCarthy's hands."[30]

Lattimore was just warming up. In March a special foreign relations subcommittee, the Tydings Committee, had opened an investigation into Joe McCarthy's charges. The charges kept growing. One day in executive session McCarthy accused Johns Hopkins professor Owen Lattimore of being the top Soviet spy in the country. Drew Pearson soon broke the story, naming Lattimore to the public. The Asian expert was in Afghanistan at the time on a UN mission. "McCarthy says off record you top Russian espionage agent in United States and that his whole case rests on you," the Associated Press cabled Lattimore in Kabul. "Pure moonshine," Lattimore replied.[31]

In April, Lattimore appeared before the Tydings Committee. He denied that he was or had ever been a Communist or had ever supported the party in any way. "I shall show that his charges against me are so empty and baseless that the senator will fall and fall flat on his face . . . ," he said. "I hope the senator will in fact lay his machine gun down. He is too reckless, careless and irresponsible to have a license to use it."[32]

"For weeks the Capital has been seized and convulsed by a terror," the *Washington Post* reported later that month in an editorial that consumed most of a page. "The rising distrust, the roaring bitterness, the ranging of Americans against Americans, the assault on freedom of inquiry, the intolerance of opposition — all this malaise, it seems to this newspaper, has its roots in a deep and troubled state of the nation's mind. Fear and frustration abound — fear of the unseen struggle in which we are locked, and frustration because of our inability to get directly at it."[33]

The next day, May 23, Harry Gold was arrested for atomic espionage.

The Communists, McCarran began to tell friends, had a plan. "Someone," he explained, "would be selected to run for the Democratic nomination who would be willing to throw mud of all kinds and descriptions, and would be willing to make the campaign with no hope of election but merely to tear down my position in the state, so as to make it possible to elect a Republican."[34] As early as January rumors floated around the state and made their way into newspapers that two million dollars in eastern money was earmarked to defeat McCarran. "My idea of the thing was to emphasize the fact that the Jews were after you," Pete Petersen wrote to McCarran. "I don't think that particular race is too well thought of in this State."[35]

Proof of the plot came in May in the form of a fund-raising letter sent out by the New York–based Committee on National Affairs. The liberal group claimed credit for helping defeat reactionary senators in past elections, scorned McCarran for his stand on the displaced persons issue, and supported two liberals up for reelection, Oregon Republican Wayne Morse and North Carolina Democrat Frank Graham. McCarran had blamed his narrow win in 1944 on Communists, was convinced that what he called New York Jew money was the reason for his defeat on the DP bill, and now believed that anyone who would dare challenge him must be a front man for the evil twins of Communism and Judaism.

That, at any rate, was the role George E. Franklin Jr. walked into during the summer of 1950, when he decided to challenge McCarran. Franklin, thirty-four, had been born in the state and educated at the University of Nevada. He was a decorated fighter pilot in the war who afterward moved to Las Vegas, where he was elected chairman of the Clark County Commission, the local government body. He was virtually unknown outside southern Nevada. He told friends he was running against McCarran because he was sick of the way the senator threw his weight around. "I love public office," he once explained, "because I love government — the way it should be, not the way it is."[36]

Franklin was no stranger to McCarran. He had written McCarran for help in getting an air National Guard unit in Clark County in 1945. McCarran, of course, promised to help. The senator also sent congratulations when Franklin passed the bar the following year. "I bespeak for you success in your life's work," he wrote.[37] By the summer of 1950, however, McCarran had taken to calling Franklin "the psychopathic kid." McCarran's supporters spread the word that Franklin was a front man for sinister eastern influences that wanted to meddle in Nevada politics. "There are rumors in Winnemucca that Mr. Franklin is a Jew and a sort of shady character," Petersen reported. "You can be sure that neither Ted nor I contradicted those statements."[38]

Jay Sourwine, McCarran's chief aide, favored making the Communist issue unmistakable. He suggested that Franklin be tricked into denying that he had received even "one red cent" in New York money. Stores in Clark County would then be flooded with scarlet pennies. "Nothing would have to be said — a lot of people would get the idea and as long as those red cents stayed in circulation, every one of them would be working against Franklin," Sourwine wrote.[39]

McCarran had no need for such desperate measures. In a state of 160,000 people, where the federal government owned 86 percent of the land, the senator had an army of patronage appointments to campaign for him. A mining inspector, for one, promised to carry literature down into the shafts scattered across the far desert reaches of the state. And when a deputy sheriff at Lake Tahoe began spouting off about McCarran, the senator's loyalists were quick to call the man's boss. "Ray Root, the Sheriff," reported a correspondent, "has promised to silence him at once and to also admonish him to the fact that if he does not, he will be looking elsewhere for work."[40]

McCarran was relentless in reminding voters what he had done for them during eighteen years in Washington. He took credit for virtually everything but the sunrise: a bombing range near Tonopah, a bridge across the Truckee in Reno, airmail service for Elko, the restoration of Fort Churchill as a historic landmark, a hospital in Humboldt County, an airport in Winnemucca, electric power in Pioche, a reservoir in Duck Valley, a post office in Yerington, a park at Lake Tahoe, a road past Angel Lake, rifle ammunition for ranchers to shoot coyotes. Even though getting home for the primary was looking less and less likely, McCarran kept a tight grip on his campaign by phone and mail. From across the continent it seemed as if not even a jackrabbit could sprint across the sagebrush without McCarran hearing about it. "The wives and members of the families of those employed in your department can certainly get busy," he wrote to the head of the IRS in Reno. "I don't hear of anything doing, hence I am writing to you."[41]

If Scott Lucas needed an example of the peril of principle, Frank Porter Graham was it. The former president of the University of North Carolina had been appointed to a special term the year before. In the spring of 1950 he was the first member of the Senate to test the campaign weather. Diminutive (he stood five foot four, weighed 125 pounds, and shopped for shoes in the boys' department), deeply religious ("Jesus does not teach us to destroy the headquarters of those who agitate in an alien cause,"[42] he said after vigilantes sacked a union meeting hall and beat three Communist organizers), and decent to a fault (the only time he mentioned his primary opponent by name was to defend him against overzealous attacks by his own supporters), Graham was sixty-three, an ardent advocate for both civil rights and civil liberties. "One of the most Christ-like men I have ever met," Republican senator Wayne Morse called him.[43] Graham had been a favorite target of HUAC since the late 1930s, and his service on Truman's commission on civil rights had done nothing to endear him to southern Democrats. His politics alone would have earned the enmity of McCarran, but Graham was also in the thick of the displaced persons fight.

In March corporate lawyer Willis Smith opened his race against Graham by promising that no one would ever have any reason to question *his* loyalty. "I do not now nor have I ever belonged to any subversive organizations and, as United States senator I shall never allow myself to be duped into the use of my name for propaganda or other purposes by those types of organizations," Smith declared. "The unwary can do just as much harm as the unscrupulous in the days that are at hand."[44]

Plagued by chronic respiratory problems and bad eyes, confined to bed by pneumonia during two vital weeks of his campaign, Graham managed to win a plurality in the primary, toasting his victory with buttermilk, but was forced into a runoff against Smith. Pegged as a Communist and a race mixer (a phony photo circulated showing Graham's wife dancing with a black man, in case the implications of his election weren't clear enough), Graham frustrated his friends like Paul Douglas by his maddening refusal to respond to Smith's vicious race- and Redbaiting. "I'm not saying anything against any human being," Graham said. "I'm not attacking anybody," he added. "If I have to do that to get in the Senate I don't want to go."[45] In the June runoff Smith won by nineteen thousand votes.

McCarran was quick to congratulate him, urging the senator-elect to seek a seat on the Judiciary Committee. "Just know," McCarran wrote, "I am delighted to be able to send you this word of greeting. . . . I am engaged in a bitter primary fight myself. It is rough, and I am not sure that the temper of the times is in my favor."[46]

On Thursday, June 22, shortly before 8 P.M., Steve Spingarn walked over to Truman's temporary residence at Blair House. It was a short trip across the street from the White House, where the president's living quarters were being remodeled. But Spingarn hoped it was also the final leg of a much longer journey. For the past two years, ever since Truman had snatched him away from the Treasury Department, Spingarn had been trying to find ways for the president to reassure a jittery public that the great Communist threat was external, not internal, that the government was not full of subversives, and that the worst possible course of action would be to run pell-mell into hysteria. A one-man civil liberties bureau, a colleague called him. For months Spingarn had been urging the president to appoint a panel of distinguished citizens to examine the government loyalty program with an eye toward balancing liberty and security. "Excessive security, however, can be as dangerous as inadequate security," Spingarn warned Truman. "Excessive security brings normal administrative operations to a stand-still, prevents the interchange of ideas necessary to scientific progress, and — most important of all — encroaches on the individual rights and freedoms which distinguish a democracy from a totalitarian country."[47]

Examined calmly, Spingarn explained, there was no question that the administration was effectively combating Communism. By the beginning of the year the FBI had already finished its part of Truman's loyalty program: 2.8 million file checks and more than ten thousand full field investigations that resulted in 139 dismissals. The party itself was almost universally despised, its influence in labor and the arts at low ebb, its finances and front organizations in tatters. In the past two years membership, microscopic to begin with, had dropped 28 percent, falling to about 53,000 people from 74,000. "It therefore seems to be an appropriate time to take a searching look at the operations of the loyalty program to date and decade what its future shape should be," Spingarn suggested in January. "Now would seem to be a particularly good time to do this because a major phase of the program has just been completed and because, although the program has frequently been under attack in the past as being unfair to federal employees, this is not currently the case."[48]

The next month Joe McCarthy went to Wheeling and the country went crazy. The White House wasn't about to create a commission that would look like an answer to McCarthy's charges. But Spingarn kept pushing for an internal security and individual rights commission. "It is not enough for the men who administer the government to know that they are doing a first class internal security job," Spingarn argued. "It is necessary for the American people to *believe* just that."[49]

This Thursday evening the president had called a meeting to talk about the commission. Vice President Barkley was there. As were Speaker Sam Rayburn and House Majority Leader John McCormack. So, too, were the Democratic members of the subcommittee investigating McCarthy's charges: Tydings, Brien McMahon, and Theodore Green. Lucas was unaccountably absent. Truman explained the purpose of the commission and asked everyone what they thought. Only Tydings and McMahon were excited by the idea. The others were undecided or opposed. Attorney General Howard McGrath strongly disapproved, especially since the Justice Department was waiting for an appeals court to rule on the conviction of the Communist Party leadership for violating the Smith Act.

Truman thought that the naysayers ought to hear Spingarn's message. "Our internal security measures must be strong and sound, but they must not destroy the things we cherish most," the president read. "We cannot preserve our liberty by sacrificing it."[50] The Democratic leaders and the attorney general agreed that it was a splendid speech but still didn't think that the timing was right. Maybe next January. Truman said think about it. There was no rush.

On June 23 Edwin Broome, the superintendent of the school system in Montgomery County, Maryland, was called to the state attorney general's office in Annapolis. O. Bowie Duckett, an assistant attorney general, told the superintendent that one of his high school English teachers had been named by Elizabeth Bentley in testimony before HUAC as having once been a Communist. The teacher, William W. Hinckley, had appeared before the committee and took the Fifth Amendment. The state was considering charging Hinckley with perjury since he had signed the loyalty oath required of all public employees in Maryland swearing that he did not belong to any subversive organizations. Hinckley had been with the district for four years and was considered an excellent teacher. Broome called Hinckley at home and fired him. "I could never employ a teacher who wouldn't say what he is," Broome explained. "I'm no Red," Hinckley said, "and everybody around here knows it."[51]

Hinckley, in fact, had been a Communist in the 1930s. He had signed Bentley's party card. During the war he was hired by the Treasury, until Steve Spingarn conducted a hearing and determined that he was a security risk. "He was a likeable fellow," Spingarn recalled. "Whenever you talk to a man who is pleasant and likeable you must try not to feel too sympathetic for him but the fact remains I thought that he didn't belong with us and we fired him."[52]

Whether he was qualified to teach Shakespeare to high school students almost a decade later was another matter.

On Saturday, June 24, Truman flew home to Independence for a weekend visit. He ate a quiet dinner with his family and was ready for bed by 9 P.M. Twenty minutes later the secretary of state called: North Korea had invaded South Korea. "It looks like," Truman told his daughter, "World War III is here."[53]

Seoul fell in two days. The South Korean army was in chaos, routed and running toward the tip of the peninsula. Truman ordered U.S. troops dispatched, and on July 5 an infantry regiment confronted a North Korean column of Soviet-made T-34 tanks. In less than an hour the U.S. forces were in retreat. Within a week two U.S. regiments were in shreds, up to three thousand men dead, wounded, or missing. In seventeen days U.S. troops fell back seventy miles. Newspapers compared the situation to the Nazi blitzkrieg of France. Talk of another Dunkirk was in the air. Truman called up ninety National Guard units and the whole marine reserve and sent them by boat and plane to fight and die in the soaking rains and hundred-degree days of monsoon season in an obscure Asian country that the secretary of state had just recently placed outside the U.S. defense perimeter. The United States, Truman told the nation, must fight aggression.

In Washington the weather was almost as stormy. The Republicans were soon braying about treason. Karl Mundt demanded to know how the United States could fight Communism in Korea but not at home. McCarran joined the fray on July 12, when he called on Truman to break diplomatic relations with the Soviet Union, railed against subversives sent into the country as diplomats, and accused the State Department of tolerating Communists. "How much longer shall we betray those of our own flesh and blood who are even now baring their breasts to the cannon and tanks which were assembled in the Soviet Union?" he asked.[54] "Conditions here in the nation's capital are much worse than what people really appreciate," he wrote privately. "Every hour the scene changes, and every hour it gets just a little bit darker. . . . Curves are being pitched by individuals in high places."[55]

On July 17, after five months of hearings and internal bickering, the Tydings subcommittee released a 313-page report on McCarthy's charges, signed only by the Democratic majority. "A fraud and a hoax perpetrated on the Senate of the United States and the American people," the report concluded. ". . . Perhaps the most nefarious campaign of half-truths and untruth in the history of this Republic."[56]

In the Senate a near melee broke out. "How can we get the Reds out of Korea," William Jenner yelled across the aisle at the Democrats, "if we can't get them out of Washington?" Ken Wherry punched a Democrat who defended the report. "You dirty son-of-a-bitch," he cursed. "The most loyal stooges of the Kremlin," McCarthy sneered, "could not have done a better job of giving a clean bill of health to Stalin's fifth column in this country."[57]

McCarran agreed, charging that Tydings had overstepped his mandate. "In place of investigating for subversives and Reds in the State Department and other departments, as his resolution called for, he set about to try Senator Joseph McCarthy, and set himself up as judge, jury and executioner," he wrote. "I am afraid he has made a martyr out of McCarthy, because the report avoids the issue as to subversives, and more rather deals with it from a desultory attitude and tears into McCarthy."[58]

McCarran and McCarthy had not gotten off to a good start. In early 1947, not long after he had arrived in Washington, McCarthy was leading a hearing on selling the federal Basic Magnesium plant in Henderson, Nevada, to the state. McCarran was testifying in favor. The freshman senator was rude and insulting to his elder colleague, taking him to task for not knowing the state's credit limit. McCarran tried to pull rank; McCarthy cut him off. "Will you try and stick to the question," he snapped, "and then if you want to make a speech afterward, make it?"[59]

Despite a three-decade difference in age, the two had a lot in common. Both were poor Irish Catholic, raised in small towns. Whatever education either got was an act of will: McCarran rose before dawn to work his way through school and read law on the sheep trail; McCarthy skipped high school and later plowed his way through the course work in a year. Neither succeeded at his first career: McCarran's sheep were slaughtered at a railroad crossing; McCarthy lost his chicken flock to the heat. Both men had been judges and ran for higher office from the bench in blatant violation of their state's constitutions. Each also had to struggle against powerful local political machines to get to Washington.

Yet in the Senate the two could not have been more different. McCarran assiduously tended to his base at home, creating a great machine of his own with a stranglehold on his state; in Washington he gathered influence slowly, rising through the seniority system and mastering the intricacies of writing law and parliamentary maneuver, plotting and scheming with great determination and glacial patience. McCarthy, on the other hand, seemed to suffer from political attention deficit disorder: throwing out charges of Communism with the ease with which most senators shook hands — and with as much follow-up.

But there was one thing that the two could both agree upon: They both despised Owen Lattimore.

On the day that the Tydings report was issued, the Justice Department announced the arrest of Julius Rosenberg for atomic espionage.

Birmingham, Alabama, July 18.[60] The city outlawed the Communist Party, giving members forty-eight hours to get out of town or face arrest. Membership would be taken for granted if anyone was found in a "non-public place in voluntary association or communication with any person or persons established to be or to have been members of the Communist Party."

On Saturday, July 22, Spingarn handed Truman another memo. The country, Spingarn warned, was on the verge of hysteria. Repressive legislation was quickly picking up steam. He urged the president to send Congress a message putting the internal security issue in context, explaining that threat to individual liberty posed by some of the pending bills and the fact that there were already ample laws on the books. Since it is difficult to beat something with nothing, Truman might accept the Justice-sponsored McCarran bill that he had been resisting. And now might finally be time to announce the internal security and individual rights commission. Spingarn already had a draft of such a speech ready for Truman.

Truman said that he would read the memo,[61] but he didn't need Spingarn to tell him the country was nervous. The president promised to veto any legislation that didn't square with the Bill of Rights. Police-state tactics cannot be allowed to encroach on individual rights, he fumed. No matter how politically unpopular it was. Election year or no election year. "The president said that the situation in this respect was the worst it had been since the Alien and Sedition laws of 1798," Spingarn recorded, "that a lot of people on the Hill should know better but had been stampeded into running with their tails between their legs."

On August 1 the Senate approved a hundred-million-dollar loan[62] to Spain — despite the fact that Truman vigorously opposed sending any money to the fascist government and that the Senate had already rejected the request back in April. McCarran believed that Franco was a bulwark against Communism. So persistent was McCarran in repeating this that Drew Pearson started to call him the senator from Madrid. The year before he had lopped off a chunk of the State Department appropriations bill when Dean Acheson refused to offer Spain credit to buy U.S. commodities. Next came the loan bill in April, which narrowly lost. Undeterred, McCarran tacked an amendment onto an appropriations bill at the last minute. Truman had no choice but to sign the bill since it was tied to funding the government.

Nevada might have only twenty-three Communists, McCarran's newspaper crony Al Cahlan wrote toward the end of the primary, but they were all massed in Clark County. "You'll be astounded one of these days when the FBI starts rounding up the twenty-three — astounded when the masks are removed and you can see for yourself who they are," he wrote.[63]

"Communists, pinks and party-Reds are crawling from their hiding places to oppose Pat McCarran," listeners to Las Vegas's KENO-FM were informed in early August. "Because," another voice chimed in, "Pat McCarran since 1944 has led the fight to halt the march of Communism in this country."⁶⁴

On the horizon of McCarran's Nevada, George Franklin was almost invisible. He got virtually no press, while McCarran was constantly in the news. One publisher promised to put a McCarran slogan at the end of every story until the election. Another offered to kill a rare Franklin story in the works. And when Mississippi's James Eastland gave a speech in the Senate decrying Communist efforts to unseat McCarran, twenty-five thousand copies were mailed to Nevada at government expense. "My Dad is running that speech Eastland made about you," the son of the editor of one of the state's biggest papers told McCarran. "His only request is that the next time he talks, have him make it shorter."⁶⁵

A clerk began reading the president's message to Congress on August 8. You must remember history, Truman said. In the past the nation had betrayed its own freedoms during moments of hysteria. Members of Congress had been arrested for their opinions under the Alien and Sedition Acts. Once the Bill of Rights was breached even the most conservative groups would not be safe from the arbitrary power of government. The best defense against Communism was vigorous democracy. He asked for a longer statute of limitations for espionage and greater supervisory powers over aliens slated for deportation. And he made pointed reference to the Mundt and McCarran bills. "There are some people who wish us to enact laws which would seriously damage the right of free speech," Truman said, "and which could be used not only against subversive groups but against other groups engaged in political or other activities which were not generally popular. Such measures would not only infringe on the Bill of Rights and the basic liberties of our people; they would also undermine the very internal security they seek to protect. Laws forbidding dissent do not prevent subversive activities; they merely drive them into more secret and more dangerous channels. Police states are not secure; their history is marked by successive purges, and growing concentration camps, as their governments strike out blindly in fear of violent revolt. Once a government is committed to the principle of silencing the voice of opposition, it has only one way to go, and that is down the path of increasingly repressive measures, until it becomes a source of terror to all its citizens and creates a country where everyone lives in fear."⁶⁶

Truman's words had barely fallen in the Senate when Mundt took the floor, thanked the president for his belated endorsement, and moved that his bill be immediately placed on the consent calendar. If Truman had been a little quicker on the uptake, Mundt added, American boys might not now be dying in Korea. McCarran agreed. "We are at war, and we may be more at war tomorrow . . . ," he said. "Being at war on the outside, it is well for us to take immediate steps to protect our government and our institutions on the inside." Lucas blocked the move, insisting that the Judiciary Committee study the message before considering any action. "The importance of these bills demands unlimited debate . . . ," he said. "I am not sure that the Senator from Nevada, brilliant as he is, although he is familiar with the various measures referred to, by hurriedly reading the message submitted to us by the president, is able to give it the thorough consideration and study which it deserves and requires."[67]

Lucas's stand against McCarran did not last long. The next day one of his subversive alien bills came up on the calendar. No one objected. The State Department had urged Lucas to block the measure, but he refused. He didn't want to offend McCarran, Lucas admitted.

Mundt was elated. Earlier in the week he had appeared on *Meet the Press*, holding up a copy of an Illinois newspaper with a big headline about Lucas sitting on his internal security bill — one of numerous stories he had fed the paper. We have got them on the ropes at last, he exulted. Pour the letters on Lucas and we can finally break him, he advised a cohort. "The only thing wrong with this bill is that it has the names of two Republican members of the Senate on it," he added. "If it were a Democratic bill, I am positive that it would be enacted into law at an early date. We have been plugging for it for some time now and I feel confident that within the next week or ten days it will be voted on in the Senate."[68]

The next day, August 10, McCarran dropped his omnibus bill on the Senate. "This chamber of horrors," Spingarn called it.[69] Mundt fumed that McCarran had just torn the flyleaf off his bill and stapled on a new cover sheet with his own name. "Except for minor changes the legislation is word for word and page for page identical to the original S. 2311,"[70] Mundt complained inaccurately. After months of fruitless labor to get his measure to the floor, Mundt could only watch in horror as McCarran swallowed his legislation in his own swollen bill. It was not done growing.

—

In his Senate office Paul Douglas covered the walls with copies of Old Master paintings: Bellini, Brueghel, Piero della Francesca. Douglas had made it into his forties without ever stopping to think much about art, but when his second wife shared her love of the subject with him, Douglas took to it with the enthusiasm of a teenager and the thoroughness of a scholar. He read widely in art history and scoured Italy for glimpses of obscure paintings. Two of his favorite works hung on the wall opposite his desk: Holbein's portraits of Reformation scholars Thomas More and Erasmus. Douglas would often point to the paintings and tell visitors about how More became involved in politics and was beheaded at the age of fifty-seven, while Erasmus avoided the subject and lived to be eighty. Who was wiser? he would ask. Erasmus was the almost unanimous answer during the summer of 1950.

Douglas grew up in a log cabin in the Maine woods, where he fought forest fires as a young man. Enchanted early by Dickens, he grew to become an assiduous bibliophile, a man who relentlessly consumed books and ideas. Douglas went to Columbia and Harvard. He became an economics professor and a Quaker. He started the 1930s as a socialist and ended the decade as an alderman in Chicago, a liberal Democrat. In 1942 Douglas was clobbered in a bid for the U.S. Senate. The next day, at the age of fifty, he enlisted in the Marine Corps, his revulsion at fascism finally trumping his pacifist inclinations. By the time the white-haired scholar arrived in Okinawa, Douglas had become a major but took off his oak leaves to fight in the front lines with the enlisted men, getting seriously wounded in the left arm, which, he liked to say, was thereafter only good as a paperweight.

His next battle was a long-shot bid for the Senate in 1948. In a station wagon fitted with a loudspeaker, Douglas logged fifty thousand miles in Illinois, campaigning furiously at intersections, El stops, factory gates, and mining washhouses. A Republican congressman branded him a secret Communist, which got front-page play in the *Chicago Tribune*. Douglas still won. "For solid intellectual force he was outstandingly the ablest man in the Senate," journalists Robert Allen and William Shannon wrote.[71]

Douglas had no truck with Communists, had opposed working with them in liberal groups even before the war, but he believed that existing laws covering criminal acts and conspiracy were sufficient to deal with the party. On August 1, for example, the U.S. Court of Appeals had upheld the use of the Smith Act to convict eleven leaders of the Communist Party for conspiring to teach or advocate violent revolution. A cumbersome law

requiring party members to register with the government hardly seemed
necessary — especially when it would seem to amount to self-incrimination
under the Smith Act. But Douglas knew that the public climate of alarm
would make it almost impossible to strike down the McCarran bill without
an alternative proposal.

For Douglas the mood of near madness in the country was reminiscent
of his youthful fire-fighting days, when he battled an seemingly inevitable
force of nature. "I had seen how fires behaved," he observed. "As the initial spark spreads, a blaze is created. The blaze heats the air. Since hot air is
lighter than ordinary air, it rises. This creates a vacuum into which other
air rushes. But this in turn brings a wind that fans the flames and heats
more air, creating a further vacuum into which the colder winds rush. And
so it goes on in a cumulative fashion. . . . I became aware of impetuous
forces that, once set in motion, release latent forces until a cumulative
process of change takes place in which the final, unpredictable result is out
of all proportion to the initial cause."[72]

To stop the anti-Communist blaze of 1950 Douglas thought he might
have to set a backfire: a counterconflagration that would change the focus
of legislation from speech and association to action, the real danger of sabotage. The wartime detention of Japanese Americans might offer something of a model. During World War II more than 110, 000 Americans
whose only crime was their ethnicity had been herded into concentration
camps by the military — an act twice upheld by the Supreme Court.
Preventive detention, arresting a certain class of persons for what they
might do during an emergency, would not be a glorious alternative,
Douglas knew, but it might be the only chance to stop something worse.
He would take the idea to the president and see what he thought.

But even Douglas's experience with wildfire could not prepare him for
what was about to happen.

The midterm elections were weeks away. The *Washington Times-Herald*
predicted that if Truman didn't sign the internal security bill, McCarran
would be the only Democratic candidate in the Senate to be reelected.
"My bill will pass the Congress in the very near future," McCarran told a
friend, "and I am betting my last thirty-one cents that the president will
sign it."[73]

CHAPTER 19

The Enemy Within

When you give any man unlimited power, it is like giving
a schoolboy a gun: he wants to go out and shoot it off.[1]
— Pat McCarran

The six men in suits carrying the stretcher out of the old Supreme Court chamber off the Capitol rotunda looked like pallbearers at a funeral. Inside the half-moon-shaped room — the original home of the Senate and its temporary meeting place while its more spacious chamber was being renovated — some of the most powerful men in the country were urgently arguing about the fate of the nation, the death of freedom, and the threatened survival of the United States. The debate had been going on for twelve hours already and showed no signs of winding down. But in the predawn gloom of September 23, 1950, the greatest deliberative body in the world was inching toward a decision, a vote on the most severe peacetime sedition law in American history. Months earlier the figure covered with a blanket on the stretcher had vowed to fight that bill with every ounce of his being. And so he had, before his voice cracked and his aged and sick body succumbed to exhaustion and crumbled to the floor. He was a man who had fought all his life, who had battled political machines, big business, the federal government and courts. "He wins them all"[2] one of his many foes once marveled. Not this one. In the autumn of 1950 forces that had long been coursing through American life welled to the surface with terrible fury. Even Bill Langer, a man who swam against the flow as often as most men drifted along, could not fight this current. Some tides were just too strong.

On Tuesday, September 5, 1950, Pat McCarran stood up at the fourth desk in the first row of the U.S. Senate. If one member looked the part it was McCarran, who had the outsized features of a Daumier caricature and a profile that belonged on a Roman coin: a large hawkish nose that seemed to incline lower with age and thick, wavy white hair cresting high on his head. McCarran was short and beefy but his large head and barrel chest gave him an imposing physical presence. When he spoke he seemed to grow even larger. "McCarran," observed journalist Richard Strout, "swells with power."[3] Opening the debate on his internal security bill, McCarran explained how Congress had spent years drafting and

509

redrafting this legislation. "This bill does not contain one iota of hysteria, nor is it the cry of alarmists, nor does it contravene any of our basic constitutional concepts," McCarran said. "It is rather . . . sober evidence of faith in the vitality of our democratic institutions to meet realistically the challenge of a deadly enemy within our gates."[4]

McCarran painstakingly went through the various bills he had stitched together: the Mundt-Ferguson requirements that Communist and front groups register with the government and label their literature as propaganda, that Communists not hold passports or government jobs, and the new crime of committing any act that might contribute to the establishment of a totalitarian dictatorship in the United States; McCarran's own bill tightening espionage law; his other bill making it easier to deport subversive aliens; a House bill giving the government greater supervisory power over aliens; another McCarran bill that would deny citizenship to aliens who had joined a subversive group in the last ten years and strip citizenship from naturalized aliens who joined or associated with subversive groups within five years of becoming Americans; and finally a McCarran bill that would set up an independent bureau of passports and visas within the State Department, the head of which would be subject to Senate confirmation — a slap at Secretary of State Dean Acheson for letting subversives into the country.

As his two-hour speech drew to a close, McCarran paid tribute to his Senate colleagues Karl Mundt and Homer Ferguson and HUAC and warned that he would not tolerate any attempt to water down the measure. "I serve notice here and now that I will not be a party to any crippling or weakening amendments," he said, "and that I shall oppose with all the power at my command any move to palm off on the American people any window-dressing substitute measure in the place of sound, internal-security legislation."[5]

A week earlier, on August 29, the clerk had begun calling the roll on the House version of the bill. As yea after yea resounded, a lawmaker from California squeezed into the row behind Helen Gahagan Douglas, a liberal representative from Los Angeles, and urged her not to vote against the bill.

"You're voting against it?" she protested. "Yes, but I'm not running for the Senate against Richard Nixon," he replied. "You won't be able to get around the state fast enough to explain why you voted against the bill after he gets through telling voters that you did it because you're soft on Reds. He'll beat your brains in."

Yea.

Yea.

Yea.

The drumbeat continued as California's large congressional delegation filed by Douglas, one by one, imploring her to save her career. She stopped answering them and let the depressing noise wash over her.

Yea.

"It'll cost you."

Yea.

"Why jeopardize your campaign?"

Yea.

"Your vote won't matter."

Yea.

When the clerk called "Douglas of California," she responded with a rare "no." Nineteen others voted against the bill, while 354 rushed to support it. "How does it feel to be a dead statesman, Helen," a colleague asked afterward, "instead of a live politician?"

She would not be the new senator from California.[6]

The month it took to rush McCarran's bill to the floor had been hell. The day after McCarran introduced his legislation on August 10, White House aide Steve Spingarn curtly sent the senator marked-up copies of two pending bills. This is *all* the president wants, Spingarn said. McCarran ignored him. Then the liberals on the Judiciary Committee fought to postpone the vote on McCarran's legislation. They wanted more time to write the kind of bill Truman desired. McCarran gave them two days, but the liberal bill would never leave the committee. Instead, on August 17, the committee reported out McCarran's bill (S. 4037) — a week after its introduction.

For McCarran the Senate conservatives turned out to be a bigger headache than the liberals. Karl Mundt and Homer Ferguson should have been fast friends with McCarran. Both were longtime anti-Communists who hated liberal Democrats as much as McCarran did. Mundt had served on HUAC before coming to the Senate and helped Whittaker Chambers and Elizabeth Bentley tell their stories about Communist espionage to the American people. Ferguson was a former prosecutor who had led a Senate investigation that tried to blame Roosevelt for Pearl Harbor and had called for Truman's impeachment when the president refused to turn over loyalty files to Congress so it could investigate Bentley's charges. But McCarran had not deigned to tell either of them that he had planned to include the Mundt-Ferguson internal security bill in *his* bill. The two Republicans tried to snatch their legislation out of McCarran's grip. McCarran finally appeased the duo by agreeing to use the exact language of the Mundt-Ferguson bill in his concoction, thereby letting them claim credit.

Finally, McCarran had to goad Scott Lucas into taking up the bill, which the majority leader promised to do in a day or two. More than a week passed without any action. In the meantime the House passed the Wood bill, its counterpart measure, which now threatened to become the internal security legislation that would rob McCarran of his anti-Communist glory. Lucas kept reassuring McCarran that he would bring up the McCarran bill and not the Wood one, but McCarran didn't believe him. McCarran was seized by one of his periodic black moods; he brooded about giving up and just letting Congress enact whatever anti-Communist legislation finally bobbed to the surface. "I am a little afraid that might be construed by some folks as abandonment of his drive against Communism," aide Jay Sourwine worried, "and I would not like to see him lose the driver's seat on the deal."[7]

At 8:30 P.M., the week before the primary election, listeners in southern Nevada heard the breathless voice of Berkeley Bunker on KENO-FM. "I hold in my hand the most amazing news bulletin ever made public during a Nevada election campaign," he said. Bunker was the Las Vegas funeral home owner who had served briefly in the Senate and House. Once he had been in McCarran's good graces; then he became an enemy who went as far as flirting with the CIO organizers to run against the senator in the 1944 election. Now he wanted to get back in favor with McCarran. So he went on the radio and read a wire service story about the Senate elections subcommittee dispatching investigators to Nevada to check out reports that large sums of outside money were flooding into the state in an attempt to influence the race. "It was not difficult to determine," Bunker said, "that New York interests were out to defeat Pat McCarran because he could not be controlled."[8]

McCarran himself had started the investigation two days earlier when he asked Senator Guy Gillette to send someone to Nevada. Gillette told McCarran that he would put an investigator on a plane immediately, but he asked for an official request. McCarran didn't want his fingerprints on the paper trail, so he had a supporter dash off a letter. Attached was a copy of a May fund-raising letter from a liberal New York group, the Committee for National Affairs, which had marked McCarran for defeat.

Bunker named several members of the Committee on National Affairs who had been favorably mentioned by the *Daily Worker* in the 1930s and had in the past belonged to various front groups. George Franklin wasn't cited in the fifteen-minute speech, but the implication was clear: McCarran's opponent was the front man for Communist money — New York Jew money McCarran called it in private.

Franklin went on the radio after Bunker. His threadbare campaign, Franklin declared, was clear for all to see. Did Franklin have a campaign headquarters in Las Vegas? In Reno? A single paid worker? "Yet the senior senator has," he said, "and practically his whole Washington staff is in Nevada campaigning for him, at your expense. Has George Franklin sent out one single circular in the mail? No. Yet the senior senator has sent out thousands of propaganda circulars, many under his senator's franking privilege, for which you pay."

McCarran's own campaign spending reports, Franklin continued, indicated that 48 percent of his money in his previous primary race came from outside Nevada and that 72 percent of his contributors were Republicans. And 82 percent of the money that McCarran raised in the last general election came from outside the state "Look who is crying to the high heavens this time," Franklin huffed. He then called McCarran a coward for not doing his own dirty work, instead sending an errand boy like Berkeley Bunker, who presumably hoped to fill the senator's seat by appointment when McCarran died in office. Then he tore into Bunker. "Of course," Franklin said, "it is fitting and proper and entirely in good taste for a notorious non-veteran, who used a discharge emblem falsely on his campaign literature, to slyly, and by transcription if you noticed, imply Communism to a man who served six and a half years in the United States Air Force, who was shot down twice, who has faced hot steel over hostile lands, all in his fight to protect the principles for which his country stands. . . . I am still fighting for the rights of the people against the privileges of the machine."[9]

In the last days[10] before McCarran's bill hit the floor, Steve Spingarn got a call from Senator Harley Kilgore to come up to the Hill to make the administration's case. Most of those gathered in the office didn't need much convincing: Humphrey, Graham, Kilgore. Only Maryland's Herbert O'Conor seemed to favor the McCarran bill. Spingarn turned to Graham, who had already lost his primary fight. You've been blasted for years by right-wingers for belonging to front groups, Spingarn said. Under the McCarran immigration provisions, if you were a foreigner, you would never be allowed into the United States.

O'Conor started defending immigration restrictions, which he had voted for in McCarran's earlier bills. I'm not going to sit here and listen to twaddle like that, he said, storming out.

While McCarran, on September 5, was mocking the president and his fellow Democrats for being blind to the Communist menace, voters in Nevada were going to the polls. Odds on the street ranged from two to one on up to seven to one in McCarran's favor. "From things I hear, the Korean mess certainly punctured that attack on you by the DP lovers," publisher Don Ashbaugh told McCarran. "Naturally, on top of that your push on the subversive handcuffing met with wide approval. Which leaves them with nothing to yap at you about."[11]

George Franklin's campaign never went anywhere. McCarran had constant reports about his challenger's money woes: Franklin getting the cold shoulder from the gambling boys in Las Vegas, having to borrow from relatives, not being able to pay bills. Still, Franklin managed to raise seventy-four hundred dollars. About five thousand of this was indeed eastern money, a contribution from the Committee on National Affairs; most of the rest came from his family. But the only "New York Jew money" was a contribution to McCarran from an old friend, the financier Bernard Baruch. McCarran reported spending a mere twenty-one hundred dollars on the primary (and later another thousand on the general election), which ignored the incalculable worth of saturation news coverage, his legion of unpaid patronage workers, and his senatorial mail privileges. Not to mention the cash contributions that McCarran never reported.

The week before the primary, the *Boulder City News,* one of the few papers not beholden to McCarran, took a rare blast at the senator. "On Tuesday next," the paper said, "the fate of a man running hog-wild, drunk with power, aged and dottering at nearly eighty — the fate of that man may be in your hands. . . . Pat McCarran is leading us — this nation into complete and total destruction."[12] But the dominant sentiment was that of the *Reese River Reveille.* "There seems little point in reiterating the fact," the paper observed, "well known to everybody, that any change — remote as it is — in Nevada's present senator would be akin to trading an established and profitable ranch for an acreage of sagebrush land without water rights."[13]

When the votes were counted the results were not surprising: McCarran whipped Franklin, 23,102 to 8,461. "The greatest mistake that my friends can make is to regard the coming election as a cinch . . . ," McCarran told a supporter. "In politics there is no such thing as a cinch until you get the certificate of election in your hands. Even then somebody is liable to steal it from you."[14]

After McCarran's speech opening the debate on his internal security bill, Herbert Lehman took the floor to offer a rebuttal. If there was one of his colleagues whom McCarran hated with a passion, it was Lehman. The liberal Jewish New Yorker came from a wealthy investment banking family, serving as lieutenant governor under Roosevelt and then as the state's chief executive himself; after the war he ran the United Nations Relief and Rehabilitation Administration, which fed and housed displaced persons — a favorite target of McCarran and other conservatives, who accused the organization of coddling subversives. In 1949 Lehman beat Republican John Foster Dulles for a special seat in the Senate, where he immediately jumped into the DP fight and became one of the first Democrats to take on Joe McCarthy. Given this background, Lehman might just as well have painted TRAITOR on his forehead as far as McCarran was concerned. While McCarran would never win more than thirty-six thousand votes in any election, Lehman had been sent to Washington, after a long and distinguished public career, by 2.6 million votes. McCarran, only two years older, treated Lehman, seventy-two, like a slow office boy. "He'd come into the chamber and lay down the law," Lehman recalled. "It didn't make any difference who had the floor. He'd just take it and insist on his legislation being taken up at his will, frequently out of turn. He paid no attention to the amenities or to fair play."[15]

So it was that Lehman, before he even started speaking, momentarily yielded to a colleague who wanted to ask a question. Although it was Lehman's turn, McCarran began speaking. Lehman protested and Russell Long, who was presiding over the Senate, agreed with the New Yorker.

"Has the chair taken me off the floor?"[16] McCarran snapped. He then ignored Lehman and Long and recognized Ferguson. Lehman would not get to talk until much later.

When Lehman was finally able to speak, he first made clear his opposition to Communism. The McCarran bill, however, would do little to hamper the party and much to limit the liberty of all Americans. "If we outlaw views, and penalize persons for their thoughts and beliefs," Lehman said, "we will grant the Communists a victory which they have not won."[17]

Lehman compared the Communist Party to an iceberg that was two-thirds submerged; the McCarran bill would cause it to sink farther instead of bringing it to the surface. The real threat, he said, was not party members but professional spies who would never risk exposure by openly moving in radical circles. Instead of finding those who truly endanger the country's security the bill would divert the government's resources to chase the fifty-four thousand party members who would be required to register. And how would the FBI know if proscribed organizations were complying by labeling their material as propaganda? "The enforcement agencies will have to go through the mails, look into every letter and every piece of literature to see from what kind of organization it emanates," he said. "Privacy of the mails will be gone. And an army of snoopers will necessarily be let loose to pry into the personal and private affairs of all our citizens. . . . This is not legislation, it is a parody on legislation."[18]

It would be a black day in the history of the country, Lehman continued, if this bill passed. "Do not think that this will catch only those whose views you hate," he warned. "All of us may become victims of the gallows we erect for the enemies of freedom."[19]

McCarran had one question for Lehman.

"Is the senator from New York trying to defend Communist front organizations?" McCarran wondered.

Lehman said he wasn't. Then McCarran asked Humphrey the same question.

"May the senator from Minnesota identify who he wants to defend," Humphrey snapped, "without the able assistance of the senator from Nevada?"[20]

Spingarn was working seven days a week and most nights trying to head off the McCarran bill. He wrote to an old friend who was the chairman of the National Counter Intelligence Corps Association asking for a public statement against the legislation. Back in early August, Spingarn had spoken at the group's annual convention, bringing greetings from Truman and a warning (written by Spingarn) not to sacrifice liberty to security. But now his old army buddy wrote back that the organization would not take a position on the bill. Spingarn had no better luck getting any help from J. Edgar Hoover. The White House aide asked for an endorsement of the administration's measure. An assistant director called to say Hoover was out of town. Spingarn then tried to interest Dwight Eisenhower in the cause, but the revered general was out of the country. Spingarn met with William "Wild Bill" Donovan, the legendary head of the OSS, the wartime precursor to the CIA. But Wild Bill was not ready to take a stand against McCarran's bill, either. Spingarn kept at it, spewing out dozens of letters packed with Truman's speeches, as well asvarious documents and studies, which he rushed to cabinet members, party officials, Pentagon bureaucrats, prominent lawyers, and anyone else he could think of who might help. But his optimism was waning. "The outlook is very gloomy," he wrote. "It looks as if the president's recommendation will be badly licked and we are in for a 1950 version of the Alien and Sedition laws of 1798."[21]

On Wednesday morning, September 6, Paul Douglas and Hubert Humphrey led a delegation of liberal lawmakers to the White House. Most of the liberals didn't think much of Truman; he thought less of them. Six of the seven were freshman senators, men who in other words were expected to sit in the back row of the chamber and keep quiet. And Harry Truman was a great believer in the traditions of the Senate. When he'd arrived in Washington in 1935, a colleague advised him to be a workhorse not a show horse, and Truman had taken those words to heart. The liberals, on the other hand, had done nothing but prance and prate since coming to the Hill.

There was Douglas ("an overeducated S.O.B.," Truman called him[22]), Humphrey ("a crackpot"), Tennessee's Estes Kefauver ("Cow-fever"[23]), Lehman, the only one in the group running for reelection that fall, Frank Graham, who had already been defeated in a vicious primary fight, Connecticut's William Benton, a rich advertising man, and West Virginia's Harley Kilgore. To Truman the only adult in the group was Kilgore, a friend of his who had served in the Senate since 1940 and sat a couple of seats down from McCarran in the front row ("Kilgore," observed journalists Robert Allen and William Shannon, "gets along with almost everyone, even . . . McCarran"[24]). Although Truman and the liberals shared similar policies, most of them were more trouble than they were worth. Kefauver, especially, had been a pain in the neck since April when he launched a high-profile congressional investigation into organized crime, uncovering numerous links between various Democratic political machines and the mob (most recently in Chicago, giving Scott Lucas yet another headache). It was a group distinguished by its passion and intelligence and its utter lack of power or influence in the Senate.

But with Lucas and the rest of the party leadership floundering in their efforts to stop the McCarran bill, the liberals came to Truman with a bold proposal. The only way to head off the McCarran bill, they explained, was by offering a tough substitute measure, one that would stop spies and saboteurs without tramping on civil liberties. Douglas said that they had crafted a preventive detention measure, a law that would let the government put potential subversives in concentration camps during a national emergency.

Truman was not impressed. He had a Midwest farmer's disdain for intellectuals (professional liberals, he called them), but he also had a bedrock belief that the Bill of Rights was the most important part of the Constitution. Now these upstarts were asking him to support a law to lock people up for what they *might* do. His aides were shocked at the idea. "The substitute is worse than the Mundt bill," David Lloyd wrote to Spingarn.[25]

The president said that he would reserve judgment until the bill reached his desk. But he told the group that by all means they should try to stop McCarran. "Go ahead," he said, "and make the move."[26]

Later that day Mundt[27] was virtually calling Lehman a fool and a liar on the floor of the Senate and promising to eat the bill if anyone could show him where any line of it threatened thought control, when Harley Kilgore asked him to yield. Kilgore then introduced the emergency detention bill. Mundt barely blinked, returning to a tedious recitation of the Communist conspiracy that was consuming yet another day of Senate activity. Would the Democrats please explain, he asked, why they opposed registering Communists when American boys were dying in Korea?

"Will the senator yield?"

Joe McCarthy wanted to add his thoughts to the debate. Mundt was reading long passages from a book by ex-Communist Louis Budenz. Normally solicitous of his friend McCarthy, Mundt waved off his colleague with a promise to let him have some time later.

"Will the senator yield?" McCarthy persisted several minutes later.

"I shall be glad to yield," Mundt said, "when I have finished."[28]

McCarthy wandered off, his contribution to the great debate on the Internal Security Act over.

"I should like to know who is undermining the government of the United States?" Humphrey asked as the debate carried into Thursday. "Is it not subversive for members of the Congress continuously to brand honorable

American citizens as being Communists? . . . I submit that the irresponsible charges which have been made in the Eighty-first Congress, second session, have done more to undermine the faith of the American people in representative government than the Communist Party will ever be able to do."[29]

Later that day Truman was asked by a reporter if he would sign the McCarran bill. "That is the Mundt-Nixon bill as revised by Senator McCarran and made a little worse," he said. "I would do the same thing to it that I would do to the Mundt-Nixon bill."[30] He called the Kilgore substitute an improvement but refused to say if he would sign it.

McCarran predicted that a veto could lead to a Republican sweep at the polls.

Between the McCarran bill, the liberal alternative, and various other measures, orphaned but still kicking, the internal security issue had become an ungodly mess.[31] A comparative print of six of the bills sprawled over both sides of ninety-six pages of triple-width paper. The booklet weighted more than a pound. The number of people who actually understood all of this could fit into the Oval Office. To help others wade through the swamp of legislation, Steve Spingarn put together what he called a "portable file," including a scorecard and various items showing that the McCarran bill would harm security by driving the party underground, which the FBI had reported was already happening. On September 7 Spingarn asked Lucas to help him distribute the material to fifty senators who might have an open mind. Lucas begged off. Why don't you try Humphrey's office, the majority leader suggested. It was not a good sign.

As befitted a man who devoured the lesser-known works of Machiavelli for summer reading, Douglas took a long view of events when he spoke the next day. He sprinted through the history of free speech, past Locke and Mill, past Mason, Madison, and Jefferson, past Holmes and Brandeis and the development of the reigning constitutional doctrine of clear and present danger, finally stopping in his own troubled time. "There are some who in the name of security would have us abandon freedom while there are others who in their zeal for liberty would disregard the needs of security," Douglas said. The theory of the Constitution and its Bill of Rights, however, held that liberty and security were inseparable. Free speech was necessary for democracy to function. "For truths which are not examined are not sufficiently understood and valued," Douglas said. "It is in the conflict of ideas and under stress that men find out for themselves the bedrock truths." Milton realized this. "And though all the winds of doctrine were let loose to play upon the earth, so Truth be in the field, we do injuriously by licensing and prohibiting to misdoubt her strength," the poet wrote. "Let her and falsehood grapple: who ever knew Truth put to the worse, in a free and open encounter?"[32]

But then a tone edged into the speech that was different. "Lincoln, who was as devout a believer in civil liberties as, I suppose, any public man we have ever had, had thousands of pro-Southern advocates in the North thrown into prison," Douglas said, "and he refused to honor writs of habeas corpus which were issued by the chief justice of the United States himself to release them."[33] The Communist Party, Douglas continued, was a political organization only after it was a conspiratorial one, but since it had repeatedly demonstrated its inability to win at the ballot box the only threat it posed was through acts of sabotage and espionage. Douglas then dropped an ominous thought on the chamber. "It is not enough," he said, "to punish acts of sabotage *after* they have occurred."[34]

Douglas dissected the McCarran bill, slicing apart its eighty-one pages into their constituent measures, spending most of his time demolishing the registration section. The bill would establish a subversive activities control board to decide if a group was controlled by Communists. If so, the organization had thirty days for its members to register with the government. Front groups need only register their officers. Both must report their finances and label all literature and correspondence as Communist propaganda. Members would be ineligible for passports or government jobs. Those failing to register could face up to five years in prison for each day they didn't comply. But the appeals process built into the bill would cripple its effectiveness. Cases coming before the National Labor Relations Board, for example, averaged more than fifteen months, plus another seventeen months for court appeals, which suggested that it could take two or three years for a final determination on any group, whose members would be at large in the meantime. What if all the members of a group quit and re-formed under another name? The only ones likely to be netted by this whole laborious process were harmless progressives. "What we have heard on the floor of the Senate during the past year would be nothing, as compared to the smearing which would occur all over the country once the floodgates were opened wide," Douglas said. "We might have a large section of the political leaders of the country, including a majority of the present members of the Senate, in prison."[35]

A better alternative, Douglas argued, was to give the president the power to declare a national emergency in case the United States was invaded, threatened with imminent invasion, if insurrection broke out, if the country declared war, or if Congress passed a concurrent resolution. The attorney general could then issue warrants for the detention of those believed to be potential saboteurs, such as members of the Communist Party, who would be entitled to a hearing. Congress would also be able to monitor the status of detainees, and the president could establish a board to review complaints. The state of emergency could be ended by either the president or Congress; the whole act would expire after three years. "The Kilgore bill would make the least possible inroads upon liberty," Douglas said. ". . . But the dangerous actors would be taken out of circulation during an emergency and the country would be protected."[36]

Douglas was speaking mostly to his own liberal colleagues, with McCarran and the other conservatives wandering into the chamber only after he finished his remarks. Picking up a copy of Douglas's speech, Ferguson asked what the difference between detention and imprisonment was. "The worst part of imprisonment," Douglas replied, "is the blot upon the name which comes from conviction for a crime. Defamation of character is worse than detention. That is something which its seems to be very difficult for certain persons to understand. Defamation is really more injurious than is detention."[37]

It was after six in the evening. Douglas had been going for twelve hours, having skipped breakfast to prepare for the debate. He was wiped out. He had worked like a dog to put together an alternative to the McCarran bill; he had taken a big risk by proposing the detention bill but believed that the FBI would round up subversives in an emergency anyway. Better, he felt, that Congress set up a fair contingency program with adequate supervision than pass hysterical legislation like the McCarran steamroller. But Douglas found his idea derided with scorn and ridicule. The man who at fifty years of age had set aside his Quaker convictions and volunteered to fight fascism was now called a fascist by McCarran and Mundt, both great isolationists given to martial metaphors about battling Communists, but neither of whom had ever put on a uniform. And so Douglas, the most decent and conscience racked of lawmakers, yielded the floor to the conservatives and let their blows rain down on his reputation without interruption.

Mundt compared the detention bill to Nazi death camps. "Let us not tear the Constitution to shreds," he pleaded, "Let us not out-Hitler Hitler; let us not out-Stalin Stalin; let us not establish concentration camps in America and deprive American citizens of their freedom without some kind of charge against them or some kind of court process." Mundt claimed that the bill would create a swarm of Gestapo agents to scour the country. "Some obscure political agent reviews it," he mocked, "and says, 'No.' Perhaps by that time they will be saying, in Gestapo language, 'Nein, nein,' or as a Communist agent would say, 'Nyet, nyet.' " And he lambasted the bill's provision to compensate those wrongly detained. "I wonder," he said, "if all the printing presses in the country printing money and working twenty-four hours a day could produce enough thousand-dollar bills to indemnify the citizens of America who rightfully would have a claim against their government if they were to be locked up by Gestapo agents such as those provided in this proposed substitute bill. . . . This certainly is a way to spend the government money faster than anything the Fair Dealers have ever thought of before."[38]

Ferguson said that the bill reminded him of the Russian constitution, which guaranteed individual rights except when the government decided to violate them. "I did not think the time would ever come, Mr. President, when we would have to rise upon the floor of the Senate and defend the Constitution of the United States," he said. No one complained about making lobbyists register, Ferguson said, yet we should let the attorney general throw men in jail without trial, but not register Communists? "Why the opposition to registration?" he asked. "Is it because some men in key positions in various communities are actually Communists. . . . Is it because some of our political parties are infiltrated with these agents of Moscow, that they do not want them to be registered as Communists?"[39]

Then McCarran rose. "One of the most potent ways of destroying valuable legislation is to insert in it somewhere along the line something which on the very first test will cause it to be held unconstitutional," he rumbled. "Of course, the substitute could not be regarded in any other light."

Kilgore demanded to know if McCarran was accusing him of trying to torpedo the whole act. "I did not say that," he replied. "I say there is no better way of destroying a valuable law." McCarran then launched into a diatribe against Lehman. "I really think the senator from New York is more to be pitied than blamed," McCarran said. "It should not take a lawyer, nor even a law student, to see the absurdity of those statements. It should be apparent to anyone who understands plain English."[40]

A history teacher from the Bronx complained to both Kilgore *and* Mundt about the debate. "According to the press you are accusing each other of promoting police state tactics," she wrote. "You are *both* right. Both of you reveal that you have no faith whatsoever in American freedom and democracy. The Nazis never hatched a swarm of irresponsible and unprincipled politicians who hated democracy more than our own political stars who are now in ascendancy — such as McCarthy, McCarran, Mundt, Nixon, Ferguson, Rankin."[41]

On Monday, September 11, Humphrey took the floor for five hours. "More good names have been hurt, more good souls have been blemished by irresponsible remarks made by persons in the government of the United States in the last year than in the past twenty years of our history," he said. Behind his famously large forehead, Humphrey's personality twined moral passion and raw ambition. Sometimes, as in this speech, these two traits seemed to be slugging it out in Humphrey's soul. At other times the drive to power won, as it would when Humphrey later hitched his wagon to Lyndon Johnson's star or when he swallowed his doubts on Vietnam and became a hawk. But at this moment, his conscience triumphed. "I ask the members of the Senate to search their own souls and consciences. I ask them to think about what they are doing, before they vote for this bill. . . . [T]he Congress of the United States will regret the day that it ever passes S. 4037. It will prove to be one of the darkest pages in American history."[42]

McCarran, too, saw the detention issue in the clarifying light of moral certainty bright as the Nevada sun. "This title, Mr. President, is one of the most startling products of legislative draftsmanship which has ever been printed under the sponsorship of a United States senator," he said about the Kilgore proposal. "It is a workable blueprint for the establishment of the dictatorship of the proletariat in the United States; but it is not workable under any of the accepted standards of Americanism which include preservation of the fundamental freedoms guaranteed in the Bill of Rights. . . . How the sponsors of the substitute can rise and declare that any other bill is unconstitutional is more than I can understand."[43]

Nothing, he added, in the bill compelled the president to ever use his emergency power. McCarran did not elaborate, but the implication was clear: Some presidents could not be trusted to take action against Communists even in the event of war.

On Tuesday, September 12, shortly before the 1 P.M. deadline for the vote, Scott Lucas made a plea to the Senate to vote for the Kilgore bill instead of the McCarran one. Lucas, never much of a Fair Dealer to begin with but increasingly bitter as his reelection prospects soured and his stomach ulcers bled, worried little over the threat to individual liberties or the rights of minorities that so troubled the president and the liberal wing of his party. "One may talk about concentration camps," Lucas said, "one may talk about the Kilgore proposal as being one to create a police state, if he desires; but when we are dealing with a Communist group such as the one we know exists in this country, a group which we have seen in operation as the result of a few trials which have taken place, there is nothing too drastic, so far as the senator from Illinois is concerned, in order to meet that situation."[44]

The Kilgore substitute came to a vote and was defeated 45 to 29. Kilgore then tried to introduce the same bill as an amendment, but yielded to Lucas who now surprised the Senate by proposing to attach the liberal legislation (the Kilgore amendment) onto the end of the McCarran measure. Most of the liberals and centrists rushed to support the idea, forgetting that the plan was to kill the McCarran bill, not make it bigger. Conservatives beat back the attack with one vote to spare, 37 to 35. Even though he voted for the amendment, Lehman was furious that Lucas had not broached the idea with the bill's sponsors, cornering the majority leader in the cloakroom and telling him off.

Kilgore then tried to revive his amendment, and lawmakers started shouting at one another. "There is so much confusion in the chamber that we cannot hear what is being said," Mundt pleaded.[45] The presiding officer gaveled the Senate back to order, and Kilgore made a final appeal. "Why do they object to bringing Communists into the open?" Mundt said.[46] The amendment went down with a thud, 50 to 23.

Millard Tydings, the conservative Democratic who had led the sub-committee that investigated McCarthy's charges earlier in the year and was now locked in a savage reelection campaign, suggested that the Senate reconsider Lucas's idea to combine the two bills. The motion passed. Pandemonium engulfed the floor, senators swirling into small groups to search their consciences. McCarran and Mundt huddled with Lucas. With some detention safeguards they could drop their opposition to the com-bined measure. Douglas and Humphrey scoured their souls. Both had been battered in the furious fight, bludgeoned with their own substitute bill, now added onto the ever-swelling McCarran measure. Reluctantly they decided they should vote for the bill in the hope of trying to alter it in conference. They talked Connecticut's William Benton into doing the same. And liberal Republican Bill Langer decided likewise — although he quickly apologized to Truman.

McCarran then moved to substitute his own amendment (cosponsored by Mundt and Ferguson) in place of the Lucas one, which kept the basic concept of preventive detention but added a guarantee of habeas corpus and a provision to pay for the camps, one of those tiny but important administrative details that made McCarran such a master of parliamentary procedure. Lehman was one of the few to rise up in opposition. "I will not compromise my conscience . . . ," he said. "I am going to vote against this tragic, this unfortunate, this ill-conceived legislation. My conscience will be easier, though I realize my political prospects may be more difficult. I shall cast my vote to protect the liberties of our people."[47]

Only six others voted with Lehman. Two of them, Graham and Kefauver, had also been sponsors of the Kilgore bill and now joined Lehman in opposing it. All were stalwart liberal Democrats; none but Lehman faced reelection. Indeed, three were leaving the Senate after the session ended.

Douglas, Humphrey, Kilgore, Benton, and Langer voted with the majority, 70 to 7. "It certainly was a strange thing," Mundt chortled, "to see Senators Douglas, Lucas, Humphrey, Langer, and some of the other bleeding-heart liberals stand up and vote for my measure after they had spent so many hours on the floor of the Senate and in their own home bailiwick in condemning the registration features of this legislation."[48] None of them felt good about it. Benton said it troubled him more than any other vote he cast in the Senate. Humphrey told Kefauver that he was very proud of his colleague's vote. "I wish I could say the same for myself," he wrote.[49]

No one was more despondent than Douglas. Going home, he found his two sons dispirited by his action. Douglas didn't sleep that night, or the next, his mind troubled by visions of a reign of terror descending upon the nation, of innocents dragged before the subversive activities control board. Friends tried to assuage his guilt, but Douglas was inconsolable. He would regret that vote for the next twenty years.

The next day McCarran predicted that Truman would sign the bill. "American public opinion won't let him do otherwise," he said.[50] In the White House there was a parade of congressional leaders telling the president the same thing. Vice President Alben Barkley, Majority Leader Scott Lucas, House Speaker Sam Rayburn, House floor leader John

McCormack — all implored Truman to face the inevitable: The McCarran bill would soon be the law of the land, with or without his signature. It would be a lot easier on the party if Truman would go along with the legislative landslide. He told them he hadn't made up his mind. All year long Truman had been railing against just this type of drift-net legislation, but at his Thursday press conference the next day he sounded less certain. He said that he hadn't had a chance to analyze the bill. Phones at the White House began ringing. The twenty-seven lawmakers who had voted against the measure were worried that Truman would not veto it now; that they would be out on a limb in an anti-Communist storm. Spingarn could only say that the president was hoping for a better bill to come out of the House-Senate conference the next week. "It was theoretically possible that a reasonably good bill could emerge from the conference," he said lamely. "Consequently, the president could hardly commit himself until he saw what the conferees did."[51]

On Wednesday, September 20, both houses agreed to a conference report — which increased the criminal penalties of the act and removed the three-year expiration clause from the detention section, making it a permanent law. In the Senate Mundt pleaded for a unanimous vote, a second Declaration of Independence, this time from the tyranny of Russian Communism. The liberals fought again — and again they lost heavily, this time 7 to 51.

By the time the bill landed on the president's desk early the next afternoon, Spingarn and five other aides had already worked up three drafts of a veto message. Spingarn thought that there was at least a fighting chance of sustaining a veto in the Senate. A number of senators told him it all depended on the strength and cogency of the message. Several urged Truman to finally name an internal security and individual rights commission, even if he decided to sign the bill. Back in his August message, Truman had pulled the idea from the speech at the last moment. The timing, he felt, wasn't right. Now, when Spingarn pushed the idea once again, Truman said he would gladly propose the commission if it would help his veto.

To Spingarn the lonely moment in the White House when Truman would pick up a pen to sign either the McCarran bill or the veto was a watershed. "The signing of the bill would represent an action of moral appeasement on a matter of highest principle," he wrote. He called the bill an act of aggression akin to the North Korean invasion; sign it and there would be further calls for even more repressive measures. "The enactment of this legislation," Spingarn continued, "would furnish a green light to states, counties, cities, and towns to enact their own junior-model anti-subversive laws and ordinances. This has already started but the approval of the present legislation would, it is believed, establish an approved pattern and enormously accelerate the trend." Vigilantes would swamp the FBI with denunciations of their neighbors. "Before we finish with this business we might well go through a period that would make the period of the Alien and Sedition Laws looked like one of moderation," he concluded. "Nothing could do more serious harm to our internal security than this."[52]

Spingarn and other aides had labored until midnight on a new version of the veto text. They reworked the message yet again on Friday morning, finishing the fifth iteration just in time for the 11 A.M. cabinet meeting. In the White House support for the veto came from some surprising quarters: Justice, Defense, State, and the CIA. In the past all of these departments had taken a harder line than the president favored on internal security, but they agreed that the bill's provisions would be so cumbersome and unworkable that if only in the interest of bureaucratic efficiency, Truman should sign the veto message. Truman spent ninety minutes going over the document. "This is a totalitarian approach," the president scrawled.[53] Spingarn suggested a dramatic gesture to go along with the message: Maybe Truman could hand deliver it to Congress and arrange for a live nationwide radio hookup to carry his words to the country. In the end Truman opted for the less daring but still unprecedented step of adding a cover note urging each member of Congress to carefully read and study the message before voting. Finally, the president ordered his six-thousand-word plea to be printed double spaced on single-sided paper to make it easier to read. At 4 P.M. the message was delivered to the House. "The bill is one of the most absurd pieces of legislation passed by any Congress," Truman confided to a friend, "but I am of the opinion that my veto will be overridden."[54]

Later that day Charlie Murphy told Spingarn that the president was naming him to the Federal Trade Commission. Spingarn was shocked. He didn't want to leave the White House. The past two years had been the most fulfilling of his professional life. He loved the job and worshiped his boss. But now for some unfathomable reason he was being kicked out of the White House. His mind quickly scrolled down the possibilities. There was the time he pissed off the vice president by accidentally keeping him waiting? Or maybe it was the meeting where he offended Herbert O'Conor and the senator stomped out in a huff? Could it have been the

occasion when he handed Speaker Sam Rayburn a bill from the president
and innocently told him what committee Truman wanted it sent to?
Young man, no one tells the Speaker of the House of Representatives
where legislation is to be referred, Rayburn boomed at him. Everything
he could think of seemed so petty. Maybe it was just little things, accumulating like snow on a roof until the structure finally gave way: the miles
of memos, criticizing everything from the White House filing system and
security to suggesting how to better organize office supplies. "It is a very
delicate subject," one of the president's chief aides warned Spingarn when
he threatened to step on another bureaucrat's toes. Still, Spingarn was
dumbstruck. "There may have been some thought that I was tactless, or
that my modus operandi was not good, or something like that, I don't
know," he said. "Obviously something had happened."[55]

In the Senate the clerk began reading the president's message. "I am taking
this action only after the most serious study and reflection and after consultation with the security and intelligence agencies of the government,"
the statement began. The McCarran anti-Communist bill, unfortunately,
would not hurt the Communists but instead would help them. It would
weaken existing security and overburden the FBI; it would be a boon for
Communist propagandists, sow dissension within the United States, and
give the government vast powers to harass citizens and aliens alike. The
message denounced the registration provision as unworkable, akin to
asking criminals to check in with the sheriff. And it ringingly reasserted
the president's belief that any government stifling of free expression was a
long step toward totalitarianism. "We would betray our finest traditions if
we attempted, as this bill would attempt, to curb the simple expression of
opinion," the president wrote. "This we should never do, no matter how
distasteful the opinion may be to the vast majority of our people. The
course proposed by this bill would delight the Communists, for it would
make a mockery of the Bill of Rights and of our claims to stand for
freedom in the world." The path of prudence, under such a law, would be
to offer no opinions on controversial issues; democracy would wither.
"This is a time when we must marshal all our resources and all the moral
strength of our free system in self-defense against the threat of Communist
aggression," the message concluded. "We will fail in this, and we will
destroy all that we seek to preserve, if we sacrifice the liberties of our citizens in a misguided attempt to achieve national security."[56]

"Vote! Vote!" echoed across the House as soon as the president's message was delivered and before it could even be read. Speaker Sam Rayburn had to insist on at least letting Truman's words be heard before a roll call. Within an hour 248 members voted to override the veto. Only 48 supported the president.

The president's last hope was the Senate, where the Democratic leadership was pushing for a quick vote to meet its scheduled adjournment at midnight. At 11 P.M. Truman called Douglas and told him that if he could keep the debate going through Saturday, then the newspapers and radio could report his veto message and arouse enough public opinion to send a wave of moral suasion crashing over the Senate. Douglas rushed to the floor.

The liberals had frequently berated the southern Democrats for strangling civil rights legislation with filibusters, but Douglas thought that many senators and most of the public didn't pay much attention to important issues unless there was substantial debate. "Busy men are not convinced by a glancing reference or a subtle allusion," recalled Douglas, whose maiden speech in the Senate had been about limiting debate. "The argument has to be ample, well-documented, and sustained. . . . But there was always a basic distinction between our tactics and those of the Southern filibusterers. They wanted to prevent a vote. We wanted only to delay it until the appropriate time."[57]

Lucas had abandoned his president and was helping McCarran marshal the forces behind the bill. In the past week the majority leader had been getting hammered with headlines such as "Dirksen Says Lucas Coddles Reds."[58] Although the liberal media — led by the *New York Times* and the *Washington Post* — never wavered in its opposition to the McCarran bill or its tepid response to Kilgore's alternative, the conservative press was having a field day. "A Red Control Bill — Two Years Late," the *Washington Times-Herald* snarled. "But the Democrats fool no one in trying to claim credit of any kind for curbing subversives at home or abroad," the editorial said. "Their record of Red appeasement the world over is too long and too well known."[59]

In the old Supreme Court room, where the Senate was meeting while the ceiling in its chamber was being repaired, Humphrey rose first to speak. "Mr. President," he began, "this is a reversal for me, and it is a decision which I have thought about for many, many days. I want to say to my colleagues in the Senate that the most difficult decision I have ever had to make on a vote was on the occasion of the original passage in this body of the McCarran bill. It was one of those decisions that went deep into my conscience. . . . I can honesty say that I have never been more unhappy in my life. But this is indeed a happy moment, because it is good to be able to vote one's convictions."[60]

But what started out sounding like a declaration of conscience, a soul-clearing confession for having rushed to support an unjust bill, quickly turned into an attack on the measure for being too weak. "The authors of this bill became a little bit confused," he said. "They apparently thought they were going to register the Eagles or the Elks or the Moose. . . . But this bill requires the registration of the most sinister, deceitful, despicable people that have ever inhabited the earth." Wading farther into the swamp of paradox, Humphrey declared that the McCarran bill threatened liberty but at the same time wasn't tough enough. "I have never seen such solicitude on the part of so-called anti-Communists for the Communists . . . ," he said. "If we are in war and these despicable traitors decide to blow up every building we have, if they decide to destroy every means of communication, every port facility, and every dock, Mr. President, do you know how they would get protection? They would get it through the writ of habeas corpus, under this bill. I repeat, had Abraham Lincoln waited for a writ of habeas corpus, we would not have had the United States of America."[61]

It was a manic, almost schizophrenic, performance. Four years later there would be an equally bizarre sequel when the man whose political career would stand as an embodiment of midcentury liberalism, not least for his fight against the Internal Security Act, would sponsor and help pass a bill to ban the Communist Party.

Friday turned into Saturday, and around 2 A.M. Bill Langer stood to take his turn. Langer, a week short of sixty-four, was a diabetic, often ill, and looking particularly pale this morning. In fervor and length of opposition to every incarnation of the McCarran bill, no one in Washington could touch the square-headed, big-eared North Dakotan. The only Republican to speak against the bill, Langer was also the only lawmaker to vigorously condemn *both* the registration and detention sections of the measure. Both threatened liberty. "Tonight," he said, "we find this heritage under direct attack by forces which seek to undermine the very foundation of human freedom."[62]

William Langer was born in the Dakota territory and graduated from the University of North Dakota Law School at the age of nineteen. He then enrolled at Columbia University, where he pledged the Sigma Chi fraternity. His farm-boy clothes and hayseed haircut earned him twenty-two blackballs. Langer threw himself into school activities with furious energy, becoming class president, winning election to the fraternity that had scorned him, and graduating as valedictorian in 1910. He turned down a job at a Wall Street law firm and returned home to North Dakota. Nominally a Republican, he joined the Non-Partisan League, a group of agrarian radicals. No one in the league was bolder. In 1917 Langer, now the state's attorney general, deputized a number of local citizens in the town of Minot, ordered the telephone exchange seized at gunpoint to prevent word from spreading, and launched a series of vice raids on local bars, brothels, and gambling parlors. The governor had Langer arrested, but the charges were dropped. People started calling him Wild Bill.

With the First World War, Langer's libertarian streak began to show. Although he enforced a state law that the flag must be displayed in school, Langer, the son of Czech and Austrian immigrants, defended the rights of Germans to speak their language, study it in school, and hold church services in the tongue. In 1932 Langer was elected governor. He declared an embargo on shipping wheat out of state, ordered sheriffs not to help the banks with foreclosures, and forbade evictions during winter. Soon he was fighting his own eviction. After he required state employees to help finance the NPL newspaper by spending 5 percent of their salary to buy subscriptions, Langer was indicted by a federal grand jury for soliciting funds. Found guilty, Langer called out the National Guard to help him stay in office. A second trial ended in a hung jury. A third acquitted him. In 1940 Langer was elected to the Senate. No sooner had he taken the oath of office then the Committee on Elections and Privileges, led by Scott Lucas, tried to unseat him for moral turpitude over the solicitation charge. The full Senate voted to let him keep his seat. "He wins them all," Lucas once marveled.[63]

During the debate on his fitness for office, Langer sat on the Democratic side of the aisle chewing on a cigar still in its plastic wrapper, a harbinger of things to come. The Republican lawmaker looked like a good New Deal Democrat on most domestic issues but resembled an old-guard GOP isolationist on foreign policy. Langer was one of only two senators to vote against the United Nations; he also opposed the Marshall Plan and instead suggested that aid money would be better spent on rural America. In 1952 Langer would snub Eisenhower and travel with his friend Truman on his train trip across North Dakota in support of Adlai Stevenson. When state Republicans wanted nothing to do with Langer, he ran for a fourth term as an independent and won the contest without even having to return to North Dakota to campaign. "Whenever people were in trouble, with their backs against the wall," Paul Douglas remembered, "Bill would be on their side, swinging both arms and pouring out a stream of violent language. . . . When the chips were down, he was always on the side of the weak."[64]

Langer spoke for an hour, then two, rambling on about the Sherman Antitrust Act, among many other topics. Douglas thought that he looked ill and tried to spell him by asking a question. Langer waved him off and pushed on, condemning monopolies, the failure to bring electricity to farmers in the Northwest, the price of farm machinery. Kilgore also wanted to give the clearly exhausted senator a breathing period. "I decline to yield for any purpose," Langer said. "I am sorry . . . I would lose three or four minutes. Time is precious."[65]

Finally Langer stumbled upon the McCarran bill. "It throws our Bill of Rights out the window," he said. "For the first time in the history of America we hear about concentration camps in America. If the press does not write the kind of an article the president of the United States wants them to write, put them in a concentration camp."

Soon Langer could not even rise from his desk to fend off parliamentary challenges from his Republican brethren. He pushed on, recalling when the mood in the country was different. "We were a happy, contented, and prosperous nation," he said. "We were not worried about the Communists. If anyone had, in those days, prophesied that at this time there would be before the Senate a bill providing for concentration camps and registration for Communists, he would have been laughed at. . . . What has happened to America?"[66]

Five in the morning drew near and Langer, after three hours, began to sputter as he was reading an old speech about the UN. "The senator should continue talking if he is to keep the floor," a Republican carped.[67]

"I said I would not yield," Langer snapped. Suddenly he stopped speaking, swayed slightly, and crashed to the floor. The Republicans called for a vote. Humphrey demanded a quorum. An exasperated Lucas begged for a roll call. "Senators will not change votes by engaging in further debate on this issue, even if they do so continuously for a week," he said.

Douglas, stepping over Langer's prone body, asked to be recognized. My God, he looks dead, Douglas thought, as he began talking to prevent a vote. Langer was carried out of the chamber. Four hours later Douglas was still at it. "How long, O Lord, how long," cried Alexander Wiley.[68]

As the clock approached the twenty-four-hour mark since Truman's message was read to the Senate, the liberals finally bowed to the inevitable and gave up the floor. "Amen," someone said.[69] The conservatives fired off a few parting insults. McCarran expressed incredulity that Truman could have read the bill and written such a statement. Mundt pointed to a correspondent for the *Daily Worker* in the press gallery. "How near the Red menace has actually penetrated our own surroundings!" he exclaimed.[70]

At 4:30 P.M. the roll was called. Fifty-seven senators voted to override the president. Just ten went the other way. Only Douglas, Humphrey, Kilgore, and Dennis Chavez changed their votes and supported Truman. Glen Taylor missed the vote. And Bill Langer was resting in Bethesda Naval Hospital. "One of the most distressing political defeats my father ever suffered," Margaret Truman wrote.[71]

Lucas, at last, was free to campaign full time. He would, he said, "work every conceivable angle until the clock strikes five on election day."[72] And on that day, six weeks after the veto override, Lucas scrawled a single word on his appointment book: DEFEATED. Dirksen, not Lucas, would be the one to get a Senate office building named for him.

A few days after the vote, Spingarn lingered after the White House morning staff meeting. He had never been invited to the meetings in the first place but had just started showing up and had become a fixture. Now he tried to explain to Truman how much he loved working in the White House, how he hadn't meant to cause any problems. Truman listened patiently for several minutes and then his fingers started twitching. Spingarn knew there was no point going on. He thanked the president and left.

Spingarn spent two years at the FTC, during which time he kept in touch with his old colleagues at the White House, pinch-hitting on internal security matters. After Truman left the White House, Spingarn kept at it, trying to start up a liberal think tank to combat McCarthyism. Out of government, he continued to rise early, craft copious memos, and vent his opinions to anyone who would listen, almost as if he were trying desperately to atone for not doing more to ensure that Truman's loyalty program did not become the witch hunt it did. But Spingarn never found any outlet for his energy or frustration. His brilliance faded to eccentricity; his persistence became monomania. During Vietnam he took to showing up uninvited at Defense Secretary Robert McNamara's house on Sundays to hand his wife memos on how better to run the war. Years later he would practically stalk a revisionist historian who suggested that Truman was less than sincere on civil rights. And for the rest of his life Spingarn would wonder why Truman had kicked him out of the White House. "I think it was just this sort of overpowering personality problem," Charlie Murphy recalled years later. "Steve just couldn't keep quiet."[73]

On Sunday, despite only a few hours sleep squeezed in around the debate, McCarran showed up at the office full of pep, healthy and happy. He cleaned up his desk, packed his briefcase, and caught the evening Capitol Limited for Chicago and from there to Nevada, where the election would take place in little more than a month. McCarran was as insecure as ever. "The mud slinging of the past campaign will, in my judgement, be only a pee wee as compared with what will take place in the oncoming campaign," he complained. "My opponent in this oncoming campaign is a mud-slinger from Mudville and he knows how and he hesitates at nothing, so you can look for everything."[74]

The election, of course, would be a cakewalk.

CHAPTER 20

Burnt Offerings

Julian Sourwine: You are, as a matter of fact, one of a relatively small number of persons employed by the State Department today who do speak the Chinese language fluently, are you not?

John Paton Davies: That may be so.

Sourwine: Do you know how many others there are in the department who do?

Davies: I don't, but I could make a rough estimate of ten or fifteen.

Sourwine: Isn't it perhaps an unfortunate thing that we do not have more experts in that language?

Davies: It is a very serious matter, and it is also a serious matter that very few of them now are dealing with Far Eastern affairs.

Sourwine: Why is that?

Davies: I have my guesses.

Sourwine: Do you think you know?

Davies: They are personal guesses.

Sourwine: Do you think you know why that is?

Davies: I think it is because they have been persecuted out of the Far East.[1]

> — Subcommittee on Internal Security,
> Institute for Pacific Relations hearings

Oliver Edmund Clubb was walking down a road with his daughter. Men appeared and threw knives at him. A car tried to run him down. The driver jumped out and stabbed him in the back. He wasn't hurt. A crosslike mark appeared on his back.

Zoë Clubb recalled the dream about her father at breakfast on the morning of January 2, 1951. Edmund Clubb had heard stranger things recently. The State Department was getting to be a scary place to work, especially if you had had anything to do with China. And Clubb, fifty this year, was the director of the department's office of Chinese affairs, a career diplomat who had spent the better part of the past two decades serving in posts all over China. Many of Clubb's fellow China experts — men such as Jack Service, John Carter Vincent, and John Davies — were being publicly attacked as

Communists, flailed in the press and Congress, subjected to seemingly end-less departmental loyalty investigations. "The atmosphere of public life in Washington," State Department counselor George Kennan had warned the year before, "does not have to deteriorate much further to produce a situa-tion in which very few of our more quiet and sensitive and gifted people will be able to continue in government. . . . The margin of safety with which our country moves in the world today is not great enough to permit us to be reckless and wasteful with the talents and the idealism of those people we depend on for the generalship of our peacetime battles."[2]

At the end of the day Ed Clubb was at his desk in the State Department when a lawyer came by with a letter. "Are you, or have you ever been," it asked, "a member of, affiliated with, or in sympathetic association with the Communist Party, or any organization which is a front for, or controlled by, the Communist Party?"[3]

The snow fell on the truck's windshield faster than the wipers could clear it away. It was a good thing Don Surine knew where he was going. It was February 7, 1951, and Surine and Frank Schroeder were on the outskirts of Lee, in western Massachusetts. Surine was thirty-five, a decade veteran of the FBI until Hoover had fired him for getting to know a suspect in a pros-titution case rather too well. But Surine was an energetic investigator and an ardent anti-Communist, and Hoover had recommended him for a job to a man who didn't share the FBI director's sense of moral delicacy: Joe McCarthy. And this winter McCarthy had loaned Surine to McCarran, who needed all the help he could get.

For all the furor that McCarthy had caused in the year since his speech in Wheeling, he was what he had always been: a freshman senator from the minority party. He may have suddenly become one of the most famous faces in the country, a lightning rod for controversy and conflict, but his essential source of power was publicity. After the Tydings Committee branded his charges of Communist infiltration in the State Department a fraud and a hoax, McCarthy was at an impasse.

McCarran wasn't. McCarthy said what McCarran had been thinking for years. Ever since he had first arrived in Washington almost twenty years earlier, McCarran had seen the furrows running hither and yon across the plateau of the New Deal, an indecipherable crosshatch of suspicious trac-ings. Henry Wallace and the radicals running riot in the Ag Department. The National Labor Relations Board kowtowing to the CIO. The State Department's coddling of the Soviet Union and its implacable hostility toward anti-Communist leaders from Franco to Chiang Kai-shek. But like the plain of Nazca in Peru, the crazy lines on the ground formed a grand design when viewed from above. "McCarran believed completely that there was one being in the United States who directed the operation of the Communist Party," his friend Norm Biltz recalled. "He was completely convinced of this, and so was McCarthy. Patsy told me many, many times, he said, 'Norm, I can't get through the cloud. I can't find that person. But I feel his influence all over Washington.' . . . I wouldn't dare tell you some of the people he suspected."[4]

Unlike McCarthy, McCarran had the power to do something about his suspicions. In December 1951 McCarran asked Mississippi Democrat James Eastland to introduce Senate Resolution 366, which created the Senate Internal Security Subcommittee. On paper the Judiciary Committee panel's main charge was to look at how the McCarran Act was being carried out. "We are going to find out how the Internal Security Act has been administered," McCarran said, "and whether any efforts are being made to wreck the law or misconstrue it."[5] The last part of the resolution, however, empowered the subcommittee to investigate "the extent, nature and effects of subversive activities." In practice this meant that the only curb on the subcommittee was McCarran's own self-restraint.

McCarran appointed himself as chairman of the subcommittee. For its other members, he shunned the liberals on the Judiciary Committee and picked its three most conservative Democrats: Mississippi segregationist Jim Eastland (who addressed blacks as boy and whose idea of a subtle question was "Did you know traitor Harry Dexter White?"[6]), Maryland's hard-shelled Herbert O'Conor, and Willis Smith, who had just joined the Senate from North Carolina after an ugly attack campaign against liberal Frank Graham. Moderate Republicans were also anathema to McCarran, who selected the three most cantankerous minority members he could find: Michigan's Homer Ferguson, who attacked Democrats like some dogs chase cars; Indiana's venomous William Jenner, whose policy pronouncements often sounded like calls to armed insurrection ("Congress should lock the doors of the Capitol, haul down the flag over the dome, and go home to fight for liberty"[7]); and Utah's Arthur Watkins, a dignified Mormon with the courtly manners of a small-town judge but whose bedrock political philosophy was as dry and unforgiving as the Great Basin desert. A more ideologically cohesive subcommittee would be hard to find on the Hill. SISS wouldn't need a minority counsel.

The staff was also carefully chosen. McCarran's right-hand man remained

Judiciary Committee counsel Jay Sourwine, but the senator also hired New York lawyer Robert Morris as a special counsel. Morris had been investigating Communists since working for New York's Rapp-Coudert Committee, which had scoured the state's school system for subversives in 1940 and continued looking for them during the war with naval intelligence. In 1950 Morris was hired as the minority counsel on the Tydings Committee, where he vainly tried to expand the investigation beyond McCarthy's original charges into a wholesale probe of domestic subversion. For Morris, getting hired by McCarran was like winning the lottery. "The subcommittee was everything that the Tydings Committee was not," Morris remembered. "Senator McCarran, on the occasion of our first meeting, made it clear that all political considerations were to be kept completely out of the picture. He asked me to put aside my political accoutrements as a Republican and to plunge into the job. McCarran was the very essence of integrity at all times and he pursued the investigation with scrupulous and careful restraint."[8]

McCarran hired Ben Mandel as the subcommittee's director of research. Mandel was a former New York teacher, an ex-Communist (he had issued Whittaker Chambers his party card) and business manager for the *Daily Worker*, who turned against the party and spent years working as the chief researcher for HUAC. "A fidgety, kindly man," Chambers remembered.[9] One of Mandel's first tasks was to quietly investigate the staffs of other congressional committees. "The penetration of House and Senate committees by personnel with Communist affiliations,"[10] he explained, was pervasive on the staffs of liberals such as Kilgore and Kefauver, two Judiciary Committee members excluded from SISS.

McCarran, in short, assembled something of an all-star team of anti-subversives, combining HUAC and McCarthy stalwarts (and five ex-FBI agents) with a wide array of contacts among the government and the netherworld of disaffected party members — all operating under the patronage of one of the most powerful senators on the Hill.

Which was why Surine found himself driving four hundred miles through a snowstorm to a farm in New England. Surine and Schroeder, another subcommittee investigator, pulled up next to a tumbledown barn on the farm, dragged the caretaker out into the cold, waved a subpoena from the subcommittee, and then filled the truck with several steel filing cabinets stuffed with old documents. The farm belonged to Edward C. Carter, the retired executive secretary of a think tank called the Institute for Pacific Relations, who was storing the organization's old files. Surine and Schroeder set off through the blizzard toward New York. Treasury agents were waiting to meet them and escort them to a small room in the Senate Office Building where McCarran had just had the locks changed.

It was tedious drive. Surine had already made it several times, and the cargo held few secrets for him. He had already poked through the files. He had even carried several boxloads to New York and photocopied hundreds of the files before HUAC heard about the documents — prompting Surine to secret them back to the barn until SISS could issue a subpoena. Actually, the FBI had already beat Surine to the files and found little of interest. "None relate," the FBI concluded, "to pro-Soviet or pro-Communist sentiments or espionage."[11] It didn't matter. The FBI was looking for a legal case. McCarran's subcommittee had something else in mind.

More than a year earlier, in 1949, Mao Tse-tung had entered Peking and announced the founding of the People's Republic of China. Four years before, the U.S.-supported Nationalist government of Chiang Kai-shek had ruled China with an army twice the size of the Communist forces. But in less than half a decade the Nationalists were defeated, and the most populous country in the world turned Communist. How was such a stunning reversal possible? Who lost China?

Snow landed on the windshield. The wipers moved like metronomes. Snow fell, was almost swept away, then fell again. Surine tried to stay awake. The beams of the truck's headlights disappeared into the darkening white. The tedium had just begun. So had the storm.

In February 1941 John Carter Vincent sailed to Shanghai on the SS *Pierce*. Vincent was forty-one, a foreign service officer who had first been stationed in China in 1924 and was now on his way back for another tour of duty. One night at dinner at the captain's table, Vincent tried to liven up the meal by recounting how in 1919, most of his class at Clemson University in South Carolina had staged a walkout in support of striking student busboys. "The Bolsheviks," the rebellious students called themselves. Vincent laughed. No one else did. "We would rather have fascism than socialism," a businessman from New York named Alfred Kohlberg said finally. "The entrepreneur and property would be safer."[12]

In China, during the war, Kohlberg got his preference. China had not had a government worthy of the name for three decades, not since the

Qing dynasty had collapsed in 1911.* Much of the country had been ruled by warlords and then by an uneasy alliance between Chiang Kai-shek's Kuomintang, or Nationalists, and Mao Tse-tung's Communists — which ended in 1927 when Chiang launched a bloody purge against the Communists in Shanghai, killing thousands. The Communists eventually fled to northern China, a grueling, yearlong, fifty-six-hundred-mile trek called the Long March. Almost ninety thousand started; ten thousand finished, setting up headquarters in the caves of Yenan, south of the Great Wall. For the next decade Chiang ruled most of the country until war broke out with the Japanese in 1937.

The Nationalist army was ragged, peasants press-ganged into service, tied together by rope to prevent escape, marched to faraway provinces so they couldn't run home, given three weeks of training, a stocking filled with rice, sometimes shoes, and occasionally a gun (one in ten had rifles, John Stewart Service once estimated) — and flung into battle. The Japanese cut them down like rice. They chased the Nationalists all over the map: from Peking in the northeast, to Nanking on the Yangtze River in the middle of coastal China, down the river to Hankow in the center of the country, then through the treacherous rapids and reefs of the Yangtze gorge to Chungking in the southwest, closer to India than the Pacific. Chiang's retreating army was almost as tough on the Chinese as the brutal Japanese troops. The Nationalists blew up the dikes on the Yellow River, which slowed the Japanese but flooded eleven cities and thousands of villages, inundating crops and killing half a million Chinese. Fleeing Hankow, the Nationalists dumped hundreds of sick and wounded soldiers on the riverbank to die or be killed by the advancing enemy.

The Nationalists and the Communists resurrected a united front against the invaders, although Chiang's priorities seemed clear from the half a million troops he assigned to blockade Mao's armies in the north. In 1941 the Nationalists attacked Mao's New Fourth Army, massacring five thousand soldiers. "The Japanese are a disease of the skin," Chiang told *Time* magazine correspondent Theodore White. "The Communists are a disease of the heart."[13]

The United States gave the Nationalist government more than three billion dollars in lend-lease aid, medical supplies that almost instantly turned up on the black market, arms that were stockpiled in warehouses

---

*Chinese names in this account follow the Wade-Giles transliteration system, the system in wide use at the time.

for eventual employment against the Communists rather than being used against the Japanese. Inflation soared into the stratosphere. "China is in a mess," foreign service officer Jack Service reported to Washington from the Chungking embassy. "No military action on a significant scale is in sight. The economic crisis continues to drift and worsen. Internal unrest is active and growing."[14]

The United States also gave Chiang General Joseph Stilwell, who was the commander of the Allied forces in China. Stilwell was a wiry, blunt, buzz-cut, hatchet-faced man who had served in China for years, spoke the language, and was practically obsessed with getting Chiang to send his troops into combat against the Japanese. Chiang was obsessed with staying in power, which meant saving his military strength to fight the Communists *after* the U.S. beat the Japanese. Stilwell loathed Chiang and the Nationalists. "A gang of fascists under a one-party government similar in many respects to our German enemy," he observed.[15]

Most of the younger U.S. foreign service officers and correspondents in China shared Stilwell's opinion. "The Kuomintang aspires to a 'democracy' in which everybody votes the Kuomintang 'ticket' . . . ," embassy counselor John Vincent wrote. "They smack . . . pretty much of fascism."[16] Before long Vincent was sent back to Washington and put in charge of the China desk at the State Department, where most of the cables arriving from Chungking continued to paint a bleak picture of Chiang's government. Two of Vincent's former colleagues in the embassy were even more outspoken in their hostility toward the Nationalists: John Paton Davies and John Stewart Service, both detailed to Stilwell's staff as advisers. The two had a lot in common: They were in their thirties, children of missionaries, born a year apart in the Szechwan province not far from Chungking, fluent in Chinese.

Stilwell, Davies, and Service were all convinced that Chiang's government was too corrupt and incompetent to fight the Japanese, no matter how many billions of dollars Washington gave the Nationalists. The only military alternative, they came to believe, was the Communists. Mao had representatives in Chungking, but Chiang had not let any U.S. diplomats or reporters venture past his blockade into Communist-controlled northern China. For months Davies and Service lobbied Washington to send an observer mission to Yenan to investigate the possibility of helping the Communists fight the Japanese. Service was especially keen to go. "The Communists, from what little we know of them, also are friendly toward America," Service wrote in a report in April 1944, "believe that

democracy must be the next step in China, and take the view that economic collaboration with the United States is the only hope for speedy
postwar rehabilitation and development. It is vital that we do not lose this
good will and influence."[17]

To Service it was clear that Chiang was doomed and that the Communists
were the most vibrant political force in China. For a young, frustrated, ambitious foreign service officer, going to Yenan looked like a great chance to
make a name for himself. "To be noticed and advanced in the foreign
service," he recalled, "one had to write notable reports."[18]

Jack Service would eventually get noticed in a way that he could never
have imagined. He went to Yenan to make his career in the State
Department. Instead, he ended it.

On February 12, 1951, a year after Joe McCarthy strode onto the national
stage and five days after Pat McCarran's Senate Internal Security
Subcommittee descended upon Ed Carter's barn, a small ceremony took
place in the White House cabinet room. Truman swore in nine men and
women as the members of the President's Commission on Internal
Security and Individual Rights. Their orders were simple, the president
said: Stop McCarthyism. The group soon became known as the Nimitz
Commission, for its chairman, retired fleet admiral Chester Nimitz. It
could also have been called the Un-McCarran Activities Committee, born
just after the Senate Internal Security Subcommittee and intended to reassure the same jittery public that SISS was prepared to further unsettle.
"The president's commission," *The Nation* wrote, "is as necessary and as
promising as the McCarran subcommittee is useless and threatening."[19]

Truman was worried that the country was in the grip of a fever; that
his own loyalty program had been turned into an assault upon the Bill of
Rights he so cherished. "I have been very much disturbed with the action
of some of these boards," Truman told aide Charles Murphy, "and I want
to find some way to put a stop to their un-American activities."[20]

The idea for such a commission had, of course, been kicking around the
White House for a couple of years, but the timing never seemed right. After
the McCarran Act became law in 1950 Truman's aides made another push.

"The McCarran Act has gone into effect," Charlie Murphy told
Truman, "and is already proving to be the foolish and pernicious statute
you knew it would be. . . . A commission of outstanding citizens will be
bound to recommend repeal or substantial overhauling of the McCarran
Act. . . . If the appointment of the commission is delayed there is no telling

what investigations might be authorized, particularly in the Senate. . . . There is a real and present danger that the drive to suppress fundamental liberties, already well started with the McCarran Act, may go further and further."[21]

Truman finally decided to act. He asked Herbert Hoover to head the commission. As a Republican, a staunch anti-Communist, and the only living former president, Hoover would have given the panel unimpeachable authority. And Hoover owed Truman. Roosevelt had snubbed his predecessor, and Hoover spent years moping in the Waldorf Astoria Towers until Truman took office and invited the former president back into public life. Hoover turned Truman down cold. For one thing, he considered the New Deal (and by extension Truman's Fair Deal) a national tragedy, the usurpation of capitalism and democracy by socialism and executive authority run amok. McCarthy spoke of twenty years of treason; Hoover spent those same twenty years brooding about it, writing one unreadable book after another decrying the government's slide into totalitarianism. He told Truman as much. "I suggest," Hoover replied, "that the current lack of confidence arises from the belief that there are men in government (not Communists) whose attitudes are such that they have disastrously advised on policies in relation to Communist Russia. The suspicion is abroad that they continue in the government."[22]

Hoover wrote in the third person but he shared the suspicion, which was an article of faith among right-wing conservatives. He suggested that a better idea would be a wide-ranging inquiry into the foreign policy of the United States for the last couple of decades, as well as the men who'd shaped it. It was an inauspicious portent that Truman's first choice to head the commission implied that what was really needed was an investigation more along the lines that McCarran was about to undertake.

On January 23, the day after the Senate gave McCarran's Internal Security Subcommittee its budget, Truman signed Executive Order 10207, establishing the President's Commission on Internal Security and Individual Rights. The president's commission, unlike McCarran's subcommittee, would have access to the FBI's loyalty files. In the Senate, McCarran smoldered. "Congress hasn't had the kind of access to files that amounts to anything," McCarran said. "We have been trying to get it for years."[23]

In February, Truman welcomed the commission to the White House, telling its members that the Bill of Rights was in peril. "We must find a balance . . . ," he said. "I am anxious that this job be done in the manner that will stop witch-hunting and give us the facts."[24]

—

In early 1941 Lauchlin Currie called Owen Lattimore in Baltimore and invited him to Washington. Currie was the White House aide in charge of China's lend-lease program. He had just come back from Chungking, where Chiang Kai-shek had asked for a political adviser, and he wanted to know if Lattimore might be interested. "I have been looking for the right man," Currie wrote in a memo, "as the position is of enormous importance."*25

At the age of forty, Lattimore had spent most of his life in China. The son of an English teacher in Shanghai, Lattimore was born in Washington but moved to China as a child. He went to school in Switzerland and England, but when he failed to get a scholarship to Oxford he returned to China. Lattimore was nineteen. He worked at various jobs, traveled widely around the country, got married to the daughter of a Northwestern University professor who was living in China, and almost immediately left his new bride to make a six-month camel trek across Central Asia, a journey recounted in *Desert Road to Turkestan*, which was published in 1929.

Without a college education, Lattimore managed to turn himself into a respectable scholar. He landed a grant to study at Harvard for a year and then returned to travel in China for four years on a series of fellowships, becoming especially fascinated with Central Asia, learning to speak Mongolian and writing several books. In 1933 Lattimore went to a conference in Canada sponsored by the Institute for Pacific Relations, the Asian studies think tank headquartered in New York but with affiliates in several different countries and plenty of cash from philanthropic organizations such as the Rockefeller Foundation. "The IPR was a magnificent institution," Harvard China scholar John King Fairbank remembered. "Its conferences were held in glamorous settings. They were staffed by smart young women like Barbara Wertheim [Tuchman] and Marian Cannon [Schlesinger]."26

Lattimore landed a job as editor of IRP's quarterly journal, *Pacific Affairs*. He spent several months at IPR headquarters on East Fifty-second Street in New York before heading back to China. America was mired in the Depression, Washington was thrilled and terrified by the New Deal, the Popular Front was just around the corner. The IPR office was full of young

---

*In late 1941, Elizabeth Bentley began traveling regularly to pick up documents from Greg Silvermaster, one of whose sources was Lauchlin Currie.

people from good colleges who wanted to change the world. The organization's secretary general was Edward C. Carter, his deputy Frederick Vanderbilt Field. Carter was something of a radical; Field was the real thing, an extremely wealthy socialist on his way to becoming a Communist. "Everyone in labor or progressive politics played footsy with the Communists at some time or in some way," remembered Len De Caux, a member of IPR's board and a hidden Communist. "A rule of the game was that the Communist player should not proclaim his Communism."[27] Lattimore never asked his new associates about their politics. "I was not at all concerned about whether someone was a Communist or any other thing," Lattimore recalled late in life. "I was only interested in what he or she said or did."[28]

In 1936 Lattimore and Carter went to Moscow. For years Carter had been trying to get the Soviets to sponsor an IPR affiliate, which the Russians finally did in 1935. The government's Institute of World Economy put a sign on a room saying SOVIET COUNCIL OF THE INSTITUTE OF PACIFIC RELATIONS. Only one Soviet author ever offered Lattimore a submission, which the editor disliked ("rank propaganda") but published anyway. In Moscow, Carter was hoping to inspire the Soviets to take a more active role in the organization. "I was astonished," recalled Freda Utley, a British Communist who had married a Russian and was working at the institute, "to see how often and completely Mr. Carter . . . deferred to the Soviet view. Owen Lattimore appeared to be more independent in his attitude. . . . I concluded that he was not a Communist."[29]

Lattimore told Utley that he'd almost lost his job as editor because he published an article by a Trotskyist. It was not a mistake he would make again. Although the Soviet IPR affiliate stopped paying its dues and quit answering mail from headquarters, Lattimore still ran articles by writers fawning over the Soviet system, including one that praised Stalin's purges. When protests poured into the *Pacific Affairs* office, Lattimore defended the show trials. "That sounds to me like democracy," he wrote.[30]

In 1937 Lattimore journeyed from Peking to Yenan to meet Mao. One of his traveling companions was Philip Jaffe, the wealthy Sinophile who was starting a new journal called *Amerasia*, whose editorial board Lattimore joined. The next year Lattimore returned to the United States and began teaching at Johns Hopkins, where he became head of the Page School of International Relations, which consisted of Lattimore and two postgrad scholars.

Then in 1941 Currie called. He was impressed by Lattimore and sent him over to the Treasury for a briefing about China by Harry Dexter White.* Currie told Roosevelt about Lattimore and wrote to Chiang: The president, he said, recommends that the scholar serve as the generalissimo's civilian adviser. Chiang promptly hired Lattimore. Before Lattimore left Washington he had lunch with Soviet ambassador Constantine Oumansky. The Russian said that the Soviet Union would continue to give all its support to the Nationalists instead of the Communists. "I suppose," Oumansky added, "you know what kind of a son of a bitch you'll be working for?"[31]

Lattimore reached Chungking in July. Chiang told Lattimore what he wanted. Lattimore told Currie, who told the president. On home leave after six months in China, Lattimore pressed the case for supporting Chiang in a flurry of speeches and articles, becoming Chiang's de facto flack in America. "A land long torn by inner dissension and local prejudice has, under Chiang Kai-shek, become united," he wrote in one article, "just as our thirteen colonies once became united."[32]

When Chiang became infuriated with General Stilwell, Roosevelt sent Currie to Chungking. Currie recommended replacing Stilwell, as well as Ambassador Clarence Gauss. For the new ambassador, Currie suggested either John Vincent or Lattimore. While Currie was overseas, Lattimore used his office at the White House. Then, in 1942, Lattimore was hired to direct coverage of the Pacific region for the Office of War Information. Even decades later, when Lattimore had good reason to hate anything to do with the Nationalists, he professed admiration for Chiang. "I still think that he was a great man," he said.[33]

Exploring Asia in the 1920s Lattimore survived rampaging soldiers, water that tasted like a camel had bathed in it, body lice that would drive a dog to distraction, a guide who threatened to dump him in the Gobi, local officials who detained him for ten days, blinding blizzards, and Mongol caravan companions who thought that he was a Soviet spy. "I caught the drift of a whispered conversation," he recalled. ". . . I was being set down as a Soviet officer. . . . It annoyed me, but it was not worth denial, since denial would only strengthen the conviction."[34]

In Washington in the 1950s Lattimore would deny a similar accusation at the top of his lungs, but the United States had one weapon that the desert nomads had never thought of: the perjury trap. Lattimore would miss the lice.

———

*White was another source who gave documents to Greg Silvermaster to pass on to Elizabeth Bentley.

In March 1951 J. Edgar Hoover appeared before McCarran's appropriations subcommittee. At one point the FBI director wanted to go off the record. McCarran, of course, agreed. For years Hoover had been dribbling leaks to friendly legislators and covertly assisting the House Un-American Activities Committee with its hearings. He had helped McCarthy, too, but McCarthy kept screwing up, mixing up details, getting the numbers wrong, wildly exaggerating charges. McCarthy's Wheeling speech had infuriated the director, although Hoover was willing to continue helping McCarthy as long as the senator seemed to be aiding the cause of anti-Communism. But McCarthy's publicly citing secret FBI reports as his source was not helping the cause; the attorney general had even ordered Hoover to investigate how McCarthy was getting his information. "Hoover knew that Joe wasn't the best guy in the world to be doing this job," SISS counsel Robert Morris recalled. "We all did."[35]

A better guy to do the job, Hoover thought, was McCarran. Hoover had been helping McCarran in the same casual fashion, but now he suggested to McCarran in executive session that perhaps the FBI and the new Senate Internal Security Subcommittee could set up a more formal arrangement. "A properly constituted congressional committee," Hoover later told one of his deputies, "that properly observed the propriety of the situation can be of great assistance."[36] "The senator," Eva Adams noted, "was very jubilant over the director's attitude."[37]

A week later McCarran invited Hoover and Attorney General J. Howard McGrath to a closed session of the Judiciary Committee where a secret liaison between SISS and the FBI was officially established. Jay Sourwine would serve as the go-between. The FBI would act as a kind of private detective agency for SISS, investigating suspects and furnishing leads, while the committee would launder information for the bureau, publicly pillorying suspected subversives against whom a court case could not be made. The attorney general said that he was happy to let Hoover handle all the details of the liaison as long as his office was informed about what was going on. The White House, apparently, was not. Thus while Truman was trying to fight the McCarran Committee, his Justice Department was trying to help it. "McCarran," Adams said "commented . . . that he felt there was little likelihood of anybody ever knowing exactly what cooperation was extended by the FBI."[38]

Hoover opened his files. Before long the bureau had twenty agents working on behalf of SISS. The FBI's leaks to McCarran became a flood. "The senator," Hoover observed, "wanted to use this committee not only to strengthen internal security for the good of the United States but to help the bureau in every possible manner."[39]

Hoover was right. "McCarran," Sourwine told the FBI, ". . . would do just about anything the director asked him to do."[40]

In October 1942 the Nationalist government cleaned up Chungking. Shanties were razed, street children herded out of town, U.S. flags and welcoming banners hung everywhere. Wendell Willkie was coming. To the Nationalists it was like a visit from Santa Claus.

Roosevelt distrusted the professional foreign service ("Half the time I can't tell whether I should believe them or not," he told one of his sons[41]), preferring to deal with other heads of state himself or through his personal emissaries. The State Department had capable and courageous diplomats posted in Russia and China, men like George Kennan in Moscow and John Davies in Chungking, specialists who knew the language and culture of the countries where they served and perceptively reported to Washington about the near-criminal regimes that ruled two of America's most important allies in World War II.

Roosevelt ignored them. He considered himself something of an Old China Hand. His grandfather Warren Delano had sailed to China in 1833 and made his fortune in Canton as a trader, opium among his wares. FDR's beloved mother, Sara, had lived in Hong Kong for three years as a child. Chinese antiques filled the family home in Hyde Park; FDR collected stamps from China. Roosevelt himself, however, had never been to Asia. Chiang Kai-shek, he said, was the first *real* Oriental that he had ever met. The president picked diplomatic envoys whose knowledge matched his own; he skipped over the State Department experts, preferring to dispatch personal representatives who shared his hope that two great tyrannies whose short-term interests coincided with the United States' could become long-term partners in building a new world after the war. Wendell Willkie, then, was perfect: enthusiastic, likable, almost boyish in demeanor, much like Roosevelt himself, and equally uninformed. Willkie was the liberal Republican who ran against Roosevelt in 1940. As a consolation prize, Roosevelt sent him to China.

In Chungking, Willkie was greeted as if he had won the election. Children lined eleven miles of road from the airport to town, waving and smiling as if they had some idea who he might be. And if nothing else, Chiang certainly looked like a general, lean and austere in his high-necked military tunic, his head shaved like some sort of warrior monk, although he was actually a Methodist. He beat subordinates with a stick and had enemies buried alive. "Even bigger than his legendary reputation," Willkie gushed.[42] Madame Chiang (née Soong May-ling) was the real charmer. She had gone to school for nine years in the United States, spoke English with a southern lilt, and could flatter a bird out of a tree. "Madame would be the perfect ambassador,"[43] Willkie said, inviting her to Washington.

Willkie returned to the United States smitten. He wrote glowingly of his trip in a ten-part newspaper series and then in a book called *One World*, which became the publishing sensation of the year, selling a million copies in eight weeks. "Military China is united," Willkie claimed. "Its leaders are trained and able generals; its armies are tough fighting organizations of men who know both what they are fighting for and how to fight for it."[44]

Madame Chiang followed the next month. Officially she came for medical treatment, which took eleven weeks, although her visit lasted more than half a year. Madame Chiang stayed at the White House, bringing her own silk sheets, which she had changed four or five times a day, and clapping her hands whenever she wanted anything. Henry Luce put her on the cover of *Time*. She went on a six-week speaking tour across the country, telling audiences from Madison Square Garden to the Hollywood Bowl about China's struggles to defeat the Japanese. "A soldier unafraid to fight for justice," Willkie called her.[45]

After Pearl Harbor, the American public hated the Japanese. The Chinese had already been fighting them for four years. When the winter fog lifted from the Yangtze gorge in 1939, Japanese planes began bombing Chungking; for the next several years, whenever the skies above the city were clear, life revolved around the bomb shelters carved out of the hills above the river. Chungking, like Madrid, became an emblem of the struggle against fascism. "The early Chungking, under the bombings, was more than a legend that foreign correspondents told the world," Teddy White wrote. "The foreigners who lived with the Chinese were caught up in the spirit of the place and swept away by it. From them the illusion of a great and vibrant China made its way across the world, and by the time Pearl Harbor imposed new standards of restraint and censorship, the picture was fully established, and it was difficult to write of the changes that were falsifying it."[46]

Nationalist censorship kept U.S. correspondents from filing stories about Chiang's inept regime; about Nationalist soldiers who starved to death on the streets of Chungking while Chiang's relatives amassed great fortunes.

Instead the U.S. public heard Roosevelt and Willkie and Madame Chiang rhapsodizing about the brave Nationalist armies, millions of soldiers who just needed American arms to beat back the Japanese. It was the wartime love affair with the Soviet Union all over again. Fighting enemies on both sides of the globe, the United States could not admit that its biggest allies were almost as bad as its foes.

Eventually the United States would give China three and a half billion dollars in lend-lease aid — although critics questioned how much ever reached China. T. V. Soong, the Nationalist foreign minister and Madame Chiang's brother, moved to Washington, where his house in Chevy Chase became a regular stop on the capital dinner-party circuit for such useful friends as Treasury Secretary Henry Morgenthau. Soong set up China Defense Supplies Incorporated to handle the lend-lease largesse and strengthen his ties to the White House. The company's general counsel was Thomas Corcoran, an architect of the New Deal and still an intimate of the president; one of the company's directors was Frederic Delano, the president's uncle, while Roosevelt's cousin, the columnist Joe Alsop, was also on the payroll. This was the beginning of what would later be called the China Lobby, a loose network of influential people that reached into the White House, Congress, and the media. "There are no secrets in Washington," Soong told John Davies. ". . . No conference takes place regarding which I do not have accurate and complete information."[47]

In November 1943 the Allies gathered in Cairo for a Big Four conference: Roosevelt, Churchill, Stalin, and Chiang (with Madame Chiang at his side as his translator). In Nationalist China millions of peasants were starving to death in the Honan famine because the government was too incompetent to feed its own population; in Cairo Roosevelt praised Chiang as the undisputed leader of more than four hundred million people, who in a couple of decades created a republic akin to the United States. "What it took us a couple of centuries to attain," he said.[48]

The China experts were aghast. "The generalissimo is probably the only Chinese who shares the popular American misconception that Chiang Kai-shek is China," Davies reported to the State Department.[49]

Stilwell, as usual, was even more blunt. Madame put it over FDR, he told his diary, like a tent. "A one-man joke," Stilwell groused about Chiang. "The KMT is his tool. Madame is his front. The silly U.S. propaganda is his lever. We are his suckers."[50]

Before long Chiang would clean Stilwell out of Chungking as well.

On April 10, 1951, Dean Acheson and his deputy went to Capitol Hill to see Pat McCarran and Styles Bridges, the ranking Republican on McCarran's appropriations subcommittee. "A strange appointment," Acheson called it. McCarran and Bridges weren't sure the secretary would show up. A few months earlier they had both signed a statement calling on Acheson to resign. Inviting him to Capitol Hill then seemed a bit iffy. "So they asked Deputy Under Secretary Carlisle Humelsine to sound me out," Acheson recalled. "To their surprise I said I would be delighted to call on them."[51]

It was the day before Acheson's birthday, and he was about to give himself a small present. Acheson, fifty-seven, cut a fine figure, always neatly dressed, with great arching eyebrows thicker than his salt-and-pepper mustache. At six foot two, Acheson was a head taller than McCarran, whom he always seemed to be looking down on. "Acheson," McCarran told a friend, "is the most over-rated silk stocking I have ever known in my life."[52]

McCarran wanted to talk about Communists.[53] How many do you have in the department? McCarran asked. Acheson said that Humelsine was handling security and asked him to answer the question. Humelsine said that to his knowledge there were none. McCarran wanted to talk about Spain. Are you giving them what they want? he asked. Acheson said that he was following the loan program approved by Congress. But most of all McCarran wanted to talk about Douglas MacArthur. The general and the president had been publicly feuding over how to fight the war in Korea. McCarran wanted Truman to back down. "They pressed me to get the president to reconsider his attitude and come to an accommodation with the general," Acheson recalled. McCarran said that he had just traveled across the country and found great regard for MacArthur everywhere. Bridges nodded. "I told them," Acheson remembered, "that the president would be deeply interested in the views of such distinguished and influential senators, which I would faithfully report."

What Acheson didn't tell McCarran and Bridges was that he had just come from the State Department code room where he had transmitted Truman's order firing MacArthur. Acheson had a happy birthday. "Of course, when the next day's news of the relief broke," Acheson recalled, "they accused me of misleading them by silence — a charge not without some justification, though no other course was possible — and our relations deteriorated further."[54]

Deteriorate they did. A month later, on March 4, McCarran told the Senate that MacArthur's firing was a Communist plot. It was certainly one of Truman's least popular decisions. The general returned home to a hero's welcome, half a million people lining the streets of San Francisco to greet him. Truman was booed at a baseball game by an angry crowd, burned in effigy across the country. MacArthur addressed a joint session of Congress ("There can be no substitute for victory") and was met with a thunderstorm of applause. "If that speech had gone on much longer there might have been a march on the White House," one lawmaker said.[55] The Senate opened hearings on MacArthur's dismissal. The Democrats wanted to keep proceedings closed; the Republicans wanted them open to the public. McCarran was the only Democrat to break party ranks on the vote, but the Democrats still had a majority.

Then, while the hearings were still going on, McCarran told the Senate that closed-session testimony before the Senate Internal Security Subcommittee had revealed a plot against MacArthur. In 1945, he explained, the American Communist Party passed a resolution opposing U.S. imperialism in the Far East, which was followed by Owen Lattimore, John Carter Vincent, and Dean Acheson advocating policies to that effect, which, in turn, ultimately led to Truman's decision to recall MacArthur. McCarran's tone was calm, his words unemotional, his facts precise, names, dates, publications. It was like filling up a chalkboard with an elaborate mathematical theorem only to state at the end that two plus two equals five. "MacArthur was being opposed by officials of our own State Department on much the same grounds as were being advanced by the Communists," McCarran said. ". . . Thanks to General MacArthur, our former enemy, Japan, is now our friend. Thanks to the State Department, our former ally, China, is now our bitter enemy."[56]

Almost three months before SISS began its public hearings, McCarran had offered a glimpse of what was to come. The speech was as crazy as anything McCarthy ever said, but it received scant attention. "The son of a bitch should be impeached,"[57] McCarthy said when Truman fired MacArthur; it was front-page news across the country.

In 1943, two years after he met the young American diplomat who called himself a Bolshevik, Alfred Kohlberg went to China again. The wealthy textile importer had been traveling to Asia for thirty years. Now Kohlberg was crossing the Pacific to investigate how the American Bureau for Medical Aid to China was distributing relief supplies. White House aide Lauchlin Currie and others had told the importer that the organization was rife with corruption. As a donor to the bureau, Kohlberg wanted to see for himself. He spent weeks traveling around China by train, truck, and horse and concluded that the charges were completely false. But then, what was the motive behind the accusations? Who would want to disrupt relief efforts and contribute to the strife and instability in China? Kohlberg voiced these worries to Maurice William, a crusading former socialist, who suggested that the Communists might be trying to slander the relief bureau. The IPR, he added, was full of Communists.

Kohlberg had been a member of IPR for years, although he had never bothered to read its publications. He began to spend Saturdays and Sundays at the New York Public Library poring over back issues of *Pacific Affairs* and its sister journal, *Far Eastern Survey*. Kohlberg found himself leaving work early during the week to continue his studies. After he read through seven years of IPR's commentary on China, Kohlberg looked at the *New Masses* and *The Communist* for the same period. The IPR publications seemed to follow the Communist Party's publications like night followed day, criticizing the Nationalists but never the Communists or the Soviet Union.* Kohlberg put together an eighty-eight-page study comparing the think tank's thinking and that of the party. In 1944 Kohlberg sent the report to IPR secretary general Edward Carter and the group's trustees, asking them to fire all the Reds at the organization "I think you will find that your employees have been putting over on you a not-too-well camouflaged Communist line," Kohlberg wrote. ". . . Is it treason?"[58]

Kohlberg got nowhere. The organization's trustees dismissed him as a nut. So he started his own think tank, the China Policy Association, and his own magazine, *Plain Talk*, and, as always, he wrote letters and more letters.

During the war Alfred Kohlberg had offered to fly a kamikaze mission against the Japanese, but the navy turned him down. Instead, after the war, Kohlberg flew a kamikaze mission into the State Department.

On May 8, 1951, the Nimitz Commission resigned en bloc. In the *Washington Post* Herb Block drew a cartoon showing McCarran peering from the hatch of a submarine at a sinking ship labeled NIMITZ. McCarran

---

* That Lattimore supported Chiang at one point and the Chinese Communists later is probably explained by the fact that the Soviet Union was supporting both at the same time during the war as part of a united front.

had torpedoed the commission before it could even get started. The pioneering submariner had his own weapon turned against him. "All quiet along the Potomac," the caption read.*

Nimitz's first act in February had been to ask Truman for a routine conflict-of-interest waiver for the commission and its staff. Without the exemption, the members and its counsel would be barred from appearing before federal courts and government agencies for two years after they left the commission. Nimitz was sure that no high-powered Washington lawyer in his right mind would join the panel under such terms. Truman asked Congress for legislation. In March the House approved a bill and sent it over to the Senate. McCarran's Judiciary Committee stalled for more than a month. McCarran assigned to consider the bill a subcommittee of three conservative Republicans (all SISS members), led by Homer Ferguson, who had been fighting Truman for years over access to loyalty files and was infuriated that the president was giving the commission carte blanche to examine FBI records. Ferguson asked the commissioners if they would turn over their records to the Senate. The commissioners said no. On April 30 the Judiciary Committee spat back the waiver bill, refusing to approve the exemption. McCarran primly declared that he was against the piecemeal repeal of laws. If a law interfered with the functioning of government, he said, it should be changed. "A slick, cynical piece of obstructionism," the *Washington Post* called it.[59]

The commission then resigned. "With great respect and regret," the admiral told the president.[60] Truman refused to accept the resignations, urging the commission to serve informally until he could get the conflict-of-interest waiver approved by Congress. The president then implored

---

Washington Post cartoonist Herb Block was one of the senator's most astute critics. "McCarran," he wrote in a collection of his work the next year, "was now in the position of the cannibalistic sailor W. S. Gilbert's poem, who said:

> Oh, I am a cook and a captain bold
> And the mate of the Nancy brig
> And a bo'sun tight, and midshipmite,
> And the crew of the captain's gig.

"After disposing of the Nimitz Commission he was the Fleet Admiral too, and the chief petty officer in charge of security. But in all his many capacities he is the tireless investigator and prosecutor of Un-McCarran Activities. . . . And who can blame him for not wanting people like Admiral Nimitz poking around in the work that he and McCarthy have laid out for themselves?" (Herbert Block, *The Herbblock Book*. Boston: Beacon Press, 1952; p. 151–53.)

McCarran to reconsider. "I have sought by this means to obtain the best possible advice concerning some of the basic questions affecting the survival of our democracy," Truman wrote to McCarran. ". . . The purpose of this commission is to make recommendations concerning the problems involved in providing for the internal security of the United States and at the same time protecting the rights and freedoms of individuals. Surely there can be no quarrel with these purposes."[61]

McCarran took two weeks to reply to the president, at which point he dismissed the idea that any presidential commission was needed to investigate the country's internal security. "There can be no serious doubt," he told Truman, "that the Congress (and particularly the Senate Committee on the Judiciary) is exceedingly anxious to rid the government service of subversives."[62] On the subject of civil liberties McCarran had nothing to say.

A few weeks later McCarran sponsored a bill to exempt immigrant writer Arthur Koestler from the McCarran Act restrictions so that he could visit the United States. Koestler was a former Communist who would have normally been denied a visa — but he was also a fierce anti-Communist, so McCarran wanted to help him out. The *Washington Post* could barely contain itself. "It is particularly surprising to find Senator McCarran recommending an exemption from the McCarran Act because Senator McCarran is plainly on record as opposed to any exemption from any law," the paper editorialized. ". . . Could it be that Senator McCarran is trying to bring about the destruction of the McCarran Act? Or is it merely that he believes he is entitled to be exempted from his own principles?"[63]

As McCarran's Internal Security Subcommittee began its closed hearings that summer, Truman urged Nimitz to keep the commission going. "Information that has come to me in recent weeks has made it clearer than ever that there is a great need to do the job for which the commission was established," he told him. "The job must be done."[64]

In June 1944 the beggars disappeared from the streets of Chungking again. Another presidential envoy was coming. This time it was Vice President Henry Wallace, whom Roosevelt wanted out of the country until just before the summer Democratic convention. So Roosevelt dispatched Wallace to spend a month touring Siberia and then head to China to meet with Chiang. Wallace took two China advisers: the State Department's John Carter Vincent, and Owen Lattimore from the Office of War Information. He also took with him a glow-in-the-dark picture of Stalin as a gift for the Russian dictator and melon seeds to plant in China. On refueling stops Wallace made his entourage jog around the airfield with him to keep in shape. He spent more time playing volleyball than listening to his China experts. "Soybeans, strawberries, fruits, rainfall and irrigation,"[65] Lattimore noted, were Wallace's main topics of conversation.*

When the Wallace mission reached Chungking, the vice president spent several days meeting with Chiang, relaying to the generalissimo the president's wishes. Roosevelt wanted Chiang to start fighting the Japanese. Chiang wanted Roosevelt to recall General Stilwell. Roosevelt wanted Chiang to unify his military operations with the Communists in the north. Chiang wanted Rooseveslt to recall Stilwell. Roosevelt wanted Chiang to let the United States dispatch an observer mission to the Communist stronghold in Yenan. Chiang wanted Roosevelt to recall Stilwell.

Wallace told Chiang that Stalin had dismissed the Chinese CP as margarine Communists, not the real thing. Chiang told Wallace that the CCP was more Communist than the Russian CP. The generalissimo finally agreed to let the United States send a mission to Yenan. "I like him," Wallace told his diary, "but I do not give him one chance in five to save himself."[†66]

After Chungking, Wallace and his advisers flew to Kunming, where they spent three days as the houseguests of General Claire Chennault, head of the China Air Task Force, a bitter rival of Stilwell's who believed that air power, not ground troops, was the way to beat the Japanese. Chennault hated Stilwell almost as much as Chiang did; the general's aide Joseph Alsop hated him more. Alsop was a powerful Washington newspaper columnist and an old friend of Wallace's who happened to be living in Chennault's house. The two spent hours filling the vice presi-

---

*Wallace originally wanted to take Colonel Philip R. Faymonville, who had been in charge of Russian lend-lease, on the trip but General George Marshall objected, noting that Faymonville was considered to be practically a Communist. Lauchlin Currie and Owen Lattimore both praised Faymonville to Wallace. (See *The Price of Vision,* edited by John Morton Blum. Boston: Houghton-Mifflin, 1973; p. 314.)

†Vincent had given Wallace one of John Davies's reports about the growth of the Communist movement in Yenan. "Foreign observers (including American) who have recently visited the Communist area," Davies wrote, "agree that the Communist regime in present policy and practice is far removed from orthodox Communism; that it is administratively remarkably honest; that popular elections are held; that individual economic freedom is relatively uncurbed; that the regime appears to have strong popular support and that it is described less accurately as Communist than as agrarian democratic." (Gary May, *China Scapegoat: The Diplomatic Ordeal of John Carter Vincent.* Prospect Heights, Ill.: Waveland Press, 1979; p. 98.)

dent's ear with warnings about how China was doomed if Stilwell stayed on the job.

Lattimore spent most of the time in Kunming sick. "Pretty blank for me," he jotted in his diary, "as diarrhea all the time. Would have been lovely chances for rural photos, too, if only could have stayed a couple of hundred yards from can safely."[67]

One day Alsop took Wallace and Vincent aside for another harangue. Alsop was convinced that Stilwell's willingness to fight alongside the Chinese Communists would lead to disaster; he suggested to Wallace that he cable the president to dump Stilwell. Vincent also thought that it was best for the war effort. "Do everything one can to hold them together during this war," Vincent told his wife, "and afterwards to hell with Kuomintang!"[68] Wallace agreed to send the cable. "It was an unmanageable situation to have an American commander in China who did not enjoy the generalissimo's confidence," Wallace noted.[69]

Alsop pulled out his typewriter, and the three worked out a letter to Roosevelt, which had as much influence in the White House as any State Department dispatch, which is to say none. Later Wallace wrote a more detailed assessment of the situation for the president. "Chiang, at best, is a short-term investment," he noted.[70]

Roosevelt felt the same way about Wallace. The president responded to the stalemate in Chungking by sending another personal envoy — this time Patrick Hurley, an Oklahoma oilman who had been Hoover's secretary of war — to make peace between Chiang and Stilwell. Chiang continued to insist that he couldn't work with Stilwell. Roosevelt replied by sending Chiang a curt cable urging the generalissimo to immediately put Stilwell in charge of all Chinese forces. Stilwell personally handed the message to Chiang and watched his expression with delight. "The harpoon hit the little bugger right in the solar plexus and went right through him," Stilwell exulted.[71] Chiang raged at Hurley, who told the president that he had to choose one or the other. Roosevelt picked Chiang and fired Stilwell, replacing him with General Albert Wedemeyer. And before too long Mao would replace Chiang as the ruler of China.

Seven years later, in his fourth-floor committee room, Pat McCarran would try to draw a straight line from Stilwell's firing to Mao's triumph.

In June 1951 guards stood at the door to Room 113 on the ground floor of the Reconstruction Finance Building on Vermont Avenue. Inside were more guards. It seemed like a lot of security for a room that seldom held more than a dozen people. To John Abt it was just another sign that fascism was drawing nigh. "The hearing room was a virtual armed camp," he remembered.[72]

But sit in the room for any amount of time and you might get the idea that the guards were actually there to keep the five members of the Subversive Activities Control Board from fleeing out of sheer boredom. The board had been created by McCarran's Internal Security Act to determine if the Communist Party was a subversive organization — and, if so, to force it to register as such with the government.

Earlier in the year Abt had become the Communist Party's general counsel — which in 1951 basically meant representing it before the SACB. Every Monday morning Abt (and his cocounsel, former Harlem congressman Vito Marcantonio) flew down from New York to Washington and spent the next four days in the hearing room, flying home on Thursday evening. Most Fridays, Abt spent at party headquarters on Eleventh Street, trying to shake loose some of the money that he was owed. At one point after the party stiffed him for several months, Abt was reduced to borrowing against his life insurance. "Every party treasurer I've known," he complained, "has thought it his personal and political duty to avoid payment of bills for as long as possible, and often even longer."[73]

Delay was also Abt's legal strategy. Many in the party leadership had wanted to boycott the hearings altogether, but Abt wanted to expose the act as unconstitutional and un-American. "Nothing less than a blueprint for American fascism," Abt called it.[74] Abt hoped to drag out the appeals process long enough for the political climate in the country to change. "The SACB was simply going through the motions before it ruled against us," he recalled. "For our party, we were building a record, knowing that we would be appealing the board's rulings through the courts."[75]

Abt wasn't the only one stalling. Truman had appointed five prominent conservatives to the board in October when Congress was in recess and then submitted the nominees to the Senate for approval. McCarran insisted on examining the FBI files on the nominees before holding confirmation hearings. Truman refused. His nominees included such establishment types as Seth Richardson, a Republican lawyer and former head of the Loyalty Review Board, and Charles M. La Follette, a former Republican congressman from Indiana (and national director of the ADA who had opposed the McCarran Act). But after McCarran didn't budge for five months Truman relented and turned over the files.

McCarran still refused to hold confirmation hearings, but in April the board began its proceedings anyway. Most days the room was practically empty: Only the five board members, the three Justice Department attorneys led by Smith Act prosecutor Irving Shapiro, the two Communist Party attorneys, and the witness attended. The press table was usually empty except for the *Daily Worker's* Sender Garlin. "The press has found the proceedings undramatic," he wrote, "and this is just what the McCarranites desire."[76]

The first witness was Benjamin Gitlow, a founding member of the American Communist Party, who was kicked out in 1929; he testified about how the Russians controlled the party through the Comintern. As it happened, former party leader William Z. Foster was writing a book on the group's history from his sickbed in the Bronx. Foster was old and cantankerous and knew that if it wasn't for the heart condition that had saved him from a Smith Act trial, he, too, would be headed to prison with the rest of the party's leaders. Foster was sure his bedroom was bugged, so whenever he wanted to say something important, he reached for pencil and paper. "Illegality — inevitable," he scribbled to one visitor. "Fascism — not inevitable. War — inevitable."

Abt looked over Foster's chapters on the party's history and discovered with dismay that the manuscript agreed with Gitlow. Abt asked him to rewrite it. Foster balked. He suggested that Abt use the hearing to defend the party's kowtowing to the Comintern. Abt persisted. "I sat at the side of Bill's bed," Abt recalled, "spending several hours explaining how difficult a position we would be in if William Z. Foster's book confirmed the testimony of the renegade Benjamin Gitlow. Bill was still a very tough guy and it was difficult to persuade him otherwise when he thought he was right, as he very often was. But at the end, he agreed to make some alterations."[77]

Still, Abt unexpectedly found himself encouraging Gitlow's testimony rather than rebutting it. In May it slipped out that Gitlow (as well as another witness, Zack Kornfeder) had been reporting to SISS research director Ben Mandel about the board's hearings.

"I discussed the conduct of this case," Gitlow admitted. "I discussed the attorneys in the case. I discussed the members of the panel."

"You discussed the members of the panel?" asked board member Charles La Follette.

"That's right . . . ," Gitlow replied.

"These are very, very unpleasant answers to hear from this witness," La Follette said.[78]

La Follette stalked out of the hearing room in a huff. Abt and

Marcantonio pounced, arguing that McCarran was using the confirmation delay to keep the board on a leash; they demanded that the proceedings stop until the board was confirmed. "The panel's rulings and actions," the lawyers wrote, "are being largely controlled by the pressures arising from the lengthy pendency of the appointments without action by the Senate Judiciary Committee or Senate."[79]

The plea failed. And in June, when McCarran still hadn't scheduled a confirmation hearing after half a year, Chairman Seth Richardson quit. Richardson claimed ill health and, indeed, he almost had a coronary in talking to a *Time* magazine reporter about how McCarran had treated him. "I've been subjected to the damnest bunch of intellectual balderdash that I've seen come out of politics in a hell of a long time . . . ," he raged. "The natural thing for the committee to do if it doubted the board was to hold a meeting to find out if we were sons-of-bitches. But no. There was no hearing. The damned representative of Franco could get a hearing and sit in the committee councils but decent Americans couldn't. . . . It makes me damned mad to have the papers announced that damned scaly representative of a scaly country can have a conference with the Judiciary Committee when five men who are just as good can't have a hearing."[80]

The new chairman of the SACB, Peter Campbell Brown, was more to McCarran's liking. "He asked me to let you know that he is working on a finding for the board . . . ," McCarran's aide Don Connors reported after talking to Brown, "and thinks it will be eminently satisfactory. He asked me to say that it is his considered opinion that a finding of fact can be made that the Communist Party has advocated the forceful and violent overthrow of the government here, although he said that the evidence presented along these lines by the Department of Justice was not as strong as he had hoped it would be. He also mentioned, in confidence, that the help he has received from other members of the board has not been up to his expectation. He also asked me to give you his very best regards."[81]

On June 20, 1951, Abt was in the hearing room when he found out that the Justice Department had just rounded up another batch of Communists for prosecution under the Smith Act, including Elizabeth Gurley Flynn and one comrade arrested in a nursing home. Abt had been expecting as much. On June 4 the Supreme Court had upheld the convictions of the party's top leaders (*Dennis v. U.S.*). But what Abt didn't expect was that the second-string Smith Act arrests would include his sister Marion.

If Abt was hoping for the political climate to improve, it was starting to look like he was in for quite a wait. "I couldn't have known or even imagined," he recalled later, "that dismantling the McCarran Act would occupy my full time and energies for the next twenty-four years."[82]

On July 22, 1944, the pilot of an U.S. Army Air Force C-47 cargo plane sighted a pagoda on a hill and then landed on a rough field amid the dry, yellow hills of Yenan. Nine Americans in military uniforms climbed out of the plane and into a weird landscape of loess, rich loam hills eroded into a honeycomb of caverns and carved by wind into shapes out of an Yves Tanguy painting. "Hills like great castles, . . ." remembered journalist Edgar Snow, who had been there years earlier, " — queer, incredible, frightening shapes in a world of strange surrealist beauty."[83]

Seven years after ten thousand Red Army soldiers straggled into the Shensi province at the end of their brutal Long March, Mao's Communists now claimed to rule an area the size of Japan, governing as much as a fifth of China's population and fielding an army of half a million men. To Jack Service and the other members of the U.S. observer group, called the Dixie Mission, it quickly became clear that it wasn't only the topography that was different in Yenan from the rest of China.

"All of our party have had the same feeling — that we have come into a different country and are meeting a different people," Service reported six days after arriving " To the skeptical, the general atmosphere in Yenan can be compared to that of a rather small, sectarian college — or a religious summer conference. . . . One cannot help coming to feel that this movement is strong and successful and that it has such drive behind it and has tied itself so closely to the people that it will not easily be killed."[84]

Chungking had been weird in its own way. Although Chiang didn't speak English or have much education ("An ignorant, illiterate, superstitious, peasant son of a bitch," Stilwell called him[85]), the Nationalist government was stuffed with so many foreign-educated technocrats that journalist Theodore White had no trouble starting up a Harvard Club when he arrived. Yet the Americans found themselves walking out of their way in town to avoid passing the Kuomintang jail, where only the screams of prisoners escaped. Chiang's secret police were assumed to be everywhere, and the U.S diplomats didn't think that the machine-gun emplacements in the city were intended for either the Japanese or the Communists. "The enthronement of reaction," Jack Service called the Nationalists.[86]

In Yenan everything was different. "The people were ruddier, healthier, and the proportion of young to old was striking," Teddy White wrote.[87] In Chungking, Chiang wore a smart khaki tunic, gold buttons fastened to the chin, and shaved his head to hide his gray hair; in Yenan, Mao wore a plain blue uniform that looked like it had been made from an old blanket, his hair falling long over the nubby collar because he had more pressing concerns than his grooming. Madame Chiang seemed to spend more time abroad living in luxury hotels than she did in Chungking, where the generalissimo spent most of his time with his pregnant girlfriend — actually his first, never divorced, wife. Mao lived in a cave and tended his own vegetable patch. Chiang threw teacups at his ministers. Mao wrote poetry. After three months in Yenan, Jack Service was still impressed. "The Communist political program is simple democracy," Service reported. "This is much more American than Russian in form and spirit."[88]

The Chinese Communists were beautiful and pure as only the newborn and powerless can be. Yenan in the summer of 1944 was St. Petersburg in the fall of 1917. There were no beggars, no police in sight. Mao and other party leaders dropped by for long talks with the Americans; they all went to Saturday-night socials together, Mao spinning peasant girls around on the earthen floor. The Dixie members went native. Colonel David Barrett, the commander of the mission, began wearing a blue Mao uniform. Jack Service labored like a coolie to help rebuild the airstrip, hoisting a shoulder pole, its baskets sagging with rocks. In other parts of China children shouted "foreign devils" at westerners; in Yenan they chirped "foreign friend." "Almost too good to be true," John Davies recorded in his journal, after he joined the mission in October. "I suppose it's the party line."[89] Arriving newsmen were just as impressed. "Yenan," the *New York Times* beamed in a headline, "A Chinese Wonderland City."[90]

In one long interview Mao told Jack Service that the Communists wanted to work with Washington. Service joked that Americans were afraid of Communists. Mao laughed that they had thought of changing their name. Mao said that he wanted free enterprise and foreign investment for China. He wanted the United States to open a consulate in Yenan, which would have amounted to de facto diplomatic recognition. Service passed on Mao's message to the State Department. "Washington," John Davies recalled, "took little, if any notice of Mao's overture. And so a historic point in American-Chinese relations was passed unperceived."[91]

It wasn't because the foreign service officers in Yenan weren't trying to make Washington notice. In the fall of 1944 Davies was convinced that the United States should make an entente with the Communists. No other government, he realized, in modern Chinese history enjoyed so much widespread popular support. "We must not indefinitely underwrite a politically bankrupt regime . . . ," Davies wrote to Washington. "We must make a determined effort to capture politically the Chinese Communists rather than allow them to go by default wholly to the Russians."[92] "How Red Are the Chinese Communists?" Davies asked in another memo. "They have now deviated so far to the right that they will return to the revolution only if driven to it by overwhelming pressure from domestic and foreign forces of reaction," he answered himself.[93]

Jack Service agreed. Service came to Yenan already convinced that the Kuomintang was near collapse, that civil war was inevitable, and that arming the Communists the only way to get the Chinese to fight the Japanese. "Any new government under any other than the present reactionary control will be more cooperative and better able to mobilize the country," Service wrote to Washington. ". . . We need feel no ties of gratitude to Chiang. The men he has kept around him have proved selfish and corrupt, incapable and obstructive. Chiang's own dealings with us have been an opportunist combination of extravagant demands and unfilled promises, wheedling and bargaining, bluff and blackmail. Chiang did not resist Japan until forced by his own people. He has sought to have us save him — so that he can continue his conquest of his own country. In the process he has 'worked' us for all we were worth."[94]

In China, during the war, many U.S. diplomats thought any leader would be better than Chiang. They were wrong. Mao seized power in 1949. Eventually, he would prove as great and terrible a ruler as Stalin or Hitler, a man determined to remake his society at any cost. The Great Leap Forward, Mao called it. A great leap backward is what it really was. Mao's economic experiment proved a catastrophe. As many as thirty million Chinese died in the resulting famine. Then came the Cultural Revolution, which banned virtually all culture, closed schools, destroyed temples and other vestiges of China's ancient civilization, and unleashed gangs of thugs, called Red Guards, to terrorize intellectuals, party members, and anyone who could not demonstrate sufficient zeal during the spasm of revolutionary violence. The Middle Kingdom was a land accustomed to disasters on a colossal scale, both natural and human-made, yet Mao's reign turned out to be a cataclysm unprecedented in Chinese history.*

---

*"If someone had tried to tell me in the summer of 1944 that the time would come when Chinese boys and girls would stand up in a mass trial and ask that their parents be shot as counter-revolutionaries," Dixie commander Colonel David Barrett wrote later, "I would have laughed at him." (See David D. Barrett, *Dixie Mission*. Chine Research Monograph, Berkeley, Calif.: University of California, 1970; p. 46.)

In Yenan the Americans could see that Chiang had no future in China. But what Mao would do to the country, they had no idea. "Chinese Communists were different then," Teddy White insisted decades later. "We were not duped."[95]

Colonel David Barrett read over Jack Service's reports before sending them to State. He suggested to Service that his opinions might get him in trouble with the conservatives in government. "Dave," Service replied, "I'm a foreign service officer. What I have written in these reports and the recommendations I have made are my observations and carefully considered opinion. If they don't like them in Washington, they can throw them out."[96]

Instead, eventually, they threw Service out.

One day in July 1951, Joe Alsop went to the State Department and spoke to the loyalty board that was trying to decide if John Davies should be fired from the foreign service after twenty years of outstanding work. Alsop, an influential columnist and an ardent anti-Communist, was testifying on behalf of Davies. He was also one of the reasons that Davies was fighting for his job in the first place.

The year before, in January 1950, Alsop published a series of articles in the *Saturday Evening Post* called "Why We Lost China." John Davies's bad advice was one of the reasons; Jack Service's was another. "The American representatives there actively favored the Chinese Communists," Alsop wrote. "They also contributed to the weakness, both political and military, of the Nationalist government. And in the end they came close to offering China up to the Communists, like a trussed bird on a platter, over four years before the eventual Communist triumph."[97]

Alsop made the point that the diplomats in the U.S. embassy in Chungking were not disloyal, just wrong — a distinction that quickly evaporated in the heat of 1950. "Poor fellow," Alsop had told his editor after he spent a day interviewing Davies for the series, "he is exceedingly ashamed now of the part he played, not to say a bit fearful of the effect disclosure of this part may have on his career."[98]

At first Davies's career seemed on track. From Chungking he had gone to the Moscow embassy and then on to George Kennan's policy planning staff at the State Department. And in 1951 he was assigned to Germany. Then he was given a loyalty interrogatory and suspended from duty. Alsop was outraged. "Here was Davies . . . ," he wrote in a column, "publicly charged with doubtful loyalty and publicly suspended from duty on the eve of a most important assignment as political adviser in Germany. Here was his name blackened, his career perhaps permanently damaged, his fortune already hard-hit by all the horrible complications of a sudden change of family plans after the sale of the family house. And all for what? To make a burnt offering with a sweet savor in the peculiar nostrils of Senator McCarthy and Senator McCarran."[99]

Alsop volunteered to testify on Davies's behalf. "God knows, I thought and still think that Davies, Service and the others who shared their views were wrong," Alsop told Henry Luce. "God knows, I thought them fools, and still think the same of them, with the exception of Davies. But there is all the difference in the world between saying a man has been wrong and accusing him of being a disloyal plotter against the United States; just as there is all the difference in the world between saying that the IPR was an academic nest of silly people and falsely blowing it up into a sort of sinister directorate of American foreign policy."[100]

Kennan paid his own way back from Europe to testify for Davies as well. "One of the most excruciating aspects of these attacks on individual officials," Kennan reflected, "was the feeling on the part of those of us who were not attacked that it was only chance, rather than any superior wisdom or virtue on our part, that saved us from this fate. It gave one something akin to a sense of guilt to see other people pilloried for things that might just as well have happened to oneself."[101]

Alsop told the loyalty board that Davies had advocated a perfectly logical position in China — just one that happened to be wrong, although Davies could not have known this at the time. "For this outcome John Davies, the man being sacrificed to Senator McCarran and Senator McCarthy, had no more visible responsibility than I," Alsop wrote in his column. "As I thus reviewed the past, it struck me we would be much wiser to start loyalty investigations of the politicians who are now working all out to destroy the last vestiges of decency and fair play in our public life, than to waste time picking over the bygone views of such men as John Davies."[102]

The State Department loyalty board cleared Davies. Then he was subpoenaed by the McCarran Committee.

In November 1944 Patrick Hurley bounded off a plane in Yenan, let out a Choctaw war whoop (*Yahoo!*), and sat down with Mao to work out a deal for the Communists to fight with the Nationalists. After Mao signed the agreement, Hurley returned to Chungking. Chiang balked at the terms but made a counteroffer. This time Mao balked. "The motherfucker," Hurley exploded.[103] Turtle egg, Mao called him, which was almost as bad. "We are not like Chiang Kai-shek," Mao added. "No nation needs to prop us up."[104]

Pat Hurley was nothing if not a can-do guy. But for most of his time in China he couldn't. First Roosevelt sent him to make peace between Stilwell and Chiang; Hurley realized that it was impossible, and Stilwell was recalled. Then Hurley assigned himself the task of making peace between Chiang and Mao, which didn't turn out to be any easier. In the meantime Roosevelt appointed Hurley ambassador. The only thing worse than Roosevelt's taste in personal diplomatic envoys was Roosevelt's choice for ambassadors. He sent an ignoramus like Joseph Davies (no relation to John) to the Moscow embassy, and foreign service officers such as George Kennan considered resigning en masse. He sent Pat Hurley to Chungking, and the foreign service officers would have been better off resigning.

At sixty-one Hurley was not in his prime; his eyes were weak, his teeth hurt, his head ached. Some of the career foreign service officers thought that he was senile. Jack Service spoke Chinese so well that in the dark he could be mistaken for a native. Hurley couldn't tell Chinese first and last names apart. *Madame Shek* was what he called Madame Chiang. *Mouse Dung* he pronounced Mao Tse-tung. The China experts laughed about this for decades. When the embassy burned down one night, no one bothered to tell the ambassador.

Hurley returned the contempt. He began to suspect that the arrogant foreign service officers didn't want him to succeed. When John Davies flew to Yenan, where Hurley was trying to broker a modus vivendi between the Communists and the Nationalists, the ambassador accused the foreign service officer of trying wreck the talks. Hurley called Davies a Communist and threatened to have him kicked out of the State Department. Hurley also warned Service to stop trying to make policy or he would break him. Davies soon transferred to Moscow. "Hurley says he's a Communist,"[105] Secretary of State James Byrnes told Molotov when he introduced him to Davies in Moscow. Hurley was determined to keep a firm grip on the embassy. "Hurley has given out directions that only favorable reports of the Nationalist government be sent," Edmund Clubb wrote in his diary, "and those who think unfavorably in regard to the subject are classified as 'Communists.'"[106]

In February, Hurley left for Washington. The embassy revolted. The foreign service officers were alarmed that Hurley had been giving the State Department a wrong and misleading picture of China. Jack Service wrote a memo suggesting that Washington arm the Communists. "We could expect," he wrote, "to secure the cooperation of all of China's forces in the war, to hold the Communists to our side rather than throw them into the arms of the Russians."[107] Acting chargé d'affaires Geoge Atcheson approved the telegram, and every diplomat in the embassy signed it. In the State Department John Carter Vincent endorsed the cable and sent it to the White House. Then he showed it to Hurley.

Hurley almost had a stroke. "An act of disloyalty," he called it.[108] To Hurley the cable sounded like more insubordination from Service. "I'll get that son of a bitch if it's the last thing I do," he raged.[109] Hurley had all the diplomats in embassy transferred to other posts. Service had been back in Yenan for less than a month when he was suddenly ordered to return to the United States. There he became friendly with Philip Jaffe, the *Amerasia* publisher and de facto Communist, and walked into the middle of a FBI espionage investigation.

In November 1945 Hurley quit in a huff. "The professional foreign service men sided with the Chinese Communist armed party," he wrote to Truman. In December Hurley told the Foreign Relations Committee that he had been betrayed by his staff, including Davies, Service, and Vincent. "Disloyal to the American policy," he called them.[110]

The Foreign Relations Committee wasn't much interested in Hurley's allegations. Alfred Kohlberg was. The lace importer stuck up a friendship with the general, and his files on the State Department China experts got a little thicker. Six years after Hurley had failed to impress the Foreign Relations Committee, McCarran's Internal Security Committee would spend eighteen months investigating Hurley's charges.

Early in 1950, not long after the Communists drove the Nationalists off the Chinese mainland, Ed Clubb was the highest-ranking foreign service officer left in Peking when the new government plastered notices on all Western consulates giving diplomats six days to move out. Clubb and his family and his elderly Chinese clerks spent the next week cleaning out the three-story building and moving everything to a new location, working through the last night of a twenty-four-hour extension and leaving the keys in the lock at five minutes to midnight.

Three months later, while Clubb was transmitting a long telegram to Foggy Bottom, the Chinese cut off the embassy's radio link to Washington. On April 13 Clubb pried the U.S. government seal off the gate and lowered the flag for the last time at the American embassy. It would be more than two decades before the United States would restore diplomatic relations with the People's Republic of China. Clubb and his wife left the country the same day.

"And so, away from Communist China," Clubb wrote in his diary. "We are now on the right side of the bamboo curtain, and can breathe deeply again."[III]

A year later Clubb found himself in McCarran's hearing room.

CHAPTER 21

Names, Names

Saving face single-handedly, without the considerable collaboration of others, was the less attractive alternative. It tended to involve a preemptive attack on those who would cause the loss of face. This was almost sure to arouse inconvenient rancor, lead to an unseemly spectacle, and not be very convincing. Trying alone to save one's face was therefore a last resort.[1]

— John Davies

I always found that the worse a man's character, the better I got on with him.[2]

— Owen Lattimore

In the great river of man's knowledge all things are relative and no one can grasp absolute truth.[3]

— Mao Tse-tung

At 10:30 A.M. on July 25, 1951, Pat McCarran banged a gavel and opened the first public session of the Senate Internal Security Subcommittee. McCarran sat at the center of the table in Room 424 of the Senate Office Building, a small fourth-floor committee room. He was flanked by the rest of the panel, three Democrats to his left, three Republicans to his right, although the actual spectrum of the panel ran from conservative Democrat to extremely conservative Republican. Joe McCarthy was there, too, although McCarran told him that if he had a question for a witness he would have to write it out and pass it to McCarran. There was no doubt who was in charge. "A publicity hound," McCarran called McCarthy to Robert Morris. "A bit irresponsible."[4]

McCarran was determined to make his hearing respectable. Television cameras had recently started covering congressional hearings, but McCarran banned them from his room. He wanted to avoid spectacle, he explained, and merely gather facts. "We begin these hearings making no charges," McCarran promised. "We propose to let the evidence precede our conclusions. . . . We strive to be fair."[5]

The nominal subject of the hearing was the Institute of Pacific Relations, the Far Eastern think tank founded in 1925. Who Lost China? was the real subject. More than a year earlier, Joe McCarthy had accused Asia scholar Owen Lattimore, the longtime editor of IPR's journal *Pacific Affairs*, of being the top Soviet espionage agent in the United States, and stated that his whole case would rise or fall on that charge. Then the Tydings Committee, voting on party lines, condemned McCarthy as a liar. That might have ended things if not for McCarran's new Internal Security Subcommittee.

The Tydings Committee had been a slapdash affair, disorderly, partisan, and largely confined to narrowly refuting McCarthy's specific charges, which was not too hard to do. McCarran's committee would be different: methodical, ideologically unified, glacial in pace and power, slowly grinding across the political landscape of the past two decades, minutely exposing the lives of scores of people to a relentless investigation. "The measurement of men's motives, the assessment of the strands of thought and the elements of pressures which may have influenced another's behavior is not a task to be sought," McCarran declared that first day. "And yet if we are to do our full part to save our country and our way of life from subversion and erosion we must make the effort."[6]

Back in February, McCarran, acting on a tip from McCarthy, had dispatched Don Surine with subpoena to seize IPR's old records, which had been stored on the farm of the organization's former secretary general Edward Carter. SISS counsel Robert Morris then sequestered himself in a tiny windowless room with twenty years' worth of old IPR correspondence. Like a medieval monk diligently trying to translate crumbling documents before the past slipped away, Morris spent months burrowed in his stacks of paper, well after midnight on many occasions. "It was fascinating," Morris enthused, "so many interesting letters and papers, all bearing, with an undercurrent of intrigue, on a segment of history."[7] As the minority counsel to the Tydings Committee, Morris had come up with a couple of dozen witnesses whom he wanted to question about the making of American foreign policy, only to be thwarted by the Democrats running the investigation. Now he was working for a different sort of Democrat. In April the subcommittee began questioning Morris's witnesses in closed session. "Our policy," McCarran explained, "of taking a witness into executive session and finding out what he knows and what he is going to testify works as a safety valve so that innocent people will not be harmed."[8]

By late July the committee had taken secret testimony from nineteen people, including Lattimore, who testified for six hours and was surprised to find McCarran apparently more reasonable than McCarthy. It wasn't, he told his wife, so bad after all.

A severe-looking man with thin gray hair knelt before the altar in St. Patrick's Cathedral in New York one day in October 1945, put his hand on a Bible, and asked God to let him come home. "I Louis Francis Budenz . . . ," he began.[9]

In 1945 Budenz was fifty-four years old. He had been raised a devout Catholic, educated at religious schools, and inspired by the charity of his church to become active in the labor movement at the age of twenty. He married a divorced woman and was excommunicated. His politics grew steadily more radical; he was arrested twenty-one times on picket lines. In 1935 he joined the Communist Party, becoming the labor editor of the *Daily Worker* and later the newspaper's managing editor and a member of the party's national committee. Two years later he wrote an article attacking Monsignor Fulton J. Sheen for denouncing the party. The priest sent Budenz a manuscript to read — *Communism Answers a Communist* — which used the horrors reported in the Soviet press to indict the Soviet experiment. The two met. "Let us now talk of the Blessed Virgin," the priest finally said. "*Ave Maria, gracia plena,*" echoed in the radical's head.

Nine years later Budenz was editing the *Worker* while fingering a rosary in his pocket and sneaking off to attend Mass. He called Sheen. In October 1945 Budenz reentered the Catholic Church. "The Lord has written wisdom into my heart," Budenz said to himself.[10] He became a professor at Notre Dame. The next month Budenz sat down with two Catholic FBI agents who spent five days debriefing the apostate about his decade with the party. "He is not, however," one of the agents reported, "as well informed as expected."[11]

Budenz became a public critic of the party, giving lectures against Communism, talking to reporters, writing articles. In 1946 Budenz testified before HUAC. He became friends with Alfred Kohlberg, who gave him a complete set of *Daily Workers* from 1935 to 1945 to help him research his ever-growing output of articles and speeches. The two had lunch together every week, sometimes more often if they had something really interesting to discuss. More and more they were talking about China.

In 1947 Budenz published an autobiography, the first of several, called *This Is My Story*. The book was dedicated to the Virgin Mary, had a cross inscribed on its cover, and read more like a Bible tract than a political memoir. "I have made a religious pledge not to injure innocent people," he wrote.[12] Budenz hinted at the activities of the Communist underground ("Jacob Golos ... did much undercover work for the Soviet agents before his death"[13]) but pointedly declined to offer details about the party's secret activities. "Those who will look," he wrote, "in these pages for bitter invective against individual Communists, to the ferreting out of Reds in this place and that, to lurid accounts of countless secret conclaves will be disappointed."[14]

Not for long. "*Miserere me, Deus*," Monsignor Sheen read from Psalm 50 at St. Patrick's. "According to the multitude of Thy tender mercies: blot out my iniquity."[15]

Budenz's iniquity was just starting.

Edward Carter was the first witness. Carter had joined IPR a year after its founding in 1925; in 1933 he became secretary general of the organization, a position he held for eleven years until he retired, although he continued to serve on the group's board. The IPR was Carter's life. He built the organization up from a small Pacific Rim discussion group based in Honolulu and turned it into the major Far East think tank, headquartered in New York, with ten affiliated international councils and a budget of one hundred thousand dollars a year, funded by major American philanthropies such as the Rockefeller Foundation. "Most of the leading American students of the contemporary Far East," noted William Holland, who became the head of the organization after Carter, "have during the past twenty five years been associated with the Institute of Pacific Relations in one way or another."[16]

SISS counsel Robert Morris led the questioning, walking Carter through his résumé, taking long stops here and there: Carter's efforts to establish a Soviet IPR council, his visits to Russia, his hiring of Lattimore as an editor, his hiring of Fred Field as an assistant and then as head of the American council of IPR, his friendship with the Russian ambassador in Washington, his defense of the Moscow trials, his lack of curiosity about the evident Communist affiliations of many of his staff members. Carter had been, in other words, a fellow traveler — at the very least.

And IPR, Morris implied, followed the Communist Party line like a kite on a string. Morris had not spent weeks reading IPR's documents for nothing. "For the USSR," Lattimore had written to Carter in 1938, "back their international policy in general, but without using their slogans and, above all, without giving them or anybody else an impression of subservience."[17]

Morris read scores of names, asking Carter if the person had any connection to IPR: Edmund Clubb, Frank Coe, Lauchlin Currie, John
Davies, Len De Caux, John Fairbank, Fred Field, Mark Gayn, Alger Hiss,
Owen Lattimore, Duncan Lee, John Service, Agnes Smedley, John Carter
Vincent, and Harry White, to name a few. The list included those arrested
in the *Amerasia* case, foreign service officers, and former government officials accused by Elizabeth Bentley and Whittaker Chambers of being
secret Communists or fellow travelers. All, of course, had some ties to the
institute.

Carter, seventy-three, smiled a lot, tended to go on a bit, but vigorously
denied that he had ever been a Communist and said that he didn't think
Lattimore was, either. "A good American, a great scholar, and one of the
best authorities on Asia," Carter called him. "I still believe Lattimore is
opposed to Communism," he added.[18]

McCarran smiled somewhat less. Ten minutes into the questioning the
senator was threatening to throw Carter's attorney out of the room.

"May I have — " attorney Edgar G. Crossman started to ask.

"That is all," McCarran interrupted. "I have said the last word and that
is all there is to it."[19]

Fred Field journeyed from his new residence in New York City to
Washington, D.C., where he walked into the Senate Office Building
hearing room amid a crush of reporters and photographers. As a descen-
dant of Cornelius Vanderbilt, Frederick Vanderbilt Field might have
expected to end up in the Senate some day — but not in handcuffs.

Fred Field was the Red sheep of the family. Born to great wealth, he
squandered a third of his personal fortune and gave another third away.
Field never met a left-wing cause he couldn't support, morally as well as
financially — from the Moscow show trials ("Because Comrade Stalin
says so, we have to believe the trials are just"[20]) to supporting the Hitler-
Stalin pact. As Field recalled late in life, he became a Communist in 1934
almost by accident. "Little by little, I became aware that I was becoming a
full-fledged Communist and being treated as such," he remembered.
"There was no decision."[21]

One of Field's causes was IPR. After graduating from Harvard, Field
joined IPR in 1928 and became secretary of its American chapter in 1934,
a job he held for six years, while keeping mostly quiet about his party
membership. Field gave the group sixty thousand dollars. His office was

next to Lattimore's at the organization's New York headquarters on 129 East Fifty-second Street. Once after a trip to Outer Mongolia, Lattimore gave Field a bag of the local tobacco, which he enjoyed smoking in his pipe for a few days until the women in the office complained about the smell. Of course, Lattimore explained, it's camel dung. In 1940 Field resigned his position with IPR when Earl Browder tapped him to become the head of the party's anti-interventionist front organization, American Peace Mobilization, although he stayed on the IPR board until he was forced off in 1947 — by which time his Communism was pretty easy to infer from his frequent writings in the *Daily Worker* and the *New Masses.*

During the Tydings hearings, Field testified that Lattimore was not a Communist. When asked about himself, Field took the Fifth. A year later Field found himself in court as one of the trustees of the Civil Rights Congress, a party front group that put up an eight-thousand-dollar bond for the Communist leaders who had been convicted under the Smith Act. When four of the party leaders jumped bail and went underground, Field and three other CRC trustees (including novelist Dashiell Hammett) were ordered to produce a list of contributors to the fund. They refused and were sentenced to jail for contempt of court. Field got nine months. In jail the Vanderbilt heir was greeted with a strip search. When a guard told Field to drop his pants and bend over, the prisoner looked up from between his ankles at the guard's upside-down face. "You won't find the fugitives there," he deadpanned.[22]

Hauled before McCarran's committee, Field gave his occupation as prisoner. He took the Fifth Amendment many times. "I knew that this time I was up against the real enemy," he recalled. "In comparison to McCarran, Tydings had been a knight in white armor fighting for liberty and decency. McCarran was the pinnacle of reaction, on a par with McCarthy, but less crude. If McCarran wasn't the devil himself, he was his surrogate."[23]

The committee wasn't expecting to get much information from Field. He lived up to expectations. Field was there for display only: a Fifth Amendment Communist, a former high official of IPR serving time in jail for refusing to help his government. Field, of course, really was a Communist, and if anyone could tell the committee the truth about the party's relationship with the IPR, it was he. Neither Field nor McCarran, however, wanted to talk about what had actually transpired in the past. Field wanted to ignore it; McCarran wanted to exaggerate it. Field was happy when the marshals finally took him away. "It's hard to believe now, so many years later," Field recalled, "that I felt a sense of relief when I got back to the maximum security prison."[24]

The next day, only two witnesses into an inquiry that would last more than a year, McCarran was ready to offer an early verdict. "Certain individuals, working together, influenced government policies out of which came the predicament we are in today . . . ," he said. "You haven't seen anything yet."[25]

In early August, John Paton Davies found himself sitting in the nearly empty committee room, facing a barrage of questions from SISS in closed session. "Subjected to much hostile and suspicious interrogation," Moscow ambassador George Kennan remembered. For this, Kennan blamed himself. "The matter weighed on my conscience and my thoughts for years," he recalled.[26]

Kennan, of course, was the kind of man who would blame himself for an overcast day. He was also the most brilliant, not to mention moody and melancholy, foreign service officer of his generation. Kennan had known Davies well since 1945, when the China expert transferred to the Moscow embassy. There the Russian expert was formulating a grand strategy that would guide U.S. foreign policy for the next half century, which would become known as containment — a strategy that, in typical Kennan fashion, he later renounced. In 1949 Kennan was head of policy planning at the State Department, and Davies was on his staff. Kennan asked Davies to attend a meeting with two officials from the CIA, one of whom was Lyle H. Munson. The State Department and the CIA were looking for ways to gather intelligence inside Communist China. Davies suggested recruiting journalists and scholars who were respected by the Chinese Communists. He tossed out half a dozen names, such as Agnes Smedley, Anna Louise Strong, Edgar Snow, and John Fairbank. The plan was codenamed Tawny Pipit, a rare bird. The idea never got off the ground.

Not long afterward a journalist friend came to Kennan and told him that Davies had tried to infiltrate Communists onto the CIA payroll. Kennan complained to the CIA that one of its representatives was leaking top-secret (and distorted) information to the press. Munson was soon looking for another job. Before long he was also talking to Alfred Kohlberg and Robert Morris. Five of the six names suggested by Davies, it turned out, had links to IPR.

The matter came up during Davies's loyalty hearing in June, although he was still cleared. Then he was subpoenaed by McCarran. Kennan was the U.S. ambassador in Moscow at the time and wrote to the secretary of state, pointing out that he had been Davies's boss and deserved any blame for the idea. "I could not stand by," Kennan told Dean Acheson, "and see an officer suffer injury to his career or to his status as a citizen by virtue of actions performed by him in good faith as part of his best effort to carry out duties laid upon him by myself."[27]

Davies testified for two days before SISS. He denied trying to sneak Communists into the CIA but declined to reveal details about the meeting with the agency, citing its top-secret nature. "It touches on an operation which is only slightly less sensitive than that of atomic energy," he said. "I, therefore, am not at liberty to talk about this subject without clearance from my superiors."[28]

Sourwine quizzed Davies about the six China experts mentioned by Munson. Davies readily admitted that he was sure two of them — Agnes Smedley and Anna Louise Strong — were Communists, but he refused to say precisely what he had considered asking them to do for the CIA. "I think it indicates mysteriousness," Senator Willis Smith said. "It is a mysterious operation," Davies replied.[29]

At one point Davies pulled out a letter from the State Department files about Smedley. Sourwine wanted to know how Davies came to find it. Edmund Clubb gave it to him, Davies replied, which sent Sourwine off on a long series of questions about another foreign service officer who had served in China. Later Sourwine asked Davies about letters he had written to Edgar Snow, the first Western reporter to interview Mao, whose book *Red Star Over China* was considered by conservatives to be Communist propaganda. The diplomat said that the reporter had been curious about a young women whom he had dated in Moscow. "I remembered his inquiring about her and my writing back and saying that the NKVD had not gotten her and she was all right," Davies recalled. ". . . She was a cute dish."

Why did he say that the NKVD had not gotten her yet? Sourwine asked.

"A totalitarian state," Davies quipped, "devours its own, you know."[30]

When Lyle Munson testified, he told the committee a different story. Davies, he said, wanted the CIA to hire Communists. McCarran sent the hearing transcripts to the Justice Department, asking that it investigate Davies for perjury.

All Betty Bentley really wanted to do was sit in her new house in Connecticut with her cat on her lap and a highball within reach. But the subpoenas kept coming as relentlessly as junk mail.

Three years after Elizabeth Bentley had startled the country with her account of Soviet espionage, she was back on Capitol Hill testifying about Communism before McCarran's committee. By the summer of 1951 Bentley could find her way around the halls of Congress wearing a blindfold. She had gone to the FBI in 1945 to escape her past; six years later she was trapped in that past like a bad dream that comes back night after night. Bentley still met FBI agents almost weekly, but she spent a good part of her time retelling her story in public as well. She'd become a regular witness at congressional hearings, grand juries, and government tribunals, such as the Subversive Activities Control Board. Earlier in the year she'd testified against former Commerce Department official William Remington, who was found guilty of perjury for denying that he had been a Communist. For a while after her debut before HUAC in 1948, Bentley had tried to build herself a quiet life. She converted to Catholicism and got a teaching job at Mundelein College, a small Catholic women's school in Chicago. Her drinking and proclivity for entertaining men didn't go over well with the college, which she soon resigned from. Bentley, the college announced, had been released from her contract because she needed more time to testify "My frequent subpoenas did not help class morale," she said, "so I gave up the teaching."[31]

Bentley, instead, resigned herself to becoming a professional ex-Communist. In the United States during the 1950s this was actually a viable career. Hede Massing had recently just published her account of her Communist days (*This Deception*) and preceded Bentley before SISS (she didn't know anything about IPR per se but could identify many of its members as Communists). Whittaker Chambers, who followed Bentley before SISS, was a shy and reluctant witness; yet he was voluble enough to write an eight-hundred-page autobiography (*Witness*) that would fetch seventy-five thousand dollars from the *Saturday Evening Post* in serialization and become a runaway best-seller the next year. Louis Budenz, the professional par excellence, seemed to write a book a year.

Bentley, in fact, had recently just finished her own autobiography, *Out of Bondage*, which would be published in September. Bentley's book basically followed the account she had given over and over to the FBI, but she added some flourishes (re-created dialogue, a dash of melodrama) that tended to undermine her credibility, which had never been high in some circles to begin with. "A deep strain of phoniness runs through her whole story," columnist Joseph Alsop wrote. "This does not mean, of course, that the whole fabric is phony."*[32]

Indeed, the basic story was true enough (certainly much truer than the denials or evasions of most of those implicated by Bentley), but it did get a bit polished with constant telling, like a stone rubbed shiny. In *Out of Bondage*, for example, Bentley wrote that the evening Jacob Golos died, he was preoccupied with calling a source to find out what was going on at IPR. "They've placed several good solid people in jobs where they can effectively influence American policy on the Far East in a pro-Soviet direction,"[33] Golos told Bentley, and she remembered those words verbatim eight years later.

In August, before SISS, Bentley was more careful. She testified that Golos warned her to stay away from IPR because it was too Red. She identified Mildred Price, the head of the China Aid Council, a front group, as a Communist who worked with a party cell at IPR, which was headed by Fred Field. Bentley identified Michael Greenberg, who replaced Lattimore as the editor of *Pacific Affairs* and went to work for Lauchlin Currie during the war, as a Communist who gave information (via Mildred Price) to the party underground.

But Bentley also wandered a bit afield. She said that she didn't know anything about Lattimore, although she implicated two of his friends: Harvard China scholar John King Fairbank and Joseph Barnes, who used to work for IPR, later became the foreign editor of the *New York Herald Tribune*, and now worked in publishing. Both denied having anything to do with the party. She also said that John Davies was considered very sympathetic to the party, and after reading one of his reports she agreed. "I once asked Mr. Golos why we just didn't take on the Institute of Pacific Relations itself," she said, "and he said, 'No. They are operating much too loosely.' . . . They were operating so much in the open and they were making so many blunders that it would be a mercy if the FBI didn't get them."[34]

In the first month of testimony, McCarran's committee fairly well established that the party had a strong presence in IPR, if it didn't actually dominate the organization. IPR's leading lights were either fellow travelers (Carter, Lattimore) or Communists (Field, Greenberg), and its active membership included a suspiciously high number of people convincingly impli-

---

*Bentley's uncredited collaborator was Catholic poet John Gilland Brunini, who also happened to be the foreman of the grand jury that had reconvened to consider more indictments based on Bentley's charges.

cated by Bentley, Chambers, and Massing as working for Soviet intelligence. But the biggest names also had the least to do with the organization and were already roadkill: Harry White was dead, Alger Hiss was in jail, Lauchlin Currie had left the country. Fred Field was the highest former IPR official creditably linked to the Communist underground, but he was already serving a contempt sentence, didn't seem indictable on anything else, and had protected himself by taking the Fifth Amendment.

If SISS had stopped there, the committee might have performed a reasonable public service by adding to the catalog of Communist machinations during the 1930s and 1940s. But SISS didn't stop. McCarran and Morris weren't satisfied with further exposing the already naked. White, Hiss, and Currie had all been uncovered by HUAC. McCarran and Morris wanted to demonstrate a causality between the influence of New Deal liberals and Cold War reversals. They wanted to find *their* own Communists.

This proved harder to do. When Bentley was asked about Lattimore, for example, she replied that she didn't know anything about him.

Bob Morris called Edmund Clubb and asked him to testify before the McCarran Committee. Pretty much all Clubb was doing that summer was appearing before various committees and panels: HUAC, the State Department loyalty board, now SISS. At least it gave him something to do. In June the State Department had suspended Clubb pending the outcome of his loyalty hearing. "This is one of the first healthy indications that the State Department is becoming afraid of the McCarran committee," McCarthy said, "and is going to start cleaning house."[35]

Clubb put together an analysis of two decades of his State Department reports and gathered character statements from thirteen witnesses. But all anyone wanted to know about was why Clubb had gone to the office of the *New Masses* nineteen years earlier. Clubb had Whittaker Chambers to thank for that.

Not long after Clubb had closed down the diplomatic mission in China and returned to the United States in 1950, Chambers saw Clubb's picture in the paper. Chambers called the FBI. He remembered, Chambers told the bureau, meeting a young foreign service officer on home leave from China in 1932 who had come to the Communist magazine bearing a letter from Agnes Smedley. Had Clubb been a courier for the party? Chambers wasn't sure. "I find it impossible," Chambers admitted, "with the play of so many influences on my mind, because people are always asking me questions, bringing me information and there are areas in my experiences where I can no longer distinguish between what I once knew and what I have heard and learned in the course of testifying."[36]

At first Clubb didn't remember the meeting. Then his diary turned up with his household belongings after a slow trip from China. "Their so-called 'revolutionary organ' is a horrible rag," Clubb had written in 1932, "but Agnes had given me a let of introduction to Walt Carmon and so I went to see . . . Chambers, a shifty-eyed unkempt creature who neverthe-less showed considerable force and direction in asking me about the Red movement in China. . . . I felt too much like a stranger to show the proper 'revolutionary enthusiasm.'"[37]

Clubb spent three hours answering questions from SISS and never got to give his side of the story. Over the course of almost a quarter century in the foreign service, Clubb had been interned by the Japanese during the war for eight months, separated from his family for three years, afflicted with dysentery, harassed by the Chinese Communists. But nothing was as bad as what his own country did to him. "With this hearing before the Senate Internal Security Subcommittee," he wrote, "my experience was rounded out. I discovered, as have so many people of various nationalities in the twentieth century, how much easier it is in the end to meet an enemy in strenuous and dangerous contest, confident in the superiority of one's associates and one's government, than it is to face the slings and arrows of one's own compatriots. The difference lies in what happens to the heart."[38]

McCarran, in the end, did not go after Clubb. The State Department did.

Harry Truman left the White House one day in August and traveled a few blocks away to K Street to inaugurate the new glass-and-steel American Legion headquarters. The president praised the patriotic group. The legion-naires clapped appreciatively. Then the president warned that some of those attacking Communism were doing more to destroy freedom than the Communists themselves. The applause stopped. "You have no way of telling when some unfounded accusation may be hurled against you," the presi-dent said. "Perhaps straight from the halls of Congress."[39]

Summer in Washington was always oppressive. The past two years it had been hell. McCarran, McCarthy, Korea. Every time Truman thought it couldn't get any worse, it did. In June, McCarthy spent the better part of three hours making a wild speech in the Senate accusing General George Marshall and Secretary of State Dean Acheson of treason. "A conspiracy on a scale so immense as to dwarf any previous such venture in the history of man," McCarthy said. "A conspiracy of infamy so black that, when it is finally exposed, its principals shall be forever deserving of the maledictions of all honest men."[40]

The Democratic side of the Senate was empty, but the press gallery was full and the next day McCarthy's ridiculous charges were slapped across newspapers from one end of the country to the other. Connecticut senator William Benton introduced a resolution calling for McCarthy's expulsion from the Senate. McCarthy replied that it was just an attempt by the Democrats to deflect scrutiny from their own inability to deal with subversion. "I think they are trying to take attention away from what is coming out of the McCarran Committee," he said, "where testimony shows that Communists and fellow travelers have influenced our foreign policy."[41]

McCarthy seemed to forget that McCarran was a Democrat. He wasn't alone. "Wags are talking of gerrymandering the aisle that separates Democrats and Republicans in the Senate," reported George Dixon in the *Washington Times-Herald*, "so that the GOP side will take in Mr. McCarran's seat."[42]

In July, McCarthy nudged out McCarran to be named the worst senator in a poll of newspaper correspondents.[43] And while McCarthy could get headlines like no one else in America, McCarran was the one actually getting the Communists — or those he accused of being Communists. "There are louder voices in the United States Senate than Pat McCarran," Alan Barth noted in *The Reporter* magazine, "but none speaks with more authority — at least on the subject of American loyalty. The chairman of the Senate Judiciary Committee has, over the last six months, managed to establish himself as Grand Inquisitor and Lord High Executioner in charge of the extirpation of heresy. . . . With the Nimitz Commission out of the way, Senator McCarran will now oversee the operation of the McCarran Act, Senator McCarran will consider the methods used by the McCarran subcommittee, and Senator McCarran will determine whether Senator McCarran has found the wisest balance that can be struck between security and freedom. As for Senator McCarran's qualifications to exercise all this authority — Senator McCarran will doubtless pass upon these too."[44]

McCarran later read the *Reporter* article at an appropriations subcommittee hearing when the panel was considering giving eighty-five million dollars to the U.S. Information Service, a State Department agency charged with serving as a sort of global public relations firm for the country. The Information Service, McCarran pointed out, distributed *The Reporter* to American embassies and overseas libraries. He moved to slash the appropriation to sixty-three million. The committee agreed. McCarran also gutted another appropriations bill when he found out that the State Department had distributed abroad cartoons by the *Washington Post's* Herb Block mocking Communism. "Apparently he was mad about *any* of my stuff being sent overseas," Block recalled, "even in the fight against Communism."[45] The cartoonist was one of the senator's harshest critics. "Is there money in this appropriation," McCarran asked Deputy Undersecretary of State Carlisle Humelsine, "whereby writers and cartoonists can be employed for the purpose of traducing and tearing down the efforts of congressional committees?"[46]

Inside the new American Legion building, the audience listened to the president and sat on its hands. "Rise up and put a stop to this terrible business," Truman urged. "Expose the rotten motives of those people who are trying to divide us and confuse us and tear up the Bill of Rights."

Truman's speech was greeted with silence. McCarthy and McCarran were not quite so quiet. "Why does the president fear discussing the evidence against his planners who have been responsible for the loss of one hundred million people a year to Communism since 1945?" asked McCarthy. "There are none so blind," added McCarran, "as those who won't see."[47]

On August 22 Louis Budenz testified before SISS. He recited his résumé: managing editor of the *Daily Worker*, member of the party's national committee, three thousand hours of interviews with the FBI over the past five years, star witness in the Smith Act conspiracy trial of the party's top leaders, fourteen appearances before HUAC and various other investigative bodies, including the Tydings Committee that originally investigated McCarthy's charges against Lattimore. To the outside world, Budenz said, Communists lied as a matter of course, but on the ninth floor of party headquarters in New York telling the truth to one another was essential. "The Communist Party is an army," he declared.[48]

Did the party's leaders ever discuss IPR? Robert Morris asked. "The politburo," Budenz said, "in these discussions declared the Institute of Pacific Relations repeatedly to be a captive organization, completely under control of the party."[49]

Budenz said he had been at a meeting with Field where it was decided that the millionaire Communist would instruct Lattimore to pick writers for *Pacific Affairs* who could be trusted to parrot the party line. "Instructions were given to him as a member of the Communist cell," Budenz said. ". . . Lattimore, whom I was told by Mr. [Jack] Stachel at the time to consider a Communist."⁵⁰

Budenz testified for two days, naming forty-three people as Communists, including Lattimore and John Vincent, the highest-ranking official to have been called a Communist since Alger Hiss. "I do know that the Communists relied very strongly on Service and John Carter Vincent," he said.⁵¹ Budenz added that Vice President Henry Wallace's trip to China in 1944 had been stage-managed by the party. "It was pointed out," he said, "that Mr. Wallace was more or less under good influences from the Communist viewpoint, that is to say, that he had on one hand Mr. Lattimore and on the other John Carter Vincent, both of whom were described as being in line with the Communist viewpoint, seeing eye to eye with it, and that they would guide Mr. Wallace largely along those paths."⁵²

And Jack Service, Budenz added, was a fellow traveler if not an actual party member. "John S. Service, at least from the official information I received," he said, "had many contacts with the party. He was designated as Lattimore's pupil. . . . Service and John Carter Vincent were repeatedly mentioned as being dependable."⁵³

And so it went, Budenz naming Communists, followed by Robert Morris putting into the record a document linking them to IPR. Some of which was news to the FBI. "In this testimony," one FBI agent noted, "there are at least seven instances in which Budenz either furnished information differing from that furnished previously to the bureau or before the Tydings Committee or relative to certain occurrences gives testimony which he has never made known before."⁵⁴

The bureau asked Budenz to explain the difference between what he told the FBI and SISS. "Budenz stated that he furnishes info which he knows to be a fact," an agent reported. "However, when furnishing info to the bureau, he furnishes only that info which in his opinion he can prove to be a fact."⁵⁵

Joe Alsop came up with a simpler explanation: Budenz was lying. Alsop was a fierce anti-Communist; he didn't much care for Lattimore or Vincent, but he had actually been in China during the Wallace mission and knew quite a bit about the political backstabbing that went on during the trip — and he knew that the Communists didn't have anything to do with it. "What the McCarran Committee is really doing," he told Henry Luce, "is to put a small and rather idiotically selected group of individuals through a star chamber trial for the sins of the zeitgeist.... After the most careful study of the McCarran Committee record to date, I am convinced that this is a complexly and silly rigged attempt to deceive and befuddle."[56]

Joseph Wright Alsop V's family had come to America before it was a country. Franklin Roosevelt was a cousin. Alsop went to Groton and Harvard and moved through life with the effortless grace of one born with the wind to his back. He was a man who refused to eat in a restaurant on the Champs-Élysées because the subway vibrations shook the cellar, bruising the wine. He lived in a house that he designed himself on a huge lot in Georgetown, filled with Chinese antiques. His dinner parties resembled cabinet meetings. On the night that the Korean War erupted, for example, Pentagon and State Department operators tracked a number of high officials to Alsop's terrace, where they were enjoying cigars and brandy amid the wisteria. In Washington the outbreak of a war just barely trumped an Alsop dinner party.

Alsop devoted four of his syndicated columns to attacking McCarran and Budenz. He noted, among other contradictions, that Budenz had *not* called Vincent a Communist when he testified to the Tydings Committee; yet a year later he *was* calling him a party member to the McCarran Committee. "McCarran's Internal Security Subcommittee," Alsop wrote, "has been taking demonstrably false testimony.... The issue is whether the liberties of the citizen still have any meaning or whether interested politicians are to be allowed to run their own star chamber proceedings at will, and to round up any victims they please on any kind of evidence, however phony, they choose to admit to the record."[57]

The columnist, of course, had his own contradictions. The year before, Alsop was attacking the U.S. foreign service for losing China; now he seemed to be making a career of defending the State Department China experts who were accused by others of doing the same thing. Partly it was a tribal issue. Most of the foreign service officers were men of the Eastern Establishment, by aspiration if not by birth. The men of SISS, in contrast, were rabble, mostly from the Far and Middle West, and as contemptuous of the easterners they lived amid in Washington as the establishment was of them. John Davies, for instance, might be accused of being pro-Communist and lying under oath to a Senate panel, but he could still get invited to a dinner party at Joe Alsop's house. McCarran never would.

The antagonists: Chairman Pat McCarran (left, with his counsel, Jay Sourwine) turned the Senate Judiciary Committee into a virtual government within the government, using his power to block the president's nominations and berate his officials. President Harry S. Truman (below left) and columnist Drew Pearson didn't agree on much, but they both hated McCarran.

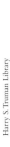

A divided government: Secretary of State Dean Acheson (top) frequently found himself accused of being soft on Communism when he had to appear before McCarran, who was chairman of the appropriations subcommittee that controlled the department's budget. FBI Director J. Edgar Hoover (bottom left) and Attorney General Howard McGrath both got along much better with McCarran, whose Senate Internal Security subcommittee eventually formed a secret liaison project with the FBI.

The 1948 election: McCarran was desperate for the Democrats to win so he could return to the chairmanship of the Judiciary Committee. When Truman stopped in Reno, McCarran campaigned with the president and gubernatorial candidate, Vail Pittman, younger brother of the senator's old nemesis Key.

Witnesses: Whittaker Chambers (top) and Elizabeth Bentley (bottom left) were alternatively hailed and ridiculed when they began testifying to congressional committees in 1948 about Communist cells operating in Washington during the New Deal and World War II. Years later Soviet archives would confirm their stories. Harvey Matusow (bottom right) also aspired to become an anti-Communist celebrity, but his testimony turned out to be less truthful.

Congressional refugee: When the Senate looked like it might consider a Displaced Persons bill that McCarran opposed he postponed the vote by going to Europe on a three-week fact-finding mission (pictured here on that trip with his wife, Birdie). Ten weeks later McCarran was still in Europe, where he found time to meet with Spanish dictator Francisco Franco (bottom) and offer U.S. financial assistance despite the fact that Franco's government was officially shunned by Washington.

Displaced legislation: McCarran managed to stall action on the Displaced Persons bill for eighteen months, as *Washington Post* cartoonist Herb Block shows, even though the White House and leaders from both parties were pushing for its enactment. With the help of Senate liberals such as Harley Kilgore and Herbert Lehman (to the left and far left of Truman) the president was eventually able to sign a bill to let more refugees immigrate to the United States. Then McCarran brought the DP program to a standstill with his Internal Security Act.

from *The Herblock Book* (Beacon Press, 1952)

Liberals: White House aide Stephen Spingarn (left) battled radicals who called Truman a fascist and reactionaries who called him soft on Communism. Senator Paul Douglas (below) spent years trying to defeat McCarran's laws.

The *-ism*: Republican Senator Joe McCarthy (right) gave his name to the cause of zealous anti-Communism in February 1950 when he accused the State Department of being full of subversives, but as a freshman member of the opposition party he had no power except for publicity. Herb Block (below) coined the term *McCarthyism* and was an astute critic of both senators.

"How Can You Sink So Low?"

"Can't Take Any Chance On Having Varmints Around"

McCarran's act: Passed over Truman's veto, the Internal Security Act (left) forced the Communist Party to register with the government, set up a network of concentration camps to hold potential subversives, and made it harder for foreigners to come to America. When the president appointed the Nimitz Commission (below) to investigate the way the government was balancing liberty and security McCarran blocked the Senate confirmation of the entire panel, sinking the idea.

All Quiet Along The Potomac

"Say, What Ever Happened To 'Freedom-From-Fear'?"

from The Herblock Book, Beacon Press, 1952

Herb Blocked: When McCarran found out that the State Department was stocking overseas libraries with some of Herb Block's cartoons, the senator cut the department's budget.

"Now, You Said You Wanted To Be Heard?"

McCARRAN COMMITTEE

The China Lobby: During World War II, Owen Lattimore was an adviser to Chiang Kai-shek. A decade later McCarthy named Lattimore as the top Soviet agent in America (Lattimore, top, center, is pictured with Chiang and Colonel Claire L. Chennault). Diplomat John P. Davies (bottom left) was also accused of undermining Chiang's government, leading to the Communist seizure of power in 1949. McCarran's Internal Security Subcommittee (cartoon bottom) spent eighteen months investigating the influence of China experts such as Lattimore and Davies on U.S. foreign policy, which led to a purge of the State Department's most experienced Asia diplomats.

Payback: In 1952 McCarran's SISS came to Salt Lake City to investigate Communists in the leadership of the International Union of Mine, Mill and Smelter Workers, which had led the fight against the senator's reelection campaign eight years earlier.

"There — That's Much Better"

MCCARRAN IMMIGRATION BILL

KEEP OUT — THIS MEANS YOU!

HERBLOCK ©1952 THE WASHINGTON POST CO.

Redefining America: The McCarran-Walter Act (left) made it harder for immigrants to come to America and made it easier for the government to kick them out; McCarran said that voting to let the United States join the UN was the worst mistake he made in twenty years in Washington. In 1952 SISS (below) investigated Communist influence in the organization.

"Why Don't You Go Back Where You Came From?"

U.N.

MCCARRAN COMMITTEE

HERBLOCK ©1952 THE WASHINGTON POST CO.

Las Vegas stripped: In the early 1950s Las Vegas had become Nevada's newest boomtown, but a proposed federal gambling tax threatened the industry and prompted McCarran to use all his influence to defeat the measure.

Snake eyes: Political novice Tom Mechling, pictured here with his wife, challenged McCarran's protégé Alan Bible in the 1952 Senate primary, but he actually seemed to be running against the senior senator. *Las Vegas Sun* publisher Hank Greenspun was McCarran's harshest critic in the state; his newspaper was the only one to back Mechling. One morning Greenspun discovered that every casino in town had mysteriously decided to stop advertising in the *Sun*.

The last years: Although McCarran welcomed Dwight Eisenhower's election in 1952, he fought the new president over his plan to let more refugees into the country. Eisenhower tried to charm McCarran by inviting him to the Oval Office. The president recalled that it had the same effect as beating an anvil with a sponge. As the Senate began considering a motion to rebuke McCarthy, McCarran continued to warn against subversive influences in American life.

Alsop was unafraid of attacking a powerful senator. Alsop's own paper, the *New York Herald Tribune*, was somewhat warier. It delayed delivery of one of the McCarran columns to other newspapers, ominously citing "legal problems," and ran an editorial the day after praising the McCarran Committee.

Then Alsop demanded that McCarran call a witness who could testify about what had actually happened in China: himself. "I had hoped to be able to regard that particular episode of my own life as over and closed," Alsop told his old mentor General Albert Wedemeyer. "The extraordinary attempt that is now going on, to rewrite the whole China story around a dark, imaginary plot, has forced me, much against my will, to plunge back into the controversy. . . . Getting a reasonable measure of justice for these men who neither of us much like."[58]

The day after Budenz finished testifying, Alfred Kohlberg asked McCarran for two thousand copies of one of the senator's speeches for his mailing list. "This inquiry is revealing step by step a vast and treasonable conspiracy," Kohlberg told McCarran.[59]

The inquiry, of course, was also repeating virtually the identical story that Kohlberg had been trying to tell people for years. Kohlberg had been accusing Owen Lattimore and the State Department's Far Eastern experts of trying to undermine the Nationalist government all during the Chinese Civil War. In 1947, for example, when John Carter Vincent was promoted by the State Department to the rank of career minister, which required Senate approval, Kohlberg rushed to Washington and convinced New Hampshire's Styles Bridges to oppose the nomination. Senate conservatives eventually extorted a deal from the State Department to permit Vincent's confirmation if he were dispatched to an unimportant post. Kohlberg kept up the attack. "A small group," Kohlberg explained in the *China Monthly* the following year, "including Alger Hiss, Owen Lattimore, Lauchlin Currie, Edgar Snow and later John Carter Vincent, planned to slowly choke to death and destroy the government of the Republic of China and build up the Chinese Communists for post-war success."[60]

In 1949, shortly after McCarran sponsored a huge loan to the dying Nationalist government, the businessman met the lawmaker at a dinner at the Institute of Chinese Culture. "It was a rare pleasure," Kohlberg beamed to McCarran, ". . . to observe the clarity with which you approached the confused Chinese situation."[61] Kohlberg was soon feeding McCarran tips about people he suspected of being Communists, names that McCarran repeated during his Judiciary Committee investigation of the United Nations later that year. But it wasn't until after Joe McCarthy made his Wheeling speech that Kohlberg met the politician who would give loudest voice to his suspicions. Kohlberg and McCarthy became friendly and one day spent eighteen hours talking about Lattimore. "It is easy to understand," Lattimore told the Tydings Committee, "the joy of Kohlberg and his associates when they found the willing hands and innocent mind of Joseph McCarthy."[62]

During the IPR hearings, observers noticed that Joe McCarthy was frequently sitting with McCarran at the committee table and concluded that the Wisconsin senator was really the guiding force behind the investigation. But McCarthy had just picked up Kohlberg's charges like a handy stick when he needed a club for his fight against the State Department. McCarthy wasn't a true believer. Kohlberg was. So was McCarran. The senator didn't let the businessman testify during the hearings, but Kohlberg kept in frequent touch with Robert Morris and sent him boxloads of documents. In the end Kohlberg was almost something of an unofficial committee member. "Your name will go down in American history for the sound and judicial inquiry you are now conducting," Kohlberg told McCarran.[63]

On September 14 Herbert Lehman stood up from his back-row desk in the Senate and asked unanimous consent to insert several columns by Joe Alsop into the *Congressional Record*. Most of the time senators could insert a volume from an encyclopedia into the *Record* without anyone complaining, but as soon as it became clear what the columns were about, McCarran was on the floor roaring objections from the front row. "He wants to sponsor a columnist who charges a committee of the Senate is guilty of subornation of perjury," McCarran said. "All the Alsops from here to perdition cannot stop this committee from going forward."

Lehman demanded an investigation into McCarran's investigation. McCarran demanded that Lehman sit down and shut up. "Overstepped every bound I have ever known in the Senate," McCarran raged at Lehman. ". . . The committee is not going to be bulldozed."[64]

Lehman sat down. Ten days later he tried again. As soon as the Senate opened on September 24, Lehman moved to put a letter from Henry Wallace to Truman into the *Record*. Wallace had denied Budenz's accusation that his trip to China was steered toward the party line by Lattimore and Vincent. "If my recommendations had been followed," Wallace modestly suggested, ". . . the chances are good the generalissimo would have been ruling China today."[65]

Lehman also wanted to include Alsop's columns. Two conservative Republicans — Owen Brewster of Maine and Herman Welker of Idaho — tried to block Lehman, but he persisted and read the columns out loud. This time Alsop's charge got into the *Record*.

On October 17 Henry Wallace walked into McCarran's committee room. Congressional decorum dictated that former high government officials should be invited to testify. McCarran had issued Wallace a subpoena ordering him to appear. "It is a humiliating experience," Wallace privately complained to SISS member Homer Ferguson, "when a man who has served his country to the best of his ability in high public office for twelve years is dragged before a Senate Committee."[66]

That was the point. McCarran had been waiting almost twenty years to embarrass Wallace. "Mr. Wallace is in fact and in reality a socialist," McCarran told a friend in 1933. "This Farm Bureau . . . is in fact and in reality a Soviet organization. . . . This growth in America threatens the democracy of this country more than anything that has ever developed in the nation."[67]

Nothing Wallace did in the next twenty years changed McCarran's opinion. In fact, McCarran's office had recently passed a tip to the FBI from a source that claimed Wallace had discussed atomic secrets with a Soviet agent during the war. "Keep after this," Hoover exhorted his agents. "We must nail it down."[68]

Alsop advised Wallace to get a good lawyer. Wallace said he didn't want one. This scared the hell out of Alsop. "I can hardly remember having been in a tighter spot," Alsop told a friend. ". . . It was perfectly clear that Wallace would be destroyed by McCarran and Wallace's destruction meant my own destruction and the destruction of the large group of in my opinion perfectly innocent men untruthfully accused by Budenz."[69]

The columnist had good reason to be worried. After Alsop's articles accused him of lying, Budenz was recalled before SISS on October 5. From the start of the hearings, McCarran and his colleagues had treated repentant party members with great deference and respect, welcoming them like returning war heroes; Communists or those so suspected were treated like child molesters. Upon Budenz's reappearance, the committee continued to be patient and indulgent. Budenz was allowed to explain away the contradictions in his story without challenge. Counsel Robert

Morris helped out by recalling that while Budenz never told the Tydings Committee that John Carter Vincent was a Communist, he had privately told Morris the information. And Morris produced a naval intelligence report he had made of the accusation at the time. "I want to ask the question, whether or not you want to change any of your testimony?" Ferguson said. "Absolutely not," Budenz replied.[70]

Budenz had already exonerated himself in front of the committee before McCarran got around to calling Wallace to testify. After much cajoling, Alsop had convinced Wallace to bring a lawyer. Finding one was another matter. Alsop called thirty lawyers in Washington; not a one would touch the case. Finally he tried a young attorney named George Ball, who didn't want to have anything to do with Wallace, either. "Though Alsop had no sympathy for Wallace, he was outraged that McCarran was rewriting history so grotesquely," Ball recalled. "Neither my partners nor I were anxious to get mixed up in Wallace's affairs, since we thought him a naive and muddled man and normally I would have refused to represent an individual touched by so much folly." But when Alsop explained how a former vice president of the United States couldn't find a lawyer willing to appear with him before a Senate committee, Ball changed his mind. "No matter how foolish Wallace may have been," Ball recalled, "he was entitled to counsel."[71]

Wallace was a difficult client. He wanted to start off by attacking the committee. Ball wanted him to offer a factual account of the trip to China. Wallace and Ball disagreed frequently, and the attorney was on the verge of quitting several times. At one point Alsop and Wallace were arguing in the columnist's house while Ball waited outside for a cab, poking his head inside every few minutes to see if he was going to represent Wallace or not. Ball stayed on the case, put Wallace through several hours of rehearsal, and escorted him into the committee room.

For almost four hours Morris and Sourwine scoured Wallace's memory for details of the trip to China seven years earlier; they were especially interested in a stop the Wallace mission had made in Russia, where one of their hosts offered a toast to the vice president's advisers. "To Owen Lattimore and John Carter Vincent," a Soviet official said, "American experts on China, on whom rests great responsibility for China's future."[72]

What did he mean? Morris demanded. Wallace said he had no idea, but he noted that the Russians toasted everything under the sun, including Roosevelt's reelection. "It was a terrible kind of thing to do," Wallace said in mock horror, "but he toasted his reelection."[73]

Eventually the hearing got around to Budenz. "Never have I seen such unmitigated gall as that of this man in coming before a committee of the United States Senate to utter such nonsense," Wallace said. "I say it is an affront to the dignity of a great and honorable body, over which I had the honor of presiding for four years."[74]

Alsop was relieved. "Wallace performed admirably," he told a friend. "The committee tried every way they knew to break him down but failed utterly. . . . A really deadly blow against the whole McCarthy-McCarran operation. For if these endless charges of treason are just once proven to have been grossly untruthful, as can be done in this case, then the same 'big doubt' will be created about the McCarthys as was created about the other side in the Hiss case. And after that, I faintly hope we may return to some sort of national sanity."[75]

Even Ball was reasonably pleased with Wallace, although looking around the committee room he was not as optimistic as Alsop. "The room," Ball recalled, "was filled with fanatical McCarthyites, principally old women exuding venom and muttering virulent curses. They were, I thought, spiritual descendants of Madame La Farge and those other scabrous crones who watched the tumbrels roll by."*[76]

The next day Joseph Alsop appeared before the committee and began to read a prepared statement. McCarran stopped him. Other members of the committee, Alsop began to explain, had told him that he could do so while McCarran had been out of the room. Alsop was used to considering senators as almost his social equals. McCarran intended to remind him otherwise.

"Whether you are running this committee or the committee is running itself is a matter to be determined very shortly," McCarran said.

"I am not trying to run the committee in the least," Alsop said.

"I think you are," McCarran replied.[77]

Alsop had the arrogance of a man who could accuse the State Department's China experts of favoring the Communists and losing China but still feel affronted when senators took him at his word. After McCarthy's attack on the State Department in 1950, Alsop became one of

---

*Wallace later complained about the fee that Ball charged, which infuriated Alsop. "You have behave almost unbelievably badly to George Ball," Alsop told Wallace. ". . . A more childishly imprudent procedure than to have gone before the McCarran Committee without legal protection, I cannot imagine." (Alsop to Wallace, 20 August 1952, Alsop Papers, Library of Congress.)

the senator's most pitiless critics. "I do not attempt to excuse or palliate the grave American mistakes in China, which I have often before denounced," Alsop wrote in a letter to the *Washington Post*. "But I submit that we may as well abandon all hope of having honest and courageous public servants if mere mistakes of judgment are later to be transformed into evidence of disloyalty to the state. And I submit further that the members of the Senate who are now persecuting these men who made, as I think mistakes in China, have far more to explain."[78]

More than a year later, Alsop was still demanding an explanation. When the columnist wrote to McCarran insisting that he be allowed to testify to the committee, McCarran invited Alsop to appear in executive session. Alsop insisted on speaking in open session. "My private war with the McCarran Committee," Alsop wrote to a friend.[79]

On October 18 Alsop finally got to testify, although McCarran didn't stay to hear it, wandering off after opening the session. Alsop launched into an attack on Budenz. "He has deceived the committee," Alsop said. ". . . Budenz should be investigated by the Justice Department to see whether a charge of perjury exists."[80]

Alsop spent a long and acrimonious day trying to explain what had happened in China seven years earlier; how Wallace had come to Kunming, where Alsop convinced him that General Stilwell needed to be replaced by someone who could get along with Chiang, and how Vincent had agreed. "The heaviest blow to the Communist cause in China that could be struck at that time," Alsop claimed. ". . . Mr. Vincent joined and concurred in the most profoundly anti-Communist act that could have been attempted in China."[81]

Senator Willis Smith was more interested in talking about Alsop's "Why We Lost China" article from the *Saturday Evening Post* the previous year, especially the reference to Davies and Service as giving bad advice to Stilwell. "It is a magazine article that I wrote some time ago," Alsop said. "I particularly did not want him to introduce Mr. Davies and Mr. Service because that is a separate and very complex subject all of its own and I think they were also, like General Stilwell, passionately loyal but mistaken Americans. Now a man is not to be denounced as disloyal because he has made a mistake."[82]

Smith kept asking Alsop about the China experts. Morris insisted on reading Alsop's own words back to him. "Throughout the fateful years in China, the American representatives there actively favored the Chinese Communists," Alsop had written.[83]

"It is very unfortunate, Mr. Chairman, to bring these men's names into this open hearing," Alsop said in exasperation, "because I do not think they were disloyal. I thought they were very mistaken."[84]

By the end of the day something strange had happened. Alsop kept insisting that Budenz had lied, but he became noticeably more deferential to SISS. "I withdraw any criticism of the committee," he said.[85] Such a retreat was out of character for Joe Alsop, normally the most fearless of men. But Joe Alsop had one secret that he desperately wanted to keep: He was gay. "In brief I have been an incurable homosexual from boyhood," he eventually told his brother and writing partner Stewart. ". . . It has not troubled me especially — it does not trouble most homosexuals — except in one respect. I have always hated the concealment I practiced with my family and friends."[86]

For most of the past two years the Alsops had been the boldest critics of McCarthy and McCarthyism. The year before, for example, the brothers published a piece in the *Saturday Evening Post* examining the growing hysteria. "Why Has Washington Gone Crazy?" they called the article, their first and last piece on McCarthyism for the magazine.

McCarthy and his allies responded with veiled threats to expose Joe's homosexuality. "I may publicly discuss any of his mental or physical aberrations which I see fit," McCarthy wrote to the *Saturday Evening Post*.[87] SISS member Senator William Jenner publicly taunted Alsop about his sexual preferences, which J. Edgar Hoover kept files on. McCarran had the head of the Washington, D.C., vice squad — which occasionally raided parks at night, arresting homosexuals, some of whom worked for the government — run name checks on witnesses who came before SISS. Alsop had once been picked up by the police in San Francisco under similar circumstances, although he'd managed to keep it quiet. McCarthy might fight dirty, but he didn't hold a grudge. McCarran did both.

So while Alsop continued to insist that Budenz was a liar, he stepped back from accusing the committee of actually suborning perjury, which if Budenz had been lying it clearly had. "I think the procedure is at fault and not the committee," Alsop said. ". . . I have withdrawn the statement, withdrawn any implication that the committee purposely encouraged this false evidence. I say now that the man who is at fault was Mr. Budenz."*[88]

---

*Harvard China scholar John King Fairbank wrote to Alsop for advice when he was subpoenaed to testify before SISS. "My own thought is to buy a football helmet and shoulder pads and take sleeping pills," he told Alsop. "I have no advice to give you except to keep your wits about you and not to let the bastards get you down," Alsop replied. (Fairbank to Alsop, 13 February 1952, and reply 19 February 1952, Alsop Papers, Library of Congress.)

Crowding into the elevator after the hearing, Alsop bumped into Joe McCarthy. The senator offered his hand. The columnist turned away. "One of the high points of my long career as a reporter," Alsop recalled.[89]

McCarran did wind up sending hearing transcripts to the Justice Department and demanding a perjury investigation. But not for Louis Budenz.

In November, McCarran suffered a heart attack. He spent the next two months in St. Mary's Hospital in Reno. "I'm going to pull out of this all right," McCarran told his wife, Birdie. "I want to live to block the Red gang that is trying to destroy this country. Acheson made such a failure in Europe I think he'll be out soon. Should be out. That will put that pink Vincent out."

Even though he was in the hospital, December turned out to be a pretty good month. The State Department loyalty board found that Clubb was a bad security risk. Vincent had to defend himself before a loyalty board that accused him of being a Communist. And then a loyalty board recommended that Jack Service be dismissed for his role in the *Amerasia* case six years earlier. Service had not been hauled before SISS but his name came up again and again, like a Rosetta stone that would explain the past to those who could read it. Acheson fired him.

"I get the Internal Security reports and I sign the statements," McCarran told his wife. "We have done things with that committee I can tell you. We got John Stewart Service and we will get others."[90]

On January 30, 1952, five months after being named before SISS as a Communist, John Carter Vincent finally appeared before the committee to defend himself in a public hearing. "Gentlemen, anyone, including Budenz, who before this subcommittee or anywhere else, testifies that I was at any time a member of the Communist Party is bearing false witness," Vincent said. "He is, to put it bluntly, lying. I am not a Communist and have never been a member of the Communist Party. I have never sympathized with the aims of Communism, on the contrary, I have worked loyally throughout the twenty-seven years of my foreign service career in the interest of our own government and people. . . . I am in full accord with the objectives of this subcommittee. . . . But we cannot defend democracy with perfidy or defeat Communism with lies."[91]

McCarran was not impressed. "It is not alone membership in the Communist Party that constitutes a threat to the internal security of this country," he said. "It is sympathy with the Communist movement that raises one of the gravest threats that we have."

"I think I said had no sympathy with the aims of the Communists," Vincent protested.[92]

Vincent had been waiting for this day for months. In October he arrived in New York from Tangier, shortly after Budenz had repeated his charge that Vincent was a Communist. Not too many years before, Vincent had been the head of the division of Far Eastern affairs, a rising star in the State Department; then the attacks mounted and Acheson sent him off to Switzerland, thence to Morocco, each post less important than the last but none far enough away to appease his enemies. After his return, Vincent wrote to McCarran, asking for a chance to defend himself in public. McCarran didn't reply. Then after the State Department released Vincent's plea to the press, McCarran promised him a hearing. Two more months passed, during which time Vincent faced a State Department loyalty board and made an appearance at a HUAC hearing. At the State Department hearing, Vincent testified for fifteen hours. It was a sprint compared to what happened when he walked into McCarran's fourth-floor committee room in late January.

"Did you ever talk over the subject of Communism with Clubb?" Ferguson wanted to know.

Vincent said that he hadn't and admitted that he didn't know much about Communism at all. "How can a man be a foreign service officer these days and not know about Communism?" Ferguson wondered.[93]

Ferguson pushed Vincent to name any books he had read about Communism, and when he couldn't the senator asked him if he could have then been following the party line without knowing it?

Ferguson was especially interested in Vincent's contribution to the Jack Service defense fund during the *Amerasia* affair. "Why would you in your position contribute to a man when you didn't know whether he was guilty or not?" the senator asked.

"Because of a matter of friendship," Vincent said.[94]

"I cannot understand why you would not make some inquiry about that before you would take such a definite stand as to make a donation," Ferguson continued. "I really cannot."[95]

Vincent's lawyers had worked hard to prepare him. They put together a thick briefing book, combing the SISS transcripts for names linked to Vincent, coming up with twenty-nine people (Clubb, Davies, Lattimore, and Service among them) and drawing up a second list of sixty-nine people who were associates of his associates. They abstracted thirty-two documents that SISS had subpoenaed. The committee still managed to fluster Vincent.

"I did not consider the IPR Communist or pro-Communist at the time I had any association with it," Vincent said. ". . . From the testimony I have heard and seen here, I would say that it certainly had a pro-Communist slant at times."

"You say that you are now convinced it is a pro-Communist organization," James Eastland pounced. "Who were those pro-Communists?"

"I have tried to think of names," Vincent said, "and I have thought of Field and I can't think of any others."

"The leaders of IPR have been referred to here," McCarran said. "Where was the policy fixed, if not in the leadership?"[96]

The briefing book was equally useless when Sourwine asked for details about a short visit Wallace and Vincent had made to Madame Sun Yat-sen in 1944. Sourwine wanted to know if the room had windows, if madame was standing or sitting, and if so was it on a divan or in a chair? Vincent was hazy.

"Do you have the same difficulty," Ferguson asked, "in your work in the State Department, advising with other officers, of remembering things that have happened, as you have here on the witness stand?"

"Senator, this all happened seven or eight years ago," Vincent said.

"Can you answer that question?" Ferguson insisted.

"You better answer that question," McCarran added.[97]

"Are you in as much doubt in conferring with State officials on things that have happened as you are before this committee?" Ferguson continued.

"It is a matter of recalling what I think of now as details," Vincent explained.

"I am asking are you usually in as much doubt?" Ferguson snapped.

"I think that is a simple question," McCarran said. "Why do you not answer it?"[98]

"Vincent all but had a light shined in his eyes and was beaten by a rubber hose," the Alsop brothers wrote.*[99] "One got the impression that the committee intended to make an object lesson of Mr. Vincent," added Lowell Mellett in the *Washington Star*, "a warning to any other persons accused by

---

*Joe Alsop still disliked Lattimore and Vincent. "They have seemed to me silly since I first knew them," he told Vera Dean. "They seem to me silly still." (Alsop to Dean, 8 January 1953, Alsop Papers, Library of Congress.)

Budenz or McCarthy that it was better to let the accusations stand."[100]

There was a method to the committee's relentless, minute probing. "Come along to the hearing, today," Ferguson said one day during a recess. "We're going to get Vincent on perjury."[101]

Vincent testified for a week, three days in executive session, four in public, a total of twenty-eight hours of questioning. "John Carter had faced death in Mukden and terrible danger in Changsha and had been cool as a cucumber," his wife, Elizabeth, said. "But this almost killed him. And the McCarran Committee was the worst experience of my life, too. Childbirth was fun compared to that."[102]

"Do you believe it was a fair hearing?" Ferguson asked on the seventh day.

"Yes, sir," Vincent replied.

Vincent committed perjury, after all. "I knew that if I'd said 'no,'" he told his wife, "they'd have started in all over again."[103]

The fourth-floor committee room was packed on February 26 at two-thirty when Pat McCarran swore in Owen Lattimore. From the committee table Joe McCarthy looked on and smiled. Almost exactly two years earlier, McCarthy had called Lattimore the top Russian espionage agent in America, an allegation that the Tydings Committee had investigated and found baseless. Then McCarran created the Senate Internal Security Subcommittee, which spent the next year investigating the Institute of Pacific Relations and for the last six months had gone into open hearings where a parade of witnesses testified that Lattimore was a Communist and a spy who had secretly influenced U.S. policy in Asia, in effect handing China to the Russians. Now Lattimore was supposed to get his turn. At the press table reporters flipped through his fifty-page statement with glee: Veteran Capitol Hill correspondents had never seen anything like it.

In front of the committee table news photographers faced the witness table crouched like gremlins waiting for a plane crash. McCarran warned them not to take pictures while the hearing was going on. "We do not think it is best to annoy or interrupt the witnesses in their testimony," he said.[104]

McCarran then announced that the committee had always expected to be attacked by Communists, and the Communists had done so with abandon. Lattimore, he continued, had released a statement to the press that was very similar to the party's attacks on the committee. "Intemperate and provocative expressions are there set out and elaborated upon," McCarran said. "This committee could exercise its rights. We could deny that statement the right to become part of the record. We realize that this is a country of free speech. . . . You may proceed, sir."

The owlish professor looked at the bulky, white-haired senator through his round glasses and then began reading. "I have asked for this public hearing," Lattimore started, "because your proceedings have resulted in serious damage to my reputation as an objective scholar and patriotic citizen, to the Institute of Pacific Relations with which I have been connected, and to our government's foreign service personnel and the conduct of its foreign policy — "

"If the chair will excuse me, please," Sourwine broke in. He wanted to challenge Lattimore before he could get to the second sentence and put into the record the correspondence between Lattimore and the committee. Sourwine then told him to continue.

"The impression," Lattimore went on, "has been assiduously conveyed in your proceedings — "

"Do you mean," Sourwine interrupted, "by 'assiduously conveyed' to make the charge that the committee has intended to convey a certain impression?"

And so it went for the rest of the day and two more after that. Sourwine, McCarran, and other committee members picked apart Lattimore's words as quickly as Lattimore could utter them. They halted Lattimore after every line, often before he could finish a sentence. It took him two and a half hours to struggle through eight lines of his fifty-page statement.

" — that I am a Communist or a Communist sympathizer or dupe," Lattimore's statement continued, "that I master-minded the Institute of Pacific Relations; that the Institute of Pacific Relations and I master-minded the Far Eastern experts of the State Department; and that the State Department 'sold' China to the Russians. Every one of these is false — utterly and completely false."

At Lattimore's side was his attorney Abe Fortas, a future Supreme Court justice, who pleaded with McCarran to let his client finish at least a single section before the committee dissected his words. More than once McCarran threatened to have the lawyer removed from the room.

"You have now for many months been publishing to the world," the statement went on, "an incredible mass of unsubstantiated accusations, allegations and insinuations. For months a long line of witnesses has set me in the midst of a murky atmosphere of pretended plots and conspiracies so that it is now practically impossible for my fellow citizens to follow in detail the specific refutation of each lie and smear. I should, in fact, be less than frank if I did not confess that I see no hope that your committee will fairly appraise the facts and I believe I owe it to you to state the reasons. To give a false impression of reality to this nightmare of outrageous lies, shaky hearsay and undisguised personal spite the subcommittee has put into the record."

By the end of the day, Lattimore had accused the McCarran Committee of unleashing a reign of terror against the State Department, of intimidating scholarly inquiry, and of acting as a goon squad against anyone who disagreed with the China Lobby. He attacked Joe McCarthy (the "Wisconsin Whimperer"), defended the State Department's China experts and IPR, and said that as editor of *Pacific Affairs* it had never occurred to him to set up a private FBI to investigate the institute's staff or the journal's writers. "If it was party strategy to infiltrate the Institute of Pacific Relations," he said, "I did not suspect it." Lattimore charged that McCarran had already prejudged the case, citing a November *U.S. News* article in which the senator said that IPR had been controlled by the Communists, and pointed out that he couldn't finish a sentence without being cross-examined while some witnesses could testify for days without challenge. "I am an innocent man," he said.

Throughout the hearing, McCarran's gavel fell like thunder. He ordered remarks stricken from the record, warned attorneys that they could be tossed out of the proceedings at any time, cut off Lattimore, and demanded yes or no answers to complex questions. "If you were in a court and said the things you said here," Arthur Watkins told Lattimore, ". . . you would promptly be in jail."

"I am not," Lattimore protested at one point, "and have never been a Communist, a Soviet agent, a sympathizer or any other kind of promoter of Communism or Communistic interests and all of these are nonsense."[105]

At 5 P.M. McCarran gaveled the hearing to a close for the day.

"My mind," Lattimore said, "is a maze now."[106]

It took Lattimore three days to stumble through his statement. "One of the most acrimonious exchanges Capitol Hill has ever heard," the *Washington Post* observed.[107] "Appearing before the forum in which for nearly a year he had been under running attack," added William White in the *New York Times*, "Professor Lattimore denounced his judges, Chairman McCarran and the members of the subcommittee, in terms rarely heard in the history of congressional investigations."[108]

Lattimore came into the hearing swinging and the committee swung back. He denounced the China Lobby. McCarran demanded that he name the alleged members of the lobby. Lattimore demurred. "Names, names," McCarran shouted.

Lattimore mentioned California senator William Knowland, whom he referred to as the senator from Formosa. Ferguson wanted to know where that term came from. Lattimore said he read it somewhere. Ferguson wanted to know where. Lattimore couldn't recall. Ferguson pointed out that the *Daily Worker* had used the term. The committee dragged more China Lobby names out of Lattimore: businessman Alfred Kohlberg (who had been feeding tips to SISS), columnist George Sokolsky (a McCarran friend and SISS supporter), and ex-Communist writer Freda Utley (who had briefly worked for SISS as a consultant). "Those are all of the names I can recall under this kind of hammering," Lattimore said.[109]

That will be stricken from the record, McCarran ordered, although it wasn't. But Lattimore's career might as well have been. In 1949 the professor had more than a hundred speaking invitations. In 1951 he had three. Once a prolific book reviewer for the *New York Times* and other prestigious outlets, Lattimore's opinions were no longer in demand. Social invitations had become almost as rare. And even the speaking engagements Lattimore did get were sometimes hard to fulfill. In December, for example, the State Department refused to issue Lattimore a passport to give a speech in London, although he did prevail on appeal. "Senators can hit a man below the belt and keep it up day after day," Lattimore complained to Vincent, "but if he hits back straight from the shoulder, that is not 'becoming.'"[110]

Then the real pain started. Over the next three weeks Lattimore was grilled by the committee for another nine days, making a dozen altogether, the longest testimony of a congressional witness to date (McCarthy sat in for seven days). Almost a year earlier, after Robert Morris had finished his detailed perusal of the IPR papers from the 1930s and 1940s, Lattimore had been closely questioned by the committee in executive session about the old correspondence, although he was not allowed to refresh his memory by seeing any of the documents. Now the committee went over Lattimore's earlier testimony, probing for discrepancies. They asked Lattimore if his lunch with Soviet ambassador Constantine Oumansky was before or after the German invasion of Russia. He thought it was *after*, although he hedged that he wasn't sure. The committee then put into the record a letter establishing that it was *before*. The committee asked Lattimore if he had ever handled Lauchlin Currie's mail when the White

House aide (and Soviet agent) was out of town. Lattimore said never. Did he ever knowingly publish an article by a Communist, other than a Russian? the committee wanted to know. No, Lattimore replied. In each case Morris pulled out a document from the IPR files proving that Lattimore was mistaken.

"Names have been mentioned of persons whom I totally failed to recall . . . ," Lattimore pleaded on day seven. "Later some document is brought out indicating that I did know them. That is one part of the whole procedure which I would very respectfully like to criticize — "

"That will be stricken from the record," McCarran ordered. "You're not here to criticize. You're here to testify under oath."[111]

In other words, to open himself up to a perjury investigation. A decade later Thurman Arnold, one of Lattimore's attorneys, was still amazed at McCarran's attempt to snare Lattimore. "As an example of unfair and oppressive procedure, the open hearings were a masterpiece of hypocritical ingenuity," Arnold wrote. ". . . I had never before seen an investigation conducted with third-degree methods. It was hard to believe that we were in the United States of America."[112]

On March 21 Lattimore walked into the committee room for his twelfth day of testimony. After the questioning was finally over, McCarran announced that he had a few words to say. "The committee has been confronted here with an individual so flagrantly defiant of the United States Senate, so outspoken in his discourtesy, and so persistent in his efforts to confuse and obscure the facts, that the committee feels constrained to take due notice of his conduct . . . ," McCarran said. "Suggestions have been made that the committee should seek to discipline Mr. Lattimore for his contumacious and contemptuous conduct. Clearly, Mr. Lattimore did, on many occasions, stand in contempt of the committee. . . . Mr. Lattimore used, toward the committee, language which was insolent, overbearing, arrogant, and disdainful. He flouted the committee, he scoffed at the committee's efforts, he impugned the committee's methods, and he slandered the committee's staff. . . . There has been no striking back on the part of the committee."

McCarran went on to abrade Lattimore at length, concluding that he knowingly lied to the committee. "That he has uttered untruths stands clear on the record . . . ," McCarran finished. "When, in the face of the record, he undertook before this committee a deliberate attempt to deny or cover up pertinent facts, this witness placed himself in a most unenviable position."[113]

In February the State Department loyalty board announced that Vincent had been cleared and sent him back to Tangier. McCarran exploded. "The clearance process is not completed," he warned.[114]

Then Acheson announced that he had reversed the loyalty board's finding that Edmund Clubb was a security risk. McCarran said he would try to cut off Clubb's pension and threatened to launch an investigation into the State Department security program.

Whatever happened, Clubb knew that his career was effectively over. After a quarter century as a foreign service officer, he was reassigned to the department's division of historical research, sent to gather dust in the archives. He resigned.

In April, Conrad Snow found himself sitting in a closed session with Pat McCarran and Joe McCarthy. This was getting to be a regular occurrence. Again and again that spring, McCarran summoned Snow, the head of the State Department's loyalty board, to executive session hearings. McCarran was the chairman of the appropriations subcommittee that handled the State Department budget. Joe McCarthy was also a member. The secret hearings resembled nothing so much as tag-team wrestling.

"You have been using a term that was coined by Owen Lattimore and is constantly used by the *Daily Worker*," McCarthy told Snow. "The term is 'McCarthyism.' I would like to get your definition of that term."

"McCarthyism," Snow replied, "is making public statements that are not based on facts."

"Where do you get the right to revile members of the Senate of the United States?" McCarran put in. "Where do you get such authority?"

"I am a citizen of the United States," Snow said. "As such, I have the con-stitutional right to say what I want to say when I want to say it. Also, I am holding a public office that entails responsibility on me to speak frankly."

"You ought to be out of that office," McCarran said.[115]

A few days later Truman wrote one of those letters that he never dared mail. "I wonder if there is not some way we can get the actions of certain committees into the courts," the president scribbled to former Senator Burt Wheeler. "They now have me in the court and I don't object at all. McCarran's committee . . . have been calling members of the administra-tion staff before them and browbeating them unmercifully. . . . Don't you think that a grand jury could support the Bill of Rights by perhaps indicting these gentlemen for tearing up the Constitution?"[116]

—

Archibald MacLeish read the newspapers and wrote a poem:

Says McCarran to McCarthy,
What's platform or party!
We sport the same feather:
Let's fight this together.
I'll tear them in two
If they criticize you.

Says McCarthy to McCarran,
Sweet Rosie of Sharon,
My truth and my honor
Shall fly to your banner.
If they light into you
They're Commies, that's who.

It's only the foreign,
It's only the dirty,
Would question McCarthy,
Says Mister McCarran.

And its worse than subversive,
It's un-American,
Says Mister McCarthy,
To talk against you.

Thank you, says McCarran,
Thank you:
But where does this nation,
He says, get the notion,
The people are free
To talk back to me?

Or to me, says McCarthy.

Who says they can grin at
Their lords in the Senate?
They're South Europeans!
They're scum beside we uns!

They're Reds, says McCarthy.
It's true, says McCarran:
There's only us two
That are red, white and blue:
There's me and there's you.

That's me says McCarthy
And how do you do![117]

In May federal judge James P. McGranery appeared before McCarran's
Judiciary Committee. Truman had just nominated McGranery to be the
new attorney general. Truman went through attorney generals like some
rich men go through wives. And each one seemed worse than the last. In
April, Truman had fired his most recent hapless attorney general, J.
Howard McGrath, and named McGranery to replace him. Conservatives
immediately went on the offensive. McGranery, after all, had been a
ranking official in the Justice Department during the *Amerasia* case, which
to the right had become a synonym for whitewash. "A cruel hoax on the
American people,"[118] HUAC's Harold Velde called the nominee.

In the Judiciary Committee hearing, Ferguson and Watkins grilled
McGranery over *Amerasia*. McCarran wanted to talk about Lattimore.
There were persistent rumors, he said, that McGranery had already talked
about not presenting the perjury case to a grand jury. "Never, never," he
assured McCarran. Are you opposed to sending the case to a grand jury?
McCarran persisted. No, sir, McGranery replied.[119]

While McCarran's soul mates on the committee remained adamantly
opposed to McGranery, however, McCarran became the judge's unexpected
champion. He led the floor fight for McGranery, who was confirmed. There
were several theories to explain McCarran's sudden solicitude for a Truman
nominee. Drew Pearson told listeners to his radio show that McCarran
extorted a promise from McGranery to make Eva Adams a judge. Harvey
Matusow, an ex-Communist witness who was temporarily the toast of conservative circles, later asserted that McCarran pressured McGranery into
promising to prosecute Lattimore in exchange for confirmation.[120] Liberal

columnist Robert Allen claimed that McCarran struck a patronage bargain with McGranery. "McCarran . . . has gotten the secret assurances he was after that he will continue to have a big voice in the dispensation of judicial patronage," Allen reported. ". . . The chunky Nevadan built up a patronage empire in the Justice Department while it was under ousted Attorney General McGrath. He gave McCarran virtually all the jobs he demanded. That's why he was so angry at McGrath's abrupt dismissal."[121] Graham Morison, an assistant attorney general and head of the antitrust division, later asserted that McCarran privately demanded that the Justice Department go easy on some of his corporate friends, such as Dollar Steamship Line, RCA, and IBM.[122]

Of course, it wouldn't have been out of character for McCarran to demand that McGranery do all of the above. And it would soon become evident that McCarran was able to wield unusual influence in McGranery's Justice Department. "McCarran," observed columnist Murray Kempton, "was de facto attorney general during the last year of the Truman Administration."[123]

On July 2 Pat McCarran told the Senate that the IPR hearings were finally over. He was the only Democrat in the chamber. "But for the machinations," McCarran said, "of the small group that controlled and activated the Institute of Pacific Relations, China today would be free and a bulwark against a further advance of the Red hordes into the Far East."[124]

The investigation had gone on for eighteen months, finally ending on June 20. The transcript ran to 5,712 pages. The day before, the Judiciary Committee had voted to approve the 226-page final report, with two liberals, Kilgore and Magnuson, declining to vote. The report found that the officials and staff of IPR were either Communist or pro-Communist. It listed eighty-seven people associated with the institute who had some Communist affiliation, many of whom were either dead or out of the country. Of those accused who testified before the committee, ten denied the allegations and eleven took the Fifth.

The report accused the institute of subverting U.S. foreign policy and helping undermine the Nationalist government in China. "The leaders of the IPR and their advisers — Lattimore, Carter, Currie, Hiss, Vincent, Jessup, Field and Fairbank — conducted their operations during the war," the report explained. "Through their influence in the White House, by reports from foreign service officers in the field and through the mission of the vice president to China; they sought to bring pressure to bear to undermine the Chinese government and to exalt the status of the Chinese Communist Party."[125]

The subcommittee urged the Justice Department to charge Davies and Lattimore ("a conscious articulate instrument of the Soviet conspiracy") with perjury. In fact McCarran had already twice tried to get the Justice Department to indict Davies. "The American Communist Party and the Soviet Union considered the IPR an instrument of Communist policy, propaganda and military intelligence," the report concluded. "Members of the small core of officials and staff members who controlled IPR were either Communist or pro-Communist. . . . The effective leadership of the IPR often sought to deceive IPR contributors and supporters as to the true character and activities of the organization. . . . IPR officials testified falsely before the Senate Internal Security Subcommittee concerning the relationships between IPR and the Soviet Union. Owen Lattimore testified falsely . . . John Paton Davies, Jr., testified falsely . . . John Carter Vincent was the principal fulcrum of IPR pressures and influence in the State Department. . . . The effective leadership of the IPR used IPR prestige to promote the interests of the Soviet Union in the United States. . . . Owen Lattimore and John Carter Vincent were influential in bringing about a change in United States policy in 1945 favorable to the Chinese Communists."[126]

The report stopped just short of blaming the loss of China on IPR (although McCarran said so in his Senate speech presenting the document) and calling its officials as well as those only vaguely associated with the institute spies and traitors, although the implication was obvious. On the Senate floor McCarran was not so cautious. "Our official secrets have been bared to agents of the Soviet," he said. "Loyal and sincere men have been driven from their diplomatic posts and under the cloak of public office messages have been written and words spoken that have tended to weaken this nation's position in world affairs."[127]

Normally the Senate printed fifteen hundred copies of a report. McCarran had an extra five thousand run off. He sent J. Edgar Hoover an autographed copy. "A perfect illustration of what can be accomplished through cooperation and proper timing," Hoover enthused.[128]

Liberals were outraged by McCarran's investigation. "The McCarran Subcommittee has given us not a report but a revision of history," the *Washington Post* wrote, "a revision compounded out of McCarthian bigotry, McCarranesque spleen and MacArthurian legend. It is an attempt to perpetuate another fraud and hoax on the American people."[129]

On the other end of the spectrum Irving Kristol, a socialist-turned-conservative and grandfather of the neoconservative movement, hailed SISS for exposing IPR and Lattimore. "He was the merchant of Stalinist ideology and the salesman of Stalinist policy to the non-Stalinist world," Kristol wrote in a journal called *The Twentieth Century*. ". . . A moral and intellectual *trahison des clercs* that, for the sheer simplicity and magnitude of it, is perhaps without parallel in history."[130]

In between, a few liberals admitted that the committee had actually unearthed some valuable information, while still deploring its methods. *The New Republic*, for example, agreed with SISS that a Communist caucus had infiltrated the Institute for Pacific Relations. "IPR officials knew of this infiltration and tolerated it," the magazine wrote. ". . . IPR gave up its objective research function and adopted the role of advocate in China policy. The record will further indicate that Owen Lattimore knowingly accepted these trends and that he erred in professing naiveté or ignorance before the committee."[131]

Anti-Communist liberals found themselves opposing McCarran but not exactly running to Lattimore's defense. "I am no admirer of Lattimore," Arthur Schlesinger Jr. wrote to Lattimore's attorney Paul Porter. "In my book, he was well on the other side from us on the fight to awaken the U.S. to the dangers of Soviet aggression. . . . But, so far as I know, he committed no crimes; and I think that the persecution of him . . . has been outrageous. I only wish that a greater candor about his own past views would make it easier for some of us to defend him."[132]

In the White House, Truman was incensed. "I do not want to prevent anyone from being prosecuted who deserves it," he told his new attorney general, James McGranery, "but from what I know of this case, I am of the opinion that Davies and Lattimore were shamefully persecuted by this committee, and that if anyone ought to be indicted as a result of these proceedings they are not the ones."[133]

CHAPTER 22

Day of the McCarrans

Mr. Pressman: Back in the early days of the New Deal, on the occasion when I joined, to be a Democrat at that time and to participate in the New Deal program under President Roosevelt was akin to being a Communist in the minds of some people in this country.

Mr. Harrison: You were both, though.

Mr. Pressman: That is correct.[1]

Mr. Matusow: You see, this was all part of this plan that McCarran and McCarthy set up.

Mr. Kahn: Well, before you were talking about McCarran. Now, you bring in the name McCarthy. Evidently it was sponsored by both?

Mr. Matusow: Correct. McCarthy was just as anxious to see these candidates elected or defeated as McCarran.

Mr. Kahn: . . . In other words, you are saying these two worked close together.[2]

$\int$alt Lake City was usually beautiful in October. The worst of the summer heat had gone, but a pleasant warmth lingered in the high-desert air. Set in a wide valley at 4,330 feet, with the Wasatch Mountains shooting up another 7,000 feet to the east, the cityscape was dominated by the copper dome of the state capitol, gleaming under the cobalt blue of the Rocky Mountain sky. The real center of power, however, was the Latter Day Saints Temple in the middle of downtown, a granite fortress crowned by six spires stretching toward heaven, the central steeple rising to 210 feet and topped by a bronze figure of the angel Moroni sounding his trumpet. Fleeing persecution, the Mormons settled in this valley, the last redoubt of ancient Lake Bonneville, which once covered parts of three states and even as a dead sea was still the largest body of water between the Great Lakes and the Pacific. In this wasteland the Mormons built a handsome city, lined with trees and enlivened with flowers and fountains. And with a different mountain peak on every compass point and all the streets laid out on a neat, north–south grid centered on the temple, Salt Lake City resembled nothing more than an idyllic American small town where you always knew where you stood and what was true and what was right. But sometimes, when the brine shrimp died and the algae rotted in the vast lake in the northwest corner of the valley, an awful scent wafted over the city.

On Monday, October 6, 1952, Room 230 of the Salt Lake City Federal Building filled up with as odd an audience as had ever gathered before a hearing of the Senate Internal Security Subcommittee. The hard wooden chairs were packed with blacks and whites and Mexicans, miners most of them, a few in ties, most in open-necked shirts, more than a few without coats at all. Virtually every lapel spotted a union button, and those without a lapel stuck the pin somewhere else. For the International Union of Mine, Mill and Smelter Workers, Salt Lake City looked like it could be the union's last stand.

At the front of the room, behind a line of desks pushed together like a barricade, sat a row of white males in suits: Pat McCarran and Arthur Watkins, flanked by McCarran's right-hand man Jay Sourwine and a burly ex-FBI agent named Don Connors. At sixty-five Watkins was a decade younger than McCarran, a Utah native and former Mormon missionary who was finishing his first term in the Senate and facing a tough reelection contest in another month against Representative Walter Granger, a liberal Democrat who had served in the House for a decade. Although Watkins was a Republican, McCarran wanted to help his colleague gain another term. Which was why SISS was holding a two-member hearing in Salt Lake City.

"McCarran and I became friends," Watkins recalled. "We were in opposite parties, of course, but in many ways alike. From our respective religious faiths, we shared a deep distrust of Communism and were both dedicated to the exposure of Communists in places of influence and their removal from places of trust. McCarran and I had also been judges. . . . We agreed that investigations would be conducted fairly, guided by the evidence and the dictates of judicial practice."[3]

But if Watkin's reelection campaign explained the venue, it was McCarran's own reelection fight eight years earlier that explained the subject: Mine-Mill. The union had led the fight against McCarran in the 1944 primary. And if McCarran had forgotten how the union felt about him (and he hadn't), he had only to look in that morning's *Salt Lake City Tribune*, where a full-page ad (previously run in the *Daily Worker*) showed a picture of a concentration camp in Arizona that could house subversives under McCarran's Internal Security Act. "He has hounded educators, writers, artists, actors, scientists, diplomats and trade unionists," the ad read. "He has struck fear in the hearts of millions of foreign born Americans. He has helped to destroy one article of the Bill of Rights after another. And for those who refuse to 'conform,' for those who see in his reign of terror the ingredients which Hitler poured into his own poison brew, McCarran has brought concentration camps to America."[4]

At 10 A.M. McCarran gaveled the hearing to order. "No honest man need fear the outcome of this investigation," he declared. "Communists may well be concerned."*[5]

When the organizing meeting in Chicago in 1947 turned ugly and the blackjacks came out, Ken Eckert was quick enough but Reid Robinson wasn't. Eckert slipped out of the melee without a bruise, but his Mine-Mill comrade Robinson took a beating. "They label me — and everyone who will not kowtow to the company — as a Red," Eckert complained afterward. "I will stack my Americanism against theirs. . . . To them everyone not yellow must be Red."[6]

Before long, however, Eckert got quite a beating — at the hands of his own comrades. Once Eckert had been a darling of the union. "Eckert," noted a dossier put together on him later by the union, "was judged as a great and militant leader." Events quickly changed that assessment. Eckert was born in 1906. ("He is probably a bastard — literally," the dossier opined. "Apparently there is no birth record.") In 1932 he joined the Communist Party and was sent to Moscow for training at the Lenin School ("Gossip has it that he spent his Moscow sojourn quite pleasantly, feminine companionship and the works"). Back in the United States he became a leader of the National Association of Die Casting Workers, which merged with Mine-Mill in 1942. Eckert earned a reputation as a good union organizer, including his audacious attempt to take Basic Magnesium away from the AFL in Las Vegas, although his relations with

---

*Mine-Mill was one of six radical unions, most of which had been expelled by the CIO, that SISS began investigating in 1951. The others were the American Communications Association; the United Public Workers (whose president, Abraham Flaxner, refused to answer questions in front of SISS and was convicted of contempt of Congress; his two-month jail sentenced was overturned by the Supreme Court); the Dining Car and Railroad Food Workers Union; the Distributive, Processing and Office Workers; and United Electrical, Radio and Machine Workers.

the party were sometimes strained. ("The CP got wind of Eckert's personal immorality — he had a wide reputation as a wolf — and ordered him to clean up his unbecoming conduct or clear out," the dossier continued. "He told CP to go to hell.") When war came, Eckert turned down a military deferment and served with the army. Unlike many party members, he saw front-line combat. ("FBI and G2 were already working on him and trying to scare him into the right camp.") After the war, Eckert became chairman of the Die Casters, although his personal life continued to generate talk among party members. ("She had an abortion. Does his wife know of this?")[7]

For years Eckert himself had been harshly critical of anyone defying the party's position. When Estolv and Angela Ward broke the party's no-strike pledge by leading a walkout at BMI, Eckert was quick to attack them. And at the union's 1947 convention he worked himself into a lather denouncing those who disagreed with the party. "The entire staff of the Casting Division had to be mobilized against the disloyal elements who were trying to wreck the union," he raged. "Dispersing the dense fog of lies, smears, distortions and character assassinations."[8]

The next year, however, Eckert found himself groping through that same dense fog. In 1947 Congress had passed the Taft-Hartley Act, which required labor leaders to sign non-Communist affidavits or risk losing the protection of the National Labor Relations Board, a potentially fatal blow for a union. Party members always said that there was no conflict between being a good Communist and being a good unionist. Taft-Hartley changed that. The CIO's position was to sign the oaths; Mine-Mill and ten other unions with Communist leaders balked. Eckert soon found that companies refused to bargain with the Die Casters because the union wasn't complying with Taft-Hartley. Rival unions raided Die Caster plants, and locals began to secede; Eckert could see the organization dissolving before his eyes. Suddenly he faced a stark choice: Follow the union or follow the party. In 1948 Eckert and the Die Casters walked away from Mine-Mill and joined up with the United Auto Workers. Eckert read in the *Daily Worker* that he had been expelled from the party. "I found out," Eckert said, "that one cannot be a good union man and a Communist Party member, too, and I preferred to be a good union man."[9]

In 1949 Mine-Mill suddenly changed its position and decided to comply with Taft-Hartley. Maurice Travis, the union's secretary-treasurer and its highest-ranking Communist, publicly resigned from the party and signed an affidavit. It was too late. In 1950 the CIO put Mine-Mill on trial to determine if the union was dominated by Communists. The star witness was Eckert, who recalled how the union's leaders used to meet with party officials and follow their instructions. "There were a very few Mine-Mill staff members who were not members of the Communist Party," he said.[10] For years the union's conventions had ritualistically praised Soviet positions and attacked U.S. policies, such as the Marshall Plan. "It is very plain," Eckert testified, "to any fair-minded person who wants to compare both records, the *Daily Worker* and the *Union* paper, that there is no difference whatsoever in any way at any time in the policies that have been advocated by the Mine, Mill and Smelter Workers and the policies advocated by the *Daily Worker.*"[11]

Mine-Mill offered no rebuttal, and its attorney Nat Witt declined to cross-examine Eckert or any other witness. In three years the union's membership had tumbled from more than one hundred thousand to forty-four thousand. "This union," the CIO report found, "had thus, by blindly pursuing the goals of the Communist Party, driven away from it the major portion of its membership."[12]

The CIO expelled Mine-Mill. The union's troubles were just beginning.

Harvey Matusow was wandering around the long hallways of the Senate Office Building. First he visited Joe McCarthy; then he poked his head into the Senate Internal Security Subcommittee office. Matusow wanted someone to talk to. For Matusow, talking was like breathing: something he did constantly and without thinking. Matusow was twenty-six, five foot eight, dark haired, pear shaped, and sullen looking. But his face lit up when he saw Don Connors, a strapping former FBI agent working as an investigator for SISS. Matusow chatted Connors up, and Connors squeezed in enough words to mention that the subcommittee was headed to Salt Lake City to hold hearings on the International Union of Mine, Mill and Smelter Workers. Then the words really poured out of Matusow: He knew some of the union's officials. Connors wanted to hear more. Matusow was happy to talk.

Matusow had been born in the Bronx, had served in World War II, and in 1946, at the age of twenty, had joined the Communist Party. He wasn't very political but he was energetic and eager for attention. He sold enough subscriptions to the *Sunday Worker* to win a trip to Puerto Rico. But Matusow was a man of quick and easily changed enthusiasms, and in 1950 he called the FBI. For a few months he reported on his party activities, then the party kicked him out. Matusow decided to go pro. He made his Washington witness debut before HUAC in February 1952, testifying about Communist activities in youth groups. Then came the call from one of McCarran's investigators. "McCarran Committee boys want to see me," Matusow wrote in his diary. "That's a good sign. I'm on my way."[13] The rest of the year was a blur of activity. Matusow made an appearance in front of SISS, claiming that the Communist Party was trying to infiltrate the Boy Scouts. Next stop was the Subversive Activities Control Board. Then it was back to SISS, where Matusow testified during the IPR hearings that when he worked in a Communist bookstore, Lattimore's books were considered official party dogma. From there Matusow went on to serve as a witness at the Smith Act trial of second-string party leaders. Then he walked into Joe McCarthy's office and volunteered to work for the senator's reelection campaign. McCarthy sent Matusow to Wisconsin during the primary to make speeches — and McCarthy won by a landslide. "There won't be enough cells in federal prisons when I get through," McCarthy told Matusow. "There won't be enough trains leaving Washington to hold them if the Republicans control the Senate."[14]

Then Matusow bumped into Connors, who mentioned the upcoming Mine-Mill hearing. For months, Connors had been researching the union and interviewing former officials such as Ken Eckert. ("He said that Mine, Mill and Smelter is still completely under the control of the Communist Party."[15])

Connors had already lined up five former Mine-Mill officials to testify as friendly witnesses. He added Matusow to that list. In August the subcommittee subpoenaed four union officials to appear at a hearing in Salt Lake City in October. Connors didn't expect the union leaders to say much other than that they were taking the Fifth Amendment, which was fine with the subcommittee. "I am rather certain that these hearings will be successful," Connors told Jay Sourwine. "At any rate, we have subpoenaed a number of really hostile witnesses and highly articulate and well-informed friendly witnesses, all of which makes for a nice contrast and a spirited public hearing."[16]

Sourwine advanced Matusow fifty dollars for airfare. Matusow was going to get to do a lot of talking.

In New York, in September, Mine-Mill vice president Orville Larson stood up before the union's convention and lamented the fact that Pat McCarran was not in attendance. "It is unfortunate," Larson began, "that that poor, old, frightened gentleman in Nevada, Mr. McCarran, could not have been here yesterday and today and see a real American trade union in action."[17]

The union's major action in the summer of 1952 was its "Stop McCarran" campaign. Issue after issue of Mine-Mill's *The Union* newspaper was filled with attacks against McCarran and his policies. *The Union* editor Graham Dolan drove out to Nevada and wrote a booklet ("Sagebrush Caesar") that compiled virtually every slur and innuendo that McCarran's enemies had ever hurled at the senator. Mine-Mill also published a special newsletter called "Facts to Fight McCarran." One hundred twenty locals circulated petitions demanding that McCarran call off the union hearings. Mine-Mill invited hundreds to a Political Action Conference in Salt Lake City the day before the SISS hearing was scheduled. And the union even asked McCarran to come to its national convention. "Answer our charge that you, Senator McCarran, are an enemy of American labor," the invitation went.[18]

Perhaps not surprisingly, McCarran declined. Larson called that a victory. "Now, we have licked McCarran and all he stands for in this convention but that is only part of the job," he said. "The real job is to go back into our local unions, go back into our communities and lick McCarranism there, lick McCarranism on the North American continent."

Larson noted that some union members might be sick of defending its leaders from constant attacks. "If you are tired," he said, "Mr. McCarran has provided a home for you tired people, where you get a good, long rest."

He showed a picture of the government camp in Arizona for detaining subversives. "Nothing less than a complete end to McCarthyism, McCarranism and Smithism, will satisfy us," Mine-Mill declared in stating its political platform.

"We were born in a jail cell but we're telling McCarran that we are not going to rot and die in a McCarran concentration camp," Larson went on. "The day of the McCarrans is over in America."[19]

McCarran skipped Mine-Mill's convention, but later in September he spoke to the American Mining Congress in Denver. McCarran didn't mention Mine-Mill. He didn't have to. McCarran decried a four-day copper strike the summer before that had virtually shut down the industry until Truman invoked the Taft-Hartley Act provisions to order the miners back to work. It was, McCarran said, a threat to national security to have unions in defense-related industries run by Reds. And everyone at the mining industry convention knew which union was to blame for that strike.

On October 3, the day before he was supposed to head to Salt Lake City to testify before SISS, Harvey Matusow bumped into Elizabeth Bentley at the Devin-Adair office. Matusow was trying to pitch the publishing house on a book about the Communist youth movement. "Red Rocks the Cradle," he called the idea. The year before Devin-Adair had published Bentley's memoir, *Out of Bondage.* Now, in the fall of 1952, it was all Bentley could do to keep from crying.

Matusow thought Bentley looked lonely. She was. Bentley was forty-four, with short, curly brown hair, and a potato-sack figure, looking like nothing so much as the middle-aged schoolmarm that she longed to be. Instead she was, as the *New York Telegram* indelibly labeled her, the Blond Spy Queen. And that was hell. The only people who seemed to want to have much to do with her were the FBI agents who called weekly with questions and the investigators from the congressional committees and the government prosecutors who always wanted to put her on the witness stand. Come to dinner with me, Matusow suggested. It's my birthday.

While Chambers was a reluctant witness, an intellectual tortured by his unwanted role as a prophet to a doomed world, Bentley was more willing and talkative, a wounded soul looking for approval and acceptance. Their memoirs sharpened the contrast. Chambers wrote an eight-hundred-page funeral oration for Western civilization (*Witness*); Bentley penned a valentine to the only man she had ever loved, who was fated to have been a Soviet spy runner (*Out of Bondage*). But Bentley soon learned, as Matusow never would, that not all attention is good.

Matusow took Bentley to the Rochanbeau Restaurant on Eleventh Street. "Everybody was all awe-impressed at the sight of Elizabeth Bentley . . . ," Matusow recalled. "And of course, Bentley-Matusow sitting at one table was too much for most people to take."[20] Matusow had bragged to his roommate Llewellyn Watts that he was having dinner with Bentley. Watts showed up at the restaurant with a date to gawk at Bentley like they were going to the theater. Watts stopped by the table, said that he recognized Bentley from her pictures in the paper, and asked her about being a Communist courier. Before Bentley could answer, Matusow started talking about *his* days as a Communist. Bentley opened her mouth. Then Matusow starting tossing off the names he planned to drop in future congressional testimony. Band leader Artie Shaw was one. Practically everyone in show biz, in fact, is tinged with Communism, he said. A third acquaintance happened by the table. Matusow liked nothing better than an audience.

Matusow kept talking. Bentley smiled, but her despair was beyond words. Her life had been pretty much downhill ever since Jacob Golos died in 1943. Who could have guessed that the best boyfriend Bentley would ever have would be a married Russian spy half a foot shorter than her? For the past seven years Bentley had been in almost daily contact with the FBI. It was the longest relationship of her life. To Bentley the bureau's agents became something of a surrogate family. When she got in trouble she turned to them. In 1952 Bentley got in trouble a lot. In April she was drunk and got in a fight with John Burghardt Wright, her boyfriend-handyman, as they were driving from New Haven to Madison, Connecticut. She hit him with her gloves. He struck her. She told the FBI. Some days it seemed like the whole world was beating up on Betty Bentley. She was broke, spiritually as well as financially. She was out of work, out of money, and drinking too much. She started hanging out at the Devin-Adair office because she had no place better to go.

Occasionally the publisher gave her some money, although Bentley had already gone through her three-thousand-dollar advance, which she had spent on a house in Madison. She had also gone through the two thousand dollars that the KGB had given her in 1945, which she subsequently turned over to the FBI, only to ask for it back when things got rough. More and more, Bentley was asking the bureau for money. "She indicated that if the lump sum payment referred to above was not forthcoming in the immediate future," one FBI agent noted, "she would feel disinclined to cooperate in future interviews or to make further appearances as a witness."[21] And with Bentley as the crucial witness in three pending trials and a Subversive Activities Control Board hearing, Hoover wanted to keep her happy. The FBI gave her five hundred dollars and put her on a fifty-dollar-a-week retainer to help out.

Things only got worse. Bentley crashed her car three times, wrecking it in September. A young assistant U.S. attorney named Roy Cohn became Bentley's helpmeet. Cohn handed Bentley's abusive boyfriend a grand jury subpoena and warned him not to interfere with a government witness. Then one day Bentley went to Cohn's office and staged a sitdown strike, refusing to leave until the government provided her with another auto. Cohn found Bentley a car, and bureau agents began driving her around. Her FBI handlers worried about her drinking. "She is probably cracking up emotionally," one agent wrote.[22] Others suggested that it was menopause. Whatever it was, Bentley was becoming a huge pain. "A spoiled child," Cohn called her.[23]

Several weeks after her dinner with Matusow, Bentley met him for lunch, along with Ruth Matthews, the wife of J. B. Matthews. Every time she found a potential job, Bentley said, she was called to testify about something and the employer lost interest. The two women walked out of the restaurant together. "It just doesn't seem worth the struggle," Bentley sighed. "Sometimes I think I should step out in front of a car and settle everything."[24]

Three years later Matusow recalled that he spent the evening of October 3 listening to Bentley's problems. She certainly had problems. But listening to other people, as anyone who knew Matusow could attest, was not his strong point. Matusow remembered that Bentley cried most of the night, complaining about her financial problems, lack of job prospects, and the need to come up with more information for the government — whether or not it was true. Bentley, when the FBI interviewed her in 1955, could not remember the dinner; the three other guests could remember nothing but Matusow's ceaseless chattering.

Doris Hibbard, the date of Matusow's roommate, figured out after an evening with Matusow that he was whacked. "She described him as unstable mentally," reported a FBI agent who interviewed her, "an egomaniac, and an intense individual who demands everyone's attention."[25]

It took years for the ex–FBI agents and other hardened investigators working for McCarran's Internal Security Subcommittee to reach a similar conclusion. Harvey Matusow wanted to be as famous a witness as Elizabeth Bentley. The only difference, for all Bentley's tears and drama, was that she was telling the truth. Matusow was lying.

On Saturday, October 4, McCarran drove from Las Vegas to Salt Lake City and checked into the Hotel Utah. The hotel sat across the street from Temple Square and was the finest in the city, ten stories of white terracotta topped by the state emblem of a beehive, which was lit up in a neon rainbow at night. The beehive sign gave a fair indication of the activity within. The hotel dining room resembled a SISS field office with counsel Jay Sourwine and Richard Arens going over last-minute details at tables beside committee staffers like Don Connors and friendly witnesses such as J. B. Matthews.

Four blocks south on Main Street sat the imposing federal courthouse; across the street was the Hotel Newhouse, filled with hundreds of Mine-Mill members who were holding a Political Action Conference to protest the SISS hearing before it even started. Everyone in the street seemed to be wearing a union pin.

On Monday, McCarran opened the hearing. "If a man comes here,"

McCarran said, "and he is asked, 'Are you a horse thief?' and he is not a horse thief, all he has to do is say, 'No. I am not.' If he comes here and he is asked if he is a Communist and he is not a Communist, all he has to do is say, 'No. I am not.' But when he resorts to the Fifth Amendment and says, 'It might incriminate me if I answered,' his attitude and his conduct must be judged by his answer."[26] Utah's Arthur Watkins was the only other SISS member present. The day passed mostly in executive session, the committee rehearsing the show before raising the curtain to the public.

Tuesday started with J. B. Matthews testifying that Mine-Mill's newspaper had been marching in lockstep with the party line for fourteen years. Ken Eckert recalled his experience as a Communist who met with other party members in the union (Al Skinner, Maurice Travis, and Chase Powers) and took orders from CPUSA leaders such as Gil Green and John Williamson. He named other secret Communists active in the union, such as Clinton Jencks and lawyer Nat Witt. Eckert said that he was a reluctant witness and urged the subcommittee to let labor clean its own house. "We in the labor movement," he said, "are best able to eliminate the control that the Communists have been able to seize in some of these unions."[27]

Maurice Travis was an even more reluctant witness. Travis, the union's secretary-treasurer, wore a patch over his right eye, which he had lost in a fight with rival unionists. "The real boss of the whole outfit," Don Connors called him.[28] In 1949 Travis had publicly resigned from the party in order to sign the Taft-Hartley anti-Communist oath required of union officials. "This has not been an easy step for me to take," Travis wrote in a statement. "Membership in the Communist Party has always meant to me . . . that I could be a better trade unionist."[29]

Travis, as expected, took the Fifth frequently.

"Explain to the subcommittee," Don Connors asked, "why you believe that Communism is consistent with the best interests of the American people or of the Mine, Mill and Smelter Workers Union?"

"I refuse — " Travis said.

"Do you know that it is an old Commie trick to come before a congressional committee and invoke the Fifth?" counsel Richard Arens asked.

"I refuse to answer that question on the grounds — " he replied.

Jay Sourwine tried to question Travis about his membership in the Communist Political Association, also known as the CPA, a photostat of which he waved around. Are you now or have you ever been, Sourwine asked, a certified public accountant?

This time Travis answered directly. No, he said.[30]

Jay Sourwine had just asked Travis a question about the union's counsel Nat Witt when the lawyer stood up and announced that he was in the room and willing to testify without being subpoenaed. Witt had been one of the most powerful men in the union movement, a catalyst that had helped the CIO to become a great force in American politics. In private practice Witt became counsel for Mine-Mill, which had recently been kicked out of the CIO that both Witt and the union had helped to build. McCarran immediately slapped Witt with a subpoena, swore him in as a witness, and then threw him out of the hearing room.

Later McCarran called Witt, forty-nine, back to testify. Pat McCarran and Nat Witt had both arrived in Washington in 1933; their paths to the capital had been as different as their journeys since. McCarran never finished college; Witt graduated from Harvard Law. McCarran opposed the New Deal from its first week, fighting to keep his country the way it was the day he was born; Witt burned with passion to use the New Deal to radically alter his country, to make a revolution in America. McCarran charged that the government was full of Communists; Witt was one.

Witt had followed his friend and fellow Harvard Law alum Lee Pressman to Washington, where they worked in the Agricultural Adjustment Administration. Witt then followed Pressman into the Ware Group, a secret Communist cell of New Dealers. So did their colleagues and friends John Abt and Charlie Kramer. The four friends were joined in the Ware Group by another young man of great promise and hidden passion, Alger Hiss, aloof even during the great days of camaraderie in the early New Deal, doomed to become more alone later.

Witt spent seven years in Washington, rising to become the secretary for the National Labor Relations Board during the glory days of the CIO's massive union-organizing campaign. Forced out of the NLRB, Witt joined his friends who had also left government service for the labor movement. Witt went into private practice with Lee Pressman, representing Mine-Mill and other left-wing unions. In 1948 the four friends threw themselves into Henry Wallace's campaign for president, the last great fling of the hard left in American politics. "The four of us," Abt recalled, "had been best friends and the closest of co-workers for thirty years."[31]

Twenty years earlier Witt and his friends joined the New Deal and could see history flowing their way like a swiftly moving stream. Two decades later the stream was running in the opposite direction and they were struggling to keep their heads above water. After the FBI began seriously investigating Whittaker Chambers's account of the Ware Group, the four friends were interviewed by the bureau, subpoenaed by the New York grand jury, and hauled before HUAC. Invoking the Fifth Amendment was the only thing they had to say to the government they once worked for.

Then, in the summer of 1950 after the outbreak of the Korean War, HUAC summoned the friends back. Lee Pressman was called first. He stunned his friends. He admitted to having been a secret Communist during the early days of the New Deal. He admitted to one year of party membership and fifteen years of fellow traveling. And he named his three friends as secret party members as well, although he denied that Hiss had been part of the Ware Group. The Korean War, he said, had finally convinced him to fully break with the party. His former friends did not believe him. "Lee," Abt complained, "simply found in the war a convenient rationalization for betraying his closest co-workers and his own life's work. . . . His three best friends, perhaps his only three friends."[32] Nor did his enemies. "Pressman was a phony . . . his conversion was not sincere, and I felt it was largely an act that might be put on in order to help Hiss on the appeal case," J. Edgar Hoover wrote.[33] Not long after his HUAC appearance, Witt saw Pressman walking down Broadway. They had been friends, colleagues, and comrades for two decades; law partners who summered in neighboring cottages in Vermont. Witt turned his head away.

In Salt Lake City, Don Connors asked Witt who Lee Pressman was. A lawyer, he replied. When Connors asked Witt if he had ever been a law partner with Pressman, he took the Fifth. Maybe Witt was trying to protect himself. Maybe it all was just too painful.[34]

The U.S. marshal mispronounced his name. Harvey Matusow was in the marshal's office when he was finally called into the crowded hearing room. If his appearance was successful, no one would ever get his name wrong again.

Matusow moved through the mass of Mine-Mill supporters, sure that everyone in the audience was looking at him, afraid to look at their faces in case they weren't. McCarran administered an oath. Matusow, as usual, couldn't hear a word. It didn't matter. I do, he said.

Matusow talked about his favorite subject: himself. How he had joined the Communist Party, how he began to work for the FBI in February 1950, how that summer he spent a week at the San Cristobal Valley Ranch, a former boarding school in the folds of the Sangre de Cristo Mountains near Taos, New Mexico, sort of a dude ranch for comrades. At the ranch, Matusow recalled, he met a Mine-Mill organizer named Clinton Jencks who said that the party was going to stage a strike in a local copper mine to hinder the U.S. war effort in Korea. Most of what Matusow had to say about Mine-Mill had been said already by other witnesses, but he added two key allegations: that Jencks was a party member in June 1950, *after* he had signed a Taft-Hartley anti-Communist oath, and that he'd bragged about calling a strike to hurt the defense industry.

That was enough to make Matusow the star of the show. "I think it will be a dramatic ending," Don Connors wrote in outlining the hearing, "if we have a confrontation between Matusow and Jencks."[35]

It would also make Matusow more famous than he could imagine — and send someone to prison.

Clinton Jencks walked into the hearing room with Nat Witt. Jencks was thirty-four, tall and blond, a veteran of World War II and of the Grant County Jail in Silver City, New Mexico, where he had been served a sub-poena to appear before SISS. Jencks had grown up in a mining town, Colorado Springs, then gone to the University of Colorado, where he was a leader of the radical antiwar American Student Union before the Soviet Union was invaded by the Nazis, at which point Jencks became very pro-war, joining the air force, where he served as a bomber-navigator and won the Distinguished Flying Cross. Afterward he went to work in a smelter, joining Mine-Mill; in 1947 the union assigned him to Silver City, in southwest New Mexico.

Jencks loaded his household belongings into a cattle trailer and with his wife and two children drove south into Grant County, close to the Continental Divide. In Silver City, Jencks found five small locals that had chipped in to hire an organizer. The union hall was a log cabin that could hold a dozen people. Almost all of the miners were Mexican Americans. Few spoke English. The only Spanish words Jencks knew were profanities. A railroad cleaved the town in half; on one side lived Anglos, on the other Mexicans. "Down there," Jencks recalled, "discrimination against Spanish-speaking workers was at least as bad in the Deep South for the black workers. . . . Spanish-speaking workers could only rise to about the level of helper, even if they'd been working there thirty, forty years. They would bring in Anglos, whom these guys would have to train, and then the Anglos would go on up the scale and become journeymen."[36]

The miners nicknamed Jencks *El Palomino*. Sometimes they called him other things. "I hate you," a drunk miner once slurred at Jencks. "All of you with blue eyes."[37] He didn't take it personally. "I was knocking my guts out, working every day, every night," Jencks said. "But I'm fighting two, three hundred years of prejudice and exploitation."[38]

Jencks threw himself into his work. The five locals became one, Mine-Mill 890, moved into a new hall, started a bilingual newspaper and a radio show. In 1950 the union walked out of an Empire Zinc mine in the town of Hanover. When the mine operator got an injunction forbidding the union from setting up a picket line, the miners sent their wives to march. The sheriff arrested more than sixty women and children and threw them into jail. The strike dragged on for fifteen months, finally ending with a settlement in January 1952. In September the local police arrested six union officials, including Jencks, who were given ninety days for contempt of court for violating the injunction. But Jencks could at least take pride in his accomplishments: In seven years daily wages had jumped from three dollars a day to eighteen.

During the strike Jencks took his family on a vacation to the San Cristobal Valley Ranch, outside Taos. It was a well-earned rest. His wife had been beaten up, his daughter arrested, his son tear-gassed. Jencks became friendly with another guest, Paul Jarrico, a Communist screen-writer who had made a film about the Hollywood Ten and then found himself summoned before HUAC. Given the choice between crawling through the mud with informers or going to prison like the Hollywood Ten, Jarrico told reporters, he would rather go to prison. He didn't. He took the Fifth. In Stalin's Russia, blacklisted writers went to the gulag; in Truman's America, blacklisted screenwriters lost two-thousand-dollar-a-week jobs and went square dancing at a dude ranch in New Mexico.

Jarrico was captivated by Jencks's tales about the striking zinc workers in Grant County. "This is a story that's got everything," he enthused. "It's got labor's rights, women's rights, minority rights, all in a dynamic package."[39] Along with Hollywood Ten director Herbert Biberman, who also had time on his hands, Jarrico started working on a movie about the union struggle against Empire Zinc called *Salt of the Earth*. Clint Jencks would play himself. It wasn't too much of a stretch. Mine-Mill organizers had been acting for years.

In Salt Lake City, for instance, Jencks played an outraged civil libertarian. "The intentions and the procedures of this committee are arbitrary and tyrannical," he told McCarran.[40]

"Are you innocent of being a Communist?"[41] McCarran asked.

McCarran, of course, already knew the answer. The committee had FBI dossiers on Mine-Mill's leaders. McCarran knew that Jencks had joined the party in 1940; at his fingertips he had dates and places where the organizer had attended meetings. Jencks, like the rest of the union officials, took the Fifth, including when he was asked if he knew Matusow. When Witt interrupted Jencks because he didn't state that he was taking the Fifth, McCarran cut him off. "I withdraw as counsel because I am not being allowed to act as this man's counsel," Witt said.

"I'm sorry to lose you," McCarran said. "Come back whenever you feel like it."

"You are denying this witness counsel," Witt said.

"Mr. Marshal," McCarran commanded, "remove the gentleman from the room."[42]

Once again, McCarran had Nat Witt thrown out of the hearing room.

McCarran called Matusow back into the room. He stood three feet from Jencks. He repeated his charges.

Afterward Matusow moved through the hallway crowded with Mine-Mill members. He could feel the hostility in the air. "I heard their talk and felt their cursing and I felt their pushing," he recalled.[43]

Someone shoved him. He turned around and threw his knee into a man's groin. Or at least that was his story later. With Matusow you could never be sure.

One day during the hearings Eva Adams called Matusow and asked him to come to McCarran's suite. Adams ushered Matusow into the room, where he found the senator in a chair. McCarran asked him if he knew Hank Greenspun, the feisty editor of the *Las Vegas Sun*, whose newspaper had gone on a crusade against McCarran and McCarthy. "McCarran said he thought Greenspun was a Communist or a Communist fronter," Matusow recalled. "He wanted to know if I, through my connections, could establish this fact. I was elated at the thought of McCarran's coming to me for help and was over-eager as I accepted his invitation."[44]

McCarran, Matusow recalled, asked him to campaign in Nevada on behalf of Molly Malone, the Republican candidate for the Senate. Four days before the election, Matusow arrived in Las Vegas. "My instructions included eavesdropping on bartenders, card-dealers and stickmen at the dice tables, to see if they were supporting McCarran's machine, which was supporting Malone," he later wrote. "I also had a few rumors to spread."[45]

For the next few days Matusow talked his heart out.

—

On Wednesday, McCarran closed the Salt Lake City hearing with an impassioned speech. McCarran pointed out that he had helped write the first law limiting the hours in mines and mills in the country in 1903. "The chairman . . . ," he said, "came from the loins of labor. He was born and reared in a labor home. Everything that surrounded him in his boyhood days was labor." McCarran urged the union rank and file to throw out their Communist leaders. He mentioned a bill he had sponsored (S. 2548) that would prevent a party member from holding a union office or being employed by a union. He mentioned that he was sending a copy of the hearing report to the attorney general for a perjury investigation. "In God's name," McCarran cried, "and in the name of the country to which you belong, to which you give your loyalty as a citizen, your union having been read out of the CIO, your union having its lead membership brought here yesterday who refused to deny under oath that they belonged the Communist Party and followed the Communist line, in God's name as American citizens awaken to the situation that you may cleanse yourself of this situation and not wait for law to deal with these individuals."[46]

The night that the hearings ended McCarran and the SISS staff with their FBI escorts drove over to the Alta Club for a reception and dinner in the senator's honor. Senator Arthur Watkins and Mayor Earl J. Glade toasted McCarran. Harvey Matusow and J. B. Matthews gave quick talks on how the Communists were trying to subvert America. Then Gardner Osborne, the president of the American Coalition of Patriotic Societies, pinned a medal on McCarran's lapel. McCarran thanked the society for the honor and announced that on Monday the Senate Internal Security Subcommittee would open hearings in New York on Communists working for the United Nations. "When we set up the United Nations we thought we were setting up an organization for the peace of the world," McCarran said. "Little did we believe the United Nations would be a vantage ground for the infiltration of the United States."[47]

The United Nation's striking new high-rise on Manhattan's East Side was two weeks away from a gala inaugural bash. McCarran wanted to shut it down before it ever opened.

—

Not long after the Salt Lake City SISS hearings, a group of Mine–Mill representatives from locals in Tennessee met with Senator Estes Kefauver for an hour. Kefauver was one of the few liberals on the Judiciary Committee, and Mine–Mill was hoping to spark some opposition to McCarran on the committee. "My thought here is that they might be persuaded to undertake a campaign within the Judiciary Committee against the procedures and activities of the subcommittee," explained Rod Holmgren, the union's public relations director.[48]

The union was desperate to fight McCarran. Mine–Mill was already active in the Committee to Repeal the McCarran Act, a front group fighting the Internal Security Act and its provisions to make the party register with the government and deport foreign-born Communists. "A continual drumfire of information about McCarranism should be gotten out," Holmgren urged.[49]

After the Salt Lake City hearing, Mine–Mill's leaders had hoped to build a Popular Front revival against McCarran and McCarthy. Half a year later those hopes had collapsed. Estes Kefauver had told the union delegation as much. "Kefauver was genuinely sympathetic to our position on McCarran," the union's Alton Lawrence noted, "but seemed to doubt there was very much he could do. He stated that there was no way he knew of to block a report or to get a minority report out of the subcommittee since it was completely dominated by McCarran."

Kefauver and his liberal friends in the Senate hated McCarran. "McCarran," Kefauver told the Mine–Mill reps, "is nothing but a little Franco." But he saw scant hope of things changing anytime soon. "If he were to vote according to the correspondence and pressure brought to bear on him from Tennessee," Lawrence reported Kefauver as saying, "he would vote with McCarran and McCarranism all the way down the line."[50]

In early 1953 Clint Jencks was getting ready to play the role of a mine union organizer who battles company thugs one morning when actual thugs showed up on the movie location in the small town in Grant County, New Mexico. The beating they gave him, too, was real.

After a year of difficulties and delays, Paul Jarrico and Herbert Biberman were finally making their film about the Mine–Mill strike against Empire Zinc: *The Salt of the Earth*. In the 1950s it would be hard to think of a less commercial enterprise: a group of blacklisted Hollywood Communists making a movie about a radical, Communist-led union going on strike in a defense-related industry during the Korean War. But the script (by party member Michael Wilson) eliminated the Cold War background and context of the strike, stripping it down to a parable about miners who wanted better wages and conditions and a callous company that treated its workers like shovels and picks, tools to extract profit from the earth, not men to be treated with dignity and respect. "The fantastic aspect of this work," Biberman enthused, "is that it makes so real what we have believed for so long . . . that the talent hidden in the vast majority of the world's people is monumental beyond estimation and that as it is exploded into life we will have a world beyond all the calculations of men and women. This is the inspiriting aspect of this work . . . the vast and unmeasured power and dignity of the working multitudes of this earth."[51] Clint Jencks was more blunt. "A weapon," he called the film.[52]

Making the movie would turn out to be almost as arduous as the fifteen-month strike itself. In Hollywood the anti-Communist production union, the International Alliance of Theatrical Stage Employees and Moving Picture Operators, boycotted the project. Jarrico couldn't find many professional actors willing to work on the film, so he cast miners and their wives to play themselves.

In January 1953 Jarrico arrived in New Mexico with his ragtag collection of actors and production people; Mine-Mill Local 890 issued union cards to the crew. Before long conservative columnists were complaining about Communists making a propaganda picture in New Mexico, not far from the nuclear weapons lab at Los Alamos. In February, HUAC's Donald Jackson denounced the film on the House floor. "A new weapon for Russia," Jackson called the movie. ". . . Deliberately designed to inflame racial hatreds and to depict the United States as the enemy of all colored peoples."[53]

The next day two INS agents showed up on the set and arrested Rosaura Revueltas, the Mexican actress playing the female lead. She was deported on a passport technicality. A film-processing lab in Hollywood canceled its contract to process the rushes. The producers couldn't find another lab, so they had to make the second half of the film without reviewing what they were shooting. In the final film you can see light stands in one scene.

Early one morning Biberman drove into the town of Central with a small crew. They set up their equipment in the street. Eight men, some with guns, walked up. "Get going," one said.[54] Biberman offered to show them a letter from the mayor. The mayor doesn't run the town, one man said. We do. You can leave on your own or we can help you leave. The crew decided to pack up.

Another day the crew tried to shoot a scene of a car driving through town. This time they hastily set up in front of the Silver City union hall. As soon as Biberman finished his shot, two cars screeched to a stop and a dozen men jumped out. They knocked over the camera and threw punches. "We don't wan' no Roosian Commonists," one of the men said.[55]

One night someone put five bullets into Jencks's car. The union hall was set afire. A Mine-Mill official's house was burned down. Production was wrapped up with state troopers standing guard. Postproduction didn't go much easier, and the film wasn't released until 1954. Distributors and theater owners shunned the movie. Newspapers and radio stations wouldn't take advertising for it. The American Legion protested at the few venues that did show *The Salt of the Earth*. Reviewers called it propaganda. "Aside from possibly some pornographic films," Jarrico recalled, "it was the only film ever made underground in the United States or at least completed underground."[56]

Back in 1951, when the House Un-American Activities Committee reopened its probe of Communists in the movie industry and the Hollywood blacklist began, a number of conservatives in the industry tried to interest McCarran in bringing his new Senate Internal Security Subcommittee to town. McCarran's aide Don Connors met with MGM's Louis B. Mayer, who couldn't say enough good things about SISS. "Mayer was very frank and open and indicated that he was an extremely warm admirer of Senator McCarran and had considerable faith in the Internal Security Subcommittee," Connors reported to Eva Adams.[57] "A whole group of people headed by Adolphe Menjou began to build up a campaign that the McCarran Committee take over the motion picture investigation because of the inadequacy of the House job," Robert Morris told Jay Sourwine several months later. "Apparently this is a definite growing demand."[58] HUAC's return to Hollywood was giving the committee its biggest headlines since Chambers-Hiss three years earlier, but however attractive the publicity seemed, McCarran's committee had more serious business to pursue. "Right now we are so tied up with IPR we can not possibly come near to that," Morris told Sourwine.[59]

But by late 1952 Jay Sourwine thought that it might be time for SISS to launch yet another probe of Communist influence in the movie industry. "It would be possible," he told Eva Adams, "to go into Hollywood and hold a series of hearings which would put the House Un-American Activities Committee hearings in that connection in complete shade."[60]

Hollywood was only one item on Sourwine's wish list of investigations. He jotted down some possibilities for McCarran: Communism in education ("a tremendous field here"), subversive writing ("who writes for a particular magazine or for a particular publisher"), Communism in Hawaii ("The House Un-American Activities Committee has taken five volumes of testimony in the Islands. . . . We should be careful to avoid any suggestion or appearance of following in the footsteps of the House committee"), Communism in San Francisco Bay Area ("the domination of Harry Bridges"), the CIO PAC ("it may turn out to be one of the most important tasks the committee could undertake, reaching some dangerous subversive characters who probably could not be reached any other way, and who certainly could not be attacked frontally at this time"), labor unions ("Loose charges must be avoided and a shotgun approach must be avoided").

The problem was that there weren't enough senators to go around. SISS had started breaking into one-man subcommittees, such as in September when Homer Ferguson spent a week investigating Communists in New York City schools. Thirty teachers took the Fifth and were summarily dismissed by the school board. But there were more investigative possibilities than even SISS could go after. "One of the most difficult problems during this period was to arrange for a senator to be present," Bob Morris recalled. ". . . We could have had two or three times as many teachers as witnesses if we had been able to secure the presence of a senator."[61]

The day was warm and clear in Silver City, and Clint Jencks didn't bother to put on shoes when he went into his front yard with his son to play. It was April 1953; the Hollywood people were gone, and life had returned to normal in Grant County.

Then the FBI agents arrived. They told Jencks that they had a warrant for his arrest for perjury. Jencks wanted to go inside and get his shoes. The agents said no, they couldn't let him out of their sight. Jencks hollered into the house at his wife, who came out with her husband's shoes. Jencks went to jail.

Harvey Matusow had repeated his SISS testimony to an El Paso grand jury, charging that Jencks had been in the party in June 1950, *after* he had signed a Taft-Hartley affidavit declaring that he was not a Communist. Matusow testified at the trial; Jencks didn't take the stand to deny the charges. The jury took twenty minutes to find him guilty, and the judge gave him five years in prison.

Matusow's career as a professional ex-Communist witness was really taking off. Whittaker Chambers had sent Alger Hiss to jail. Elizabeth Bentley had done the same to William Remington. Now Matusow had gotten Jencks.[62]★

★The case of Jencks and other Mine-Mill officials accused of lying when they signed their Taft-Hartley non-Communist affidavits dragged on until 1966, when the Supreme Court threw out the convictions.

CHAPTER 23

Keep Out

> **Reporter:** "You seem closer to the Republicans than to
> the Democrats."
> **McCarran:** "I'm not certain, maybe I am."[1]

On November 13, 1952, the SS *Uruguay* slipped away from the pier at Fifty-fifth Street in Manhattan and sailed down the East River on its way to South America. In the ship's finest suite, Pat and Birdie McCarran enjoyed a private balcony from which they could watch the magnificent New York skyline slide by. Before long, around Forty-eighth Street, a thirty-nine-story slab of glass and steel rose over the river. The building was the office of the United Nations secretariat, fittingly designed by Le Corbusier in the International Style, finished just three weeks earlier and already an icon of Cold War diplomacy. After clearing the tip of Manhattan, the ship nosed into New York Harbor, where to starboard the Statue of Liberty raised her torch to the world, a beacon of hope held aloft three hundred feet into the sky. From the ship the statue looked so small.

Recently *Washington Post* cartoonist Herb Block had begun to lampoon McCarran's efforts to reshape the New York skyline. In one drawing McCarran forces the Statue of Liberty to drop her torch and bend over backward, kicking one leg out to the world in a gesture of hostility instead of welcome. KEEP OUT is scrawled on the statue's pedestal. THIS MEANS YOU![2] In another, McCarran pitches bricks at the UN building, pocking its smooth skin with broken windows. WHY DON'T YOU GO BACK WHERE YOU CAME FROM?[3] McCarran bellows.

In the fall of 1952 McCarran broke much more than glass.

Shortly after the McCarran Internal Security Act took effect in September 1950, Waclaw Furtha[4] received a summons from the Immigration and Naturalization Service. Furtha had been born in Poland, lost his entire family during the war, and in 1948 arrived in New York on the steamship *Batory*. At the age of thirty-seven he was still young enough to start a new life in the land of opportunity. He settled in Plainfield, New Jersey, and found a job in a hat shop. Then came the McCarran Act, and suddenly anyone who came from a Communist country had to establish that he had never been a member of the party or face deportation. The INS ordered

Furtha to appear at a hearing. Furtha wrote a letter, explaining that he had never been a Communist, that the Communist government ruling his homeland would kill him, and that he would rather die in his adopted country with honor.

So he cut an artery in his leg and bled to death.

Ellen Knauff first saw the Statue of Liberty from the deck of an army transport ship steaming toward a Manhattan pier after crossing the Atlantic in August 1948. Several hours later she saw Lady Liberty again, this time from an army tugboat that pulled up to a patch of landfill in the statue's shadow, just off the New Jersey coast. A stately Victorian building fronted by two peaked towers rose from the island, surrounded by a fence topped with barbed wire. A series of boxy outbuildings reminded Knauff of dog kennels. For most of the next three years this was home: Ellis Island.

On Ellis Island a series of bells tolled away throughout the day: time to rise, time to eat, time to go to sleep. But most of the time life at the immigration detention center was unhurried. Then the McCarran Act went into effect and the island was overrun. "Ellis Island began to bulge at the seams with a sudden influx of travelers from Germany and Italy . . . ," Knauff recalled. "The noise became unbearable and the establishment was a complete madhouse."³

Knauff (née Raphael) was born in Germany; her parents died in a concentration camp. She fled to England, worked for the Royal Air Force during the war, and afterward went back to Germany with the American Military Government. In 1948, when she was thirty-three, she married Kurt Knauff, a U.S. soldier stationed in Germany. Five months later she sailed by herself on an army transport ship named the *Comfort* to New York to beat the deadline for war brides to immigrate to the United States. After the ship docked, immigration authorities diverted Knauff to Ellis Island. Knauff's name, it turned out, was on a list of people not to let into the country. In America in midcentury this was a very long list.

Immigration authorities would not tell Knauff why, only that her admission would be prejudicial to the best interests of the country — a threat, in other words, to national security. The Justice Department wanted to send Knauff back to Germany; she spent the next nine months on Ellis Island. In 1949 the Supreme Court granted Knauff bail and let her into Manhattan while it considered her case. In January 1950 the Court upheld the government's authority to keep people out of the country without granting them a hearing. "The exclusion of aliens is a fundamental act of sovereignty," Justice Sherman Minton wrote in *U.S. ex rel. Knauff v. Shaughnessy*.[6] Robert Jackson (with Black and Frankfurter joining) dissented. "Security is like liberty in that many are the crimes committed in its name," he wrote. "The menace to the security of this country, be it great as it may, from this girl's admission is as nothing compared to the menace to free institutions inherent in procedures of this pattern."[7]

The next month Knauff was back on the island. In April the House Judiciary Committee unanimously reported a private bill to admit Knauff to the country, which was passed in May. Then the Justice Department tried to deport Knauff, taking her to the airport. Knauff won a last-minute Supreme Court reprieve, although her luggage still went to Germany.

Knauff's attorney went to see Pat McCarran, the chairman of the Senate Judiciary Committee, who promised to quickly take up the private immigration bill. Then McCarran changed his mind. "I never heard of the case," he told a reporter. "What's all the hullabaloo about?"[8] Knauff was still optimistic. "At the time this did not worry me," she recalled. "Nor did I realize the weight Senator McCarran was to carry and soon to use."[9]

In July, two and a half months after the House passed a bill admitting Knauff into the country, McCarran's immigration subcommittee finally took up the matter. "*NO!*"[10] McCarran scrawled over the proposal. "The exclusion of the alien appears fully warranted," the subcommittee concluded.[11]

In the White House, Truman asked Steve Spingarn to try to resolve the case. "I wish you would look into it," Truman told him, "and see if anything can be done to straighten it out."[12] Once again Spingarn asked the attorney general for a file. It took six weeks of complaining before he finally saw the Justice Department record on Knauff. It turned out that a week before Knauff had arrived in New York, the Immigration and Naturalization Service decided to bar Knauff the United States based on an FBI report that she had secretly worked for the Communist government of Czechoslovakia while employed by the U.S. Military Government in Germany. The Justice Department evidence — unsupported allegations from two sources of unknown reliability — did not impress Spingarn. "It seems to me most meager despite the seriousness of the allegations," he wrote.[13]

A month after the McCarran Act became law, the two-story great hall at Ellis Island was crowded with more than six hundred people, more than twice the usual number, some sitting on hard benches, more on the ground, all waiting for an interview with an immigration inspector. Austrian Friedrich Gulda, twenty, was stopped when he landed at Idlewild Airport in Queens in October 1950 on his way to give a piano recital at Carnegie Hall. A decade earlier Gulda had belonged, as all Austrian boys and girls did, to Hitler Youth. He was shipped to Ellis Island, where he entertained his fellow internees by practicing on a battered old piano.[14] When the *Saturnia*, docked in New York in November 1950, more than a quarter of the foreigners on board, 130 people, were ferried over to Ellis Island, where they joined a group of Italian singers who had been headed to the Metropolitan Opera and eighty-six foreign-born American Communists whom the Justice Department was trying to deport — the first names on a list of thirty-four hundred resident alien party members slated for ejection from the country. Thirty-eight German war brides and seven children were pulled off another ship, as well as fourteen Germans who were on a U.S. government junket to see how democracy works. "We'd be ashamed if such a thing happened in our country," one of the Germans told Knauff.[15] A reporter noted that many of the detained looked bewildered. "Yes," quipped Immigration Commissioner Edward J. Shaughnessy, "it's a bewildering law."[16]

The immigration service even stopped visitors who had been drafted into the German or Italian armies during the war. Refugees who had been cleared by U.S. security authorities in German displaced persons camps reached New York only to be interned on the island, which began to resemble a DP camp with a better view. "This interpretation," wrote White House aide David Lloyd, "has, I am told, brought the operation of the Displaced Persons Act almost to a standstill."[17]

That, as the *Washington Post* noted, was the point. "Manifestly this law cannot be enforced without making the United States look ridiculous," observed the *Post*. ". . . As long as this piece of panic legislation remains on the statute books, it will subject the United States to the laughter and the contempt of the civilized world. It drops, and was intended to by its authors to drop, an asbestos curtain against supposedly inflammatory ideas around this country's ports of entry. It will require an examination of the present and past political beliefs of all sorts of nonpolitical persons — artists, businessmen, tourists — who are not in the most remote sense dangerous to the security of the United States. There is no way to make it rational by administrative regulations. Only Congress can correct this fiasco for which it is responsible."[18]

Then immigration authorities went too far: They stopped a contingent of Basque sheepherders heading to Nevada on the grounds that they had been members of Franco's fascist party. McCarran amended the act to make it easier for people who had involuntarily joined totalitarian organizations to enter the country.

When it came to Ellen Knauff, McCarran refused to budge. In 1951 Knauff's husband, Kurt, visited Washington and spoke to Democratic representative Francis Walter and Republican senator William Langer, who had introduced new bills in both houses to admit Knauff to the country. The lawmakers assured Knauff that the membership of both judiciary committees supported the legislation — with one noteworthy exception. "All but McCarran on our side," Kurt Knauff wired his wife.[19]

In January 1951 the attorney general again released Knauff, granting her bail while her case dragged on. In March the INS finally gave Knauff a hearing and ruled against her. In May she was sent back to Ellis Island. Knauff's last chance was the Board of Immigration Appeals, which examined her case and concluded in August that there was no evidence to justify keeping her out of the country; it sent the decision to Attorney General Charles McGrath for approval. "There is no charge that Mrs. Knauff is or has been a Communist," the board ruled. "There is not the faintest thread of traditional party line thinking or Marxist philosophy apparent in her background."[20] In November 1951, more than three years after Ellen Knauff arrived in New York married to a citizen and a war veteran, she was finally officially admitted to the United States.

By then McCarran had already started to work on a new immigration bill so that it wouldn't be so easy to get into the country.

On March 7, 1951, Pat McCarran opened a joint Senate-House hearing by declaring that it was time for the first systematic revision of the nation's immigration law since the republic's founding. For the last four years no subject had been more important to McCarran, who had appointed himself chairman of the Judiciary's immigration subcommittee, which had spent almost three years studying the matter and produced a bill the size of the Washington phone book. Joining McCarran was Francis Walter, a conservative Democrat from Pennsylvania who was chairman of the House Judiciary Committee's immigration panel. Both lawmakers had sponsored omnibus immigration bills that attempted to codify and smooth out a rough patchwork of laws and regulations stitched together over the last 150 years. While not identical, the two bills were close enough, in both spirit and detail, that *McCarran-Walter* soon tripped off the tongue as shorthand for the proposed legislation. McCarran called the first witness.

"I asked to be heard," interrupted New York representative Emmanuel Celler.

"I know you want to be heard," McCarran responded. Celler, he added, could talk later.

Celler was McCarran's counterpart on the south side of the Capitol, the chairman of the House Judiciary Committee, a Democrat with twenty-eight years of seniority. In every other aspect, Celler was McCarran's exact opposite: an urban liberal, a Brooklyn Jew — and author of his own immigration bill, which was as different from McCarran's as McCarran was from Celler. The congressman had already publicly blasted McCarran's bill as a thought-control measure because of its numerous restrictions against alleged subversives.

McCarran slammed his gavel down. "I am the chairman of this committee," he said.

Celler claimed that he had just as much right to be chairman of a joint hearing.

"You couldn't get away with it," McCarran snapped.

McCarran and Celler glared at one another. Finally, McCarran granted Celler three minutes. The congressman ran through a statement about the need to liberalize immigration law and finished in eight minutes. McCarran icily called the first witness. Celler slapped on his hat and walked out of the room. Then the hearing went on as McCarran had planned.[21]

For the next fifteen months conservatives and liberals would shout themselves hoarse over immigration policy — but in the end McCarran would dominate the legislation as thoroughly as he controlled the hearing on that first day.

If you wanted to leave the country in 1952, you had to ask Ruth Shipley. Shipley was a sixty-seven-year-old widow who lived with her sister in a large old house in Chevy Chase called the Parsonage because it had belonged to their father, a Methodist minister. At work they called her Ma. Work happened to be the State Department's division of passports.

Shipley was the most powerful woman in Washington. She was one of those bureaucrats who, like J. Edgar Hoover, went to work for the federal government straight out of school and stayed for life, becoming virtually synonymous with her domain and growing impervious to the dictates and importunings of her nominal superiors, including the president. Shipley (née Bielaski) joined the Patent Office at the age of eighteen in 1903; twenty-five years later she became chief of the State Department's passport division, a job she held until she retired in 1955. "The Queendom of Passports," Dean Acheson called it.[22] "Old Mrs. Bottleneck," others called her. "No office in Washington carries such impenetrable armor," wrote columnists Robert S. Allen and William V. Shannon.[23]

Every day for a quarter century Shipley was at work by nine-thirty. Her huge desk was piled high with two stacks: letters asking for passports and the little green books themselves, which she signed R. B. SHIPLEY — if she signed at all. More and more often she didn't. For years Shipley had been refusing to give passports to people she suspected of disloyalty to the United States. If she had any doubts, she could go to her records: twelve hundred filing cabinets filled with dossiers on some twelve million citizens. If she still had questions, she could ask her friend FBI director J. Edgar Hoover. Or two of her brothers, who had worked for the FBI and the OSS and were now private investigators. Or her retired sister, who had worked for the CIA and military intelligence. "One of the things I believe in is refusing passports to Communists," Shipley said once. "They've been working against us for a long time."[24]

But in the 1950s even anti-Communists could have trouble getting permission to go abroad. Joe Lash, for example, was a founding member of the staunchly anti-Communist ADA, although years earlier during the Popular Front he had been a fellow traveler. When Lash applied to go to Europe as a correspondent for the liberal *New York Post*, he couldn't get a passport. "Back in the thirties Joe was guilty of association with some dangerous characters, just as much as most of us were," *Post* editor James Wechsler complained to his friend Adrian Fisher, the State Department legal adviser. "For at least the last twelve years — I believe somewhat longer — Joe has been one of the guys whom the Commies hate most and they have said so in any number of printed documents. . . . If Joe McCarthy were running the State Department, this would be perfectly understandable. But I'm damned if I can understand how Dean Acheson's State Department can operate this way. Day after day for the past few months the *Post* has been one of the few papers in the country fighting the State Department's battle — against both McCarthy and the Commies. I dread to find myself in the ludicrous position of having to inform our readers that this great department won't give our UN correspondent a passport."[25]

Lash finally got a passport. Others were less lucky, such as Truman's friend Max Lowenthal, who had infuriated J. Edgar Hoover with a critical book about the FBI. Truman wrote a letter to Shipley complaining about some of the people she had given passports to, such as hyperconservative columnist Westbrook Pegler ("a louse"[26]) and Alfred Kohlberg ("next door to a number one traitor"[27]). "I want a report in writing," the president ordered, "and I want it *promptly* as to why an honorable decent citizen is refused a passport and a couple of crumbs can receive passports."[28]

Truman never mailed the letter. Even the president didn't want to tussle with Shipley. But in June 1952, Oregon's Wayne Morse attacked Shipley on the Senate floor when Nobel Prize winner Linus Pauling couldn't get a passport to go to a scientific conference in London because he had belonged to several front groups. "This was government by a woman rather than by law," Morse said.[29]

McCarran came to Shipley's defense. He was a big fan of hers. In 1950 McCarran's Internal Security Act had banned members of the Communist Party or its front groups from applying for or using passports. "All the protective measures against subversives," McCarran said, "came from the mind of Mrs. Shipley."[30] Morse, McCarran said, was trying to help the Communists. "Instead of being criticized, Mrs. Shipley should be commended for efficiency, courtesy and fair play," McCarran said. "No greater service could be rendered the Kremlin than to publicly disclose the security information of our intelligence agencies respecting the identity and operations of the Communist conspiracy in the United States." And the fact that three hundred Americans had been denied passports in the past few months was nothing to complain about. "If passports have been denied in certain cases in which the senator from Oregon is interested," McCarran said, "then the embarrassment is his and not the passport division of the State Department."[31]

After McCarran left the chamber, Morse lashed back. "I am not embarrassed," Morse yelled. ". . . There is nothing omnipotent or infallible about Mrs. Shipley that causes me to think she should be given unchecked power over the rights and liberties of American citizens. I propose to keep up this fight and the senator from Nevada cannot stop me."[32]

The State Department eventually created a Board of Passport Appeals, which required the appellant to sign a non-Communist oath. Although in its first nine months the board never met to consider a case, Pauling eventually got a passport, albeit one restricted to two scientific conferences.

The Queendom of Passports was not threatened. "By all means, complain to the president himself," Shipley bragged to a reporter, "but he'll refer you right back to me and I'll say no."[33]

On May 13, 1952, Pat McCarran opened one of the most momentous legislative battles in U.S. history, a debate over what kind of country America was and what kind of nation it would be for decades to come. "A sound immigration and naturalization system is essential to the preservation of our way of life," McCarran said.[34]

Herbert Lehman asked McCarran to yield so that he could say something. McCarran refused. Again and again on this day Lehman tried to interrupt McCarran; again and again McCarran refused to let Lehman speak. The immigration debate was turning out to be less a battle than a massacre. Immigration had become McCarran's white whale, a submerged beast threatening doom. Whether refugees from displaced persons camps or UN diplomats, foreigners had become synonymous with subversives to McCarran. For the last five years he had been trying to tighten immigration policy every chance he could get: The Displaced Persons Act and the McCarran Internal Security Act, for example, both made it harder for people to immigrate to America or even visit the country. "This was the thing that he worked on and dreamed of day and night," McCarran's friend Norm Biltz recalled, "to block it every way possible."[35]

Now McCarran had a new bill: the Immigration and Nationalities Act of 1952, soon to be known as the McCarran-Walter Act, which codified and strengthened decades of law. McCarran's bill left intact the essential feature of U.S. immigration policy: the quota system put in place during the last major overhaul, the 1924 immigration act, which granted visas to countries based on their representation in the U.S. population in 1920. The result was a system that allotted generous quotas to Britain, which couldn't use them all, and very small ones to countries such as Italy, which had a huge visa backlog. Unused quotas could not be transferred from one country to another.

McCarran's bill did make one huge change in the law: It let Asians become citizens. In recent years immigrants from some Asian countries had become eligible for nationalization: China in 1943, followed by India and the Philippines in 1946. But even while American troops were dying to protect Korea, its nationals could not become U.S. citizens. Removing the last racial bar to citizenship (Africans became eligible in 1871, American Indians in 1924) was so important to U.S. foreign policy that Dean Acheson urged Truman to sign the bill for that reason alone.

"McCarran had pulled a slick one in getting this inserted into the legislation," Senator William Benton told Acheson.[36]

Benton went to the secretary on behalf of the Senate liberals who were outraged that Acheson supported the McCarran bill. Benton said that poor Herbert Lehman was devastated by the blow, which he thought had cost the liberals the margin of votes that could have sustained a presidential veto. "He was extremely upset at the knowledge which he had of the department's recommendation," Acheson's aide Lucius Battle noted. "He said he was shocked at our support and thought we had made a great mistake." Acheson showed Benton cables from the ambassador in Tokyo explaining how important the measure was to the Japanese. "It was our obligation to report to the president the views of our Far Eastern friends on this subject," Acheson explained.[37]

To the White House that was the *only* good thing about the proposal. The McCarran-Walter bill also sharpened the ideological teeth on immigration law, allowing potential subversives, loosely defined, to be more easily banned from visiting the country or deported after arrival, as well as making appeals more difficult. "The McCarran bill," White House aide David Lloyd told Truman, "embodies Senator McCarran's philosophy of how to treat aliens and naturalized citizens."[38]

Liberals were so aghast at the bill's restrictions that they lined up to tell Truman that the price of removing racial discrimination from immigration law was simply too steep; that no new law would be far better than McCarran's. "It would be a repudiation of all you have accomplished, over Senator McCarran's bitter opposition, on the Displaced Persons program," Harry N. Rosenfield, head of Truman's Displaced Persons Commission, told the president.[39] "We might as well send the Statue of Liberty back to France," added Drew Pearson.[40]

The liberals furiously drafted a substitute bill sponsored by Lehman, Hubert Humphrey, and a host of their colleagues who had fought McCarran on one immigration bill after another over the years. The liberal substitute would allow immigration quota pooling as well as removing racial bars to citizenship and easing ideological restrictions. "An excellent bill in most respects," David Lloyd told Truman.[41]

McCarran noted that every senator who voted against the Internal Security Act was listed as a sponsor of the Humphrey-Lehman substitute. He as much as accused the liberals of being Communists. "I know that this bill," he said, "is wholly unsatisfactory to and is vigorously opposed by certain elements which are bent upon the destruction of our protective immigration and naturalization system."[42]

After ignoring Lehman eight times, McCarran finally yielded. Lehman took the floor. McCarran left the chamber, followed by most of the remaining senators. "The senator from Nevada," Lehman said, "has questioned, at least by implication, the loyalty and patriotism of the senators who oppose the enactment."[43] McCarran, Lehman continued, had refused to hold hearings on the liberal immigration bill for eight months. The senator, he said, would accept no bill except his own. But the McCarran bill was vile. "This philosophy is a xenophobic philosophy," Lehman said. "It is a racist philosophy. It is a philosophy of fear, suspicion and distrust of foreigners outside our country and of the aliens within our country. It is a philosophy which is plainly prejudiced against immigration. It is a philosophy which accepts or rather tolerates a trickle of immigration, but surrounds it with such hedges, barriers and obstacles as to make it a virtually impossible course to follow."[44]

Lehman was right on every point, but the votes had walked out of the chamber with McCarran. In the Senate press gallery, Hank Greenspun watched McCarran's treatment of Lehman during the immigration debate and boiled. Greenspun was the publisher of the *Las Vegas Sun*. He was also a New York Jew who had fought the Nazis during World War II and the Arabs during the Israeli war for independence, and he considered McCarran an enemy of the same magnitude as either. "I think we all know where the opposition to his bill comes from," McCarran had said, looking at Lehman. "It's a gang of cloak and suiters from New York."

Greenspun went down to the Senate cloakroom after the debate to find Lehman. "For what that man said out there today," Greenspun promised, "I'm going to hound him to his death."[45]

McCarran was the only senator who spoke in favor of his bill. For ten days he fought the liberals single-handedly. Herbert Lehman, Paul Douglas, Hubert Humphrey, William Benton, and liberal Republican Wayne Morse spelled each other on the floor. They tried McCarran's own tricks against him, moving to recommit the bill to the Judiciary Committee for further study, making a motion to substitute their own bill, heaping 189 amendments on McCarran's. "We have a story to tell," Lehman said. "We have logic, justice, fair play and humanity on our side. And we are going to tell that story. I think we may be debating this bill for a long, long time."[46]

Three days later it was all over. The vote to recommit failed. The substitute maneuver failed. The amendments failed. Although liberal and moderate Republicans crossed party lines to vote with the liberal Democrats, the southern Democrats followed McCarran as if he were Robert E. Lee. On May 22 the Senate passed McCarran's bill. McCarran appointed the conference committee, packing it with six members of SISS (including himself) and excluding liberals and moderates altogether. On June 11 the Senate took up the revised McCarran-Walter bill, with fewer than a score of lawmakers on the floor. The Senate passed the bill by a voice vote and sent it to the White House. "I don't know what is happening to the committess in the Congress," Truman fumed. "I sent a message to the Congress with the bill for the admission of some three hundred thousand more refugees and all I got was this terrible McCarran bill."[47]

Would Truman sign it? "Even for the president of the United States," Displaced Persons Commission head Harry Rosenfield noted, "it took guts to stand up against McCarran."[48]

On June 25, Truman sent the bill back, unsigned. The president called the bill's ideological provisions worse than the Alien and Sedition Acts. "Seldom has a bill," he wrote, "exhibited the distrust evidenced here for citizens and aliens alike   at a time when we need unity at home, and the confidence of our friends abroad."[49] McCarran accused Truman of following the Communist Party line. "One of the most un-American acts I have witnessed in my public career," McCarran called the veto.[50] Two days later Congress overruled the president once again and the McCarran-Walter bill became law. "That McCarran-Walter bill I think is about the worst piece of legislation that has ever been placed on the books of the government of the United States," Truman told his friend Max Lowenthal.[51]

Truman had one trick left. One of McCarran's pet provisions in the new law elevated the State Department's Office of Security and Consular Affairs to a quasi-independent bureau, thus taking away control of issuing visas and passports from Foggy Bottom and putting it into the hands of a new agency that owed its creation and survival to Congress in general and to McCarran specifically. The head of the bureau, in McCarran's original version, would have to be a native-born citizen. White House aide David Lloyd was convinced that McCarran had already virtually taken over the passport and visa offices, which were headed by his ideological allies Ruth

Shipley and Herve L'Heureux. "We already had trouble in the field of immigration policy because the Visa Division in the State Department under Mr. L'Heureux plays footsie with McCarran and is practically outside the control of the secretary of state," Lloyd told Truman in May.[52] "Certain personnel in of the Office of Security and Consular Affairs, particularly in the Visa Division, have been working in close conjunction with Senator McCarran," Lloyd added a few months later, "and are really not responsive to executive control. These people have tried to carry out the wishes of Senator McCarran and they have little or no sympathy with the administration program."[53]

It was even worse than Lloyd thought. The immigration regulations to implement the McCarran Internal Security Act, for example, had been largely drafted in McCarran's office by Richard Arens, the immigration subcommittee counsel. "The new visa regulations which will be issued soon have been prepared more or less with Dick Arens' collaboration," Jay Sourwine told McCarran just after the Internal Security Act passed in 1950. ". . . It was entirely satisfactory."[54]

Lloyd had an idea. Since the president had to name another assistant secretary of state to head the new bureau, Lloyd suggested to Truman that he nominate Harry Rosenfield from the Displaced Persons Commission. Rosenfield, of course, was one of McCarran's major antagonists, a Jew who had stretched McCarran's restrictive DP law as far as he could to admit as many refugees as possible. Rosenfield had shadowed McCarran on his European inspection trip of refugee camps, had challenged him during committee hearings, and had plotted with Herbert Lehman and other Senate liberals to push for a more humane alternative to the McCarran-Walter Act. McCarran would never let Rosenfield get a confirmation hearing, although the mere fact of his nomination might give McCarran a heart attack.

Truman had another job for Rosenfield. He wanted him to head a commission to investigate U.S. immigration law and recommend improvements. Yes, Congress had just overhauled immigration law for the first time in twenty years, but Truman wanted Congress to go back to the drawing board and come up with a decent law this time. The President's Commission on Immigration and Naturalization, Truman called the group. The Commission to Repeal the McCarran-Walter Act was what it really was. Rosenfield didn't need to investigate the law to know what he thought of it. "I bitterly resisted this act," Rosenfield recalled. "A dreadful immigration law."[55]

That fall about the only thing the Democrats and Republicans could agree upon was that the McCarran-Walter Act needed to be revised. "It's true this new law bears the name of a Democrat, Pat McCarran, but he's not my kind of a Democrat," Truman said. "The McCarran Act must go."[56] General Dwight D. Eisenhower, the Republican presidential candidate, concurred. "A new immigration law was certainly needed," Eisenhower said, "but with leadership, rather than vetoes, we should have had, and we must get, a better law than this McCarran Act. . . . Yet to the Czech, the Pole, the Hungarian who takes his life in his hands and crosses the frontier tonight — or to the Italian who gets to some American consulate — this ideal that beckoned him can be a mirage because of the McCarran Act. We must develop a system of immigration in line with our concept of America as the great melting pot of free spirits."[57]

In January, Truman welcomed Rosenfield and the rest of the immigration commission to the White House to present its three-hundred-page report. In less than half a year Rosenfield and his colleagues had conducted hearings all over the country. McCarran aide Richard Arens had suggested that McCarran haul Rosenfield in front of the Senate Internal Security Subcommittee before the commission could release its report. "It should help blow them out of the water," Sourwine agreed.[58]

The commission, in effect, urged Congress to ditch McCarran-Walter and replace it with a liberal immigration policy similar to the substitute bill that had been defeated six months earlier. "An arrogant, brazen instrument of discrimination based on race, creed, color and national origin," the commission called the McCarran-Walter Act.[59] McCarran didn't bother to read the report. "A rehash," he said nonetheless, "of the line that was parroted by the radical left wing clique in Congress."[60]

The report was too late. The Democrats were losing Congress and any hope they had of passing a liberal immigration law. The Democratic leadership resigned itself to simply making the law less worse than it was. "It has seemed to me that the way to handle this issue is to begin nibbling at it," Lyndon Johnson told Lehman. "If we nibble long enough, we will break its back."[61]

Congress would nibble at the McCarran-Walter Act for half a century before it could significantly change it.

In September the Civil Service Commission suspended a lawyer on its staff, Miriam M. de Haas, when she refused to answer questions about whether she had leaked files from the loyalty board to McCarran and McCarthy. The Justice Department opened a criminal investigation. "Much of the information that was removed from the files of the Loyalty Review Board ultimately and by a circuitous route found its way into the possession of Robert Morris and Benjamin Mandel of the staff of your Subcommittee on Internal Security," Assistant Attorney General Charles B. Murray told McCarran.[62] Murray asked McCarran for permission to examine SISS files. Three months later Murray was still asking. By that time McCarran was sailing around South America and a new attorney general was about to come into office.

In the fall of 1952 the New York City skyline had a new addition: a low, swayback building topped by a small dome, next to which rose a thirty-nine-story slab of glass and steel flying a blue-and-white flag. This was the new headquarters of the United Nations. "In contrast to the disappointments and the deterioration of the world political scene," UN secretary general Trygve Lie recalled, "the sight of headquarters rising day by day was a source of strength and confidence."[63]

The year after its founding in San Francisco in 1945, the UN set up temporary headquarters in an old Sperry Gyroscope factory in the village of Lake Success, outside Queens on Long Island. For the next five years the UN secretariat and Security Council worked out of the former defense factory while the General Assembly sat in a building on the site of the 1939 World's Fair in nearby Flushing Meadows. In the meantime the UN started building a permanent headquarters on Manhattan's East Side, an area called Turtle Bay, half a dozen blocks along the river between Forty-second and Forty-eighth Streets, a warren of slaughterhouses and slums. The Rockefeller family gave the UN eight and a half million dollars to buy the eighteen acres of land, New York parks commissioner Robert Moses tore down the tenements and lavished twenty-five million dollars on improvements, and a stellar team of architects (including Oscar Niemeyer and Charles Le Corbusier) designed a complex of buildings, including the boxy General Assembly meeting hall and the office tower for the staff and various international agencies, such as the International Monetary Fund. "This workshop for peace," Lie called it.[64]

Pat McCarran called it something else. "A vantage ground for the infiltration of the United States,"[65] he said in Salt Lake City in early October, two weeks before Truman was scheduled to attend the gala opening of the UN headquarters. For years McCarran had been haunted by the fear that foreign Communists were slipping into the country, whether as displaced persons or as diplomats. When McCarran regained control of the Judiciary Committee in 1949 he used its immigration subcommittee to investigate the UN, which struck pay dirt when the FBI found Judith Coplon passing government secrets to a Russian employed by Lie's secretariat. "Several important officials of the United Nations are Communists," subcommittee counsel Richard Arens reported to McCarran, "and are using their official positions to further Communist objectives and that the United Nations desk in our own State Department definitely is Communist-dominated."[66] At one McCarran hearing, an unidentified witness claimed that Communists in the UN were terrorizing the secretary general, promptingthe UN to file an official protest with the State Department. McCarran didn't back down. "The U.S. should pull out of the UN quickly while there is yet time to save this country," he said in early 1951.[67] "I made an error which I shall regret all the days of my life when I voted for the United Nations," he added in May.[68]

While McCarran had been looking for Communists in the UN for years, Trygve Lie had been looking even longer. Lie was a Social Democrat who had fought Communists in the Norwegian labor movement, and when he became the first secretary general of the UN he was determined to fight them there as well. "I would never knowingly have employed a member of the American Communist Party," Lie wrote. ". . . If there was even one American Communist in the secretariat I wished to get rid of him. I would do it quietly and in accordance with the staff regulations, in the ways to which I had been accustomed in Norway. Western European governments do not make a public row, nor destroy a man's future chance to make a living, when they find a Communist."[69]

But finding American Communists in the UN wasn't that easy. In less than a year the secretariat had hired more than three thousand employees. In 1946 Lie informally asked the State Department for any information it had about American citizens who might be Communists (Communists from Communist countries, of course, were okay). Secretary of State James Byrnes told Lie that the United States didn't want to influence personnel selection at the UN. Lie went back to the State Department the next year and again got nothing. Then, in 1948, Lie tried a different strategy: He gave the State Department a list of 377 Americans who might need official passports to travel to a General Assembly session in Paris. Lie figured that if any of the Americans were denied passports, he should investigate them as possible Communists. "I did not know there were any," Lie recalled. "I only had the uneasy feeling there might be a few."[70]

Lie went to the FBI in 1949 and asked for help. The bureau declined. Finally that fall the State Department agreed to check U.S. records. But the

State Department simply forwarded its own evaluations to Lie, instructing him to fire thirty-eight employees without giving any reasons or evidence. It was enough to drive a fair man nuts. Like Steve Spingarn before him, Lie was learning that U.S. security officials expected him to get rid of people based on their oracular pronouncements. In 1950 Lie sacked several temporary staffers. He was overruled by the UN's administrative tribunal. The following year Lie got the General Assembly to give him the authority to fire temporary employees without a hearing if the termination was in the interest of the organization — the UN's version of the McCarran rider, which gave the State Department the same power.

By the fall of 1952, after years of pleading with the United States for help in screening his staff, Lie still had little idea if there were any American Communists working for him, although he had his suspicions about a score of employees. "I was making the customary careful and confidential inquiries in these doubtful cases," Lie recalled, "when the storm clouds that had been gathering on the American scene burst in all their fury."[71]

Homer Ferguson needed a ride to the airport one fall day in New York. Roy Cohn volunteered to give him one. Cohn was always eager to help someone who could help him. Ferguson was the ranking Republican on SISS and quite possibly its next chairman, a fierce critic of the New Deal who blamed Roosevelt for Pearl Harbor and Truman for losing China. Cohn, twenty-five, was an anti-Communist enfant terrible. "Cohn is smart beyond comprehension,"[72] marveled FBI assistant director Lou Nicols. He was also cocky beyond comprehension. "The most arrogant little son of a bitch," said federal judge Sam Kaufman, "I've ever met in my life."[73]

The son of a New York Supreme Court judge, Cohn had graduated from Columbia Law School at the age of nineteen but had to wait two years until he was old enough to take the bar exam. It was the last time that Cohn was willing to wait for anything. The same day that Cohn became a lawyer he was sworn in as an assistant U.S. attorney; during the next four years he took part in a series of high-profile cases, from the Smith Act trial of the leaders of the American Communist Party to the prosecution of Julius and Ethel Rosenberg for atomic espionage. Cohn loved power and publicity. Like a horticulturist with a prize rose garden, he cultivated powerful allies. McCarran was one, Homer Ferguson another. But McCarran wasn't much of a social animal; Ferguson, on the other hand, liked a good night out on the town. The Republican senator and the young lawyer became friendly, meeting sometimes for drinks at SISS counsel Bob Morris's New York apartment, other times hanging out together at the Stork Club, where Cohn worked the room late at night as relentlessly as he grilled witnesses during the day.

On the drive to the airport Cohn and Ferguson had a lot to talk about. For one thing, there was Cohn's new job as a special assistant to the attorney general for internal security. In May, McCarran had pressed James McGranery at his confirmation hearing about prosecuting Owen Lattimore. McGranery assured McCarran that he would strictly enforce the law. Roy Cohn was supposed to be the enforcer. Harvey Matusow recalled being at a party where conservative columnist George Sokolsky, who was friends with both McCarran and McGranery, claimed credit for arranging the deal. "Sokolsky said he had contacted McGranery and told him there would be no problem with his confirmation as attorney general if he agreed to appoint Roy Cohn as special assistant to the attorney general to bring the Lattimore case before a grand jury," Matusow remembered.[74]

In August, while he was still working in the U.S. attorney's office, Cohn went to Lisbon on vacation. For beach reading he lugged with him Lattimore's testimony before SISS. From Europe, Cohn called the attorney general asking for more material on Lattimore. McGranery told James McInerney, the head of the criminal division, to send Cohn the files. McInerney was shocked. "It was the first inkling he knew that Cohn was to come to Washington," one FBI agent noted.[75] McInerney protested, saying that it was a bad idea to have confidential government files shipped all over Europe. The attorney general said that he agreed but that he had been overruled (by whom is blacked out in the FBI files). McInerney was soon transferred to a different division.

Back from his vacation, Cohn showed up at the Justice Department for his swearing-in. Normally this wasn't much of a ceremony. Cohn arrived with his parents and a small entourage of reporters and photographers. Then he saw the press release that the Justice Department was about to send out: The department announced Cohn's appointment as *an* attorney in the internal security section, not the section's head. "The attorney general," recorded the FBI's Alan Belmont, "told Cohn that he is a young man and although he had a good record in New York he was concerned about putting him officially in charge of a division in the Department of Justice, as the reaction throughout the country might not be good."[76] Cohn's reaction (in his own recollection) wasn't good, either. He threw a fit. He stormed out and called George Sokolsky, who told him to tear up the press release and announce that he was headed back to New York. Do I just leave then? Cohn wondered. No, Sokolsky assured him, the attorney general will call me to straighten it out. Cohn followed the columnist's advice, and McGranery asked Cohn to wait while the attorney general disappeared into his inner office. Ten minutes later Sokolsky called Cohn into the attorney general's outer office and told him to go see McGranery. Cohn got his title. More importantly, he got power. "All important cases are to go to Cohn," McGranery told one of his subordinates.[77]

Although Cohn had been transferred from New York to Washington, he was still spending four days a week in Manhattan working feverishly on two cases: a grand jury investigation into the UN and the Lattimore perjury case. The cases were related — a suspected Communist at the UN (David Weintraub) had once appointed Lattimore as the head of an economic mission to Afghanistan — and both were dear to the heart of Pat McCarran. Neither was going especially well. In May the grand jury had subpoenaed a number of American employees at the UN to testify (including a few linked to the Communist underground by Chambers and Bentley); fifteen refused to answer questions and were fired by Secretary General Trygve Lie for not cooperating with a government inquiry. But months later the grand jury was no closer to returning an indictment, and McGranery was considering ending the inquiry. "To call a halt to this investigation at this time would, in my opinion, be unconscionable from every standpoint," Cohn pleaded with McGranery. ". . . I cannot understand why a point is suddenly raised now as the investigation is crowned with such great success and approval."[78]

The Lattimore investigation wasn't looking much more promising. Justice Department attorney Edward J. Hummer wrote a forty-page analysis of a possible perjury case, finding it extremely weak. "To charge technical perjury on minor questions," he concluded, "is to invite a full acquittal and thus place Lattimore on a pedestal and make him a martyr, a role he would relish but does not deserve."[79]

McGranery was in a tough position. The president was against prosecuting Lattimore, but McCarran was insistent. "The attorney general received two 'very nasty' letters from Senator McCarran on the Lattimore case," the FBI's L. Laughlin told Assistant Director Alan Belmont. ". . . Senator McCarran was described . . . as being particularly vicious."[80] Then Roy Cohn took over the investigation. Cohn wrote a ten-page memo rebutting Hummer and making the case for a perjury prosecution.

The two attorneys clashed from the minute they met. "People who were fifty, sixty or something like that were sitting around the department reading newspapers for twenty years and here I come full of action," Cohn said. "And you know my light was on hours after they had gone home in the afternoon and I was there hours before they got there in the morning. And I was just, as my friend Senator Jenner once put it, 'I was the kid who went to the party and peed in the lemonade.' "[81]

Hummer was no anti-Communist slouch. He was a former FBI agent who had been in charge of leaking the bureau's files on Alger Hiss to Richard Nixon. "I was investigating Communism for the bureau when Cohn was a mere lad of fifteen," Hummer said.[82] Before long Hummer was complaining to his superiors that Cohn seemed to be working for McCarran and not the Justice Department. "Cohn was reporting regularly to members of the McCarran Committee," Hummer told Assistant Attorney General William Tompkins. "His reputation for leaking confidential information to outsiders was so notorious."[83]

For the attorney general it was coming down to a contest between Truman and McCarran, between Hummer and Cohn. Whom did McGranery least want to displease? Who would make his life more miserable? The FBI had no doubt who would be more wrathful. "If the department advises the McCarran Committee of the results of [Hummer's] analysis," the FBI's Alan Belmont noted, "the McCarran Committee, with widespread publicity, will claim that the department has whitewashed the Lattimore case."[84]

Half a year after he had first asked the Justice Department to investigate Lattimore for perjury, McCarran was getting impatient. After Cohn drove Ferguson to the airport, for example, the young lawyer made sure that his less enthusiastic colleagues at Justice knew that McCarran was not happy with the department. "The senator reported that he and Senator McCarran were very displeased with the department over the Miriam de Haas case which, as you know, involved an employee of the Civil Service Commission who was sending loyalty reports to the McCarran Committee and to Senator McCarthy," Assistant Attorney General Charles Murray told McGranery. "Cohn reported that Senator Ferguson stated that he and Senator McCarran were going to renew their demands on the Department of Justice to prosecute Davies and Lattimore."[85]

UN secretary general Trygve Lie asked SISS counsel Bob Morris to come to New York to see him. Judiciary Committee chief counsel Jay Sourwine told Morris to forget it. "If Lie thought it urgent enough," Sourwine snapped, "he could come down here."[86]

McCarran's committee was in the middle of investigating the UN, but it wasn't really interested in talking to the head of the organization. "The whole secretariat is shot through with Communists," Bob Morris told Eva Adams. "In fact it reaches the proportion of uniformity and the statements of some witnesses that they haven't noticed any Communist activity stems from this uniformity, namely that it couldn't be recognized in the entire activity. Of course, most of this evidence we will not present, because it is not nearly as conclusive as the officials invoking their constitutional privilege which I believe in today's market is the most convincing proof that we can present."[87]

On October 13, eleven days before the UN's opening ceremony, the Senate Internal Security Subcommittee began public hearings in the federal courthouse in Foley Square in Lower Manhattan. Ten hearings eventually stretched out over six weeks. Thirty-three UN employees were subpoenaed. Twenty-six took the Fifth. "The UN," said committee member Willis Smith, "should not be allowed to sit in America."[88]

Whittaker Chambers was the star witness. He testified that David Weintraub, who was director of the National Research Project, had gotten Chambers a job working for the federal government in 1937 at the request of the Communist Party. At the time Chambers said he knew that Weintraub's deputy Irving Kaplan was a party member. Weintraub was now the director of the economic stability and development section of the UN, where Kaplan was once again hired as his deputy. Weintraub was also the person responsible for appointing Owen Lattimore to a UN mission. Chambers was not an eager witness. "I would like the record to show clearly that I am testifying here today solely in response to subpoena power of the committee," Chambers said, "and that I myself solicited in no way this unpleasant privilege. The nature of the matters you asked me I have already testified to at considerable length at least before one grand jury and my statements about them rest in the files of the government. I was going to say rest in peace."[89]

Weintraub denied that he was a Communist but acknowledged that he knew members of both the Ware and Perlo Groups. Kaplan took the Fifth. Weintraub kept his job; Kaplan didn't. Virginius Frank Coe was also subpoenaed. Coe had worked for Harry Dexter White at the Treasury and followed White to the International Monetary Fund when White became director of the UN agency in 1946. Both Chambers and Bentley had identified Coe as a Communist. He took the Fifth before SISS. A few days later he was fired.

A number of State Department officials also testified. The committee asked

Deputy Undersecretary Carlisle H. Humelsine for the names of the State officials who had done the screenings for the UN. Humelsine refused to disclose
that information. "The evaluation made by the State Department," the SISS
report concluded, ". . . was so faulty and so delinquent from a security standpoint as prima facie to justify if not actually require an interrogation to determine if it was the result of any subversive influence."[90]

When SISS came to New York, Lie announced that he would fire any
employees who refused to cooperate with the committee. He eventually
fired three dozen employees for taking the Fifth. "I felt strongly," he
recalled, "that a United Nations official should cooperate fully with investigations conducted by an official agency of his own government."[91]

But Lie could never fire enough people to keep McCarran happy. Lie
wanted to get rid of any party members working for the UN. McCarran
wanted to get rid of the UN itself.

On November 10 Trygve Lie announced to the UN General Assembly that
he was resigning. For more than a year the Soviet Union and the rest of the
Eastern bloc — upset over the secretary general's support of UN action in
Korea — had refused to recognize Lie as the organization's chief executive.
Tass, the Soviet news agency, rejoiced. So did McCarran, who attributed
Lie's resignation to the disclosures made during the SISS hearings. In the
Washington Post Herb Block drew a cartoon of McCarran and Soviet ambas-
sador Andrei Vishinsky (who was also the prosecutor at the Moscow purge
trials) both rubbing their hands in glee. "The fierce Soviet campaign against
Lie has been a matter of record for many months," noted the *New York Post*.
"Pat McCarran's attempt to steal credit for this Russian victory is as absurd
as it is unconvincing. . . . As Americans we are humiliated by McCarran's
claim that a U.S. senator did the work of the Soviet firing squad."[92]

In late November, after the Democrats took a drubbing in the 1952 election and lost the White House, Attorney General McGranery decided to
send the Lattimore case to the grand jury. But he pulled Roy Cohn off
the case and put Ed Hummer in charge of the presentation. McGranery
instructed other officials in the department not to tell Cohn about the
decision until the press release went out. "He just could not be trusted,"
Hummer crowed. "In addition, he is a pathological liar."[93]

In less than three months Cohn had managed to alienate just about
everyone he worked with in the Justice Department. Although the grand

jury investigation of the UN didn't result in any indictments, Cohn persuaded the foreman to release an unusual presentment. "The employment of so many of our disloyal nationals in the secretariat," the grand jury concluded, ". . . constitutes a menace to our government."[94] Since grand jury proceedings are supposed to be secret, Assistant Attorney General Charles Murray reprimanded Cohn for recklessness. U.S. Attorney Myles Lane, under whose jurisdiction the investigation started, wanted to fire Cohn. "That little son of a bitch is riding for a fall," Lane said.[95]

Even Cohn's supporters, such as J. Edgar Hoover, were growing concerned. "While I had great admiration for his enthusiasm and aggressiveness I thought he needed to be less spectacular," Hoover noted. ". . . I would like to see someone a little older and more mature just caution Cohn to kind of watch his step and not be so flamboyant because I felt he had a great future and could go far."[96]

And Jay Sourwine warned McCarran to be careful about his dealings with Cohn. "While it is desirable to work very closely with Cohn, and while we appreciate Cohn's cooperation," Sourwine told McCarran, "I do not think there should be too much of the appearance that the committee and the Department of Justice are working hand and glove."[97]

Hoover was right. Roy Cohn would go far. Too far for even his powerful friends to save him.

Several weeks later McCarran introduced a bill to require that American citizens employed by the UN receive a security clearance from the attorney general. Failure to comply with the law would be punishable by five years in prison and a ten-thousand-dollar fine. "The only precedent I could discover for such a law was the edict promulgated by Fascist Italy," Lie recalled, ". . . though the penalties for violation were less severe than those Senator McCarran found appropriate."[98] Two days later, on January 9, Truman took the matter out of McCarran's hands, signing an executive order that placed Americans employed by the UN under the government's loyalty program. "It is a sad commentary on the character of the present administration," McCarran said, "that only after nearly a decade of inattention or worse, our State Department only now announces it is preparing 'security' arrangements to provide the United Nations with a loyalty check. . . . This deathbed conversion, reached less than a month before a new administration takes over, would be ludicrous but for the unpleasant fact that disclosures of our subcommittee that scores of persons of questionable loyalty have been allowed to pose as honest and loyal representatives of this country."[99]

Ten days later McCarran used the occasion of Herbert Brownell's confirmation hearing to once again pressure an incoming attorney general into prosecuting Lattimore. McCarran referred to Ed Hummer by name and urged Eisenhower's attorney general nominee to replace him. "Do you believe," McCarran asked, "that a man who has evinced his attitude as against the indictment should have charge of the prosecution before a trial jury?"[100]

Brownell assured McCarran that he would rigidly enforce the law, even assigning another attorney to the case if necessary. Hummer's friends were outraged. He was, after all, a firm anti-Communist; if there were a case against Lattimore, he would certainly make it. "You were deceived by someone who was ill-informed, malicious or both,"[101] Father John F. Cronin told McCarran.

McCarran was informed by Roy Cohn. After Cohn was replaced on the Lattimore case by Hummer, the young attorney began bragging that he would become the new chief counsel of the Judiciary Committee. And he took Hummer's old memo arguing against prosecuting Lattimore to McCarran, who was predictably outraged.

After McCarran's outburst, Hummer met with Sourwine, who along with Eva Adams finally prevailed upon McCarran to issue an apology. "I am sorry if you have been hurt by the interpretation placed upon my remarks," McCarran wrote to Hummer. "I had no purpose of injuring you and there was nothing of personal vindictiveness in what I said."[102]

If he had been under oath, McCarran would have been courting a perjury indictment himself.

Abraham H. Feller sat on the couch in the living room of his apartment across from Central Park with his wife, Alice. He wore a tie and slippers, a man almost dressed for work but not wanting to go. Before him a vast tableau of wide park and soaring skyline filled the apartment's windows, but all Feller could see was darkness.

It was November 13, 1952. Feller was forty-eight, a slight man with thinning hair and thick glasses, a Harvard Law School graduate, who had worked as a special assistant to the attorney general during the New Deal, served as general counsel for the Office of Wartime Information, and joined the UN at its founding. He was Trygve Lie's general counsel, the secretary general's right-hand man. Feller had given the past seven years of his life to the international organization. He had just published a book, *United Nations and the World*, which the *New York Times Book Review* had praised on Sunday.

And his life was hell. For months Roy Cohn's grand jury and Pat McCarran's Internal Security Subcommittee had been making life miserable for the UN's head lawyer. Lie wanted to get rid of Communists in the UN, but he insisted on an orderly and fair process. McCarran and Cohn just wanted them out. Feller was in the middle. The never-ending subpoenas, the secretariat employees refusing to testify, and the calls from reporters were filling his days with frustration. When Lie agreed to fire anyone who wouldn't cooperate with SISS, Feller became the one who actually did the dirty work. SISS would call another hearing, some UN employee would take the Fifth, and Feller would have to ask the person to clear out his desk. Privately Lie and Feller knew that there were some Communists working for the UN. Publicly McCarran and Cohn kept saying that no one but Communists seemed to be working at the UN. At home at night, Feller couldn't shake the sense of dread that enveloped every day at the office. He couldn't focus enough to help his daughter with her high school homework. After lunch with Alice the day before he'd walked across a New York street like a man who didn't notice the honking cars. Only the sleeping pills offered any peace.

Alice was worried. She called the family doctor and a psychiatrist and sat on the couch with her husband. "Doctors can't help me," Feller muttered, over and over again.[103] Feller jumped up and ran through the apartment. Alice chased him through the dining room and kitchen and into the den. She grabbed an arm, a leg, anything she could reach. She clutched at his shirt and it pulled out of his pants and slipped out of her grip. Feller opened a window and jumped to his death. She screamed.

Lie was at a luncheon with Dean Acheson at the Metropolitan Club when he heard the news. He rushed to Feller's apartment. He knew that Feller had recently spoken with Robert Morris and Roy Cohn, and the secretary general told reporters that McCarran's committee and Cohn's grand jury had driven Feller to suicide. "Indiscriminate smears and exaggerated charges," Lie said.[104] "No doubt Abe Feller was a victim of the witch hunt," Lie wrote later, "of the awful pressure of the hysterical assault upon the United Nations that reactionaries were promoting and using for their own ends. Day after day, he followed the Senate hearings and saw the tragedy unfold. He saw the hysteria invade high places and sweep his country in violation of fundamental principles of fair play and orderly justice by which he had lived all his life. The strain finally grew too strong and he broke."[105]

At Feller's funeral the UN's Ralph Bunche blamed his boss, Trygve Lie. "Hard as it must be to stand up against the demands of Washington," Bunche said, "a strong secretary general would surely have refused to enter into a secret pact with the State Department under which he agreed not to employ any American citizen who was, or appeared to be, a Communist. . . . Abe Feller, as general counsel, tried desperately to substitute decent legal procedures for such miserable capitulation."[106]

On November 10, 1952, McCarran and Birdie got off a train in New York at Penn Station. Bob Morris and a State Department official were waiting to drive the McCarrans to the Plaza Hotel, where a suite had been reserved. Three days later McCarran and his wife had reservations to sail for South America on the SS *Uruguay*. The McCarrans loved to take cruises. They didn't especially like to pay for them. This time the State Department was picking up most of the tab. Usually it was Stanley Dollar, the shipping magnate who had inherited the Dollar Steamship Company from his father in 1932.

Over the years McCarran and Dollar had become close. When McCarran was in the hospital in Reno after his heart attack in 1951, only dear friends such as Pete Petersen and Norm Biltz visited—and Stanley Dollar. The next year when Sister Margaret got her Ph.D. at Catholic University in Washington, McCarran invited Dollar to the ceremony. When the senator needed a place to stay in New York, Dollar often offered his apartment at the Drake. And when McCarran wanted to take a cruise, Dollar was always the first person he called.

It hadn't always been that way. When McCarran first arrived in the Senate in 1933 he was chairman of the Special Investigating Committee on Ocean and Air Mail Subsidies. "McCarran declares that beside this scandal, Teapot Dome was as pure as a lily . . . ," *Las Vegas Review-Journal* editor Al Cahlan wrote after visiting McCarran. "He tells you evidence shows that big shipping interests including the Dollar lines purchased ships from the shipping board, which had built them with your money and mine . . . the consideration was some sort of promissory note which has never been paid and never will . . . the Dollar interests invested no money in their company, got the ships from the government and has made a net profit over a period of years of several million dollars."[107]

Twenty years later McCarran and Dollar were good friends. In late 1952, for example, Dollar called McCarran. "I talked to Stanley Dollar on the phone yesterday," McCarran told Birdie. "He called me from San

Francisco. They are getting along all right with this ship deal with the government."[108] That was a bit of an understatement. In 1938 Stanley Dollar had run his father's shipping business into the ground. The company was worth eleven million dollars but was in default to the government for almost eight million. The U.S. Maritime Commission, headed by Joseph P. Kennedy, took over the company, renaming it the American President Lines and putting more than four million dollars into the operation. In turn the government forgave Dollar's personal debt of close to two million and the tycoon took a tax write-off for the stock he sold to the government. In 1945, after the government had added thirty-two ships to the fleet and turned the company into a forty-million-dollar business, Dollar filed suit to get the company back, claiming that he had only pledged it to the government, not sold it outright. The suit dragged out for seven years, but now the government was about to give half of the company back to Dollar. "If this deal goes through," fumed reporter Tom McNamara to his boss, columnist Drew Pearson, "the taxpayers will be shaken down for about $20 million."[109]

The person doing the shaking, Pearson's legman thought, was McCarran. "The Dollars are from California and therefore not constituents of Senator Pat McCarran," McNamara continued, "but by 1945 he suddenly began to take an unusually keen interests in the Dollar campaign to get control of the American President Lines. . . . The senator made the Dollar fight almost a personal project."[110]

McNamara told Pearson that it was the most significant influence-peddling case of the Truman administration, which had been plagued by a series of scandals, but that neither party wanted to touch it. The Republicans didn't want to embarrass Stanley Dollar; the Democrats didn't want to embarrass themselves. "Senators are ever fearless to investigate others," McNamara told Pearson, "but they rarely investigate a 'member of the club.' And if the Dollar case ever got a thorough airing it would reveal some interesting backstage pressure maneuvers by one Pat McCarran."[111]

On the floor of the Senate, McCarran took to attacking the Maritime Commission, calling it an "unlawful outfit," and praising Dollar. "That great pioneer of steam shipping on the Pacific Ocean," he called him.[112] McNamara told Pearson that McCarran was clearly trying to pressure the courts with his speeches. "The man who decides what judges shall be appointed to the bench and which ones should be promoted," he observed, "was bluntly plain in telling his colleagues — as well as any judges who happened to read his remarks — how the Dollar case should be decided."[113]

Years later Graham Morison, an assistant attorney general and head of the antitrust division, claimed that McCarran had demanded that James P. McGranery drop the Dollar case in exchange for being confirmed as attorney general. "McGranery without hesitation said he would comply to McCarran's demands,"[114] Morison said, citing as his source an unnamed staff member on the Judiciary Committee.

Morison soon resigned from the Justice Department. Later, he recalled that Hank Greenspun told him that Dollar had bribed McCarran. "McCarran was paid off," Morison remembered. "He would not go to Las Vegas, he would go to Reno. There would be on this occasion — one table cleared, and he would play roulette, and would win maybe a hundred thousand dollars, and even though the Internal Revenue people were right there, that's how he got paid off."[115]

Pearson, however, could never put much into print. Other columnists also tried to raise questions about McCarran and Dollar, but neither the White House nor Congress seemed very interested in looking into the matter. "How closely is the mess in the administration," wondered columnist Marquis Childs, "linked to the controls exercised by certain powerful Democrats in Congress?"[116]

Stanley Dollar spent a lot of time in Reno. He had a house at Lake Tahoe, where he was a major real estate developer, and he was also partners with McCarran's close friend Norm Biltz in a five-million-dollar resort being built downstream from the Riverside Hotel in Reno. The new development was called the Holiday Hotel, and its claim to fame was that it would be the first major resort in Nevada *not* to have a casino. Stanley Dollar didn't like to gamble. He only liked to bet on a sure thing.

On November 13 Pat and Birdie were on the dock getting ready to board the SS *Uruguay* when reporters came panting after them. For the past four years McCarran had been a terror to his president and his party, amassing more power and using it more ruthlessly than any but a handful of senators in American history. From his oversized chair in the Judiciary Committee room McCarran ran a virtual government-in-opposition, even while his own party controlled the White House and both wings of the Capitol. He bullied the State and Justice Departments into subverting their leaders; he created and unleashed the Senate Internal Security Subcommittee, which quickly became the most fearsome congressional investigating committee of the early McCarthy years, scouring the federal government, the United Nations, academia, unions, and the entertainment industry for subversives. With the McCarran and McCarran-Walter Acts, he fortified an immigration wall around the United States, keeping out refugees and Communists alike and ejecting non-native citizens for their politics, even some who had long since repudiated their pasts.

It was time for a vacation. Officially McCarran was going to inspect security programs at the U.S. embassies in Brazil, Colombia, and Venezuela. In reality Birdie wanted to practice her Spanish, which she had been studying for years. McCarran summoned Carlisle Humelsine, the deputy undersecretary of state, to his house to serve as his travel agent. Humelsine assured McCarran that the department would pay the maximum first-class fare for him, while the cruise line would charge the minimum fare for Mrs. McCarran. The best suite on the ship had already been booked, but at McCarran's insistence the couple were moved to lesser quarters. The McCarrans, of course, had no trouble getting passports from Ruth Shipley. "I have always known you wanted to see South America," McCarran told his wife, "so this trip is for my sweetheart so you just get ready."[117]

At the dock the reporters told McCarran about Abe Feller's suicide that day and asked about the United Nations probe. Was Feller under subpoena from SISS? Yes, McCarran said, he was. Then Robert Morris whispered into McCarran's ear. No, McCarran corrected himself, he wasn't. "If Feller's conscience was clear," McCarran said, "he had no reason to suffer from what he expected of our committee."[118]

The *Uruguay* pulled away from the East River pier, slid by the new UN building, and entered New York Harbor, where the crowded Ellis Island detention center squatted low against the New Jersey horizon in the shadow of Lady Liberty's torch. Then the ship steamed into the Atlantic Ocean, leaving the Statue of Liberty standing on her pedestal like the last survivor of some great flood. Four weeks later, a radiogram from Washington reached the ship in the South Atlantic: A grand jury had indicted Owen Lattimore.

CHAPTER 24

The Dead

We came to the great gambling and marriage destruction
hell, known as Nevada. To look at it from the air it is just
that — hell on earth. There are tiny green specks on the
landscape where dice, roulette, light-o-loves, crooked
poker and gambling thugs thrive. Such places should be
abolished and so should Nevada. It never should have been
made a state. A county in the great state of California
would be too much of a civil existence for that dead and
sinful territory. Think of that awful, sinful place having two
senators and a congressman in Washington, and Alaska and
Hawaii not represented. It is a travesty on our system and
a disgrace to free government.[1]

— Harry Truman

Lunched with Governor Pittman. . . . He gave me a long
story of the despotism of Senator McCarran. It was so
shocking that it was hard to believe — more like a story
happening in Russia.[2]

— Drew Pearson

During an unusually cold winter, a '51 Chevy coupe pulling a trailer
crawled into Las Vegas. The young couple in the front seat had seven
thousand dollars and a plan. In Las Vegas this wasn't exactly unheard of,
but Tom Mechling's plan was more audacious than most. He wanted to
run for the U.S. Senate against Pat McCarran — only McCarran wasn't
up for reelection for another four years. So Mechling, a Washington journalist with no political experience whose only tie to the state was the fact
that his wife had been born there, had to settle for running against
McCarran's protégé and former law partner, Alan Bible, whom McCarran
had been grooming for the job for years.

"No candidate in Nevada," Mechling recalled, "within the past decade
had ever run for high office with even a hope of making a creditable
showing unless he had behind him the McCarran political machine, a good
deal of millionaire gambling money, and Nevada birth. I had none of these."[3]

With the postwar boom, Nevada finally had more people than square miles — but just barely. Mechling and his wife planned to spend eight months and their life's savings driving around Nevada, going door to door across the state, bypassing the newspapers that printed only what McCarran wanted them to print and taking his candidacy straight to the voters. "Don Quixote in a trailer," people called him. "That a boy's a gonna surprisa a lotta peeple,"[4] his father-in-law Johnny Di Grazia said.

Even in Las Vegas you couldn't find someone to take that bet.

Across the room the phone kept ringing. It was March 24, 1952, and Hank Greenspun, the owner and publisher of the *Sun*, was pounding away with two fingers at his typewriter, writing his column for the next day's paper, railing against a prominent brothel on the outskirts of town. Since the town was Las Vegas he might as well have complained about the dawn, but Greenspun, forty-three, was nothing if not pugnacious. Standing trim, just over six feet tall, with a brawler's nose and a mouth full of gold teeth (usually clamped on a cigar), Greenspun could have passed for a former boxer. Indeed, he approached journalism like a barroom fight; he threw words like punches and he wrote to hurt. He ignored the ringing.

Norman White, the paper's ad manager, walked over.

"We're in trouble," he said.

In thirty minutes, he explained, three big casinos had pulled their business from the *Sun:* the Thunderbird, El Rancho, and the Last Frontier.

White's phone rang again. Greenspun followed him back to his desk. The Flamingo canceled its ads. Then the morning got *really* bad. Another eight casinos walked away from the *Sun*. Almost a third of the paper's revenue had disappeared before lunch. Not a single large casino on the Strip or downtown wanted anything to do with the publication.

Greenspun rushed out of his office on Main Street, jumped into his red convertible, and drove south for a few blocks until the road merged into the Strip. On his right he passed a low-slung building topped by a neon windmill: El Rancho, a glorified motel built in 1941, the first casino to open just outside the city limits on the highway stretching toward Los Angeles. Across the way sprawled a two-story casino dwarfed by a tower rising from its lobby on which perched something that looked like a giant chicken: the Thunderbird, briefly the most luxurious place on the Strip, which had opened in 1948 and expanded six times in three years. Next door was a dusty construction site where the five-and-a-half-million-dollar Sahara was rising from the desert.

Another mile and Greenspun reached the Last Frontier, the Strip's second casino, a motor court now duded up as a western theme park crammed with covered wagons, railroad cars, and a ghost town's worth of old buildings from all corners of the state (including a framed poster from the 1932 Senate race: A NEW DEAL FOR AMERICA, ROOSEVELT, GARNER AND McCARRAN). Down the way yet another huge new casino was going up: the Sands. Beyond that slunk the last casino on the Strip, where a tall, thin sign topped by a pink bird towered above a low-rise building. FLAMINGO, it glowed at night in soft pink neon.

Six years earlier when Greenspun first drove down this road there where only two motels and fewer than two hundred rooms on the Strip. Greenspun came to town to promote a racetrack; instead he wound up as a flack, a publicity agent for mobster Bugsy Siegel, whose Flamingo set off the Strip's building boom in 1946. This year the Strip was gaining another five hundred hotel rooms — and it wouldn't be nearly enough for the prosperous hordes of tourists. In a decade the town's population had tripled, and Las Vegas showed no sign of slowing down.

Greenspun wheeled left and pulled into a circular driveway, wrapping around a fountain spraying water sixty feet into the air. In the center of the drive stood a tower topped by a cloud-shaped sign (it was supposed to be an artist's palette) proclaiming WILBUR CLARK'S DESERT INN.

Actually it was Moe Dalitz's Desert Inn. Clark ran out of money during construction and had to give up three-quarters of his stake to Morris Dalitz, who got his start in the dry-cleaning business in Michigan but found his real métier as a rumrunner and casino operator in Ohio and Kentucky. In the sunny years after the war, Dalitz was one of many who discovered that moving to Las Vegas could change him overnight from a criminal to a businessman. But the old way of doing things died hard. When boxer Sonny Liston tried to pick a fight with Dalitz, the casino owner didn't blink. "If you hit me, nigger," Daltiz said, "you'd better kill me, because if you don't, I'll make one telephone call and you'll be dead in twenty-four hours."[5] Liston kept his fists at his side. "Tough times," Dalitz liked to say, "call for tough people."[6]

Greenspun went into the front door of the Desert Inn (the DI, everyone called it) and straight out the back. He knew his way around. Greenspun had put his savings into the casino and worked as its PR man only to find, like his friend Wilbur Clark, that his role was being reduced to insignificance. Clark was content to see his name on the marquee. Greenspun went out and brought a newspaper, putting his opinions on the front page every day. "Where I Stand," Greenspun called his column.

Behind the casino Greenspun found Dalitz talking with an architect about an eighteen-hole golf course they were building. Daltiz loved golf. He also loved guns. "Subject is known to have registered seven guns with the Clark County, Nevada, sheriff's office," the FBI noted, "and therefore should be considered armed and dangerous."[7]

What's going on? Greenspun interrupted.

"You should know," Dalitz said (in Greenspun's recollection). "Why did you have to attack the Old Man."[8]

"What business is it of the Desert Inn, or any other hotel, what I print in my paper?" Greenspun insisted.

"You've put us in a terrible position," Dalitz replied. "You know as well as I that we have to do what he tells us. You know he got us our licenses. If we don't go along, you know what will happen to us."

When Dalitz first came to the state in 1949 he couldn't get a gambling license, something usually only slightly harder to get in Nevada than a driver's license. McCarran took an interest in his new constituent's problem. Dalitz got his license. Then in 1951 McCarran had saved Nevada's gambling industry from federal taxation; now the senator wanted the industry to squash his loudest critic in the state. Dalitz knew whom to put his money on. "He was a good investor," a friend recalled. "Moe never went against the tables."[9]

Behind the men the Desert Inn sign rose above a three-story tower, the tallest building on the Strip, which held the Sky Bar, a favorite place for people to watch the mushroom clouds that occasionally erupted on the edge of the desert. For a year the federal government had been exploding atomic bombs at the Nevada Test Site, sixty-five miles northwest of town. In Las Vegas the ground could shake and the sky turn to fire and someone would make book on how long the world would last.

Greenspun glared down at Dalitz, half a head shorter and a decade older. Greenspun hated him. During the Arab-Israeli war Greenspun had smuggled arms for Israel, Dalitz for the Arabs. Now the mobster was trying to kill his newspaper. The *Las Vegas Sun* was approaching its second anniversary. It might not see a third. Greenspun stuck his fists into his pockets. "If I hadn't," he remembered, "I probably would have used them."[10]

At the Thunderbird — where the neon chicken above the marquee spat gas flames from its mouth, nude ice skaters cavorted in the showroom, and millionaire Howard Hughes was a regular guest (washing his own shirts in the sink) — there was always a booth reserved for McCarran and a suite waiting for him or his family. And when McCarran asked for the check, it never came. "Thank you again for the wonderful vacation in Las Vegas and the southwest," Sam McCarran told his father. "Mr. Hicks was very nice to us."[11]

The casino knew how to treat politicians. It should. One of its owners was Cliff Jones, forty, the state's lieutenant governor, whose idea of business dress was a calfskin vest with cowboy boots and who held eleven points in the hotel. Jones didn't smoke, drink, or gamble, but he made a good living off those who did. Jones had been a McCarran supporter since his 1932 Senate campaign (before Jones was old enough to vote). You'd make a good lieutenant governor someday, McCarran once told Jones. He'd paid for law school by working on Boulder Dam and then opened an office above a clothing store on Fremont Street in downtown Las Vegas. Most of his legal business involved helping clients get gambling licenses, and Jones soon realized that taking a percentage of a casino was more lucrative than billing by the hour. When the cleaning store below his office turned into the Pioneer Club, Jones took five points in the deal. At one time he had interests in seven different casinos, mostly remuneratively the Thunderbird, which opened in 1948, the year after Jones became lieutenant governor. The twin endeavors made Jones a very useful person to know in Las Vegas. The Big Juice, people called him. *Juice*, in local parlance, was the ability to make things happen. In Nevada, only McCarran had more juice.

The majority owner of the Thunderbird was Marion Hicks, who went from running a gambling boat off the California coast to building casinos in Las Vegas, and who owned 51 percent of the venture. McCarran was fond of Hicks. ("He really knows the game and has a nice personality. He is neither boastful, nor is he pessimistic. He was a fine assistant."[12]) Together Jones and Hicks owned almost two-thirds of the Thunderbird. The rest belonged to the mob.* In Las Vegas in the 1950s lawmakers and lawbreakers rubbed shoulders with a nonchalance remarkable even for a frontier boomtown. And Nevada had finally found its true bonanza, a gold mine that could never be dug dry: legal gambling.

Nearly a century after Brigham Young had tried to claim Las Vegas for the Mormons, the town more closely resembled Sodom and Gomorrah than Salt Lake City. Las Vegas was not yet fifty years old, but it was the

---

* In 1955 the Nevada Tax Commission tried to revoke the gaming licenses of Hicks and Jones. The pair won on appeal, although the case helped spur the creation of the Gaming Control Board, which tried to keep mobsters out of gambling. The state came up with a List of Excluded Persons, reputed organized crime figures who were not allowed to enter casinos — the Las Vegas blacklist.

fastest-growing city of its size in the United States. The population grew
from 8,422 in 1940 to 24,624 in 1950 and would jump to 64,405 in
another decade. At the end of World War II there were two casinos on the
Strip. Before 1952 was over there would be seven. And the three-block
stretch of Fremont Street downtown already housed the densest concentration of gambling on the planet. Only three establishments weren't
casinos: a drugstore (which had slot machines), a bank, and a twenty-four-
hour Western Union office. "We give 'em what they can't get in Grand
Rapids," crowed one local booster, "and we give it to 'em twenty-four
hours a day."[13]

At first glance, Las Vegas seemed too good to be true, some sort of
mirage simmering in the desert: palm trees shading pools that curved like
a women's hips, showgirls sunning themselves by day, mingling in casinos
at night, cheap rooms and cheaper buffets piled high with shrimp on ice
and endless slices of prime rib, showrooms where you could watch Frank
Sinatra or Eartha Kitt or Liberace, no cover, no minimum. On Saturdays
and Sundays there were three shows a night, which meant, as A. J. Liebling
noted, that you could see six top acts over a weekend for free.

Of course, nothing was really free. Conventioneers might be greeted
with a clanging bag of twenty-five silver dollars, but few left town with
much change jingling in their pockets. From the gauntlet of slot machines
lining the way out of the adobe terminal at McCarran Airport to the gro-
cery stores that took casino chips as cash, Las Vegas was growing rich on a
single, ineluctable proposition: The house, on average, never loses. And Las
Vegas was nothing but one big house. Liberace might earn fifty grand a
week for playing to crowds that paid nothing, but to get to the showroom
thousands had to funnel through casinos where the slot machines pulled
in pennies and nickels and dimes and quarters and silver dollars like magnets but returned only a few pounds on the ton — and after little more
than an hour of diversion guests were herded back into the casinos, where
dice tumbled, roulette balls bounced, and blackjack dealers turned over
each card like a personal favor. Just to find a hotel lobby you had to nav-
igate a maze of green felt tables and narrow passageways of winking slot
machines. Whatever a casino spent on attracting traffic came back in waves
of profit. A multimillion-dollar establishment paid for itself in half a year.
A single casino wore out eighty pairs of dice in a day. The promise of the
Strip was that its carpet-joint casinos were somehow qualitatively different
than the downtown sawdust joints; that gambling (*gaming* in the vernac-
ular) was a wholesome recreational activity to be enjoyed by Americans in

the postwar boom, sort of like television with odds. The reality was that it was just the same sucker's game dressed up as family entertainment. "I used to be a star on Broadway," Tallulah Bankhead admitted from the stage at the Sands, where she was earning twenty thousand dollars a week. "But now you see me reduced to a shill for a gambling joint."[14]

Gambling was changing Nevada. Reno was still the state's largest city, but Las Vegas, which accounted for two-thirds of the gambling business, was quickly catching up. And population meant votes, which meant power, which, too, was shifting southward. Nineteen fifty was the first year that Nevada made more from gambling than from mining; a decade later gambling was almost two and a half times bigger than mining. In 1952 seven million tourists dropped forty-three million dollars in Las Vegas; the next year ten million visitors left behind fifty million, and the year after that eleven million tourists lost sixty-five million — and that was just the *reported* revenue, of which the state asked for a mere 1 percent in taxes (soon to be raised to 2 percent). The skim — the cash that gushed into the counting rooms but never made it onto the official books — was the real jackpot, a source of untaxed wealth as limitless as human optimism and gullibility.

But for McCarran there was a paradox behind this prosperity. When he settled into his booth at the T-bird's Pow Wow room and the steaks came and the tab didn't, McCarran was acutely aware that for all the visitors who shuffled through the casinos (and more people than the population of the state passed through just the Golden Nugget in a year), Nevada's latest bonanza was less the functioning of a real economy than the exploitation of yet another extractive industry. Digging rocks out of the earth, sundering the vows of marriage, and taking the coins out of the pockets of visitors — this was how Nevada sustained itself. For years McCarran had struggled to attract manufacturing and respectable commerce to Nevada. A decade earlier the Basic Magnesium plant outside of town had seemed to herald an era of industrial production, but after the war the federal government could barely give away the largest magnesium plant in the world. "We're going to build a great industrial center in Clark County,"[15] McCarran had beamed in 1947, but five years later when the plant had been turned over to private industry it employed fewer than three thousand people — less than half the number that worked in casinos. The only industry, in the end, that was really able to flourish in the desert soil was gambling. McCarran had helped nurture that industry, in ways that he was glad to declare and in ways that he would never acknowledge. For McCarran, then, the Las Vegas boom was both an accomplishment to claim credit for and a personal failure to lament, a source of pride and a badge of shame.

"I'm afraid we have blinked our eyes at that which to my mind is the stronger form of economy, namely payrolls on legitimate business . . . ," McCarran had recently confessed to his friend Joe McDonald. "I hope the time will come when the financial structure of the state of Nevada will not rest upon gambling. I hope the time will come when we point with pride to industries of all kinds in the state of Nevada, with payrolls that will sustain the economy of Nevada. But that isn't today, Joe, and it won't be tomorrow."[16]

That day would never come.

Bugsy Siegel was furious.

"Bring Hoover in front of me and let that cocksucker tell me where he got it from," Siegel shouted.[17]

Columnist Walter Winchell had recently printed an item that the FBI was concerned about the mob moving into Las Vegas. Privately, Winchell told his friend Siegel that the tip had come from FBI director J. Edgar Hoover.

"Honest to Christ," Siegel muttered.

Siegel was forty-two, five foot nine and trim, a natty dresser whose only outward sign of having some rather rough friends was a scar on his head from where a brick had hit him after a bomb was tossed down a chimney at a business meeting years earlier. Siegel looked more like an actor than his friend George Raft, who often played a gangster. "Baby-blue eyed Benjamin," Hank Greenspun called him.[18]

"I said," Siegel fumed, "tell that dirty son of a bitch. . . ."[19]

The story was *slightly* inaccurate. Siegel was in the mob, but he was *already* in Las Vegas. In Room 401 at the Last Frontier, to be precise. And in July 1946, the FBI was listening to every word that he yelled at his girl-friend Virginia Hill.

Siegel got mad a lot. "You're crazy"[20] were the first words his boyhood friend Meyer Lansky said to him when they met. It was one of the reasons that his friends called him Bugsy. That nickname made him really mad. "The name is Ben," Siegel told a man who greeted him with the wrong name and found himself on the floor with a bleeding nose. "B-e-n," Siegel said, adding a kick in the ribs for emphasis.[21] When Siegel got angry, other people tended to get hurt. The FBI estimated that he'd had at least thirty people killed. But the only crime Siegel was ever convicted of was a bookmaking charge in 1944 that cost him a $250 fine. That, too, made Siegel mad. "A source of constant irritation to him," the FBI noted.[22]

Recently the federal government had been making Siegel very upset. Siegel lived in Los Angeles but had been coming to Las Vegas regularly since 1941, when Nevada legalized betting on horses and Siegel arrived to persuade bookmakers that they should subscribe to his racing wire service. Bookmaking was a good business, but casinos looked even more lucrative. Siegel tried to buy El Rancho. It wasn't for sale. El Cortez was. In 1945 Siegel and a group of investors, including mobster Meyer Lansky, paid six hundred thousand dollars for the casino. They sold it six months later for a $166,000 profit.

Then Siegel found another investment that looked even better: the Flamingo, which was going up on the edge of the Strip, a mile past the Last Frontier. The only thing farther out was McCarran Airport. The Flamingo was the brainchild of Billy Wilkerson, who owned a number of Los Angeles nightclubs as well as the *Hollywood Reporter*. Wilkerson decided to build a casino because he seemed to spend most of his time in one anyway, more than once betting his business empire to the brink of bankruptcy. Wilkerson didn't like Nevada but it didn't matter. "People will endure almost anything," he told Siegel, "go anywhere where there is legal gambling."[23] Wilkerson had purchased thirty-three acres on the Strip with the idea to build a luxurious casino-resort that would shame the motels-*cum*-dude-ranches that dominated the town's tourist trade: 250 rooms, a plush showroom, a top-notch restaurant, and a spa. Then he ran out of money. Howard Hughes staked him two hundred thousand but Wilkerson lost it on the gambling tables and was forced to look for other investors, among them Siegel, who quickly became obsessed by the project. Wilkerson found himself squeezed out of the Flamingo and his involvement limited to having his name on the sign at the building site.

Construction started on March 21, 1946. Five days later the federal government told Siegel to stop. The Civilian Production Administration ordered a halt to virtually all new civilian building projects so that construction materials could used to make homes for veterans. Projects that were well under way could get an exemption. Siegel's casino had stakes driven into the ground to mark where to pour the concrete. He got an exemption. "We will not stop construction," Siegel said. "We will go to jail first."[24]

In Los Angeles one explanation for the CPA reversal was suggested to an FBI agent. "Funds were made available to Senator Pat McCarran of

Nevada," claimed the informant, name blacked out in the FBI files, who admitted that he was just passing on gossip, "and shortly thereafter construction was authorized."[25]

The FBI opened an investigation, bugging Bugsy's room at the Last Frontier. The bureau was eager to nail Siegel for anything: murder, pandering, drug running, committing perjury to get a building permit. The bureau was somewhat less eager to investigate Hoover's friend McCarran. "The allegation of a bribe payment to Senator Pat McCarran is rather nebulous," one agent noted.[26]

Hoover agreed. "The inquiries relating to the alleged participation of Senator McCarran," Hoover commanded, "or other prominent people should be handled on a discrete basis in order that no rumor will be circulated that the bureau is investigating the senator or other officials until such time as definite information has been received indicating some possible irregularity on their parts."[27]

Siegel had other problems. In August the Clark County commissioners declined to give him gambling and liquor licenses. Normally these weren't much harder to get in Las Vegas than a wedding license. "If they refuse to give me a gambling license, what am I gonna do with the hotel, stick it up my ass?"[28] Siegel barked at his girlfriend.

Siegel appeared in person before the commissioners, and they granted him the licenses. Siegel then called Meyer Lansky and asked him to send a railcar of booze out to Nevada to thank the commissioners. "I should have busted a leg before I got into this thing . . . ," Siegel told his friend. "I had to go up to get nine sons-of-bitches to make an appearance. Bawled the Jesus out of them, granted the license for liquor and gambling. . . . I'm not going to quit working, they can send me to jail. Those rats. Goddamn."[29]

Siegel also had his hands full with Hill. "A fabulous woman of mystery," the FBI called her. Hill was twenty-eight, five foot four, good looking enough to be a consort to numerous mobsters but not good looking enough to parlay her talents into a career in Hollywood. "Buxom," the FBI described her. "Wears daring clothes, smokes and drinks excessively, uses foul language and considerable makeup, spends money freely. Bad, promiscuous."[30]

Hill had a temper to match Siegel's. Although neither was much for monogamy (as Siegel's wife could attest), each was incensed by the other's infidelity. Keeping Hill under surveillance was also difficult for the FBI. "Hill frequently dyes hair and changes hair style," complained one agent. "During first four opening nights of Flamingo Hotel, December 26 to 29, Hill's hair was platinum blonde with upswept hairdo first night, jet black with long bob second night, and red with long **BLACKED OUT** fourth night."[31]

In September, Siegel and Hill flew to San Francisco for a CPA hearing on the Flamingo. McCarran, FBI agents noticed, also happened to be in the city for a judicial conference. Siegel won his case, but that was just the start of his problems. Siegel had promised his partners that the Flamingo would be a cash gusher. It turned into a sinkhole. Construction materials were scarce. Siegel demanded rare wood paneling inside and imported trees outside. His own suite at the hotel had to be kingly yet built to bunker specs, including a trapdoor and escape tunnel. Bribes were needed to get many of the materials that Siegel wanted, which were then stolen from the construction site almost as soon as they were delivered. By December 1946 the one-million-dollar dream investment had become a six-million-dollar nightmare.

The grand opening took place on the day after Christmas. "The world's most lavish conception of hotel resort, casino, cafe and playground all rolled into one," wrote Siegel's new PR man, Hank Greenspun.[32] Siegel leased two planes to fly celebrities out from Hollywood. The airport was fogged in. They came by car — those who came at all. Jimmy Durante and Xavier Cugat performed. The inexperienced dealers let the guests walk away with hundreds of thousands of dollars — and since the hotel rooms weren't ready, the guests decamped for the night to the Last Frontier and El Rancho. Less than a month later the casino shut its doors.

Things weren't going much better for the FBI. After half a year of heavy surveillance with ten agents on the case, the bureau was picking up lots of information, but didn't have enough evidence to bust Siegel for a parking ticket. "After six months of almost constant coverage, we still have nothing," Assistant Director Edward Tamm complained to Hoover.[33]

In January 1947 Hoover canceled the investigation. According to one of Hoover's top aides, Cartha D. DeLoach, the order came down from Attorney General Tom Clark himself. "Agents in the field were stunned," he recalled. "They were in the middle of a gold mine, picking up nuggets every hour. But the attorney general's office pointed out that we had no business investigating activities that could not be construed as violating federal law. We later heard that a complaint had been filed by Senator Pat McCarran of Nevada, claiming that our activities were designed to damage the economy of his state."[34]

The Flamingo reopened in March. A few months later Hill exploded at Siegel when he seemed to be paying too much attention to a cigarette girl. He beat her badly enough that she was bruised for weeks, and she gulped down enough sleeping pills to wind up in the hospital. When she recovered, Hill lit off for Paris, while Siegel returned to her house in Beverly Hills. On the night of June 19, 1947, Siegel was looking over the *Los Angeles Times* on the sofa in Hill's living room when a marksman fired nine shots through the window, six of which hit their target. When a Los Angeles detective showed up in Las Vegas to ask about Siegel's enemies, no one could think of any.

Although the FBI must have gone through cartons of black markers before it released Siegel's file, the pages that weren't completely redacted include numerous intriguing mentions of McCarran:

> During a temporary recess in the hearing, he overheard the name of Senator McCarran of Nevada mentioned. At the time he heard **BLACKED OUT** remark that McCarran would come into this matter "over my dead body."
>
> McCarran of Nevada was in San Francisco during first hearing and wanted to come to the hearing. **BLACKED OUT** refused to allow his doing so.
>
> **BLACKED OUT** also mentioned that Siegel stated that Senator McCarran of Nevada either had or was going to personally "pound the table with his fists" and impress upon **BLACKED OUT** that the state of Nevada wanted the hotel constructed.
>
> Siegel asked [Moe] Sedway if McCarran is a friend of **BLACKED OUT** and Sedway replied that **BLACKED OUT** and Pat were very good friends.
>
> Siegel . . . remarked that he is getting very good cooperation at the present time from United States Senator Patrick McCarran and **BLACKED OUT** [probably Nevada senator George Malone]. Siegel remarked that he had given **BLACKED OUT** $500 as a campaign contribution.
>
> [Gus] Greenbaum stated that he overheard a conversation at Del Mar indicating that Senator McCarran is the person responsible for the "heat."
>
> **BLACKED OUT** then suggested that arrangements be made through United States Senator Pat McCarran to apply for a loan from the Reconstruction Finance Corporation. blacked out then sug-

gested to Siegel to advise McCarran that it would "be good for McCarran to play dumb about the money going into the place" in the event McCarran should be questioned about the original financial arrangements in the Flamingo Hotel.[35]

Five years after Siegel was killed, McCarran was asked in a sworn deposition for a civil suit if he had helped Siegel with his casino.

"I never saw Siegel in my life," he said.[36]

In September 1946 Herman Greenspun and a friend drove into Las Vegas in Greenspun's red Buick convertible looking for a business opportunity. Greenspun was thirty-six, Brooklyn born, and a fierce Zionist, a lawyer by night school, a street fighter by temperament. He had worked in the law office of Vito Marcantonio, the closest thing the United States ever had to a Communist member of Congress, before deciding that the law did not suit him. He served with distinction in World War II but afterward found himself at loose ends. So when his wife got pregnant, he drove out west. Greenspun checked into the Last Frontier, went for a swim in the pool, and then called his wife. "Come on out," he told her. "I'm never coming back."[37]

Greenspun put out a promotional magazine called *Las Vegas Life*, which published a story about Ben Siegel's new casino, the Flamingo. Siegel stopped by the office, purchased the advertising rights to the back cover for a year, and then hired Greenspun to flack for the Flamingo. When Siegel was killed, some suspected it was Greenspun's idea of a publicity stunt. Greenspun quickly disassociated himself from the Flamingo and put his family's savings (seven thousand dollars) into Wilbur Clark's Desert Inn project, taking over the publicity duties for the new casino. He soon went AWOL. A childhood friend showed up in Las Vegas one day in late 1947 asking for help in smuggling arms to Israel, which was fighting for independence. The next thing Greenspun knew, he was in Hawaii labeling crates of machine guns AIRCRAFT ENGINES and then on a yacht off the California coast pressing a gun to the head of a reluctant skipper.

By the time Greenspun was back in Las Vegas more than a year later, Wilbur Clark's role in the Desert Inn was reduced to a spot on the sign and mobster Moe Dalitz was running the casino. Greenspun cashed out and found another investment: the *Free Press*, a newspaper started up by striking typesetters who had been locked out of the *Las Vegas Review-Journal*, whose longtime editor was Al Cahlan, McCarran's satrap in southern Nevada. Greenspun borrowed a thousand-dollar down payment, took over the newspaper, found that it had twenty-eight hundred dollars in cash, and promptly repaid his loan. He changed the name to the *Sun*, which published its first issue on July 1, 1950.

Two weeks later Greenspun met with Guernsey Frazer, who was running McCarran's reelection campaign in Las Vegas. "Greenspun has just left," Frazer reported to McCarran. "He feels very 'friendly' to you and advised that all of his backers are for you, so that he will go along with them."[38]

Later that month Greenspun found himself in federal court in Los Angeles pleading guilty to violating the Export Control and Neutrality Act for his gun-running stint — on one condition, he insisted, that he not enter his plea until the afternoon. Once the morning *Review-Journal's* deadline had passed, Greenspun entered his plea and filed a story to the *Sun*, which led the paper above the fold: "Greenspun Guilty."

Greenspun was given a suspended sentence — something McCarran later took credit for, claiming that he had spoken to the Justice Department on the publisher's behalf. "Your honor," Greenspun told the court, "I wear my guilt of supplying arms to Israel as a badge of honor."[39]

As a newsman Greenspun was a neophyte, but he certainly knew how to make headlines. He was about to get the biggest of his life.

In the summer of 1951 a shadow much more ominous than the mushroom clouds on the edge of the desert fell over Las Vegas: a proposed federal gambling tax. Senator Estes Kefauver and other lawmakers were pushing bills through Congress to levy a 10 percent gross tax on all gambling revenue — a tax that would, of course, apply only to Nevada. If it passed, McCarran told his friend Joe McDonald, every gambling house in the state would shut. "Virginia Street would be in mourning, and the gleaming gulch of Las Vegas would be a glowing symbol of funereal distress . . . ," McCarran complained. "In the last few years the state of Nevada has woven gambling in its various forms into the warp and woof of the state's economic structure."[40]

Estes Kefauver was becoming a real pain in the ass. The year before, on November 15, Kefauver had flown into Las Vegas for the day, a brief stop on a fourteen-city, ten-month grand tour of the American underworld. Like Orpheus with a southern accent, Kefauver descended into a desert netherworld where the sinful became respectable, other state's criminals were reborn as businessmen, and vice was a legitimate trade. "As a case history of legalized gambling," Kefauver later observed, "Nevada speaks eloquently in the negative."[41]

Born in a small town in Tennessee, Kefauver was educated at the University of Tennessee and Yale Law School. He returned home to practice law, and in 1939 went as a congressman to Washington, a liberal representative from a region that generally abhorred liberals. In 1948 Kefauver won election to the Senate after a nasty campaign where his stands against HUAC and on behalf of civil rights were used to paint him as a Communist. When his opponents accused Kefauver of being as sneaky as a coon, he started campaigning with a live raccoon. ("The most American of all animals has been defamed. You wouldn't find a coon in Russia."[42]) But crowds scared the raccoon and made it bite, so he replaced the animal with a coonskin cap. Kefauver was part of great Class of '48 that included such liberals as Paul Douglas and Hubert Humphrey, who formed the core of opposition to McCarran's Internal Security Act in 1950. That alone was reason enough for McCarran to detest Kefauver. Trying to strangle his state's economy was another.

In January 1950 Kefauver proposed Senate Resolution 202, which called for the Judiciary Committee to launch an investigation into organized crime's role in gambling and racketeering. McCarran sat on the idea for two months before diluting the proposed investigation by requiring the subcommittee to inquire into *all* aspects of organized crime, such as prostitution, narcotics, and murder, and refrain from recommending any changes in state gambling laws. Senate majority leader Scott Lucas, who was facing reelection in Illinois, wasn't any happier than McCarran about having the annoyingly persistent Kefauver poking around cities (say, Chicago) where Democratic party bosses had more than a passing familiarity with organized crime figures. So it took another two months of haggling before the resolution finally came to a vote in May, by which time the proposed panel had been pried out of McCarran's grip in the Judiciary Committee. The vote was a tie, broken by the vice president in Kefauver's favor. McCarran missed the roll call — and his chance to kill the committee.

That summer the Kefauver Committee (formally, the Special Committee to Investigate Organized Crime in Interstate Commerce) set off on a fifty-two-thousand-mile odyssey across America, listening to eight hundred witnesses and compiling 11,500 pages of testimony. The committee reached Las Vegas in November 1950 and set up shop on the second floor of the federal courthouse on Stewart Avenue, two blocks over from Glitter Gulch on Fremont, where a parade of casino owners passed before Kefauver and his colleagues.

There was Bill Moore, owner of the Last Frontier and also a member of the state tax commission, which was the agency in charge of regulating casinos. His first job earned him eighty thousand dollars a year, the second less than eight thousand. There was Cliff Jones, owner of the Thunderbird and the state's lieutenant governor, who noted that many of the gambling operators drawn to Las Vegas in recent years had not formerly been Sunday school teachers. There was Wilbur Clark, who had a vague idea that he had sold three-quarters of the DI to investors with less-than-sterling reputations but wasn't really worried about it. There was Moe Sedway, who had taken over the Flamingo after Bugsy Siegel was killed but insisted that the mob had nothing to do with the place now. (Later the committee caught up with Siegel's old girlfriend Virginia Hill. "You bastards," she cursed. "I hope a goddamn atom bomb falls on every goddamn one of you."[43]) By the end of the day the committee hadn't exactly broken any news, but it had publicized Nevada's half-assed regulation of its leading industry as well as the ample ties between the gambling community and organized crime figures. This was, Hank Greenspun observed, something a sharp ten-year-old boy could have figured out.

On January 23, 1951, Kefauver introduced a list of nine committee witnesses whom he wanted to cite for contempt. McCarran jumped up to block the action, citing a Supreme Court ruling in favor of a woman who refused to answer questions about being a Communist. McCarran suggested sending the resolution to his Judiciary Committee for further study. McCarran lost the vote.

The Kefauver Committee became a sensation, especially after its New York hearings were broadcast live on television and became an unlikely daytime hit, getting better ratings than the World Series. Kefauver was suddenly one of the most recognized politicians in the country. He appeared on *What's My Line*, then put his name on a four-part series in the *Saturday Evening Post* and his face on the cover of *Time*.

In May 1951 the committee released its final report, which devoted four pages to Nevada. "Where gambling receives a cloak of respectability through legalization," the report said, "there is no weapon which can be used to keep the gamblers and their money out of politics."[44]

That summer the federal gambling tax bills came like furies. McCarran summoned help to Washington: his friend Republican millionaire Norm Biltz, lobbyist Johnny Mueller, and T-bird owner Marion Hicks. "For ten days we went round and round," McCarran told Pete Petersen. "I pulled on every string that I had ever known of. . . . Everyone for whom we have ever turned a hand in the Congress or in the Senate was called upon."[45]

McCarran made a personal plea before the Senate Finance Committee. Almost a third of the state's budget came from its 1 percent gambling tax. A federal tax would cripple the industry and might drive away 40 percent of the state's population. "It will kill the goose that lays the golden eggs, so far as federal tax collections from Nevada are concerned," McCarran said. ". . . The cumulative results would spell tragedy for the state."[46]

McCarran admitted to his friend Joe McDonald that he wasn't thrilled that gambling had come to dominate the state's economy, but he had little choice except to fight the tax proposal. "It isn't a very laudable position for one to have to defend gambling," he told McDonald. ". . . One must lay aside pride and put on the hide of a rhinoceros and go to it. . . . When Kefauver and Douglas and Humphrey and all the other puritanically-inclined gentlemen are clamoring to put gambling out of business, upon whom shall I call for assistance?"[47]

The tax bill died in committee. McCarran had helped save the gambling industry. And when McCarran needed a favor, he knew who he could call.

March was freezing in Nevada. The winter of 1952 was the worst in sixty years. The northern part of the state was walloped by storm after storm. The roads across the Sierra disappeared under snow. On Mount Rose, near Reno, a couple got caught in a snowdrift in their car and froze to death. Planes didn't fly and transcontinental trains didn't move. On the winter range ten thousand cows and sheep were out of food and out of reach. Washington dispatched eight C-54 cargo planes to Elko to drop feed, but the weather was too fierce to fly for several days. Even in Las Vegas the temperature plunged into the twenties and more than an inch of rain fell, a monsoon for the city, while twenty miles away on Mount Charleston snow drifted fifteen feet deep. So much rain fell near Yucca Flat at the Nevada Test Site that a dry lake became a real lake as deep as six inches, forcing the Atomic Energy Commission to postpone a series of spring bomb blasts. It was so cold that the public utility commission banned space heaters in Las Vegas for fear that the city's population would overload the county's electrical system.

In these chill desert mornings few early risers were tempted to linger. Still, if you were on the street that winter in Clark County before stores opened, sooner or later you were probably approached by a tall, skinny young man in a suit and tie, holding a large book in one hand, extending the other to shake. Even the Mormons didn't get up this early. Tom Mechling, the man introduced himself, I want to be your senator.

Six days a week Tom Mechling woke up at six, ate breakfast with his wife, Margaret, in the trailer that they called home, and then walked around for a couple of hours, introducing himself to milkmen, bus drivers, and anyone else who would stop to talk to him. At nine he pulled out a well-seamed Las Vegas street map and started knocking on the doors he had not knocked on the day before. House by house, street by street, block by block, Mechling worked his way across Las Vegas. At noon he spoke at a luncheon or two and then went back to his map until dark. Nights were given to dinner speeches and club meetings. Some evenings Mechling made half a dozen appearances, speaking for five minutes, then taking questions. Then he hit the streets downtown before winding up in a diner for a midnight snack and some chatting with the late-shift waiters. Everywhere Mechling went he carried his big book, writing down the name and address of everyone he met, and each night in the trailer Margaret typed up hundreds of postcards that Mechling mailed off the next day. "He seems to be," one of Drew Pearson's researchers gushed, "the most purposeful young man we have heard about in years."[48]

Some men run for office. Mechling walked. He'd arrived in Las Vegas with his wife, their savings, a car and trailer, a dozen pairs of dress shoes, and four spare tires. Mechling was thirty-one, almost six foot three, barely 170 pounds, with blond hair and blue eyes. Born in Colorado, he had worked for the last few years as an associate editor in the Washington office of *Kiplinger*, the personal finance magazine. The man he most admired in Washington was Senator Paul Douglas. His wife, unfortunately, worked for the senator least like Douglas: Pat McCarran. Margaret Mechling (née Di Grazia) grew up in Wells, where her father owned a big ranch and was active in Democratic politics. In 1950 she was hired by McCarran's immigration subcommittee as a stenographer. At night she often came home smoldering over her boss's fixation with subversive aliens. "He doesn't want anybody here who arrived after his parents got to this country," she fumed to Tom.[49]

On December 31, 1951, Margaret quit McCarran's staff. A month later Tom announced that he was running for the Senate. In between he had become a resident of Wells. In February, Mechling hit the streets of Las Vegas. "I don't know whether to admire Tom Mechling," Hank Greenspun wrote, ". . . or to dismiss him as a presumptuous upstart."[50]

Greenspun didn't take long to decide. The *Sun* became the only newspaper to back his candidacy, in fact one of the few newspapers in Nevada to even acknowledge it. "Maybe Tom doesn't know too much about our senior senator and should be briefed on the subject . . . ," Greenspun wrote in his column. "His spirit of vindictiveness has instilled such fear in the hearts of his henchmen that he will still control the thoughts and actions of many Nevada politicians after his retirement from public life. . . . There is only one McCarran, stronger and more powerful than Samson and I doubt if Tom Mechling has the price of a good slingshot."[51]

Greenspun was a willing slingshot. While Mechling walked his heels thin across Clark County, Greenspun burrowed into the twelve thousand pages of the Kefauver Committee report and began printing excerpts that accused McCarran of trying to cover up a scandal in the Bureau of Internal Revenue. McCarran had appointed as the state's field director Pat Mooney, who in turn shook down people to invest in a sham mining company of his or face hostile audits. Mooney wound up in jail, and one of his henchmen accused McCarran of whitewashing the whole incident. It was a murky allegation but it was good enough for Greenspun, especially since Kefauver had ridden his committee's fame to become the front-runner for the Democratic presidential nomination. "I am certain that McCarran would not relish the prospect of the six-foot-three crimebuster sitting in the White House and having knowledge of the supposed activities that tied Silvertip in with Mooney," Greenspun wrote in March. ". . . I know that Kefauver is on the McCarran list because word has come from the office of Pat that if the Tennessean is elected, he will kill gambling in the state of Nevada."[52]

The next day Tom Mechling finished two months of campaigning in Las Vegas, hooked up his trailer, climbed into his Chevy with his wife, and headed north into the mountains toward Tonopah.

The following afternoon, Greenspun walked into the Flamingo and met with its owner Gus Greenbaum and Benny Binion, who ran the Horseshoe on Fremont. These were the last two guys in Las Vegas you wanted to get on the wrong side of. Greenbaum was less given to pistol-whipping employees than Bugsy Siegel had been but one still didn't want to make him mad; in 1951, for instance, two thieves stole thirty-five hundred dollars from the Flamingo and the next month were found in a car in Los Angeles, shot in the head. Binion once beat fourteen men into a pulp with a car bumper and killed at least two men in Texas before arriving in Las Vegas with a suitcase full of cash.

"You'll ruin us by attacking the senator," Greenbaum told Greenspun. "He has been burning up the wires from Washington and you must stop."

Greenspun agreed to lay off McCarran. "Until he irritates me again," he added.

"I'm afraid," Greenbaum said, "you have already gone too far."[53]

Three days later almost every casino in town pulled its advertising from the *Sun*. That afternoon the temperature climbed into the sixties. But Greenspun was out in the cold.

The *Sun* lost a third of its business on Monday. On Wednesday, Greenspun ran a cryptic column. "Evil is entrenched in Nevada politics," he declared oracularly. ". . . Men must indeed be devoid of all moral qualities if they permit themselves to be enticed into a position where one tyrannical person can command their complete obedience. . . . This newspaper will go on writing, reporting and printing the news as it is made, instead of through the tyranny-beclouded eyes of one man who has dedicated his life to rule or ruin."[54]

That evening the city's crusty mayor, C. D. Baker, summoned Greenspun and three casino representatives to his office. Baker was a rarity in Nevada: a politician unbeholden to McCarran, and furthermore had come to office by defeating Ernie Cragin, a McCarran acolyte. Baker was blunt, a surveyor by training who was used to finding the straightest line between two points and an ex-military man who never got out of the habit of barking orders. "Sit down and shut up" was his customary way of starting city commission meetings. Now, he wanted to know, what on earth is going on between the casinos and the *Sun*? Nothing, averred Lieutenant Governor and Thunderbird owner Cliff Jones, the casinos just decided to save money by not advertising in the paper. But Monte Carlo Club owner Fred Soly and the Boulder Club's J. Kell Houssels finally admitted that the decision was prompted by McCarran.

Baker blew his top. "Neither the gambling industry nor any politician in Washington will be permitted to destroy a legitimate enterprise in this community," he said.[55]

Greenspun went home and sat at his kitchen table typing up the next morning's column, in which he accused McCarran of trying to kill the *Sun* with an advertising boycott. There was, Greenspun wrote, a phone call from McCarran's office in Washington to Marion Hicks at the Thunderbird, who then organized a meeting of casino owners to spread word of the senator's displeasure with the *Sun*. "A man who has gone so power-mad that he has threatened to wreck the industry unless it withdraw all support of this newspaper," Greenspun wrote of McCarran.[56]

Over the weekend Drew Pearson repeated the story on his national radio show. A small Las Vegas newspaper was about to become the center of a very big fight.

—

On the night of May 20 high winds scoured the Las Vegas valley and formed into a twister that touched down on the far edge of the Strip, past the Flamingo, at McCarran Airport. The whirlwind picked up a small private plane and hurled it into a transformer, snapping power lines and flinging a cascade of sparks across the night sky. The plane's fuel tank exploded and the airport lights went off, the field plunging into darkness except for the burning plane. The Strip, too, fell black. It was as if the gods were angry.

Earlier in the day thirteen attorneys had crowded into a room at the federal courthouse for a preliminary hearing on the *Herman Greenspun v. Patrick A. McCarran, et al.* After Greenspun lost his gambling ads, he went looking for an attorney. There were a lot of lawyers in Las Vegas; almost none were interested in his case. Finally he hired George Marshall, a Republican who had challenged McCarran for the Senate in 1950. Then the pundits called.

Washington columnists Drew Pearson and Robert Allen were friends and former partners. Pearson's column ran in the *Review-Journal;* Allen's in the *Sun.* Both despised McCarran. "This old son-of-a-bitch has got a thumping due him," Allen told Pearson. ". . . There is no question he's no different or better than McCarthy, they are both out of the same outhouse."[57] Pearson was even less fond of McCarran. The columnist had tried to help defeat McCarran during the tough 1944 primary fight. McCarran paid Pearson back by exposing his legman Dave Karr as a former Communist in a 1949 Judiciary Committee hearing. Pearson publicly denied that Karr had been a party member but was more candid in his diary. "If I am any judge of human nature, he was cured of this long ago,"[58] Pearson wrote. McCarran called Pearson a skunk. Pearson called McCarran a fascist. "If Senator Pat McCarran wasn't in a position to do so much damage to our free institutions, I'd feel a little sorry for him," Pearson said once. "The years are creeping up on him and atrophy may be taking a toll on his imagination no less than his arteries. But I have an idea that the Kremlin must be getting some belly laughs out of Pat's reasoning that anyone who disagrees with him is a Communist traveler."[59]

Pearson recommended that Greenspun hire his attorney William A. Roberts, who flew out to Las Vegas and took over the case. Greenspun filed a million-dollar lawsuit against McCarran, Eva Adams, and fourteen casino owners, charging that they had conspired to drive the *Sun* out of business. Bookmakers put the odds on Greenspun winning at twenty to one against.

Then the trial judge was assigned: Roger T. Foley, a McCarran appointee. The odds went into orbit. "You will never have cause to feel that I am ungrateful or that I am one to go back on my friends or on my word,"[60] Foley had written to McCarran when he was named to the bench in 1945.

In the hearing room a procession of casino owners denied that they were out to get Greenspun. The owners did admit to meeting in two different groups on March 22 — first at the Flamingo and then at the Golden Nugget, where they decided to stop advertising in the *Sun* — but they insisted that they were acting on their own accord, not at McCarran's behest. Moe Dalitz disputed Greenspun's version of their conversation at the Desert Inn. Greenspun lunged at Dalitz. Then Mayor Baker took the stand and recounted how two of the defendants had admitted to him in his office that McCarran had pressured them into the boycott.

Foley threatened to find Greenspun in contempt for his column, which had intimated that the gamblers were guilty of perjury. Someone obviously had committed perjury, the judge said, ruling that the suit could go to trial and ordering the casinos to resume advertising with the *Sun* in the meantime.

McCarran denied having anything to do with the fracas. "The whole thing is ridiculous," he sniffed.[61]

One day in July, Nevada's U.S. attorney Miles Pike suddenly resigned — a fact that McCarran seemed to know before Pike. Hours later McCarran suggested a replacement: James Johnson Jr., one of the Nevada boys who had worked for McCarran in Washington and whom he had later made the Democratic state chairman. The nomination raced through the Judiciary Committee in two days, even before the usual FBI background investigation was done, and was sent to the White House for the president's signature. At that point it turned out that Truman had no idea who Johnson was. Normally the president and the attorney general had *some* say in who was named as the highest federal law enforcement official in a state, even if they usually deferred to patronage considerations. "Doubt now exists," Drew Pearson reported, "as to whether Johnson's name actually was ever sent to the Senate by the White House."[62]

Greenspun wrote to the White House (and fulminated in the *Las Vegas Sun*) that McCarran was trying to install a dependable political hack as the U.S. attorney to insulate himself from possible prosecution in case Judge Foley's perjury inquiry in Greenspun's lawsuit led back to the senator. Greenspun urged Truman not to sign the appointment. Truman didn't need much encouragement. "This, of course, is a very serious matter," Truman told his new attorney general, James McGranery, "if there is any foundation for it and I would like to have you examine the record in the *Las Vegas Sun* case and make such other investigation as may be necessary to get to the bottom of this."[63]

At the Democratic convention in Chicago in July, McCarran almost got into a fistfight.[64] A parade for Estes Kefauver broke loose on the convention center floor, and Nevada delegate William Ruymann grabbed the Silver State's sign to join the procession. McCarran stepped in his way, called him a punk, and threw a punch. Ruymann said that he'd fight McCarran if he weren't so old. Another delegate stepped between them. You double-crossing skunk, McCarran began. You son of a bitch.

The double cross was that the twenty members of the delegation were supposed to support Georgia senator Richard Russell. Not because they wanted to, but because McCarran told them to. Harry Truman had decided not to run for another term. Truman's favored successor was Illinois governor Adlai Stevenson. Bald, brainy, and beloved by anti-Communist liberals, Stevenson had been playing Hamlet for months, coming into the convention with the second largest number of delegates even through he professed not to be a candidate. The front-runner for the nomination was Estes Kefauver, who trudged through the snow of New Hampshire in March in his coonskin cap and trounced Truman in the primary. Kefauver, a folksy southern liberal, was the candidate most like Truman. Stevenson, a coy patrician, the least. Truman didn't like Kefauver: He never stopped looking for the main chance, couldn't hold his liquor, and, worst of all, was a damn show horse. He thought he liked Stevenson.

McCarran couldn't stand either. Kefauver had dragged Nevada's name through the mud with his organized crime hearings, making Las Vegas look like a retirement community for gangsters and hoods, and then he tried to tax gambling to extinction. And just the past month Kefauver had joined with the Senate's other liberals to fight the McCarran-Walter bill, calling it a thought-control law. Stevenson was a lesser-known quality. But he had worked in the Triple A at the start of the New Deal when the agency was crawling with Ivy League Communists and now his most passionate backers were Cold War liberals, which was all McCarran needed to know. McCarran's own candidate was Georgia senator Richard Russell, one of the giants of the Senate, for whom McCarran made a seconding speech at the convention. McCarran also made speeches to the Nevada delegation, of which he was chairman. "You will vote for Russell," McCarran roared at Representative Walter Baring on the convention floor, "or I will personally see to it that you're beaten in this fall's election."★[65]

On the first ballot Kefauver won, followed by Stevenson, closely trailed by Russell. Several of the Nevada delegation voted for Stevenson but were surprised to hear McCarran count their votes with Russell's when he reported the tally into the floor microphone. "A Russell election would have given our senator more power than any one man could absorb," Greenspun wrote in the *Sun*, "which would have certainly made it most unhealthy for me. I definitely would have had to leave Nevada and I doubt if there would have been any place in the country where I could have found haven."[66]

Stevenson was nominated on the third ballot. McCarran was the only member of the delegation who refused to sign a pledge to support the nominee. A few weeks later he was hinting that he might bolt the party. "I want to support the Democratic nominee but I am waiting to see what Governor Stevenson will do before I pledge myself to him," McCarran told the *San Francisco Examiner*. "I hate to think that he's pursuing the ADA line, but there is some indication of it. People will turn away from both Stevenson and Eisenhower if they fail to back the principles on which the country was founded. Of course, it's too late to form another party for this election, but one may be organized in the future."[67]

A group of Las Vegas Democrats wired Stevenson urging him to name Alan Bible as the state party chief in place of McCarran. Two days later McCarran endorsed Stevenson. McCarran had wired Stevenson a complaint about his campaign manager Wilson Wyatt, who had been active with ADA. The governor said he had never belonged to the ADA. McCarran was satisfied. For the moment.

The day had hit 106 degrees but by seven in the evening you could walk the streets of downtown Las Vegas without wanting to die. On the corner of Third and Fremont, at the edge of Glitter Gulch, stood a tall young man whose thin frame seemed too insubstantial to hold up his sand-colored suit, speaking into a microphone atop a stand almost as wide as he was. Next to him a pretty young brunette sat at a small table smiling into a phone. In a town full of shills and touts who hired pretty girls by the busload, this looked like one of the least imaginative promotions that the

---

★He was.

gulch had seen for a while. THE OPEN BOOK CAMPAIGN, read the banner behind the lanky man. TOM MECHLING FOR U.S. SENATOR.[68]

Mechling had spent four months in Las Vegas and Reno, where his appendix burst and Margaret carried on for him while he recovered in the hospital, and then the couple made a lap of the cow counties. Now, in August, Mechling was back in Las Vegas, where every evening for a week he stood on the corner broadcasting over the radio. Mechling talked about civil rights, public disclosure of campaign financing, and supporting Truman's foreign policy. Mostly, though, he talked about McCarran's machine. "What I saw up close," he said, "of self-serving politicians in Washington made me mad — mad enough to jump down out of the press gallery and into politics with both feet."[69]

To listen to Mechling, you'd never know that McCarran wasn't actually running for office this year. Alan Bible, on the other hand, wasn't doing much to remind voters that he *was*. Although Bible had been forced to declare for the race in February, a week after Mechling did, he didn't actually start campaigning until late May, almost five months after his rival.

No one ever accused Alan Bible of being overeager. He was forty-one, with a huge square head, thick glasses, and a face as lumpy and rough as a dry riverbed. He was only a decade older than Mechling but looked two. Friends never met anyone less physically active. He'd go on a fishing trip to Mexico, hook a marlin, and then hand the pole to a crewman to take care of the rest. On a duck-hunting trip a friend found him sitting in car listening to the radio when he was supposed to be flushing birds out of the bush. Bible had no reason to rush. He was liked and respected, and most people just figured that he'd run for the Senate and win. After all, he was the first McCarran boy.

Two decades earlier, in March 1933, Bible had walked into McCarran's office in Washington. The senator had just been sworn in. Bible, born in Lovelock (population fourteen hundred), was going to Georgetown Law School and needed a part-time job. He visited both McCarran and Key Pittman looking for work. McCarran's office called with a job to run the elevator in the Capitol. The next day Key Pittman's office called with the same offer. Bible was the first of the long line of young men from Nevada who worked their way through law school in Washington under McCarran's patronage.

After Bible graduated from law school, he joined McCarran's Reno law firm. Later Bible served two terms as the state's attorney general and declined to run for a third in 1950 — largely, most folks believed, because there was a Senate seat coming up for grabs two years later. The seat was held by George "Molly" Malone, a Republican who'd slipped into office when McCarran's machinations split the Democratic ranks in 1946. Malone was generally considered one of the worst members of the Senate. "Malone's record in Congress is virtually indistinguishable from McCarran's," noted the *Washington Post*, "except that Malone has not wielded the power for evil that is the hallmark of the senior senator."[70] And in overwhelmingly Democratic Nevada no one expected that Alan Bible would have any problem beating him. Then Tom Mechling registered to vote in Nevada and proceeded to shake more than sixty thousand hands — three-quarters of the number of voters who would go to the polls.

If Mechling resembled nothing so much as an overgrown Boy Scout, then Bible looked like the second-choice speaker for a Kiwanis luncheon. Bible ran a plodding campaign on a platform of platitudes. He was McCarran's protégé. Mechling might not have any experience but he was young and energetic and proudly announced himself as an independent liberal. He was the anti-McCarran. Bible was an expert on water law. No one in the state could talk more knowledgeably about the in-lieu tax dispute between Carson City and Clark County. Mechling had a hot wife.

In the final week of the primary race, Bible was finally roused. He tried to steal Mechling's anti-machine strategy, accusing his opponent of being a paid spoiler for the Republicans, calling him part of the Mechling-Malone Alliance. "Democrats Don't Be Suckers," one ad cried. "The machine smears legitimate candidates by entering mud-slinging opponents against them in the primary races."[71] "They are selling you another Republican," charged another.[72] On August 28 McCarran endorsed Bible — something he had never done publicly in a primary before. "He is no carpetbagger," McCarran said.[73]

Greenspun flung the endorsement back in McCarran's face, calling it a diktat to purge Mechling. "Defeat this young fellow," Greenspun wrote, "and you doom the state to continual vicious machine politics, because no other young man will ever dare run again without boss permission."[74]

Primary day, September 2, was a scorcher, 107 degrees with cold beer nowhere to be found in Las Vegas during polling hours. Bible had the endorsement of virtually every newspaper in the state, while those that took notice of Mechling did so mainly to heap scorn upon him. "An unknown carpetbagger who came to the state of Nevada as a snake oil salesman," the *Review-Journal* called him.[75] The *Sun* was the only exception. The top of that morning's paper featured photos of McCarran, Bible, and Lieutenant

Governor Cliff Jones versus one of Mechling. "Mechling," the headline read, "Faced by 'Unholy Alliance.'" "Are the people of the state to be saddled with the McCarran machine for another six years," Greenspun asked in his column, "or has the time come when the yoke will be cast off?"[76]

Almost no one (including Greenspun) expected Bible to lose. Mechling won by 475 votes. Adlai Stevenson soon came out for Mechling. "From what I have read and heard about it," he told a press conference, "he seems to me a splendid man. I am very gratified that the Democratic Party has such a good candidate up in Nevada."[77]

McCarran was more coy. "I always back bona fide residents of Nevada," he said.[78]

In September two dozen of McCarran's boys threw a dinner for him at the Riverside Hotel in Reno. "They drove in from all over the state to be there," McCarran told his wife. "I thought it was awful fine."[79]

The McCarran boys were working their tails off to help elect Malone. "We all had to come out to Nevada to do whatever we could in the campaign," Ralph Denton recalled. "I say had to. God, I wanted to."[80]

Even those who couldn't abide McCarran's politics helped him work against his own party that fall. One young lawyer crisscrossed five counties on McCarran's behalf and then after the election went back to Washington and quit the senator's staff. He told Eva Adams he had paid his debt for what McCarran had done for him but he couldn't work for him any more and still sleep at night. "I admired McCarran so greatly as a man, but disagreed with his political philosophy," added Denton. "Yet I was proud of him that he was not reading the polls, deciding what to vote. He was a believer."[81]

The old man sat in the middle of the table, surrounded by the young men who would be the future of Nevada. "My God, here I am," McCarran said, "and they call you guys a machine."[82]

On October 13 Joe McCarthy and Molly Malone stood together on the stage of the packed Las Vegas War Memorial Auditorium at a Republican campaign rally. WE LIKE IKE, a banner behind them read. McCarthy then named a couple of other people whom he liked: Molly Malone and Pat McCarran. "Two great Americans," he called them. Then McCarthy mentioned one he didn't like. "You have a man who pretends to be a newspaper man," he said and his voice was carried live to radio stations all across Nevada. "He's in the audience —"

Faces turned to look at Greenspun and his wife, Barbara. "Greenspun, to begin with, spouts all the usual mouthings of the *Daily Worker*," McCarthy continued. "He doesn't even have the intelligence to think up anything new for himself. Everything he writes is taken verbatim from the *Daily Worker*."

"Liar," Barbara Greenspun shouted. McCarthy went on to attack the publisher's war record and make note of his arms-smuggling conviction.[83]

"I wish his name wasn't Greenspun," McCarthy shouted. "He's a disgrace to a fine race. He smears anyone. One of them is a man I love dearly, Senator Pat McCarran."[84]

"Women shuddered and strong men controlled their emotions with difficulty as the attack continued," the *Sun* reporter wrote. "They had never heard such disgraceful language from a Nevada rostrum. Their sense of fair play, their love of truth was outraged to the breaking point, as the Las Vegas publisher was excoriated by the tongue of a man whose like had never before been seen or heard."[85]

"Greenspun is here," McCarthy declared. "Let him stand up and be seen."

Greenspun stood up. "There he is," McCarthy cried, "the admitted ex-Communist." Greenspun walked to the stage. "If you want to listen to the editor of the local *Daily Worker* you can," McCarthy said, "but I'm going."[86]

McCarthy reached for his hat and headed for the door, followed by Malone and a number of supporters. Greenspun grabbed the microphone. He yelled at the senator to come back. "Debate with me, if you're not afraid of the truth, senator," Greenspun cried.[87] McCarthy moved through the crowd and slipped out the door into the warm desert night. Greenspun spent the next half an hour attacking McCarthy over the radio.

"Decent men do not run from a free and open debate, American style," Greenspun started his column the next morning. "McCarthy . . . ran as he does from all truth. McCarthy is afraid to debate openly. He knows the truth will find him out and show him to be the lying scoundrel history will prove him. . . . Never in his disreputable career has he ever made so untruthful a statement as he made last night when he said I was an admitted ex-Communist. If there was a shred of truth in that, his twin brother in the ranks of bigotry, Senator Pat McCarran, would have found it out by this time."[88]

Greenpsun swore out an affidavit that he had never been a Communist, put it on his front page, and offered a thousand-dollar reward to anyone who could prove otherwise. And since McCarthy had clearly libeled Greenspun by calling him an admitted ex-Communist (he probably meant *ex-convict*), Greenspun felt free to say anything he wanted to about

McCarthy — and unlike most of the journalists in the country who felt bound to treat McCarthy's ridiculous charges with professional neutrality, Greenspun lunged for the senator's neck. Earlier in the year McCarthy had tried to get the Justice Department to indict Drew Pearson under the McCarran Act for publishing government secrets in his column. Pearson responded by threatening to print an affidavit from a man who claimed to have had sex with McCarthy in a Wisconsin hotel room. Pearson never printed the material, but he gave it to Greenspun — who did. "It is common talk among homosexuals in Milwaukee who rendezvous at the White Horse Inn that Senator Joe McCarthy has often engaged in homosexual activities," Greenspun wrote in one column. "The persons in Nevada who listened to McCarthy's radio talk thought he had the queerest laugh. He has. He is."*[89]

Years later Greenspun admitted that he had no idea if any of that was true. "The most immoral, indecent, and unprincipled scoundrel to ever sit in the United States Senate," the newspaperman called the lawmaker.[90] "Sure I called him a faggot," Greenspun said. "Maybe he was. He was as much a homosexual as the hundred homosexuals he said worked in the State Department, which he never produced. It was fighting the devil with fire."[91]

McCarran and his friend Norm Biltz were walking across the Sierra Street Bridge in Reno when they stopped over the middle of the river. McCarran started to cry. Did you think you'd ever see the day I'd go on the radio for Malone? McCarran asked.

Mechling had just made a radio broadcast in which he claimed that McCarran had sent two unnamed minions to him four days after the primary to make him an offer. "McCarran wanted me to clear every political decision with him, just as if I were one of his errand boys," Mechling recalled. "In short, I was to help him rebuild the machine we had wrecked in the primary. With McCarran it was either rule or ruin. . . . I couldn't believe the senator had so much gall. . . . My unforgivable mistake was that I had never asked McCarran whether it was all right to run for United States senator."[92]

McCarran was livid. "Mechling is going wild with his lies about me," McCarran told his wife, "and I'm going to answer him on the radio. He too is being led by Eastern Jews, and Commies."[93] McCarran was going to

---

*"Was it part of a Commie plot to smear Joe McCarthy?" Hoover wondered. (See Hoover to Tolson, 23 January 1952 and 19 May 1953, both FBI 62-96332.)

come out in public and support Molly Malone, the Republican candidate.
In the past McCarran had helped Republicans but never so openly. "This
little boy won't light his way into the Senate with my consent," McCarran
told his daughter Margaret. "I may not think very much of the other fellow
but at least he won't vote with the ADA and that is something."[94]

Standing over the Truckee River McCarran and Biltz both knew that
McCarran might be committing political suicide.

Do you want me to walk to the radio station with you, Patsy? Biltz
asked.

No, McCarran said, I think I can stand it better alone.[95]

On October 23 McCarran spoke into a radio microphone and urged his
friends across Nevada to vote for the Republican candidate in the election
two weeks away. "I have been," McCarran said, "the target of certain elements in America and from abroad who seek either to destroy me personally or to discredit me." The senator then pointed out that he would lose
his chairmanship if the Republicans took over the Senate ("a single seat
may decide it") but insisted that Mechling must be defeated, whatever the
costs. "Mechling," McCarran concluded, "is untrustworthy, untruthful, and
unfit to represent the people of the Nevada in the United States Senate."[96]

The next day Mechling blasted back. "Malone has accepted the deal
which I rejected seven weeks ago and has paid the high price of servitude
for the senior senator's endorsement,"[97] he said. Mechling named McCarran's
henchmen who'd come to him with a deal: Norman Biltz and John Mueller,
two of the most powerful men in the state. Biltz was, of course, a millionaire
Republican who lived in Reno, and one of McCarran's strongest supporters.
Mueller was a Carson City lobbyist (known as Nevada's eighteenth state senator) and just as big a McCarran backer. "If Norman Biltz and Johnny
Mueller did not offer Tom Mechling a deal," Greenspun wrote, "then he is
the first person running for political office they missed."[98]

But Biltz and Mueller had alibis for September 6, the day Mechling
claimed they offered him a deal. Biltz then produced excerpts of a tape
recording made without Mechling's knowledge on September 27, in which
the candidate appeared to be the one seeking a rapprochement. "I need
somebody back there to show me around," he said, "and I hope to hell it's
my own senator. I don't want to go out and have somebody else like Paul
Douglas or another of my friends show me around. I mean it would be
better if we worked together."[99]

Mechling said that the tape had been doctored and offered to pay for radio time to play the whole recording — an offer not likely to be taken by any station, since Biltz used profanity as punctuation in his speech. Instead, Biltz invited reporters to his office to listen to the whole tape. Most of them came away convinced that he was telling more of the truth than Mechling.

Even Mechling's admirers began to have doubts. Running on little more than his integrity, Mechling suddenly seemed slippery with the truth himself. One of his primary ads showed a picture of the sign for the McCarran and Bible law office, without disclosing that the photo was a decade old or that Bible had left the firm years ago. Mechling always proclaimed that he got into politics because he got so mad covering Washington as a reporter that he felt compelled to do something; actually, he wrote for a personal finance publication and covered trade associations instead of Congress, as he seemed to imply.

Ralph Denton, for example, had been a McCarran boy in Washington and was now an assistant district attorney in Elko. Denton promised Mechling his support after he won the primary. But then Mechling's hammering at McCarran changed his mind. "I resent greatly the implication contained in your ads and speeches to the effect that I, like many other young Democrats in the state of Nevada, are nothing but pawns on a chess board to be moved into position by the player," Denton wrote to Mechling. "If you feel that we are all part of the McCarran machine . . . please permit me to advise you that I deem it an honor to be considered a member of such a machine and shall be proud to my dying day that I was one of those whom Senator McCarran chose to assist in obtaining a legal education, and shall likewise be proud of my relationship with him and shall ever treasure it as one of my choicest memories, and shall forever be grateful to him."[100]

The alternative to sending Mechling to the Senate was the Republican candidate: George Malone, a mossbacked conservative who didn't like to work too hard or think too much. If even liberal Democrats were thinking of voting for Malone, Mechling was in trouble.

One morning McCarran got up at five at his suite at the Riverside, climbed into a car with some friends, and set off east from Reno toward Winnemucca, where they drove north for 175 miles to cross into Hornby County, Oregon. McCarran's traveling companions were Norm Biltz and

C. R. Smith, the president of American Airlines. "They say ducks and geese are so thick you can knock them down with a stick," McCarran told his wife.[101]

When they got back to Reno after thirty-six hours without phone calls or newspapers, McCarran learned that Stevenson had attacked him. "McCarran used to be a Democrat," Stevenson told a crowd in New Haven, "but in his own state he is backing a reactionary Old Guard Republican against a progressive young Democrat, Tom Mechling."[102]

"Stevenson," McCarran replied, "has been consorting so long with the Americans for Democratic Action that he wouldn't know a Democrat if he saw one. . . . Stalin and all he stands for is anathema to me. I wonder if Mr. Stevenson can say the same?"[103]

Four days before the election Harvey Matusow flew from Salt Lake City to Las Vegas. Matusow had just come off a speaking trip through the mountain states, assailing Democratic candidates in Idaho, Montana, and Utah as soft on Communism. "I was like a junior McCarthy," he beamed.[104]

A month earlier McCarran had summoned Matusow to his hotel room in Salt Lake City during the Mine-Mill union hearings. McCarran wanted to talk about Greenspun and Mechling. The publisher's lawsuit against the senator was coming to trial soon, and Mechling's brazen challenge to McCarran's authority in Nevada was coming to a head in the election. The two attacks, McCarran was sure, were related. If Mechling won, Greenspun would practically be sitting in the Senate. He wanted to know if Matusow had any information on Greenspun. Matusow suggested that he could check the *Sun's* staff to see if any were Communists. McCarran thought that was a good idea. Then he asked Matusow to go to Las Vegas for him. He had, McCarran said, a little job he wanted Matusow to do.

Matusow was McCarran's last chance. For months the Senate Internal Security Subcommittee investigators had chased every lead they could find about Greenspun: that he'd fought in the Spanish Civil War with the Loyalists, that he kept two sets of books at the *Sun* to cheat on his taxes, that Drew Pearson was paying his legal bills. They pored over Greenspun's passport records, old HUAC hearings, the FCC license for a radio station he owned. Nothing panned out. Mechling was even cleaner.

Then Don Connors hit what he thought was a jackpot. Seth Pope, who worked for the General Services Administration in Washington, told Connors that Greenspun had offered him twenty-five thousand dollars to fix his arms–running case (and he'd throw in a stay at the Flamingo, gambling money, and a woman). "Pope said he would swear to this conversation and that he would be very happy to testify in Las Vegas if necessary," Connors told McCarran.[105]

McCarran sent Connors to Lou Nichols at the FBI with the tip. "He assures me that an active investigation is underway, looking toward prosecution of Greenspun for bribery," Connors reported to McCarran, "although he is not confident that a case can be made since the bribe was offered to a man outside the Justice Department."[106]

But when the FBI, HUAC, and the IRS all failed McCarran, he turned to Matusow. "The senator wanted me to go to Las Vegas and spread some anti-Mechling rumors among the Strip and Fremont Street casino employees," Matusow recalled.[107]

McCarran was like Lear amid the sagebrush, spiritually naked and howling, tearing at his hair, raging against ingratitude and betrayal.

Mechling is a Commie plant in Nevada but people don't seem to catch on, he told his wife. *Clark County is the worst mess I ever saw.*[108]

His influence had never been greater. He was one of the most powerful committee chairman Congress had ever seen. The McCarran Internal Security Act was terrorizing the Communist Party. The McCarran–Walter bill was about to take effect, remolding U.S. immigration policy into the shape of his obsessions for generations to come. The Justice Department was about to indict Owen Lattimore for perjury. The Senate Internal Security Subcommittee had just assailed the Mine-Mill union, avenging an eight-year-old grievance, and the Justice Department was looking at indictments. Men were in jail, facing prison or deportation because of McCarran's laws. More would follow. His resentment and wrath were matters of concern to the president, the secretary of state, the attorney general. With the possible exception of Huey Long, his power over Nevada was as vast as any politician had ever exercised over any state. And his power in national affairs was scarcely less.

It seems both Stevenson and Eisenhower are dumb as to law. They both show gross ignorance as to my bill. They don't even read the bill. The Jews are misleading both of them.[109]

Yet everywhere McCarran looked he saw treachery.

Truman will go down in history as the dirtiest as well as the most ignorant of all presidents. This pissant in human form is a disgrace to his country.[110]

In his anger and despair McCarran would do anything to lash out at his enemies.

I think Eisenhower will carry this state. I hope he carries the nation. There's no hope for democracy with Stevenson.[111]

Including bringing down the temple upon himself.

It's a stormy time for me but these storms make us strong when we know we are right, and I'm right. These Commie rats can't cower me with their threats; this land is worth fighting for, and should not be turned over to the criminal and the insane of the weak decrepit old world of graft and slavery. So we fight on.[112]

Matusow arrived in Las Vegas on the Friday before Election Day and caught a cab from the airport down the Strip to the Thunderbird. He had called the hotel from Salt Lake City to make a reservation but was told that it was filled for the weekend. He called back and dropped Eva Adams's name. A room appeared. Matusow made the rounds of the casinos. Always gregarious, he talked more than usual. He talked to bartenders, stickmen, and pit bosses — anyone who couldn't move away. He said bad things about Mechling and hinted at worse but somehow the monologues always veered back toward his favorite subject: Harvey Matusow. Even later — even after he had passed through a suicidal funk and come to hate everything that he had once been — Matusow could not recall those four days of spreading slurs and innuendo without remembering how poorly compensated he was for his services. "You know what McCarran paid me for my trouble during the '52 election?" he griped. "A measly plane ticket. That's all. And McCarthy? Nothing."[113]

On Election Day Matusow got on a plane at McCarran Field and flew home to New York. The person sitting next to him had never been on a longer flight.

McCarran slipped between the sturdy columns of the Washoe County Courthouse. On Election Day in Reno, McCarran woke up in his room at the Riverside Hotel, took the elevator to the lobby, and walked into the courthouse next door, where he descended to the basement to vote for Eisenhower and Malone. "Today is the day," McCarran told his wife, "and only God knows what it will bring."[114]

And Samson said unto the lad that held him by the hand, Suffer me that I may feel the pillars whereupon the house standeth, that I may lean upon them.

Down in Las Vegas the *Sun* put pictures of Biltz, McCarran, and Malone on the top of its front page across from one of Mechling. "Malone

Bosses Vs. Mechling," the headline read. "McCarran, Norman Biltz, John Mueller and the little jackals who comprise the kit and kaboodle of selfish, grasping men are busying slinging mud at a decent person, whose only desire is to represent all the people of the state instead of the privileged few," Greenspun wrote. ". . . Mueller and Blitz have offered every living human who can do them the slightest bit of good a deal. When Biltz spoke to me about a deal, he placed his remarks off the record, which is the only thing saving him now. . . . If the average person knew what is taking place in this state today, not only would Malone be soundly defeated, but McCarran would be impeached and his henchmen thrown in jail."[115]

Now the house was full of men and women; and all the lords of the Philistines were there; and there were upon the roof about three thousand men and women, that beheld while Samson made sport.

The 1952 election was turning out very strange in Nevada. McCarran and most of the rest of the bigwigs of the Democratic Party were supporting Republicans for the Senate and the White House. "Well Eisenhower would at least clean out the rats from the White House," McCarran told his wife. "But I'm saying nothing, only shaking hands with my friends and being seen."[116] Hank Greenspun, a nominal Republican, was supporting Democrats. "The *Sun* was one of the first newspapers to climb aboard the Eisenhower bandwagon," Greenspun wrote. ". . . But when the bandwagon rolled into Nevada with Joe McCarthy in the driver's seat, we must reluctantly come to the conclusion that it is high time we got off. . . . Our disillusionment is complete."[117]

And Samson called unto the Lord, and said, O Lord God, remember me, I pray thee, and strengthen me, I pray thee, only this once, O God, that I may be at once avenged of the Philistines for my two eyes.

There were twice as many Democrats registered in Nevada as Republicans, but most of them crossed party lines that day. Eisenhower beat the tar out of Stevenson across the country and carried Nevada by almost nineteen thousand votes. Malone squeaked past Mechling, wining by 2,722 votes. In less than a year Mechling had come from nowhere to win a nomination that no one thought he could win and then lose an election that no one thought he could lose. Like Icarus, Mechling soared too close to the sun — both of his own hubris and of McCarran's malice — and fell to earth.

And Samson took hold of the two middle pillars upon which the house stood, and on which it was borne up, of the one with his right hand, and of the other with his left.

And when the walls came down, Eisenhower went to the White House and the Republicans seized control of both houses of Congress for the first time since 1930, and Patrick McCarran lost the chairmanship of his beloved Judiciary Committee. The Republicans took the Senate by one seat — a seat McCarran helped keep a Democrat out of.

And Samson said, Let me die with the Philistines. And he bowed himself with all his might; and the house fell upon the lords, and upon all the people that were therein. So the dead which he slew at his death were more than they which he slew in his life.[118]

McCarran sat as imperturbable as Buddha. The still-great head of white hair, the small, piercing blue eyes, and the dark, double-breasted suit all hinted at his power and drive, but everything else spoke of decay: the sagging hook of a nose, the enfolding jowls, the spreading girth, the voice as dry and brittle as old paper.

The lame-duck chairman of the Senate Internal Security Subcommittee was in an unusual position: being a witness. At eleven o'clock on December 29 McCarran took a seat in the Washington office of his attorney William Leahy. Across a table Greenspun's attorney William Roberts sat down to take McCarran's pretrial deposition.

"You didn't have lunch at the Desert Inn with Mr. Jake Lansky and with Mr. Marion Hicks?" Roberts asked.

"I don't recall it at all," McCarran replied.

McCarran didn't recall a lot that morning. He didn't recall sending Guernsey Frazer and James Johnson to visit Greenspun during the 1950 election to win the publisher's support. He didn't recall asking Reno Bank Club owner Billy Graham to give Greenspun advertising business — then withdraw it when the publisher didn't support McCarran. He didn't recall having lunch with Moe Dalitz in Florida. He didn't recall helping Flamingo owners Gus Greenbaum and Moe Sedway win a tax case with the IRS. He didn't recall writing a letter to another editor saying that some way had to be found to muzzle Greenspun.

What McCarran wasn't hazy about he denied outright. He denied drawing cash advances at the Thunderbird. He didn't know that Cliff Jones collected one hundred thousand dollars in Las Vegas for political campaigns. He didn't know Marion Hicks had come to Washington to lobby against the federal gambling tax the previous summer with a war chest of fifty thousand dollars. He didn't read Greenspun's excoriating column of March 18 until long after it ran, certainly after the *Sun* had lost all its casino ads. He didn't see Greenspun's FBI record or turn SISS investigators loose on the newspaperman. He wasn't on bad terms with the Mine-Mill union, which just two months earlier he had flayed in Salt Lake City. ("I have always been a friend of that union. . . . It is the heads of the union who refuse to answer questions as to whether or not they were Communists.") He didn't have anything to do with persuading advertisers to shy away from the *Nevada State News,* which was run by Denver Dickerson, helping tip the paper into bankruptcy — or getting Dickerson a job with the State Department that conveniently sent one of his harshest critics to Burma. He didn't arrange for Joe McCarthy to come to Las Vegas to attack Greenspun. He denied that Pete Petersen was a political henchman ("Postmasters are not very useful to you") and claimed that he exerted no real influence in Nevada politics. "I have no control of Democratic organizations in the state," he declared.

McCarran denied, above all, that he felt ill will toward Greenspun. "If you, Mr. Roberts, attribute antagonism or animosity because a man is criticized or reviled or even abused in the press who holds a public office, you are very much mistaken," McCarran said. "We had to take those things. It comes to us. You have got to take it in stride. And you will outgrow it after a while if you will just be patient. . . . If that were true, you would be destroying papers many times."

For six hours McCarran lied. He denied the obvious, he denied that friends were really friends and that enemies were enemies; he almost denied that the sun rose in the east. McCarran committed perjury again and again, certainly more than Owen Lattimore ever had and much more brazenly than the China scholar who had just been indicted two weeks earlier on seven counts of lying to McCarran's Internal Security Subcommittee. McCarran had badgered and bullied Lattimore for not being able to recall minute details from a dozen years past; McCarran couldn't remember things from barely twelve months before.

One thing that McCarran did remember was that he'd kept Greenspun out of prison. "Frazer talked to me about Mr. Greenspun either going on trial or being on trial," McCarran recalled. "He says he has a paper here. He is a pretty good scout. If you could help him to keep out of the penitentiary, it would be worthwhile. I took it up with the Department of Justice as to whether or not they had a case that would warrant the penitentiary, and if they didn't would it not be well to arrange that Mr. Greenspun take a fine in place of going to the penitentiary. He was a young man. He was just starting out in the newspaper business there in

Nevada. I didn't know the nature of the charge particularly. . . . Had it not
been for that, in my judgement, Mr. Greenspun would be in the penitentiary today."

Roberts did elicit a couple of nuggets of information: McCarran never
paid for hotels or restaurants in Las Vegas and he did all sorts of favors for
questionable characters without looking very closely at their cases. And
Roberts clearly had a good time grilling the griller.

"Don't put words into my mouth," McCarran snapped at one point.

"I'm all too conscious," Roberts replied, "of the way that is done sometimes in other places."[119]

In January, one week before Truman left office, Lyndon Johnson went to
the White House to ask the president a favor on behalf of his least favorite
Democrat. McCarran, the new Democratic minority leader explained to
Truman, wanted a seat on the Government Operations Committee. The
committee was something of a backwater, but since its wide purview
included the functioning of any part of the federal government, the potential for causing trouble was great, especially considering its Permanent
Subcommittee on Investigations. And the committee's new chairman
would be Joseph McCarthy. Given McCarran's seniority, the assignment
should have been his for the asking.

But Johnson told Truman that McCarran would give up his claim to
the seat if Truman would finally sign the commission for James Johnson,
McCarran's choice for Nevada's U.S. attorney. McCarran had sent the
commission to Truman to sign in July. When Hank Greenspun complained that McCarran was trying to save himself from possible indictment by installing a political hack in the U.S. attorney's office, the
president ordered Attorney General James McGranery to investigate.
McGranery told the FBI to look into the matter, which the bureau did
and found nothing.

McCarran had already enlisted the attorney general to lobby the president regarding Johnson's commission. "Just talked with McGranery," one
of McCarran's staffers reported in October, "and he said that he had seen
president on Jim. He said he recommended that Jim assume office. He said
that he holds little hope that anything will be done before the election,
although he is fully aware of spot senator is on. He said that he will do
everything possible to get president to sign and to bear with him."[120]
Truman didn't budge. After the election Jay Sourwine tried to get White
House aide Charlie Murphy to work on the president, making the case

that it was better to get a Democratic U.S. attorney while they could before the Republicans would be in a position to give the job to one of their own. Nothing. Then McCarran pressed McGranery to try one more time. The attorney general went to the army-navy football game with the president and again tried to persuade him to relent. Truman held firm. "As usual, Harry is petty," Eva Adams told McCarran. ". . . I dunno. But at least folks are seeing why the Democratic administration was getting too bad to endure when the top man acts childish in this fashion."[121]

McCarran turned to Lyndon Johnson for help. Johnson, forty-four, was a fiercely ambitious Democrat who arrived in the Senate in 1949 and rapidly rose to become majority whip. Almost six foot four, Johnson towered above most of his colleagues; his personality was even more outsized. At underlings he threw books, but to his colleagues he was all Texas charm, full of Hill Country stories and bonhomie. Johnson was quickly gaining a reputation as a master politician, especially for his keen vote-calling ability. Before any important roll call, Johnson sent an aide to visit other senators and find out how they were planning to cast their ballots. McCarran was the only senator to send the aide back to Johnson with instructions never to call again. "A young fellow who maybe one day may make a leader," McCarran later told Pete Petersen about Johnson, "but at the present time is not very strong."[122] Johnson never gave up trying to court McCarran. "There are some men who grow in stature and wisdom with each passing year," Johnson told McCarran on his birthday. "To such men it is always a special pleasure to extend birthday greetings."[123]

After the election debacle Johnson wanted to become minority leader, and he wanted it to be a unanimous vote. McCarran said that he would gladly give Johnson his support — if he would talk to Truman about the U.S. attorney commission. Johnson did, but Truman remained unmovable. Then, during Truman's last week in the White House, Johnson went back to Truman and offered him a deal: McCarran would stay off McCarthy's investigative committee if the president would sign the commission that had been sitting on his desk for six months.

To Truman it was a distasteful offer. He hated McCarran. "He is always for something where he can get his hand in the money barrel," Truman later groused.[124] For years the senator had been one of the president's biggest torments. McCarran's laws and his opposition to the president's program were bad enough; even more insidious was the way McCarran had managed to infiltrate Truman's own government. In both the State Department and the Justice Department McCarran either cowed or cajoled senior officials into working with him — and in the case of the latter this included a string of attorney generals. Truman had a deep and abiding respect for civil liberties, yet again and again he had to watch as his own government traduced these very traditions. "McCarran . . . ," Truman once sputtered, "whose record for obstruction and bad legislation is matched by that of only a few reactionaries."[125]

Johnson, however, was able to point out to Truman that it might be worse to let both McCarran and McCarthy serve on the same investigations subcommittee. A great deal of potential trouble had already been averted with the Senate Internal Security Subcommittee. Twice, in fact. First, McCarran had desperately tried to cling to the chairmanship, even through it would normally pass to the majority party. "McCarran," William S. White observed in the *New York Times*, "is a measurable force within the Republican Party as well as in his own and there has been a good deal of private talk in the Senate about the possibility of keeping him at the head of the Internal Security Subcommittee."[126] Sourwine, for instance, had sounded out other Senate staffers. "I have talked with several administrative assistants on the subject of retaining you as chairman of the Internal Security Subcommittee," Sourwine told McCarran. "It looks as though there may be a majority of the committee in favor of that — possibly a very solid majority."[127] New Judiciary chairman William Langer was in favor of keeping McCarran but was persuaded by GOP leaders to pick a Republican.

Second, the ranking Republican claiming the chairmanship was McCarthy, which would have been like putting an arsonist in charge of a match factory. Even the Republicans were worried about *that* possibility. So the party leaders gave McCarthy the chairmanship of the Government Operations Committee, while SISS veteran William Jenner took the center seat on the internal security subcommittee. "We've got McCarthy," Majority Leader Robert Taft said, "where he can't do any harm."[128]

Now Johnson wanted Truman to yield, to give in to McCarran one last time, to let the senator win the final confrontation between them. "Some day I'll have an opportunity to level him off," Truman had fumed to his wife about McCarran early in his first term. "Probably won't do it but it should be done."[129]

The big young Texan was persuasive. "All right," the president told Johnson, "I'll give this to you, Lyndon."

Truman had a courier deliver the signed nomination to Johnson's office

— not McCarran's. "As you know," the president wrote, "I am doing this under protest. It is your 'baby' from now on."[130]

Truman had signed. McCarran stayed off McCarthy's committee — and McCarthy stayed off McCarran's. What mischief the two might have created on the same investigative committee was avoided. What they created on their own was enough.

On February 4, 1953, *Greenspun v. McCarran, et al.* came to trial in federal court in Las Vegas. Norm White, the *Sun* business manager, testified about the morning that every ad in town walked away from the paper. Next came Charlotte Furer, a telephone operator at the Thunderbird, who took the stand prepared to talk about a flurry of calls between Washington and Las Vegas the previous March. Then, before Furer could testify, the trial adjourned for the weekend.

The following week when court reconvened it was to approve a settlement. The casino owners agreed to pay Greenspun $80,500 and to return to advertising in his paper. McCarran said that he had no part in the deal and claimed vindication. "I consider the fact that this action had been dismissed as an open admission by the plaintiff that the charges which he brought against me during the recent political campaign were entirely unfounded."[131]

Greenspun demanded to be paid in cash. The day he collected the money he jumped into his red convertible and drove along the Strip, waving a fistful of bills as he drove past the casinos. Greenspun had done something that almost no one ever got away with in Las Vegas: He'd bet against the house and won.

Tom Mechling, on the other hand, had lost the Senate race. But then the state sent a Republican to Washington and McCarran lost the chairmanship of the Judiciary Committee. Mechling, too, did something that almost no one in Nevada ever did: He beat McCarran.

CHAPTER 25

Caught in the McCarran Act

Interviewer: There is a real history to be told. If you use
different names, then you're not telling the history. I
can understand you not wanting to use the names,
because you're worried about family members, but in
another twenty years it might be different.

Estolv Ward: It wouldn't mean that much. Very few of
these things standing alone are really important. It's
the mass of stuff.[1]

A lot of us would be out of luck if all the sins of our
youth were held against us.[2]

— Drew Pearson

Angela and Estolv Ward drove through the woods and hills of Sonoma
County, a fragrant journey in their convertible. They crossed a lovely
valley, passed twisting oaks and spreading bays, and then climbed into hills
shaded by tall groves of pine and redwood before rolling down another
grade and back into the California sunlight. The rear of the car rode low,
occasionally scraping the road. Driving out of San Francisco earlier in the
day they had been rear-ended; gas dribbled from the heavily loaded car,
but they weren't going to stop until they reached the ranch where their
comrades were waiting. They were almost there, at the bottom of the last
hill, when the car gave out.

Ward tried to open the trunk, but the accident had jammed it shut. A
comrade fetched a jack and they popped open the lid. A cascade of books,
pamphlets, and flyers poured out. Amid the theoretical tracts and yellowed
back copies of the *Worker* were papers that meant more to them: faded
union mimeographs from the campaign at Basic Magnesium a decade earlier. Broadsides against McCarran in his 1944 Senate race. A cartoon of
Estolv in a coffin that the AFL circulated around Las Vegas. The tumble of
old paper was a personal archive of the glory days of the couple's commitment and struggle. Angela wanted to weep. "We had a marvelous
Marxist library," she recalled. "We were going to put all this stuff in a secret
place until times got better and we could give it to the labor libraries."[3]

The 1950s were not a great time to be Communists. Every day after work, whichever Ward got home first would stand on the doorstep watching the streetcar to see if the other was coming home or had been arrested. "You couldn't go out our front door without running into an FBI agent," Estolv remembered.[4]

After their failed organizing drive in Las Vegas and the frustrated attempt to defeat McCarran, the Wards had returned to San Francisco. He went to work for the Utility Workers Union but was fired for refusing to take the Taft-Hartley anti-Communist oath. He was offered a job in the state unemployment office but scoffed at taking California's Levering oath ("I will not advocate or become a member of any party or organization, political or otherwise, that advocates the overthrow of the government of the United States or the state of California by force or violence or other unlawful means").

Ward finally landed a job in an electrical manufacturing plant, lugging about steaming pans of hot plastic dies. "It was a low-paid, miserable, lousy job,"[5] he said. The plant was an AFL local. Ward discovered three other comrades in the shop and organized a party unit. He was offered the post as shop steward but turned it down. "I should have taken it," he said, "but in a practical sense I couldn't see any possible chance of success."[6]

After the Smith Act trials started putting party leaders in prison, many prominent Communists went underground; Ward found himself sneaking around. "After working in the plastic factory all day I would come home and take a shower and eat dinner, get in the car and drive to help transport these underground people to attend to their needs," he recalled. "A guy needs a dentist, has a hell of a toothache, and he's underground. I'm the guy who knows the kind of a dentist who will pack up a kit of tools and come out at night to his hiding place."[7]

You couldn't be too careful. When a couple of New York leaders were hiding out in a cabin in the Sierra Nevada, they sent their housekeeper to town to find bagels and lox. The FBI soon sniffed them out.

Standing behind their broken car at the bottom of the hill in the woods, the Wards raked their papers and books into a pile like so many leaves. "It was the considered judgement of everybody that we should get rid of it right away . . . ," Estolv Ward said. "We didn't want this material to get into the hands of anyone if we got arrested or whatever."[8]

Then Ward burned his own books.

On January 20 Dwight D. Eisenhower stood atop the east steps of the Capitol and was sworn in as the thirty-fourth president of the United

States. It was, the new president acknowledged, a tremulous moment in history.

"Are we nearing the light — a day of freedom and of peace for all mankind?" he asked. *"Or are the shadows of another night closing in upon us?"*[9]

At sixty-two Eisenhower was one of the most admired living Americans. He radiated reassurance. "He was," George Kennan recalled, "the nation's number one Boy Scout."[10] Born in Abilene, Kansas, educated at West Point, named the supreme commander of the Allied forces by army chief George Marshall, Eisenhower was the hero who led the European invasion on D-Day. He became army chief of staff himself, president of Columbia University, and then the first NATO supreme commander. As genial as he was bald, apparently apolitical, Eisenhower was seemingly progressive enough for ADA liberals to prefer him to Truman on the Democratic ticket in 1948 but conservative enough to get the Republican nomination in 1952. He won by a landslide.

"The strength of all free peoples lies in unity," Eisenhower continued, *"their danger, in discord."*

Eisenhower had only a nodding familiarity with domestic policy. After a life in the army, including long stints overseas, the president didn't know how to dial a phone number, rarely carried any money, and had never been in a supermarket. Eisenhower devoted his inaugural speech to foreign affairs.

"We face the threat not with dread and confusion," Eisenhower said, *"but with confidence and conviction."*

Eisenhower was somewhat less confident in displaying his own convictions. On the campaign trail in September he appeared on a platform in Indiana with Senator William Jenner, one of McCarthy's loudest supporters, a member of SISS who had called Eisenhower's mentor General George Marshall "a living lie" and a "front man for traitors." Jenner embraced Eisenhower, who privately said he felt dirty from the touch of the man but did nothing to convey that to the public. Later that month, Eisenhower came to Wisconsin with a tough speech defending General Marshall and implicitly attacking Joe McCarthy, who had spent three hours in the Senate calling Marshall a traitor. "A sobering lesson in the way freedom must not defend itself," the speech said.[11] Eisenhower never delivered those lines. Instead he assailed the Truman administration for being infiltrated with Communists. When the speech was over Eisenhower shook McCarthy's hand.

"For history does not long entrust the care of freedom to the weak or the timid,"

Eisenhower concluded. "We must acquire proficiency in defense and display stamina in purpose."

John Carter Vincent sat outside the office of John Foster Dulles on the seventh floor of the new State Department building wondering if he still had a job. It was February 23, and the new secretary had summoned Vincent back from Morocco to decide his fate. At fifty-two, Vincent had served the department with distinction for almost thirty years. "Reason and justice may prevail," Vincent told his wife, "but not necessarily."[12]

For six years Vincent had been under fire. In 1947 Alfred Kohlberg's began attacking Vincent. In 1950 McCarthy joined in, calling Vincent a spy and a Communist. The next year McCarran made Vincent one of the targets of the IPR investigation. Louis Budenz testified before SISS that he had heard in party circles that Vincent was a Communist. Vincent had to wait almost half a year to defend himself before the committee, whereupon he was grilled for the better part of seven days. "That pink Vincent," McCarran called him.[13]

McCarran wanted to charge Vincent with perjury. The loyalty board got to him first. After the State Department loyalty board cleared Vincent for a fourth time, the decision was forwarded to the Loyalty Review Board for a routine evaluation. Truman had created the review board to strike a balance between liberty and security, but McCarran managed to oust its first chairman, Seth Richardson, by blocking his confirmation. The next chairman was Hiram Bingham, a former governor of Connecticut and U.S. senator, who tilted the panel toward a stricter definition of loyalty. Bingham came to the board in 1951 acutely aware of the pressure he was facing from Congress. "The board is under fire," he said at one meeting. "I have had conferences with four of the senators who have attacked us on the floor of the Senate. I had very pleasant meetings with Senator Ferguson, Senator McCarran, Senator McCarthy and Senator Hickenlooper. . . . They didn't know what they were talking about, really. So I hope that the matter is straightened out."[14]

The new chairman also met with Secretary of State Dean Acheson. Bingham pointed out that some government loyalty boards, such as the post office board, were finding as many as 10 percent of those employees reviewed worthy of discharge. The average was 6 percent. The State Department board was at zero. "I called his attention to the fact that his board was out of step with all other agency boards,"[15] Bingham recalled. Bingham asked Truman to *decrease* the standard of proof needed to find an employee disloyal. Truman complied. Bingham defended the increased severity of the loyalty program before the American Bar Association, and McCarran put the speech into the *Congressional Record*. "One of the finest that it has been my privilege to read," McCarran said.[16]

When Vincent's case was forwarded to the loyalty board, Bingham took an unusual personal interest in the matter, assigning himself chairman of the panel. Vincent returned from Morocco and testified for eight hours over two days. The panel reviewed his decades of service, as well as his week of testimony before SISS. The debate was bitter, especially when it came to considering the McCarran Committee's findings ("John Carter Vincent was the principal fulcrum of IPR pressures and influence in the State Department"[17]). John Harlan Amen said that it would be impossible to clear Vincent without criticizing McCarran. The panel split 3 to 2 (Bingham and Amen) in favor of Vincent, then one member changed her mind and voted to find the diplomat a risk because he had demonstrated a sympathy for Communism by contributing to the Jack Service defense fund. The two Vincent supporters filed a nineteen-page dissent. One of the holdouts, Harry Blair, thought that Bingham was trying to curry favor with McCarran. "McCarran was chairman of the powerful Judiciary Committee in the Senate," Blair noted. "He was courted and kow-towed to by Republicans in the Senate and generally . . . Bingham was a politician and a Republican and . . . was interested in keeping McCarran happy and . . . to back up the findings of the McCarran Committee."*[18]

In December 1952 the Loyalty Review Board released its decision and the State Department suspended Vincent. Acheson could have overruled the board but was afraid of creating more controversy. Instead Acheson talked Truman into appointing a distinguished commission chaired by retired judge Learned Hand to investigate the case — a move that McCarran called illegal. Acheson consulted Dulles about the commission; he was noncommittal. The commission concluded that Vincent was not a risk but before it could file a report Dulles took over as secretary of state and promptly dismissed the panel. Dulles said that he would decide the matter himself.

Nearing sixty-five, John Foster Dulles was tall, gray haired, and dour. He had a constitutional aversion to wasting time; at diplomatic meetings he

---

*State Department legal adviser Adrian Fisher thought that Bingham was trying to protect his son Woodbridge, a professor of Chinese history at the University of California, a potential target for McCarran. (See Gary May, *China Scapegoat: The Diplomatic Ordeal of John Carter Vincent*. Prospect Heights, Ill.: Waveland Press, 1979; p. 258.)

often sharpened pencils with a pocketknife. One of his favorite forms of relaxation was swimming in frigid water. To many of those who met Dulles, he always seemed like a man who had just climbed out of an icy lake. On his first day as secretary, Dulles walked into an already demoralized State Department and made the career foreign service officers feel worse. For the better part of a decade foreign service officers had endured attacks from outsiders accusing the department of being full of Communists; now the suspicions were being raised from within. "Dulles' words were as cold and raw as the weather that February day," Charles Bohlen recalled. "He said that he was going to insist that every member of the department extend not just loyalty but 'positive loyalty.' He did not define the difference, but his intent was clear. It was a declaration by the Secretary of State that the department was indeed suspect. The remark disgusted some foreign service officers, infuriated others, and displeased even those who were looking forward to the new administration."[19]

A lawyer by training, a diplomat by preference, Dulles was the son of a Presbyterian minister and the grandson of a former secretary of state. For years he had been an emblem of bipartisan foreign policy, part of the U.S. delegation to the founding UN conference and the chief negotiator of the peace treaty with Japan in 1951. "He was," Dean Acheson remembered, "competent, ambitious particularly to succeed me — close to Vandenberg and in good standing with both the Dewey and Taft wings of the Republican Party."[20]

That changed in 1952 when Dulles threw his support to Eisenhower. For years Dulles had been Tom Dewey's foreign policy adviser (and he had even gotten Alger Hiss his job at the Carnegie Endowment), but in that election year he lurched right. He wrote the rabid GOP foreign policy plank, bad-mouthed Truman's containment policy ("negative, futile and immoral"[21]), and hinted that an Eisenhower administration would not tolerate the status quo but would actually roll back the Communist advances of the past several years, seeking to liberate the captive nations of Eastern Europe.* Rollback, it turned out, started in the State Department.

Dulles called Vincent into his office. Three days before, the secretary had received Vincent's file: six volumes of testimony and dozens of FBI reports.

*Even before Dulles began attacking the Democratic foreign policy, he was one of three Republicans to whom the Chinese ambassador V. K. Wellington Koo leaked confidential Nationalist documents. A fourth person who was given the information was McCarran. (See Robert P. Newman, *Owen Lattimore and the "Loss" of China.* Berkeley, Calif.: University of California Press, 1992; p. 315.)

Dulles seemed nervous, playing with his hands, with his tie, wishing that he had some pencils to sharpen. He told Vincent that he didn't think he was a security risk, but that he should resign anyway if he wanted to keep his pension. He then asked Vincent to come to his house on the weekend to work out the details. Oh, Dulles added, use the back door.

Five days later Vincent slipped into Dulles's house. Vincent asked if he could retire in May, the twenty-ninth anniversary of his joining the foreign service. Dulles gave him three days to leave. Vincent asked the secretary to use his influence to stop the SISS investigation. "There is still talk of a perjury action,"[22] Dulles noted, but he said the Justice Department would stop any criminal probe.

Dulles was unusually talkative. He was puzzled, he said. How could so many people have underestimated the threat of Communism? He pulled out his worn copy of Stalin's *Problems of Leninism* and asked Vincent if he had read the book. No, Vincent replied. If you had read it, Dulles lectured, you would not have advocated the policies you did in China.

Vincent tried, one more time, to explain how things had looked in the embassy during the war when nothing seemed more important than fighting the Japanese and the only Chinese forces willing to do so were the Communists. He might as well have been speaking Chinese for all the comprehension Dulles displayed. "Vincent's reporting of the facts, evaluation of the facts, and policy advice during the period under review show a failure to meet the standard which is demanded of a foreign service officer," Dulles would say in a statement to the press. "I do not believe that he can usefully continue to serve the United States as a foreign service officer."[23]

In his study Dulles asked Vincent his opinion about Chinese politics. Dulles was firing Vincent for being incompetent. Now he was asking his advice. Vincent gave it.

McCarran was enraged that Vincent had been allowed to resign. "A subterfuge on the part of the secretary of state," McCarran fumed, "and the fact that Mr. Dulles sees fit to follow in the footsteps of Mr. Acheson doesn't do much credit to him, nor does it change my view of the situation."[24]

On March 19 Pat McCarran took the floor in the Senate and declared war on the Eisenhower administration. Soon after taking office, Foster Dulles had made two important appointments. First he named Scott McLeod as the State Department's security chief. Then he named Chip Bohlen as ambassador to the Soviet Union, a post that had been vacant for almost half a year and was even more critical now that Stalin had just died, leaving

Russia without a clear leader for the first time in more than two decades. McLeod, thirty-eight, was a former FBI agent who had worked for New Hampshire senator Styles Bridges, a friend of McCarran's. As the department's new security chief, McLeod's mandate was to clean house, which he started to do by going through desks and listening in on phone calls. Within three weeks, McLeod bragged, he had fired twenty-four homosexuals — who were considered ipso facto security risks. Charles Eustis Bohlen, forty-eight, the grandson of a senator who became the first U.S. ambassador to France, went to St. Paul's prep school and then Harvard. He joined the foreign service in 1929, worked in the Moscow embassy, and became one of the top Russian experts in the department, serving as Roosevelt's translator and adviser at Yalta — now a synonym, to conservatives, for sellout. Bohlen was also, McLeod suspected, a homosexual.

In the Senate, McCarran said that security chief McLeod had opposed Bohlen's confirmation but had been overruled by Dulles. The day before, Dulles told the Foreign Relations Committee that the FBI had found Bohlen above reproach. "There is no derogatory material whatsoever," Dulles said.[25] The committee then unanimously approved Bohlen. Now McCarran was calling Dulles a liar and urging the Senate not to vote on the nomination until lawmakers could personally inspect the diplomat's FBI file. Bohlen, McCarran continued, had become an acid test of whether the administration would finally clear the subversives out of the State Department. "I am sorry to say," McCarran added, "it is clearly apparent this clique has not yet been defeated, but has, on the contrary, just won one of its greatest victories."[26]

After McCarran finished his speech, Joe McCarthy joined in on the attack. "My information is in accord with what Mr. McCarran said," McCarthy told the Senate. He also called Dulles a liar. "I know what's in Bohlen's file," McCarthy added, "and to say that he is a security risk is putting it too weak."[27]

Dulles called a press conference that afternoon and again denied that there was anything to give a reasonable person pause about Bohlen, only three or four unsubstantiated rumors. "An acid test of the orderly process of our government," Dulles called the confirmation.[28] "This," the Alsop brothers wrote, "is war and no mistake about it."[29] Liberal opinion was outraged. "The Bohlen case," the *Washington Star* editorialized, "is the acid test of whether a corporal's guard of reckless senators is going to be able to butcher the reputation of a respected public servant — and get away with it."[30]

"Dulles Vs. McCarran," the *Washington Post* editorial page called it. "The issue raised by Senators McCarran and McCarthy is plainly a test of who is running the State Department. . . . Dulles had better be on the lookout for a new kind of fifth column — the person or persons who may have been feeding Senators McCarran and McCarthy."[31]

The person who told McCarran and McCarthy about the FBI report was J. Edgar Hoover. The day before they denounced the diplomat in the Senate, McCarthy called Hoover to inquire about Bohlen. How bad is he?

The FBI had finished its investigation the day before, but rumors about Bohlen had been circulating for weeks. On March 5 FBI agents had visited columnist Drew Pearson. "I was amazed when they asked me whether he was a homo and then quoted me as having once said he was," Pearson wrote in his diary. "I disabused them as far as any statements by me were concerned and told them further that I had never had the slightest suspicion or thought along this line."[32]

A number of people had bad things to say about Bohlen. His former boss William Bullitt, the first ambassador to Soviet Union, complained that Bohlen drank too much twenty years earlier ("Bullitt has the utmost contempt for Bohlen"[33]). Ex-Communist Jay Lovestone questioned Bohlen's judgment for defending Yalta. Conservative journalist Isaac Don Levine also feared that Bohlen would be too easy on the Soviet Union. But the only real negative information (from the FBI's point of view) about Bohlen was that he might be gay. One apparent friend (name withheld by the FBI) told the bureau that he was homosexual and said that he thought Bohlen was, too. "He stated Bohlen acts, walks and talks like a homosexual," the agents reported.[34]

That was enough for Hoover. On March 17 Eisenhower asked Dulles to talk to Hoover. "The director would not be inclined, if he were passing on the question of security, to give Bohlen a complete clearance," Assistant Director Lou Nichols recorded. "The director pointed out that there was no direct evidence that Bohlen had engaged in homosexual activities, but it was a fact that several of his closest friends and intimate associates were known homosexuals."[35] McLeod felt the same way. He told Hoover that Dulles also was opposed to Bohlen but that Eisenhower, who knew Bohlen personally, was insistent that he go to Moscow. "McLeod seemed to be quite depressed," Hoover noted. ". . . He could not conscientiously give Mr. Bohlen a security clearance."[36]

Then McCarthy called Hoover and asked him if Bohlen were gay. "We had no evidence to show any overt act," Hoover recalled. "But he, Bohlen, had certainly used very bad judgement in associating with homosexuals. The senator stated this was a matter that he was almost precluded from discussing on the floor, that it was so easy to accuse a person of such acts but difficult to prove. I agreed and stated that it was often a charge used by persons who wanted to smear someone."[37]

George Kennan walked into Foster Dulles's office one day in March more nervous than usual. Kennan was a twenty-seven-year veteran of the State Department, the most brilliant foreign service officer of his generation, an architect of Truman's containment policy toward the Soviet Union. He was also, in the best of times, moody, high-strung, and overly sensitive. These were not the best of times. "The McCarran Committee has stumbled over me in its pursuit of Davies and there is plenty of trouble ahead for me . . . ," he'd told his sister back in January. "McCarthy and McCarran will do a job on me in this coming period and whenever they're through, whatever reputation I had will be pretty well shattered."[38]

In 1946 Kennan was in the Moscow embassy, filling in for the absent ambassador, when he sent Washington an eight-thousand-word treatise on Soviet behavior, which came to be known as the Long Telegram, one of the most influential diplomatic cables ever composed. Kennan urged a firm resistance to Soviet expansionism but also to warned against overreacting. "We must have courage and self-confidence to cling to our own methods and conceptions of human society," he wrote. "After all, the greatest danger that can befall us in coping with this problem of Soviet Communism is that we shall allow ourselves to become like those with whom we are coping."[39]

Kennan went on to become head of policy planning at the State Department, and Truman named him ambassador to the Soviet Union, where some undiplomatic remarks comparing Stalin's Russia to Hitler's Germany got him declared persona non grata in October. McCarthyite Washington wasn't that much different. Kennan was dismayed that any crackpot charge seemed to trigger a full-blown loyalty investigation. He thought the State Department ought to investigate the charge instead asking the accused to prove it false. "I would have suspected pusillanimity, except that this was the last thing one could suspect in Dean Acheson," Kennan remarked. "I can only conclude that he was badly advised."[40]

Kennan wrote a letter to *Time* defending John Paton Davies, whom McCarran still wanted charged with perjury. Two weeks later SISS subpoenaed Kennan to a hearing without telling him why. "The experience was a traumatic one," he remembered. ". . . Only gradually did it become evident to me that the affair was in connection with the Davies case. I was placed under oath, and in this condition, wholly without preparation, without counsel, without the possibility of forethought, yet vulnerable to a charge of perjury if I made the slightest slip, I endured an hour or so of cryptic and carefully prepared questioning. It included, at one point, what I could only take to be a deliberate attempt to entrap me, one of them so shameless and egregious that I could hardly believe it. It was a matter of dates, in which point I have one of the world's worst memories; and only the presence of some real but invisible guardian angel can have saved me from falling into the apparent snare."[41]

Eisenhower took office the next week. Two months later Kennan was still waiting for a new assignment from Dulles when the secretary asked him to come to his office on March 13. That morning Kennan read about his own retirement in the *New York Times*. In his office Dulles made it official. He told Kennan there was no place in the department for him, that he feared that the diplomat would have problems with any post requiring Senate confirmation. Then, after severing Kennan's connection to the institution to which he had devoted his adult life, Dulles asked the cashiered diplomat for his views on the Soviet Union. If nothing else, Dulles was consistent.

It was just as well, Kennan thought, for he would have been forced to resign sooner or later. Kennan had worked at State for almost thirty years, but on his last day on the job, he couldn't find anyone to say good-bye to. "The housecleaning conducted by Mr. Dulles' minions as a means of placating congressional vindictiveness had been thorough and sweeping," Kennan recalled. "The place was of full of new faces — many of them guarded, impassive, at best coldly polite, faintly menacing."[42]

The only person Kennan said good-bye to was the receptionist. Then he drove out of Washington, across Maryland, and into Pennsylvania, where he had a farm. He sat on the porch and for two hours just stared into space.

On March 27 the Senate voted on Bohlen. McCarran and McCarthy and other conservatives had continued their attacks on him, and the Senate dispatched Robert Taft and John Sparkman to read the FBI report on the diplomat in Dulles's office. Dulles showed the senators a summary FBI memo; they asked for the raw reports. Dulles called Hoover. The director told the secretary that the raw reports had never been made available to anyone. "Dulles then referred to Senator McCarran's claim that such raw reports were made available to him," Lou Nichols recorded. "The director referred to the department policy of furnishing summaries to the chairman of the Judiciary Committee and in response to the secretary of state's inquiry the director stated these summaries are similar to the summary presented in the Bohlen case."[43]

Taft and Sparkman went back to the Senate and assured their colleagues that there was nothing to worry about. The Senate voted 74 to 13 to confirm Bohlen. McCarran and Edwin Johnson of Colorado were the only Democrats voting against him. More ominous for the president: Eleven Republicans, including Joe McCarthy, wouldn't support his nominee.

Before reporting to his new post, Bohlen visited the White House. He mentioned to Eisenhower that he was president of the Foreign Service Association, and that morale in the State Department was low. Oh, you're talking about that McLeod fellow, Eisenhower offered. He was a mistake, the president admitted, but it would be a worse mistake to fire him.

Bohlen concluded by telling Eisenhower that some of the most respected foreign service officers were thinking of resigning instead of putting up with persecution. Stand firm, Eisenhower offered. Let the storm pass. Bohlen gave up. "For Dulles," Bohlen observed later, "the victory also meant that he — and not McCarthy or McCarran or McLeod — would control the State Department."[44]

For John Carter Vincent, George Kennan, and a host of other dedicated foreign service officers that was no victory at all.

In April, Eisenhower sent an urgent request to Capitol Hill for emergency refugee legislation. On the campaign trail Eisenhower had attacked the McCarran-Walter Act; in the White House, he told Congress that a more liberal immigration bill law was vital for U.S. foreign policy. Elections were coming in Italy, where unemployment was high and the Communist Party was threatening to make a strong showing at the polls. A gesture by the United States to accept more Italian immigrants, the president suggested, would help pro-Western premier Alcide De Gasperi. Immigration subcommittee chairman Arthur Watkins promptly sponsored a bill that would admit to the country an extra 120,000 refugees a year for two years. "The administration," Eisenhower recalled, "once again had to take on Senator Pat McCarran."[45]

Cedric Belfrage walked into his office to a hero's welcome on May 15. The staff of the *National Guardian* gave him two huge bouquets of flowers. Like a good pull from his beloved pipe, this was a moment to savor. The day before, Belfrage had taken the train to Washington and faced down Joe McCarthy. To much of America this made him a Fifth Amendment Communist; to the staff of the *Guardian* this made him a hero. "Daddy talks only to them these days," his daughter Sally recalled. "The world is so black and white and scared of crossing boundaries that he rarely has the chance to see anyone who doesn't agree with him. Some of them go a lot further than agreement; they worship him."[46]

In Belfrage's circle you could dine out on a good McCarthy confrontation story for years. And even Belfrage didn't know how good his McCarthy story was about to get.

Belfrage was enjoying the adulation of his staff when the elevator opened and two FBI agents stepped off. They arrested Belfrage under the McCarran–Walter Act as a dangerous alien. They took him to Ellis Island. In 1937 Belfrage wrote a piece for the *New Masses* called "Politics Catches Up with the Writer." In 1953 it did.

Belfrage was forty-nine, tall and thin, a man whose essential possessions were one suit, two pipes, and a typewriter. Born in London, educated at Cambridge, he'd been a journalist in Hollywood during the heyday of the Popular Front when he joined the Communist Party. He quit, Belfrage later claimed, after three months, although he never moved far from the party's orbit. "My fellow-travelling has continued," Belfrage wrote later, "because Communist parties are moving in the direction of history; because they believe that history does not just happen but that men and women make it, however blunderingly — and if I did not believe that, my life would be pointless."[47]

In 1941 Belfrage moved to New York, where he worked for British Security Coordination out of its Rockefeller Center office. He also worked for Jacob Golos, passing secret information to the Russians. "Although passionately devoted to the cause," Golos told Elizabeth Bentley, "he said he considered himself a patriotic Britisher and hence he would give us no information that showed up England's mistakes or tended to make her a laughingstock."[48] When Golos shared some of Belfrage's information with Earl Browder, the Communist Party boss leaked it to a Popular Front publication, and the resulting story threatened to expose Belfrage as the source. Belfrage broke off his relationship with Golos. Later the Soviets asked Bentley to contact Belfrage again. She approached Browder about talking to him. "He is out of the racket now," Browder told Bentley. "Let him stay out."[49]

In 1947 the FBI interviewed Belfrage. He denied that he had ever been a Communist, a claim that he repeated in front of a grand jury. In 1949 Bentley named Belfrage publicly for the first time in testimony to McCarran's Judiciary Committee. "I had been one of dozens of leftists 'named' by an alcoholic lady whom it was my good fortune not to know," Belfrage wrote later.[50]

Some people might have kept a low profile after being named as a Soviet spy by Elizabeth Bentley. Belfrage raised his. In 1948 he founded a weekly newspaper, the *National Guardian*, to support Henry Wallace and the Progressive Party. The *Guardian* became the leading publication of what soon became the Unpopular Front. When Joe McCarthy started his crusade, the *Guardian* considered him so ineffective that it didn't pay much attention to the senator. "The other Macs needed coverage more urgently," Belfrage wrote, "especially the Nevada senator."[51] In 1951 McCarran tried to get Defense Secretary Robert Lovett to prosecute Belfrage because the *Guardian* was running a list of U.S. soldiers held in North Korean prisons and urging their families to write to them. This might be a sinister scheme, McCarran suggested, to spread panic and hysteria among their relatives. "It appears that the *National Guardian* has made no overt attempts to force the parents to subscribe to the publication," Army Secretary Frank Pace Jr. reported back to McCarran, "although from time to time the *National Guardian*'s replies to such inquiries have included information as to subscription rates."[52]

In 1952 the *Guardian* (circulation seventy-five thousand) and its editor campaigned against the McCarran-Walter Act. "If there is something that needs subverting, what is wrong with subverting it?" Belfrage said at one rally. "... What we should rather fear is to be called conservative if Senators McCarran and McCarthy, and Whittaker Chambers and a national policy based on the atom bomb, are the things to be conserved. Heaven spare us the shame of being smeared as that."[53]

The next year HUAC subpoenaed Belfrage. He took the Fifth Amendment. A week later, on May 14, Belfrage again took the Fifth before McCarthy's subcommittee. McCarthy nodded toward an INS official in the room. "I assume they will take the necessary action after your evidence has been reviewed," he said.[54]

The next day Belfrage was taken off to Ellis Island, where he spent six weeks before being released on bail. One of his first stops back on mainland Manhattan was the Capitol Hotel, where he spoke at a rally for the Nonpartisan Committee against the Walter-McCarran Act. "I wish," he said, "there were some way of making Americans understand this shameful thing in terms of the flesh-and-blood victims: of the broken lives, the families torn apart; of the children wondering how in God's name to make sense out of a life in which their parents can be held in a cage without charges or court trial, and finally forced to go to countries they may not even know — in a land which, their teachers tell them, is dedicated to freedom and the rule of constitutional law. The issue is not one of politics. It is one of humanity and ordinary decency."[55]

McCarran and McCarthy kept hounding him, and in 1955 Belfrage gave up his fight and accepted voluntary deportation back to England.

On June 17 Supreme Court justice William O. Douglas granted convicted atomic spies Julius and Ethel Rosenberg a stay of execution. The next day the Court hurried into a special session to overturn the ruling. On June 19 the Rosenbergs were executed. The following month McCarran introduced a bill to prevent a single judge from staying a death sentence.[56]

McCarran had a suggestion. Only ten members of the Judiciary Committee had straggled into the meeting on June 22. The missing third of the committee, McCarran pointed out, undoubtedly had more pressing matters to attend to. Congress was racing toward adjournment at the end of next month, and the appropriations subcommittee, for example, was bogged down in hearings. McCarran said that he and other members who were also on appropriations needed to devote themselves to budget business. He proposed that Judiciary not hold any more hearings until July 2. McCarran's motion passed. "It looked," remembered one senator, "so innocent."[57]

What McCarran had actually done, his colleagues soon learned, was to pour sand into the Judiciary Committee's gears. In May, when Arthur Watkins tried to take up the president's refugee bill in the immigration subcommittee, McCarran asked for a ten-day delay to visit his wife in the Mayo Clinic in Minnesota. Watkins, who had been supported in his reelection campaign the previous fall by McCarran, agreed. From the hospital McCarran wired Watkins asking for an additional delay of three weeks, noting that SISS chairman William Jenner wanted him to conduct a hearing in California. This time Watkins refused.

Now McCarran's resolution tabled everything that the committee might do — such as work on the emergency refugee bill for the president — for two weeks. Once again Congress was trying to pass a displaced persons bill. And once again McCarran was determined to stop the bill — or at least drag out the process as long as humanly possible. "It's an attempt by Pat McCarran to block the refugee bill," snapped New Jersey's Robert Hendrickson, who had voted for McCarran's motion then claimed that he hadn't understood what it meant. "It's a slap at the administration any way you look at it."[58]

A majority of the committee petitioned Chairman Bill Langer for a reconsideration of the vote, which was reversed a week later. But McCarran had added seven days to the months of roadblocks he had already heaped in the bill's path. He was only the ranking minority member of the committee, but he acted as if he were still chairman. "McCarran's rule," wrote columnist Marquis Childs in the *Washington Post*, "appears today nearly as complete as it was before November 4."[59]

On June 30 McCarran went to the White House, a place he had not been invited in four years. Eisenhower was signing a bill that would let Korean veterans who fought with U.S. forces become citizens. The president made sure that the congressional leaders on immigration policy were all there. From the Senate: Judiciary chairman Bill Langer, immigration subcommittee chairman Arthur Watkins, and McCarran. From the House: Judiciary chairman Francis Walter and ranking minority member Emmanuel Celler. Eisenhower and McCarran both put on their glasses for the signing. The president autographed a photo of himself (TO MY GOOD FRIEND, SENATOR MCCARRAN, A DISTINGUISHED AMERICAN[60]) and handed the pen to McCarran as a souvenir.

Some presidents might use such an occasion to lobby for their own pending legislation. Eisenhower liked to stay above the fray. After a lifetime in the army he expected the White House to operate the same way: He would decide policy; his staff would implement it. So when Eisenhower found himself in the Oval Office with the five most influential lawmakers on immigration policy, he decided to talk about golf. As the group broke up, McCarran hung around for a quick private chat. "The president didn't ask me to do anything," McCarran told reporters.[61]

Two weeks later, on July 14, McCarran was back in the White House. Eisenhower had invited him and Watkins to the Oval Office to talk about the immigration bill. McCarran was charmed by the genial, easy-smiling president, so different from the sharp, snappy Truman. "I would be proud if the years to come could let us get better acquainted," McCarran wrote to Eisenhower a few days later. "I think we might be good friends."[62]

Back in the subcommittee room, McCarran quickly reverted to form.

Watkins hadn't been able to drag McCarran to a meeting for weeks, and when he finally did show up McCarran objected to considering the refugee bill since counsel Richard Arens was sick. Watkins overruled the objection. "McCarran was furious," wrote *Time*. "He showered Watkins with such abuse that Watkins turned pale and finally became ill."[63]

Being invited to the White House again did nothing to make McCarran more receptive to the president — *any* president. "I tried to persuade him to go along," Eisenhower remembered. "I made about as much impression on him as beating on an anvil with a sponge."[64]

July 27, 1953. The Korean War ended. "McCarran alone among senators," reported the *Orlando Evening Star*, "says he would rather go on fighting than accept the proposed Korean armistice, which he calls 'a perpetuation of a fraud on this country and the United Nations.'"[65]

The portly, white-haired figure lingered in the long, dim hallway of the Senate Office Building like a ghost. McCarran would not go into the hearing room if doing so would give the committee a quorum. Then work on the refugee bill would have to be postponed until the next meeting. But if enough members turned up to achieve a quorum, McCarran would cross the doorway — and proceed to stall the hearing as best he could. "His persistence is in itself remarkable," marveled columnist Marquis Childs.[66]

One day when McCarran did go into the hearing room he almost got in a fight with Everett Dirksen. McCarran blasted the refugee bill, saying that it had been written by the displaced persons lobby that he had been fighting for years.

"There is no proof of that and I think it is untrue," Dirksen said.

"I consider that a personal insult," McCarran replied.

McCarran offered to settle the matter outside with his colleague, twenty years his junior. "I am not going to take this," he yelled.

"I'm too much of a gentleman to take you on," Dirksen replied. "If any language of mine was interpreted as casting aspersions on the distinguished senator from Nevada I am sorry."[67]

Even McCarran could stall for only so long. On July 23 the committee reported out a bill allowing 215,000 additional refugees into the country over three years, close to the president's original request. McCarran went to the White House for the third time in as many weeks. He offered Eisenhower a deal: Cut another twenty thousand refugees from the bill and McCarran would not fight it on the floor. "I refused," Eisenhower recalled.[68]

Less than a week later the bill passed. "America has once again demonstrated to the world that she is a symbol of freedom, opportunity and one man's concern for another," the *New York Herald Tribune* said. "Congress has done a good day's work."[69]

On August 7 Eisenhower signed the Refugee Act of 1953. "We haven't lost yet," one of McCarran's aides boasted. "We're going to administer the act."[70]

Three months later no refugees had been granted visas yet. McCarran, according to Drew Pearson, had cut a secret deal with the White House to put the State Department's Scott McLeod in charge of screening refugees in exchange for dropping his opposition. "McLeod seems to be carrying out the precise wishes of Senator McCarran," Pearson wrote. "He has been proceeding as though his job is to obstruct rather than to admit refugees into this country."[71]

Lewis and Esther Corey were at a dinner party in New York. One of the guests, a doctor named Morris Greenberg, started defending the Soviet Union. He sounded, Corey thought, like a Stalinist. Corey should know. More than three decades earlier Corey had helped found the American Communist Party. These days, however, there was no more fervent anti-Communist than Lew Corey. And he was not a man to suffer fools lightly. "He wasn't the most serene of men," Daniel Bell recalled. ". . . My visual recollections are primarily of his head thrust out, cocked to a side, eyes squinting, impatient to talk and arguing back with an emotional force."[72] Once when a magazine editor was slow getting back to Corey about a submission, the writer called him up. "I'm returning to you the book you sent me for review," he said. "You can take the book, your magazine and yourself and stick them up your arse."[73]

At the dinner party, Corey had a heart attack. Greenberg, the physician, didn't move. "I was shocked by your behavior as a doctor and as a human being," Esther Corey later raged to Morris. "I thought these things only happen in Germany or Russia."[74]

The Coreys were not having a good year. Since coming to New York from Italy with his mother at the age of three, Lewis Corey had lived fifty-seven of his sixty years in the United States. Then, on December 24, 1952, the McCarran-Walter Act went into effect. That same day government agents served Corey with deportation papers and arrested him for being an illegal alien. "He was caught," Esther complained, "in the McCarran Act."[75]

Lewis Corey once thought that he knew which direction history was moving. Then he changed his mind and changed his name. Now history was catching up. Corey was hardly alone. Under the McCarran-Walter Act deportations would peak in 1954, a year when 26,951 people were thrown out of the country, although only 61 were actually removed as subversives. Exclusions had already peaked earlier in 1951 (under the McCarran Internal Security Act), when 5,647 people were prevented from entering the country.[76]

His real name was Louis Fraina (né Luigi Carlo Fraina). Fraina grew up on New York's Lower East Side, working almost as soon as he could walk, dropping out of school at thirteen. He became a socialist; he spent a month in jail as a conscientious objector — which got in the way of his first application for citizenship. In 1919 he helped form the American Communist Party and went to Moscow to meet with Lenin, who dispatched him to Mexico to found a party there (along with his Russian wife, Esther). In 1922 he quit the party and the following year he moved back to New York — entering the country on a Czech passport as Joseph Charles Skala, an illegality that would not bother the government for another thirty years. He reemerged in public as Lewis Corey, who in 1931 published *The House of Morgan*, the first of five books, and tried to rejoin the Communist Party. "I deserted the party," Corey wrote Earl Browder. ". . . I want to work with the party and the Comintern. But when a man has left the party as I did, he does not come back with empty hands. He comes back with work, with concrete evidence that he has not abandoned his former ideas and that he can do work for the party which the party needs."[77]

But by 1940 Corey had completely given up on socialism. "The Marxist way, history now shows," he concluded in *The Nation*, "ends in totalitarian nightmare."[78] That same year Corey joined with Reinhold Niebuhr and Jim Loeb to found the Union for Democratic Action, the first liberal organization to stand firmly against the totalitarians of both the right and the left.

In 1947 the FBI tried to debrief Corey. Five days later the exhausted agents gave up. "It is extremely difficult to conduct an efficient and logical interview with him," a frustrated agent reported to Hoover. "He describes himself as a 'theoretician,' and he obviously loves to theorize. When asked a question he will start talking with the apparent thought of answering the question. However, he is literally full of parenthetical ideas, and the attachment will reflect that he frequently wanders far afield. . . . He is very emotional by nature. . . . It was necessary to allow him to theorize, wander, and expound, in spite of the fact that he was frequently well off of the subject."[79]

Two years later Corey applied again for citizenship. He had heard nothing from the Immigration Service for three years. Then the McCarran-Walter Act went into effect and Corey was arrested. "The proceedings, of course, are ridiculous," he told Norman Thomas. "A law to get Communists starts on an anti-Communist. The deportation warrants alleges only the 'crime' of CP membership from 1919 to 1922 and nothing else."[80]

That summer Corey had a deportation hearing. "I want to state categorically that I never, directly or indirectly, applied for re-admission to the Communist Party," Corey lied.[81] The main witness against Corey was Benjamin Gitlow, an old comrade and former rival who had become a well-known ex-Communist. "A bundle of pompous vanity and egotism," Gitlow called Corey. [82] Gitlow testified about what Corey had done in the party thirty years before. "No heart, no vigor," thought Corey, "not even any viciousness, testified like a somnambulist."[83] Gitlow didn't even look at Corey, who glared at him the whole time. "He's still a filthy Stalinist," Corey fumed, "in morals if not in political affiliation."[84]

On the evening of September 15, 1953, Corey was hard at work at his desk. He had so many ideas. There was the book about his adopted country, *On an Understanding of America*, for which he had written a seven-thousand-word outline. There was the biography of Frances Wright, a nineteenth-century reformer. And then there was his autobiography. *One Rebel's Years*, he planned to call it. In a month he would be sixty-one.

Corey slumped over his desk. Half a year after his heart attack, a blood vessel burst in his brain. He was in a coma for a day before he died. Two months later a letter came from the INS: Corey could apply for legal reentry.

On November 6 Attorney General Herbert Brownell spoke to the Executive Club in Chicago. For most of the year McCarran and the conservatives had carped about the Eisenhower administration's laxity, even as Dulles cleaned out the State Department and the president invited Bill Jenner and Joe McCarthy into the Oval Office for a photo op in April when he signed Executive Order 10450, increasing the government loyalty standard. Now the attorney general was about to demonstrate unequivocally where the Eisenhower administration stood.

Brownell said that he wanted to talk about Harry Dexter White, the assistant secretary of the treasury who had been accused of being a Soviet espionage agent and had died days after publicly denying the charge in 1948. "I can now announce officially, for the first time in public," Brownell said in a speech that he had cleared with the White House, "that the records in my department show that White's spying activities for the Soviet government were reported in detail by the FBI to the White House . . . in December of 1945."[85]

That was a month *before* Harry Truman nominated White to become head of the International Monetary Fund. In other words, what McCarran and McCarthy had been saying for years about the Democrats being soft on Communism was true. Before Brownell's speech, White had been the highest-ranking government official ever accused of betraying his country. Now, Brownell suggested, that dishonor belonged to the former president.

Ten days later, on November 16, Truman went to a small television studio in Kansas City and spoke to the nation, an American flag behind him, another on his American Legion lapel pin. "I have been accused, in effect," the former president said, "of knowingly betraying the security of the United States. This charge is, of course, a falsehood."[86]

Truman said that he had seen the FBI report against White, that the allegations were serious but unsupported, and that the information had reached his desk too late to stop the appointment. Truman then suggested that he had sent White to the IMF to get him out of Treasury, a stratagem that the FBI had agreed with. At best Truman was trying to cover his ass; at worst, he was lying. But he was absolutely correct when he analyzed Brownell's motives for bringing up the incident.

"It is now evident," Truman concluded, "that the present administration has fully embraced, for political advantage, McCarthyism. I am not referring to the senator from Wisconsin. He is only important in that his name has taken on a dictionary meaning of the word. It is the corruption of the truth, the abandonment of the due process of the law. It is the use of the big lie and the unfounded accusation against any citizen in the name of Americanism or security. It is the rise to power of the demagogue who lives on untruth; it is the spreading of fear and the destruction of faith in every level of our society."[87]

But in attacking the attorney general, Truman had offended someone even more powerful: J. Edgar Hoover.

Robert Lamphere was sweating like crazy. It was November 17, 1953, the day after Truman's television appearance. Lamphere was sitting in assistant FBI director Mickey Ladd's office starring at a blank TV. He was waiting for J. Edgar Hoover's televised testimony before SISS. Hoover would read a prepared statement, but if he was then asked a question he couldn't answer, he would give a discreet hand signal. Lamphere was supposed to provide the answer, which would be relayed over a live phone line to an agent in the hearing room, who would whisper the information to Hoover.

Lamphere could feel the sweat running down his back and chest, soaking his undershirt. Months earlier Hoover had ordered Lamphere to write a memo for the new attorney general, Herbert Brownell, about Harry Dexter White. Then Hoover asked for a second memo. "The period was the most nerve-wracking I ever experienced in the FBI," Lamphere recalled. "I worked without a day off for six weeks, and averaged about eighteen hours a day, feverishly writing memoranda about White. I hated it. I wasn't developing a new spy case — Harry Dexter White had been dead for five years."[88]

The White case had been mishandled from the beginning. Whittaker Chambers had named White as a fellow traveler and source of information in 1939. FBI agents didn't interview White until 1942. He denied the charges. In November 1945 Elizabeth Bentley, who'd never met White, implicated him in Soviet espionage. Hoover immediately alerted the White House to the charges. Although the FBI couldn't find any evidence against White, Hoover sent Truman another warning in December. Nevertheless, Truman nominated White to become head of the International Monetary Fund in 1946, which infuriated Hoover, who then dashed off a twenty-eight-page memo on White. This, Truman later claimed, was the first he had actually heard of the matter. By then it was too late to stop the nomination. White was confirmed, only to retire after a year. In 1948 Bentley and Chambers appeared before HUAC and testified that White had been involved with Soviet espionage. White forcefully denied the charges and days later died of a heart attack.

After Brownell dug up White's corpse to attack Truman, HUAC served the former president with a subpoena. Truman ignored it. William Jenner, the new SISS chairman, also wanted to haul Truman before his committee. "A grave mistake," McCarran advised Jenner.[89] "Absolutely inadvisable," McCarran added a week later when Jenner was still considering the idea. "I assure you it would bring about disastrous reaction to subcommittee now in dignified position and it would do irreparable damage in every regard."[90]

Jenner didn't subpoena Truman. Instead he gave J. Edgar Hoover a platform to attack the former president. The director had never liked Truman, but five years earlier the White debacle had infuriated him to the point of recklessness. "He was blind to the Communist menace," Hoover fumed about Truman.[91] So Hoover began a campaign of leaks to HUAC, McCarran, and McCarthy that did much to turn what Truman wanted to handle as a law enforcement problem into a national nightmare in which liberals and conservatives questioned each other's motives and good faith. No committee proved more trustworthy than McCarran's, which was why Hoover established a formal program of cooperation with SISS in 1951, a privilege that neither HUAC nor McCarthy enjoyed. "The reason the SISS did such a good job," Joe McCarthy complained to Assistant Director Lou Nichols, "was because of the help they got from the bureau."[92] In fact, Hoover decided to cut HUAC off from any assistance in 1952, and the following July he did the same to McCarthy. When Roy Cohn, McCarthy's new counsel, came to the bureau for help, the director ordered his former ally scorned. "Cohn gets nothing," Hoover commanded.*[93]

At two-thirty in the afternoon of November 17, Hoover strode into the SISS hearing room. "The custodian of the nation's security," Jenner called him. "There is more involved here than the charges against one man ...," Hoover said. "Some thirty-five years of infiltration of an alien way of life ... the Godless forces of Communism."[94]

Brownell had declassified the FBI reports about White for the occasion, so Hoover was able to give a detailed account of the case. He defended Elizabeth Bentley. "All information furnished by Miss Bentley, which was susceptible to check, has proven to be correct," he said. "She has been subjected to the most searching of cross-examinations; her testimony has been evaluated by juries and reviewed by the courts and has been found to be accurate." And Hoover called the former president of the United States a liar. "The FBI," he said, "called to the attention of the appropriate authorities the facts, as alleged by reliable sources, which were substantial in pointing to a security risk, as they occurred. It is equally clear that the FBI did not depart from its traditional position of making no evaluation and was not a party to any agreement to keep White in public service."[95]

---

*William Jenner also proved too adventurous for Hoover's taste, and in June 1954 the director ended the liaison program between the FBI and SISS.

In FBI headquarters Lamphere kept his eyes glued to Hoover's hands, but the director talked for thirty minutes and never gave the signal. "To say that I was relieved is an understatement," Lamphere recalled. "I was also wringing wet."[96]

Back in the office Hoover wrote a note to McCarran, who was ill in Reno. "My one regret was that you were not there," Hoover told McCarran. ". . . You take care of yourself because we will be counting on you when the session opens up in January."[97]

On the evening of November 24 Joe McCarthy went on national television for half an hour. The Eisenhower administration had not demanded equal time from the networks for a response to Truman's charges. McCarthy did. He threatened to ask the FCC to review the license of any station that failed to carry his broadcast. Truman had attacked McCarthyism. McCarthy attacked Trumanism. But, like the former president, he saved his real ire for Eisenhower. He attacked Dulles's State Department for still employing John Davies, for betraying American POWs, and for not cutting off aid to American allies that continued to trade with Communist China. "Once a nation has allowed itself to be reduced to a state of whining, whimpering appeasement," he said, "the cost of retaining national honor may be high. But we must regain our national honor regardless of what it costs."[98]

Eisenhower responded by inviting McCarthy to the White House to talk about internal security; Dulles responded by firing more State Department officials. Some White House aides were furious, wanting the president to attack McCarthy directly. "I will not get in the gutter with that guy," Eisenhower told his cabinet.[99]

Not long after Stalin died the guards opened the door to a basement cell in a Budapest prison and let Noel Field out. He didn't know what year it was. When Field found out that Stalin was dead, he started to cry. Stalin was one of the reasons Field had become a Communist — and the reason he had spent five years in solitary confinement.

Field was a man idealistic enough to try to sing the "Internationale" in Russian from the steps of the Lincoln Memorial when he worked in the State Department in the 1930s, but cautious enough to flee the U.S. in 1948 when his old friend Alger Hiss was exposed as a Soviet spy. Then one day in 1949, Field left his hotel in Prague and disappeared. So did his wife, brother, and foster daughter.

Then Hungarian authorities arrested Foreign Affairs Minister Laszlo

Rajk and charged the long-time Communist with treason — the first of a long line of Eastern bloc party members accused of betraying the revolution. Field was the chief prosecution witness. During World War II, Field had traveled around Europe working for the Unitarian Service Committee saving refugees — and also operating as a courier for the Communist underground and the OSS. Now anyone who had anything to do with Field was suddenly considered a traitor. Rajk was executed. Thousands more were purged.

As bad as McCarthyism was in the United States, the Communist version was much, much worse. In America, Hollywood radicals found themselves closed out of their chosen trade and forced to sell homes in Beverly Hills and move to the San Fernando Valley. In Eastern Europe accused subversives sat in jail cells, like Noel Field, or were sent to Arctic labor camps, like his step-daughter Erika Wallach (whose death sentence had been commuted after Stalin's death). When Wallach was eventually released she tried to join her husband in the U.S. but was ineligible for a visa under the McCarran-Walter Act. Representative Francis Walter intervened and got her into the country under a loophole for defectors.

When Field was finally released he discovered that his wife, Herta, had been sitting in a cell just a few doors away. Together they wept over the dictator's death. They never stopped believing in Communism.

"My accusers essentially have the same convictions that I do," Field later wrote. "They hate the same things and the same people I hate — the conscious enemies of socialism, the fascists, the renegades, the traitors. Given their belief in my guilt, I cannot blame them, I cannot but approve of their detestation. That is the real horror of it all."

Field, for once in his life, was right.[100]

At eight-thirty one morning in 1953, A. J. Liebling walked into the Chuck Wagon restaurant at the Riverside Hotel in Reno, half an hour early for an appointment with Pat McCarran. Liebling spotted the senator already ensconced in a booth, surrounded by cronies. Liebling sat down at a table near the bar, where the tender was busy mixing whiskey sours and Bloody Marys. Liebling ordered breakfast. Coins clanged in the background. In the Riverside, Liebling had become accustomed to hearing two sounds all the time: slot machines disgorging change and an almost equally metallic voice paging the hotel's most famous resident. *"Senator McCarran is wanted on the long-distance telephone,"* the tinny voice jangled day and night.

Liebling was a writer for the *New Yorker* magazine who had first come to Reno in 1949. He planned to stay for six weeks, long enough to become a legal resident and get a divorce. He lasted for two days. "I had counted on doing a bit of writing while in limbo," he recalled, "and so far it had all been on American Express checks." Liebling fled Reno, driving out thirty miles along the Truckee River until the stream turned into Pyramid Lake, where he found a guest ranch filled with aspiring divorcées. "I have never been reluctant to buy a lady a drink," Liebling wrote, "but there were thirty-eight ladies in residence at the ranch." Liebling struck up a conversation with a Paiute Indian. The land, Liebling learned, was part of an Indian reservation.

Pyramid Lake is the terminus of the Truckee River, thirty-one miles long, ten miles wide, 120,000 acres of blue water smack in the middle of the Nevada desert. John C. Frémont was the first explorer to record seeing the lake, where weirdly shaped tufa pillars stuck out of the surface, barometers of how much the water level had fallen over the ages. One tufa formation reminded Frémont of the Great Pyramid, hence the name. Pyramid Lake is the home to a species of fish (*Chasmistes cujus*) that exists nowhere else. The Paiute Indians who lived nearby called the fish cui-ui. The Indians themselves were known as cui-ui eaters. "The Lake of the Cui-ui Eaters," Liebling called his four-part *New Yorker* series, which was published in 1955.

In a bookcase on the ranch Liebling found a 1944 government report about Washington's effort to evict five families of white squatters from the reservation. In 1949 Liebling figured that the skirmish must have been over for a while. Actually the eviction fight went back to 1909 — and it wasn't close to ending. When Liebling was back in Reno four years later, in 1953, the case seemed no closer to being resolved than it had before. The central figure in the story, like the Riverside's restaurant, was Pat McCarran. "It may be that the Paiute Indians once had to contend with the American mastodon," Liebling observed. "A workout with a mastodon would have been a useful form of training for the struggle I found them engaged in with . . . McCarran."[101]

Liebling was drinking his second cup of coffee went McCarran came to his table and sat down. The night before Liebling had caught his first glimpse of the senator. "It was useless to pretend I did not see him," he wrote. "It would have been like pretending not to notice Louis XIV at Versailles. As I studied him, I saw that he had a fine, witty face, like that of a John Barrymore grown old — a Roman profile half buried in suet.

Newspaper photographs coarsen most subjects and in the case of such a man as McCarran, they sometimes induce a dangerous contempt. I had thought of him as a beefy ward-heeler type, but now I perceived that he was really a beautiful old rogue, with a mobile, calculating mask."[102]

McCarran began talking about the Pyramid Lake controversy — something he had been doing for years to anyone who would listen. "I've been trying for a long time to get justice for those white people down there on the reservation," McCarran had explained to Pete Petersen back in 1949. ". . . I am deeply sympathetic with these men. As I say, the justice is all in their favor."[103]

"Perhaps it will do no harm if I go into a little history of this case,"[104] McCarran told Liebling.

For McCarran it would be harder to imagine a more personal fight. In 1862 his Irish immigrant father carved out a homestead ranch from the sagebrush alongside the Truckee. Twenty miles farther down the river, where it emptied into Pyramid Lake, five Italian immigrant families were doing the same thing. The only problem was that in 1859 the federal government had marked the land around the lake for an Indian reservation, although Washington didn't officially declare it as such until 1874. The Italians owned the property they lived on but dug irrigation ditches across a few hundred acres of the three-hundred-thousand-acre reservation. In 1909 the federal government first tried to evict the Italians. They called themselves settlers; the Indians called them squatters. The process moved about as quickly as the case of *Jardyce v. Jarndyce* in *Bleak House*. At one point the settlers agreed to buy the land from the Paiutes, made a single payment in 1925, and promptly went into default, claiming that the Depression had wiped out the appraised value of the property.

Then, in 1933, John Collier became the commissioner of the Bureau of Indian Affairs, part of Harold Ickes's Interior Department. Collier was an activist and mystic with a long interest in Native American culture — and he soon became one of McCarran's great antagonists. Collier pushed for an Indian New Deal (the Indian Reorganization Act of 1934), which gave the federal government the power to buy land for reservations and granted tribes the authority to form self-governing councils.* And Collier appointed Alida C. Bowler, whom he had worked with in an activist organization called the American Indian Defense Association, as the superin-

---

*The main drafter of the law was Ickes's solicitor, Nathan Margold, whose later nomination to the federal bench was blocked by McCarran.

tendent of Nevada reservations. Bowler encouraged the new Paiute tribal council to complain to Washington about the squatters. John Collier and Harold Ickes championed the Indians, and the government resumed eviction proceedings against the five families. The Italians went to McCarran.

In 1937 McCarran introduced a bill to give the settlers title to the land without having to resume payments. "This question involves the homes and hearthfires of these five poor, unfortunate families," McCarran testified. "And when I say they are poor, I say it emphatically, because for years I have lived by their side and I know what I am talking about. This whole question is one of fair play, justice, and equity. It is not one of cold-blooded, heartless law. We can oust these settlers. . . . Or we can let them live as they have lived for years and years, in neighborly friendliness with these Indians."*[105]

McCarran publicly attacked Bowler for inciting "class hatred between races" and pressured the Interior Department into having her transferred. "As if you could be too prejudiced in favor of the people it is your duty to protect," she told Liebling years later. "It's like a policeman being prejudiced in favor of the law."

"I'm not saying she had leftist tendencies or anything," McCarran told Liebling at breakfast. "But these Paiutes turned up at hearings in Washington using the expression 'minority group.'"

"Well?" Liebling said.

"They were stimulated," McCarran went on.[106]

McCarran's bill passed the Senate but died in the House, which became an annual occurrence, like the swallows returning to Capistrano. On the first day of each new legislative session McCarran introduced another bill to give the disputed land to the squatters for a small fee — nine bills from 1937 to 1953. And as long as legislation was pending, the Justice Department could not evict the families. So McCarran made sure that some legislation was always pending. It took him only a dozen years to wear out Collier and Ickes, although they continued to champion the Paiutes from the sidelines. In a bizarre inversion of his obsession with foreign Communists, the Nevada aboriginal people became to McCarran an alien presence on their own

---

*The Indians had a different view. "Does Senator McCarran consider himself setting good example by representing people who are continuously disobeying government and state laws," wrote Lawrence Williams, chairman of the tribal council. ". . . It is purely a racial hatred that the McCarrans had for the Indians of Pyramid Lake reservation years ago." (Jack Forbes, *Nevada Indians Speak*. Reno, Nev.: University of Nevada Press, 1967, p. 191.)

land. "You are the senator for the Indians, too, not just the white people,"[107] the Paiute tribal council once pointed out to McCarran, to no avail. "It grieves me much to see an injustice wrought upon innocent citizens such as has been wrought on these white settlers," McCarran told Pete Petersen.[108]

In 1947 the tribe hired James Curry, the counsel for the National Congress of American Indians, as its Washington attorney (in Reno the tribe's local attorney was E. P. Carville, a former governor and McCarran ally-turned-enemy). Curry manged to be both a crusader and an opportunist and tried to make the dispute into a national cause célèbre. He encouraged the Indians to seize the disputed land by fencing it off, which they did. The Italians then turned off the water that irrigated the land — since the courts recognized that the squatters owned the water rights and the ditches that crossed the reservation even if they didn't own the land itself. Curry then advised the Indians to seize control of the water, although reservation superintendent Reeseman Fryer pointed out that seizing another man's water in Nevada was akin to murder. Fryer was sympathetic to the Paiutes — too much so for McCarran, who pressured the Interior Department into transferring him. "It is shocking to think that Oscar Chapman, or any of his appointees, could possibly be dominated by a man like McCarran," Curry complained.[109] Harold Ickes also railed against the transfer and convinced Senator Harley Kilgore to take the matter up with Truman. The transfer was canceled, although McCarran then arranged for Reeseman to be promoted out of the Interior Department into the State Department's foreign aid program, whose budget he controlled. Then McCarran got sick. "McCarran is in the Mayo Clinic Hospital," Curry wrote. "Some people here hope it is nothing trivial and would like to send him some flowers [a funeral wreath]. . . . If the old man lives I think he will have a fight on his hands."[110]

McCarran recovered, but Curry was able to enlist the Senate liberals in the fight. For a dozen years before 1949 McCarran never had any trouble getting his Pyramid Lake bills through the Senate; it was always the House where they died. But when the Eighty-first Congress opened and McCarran introduced his usual bill to give the Italians title to the disputed land, Montana senator James Murray blocked the legislation. Over the next two years Paul Douglas, Harley Kilgore, Hubert Humphrey, Herbert Lehman, and others liberals took turns stopping the bill every time McCarran tried to bring it up. During the same period that McCarran was tormenting the liberals by stalling the displaced persons bill and forcing his Internal Security Act upon Congress they were able to take small satisfaction in blockading one of his pet causes. The liberals and Paiutes even talked about trying to topple McCarran from the Senate in 1950. "McCarran is fighting a dubious battle for reelection," John Collier told Interior Secretary Oscar Chapman. "His defeat would benefit the Truman administration and the human race."[111] McCarran exploded on the floor one day. "I happen to know where the objection comes from," McCarran sputtered. "It comes from a mind that should not be given the consideration of the people of America. It comes from one Harold Ickes, formerly the secretary of the Interior. The sooner we quit listening to that individual, the better off America will be in every respect."[112]

Again McCarran outlasted his opponents. He easily won reelection. Ickes died. Curry got into trouble with a Senate subcommittee for taking advantage of the Indians he was supposed to be representing. ("With little concern for the standard laid down by the American Bar Association to guide the ethics of his profession," a report concluded, "Mr. Curry has misled the Indians, improperly solicited their claims, assumed legal responsibilities toward the Indians for the presentation of their claims which he could not possibly fulfill and bartered for his own gain the valuable claims which the Indians had entrusted to his professional care."[113]) Curry lost his Indian clients and came down with a rare disease that paralyzed him from head to foot. "I think the thing that kept me alive," Curry told Paiute leader Avery Winnemucca, "was the fear, if I died, that I might join Pat McCarran, down there with old Lucifer."[114]

McCarran even outlasted most of the Italians. By the time Liebling caught up with him in 1953, the senator had been fighting for the ranchers for almost twenty years; the five original families had dwindled down to two. And once again in the beginning of the legislative session McCarran had introduced yet another bill on behalf of the remaining Italians, whose history he traced for Liebling back to the days when his father had arrived in the Truckee Meadows back in 1862.

"The senator's talks on Pyramid Lake, I knew from my reading of the congressional hearings, usually ran to around twenty-two and a half pages," Liebling recalled, "and since I could see that he was following the traditional script, I attempted to halt him at about page ten."

Liebling asked McCarran if he thought that his most recent bill had any chance.

"I've given up," McCarran sighed. "You can't win 'em all."*

Liebling almost spat out his coffee. "I felt as if I were witnessing the withdrawal of the Roman legions from Britain," he wrote, " — the first backward step of an empire."[115]

That was, Liebling later realized, the beginning of the end for McCarran.

---

* Indeed, the next year one of the last two squatters, Mrs. M. P. De Paoli, agreed to sell her land and the ditches she owned on the Indian reservation to the government for thirty-one thousand dollars. McCarran introduced a bill to get the money; it sailed through both houses and was signed by the president.

CHAPTER 26

Beset with Enemies

Means are more important than ends, because means
mould institutions which frame ways of behaving, while
ends are never in any man's lifetime attained.[1]
— John Dos Passos, *Adventures of a Young Man*

I don't understand your politics these days. . . . But I do
understand what you say of the institutions of the
republic and bless you for it. They do indeed have to be
saved from those who would save them to destroy them.
And to talk of these things is to skate on very thin ice
indeed for the words turn mush as you say they do. Not
only in the Commies' mouths but in McCarthy's and
McCarran's even more for more men listen to them.[2]
— Archibald MacLeish to John Dos Passos

From nowhere the car appeared, and to nowhere it seemed to head. The
lonely highway had not existed when the old man was a boy. Then it
took the better part of a day to make the thirty-mile journey on a pony
to town and back. Everything else looked the same: the train tracks spanning the hardpan little valley, the river bubbling down from the unseen
mountains in the west, the fringe of cottonwoods and willows clinging to
the riverbank. And the sagebrush — dry and brittle now late in the year,
leached of what thin color it had in the spring — covered everything else,
the flat land stretching away from the river toward the hills, looking
smooth as old bones from the distance.

Once he had trailed sheep up those hills and those past them, all the
way into California. Today he fell asleep in the car driven by his young
assistant, and when he awoke he fumbled to take his pills. Many years ago
he read law books by the light of a campfire; now the books were full of
his laws.

The old house, too, looked the same when it came into view, down the
slope from the highway and the railbed, near the river. Not much bigger
than a garage, a shamrock nailed above the front door, the house had been
rented out for years. He wanted to see it one last time. Sixty years earlier

a boy left that house to go to school in the city, where he was four years older than his classmates and they laughed at his farmer's overalls and chinchilla coat. In Washington no one laughed at him now.

The car pulled over, but the old man didn't move from his seat. His small blue eyes peered down at the ranch for a while and then he nodded. The car moved on. They had a long drive ahead of them. It wasn't a trip that the old man especially wanted to take. But something needed fixing and he was the only one who could put it back together. After all, he had broken it in the first place.

In January 1954 Pat McCarran gently, if publicly, chided McCarthy's Permanent Investigations Subcommittee for stepping into the internal security field that was supposed to be the province of SISS. "I don't think it hasn't done some good work, because I think it has," McCarran said. "I have no argument with Pat McCarran," McCarthy replied. "Pat is one of the greatest senators we've ever had."[3]

In February, McCarran walked into the room where the formal dinner was being held for the president of Turkey, took one look at the seating arrangement, and almost walked out. Mayor C. D. Baker was hosting the banquet at the Las Vegas Chamber of Commerce for President Celal Bayar. McCarran pointed out that Baker, who had supported Hank Greenspun in his suit against the senator, was sitting next to the president. "Since when," McCarran growled, "does the mayor of a city come before a U.S. senator?"

State Department officials tried to sooth McCarran's feelings. The senator, after all, had the honor of introducing the president. "I will not," McCarran hissed. "I'll walk out first."

The Turkish foreign minister, who was also serving as the president's interpreter, offered McCarran his seat on the other side of Bayar. McCarran sat next to the president. The foreign minister sat on a stool behind his boss.[4]

In March, McCarran lumbered into the Senate chamber and read a short statement from his desk. He didn't stand up as he was supposed to do, and after fifteen minutes he was sweating like crazy. It was all McCarran could do to get back to Room 409 of the Senate Office Building. "Your father, to be frank with you, hasn't picked up at all so far as I can see," Eva Adams told his daughter Mary. ". . . He told me when he came back to the office that he just simply wasn't getting his strength back."[5] Some days McCarran felt every one of his seventy-seven years.

In April, McCarran was feeling better. "Your father seems to be getting back to his old self again," Adams reported to his daughter Margaret. "It actually is a thrill to us to see him looking better and seeming more relaxed. He had a little spell of some kind last week but he was sensible as could be and stayed in bed for a day or so. We kidded him and told him we thought he just wanted to look at the McCarthy hearings on the television."[6]

Like twenty million other Americans, McCarran was enthralled by the thirty-six days of live broadcasts that dominated daytime television for two months. Three months earlier McCarran had lectured McCarthy about overstepping his boundaries. Now it was time to defend him.

Roy Cohn just couldn't help showing off his new friend. In the Senate dining room Cohn bounded up to McCarran one day when he was having lunch with Jay Sourwine. Cohn introduced the senator to Dave Schine. In a room full of old men, the young and handsome Schine looked like a Hollywood star. Before long, as it turned out, Schine would have a cameo role in a daytime drama that griped the nation: the army-McCarthy hearings.

Cohn and Schine were both twenty-six but as different as night and day. Roy Cohn was slight but intense, hound-dog eyes hiding a quick mind and a burning desire to succeed; as Joe McCarthy's energetic chief counsel he could seem both older than his years and at the same time impossibly young, his hairline already in retreat but his suits just a little too big, like a boy trying on his father's clothes. G. David Schine, on the other hand, never had to try a day in his life. The son a millionaire businessman who owned a chain of hotels and theaters, Schine was strikingly handsome, good looking enough to be a leading man in the movies but far too shallow. He went to Harvard to stay out of the Korean War. He wrote an anti-Communist pamphlet (although he couldn't quite get the date of the Russian Revolution right), and his father put it in every hotel room in the chain, right next to the Bible. And when Cohn first saw Schine in one of his father's hotels in Florida, it was like Jove looking at Ganymede. "The king of the gods once loved a Trojan boy named Ganymede," wrote Ovid. "For once, there was something found that Jove would rather have been than what he was."[7]

The young anti-Communist star swept up the feckless young man and brought him back to Washington.*

Cohn gave Schine an unpaid job on the Permanent Investigations Subcommittee ("We must create a 'Demiform,' or association of democratic parties on the basis of mutual cooperation free of the charge of American imperialism," Schine wrote in one proposal[8]). Cohn took Schine to Europe, where they went looking for subversive books in the State Department's overseas libraries. They stayed in adjoining hotel rooms wherever they traveled. Every Friday they fled Washington together, flying to New York, where the famous prosecutorial prodigy and the dashing millionaire's son socialized at the Stork Club. "The sensitive liberals who decried 'McCarthyism,' spread the rumor that Cohn and Schine were Jack and Jill," Cohn recalled later, "a slander that continues to this day, no matter that Dave married Miss Universe and is the father of seven children."[9] Cohn, however, never married and died of AIDS.

Whatever else they shared, the two young friends were both committed to fighting Communism in America, although they were somewhat less interested in fighting Communism in Korea, at least in uniform — a fact that drew the attention of columnist Drew Pearson. Jack Anderson, a Pearson legman, managed to get a copy of Schine's draft record, which detailed his myriad deferments and 4-F classification. Pearson began hounding the draft board and writing about Schine's good fortune, which soon ended with Schine reclassified as 1-A. Cohn tried to get Schine a commission as an intelligence officer in every branch of the service, and when that failed he managed to delay Private Schine's reporting to boot camp by getting the army to temporarily assign him to McCarthy's committee. Eventually, however, Schine arrived at Fort Dix. Cohn was constantly on the phone, calling Secretary of the Army Robert Stevens, the commander of Fort Dix, and anyone else who could grant Schine weeknight passes to leave the base and weekend furloughs. Boot camp did not greatly interfere with Schine's social life at the Stork Club.

Drew Pearson smelled blood. In 1950 Pearson had broken the story about McCarthy's claim in executive session during the Tydings hearing

---

*Cohn proved to be no more popular as the McCarthy Committee counsel than he'd been in the Justice Department. In January a majority of the committee wanted to fire the young attorney, until McCarran, who wasn't even a member, came to his rescue. "McCarran intervened on behalf of Roy and finally Joe won out with the rest of the committee and Roy stayed as counsel," noted FBI assistant director Lou Nichols. (See Nichols to Tolson, 27 January 1954, Cohn FBI file.)

that Owen Lattimore was the top Soviet spy in the United States. McCarthy responded by kneeing the columnist in the groin at his fifty-fourth birthday party. Senator Arthur Watkins told McCarthy that he had heard two different versions of where McCarthy hit Pearson and hoped that they were both true. "The only good thing McCarthy ever did," Truman added.[10]

Pearson kept after McCarthy, exposing his bogus claims to having been a tail gunner in World War II. Then Pearson detailed his questionable financial dealings. Nothing stuck. In June 1953 Pearson began writing about Schine's charmed stint in the army; he kept writing about it until the military began its own investigation, which was leaked to the press in March. The army report detailed forty-four occasions over eight months when McCarthy and Cohn had pressed for preferential treatment for Schine, with Cohn going as far as to threaten to wreck the army. McCarthy responded by claiming that the army had held Schine as a hostage to get the subcommittee to call off its investigation of the military, which included a probe of Fort Monmouth in New Jersey and the case of a Communist dentist named Irving Peress who got promoted to major. McCarthy's own committee decided to hold hearings, with McCarthy stepping aside and turning over the chairman's gavel to Karl Mundt.

During the army's investigation of Cohn's behavior it turned out that Schine had dropped McCarran's name. "Schine has given you as a reference and has said that he 'worked with McCarran in 1952,'" Sourwine told McCarran. "Eva says there is a request from a Army Criminal Investigation Division officer for an interview with you about Schine."[11]

Sourwine reminded McCarran about Cohn introducing Schine to him at lunch and another time when the two dropped by McCarran's office. "You have neither anger nor warmth," Sourwine told McCarran, suggesting how he answer any questions about Schine, "but there is not much you can say about him. He was introduced to you by a young man [Cohn] whom you know to be brilliant and definitely anti-Communist. But otherwise, you know nothing about Schine or his background or his abilities. That is the whole story."[12]

On April 22 four hundred spectators and a hundred reporters packed the rococo Caucus Room on the third floor of the Senate Office Building and millions more across the country watched on live television as the army-McCarthy hearings started. For the next seven weeks, the hearings were a national sensation. "Point of order," McCarthy interrupted again and again. Army Secretary Robert Stevens testified for thirteen straight days, breaking Owen Lattimore's record.

In May, McCarran spoke to the annual convention of the Catholic War Veterans in New Hampshire. Senator Styles Bridges and Senate candidate Wesley Powell were also at the dinner. McCarran praised both Republicans, but the person he really wanted to talk about was absent. "Joe McCarthy," McCarran said, "has done one thing and that is he has routed a lot of Communists in this country."[13]

The applause was terrific. "The rank and file of people of America today are behind McCarthy," McCarran had told reporters earlier in the day at a press conference. "Party lines must be forgotten when we come to deal with enemies of America. Anyone who fights Communism should have the support of both parties. McCarthy has done a good job and while his methods may not be all that we would commend, the results of his activity have been good. He has said there were Communists in government and he proved it. He has investigated into many phases of government and in every instance, he has brought up results. Every Communist claims he's liberal. You have to look to find out what is his thought and whether he has another doctrine in his head."[14]

For the next several months McCarran went on a self-assigned speaking tour to defend McCarthy and his — *their* — cause. The fight seemed like a tonic, restoring his strength. "The senator is remarkable," Eva Adams gushed to Norm Biltz. "He has been coming early in the morning and staying, as he did last night, until almost eleven o'clock."[15]

For years McCarran had been concerned that adverse publicity could wound the anti-Communist cause, the way Martin Dies made himself into a laughingstock a decade before with charges that HUAC could not possibly back up. That was why McCarran made his staff (and the FBI) work so hard to dig up material to support *his* cases. You could argue with the interpretation but you couldn't dismiss the whole cause as a mere vendetta the way McCarthy had opened himself up to being portrayed.

"The tragedy of this situation is that through these hearings just completed," McCarran said in the Senate, "it has appeared to millions of Americans, and to millions abroad, that anti-Communism was here under attack . . . that congressional investigating committees were being exposed as fumbling, publicity-seeking, unfair, ineffective road-shows. What a tragedy!"[16]

There was nothing like being mad to make McCarran feel alive.

In June army counsel Joseph Welch put Roy Cohn in the witness chair for six days and demanded that he tell the committee anything that he knew about *real* Communists or spies. McCarthy interrupted to mention Fred Fisher, a lawyer who worked for Welch's law firm Hale and Dorr.

Cohn's face dropped. Welch had originally picked Fisher to work on the case but then pulled him off when Fisher admitted that he had once belonged to the National Lawyers Guild, a front group. The story made the *New York Times* but Welch and Cohn had cut a deal: Cohn and McCarthy wouldn't bring up Fred Fisher if Welch didn't bring up the fact that Cohn had avoided the draft by enlisting in the National Guard.

Welch told McCarthy that he had never realized how reckless the senator was until that moment. McCarthy kept at it and then Welch uttered words that became famous as soon as they fell from his mouth.

"Let us not assassinate this lad further, Senator," Welch said. "You have done enough. Have you no sense of decency, sir, at long last. Have you left no sense of decency?"[17]

The Caucus Room exploded into applause. "You can only measure what that applause meant when you knew that two press photographers were clapping," Murray Kempton wrote, "and I have never believed before that a press photographer cared whether any subject lived or died."[18] The hearings would be over in a few more days. Joe McCarthy was nearly finished.

The month after Communist Vietnamese guerrillas defeated the French at Dien Bien Phu, McCarran made a speech in the Senate warning that the United States should not get sucked into another war. "Hour by hour we are being drawn closer and closer to active involvement in a bloody war in Indochina which could turn out to be the greatest disaster this country has ever known," he said in June. "Day by day steps are being taken which bring us nearer to the point of no return. Sooner or later, I am very much afraid, the administration will come before us to ask us to approve the sending of our boys into the swamps and jungles of Indochina."[19]

The State Department had once employed a number of China specialists who might have echoed McCarran's warnings about the folly of getting mired in a land war in an Asian country where Communist designs and nationalist aspirations could combine to wreck any U.S. attempt to preserve the status quo. But most of the China experts were gone. Jack Service had been fired in 1951. Ed Clubb had been forced out the following year. John Carter Vincent had been sacked the year after that. Now one of the last China Hands in the foreign service was John Davies, an expert on both the Chinese and Russian variants of Communism. Until the State Department suspended him again.

In June, Joe Alsop appeared as a witness for John Davies at a loyalty hearing in Washington. For Alsop this had become a regular occurrence since he'd testified at Davies's first hearing in 1951. This was the diplomat's ninth. "Surely there is something wrong with a system of checking which has already subjected an official's career and reputation to octuple jeopardy and which now compels him to undergo a ninth ordeal . . . ," the *Washington Post* observed. "This case long ago became much more than a test of Mr. Davies. It became a test to determine whether a nonpolitical career service can function."[20]

Davies had become a cause célèbre. "The Strange Case of John P. Davies," *U.S. News & World Report* headlined a long story in 1953. "Investigated Since 1945, He's Still a Diplomat."[21] Actually in 1945 Davies had just been denounced, not investigated. That was when Patrick Hurley, the former U.S. ambassador to China, told the Senate Foreign Relations Committee that Davies had been disloyal during his stint in Chungking. In early 1950 Joe Alsop published a series in the *Saturday Evening Post* called "Why We Lost China," which didn't call Davies disloyal but still blamed his bad advice for the Communist takeover. Soon Joe McCarthy was calling Davies pro-Communist. In 1951 the State Department loyalty board investigated and cleared him. A week later McCarran subpoenaed him to appear before SISS during the Institute of Pacific Relations hearings. When the IPR report came out in 1952, the committee devoted four pages to Davies and asked the Justice Department to open a perjury investigation. In January 1953 SISS held eleven days of secret hearings on Davies. On April 14 McCarran made his fourth request to the Justice Department for a perjury investigation. Three days later the State Department announced that it was transferring Davies from Germany to Peru. Two more times that summer McCarran and Jenner badgered Justice about Davies, as well as rehashing his case in the committee's report on "Interlocking Subversion of Government Departments." In November Joe McCarthy went on national television and attacked Davies again. "Part and parcel of the old Acheson-Lattimore-Vincent-White-Hiss group which did so much toward delivering our Chinese friends into the Communist hands . . . ," McCarthy called him. "Why is this man still a high official in our government after eleven months of Republican administration?"[22] A week later Secretary of State John Foster Dulles announced the department's loyalty board had reopened Davies's case.

Alsop, who was on a first-name basis with Dulles, pleaded with the secretary not to fire the diplomat. "An unfavorable verdict on Davies will be a tragic mistake," Alsop told Dulles. ". . . And you place all the subordinate officers of the foreign service on notice that they may subject themselves to the gravest future pains and penalties if they venture to form views and make observations of their own, instead of following like humble dogs in the footsteps of their seniors. . . . You and the president will be the next victims if the administration continues to build up McCarthy by surrenders and seeming surrenders to him. . . . Davies is the victim, as it were, that the high priest of Moloch has requested. It does not matter what you say or do; if Davies is now dropped from the department, you and the administration will be universally regarded as bowing down in Moloch's temple in the most public and decisive manner."[23]

By this time Davies's loyalty file stretched to a yard. Most of it covered the same ground again and again: that he had favored the Chinese Communists during the war and had tried to slip American Communists into the CIA afterward. And in June when Alsop again testified on behalf of Davies, the only thing anyone on the loyalty board wanted to talk about was the columnist's "How We Lost China" article from four years earlier. "My experience in China, was, in many respects, a very bitter one," an exasperated Alsop explained to Lieutenant General Daniel Noce, the chairman of the board. ". . . It took a long time for the personal bitternesses to wear away and to give place to cool judgement. . . . I am quite sure that my judgement is more just and accurate today than it was when I left China and than it was in 1950."[24]

In July his ninth loyalty hearing concluded and John Davies waited for the decision. Over the next two months Dulles passed several suggestions to Davies through intermediaries that he should resign. If Dulles wants to get rid of me, Davies told one person, he'll have to fire me.

On July 29 the Democratic Policy Committee met to talk about Joe McCarthy. "Every man in the Senate has a responsibility," Herbert Lehman said. "Senator McCarthy has shown himself dangerous and unworthy. . . . I very much hope that Senator Johnson will take the lead in censuring Senator McCarthy. I think the Democratic Party will suffer if it does not take a stand."

Minority Leader Lyndon Johnson, of course, wanted the Democrats to avoid taking a stand at all costs. "I have done what I could to prevent this from becoming a partisan issue," Johnson said. McCarthy, added Rhode

Island's Theodore Green, was a Republican problem. "They can remove him if they want to," he said.

The next day in the Senate Vermont Republican Ralph Flanders introduced a motion to censure McCarthy.[25]

One morning in July an ocean liner pulled up to the dock in New York. Pat and Birdie McCarran and their daughter Patty were standing there to greet it, waving their arms in the air. Technically, you weren't allowed to wait on the dock, but when the senator asked the immigration authorities for a favor he usually got it. McCarran searched the crowd coming off the boat, looking for the black-shrouded figure. Sister Mary Mercy was coming back to the United States after spending a year studying art in Florence. The nun was overjoyed to see her father waiting, shocked to see how much he seemed to have aged in a year. "We found him so sweet always," she recalled. "But he seemed so lonely to me."[26]

Cardinal Francis Spellman had given Mary a scholarship to study in Florence and then flew to Montreal to personally ask the mother superior of the Holy Names order to let the nun accept it. From across the Atlantic, McCarran did his best to make sure Mary had a good time. He asked Clare Boothe Luce, the new American ambassador in Rome, to look after her. Luce threw a tea for the sister. He asked J. Edgar Hoover to assign FBI agents to guide Mary around on sight-seeing tours of London and Paris. When Mary wrote home that she had a bad hangnail, McCarran had the State Department send someone to visit her. McCarran asked Franco to give his daughter an audience. "Thank you for writing to generalissimo Franco," Mary told her father. "I surely like him — and he surely likes you Pops!"[27]

Mary cried when she saw her father. They took the train to Washington, where she stayed with her parents while McCarran tried to get Catholic University to let her study there for a doctorate in art history, despite the fact that they offered none. Cardinal Spellman suggested to McCarran that Mary study art history at Johns Hopkins instead. McCarran suggested that the cardinal try harder with Catholic University. Obstacles, as usual, did not greatly concern McCarran. "Keep your head high," he told Mary, "your eyes to the stars and never be afraid to walk alone."[28]

Walking alone, however, had its price. The sadness in the big house in Washington was palpable. Birdie despaired of her husband's constant absence. He worked all the time. They rarely took part in Washington's social life. "In the last twenty-one years I saw so little of Patsy — the public really stole him from me," she complained to her children. "Sometimes I cannot help but resent the fact."[29]

The children were gone, except for Norine, who still worked paging books in the Library of Congress. Alone among the children, Norine asked McCarran for nothing. Her life seemed more cloistered than that of the two nuns. "Be careful dear," McCarran told her, giving her the only thing that he could offer her, "the world is full of sharks in human form. Be careful."[30]

Birdie passed the long hours of the day going out to Delaware for the horse races, escorted by FBI agents who drove her to the track and back. Sometimes McCarran took her along on his official trips, such as when he went to Florida to conduct a one-man SISS hearing. There, too, Birdie went to the races, alone except for the local FBI agents who drove her. Most women's husbands would have retired a decade earlier. Yet night after night, McCarran's dinner was warmed over and finally put away when he didn't come home from the Hill until late at night. In her twilight years with Patsy, Birdie had little to look forward to except the daily double.

Mary begged her father to stop working so hard. Birdie made him promise to spend two weeks resting in Walter Reed Hospital in a room with no phone as soon as Congress adjourned. This may have been a bit of sly revenge on Birdie's part. For McCarran solitude and inaction were less a reprieve from work than a punishment. "He could not leave the hospital fast enough," Mary recalled.[31] "A life of quiet and peace," Mary added, "was not for him."[32]

Melvin Belli nudged Ed Olsen.[33] They were having a drink at the bar in the Riverside Hotel. Isn't that your senator? Belli asked. Across the room a bulky man wearing dark glasses was sitting at a table having dinner by himself. The great head of white hair was unmistakable. It was Pat McCarran.

Olsen went over to introduce himself. As a reporter for the Associated Press in Reno, he had met McCarran dozens of times. "I could never get anything but pomposity out of him and gobbledygook most of the time," he recalled. This time he got more than he expected.

What do you want? McCarran growled.

Up close, Olsen could see that the white hair was thinning considerably at the temples, but there was still enough for a wavy tuft on top. The face remained remarkably unlined, although gravity tugged at the jowls and nose and his skin was as splotchy as an old piebald dog's.

Olsen said that he wanted to know what the senator was up to.

How do I know you're who you say you are? McCarran said.

Olsen dug into his pockets. He didn't have a press card but he pulled out his driver's license and a gas station credit card and put them in front the senator. McCarran looked at the cards and then shoved them back across the table.

You're nothing but a goddamn Communist that's been following me across the country, McCarran bellowed. He stood up, grabbed the edge of the table, and tipped it toward Olsen, sending his steak and silverware and everything else crashing to the floor in the middle of the dinning room. He stomped out.

McCarran's behavior could remind people of a chronic alcoholic's: wild mood swings, mysterious illnesses, outrageous actions. But the only thing McCarran was drunk on was power.

On Friday, August 6, at four-thirty a birthday party broke out in Room 409 of the Senate Office Building. McCarran would be seventy-eight years old in two days. Eva Adams went into McCarran's private office to drag him out. McCarran was at his desk, which was heaped with airline memorabilia: a Lockheed ashtray, model planes from Pan Am and United Airlines, a Northwest Airlines letter opener (which McCarran liked to twirl as he spoke), and a Pan Am globe. There was also a pen set that Joe McCarthy had given him ("To a star-spangled American"). The walls were full of signed photos: McCarran and Amelia Earhart; McCarran and his mentor, progressive Republican William Borah; McCarran and Lyndon Johnson; McCarran and Jay Sourwine. Sister Margaret's Ph.D. hung on one wall, a photo of a sheepherder and a burro on another. There were no photos of presidents: no Roosevelt, Truman, or Eisenhower. To McCarran's right the window looked over the park across the street and to the west the great dome of the Capitol filled the frame.

McCarran lumbered into the party. The Capitol chef had baked a big cake in the shape of Nevada. Birdie, Mercy, and Norine were there. The Senate guests were mostly conservatives: extreme Republicans such as Styles Bridges, Bill Jenner, and Herman Welker and Democrats who would have been Republicans anywhere outside of the South, such as James Eastland and Florida's George Smathers. Minority Leader Lyndon Johnson was the closest thing to a liberal. Also there was K. C. Li, a Chinese millionaire and Nationalist supporter living in New York.

McCarran didn't much feel like celebrating. The year before, the Las Vegas casino owners had reached an out-of-court settlement with Hank Greenspun, and Greenspun hadn't shut up since. The publisher had been using his *Las Vegas Sun* column to suggest that the only thing keeping McCarran from being indicted was his position on the Judiciary Committee. "If truth be known," Greenspun wrote, "the senator should have spent a good part of his long life behind bars."[34] Jay Sourwine wanted McCarran to sue Greenspun for libel. "We have been quietly working, trying to find a way to silence Greenspun," Eva Adams told McCarran's daughter Margaret. ". . . The senator feels that all the people in Las Vegas have sold him down the river."[35]

Drew Pearson was also keeping up his attacks, assisted more and more by Greenspun. "If you are interested in a tie-in between politics and crime with the politics being represented by the senior senator from the state of Nevada it wouldn't be very difficult to uncover," Greenspun told Pearson. "It is common knowledge here and the proof is available. . . . I keep hinting at his connections with the hood element and the necessity for getting permission from him in order to get a gambling license. . . . The mess wouldn't really be cleaned until the McCarran hold on the state is broken or the old bum dies."[36]

Nineteen fifty-four, in fact, was turning out to be a terrible year. Slowly, almost imperceptibly at first, the barometric pressure in the country seemed to be changing. First, in May, an appellate court threw out four of the seven counts in the Owen Lattimore perjury indictment and ruled that the remaining three were doubtful.

Then, in June, liberal bishop G. Bromley Oxnam announced that Harvey Matusow had come to him to renounce the testimony he had given before congressional committees and grand juries, including McCarran's SISS. Matusow, Oxnam claimed, admitted that he'd made most of it up. Joe Alsop had heard a similar confession from Matusow several weeks earlier when the pudgy ex-Communist showed up at the columnist's door. The last time Alsop had heard from Matusow was when the professional witness had threatened to sue the journalist for libel for pointing out that Matusow's claim that more than a hundred Communists worked for the Sunday section of the *New York Times* was unlikely to be true since the section employed fewer than a hundred people. "He now explained," Alsop recalled, "that he had abandoned what he called 'the blacklisting business' and was writing a memoir of his experience as an ally of Senator McCarthy under the title 'Blacklisting Was My Business.' He showed me an outline of his projected book together with the manuscript of one chapter, which I found over-written and uninteresting. He also showed me his poetry, which was unspeakably bad; favored me with his views on the world, which were singularly half-baked; and ended by asking me for a loan of seven hundred and fifty dollars to finance the completion of his book. I regretfully refused this incredible request."*[37]

In July Matusow appeared before HUAC and retracted his retraction, but Communists and liberals were giddy in a way they had not been for years. "Some of these people are now saying that Matusow was a Communist plant inside the loyal legion of the dedicated," columnist Murray Kempton observed in the *New York Post*. "Normally I would think this nonsense, but, if they want to say that he made a fool of the whole batch of them from Pat McCarran through *Counterattack*, I'll have to accept their verdict and they'll have to accept its implications on their credentials as persons gifted with special insight into subversive infiltration. They were anxious to use Matusow to send people to prison. They are indignant now because he is trying, for whatever obscure reason he may have, to get people out of jail. By their standards, it is honorable and patriotic to testify against an accused person, and it is treason to testify on his behalf."†[38]

And now, just a week before his birthday, that ass Ralph Flanders had introduced a motion in the Senate to censure Joe McCarthy. In the courts, the Senate, the press — anti-Communism seemed under attack as it had not been for years. "The senator," Eva Adams told Norm Biltz, "is a little irritated about having another birthday."[39]

Hubert Humphrey bobbed up in the Senate chamber as soon as Congress opened at ten on August 12, looking both weary and energized, like a preacher at the end of a long revival meeting. And indeed, Humphrey seemed to be on some kind of manic mission, urging and pleading with his colleagues to consider a new bill that no committee had ever discussed, a bill that, in fact, had just been written in an hour around midnight and rushed

---

*Matusow ultimately finished his book with the financial assistance of the International Union of Mine, Mill and Smelter Workers, which placed a large pre-order of books from Cameron & Kahn, a pro-Communist publishing house run by Angus Cameron and Albert Kahn. The union was interested in subsidizing the publication in order to get the perjury conviction of organizer Clinton Jencks overturned.

†Matusow's change of heart led to a SISS investigation in 1955; the committee labeled his confession a Communist plot to discredit the government's security program. Matusow was convicted of perjury — for lying when he recanted — and served five years in prison.

to the Government Printing Office this morning and that Humphrey now passed out like a religious tract: the Communist Control Act. Hubert Humphrey, the great champion of civil rights, wanted to ban the Communist Party. "I am tired," Humphrey said, "of reading headlines about being 'soft' toward Communism."[40]

"Welcome to the fold," snapped Homer Ferguson.[41]

Humphrey's bill was an attempt to derail more damaging legislation. Maryland's John M. Butler, a member of SISS, had a bill pending to amend McCarran's Internal Security Act to make it possible for the government to declare unions Communist-dominated and strip them of their legal rights. (McCarran himself had introduced a similar bill earlier in the year.) Humphrey and other liberals feared that the Butler bill could be used as a club to beat unions. "A powerful weapon to cripple labor," Herbert Lehman called it.[42] Humphrey thought that it would be better just to declare the party itself illegal, thereby protecting unions.

The Senate liberals were once again trying to wrest the internal security issue back from the conservatives. When the Americans for Democratic Action formed in 1947, liberal anti-Communism began its brief heyday. The Truman Doctrine announced America's determination to fight Communism abroad; the president's loyalty order did the same at home. The Marshall Plan proclaimed the country's commitment to help rebuild the economies of its allies, and NATO signaled the willingness to defend those friends by force if necessary. The triumph of liberal anti-Communism was the 1948 election, when Truman defeated the Republicans to stay in the White House and crushed Henry Wallace and the Progressives as a viable force on the left. But at almost precisely the same time, HUAC was introducing Elizabeth Bentley and Whittaker Chambers to the world and making *liberal anti-Communism* sound like an oxymoron. The perjury trial of Alger Hiss, China going Communist, Russia testing an atomic bomb, Joe McCarthy's charges of treason — the revelations and crises came like winter storm waves, battering and battering, destroying confidence and bestirring doubt. And the liberals, try as they might, could barely keep their heads above water. Earlier in the year, for example, Paul Douglas had introduced a bill to create a joint Senate-House committee to take control of all congressional internal security investigations, along with a bill of procedures designed to ensure fair treatment of witnesses. It was a fine idea and an utter failure, which sank from sight as soon as Douglas dropped it into the Senate chamber.

Now, heading into an election season, the liberals were yet again trying to reestablish their bona fides on the Communist issue while defeating a more pernicious proposal. Of course the last time the liberals tried to derail an internal security bill was when they introduced a concentration camp substitute for the registration provisions of the McCarran Act, which McCarran bundled up together, making the bill that much worse. This time the conservatives balked. They believed that the liberals were trying to make the Butler bill unconstitutional so that it could never be enforced and would thereby undermine the Internal Security Act. "A monstrosity," McCarran called the Humphrey bill.[43]

After much arguing and amending the Senate passed the Humphrey bill with only a single member voting against it: Estes Kefauver. In the conference committee McCarran gutted the criminal penalties for individuals joining the party from the bill (which would have triggered a constitutional challenge) and instead added language to deprive the party of rights as a legal body. Eisenhower signed it.

What the bill wound up actually doing to the Communist Party was hard to say. New York eventually used the act to deny laid-off party workers from getting unemployment. What the act did to the Democrat Party was another story: Humphrey, Paul Douglas, James Murray, Clinton Anderson, and other liberals were able to campaign that fall boasting of having supported something called the Communist Control Act and complaining that the Republicans had watered it down. "We have closed all the doors," Humphrey said. "These rats will not get out of the trap."[44]

Outside of Congress most liberals were aghast, more by what the bill claimed to do (outlaw the party) than by the cynical natural of what it actually did (let Democrats call Republicans soft on Communism). "The Humphrey madness,"[45] *New York Post* editor Jimmy Wechsler called it to his friend Joe Rauh. "Legislation by stampede," Rauh called it.[46] Years later even Humphrey seemed to regret the bill. "Not one of the things I'm proudest of," he admitted.[47]

After Congress adjourned on August 20, McCarran had begged off his promise to Birdie to take a break immediately. Bill Jenner, he explained, needed him to go to Florida for three days to conduct an SISS hearing. When McCarran returned to Washington he checked into Walter Reed Hospital for two weeks of rest. Then, in September, McCarran and Birdie took the Capitol Limited to Minnesota, where she had a checkup at the Mayo Clinic. They continued on to San Francisco, where McCarran spoke to a mining convention, touting the continuing SISS investigation into how the Treasury's Harry Dexter White had manipulated U.S. policy to undermine the Chinese Nationalists during the war and bring the Communists to power.

The main point of the trip, however, was across the bay in Oakland, where Sister Margaret McCarran was teaching at the Holy Names College. She should have been teaching at the Catholic University in Washington, McCarran thought. It wasn't as if he hadn't tried. For months McCarran had been badgering his friend Cardinal Spellman to get his first child a teaching position at Catholic University, where Margaret had gotten her Ph.D. in history in 1952, and where she would be closer to her parents. McCarran wasn't having much luck, but at least he had found a publisher to turn his daughter's unreadable thesis into a book. In "Fabianism in the Political Life of Britain, 1919–1931" Margaret traced the intellectual history of evolutionary socialism to the point at which it was ready to infect American politics. Margaret was already hard at work on a sequel about Fabianism in America (in other words, the New Deal), much to the dismay of McCarran's office staff, which was spending a lot of time at the Library of Congress doing research for her. "It would be impossible to copy all the material contained in two books," Eva Adams delicately suggested to Margaret one day. "Perhaps in this instance you could arrange to spend a few hours in the university library."[48]

None of McCarran's children was more like him than Margaret. I have a perfectly even temper, she liked to say: I'm always angry. McCarran in drag, Jerome Edwards called her. [49] "She was born a politician," McCarran said, "but God made her a nun."[50] Margaret was actually to the right of her father. She distrusted some of the former Communists that he had hired on SISS, such as research director Ben Mandel. "I am convinced that the internal security committee ought to make a study of the infiltration of the gulliberals," Margaret told her father. "I don't think any committee can come to grips with the gradualist socialism unless they are willing to establish a basic American philosophy from which socialism is a deviation. It is hard to avoid bringing the investigatory power into the field of thought control."[51]

Margaret was especially concerned about subversive influences in education. When the Reece Committee in the House began investigating foundations to see if they were funding un-American activities, Margaret told her father to encourage the probe. He soon introduced a bill to deprive a foundation of its tax-exempt status if it gave *any* money to *any* subversive individual or group. "There is no question but that the Ford money is to be used to smear Senators McCarthy, McCarran and Jenner,"

columnist George Sokolsky warned Margaret when the foundation created the Fund for the Republic and announced a series of books about
the Communist problem. "This is the latest refuge for the Communists. It
gives the anti-anti-Communists a huge treasury to do their dirty work."[52]

Sister Margaret's name came up during one of the Reece Committee
hearings. One member approvingly cited her book on Fabianism. That
was too much for Ohio Democrat Wayne Hays. "I happen to know something about the background of the author of that book," Hays said, "how
long it took her to get a degree, and so forth, and even that there was a
little pressure used or she would not have it yet."[53]

Eva Adams had the unpleasant duty of telling McCarran. "I could feel
fur rising and his voice became very angry," Adams recalled to Margaret,
"so I told him it wasn't anything to worry about now."[54]

On a beautiful autumn day, in the tranquillity of the Holy Names convent, near sparkling Lake Merit, Margaret and her father went for a walk.
She told him about her new book. He told her about the SISS hearings
in Florida. "It was very hot," McCarran recalled, "maybe just a taste of
what is in store for most of us."[55]

Chester Smith stopped the green Buick in front of 401 Court Street. It
was September 28, a warm fall afternoon in Reno. Smith had only driven
a few blocks from downtown, yet it looked like he was already in a different city. THE BIGGEST LITTLE CITY IN THE WORLD, the neon arch spanning Virginia Street proclaimed. From the train station to the river every
building in downtown seemed to be a casino, although the entire length
of downtown was less than three blocks. Then came the city's glory, the
Truckee River, bubbling over and around granite boulders, tiny chunks of
the great Sierra Nevada washed down the mountain by the force of
snowmelt. By late fall there was always more riverbed than river, but if you
stopped on the Virginia Street Bridge and peered over the rail into the
deeper pockets of water you could still see the shimmering silver shapes,
upside-down trout grubbing for worms on the undersides of rocks. Reno
was, A. J. Liebling said, the only city he knew where you could see fly fish-
ermen casting away in the middle of downtown.

Smith waited for McCarran while he said good-bye to his family.
McCarran apologized to Sam for having to leave town just before his son's
thirty-third birthday. Birdie told Patsy that if he didn't rest more, he would
drop dead in his tracks. That's just the way I want to go, he said. Smith
tried to pick up McCarran's suitcase. McCarran said he could take it him-

self. Smith knew better than to argue with the senator. They climbed into the car. Smith got behind the wheel. McCarran sat next to him. Later Birdie would blame Smith for letting McCarran carry his bag.

They drove out of town, heading east on the new highway, following the Truckee and the transcontinental railroad tracks as they descended into Wadsworth Canyon. The Truckee meandered through the valley, running straight here, oxbowing there, forming islets where the trees thickened, the cottonwood and willow leaves a pallet of fall colors, their branches full of yellow warblers and ash-throated flycatchers trying to outsing one another. Huge osprey nests topped dead trees like crowns of thorns. In the mornings mule deer came down to the river, where wood ducks floated in the shallows and sailed through the reeds.

Pull over, McCarran said. There by the ranch. Smith stopped at the side of the road. McCarran looked out the window, down at the ranch, where the summer hay was still green and the new mowing machine sat perched at the edge of the field like a bird of prey. Smith drove on until they reached Fallon, where the U.S. Naval Air Station kept the small town alive — one more thing McCarran had given to his state. They stopped at the barbershop. McCarran wanted to get a haircut. Someone else was already in the barber's chair. McCarran paid his way to the front of the line and sat for a trim. He was on his way to Hawthorne, where the Democratic Party would start the fall campaign with a rally and then a tour of the state. He wanted to look good for the evening.

They headed south on the road to Las Vegas. The Carson River trickled under a bridge.

Salt flats stretched off to the distance in the east. Half a century earlier McCarran had left the ranch as a newly minted lawyer and traveled this way by train, headed toward the boomtown of Tonopah. He became a great defense lawyer and later a good judge, an eloquent advocate for the weak against the powerful. He bucked public opinion to speak up for the rights of radical miners to demand better conditions. Now he hounded the same miners' union and brought against it all the force of the federal government. The road threaded between Walker Lake and the mountains to the west. Finally they reached Hawthorne, 130 miles from Reno. Hawthorne was the home of the Naval Weapons Depot. The town wasn't much, but it had fifteen hundred residents — and in Nevada that was a lot of votes. The base commander was waiting to take McCarran to dinner.

At seven they went to the Mineral County Courthouse to wait for the open car. When he sat on the Nevada Supreme Court, McCarran took a dim view of overzealous prosecutors. "When a prosecuting officer seeks to take advantage of public sentiment to gain an unjust conviction or seeks to take an unfair advantage in the introduction of evidence or in any other respect, he is failing in his duty as the state's representative," he wrote. "The duty of district attorneys to be fair to defendants on trial is scarcely less obligatory than the duty which rests upon the courts, whose officers they are."[56] In the Senate, McCarran made himself both the judge and jury of men such as Owen Lattimore and John Davies.

The weather was cooling. The state Democratic chairman offered to put McCarran in a warmer vehicle. "I feel fine," McCarran said. "Just fine."[57]

Two Boy Scouts waved flags. What are you holding? McCarran asked. The American flag, the boys chirped. At the height of his influence McCarran was almost wholly a negative force, instinctually and implacably opposed to whoever was in the White House, vindictive in the extreme to anyone who dared to cross him, and willing to pull down the whole structure of government to satisfy his pique. Always, McCarran had grasped for power like a Nevada rancher amassing water rights: He could never have enough. Once he could have told himself that he wanted power to help the people of his state. Now it was clear that he helped the people of his state so he could keep his power. His immigrant parents carved a garden out of the desert; he helped build a legislative wall around the country to keep out immigrants. He bullied and besmirched dedicated public servants and intimidated high government officials into prosecuting them on specious charges. His actions caused people to lose their jobs, sometimes careers, to sit in jails awaiting deportation, to sit in refugee camps denied entry to the United States. Power, like money, has a way of altering one's perceptions, but the sight of the flag never failed to move McCarran. To the end, symbols still affected him in a way that people no longer did.

You're holding the greatest thing in the world, McCarran told the Boy Scouts. Remember that.

As night fell on Hawthorne, a slight chill crept into the autumn air. Yet inside the crowded hall the temperature was rising. For forty minutes speaker after speaker assailed the Republicans and praised the Democrats and the audience jeered and whooped. Then, at eight-forty, the portly white-haired man walked to the podium.

"Every man on the ticket is my candidate," Pat McCarran said.[58]

In the back of the room John McCloskey chuckled. For years McCarran had run the Democratic Party in his state like Stalin ran the Communist Party in Russia. Loyal Democrats were purged if they weren't loyal enough and first of all to McCarran. Standing on the stage with McCarran were Vail Pittman and Walter Baring. Pittman was Key Pittman's younger brother, as great an enemy as McCarran had ever had, who had almost beaten the senator in the 1944 primary — an election that many people believed McCarran stole. Pittman went on to become governor, but McCarran worked against him in the 1950 campaign and Pittman lost. Baring, too, had angered McCarran, who publicly threatened to see that he was defeated for reelection to the House when he refused to support McCarran's choice for the presidential nomination in 1952.

Now McCarran wanted both men to win the election in November. McCarran wanted a Democratic sweep this year. He wanted to be chairman of the Judiciary Committee again. He wanted to run for a fifth term in two more years when he would be eighty. Tom Mechling had been making noise about running against McCarran himself. "There are now only two political factions in Nevada," Mechling said after losing his campaign for Senate in 1952, "— the McCarranites and the Mechlingites and the battle didn't stop on election day."[59] No, the battle stopped this year, when the Nevada legislature passed a law requiring a residency period to run for Senate, which coincidentally was longer than Mechling had lived in the state. "The damage done to our party by the machinations of McCarran and his gang was almost irreparable," Denver Dickerson told Vail Pittman years later.[60] Everyone in the room, for instance, knew that McCarran had given the Senate to the Republicans in the last election. "If he doesn't stop it, he's gonna choke to death," McCloskey said to Smith in the back of the room. "He won't vote for a damn one of 'em and you know it."[61]

"It is imperative that a Democratic Congress be elected in order that your senior senator may resume his position as head of the Judiciary Committee of the Senate and continue his fight against Communism."

Before Eisenhower took office, McCarran had praised the president-elect for his plans to get tough with subversives. "The one great thing accomplished by this change of administration," McCarran had said, confident enough to use the past tense even before the inauguration, "will be the removal from the United States government agencies of all Communist sympathizers."[62] Two years later Dulles had purged the State Department of many career diplomats, but McCarran had become convinced that Eisenhower was just another Truman or, as he called him, a Dewey — in either case, a liberal in thrall to the Communists. "This Dewey administration is not a very happy one," McCarran told Petersen. "The general, called president, is a captive in the hands of one of the most ruthless groups of political masters that I have ever seen. It's really too bad. I believe the fellow is a good fellow with some sound military sense, but being a captive of the Dewey regime he doesn't get very far."[63]

"At no day in history has the U.S. been in such jeopardy as it is today."

The day before, on September 27, the bipartisan Watkins Committee had released a unanimous report calling for the censure of Joe McCarthy for conduct unbecoming a member of the Senate. A few senators greeted the report with glee, a few with outrage. Most reserved judgment, an indication that the tide in the nation was changing. McCarran was one of the few senators to announce that he would vote against the censure resolution. McCarthy, he said, should never have been put on trial in the first place. Even as he was stumping for his party in Nevada, McCarran was standing more alone than ever. In the Eighty-third Congress, for example, McCarran introduced enough bills to fill fifteen pages. A bill for the government to buy the water rights from the white squatters on the Pyramid Lake Indian reservation, a bill to exempt Basque sheepherders from immigration quotas, a bill to bar U.S. citizens of questionable loyalty from employment at the UN, a bill to revoke the tax exemption from organizations that gave money to subversives, a bill to force witnesses to testify before congressional committees, a bill to ban Communists from holding union offices, a bill to amend the Internal Security Act so that government departments would have to provide quarterly reports on the number of security risks they fired, a bill to protect the FBI's name from commercial exploitation, a bill to investigate the loyalty of Senate employees, a resolution to break diplomatic relations with the Soviet Union and to pull the United States out of the UN. It was a legislative agenda that would have been as objectionable to Truman as to Eisenhower. "He is neither a Democrat nor a Republican," observed Edward Carville, who had been governor as a McCarran protégé and then an ex-governor as a McCarran apostate. "Just a McCarrancrat."[64]

"It is beset with enemies from within and from abroad in greater numbers than ever before."

Walking off the platform after twenty minutes, McCarran was engulfed by the crowd. A woman came up to him to ask for a favor; he spoke to her for a minute and told her that Chet Smith would take down her name and make sure she got some help. Then he turned away. McCarran's eyes suddenly rolled back in his head. His knees buckled. He fell backward to the floor. Smith knelt down by McCarran's side, then jumped up on a chair to shout for a doctor and a priest. McCarran's pale face turned a dark gray. He was dead.

The next day the Democrats were supposed to convoy to Tonopah to continue their campaign swing around the state. The tour was canceled. Even in death, McCarran disrupted the Democrats.

He Who Raised Up the Walls
and Set Up the Gates and Bars

From Peter I keep these keys and he told me, rather to
err in opening than in closing, if souls but cast themselves
down at my feet.

— Dante, *Purgatorio,* Canto IX

On Saturday morning, October 2, 1954, six hundred people packed the redbrick St. Thomas Aquinas Church in Reno to listen to Bishop Robert J. Dwyer read from Ecclesiasticus. "And let Nehemias be a long time remembered," the priest said, "who raised up for us our walls that were cast down and set up the gates and the bars, who rebuilt our houses."[1]

Afterward the Knights of Columbus, dressed in black and white and carrying swords, marched out from beneath the twin cross-topped towers of the church, turned onto Arlington Street, and headed toward the Truckee River. Behind them one hundred cars formed a cortege as long and as sad as any the state had ever seen. "McCarran commanded either unquestioning loyalty or black hatred in Nevada," the *Reno Evening Gazette* noted. "There was no neutral ground. And he likewise bestowed his complete friendship or loosed implacable fury. There was no middle ground for him, either."[2]

The funeral procession crawled across the bridge, passing through Wingfield Park on the islet in the middle of the river, where the trees glowed gold in the slanting autumn light. Up the slope of the opposing bank the cavalcade climbed to the McCarran house on Court Street, where the mourners turned left. Three blocks later they stopped at the state building across from the courthouse on Virginia Street. More than twenty-five hundred people jammed into the auditorium. The overflow crowd spilled into the park next door. Troops from Stead Air Force Base stood watch over the bronze coffin, laid at the foot of the stage and flanked by flower arrangements in the shape of an American flag and a shamrock. A long row of mourners filed past, some kneeling to pray, others crying. "McCarran was dead," Clel Georgetta wrote in his diary. "Well, at least he died with his boots on, as the old fighter would have preferred to die. He was a very controversial figure to be sure, but he was truly a very great man, by far the greatest man Nevada has ever produced and one of the truly great Americans in our national history."[3] Others came just to be sure that he was really dead. "McCarran," grumbled one local reporter, "was a son of a bitch alive and he's a son of a bitch dead."[4]

The stage looked like God's waiting room, filled with flowers and old men. On the platform sat seven members of the U.S. Senate, five of whom were Republicans: Majority Leader William Knowland, Arizona's Barry Goldwater, Idaho's Herman Welker, Nevada's George Malone, New Hampshire's Styles Bridges, Mississippi's James Eastland, and Kentucky's Earle Clement, the last two nominally Democrats. "McCarran's death removes from the Senate one of its most formidable influences — a controversial man of passionate convictions made effective by extraordinary force of personality and an adroit wielding of political power," commented the *Washington Post*. ". . . He often used his power short-sightedly and for narrow ends. But no one, even while disagreeing with him, could challenge his sincerity of purpose. His granitic strength commanded prestige even among his critics."[5]

Floral arrangements crowded the stage and cascaded onto the floor, where a pile of red roses covered the coffin. The Spanish embassy sent a huge bouquet ("McCarran," wrote Madrid's *El Mundo Visto*, "era un gran amigo de espana"[6]), so did the American Federation of Labor. At the end of the day it took seven trucks to haul the flowers away.

"Last Tuesday, the 28th day of September, was a tragic day for this nation," Bridges said. ". . . A day of relief for the enemies who opposed his fight for America. Any person with a personality can acquire friends, but only great men with the characteristics of Pat McCarran acquire enemies. I admired him for a great many things, not the least of which was the cluster of enemies he had."[7]

"The nation has lost its greatest patriot," Welker said.[8]

"He wore the collar of no political party," Eastland said. "I think when the history of the 20th century is written, historians will agree that Pat was one of the greatest statesmen of the century."[9]

Even some of those enemies who had yearned for his death were gracious when it finally came. "McCarran," Hank Greenspun wrote in the *Las Vegas Sun*, "died as he lived — fighting. He could fight in fierce anger, courageously, with the power of a lion or he could do battle shrewdly, vindictively, with the cunning of a fox. And it mattered not whether the cause be just or popular. If he had taken a stand to defend it, he fought. And who today can say what his motives were, because though we may examine a man while he lives, it is beyond our power to judge him after death."[10]

Late in the afternoon the Knights of Columbus began to march again. The procession crossed the Truckee back into downtown, where businesses and offices stood closed and empty and people lined Virginia Street to watch the cortege move under the Reno arch instead of the New York Giants beating the Cleveland Indians in the final game of the World Series. "I hated that man and I spent my life fighting him," one local pol told newsman Robert Laxalt. "He was a politician and he played the game the way he saw it. When you fought him, you knew you'd been in a fight, mister. Things aren't going to be the same around here now."[11]

The line of cars turned west into the foothills, where the higher peaks were already fading into blue as the day ebbed away. At Mountain View Cemetery the procession finally stopped. Nine pallbearers heaved their load off the hearse and walked toward the plot where McCarran's parents were buried. "For twenty-two years I have loved and respected this man," Fulton Lewis said on his radio show. "He told me once . . . that it was more important to be hated by the right people, than it was to be admired by others."[12]

On the hillside overlooking Reno, they put Patrick Anthony McCarran into a crypt. "Neither in Nevada nor in Washington was Pat McCarran widely or warmly loved," observed *Time* magazine. "But he made his mark on political history — and he was widely feared. That seemed to be what he wanted."[13]

The sun edged below the Sierra Nevada. Down in the valley the Truckee caught the last light of the day and then let it go. The river darkened like a spreading stain.

Five days later, on October 7, a grand jury issued a second indictment against Owen Lattimore — although the vote had actually been taken on September 27, the day before McCarran died. The new indictment accused Lattimore of two counts of perjury, lying when he denied that he had either followed the Communist line or promoted Communist interests. In January a federal judge tossed out the indictment. "To require a defendant to go to trail for perjury under charges so formless and obscure as those before the court would be unprecedented," ruled Judge Luther Youngdahl, "and would make a sham of the Sixth Amendment and the federal rule requiring specificity of charges."[14]

Almost five years after Joe McCarthy first accused the Johns Hopkins professor of being the top Soviet espionage agent in the United States and four years after McCarran began his relentless persecution of the scholar, Lattimore was finally absolved. Then the IRS, at McCarran's behest, revoked the tax-exempt status of the Institute of Pacific Relations, which wound up moving its headquarters from New York to British Columbia. Lattimore, too, left the country. Johns Hopkins abolished the Page School of International Relations that Lattimore had directed, and he moved to England.

On November 5, 1954, John Paton Davies walked into the office of John Foster Dulles at the State Department. Dulles told the diplomat that the ninth loyalty board had ruled against him. Dulles fired him. Davies, Dulles announced in a three-page press release, had shown a lack of judgment, discretion, and reliability. A few days later, the secretary offered to serve as a reference if Davies needed one for a new job. Davies decided to stay in Peru, where he opened a furniture store.

In 1964 Davies moved back to Washington and began a campaign to salvage his reputation. In 1969 the government restored his security clearance so he could work as a consultant. In 1973 — the same year that President Richard Nixon went to the People's Republic of China — an unofficial luncheon took place at the State Department in honor of the China experts who had been fired years earlier for being pro-Communist. "I think," Davies said, "a prudent young man would enter the foreign service knowing another trade."[15]

On December 2, 1954, the Senate voted 67 to 22 to censure Joe McCarthy, the third time in the nation's history that the body had so admonished a member. It was, in the end, the Republicans who took him down. Vermont's Ralph Flanders had introduced the censure resolution the year before. "My good friend, Pat McCarran, as you know, had planned to rip the hide off you on constitutional grounds," columnist George Sokolsky wrote in an open letter to Flanders. "Each man to his tastes: Pat McCarran enjoyed fighting Communists and you enjoy fighting Joe McCarthy."[16]

Utah Republican Arthur Watkins, the member of SISS whom McCarran had supported in his reelection campaign, led the committee that investigated McCarthy and unanimously recommended the rebuke. "Watkins went on to remember the times he had praised McCarthy in the past," Murray Kempton noted while watching the censure debate. "He had his own credentials in the Communist hunt, and he read in his flat voice a letter of recommendation from Pat McCarran. No one could have thought that the rock upon which Joe McCarthy broke would be a man proud of a reference from Pat McCarran."[17]

For McCarthy the admonishment really changed nothing — he still had his seat in the Senate and his committee chairmanship — but suddenly everything was different. McCarthy found himself in a strange, new world where reporters no longer tripped over one another to record his every word. Publicity, to McCarthy, was like Samson's hair: Without it he was nothing. As McCarthy's profile plummeted, so too did his spirits. He drank himself to death within three years.

In 1957 the Supreme Court issued several important decisions, ruling that John Stewart Service had been improperly fired by the State Department and ordering him reinstated, overturning the Smith Act convictions of Communist leaders, and limiting the power of congressional committees to punish witnesses for contempt. The next year the court held that the government couldn't deny passports to citizens on ideological grounds.

After McCarran's death Birdie stayed in Reno with Sam, his wife, Betty, and their children in the house on Court Street. It was not a harmonious household. "Thanksgiving day is about over and I am glad," Birdie wrote to Mary. "Sam came in and finding that Betty was not here he was beside himself. Didn't want any dinner, but went out to hunt Betty. Well, I ate my dinner and went to bed to worry all night. Sam came in about five o'clock. He had been drinking and he talked to me about an hour and I went to bed again. He did and slept until three o'clock this afternoon."[18]

Sam told his mother that his wife had called and explained that she had stayed at a motel and wouldn't come home until Birdie left. Sam begged Birdie not to tell Betty that he drank, and he promised never to do it again. Birdie told Sam to take all the money out of the couple's joint checking account and then tell Betty to come home whenever she felt like it. "He tells me his whole ten years of married life has been one hell," Birdie told Mary. "He blames her. She blames him. It is a sad mess."[19]

Toward the end of McCarran's life, Sam had moved into the family home in Reno and gone into medical practice with his father's physician. Not long after McCarran's death the practice broke up. So did Sam. The young man who had once taken his father's Senate license plates and put them on his own car so he could drive cross-country without getting any speeding tickets found himself at sea without the old man. "Your father had such great hope for him, and such tremendous faith in him, that I feel

Sam is overwhelmed by this knowledge, when life seems hard and he feels he progresses very slowly," Eva Adams told Margaret. "Your father loved him so that he perhaps unwittingly provided a 'leaning post' which Sam never was without. When it was suddenly jerked away, he was bewildered, and I have a felling that he is, still. . . . I just feel so deeply that he is a rather little boy with a burden too big for him to carry alone."[20]

Birdie went back to Washington, where she complained to Eva Adams that the FBI would no longer drive her to the horse races in Delaware. Occasionally Birdie would hear from her youngest daughter, Patricia, whose life on Long Island was as turbulent as ever. Sometimes it was the grandchildren. "Please help my mom,"[21] pleaded her grandson Richard Hay, explaining that the family needed money to keep from losing the car and house.

Sister Mary Mercy left her order after thirty years, getting a papal dispensation to become Mary McCarran again, and taking care of her mother and Norine. Mary had long been unhappy as a nun; now she became a stockbroker, and after Sam's marriage finally fell apart she took care of his four children. She wrote a memoir called *Once There Was a Nun*. Birdie died in 1963. Mary died in 1966 at the age of fifty-nine. Poor Norine's death, whenever it occurred, didn't even make the papers.

Sam moved to Eureka, in the middle of Nevada, where he practiced medicine and hid from his wife. "Her highness will never touch me here," he told Mary. "The sheriff and district attorney are patients and pals of mine."[22]

Margaret's career as a historian didn't flourish after her father's death. "Mother General forbids you to publish your book,"[23] a sister told Margaret. She continued to teach at the College of Holy Names in Oakland and devoted herself to preserving her father's reputation. She wrote a long manuscript about his life, collected his papers, and traveled around the country to gather other archival material about his career. When she retired, she moved to the family ranch along the Truckee, where Sam also eventually ended up after losing his medical license. Sam seldom left the ranch, but people in town noticed that the old nun seemed to be buying awfully large bottles of vodka with her groceries after her brother moved home.

McCarran's last two surviving children reached old age together living on the ranch, each still in her or his own way transfixed by their father's long shadow: Margaret obsessed with McCarran's accomplishments, Sam upset with his own. Samuel P. McCarran died in 1997 at the age of seventy-six. Sister Margaret Patricia McCarran died on New Year's Eve in 1998 at the age of ninety-four.

On June 7, 1962, about twenty-five hundred people gathered at the Manhattan Center in New York City under the auspices of a Communist front group called the Citizens Committee for Constitutional Liberties, which was protesting the U.S. government's continuing attempt to force the party to register under the McCarran Act. At eight twenty-four, FBI agents reported to J. Edgar Hoover, the rally started with the singing of "The Star Spangled Banner." "McCarranism," declared committee executive secretary Miriam Friedlander, is "the gravest threat to our democratic guarantees since the days of McCarthy."[24]

The phenomenon of McCarthyism reached its high water during the first year of the Eisenhower administration, when McCarran and McCarthy attacked Chip Bohlen as a security risk and John Foster Dulles purged the State Department of men like George Kennan and John Paton Davies. The first excess was to be expected; the second, to be lamented. Harry Truman, for all his impulsiveness and early lackadaisical attitude toward security, clearly recognized the moral imperative involved in protecting civil liberties and combating hysteria and fought as best he could. Dwight Eisenhower occasionally caught sight of the principle at stake but more often averted his gaze. Some historians have commended Eisenhower's reluctance to make an issue of McCarthy as a deliberate strategy to deprive the senator of the oxygen of publicity, which hastened his demise. But this confuses the man with the ism and slights what seems to be the far more likely reason for McCarthyism's waning: the end of the Korean War.

McCarthyism, seen in this light, was less a volcano, something that erupted into being, than a coral reef, a slow accretion of beliefs and suspicions that built up a structure of laws and institutions, official and otherwise, on which the ship of domestic Communism would ultimately run aground. Many men over many years labored to construct the anti-Communist edifice. Joseph McCarthy wasn't one of them. McCarran did not create American anti-Communism alone, but his role was bigger and more important than that of his colleague.

Why has McCarthy's name dominated the history of the era? Pure drama is the main reason. McCarthy gave good copy. He could venture onto the Senate floor and spend three hours denouncing George Marshall as a traitor, and the story wrote itself. McCarran, on the other hand, defied easy summation. He had the persistence of a glacier: a seemingly immovable object that changed the landscape. His influence was often subterranean, burying bills, blocking nominations, coercing bureaucrats, bullying attorney generals, thwarting presidential commissions. Much of McCarran's power was negative: he prevented things from happening. McCarthy might berate Jimmy Wechsler for writing a book that turned up in a State Department library; McCarran lopped twenty million dollars off an appropriations bill when he found out the department was distributing a magazine that had written a story about him that he didn't like.

McCarthy spoke of twenty years of treason. McCarran spoke of treason for twenty years. The difference is that McCarran did something about it. McCarthy left no legislative legacy. McCarthy did not even get the chairmanship of his investigating committee until 1953, and after barely a year he was already in hot water. His hearings, for all their flash and theatrics, uncovered little. Perhaps McCarthy's biggest discovery was the presence of Communists in the Government Printing Office. McCarthy may have called an INS agent to Cedric Belfrage's hearing, but it was the McCarran-Walter Act that the British immigrant was deported under.

McCarran, in contrast, left his fears and obsessions embedded in a stack of laws. He sank the Nimitz Commission and launched the Senate Internal Security Subcommittee. He almost single-handedly forced Owen Lattimore's indictment and pursued John Davies almost as unrelentingly. He got almost a score of officials fired from the UN. He helped cripple the Mine-Mill union. His Internal Security Act (a group project, to be sure) tormented the Communist Party for years, until a 1967 appellate court ruled that the registration provision was unconstitutional and the Supreme Court declined to hear the case. In 1971 Congress repealed the concentration camp section of the law. President Richard Nixon formally killed the Subversive Activities Control Board two years later. In 1975 Congress abolished HUAC, which had changed its name to the House Internal Security Committee; SISS died two years later (Jay Sourwine remained counsel until almost the very end, retiring in 1975). The McCarran-Walter Act lasted even longer. Congress liberalized the immigration provisions in 1965, but the ideological restrictions proved harder to remove. It wasn't until 1990 — a year after the Berlin Wall fell — that Congress finally stopped asking people seeking a visa to the United States if they were or had ever been a Communist.

The Communist Party presented a unique challenge to American liberty. The party was simultaneously a movement and a conspiracy that enjoyed the constitutional protections of a society it despised and was trying to destroy. Anti-Communism, then, was both a rational and necessary response. Anti-Communism run amok was something altogether different.

At the "End McCarranism" rally, for example, one of the few non-Communists was columnist Murray Kempton. "Domestic anti-Communism has an old and honorable history in the United States," Kempton once observed. "In the last five years, it has become, when least malevolent, the flagellation of dead horses. Worse than that, it has become, on every level, a war on the weak and their children. Throughout the fifties, as the American Communists have grown steadily weaker, their enemies in every camp have become more violent, more cruel and more irresponsible. As an organized political group, the Communists have done nothing to damage our society a fraction as much as what their enemies have done in the name of defending us against subversion. The authors of this damage are named Harry Truman and Joe McCarthy. They are, if you please, you and I even to the extent that we simply kept quiet and rode with the times. There are few Americans who have no part in this shame and no hostage to the policy which produced it. It is a thing which has infected our whole society."[25]

Kempton told the rally that he was proud to live in a society where Communists were free to give speeches denouncing the government, but ashamed to live in one where there were probably FBI agents taking notes that might someday come back to haunt people in the audience. "Kempton," one FBI agent at the rally told J. Edgar Hoover the next day, "expressed sympathy for sufferings being endured by Communists in America."[26]

"He is a real stinker," Hoover fumed.[27]

At the Vatican, in 1949 when McCarran was in Europe on his crusade to keep refugees from immigrating to America, the pope gave him an indulgence. "Senator and Mrs. Patrick A. McCarran and family," the document stated, "humbly prostrate at the feet of Your Holiness and beg the apostolic benediction and a plenary indulgence to be gained at the hour of death on condition that being truly sorry for their sins even though unable to confess them and to receive the holy viaticum they shall at least invoke with their lips or heart the holy name of Jesus."[28]

It was good to have a papal dispensation. At Saint Peter's gate everyone is a refugee.

AUTHOR'S NOTE

In 1990 I graduated from college and spent the summer working on the national desk of the *Washington Post*. One of my assignments was to write a piece about some pending immigration legislation, which turned out to be the latest in a long line of attempts to revise the McCarran-Walter Act, a controversial 1952 bill that had passed over the veto of President Harry Truman, who called it the worst law ever enacted by Congress. The signature feature of the McCarran-Walter Act was the extraordinary power it gave the government to bar foreigners from visiting the United States, to deport immigrants, and to strip citizenship from those already nationalized because the person had once been a member of the Communist Party. Nobel Prize–winning novelist Gabriel Garcia Marquez was just one of many foreigners who had trouble getting into the United States because of the law. Liberals had been trying to repeal McCarran-Walter since the day it passed. In 1990 they finally succeeded, although even after the fall of the Berlin Wall it required a fight.

A year later I had pretty much forgotten about the whole thing when I was working for the *Wall Street Journal* and happened to write a story about a group of Palestinian activists fighting deportation in Los Angeles (under the supposedly defanged McCarran-Walter Act) because of their alleged financial support of a terrorist group.

I became interested in the challenge of how a free society can protect itself and its values at the same time. Reading up on the subject led back to the McCarthy era in the 1950s, the milieu that produced the McCarran-Walter Act. Senator Joseph McCarthy stood out in most accounts as the symbol of a frightening time when America seemed menaced not just by enemy bombs but also by a fanatical group of idealogues who had infiltrated her society and were determined to destroy it. A number of writers remarked, more or less in passing, that Senator Patrick McCarran actually had done a lot more to shape the period than McCarthy. The more I learned about the author of the McCarran-Walter Act, the more I agreed. The result is this book.

I conceived this work after the end of the Cold War largely as a historical project to examine how a democracy balanced freedom and security at a perilous moment. As I write now — at the beginning of what looks like another protracted conflict between two opposing ideals of human organization — the dilemma, alas, looks all too current.

Since starting this book in 1995 I have incurred numerous debts, many of which I put on my credit cards. Others will be less easy to repay. Foremost among them is to Jerome Edwards, whose pioneering book *Pat McCarran: Political Boss of Nevada*, was an invaluable road map to McCarran's life as well as the Silver State's political labyrinth. Jerry was also a careful reader of the manuscript, went beyond the call of scholarly courtesy to help with the photo research, and even picked up the tab for breakfast. At the University of Nevada Historical Society, manuscript curator Eric Moody and the rest of the staff were indefatigable in their help and assistance. One of the reasons they had to remodel the reading room, I suspect, is because of the path I wore in the carpet walking to the information desk with requests. Bob Blesse and the staff at the University of Nevada Special Collections Department were also more than commonly generous. Chester Smith, one of the last McCarran boys, was kind enough to grant me an interview and give me a ride from the metro station. The late Sister Margaret would probably not appreciate much of what I have to say about her father, but she was nice enough to let me into her house, and her long hours researching McCarran's life made my job easier. The staff at the San Francisco Public Library interlibrary loan desk was nothing less than heroic in finding and borrowing a vast amount of obscure material. Archivists and librarians around the country were of enormous help, especially Dennis Bilger at the Truman Library. Many real scholars took time to help an obscure grad-school dropout they had never met, including Michael Green, Athan Theoharis, Robert Kutler, Alonzo Hamby, and Richard M. Fried. Thanks also to Victor Navasky and Tom Petzinger. My former professor at Berkeley's Boalt Hall Law School, Robert Post, was generous long after I left his classroom. Robert P. Newman was unstinting in his help. Gene, Joyce, Gary, and Suzanne Ybarra all helped in ways I'll never be able to adequately express. Darcy Padilla thought it was a book before I did. My agent Jay Mandel was enthusiastic from the start. Tom Powers, Kristin Sperber, and Chip Fleischer at Steerforth were pillars of editorial excellence and support. Bret Israel was helpful in numerous ways, including trying to read the manuscript and buying as many drinks as any journalist could want. The Truman, Roosevelt, and Hoover Libraries and the Rockefeller Archive Center gave me travel grants and able research assistance. The Dirksen Congressional Center and the Redd Center at Brigham Young University also provided financial assistance. My FBI bathroom escorts never complained. Editors at a number of publications helped me to feed myself and also sent me on assignment to many cities where I coincidentally needed to visit archives or libraries. Some of those still returning my calls include David Bailey, Jerry Borrell, Dale Conour, Elena Howe, and Ken Yamada. I hope the statute of limitations on expense account fraud has expired. My appreciation hasn't.

San Francisco, Reno, Washington
April 2003

NOTES

Abbreviations for frequently cited sources:

AWOH, EWOH, Angela Ward, Estolv Ward Oral History (UCB)

CR, *Congressional Record*

CU, Columbia University Rare Book and Manuscript Collection

CUOH, Columbia University Oral History Collection

EA, EAP, Eva Adams, Papers (UNR)

FBI, Federal Bureau of Investigation, files

FDR, FDRL, Franklin D. Roosevelt, Library

GJ, GJP, GJOH, Gardner (Pat) Jackson, Papers (FDRL), Oral History (CUOH)

HH, HHL, Herbert Hoover, Library

HST, HSTL, Harry S. Truman, Library

IPR, Institute of Pacific Relations, hearings and report, U.S. Senate, Judiciary
   Committee, SISS, July 24, 1951, through June 20, 1952, Eighty-second Congress, first
   and second session

KP, KPP, Key Pittman, Papers (LOC)

LBJ, LBJL, Lyndon B. Johnson Library

LOC, Library of Congress, Washington, D.C.

LVRJ, *Las Vegas Review-Journal*

LVS, *Las Vegas Sun*

Mine-Mill, Communist Domination of Union Officials in Vital Defense Industry.
   International Union of Mine, Mill and Smelter Workers, hearings, SISS, October
   6–8, 1952, Eighty-second Congress, second session

NARA, National Archives and Records Administration, Washington, D.C.

NHS, NHSQ, Nevada Historical Society, Quarterly

NSJ, *Nevada State Journal*

NYHT, *New York Herald Tribune*

NYT, *New York Times*

PM, PMP, Patrick McCarran, Patrick McCarran Papers (NHS)

PMA, Patrick McCarran Autobiography, unpublished (EAP)

PP, PPP, Pete Petersen, Papers (UNR)

REG, *Reno Evening Gazette*

SISS, Senate Internal Security Subcommittee

SJS, Stephen J. Spingarn, Papers (HSTL)

SU, Stanford University, Hoover Institution

TB, *Tonopah Bonanza*

TDS, *Tonopah Daily Sun*

TNR, *The New Republic*

TO, TOP, Tasker Oddie, Papers (NHS)

UCB, University of California, Berkeley, Bancroft Library

UN, Activities of the U.S. Citizens Emplyed by the UN, hearings and report, SISS,
   October 23, 1952, Eighty-second Congress, second session

UNOHP, University of Nevada Oral History Program

UNR, University of Nevada, Reno, special collections

VP, VPP, Vail Pittman, Papers (UNR)

WAP, *Washington Post*

WFM, Western Federation of Miners (Mine-Mill Union), Papers (University of
   Colorado, Boulder)

WSHS, Wisconsin State Historical Society, Madison

Prologue: The Road to Wheeling

1. This account is taken from the transcript of the SISS/Mine-Mill hearings, pp. 114–120.
2. *Washington Times-Herald*, 9 August 1949.
3. *Salt Lake City Tribune*, 6 October 1952.
4. Hank Greenspun, *Where I Stand* (New York: David McKay, 1966), p. 195.
5. Sister Margaret P. McCarran, "Patrick Anthony McCarran, 1876–1954," Part 1, NHSQ (fall–winter 1968).
6. Willard Shelton, "Powerful Pat McCarran," *The Progressive*, May 1952.
7. Paul Douglas, *In the Fullness of Time* (New York: Harcourt Brace Jovanovich, 1972), p. 249.
8. David D. Lloyd memo, 7 August 1952, Lloyd Files, Truman Papers, HSTL.
9. *New York Post* clip, nd but circa February 1955, Kohlberg Papers, SU.
10. David M. Oshinsky, *A Conspiracy So Immense: The World of Joe McCarthy* (New York: Free Press, 1983), p. 348.
11. George F. Kennan, *Memoirs, 1950–1963* (New York: Pantheon, 1972), p. 190.
12. Joseph and Steward Alsop, *Saturday Evening Post,* July 29, 1950.
13. Allan Nevins, *Herbert H. Lehman and His Era* (New York: Scribner's, 1963), p. 316.
14. REG, 5 January 1953.
15. Lyndon Johnson, remarks, 23 March 1960, program dedication, LBJ senate papers, LBJL.
16. Douglas, *Fullness*, p. 249.
17. *Labor,* 8 April 1944.
18. PM to PP, 19 April 1943, PPP.
19. Norman Biltz, UNOHP, p. 177.
20. Ibid., p. 169.

Part One: Struggle

1. James T. Farrell, *Young Lonigan,* in *Studs Lonigan* (Urbana, Ill.: University of Illinois Press, 1993), pp. 39–40.

Chapter 1: Unruly Spirits

1. PM to Connie Estcourt, 16 November 1915, PMP.
2. This account is taken from Sister Margaret P. McCarran, "Patrick Anthony McCarran, 1876–1954," Part 1, NHSQ (fall–winter 1968).
3. Richard H. Orton, *Records of California Men in the War of the Rebellion, 1861–1867* (Sacramento, Calif.: J. D. Young, 1890), p. 40.
4. Orton, *Records*, p. 172.
5. Ibid., p. 18.
6. Russell R. Elliott (with William D. Rowley), *History of Nevada* (Lincoln, Neb.: University of Nebraska Press, 1993), p. 3.
7. William D. Rowley, *Reno: Hub of the Washoe Country, an Illustrated History* (Woodland Hills, Calif.: Windsor Publications, 1984), p. 10.
8. Writers Program of the Work Projects Administration in the State of Nevada, *Nevada: A Guide to the Silver State* (Portland, Oreg.: Binfords & Mort, 1940), p. 25.
9. James W. Hulse, *The Silver State: Nevada's Heritage Reinterpreted* (Reno: University of Nevada Press, 1991), p. 66.

10. Twain, *Roughing*, p. 184.
11. Dale L. Morgan, *The Humboldt: Highroad of the West* (New York: Farrar & Rinehart, 1943), p. 4.
12. Shepperson, *Mirage-Land*, p. 22.
13. Twain, *Roughing*, p. 130.
14. Shepperson, *Mirage-Land*, p. 38.
15. Margaret McCarran, "McCarran," Part 1, NHSQ.
16. Ibid.
17. William Rowley, "Farewell the Rotten Borough," *Halcyon: A Journal of the Humanities* (Reno: University of Nevada Press, 1995), p. 124.
18. Shepperson, *Mirage-Land*, p. 36.
19. Jerome Edwards, *Pat McCarran: Political Boss of Nevada* (Reno, Nev.: University of Nevada Press, 1982), p. 2.
20. PMA, p. 2.
21. Ibid., p. 3.
22. Edwards, *McCarran*, p. 3.
23. PMA, p. 3.
24. Ibid.
25. Robert Laxalt, *Nevada: A Bicentennial History* (New York: Norton, 1977), p. 69.
26. Fred E. Whited Jr., "Senator Patrick A. McCarran: Orator from Nevada," NHSQ (winter 1974).
27. Edwards, *McCarran*, p. 3.
28. REG, 28 November 1903.
29. Anne Martin, "Nevada: Beautiful Desert of Buried Hopes," *The Nation*, 26 July 1922.
30. Anne Bail Howard, *The Long Campaign: A Biography of Anne Martin* (Reno, Nev.: University of Nevada Press, 1985), p. 169.
31. PM to T. L. Withers, 10 February 1915, PMP.
32. Sally Springmeyer, *The Unspiked Rail* (Reno, Nev.: University of Nevada Press, 1981), p. 241.
33. Twain, *Roughing*, 174.
34. De Quille, *Bonanza*, 356.
35. Richard Hofstadter, *The Paranoid Style in American Politics* (New York: Knopf, 1965), p. 266.
36. Hofstadter, *Paranoid*, p. 268.
37. Mary Ellen Glass, *Silver and Politics in Nevada 1892–1902* (Reno, Nev.: University of Nevada Press, 1970), p. 32.
38. Richard Hofstadter, *The Age of Reform* (New York: Knopf, 1955), p. 65.
39. Hofstadter, *Reform*, p. 74.
40. Gilman M. Ostrander, *Nevada, The Great Rotten Borough, 1859–1964* (New York: Knopf, 1966), p. 144.
41. Tasker Oddie, *Letters from the Nevada Frontier*, edited by William A. Douglass and Robert A. Nylen (Norman, Okla.: University of Oklahoma Press, 1992), p. 227.
42. Glass, *Silver*, p. 80.
43. Paul W. Glad, *McKinley, Bryan, and the People* (Philadelphia, Penn.: Lippincott, 1964), p. 249.
44. WPA, *Guide*, p. 49.
45. David D. Anderson, *William Jennings Bryan* (Boston: Twayne Publishers, 1981), p. 61.

46. Glad, *McKinley*, p. 93.

47. Hofstadter, *Paranoid*, p. 295.

48. Ibid., p. 303.

49. Clip, 30 November 1933, PMP.

50. REG, 30 January 1903.

51. Ibid.

52. REG, 3 February 1903.

53. PM to Birdie, 26 July 1942, PMP.

54. Ibid.

55. Laxalt, *Nevada*, p. 24.

56. John Muir, "My First Summer in the Sierras" (New York: Mariner, 1998), p. 97.

57. Robert Laxalt, *Sweet Promised Land* (New York: Harper and Row, 1957), p. 108.

58. PMA, p. 5.

59. Speech, December 1915, copy in PMP.

60. WAP, 21 March 1934.

61. Margaret McCarran, "McCarran," Part 1, NHSQ.

Chapter 2: To the Last Ditch

1. Max Miller, *Reno* (New York: Dodd, Mead & Co., 1941), p. 6.

2. This account is taken from Sister Margaret P. McCarran, "Patrick Anthony McCarran, 1876–1954," Part 1, NHSQ (fall–winter 1968); REG, 20 July 1905.

3. Tasker L. Oddie, *Letters from the Nevada Frontier*, edited by William A. Douglass and Robert A. Nylen (Norman, Okla.: University of Oklahoma Press, 1992), p. 3.

4. Oddie, *Letters*, p. 74.

5. Ibid., p. 136.

6. Ibid., p. 83.

7. Ibid., p. 172.

8. Ibid., p. 72.

9. Ibid., p. 225.

10. Ibid., p. 251.

11. Ibid., p. 278.

12. Mrs. Hugh Brown, "Lady in Boomtown," (Palo Alto, Calif.: American West Publishing, 1968), p. 27.

13. Robert D. McCracken, *A History of Tonopah, Nevada* (Tonopah, Nev.: Nye County Press, 1992), p. 139.

14. TDS, 12 January 1905.

15. Oddie, *Letters*, p. 282.

16. Ibid., p. 321.

17. Ibid., p. 321.

18. Fred Israel, *Nevada's Key Pittman* (Lincoln, Neb.: University of Nebraska Press, 1963), p. 18.

19. Brown, *Lady*, p. 87.

20. Betty Glad, *Key Pittman: The Tragedy of a Senate Insider* (New York: Columbia University Press, 1986), p. 115.

21. Glad, *Pittman*, p. 92.

22. Ibid., p. 281.

23. Ibid., p. 151.

24. Ibid., p. 92.

25. Ibid., p. 27.

26. Ibid., p. 116.

27. *Tonopah Bonanza*, 14 April 1906.

28. PMA, p. 8.

29. PM to John Sheridan, 16 April 1915, PMP.

30. TDS, 11 July 1906.

31. TDS, 13 July 1906.

32. Ibid.

33. Sally Springmeyer Zanjani, *Goldfield : The Last Gold Rush on the Western Frontier* (Columbus, Ohio: Swallow Press/Ohio University Press, 1992), p. 70.

34. C. Elizabeth Raymond, *George Wingfield: Owner and Operator of Nevada* (Reno, Nev.: University of Nevada Press, 1992), p. 91.

35. Jerome Edwards, *Pat McCarran: Political Boss of Nevada* (Reno, Nev.: University of Nevada Press, 1982), p. 10.

36. *May Wingfield v George Wingfield*, District Court, Nye County, August 1906, PMP.

37. Raymond, *Wingfield*, 84.

38. PM to Joe McNamara, 1914, PMP.

39. *Tonopah Bonanza*, 7 April 1906.

40. *Tonopah Bonanza*, 23 September 1906.

41. This account is taken from TDS, 19 July 1907.

42. TDS, 22 November 1907.

43. Raymond, *Wingfield*, 69.

44. John Dos Passos, *USA*, p. 91.

45. Melvyn Dubofsky, *We Shall Be All: A History of the Industrial Workers of the World* (Chicago: Quadrangle, 1969), p. 51.

46. Raymond, *Wingfield*, p. 66.

47. TDS, 13 April 1907.

48. Sally Springmeyer Zanjani and Guy Louis Rocha, *The Ignoble Conspiracy: Radicalism on Trial in Nevada* (Reno, Nev.: University of Nevada Press, 1986), p. 20.

49. Paul F. Brissenden, *The I.W.W.: A Study of American Syndicalism* (New York: Russell & Russell, 1957), p. 201.

50. TDS, 11 March 1907.

51. TDS, 15 March 1907.

52. TDS, 30 March 1907.

53. TDS, 14 March 1907.

54. Raymond, *Wingfield*, 75.

55. Russell R. Elliott (with William D. Rowley), *History of Nevada*, 2nd ed. (Lincoln, Neb.: University of Nebraska Press, 1993), p. 222.

56. TDS, 6 December 1907.

57. TDS, 9 December 1907.

58. *Rhyolite Bullfrog*, 18 January 1908.

59. TDS, 6 August 1908.

60. TDS, 5 August 1908.

61. Edwards, *McCarran*, p. 9.

62. TDS, 3 June 1908.

63. *Rhyolite Daily Bullfrog*, 15 April 1908.

64. TDS, 30 June 1908.

65. TDS, 5 August 1908.
66. KP to Rice, 15 August 1908, KPP.
67. TDS, 1 September 1908.
68. KP to Frank Mannix, 15 August 1908, KPP.
69. *Tonopah Bonanza*, 6 September 1908.
70. Sam Davis to KP, 13 August 1908, KPP.
71. Loren Briggs Chan, *Sagebrush Statesman: Tasker L. Oddie of Nevada* (Reno, Nev.: University of Nevada Press, 1973), p 44.
72. Chan, *Statesman*, p. 43
73. Brown, *Lady*, p. 116.

Chapter 3: Night, Noon, and Morning

1. PM, *State v Comisford*, in Jerome Edwards, "Patrick A. McCarran: His Years on the Nevada Supreme Court, 1913–1918," NHSQ (winter 1975).
2. This account is taken from NSJ, 31 October 1914.
3. Fred Israel, *Nevada's Key Pittman* (Lincoln, Neb.: University of Nebraska Press, 1963), p. 24.
4. KP to Gil Ross, 22 December 1914, KPP.
5. Jerome Edwards, *Pat McCarran: Political Boss of Nevada* (Reno, Nev.: University of Nevada Press, 1982), p. 14.
6. Joseph F. McDonald, UNOHP.
7. KP to PM, 7 October 1911, KPP.
8. PM to KP, 3 April 1912, KPP.
9. KP to PM, 4 April 1912, KPP.
10. NSJ, 1 September 1912.
11. NSJ, 20 October 1912.
12. NSJ, 8 October 1912.
13. NSJ, 13 October 1912.
14. REG, 21 October 1912.
15. REG, 4 November 1912.
16. NSJ, 17 October 1912.
17. NSJ, 29 October 1912.
18. REG, 31 October 1912.
19. NSJ, 23 October 1912.
20. REG, 4 November 1912.
21. Ibid.
22. PM to J. A. Buchanan, 13 March 1913, PMP.
23. For more on Newlands, see William D. Rowley, *Reclaiming the Arid West: The Career of Francis G. Newlands* (Bloomington, Ind.: Indiana University Press, 1996), p. 154.
24. Quoted in REG, 10 March 1914.
25. PM to Joe McNamara, 19 January 1914, PMP.
26. PM to James Finch, 6 January 1914, PMP.
27. W. D. Jones to PM, 28 February 1914, PMP.
28. PM to Jones, 2 March 1914, PMP.
29. Clay Tallman to Newlands, 20 April 1914, Newlands Papers, Yale.
30. A. B. Gray to KP, 1914, KPP.
31. William Woodburn to KP, 24 June 1915, KPP.
32. PM to H. M. Standerwick, 30 September 1915.

33. PM to Adams Brown, 27 October 1914, PMP.

34. REG, 23 July 1915.

35. William Woodburn to KP, 24 June 1915, KPP.

36. KP to Woodburn, 11 April 1916, KPP.

37. REG, 23 July 1915.

38. Israel, *Pittmann*, p. 31.

39. Ibid., p. 32.

40. Ibid.

41. Ibid., p. 33.

42. REG, 23 July 1915.

43. KP to Ross, 22 December 1914, KPP.

44. Frank Curran to PM, 4 August 1915, PMP.

45. PM to Jane Gurney Yoakum, 1 September 1915, PMP.

46. Gray to KP, 23 June 1916, KPP.

47. Jerome Edwards, "McCarran: His Years on the Nevada Supreme Court," NHSQ (winter 1975)' PM to M. Ethel Berlin, 19 June 1916, PMP.

48. PM to KP, 10 August 1916, KPP.

49. KP to Woodburn, 11 April 1916, KPP.

50. Woodrow Wilson, *Constitutional Government in the United States* (New York: Columbia University Press, 1908), p. 70.

51. Robert H. Ferrell, *Woodrow Wilson and World War I, 1917–1921* (New York: Harper & Row, 1985), p. 2.

52. Bert Wolfe, State Department loyalty interrogatory, nd, Corey Papers, CU.

53. PM to Connie Estcourt, 16 November 1915, PMP.

54. PM to illegible, 25 April 1917, PMP.

55. PM to McNamara, 1913, PMP.

56. PM to McNamara, 14 January 1918, PMP.

57. PM to McNamara, 28 June 1918, PMP.

58. Arthur S. Link, *Wilson* (Wheeling, W.Va.: Harlan Davidson, 1979), p. 107.

59. Marian C. McKenna, *Borah* (Ann Arbor, Mich.: University of Michigan Press, 1961), pp. 145–146.

60. William Borah in CR, 66th Congress, 1st Session, pp. 8781–8784, in Robert C. Byrd, *The Senate* (Washington, DC: Government Printing Office, 1989), p. 573.

61. McKenna, *Borah*, p. 164.

62. PM to PP, 9 April 1947, PPP.

63. PM to George Ackerman, 16 November 1916, PMP.

64. Ibid.

65. Richard Gid Powers, *Not Without Honor: The History of American Anticommunism* (New York: Free Press, 1995), p. 19.

66. Murray, *Scare*, p. 63.

67. Ibid., p. 202.

68. Powers, *Honor*, p. 26.

69. Murray, *Scare*, p. 219.

70. PM to J. H. Causten, 18 April 1918, PMP.

71. *State v. Scott*, in Edwards, "McCarran."

72. PM to Joe McDonald, 14 January 1918, PMP.

73. PM to H. M. Standerwick, 28 March 1917, PMP.

74. Edwards, "McCarran," p. 24.

75. PM to J. H. Causten, 18 April 1918, PMP

76. REG, 4 November 1912.
77. PM to McDonald, 6 June 1918, PMP.
78. PM to Harry Dunseath, 18 November 1918, PMP.
79. Gray to KP, 12 November 1918, KPP.
80. PM to J. G. Thompson, 19 November 1918, PMP.

Chapter 4: Where Is Your Blood?

1. Sinclair Lewis, *Babbitt* (New York: Penguin, 1996), p. 138.
2. Wilbur S. Shepperson, *Mirage-Land: Images of Nevada* (Reno, Nev.: University of Nevada Press, 1992), p. 104.
3. Richard G. Lillard, *Desert Challenge: An Interpretation of Nevada* (New York: Knopf, 1949), p. 345.
4. George Bartlett, *Men, Women and Conflict: An Intimate Study of Love, Marriage & Divorce* (New York: G. P. Putnam's Sons, 1931), p. 53.
5. This and the following quotes are taken from the transcript of *Moore v Moore*, PMP.
6. REG, 3 March 1920.
7. REG, 5 March 1920.
8. Mary Pickford, *Sunshine and Shadow* (New York: Doubleday, 1955), p. 122.
9. REG, 31 March 1920; see also Jerome Edwards, "Mary Pickford's Divorce," NHSQ (fall 1976).
10. Margaret McCarran, "Patrick McCarran," Part 1, NHSQ.
11. Edwards, *McCarran*, p. 32.
12. PM to Margaret, 29 August 1923, PMP.
13. Ruth Montgomery, *Once There Was a Nun: Mary McCarran's Years as Sister Mary Mercy* (New York: G. P. Putnam's Sons, 1962), p. 14.
14. Montgomery, *Nun*, p. 72.
15. John Sanford Oral History, UNOHP.
16. C. Elizabeth Raymond, *George Wingfield: Owner and Operator of Nevada* (Reno, Nev.: University of Nevada Press, 1992), pp. 153–154.
17. Loren Briggs Chan, *Sagebrush Statesman: Tasker L. Oddie of Nevada* (Reno, Nev.: University of Nevada Press, 1973), p. 96.
18. NSJ, 22 August 1926.
19. PM for U.S. Senate pamphlet, PMP.
20. William McKnight to KP, 12 July 1926, KPP.
21. NSJ, 15 August 1926.
22. Quoted in NSJ, 29 August 1926.
23. William Woodburn to KP, 19 July 1926, KPP.
24. NSJ, 15 August 1926.
25. NSJ, 14 August 1926.
26. NSJ, 15 August 1926.
27. NSJ, 5 September 1926.
28. McKnight to KP, 12 July 1926, KPP.
29. James Farley to Louis Howe, 1931, DNC Papers, FDRL.
30. NSJ, 7 September 1927.
31. NSJ, 8 August 1927.
32. REG, 7 May 1927.
33. Raymond, *Wingfield*, p. 177.
34. NSJ, 7 September 1927.

35. REG, 25 August 1927.
36. Ibid.
37. NSJ, 8 August 1927.
38. NSJ, 11 September 1927.
39. Ibid.
40. Ibid.
41. Ibid.

Chapter 5: A Time for Surprises

1. William Boyle to FDR, 23 September 1932, DNC 369, FDR.
2. Clel Georgetta, Diary, 6 November 1932, NHS.
3. This account is taken from PP, EA UNOHP.
4. NSJ, 3 January 1932.
5. W. A. Kelly to KP, 15 November 1931, KPP.
6. Russell R. Elliott (with William D. Rowley), *History of Nevada* (Lincoln, Neb.: University of Nebraska Press, 1993), pp. 289, 406.
7. Israel, *Pittman*, p. 70.
8. Smith, *Uncommon*, p. 73.
9. Arthur M. Schlesinger Jr., *The Crisis of the Old Order* (Boston: Houghton Mifflin, 1957), p. 83.
10. Schlesinger, *Crisis*, p. 89.
11. Smith, *Uncommon*, p. 106.
12. Schlesinger, *Crisis*, p. 80.
13. Ibid., p. 165.
14. Ibid., p. 23.
15. Smith, *Uncommon*, p. 17.
16. Ibid., p. 29.
17. J. H. Fulmer to TO, 2 May 1932, TOP.
18. E. M. Steninger to TO, 24 March 1932, TOP.
19. Noble Getchell to TO, 2 July 1932, TOP.
20. Loren Briggs Chan, *Sagebrush Statesman: Tasker L. Oddie of Nevada* (Reno, Nev.: University of Nevada Press, 1973), p. 80
21. Chan, *Statesman*, p. 96.
22. PM to TO, 1 September 1911, Oddie Papers, Huntington Library, San Marino, California.
23. Chan, *Statesman*, p. 111.
24. Sally Springmeyer, *The Unspiked Rail* (Reno, Nev.: University of Nevada Press, 1981), p. 181.
25. Springmeyer, *Rail*, p. 181.
26. TO to PM, 2 April 1932, PMP.
27. PM to TO, 10 May 1932.
28. PMA, page 9.
29. NSJ, 21 May 1932; see also Eugene P. Moehring, *Resort City in the Sunbelt: Las Vegas, 1930–1970* (Reno, Nev.: University of Nevada Press, 1995), p. 15.
30. Kevin Starr, *Endangered Dreams: The Great Depression in California* (New York: Oxford University Press, 1996), p. 301.
31. Edmund Wilson, *The American Earthquake* (New York: Da Capo, 1996), p. 373.
32. NSJ, 24 May 1932.
33. Ibid.

34. NSJ, 22 May 1932.
35. PM to Margaret, 12 February 1933, PMP.
36. PP, UNOHP.
37. Schlesinger, *Crisis*, p. 314
38. Ibid., p. 290.
39. Ibid., p. 417.
40. Ibid., p. 416.
41. Frances Perkins, *The Roosevelt I Knew* (New York: MacMillan, 1946), p. 29.
42. Schlesinger, *Crisis*, p. 291.
43. Ibid., p. 291.
44. Ibid.
45. Ibid., p. 265.
46. Getchell to TO, 6 August 1932, TOP.
47. Claude Smith to TO, 14 July 1932.
48. TO to Wingfield, 18 May 1932.
49. TO to H. Lawrie, 26 August 1932.
50. Illegible to TO, 12 September 1932.
51. Johnnie Thompson to TO, 15 August 1932.
52. TO to Ernest Smout, 23 August 1932.
53. REG, 8 June 1932; PM to Margaret, 12 February 1933, PMP.
54. REG, 29 October 1932.
55. Clel Georgetta, Diary, 5 November 1932, NHS.
56. REG, 1 October 1932.
57. LVRJ, 28 October 1932.
58. TO to HH, 9 August 1932, TOP
59. TO to HH, 12 August 1932.
60. HH to TO, 13 August 1932.
61. TO to H. Lawrie, 26 August 1932.
62. NSJ, 18 October 1932.
63. REG, 15 October 1932.
64. PM speech transcript in TOP.
65. NSJ, 20 October 1932.
66. TO to H. Lawrie, 20 October 1932, TOP.
67. Eleanor Tientz to H. Lawrie, 26 September 1932, TOP.
68. B&B Publishing Co. to PM, 15 January 1914, PMP.
69. NSJ, 29 October 1932; REG, 7 November 1932.
70. TO to H. Lawrie, 24 October 1932, TOP.
71. TO to Lawrie, 23 September 1932, TOP.
72. TO to Wingfield, 3 May 1932, TOP.
73. NSJ, 2 November 1932.
74. Raymond, *Wingfield*, p. 212.
75. PM to Margaret, 12 February 1933, PMP.
76. Raymond, *Wingfield*, p. 215.
77. Catherine B. (illegible) to H. Lawrie, 10 November 1932, TOP.
78. *Tonopah Daily Times & Bonanza*, 2 November 1932.
79. REG, 31 October 1932.
80. *Fallon Standard*, 23 September 1932.
81. TO to R. H. Leigh, 15 October 1932, TOP.
82. Bi Barlow to TO, 1 November 1932.

83. E. M. Steninger to TO, 20 October 1932.

84. J. Crawford to TO, 15 October 1932.

85. TO to Willard Smith, 3 November 1932.

86. TO to Ferry Heath, 17 October 1932, TOP.

87. TO to Ferry Heath, 18 October 1932.

88. H. Lawrie to TO, 26 October 1932, TOP.

89. McDonald Construction Co. to TO, 4 November 1932, TOP.

90. NSJ, 6 November 1932.

91. Schlesinger, *Crisis*, p. 429.

92. Smith, *Uncommon*, p. 144.

93. *Ibid.*

94. REG, 7 November 1932.

95. Ibid., 8 November 1932.

96. REG, 8 November 1932.

97. Geb Ray to FDR, 10 October 1932, DNC Papers, FDRL.

98. J. P. Liddell to TO, 1 September 1932, TOP.

99. NSJ, 9 November 1932.

100. *Las Vegas Age*, 9 November 1932.

101. REG, 13 November 1932.

102. LVRJ, 9 November 1932.

103. PM to Margaret, 12 February 1933, PMP.

104. Ibid.

105. Ruth Montgomery, *Once There Was a Nun: Mary McCarran's Years as Sister Mary Mercy* (New York: G. P. Putnam's Sons, 1962), p. 120.

Part Two: Opposition

1. Ovid, *Metamorphoses*, translated by Rolfe Humphries (Bloomington, Ind.: Indiana University Press, 1983), p. 35.

Chapter 6: The Awakening Comes

1. Gore Vidal, *Washington, D.C.* (New York: Modern Library, 1999), p. 84.

2. PM to Margaret, 12 February 1933, PMP.

3. Arthur M. Schlesinger Jr., *The Crisis of the Old Order* (Boston: Houghton Mifflin, 1957), p. 7.

4. Kenneth S. Davis, *FDR: The New Deal Years, 1933–1937: A History* (New York: Random House, 1986), p. 36.

5. Schlesinger, *Crisis*, p. 8.

6. *New York Times*, 5 March 1933.

7. Fred Israel, *Nevada's Key Pittman* (Lincoln, Neb.: University of Nebraska Press, 1963) p. 27.

8. Israel, *Pittman*, p. 132.

9. Donald R. Matthews, *U.S. Senators and Their World* (Chapel Hill, N.C.: University of North Carolina Press, 1960), p. 93.

10. Israel, *Pittman*, p. 28.

11. Joseph S. Clark, *The Senate Establishment* (New York: Hill and Wang, 1963), p. 22.

12. Matthews, *Senators*, p. 94.

13. Ibid.

14. PM to Margaret, 12 February 1933, PMP.
15. PMA.
16. Ibid.
17. Ray Tucker and Frederick R. Barkley, *Sons of the Wild Jackass* (Boston: Page & Co., 1932), p. 70.
18. Marian C. McKenna, *Borah* (Ann Arbor, Mich.: University of Michigan Press, 1961), p. 128.
19. McKenna, *Borah*, p. 211.
20. PM to Margaret, 12 February 1933, PMP.
21. Senate history Web site, www.senate.gov.
22. H. W. Laidler and Norman Thomas, editors, *The Socialism of Our Times* (New York: Vanguard Press, 1929), p. 51.
23. Laidler and Thomas, *Socialism*, p. 57.
24. Paul Douglas, *In the Fullness of Time: The Memoirs of Paul H. Douglas* (New York: Harcourt Brace Jovanovich, 1972), p. 32.
25. Daniel Aaron, *Writers on the Left* (New York: Columbia University Press, 1992), p. 144.
26. Laidler and Thomas, *Socialism*, pp. 95–96.
27. Harvey Klehr, *The Heyday of American Communism: The Depression Decade* (New York: Basic Books, 1984), p. 3.
28. Granville Hicks, *Where We Came Out* (New York: Viking, 1954), p. 32.
29. Schlesinger, *Crisis*, p. 7.
30. TNR, 14 January 1931.
31. Hicks, *Where*, p. 36.
32. Ibid.
33. Laidler and Thomas, *Socialism*, p. 77.
34. CR, 13 March 1933, p. 252.
35. *Washington Herald*, 20 March 1933.
36. Raymond Moley, *After Seven Years* (New York: Da Capo Press, 1972), p. 155.
37. CR, 13 March 1933, p. 252.
38. CR, 13 March 1933, pp. 253–254.
39. CR, 14 March 1933, p. 343.
40. PMA.
41. CR, 14 March 1933, p. 347.
42. CR, 15 March 1933, p. 434.
43. Alan Brinkley and Davis Dyer, editors, *The Reader's Companion to the American Presidency* (Boston: Houghton Mifflin, 2000), p. 371.
44. Alexander Hamilton, John Jay, James Madison, *The Federalist* (New York: Modern Library, nd), p. 229.
45. Brinkley and Dyer, *Companion*, p. 168.
46. Alexis de Tocqueville, *Democracy in America*, translated by George Lawrence, edited by J. P. Mayer (New York: Perennial Library, 1988), p. 126.
47. Brinkley and Dyer, *Companion*, p. 187.
48. Ibid., p. 200.
49. Ibid., p. 211.
50. GJ, CUOH, p. 694.
51. John Dos Passos, *USA* (New York: Library of America, 1996), p. 1147.
52. Sinclair in Arthur M. Schlesinger Jr., *The Coming of the New Deal* (Boston: Houghton Mifflin, 1959), p. 51.

53. Dos Passos, *USA*, pp. 1156–1157.

54. Murray Kempton, *Part of Our Time* (New York: Simon & Schuster, 1955), p. 53.

55. Gilbert J. Gall, *Pursuing Justice: Lee Pressman, the New Deal, and the CIO* (Albany, N.Y.: SUNY Press, 1999), p. 17.

56. Gall, *Pursuing*, pp. 21–23.

57. GJ, CUOH, p. 561.

58. GJ to Helen Jackson, 15 October 1932, GJP, FDRL.

59. GJ to William Jackson, 3 November 1932, GJP, FDRL.

60. FF to GJ, 4 May 1932, GJP, FDRL.

61. GJ, CUOH, p. 411.

62. Schlesinger, *Crisis*, p. 176.

63. Kenneth S. Davis, *FDR: The New Deal Years, 1933–1937: A History* (New York: Random House, 1986), p. 69.

64. Schlesinger, *Coming*, p. 40.

65. Ibid.

66. Ibid., p. 44.

67. CR, 19 April 1933, p. 1947.

68. Hope Hale Davis, *Great Day Coming: A Memoir of the 1930s* (South Royalton, Vt.: Steerforth Press, 1994), p. 35.

69. John J. Abt (with Michael Myerson), *Advocate and Activist: Memoirs of an American Communist Lawyer* (Urbana, Ill.: University of Illinois Press, 1993), p. 25.

70. GJ to FF, 23 May 1933, GJP, FDRL.

71. Robert Jerome Glennon, *The Iconoclast as Reformer: Jerome Frank's Impact on American Law* (Ithaca, N.Y.: Cornell University Press, 1985), p. 70.

72. George Peek with Samuel Crowther, *Why Quit Our Own* (New York: D. Van Nostrand Company, 1936), p. 20.

73. Abt, *Advocate*, p. 28.

74. Alger Hiss, *Recollections of a Life* (New York: Seaver Books/Henry Holt, 1988), p. 62.

75. Abt, *Advocate*, p. 25.

76. Schlesinger, *Coming*, p. 98.

77. Ibid., p. 102.

78. Ibid., p. 120.

79. CUOH, p. 24.

80. GJ to Brandeis, 21 December 1934, GJP, FDRL.

81. M. C. Migel to Borah, 21 February 1933, Borah papers, LOC.

82. Borah to Migel, 22 February 1933.

83. Borah to Hunter Woodson, 1 May 1933.

84. Schlesinger, *Crisis*, p. 324.

85. Ibid., p. 359.

86. Ibid., p. 455.

87. Frances Perkins, *The Roosevelt I Knew* (New York: MacMillan, 1946), p. 330.

88. TB, 16 March 1933.

89. REG, 15 March 1933.

90. *Elko Independent*, 3 July 1933.

91. REG, 4 July 1933.

92. Ella Reeve Bloor, *We Are Many: An Autobiography* (New York: International Publishers, 1940), p. 266.

93. Gall, *Pursuing*, p. 21.
94. Davis, *Great*, p. 46.
95. GJ, CUOH, p. 467.
96. Abt, *Advocate*, p. 17.
97. Ibid., p. 40.
98. Gall, *Pursuing*, p. 30.
99. Bloor, *We*, p. 160.
100. Ibid., p. 161.
101. Whittaker Chambers, *Witness* (New York: Random House, 1952), p. 348.
102. Bloor, *We*, p. 244.
103. PM, "The Growth of Federal Executive Power," speech, 31 August 1933, PMP.
104. PMA.
105. PM to Joe McDonald, 19 August 1933, PMP
106. PM, "The Growth" *American Bar Association Journal*, ND, Copy PMP.

Chapter 7: Rise Up and Stamp This Thing Out of Existence

1. Frankfurter to Frank, 6 June 1933, Frank Papers, Yale University.
2. Pressman, interview, Daniel Bell Papers, New York University.
3. *Machinists' Monthly Journal*, May 1934.
4. *Washington Herald*, "Merry Go Round" column, 4 April 1934.
5. *Government Standard*, clip, nd, PMP.
6. *Time*, 5 March 1934.
7. *Washington Herald*, 15 March 1934.
8. *Washington Times*, 26 March 1934.
9. WAP, 29 March 1934.
10. John J. Abt (with Michael Myerson), *Advocate and Activist: Memoirs of an American Communist Lawyer* (Urbana, Ill.: University of Illinois Press, 1993).
11. Abt, *Advocate*, p. 41.
12. Herbst, FBI interview, 8 January 1949, Alger Hiss file, copy in Tanenhaus Papers, SU.
13. Hope Hale Davis, *Great Day Coming: A Memoir of the 1930s* (South Royalton, Vt.: Steerforth Press, 1994), p. 75.
14. Arthur M. Schlesinger Jr., *The Coming of the New Deal* (Boston: Houghton Mifflin, 1959), p. 458.
15. Select Committee to Investigate Charges Made by Dr. William A. Wirt, Hearings, 73 Congress, 2nd session (1934), pp. 26–27.
16. Wirt hearings, p. 39.
17. George Wolfskill and John A. Hudson, *All But the People: Franklin D. Roosevelt and His Critics, 1933–39* (New York: MacMillan, 1969), p. 100.
18. Wolfskill and Hudson, *All*, p. 101.
19. Schlesinger, *Coming*, p. 460.
20. Wirt hearings, p. 48.
21. Ibid., p. 69.
22. Ibid., p. 106.
23. FBI interview, copy in Gardner Jackson file, Tanenhaus Papers, SU.
24. FDR, "Review of the Achievements of the Seventy-third Congress," speech, 28 June 1934 (www.fdrlibrary.marist.edu/062834.html).
25. Herbst, FBI interview, 8 January 1949, Alger Hiss file, copy in Tanenhaus Papers, SU.

26. LVRJ, 28 September 1934.

27. Jerome Edwards, *Pat McCarran: Political Boss of Nevada* (Reno: University of Nevada, 1982), p. 67.

28. *Elko Daily Free Press*, 29 September 1934.

29. LVRJ, 28 September 1934.

30. KP to E. J. Trenwith, 18 September 1934, KPP, LOC.

31. Farley, Diary, 22 July 1934, LOC.

32. William O'Donnell to GJ, circa October 1934, GJP, FDRL.

33. Lester B. Granger, "The Negro Joins the Picket Line," *Opportunity, Journal of Negro Life* (August 1934), National Urban League.

34. O'Donnell, nd, circa October 1934, GJP, FDRL.

35. Ibid.

36. Rita James Simon, editor, *As We Saw the Thirties: Essays on Social and Political Movements of a Decade* (Urbana, Ill.: University of Illinois Press, 1967), p. 116.

37. Simon, *Thirties*, p. 20.

38. GJ to Pelham Glassford, 9 November 1934, GJP, FDRL.

39. Warren C. Montross, "Stepchildren of the New Deal," *The Nation*, 12 September 1934.

40. GJ to Pelham Glassford, 9 November 1934, GJP, FDRL.

41. Chester Davis to Jerome Frank, 3 July 1934, Frank Papers, Yale University.

42. GJ to James Myers, 25 January 1935, GJP, FDRL.

43. GJ to Robert Wohlforth, 29 July 1936, GJP, FDRL.

44. Frank to Felix Frankfurter, 21 January 1938, Frank Papers, Yale University.

45. Meyer A. Zeligs, *Friendship and Fratricide: An Analysis of Whittaker Chambers and Alger Hiss* (New York: Viking Press, 1967), p. 193.

46. GJ to Wohlforth, 29 July 1936, GJP, FDRL.

47. TNR, 4 June 1965.

48. GJ to Louis Brandeis, 21 December 1934, GJP, FDRL.

49. GJ to Walter Gelhorn, 16 March 1935, GJP, FDRL.

50. *Washington Star*, 10 February 1935.

51. NYHT, 21 February 1935.

52. *The Federal Employee*, October 1935.

53. *Washington Herald*, 8 February 8 1936.

54. *Today*, 4 May 1935.

55. *Washington Herald*, 25 February 1935.

56. NYHT, 28 February 1935.

57. Chester Davis to GJ, 5 February 1935, GJP, FDRL.

58. GJ, CUOH, p. 616.

59. Letter, 21 March 1935, GJP, FDRL.

60. Abt, *Advocate*, p. 37.

61. *The Nation*, 20 February 1935.

62. *Boston Globe*, 4 March 1935.

63. GJ, CUOH, p. 618.

64. T. Harry Williams, Huey Long (New York: Vintage, 1981), p. 626.

65. *Boston Transcript*, 4 May 1935.

66. *Washington Daily News*, 15 March 1935.

67. WAP, 16 March 1935.

68. CR, 74th Congress, 1st Session, 15 March 1935, p. 3722.

69. Ibid.

70. *Cleveland Plain Dealer*, 4 July 1935.

71. *Washington Herald*, 15 August 1935.

72. *Federal Employee*, October 1935.

73. James G. Ryan, *Earl Browder: The Failure of American Communism* (Tuscaloosa, Ala.: University of Alabama Press, 1997), pp. 83–84.

74. Ryan, *Browder*, p. 96.

75. Ryan, *Browder*, p. 104.

76. PM to Mary, 20 April 1936, PMP.

77. Clip, nd, circa April 1936, PMP.

78. Sister Margaret P. McCarran, "Patrick Anthony McCarran, 1876–1954," Part 1, NHSQ (fall–winter 1968).

79. Margaret to PM, 7 August 1934.

80. Margaret to PM, 3 February 1934.

81. PM to Mary, 23 August 1936.

82. Ibid.

83. PM to Mary, 27 August 1937.

84. Ibid.

85. Patricia to PM, 13 May 1936.

86. REG, 1 September 1936.

87. PM to Mary, 24 May 1937, PMP

88. PM to Margaret, 10 September 1937, PMP.

89. PM to Mary, 3 July 1937, PMP.

90. PM to Margaret, 10 September 1937, PMP.

91. PM to Mary, 23 August 1936, PMP.

92. Hede Massing, *This Deception* (New York: Duell, Sloan and Pearce, 1951), p. 171.

93. Massing, *Deception*, p. 154.

94. Flora Lewis, *Red Pawn: The Story of Noel Field* (New York: Doubleday & Co., 1965), p. 67.

95. Massing, *Deception*, p. 171.

96. Ibid., p. 172.

97. Hermann to Herbst, Herbst file, Tanenhaus Papers, SU.

98. "A Little Page on The Internationale," (www.ifa.hawaii.edu/~yan/int/int.html).

99. PM to Mary, 26 May 1936, PMP.

100. *Pioche Record*, 28 May 1936.

101. PM to FDR, 1 June 1936, PPF, FDRL.

102. *Panama Star and Herald*, 10 October 1936.

103. LVRJ, 28 July 1936.

104. LVRJ, 11 September 1936.

105. REG, 26 September 1936.

106. *Wenatchee (Washington) Daily*, 28 October 1936.

107. Edwin C. Rozwenc, editor, *The New Deal: Revolution or Evolution?* (Boston: Heath, 1959), p. 52.

108. James MacGregor Burns, *Roosevelt: The Lion and the Fox* (New York: Harcourt Brace, 1984), p. 283.

109. *Salt Lake City Tribune*, 2 November 1936.

Chapter 8: Copperheads Among Us

1. Ernest Hemingway, *For Whom the Bell Tolls* (New York: Scribner's, 1968), p. 268.
2. James MacGregor Burns, *Roosevelt: The Lion and the Fox* (New York: Harcourt Brace, 1984), pp. 291–293.
3. Joseph Alsop and Turner Catledge, *The 168 Days* (New York: Doubleday, Doran, 1938), p. 71.
4. FDR, speech, 4 March 1937, in Edwin C. Rozwenc, editor, *The New Deal: Revolution or Evolution?* (Boston: Heath, 1959), p. 59.
5. *Washington Star*, 11 February 1937.
6. Ronald Radosh, Mary R. Habeck, and Grigory Sevostianov, editors, *Spain Betrayed* (New Haven, Conn.: Yale University Press, 2001), p. 109 (proof).
7. George Orwell, *Homage to Catalonia* (New York: Harvest/HBJ, 1980), p. 4.
8. Hemingway, *Bell*, p. 254.
9. Radosh et al., *Spain*, p. 110.
10. Loeb, Confessions of an Egghead manuscript, p. 16, Loeb Papers, WSHS.
11. W. H. Auden, in *The Norton Anthology of English Literature*, Vol. 2, 5th ed. (New York: Norton, 1986), p. 2296.
12. Richard H. Crossman, editor, *The God That Failed* (Chicago: Gateway, 1987), pp. 219–220.
13. Loeb, Egghead, p. 17.
14. Loeb to Baldwin, 22 November 1937, Loeb Papers, WSHS.
15. *Washington Times*, 18 February 1937.
16. Cardozo concurring in *A. L. A. Schechter Poultry Corp. v United States*, 295 U.S. 495 (1935).
17. REG, 28 May 1935.
18. LVRJ, 28 July 1936.
19. KP to John Robbins, 19 April 1937, KPP.
20. *Boston Globe*, 4 March 1937.
21. George Wolfskill and John A. Hudson, *All But the People: Franklin D. Roosevelt and His Critics, 1933–39* (New York: MacMillan, 1969), p. 260.
22. James T. Patterson, *Congressional Conservatism and the New Deal: The Growth of the Conservative Coalition in Congress, 1933–1939* (Lexington, Ky.: University of Kentucky Press, 1967), p. 87.
23. NYHT, 8 February 1937.
24. "This Is No Lawyer's Dispute Over Legalisms," Herbert Hoover, 15 February 1937, in *Vital Speeches of the Day*, p. 315 (newdeal.feri.org/court/hoover.htm).
25. Patterson, *Conservatism*, p. 22.
26. Wheeler, 10 March 1937, in *Vital Speeches of the Day* 3, no. 11 (15 March 1937), p. 614 (newdeal.feri.org/texts/673.htm).
27. Mary McCarthy, *On the Contrary: Articles of Belief, 1946–1961* (New York: Farrar, Straus and Cudahy, 1961), p. 87.
28. McCarthy, *Contrary*, p. 100.
29. Ibid.
30. Frank A. Warren III, *Liberals and Communism: The ìRed Decadeî Revisited* (Bloomington, Ind.: Indiana University Press, 1966), pp. 172.
31. Ella Reeve Bloor, *We Are Many: An Autobiography* (New York: International Publishers, 1940), pp. 299–300.
32. Hede Massing, *This Deception* (New York: Duell, Sloan and Pearce, 1951), p. 222.
33. Massing, *Deception*, p. 219.
34. Ibid., p. 250.

35. Alsop and Catledge, *168 Days*, p. 194.

36. WAP, 12 March 1937.

37. David M. Kennedy, *Freedom from Fear: The American People in Depression and War, 1929–1945* (New York: Oxford University Press, 1999), p. 333.

38. Burns, *Roosevelt*, p. 305.

39. Gilbert J. Gall, *Pursuing Justice: Lee Pressman, the New Deal, and the CIO* (Albany, N.Y.: SUNY Press, 1999), p. 55.

40. Saul Alinsky, *John L. Lewis: An Unauthorized Biography* (New York: Putnam, 1949), pp. 152.

41. Alinsky, *Lewis*, p. 154.

42. Pressman, CUOH, p. 171.

43. Gall, *Pursuing*, p. 61.

44. *New York Daily News*, 16 April 1937.

45. *Washington Herald*, 15 April 1937.

46. *Baltimore Sun*, 29 April 1937.

47. WAP, 16 May 1937.

48. James Farley, *Jim Farley's Story: The Roosevelt Years* (New York: Whittlesey House, 1948), p. 88.

49. NYT, 18 May 1937.

50. PM memo, Suggestions for Report on S. 1392, PMP.

51. *Washington Herald*, 19 May 1937.

52. Reorganization of the Federal Judiciary, Adverse Report, 75th Congress, 1st. sess., copy PMP.

53. PM to Mary, 24 May 1937, PMP.

54. Len De Caux, *Labor Radical* (Boston: Beacon Press, 1970), pp. 267–268.

55. John J. Abt (with Michael Myerson), *Advocate and Activist: Memoirs of an American Communist Lawyer* (Urbana, Ill.: University of Illinois Press, 1993), pp. 302–303.

56. NYT, 11 July 1937.

57. Alsop and Catledge, *168 Days*, p. 294.

58. PMA, p. 9.

59. *Washington Herald*, 18 August 1937.

60. PM to Margaret, 10 September 1937, PMP.

61. De Caux, *Radical*, p. 515.

62. Abt, *Advocate*, p. 35.

63. James Gross, *The Reshaping of the National Labor Relations Board: National Labor Policy in Transition, 1937–1947* (Albany, N.Y.: SUNY Press, 1981), pp. 111.

64. Gross, *Reshaping*, p. 121.

65. Ibid., p. 93.

66. GJ, CUOH, 767.

67. Lombard, *Waltz*, p. 87.

68. Elinor Langer, *Josephine Herbst: The Story She Could Never Tell* (Boston: Little, Brown, 1984), p. 156.

69. GJ, CUOH, p. 716.

70. Charles Bohlen, *Witness to History, 1929–1969* (New York: Norton, 1973), p. 46.

71. Whittaker Chambers, *Witness* (New York: Random House, 1952), p. 408.

72. Chambers, *Witness*, p. 36.

73. Robert Conquest, *The Great Terror: Stalin's Purge of the Thirties* (New York: Collier Books, 1973), pp. 562–565.

74. Farley, *Story*, p. 146.

75. Ibid., p. 133.

76. FDR, The Democratic Party Primaries, June 24, 1938, Works of Franklin D. Roosevelt (newdeal.feri.org/texts/391.htm).
77. Farley, *Story*, p. 133.
78. REG, 9 May 1938.
79. REG, 26 May 1938.
80. Al Hilliard to Joe McDonald, 5 May 1938, McDonald Papers, UNR.
81. REG, 13 July 1938; NYHT, 14 July 1938.
82. FDR, *F.D.R.: His Personal Letters, 1928–1945, Volume II* (New York: Duell, Sloan and Pearce, 1950), p. 796.
83. *Humboldt Star*, 13 July 1938.
84. *Washington Herald*, 14 July 1938.
85. REG, 27 May 1939.
86. REG, 14 July 1938.
87. FDR, *Letters*, , p. 798.
88. WAP, 24 August 1938.
89. Harry Hopkins to FDR, 20 July 1938, PPF, FDRL.
90. FDR to Hopkins, 21 July 1938, PPF, FDRL.
91. NSJ, 26 July 1938.
92. NSJ, 8 August 1938.
93. Humboldt Star, 25 August 1938.
94. Patterson, *Conservatism*, p. 281; Wolfskill and Hudson, *All*, p. 290.
95. Jerome Edwards, *Pat McCarran: Political Boss of Nevada* (Reno, Nev.: University of Nevada Press, 1982), p. 86.
96. Edwards, *McCarran*, p. 87.
97. Joseph P. Lash, *Eleanor and Franklin, The Story of Their Relationship* (New York: Norton, 1971), p. 569.
98. *New York World Telegram*, 11 January 1939.
99. Ibid.
100. Lash, *Eleanor and Franklin*, p. 570.
101. Crossman, *Failed*, p. 218.
102. Loeb to Baldwin, 8 February 1939, Loeb Papers, WSHS.
103. Loeb memo, nd, Loeb Papers, WSHS.
104. Crossman, *Failed*, p. 221.
105. Nomination of Felix Frankfurter, Senate Judiciary Committee hearings (10 January 1939), p. 6.
106. Ibid., p. 8.
107. Ibid., p. 30.
108. James F. Simon, *The Antagonists: Hugo Black, Felix Frankfurter and Civil Liberties in Modern America* (New York: Simon & Schuster, 1989), p. 17.
109. Frankfurter hearings, p. 42.
110. Ibid., p. 108.
111. Ibid., p. 113.
112. Ibid., pp. 123–128.
113. Felix Frankfurter, *Felix Frankfurter Reminisces: Recorded in Talks with Dr. Harlan B. Phillips* (New York: Reynal, 1960), p. 285.
114. Frankfurter hearings, pp. 123–128.
115. Dean Acheson, *Morning and Noon* (Boston: Houghton Mifflin, 1965), p. 209.
116. See *Washington Star*, 12 January 1939, and Pearson Merry Go Round, WAP, 18 January 1939.

Chapter 9: Mass Murder Again

1. John Dos Passos, *The Grand Design, District of Columbia* (Boston: Houghton Mifflin, 1952), p. 127.
2. James G. Ryan, *Earl Browder: The Failure of American Communism* (Tuscaloosa, Ala.: University of Alabama Press, 1997), p. 160.
3. John E. Wiltz, *In Search of Peace: The Senate Munitions Inquiry, 1934–36* (Baton Rouge, La.: Louisiana State University Press), p. 38.
4. A. Scott Berg, *Lindbergh* (New York: Putnam, 1998), p. 394 (proof).
5. FDR speech to joint session of Congress, 21 September 1939.
6. *The Tablet,* 30 September 1939.
7. Ibid.
8. Arthur M. Schlesinger Jr., *A Life in the Twentieth Century: Innocent Beginnings, 1917–1950* (Boston: Houghton Mifflin, 2000), p. 241 (proof).
9. James MacGregor Burns, *Roosevelt: The Lion and the Fox* (New York: Harcourt Brace, 1984), p. 61.
10. David M. Kennedy, *Freedom from Fear: The American People in Depression and War, 1929–1945* (New York: Oxford University Press, 1999), p. 405.
11. Kennedy, *Freedom,* p. 406.
12. *Cincinnati Enquirer,* 9 March 1941.
13. Manfred Jonas, *Isolationism in American, 1935–1941* (Ithaca, N.Y.: Cornell University Press, 1966), p. 228.
14. Jonas, *Isolationism,* p. 81.
15. Michele Flynn Stenehjem, *An American First: John T. Flynn and the America First Committee* (New Rochelle, N.Y.: Arlington House, 1976), p. 32.
16. Jonas, *Isolationism,* 268.
17. September 1, 1939, Auden, *Another Time* (New York: Random House, 1940).
18. C. Day Lewis, "Where Are the War Poets," in *The Norton Anthology of English Literature, Vol. 2* (New York: Norton, 1986), p. 2320.
19. LVRJ, 11 November 1939.
20. Jonas, *Isolationism,* p. 76.
21. Schlesinger, *Life,* p. 241 (proofs).
22. Harvey Klehr, John Earl Haynes, and Kyrill M. Anderson, *The Soviet World of American Communism* (New Haven, Conn.: Yale University Press, 1998), p. 82.
23. Maurice Isserman, *Which Side Were You On?: The American Communist Party During the Second World War* (Middletown, Conn.: Wesleyan University Press, 1982), p. 26.
24. Philip J. Jaffe, *The Rise and Fall of American Communism* (New York: Horizon Press, 1975), p. 43.
25. Jaffe, *Rise,* p. 48.
26. Isserman, *Side,* p. 55.
27. Ibid., p. 38.
28. Klehr et al., *Soviet,* p. 83.
29. Isserman, *Side,* p. 43.
30. LVRJ, 11 November 1939.
31. Joseph P. Lash, *Eleanor and Franklin: The Story of Their Relationship* (New York: Norton, 1971), p. 599.
32. Lash, *Eleanor and Franklin,* p. 600.
33. Ibid.

34. Walter Goodman, *The Committee: The Extraordinary Career of the House Committee on Un-American Activities* (New York: Farrar, Straus and Giroux, 1968), p. 65.

35. Lash, *Eleanor Roosevelt* (New York: Doubleday, 1964), p. 76.

36. Goodman, *Committee*, p. 81.

37. Lash, *Eleanor and Franklin*, p. 601.

38. Ibid., pp. 604–605.

39. Pat Jackson to Arthur Garfield Hays, 4 January 1940, GJP, FDRL.

40. GJ to Morris Ernst, 28 November 1939, GJP, FDRL.

41. Ibid.

42. GJ to Hays, 4 January 1940, GJP, FDRL.

43. Ernst to GJ, 21 November 1939, GJP, FDRL.

44. GJ to Ernst, 28 November 1939, GJP, FDRL.

45. "Rebel Girl" in Industrial Workers of the World, *Little Red Songbook* (www.fortunecity.com/tinpan/parton/2/rebgirl.html).

46. Elizabeth Gurley Flynn, *Words on Fire: The Life and Writing of Elizabeth Gurley Flynn*, edited by Rosalyn Fraad Baxandall (New Brunswick, N.J.: Rutgers University Press, 1987), p. 125.

47. Harry Kalven Jr., *A Worthy Tradition: Freedom of Speech in America*, edited by Jamie Kalven (New York: Harper & Row, 1989), p. 155.

48. Kalven, *Tradition*, p. 160.

49. Corliss Lamont, editor, *The Trial of Elizabeth Gurley Flynn by the American Civil Liberties Union* (New York: Horizon Press, 1968), p. 149.

50. Lamont, *Trial*, p. 187.

51. Ibid., p. 99.

52. Ibid., p. 100.

53. Ibid., p. 102.

54. Ibid., p. 123.

55. Ibid., p. 139.

56. Doris Kearns Goodwin, *No Ordinary Time, Franklin & Eleanor Roosevelt: The Home Front in World War II* (New York: Touchstone, 1994), p. 44.

57. Curt Gentry, *J. Edgar Hoover: The Man and the Secrets* (New York: Norton, 1991), p. 225.

58. Athan G. Theoharis and John Stuart Cox, *The Boss: J. Edgar Hoover and the Great American Inquisition* (New York: Bantam, 1990), p. 175.

59. Francis Biddle, *In Brief Authority* (New York: Doubleday, 1962), p. 166.

60. Gentry, *Hoover*, p. 226.

61. Theoharis and Cox, *Boss*, p. 187.

62. Ibid., p. 192.

63. Burns, *Roosevelt*, p. 427.

64. Ibid., p. 409.

65. Ibid., p. 425.

66. Fred Israel, *Nevada's Key Pittman* (Lincoln, Neb.: University of Nebraska Press, 1963), p. 172.

67. Wayne S. Cole, *Roosevelt & the Isolationists, 1932–45* (Lincoln, Neb.: University of Nebraska Press, 1983), p. 393.

68. NSJ, 17 July 1940.

69. *Carson Appeal*, 19 July 1940.

70. John C. Culver and John Hyde, *American Dreamer: A Life of Henry A. Wallace* (New York: Norton, 2000), p. 218.

71. *Washington Times-Herald*, 18 July 1940.
72. T. H. Watkins, *Righteous Pilgrim: The Life and Times of Harold Ickes, 1874–1952* (New York: Henry Holt, 1992), p. 690.
73. PM to Joe McDonald, 19 August 1933, PMP.
74. Culver and Hyde, *Dreamer*, p. 221.
75. Ibid., p. 133.
76. FDR to George Norris, FDR, *F.D.R.: His Personal Letters*, edited by Elliott Roosevelt (New York: Duell, Sloan, and Pearce, 1947), p. 1046.
77. Roy Hoopes, *Ralph Ingersoll* (New York: Atheneum, 1985) p. 137.
78. Dr. Seuss cartoon posted online (www.ksu.edu/english/nelp/purple/miscellaneous/pm.html).
79. Richard Norton Smith, *The Colonel: The Life and Legend of Robert R. McCormick* (Boston: Houghton Mifflin, 1997), p. 375.
80. Charles A. Lindbergh, *The Wartime Journals of Charles A. Lindbergh* (New York: Harcourt, Brace, Jovanovich, 1970), p. 375.
81. LVRJ, 5 August 1940.
82. Ibid.
83. Kennedy, *Freedom*, p. 461.
84. Burns, *Roosevelt*, p. 443.
85. Harvey Klehr, *The Heyday of American Communism: The Depression Decade* (New York: Basic Books, 1984), p. 397.
86. Klchr, *Heyday*, p. 406
87. Watkins, *Righteous*, p. 695.
88. Stenehjem, *First*, p. 39.
89. Kennedy, *Freedom*, p. 463.
90. PM to EA, 4 November 1940, EAP.
91. EA to PM, EAP.
92. Lash, *Eleanor*, p. 194.
93. Israel, *Pittman*, p. 280.
94. Ibid., p. 170.
95. Jerome Edwards, *Pat McCarran: Political Boss of Nevada* (Reno, Nev.: University of Nevada Press, 1982), p. 98.
96. EA to PM, 2 November 1940, EAP.
97. PP, UNOHP, p. 41.
98. CR, 25 April 1941, p. 3312.

Chapter 10: An Act of War

1. Wayne S. Cole, *America First: The Battle Against Intervention 1940–1941* (Madison, Wisc.: University of Wisconsin Press, 1953), p. 44.
2. *The Public Papers and Addresses of Franklin D. Roosevelt, Vol. 5, 1936* (New York: Random House, 1938), p. 8.
3. *Washington Times-Herald*, 11 January 1941.
4. Michele Flynn Stenehjem, *An American First: John T. Flynn and the America First Committee* (New Rochelle, NY: Arlington House, 1976), p. 25.
5. Ibid., p. 30.
6. PM, 13 January 1941.
7. Wayne S. Cole, *Roosevelt & the Isolationists, 1932–45* (Lincoln, Neb.: University of Nebraska Press, 1983), p. 415.

8. James MacGregor Burns and Susan Dunn, *The Three Roosevelts: Patrician Leaders Who Transformed America* (New York: Atlantic Monthly Press, 2001), p. 411 (proof).

9. FDR to White, 14 December 1939, in FDR, *F.D.R.: His Personal Letters*, edited by Elliott Roosevelt (New York: Duell, Sloan, and Pearce, 1947), p. 968.

10. *Elko Independent*, 20 June 1941.

11. Stenenhjem, *First*, p. 160.

12. Doris Kearns Goodwin, *No Ordinary Time, Franklin & Eleanor Roosevelt: The Home Front in World War II* (New York: Touchstone, 1994), p. 48.

13. *New York Sun* and NYHT, 22 February 1941.

14. *Hearst American*, 5 February 1941.

15. *Chicago Daily News*, 8 February 1941.

16. PM to Margaret, 5 April 1941, PMP.

17. *Indianapolis Star*, 2 February 1941.

18. *Washington Daily News*, 18 January 1941.

19. NSJ, 30 January 1941.

20. *Washington Herald Tribune*, 18 January 1941.

21. PM to Margaret, 20 December 1941.

22. Thomas to John Flynn and Douglas Stuart, 25 June 1941, America First Papers, SU.

23. Wayne S. Cole, *America First: The Battle Against Intervention 1940–1941* (Madison, Wisc.: University of Wisconsin Press, 1953), p. 112.

24. Stenehjem, *First*, p. 159.

25. Berg, *Lindbergh* (proof), p. 415.

26. Ibid., p. 413.

27. Ibid., p. 431.

28. Ibid., p. 405.

29. Cole, *Roosevelt*, p. 486.

30. Thomas E. Mahl, *Desperate Deception: British Covert Operations in the United States, 1939–44* (Washington, D.C.: Brassey's, 1998), p. 30.

31. Kenneth S. Davis, *FDR: The War President, 1940–1943* (New York: Random House, 2000), p. 153.

32. Mahl, *Deception*, p. 59.

33. Francis Biddle, *In Brief Authority* (New York: Doubleday, 1962), p. 189.

34. REG, 6 May 1941.

35. Kearns, *No Ordinary*, p. 238.

36. This account is taken from Davis, *FDR*, p. 167.

37. Frederick Vanderbilt Field, *From Right to Left: An Autobiography* (Westport, Conn.: L. Hill, 1983), p. 187.

38. This account is taken from NYT, 15 May 1941.

39. Harvey Klehr, John Earl Haynes, and Kyrill M. Anderson, *The Soviet World of American Communism* (New Haven, Conn.: Yale Unversity Press, 1998), p. 85.

40. Ibid., pp. 85–86.

41. Maurice Isserman, *Which Side Were You On?* (Middletown, Conn.: Wesleyan University Press, 1982), p. 110.

42. Goodwin, *No Ordinary*, p. 256.

43. CR 87, 77th Congress, 1st session, 4 September 1941, p. 7305.

44. Raymond H. Dawson, *The Decision to Aid Russia, 1941: Foreign Policy and Domestic Politics* (Chapel Hill, N.C.: University of North Carolina Press, 1959), p. 86.

45. Dawson, *Decision*, p. 83.
46. Ibid., p. 82
47. Cole, *Roosevelt*, p. 433.
48. FDR, *Letters*, p. 1205.
49. Dawson, *Decision*, p. 160.
50. An Inventory to the Robert Marshall Papers, American Jewish Archives (www.huc.edu/aja/R-Marsha.htm).
51. GJ to Edith Jackson, 16 May 1941, GJP, FDRL.
52. Ibid.
53. GJ to Edith Jackson, 17 April 1941, GJP, FDRL.
54. GJ to Schlesinger, 2 June 1941, GJP, FDRL.
55. GJ to Frankfurter, 29 October 1935, GJP, FDRL.
56. GJ to Jerome Frank, 14 February 1941, Frank Papers, Yale University.
57. Eugene Lyons, *The Red Decade: The Stalinist Penetration of America* (Indianapolis, Ind.: Bobbs-Merrill Co., 1941), p. 17.
58. Richard Wightman Fox, *Reinhold Niebuhr: A Biography* (New York: Pantheon, 1985), p. 197.
59. GJ to James Loeb, 9 June 1941, GJP, FDRL.
60. *Washington Times-Herald*, 27 August 1941.
61. Ibid.
62. Cole, *America First*, p. 144.
63. Ibid., p. 146.
64. Ibid., p. 147.
65. A. Scott Berg, *Lindbergh* (New York: Putnam, 1998), p. 429 (proof).
66. Ronald Radosh, *Prophets on the Right: Profiles of Conservative Critics of American Globalism* (New York: Simon & Shuster, 1975), p. 50.
67. On the British intelligence deception, see Christopher M. Andrew, *For the President's Eyes Only: Secret Intelligence and the American Presidency from Washington to Bush* (New York: HarperCollins, 1995), pp. 102–103.
68. This account is taken from Paul Douglas, *In the Fullness of Time: The Memoirs of Paul H. Douglas* (New York: Harcourt Brace Jovanovich, 1972), p. 109.
69. Cole, *America First*, p. 160.
70. PM to Margaret, 20 December 1941, PMP.

Chapter 11: Crude Enough for McCarran

1. Saul Bellow, *Dangling Man* (New York: Penguin, 1996), p. 56.
2. PM to MacDonald, 26 December 1941, PMP.
3. MacDonald to PM, 27 December 1941, PMP.
4. David Brinkley, *Washington Goes to War: The Extraordinary Story of the Transformation of a City and a Nation* (New York: Knopf, 1988), p. 98.
5. *Washington Star*, 14 January 1942.
6. Ibid., 15 January 1942.
7. *Washington Times-Herald*, 15 January 1942.
8. Alan Brinkley, *The End of Reform: New Deal Liberalism in Recession and War* (New York: Vintage, 1995), p. 180.
9. Alan Brinkley, *End*, p. 157.
10. PM to EA, 12 December 1942, EAP.
11. SJS to John Pehle, 4 May 1942, SJS Papers, HSTL.
12. SJS to Klaus, 14 April 1942, SJS Papers, HSTL.

13. SJS to Pehl, 4 May 1942, SJS Papers, HSTL
14. Hinckley to SJS, 24 February 1942, SJS, HSTL.
15. SJS memo to Morgenthau, March 1942, SJS Papers, HST.
16. Rowe memo, 10 July 1941, Official File, FDRL.
17. Rowe memo.
18. Jerome Edwards, *Pat McCarran: Political Boss of Nevada* (Reno, Nev.: University of Nevada Press, 1982), p. 106.
19. PM to PP, 1 August 1941, PPP.
20. PM to EA, 6 September 1941, EAP.
21. *Washington Daily News*, 9 October 1941.
22. *Washington Daily News*, 31 October 1941.
23. Joseph Davies, *Mission to Moscow*, edited by David Culbert (New York: Simon & Schuster, 1941), p. 280.
24. David Brinkley, *Washington*, p. 155.
25. Beatrice Farnsworth, *William C. Bullitt and the Soviet Union* (Bloomington, Ind.: Indiana University Press, 1967), p. 91.
26. Jackson to Frankfurter, 13 June 1933, GJP, FDRL.
27. Farley Diary, 26 December 1933, LOC.
28. Farnsworth, *Bullitt*, p. 100.
29. Dennis J. Dunn, *Caught Between Roosevelt and Stalin* (Lexington, Ky.: University Press of Kentucky, 1998), p. 149.
30. George F. Kennan, *Memoirs, 1925–1950* (Boston: Atlantic, Little, Brown, 1967), p. 83.
31. Davies, *Mission*, p. 49.
32. Dunn, *Caught*, p. 75.
33. Ibid., p. 119.
34. Kennan, *Memoirs*, p. 84.
35. Charles Bohlen, *Witness to History, 1929–1969* (New York: Norton, 1973), p. 125.
36. David Brinkley, *Washington*, p. 155.
37. PM to Mary, 9 August 1942, PMP.
38. PM to Mary, 20 August 1942, PMP.
39. PM to Birdy, 26 July 1942, PMP.
40. Sam Tanenhaus, *Whittaker Chambers* (New York: Random House, 1997), p. 170 (proof).
41. Ibid.
42. EA to Mary, 8 September 1943, EAP.
43. Margaret to Birdy, 26 July 1943, EAP.
44. "Our American Constitutional Commonwealth—Is It Passing?," CR, appendix, ND, PMP, p. A3820.
45. Mary to EA, 13 September 1943, EAP.
46. Ibid.
47. Douglas to Ickes, 28 December 1942, Ickes Papers, LOC.
48. Douglas to Ickes, 14 August 1943, Ickes Papers, LOC.
49. Paul Douglas, *In the Fullness of Time: The Memoirs of Paul H. Douglas* (New York: Harcourt Brace Jovanovich, 1972), p. 123.
50. Allen Drury, *A Senate Journal, 1943–1945* (New York: McGraw-Hill, 1963), p. 59.
51. Ibid.
52. PM to Mary, 2 March 1944, PMP.
53. PM to Margie, 2 March 1944, PMP.

54. PM to Mary, 2 March 1944, PMP.

55. Drury, *Journal*, p. 28.

56. *Washington Times*, 2 March 1944.

57. Ickes, diary, 12 February 1944, LOC.

58. Frank Freidel, *Roosevelt: A Rendezvous with Destiny* (Boston: Back Bay Books, 1990), p. 501.

59. Drury, *Journal*, p. 86.

60. Ibid., p. 12.

61. Joseph P. Lash, *Eleanor and Franklin: The Story of Their Relationship* (New York: Norton, 1971), p. 695.

62. Alan Brinkley, *End*, p. 142.

63. Drury, *Journal*, p. 87.

64. Francis Biddle, *In Brief Authority* (New York: Doubleday, 1962), p. 315.

65. Biddle, In Brief, p. 318.

66. Ibid., p. 321.

67. Ibid., p. 318.

68. WAP, 29 May 1944.

69. Biddle, *In Brief*, p. 318.

70. Ibid.

71. Edwards, *McCarran*, p. 123.

72. Ibid., p. 124

73. Ibid.

74. Ibid.

Chapter 12: Hell Popping

1. PM to Tom Miller, 6 July 1946, PMP

2. LVRJ, 13 July 1943.

3. Watson to PM, 16 October 1941, FDRL.

4. LVRJ, 6 January 1942.

5. Ken Eckert to Allan McNeil, 21 October 1942, WFM Papers, University of Colorado, Boulder.

6. Robert Hollowwa, 12 November 1942, WFM.

7. The following account is taken from Isaac F. Marcosson, *Anaconda* (New York: Dodd, Mead, 1957), p. 240.

8. Max M. Kampelman, *The Communist Party v. the CIO* (New York: Arno, 1971), p. 179.

9. Robert Hollowwa to Allan McNeil, 24 November 1942, WFM; *The Union*, 12 October 1942.

10. Fyhen, Labor Notes, NHS, Las Vegas.

11. Hollowwa to McNeil, 24 November 1942, WFM.

12. Hollowwa to Eckert, 1 December 1942, WFM.

13. LVRJ, 7 February 1943.

14. Biltz, UNOHP.

15. Berkeley Bunker, UNOHP.

16. PM to EA, 5 November 1941, EAP. See also Las Vegas Strip History Web site, www.lvstriphistory.com.

17. This account is taken from Reid Robinson to Wendell Berge, 9 March 1943, WFM.

18. Abe Isserman to Reid Robinson, 12 March 1943, WFM.

19. Fyhen, Labor Notes.
20. PM to PP, 23 February 1943, PPP; *The Union*, 22 February 1943.
21. Vernon Jensen, *Nonferrous Metals Industry Unionism, 1932–1954* (Ithaca, N.Y.: Cornell University Press, 1954), p. 62.
22. Kampelman, *Party*, p. 179.
23. Jensen, *Unionism*, p. 64.
24. Ibid., p. 96.
25. EWOH, p. 124
26. AWOH, p. 32.
27. AWOH, p. 132.
28. LVRJ, 10 May 1943.
29. King to Walgren, 11 May 1943, Special Committee Investigating the National Defense Program, Subcommittee on Aviation and Light Metals, BMI hearings, p. 8507.
30. LVRJ, 11 May 1943.
31. LVRJ, 26 April 1943.
32. LVRJ, 5 May 1943.
33. Andrew J. Dunar and Dennis McBride, *Building Hoover Dam* (New York: Twayne Publishers, 1993), p. 59.
34. Rhine to Ward, 13 Juy 1943, WFM.
35. SISS/Communist Domination of Union Officials, Mine-Mill, p. 143.
36. Robinson to Ward, 29 June 1943, WFM.
37. Rhine to Ward, 13 July 1943, WFM.
38. James Gross, *The Making of the National Labor Relations Board* (Albany, N.Y.: SUNY Press, 1974), pp. 246–247.
39. Robinson to Hollowwa, 19 April 1943, WFM.
40. Earl Latham, *The Communist Controversy in Washington* (Cambridge, Mass.: Harvard University Press, 1966), p. 144.
41. Rhine to Ward, 13 July 1943, WFM.
42. Fyhen, Labor Notes.
43. Special Committee Investigating the National Defense Program, Subcommittee on Aviation and Light Metals, BMI hearings, p. 8345.
44. Hearings, p. 8347.
45. Ibid., pp. 8350–8351.
46. Ibid., p. 8505.
47. Senate Report No. 10, Part 17, 78th Congress, 2nd Session, Report of the Special Committee Investigating the National Defense Program, 18 August 1943.
48. Harry Aubrey Toulmin, *Diary of Democracy: The Senate War Investigating Committee* (New York: R. R. Smith, 1947), p. 99.
49. Rhine to Pressman, 5 August 1943, WFM.
50. Ward, EWOH.
51. Rhine to Ward, 13 July 1943, WFM.
52. Ward to Carey McWilliams, 30 September 1952, WFM.
53. Ward, EWOH.
54. The following account is taken from AWOH.
55. www.geocities.com/Nashville/3448/whichsid.html.
56. Wilson, UNOHP, p. 32.
57. Statement on Discrimination Against Negroes at BMI, August 1943, WFM.

58. Hollowwa to Tom Burns, 11 December 1942, WFM.
59. Hollowwa to H. A. Millis, 15 April 1943, WFM.
60. Hollowwa to Allan McNeil, 11 December 1942, WFM.
61. Ibid.
62. Kampelman, *Party*, p. 181.
63. *The Union*, 13 September 1943.
64. AWOH, p. 76.
65. Ibid., p. 82.
66. The following account is taken from Gilbert J. Gall, *Pursuing Justice: Lee Pressman, the New Deal, and the CIO* (Albany, N.Y.: SUNY Press, 1999), p. 187.
67. John J. Abt (with Michael Myerson), *Advocate and Activist: Memoirs of an American Communist Lawyer* (Urbana, Ill.: University of Illinois Press, 1993), p. 94.
68. Abt, *Advocate*, p. 85.
69. Ibid., p. 77.
70. Ibid., p. 102.
71. LVRJ, 22 November 1943.
72. *The Union*, 3 January 1944.
73. AWOH, .p. 83.
74. Ibid., p. 81.
75. Ward to McWilliams, 30 September 1952, WFM.

Chapter 13: Who Will Rule Nevada?

1. A. J. Liebling, *The New Yorker*, 13 May 1950.
2. The American Forum of the Air, 13 March 1944, "What Should be America's International Commercial Air Policy?"
3. PM to Mary, 2 March 1944, PMP.
4. American Forum, ibid.
5. Walter Goodman, *The Committee: The Extraordinary Career of the House Committee on Un-American Activities* (New York: Farrar, Straus and Giroux, 1968), p. 159.
6. Tom Amlie to Hillman, 8 November 1944, Amlie Papers, WSHS.
7. See Harvey Klehr and John Earl Haynes, *Venona* (New Haven, Conn.: Yale University Press, 1999), p. 132.
8. John J. Abt (with Michael Myerson), *Advocate and Activist: Memoirs of an American Communist Lawyer* (Urbana, Ill.: University of Illinois Press, 1993), p. 103.
9. Abt, *Advocate*, p. 101.
10. *The Union*, 10 April 1944.
11. Ibid.
12. *The Union*, 22 May 1944.
13. *The Union*, 11 October 1943.
14. Ward, memo on Nevada's political prospects, nd, WFM.
15. NSJ, 1 June 1944.
16. Berkeley Bunker, UNOHP, p. 140.
17. Ibid., p. 267.
18. Ibid. p. 37.
19. Ibid., p. 80.
20. Ibid., p. 85.

21. On Bunker, see the LVRJ Web site: www.1st100.com/part2/bunker.html.
22. Ward, politcal memo, nd, WFM.
23. Bunker, UNOHP, p. 140.
24. Ibid., 137.
25. PM to PP, 8 November 1941, PPP.
26. Ward, political memo, nd, WFM.
27. Bunker, UNOHP, p. 225.
28. Freeman Lincoln, "Norman Biltz, Duke of Nevada," *Fortune*, September 1954.
29. Lincoln, "Biltz."
30. Ibid.
31. PP, UNOHP.
32. Baruch to PM, 3 August 1944, PMP.
33. PM to Baruch, 7 August 1944.
34. Biltz, UNOHP, p. 132.
35. Max Fleischmann to Biltz, 5 July 1944, EAP.
36. Jerome Edwards, *Pat McCarran: Political Boss of Nevada* (Reno, Nev.: University of Nevada Press, 1982), p. 184.
37. Lincoln, "Biltz."
38. Eric Moody, *Southern Gentleman of Nevada Politics: Vail M. Pittman* (Reno, Nev.: University of Nevada Press, 1974), p. 22.
39. Betty Glad, *Key Pittman: The Tragedy of a Senate Insider* (New York: Columbia University Press, 1986), p. 308.
40. VP to Frank Bartholomew, 26 April 1944, VPP.
41. Boyle to VP, 1 May 1944, VPP.
42. VP to Frank Bartholomew, 26 April 1944, VPP.
43. REG, 13 May 1944.
44. *Ely Daily Times*, 3 May 1944.
45. *Ely Daily Times*, 18 April 1944.
46. *The Union*, 8 May 1944.
47. The following account is taken from *CIO News*, May–July 1944.
48. *Ely Daily Times*, 9 June 1944.
49. *The Union*, 19 June 1944.
50. LVRJ, 24 June 1944.
51. REG, 26 June 1944.
52. Ibid.
53. Ibid.
54. Ibid.
55. Ibid.
56. PM to Rex Nicholson, 14 July 1944, PMP.
57. Ralph H. Rasmussen to members, 21 June 1944, WFM.
58. LVRJ, 24 June 1944.
59. Robert H. Ferrell, *The Dying President: Franklin D. Roosevelt, 1944–1945* (Columbia, Mo.: University of Missouri Press, 1998), p. 16 (proof).
60. Alonzo L. Hamby, *Man of the People: A Life of Harry S. Truman* (New York: Oxford University Press, 1995), p. 284.
61. Hamby, *Man*, p. 282.
62. REG, 29 July 1944.
63. *Salt Lake Tribune*, 22 July 1944.
64. George W. Lynn to Early, 30 June 1944, VPP.

65. Early to Lynn, 4 July 1944, VPP.
66. *CIO News*, 24 July 1944.
67. William Green to PM, 27 July 1944, PMP.
68. *Ely Daily Times*, 29 July 1944.
69. NSJ, 19 July 1944.
70. Ibid.
71. *Ely Daily Times*, 29 July 1944.
72. Ibid.
73. Ozanic Oral History, University of Illinois at Springfield, p. 164.
74. Ibid., pp. 283–284.
75. PP to PM, 14 July 1944, PPP.
76. LVRJ, 15 June 1944.
77. Moody, *Gentleman*, p. 37.
78. *Chicago Tribune*, 7 September 1944.
79. *Labor*, 21 November 1944.
80. Moody, *Gentleman*, p. 31.
81. Ibid., p. 41.
82. REG, July 1929.
83. Jerome Edwards, *Pat McCarran: Political Boss of Nevada* (Reno, Nev.: University of Nevada Press, 1982), p. 120.
84. Len De Caux, *Labor Radical: From the Wobblies to CIO* (Boston: Beacon Press, 1970), pp. 440 441.
85. Ward to Carey McWilliams, 30 September 1952, WFM.
86. WAP, 24 August 1944.
87. LVRJ, 18 August 1944.
88. Mrs. Pittman to Stephen Early, 30 August 1944, FDRL.
89. Ibid.
90. *Eureka Sentinel*, 2 September 1944.
91. VP to J. T. Myles, 4 December 1944, VPP.
92. *Salt Lake City Tribune*, 27 August 1944.
93. Ibid.
94. *Elko Daily Press*, 29 August 1944.
95. Woodrow Wilson, UNOHP, pp. 34, 37.
96. LVRJ, 24 September 1943.
97. Ward to Frank Allen, 26 August 1943, WFM
98. LVRJ, 29 May 1944.
99. Wilson, UNOHP, p. 34.
100. Ward, memo.
101. *CIO News*, 5 June 1944.
102. LVRJ, 14 August 1944.
103. Frazer to PM, 1 August 1950, EAP.
104. Frazer to PM, 23 May 1948, EAP.
105. Flyers, PMP.
106. Biltz, UNOHP, p. 164.
107. *Ely Daily Times*, 5 September 1944.
108. Biltz, UNOHP, 165.
109. NSJ, 6 September 1944.
110. VP to Mortimer J. P. Moore, 2 December 1944, VPP.
111. Ward to Carey McWilliams, 30 September 1952, WFM.

112. Frazer to PM, nd, ca. 1950, EAP.
113. VP to H. W. Buntin, 14 September 1944, VPP.
114. Middleton to VP, 6 September 1944, VPP.
115. Richards to FDR, 22 November 1944, Official File 300, FDRL.
116. Biltz, UNOHP.
117. PM to PP, 27 December 1944, PPP.
118. PM to HST, 5 April 1949, HST Official File, HSTL.
119. *Carson City Chronicle*, 20 October 1944.
120. *Pioche Record*, 26 October 1944.
121. EWOH, p. 151.
122. James Caldwell Foster, *The Union Politic: The CIO Political Action Committee* (Columbia, Mo.: University of Missouri Press, 1975), p. 16.
123. PM to EA, 16 December 1944, EAP.
124. Doris Kearns Goodwin, *No Ordinary Time, Franklin & Eleanor Roosevelt: The Home Front in World War II* (New York: Touchstone, 1994), p. 587.

Part III: Power

1. Memo, EA, nd, EAP.

Chapter 14: The Edge of Hell

1. Alger Hiss, *Recollections of a Life* (New York: Seaver Books/H. Holt, 1988), p. 119
2. Dean Acheson, *Present at the Creation: My Years in the State Department* (New York: Norton, 1969), p. 104.
3. Walter Isaacson and Evan Thomas, *The Wise Men* (New York: Simon & Schuster, 1986) p. 465.
4. Clark Clifford, *Counsel to the President* (New York: Random House, 1991), p. 141.
5. Acheson, *Present*, p. 105.
6. PM to PP, 19 April 1943, PPP.
7. Harold Ickes, diary, 4 March 1945, LOC.
8. Ickes, diary, March 3, 1945.
9. Bunker to VP, 5 March 1945, VPP.
10. Acheson, *Present*, p. 104.
11. Alfred Steinberg, "McCarran, Lone Wolf of the Senate," *Harper's*, November 1950.
12. WAP, 14 May 1938.
13. Acheson, *Present*, p. 105.
14. HST, *Memoirs, Volume 1: Year of Decisions* (Garden City, NY: Doubleday, 1955), p. 6.
15. E. J. Kahn Jr., *The China Hands: America's Foreign Service Officers and What Befell Them* (New York: Viking, 1975), p. 84.
16. Ibid., p. 165.
17. Harvey Klehr and Ronald Radosh, *The Amerasia Spy Case: Prelude to McCarthyism* (Chapel Hill, N.C.: University of North Carolina Press, 1996), p. 77.
18. Klehr and Radosh, *Amerasia*, p. 77.
19. Ibid., p. 140.
20. John Paton Davies Jr., *Dragon by the Tail: American, British, Japanese, and Russian Encounters with China and One Another* (New York: Norton, 1972), p. 405.

21. Cabell Phillips, *The Truman Presidency: The History of a Triumphant Succession* (New York: MacMillan, 1966), p. 82.
22. I. F. Stone, *The Truman Era, 1945–1952* (Boston: Little, Brown, 1972), p. 7.
23. Charles Bohlen, *Witness to History* (New York: Norton, 1973), p. 213.
24. Bohlen, *Witness*, p. 214.
25. Isaacson, *Wise Men*, p. 268.
26. Stone, *Truman Era*, p. 11.
27. Allen Weinstein, *Perjury* (New York: Vintage, 1979), p. 355.
28. Weinstein, *Perjury*, p. 361.
29. Phillips, *Truman*, p. 82.
30. PM, "The Parade That Nothing Can Stop," *Phi Kappa Phi Journal*, September 1945.
31. On Arlington Hall and the UN, see James Bamford, *Body of Secrets* (New York: Doubleday, 2001).
32. Ickes, diary, 27 January 1945, LOC.
33. T. H. Watkins, *Righteous Pilgrim* (New York: Henry Holt, 1990), p. 823.
34. Alonzo L. Hamby, *Man of the People: A Life of Harry S. Truman* (New York: Oxford University Press, 1995), p. 306.
35. PM to Joe McDonald, 19 August 1933, PMP.
36. Ickes, diary, 26 February 1939.
37. Ibid., 25 December 1937.
38. Francis Biddle, *In Brief Authority* (New York: Doubleday, 1962), p. 177.
39. Ickes, diary, 4 March 1945.
40. Ibid., 29 April 1945.
41. Ibid., 6 May 1945.
42. Ibid., 1 July 1946.
43. Ibid., 28 July 1946.
44. WAP, 2 August 1945.
45. *St. Louis Post Dispatch*, 31 January 1946.
46. Ickes column, "Man to Man," *Atlantic City (New Jersey) Home News*, 15 May 1946.
47. WAP, 29 December 1947.
48. Harvey Klehr, John Earl Haynes, and Kyrill M. Anderson, *The Soviet World of American Communism* (New Haven, Conn.: Yale University Press, 1998), p. 96.
49. Klehr et al., *Soviet World*, p. 99.
50. On Elizabeth Bentley, see Kathryn. S. Olmsted, *Red Spy Queen* (Chapel Hill, N.C.: University of North Carolina Press, 2002).
51. PM to Mary, 25 February 1945, PMP.
52. Mary to Margaret, 20 August 1946, PMP.
53. PM to Mary, 25 February 1945, PMP.
54. Ed Hay to PM, 20 October 1945, PMP.
55. Ibid.
56. Hay to PM, 23 November 1946, PMP.
57. Patricia to PM, 19 September 1945, PMP.
58. Ibid.
59. PM to Mary, 25 February 1945, PMP.
60. Igor Gouzenko, *The Iron Curtain* (New York: E. P. Dutton, 1948), p. 241.
61. *The Gouzenko Transcripts*, edited by Robert Bothwell and J. L. Granatstein (Montreal: Deneau, 1982), p. 141.
62. Dick Cooke to PM, 15 June 1946, PMP.

63. Jay Carpenter to EA, 24 June 1946, PMP.
64. PM to H. R. Cooke, 19 June 1946, PMP.
65. PM to Cooke, 26 June 1946, PMP.
66. Dick Cooke to PM, 21 June 1946, PMP.
67. Frank Aldrich, memo, 28 July 1955, Silvermaster file, FBI 65 56402.
68. Olmsted, *Spy Queen*, p. 100.
69. Curt Gentry, *J. Edgar Hoover* (New York: Norton, 1991), p. 343.
70. Elizabeth Bentley, *Out of Bondage* (New York: Devin-Adair, 1951), p. 7.
71. Bentley, *Bondage*, p. 99.
72. Ibid., p. 177.
73. Venona, 13 May 1944, www.nsa.gov/docs/venona.
74. Olmsted, *Spy Queen*, p. 116; Silvermaster file, FBI 65 56402.
75. Gentry, *Hoover*, p. 321.
76. Ibid., p. 323.
77. Ladd to Hoover, 26 March 1952, Hoover official personnel file, 67 561.
78. Ibid.
79. Robert J. Lamphere and Tom Shachtman, *The FBI-KGB War: A Special Agent's Story* (Macon, Ga.: Mercer University Press, 1995), p. 69.
80. Lamphere and Schactman, *FBI-KGB*, p. 70.
81. HST, *Dear Bess: The Letters of Harry to Bess Truman, 1910–1959*, edited by Robert H. Ferrell (New York: Norton, 1983), p. 550.
82. Gentry, *Hoover*, p. 321.
83. Klehr and Radosh, *Amerasia*, p. 128.
84. Athan G. Theoharis and John Stuart Cox, *The Boss: J. Edgar Hoover and the Great American Inquisition* (New York: Bantam, 1990), pp. 192.
85. Theoharis and Cox, *Boss*, p. 238.
86. WAP, 19 June 1946.
87. PM to PP, 1 June 1946, PMP.
88. Bentley to FBI, 16 November 1945, Silvermaster file, FBI 65-56402.
89. *New York Journal American*, 1 December 1945.
90. Ladd to Hoover, 28 May 1946, Silvermaster file.
91. Roach to Ladd, 14 March 1946, Silvermaster file.
92. E. A. Tamm to Hoover, 3 June 1946, Silvermaster file.
93. Isaac Don Levine, editor, *Plain Talk: An Anthology from the Leading Anti-Communist Magazine of the 40s* (New Rochelle: Arlington House, 1976), p. 177.
94. James F. Byrnes, *All in One Lifetime* (New York: Harper & Bros., 1958), p. 323.
95. Levine, *Plain Talk*, p. 5.
96. *San Francisco Call Bulletin*, 6 September 1946.
97. Jerome Edwards, *Pat McCarran: Political Boss of Nevada* (Reno, Nev.: University of Nevada Press, 1982), p. 135.
98. Berkeley Bunker, UNOHP, pp. 180–181.
99. PM to PP, 9 April 1947, PPP.
100. HST, *Dear Bess*, p. 526.

Chapter 15: On All Evidence

1. Wolfe interrogatory, nd, Corey Papers, CU.
2. *Pioche Record*, 23 September 1948.
3. Ibid.
4. Cabell Phillips, *The Truman Presidency: The History of a Triumphant Succession* (New York: MacMillan, 1966), p. 214.

5. *Pioche Record*, 23 September 1948.

6. Pearson in *Philadelphia Record*, 18 January 1947.

7. SJS to O'Connell, 29 January 1947, SJS Papers, HSTL.

8. SJS OH, HSTL.

9. SJS (with Milton Lehman), "How We Caught Spies in World War II," *Saturday Evening Post*, 11 December 1948.

10. Clark memo, 14 February 1947, in Alan D. Harper, *The Politics of Loyalty* (Westport, Conn.: Greenwood Publishing, 1969), p. 35.

11. SJS OH, HSTL.

12. SJS OH.

13. SJS OH.

14. Goodrich and SJS memo, 12 February 1947, SJS Papers.

15. SJS to Foley, 30 January 1947, SJS Papers.

16. SJS to O'Connell, 3 February 1947, SJS Papers.

17. Report, in Francis H. Thompson, *The Frustration of Politics* (Rutherford, N.J.: Associated University Presses, 1979), p. 197.

18. SJS to Lynch, O'Connell, 19 February 1947, SJS Papers.

19. Schlesinger to Wilson Wyatt, 21 February 1947, GJ Papers, FDRL.

20. Arthur M. Schlesinger Jr., *A Life in the Twentieth Century: Innocent Beginnings, 1917–1950* (Boston: Houghton Mifflin, 2000), p. 252 (proof).

21. James A. Wechsler, *The Age of Suspicion* (New York: Primus, 1985), p. 213.

22. Schlesinger, *Life*, p. 54.

23. Schlesinger to GJ, 3 November 1944, GJP, FDRL.

24. TNR, 13 May 1946.

25. UDA memo, Loeb Papers, WSHS.

26. Notes on ADA, Loeb Papers.

27. *Life*, 29 July 1946.

28. Schlesinger, *Life*, p. 412.

29. Draft, Schlesinger Papers, LOC.

30. Schlesinger to Wilson Wyatt, 21 February 1947, GJP.

31. John C. Culver and John Hyde, *American Dreamer: A Life of Henry A. Wallace* (New York: Norton, 2000), p. 82.

32. John J. Abt (with Michael Myerson), *Advocate and Activist: Memoirs of an American Communist Lawyer* (Urbana, Ill.: University of Illinois Press, 1993), p. 155.

33. Curtis D. MacDougall, *Gideon's Army* (New York: Marzani & Munsell, 1965), p. 127.

34. Culver and Hyde, *Dreamer*, p. 433.

35. Ibid., p. 434.

36. Schlesinger to Wyatt, 21 February 1947, GJP.

37. Ibid.

38. Phillips, *Truman*, p. 175.

39. *Washington Star*, 12 March 1947.

40. PM to PP, 22 April 1947, PPP.

41. Culver and Hyde, *Dreamer*, p. 436.

42. Alonzo L. Hamby, *Man of the People: A Life of Harry S. Truman* (New York: Oxford University Press, 1995), p. 393.

43. Clark Clifford (with Richard Holbrooke), *Counsel to the President: A Memoir* (New York: Random House, 1991), p. 180.

44. Thompson, *Frustration*, p. 27.

45. Clifford, *Counsel*, p. 181.
46. Ibid., p. 175.
47. *Washington Evening Star*, 25 July 1947.
48. Kansas City Vote Fraud Report, July 1947, on SR 116, copy in PMP.
49. *Washington Evening Star*, 25 July 1947.
50. Clark to PM, 31 March nd, EAP.
51. The following account is taken from *Tonopah Times*, 29 August 1947.
52. PM to EA, 28 October 1946, EAP.
53. PM to Patricia, 16 July 1947, PMP.
54. PM to George Dewey, 6 January 1947, PMP.
55. Patty to parents, 25 October 1947.
56. Spellman to PM, 10 February 1947.
57. PM to Birdie, 8 November 1948.
58. PM to EA, 28 October 1947, EAP.
59. Walter Goodman, *The Committee: The Extraordinary Career of the House Committee on Un-American Activities* (New York: Farrar, Straus and Giroux, 1968), p. 212.
60. Culver and Hyde, *Dreamer*, p. 456.
61. Theodore H. White, *In Search of History: A Personal Adventure* (New York: Harper & Row, 1978), p. 257.
62. Abt, *Advocate*, p. 144.
63. NSJ, 10 July 1948.
64. McCullough, *Truman*, p. 632.
65. PM to PP, 9 April 1948, PPP.
66. Gary A. Donaldson, *Truman Defeats Dewey* (Lexington: University of Kentucky, 1999), p. 163.
67. Donaldson, *Defeats*, p. 121.
68. McCullough, *Truman*, p. 642.
69. Ralph de Toldedano and Victor Lasky, *Seeds of Treason* (New York: Funk & Wagnalls, 1950), p. 139.
70. SJS, memo, 14 October 1947, SJS Papers.
71. MacDougall, *Gideon's*, p. 537.
72. Ibid., p. 549.
73. Ibid., p. 565.
74. Ibid., p. 566.
75. Ibid., p. 571.
76. I. F. Stone, *The Truman Era* (Boston: Little, Brown, 1972), p. 67.
77. NYT, 31 July 1948.
78. NYT, 1 August 1948.
79. NYT, 3 August 3 1948.
80. NYT, 4 August 1948.
81. NYT, 5 August 1948.
82. NYT, 6 August 1948.
83. HST, *Dear Bess*, p. 536.
84. Clifford to HST, 4 August 1948, Elsey Papers, HSTL.
85. Phillips, *Truman*, p. 228.
86. Roger Morris, *Richard Milhous Nixon* (New York: Henry Holt, 1990), p. 402.
87. Morris, *Nixon*, p. 402.
88. Ibid., p. 332.

89. Sam Tanenhaus, *Whittaker Chambers* (New York: Random House, 1997), p. 277 (proof).

90. Morris, *Nixon*, p. 425.

91. Murphy OH, HSTL.

92. *Chicago Tribune*, 4 August 1948.

93. SJS OH, HSTL.

94. SJS OH.

95. SJS OH, HSTL.

96. WAP, 16 August 1948.

97. Elsey, Random Thoughts, 26 August 1948, Elsey Papers, HSTL.

98. SJS to Clifford, 16 September 1948, SJS Papers, HSTL.

99. MacDougall, *Gideon's*, p. 712.

100. Ibid., p. 717.

101. Culver and Hyde, *Dreamer*, p. 470.

102. MacDougall, *Gideon's*, p. 730.

103. McCullough, *Truman*, p. 656.

104. Clifford, *Counsel*, p. 235.

105. Richard N. Smith, *Thomas E. Dewey and His Times* (New York: Simon & Schuster, 1982), p. 508.

106. Smith, *Dewey*, p. 526.

107. McCullough, *Truman*, p. 673.

108. Morris, *Nixon*, p. 441.

109. Donaldson, *Defeats*, p. 175.

110. HST, speech, 28 September 1948, copy in SJS Papers, HSTL.

111. Tanenhaus, *Chambers*, p. 249.

112. HST, speech.

113. Margaret Truman, *Harry S. Truman* (New York: Morrow, 1973), p. 21.

114. Alfred Steinberg, "McCarran, Lone Wolf of the Senate," *Harper's*, November 1950.

115. PM, radio speech, 4 October 1948, copy in PMP.

Chapter 16: A One-Man Un-American Activities Committee

1. HST, *Memoirs, Volume 1: Years of Decision* (New York: Doubleday, 1955), p. 189.

2. Frank McNaughton, memo, 26 July 1949, McNaughton Papers, HSTL.

3. Stephen K. Bailey and Howard D. Samuel, *Congress at Work* (New York: Henry Holt, 1952), p. 237.

4. Paris Beltran, *Beltran: Basque Sheepman of the American West* (as told to William A. Douglass) (Reno, Nev.: University of Nevada Press, 1979), p. 157.

5. PM to Tom Wilson, 29 January 1949, PMP.

6. Alonzo L. Hamby, *Man of the People: A Life of Harry S. Truman* (New York: Oxford University Press, 1995), p. 488.

7. Cabell Phillips, *The Truman Presidency: The History of a Triumphant Succession* (New York: MacMillan, 1966), p. 214.

8. Robert A. Caro, *The Years of Lyndon Johnson: Master of the Senate* (New York: Knopf, 2002), p. 89.

9. PM to Sam McCarran, 25 November 1938, PMP.

10. Ralph Denton, *A Liberal Conscience: The Oral History of Ralph Denton* (Reno, Nev.: University of Nevada Oral History, 2002), p. 79.

11. PM to Florine Maher, 12 November 1939, PMP.

12. Denton, *Conscience*, pp. 63, 69.

13. Ibid., p. 42.

14. Felix Frankfurter, *Felix Frankfurter Reminisces: Recorded in Talks with Dr. Harlan B. Phillips* (New York: Reynal, 1960), pp. 285–287.

15. PM to EA, 4 January 1945, EAP.

16. Joseph Keeley, *The China Lobby Man: The Story of Alfred Kohlberg* (New Rochelle, N.Y.: Arlington House, 1969), p. 22.

17. Barbara W. Tuchman, *Stilwell and the American Experience in China* (New York: Grove Press, 1985), p. 188.

18. Keeley, *China Lobby*, p. xvii.

19. Ibid.

20. Ibid., p. 22.

21. Agnes Smedley, *Battle Hymn of China* (New York: Da Capo Press, 1975), p. 57.

22. John King Fairbank, *Chinabound* (New York: Harper & Row, 1982), p. 67.

23. Freda Utley, *Odyssey of a Liberal* (Washington, D.C.: Washington National Press, 1970), p. 200.

24. John Paton Davies Jr., *Dragon by the Tail: American, British, Japanese, and Russian Encounters with China and One Another* (New York: Norton, 1972), p. 195.

25. Janice R. MacKinnon and Stephen R. MacKinnon, *Agnes Smedley: The Life and Times of an American Radical* (Berkeley, Calif.: University of California Press, 1988), p. 193.

26. MacKinnon and MacKinnon, *Smedley*, p. 161.

27. Robert P. Newman, *Owen Lattimore and the ìLossî of China* (Berkeley, Calif.: University of California Press, 1992), p. 23.

28. Harvey Klehr, John Earl Haynes, and Fridrikh Igorevich Firsov, *The Secret World of American Communism* (New Haven, Conn.: Yale University Press, 1995), p. 69.

29. Keeley, *China Lobby*, p. 321.

30. PM to Alexander Smith, 26 February 1949, PMP.

31. Dean Acheson, *Present at the Creation: My Years in the State Department* (New York: Norton, 1969), p. 257.

32. Acheson, *Present*, p. 305.

33. Ibid., 306.

34. Acheson to Connally, cited in PM press release, 16 April 1949, PMP.

35. Mary to PM, 11 January 1949, PMP.

36. PM press release, 16 April 1949, PMP.

37. Frank McNaughton, memo, 26 July 1949, McNaughton Papers, HSTL.

38. Drew Pearson, *Diaries, 1949–1959*, edited by Tyler Abell (New York: Holt, Rinehart and Winston, 1974), p. 209.

39. Notes of a conversation with Senator PM, 31 March 1949, Wellington Koo Papers, CU.

40. Pearson, *Diaries*, p. 8.

41. William S. White, *Citadel: The Story of the U.S. Senate* (New York: Harpers & Bros, 1957), p. 68.

42. PM to EA, 11 December 1942, PMP.

43. PM to Richard Russell, 22 July 1949, PMP.

44. Russell to PM, 25 July 1949, PMP.

45. Caro, *Master*, p. 448.

46. Ibid., p. 449.

47. The following account is taken from Pierre J. Huss and George Carpozi Jr., *Red Spies at the UN* (New York: Coward-McCann, 1965), pp. 16–40.

48. The following account is taken from Robert J. Lamphere and Tom Shachtman, *The FBI-KGB War: A Special Agent's Story* (Macon, Ga.: Mercer University Press, 1995).

49. *Washington Star*, 12 May 1949.

50. Ibid.

51. WAP, 19 July 1949.

52. Huss and Carpozi, *Red Spies*, p. 41.

53. Sourwine to PM, 2 November 1948, PMP.

54. WAP, 13 May 1949.

55. *Washington Star*, 22 May 1949.

56. *Washington Times-Herald*, 2 June 1949.

57. WAP, 26 July 1949.

58. *Washington Times-Herald*, 9 August 1949.

59. Kohlberg to PM, 25 March 1949, Kohlberg Papers, Hoover Institution, SU.

60. *Washington Times-Herald*, 9 August 1949.

61. WAP, 7 June 1949.

62. Bailey and Samuel, *Congress*, p. 238.

63. EA, UNOHP, p. 153.

64. Biltz UNOHP, p. 134.

65. Frank Donner, *The Age of Surveillance* (New York: Knopf, 1980), p. 408.

66. Carl Bernstein, *Loyalties* (New York: Simon & Schuster, 1989), p. 58.

67. Chester Smith, author interview.

68. EA to PM, 31 October 1940, EAP.

69. PM to EA, 10 November 1940, EAP.

70. Chester Smith, author interview.

71. EA, UNOHP, p. 151.

72. Morison OH, HSTL, p. 206.

73. EA to PP, 3 July 1944, EAP.

74. Denton, *Conscience*, p. 85.

75. Smith interview.

76. Sourwine to PM, 17 February 1949, EAP.

77. Sourwine to EA, 31 August 1943, EAP.

78. PP to PM, 28 February 1950, PPP.

79. PM to PP, 7 July 1944, PPP.

80. PM to EA, 26 October 1949, EAP.

81. PM speech, 14 June 1949, PMP.

82. James Chace, *Acheson* (New York: Simon & Schuster, 1998), p. 220.

83. Chace, *Acheson*, p. 220.

84. Ibid.

85. NYT, 17 June 1949.

86. The following account is taken from Chester Smith interview.

87. Margaret Truman, *Harry S. Truman* (New York: Morrow, 1973), p. 474.

88. Joseph G. Feeney, OH, HSTL.

89. Smith interview.

90. Alfred Steinberg, "McCarran, Lone Wolf of the Senate," *Harper's*, November 1950.

Chapter 17: Turbulent Populations

1. Pope Pius XII, *Quemadmodum, A Plea for the Care of the World's Destitute Children*, 6 January 1946.
2. *Life Reborn : Jewish Displaced Persons, 1945–1951*, edited by Menachem Z. Rosensaft (Washington, D.C.: U.S. Holocaust Memorial Museum, 2001), p. 101.
3. PM, testimony, Munich, 1949, EAP.
4. Leonard Dinnerstein, *America and the Survivors of the Holocaust* (New York: Columbia University Press, 1982), p. 229.
5. WAP, 11 July 1949.
6. Frank McNaughton, memo, 26 July 1949, McNaughton Papers, HSTL.
7. Dinnerstein, *Holocaust*, p. 229.
8. *Life Reborn*, p. 6.
9. Dinnerstein, *Holocaust*, p. 43.
10. Truman memo, 22 December 1945, copy in PMP.
11. Dinnerstein, *Holocaust*, p. 132.
12. Ibid., p. 173.
13. Ibid., p. 169.
14. Ibid., p. 173.
15. Ibid., p. 169.
16. NSJ, 3 August 1947.
17. Dinnerstein, *Holocaust*, p. 217.
18. PM, speech, 26 April 1949, PMP.
19. Ibid.
20. Rowe memo, 10 July 1941, OF 516, FDRL.
21. WAP, 29 December 1947.
22. PM to Mary, 29 January 1954, PMP.
23. CR, 2 February 1950, p. 1369.
24. Biltz UNOHP, p. 169.
25. PM speech, ibid.
26. Pearson column, WAP, 28 July 1949.
27. PM to PP, 1 April 1949, PPP.
28. Pearson column, WAP, 28 July 1949.
29. SJS to Murphy, 19 July 1949, SJS Papers, HSTL.
30. Memo, 26 July 1949, McNaughton Papers, HSTL.
31. CR, 12 September 1949, pp. 13,005–13,006.
32. PM to Mary, 25 September 1949, PMP.
33. Birdie to Mary, nd; PM to Margaret, 22 October 1949; Birdie to Mary; PM to Margaret, 9 October 1949; all PMP.
34. Cutler testimony, Munich, 3 October 1949, copy in EAP.
35. PM to EA, 26 October 1949, EAP.
36. PM to Eastland, 7 October 1949, EAP.
37. Dinnerstein, *Holocaust*, p. 231.
38. Kathryn Hulme, *The Wild Place* (Boston: Little, Brown, 1953), pp. 250–251.
39. Rosenfield OH, HSTL.
40. WAP, 16 October 1949.
41. WAP, 30 August 1949.
42. Stephen K. Bailey and Howard D. Samuel, *Congress at Work* (New York: Henry Holt, 1952), p. 253.
43. WAP, 14 October 1949.

44. WAP, 16 October 1949.
45. Ibid.
46. Ibid.
47. *Newsweek*, 24 October 1949.
48. *Ibid.*
49. Alfred Steinberg, "McCarran, Lone Wolf of the Senate," *Harper's*, November 1950.
50. PM to Mary, 27 October 1949, PMP.
51. PM to Mary, 20 October 1949, PMP.
52. Pope Pius XII, *Quemadmodum.*
53. PM to Mary, 27 October 1949, PMP.
54. PM to EA, 9 November 1949, EAP.
55. Paul Preston, *Franco* (New York: Basic Books, 1994), p. 562.
56. Preston, *Franco*, p. 619.
57. PM to EA, 9 November 1949, EAP.
58. "R. Richard Rubottom and J. Carter Murphy, *Spain and the United States* (New York: Praeger, 1984), p. 17.
59. Preston, *Franco*, p. 601.
60. *Washington Star*, 4 May 1949.
61. Ibid.
62. CR, 10 May 1949, p. 6069.
63. Willard L. Thorp, OH HSTL.
64. Acheson, memo, 10 April 1951, Acheson Papers, HSTL.
65. PM to HST, 9 November 1950, EAP.
66. *The Reporter*, 13 September 1949.
67. PM to EA, 9 November 1949, EAP.
68. Preston, *Franco*, p. 592.
69. *Washington Times-Herald*, 26 August 1952.
70. *El Mundo Visto*, 29 September 1954.
71. Preston, *Franco*, p. 592.
72. PM to Margaret, 9 November 1949, PMP.
73. PM to Mary, 22 November 1949, PMP.
74. PM to EA, 26 October 1949, EAP
75. Hulme, *Wild Place*, p. 245.
76. Displaced Persons Commission, Second Semiannual Report to the President and the Congress, 1 August 1949, copy in PMP.
77. Hulme, *Wild Place*, p. 240.
78. PM to Mary, 22 November 1949, PMP.
79. WAP, 8 October 1949.
80. Bailey and Samuel, *Congress*, p. 257.
81. *Time*, 9 January 1950.
82. CR, 6 January 1950.
83. Dinnerstein, *Holocaust*, p. 234.
84. WAP, 15 February 1950.
85. WAP, 17 August 1949.
86. WAP, 17 April 1950.
87. Dinnerstein, *Holocaust*, p. 241.
88. Ibid.
89. WAP, 1 February 1950.

90. Dinnerstein, *Holocaust*, p. 243.
91. Allan Nevins, *Herbert H. Lehman and His Era* (New York: Scribner's, 1963), p. 317.
92. Dinnerstein, *Holocaust*, p. 244.
93. Bailey and Samuel, *Congress*, p. 261.
94. Ibid., p. 263.
95. Ibid.
96. Dinnerstein, *Holocaust*, p. 238.
97. Bailey and Samuel, *Congress*, p. 262.
98. Ibid., p. 264.
99. Ibid., p. 265.
100. CR, 5 April 1950, p. 4724.
101. Dinnerstein, *Holocaust*, p. 248.
102. NYT, 8 June 1950.
103. PM to Mary, 7 April 1950, PMP.
104. Hulme, *Wild Place*, p. 255.
105. Ibid., p. 257.
106. Dinnerstein, *Holocaust*, p. 251.
107. PP to PM, 16 January 1950, PPP.

Chapter 18: Chamber of Horrors

1. Alfred Steinberg, "McCarran, Lone Wolf of the Senate," *Harper's*, November 1950.
2. CR 96, 81st Congress, 2nd Session: 10 August 1950, p. 12,146.
3. Sourwine to EA, 9 August 1950, EAP.
4. Sourwine to EA, 10 August 1950, EAP.
5. Cedric Belfrage, *The American Inquisition, 1945–1960* (New York: Thunder's Mouth Press, 1989), p. 130.
6. Thomas C. Reeves, *The Life and Times of Joe McCarthy* (New York: Stein and Day, 1982), p. 221.
7. Richard L. Strout, *TRB: Views and Perspectives on the Presidency* (New York: Macmillan, 1979), p. 81.
8. Dean Acheson, *Present at the Creation: My Years in the State Department* (New York: Norton, 1969), p. 361.
9. PM to Mary, 17 August 1950, PMP.
10. Proceedings, 28–29 January 1950, Mundt Papers, Dakota State University, Madison, South Dakota.
11. For Mundt's biography, see Scott N. Heidepriem, *A Fair Chance for a Free People* (Madison, Wisc.: Karl Mundt Historical and Educational Foundation, 1988).
12. Richard M. Fried, *Men Against McCarthy* (New York: Columbia University Press, 1976), p. 48.
13. Mundt to Otto Kundert, 18 February 1950, Mundt Papers.
14. *U.S. News & World Report*, 23 June 1950.
15. Reeves, *McCarthy*, p. 224.
16. David Halberstam, *The Fifties* (New York: Villard, 1993), p. 51.
17. Edwin R. Bayley, *Joe McCarthy and the Press* (Madison, Wisc.: University of Wisconsin Press, 1981), p. 29.
18. Bayley, *McCarthy and the Press*, p. 68.

19. Joe F. McDonald Jr. to PM, 10 August 1950, EAP.

20. Biltz, UNOHP.

21. Angelina Angelides to PM, circa 1950, PMP.

22. PM to Arthur Sorensen, 22 July 1950, PMP.

23. PM to PP, 19 January 1950, PPP.

24. PM to Les Leggett, 3 April 1950, EAP.

25. Guernsey Frazer to PM, 1 March 1950, EAP.

26. CR, 7 September 1950, pp. 14,319–14,321.

27. Edward Schapsmeier and Frederick Schapsmeier, "Scott W. Lucas of Havana: His Rise and Fall as Majority Leader in the United States Senate," *Journal of the Illinois State Historical Society*, November 1977.

28. Mundt to Dirksen, 28 April 1950, Mundt Papers.

29. Mundt to Dirksen, 4 August 1950, Mundt Papers.

30. Owen Lattimore, *Ordeal by Slander* (Boston: Little, Brown, 1950), pp. 63–64.

31. Robert Newman, *Owen Lattimore and the ìLossî of China* (Berkeley, Calif.: University of California Press, 1992), pp. 217–218.

32. Lattimore, *Ordeal*, p. 65.

33. WAP, 22 May 1950.

34. PM to Gladys Dula, 9 August 1950, EAP.

35. PP to PM, 16 January 1950, PPP.

36. LVRJ, 23 April 1988.

37. PM to Franklin, 1946, EAP.

38. PP to PM, 1 August 1950, PPP.

39. Sourwine to EA, 18 July 1950, EAP.

40. PP to PM, 10 August 1950, PPP.

41. PM to Robert Douglass, 11 August 1950, EAP.

42. Warren Ashby, *Frank Porter Graham* (Winston-Salem, N.C.: John F. Blair, 1980), p. 81.

43. Ashby, *Graham*, p. 245.

44. Ibid., p. 258.

45. Ibid., p. 267.

46. PM to Smith, 29 July 1950, EAP.

47. SJS to HST, 16 May 1950, SJS Papers, HSTL.

48. SJS to HST, 9 January 1950, SJS Papers, HSTL.

49. SJS memo, 26 June 1950, SJS Papers, HSTL.

50. Copy in SJS Papers.

51. WAP, 24 June 1950.

52. SJS, OH, HSTL.

53. Margaret Truman, *Harry S. Truman* (New York: Morrow, 1973), p. 172.

54. Speech, PMP, in CR, 12 July 1950, p. 9992.

55. PM to Don Ashbaugh, 5 August 1950, EAP.

56. David M. Oshinsky, *A Conspiracy So Immense* (New York: Free Press, 1985), pp. 168–170.

57. Reeves, *McCarthy*, p. 307.

58. PM to Alan Bible, 21 July 1950, PMP.

59. Oshinsky, *Conspiracy*, p. 61.

60. The following account is taken from WAP, 19 July 1950.

61. SJS, memo, 22 July 1950, SJS Papers, HSTL.

62. Pearson, WAP, 7 August 1950.

63. LVRJ, clip, nd, EAP.

64. Radio transcript, 11 August 1950, EAP.

65. Joe F. McDonald Jr. to PM, 15 July 1950, EAP.

66. HST in CR, 8 August 1950, p. 12,020.

67. PM in CR, 8 August 1950, p. 11,966.

68. Mundt to Jack B. Tenney, 9 August 1950, Mundt Papers.

69. SJS, memo, 17 August 1950, SJS Papers.

70. Mundt to Bechtold, 11 August 1950, Mundt Papers.

71. Robert S. Allen and William Shannon, *The Truman Merry-Go-Round* (New York: Vanguard Press, 1950), p. 281.

72. Paul Douglas, *In the Fullness of Time: The Memoirs of Paul H. Douglas* (New York: Harcourt Brace Jovanovich, 1972), p. 14.

73. PM to Gladys Dula, 16 September 1950, EAP.

Chapter 19: The Enemy Within

1. CR, clip, nd, PMP.

2. Agnes Geelan, *The Dakota Maverick: The Political Life of William Langer* (Fargo, N.D.: Kaye's Printing, 1975), p. 2.

3. Richard L. Strout, *TRB: Views and Perspectives on the Presidency* (New York: Macmillan, 1979), p. 81.

4. CR, 5 September 1950, p. 14,170.

5. Ibid., p. 14,171.

6. Helen Gahagan Douglas, *A Full Life* (New York: Doubleday, 1982) pp. 304–305.

7. Sourwine to EA, 30 August 1950, EAP.

8. Bunker transcript, 30 August 1950, EAP.

9. Franklin transcript, 30 August 1950, EAP.

10. The following account is taken from SJS OH, HSTL.

11. Don Ashbaugh to PM, 10 August 1950, EAP.

12. *Boulder City News*, 31 August 1950.

13. *Reese River Reveille*, clip, nd, EAP.

14. PM to Frank Evans, 16 September 1950, EAP.

15. Allan Nevins, *Herbert H. Lehman and His Era* (New York: Scribner's, 1963), p. 323.

16. CR, 5 September 1950, p. 14,186.

17. Ibid., p. 14,190.

18. Ibid., p. 14,192.

19. Ibid., p. 14,194.

20. Ibid., pp. 14,195–14,196.

21. SJS to General Landry, 24 August 1950, SJS Papers.

22. Douglas, *Fullness*, p. 222.

23. *Harry Truman: Strictly Personal and Confidential*, edited by Monte M. Poen (Boston: Little, Brown, 1982), p. 121.

24. Allen and Shannon, *Merry-Go-Round*, p. 275.

25. Lloyd to SJS, 17 August 1950, SJS Papers.

26. SJS, memo, 6 September 1950, SJS Papers.

27. The following account is taken from CR, 6 September 1950, p. 14,236.

28. Ibid., pp. 14,247–14,249.

29. CR, 7 September 1950, p. 14,322.

30. HST press conference, excerpt, 7 September 1950, SJS papers.

31. The following account is taken from SJS to Elsey, 7 September 1950, SJS Papers.

32. CR, 8 September 1950, p. 14,401.

33. Ibid., p. 14,403.

34. Ibid., p. 14,405.

35. Ibid., p.14,413.

36. Ibid., p.14,420.

37. Ibid., p.14,424.

38. Ibid., p.14,439.

39. Ibid., p.14,439.

40. Ibid., p.14,441.

41. Charles J. Hendley to Mundt and Kilgore, 5 September 1950, Mundt Papers.

42. CR, 11 September 1950, p. 14,489.

43. Ibid., p. 14,548.

44. CR, 12 September 1950, p. 14,577.

45. Ibid., p. 14,594.

46. Ibid., p. 14,598.

47. Ibid., p. 14,627.

48. Mundt to George Robnett, 15 September 1950, Mundt Papers.

49. Robert Griffith and Athan Theoharis, *The Specter* (New York: New Viewpoints, 1974), p. 186.

50. PM press release, 13 September 1950, PMP.

51. SJS, memo, 25 September 1950, SJS Papers.

52. SJS, memo, 20 September 1950, SJS Papers.

53. Ferrell, Robert S. *Harry S. Truman* (Columbia, Mo.: University of Missouri Press, 1994), p. 304

54. HST, SJS Papers.

55. David Lloyd to SJS, 3 July 1950, SJS Papers.

56. Veto message, Francis H. Thompson, *The Frustration of Politics* (Cranberry, NJ: Associated University Presses, 1979), p. 277.

57. Douglas, *Fullness*, p. 219.

58. Edward Schapsmeier and Frederick Schapsmeier, "Scott W. Lucas of Havana: His Rise and Fall as Majority Leader in the United States Senate," *Journal of the Illinois State Historical Society*, November 1977.

59. *Washington Times-Herald*, 3 September 1950.

60. CR, 22 September 1950, p. 15,520.

61. Ibid., p. 15,522.

62. CR, 23 September 1950, p. 15,647.

63. Geelan, *Maverick*, p. 2; also see John M. Holzworth, *The Fighting Governor* (Chicago: Pointer Press, 1938), and Glenn H. Smith, *Langer of North Dakota* (New York: Garland Publishing, 1979).

64. Douglas, *Fullness*, p. 178.

65. CR, 23 September 1950, p. 15,648.

66. Ibid., p. 15,654.

67. Ibid., p. 15,667.

68. Ibid., p. 15,679.

69. Ibid., p. 15,714.

70. Ibid., p. 15,724.

71. Margaret Truman, *Harry S. Truman* (New York: Morrow, 1973), p. 474.

72. Schapsmeier and Schapsmeier, "Lucas."
73. Murphy OH, HSTL.
74. PM to Frank Evans, 16 September 1950, PMP.

Chapter 20: Burnt Offerings

1. SISS/IPR hearings, 82nd Congress, 1st and 2nd Sessions, p. 5480.
2. WAP, 22 May 1950.
3. O. Edmund Clubb, *The Witness and I* (New York: Columbia University Press, 1974), p. 29.
4. Biltz, UNOHP.
5. *Washington Times-Herald*, 25 January 1951.
6. Robert P. Newman, *Owen Lattimore and the ¡Loss¡ of China* (Berkeley, Calif.: University of California Press, 1992), p. 346.
7. Jenner to Herbert Hoover, 26 September 1951, Hoover Papers, HHL.
8. Robert Morris, *No Wonder We Are Losing* (New York: The Bookmailer, 1958), p. 117.
9. Whittaker Chambers, *Witness* (New York: Random House, 1952), p. 207.
10. Mandel to Arens, 25 April 1951, SISS Papers, NARA.
11. Newman, *Lattimore*, p. 317.
12. Gary May, *China Scapegoat: The Diplomatic Ordeal of John Carter Vincent* (Prospect Heights, Ill.: Waveland Press, 1979), p. 61.
13. Theodore H. White, *In Search of History: A Personal Adventure* (New York: Harper & Row, 1978), p. 116.
14. John S. Service, *Lost Chance in China: The World War II Despatches of John S. Service*, edited by Joseph W. Esherick (New York: Random House, 1974), p. 91
15. Barbara W. Tuchman, *Stilwell and the American Experience in China, 1911–45* (New York: Grove, 1985), p. 320.
16. May, *Scapegoat*, p. 67.
17. Service, *Lost*, p. 128.
18. Ibid., p. 169.
19. Francis H. Thompson, *The Frustration of Politics* (Rutherford, N.J.: Associated University Presses, 1979), p. 169.
20. HST to Murphy, 24 May 1951, Murphy Papers, HSTL.
21. Murphy to HST, 15 November 1950, Murphy Papers.
22. Hoover to HST, 26 November 1950, HST Papers.
23. *Washington Star*, 26 January 1951.
24. HST remarks, 12 February 1951, HST Papers.
25. Newman, *Lattimore*, p. 57.
26. John King Fairbank, *Chinabound* (New York: Harper & Row, 1982), p. 323.
27. Len De Caux, *Labor Radical: From the Wobblies to CIO* (Boston: Beacon Press, 1970), p. 245.
28. Owen Lattimore, *China Memoirs*, compiled by Fujiko Isono (Tokyo: University of Tokyo Press, 1990), p. 40.
29. Freda Utley, *Odyssey of a Liberal* (Washington, D.C.: Washington National Press, 1970), p. 133–134.
30. Newman, *Lattimore*, p. 40.
31. Ibid., p. 59.
32. Ibid., p. 89.
33. Lattimore, *Memoirs*, p. 135.

34. Owen Lattimore, *The Desert Road to Turkestan* (New York: Kodansha, 1995), p. 33.
35. David M. Oshinsky, *A Conspiracy So Immense* (New York: Free Press, 1985), p. 258.
36. Hoover to Tolson, 25 November 1952, FBI 62-88217-854.
37. Nichols to Tolson, 30 March, 1951, FBI 62-88217-854.
38. Ibid.
39. Athan G. Theoharis and John Stuart Cox, *The Boss: J. Edgar Hoover and the Great American Inquisition* (New York: Bantam, 1990), p. 307.
40. Nichols to Tolson, 22 March 1951, FBI 62-88217-854.
41. May, *Scapegoat*, p. 109.
42. Tuchman, *Stilwell*, p. 334.
43. May, *Scapegoat*, p. 85.
44. Tuchman, *Stilwell*, p. 333.
45. Sterling Seargrave, *The Soong Dynasty* (New York: Harper & Row, 1985), p. 388.
46. Theodore H. White and Annalee Jacoby, *Thunder Out of China* (New York: Da Capo, 1980), pp. 18–19.
47. John Paton Davies Jr., *Dragon by the Tail: American, British, Japanese, and Russian Encounters with China and One Another* (New York: Norton, 1972), p. 266.
48. Tuchman, *Stilwell*, p. 360.
49. Davies, *Dragon*, p. 299.
50. Tuchman, *Stilwell*, p. 369.
51. Dean Acheson, *Present at the Creation: My Years in the State Department* (New York: Norton, 1969), p. 523.
52. PM to Vern Adams, 2 September 1950, PMP.
53. Acheson, memo, 10 April 1951, Acheson Papers, HSTL.
54. Acheson, *Present*, p. 523.
55. Robert A. Caro, *The Years of Lyndon Johnson: Master of the Senate* (New York: Knopf, 2002), p. 370.
56. CR, 4 May 1951, p. 4982.
57. Thomas C. Reeves, *The Life and Times of Joe McCarthy* (New York: Stein and Day, 1982), p. 370.
58. Newman, *Lattimore*, p. 126.
59. WAP, 2 May 1951.
60. Nimitz to HST, 8 May 1951, Truman Papers, HSTL.
61. HST to PM, 12 May 1951, PMP.
62. PM to HST, 26 May 1951, PMP.
63. WAP, 24 June 1951.
64. HST to Nimitz, 16 July 1951, Truman Papers, HSTL.
65. John C. Culver and John Hyde, *American Dreamer: A Life of Henry A. Wallace* (New York: Norton, 2000), p. 337.
66. Culver and Hyde, *Dreamer*, p. 337.
67. Newman, *Lattimore*, p. 117.
68. May, *Scapegoat*, p. 75.
69. Ibid., p. 104.
70. Culver and Hyde, *Dreamer*, p. 337.
71. Tuchman, *Stilwell*, p. 494.
72. John J. Abt (with Michael Myerson), *Advocate and Activist: Memoirs of an American Communist Lawyer* (Urbana, Ill.: University of Illinois Press, 1993), p. 194.

73. Abt, *Advocate*, p. 238.

74. Ibid., p. 184.

75. Ibid., p. 197.

76. Garlin, *Red Tape and Barbed Wire* (New York: The Civil Rights Congress, 1952).

77. Abt, *Advocate*, p. 195.

78. Alan Barth, "McCarran's Monopoly," *The Reporter*, 21 August 1951.

79. WAP, 5 June 1951.

80. Time, 18 June 1951.

81. Don Connors to PM, 18 September 1952, SISS Papers, NARA.

82. Abt, *Advocate*, p. 187.

83. Edgar Snow, *Journey to the Beginning* (New York: Random House, 1958), 155.

84. Service, *Lost*, p. 179

85. E. J. Kahn Jr., *The China Hands: America's Foreign Service Officers and What Befell Them* (New York: Viking, 1975), p. 82.

86. Service, *Lost*, p. 140.

87. White and Jacoby, *Thunder*, p. 226.

88. Service, *Lost*, p. 312.

89. Davies, *Dragon*, p. 349.

90. Tuchman, *Stilwell*, p. 477.

91. Davies, *Dragon*, p. 322.

92. Ibid., p. 371.

93. Ibid., p. 362.

94. Service, *Lost*, p. 163–164.

95. White and Jacoby, *Thunder*, p. 182.

96. David D. Barrett, *Dixie Mission*, Chine Research Monograph (Berkeley, Calif.: University of California, 1970), p. 46.

97. Robert W. Merry, *Taking on the World: Joseph and Stewart Alsop ó Guardians of the American Century* (New York: Penguin, 1997), p. 10.

98. Merry, *Taking*, p. 209.

99. WAP, 25 July 1951.

100. Alsop to Luce, 8 September 1951, Alsop Papers, LOC.

101. George F. Kennan, *Memoirs, 1950–1963* (New York: Pantheon, 1972), p. 218.

102. WAP, 25 July 1951.

103. White and Jacoby, *Thunder*, p. 205.

104. Davies, *Dragon*, p. 381.

105. Ibid., p. 422.

106. Kahn, *China Hands*, p. 147.

107. Service, *Lost*, p. 363.

108. May, *Scapegoat*, p. 125.

109. Kahn, *China Hands*, p. 152.

110. Davies, *Dragon*, p. 418.

111. Kahn, *China Hands*, p. 211.

Chapter 21: Names, Names

1. John Paton Davies Jr., *Dragon by the Tail: American, British, Japanese, and Russian Encounters with China and One Another* (New York: Norton, 1972), p. 54.

2. Owen Lattimore, *The Desert Road to Turkestan* (New York: Kodansha, 1995), p. 117.

3. Edgar Snow, *Journey to the Beginning* (New York: Random House, 1958), p. 166.

4. David M. Oshinsky, *A Conspiracy So Immense* (New York: Free Press, 1985), p. 208.

5. SISS/IPR hearings, p. 4.

6. Ibid., p. 3.

7. Robert Morris, *No Wonder We Are Losing* (New York: The Bookmailer, 1958), p. 118.

8. Robert P. Newman, *Owen Lattimore and the "Loss" of China* (Berkeley, Calif.: University of California Press, 1992), p. 324.

9. Louis Francis Budenz, *This Is My Story* (New York: Whittlesey House, 1947), p. 163.

10. Budenz, *Story*, p. 314.

11. Newman, *Lattimore*, p. 266.

12. Budenz, *Story*, p. 262.

13. Ibid., p. 238.

14. Ibid., p. x.

15. Ibid., p. 347.

16. SISS/IPR hearings, p. 63.

17. Ibid., p. 40.

18. Ibid., p. 59.

19. Ibid., p. 18.

20. Frederick Vanderbilt Field, *From Right to Left* (Westport, Conn.: L. Hill, 1983), p. 172.

21. Field, *From Right*, p. 169.

22. Ibid., p. 246.

23. Ibid., p. 233.

24. Ibid., p. 238.

25. Newman, *Lattimore*, p. 331.

26. George F. Kennan, *Memoirs, 1950–1963* (New York: Pantheon, 1972), pp. 205–206.

27. Kennan, *Memoirs*, p. 208.

28. SISS/IPR hearings, p. 5448.

29. Ibid., p. 5444.

30. Ibid., pp. 5463–5464.

31. *New Haven Register*, 16 October 1951.

32. Elizabeth Bentley, *Out of Bondage* (New York: Ivy Books, 1988), afterword by Hayden B. Peake, p. 234.

33. Elizabeth Bentley, *Out of Bondage* (New York: Devin-Adair, 1951), p. 194.

34. SISS/IPR hearings, p. 412.

35. O. Edmund Clubb, *The Witness and I* (New York: Columbia University Press, 1974), p. 137.

36. SISS/IPR hearings, p. 496.

37. Clubb, *Witness*, p. 110.

38. Ibid., pp. 219–221.

39. HST, speech 14 August 1951, PPF 200, HST Papers, HSTL.

40. Thomas C. Reeves, *The Life and Times of Joe McCarthy* (New York: Stein and Day, 1982), p. 372.

41. *Washington Star*, 8 August 1951.

42. *Washington Times-Herald*, 10 May 1951.

43. *Washington Star*, 26 July 1951.

44. *The Reporter*, 21 August 1951.

45. Herbert Block, *The Herblock Book* (Boston: Beacon Press, 1952), p. 25.

46. Robert Allen column, LVS, 25 June 1952.

47. WAP, 15 August 1951.

48. SISS/IPR hearings, p. 552.

49. Ibid., p. 516.

50. Ibid., p. 521.

51. Ibid., p. 552.

52. Ibid., pp. 624–625.

53. Ibid., pp. 678–679.

54. Newman, *Lattimore*, p. 339.

55. Ibid.

56. Alsop to Harry Luce, 8 September 1951, Alsop Papers, LOC.

57. WAP, 26 September 1951.

58. Alsop to Wedemeyer, 23 September 1951, Alsop Papers, LOC.

59. Kohlberg to PM, 24 August 1951, PMP.

60. E. J. Kahn Jr., *The China Hands* (New York: Viking, 1975), p. 50.

61. Kohlberg to PM, 3/25/49, Kohlberg Papers, Hoover Institution, SU.

62. Reeves, *McCarthy*, p. 273.

63. Kohlberg to PM, 24 August 1951, PMP.

64. WAP, 15 September 1951.

65. WAP, 25 September 1951.

66. John C. Culver and John Hyde, *American Dreamer: A Life of Henry A. Wallace* (New York: Norton, 2000), p. 513.

67. PM to Joe McDonald, 19 August 1933, PMP.

68. Culver and Hyde, *Dreamer*, p. 516.

69. Alsop to Ben Hibbs, 10 October 1951, Alsop Papers, LOC.

70. SISS/IPR hearings, p. 1081.

71. George Ball, *The Present Has Another Pattern* (New York: Norton, 1982), p. 108.

72. Newman, *Lattimore*, p. 347.

73. SISS/IPR hearings, p. 1329.

74. Ibid., p. 1368.

75. Alsop to Hibbs, 10 October 1951, Alsop Papers, LOC.

76. Ball, *Present*, p. 109.

77. SISS/IPR hearings, p. 1406.

78. Robert W. Merry, *Taking On the World* (New York: Penguin, 1997), p. 214.

79. Alsop to Hibbs, 10 October 1951, Alsop Papers, LOC.

80. SISS/IPR hearings, p. 1405.

81. Ibid., p. 1455.

82. Ibid., p. 1436.

83. Merry, *Taking On*, p. 210.

84. SISS/IPR hearings, p. 1454.

85. Ibid., p. 1436.

86. Alsop, letter, circa 1959, in J. Edgar Hoover, Official & Confidential file, #26, FBI.

87. Merry, *Taking On*, p. 217.

88. SISS/IPR hearings, pp. 1488–1489.

89. Newman, *Lattimore*, p. 351.

90. PM to Birdie, 14 December 1951, PMP.

91. SISS/IPR hearings, p. 1688.
92. Ibid., p. 1689.
93. Ibid., p. 1705.
94. Ibid., p. 1750.
95. Ibid., p. 1754.
96. Ibid., p. 1910.
97. Ibid., p. 1934.
98. Ibid., p. 2021.
99. Gary May, *China Scapegoat: The Diplomatic Ordeal of John Carter Vincent* (Prospect Heights, Ill.: Waveland Press, 1979), p. 224.
100. Ibid.
101. Ibid., p. 228.
102. Ibid., p. 224.
103. Ibid., p. 230.
104. SISS/IPR hearings, pp. 2897–2905.
105. Ibid., p. 2898.
106. WAP, 27 February 1952.
107. WAP, 27 February 1952.
108. NYT, 27 February 1952.
109. NYT, 29 February 1952.
110. Newman, *Lattimore*, p. 380.
111. WAP, 5 March 1952.
112. Thurman Arnold, *Fair Fights and Foul* (New York: Harcourt, Brace & World, 1965), p. 216.
113. SISS/IPR hearings, pp. 3674–3679.
114. May, *Scapegoat*, p. 231.
115. Robert Allen column, LVS, 22 April 1952.
116. HST, *The Letters Harry Truman Never Mailed*, edited by Monte M. Poen (Boston: Little, Brown, 1982), p. 75.
117. *ADA World*, July 1952.
118. *Washington Star*, 4 April 1952.
119. Judiciary Committee hearing, 6 May 1952, excerpt, PMP.
120. Harvey Matusow, *False Witness* (New York: Cameron & Kahn, 1955), p. 107.
121. Robert Allen column, LVS, 10 April 1952.
122. Morison, OH, p. 203, HSTL.
123. *New York Post*, clip, nd, Kohlberg Papers, SU.
124. NYT, 3 July 1952.
125. SISS/IPR Report, p. 197.
126. SISS/IPR Report, pp. 223–225.
127. NYT, 3 July 1952.
128. Hoover to PM, 14 July 1952, FBI 100-64700-1094.
129. May, *Scapegoat*, p. 236.
130. Kristol, "Ordeal by Mendacity," *The Twentieth Century*, October 1952.
131. TNR, 14 July 1952.
132. Schlesinger to Porter, 4 February 1953, Schlesinger Papers, LOC.
133. HST to McGranery, 5 July 1952, cited in Newman, *Lattimore*, p. 398.

Chapter 22: Day of the McCarrans

1. Testimony before the House Un-American Activities Committee on 28 August

1950, The Alger Hiss Story Web site, homepages.nyu.edu/~th15/home.html.

2. Matusow transcript, p. 38, SISS Papers, NARA.

3. Arthur V. Watkins, *Enough Rope* (Engelwood Cliff, N.J.: Prentice Hall, 1969), p. 14.

4. *Salt Lake City Tribune*, 6 October 1952.

5. SISS/Mine-Mill, p. 3.

6. Eckert, open letter, 4/20/47, WFM Papers.

7. Notes on Eckert, April 13, 1951, WFM Papers.

8. Eckert Report, July 23, 1947, WFM Papers.

9. Vernon H. Jensen, *Nonferrous Metals Industry Unionism, 1932–1954* (Ithaca, N.Y.: Cornell University Press, 1954), p. 223.

10. Eckert, testimony before the CIO investigating committee, January–February 1950, p. 9, copy, WFM Papers.

11. Ibid., p. 1.

12. Why the CIO Expelled Mine Mill: Excerpts from the Report, WFM Papers.

13. Harvey Matusow, *False Witness* (New York: Cameron & Kahn, 1955), p. 146.

14. Matusow, *False*, p. 77.

15. Connors to Arens, 7 April 1952, SISS Papers, NARA.

16. Connors to Sourwine, 20 August 1952, EAP.

17. *The Union*, 22 September 1952.

18. Ibid., 25 August 1952.

19. Ibid., 22 September 1952.

20. Matusow transcript, SISS Papers.

21. FBI Bentley file, 134-435-66.

22. Ladd to Belmont, 26 September 1952, FBI Bentley file, 134-435-67.

23. Memo, Silvermaster file, 65-14603-4417.

24. Matthews interview, 23 February 1955, Bentley file, FBI 134-435.

25. Tompkins to Hoover, 9 March 1955, FBI 134-435. Also see Kathryn. S. Olmsted, *Red Spy Queen* (Chapel Hill, N.C.: University of North Carolina Press, 2002).

26. SISS/Mine-Mill hearings, pp. iii–iv.

27. SISS/Mine-Mill, p. 45.

28. Connors to Arens, 24 March 1952, SISS Papers, NARA.

29. *The Union*, 15 August 1949.

30. SISS/Mine-Mill, p. 80.

31. John J. Abt (with Michael Myerson), *Advocate and Activist: Memoirs of an American Communist Lawyer* (Urbana, Ill.: University of Illinois Press, 1993), p. 173.

32. Abt, *Advocate*, p. 173.

33. Gilbert J. Gall, *Pursuing Justice: Lee Pressman, the New Deal, and the CIO* (Albany, N.Y.: SUNY Press, 1999), p. 283.

34. SISS/Mine-Mill, pp. 114–120.

35. Connors, memo, 18 September 1952, SISS Papers, NARA.

36. Griffin Fariello, *Red Scare* (New York: Norton, 1995), pp. 381–382.

37. Fariello, *Red*, p. 383.

38. Ibid., p. 382.

39. James J. Lorence, *The Suppression of Salt of the Earth* (Alburquerque, N.M.: University of New Mexico Press, 1999), p. 58.

40. SISS/Mine-Mill, p. 169.

41. Ibid., p. 170.

42. Ibid., p. 172.
43. Matusow transcript, p. 44, SISS Papers, NARA.
44. Matusow transcript, p. 45.
45. Matusow, *False*, pp. 160–161.
46. SISS/Mine-Mill, pp. iii–iv.
47. *Salt Lake City Tribune*, 9 October 1952.
48. Holmgren to John Clark, 27 October 1952, WFM Papers.
49. Ibid.
50. Alton Lawrence, memo, 2 December 1952, WFM Papers.
51. Lorence, *Supression*, p. 77.
52. Ibid., p. 104.
53. Ellen Schrecker, *Many Are the Crimes* (Boston: Little, Brown, 1998), p. 333 (proof).
54. Herbert J. Biberman, *Salt of the Earth* (Boston: Beacon Press, 1965), p. 86.
55. Biberman, *Salt*, p. 91.
56. Fariello, *Red*, p. 282.
57. Connors to EA, 9 August 1951, SISS Papers, NARA.
58. Morris to Sourwine, 13 November 1951, SISS Papers.
59. Ibid.
60. Sourwine to EA, 8 July 1952, SISS Papers, NARA.
61. Robert Morris, *No Wonder We Are Losing* (New York: The Bookmailer, 1958), p. 145.
62. See Fariello, *Red*.

Chapter 23: Keep Out

1. *Brazil Herald*, 27 November 1952.
2. Herb Block, WAP, 8 June 1952.
3. WAP, 18 November 1952.
4. The following account is taken from NYT, 25 October, 1950.
5. Ellen Knauff, *The Ellen Knauff Story* (New York: Norton, 1952), pp. 162–163.
6. Knauff, *Story*, p. 93.
7. Ibid., p. 94.
8. Ibid., p. 151.
9. Ibid.
10. Statement by the Immigration and Naturalization Subcommittee, re: HR 7614 and S. 2979, EAP.
11. Ibid.
12. HST to SJS, 17 June 1950, SJS Papers, HSTL.
13. SJS to Peyton Ford, 25 September 1950, SJS Papers.
14. NYT, 9 October 1950.
15. Knauff, *Story*, p. 165.
16. NYT, 23 November 1950.
17. Lloyd to Charles Murphy, 25 January 1951, Murphy Papers, HSTL.
18. WAP, 12 October 1950.
19. Knauff, *Story*, p. 176.
20. The Decision of the Board of Immigration Appeals, p. 17, cited in Knauff, *Story*, appendix.
21. WAP, 8 March 1951.
22. Dean Acheson, *Present at the Creation: My Years in the State Department* (New York: Norton, 1969), p. 16.

23. Robert S. Allen and William V. Shannon, *The Truman Merry-Go-Round* (New York: Vanguard Press, 1950), p. 412.

24. Stanley I. Kutler, *The American Inquisition* (New York: Hill and Wang, 1982), p. 93.

25. Wechsler to Adrian S. Fisher, 28 June 1951, Wechsler Papers, WSHS.

26. HST, *Strictly Personal* (Boston: Little, Brown, 1982), p. 83.

27. HST, *Personal*, p. 83.

28. Ibid.

29. Helen Worden Erskine, "You Don't Go, If She Says No," *Collier's*, 11 July 1953.

30. Erskine, "You Don't Go."

31. WAP, 14 June 1952.

32. *Washington Times-Herald*, 14 June 1952.

33. Erskine, "You Don't Go."

34. CR, 13 May 1952, p. 5089.

35. Biltz, UNOHP, p. 169.

36. Acheson, memo, 20 June 1952, Acheson Papers, HSTL.

37. Acheson, memo, 18 July 1952, Acheson Papers.

38. Lloyd to HST, 3 May 1952, Lloyd Files, HST Papers, HSTL.

39. Rosenfield to HST, 12 June 1952, Lloyd Files.

40. Pearson, WAP, 23 March 1952.3/23/52.

41. Lloyd to HST, 3 May 1952, Lloyd Files, HST Papers, HSTL.

42. CR, 13 May 1952, p. 5093.

43. Ibid., p. 5100.

44. Ibid., p. 5102.

45. Joseph Dalton, "The Legend of Hank Greenspun," *Harper's*, June 1982.

46. WAP, 20 May 1952.

47. HST to John O'Grady, 28 May 1952, Official File, HSTL.

48. Rosenfield OH, HSTL.

49. NYT, 26 June 1952.

50. Ibid.

51. HST to Lowenthal, 8 July 1952, Lowenthal Papers, HSTL.

52. Lloyd to HST, 3 May 1952, Lloyd Files, Truman Papers, HSTL.

53. Lloyd to HST, 7 August 1952.

54. Sourwine to PM, 20 October 1950, EAP.

55. Rosenfield, OH.

56. REG, 11 October 1952.

57. Newspaper clip, nd, PMP.

58. Sourwine memo, nd, EAP.

59. REG, 5 January 1953.

60. REG, 5 January 1953.

61. Alfred Steinberg, *Sam Johnson's Boy* (New York: MacMillan, 1968), p. 412.

62. Murray to PM, 17 September 1952 and 12 December 1952, McGranery Papers, LOC.

63. Trygve Lie, *In the Cause of Peace* (New York: MacMillan, 1954), p. 115.

64. Lie, *Peace*, p. 120.

65. *Salt Lake City Tribune*, 9 October 1952.

66. Sourwine to PM, 2 November 1948, EAP.

67. *New York Journal American*, 23 January 1951.

68. *Washington Times-Herald*, 23 May 1952.

69. Lie, *Peace*, p. 388.

70. Ibid., p. 389.

71. Ibid., 390.

72. Nichols to Tolson, 27 January 1954, Cohn file, FBI 62-97564.

73. Nicholas von Hoffman, *Citizen Cohn* (New York: Doubleday, 1988), p. 122.

74. Harvey Matusow, *False Witness* (New York: Cameron & Kahn, 1955), p. 107.

75. Laughlin to Belmont, 5 September 1952, Cohn file.

76. Belmont to Ladd, 29 August 1952, Cohn file.

77. Ibid.

78. Cohn to McGranery, 20 November 1952, McGranery Papers, LOC.

79. Robert P. Newman, *Owen Lattimore and the ìLossî of China* (Berkeley, Calif.: University of California Press, 1992), p. 403.

80. Laughlin to Belmont, 5 September 1952, Cohn file.

81. Newman, *Lattimore*, p. 407.

82. Name redacted (but obviously Edward Hummer) to William Tompkins, 23 December 1954, Cohn file.

83. Ibid.

84. Newman, *Lattimore*, p. 408.

85. Charles Murray to McGranery, 26 September 1952, McGranery Papers, LOC.

86. Sourwine to EA, 18 November 1952, EAP.

87. Morris to EA, 19 November 1952, EAP.

88. Smith, *Nevada Appeal*, 12 November 1952.

89. SISS/UN hearings, p. 140.

90. Ibid., p. 15.

91. Lie, *Peace*, p. 395.

92. *New York Post*, 13 November 1952.

93. Name redacted (but obviously Edward Hummer) to William Tompkins, 23. December 1954, Cohn file.

94. SISS/UN hearings, p. 409.

95. Von Hoffman, *Cohn*, p. 122.

96. Hoover, memo, 24 November 1952, Cohn file.

97. Sourwine to EA, 18 November 1952, EAP.

98. Lie, *Peace*, p. 401.

99. LVRJ, 13 January 1953.

100. Newman, *Lattimore*, p. 418.

101. Ibid., p. 419.

102. Ibid., p. 20.

103. Von Hoffman, *Cohn*, p. 117.

104. *Washington Star*, 14 November 1952.

105. Lie, *Peace*, p. 399.

106. Von Hoffman, *Cohn*, p. 119.

107. LVRJ, 9 December 1933.

108. PM to Birdie, 2 October 1952, PMP.

109. McNamara, memo, nd, Pearson Papers, LBJL.

110. Ibid.

111. Ibid.

112. CR, 24 June 1949, p. 8328.

113. McNamara, memo, nd, Pearson Papers, LBJL.

114. Morison, OH, HSTL, p. 203.

115. Ibid., 190.
116. *The Union*, 22 September 1952.
117. PM to Birdie, 20 October 1952, PMP.
118. *Humboldt Star*, 13 November 1952.

Chapter 24: The Dead

1. Wilbur S. Shepperson, *Mirage-Land: Images of Nevada* (Reno, Nev.: University of Nevada Press, 1992), p. 10.
2. Drew Pearson, *Diaries, 1949–1959*, edited by Tyler Abell (New York: Holt, Rinehart and Winston, 1974), p. 199.
3. Mechling, "I Battled McCarran's Machine," *The Reporter*, 9 June 1953.
4. Ralph Denton to EA, 25 February 1952, EAP.
5. Jack Sheehan (editor), *The Players* (Reno, Nev.: University of Nevada Press, 1997), p. 46.
6. Sheehan, *Players*, p. 46.
7. Dalitz file, FBI 92-30368.
8. Hank Greenspun, *Where I Stand* (New York: McKay, 1966), p. 200.
9. Sheehan, *Players*, p. 44.
10. Greenspun, *Stand*, p. 200. See also Las Vegas Strip History Web site, www.lvst-riphistory.com/.
11. Sam McCarran to PM, 8 November 1951, PMP.
12. PM to PP, 23 June 1951, PPP.
13. Katharine Best and Katharine Hillyer, *Las Vegas: Playtown U.S.A.* (New York: D. McKay Co., 1955), p. 166.
14. Best and Hillyer, *Vegas*, p. 92.
15. PM to PP, 11 June 1947, PPP.
16. PM to Joe McDonald, 3 July 1951, PMP.
17. Transcript, Siegel file, FBI 62-81518.
18. Sheehan, *Players*, p. 87.
19. Transcript, Siegel file.
20. Robert Lacey, *Little Man* (Boston: Little, Brown, 1991), p. 34.
21. Lacey, *Little Man*, p. 155.
22. Hoover, memo, 7 August 1946, Siegel file.
23. W. R. Wilkerson III, *The Man Who Invented Las Vegas* (Beverly Hills, Calif.: Ciro's Books, 2000), p. 76.
24. Rosen to Tamm, 13 August 1946, Siegel file.
25. (Blacked out) to Rosen, 26 August 1946, Siegel file.
26. Rosen to Tamm, 1 August 1946, Siegel file.
27. Hoover, 7 August 1946, Siegel file.
28. Transcript, Siegel file.
29. Memo, 12 August 1946, Siegel file.
30. Siegel file.
31. Memo, 9 January 1947, Siegel file.
32. Sheehan, *Players*, p. 87.
33. Tamm to Hoover, 16 January 1947, Siegel file.
34. Cartha D. DeLoach, *Hoover's FBI* (Washington, D.C.: Regnery, 1995), p. 303.
35. Siegel file, FBI 62-81518.
36. PM deposition, EAP.
37. Joseph Dalton, "The Legend of Hank Greenspun," *Harper's*, June 1982.

38. Frazer to PM, 14 July 1950, EAP.
39. Dalton, "Greenspun."
40. PM to Joe McDonald, 3 July 1951, PMP.
41. Kefauver Committee Report on Organized Crime (New York: Didier, 1951), p. 75.
42. Joseph Bruce Gorman, *Kefauver* (New York: Oxford University Press, 1971), p. 48.
43. David McCullough, *Truman* (New York: Simon & Schuster, 1992), p. 864.
44. Kefauver Committee Report on Organized Crime (New York: Didier, 1951), p. 74.
45. PM to PP, 23 June 1951, PPP.
46. NSJ, 21 August 1951.
47. PM to McDonald, 3 July 1951, PMP.
48. Background memo, nd, Pearson Papers, LBJL.
49. Ibid.
50. LVS, 19 February 1952.
51. Ibid.
52. LVS, 18 March 1952.
53. LVS, 20 May 1952.
54. LVS, 26 March 1952.
55. LVS, 27 March 1952.
56. LVS, 21 May 1952
57. Robert Allen to Pearson, 28 March 1952, Pearson Papers, LBJL.
58. Pearson, *Diaries*, p. 74.
59. Column copy, nd, Pearson Papers.
60. Foley to PM, 5 March 1945, EAP.
61. Jerome Edwards, *Pat McCarran: Political Boss of Nevada* (Reno, Nev.: University of Nevada Press, 1982), p. 160. See also LVS, 23 May 1952.
62. WAP, 12 September 1952.
63. HST to McGranery, 12 July 1952, McGranery Papers, LOC.
64. The following account is taken from LVS, 25–26 July 1952.
65. Edwards, *McCarran*, p. 171.
66. LVS, 28 July 1952.
67. LVS, 27–28 August 1952.
68. LVS, 25 August 1952.
69. Edwards, *McCarran*, p. 171.
70. WAP, 5 September 1952.
71. LVS, 27 August 1952.
72. LVS, 26 August 1952.
73. Edwards, *McCarran*, p. 172.
74. LVS, 28 August 1952.
75. LVS, 29 August 1952.
76. Gary Elliott, *Senator Alan Bible and the Politics of the New West* (Reno, Nev.: University of Nevada Press, 1994), p. 33.
77. LVS, 16 September 1952.
78. LVS, 17 September 1952.
79. PM to Birdy, 23 September 1952, PMP.
80. Denton, UNOHP, p. 82.
81. Ibid., p. 101.

82. Ibid.

83. Greenspun, *Stand*, pp. 211–213.

84. NSJ, 15 October 1952.

85. LVS, 14 October 1952.

86. NSJ, 15 October 1952.

87. LVS, 14 October 1952.

88. Ibid.

89. Greenspun, *Stand*, p. 221.

90. LVS, 14 October 1952.

91. Dalton, "Greenspun."

92. Mechling, "Battled."

93. PM to Birdie, 20 October 1952, PMP.

94. PM to Margaret, 23 October 1952, PMP.

95. Biltz, UNOHP.

96. *Reese River Revelle*, 1 November 1952.

97. LVS, 25 October 1952.

98. LVS, 27 October 1952.

99. Excerpts, EAP.

100. Denton, UNOHP, p. 379.

101. PM to Birdie, 25 and 28 October 1952, PMP.

102. LVS, 28 October 1952

103. Ibid.

104. Matusow, transcript, p. 39, SISS Papers, NARA.

105. Connors to PM, 18 July 1952, EAP.

106. Connors to PM, 30 July 1952, EAP.

107. LVS clip, nd, circa 1955, EAP.

108. PM to Birdie, 23 September 1952, PMP.

109. PM to Birdie, 20 October 1952.

110. PM to Birdie, 25 October 1952.

111. PM to Birdie, 4 November 1952.

112. PM to Birdie, 20 October 1952.

113. Matusow transcript, SISS Papers, NARA.

114. PM to Birdie, 4 November 1952, PMP.

115. LVS, 3 November 1952.

116. PM to Birdie, 2 October 1952, PMP.

117. LVS, 30 October 1952.

118. Judges 16.

119. PM, deposition, EAP.

120. Joe McDonnell to EA, 20 October 1952, EAP.

121. EA to PM, 30 November 1952, EAP.

122. PM to PP, 29 July 1954, PPP.

123. LBJ to PM, 6 August 1942, LBJ Senate Papers, LBJL.

124. Memoirs file, HST Papers, HSTL.

125. HST, *Memoirs, Volume 2: Years of Trial and Hope* (New York: Doubleday, 1956), p. 287.

126. NYT, 28 December 1952.

127. Sourwine to PM, 18 November 1954, EAP.

128. David M. Oshinsky, *A Conspiracy So Immense* (New York: Free Press, 1985), p. 251.

129. HST, *Dear Bess: The Letters of Harry to Bess Truman, 1910–1959*, edited by Robert H. Ferrell (New York: Norton, 1983), p. 526.

130. Robert A. Caro, *The Years of Lyndon Johnson: Master of the Senate* (New York: Knopf, 2002), p. 501.

131. Edwards, *McCarran*, p. 166.

Chapter 25: Caught in the McCarran Act

1. EWOH, pp. 75–76.

2. Drew Pearson, *Diaries*, edited by Tyler Abell (New York: Holt, Rinehart and Winston, 1974), p. 74.

3. Angela Ward in EWOH, p. 149.

4. EWOH, p. 149.

5. EWOH, p. 177.

6. EWOH, p. 177.

7. EWOH, p. 179.

8. EWOH, p. 149.

9. This and the following excerpts are taken from *The Inaugural Addresses of the Presidents of the United States* (Washington, D.C.: U.S. Government Printing Office, 1989).

10. George F. Kennan, *Memoirs, 1950–1963* (New York: Pantheon, 1972), p. 185.

11. David M. Oshinsky, *A Conspiracy So Immense* (New York: Free Press, 1985), p. 236.

12. Gary May, *China Scapegoat: The Diplomatic Ordeal of John Carter Vincent* (Prospect Heights, Ill.: Waveland Press, 1979), p. 273.

13. PM to Birdie, 14 December 1951, PMP.

14. Loyalty Review Board minutes, 13–14 February, 1951, copy in SISS papers, NARA.

15. Ibid.

16. May, *Scapegoat*, p. 241.

17. SISS/IPR report, page 224.

18. May, *Scapegoat*, p. 259.

19. Charles Bohlen, *Witness to History, 1929–1969* (New York: Norton, 1973), p. 311.

20. Dean Acheson, *Present at the Creation: My Years in the State Department* (New York: Norton, 1969), p. 432.

21. Stephen Ambrose, *Eisenhower, Volume 1* (New York: Touchstone, 1983), p. 543.

22. May, *Scapegoat*, p. 274.

23. Ibid., p. 276.

24. Ibid., p. 277.

25. Bohlen, *Witness*, p. 325.

26. *Washington Evening Star*, 20 March 1953.

27. WAP, 21 March 1953.

28. Ibid.

29. WAP, 23 March 1953.

30. *Washington Evening Star*, 21 March 1953.

31. WAP, 22 March 1953.

32. Pearson, *Diaries*, p. 252.

33. Memo, 16 March 1954, Official & Confidential File, FBI.

34. Ibid.

35. Nichols to Hoover, 16 March 1954, O&C File.

36. Hoover, memo, 16 April 1953, O&C File.
37. Ibid.
38. Walter Isaacson and Evan Thomas, *The Wise Men* (New York: Simon & Schuster, 1986), pp. 565–566.
39. George F. Kennan, *Memoirs, 1925–1950* (Boston: Little, Brown, 1967), pp. 557–559.
40. Kennan, *Memoirs*, p. 208.
41. Ibid., p. 210.
42. Ibid., p. 188.
43. Nichols to Hoover, 16 March 1954, O&C File, FBI.
44. Bohlen, *Witness*, p. 334.
45. Dwight D. Eisenhower, *Mandate for Change, 1953–1956* (New York: Doubleday, 1963), p. 216.
46. Sally Belfrage, *Un-American Activities* (New York: HarperCollins, 1994), p. 123.
47. Cedric Belfrage, *The Frigthened Giant* (New York: Weekly Guardian Associates, 1957), p. 112.
48. Elizabeth Bentley, *Out of Bondage* (New York: Devin-Adair, 1951), p. 202.
49. Report 3 January 1946, p. 320, Silvermaster file, FBI 65-56402.
50. Cedric Belfrage and James Aronson, *Something to Guard* (New York: Columbia University Press, 1978), p. 8.
51. Ibid., p. 115.
52. Pace to PM, 13 February 1952, SISS Papers, NARA.
53. Belfrage, *Giant*, p. 21.
54. Belfrage and Aronson, *Guard*, p. 183.
55. Belfrage, *Giant*, p. 62.
56. WAP, 16 July 1953
57. NSJ, 26 June 1953.
58. Ibid.
59. WAP, 25 June 1953.
60. *Carson Appeal*, 14 July 1953.
61. WAP, 1 July 1953.
62. PM to Eisenhower, 6 July 1953, Eisenhower Papers, Dwight D. Eisenhower Library.
63. *Time*, 13 July 1953.
64. Eisenhower, *Mandate*, p. 217.
65. *Orlando Star*, 30 June 1953.
66. WAP, 21 July 1953.
67. Pearson, NSJ, 2 August 1953.
68. Eisenhower, *Mandate*, p. 218.
69. NYHT, 30 July 1953.
70. WAP, 22 November 1953.
71. Ibid.
72. Daniel Bell to Olga Corey, nd, Corey Papers, CU.
73. Lewis Corey to Elliot Cohen, 6 August 1948, Corey Papers.
74. Esther Corey to Greenberg, 7 March 1953, Corey Papers, CU.
75. Esther Corey to Norman Thomas, 24 June 1954, Corey Papers.
76. Harvey Klehr, John Earl Haynes, and Kyrill M. Anderson, *The Soviet World of American Communism* (New Haven, Conn.: Yale University Press, 1998), p. 199.
77. M. Albert Dimmitt, "The Enactment of the McCarran-Walter Act of 1952," Ph.D. dissertation, University of Kansas, 1970.

78. Esther Corey, "Marxism Reconsidered," *The Nation*, 2 March, 1940.

79. Cincinnati to director, 7 October 1947, Corey file, FBI 100-3-74-1130.

80. Corey to Thomas, 2 May 1953, Corey Papers.

81. Deportation hearing notes, nd, Corey Papers.

82. Benjamin Gitlow, *The Whole of Their Lives* (New York: Scribner's Sons, 1948), pp. 14, 25.

83. Deportation notes, nd, Corey Papers.

84. Corey to Eastman, unsent letter, 1952, Corey Papers.

85. Curt Gentry, *J. Edgar Hoover* (New York: Norton, 1991), p. 428.

86. Margaret Truman, *Harry S. Truman* (New York: Morrow, 1973), p. 563.

87. David M. Oshinsky, *A Conspiracy So Immense* (New York: Free Press, 1985), p. 348.

88. Robert J. Lamphere and Tom Shachtman, *The FBI-KGB War* (Macon, Ga.: Mercer University Press, 1995), p. 283.

89. PM to Jenner, 12 November 1953, EAP.

90. PM to Jenner, 22 November 1953, EAP.

91. Gentry, *Hoover*, p. 430.

92. Memo, Nichols to Tolson, 9 March 1953, FBI 62-88217.

93. Belmont to Ladd, 18 January 1954, Cohn file, FBI 62-97564.

94. Gentry, *Hoover*, p. 429.

95. Hoover statement, 17 November 1953, EAP.

96. Lamphere and Schactman, *FBI-KGB*, p. 287.

97. Hoover to PM, 17 November 1953, EAP.

98. Thomas C. Reeves, *The Life and Times of Joe McCarthy* (New York: Stein and Day, 1982), p. 530.

99. Oshinsky, *Conspiracy*, p. 352.

100. Flora Lewis, *Red Pawn: the Story of Noel Field* (New York; Doubleday & Co., 1965) p. 235.

101. A. J. Liebling, "The Lake of the Cui-ui Eaters, Part I," *New Yorker*, 1 January 1955.

102. A. J. Liebling, "The Lake of the Cui-ui Eaters, Part IV," *New Yorker*, 22 January 1955.

103. PM to PP, 11 May 1949, PPP.

104. Liebling, "Part IV."

105. Stanley James Underdal, "On the Road Toward Termination," Ph.D. dissertation, CU, 1977, p. 69.

106. Liebling, "Part IV."

107. Underdal, "Road," p. 65.

108. PM to PP, 25 May 1951, PPP.

109. Underdal, "Road," p. 169.

110. Curry, memo, 24 August 1949, copy in PMP.

111. Underdal, "Road," p. 169.

112. Ibid., p. 147.

113. Ibid., p. 224.

114. Ibid., p. 232.

115. Liebling, "Part IV."

Chapter 26: Beset with Enemies

1. John Dos Passos, *District of Columbia* (Boston: Houghton Mifflin, 1952), p. 342.
2. MacLeish to Dos Passos, nd, Dos Passos Papers, University of Virginia.
3. NYHT, 2 January 1954.
4. *Time*, 22 February 1954.
5. EA to Mary, 31 March 1954, PMP.
6. EA to Margaret, 28 April 1954, PMP.
7. Ovid, *Metamorphoses*, translated by Rolfe Humphries (Bloomington, Ind.: Indiana University Press, 1983), p. 239.
8. Sidney Zion, *The Autobiography of Roy Cohn* (Seacaucus, N.J.: L. Stuart, 1988), p. 156.
9. Zion, *Cohn*, p. 91.
10. Jack Anderson and James Boyd, *Confessions of a Muckraker* (New York: Random House, 1979), p. 223.
11. Sourwine to PM, 17 March 1954, EAP.
12. Ibid.
13. *New Hampshire Sunday News*, 2 May 1954.
14. Ibid.
15. EA to Biltz, 31 July 1954, EAP.
16. Senate speech, 22 June 1954, copy in PMP.
17. Thomas C. Reeves, *The Life and Times of Joe McCarthy* (New York: Stein and Day, 1982), p. 631.
18. Murray Kempton, *America Comes of Middle Age* (Boston: Little, Brown, 1963), p. 310.
19. CR, 83rd Congress, 2nd Session, clip cira 1954, in PMP, p. 8591.
20. WAP, 4 January 1954.
21. *U.S. News & World Report*, 11 December 1953.
22. Ibid.
23. Alsop to Dulles, 27 February 1954, Alsop Papers, LOC.
24. Alsop to Noce, 25 June 1954, Alsop Papers.
25. Account from Minutes, Democratic Policy Committee, 29 August 1954, Senate Papers, LBJL.
26. Mary to sisters, 4 November 1954, PMP.
27. Mary to PM, 3 February 1954, PMP.
28. Ruth Montgomery, *Once There Was a Nun: Mary McCarran's Years as Sister Mary Mercy* (New York: G. P. Putnam's Sons, 1962), p. 301.
29. Birdie to Dear Ones, 15 November 1954, PMP.
30. PM to Norine, 19 November 1952, PMP.
31. Mary to sisters, 4 November 1954, PMP.
32. Montgomery, *Nun*, p. 292.
33. The following account is taken from Edward Olsen, UNOHP.
34. LVS, clip, nd, in Pearson Papers, LBJL.
35. EA to Margaret, 25 March 1953, PMP.
36. Greenspun to Pearson, nd, Pearson Papers, LBJL.
37. Alsop to Frank Wisin, 6 May 1954, Alsop Papers, LOC.
38. Kempton, *New York Post*, nd, clip, Kolhberg Papers, SU.
39. EA to Biltz, 31 July 1954, EAP.
40. Mary Sperling McAuliffe, *Crisis on the Left* (Amherst, MA: University of Massachusetts Press, 1978), p. 139.

41. McAuliffe, *Crisis*, p. 140.

42. Ibid., p. 134.

43. Ibid., p. 136.

44. Ibid., p. 139.

45. Wechsler to Rauh, 23 September 1954, Wechsler Papers, WSHS.

46. Rauh to Humphrey, 14 September 1954, Wechsler Papers.

47. McAuliffe, *Crisis*, p. 140.

48. EA to Margaret, 28 April 1953, PMP.

49. Jerome Edwards, e-mail to author.

50. *Independence*, August 1953.

51. Margaret to PM, 10 June 1954, PMP.

52. Sokolsky to Margaret, 27 March 1953, Sokolsky Papers, SU.

53. *Chicago American*, 18 September 1954.

54. EA to Margaret, 26 May 1954, PMP.

55. PM to Margaret, 30 August 1954, PMP.

56. Jerome Edwards, *Pat McCarran: Political Boss of Nevada* (Reno, Nev.: University of Nevada Press, 1982), p. 17.

57. Chester Smith interview with author, Washington, D.C., October 2002.

58. This and the following excerpts are taken from NSJ, 28 September 1954.

59. WAP, 4 January 1953.

60. Dickerson to Vail Pittman, 19 December 1958, VPP.

61. McCloskey, UNOHP.

62. *Brazil Herald*, 27 November 1952.

63. PM to PP, 29 July 1954, PPP.

64. A. J. Liebling, "Lake of the Cui-Cui Eaters," *New Yorker*, 22 January 1955.

Epilogue: He Who Raised Up the Walls and Set Up the Gates and Bars

1. CR, 9 November 1954, p. 15,900.

2. REG, 29 September 1954.

3. Georgetta Diary, 29 September 1954, NHS.

4. Jerome Edwards, *Pat McCarran: Political Boss of Nevada* (Reno, Nev.: University of Nevada Press, 1982), p. 198.

5. WAP, 30 September 1954.

6. *El Mundo Visto*, 29 September 1954.

7. Bridges statement, copy in PMP.

8. NSJ, 3 October 1954.

9. Ibid.

10. Edwards, *McCarran*, p. 198.

11. NSJ, 3 October 1954.

12. Lewis transcript, EAP.

13. *Time*, 11 October 1954.

14. Robert P. Newman, *Owen Lattimore and the "Loss" of China* (Berkeley, Calif.: University of California Press, 1992), p. 484.

15. E. J. Kahn Jr., *The China Hands* (New York: Viking Press, 1975), p. 33.

16. Sokolsky, column, 17 November 1954, clip, EAP.

17. Murray Kempton, *America Comes of Middle Age* (Boston: Little, Brown, 1963), p. 358.

18. Birdie to Mary, 25 November 1954, PMP.

19. Ibid.
20. EA to Margaret, 8 September 1955, PMP.
21. Richard Hay to Birdie, 1 August 1962, PMP.
22. Sam to Mary, 22 June 1960, PMP.
23. Jeanne de la Vistation to Margaret, 15 February 1957, PMP.
24. Phamphlet, UCB, "End McCarranism," (New York: The Committee, 1962).
25. Kempton, *America*, p. 324.
26. Memo, 8 June 1962, Kempton file, FBI 100-412326.
27. Kempton file, FBI 100-412326, memo 29 October 1958.
28. Copy, PMP.

INDEX

Throughout this index, the initials *PM* indicate references to Senator Pat McCarran. Page numbers preceded by letters indicate photos in photo sections A, B, and C. Page numbers higher than 764 indicate material in the Notes section, which includes bibliographical information (titles and authors).

A

Aaron, Daniel, 775
Abt, Jessica, 204, 416
Abt, John
  Advocate and Activist, 776–778, 781, 791, 797–798, 809–810, 814
  and CIO, 329–334, 349, 389, 394
  commitment to New Deal, 154
  as counsel to La Follette Committee, 210–211, 319
  as counsel to Communist Party, 558–561
  discovery of Ware Group, 165–166
  during AAA purge, 180–181
  naming of, by Chambers, 421
  on Peck, 160
  subpoenaed by the FBI, 418
  and Wallace campaign, 415–416, 432
  White House accusation of, 390
  on Witt, 213
Abt, Marion, 560
Acheson (Chace), 801
Acheson, Dean, C-2, 369–372, 816
  as counsel for Frankfurter, 225, 228
  on Dulles, 703
  and Fight for Freedom, 252
  and McCarran-Walter bill, 636
  Morning and Noon, 782
  and PM, 487–488, 510, 551, 552
  Present at the Creation, 794, 800, 804, 809, 815, 821
  and relations with Spain, 474, 504
  as secretary of state, 442–443
ACLU. *See* American Civil Liberties Union (ACLU)
Action Conference on China Policy, 438, 440
Adams, Eva, B-1, B-6, 452–455
  helping PM's family, 453, 745
  papers of, 785, 787–788, 793, 798, 800–825
  and PM, 361, 458
  as PM's emissary, 457
  on Sam McCarran, 294, 757
  on Truman, 695
Adams, John, 144–145
Adams, Vern, 809
Adler, Solomon, 293, 426
Advocate and Activist (Abt), 776–778, 781, 791, 797–798, 809–810, 814
AFL. *See* American Federation of Labor (AFL)
After Seven Years (Moley), 775
Agar, Herbert, 261
Age of Jackson, The (Schlesinger), 406

Age of Reform, The (Hofstadter), 766
Age of Roosevelt, The (Schlesinger), 406
Age of Surveillance, The (Donner), 801
Age of Suspicion, The (Wechsler), 797
Agnes Smedley: The Life and Times of an American Radical (MacKinnon and MacKinnon), 800
Agricultural Adjustment Act, 151, 155
Agricultural Adjustment Administration (AAA; Triple A), 148, 151, 157, 159–160
  Communism in, 165–167
  and labor movement, 175, 177, 208
  PM's opinion of, 201
  purging of, 180–182
Agricultural Workers' Union, 177–178
Aldrich, Frank, 386–387, 796
Alexander, Robert C., 449
Alexeev, Kirill M., 449
Alien and Sedition Acts, 505, 527
Alinsky, Saul, 781
All-American Conference, 488
All But the People: Franklin D. Roosevelt and His Critics (Wolfskill and Hudson), 777, 780
All in One Lifetime (Byrnes), 796
Allen, Frank, 793
Allen, Leo Elwood, 300
Allen, Robert S., 251, 507, 517, 603, 634, 677, 805, 816, 819
Allis-Chalmers plant, 269
Alsop, Joseph, 5, 583–585, 765, 780–781, 824
  on Bentley, 578
  and China Lobby, 550
  and Fight for Freedom, 252
  homosexuality of, 591
  and John Paton Davies, 564–565, 736–737
  on Lattimore and Vincent, 594
  on Matusow, 741–742
  and SISS hearings, 586–592
  and Stilwell, 556–557
  "Why We Lost China," 564–565
Alsop, Stewart, 5, 407, 591, 765
Ambrose, Stephen, 821
Amen, John Harlan, 702
Amerasia case, 374–376, 393, 439, 602
Amerasia Spy Case: Prelude to McCarthyism (Klehr and Radosh), 794, 796
America and the Survivors of the Holocaust (Dinnerstein), 802–804
America Comes of Middle Age (Kempton), 824–826
America First: The Battle Against Intervention (Cole), 785–787

827

ABOUT THE AUTHOR

Michael J. Ybarra is a graduate of the University of California, Los Angeles, and UC Berkeley, where he earned a graduate degree in political science. He has been a staff reporter for the *Wall Street Journal* and has written about politics and culture for the *New York Times,* the *Los Angeles Times,* the *Washington Post,* the *New Republic,* and numerous other publications. He lives in San Francisco. This is his first book.